WESTERN
CIVILIZATIONS

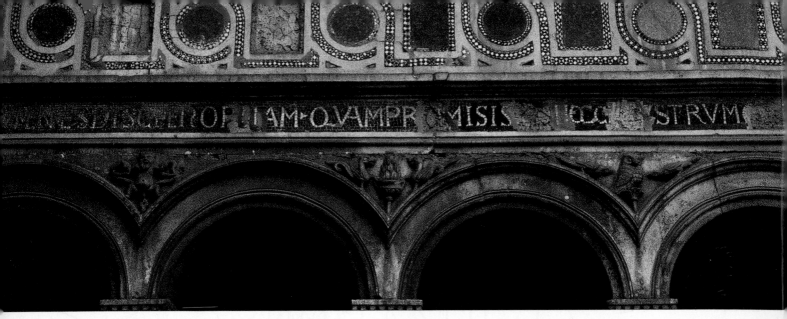

FOURTEENTH EDITION

JUDITH G. COFFIN

ROBERT C. STACEY

ROBERT E. LERNER

STANDISH MEACHAM

BASED ON THE ORIGINAL *WESTERN CIVILIZATIONS*
BY EDWARD MCNALL BURNS

W · W · NORTON & COMPANY · NEW YORK · LONDON

WESTERN
CIVILIZATIONS

THEIR HISTORY
& THEIR CULTURE

The text of this book is composed in Weiss Roman
with the display set in Bauer Text Initials and Bell Gothic
Composition by TSI
Manufacturing by Courier Corporation, Kendallville
Title page spread photo: ©2001 Paloma Pajares Ayuela, from "Cosmatesque Ornament"
Editor: Jon Durbin
Associate Managing Editor—College: Jane Carter
Director of Manufacturing—College: Roy Tedoff
Cover & Text Designer: Antonina Krass
Page layout: Carole Desnoes
Copy editor: Barbara Gerr
Project editors: Sarah Caldwell, Lory Frenkel
Photograph editor: Neil Ryder Hoos
Assistant editor: Aaron Javsicas

Library of Congress Cataloging-in-Publication Data

Coffin, Judith G., 1952–
    Western civilizations, their history and their culture / Judith G. Coffin . . . [et al.].—14th ed.
        p. cm.
    Rev. ed. of: Western civilizations, their history and their culture / Robert E. Lerner. 13th ed. 1998.
    Includes bibliographical references and index.
    ISBN 0-393-97686-6
        1. Civilization, Western. 2. Europe—Civilization. I. Lerner, Robert E. Western civilizations, their
    history and their culture. II. Title.

CB245 .C56 2002
909'.09812—dc21   2001044708

W. W. Norton & Company, Inc., 500 Fifth Avenue, New York, NY 10110
www.wwnorton.com

W. W. Norton & Company Ltd., Castle House, 75/76 Wells Street, London W1T 3QT
1 2 3 4 5 6 7 8 9 0

To our families—Robin, Will, and Anna Stacey, and Willy, Zoe, and Aaron Forbath—for their patience and support. They reminded us that books such as this are worth the work, and also that there are other things in life.

To Robert Lerner, Standish Meacham, Edward McNall Burns, and Marie Burns, our predecessors who successfully guided *Western Civilizations* for thirteen editions, spanning six decades.

About the Authors

JUDITH G. COFFIN received her Ph.D. in modern French history from Yale University. She has taught at Harvard University and the University of California, Riverside, and is currently associate professor of history at the University of Texas at Austin, where she won a 1999 University of Texas President's Associates' Award for Teaching Excellence. Her research interests focus on the social and cultural history of gender, mass culture, slavery, race relations, and colonialism. She is the author of *The Politics of Women's Work: The Paris Garment Trades, 1750–1915*.

ROBERT C. STACEY is professor and chair of the history department and a member of the Jewish Studies faculty at the University of Washington in Seattle. A long-time teacher of western civilization and medieval European history, he has received Distinguished Teaching Awards from both the University of Washington and Yale University, where he taught from 1984 to 1988. He is the author or coauthor of four books, including a textbook, *The Making of England to 1399*. He holds an M.A. from Oxford University and a Ph.D. from Yale.

ROBERT E. LERNER is professor of medieval history at Northwestern University, where he has served as director of the Humanities Program. He has won awards from the National Endowment for the Humanities, the American Council of Learned Studies, the Guggenheim Foundation, and the Rockefeller Foundation. His books include *The Age of Adversity: The Fourteenth Century; The Heresy of Free Spirit in the Middle Ages;* and *The Powers of Prophecy*.

STANDISH MEACHAM is professor emeritus at the University of Texas at Austin. He has received grants from the Guggenheim Foundation, the American Council of Learned Studies, and the American Philosophical Society. His books include *Henry Thornton of Clapman, 1760–1815; Lord Bishop: The Life of Samuel Wilberforce; A Life Apart: The English Working Class, 1890–1914;* and *Toynbee Hall and Social Reform, 1880–1914*.

CONTENTS

PART II THE GREEK AND
          ROMAN WORLDS

CHAPTER 7   CHRISTIANITY AND THE TRANSFORMATION
OF THE ROMAN WORLD   222

PART III   THE MIDDLE AGES

CHAPTER 8   ROME'S THREE HEIRS: THE BYZANTINE,
ISLAMIC, AND EARLY MEDIEVAL
WORLDS   260

CHAPTER 9   THE EXPANSION OF EUROPE: ECONOMY,
SOCIETY, AND POLITICS IN THE HIGH
MIDDLE AGES, 1000–1300   300

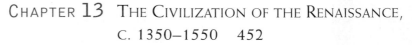

PART IV   FROM MEDIEVAL
          TO MODERN

CHAPTER 14   THE PROTESTANT REFORMATION   486

CHAPTER 15   RELIGIOUS WARS AND STATE BUILDING, 1540–1660   518

PART V   EARLY MODERN EUROPE

CHAPTER 16   THE ECONOMY AND SOCIETY OF EARLY MODERN EUROPE   556

CHAPTER 17   THE AGE OF ABSOLUTISM, 1660–1789   592

PART VI THE FRENCH AND INDUSTRIAL REVOLUTIONS AND THEIR CONSEQUENCES

PART VII   THE WEST AT THE
                 WORLD'S CENTER

CHAPTER 26   THE CHALLENGE OF THE MODERN WEST   876

CHAPTER 27   THE FIRST WORLD WAR   920

CHAPTER 28   TURMOIL BETWEEN THE WARS   954

CHAPTER 29   THE SECOND WORLD WAR   988

PART VIII   THE WEST AND THE WORLD

CHAPTER 30 COLD WAR POLITICS, ECONOMIC BOOM, AND CULTURAL CHANGE 1032

CHAPTER 31 FRAGMENTATION AND CHANGE IN CONTEMPORARY EUROPE 1056

CHAPTER 32 DECOLONIZATION AND THE TWENTY-FIRST-CENTURY WORLD 1078

MAPS

CHRONOLOGIES

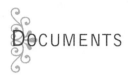

DOCUMENTS

PREFACE

SINCE THE 1920s, the western civilization survey course has held a central place in the curricula of American universities and high schools. Yet the concept of "western civilization" can be elusive. As this textbook begins its seventh decade of life, in the hands of a new team of authors, it seems appropriate to define our terms. At the beginning of the twenty-first century, how now do we conceive of our subject?

"Western" civilization was long considered to mean the civilization of western Europe, to which the earlier history of the Ancient Near East was somewhat arbitrarily attached. Western European civilization was thus presented as beginning at Sumer, developing in Egypt, and then flowering in Greece. Rome acquired it from Greece, and in turn passed it on to France, Germany, England, Italy and Spain, whose emigrating colonists transferred it to the Americas, beginning in the sixteenth century. Rather like a train passing through stations, western civilization was thus conceived as picking up "cargo" at each of its stops, but always retaining the same engine and the same baggage cars.

This vision of western civilization is not only selective, it is often tied to a series of contentious assumptions. It casts the worldwide dominance of the European imperial powers between roughly 1800 and 1950 as the culmination of several thousand years of historical development, which it is the obligation of historians to explain. Behind this assumption there frequently lies another: that European global dominance in the nineteenth and twentieth centuries reflected and demonstrated the inherent superiority of western European civilization over the African, Asian, and Native American civilizations the Europeans conquered during the heyday of their imperial expansion.

Historians today are keenly aware of how much such an account leaves out. It slights the use of force and fraud in European expansion. It ignores the sophistication, dynamism, and humanity of the many cultures it sidelines. By neglecting the crucial importance of Byzantium and Islam, it gives a misleadingly narrow account of the development of European civilization. It also misleads us about the western civilizations created in North and South America after the conquest, which were creole, or hybrid, cultures, not simply European cultures transplanted to other shores. This is not to argue that a study of western civilization must give way to a study of world civilization. It is merely to insist that understanding the historical development of western civilization requires us to place it in a much wider context.

In this textbook, we will argue that western civilization is not a single historical culture with uniform and unchanging characteristics. It is not a single train, making stops at selected stations. Rather, there have been a number of western civilizations, whose fundamental characteristics have changed markedly over time. We mean, therefore, for our title, *Western Civilizations*, to be taken seriously. In this book, we will treat "western" as a geographical designator, to refer to the major civilizations that developed in and around the Mediterranean Sea between 3500 B.C.E. ("Before the Common Era," equivalent to the Christian dating system B.C., "Before Christ") and 500 C.E. ("Common Era," equivalent to the Christian dating system A.D., "Anno Domini," "the Year of the Lord"). We will also treat as "western" the civilizations that developed out of the Mediterranean world in the centuries after 500 C.E., as the Greco-Roman world of antiquity divided into Islamic, Byzantine, and Latin Christian realms. The interdependence and mutual influence of these three western civilizations upon each other will be a recurring theme of this book.

From the twelfth century C.E. onward, however, we focus more intensively upon the evolving culture of the European continent. Between 1100 and 1500, Europe's distinctive social, economic, political, and religious characteristics combined to make it the most powerful and expansive of the three civilizations. From the sixteenth century on, Europeans turned these expansionist impulses outward, away from the Mediterranean world and into the Atlantic and Indian Oceans, becoming the first global imperial power in history. Today, we live in the shadow of that world. We need to understand the unpredictable and surprising ways in which that world took shape. To do so, we must pay attention to both the internal conflicts in which expansion was entwined and the political, economic, and cultural transformations that it entailed.

In undertaking to revise this book, we have been constantly reminded of the very high quality of the work upon which we are building. Between 1941 and 1973, Edward McNall Burns constructed a textbook with enduring features—a vigorous narrative style, and a wide-ranging attention to the diverse ways in which humans have organized their lives in response to changing environments, visions, and goals—that were

expertly carried on and updated by Robert Lerner and Standish Meacham. In preparing the fourteenth edition of their work, we have tried to retain the book's traditional strengths by remaining attentive to narrative; by aiming for clarity and accessibility without "talking down" to our audience; and by bringing together "high" politics and culture with the everyday experiences and beliefs of ordinary people.

At the same time, we have made some significant changes in this new edition, devoting, for example, more attention to the world outside northwestern Europe. We have taken a more historical approach to our story, presenting artistic and cultural developments as firmly rooted in the circumstances and conditions of their age, rather than expressions of timeless genius. We have continued to integrate new scholarly work in social and cultural history and the history of gender into our narrative, but we have also substantially increased the attention we pay to economics, religion, and military history. In addition to shortening the text by about 15 percent, we have also changed the book's design, using a two-column layout for the text, adding boxes with primary source documents, redesigning the maps, and increasing the size of the illustrations.

We have substantially revised many of the individual chapters. Parts I and II, which cover the Ancient Near East and the Mediterranean world up to c. 500 C.E., have been completely reconceived and rewritten. In keeping with our emphasis on the historical interactions and interdependence of western civilizations, we no longer present Mesopotamian, Egyptian, Myceneaean, Minoan, Persian, and Hebrew history in separate chapters as if these cultures were isolated from one other. Instead, we take a more directly chronological and comparative approach. Chapter 1 traces human history in the Mediterranean and Near Eastern world from its Stone Age origins up to c. 2000 B.C.E. Chapter 2 considers the impact of the developing empires of the ancient Near East upon Mesopotamia, Egypt, and the Aegean Sea region between roughly 2000 B.C.E. and 1200 B.C.E. Chapter 3 examines the early Iron Age, from roughly 1200 B.C.E. to 500 B.C.E., emphasizing the religious imperialism of the era and the impact of that imperialism upon the development of Hebrew monotheism.

In Part II, Chapter 4 deals with Greece from roughly 1200 B.C.E. until 400 B.C.E., while Chapter 5 treats the extension of Greek cultural influence throughout the Mediterranean world between c. 400 B.C.E. and the mid-second century B.C.E. In both these chapters, we have tried to pay particular attention to the political, social and economic context for the important cultural and intellectual developments of these eras. Chapter 6 deals with republican and imperial Rome from its origins until the mid-third century C.E. Readers will find here a new discussion of the early history of Rome, and a significantly revised presentation of Roman religion. Chapter 7 traces the impact of Romanization and Christianization upon the late antique world, paralleling the discussion of Hellenization in Chapter 5 and complicating conventional ideas about the "fall" of Rome.

Part III, "The Middle Ages," has also been reorganized and revised. Chapter 8, "Rome's Three Heirs," discusses Byzantium, the Islamic world, and Europe up to the year 1000, emphasizing that all three civilizations drew heavily upon Greek and Roman traditions. The section on early medieval Europe has been rewritten. Coverage of Byzantine and Islamic history after 1000 has been expanded and moved to Chapter 9, with significantly increased attention to the Byzantine revival, the crusades, and the economic relations between the three civilizations. Chapter 11 contains a revised section on medieval Russia and its connections with Byzantium. Throughout Part III, long-time users will also note smaller revisions and alterations in emphasis where the authors determined that new work has significantly altered earlier views.

Part IV, "From Medieval to Modern," now begins with a new chapter (12) on "Commerce, Conquest, and Colonization, 1300–1600." This chapter starts with the Mongol conquests of central Asia, then discusses the rise of the Ottoman Empire and the growth of European colonial enterprises in the Mediterranean and along the Atlantic coast of Africa. It concludes with the sixteenth century expansion of European commerce and military conquest into the Indian Ocean and across the Atlantic in the Americas. Chapter 13 offers a revised discussion of Machiavelli, and carries further the previous emphasis on the medieval roots of the Renaissance. Chapter 14 now focuses exclusively on the reformations of the sixteenth century. Coverage of the European voyages of discovery, previously found here, has been moved to Chapter 12 on "Commerce, Conquest, and Colonization." We have also tried to sharpen the focus of Chapter 15, linking the cultural developments of the era more directly with the tensions in European life that arose out of the religious conflicts of the sixteenth and seventeenth centuries.

In Part V, the most important changes are two new chapters (18 and 19) on the Scientific Revolution and Enlightenment. Both chapters are concerned with the context in which new ideas were forged and with how those ideas came to matter for a range of people, from philosophers, rulers, and bureaucrats to explorers, artists, and artisans. Chapter 19 highlights the international setting of Enlightenment thought. Here and throughout, we have expanded the treatment of gender. That has meant adding more material concerning women but also, more importantly, showing the ways in which family, sexuality, models of femininity, and the rights and duties of men and women became central to politics and culture at different historical moments.

In Part VI, Chapter 20 contains a new section on slavery and anti-slavery movements, including the Haitian Revolution. Chapters 21 and 22 set the industrial revolution in its international economic context. In Chapters 23 and 24, we have tried to clarify the many meanings and uses of nationalism.

In Part VII, we have added an entirely new chapter (25) on nineteenth-century imperialism. It begins with the relationship between the "new imperialism" and earlier moments of expansion, in keeping with the book's overall theme of outward expansion and inner conflict. It analyzes the forces that drove European imperialism in different regions and the resistance those forces encountered, resistance that shaped colonial culture and European rule. Next, the thirteenth edition's two chapters on the late nineteenth century have been condensed into one, focusing on the key events of late-nineteenth-century politics and culture. Those cuts allowed us to expand our treatment of war, spending more time on the battlefield as well as on the home front. The chapters on World Wars I and II (27 and 29) include more military history and more discussion of the world arena in which political and military battles were fought.

In Chapter 28 we have revised the treatments of Nazism and Stalinism, and added a new section on mass culture, tying it to mass politics and underscoring its democratic as well as authoritarian potential. Chapter 29 includes a short discussion of the Pacific war, and a new section, with documents, on the Holocaust.

In Part VIII, "The West and the World," Chapter 30 includes more analysis of developments in Eastern Europe. The section on culture is more attentive to the "Americanization" of popular culture in particular. Chapter 31 includes a new section on changes in consumption, youth culture, and new social movements. In Chapter 32, we have expanded the analysis of decolonization, especially the collapse of the British and French empires.

INNOVATIVE PEDAGOGICAL PROGRAM

Western Civilizations, Fourteenth Edition is designed for maximum readability. The crisp, clear, and concise narrative is also accompanied by a highly useful pedagogical program designed to help students study while engaging them in the subject matter. Highlights of this innovative program include:

- **In-Text Documents.** Designed to add depth to the more focused narrative of *Western Civilizations*, each chapter contains five primary sources, two of which are paired together to convey a sense of historical complexity and diversity.

- **Map Program with Enhanced Captions:** Over one hundred beautiful maps appear throughout the text, each accompanied by an enhanced map caption designed to engage the reader analytically, while conveying the key role that geography plays in the development of history and the societies of the world.

- **In-Chapter Chronologies.** Several brief chronologies built around particular events, topics, or periods appear throughout each chapter and are designed to provide road maps through the narrative detail.

- **Focus Question System.** Ensures that readers remain alert to key concepts and questions on every page of the text. Focus questions guide students' reading in three ways: (1) a focus question box appears at the beginning of the chapter to serve as a preview of the chapter's contents; (2) relevant questions reappear at the start of the section where they are discussed; and (3) running heads on the right hand pages keep these questions in view throughout the chapter.

- **Pull-Quotes.** Lifted directly from the narrative, pull-quotes appear throughout each chapter and are designed to highlight key thoughts and keen insights, while keeping students focused on larger concepts and ideas.

OUTSTANDING ANCILLARIES FOR BOTH INSTRUCTORS AND STUDENTS

Western Civilizations Online Tutor
www.wwnorton.com/wciv
by Steven Kreiss, Wake Technical College
This online resource for students—designed specifically for use with *Western Civilizations*—provides free access to online review and research materials. Included are online quizzes, Norton iMaps, world history excursion exercises, electronic versions of the Global Connections/Disconnections feature boxes, images from the text, audio and video clips, and Norton e-Reserves.

Norton Media Library with PowerPoint Slides
This CD-ROM contains a presentation program designed to assist instructors who want to make multimedia presentations in lecture. The easy-to-use program includes all the maps in the text, dynamic Norton iMaps, various images from the book.

Instructor's Manual and Test-Item File
by Maarten Ultee, University of Alabama, Tuscaloosa
The Instructor's Manual includes lecture outlines, ideas for launching lectures, sample lecture topics, classroom exercises, suggested films and readings, and recommended web links. The Test-Item File contains multiple-choice, short-answer, and essay questions for each chapter of the text.

Study Guide
by Stephen Wessley, York College of Pennsylvania
This valuable guide contains chapter objectives, chapter outlines, chronologies, key terms, multiple-choice questions, map exercises and a highly useful collection of primary sources tied directly to *Western Civilizations, Fourteenth Edition.*

ACKNOWLEDGMENTS:

The final version of the manuscript was greatly influenced by the thoughts and ideas of a select group of instructors to whom we are greatly indebted and wish to express our sincere thanks:

- James Brophy, University of Delaware;
- Lawrence Duggan, University of Delaware;
- Janusz Duzinkiewicz, Purdue University, North Central Campus;
- Stephen Epstein, University of Colorado at Boulder;
- William Jordan, Princeton University;
- Stephen Kreiss, Wake Technical College;
- Harry Liebersohn, University of Illinois, Urbana-Champaign;
- Thomas Max Safley, University of Pennsylvania;
- Jeffrey Merrick, University of Wisconsin-Milwaukee;
- Ian Morris, Stanford University;

- Cat Nilan;
- John Robertson, Central Michigan University;
- Evan A. Thomas, Grandview College;
- and Maarten Ultee, University of Alabama, Tuscaloosa.

We want to thank Steve Forman and Jon Durbin at W. W. Norton for their faith in this project, and Jon Durbin, Aaron Javsicas, and Sarah Caldwell for their help in seeing it through to completion. Without these friends and supporters, we could not have done it. We also want to thank Toni Krass for creating a beautiful new design, Carol Desnoes for her eye-catching page layout, and Neil Hoos for finding the images for the covers.

We are grateful for the helpful criticisms and suggestions of a large number of scholars, some of whom reviewed the thirteenth edition, and others who reviewed earlier drafts of this one.

Robert Stacey has been principally responsible for revising Chapters 1–17. He owes special thanks to Carol Thomas and Joel Walker of the University of Washington for advice on early Greek and late antique matters respectively; to Daniel Waugh (University of Washington) for his searching criticisms of Mongol, Ottoman, and early Russian matters; and to Lawrence Duggan (University of Delaware) for his help with the Renaissance chapter and for many valuable discussions on the Reformation over many years. His greatest debt, however, is to Dr. Jason Hawke, now of the University of Iowa, without whose assistance in both research and writing the revisions to Chapters 1 through 6 could not have been accomplished.

Judith Coffin is principally responsible for the revisions to Chapters 18–32. Many of her colleagues have supplied advice and expertise, but she is especially grateful to Caroline Castiglione, David Crew, Paul Hagenloh, Standish Meacham, John Merriman, Gail Minault, Joan Neuberger, Paula Sanders, Daniel Sherman, James Sidbury, Robert Stephens, Michael Stoff, and Charters Wynn. James Brophy of the University of Delaware deserves special thanks for rewriting the chapters on the late nineteenth century. Cori Crider, Patrick Timmons, Marion Barber and, especially, Justin Glasson, were terrific research assistants. Her greatest debt is to Geoffrey Clayton, whose research, writing, and energy were critical in nearly every chapter.

WESTERN
CIVILIZATIONS

PART I
THE ANCIENT NEAR EAST

THE HUMAN HISTORY of the Mediterranean world begins only about 40,000 years ago, with the completed evolution of homo sapiens sapiens, the fully modern human species to which we all belong. Civilization is an even more recent development. To the peoples of the ancient world, civilization—government, literature, science, and art—was necessarily a product of civic life. But cities only became possible as a result of the agricultural and technological discoveries that emerged between the end of the last Ice Age, about 13,000 years ago, and the appearance, in Mesopotamia, of the first true cities approximately 5,000 years ago. The story of western civilizations is thus a short one. In geologic time, it is but a momentary blip on a radar screen.

From their origins between the Tigris and Euphrates Rivers in modern-day Iraq, cities grew up throughout the Near Eastern world. Independent cities gave way to empires that rose and fell in turn. Around 1200 B.C.E. the imperial system of the entire Mediterranean world collapsed in cataclysm, to be replaced, by the middle of the first millennium B.C.E., by new empires that were larger, better armed, and more aggressively imperialistic than any of their predecessors.

At the same time, dramatic developments were occurring in religious and cultural life. The pyramids of Egypt, the Epic of Gilgamesh, the works of Homer, and the religious traditions of Zoroastrianism and Judaism had all taken shape by the time our period closes around 500 B.C.E. Upon these foundations, all the subsequent civilizations of the western, Mediterranean world have continued to rest.

	POLITICS	SOCIETY AND CULTURE	ECONOMY	INTERNATIONAL RELATIONS
B.C.E. 40,000		Paleolithic Era (40,000–11,000 B.C.E.)		
		End of the Ice Age, beginning of the Neolithic Era (11,000 B.C.E.)		
			Grain storage begins (9500 B.C.E.)	
		Settled agriculture in Fertile Crescent (8500–7000 B.C.E.)		
8000		Stone walls and tower of Jericho (8000 B.C.E.)	Emergence of pottery in Jericho (8000–7000 B.C.E.)	
			Domestication of animals, raising of crops (7000 B.C.E.)	
6000	Ubaid culture governed by priestly class (5900 B.C.E.)		Ubaid culture builds irrigation channels of stone (5900 B.C.E.)	Ubaid culture (Mesopotamia) (5900 B.C.E.)
		Agriculture established in Egypt and the Balkans (5000 B.C.E.)	Long-distance trade emerges (5000 B.C.E.)	
		Increased trade engenders social stratification (5000 B.C.E.)		
		First-known settlement in Egypt (4750 B.C.E.)		
4000		Uruk Period (4300–2900 B.C.E.)		
		End of the Stone Age (4000 B.C.E.)	Copper tools appear (4000 B.C.E.)	
		Cities form in fertile Mesopotamia (3500–3000 B.C.E.)	Building of the White Temple at Uruk (3500–3300 B.C.E.)	
			Pottery-throwing wheels (3500 B.C.E.)	
			Ubaid/Sumerians begin inscribing symbols on tablets (3300 B.C.E.)	
			Wheeled chariots (3200 B.C.E.)	
			Egyptians build fortifications, temples, settlements (3200 B.C.E.)	
			Appearance of cuneiform script (3100 B.C.E.)	Sumerian civilization (3100 B.C.E.)
3000	The Archaic Period in Egypt (3000–2715 B.C.E.)	Beginning of the Bronze Age (3000 B.C.E.)	Discovery of bronze (3000 B.C.E.)	
		Egyptians develop hieroglyphs and hieratic script (3000 B.C.E.)		
	Emergence of lugal leadership in Mesopotamia (2900–2500 B.C.E.)			
	Early Dynastic Period (I & II) (2900–2500 B.C.E.)			
	The Old Kingdom in Egypt (2715–2170 B.C.E.)	Great Pyramids of Giza (2640–2510 B.C.E.)		
	The Third through Sixth Dynasties in Egypt (2715–2205 B.C.E.)	Royal Tombs of Ur (2550–2450 B.C.E.)		
	Early Dynastic (III) (2500–2350 B.C.E.)	Epic of Gilgamesh (2500 B.C.E.)		Elamite (present-day Iran) culture (2500 B.C.E.)
	The Akkadian Period (2350–2160 B.C.E.)			
	Sargon organizes Mesopotamia (2350 B.C.E.)			Sargon of Akkad conquers Mesopotamia (2360 B.C.E.)
	Unity of Egypt dissolves (2150 B.C.E.)			Gutians conquer Sumer and Akkad (2160 B.C.E.)
	Ur Dynasty III (2100–2000 B.C.E.)			

POLITICS	SOCIETY AND CULTURE	ECONOMY	INTERNATIONAL RELATIONS	
				B.C.E. 2000
The Middle Kingdom in Egypt (2000–1683 B.C.E.)	Indo-European linguistic forms appear (2000 B.C.E.)	Horses introduced to Near East (2000–1700 B.C.E.)		
The "Palace Age" in Minoan culture (1900–1700 B.C.E.)		Major expansion of trade (1900–1700 B.C.E.)	Minoan civilization flourishes in Crete (1900–1500 B.C.E.)	
Hammurabi unifies Sumero-Akkadian area (1792–1750 B.C.E.)	Code of Hammurabi (1750 B.C.E.)	Minoan trade with Egypt, Anatolia, and Cyprus (1700 B.C.E.)		
			The Hyksos overrun Egypt (1650–1550 B.C.E.)	
			Hittites capture Babylon (1595 B.C.E.)	
The New Kingdom (1550–1075 B.C.E.)	Appearance of Linear B in Mycenaean Greece (1500 B.C.E.)	Trade surges with new internationalism (1500 B.C.E.)	The Mitannians adopt cavalry and chariot technology (1500 B.C.E.)	1500
			Mycenaean civilization established (1500 B.C.E.)	
Thutmosis III and Hatshepsut take the throne (1479 B.C.E.)			Age of internationalism begins (1500 B.C.E.)	
			Hittite empire (1450 B.C.E.)	
			Mycenaeans subjugate Crete (1400 B.C.E.)	
Reign of Amenhotep III, the Magnificent (1387–1350 B.C.E.)			Complex societies developed at Mycenae, Thebes, Athens, etc. (1400–1200 B.C.E.)	
Middle Assyrian Period (1362–859 B.C.E.)				
Amenhotep IV, later Akhenaton, takes the throne (1350 B.C.E.)	Rise of Amon as Egyptian national god (1350 B.C.E.)			
			Treaty between Egypt and Hittite Empire (1286 B.C.E.)	
			Rise of Phoenicians (Canaanites) (1200 B.C.E.)	
			Mycenaean civilization implodes (1200 B.C.E.)	
			Sea Peoples ravage Near East (1200–1179 B.C.E.)	
			Ramses III defeats Sea Peoples (1179 B.C.E.)	
		Philistines introduce vine and olive tree to the Levant (1050 B.C.E.)	Philistine preeminence in the Levant (1050 B.C.E.)	
Saul becomes first Hebrew king (1025 B.C.E.)				1000
Reign of King David (1000–973 B.C.E.)			Egypt collapses (1000 B.C.E.)	
Hebrew kingdom splits upon death of King Solomon (c. 933 B.C.E.)				
Neo-Assyrian Empire (883–859 B.C.E.)			Phoenicians establish Carthage (800 B.C.E.)	
Reign of Sargon II (722–705 B.C.E.)		Assyrians master iron-smelting (700 B.C.E.)	Assyrian Empire expands (800–700 B.C.E.)	700
	Zoroaster, founder of Zoroastrianism (600 B.C.E.)		Hebrew captivity in Babylon begins (587 B.C.E.)	
Reign of Darius I of Persia (521–486 B.C.E.)			Athens defeats Darius I at Battle of Marathon (490 B.C.E.)	
			Alexander the Great invades Persia (334 B.C.E.)	

CHAPTER ONE

CHAPTER CONTENTS

THE ORIGINS OF WESTERN CIVILIZATIONS IN THE ANCIENT NEAR EAST

CATHERINE MORLAND, the heroine of Jane Austen's novel *Northanger Abbey*, complained that history "tells me nothing that does not either vex or weary me. The quarrels of popes and kings, with wars or pestilences in every page; the men all so good for nothing, and hardly any women at all, it is very tiresome." Although Jane Austen's heroine said this around 1800, she might have lodged the same complaint until quite recently, for until deep into the twentieth century most historians considered history to be little more than "past politics"—and a dry chronicle of past politics at that. The content of historical study was restricted primarily to battles and treaties, the personalities and politics of statesmen, the laws and decrees of rulers. But important as such data are, they by no means constitute the whole substance of history. Especially within the last few decades historians have come to recognize that history comprises a record of past human activities in every sphere—not just political developments, but also social, economic, and intellectual ones. Women as well as men, the ruled as well as the rulers, the poor as well as the rich are part of history. So too are the social and economic institutions that women and men have created and that in turn have shaped their lives: family and social class; manorialism and city life; capitalism and industrialism. Ideas and attitudes, too, not just of intellectuals, but also of people whose lives may have been virtually untouched by "great books," are all part of the historian's concern. And most important, history includes an inquiry into the causes of events and patterns of human organization and ideas—a search for the forces that impelled humanity toward its great undertakings, and the reasons for its successes and failures.

As historians have extended the scope of their work, they have also equipped themselves with new methods and tools, the better to practice their craft. No longer do historians merely pore over the same old chronicles and documents to ask whether Charles the Fat was at Ingelheim or Lustnau on July 1, 887. To evaluate quantitative data, they learn the methods of the statistician. To interpret the effect of a rise in the cost of living, they study economics. To deduce marriage patterns or evaluate the effect on an entire population of wars and plagues, they master the

FOCUS QUESTIONS

• Why do we know so little about early nomadic life?

• What changes allowed the transition from nomadic to sedentary societies?

• How did irrigation and temple building figure in early Mesopotamian civilization?

• Why did a common religion not create peace among the Sumerians?

• How was the Nile River central to the development of Egyptian civilization?

skills of the demographer. To explore the phenomena of cave dwelling or modern urbanization, they become archaeologists, studying fossil remains, fragments of pots, or modern city landscapes. To understand the motives of the men and women who have acted in the past, they draw on the insights of social psychologists and cultural anthropologists. To illuminate the lives and thoughts of those who have left few or no written records, they look for other cultural remains such as folk songs, folk tales, and funerary monuments.

Of course with all their ingenuity historians cannot create evidence. An almost infinite number of past events are not retrievable because they transpired without leaving any traces; many others are at best known imperfectly. Thus some of the most fundamental questions about "how things were" in the past either can never be answered or can be answered only on the grounds of highly qualified inferences. Questions regarding motives and causes may not have definite answers for other reasons. Since individual humans often hardly understand their own motives, it is presumptuous to think that anyone can ever be entirely certain about establishing the motives of others. As for the causes of collective developments such as wars, economic growth trends, or changes in artistic styles, these are surely too complex to be reduced to a science. Nonetheless, the more evidence we have, the closer we come to providing valid reconstructions and explanations of what happened in the past. Moreover, the difficulties inherent in assembling and interpreting all sorts of data for the purposes of historical analysis should not be regarded with despair but looked on as stimulating intellectual challenges.

Should we go to the past to celebrate one or another lost age or seek to learn how we got to be the way we are now? Obviously neither one of these extremes is satisfactory, for nostalgia almost invariably leads to distortion, and at any rate is useless, whereas extreme "present-mindedness" also leads to distortion, and at any rate is foolish in its assumption that everything we do now is better than whatever people did before. It seems best, then, to avoid either revering the past or condescending to it. Instead, many historians seek to understand how people of a given era strove to solve their problems and live their lives fruitfully in terms appropriate to their particular environments and stages of development. Other historians look for change over time without postulating a march of progress to a current best of all possible worlds. Such historians believe (and let us hope they may be right) that identifying patterns and mechanisms of change will allow a better

understanding of the present and a greater possibility of plotting prudent strategies for coping with the future.

THE STONE AGE BACKGROUND

Why do we know so little about early nomadic life?

"Prehistory," the era before the appearance of written records around 3000 B.C.E. (Before the Common Era), is a period of much greater duration than human history. Humanlike ancestors first appeared in eastern Africa roughly four million years ago, and tool-making hominids (species belonging to the genus *Homo*, to which we as *Homo sapiens sapiens* belong) approximately two million years ago. The materials these early hominids employed were made principally out of stone, and from their use of stone tool technologies all human cultures down to the fourth millennium B.C.E. are referred to as belonging to the "Stone Age."

UPPER PALEOLITHIC ERA

The Stone Age is divided into various stages. Dominating the period is the Paleolithic ("Old Stone" Age), which most anthropologists would extend down to roughly 11,000 B.C.E. Within this vast expanse of time, however, scholars also speak of an Upper Paleolithic Era beginning around 40,000 B.C.E. Around this benchmark date archaeologists discern some stunning departures in human behavior, which may be associated with the appearance of anatomically modern humans in the Near East, North Africa, and Europe (though the correspondence here, if any, is highly controversial).

Among these Upper Paleolithic departures is the appearance of sophisticated figurative artwork (such as the cave paintings from Spain and southern France), which may have served religious or magical purposes for the people who created it. Archaeological finds also reveal the diffusion of microlith technologies, that is, the replacement of rather clumsy and cumbersome stone tools with smaller, more effective and increasingly fine implements (fishhooks, arrowheads, sewing needles, and so forth), usually made of stone but also of other materials such as animal bone. The development of such technologies reflects an increasing capacity to

Cave Paintings from Southern France. On the left, one of the many cave paintings discovered in 1994. On the right, a stylized depiction of reindeer by an inspired artist "of the French school" who worked about fifteen thousand years ago.

work with perishable materials (wood, antlers, and so on) that are only rarely preserved for archaeologists.

As fundamental as some of these changes were, the basic pattern of human life seems to have remained largely unchanged in the Upper Paleolithic Era. Virtually all human societies before 11,000 B.C.E. were nomadic; small bands of people, probably never exceeding more than a few dozen individuals, moved incessantly from place to place, hunting and gathering their food. Because they depended entirely on what the local environment provided for their survival, they could not stay in any one location for long. As a result, such societies leave no continuous archaeological record whereby we might trace the development of their culture. Our knowledge of these early human societies is therefore very limited.

The social, economic and political consequences of Paleolithic nomadism were profound. Because humans had no domestic animals to transport their goods, they could have no significant material possessions— wealth—aside from basic tools they could easily carry on their persons. Without the ability to accumulate goods over time, disparities in individual wealth, with their attendant distinctions of rank and status, were unlikely to develop. Such societies may well have been highly organized—it is a gross error to presume that early societies were necessarily primitive—but hierarchical structures of leadership were uncommon, and possibly unknown. When conflicts arose within a group, the usual solution was probably to divide and

separate—a process that might also have been necessary simply to keep the total numbers in the band commensurate with what the natural resources of the local area could support.

We do not know how labor was divided between the members of these Paleolithic bands. Although scholars once assumed that men did the hunting and women the gathering, such gendered presumptions do not reflect the complex realities of modern nomadism, and they may not be applicable to the Paleolithic period either. It is more likely that all members of a Paleolithic band (except for the very young and the very

Bison Carved from a Reindeer Horn. Perhaps the most graceful of all known European prehistoric carvings, this bison was carved from a piece of antler between fifteen thousand and twelve thousand years ago. Whatever its use might have been no one quite knows.

old) engaged to some extent in all the basic activities of the group. Acquiring food and tools must have been the first concern of nearly every member of the group. Specialization—the process by which some members of the group are freed up to engage in activities other than food acquisition—was nearly impossible. Specialization requires the accumulation of storable surpluses, and this was something Paleolithic nomads lacked the technology to accomplish.

THE NEOLITHIC REVOLUTION

What changes allowed the transition from nomadic to sedentary societies?

Significant changes in the patterns of human existence began to take shape only around 11,000 B.C.E., the dawn of the Neolithic or "New Stone" Age. These breakthroughs included the development of managed food production, the beginnings of semipermanent and permanent settlements, and the rapid intensification of trade, both local and long distance. For the first time, it became possible for individuals and communities to accumulate and store wealth on a large scale. The results were far reaching. Communities became more stable, and human societies more complex. Specialization developed, along with distinctions of status and rank. The "revolution" represented by the innovations of the Neolithic Era was a necessary step before cities in the truest sense could appear toward the end of the fourth millennium B.C.E.

THE ORIGINS OF FOOD PRODUCTION

During the Upper Paleolithic "Ice Age" (c. 40,000–11,000 B.C.E.) , daytime temperatures in Mediterranean Europe and Asia averaged about 60°F (16°C) in the summer and about 30°F (–1°C) in the winter. Accordingly, cold-loving game species such as reindeer, elk, wild boar, bison, and mountain goats roamed the hills and valleys. But as the last glaciers receded northward such species retreated with them. Some humans may have moved north with the game, but others stayed behind, creating an extremely different sort of world.

Specifically, within about three thousand to four thousand years after the end of the Ice Age, the peo-

ples living at the eastern end of the Mediterranean Sea accomplished one of the most momentous revolutions in human history: a switch from subsistence by food gathering to producing food for themselves. Substantial numbers of humans now began to domesticate animals and raise crops, thereby making possible greater permanence and stability in their settlement patterns. Stable settlements ultimately paved the way for other developments we associate with civilization: the emergence of cities, the development of writing, and the growth of scholarship. Although a process that takes several thousand years may seem less than "revolutionary" to our current sensibilities, it is important to remember that humans in a few small areas of the globe fundamentally altered, in a relatively short time, a pattern of survival that had existed for millions of years.

The story is roughly as follows. Around 11,000 B.C.E. most of the larger game herds had left southwestern Asia, part of the region (together with Egypt) known as the Near East. Yet people in territories that today lie in Turkey, Syria, Israel, and western Iran were not starving because the warmer and wetter climate created a nurturing environment for plentiful fields of wild grain. Because of the abundant natural food resources of the region (and its related agricultural productivity in later historical times), this arc through western Asia is often referred to as the Fertile Crescent. For at least part of the year, a society of humans could now count on plant resources plentiful enough to sustain a seasonal or permanent settlement. The shift from a nomadic to a sedentary existence had begun.

The emergence of semipermanent and permanent settlements, combined with attendant increases in overall food supply, had profound effects on human life. Most important, it produced a rapid increase in human numbers. By around 8000 B.C.E., however, the human population was beginning to exceed the natural carrying capacity of the land. To support this growing population, humans now had to take steps to increase the food-growing capacity of the land. This marked the beginnings of deliberately managed agriculture.

But the systematic and managed production of plant food also required a crucial intermediary step: storage. Even when plentiful, grain does not grow during the winter. By around 9500 B.C.E., however, peoples along the eastern coast of the Mediterranean (known as Natufians to prehistorians) had learned how to preserve their grain by digging storage pits. This strengthened their sedentary way of life: no longer were they forced to move away from their settled communities

WHAT CHANGES ALLOWED THE TRANSITION FROM NOMADIC TO SEDENTARY SOCIETIES?

THE NEOLITHIC REVOLUTION   11

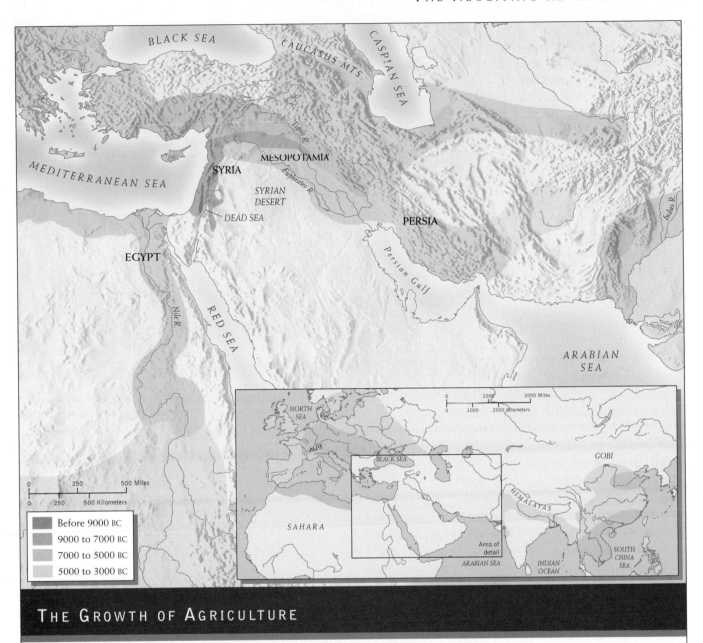

THE GROWTH OF AGRICULTURE

Examine the chronological progression of regions engaging in agriculture. What areas began practicing agriculture first? Consider why agriculture in the Asian Near East did not begin along river valleys, but spread there later. Notice the relationship of major rivers to the advance of agriculture. How might rivers have played a crucial role in the spread of farming technologies?

during the parts of the year when grain was not ready for harvesting. This in turn encouraged some Natufians to build more permanent, circular dwellings on stone foundations, although others continued to live in caves and other natural rock shelters.

Storage did more than simply reinforce a reluctance to move away from "home": after constructing their storage pits, the Natufians (and other early Neolithic peoples) probably also began to notice how grain began sprouting and rooting in or near the pits at the start of the spring rains. Once the importance of this observation impressed itself on the inhabitants of a sedentary community, they could begin to store grain not only for future consumption, but also to provide seed with which to produce more grain in the following year. This revelation had three important effects. First, humans could deliberately plant crops in a more concentrated fashion, thus producing the higher yields necessary to support a higher population (with the effect of growing the population even faster). Second, should nature fail to produce its usual abundance in a given year, both the grain and the seed needed to avert famine and the dissolution of the community would be at hand. Third, with intensification and storage, humans now had the surpluses they needed to support domestic animals, which they could now afford to feed all year.

The earliest archaeological evidence for fully sedentary agriculture comes from several areas in the Fertile Crescent between roughly 8500 and 7000 B.C.E. By 6000 B.C.E. much of the Near East (especially within the Fertile Crescent) had adopted agriculture as its primary mode of survival. In all these areas agriculture

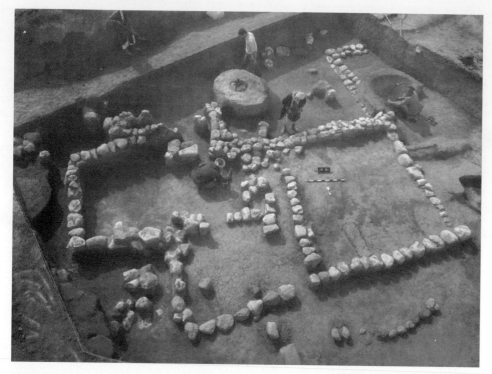

Stone Foundation of a Sedentary Dwelling. Once people in western Asia became agriculturalists, they began to build homes for year-round habitation. This stone foundation for a prehistoric house was found at the site of the village of Jarmo (in Iraq) and dates from about 6000 B.C.E.

was supplemented by domestic livestock, which by 7000 B.C.E. included cattle and pigs as well as sheep and goats. Animal protein was, of course, an ancient feature of human diet. Domestication, however, brought a host of benefits, guaranteeing not only a more reliable supply of meat, but also providing milk, leather, wool, bone, and horn for handicrafts.

Exactly how the shift to agriculture and the domestication of animals became so widespread so quickly is a matter of debate. It may be that similar demographic and environmental conditions around the region created a spontaneous shift to agriculture in several places at once. Some scholars have argued that large-scale migrations of populations with knowledge of agricultural methods spread the new technology. Still others believe that the spread was due to a slow but steady wave of new agriculturally based communities, founded beyond the "mother" settlements when the higher carrying capacity of the land, improved through agricultural technologies, still proved inadequate to growing populations. Other scholars see the role of trade networks as crucial to the diffusion of ideas about agriculture across the region. As is so often the case when dealing with such profound and fundamental change in human history, no single explanation suffices. All of these factors

must have played a role in the spread of agriculture across the Fertile Crescent and beyond, to Egypt and even the Balkans, by 5000 B.C.E.

THE GREAT VILLAGES OF THE NEAR EAST

The next steps in the Near East's accelerating evolution toward civilization were the emergence of villages and the concurrent rise of handicrafts, long-distance trade, and warfare, all made possible by the development of some degree of specialization. Villages constituted the most advanced form of human organization in western Asia from about 6500 to about 3500 or 3000 B.C.E., when some villages began to evolve into cities. A typical Near Eastern village numbered around one thousand inhabitants, but numbers could vary greatly. At first almost all of the able-bodied men and women engaged in field work, and all the women additionally in cloth production, but gradually there came to be full-time specialists in handicrafts, as well as a few full-time traders.

One of the first examples of the transition from preagricultural communities to fully agricultural and

WHAT CHANGES ALLOWED THE TRANSITION FROM NOMADIC TO SEDENTARY SOCIETIES?

THE NEOLITHIC REVOLUTION   13

completely sedentary settlements comes from Jericho in what is today northern Israel. The first continuous sequence of settlements at Jericho is associated with the preagricultural Natufians and typifies the trends we have already noted. Jericho emerged as a seasonal settlement around 9000 B.C.E., probably due to its abundant freshwater springs. Around 8000 B.C.E., however, the inhabitants of Jericho undertook a spectacular building program. Many new dwellings were built on stone foundations, and a massive, skillfully dressed stone wall was constructed around the entire settlement. Built into this perimeter wall was a circular tower, the excavated remains of which still reach to a height of thirty feet.

The precise function of this wall is impossible to know, but most likely it was intended as some sort of defense, perhaps as much against nature as human threats (Jericho lies several hundred feet below sea level and is thus vulnerable to flash floods and mudslides). The "watchtower" is even more puzzling and illustrates how difficult it is to interpret archaeological remains in the absence of written documents. Was the tower meant as a lookout post against foreign enemies and marauders, or did its ambitious height extend toward the heavens for some religious purpose? Whatever the case, the wall and its tower encircled and served an impressive population: the early site of Jericho covered 8 acres (almost 3.25 hectares) and supported a population of two to three thousand people. This population was sustained by the intense cultivation of recently domesticated strains of wheat and barley, irrigated by water from the nearby springs.

Starting in the eighth millennium B.C.E., Jericho's inhabitants also produced some of the earliest known pottery. The importance of this breakthrough, both for ancient culture and modern scholarship, cannot be overstated. For the settlers at Jericho, the invention of pottery enabled them to store more goods than ever before. Liquids in particular could now be preserved as an important part of the community's surplus. Pottery also made possible long-distance trade in such desirable commodities as beer, wine, and various oils. Pottery now provides archaeologists with a more precise means for dating prehistoric sites. Although individual ceramic objects are extremely fragile, fragments (shards) of broken pottery are virtually indestructible. Because styles of pottery changed very rapidly in the ancient world, archaeologists have been able to use pottery shards to create a more accurate (but still relative and rough) chronology for the world before recorded history.

Early Village Pottery. A shallow bowl from a western Asian village site dating from about 5000 B.C.E.

No less impressive than Jericho is Çatal Hüyük in the south central part of the Anatolian Plateau in modern Turkey. A somewhat later site than Jericho, Çatal Hüyük had its preeminence from 6500–5500 B.C.E. The agricultural technology of the inhabitants was quite advanced. They produced a wide range of vegetable foods, from peas and lentils to cereal crops. They also cultivated fruits and nuts. Meat and dairy products were also an important part of their diet; among much else, Çatal Hüyük provides us with our earliest indisputable evidence of domesticated cattle herds. But although their diets were relatively healthy, the people's life expectancies were short. Men died on average around the age of thirty-four, and women around the age of thirty.

Agricultural surpluses had important social consequences. Unlike hunter-gatherer societies, settled communities engaged in agriculture accumulated surpluses and stored commodities. This in turn allowed differences to arise in the amount of surplus wealth that individuals in a community could acquire and stockpile for themselves. Moreover, once humans became accustomed to sedentary agriculture, they found it much more difficult to split off from the community, even when the consequences of social and economic differentiation became oppressive. With agriculture, significant social and economic distinctions emerged within human societies for the first time.

At Jericho and Çatal Hüyük villagers speculated on

the supernatural powers they believed ruled their world, and how they might relate to those powers. This too was an immensely important step in the evolution of human culture. Further, the fact that humans believed these forces required special services and gifts in the form of ritual and sacrifice allowed for the emergence over time of a "priestly class," individuals uniquely qualified to commune with the supernatural forces that governed the life of the community. Such religious leadership was a natural bridge to more obviously "political" forms of authority: leading war bands, constructing defenses, and extracting resources from those subject to their authority. Through their command of the community's religious, military, and economic resources, village elites began to establish themselves as a self-justifying ruling class.

Trade was another important development in these early Neolithic villages. By 5000 B.C.E. a series of important long-distance trade networks had arisen across the Near East; local trade routes were undoubtedly even older, but are impossible to trace. Exotic goods were frequent objects of exchange: obsidian from Çatal Hüyük was an important commodity, as were precious stones such as turquoise, lapis lazuli, and jadeite. Marine shells were also prized across the region. Long-distance trade accelerated the exchange of commodities and ideas throughout the Fertile Crescent. At the same time, however, it also increased the degree of social stratification within these village communities. Long-distance trade was generally controlled by local elites, whose status was enhanced by their special access to high-prestige luxury goods. As a result, a self-perpetuating cycle developed. Trade encouraged the further stratification of society; elites, anxious to enhance their power and status, encouraged further trade as a way of acquiring even more economic and social power. Elites sought to control overland and overseas trade more effectively, and to organize the production of marketable goods within their own communities. As a result, control over specialist artisans emerged as an important feature of elite social status in these Neolithic village communities.

As this last example may suggest, what underlay all these social and economic changes was the economic specialization that agricultural surpluses made possible. In hunter-gatherer societies, every member of the community participated in the basic business of food

> What underlay all these social and economic changes was the economic specialization that agricultural surpluses made possible.

acquisition. In an organized agricultural community, however, certain people could devote at least a portion of their labor to pursuits other than agriculture: the making of pottery or cloth, the manufacture of weapons and tools, the design and construction of fortifications, the conduct of long-distance trade. Surpluses and specialization also permitted the emergence of social elites, who by organizing and exploiting the labor and production of others, were able to turn ruling into yet another specialist occupation. As villages grew larger and more sophisticated, the amount of specialization increased, until a significant fraction of the population could become full-time nonagriculturalists. This was the essential first step in the development of true urban-based civilizations.

CHRONOLOGY

FROM PREHISTORY TO HISTORY

Appearance of figurative artwork	40,000 B.C.E.
Origin of food production	11,000 B.C.E.
Beginnings of sedentary agricultural societies	7000 B.C.E.
Emergence of villages	6500–3000 B.C.E.
Development of writing	3300–2500 B.C.E.
Emergence of cities	3100 B.C.E.

MESOPOTAMIA: THE EMERGENCE OF THE FIRST CITIES AND PRIMARY CIVILIZATIONS

How did irrigation and temple building figure in early Mesopotamian civilization?

Surprisingly, the initial transition from prehistory to history, and the shift from village to city, did not take place in the Fertile Crescent. Rather, the first true cities

HOW DID IRRIGATION AND TEMPLE BUILDING FIGURE IN EARLY MESOPOTAMIAN CIVILIZATION?

MESOPOTAMIA   15

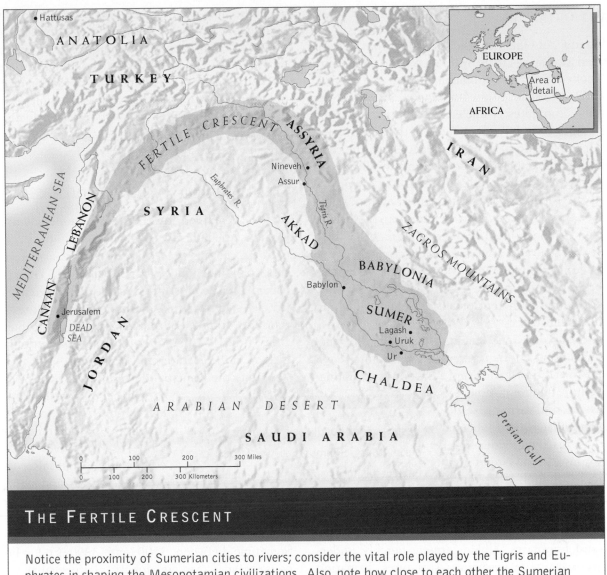

THE FERTILE CRESCENT

Notice the proximity of Sumerian cities to rivers; consider the vital role played by the Tigris and Euphrates in shaping the Mesopotamian civilizations. Also, note how close to each other the Sumerian city-states were. What challenges and opportunities did this phenomenon present? In what directions might Sumerian influence expand most quickly? Why?

developed in one of the most inhospitable environments imaginable—an area known later to the Greeks as Mesopotamia, "the land between the rivers." Corresponding roughly to the area of modern Iraq, Mesopotamia does not enjoy much rainfall, and summer temperatures routinely exceed 110°F. The soils of the region are sandy and infertile unless they are irrigated. And the two rivers that supply this flat and largely featureless plain with water—the Tigris and the Euphrates—are notorious for their violence and unpredictability. Both rivers are prone to flooding, and the Tigris could in ancient times jump its banks and

change course from one year to the next. Nevertheless, it was in this most uninviting of environments where the first true cities emerged. The civilization and people that arose in southern Mesopotamia are called Sumerian, and the area they inhabited known as Sumer. By 3100 B.C.E., the Sumerians had created one of the world's first primary civilizations, that is, a culture that "invented" the city without having adapted it from a previously established civilization. In order to understand how the Sumerians forged their civilization, we must therefore examine the roots of urban development in southern Mesopotamia.

UBAID CULTURE

The founders of Ubaid culture (so called from its best-described site at al-Ubaid in modern Iraq) appear to have moved into Mesopotamia around 5900 B.C.E. What attracted them to the unfriendly confines of the Tigris and Euphrates is unclear. Growing population densities may have forced them out of the Fertile Crescent. Or they could have been refugees from the catastrophic flooding that occurred around the Black Sea at this time, when the land bridge that had previously divided the Mediterranean Sea from what is now the Black Sea (but what was then an enormous freshwater lake) burst, inundating lakeshore settlements with a cascade of seawater. But whatever compelled the Ubaid peoples to move into Mesopotamia, it appears they brought their village culture with them. They were not hunter-gatherer nomads who had fallen into difficult circumstances.

The most consistent features of Ubaid life were ever-intensifying efforts to control their natural environment through irrigation and a pronounced emphasis on temple building. Almost as soon as we find farming settlements in what would become Sumer, we discover evidence for fairly sophisticated systems of irrigation. Although these may have begun as simple channels and collection pools to harness the excess waters from the periodic flooding of the Tigris and Euphrates, Ubaid farmers quickly undertook to create more permanent structures. Irrigation canals and ponds were excavated; soon thereafter, Ubaid peoples began lining them with stone so they would last from one season to the next. They also constructed dikes and levees to control the seasonal flooding of the rivers, and to direct the flow of water into the canals they had built for irrigation. Despite the hostile environment, Ubaid agricultural communities were soon producing surpluses sufficient to support specialists in weaving, pottery making, metalwork, trade, and construction—the typical attributes of a Neolithic village.

The inhabitants of these settlements also established central structures that served religious functions. Starting out as simple and fairly humble shrines, the edifices they erected soon evolved into impressive temples built of dried mud brick: the scarcity of stone in the region compelled them to save that material for tools. Each larger settlement had such a building,

Despite the hostile environment, Ubaid agricultural communities were soon producing surpluses sufficient to support specialists.

which became progressively larger with successive rebuildings. From these temples, a priestly class served both as the officiants of religious life in the settlements and as managers of the economic resources of the community. In this latter role, they organized not only the construction of ever-larger temples, but also developed and maintained the complex irrigation systems that made village life possible in the Mesopotamian desert.

URUK PERIOD (4300–2900 B.C.E.)

By the beginning of the fourth millennium B.C.E., Ubaid settlements were coalescing into larger and more prosperous sites, with ever more elaborate temples, buildings and village planning. This period, named after its most impressive site, the great Sumerian city-state of Uruk (modern Warka), witnessed the transition from Neolithic Ubaid villages to Sumerian cities. It marks, therefore, the true beginnings of civilization in the Mediterranean world.

Among the principal developments of the period is the further elaboration of temple architecture. This trend reflects not only the centrality of religion in the lives of these communities, but also the increasing wealth and control of the priestly class over communal life. The White Temple at Uruk provides a stunning example of this general trend. Sometime between 3500 and 3300 B.C.E., builders constructed a massive sloping platform that towered nearly forty feet above the surrounding flatlands. The platform, with its four corners at the cardinal points of the compass, was dressed in brick. Atop the platform stood another structure, the shrine or temple proper, also dressed in brick but painted a brilliant white. Per-

C H R O N O L O G Y

ORIGINS OF MESOPOTAMIAN SOCIETY

Ubaid Period	5900–4300 B.C.E.
Uruk Period	4300–2900 B.C.E.
Early Dynastic Period	2900–2500 B.C.E.
Akkadian Period	2350–2160 B.C.E.
Ur Dynasty	2100–2000 B.C.E.

HOW DID IRRIGATION AND TEMPLE BUILDING FIGURE IN EARLY MESOPOTAMIAN CIVILIZATION?

MESOPOTAMIA   17

haps dedicated to the sky god known in later Sumerian sources as An, the temple betrays an ambition to serve the gods with increasing monumentality, and—it has been suggested—to provide them with "mountaintop" homes in a part of the world conspicuous for its absence of mountains.

Such temples (which grew up across Sumer) reflect the increasingly urbanized character of Sumerian life. Throughout the region, smaller, satellite villages were falling under the control of the greater sites. Uruk, for example, organized under its management the various settlements and their separate irrigation systems extending for six miles in every direction. The larger villages were also growing rapidly, their teeming economic activity almost certainly attracting immigrants. Uruk and other principal centers were now characterized by densely packed dwellings accessed by winding streets. By the end of the Uruk Period Sumer also shared a common language, a fact made clear thanks to the invention that moves the Sumerians fully into the light of history: writing.

THE DEVELOPMENT OF WRITING

Like many of the breakthroughs we have considered in this chapter, the invention of writing did not occur overnight. For millennia, the villagers of the Near East had been using clay tokens to represent various commodities, perhaps to help them keep track of inventories and to facilitate the burgeoning trade of the region. Such tokens were cumbersome, however, especially for long-distance trade: imagine having to carry a different clay token to represent each piece of obsidian you carried as well as the obsidian itself! Merchants therefore began to create single tokens specifying both the nature and the number of their trade goods. Ultimately, the practice developed of placing all the tokens from a single transaction inside a hollow clay ball, and inscribing, on the outside of the ball, the shapes of all the tokens it contained. This helped not only to ensure accuracy of exchange, but probably also discouraged dishonest middlemen from skimming off the top of their cargos.

In its earliest phases, writing thus evolved as a means of record keeping in connection with economic pursuits. This origin meant it was natural and well suited for keeping track of the growing wealth of the Uruk Period protocities. By 3300 B.C.E., the priestly class (or those working for them) realized that they could dispense with the clumsy token-and-ball system and replace it with flat clay tablets, on which they could note the desired information by inscribing the appropriate symbols. For some time, this system remained purely pictographic: the symbols

Cuneiform Writing. On the left, a Sumerian clay tablet from about 3000 B.C.E. Here standardized pictures are beginning to represent abstractions. On the right, carvings on limestone from about 2600 B.C.E. The evolution of standardized cuneiform writing is now complete: the inscription proclaims that a king of Ur has built a temple.

marked into the clay represented physical objects, and often in some crude way resembled the objects in question. Over the course of time, however, the same symbol might be used to evoke not only a physical object, but an idea associated with that object. The symbol for a bowl of food, *ninda* (a noun) might thus be used to express a more abstract notion such as bread or sustenance—an idea not otherwise easily represented by a quick sketch into soft clay. Each symbol also came to be associated with a particular phonetic sound. The next stage in the evolution of writing was then to use a particular symbol not to evoke the thing it represented, but the sound with which it was associated. Thus any time a Sumerian scribe needed to employ the sound *ninda*, even as part of another word or name, he would use the symbol for a bowl of food. Later, special marks were added so that the reader could discern whether the writer intended the object itself or the *phonogram* (the sound represented by the symbol).

By 3100 B.C.E. scribes had largely abandoned writing with pointed sticks. Instead, they now used a more durable reed stylus to make symbols in clay, a stylus which left an impression shaped like a wedge (the Latin word for which is *cuneus*). We refer to the script rendered with this new writing implement as *cuneiform*. Cuneiform symbols could be impressed more quickly and efficiently into the soft clay, and the reeds themselves were less likely to break than were sticks. However, the new stylus made it more difficult to draw pictograms that accurately reflected the original shape (such as a bowl of food) they were meant to represent. As a result, the symbols of the language became more and more abstracted, until they barely resembled the original pictograms at all.

Symbols ultimately were invented for every possible vowel-consonant combination in the Sumerian language, and the symbols therefore ran into the hundreds. Understandably, it took many years to learn to read and write cuneiform, and only a small minority of the population ever did so. Those who did, however, became important and influential people in Sumerian society. For the entirety of the third millennium, it was largely the sons of the elite who attended the "Houses of the Tablet," as the scribal schools were called. But despite the wide variety of symbols and the complicated nature of the script, cuneiform proved remarkably durable. For over fifteen hundred years after its development, it remained the principal writing system of the Asian Near East, even in societies that no longer spoke the Sumerian language.

THE SUMERIANS ENTER HISTORY

Why did a common religion not create peace among the Sumerians?

After about 2500 B.C.E., the Sumerians used writing for a wide variety of economic, political, and religious purposes. Tens of thousands of these records survive, mostly in the form of clay tablets. These records make it possible for us to know a great deal more about the Sumerians than we do about any other human society of the time. We can begin to understand their political relationships, their feelings about their gods, and the social and economic structure of their society. The Sumerians are, in this sense, the first historical—as opposed to prehistorical—society.

The great centers of Sumerian culture—Uruk, Ur, Lagash, Eridu, Kish, and others—shared a common culture and a common language. The Sumerian language, however, appears not to be related to any other known language in the world. Attempts to relate it to the languages of the Asian subcontinent or those of western Asia have failed. This has led to bitter scholarly arguments over whether the Sumerians—a label applied to them by their neighbors—moved into southern Mesopotamia from elsewhere, or whether their unique culture (language included) developed out of Ubaid culture. The continuity of cult activity supports the latter view, as does the lack of any significant evidence for invasion; but ultimately, the question is unanswerable given the current state of knowledge on the subject.

Like language, religion was another shared element of Sumerian culture. The primacy accorded to temple building and the preeminence of the ruling priestly class continued down to the end of the Uruk period (c. 2900 B.C.E.). This common religion did not produce peace between the Sumerian cities, however. Although all Sumerian communities recognized the totality of the Sumerian pantheon (some fifteen hundred gods), the citizens of each city-state saw their city as the estate of one particular god, and sought through their endeavors to glorify their patron deity. The result was intense competition, which could easily escalate into open warfare.

A significant proportion of the cultivable land of each city belonged outright to the temple of the pa-

WHY DID A COMMON RELIGION NOT CREATE PEACE AMONG THE SUMERIANS?

THE SUMERIANS ENTER HISTORY   19

tron god, and much of the economic produce of the city was brought into the great temple-warehouse complexes. There the priests and their officials would determine the redistribution of the city's food and other goods. Each Sumerian city had a ruling aristocracy, from which the priests and important officials of the temples no doubt came; but it was the priests who stood at the top of these highly theocratic societies. In this early period of Sumerian civilization perhaps as much as half the population consisted of commoners, free persons who held small parcels of land sufficient to sustain themselves and make any required payments to the temple complex. The temples also had large numbers of legally free dependents engaged in activities ranging from the artisan workshops of the city's god (making pottery, working as smiths) to undertaking agricultural labor on temple lands. But the elites held the lion's share of nontemple land and exercised political and economic power. Commoners had few if any political rights, and their social and economic position seems to have eroded over time.

There were also large numbers of slaves in Sumerian society. The high degree of urbanization in many ancient civilizations required the production of surpluses substantial enough to support sizable numbers of priests, aristocrats, poets, artists and the like. Often such surpluses were produced through the labor of unfree persons. In Sumer, as elsewhere in the ancient world, slaves were often prisoners of war. If the slave came originally from another Sumerian city, there were strict limits on the master's power over him or her, and he or she had to be released after three years. Non-Sumerians could be held indefinitely, although there were means by which slaves might buy their freedom. Despite these safeguards, slaves in Sumer were still the chattel property of their owners. They could be beaten, punished, branded like animals, or bought and sold on their owner's whim. Although ancient slavery may not have been quite so horrible as more modern examples (such as that practiced in the New World), it was still a highly undesirable thing to be a slave.

Although the Sumerians shared a common language and religion, individual city-states were fiercely independent and frequently hostile to one another. Because the great centers identified themselves with particular gods, and the populations of those cities conceived of their activities as being dedicated to their patron deity, intense jealousy and competition among the Sumerian city-states resulted. The members of a Sumerian city would have considered any political submission or military defeat a disgrace and a failure; they had disappointed their patron deity and allowed him or her to be humiliated by the members of a community serving another god. Thus there was little possibility of greater political unification in Sumer once the pattern of domination by twelve great cities became set. Of course the tension between the Sumerian city-states also had an economic dimension: water rights and access to both arable land and trade routes were at stake. But the organization of Sumerian society meant that conflicts over economic resources by definition inevitably involved a religious dimension. To allow another god's city to encroach on the estate of your own patron deity was unthinkable. The Sumerians shared a common culture, but a common government was impossible.

> Commoners had few if any political rights, and their social and economic position seems to have eroded over time.

THE EARLY DYNASTIC PERIOD, PHASES I AND II (2900–2500 B.C.E.)

As we have seen, Mesopotamian society was dominated by the religious elite from the Ubaid period until the early part of the third millennium. Religion remained central to Sumerian thought and experience throughout the history of this people. However, the intense competition and rivalry between the Sumerian city-states allowed for the emergence of a new type of leadership that would compete for preeminence with the priesthood within Sumerian cities: war leadership and, as it evolved, something we might recognize as kingship. This has led historians to term this phase of Sumerian civilization the Early Dynastic Period.

Around 2900 B.C.E. conflicts between the great centers of Sumerian civilization intensified. As each city-state grew larger (with anywhere from ten thousand to fifty thousand inhabitants), it invariably found its frontiers colliding with those of other cities and, with its population still expanding, was more desperate than ever to secure the necessary resources to survive. In the harsh deserts of southern Mesopotamia, threats to irrigation rights and access to cultivable land were life-and-death matters. Warfare now became a regular feature of Sumerian life, and those individuals who could most successfully lead armies into battle and defend the interests of the city and its god acquired tremendous prestige and power. A variety of titles denoted authority in Sumerian society: *en* ("lord"), *ensi* ("governor"), and *lugal* (literally, "big man"). The last of these, *lugal*, became the favorite choice of those men who managed to put themselves in positions of authority by way of their martial ability.

Within Sumerian society the *lugal* soon eclipsed the power of the temple priesthood, but we should not think of his role as secular. Far from it: the *lugal* led the armies of the city's god into battle, and once the position of *lugal* became institutional, hereditary, and supreme, these men were careful to surround their power with the approval and holiness of the city's patron deity. Sumerian kingship was no more "secular" than the temple—with all of its political and economic pursuits—was purely "religious." Rather than a struggle between "religious" and "secular" authority, what developed was a certain tension between the power of the temple and the power of the palace, with the officials of each believing they should hold chief importance in the lives of the community. In practice, however, the power of the *lugal* grew throughout the Early Dynastic Period, as demonstrated by two important documents, the Sumerian King List and the Epic of Gilgamesh.

The Sumerian King List was originally composed toward the end of the third millennium, perhaps c. 2125 B.C.E.; but it draws on earlier sources and is clearly an attempt, probably by the priests at the important city of Eridu, to identify the origins of kingship and the individuals who had exercised such authority in the past. It is characteristic of the King List, as with much Near Eastern literature, that its authors attempted to recapture and rationalize a long-lost and mythical past, ascribing impossibly long reigns (tens of thousands of years, in some cases) to their ancient kings. The King List does, however, preserve some historically credible information. It begins with a story about a Great Flood, just possibly a memory of the great inundations that resulted around 5500 B.C.E. when the land bridge between the Mediterranean and the Black Sea collapsed. The King List's primary concern, however, is to demonstrate the continuity of Sumerian kingship as an institution handed down from heaven. As a result, the King List creates the impression that Sumer was more politically unified than it actually was: no Sumerian *lugal* extended his domain over a city other than his own until

at least 2600 B.C.E., although the King List would have its readers believe otherwise. Nonetheless, its concern to demonstrate the continuity and power of *lugal*-ship is itself telling; by the later third millennium, when the King List was composed, real power was perceived as residing with the *lugal*, not with the heads of the temple priesthood.

The Epic of Gilgamesh is a very different kind of source. It is a literary document, the first of its kind in world history, that recounts the exploits of a legendary king of Uruk named Gilgamesh. The epic enjoyed tremendous popularity and staying power throughout the Near East, being translated and copied for well over two thousand years after the original Sumerian version was composed. Scholars have reconstructed a significant proportion of the tale from the various fragments— some lengthy, some meager— discovered over the course of the last century. Although the composite nature of the epic as it exists today means that we may not have a "version" of the Gilgamesh story exactly like that read in ancient Sumer, most experts agree that the epic as we have it largely reflects Sumerian society and culture around the middle of the third millennium B.C.E.

> The King List's primary concern is to demonstrate the continuity of Sumerian kingship as an institution handed down from heaven.

The character Gilgamesh was a powerful *lugal* who had won his reputation through military conquest and general heroism, particularly against barbarians. (One occupational hazard of city-dwellers was that their collections of "fixed assets" made them attractive and tempting targets not only for other cities, but for nomads.) Through the fame and prestige he acquired, he became so powerful that he could surmount many of the conventions of his day. We hear at the start of the epic how the people complained about their king, even though they still revered him: he kept their sons away at war for too long; he showed no respect for the nobles, carousing with their wives and daughters as he pleased; he disappointed them by his sacrilegious conduct. They prayed to the gods for relief, and ultimately a wild man named Enkidu was fashioned by the deities to challenge Gilgamesh.

The confrontation between Gilgamesh and Enkidu is rich with historically useful information. Gilgamesh is a creature of the city, but his challenger is of the wilderness, barely more than a beast himself until he is "civilized" by a sexual tryst with a temple prostitute— an urban, specialist profession to say the least. After his contact with her, Enkidu is unable to return to the sim-

WHY DID A COMMON RELIGION NOT CREATE PEACE AMONG THE SUMERIANS?

THE SUMERIANS ENTER HISTORY   21

ple life, and the animals of the wilderness no longer speak to him; in Sumerian terms, his urbanization had literally made a man out of him.

This episode reflects the dichotomy the Sumerians perceived between city and wilderness, between what was "civilized" and what was not. We recognize in Enkidu the hunter-gatherer who was doubtless far more intimate with nature than were the Sumerians after centuries of civic life; but such "naturalness" was not a quality the Sumerians admired. The epic does not intend to provoke sympathy for Enkidu's loss of innocence; instead, that loss allows him to fulfill his destiny—to become human so he can first fight and then befriend the king of Uruk. Such disdain on the part of the urbanized and civilized toward those who were uncivilized is voiced in almost every ancient civilization. Even Aristotle's famous dictum that "Man is a political animal" means, in essence, that humans are creatures who must live in cities; otherwise, they cannot be fully human.

The episode following the friendship forged between Gilgamesh and Enkidu illustrates the hostility and fear Sumerians felt toward the wilderness. The two men set off into the forest to do battle with a terrifying nature demigod named Humbaba, who nearly bests the heroes. In the end, however, they prevail, another triumph of civilized humanity over a natural world that would destroy humanity and its creations if it gained the upper hand. Given the harsh climate and unpredictable environment in which the Sumerians lived, their adversarial relationship with the natural world is understandable. Battling uncooperative rivers, searing heat, salinization of the soil, and the raids of less civilized folk, the Sumerians developed a pessimistic attitude toward their natural environment that is mirrored not only in their general view of life, but also in their view of the gods.

SUMERIAN RELIGION

One of the Sumerian creation stories held that people had been created when the powerful god Enlil used the wind to separate the male heaven from the female earth, and then fashioned a pickax with which he broke open the earth. Through this fissure, humankind—already created inside the earth—was able to emerge and populate the surface of the world. The Sumerians thus believed that humanity itself had been

wrested from the inhospitable earth and created for one purpose, to serve the gods. Every aspect of Sumerian society and culture was thus imbued with religiosity. Their art, architecture, and literature all reflected the Sumerians' concern with fulfilling their duties. Throughout the third millennium, much of any Sumerian city's economy continued to be centered on the chief temple and administered by the huge hierarchy of priests and priestesses, entertainers and seers, eunuchs and temple slaves who kept the temples teeming with sacred activity. However much a powerful *lugal* might distance himself from the temple priesthood, it was axiomatic that his authority was also divinely inspired and bestowed, his kingship a gift from heaven.

We should not assume, though, that relations between humans and gods were warm. Gods were on the one hand to be exalted; massive temples called ziggurats, made of dried mud brick and reaching into the sky, evolved out of the increasingly elaborate shrines of the Uruk Period. The great ziggurat to a city's patron deity would have been the central architectural feature of the community—a *lugal's* palace might rival it in splendor, but for sheer awe-inspiring conspicuousness, the ziggurat was unmatched. That such effort and expense continued to be poured into honoring the gods tells us that however much a king might have eclipsed the temple priesthood, the latter was by no means weak. The gods remained a critically important part of the lives of Sumerians, who went to great pains to honor their gods dutifully with temples, festivals, and sacrifices.

> The Sumerians thus believed that humanity itself had been wrested from the inhospitable earth and created for one purpose, to serve the gods.

Affection for the gods, however, was not the primary motivation. Fear and suspicion characterized the Sumerian attitude toward divinity. They expected the gods to be cruel, mean-spirited, and capricious, attending to their own whims with little care for the effect those whims might have on humanity, whether positive or negative. Like most ancient peoples, the Sumerians sought primarily to appease their gods through the proper performance of rituals and sacrifices, in hopes the gods would remain favorable to the city and its inhabitants. A benign detachment toward humanity was what most Sumerians sought from their gods. To ask for more could be dangerous. Appeals to the gods for help were a last resort in desperate circumstances, for inviting the gods to involve themselves directly in human life could have unforeseen and often unpleasant consequences.

Sumerian Ziggurat. This edifice, built in Ur around 2100 B.C.E., is the best-preserved surviving ziggurat. As can be seen from the diagram of its original form at left, a shrine, reached by climbing four stories and passing through a massive portal, was the goal of the worshiper's ascent and the most sacred part of the temple.

The Sumerian view of an afterlife was similarly grim. Whatever devotion one might pay to the gods in this world, it was only in this world that one might enjoy the benefits. The Sumerians, despite their complex pantheon and sophisticated theology, never developed a refined sense of an afterlife. They expected neither eternal punishment nor reward. Instead, the dead simply crossed a man-eating river into the "Land of No Return," a gloomy place which enjoyed no light. Relatives might bury the dead with basic articles such as food and clothing, and diversions such as musical instruments and games, in the hope of making the glum, unhappy underworld a bit more bearable for the departed. In many ways, the afterlife was thus a continuation of the anxious, pessimistic existence of this world, only worse.

With such pessimism came a degree of quiet resignation toward the unpleasantness and ultimate futility of life. When his friend Enkidu is killed by the goddess

Inanna (whom both Gilgamesh and Enkidu have mocked), Gilgamesh's horror at Enkidu's death propels him to seek immortality for himself. Against the advice of other characters, he continues his quest until he learns of a plant of eternal life at the bottom of a

Sumerian Praying Figures. These statues dating from about 2700 B.C.E. show Sumerians praying for the gods to bring them prosperity.

THE FLOOD: TWO ACCOUNTS

The Epic of Gilgamesh preserves a traditional account of a destructive flood sent by the gods to punish humanity. As we have seen, the tale of Gilgamesh originated in the early third millennium B.C.E., meaning that it predates biblical accounts by at least fifteen hundred years, if not more. The stunning similarity between the versions of Gilgamesh and the Book of Genesis is evidence of the strong cultural influence exerted by older Near Eastern civilizations on the early Hebrews.

THE EPIC OF GILGAMESH

[Utnapishtim said to Gilgamesh]: "High up the constant Euphrates there rests a place you call Shurrupak, where gods and goddesses recline. Then came the flood, sent by gods' intent. . . . [The god] Ea [gave] me this advice: 'Arise and hear my words: abandon your home and build a boat. Reject the stinking stench of wealth. . . . Take the seed of all you need aboard with you and carefully weigh anchor after securing a roof that will let in no water.' . . . By week's end I engineered designs for an acre's worth of floor upon the ark we built . . . 120 cubits measured its deck. . . . Pitch for the hull I poured into the kiln. . . . My clan brought on the food they'd eat and all the things we thought we'd need. At last it was my turn just then to shepherd beasts and birds and babies wet and loud. . . . The sky screamed and storms wrecked the earth. . . . Flood ended. . . . I released the watch-bird, to soar in search of land. The bird came back within a day exhausted,

unrelieved from lack of rest. I then released a swallow, to soar in search of land, [which also returned]. I then released a raven, to soar in seach of land. The bird took flight above more shallow seas, found food and found release and found no need to fly back to me. . . . [I] offered sacrifice [spreading] the scents that gods favored. When [the god] Enlil saw the boat, he released his calm reason and released the Igigi, monsters of blood. 'What force dares defy my anger? How dare a man still be alive?' . . . Then with these words Ea himself said to Enlil: 'How dare you drown so many little people without consulting me? Why not just kill the one who offended you, drown only the guilty?' . . . [Enlil] gently raised me from the slime, placed my wife beside my kneeling form, and blessed us both at once with hands upon our bowed heads."

Danny P. Jackson, trans. *The Epic of Gilgamesh*, Tablet XI, Columns I–IV. (Wauconda, Ill.: Bolchazy-Carducci Publishers, 1997), pp. 78–82.

BOOK OF GENESIS

The Lord saw that the wickedness of humankind was great in the earth and . . . said "I will blot out from the earth the human beings I have created . . . for I am sorry I have made them." But Noah found favor in the

sight of the Lord. . . . God saw that the earth was corrupt and . . . said to Noah, "I have determined to make an end to all flesh. . . . Make yourself an ark of cypress wood; make rooms in the ark, and cover it inside and out with pitch. . . . Make a roof for the ark, and put the door of the ark in its side. . . . For my part I am going to bring a flood on the earth, to destroy from under heaven all flesh. . . . But I will establish a covenant with you; and you shall come into the ark, you, your sons, your wife, and your sons' wives with you. And of every living thing you shall bring two of every kind into the ark, to keep them alive with you. . . . Also take with you every kind of food that is eaten." . . . All the fountains of the great deep burst forth, and the windows of the heavens were opened. . . . The waters gradually receded from the earth. . . . At the end of forty days, Noah opened a window of the ark . . . and sent out the raven, and it went to and fro until the waters were dried up from the earth. Then he sent out the dove from him, to see if the waters had subsided from the

face of the ground, but the dove found no place to set its foot, and it returned. . . . He waited another seven days, and again sent out the dove [which] came back to him . . . and there in its beak was a freshly plucked olive leaf; so Noah knew the waters had subsided from the earth. Then he . . . sent out the dove, and it did not return to him anymore. . . . Noah built an altar to the Lord . . . and offered burnt offerings. And when the Lord smelled the pleasing odor, the Lord said in his heart, "I will never again curse the ground because of humankind . . . nor will I ever again destroy every living creature as I have done.". . . God blessed Noah and his sons.

Genesis 6:5–9:1, *The New Oxford Annotated Bible.* (Oxford: Oxford University Press, 1994).

deep pool. Gilgamesh swims to the bottom and retrieves it, only to have it stolen from him as he surfaces by a serpent, who then disappears below with Gilgamesh's only chance for immortality. In the end, Gilgamesh, the great king of Uruk, ponders the futility of all human endeavor. Reflecting on the impermanence of his own deeds, even of Uruk's walls, he asks, "Why do I bother working for nothing? Who even notices what I do?"

SCIENCE, TECHNOLOGY, AND TRADE

Despite their doubt and gloominess, the Sumerians were not paralyzed by their uncertainties. Indeed, their general suspicion of the gods and their adversarial relationship with the environment seem to have inculcated in the Sumerians a high degree of self-reliance, and a number of indispensable inventions—beyond writing—are the result of Sumerian ingenuity.

The Sumerians were first-rate metallurgists, despite the fact that their land had no natural mineral resources. By the end of the Neolithic Age, a number of cultures throughout the Near East had learned how to produce copper weapons and tools. Mesopotamia itself had no copper, but by the Uruk Period (4300–2900 B.C.E.), trade routes were bringing raw copper into Sumer, where the Sumerians processed it and hammered it into weapons and tools. Shortly before 3000 B.C.E., perhaps starting in eastern Anatolia, people discovered that copper could be alloyed with arsenic (or later, tin) to produce bronze. Bronze is almost as malleable as copper, but pours more easily

Sumerian War Chariots. The earliest known representation of the wheel, dating from about 2600 B.C.E., shows how wheels were carpentered together from slabs of wood. (For a later Mesopotamian wheel with spokes, see the illustration on p. 59.) We can also observe that at the dawn of recorded history, military aims stimulated technological innovation, as they have ever since.

WHY DID A COMMON RELIGION NOT CREATE PEACE AMONG THE SUMERIANS?

THE SUMERIANS ENTER HISTORY   25

into molds and, when cooled, maintains its rigidity and shape better than copper. Because of the widespread use of bronze in which the Sumerians and the neighboring cultures engaged, we refer to a Bronze Age beginning around 3000 B.C.E.

Alongside writing, the invention of the wheel stands at the top of any list of fundamental advancements in human technology. The Sumerians were using potters' wheels by the middle of the fourth millennium B.C.E., allowing for the production of high-quality clay vessels in greater quantity than ever before. By around 3200 B.C.E., the Sumerians were also using two-wheeled chariots and four-wheeled carts drawn by donkeys. (Horses were unknown in western Asia until they were introduced by eastern invaders sometime between 2000 and 1700 B.C.E.). The chariots and carts were mounted on wheels that were solid, not spoked: two or three slabs of wood were shaped into a circle and fastened together with studs or braces. Wheeled chariots were used mainly in warfare; surviving illustrations from about 2600 B.C.E. depict them trampling the enemy. Wheeled carts were an even more important advance, however, because they dramatically increased the productivity of the Sumerian work force.

The use of the wheel in pottery may have suggested its application for transport, but such a connection is far from inevitable. The Egyptians were using the potter's wheel by at least 2700 B.C.E., but they did not use the wheel for transport until a millennium later, and even then they probably learned of it from Mesopotamia. In the Western Hemisphere, wheeled transport was unknown (except for children's toys) until the sixteenth century C.E. We should not underestimate, therefore, either the importance or the uniqueness of Sumerian wheel technology.

The Sumerians were also pioneers in the study of mathematics. Their mathematical interests may have been encouraged by the nature of Sumerian agriculture: to construct their elaborate systems of irrigation canals, dikes, and reservoirs, they had to develop sophisticated measuring and surveying techniques, as well as the art of map making. Agricultural concerns probably also lay behind the lunar calendar they invented, which consisted of twelve months, six lasting thirty days, and six lasting twenty-nine days. Since this produced a year of only 354 days, the Sumerians eventually discovered that they had to add a month to their calendars every few years in order to predict the recurrence of the seasons with sufficient accuracy. But the Sumerian practice of dividing time into multiples of sixty has lasted to the present day, not only in our notions of the thirty-day month (which corresponds approximately with the phases of the moon), but also in our division of the hour into sixty minutes, and the minute into sixty seconds. Mathematics also contributed to Sumerian architecture, allowing the people to build domes and arches thousands of years before the Romans would rediscover them.

An assortment of other breakthroughs are also credited to the Sumerians. They developed the bronze plow, complete with attachments for depositing seed as the ground was broken, a labor-saving device that increased the efficiency and productivity of Sumerian agriculture. Sumerians developed the first sailboats, crucial for their quest to exploit overseas trade along the shores of the Persian Gulf and beyond. They used the raw materials of other lands to manufacture textiles, paints, perfumes, and medicines. Indeed, by the

A Sumerian Plow with a Seed Drill. Such plows were still being used in the seventh century B.C.E., when this black stone tablet was engraved.

middle of the third millennium, the Sumerians had invented something like a science of pharmacology, producing drugs to cure ailments they had once ascribed to divine displeasure or possession.

The Sumerians' ability to engage in these activities depended, however, on the acquisition of raw materials through trade, for their homeland was almost completely devoid of natural resources. The Sumerians therefore pioneered trade routes up and down the Tigris and Euphrates and into the hilly flanks of Mesopotamia, following the tributaries of these great rivers. They blazed trails across the deserts toward the west, where they interacted with and influenced the Egyptians. By sea, they traded with the peoples of the Persian Gulf and, directly or indirectly, with the civilizations of the Indus Valley. Like the Neolithic traders who conveyed goods from village to village, the Sumerians carried their ideas with them along with their merchandise: their literature, their art, their use of writing, and the whole cultural complex that arose from their urban way of life. From its Sumerian roots, the idea of civilization thus spread throughout the ancient Near Eastern world.

THE DYNAMISM OF THE EARLY DYNASTIC PERIOD, PHASE III (2500–2350 B.C.E.)

Contemporary records from the final phase of the Early Dynastic Period allow us to describe it in more detail than earlier epochs of Sumerian history. Competition among the Sumerian city-states for prestige, power, and resources now reached a fever pitch. Intercity warfare intensified, as did attempts by ambitious *lugal*s to magnify the standing of themselves and their cities. At the same time, the tensions that had once existed between temple aristocracy and royal power were lessening, leaving *lugal*s freer to exercise their authority than they had been in earlier ages. *Lugal*s now included the priesthood more extensively than ever before in the process of choosing and legitimating successors, while the priestly aristocracy gave greater religious function and sanctification to the kingship.

The coalescence of a more politically and religiously unified elite, however, meant that the wider population had even less of a voice than before. More and more

Objects from the Royal Tombs at Ur. On the right, a queen's headdress, made of gold leaf, lapis lazuli, and carnelian. On the left, a helmet made of an alloy of gold and silver. Its cloth lining would have been attached through the holes visible around the edges of the helmet.

WHY DID A COMMON RELIGION NOT CREATE PEACE AMONG THE SUMERIANS?

THE SUMERIANS ENTER HISTORY   27

commoners fell into debt slavery as their economic, social, and political standing declined. Once useful allies to both royal and priestly authority, the commoners no longer had any political value to either side, now that kings and priests no longer vied with one another for supremacy. So diminished had their lot become that by the close of Early Dynastic (ED) III, a *lugal* of Lagash named Urukagina set down rules to try to protect the downtrodden commoners.

Such attempts at reform were ineffective. The final phase of the Early Dynastic period witnessed a tremendous concentration of wealth and power at the top of Sumerian society. The royal tombs of Ur, dating from 2550 B.C.E. to 2450 B.C.E., provide a breathtaking demonstration of this phenomenon. Within these tombs are found the fruits of virtually every Sumerian cultural advance. Striking architectural features surrounded astonishing displays of wealth, including trade goods, ceremonial chariots, oxen, and most surprising of all, the bodies of scores of members of the royal household, from ladies-in-waiting to guards to entertainers. The presence of so many people in the royal tombs has inspired heated debate as to whether the Sumerians practiced human sacrifice. The excavator of the tombs believed that they had willingly gone to their deaths by drinking poison, a self-sacrifice so they could remain with their masters. At present, however, the question remains unresolved.

The wealth displayed in these tombs—both human and material—indicates the growing stature of the royalty, and points also to a shift in Sumerian ideas about the afterlife. It appears that at least a few members of Sumerian society—namely the kings and their supporters—now believed they would enjoy a different, better kind of afterlife, and that their tombs were stocked specifically for this purpose. Could this have been an idea the Sumerians borrowed from the pharaohs of Egypt? At present, we can only speculate. Such practices do give us some sense, however, of just how lofty the power of the *lugal* had become, and of the divide that had by now opened up between leaders and followers in Sumerian society.

The relatively rich documentary evidence from this period concerns itself largely with the military exploits of these powerful kings. We learn of a cycle of brutal warfare among the leading city-states, as the *lugal* of each sought to establish his supremacy over the others. In and of itself, this was nothing new; the great *lugals*

of earlier ages had also claimed dominion on the basis of military victories over both barbarian and rival Sumerian armies. During ED I the king of Kish had established such dominion, and later strongmen of Sumer—regardless of their actual seat of power—would arrogate to themselves the title of "king of Kish." In ED III, however, the pattern intensified as the struggle to maintain access to resources and trade routes became ever more desperate.

An emerging secondary civilization to the east of Sumer—the Elamites of present-day southwest Iran—also played a pivotal if indirect role in the story of ED III. Under the influence of their Sumerian neighbors, the Elamites had become increasingly urbanized and specialized, and therefore more dangerous. Indeed, the final phase of the Early Dynastic period sees increasing aggression on the part of the Elamites toward Sumer. Most exposed to the danger were the eastern Sumerian city-states of Umma and Lagash. But both communities were galvanized by the threat, and produced dynamic leaders in response to it.

By defeating the Elamites, the armies of Umma and Lagash became the most powerful in Sumer, and the *lugals* of these two cities vied for the title of "king of Kish". Around 2450 B.C.E., the *lugal* Eannatum of Lagash expelled the Elamites and even claimed to have conquered Elam, thus safeguarding Sumer for the foreseeable future. He then turned his attention on Umma, Lagash's nearby rival, only eighteen miles away. After humbling his powerful neighbor, Eannatum extended his dominion over the rest of Sumer, declaring himself not only king of Kish but also "He Who Subjects All the Lands."

Eannatum is a particularly interesting figure because we have contemporary documentation for his actions and claims, found on the Stele of the Vultures, a limestone slab that survives in fragments. On the stele (inscribed stone monument), Eannatum describes in both words and pictures his victory over Umma and the peace terms he imposed on the city. The document thus records in vivid detail the issues between the cities, and testifies to the vicious nature of the resulting warfare. One register on the stele portrays Eannatum in military dress leading well-armed troops in formation, trampling the bodies of his foes. Another scene, from which the stone takes it name, shows vultures carrying away the severed heads and limbs of Eannatum's defeated enemies. Sumerians shared a common

> Sumerians shared a common culture and religion, but this did not deter them from brutalizing one another pitilessly.

culture and religion, but this did not deter them from brutalizing one another pitilessly.

Umma would have its revenge roughly a century later, when it came under the rule of the forceful Lugalzagesi. This man had usurped the throne of Umma, and had incorporated his new title into his name as a way of legitimating his position. Like Eannatum, he led the battle-hardened armies of his home city to victory over the rival states of Sumer, and by 2360 B.C.E. could lay claim to the title of King of Kish. Although he claimed to have conquered "from the Lower Sea to the Upper Sea" (by which he meant from the Persian Gulf to the Mediterranean), the truth was rather different. Like most Sumerian strongmen before him, he had defeated his enemies in war and forced them to acknowledge his supremacy by paying him tribute. He did not claim direct sovereignty over them, however, probably because he could not imagine doing so.

One of the fundamental strengths of Sumerian civilization—the self-reliant and independent dynamism of the powerful city-states—would prove to be one of its basic shortcomings by the twenty-fourth century B.C.E. The interwoven nature of Sumerian politics and religion meant that to destroy another Sumerian city or completely subject it to the will of another necessarily humiliated the patron god of that city. As the Sumerians recognized a pantheon in common, they seem to have been uneasy about denigrating any god so blatantly. Their ingrained competition and will to self-determination prompted the Sumerians to innovate technologically, but it also precluded any meaningful attempt at greater political unification or integration. Left to its own devices, Sumer would probably have remained a collection of independent city-states, each one forced periodically to acknowledge the domination of one of its rivals.

THE AKKADIAN PERIOD (2350–2160 B.C.E.)

But Sumer was not left to its own devices. The impulse toward unification came from within Sumerian civilization, but the energy that made unification possible came from an "outsider," Sargon of Akkad. Sargon was not Sumerian but rather Akkadian. The Akkadians were the predominant people of central Mesopotamia to the north of Sumer, and by the 2400s had been greatly in-

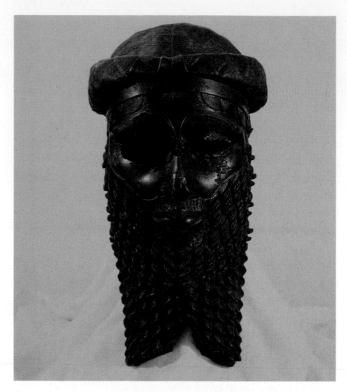

Naram-Sin. A bronze head thought to depict Sargon's grandson and successor.

fluenced by them. The Akkadians preserved their own language, however, a member of the Semitic family of tongues (which includes such languages as Assyrian, Aramaic, Hebrew, Arabic, and Ethiopic; we will have occasion to consider Semitic speakers more fully in the next chapter). As an "outsider," Sargon seems not to have been bound by the traditional assumptions and conventions of Mesopotamian warfare. Instead, he launched a systematic program of conquest, beginning around 2360 B.C.E. while Lugalzagesi was still establishing his own sway over Sumer itself. Within a decade, Sargon had subjected all of the areas around Sumer, completely surrounding the region. Unlike Lugalzagesi, Sargon did in fact campaign from the Upper to the Lower Sea, gaining control of vital trade routes. Around 2350 B.C.E., he defeated Lugalzagesi of Umma. Only when it was too late did the Sumerians realize that Sargon now had their land by the throat.

After ruthlessly organizing all of Mesopotamia under his centralized rule, Sargon founded a new capital which he called Akkad, just north of Kish. From there he appointed mostly Akkadian-speaking governors to

> The Sumerians' ingrained competition prompted them to innovate technologically, but it also precluded any meaningful attempt at greater political unification.

WHY DID A COMMON RELIGION NOT CREATE PEACE AMONG THE SUMERIANS?

THE SUMERIANS ENTER HISTORY   29

rule the cities of Sumer, pull down fortifications, collect taxes, and do the will of the new king. Sargon had, for the first time in history, supplanted the city with a much larger political unit as the basis for organization: a kingdom or empire. Sargon supported his empire (arguably the first true empire in human history) by managing and exploiting the network of trade routes that crisscrossed the Near East. As a result, his economic influence stretched from Ethiopia to the Indus Valley. Sargon made his capital the most splendid city in the world, and he exercised unprecedented power for fifty-six years.

Sargon was eventually succeeded by his talented grandson, Naram-Sin, who reigned, like his grandfather, for over a half century. Naram-Sin extended the Akkadian conquests, and consolidated caravan and overseas trade routes. An energetic promoter of culture and a patron of the arts, Naram-Sin encouraged literary and artistic endeavors throughout his realm. By dint of conquest and the quickened pace of commerce, he also helped to stimulate the growth of cities throughout the Near East. Like many conquerors in the ancient world, Sargon and Naram-Sin were products of urban life who found it easier to rule cities and to rule from them. Cities also facilitated trade, making it more convenient and more profitable. For all these reasons, these Akkadian rulers saw the proliferation of urban settlements as advantageous.

> Although the Akkadians worshiped their own Akkadian deities, they were careful to respect and revere the gods and practices of the Sumerians.

Although the Akkadians' emphasis on political centralization and imperial organization represented a clear break with the Sumerian past, culturally the Sumerians and Akkadians differed little from one another. By the twenty-third century B.C.E. most people in central and southern Mesopotamia would have been able to converse in either language. Much of Akkadian literature and art was at its root Sumerian, translated and slightly transformed to appeal to Akkadian tastes. And although the Akkadians worshiped their own Akkadian deities, they were careful to respect and revere the gods and practices of the Sumerians. Scholars speak of a Sumero-Akkadian cultural synthesis, and indeed after the reign of Sargon the two civilizations were virtually indistinguishable except for their different languages. Despite its new imperial trappings, the urban model Sargon and Naram-Sin helped to promote was still essentially the urban model of the Sumerians.

A SUMERIAN "RENAISSANCE": UR DYNASTY III (2100–2000 B.C.E.)

Court intrigue and a series of weak successors followed the long reign of Naram-Sin. By around 2160, most of Sumer and Akkad were under the rule of an invading

A Sumerian Banquet. This fine inlay, made of shell and lapis lazuli, shows animals and foodstuffs (lower two levels) being carried to a banquet (top level), perhaps held to celebrate the military victory illustrated on the opposite side.

hill people from the Iranian Plateau, the Gutians. When Sumerian civilization later recovered and re-asserted itself, Sumerians and Akkadians alike would view this period as a "Dark Age," a shameful period of foreign domination. But although the Gutians may have been uncivilized when they arrived, they quickly adapted themselves to Sumero-Akkadian culture. So thoroughly did they assimilate that they have left no archaeological remains to distinguish them from the Sumerians and the Akkadians whom they conquered. For all of its drawbacks, urban life as it had developed in Mesopotamia was simply too attractive for most invaders to resist.

After the Gutian interlude, Sumer became once again a constellation of rival, independent city-states. Around 2100 B.C.E., however, a new dynasty from Ur, the so-called Ur Dynasty III, established itself under the rule of its first king, Ur-Nammu, and his son Shulgi. Ur-Nammu was responsible for the construction of the great ziggurat at Ur, which towered seventy feet above the surrounding plain, and for many other architectural marvels. Shulgi promulgated something like a law code, which called (among much else) for fair weights and measures, the protection of widows and orphans, and checks on the power of the mighty. In a striking departure from previous practice, he also tried to limit the application of the death penalty, reserving death or mutilation for serious crimes only. Together, Ur-Nammu and Shulgi modeled their kingship on that of Sargon and Naram-Sin, pursuing military conquests, the centralization of Sumerian government, commercial expansion and consolidation, and the patronage of art and literature. Together, the Akkadian rulers and Ur Dynasty III thus established a pattern of rule that would influence the region for centuries to come.

Although the rulers of Ur Dynasty III issued their official documents in Sumerian and consciously asserted "Sumerian" culture, Mesopotamia was now a much different place from what it had been even in ED

III. The influence of Semitic speakers on the political and religious affairs of Ur Dynasty III was significant, just as it was in Sumerian culture generally. This Semitic influence became increasingly important as time wore on. As we will learn in the next chapter, the growing influence of one particular Semitic people, the Amorites, would prove instrumental in the overthrow of Ur Dynasty III (the last Sumerian rulers of Mesopotamia) and the establishment of a new era in Near Eastern history.

EARLY EGYPT

How was the Nile River central to the development of Egyptian civilization?

The other primary civilization of the Mediterranean world arose in Egypt, roughly contemporaneous with the Sumerians. Unlike the inhabitants of Mesopotamia, however, the Egyptians did not have to wrest their survival from an unwilling and unpredictable environment. Instead, their land was constantly nourished by the predictable annual summer flooding of the Nile River. The rich black soil the river left behind made the Nile valley and delta the richest agricultural region in the entire Mediterranean world. Much of the distinctiveness of Egyptian civilization rests upon this fundamental ecological fact.

Ancient Egypt was a narrow, elongated land, snaking north from the First Cataract (a series of rocks and rapids in the river at the ancient city of Elephantine) along both banks of the Nile toward the Mediterranean Sea for a distance of almost seven hundred miles (1200 km). Outside this narrow band of territory—which ranged in breadth from a few hundred yards to no more than fourteen miles (23 km)—lay an uninhabitable desert, where rain almost never falls. This contrast between the fertile, "Black Land" along the Nile and the dessicated "Red Land" beyond deeply influenced the way the Egyptians viewed their world. Egypt itself they saw as the center of the cosmos. The lands beyond Egypt, however, they regarded as lying utterly beyond the boundaries of civilized life.

As a land, a nation, and a civilization, Egypt has enjoyed remarkable continuity. The roots of Egyptian culture extend into prehistory, and Egypt continued to thrive as an independent and distinct culture until its

CHRONOLOGY	
EARLY EGYPTIAN KINGDOMS AND PERIODS	
Predynastic Period	5000–3000 B.C.E.
Archaic or Early Dynastic Period	3000–2715 B.C.E.
Old Kingdom	2715–2170 B.C.E.
First Intermediate Period	2170–1983 B.C.E.

HOW WAS THE NILE RIVER CENTRAL TO THE DEVELOPMENT OF EGYPTIAN CIVILIZATION?

EARLY EGYPT   31

ANCIENT EGYPT AND THE NEAR EAST

Notice the peculiar geography of Egypt and the role played by the Nile. How did the lands on either side of the Nile help to isolate Egyptian culture from outside influences? Consider how the Nile helped to forge Egypt into a unitary state under a powerful centralized government. How was Egypt's relationship to the Nile as potentially hazardous as it was beneficial?

assimilation into the Roman Empire after 30 B.C.E. To speak of ancient Egypt therefore requires us to survey over three thousand years of history and development. For convenience, historians divide this history into "Kingdoms" and "Periods," as shown in the accompanying box. Generally, the "Kingdoms" were phases of strength, prosperity, and unity; during the Intermediate Periods Egypt suffered from a variety of woes, out of which a unified Egypt would then reemerge. The final two phases (the Late and Hellenistic Periods) were characterized by foreign domination by Assyrians, Persians, and lastly Greeks.

PREDYNASTIC EGYPT
(C. 5000–3000 B.C.E.)

Prehistoric Egypt is often referred to as Predynastic Egypt, that is, the period prior to the rise of the pharaohs. Using archaeology to glean information about this age is notoriously difficult. Many predynastic settlements are now buried under innumerable layers of silt, or were destroyed long ago by the waters of the Nile. Furthermore, for a long time the abundance of the Nile Valley discouraged the transition to village life that took place elsewhere in the Neolithic Near East. In the Fertile Crescent, rising population forced the Mesopotamians to adopt a settled agricultural life during the eighth millennium B.C.E. In Egypt, by contrast, a steadily increasing population was able to sustain itself through hunting and gathering until the fifth millennium B.C.E.

Egypt's population rose through a combination of natural increase—itself the product of an abundant food supply—and immigration from elsewhere. Prior to around 10,000 B.C.E., the region that is now the Sahara supported a rich variety of plant and animal life. With the retreat of the glaciers, however, the area slowly began to turn into a desert, and people as well as animals looked for better circumstances. Many found their way to the Nile Valley. By the Predynastic Period a multitude of peoples from North Africa, East Africa, and western Asia had settled in Egypt. The remarkable unity of Egyptian culture actually emerged from extremely heterogeneous roots. It was not the product of any particular ethnic or racial group.

Until recently historians believed that this multifarious collection of people had forged a "civilization without cities"—that the unique character of the Nile and its hydrology had allowed the Egyptians to avoid full urbanization, yet to enjoy the fruits of civilization. Further archaeological research has modified this assessment. The first known permanent settlement in Egypt dates to approximately 4750 B.C.E. and was situated near the modern town of Merimde Beni Salama, at the southwestern edge of the Nile Delta. It was a thriving farming community that may have numbered as many as sixteen thousand residents (although this number, based as it is on burial remains that are difficult to interpret, is open to contention). Thereafter, the Egyptian economy rapidly became more sophisticated. By around 3500 B.C.E., the residents of Ma'adi, just three miles away from Merimde Beni Salama, had extensive commercial contacts with the Levant (the east coast of the Mediterranean Sea: modern-day Lebanon, Syria, and Israel) and the Sinai peninsula—copper implements, beads, and glassware are plentiful at the site—and with the upper stretches of the Nile, several hundred miles to the south. Many other early Neolithic farming centers have also been discovered in or near the Nile Delta, where a degree of cultural unity had already developed. In later centuries, this area would be known as Lower Egypt. Comparable developments were also occuring outside the delta. By the late Predynastic Period (3500–3000 B.C.E.) the material culture and burial practices of the Egyptians were more or less uniform from the southern edge of the delta all the way south to the First Cataract, a vast length of the Nile known as Upper Egypt.

Although towns in Lower Egypt were more numerous, it was in Upper Egypt that the first true Egyptian cities developed. By 3200 B.C.E., important communities such as Nekhen, the South Town at Naqada, This, and Abydos all exhibited high degrees of occupational and social specialization. They had encircled themselves with sophisticated fortifications and had begun to build elaborate temple and shrine complexes to honor the local gods.

This last fact may be key to explaining the growth of these towns into cities. Their role as regional cult centers attracted travelers and encouraged the growth of industries. And travel in Upper Egypt was relatively easy: almost all Egyptians lived within sight of the Nile, with the great river serving as a highway binding the nation together. It was due to the Nile, therefore, that the region south of the delta, despite its enormous geographical length, managed to forge a cultural unity, with its people recognizing one another's gods and sharing common burial practices, material goods, and industries.

The Nile fed Egypt and united it. The river served as a conduit for people, goods, and ideas. It also provided a way for centralizing rulers to project their power quickly and effectively up and down its course. By the close of the Predynastic Period the cities of Upper Egypt had banded together in a confederacy under the leadership of This (the Thinite Confederacy). The pressure exerted by this confederacy in turn forced the towns of Lower Egypt to adopt their own form of

> The Nile fed Egypt and united it. The river served as a conduit for people, goods, and ideas.

HOW WAS THE NILE RIVER CENTRAL TO THE DEVELOPMENT OF EGYPTIAN CIVILIZATION?

EARLY EGYPT   33

Narmer Palette. Dating from about 3100 B.C.E., this stone carving shows Narmer subduing an enemy from the north with a mace. The falcon probably represents the god Horus, who looks with approval on the birth of Egyptian unification in violence.

loose political organization. By the close of the fourth millennium, the rivalry between these competing regions had thus given rise to the two nascent kingdoms of Upper and Lower Egypt.

THE UNIFICATION OF EGYPT: THE ARCHAIC PERIOD (3000–2715 B.C.E.)

With the rise of powerful rulers who sought to unify these two Egyptian kingdoms, we enter the dynastic phase of Egyptian history. The numbering system for the pharaonic dynasties was developed (or at least enshrined in writing) by a third-century B.C.E. Egyptian priest named Manetho. By and large, Manetho's categorizations have withstood the scrutiny of modern historians and archaeologists. Recent research has led to the necessity of recognizing a "Dynasty 0," an assortment of early kings instrumental in the unification of all Egypt. These rulers, known almost exclusively from archaeological evidence, remain shadowy figures at best. Among their number was an Upper Egyptian strongman known as "King Scorpion" from a mace head that details—in pictures—his assertion of authority over most of Egypt. One of his successors, King Narmer, appears to have been responsible for the final political unification of Upper and Lower Egypt, and might possibly be identified with the legendary king Menes or Min whom later Egyptians credited with this feat.

Following the political unification of the land, the basic features of pharaonic rule took shape, more or less along lines that would persist through all of Egyptian history. From very early on, the pharaoh was identified closely with divinity. By the first and second dynasties he was regarded as an earthly manifestation of a god. Egyptian rulers thus enjoyed a sacred nature quite different from the early Sumerian *lugal*, merely a mortal who enjoyed divine favor. We do not know how the early pharaohs established their claims to divinity. We do know that the cities of Upper Egypt were closely associated with particular patron deities. It seems probable, therefore, that local potentates in the Late Predynastic Period were already asserting their own special relationship with their city's patron god. As political power extended beyond the confines of a single city and its surrounding territory, rulers may have found it necessary to extend such claims in order to legitimate their rule. No longer was it enough merely to be the human representative of a single city's god; to exercise authority over other cities with their other gods, one now had to claim to be a god oneself.

This is speculation. We do know, however, that legitimating their rule over all of Egypt was a difficult task for the earliest pharaohs. Local loyalties remained strong, and for centuries Lower Egyptians saw themselves as distinct in some respects from their cousins to the south. Efforts to create symbols of Egyptian unity began very early, however. Crowns and other regalia were already known in the middle of the fourth millennium B.C.E. The pharaohs' claims to divinity should probably be seen in the same light. By the end of the Archaic Period, pharaohs were viewed specifically as manifestations of the sky god Horus (identified as Ra in Lower Egypt), an important deity represented by a falcon and worshiped with particular fervor around the area of This and Abydos (the probable source of Egypt's political consolidation under Dynasty 0). Whatever their personal names, pharaohs from Narmer on therefore took a "Horus name" also, to emphasize their identification with the god. By the end of Dynasty 2, pharaoh was not just the ruler of Egypt; in a sense he *was* Egypt, a symbol of the land, its people, and their connection to the divine with which all could identify. By the Old Kingdom, pharaoh was seen as a discreet and vital part of the cosmic order, the guarantor of the presence of *ma'at* (see below).

EGYPTIAN RELIGION AND WORLD VIEW

As we have seen, the Egyptians saw themselves as utterly set apart from all other civilizations. One was

The gods Isis, Osiris, and Horus.

either an Egyptian or a barbarian, and the lines between the two were absolute. Within Egypt, however, what mattered was one's "Egyptian-ness"; aside from gender, all other distinctions paled in comparison to this fundamental distinction between Egyptians and outsiders. The confidence of the Egyptians in their own superiority stemmed from their self-conscious awareness of the uniqueness of their country, nurtured by the Nile and guarded by the brutal deserts and vast seas that surrounded it. For Egyptians, it was simply self-evident that their country was the center of the world.

Although the Egyptians subscribed to a variety of creation myths about the world, they did not concern themselves greatly with how humanity came to exist. They were in this respect quite different from the Hebrews, whose creation myths were otherwise quite similar to those of the Egyptians. Instead, what mattered to the Egyptians was the means by which life itself was created and re-created. In other words, how did the cycle of life come to be? For Egyptians, this was the essential problem. Once the cycle of life had been established, it could duplicate itself endlessly. This cyclical conception gave a certain repetitive, predictable, and ultimately static cast to the way Egyp-

Funerary Papyrus. The scene shows the heart of a princess of the Twenty-first Dynasty being weighed in a balance before the god Osiris. On the other side of the balance are the symbols for life and truth.

THE EGYPTIAN BOOK OF THE DEAD

Though various versions of the Egytian Book of the Dead are known, the best preserved and lengthiest is that of the Papyrus of Ani, produced sometime in the fifteenth century B.C.E. to aid an important official of the priesthoods of Abydos and Thebes and his ka's quest to become assimilated to Osiris and gain immortality. Though this version dates to the New Kingdom, most of its formulas and incantations are believed to be ancient, dating back at least to the Old Kingdom. (Note: Italicized words indicate attempts to translate variations of the root of ma'at).

Says Thoth the righteous judge of the cycle of the great gods. . . . Verily I am justifying the name of Osiris the royal scribe Hunefer. His heart has come forth upon the scale, he has not been found an evil doer. Osiris: hear ye this decision. In very *truth* is weighed the heart of Osiris, his soul is standing as a witness for him; his sentence is just upon the great scales. Any wickedness has not been found in him; he has not wasted food offerings in the temples; he has not done harm in deed; he has not let his mouth go with evil things while he was upon the earth. Says the circle of the great gods to Thoth [dwelling] in Hermopolis: It is decreed that which comes forth from my mouth. *True* and righteous is Osiris, the scribe Ani triumphant. He has not sinned, he has not done evil in respect of us. Do not let Amemet prevail over him. Let there be given to him cakes, and a coming forth in the presence of Osiris, and a field abiding in Sekhet-hetepu ("Fields of Peace") like the followers of Horus. Says Horus the son of Isis: I have come to thee Un-Nefer, I have brought to thee Osiris Ani. His heart is *right* coming forth from the balance, it has not sinned aganst any god or any goddess. Thoth has weighed it according to the decree uttered to him by the cycle of the gods; it is very true and *righteous*. Grant that cakes and beer may be given to him, and a coming forth before Osiris; may he be like the followers of Horus forever!

Based on E. A. Wallis Budge, trans. *The Egyptian Book of the Dead: (The Papyrus of Ani).* (New York: Dover Publications, 1967), pp. 16–18.

tians perceived the cosmos. Many phenomena were seen as cyclical events, not surprising given the dependence of these people on the annual cycles of the Nile.

At the heart of Egyptian religion lay the myth of the gods Osiris and Isis, brother and sister, husband and wife, and among the "original" nine gods in Egyptian belief. Osiris was the first to hold kingship on earth, but his brother Seth wanted the throne for himself. Seth betrayed and killed Osiris, sealing him in a coffin. Through great effort, Isis retrieved the corpse, but Seth seized it once again. In no mood to take any more chances, he now hacked his brother into pieces and spread his remains throughout Egypt (thus all of Egypt could claim Osiris, and shrines to him were prevalent throughout the land). Still undeterred, Isis sought the help of Anubis, the god of mummification, and together they managed to reassemble Osiris. Isis then revived Osiris long enough to conceive a child by him, the god Horus. With the help of his mother's magic, Horus withstood the assaults of Seth and his henchmen; the image of the wounded Horus was part and parcel of many healing spells and incantations in Egyptian medicine. Horus and Seth then competed over the vacant throne of Osiris, until finally Horus prevailed and avenged his father.

This mythology was very important to the Egyptians. It served as the subject for theatrical re-enactments, and the symbolism contained in the story says much about Egyptian beliefs. The tale of Osiris is a myth about life arising out of death, but it is not a resurrection story: Osiris was revivified only temporarily. The notion of new life arising from the dead probably stretched back to the earliest farming settlements of Egypt, where already bodies were being interred with extensive grave goods and special care. The promise of the continuation of life—rhythmic, cyclical, inevitable—as embodied by Osiris made him an important agricultural deity to the Egyptians.

THE EGYPTIAN DEATH CULT

Osiris was also, however, a central deity in the death cult of the Egyptians. Unlike the Sumerians, the Egyptians did not have a bleak view of death and the underworld. Death was an unpleasant rite of passage, a necessity to be endured on the way to an afterlife that was more or less like one's earthly existence, only better. But the passage was not automatic and was full of dangers. After death, the deceased's *ka*, or otherworldly existence, would have to roam the underworld, the Duat, searching for the House of Judgment, where Osiris and forty-two other judges would decide its fate. Demons and evil spirits might try to frustrate the *ka*'s quest to reach the House of Judgment, and the journey might take some time. If successful and judged worthy, however, the deceased would then enjoy immortality as an aspect of Osiris. For this reason, the dead were often referred to as "Osiris (name of the deceased)."

Because of their beliefs about death, the Egyptians developed an elaborate ritual and cult for dealing with it. It was first of all crucial that the corpse be preserved: this is why the Egyptians developed their sophisticated techniques of embalming and mummification. The body was desiccated, all its vital organs removed (except for the heart, which played a key role in the final judgment), and the body treated with chemicals to help preserve it. A funerary portrait mask was placed on the mummy before burial, so that the corpse would still be recognizable in death despite being wrapped in hundreds of yards of linen. To sustain the deceased on his or her journey through the underworld, food, clothing, utensils, and other items of vital importance would be placed in the grave along with the body.

"Coffin texts" or "Books of the Dead" also accompanied the corpse. These writings contained much that the deceased would need on his or her journey through the Duat: magic spells, ritual incantations, and the like. Not only would this knowledge help the dead navigate the perils on the way to Osiris, but would also help them prepare their hearts for the final test. Before Osiris and the other judges, the deceased performed a "negative confession," a formulaic denial of a litany of offenses. Then the god Anubis weighed the heart of the deceased in front of the judges, placing it in the scales with the feather of the goddess Ma'at. Only if the heart and the feather were in perfect balance did the dead person achieve immortality as an aspect of the god. In the third millennium this privilege was reserved for the royal family alone, but by the Middle Kingdom participation in these death rituals had become accessible to most Egyptians.

The careful detail with which Egyptians confronted death has often led to the erroneous assumption that theirs was a "death culture," completely obsessed with the problem of death. In fact, Egyptian practices and beliefs were mostly life affirming, and the role of Osiris (also, remember, a god of returning life) and the underworld were viewed not with horror, but with hope. Egyptian confidence in the cyclical nature of the cosmos and the resilient power of life is also evidenced by their interpretation of the solar cycle. Each morning the sky, personified as the goddess Nut, literally "gave birth" to the sun (often identified with the god Ra). The sun made his way westward across the celestial waters of the sky in his day boat (toward the direction of Duat, the land of death; Osiris was often called "He Who Rules the West," that is, the land of the dead). The sun's journey in his day boat was observable, a peaceful and orderly course across the sky. His trip through the Duat in his night boat could only be imagined, and the Egyptians believed that a giant serpent tried to block the sun on his journey through the underworld. In the deepest part of the night, the sun reached the mummified body of Osiris and the two gods became one, giving the sun the power to continue his journey until his mother Nut could once again give birth to him. Life always triumphed.

Binding together this great cycle of life, death, and the return of life was *ma'at*. Like many words in the Egyptian language, it has no exact English equivalent. Our concepts of harmony, order, justice, and truth

HOW WAS THE NILE RIVER CENTRAL TO THE DEVELOPMENT OF EGYPTIAN CIVILIZATION?

EARLY EGYPT   37

would all fit comfortably within *ma'at*, though none of these words captures its entire sense. Both the abstract notion and its personification as a female deity named Ma'at were what kept the universe running in its serene, repetitive, predictable fashion. Thus, unlike the Sumerians, the Egyptians of the Archaic Period and Old Kingdom were a supremely confident and optimistic people. They believed that they lived at the center of the created universe, a paradise where stability and peace were guaranteed by *ma'at* and their connection to it through the earthly manifestation of a god who ruled them, their pharaoh. For most of the third millennium, thanks to a long period of successful Nile floods and Egypt's geographical isolation from the outside world, the Egyptians were able to maintain their belief in this perfectly ordered paradise, in which they perceived that little if anything ever changed.

LANGUAGE AND WRITING

Among the many facets of Egyptian culture which have fascinated and mystified later observers is their system of pictographic writing. Called *hieroglyphs* ("sacred carvings") by the Greeks, these strange and elaborate symbols remained completely impenetrable and therefore all the more mysterious until the nineteenth century, when a French scholar named Champollion deciphered them with the help of the newly discovered Rosetta Stone. This document contains three versions of the same text, written in ancient Greek, demotic (the script of a later version of the Egyptian language), and hieroglyphics. Because he could read the text in Greek and demotic, Champollion was able to unravel the hieroglyphic text as well. From this beginning, generations of scholars have added to and refined our knowledge of ancient Egyptian society and language.

The development of writing in Egypt dates to the later phases of the Predynastic Period, and its pictographic nature may betray an influence from Mesopotamia. If so, this would represent by far the most significant cultural exchange between the two regions. Unlike Sumerian cuneiform, however, Egyptian hieroglyphics did not evolve toward a system of phonograms. Rather, the Egyptians developed a simpler, faster, cursive script for representing hieroglyphics, a system of

The development of writing in Egypt dates to the later phases of the Predynastic Period, and its pictographic nature may betray an influence from Mesopotamia.

writing called *hieratic*, which they employed for the everyday business of government and commerce.

Little early hieratic writing remains, due largely to the perishable nature of the medium on which it was usually written: papyrus. Produced by hammering, drying, and processing river reeds, papyrus was lighter, easier to write on, and more transportable than the clay tablets used by the Sumerians. When sewn together into scrolls, papyrus also made it possible to record and store large quantities of information in a very small space. Production of this versatile writing material remained one of Egypt's most important industries throughout ancient times, and papyrus became a valuable export item. Even in the sandy and arid conditions of Egypt, however, papyrus is fragile and subject to decay. In wetter climates, it almost never survives for archaeologists to unearth. The vast majority of papyrus documents have therefore been lost, a fact which significantly affects our understanding of Old Kingdom Egypt, when so many records were kept on papyrus.

The language of the ancient Egyptians has long been a matter of debate. Early Egyptian exhibits features that tie it both to the Semitic languages of the Near East and to a number of African language groups, all of which belong to a linguistic "superfamily" known as Afro-Asiatic. Some historical linguists have postulated that early Egyptian might represent the survival of a "root" language from which the other languages of the Afro-Asiatic group evolved. Given the movements of people in and out of and through the Nile Valley in the prehistoric period, this theory is a distinct possibility. But whatever its origins, the Egyptian language has enjoyed a long history. The language of the Old Kingdom survived and evolved over thousands of years, becoming the tongue known as Coptic in classical antiquity; it is still used today in the liturgy of the Coptic Christian Church.

THE OLD KINGDOM (2715–2170 B.C.E.)

Because so few of the routine business documents of the Old Kingdom survive, writing a history of this period is a difficult venture. Although funerary texts from the tombs of the elite allow us to say something about the achievements of particular individuals and to gain an impression of everyday life, we know little about

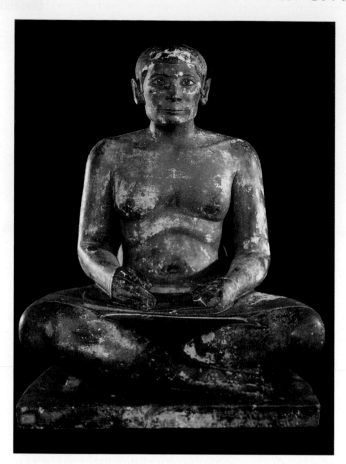

An Egyptian Scribe, c. 2400 B.C.E.

their kingdom and extract resources from it. During most of the Old Kingdom period, these governors remained closely bound to the central government. Pharaohs moved the nomarchs and other important officials around the kingdom, lest they be tempted to build up a local power base or conceive of their administrative districts (*nomes*) as personal possessions to be passed down to their descendants. Only in times of pharaonic weakness were these officials allowed to establish local roots in the territories they administered.

Nomarchs were part of an extensive pharaonic bureaucracy. Scribal literacy was widespread in Old Kingdom Egypt, because writing was critical to the management and exploitation of Egypt's vast wealth. Precisely because pharaoh was Egypt, he could call on the resources of the land for his glorification and exaltation; by doing so, he glorified and exalted Egypt. Managing and organizing enormous resources of labor as well as mineral, industrial and agricultural wealth—to say nothing of extensive trade within and beyond Egypt—necessitated a highly skilled and effective administration. Because these literate bureaucrats were absolutely essential to government at the national and local level in Egypt, they enjoyed power, influence, and status. A Middle Kingdom document called "The Satire of the Trades" reminded the scribe in training how much his long and difficult education would benefit him in the end, and how much better his life would be in comparison with the practitioners of other trades. Even a child just beginning his scribal education was considered worthy of great respect.

the lives of the great majority of ordinary Egyptian people. Further complicating our problem is the attitude of the Old Kingdom Egyptians themselves. Because of their belief in *ma'at* and the unchanging, cyclical nature of the universe, Old Kingdom Egyptians had little interest in history and historical events as we think of them. For all these reasons, it is unlikely we will ever be able to reconstruct their history in any detailed way.

Nevertheless, rich documentation about individuals, practices, and beliefs is available to us through the texts and art of this period. One feature that emerges clearly by the Third Dynasty (c. 2715–2640 B.C.E.) is the degree to which the pharaohs had successfully centralized their power and administration. There are few signs in this period of the earlier divisions between Upper and Lower Egypt. Instead, the pharaohs used centrally appointed local governors (known to the Greeks as *nomarchs*) to control

> Because of their belief in *ma'at* and the unchanging, cyclical nature of the universe, Old Kingdom Egyptians had little interest in history and historical events as we think of them.

IMHOTEP AND THE "STEP PYRAMID"

At the dawn of the Old Kingdom, we meet one of the greatest administrative officials in the history of Egypt: Imhotep. Imhotep rose through the ranks of the pharaoh's administration to become a sort of vizier, a right-hand man to Djoser, an early pharaoh of the Third Dynasty. Imhotep's learning and education spanned a variety of disciplines: medicine, astronomy, theology, mathematics, but above all architecture. It was Imhotep, sometime in the twenty-seventh century B.C.E., who decided that pharaoh needed a great monument to his person, power, and position in Egyptian society, and so designed the "Step Pyramid," the first great monument in world history built entirely

HOW WAS THE NILE RIVER CENTRAL TO THE DEVELOPMENT OF EGYPTIAN CIVILIZATION?

EARLY EGYPT   39

of dressed stone. It was not only to be the final resting place of Djoser, but a symbol and expression of his transcendent power as pharaoh.

Built west of the capital at Memphis at the site of modern Saqqara, the Step Pyramid consists of a series of platforms of decreasing size that towers over the desert to a height of 200 feet (63 meters). The design of the monument itself was based on an older form of burial monument, the *mastaba*, a low rectangular building built entirely of brick with a flat top and sloping sides. Imhotep probably began with the mastaba pattern in mind, but he radically altered it by stacking one smaller mastaba on top of another, and constructing each entirely of limestone. Surrounding this impressive monument was a huge temple and mortuary complex, perhaps modeled after Djoser's palace in the capital. These buildings served two purposes. Djoser's *ka* would have what it needed to rule in the afterlife, and the many buildings with their immovable doors and labyrinthine passageways would (it was hoped) frustrate tomb robbers, a chronic problem as pharaonic burials became richer.

Imhotep may have intended his pyramidal design to evoke the descending rays of the life-giving sun; or perhaps the pyramid was meant as the means for the pharaoh's ka to ascend into the sky and incorporate itself with the sun on its journey west after death. But whatever the theological import of the design, no one could miss the pharaonic power that lay behind its construction. Imhotep had set a precedent to which pharaohs throughout the Old Kingdom would aspire. Ultimately, the competition to build ever larger and more elaborate pyramids would ruin them.

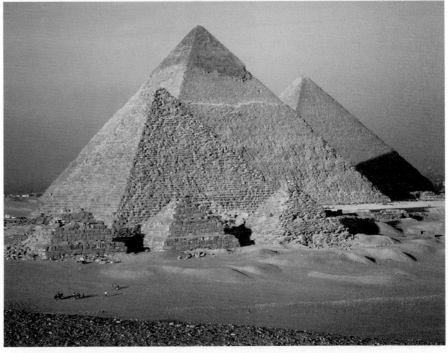

Top: **Step pyramid of King Djoser,** c. 2680 B.C.E.
Bottom: **Pyramids at Giza,** with the Great Pyramid of Khufu (Cheops) on the left, c. 2590 B.C.E.

THE INSTRUCTION OF PTAH-HOTEP

Egyptian literature often took the form of "instructions" to important personages, meant to inculcate behaviors and ideals that would lead to success. This document, authored around 2450 B.C.E. by the vizier of a Fifth Dynasty pharaoh, sought to instruct the vizier's son and eventual successor as to the proper conduct of a high-born Egyptian official. Note the emphasis placed on ma'at *in this Old Kingdom document.*

Be not arrogant because of your knowledge, and be not puffed up because you are a learned man. Take counsel with the ignorant as with the learned, for the limits of art cannot be reached, and no artist is perfect in his skills. Good speech is more hidden than the precious greenstone, and yet it is found among slave girls at the millstones. . . . If you are a leader commanding the conduct of many seek out every good aim, so that your policy may be without error. A great thing is *ma'at,* enduring and surviving; it has not been upset since the time of Osiris. He who departs from its laws is punished. It is the right path for him who knows nothing. Wrongdoing has never brought its venture safe to port. Evil may win riches, but it is the strength of *ma'at* that endures long, and a man can say, "I learned it from my father.". . . If you wish to prolong friendship in a house which you enter as master, brother or friend, or any place that you enter, beware of approaching the women. No place in which that is done prospers. There is no wisdom in it. A thousand men are turned aside from their own good because of a little moment, like a dream, by tasting which death is reached. . . . He who lusts after women, no plan of his will succeed. . . . If you are a worthy man sitting in the council of his lord, confine your attention to excellence. Silence is more valuable than chatter. Speak only when you know you can resolve difficulties. He who gives good counsel is an artist, for speech is more difficult than any craft.

Nels M. Bailkey, ed. *Readings in Ancient History: Thought and Experience from Gilgamesh to St. Augustine,* 5th ed. (Boston: Houghton Mifflin, 1995), pp. 39–42.

FOURTH DYNASTY (2640–2510 B.C.E.)

Old Kingdom Egypt reached its height in the Fourth Dynasty (2640–2510 B.C.E.), the period during which the great pyramids of Giza were built. These were true pyramids and have become timeless symbols of Egyptian civilization. Impressive as they are today, they were even more so in ancient times. The Great Pyramid, built for the pharaoh Khufu (or Cheops in the Greek tradition), was originally 481 feet high and 756 feet along each side of its base, consisting of over 2.3 million limestone blocks and enclosing a volume of about 85 million cubic feet. With the exception of a few airways, passages, and burial chambers, the structure is completely solid. The entire pyramid was encased in gleaming white limestone and topped by a massive capstone gilded in gold, as were the two massive but slightly smaller pyramids at the site built for Khufu's successors Khafre (Chephren) and Menkaure (Mycerinus). In the Middle Ages, the builders and

HOW WAS THE NILE RIVER CENTRAL TO THE DEVELOPMENT OF EGYPTIAN CIVILIZATION?

EARLY EGYPT   41

Pharaoh Menkaure and His Queen. Left: A sculpture from the Fourth Dynasty, c. 2500 B.C.E.—an example of the impassive, stately style. Right: A comparison of their profiles leaves little doubt that they were brother and sister as well as husband and wife.

rulers of the great Muslim capital of Cairo stripped the casing stones from these pyramids and used them to construct and fortify their new city. The gold cap-stones had probably disappeared already. But in antiquity these pyramids, with their gleaming limestone facing, would have glistened brilliantly in the bright Egyptian sunshine, making them visible for miles in all directions.

The Greek historian Herodotus, who toured Egypt more than two thousand years after the pyramids were built, claimed that it took one hundred thousand laborers twenty years to build the Great Pyramid. This is probably an exaggeration. Then as now, Egyptian guides enjoyed telling visitors tall tales. The impression these monuments made on him, however, may be judged by the fact that Herodotus believed what his Egyptian guides were telling him. Once thought to have been the work of slaves, the pyramids were in fact raised by tens of thousands of peasant workers, who labored most intensively on the pyramids while their fields were under water. These workers probably participated willingly in the building projects, which glorified the living god who ruled them and served as their link to *ma'at*.

The monuments of the Third and Fourth Dynasty pharaohs testify to the tremendous administrative and religious power they wielded. The pharaohs were at once the head of state—indeed, the state itself—and the link between their people and the cosmos. With such authority at their disposal, and assisted by an extensive and efficient bureaucracy, the governments of these pharaohs raised Egypt to new heights. They exploited natural resources as never before and ensured an era of prosperity and internal peace, thus demonstrating their importance as the living, divine link to *ma'at*. These powerful pharaohs also extended Egyptian power south beyond the First Cataract into Nubia, with its rich deposits of gold.

FIFTH AND SIXTH DYNASTIES (2510–2205 B.C.E.)

For reasons that are not entirely clear, the Fifth and Sixth Dynasties (2510–2205 B.C.E.) witness the slow erosion of pharaonic power. Although pyramid construction continued, the monuments of this period were less impressive in terms of architecture, craftsmanship, and size. During these two dynasties, a series of developments undermined the power of pharaoh. The priesthood of Ra at Heliopolis asserted itself and its influence against certain weaker pharaohs. Ultimately, these priests demoted pharaoh from being an incarnation of Horus/Ra to being merely the god's son. Also, whether through the actions of ambitious officials, the laziness of certain pharaohs, or both, the nomarchs began to evolve into precisely the type of hereditary nobility that the vigorous Third and Fourth Dynasty kings did not allow. These men had become so powerful and influential that a pharaoh of the Sixth Dynasty, Pepy I, even married the daughters of nomarchs and produced successors by these marriages.

Scholars are uncertain as to how these local officials and powerful priests wrested control and prestige from the pharaonic center. It may be that the extraordinarily costly building efforts of the Fourth Dynasty had overstrained the economy, leading to shortages in labor and material vital to other sectors of Egyptian society and commerce. Other evidence points to changing climatic conditions that may have resulted in increasingly poor or even failed inundations. Egyptians could guard against the worst consequences of this in the short term, but prolonged periods of failure would ultimately spell disaster, as stores of food would be consumed and famine occurred. A relief sculpture from the Seventh Dynasty shows a line of wailing Egyptians, their eyes protruding from their faces and their ribs clearly visible under their skin. Such haunting images are evocative of the type of famine and suffering that can ravage northeastern Africa even today.

In such straitened and desperate circumstances, peo-ple could and did resort to banditry and violence to survive. Furthermore, perhaps in response to Egyptian aggression, small states began to form in Nubia; with better organization and equipment, the Nubians became a greater menace than ever before and may have restricted Egyptian access to precious metal deposits in and around the First Cataract, with predictable effects on the economy.

With Egypt suffering these woes, the rightful claim of pharaoh to be a link to *ma'at* diminished accordingly. From the Fifth Dynasty on, therefore, local governors and religious authorities took it upon themselves to provide what measure of stability and order they could. Their power, authority, and prestige increased at the expense of the pharaonic government. A significant turning point was the astonishing reign of the long-lived but otherwise weak Sixth Dynasty pharaoh, Pepy II. Pharaoh for ninety-six years, Pepy II came to the throne at the age of six. During his minority, priests and nomarchs took advantage of his youth to increase their prerogatives greatly. Though Pepy II was competent enough once he came of age, the damage had been done. Furthermore, his advanced age at death meant he had outlived all the clear successors to his authority, and the ensuing confusion provided even greater scope for the growing independence of local power.

SEVENTH AND EIGHTH DYNASTIES

The Seventh and Eighth Dynasties represent the close of the Old Kingdom. These pharaohs are very obscure; many attempted to rule from Memphis, but insofar as we know anything about them, they were clearly powerless in the face of the nomarchs of Upper Egypt, each virtually independent. By the middle of the twenty-second century, Egypt had ceased to exist as a united country. Instead, it descended into a period of anarchy known as the First Intermediate Period. A century and a half would pass before one man could again legitimately call himself pharaoh of all Egypt. But although unity returned after the upheavals of the First Intermediate Period, the confidence and optimism of Old Kingdom Egypt did not return with it.

SOCIETY IN OLD KINGDOM EGYPT

The social pyramid of Old Kingdom Egypt was extremely steep. At its apex was of course the pharaoh and the royal family. During the Third and Fourth Dynasties their status, prestige, and power were so great as to set them quite apart from any other Egyptians. There was a class of nobles, but until the Fifth Dynasty the nobility's social and political position was clearly subordinate; their role was to serve as priests and officials of pharaoh's government. Because of the vaunted position of scribes, these were usually recruited and trained from among the sons of the greater families. The economic and social standing of the Egyptian elites allowed them scope for significant luxury. They owned extensive estates with exotic goods and fine furniture. They kept dogs and monkeys as pets, and hunted and fished for sport.

Beneath the tiny minority represented by royalty and nobility was everyone else. Most Egyptians were poor, living in crowded conditions in simple mud-brick dwellings. During the period of prosperity, however, skilled artisans—jewelers, goldsmiths, and the like—could elevate themselves and enjoy more comfortable surroundings, though we should not think of them as anything like a "middle class." Potters, weavers, masons, bricklayers, brewers, merchants, and schoolteachers also enjoyed some measure of respect and prestige, as well as a higher standard of living than most. Among the peasants of Egypt, however, a significant majority would have been unskilled laborers, who provided the brute force necessary for agriculture and construction. Beneath them were slaves, typically captives from foreign wars rather than native Egyptians. But despite the theocratic nature of pharaonic rule and the enormous demands the pharaohs placed on Egypt's wealth, Egyptian society does not appear to have been particularly oppressive. Even slaves had certain legal rights, including the ability to own, dispose of, and bequeath personal property.

WOMEN IN THE OLD KINGDOM

Egyptian women also enjoyed an unusually high degree of legal status and protection by the standards of the ancient world. They were not allowed to undergo scribal training or serve as important officials, but short personal notes between women of social standing suggest at least some degree of female literacy. In times of crisis, as in the case of Queen Nitocris at the close of the Sixth Dynasty, a woman of the royal family might assume pharaonic authority (although usually she would be careful to represent herself in rather mannish fashion). Egyptian women had standing before the courts as their own persons; they could initiate complaints (including suing for divorce), defend themselves, bear witness, and possess property on their own,

without the male guardian or representative that was typically required of women in other ancient societies.

None of this should obscure the fact that Egypt was, at its heart, a rigidly patriarchal society. Aside from the role of priestess, women were barred from state office. Although most Egyptians practiced monogamy, important and powerful men could and did keep harems of lesser wives, concubines, and female slaves. Furthermore, any Egyptian man could practice sexual freedom, married or not, with legal impunity; a wife who did so was subject to severe legal punishments. Gender divisions may have been less clearly defined among the peasantry. Peasant women often worked in the fields during the harvest and carried out a number of menial but vital but labor tasks. As usual in the ancient world, however, we can only glimpse the lives of Egyptian peasants through the eyes of their social superiors.

SCIENCE AND TECHNOLOGY

Their monumental architecture notwithstanding, the Egyptians lagged behind the Sumerians and Akkadians in science and mathematics, as they did in technology generally. Only in the calculation of time did the Egyptians make notable advances. Their astronomy was largely devoted to the observation of the sun for obvious religious and agricultural reasons, and the solar calendar they developed was far more accurate and sophisticated than the Mesopotamian lunar calendar. The Sumerians have bequeathed to us their means of dividing and measuring the day, but the Egyptian calendar, adopted for Rome by Julius Caesar, is the direct ancestor of our modern western calendar. Otherwise, education was mostly restricted to reading and writing, making the ingenious polymath Imhotep all the more impressive and unusual. Although the Egyptians did devise effective irrigation and water-control systems, they did not adopt such labor-saving devices as the wheel until much later than the Sumerians, perhaps because the available pool of peasant labor seemed virtually inexhaustible in densely populated Egypt.

CONCLUSION

Starting around 11,000 B.C.E.—the dawn of the Neolithic, or New Stone Age—human beings in the eastern Mediterranean world began to make a slow transition from nomadic, hunter-gatherer societies into settled agricultural and pastoral communities. With the ability to produce and store surpluses, larger villages and cities began to emerge, allowing both a greater degree of functional specialization and a wider differentiation in wealth and status between individuals and families. In Mesopotamia, where the first cities emerged during the fourth millennium B.C.E., cities served also as religious centers, with elaborate temple complexes and shrines to the city's gods. By around 2500 B.C.E., a sophisticated form of writing, known as cuneiform, had emerged as an important tool in trade and in the management of these temple complexes.

The third millennium B.C.E. saw the emergence of larger city-states with more intense warfare between them. The Mesopotamian city-states were now led by kings who claimed divine sanction for their rule, and whose power and wealth set them further and further apart from their subjects. Around 2300 B.C.E., Sumerian political life was transformed by the emergence of a new, Semitic-speaking people, the Akkadians, whose conquests resulted in the creation of the first true empire in world history. This empire would become the model future rulers of Mesopotamia would aspire to emulate.

In Egypt, the other major center of Near Eastern civilization during these centuries, political consolidation occurred at the beginning of the third millennium, a process assisted by the unique importance of the Nile River system. But Egypt during these centuries was not an empire maintained through conquest. Instead, it was a highly unified society, capable of mobilizing resources on a massive scale to support enormous building projects glorifying the pharaohs, who were conceived by Egyptians to be god-kings. Unlike the Sumerians, the Egyptians did not have to struggle to wrest a precarious living from a forbidding environment. So long as the annual flooding of the Nile occurred, Egyptians could feed themselves easily, with a relative minimum of social tension. This fact lent an air of confidence and ease to Egyptian art that is wholly lacking in Mesopotamian art.

There are many similarities between these two primary civilizations. During the third millennium, both underwent a process of political consolidation, an elaboration of religious life, and a melding of religious and political leadership. Both engaged in massive building projects; both mobilized resources on an enormous scale for temples, monuments, and irrigation projects. At the same time, however, each of these two civilizations developed an inward focus, verging on

parochialism. Although they had some trade relations with each other, and some technology transfers took place, there were no signficant political or cultural interactions between them. For all intents and purposes, they inhabited separate worlds. This relative isolation was about to change, however. The second millennium would see the emergence of large-scale, land-based empires in the Near Eastern world that would transform life in both Egypt and Sumer. These are the developments we will examine in Chapter Two.

SELECTED READINGS

Aldred, Cyril. *The Egyptians*, 3d ed. London, 1998. An indispensable, lively overview of Egyptian culture and history by one of the great masters of Egyptology.

Baines, J., and J. Málek. *Atlas of Ancient Egypt*, rev. ed. New York, 2000. A reliable, well-illustrated survey, with excellent maps.

Bottéro, Jean, Clarisse Herrenschmidt, and Jean-Pierre Vernant. *Ancestor of the West: Writing, Reasoning, and Religion in Mesopotamia, Elam, and Greece.* Chicago, 2000. A stimulating assessment of the impact of writing on the world views of the Sumerians, the Akkadians, the Elamites, the Hebrews, and the Greeks.

Butzer, Karl W. *Early Hydraulic Civilization in Egypt: A Study in Cultural Ecology.* Chicago, 1976. A lucid examination of the Nile's impact on early Egyptian history.

Crawford, Harriet. *Sumer and the Sumerians.* New York, 1991. A solid and reliable survey, up to date on both history and archaeology.

George, Andrew, trans. *The Epic of Gilgamesh: A New Translation. The Babylonian Epic Poem and Other Texts in Akkadian and Sumerian.* New York and London, 1999. The newest and most reliable translation, which carefully distinguishes the chronological "layers" of this famous text; also includes a great many related texts.

Hallo, W. W., and W. K. Simpson. *The Ancient Near East: A History*, rev. ed. New York, 1998. A reliable but somewhat dull survey; a good place to look things up.

Hoffman, Michael A. *Egypt before the Pharaohs: The Prehistorical Foundations of Egyptian Civilization.* New York, 1979. An outstanding guide to the predynastic period of Egyptian history, accessible to students but useful to scholars.

Hornung, Erik. *History of Ancient Egypt: An Introduction.* Ithaca, N.Y., 1999. Concise and authoritative.

James, T. G. H. *An Introduction to Ancient Egypt.* London, 1979. Informative survey with an emphasis on material culture.

Kemp, Barry J. *Ancient Egypt: Anatomy of a Civilization.* London, 1989. An imaginative and probing examination of Egyptian social and intellectual history.

Lichteim, Miriam. *Ancient Egyptian Literature: A Book of Readings.*

3 vols., Berkeley, 1973–1980. A wide-ranging compilation used by students and scholars alike.

Mertz, Barbara. *Red Land, Black Land: Daily Life in Ancient Egypt*, rev. ed. New York, 1990. A reliable guide that emphasizes the role of the Nile and the forbidding natural environment of Egypt.

Neugebauer, Otto. *The Exact Sciences in Antiquity*, 2d ed. New York, 1969. Includes, among much else, the standard account of Mesopotamian mathematical accomplishments.

Postgate, J. N. *Early Mesopotamia: Society and Economy at the Dawn of History*. London, 1992. An excellent, up-to-date, but challenging survey that reaches up to the middle of the second millennium B.C.E.

Redford, Donald B. ed. *The Oxford Encyclopedia of Ancient Egypt*. 3 vols. New York, 2001. An exhaustive reference work, intended for both specialists and beginners.

Roaf, Michael. *Cultural Atlas of Mesopotamia and the Ancient Near East*. New York, 1990. An informative, authoritative, and lavishly illustrated guide, with excellent maps.

Robins, Gay. *The Art of Ancient Egypt*. London, 1997. An excellent, up-to-date survey, likely to become the standard account.

Shafer, Byron E., ed. *Religion in Ancient Egypt: Gods, Myths, and Personal Practice*. London, 1991. A scholarly examination of Egyptian belief and ritual, with contributions from some of the leading modern authorities. Excellent bibliographies.

Shaw, Ian, ed. *The Oxford History of Ancient Egypt*. Oxford, 2000. The best survey of Egyptian history from the Stone Age to the early fourth century of the Common Era, with chapters written by the leading international specialists and excellent, chapter-by-chapter bibliographical essays.

Simpson, William Kelly, ed. *The Literature of Ancient Egypt: An Anthology of Stories, Instructions, and Poetry*, rev. ed. New Haven, 1973. Lichteim is fuller, but Simpson's collection is more widely available, including in paperback.

Spencer, A. J. *Early Egypt: The Rise of Civilisation in the Nile Valley*. London, 1993. More up to date than Hoffman, but less accessible to beginners.

CHAPTER TWO

THE GROWTH OF
EMPIRES IN
THE ANCIENT
NEAR EAST

I N THE SECOND MILLENNIUM B.C.E., the civilizations of the ancient Near
East were transformed by the arrival of new population groups and by the emergence of extensive empires built up through systematic military conquest. The
growth of these new empires was accompanied by widespread cultural assimilation,
deepening economic integration, and the emergence of an international diplomatic
system that encompassed almost the entire eastern Mediterranean world.

These migrations and conquests left a great deal of destruction and upheaval in
their wake; indeed, Sumerian civilization ceased to exist as a living culture in the
early part of the second millennium. However, the new inhabitants of the Asiatic
Near East typically assimilated themselves to the older traditions of the area, forging
new societies that drew heavily on the cultural legacy of the Sumero-Akkadian past.
Even the peoples who moved into the remote limits of the Near East, such as Anatolia (roughly the area of modern-day Turkey), adopted much of the practice and heritage of the region's older civilizations.

Egypt too was transformed by the dynamic changes of the second millennium.
During the weakness and division of the First Intermediate Period, foreigners from
western Asia and Nubia penetrated the "center of the cosmos" in large numbers.
Some came as immigrants; others were brought to Egypt as mercenaries to protect
the land from invaders. This strategy was largely successful. Even in the wake of the
Old Kingdom's collapse, Egypt did not suffer large-scale armed invasion. But when
Egypt recovered its strength in the early second millennium, the confidence in *ma'at*
had been shattered. Their optimism dampened, Egyptians became far more suspi-
cious and took a much greater interest in what happened beyond their frontiers.
This concern only deepened after the middle of the millennium, in the aftermath of
Egypt's subjugation by a foreign army called the Hyksos.

The Late Bronze Age (1500–1200 B.C.E.) was a period of intensifying diplomacy,
trade, and internationalism. Once the movements of people died down after the
midpoint of the millennium, a balance of power developed between the Egyptians
of the New Kingdom and the Hittite Empire of Anatolia. Between them was a

FOCUS QUESTIONS

• What are the origins of Indo-European languages?

• How did Hammurabi bind his empire together?

• How did trade help spread urbanism in the
kingdoms of the north?

• What distinctions characterize New Kingdom
Egyptians?

• What factors facilitated the creation of the
Late Bronze Age international system?

• How did Minoan culture affect Mycenaean
culture?

constellation of smaller but astonishingly prosperous and powerful states, fully engaged in the burgeoning trade and cosmopolitan culture of the age. Through their endeavors they influenced societies beyond the Near East, spreading the urban idea and its trappings to the eastern Mediterranean—the islands of Cyprus (ancient Alashiya) and Crete, and through these areas to the mainland of Greece. By the thirteenth century, nations from the southern Balkans to the western fringes of Iran were influencing each other in meaningful ways, resulting in a wide-ranging cultural synthesis. By 1250 B.C.E., the politics and economies of these early states depended in great measure on each other.

This international system proved more fragile than its participants had imagined. Around 1200 B.C.E., a new wave of invasions emanating from the Aegean Sea brought political and economic collapse from Greece to Egypt, and led to the destruction of nearly every great empire of the Late Bronze Age. But although this integrated world collapsed, the cultural and commercial impact of these societies on one another would continue to resonate in the centuries that followed, laying the groundwork for the Greek civilization of the archaic and classical age.

> The first truly consequential invasions of Sumer had come near the end of the third millennium B.C.E. at the hands of Sargon and his Akkadians.

MIGRATION AND LANGUAGE

What are the origins of Indo-European languages?

The second millennium B.C.E. began with the migration of two new groups of peoples into the Near Eastern world: Semitic-speaking peoples such as the Amorites and the Assyrians; and Indo-European-speaking peoples such as the Hittites and the early Greeks. The interactions between these two groups of peoples would help to determine the history of the ancient Near East for the next one thousand years.

SEMITIC-SPEAKERS

The first truly consequential invasions of Sumer had come near the end of the third millennium B.C.E. at the hands of Sargon and his Akkadians. Although Sumerians and Akkadians created a new culture not far re-

moved from Sumerian forms, Sargon's imperial ventures began the infiltration of Sumerian civilization by Semitic-speakers closely related to the Akkadians. This paved the way for the further influence of Semitic speakers, until finally Sumerian civilization was completely eclipsed.

The various Semitic speakers of the Near East were a diverse group. On the one hand were the Akkadians, extensively assimilated into Sumerian civilization. There were also the Amorites, nomads who ultimately came to dominate Mesopotamia, urbanizing in the process but retaining much that reflected their rough-and-tumble roots. In northern Mesopotamia were the Assyrians, early caravaners who pioneered trade routes into Anatolia during the early second millennium. Deeply influenced by Sumero-Akkadian culture, the Assyrians would go on to found an important, independent, and long-lasting civilization in their own right. The Phoenicians and their Bronze Age ancestors on the Syro-Palestine coast were the greatest seafarers and merchants of Mediterranean antiquity; their inland cousins, the Canaanites, were warlike seminomads who were one of the great national enemies of another Semitic people very much like themselves, the Hebrews.

As we saw in Chapter One, the rulers of Ur Dynasty III tried to reassert the primacy of Sumerian civilization in the face of the increasing influence of Semitic languages. The dynamic king Shulgi died around 2047 B.C.E., and was succeeded by two competent sons who both died young. As a result the throne fell to Shulgi's grandson, Ibbi-Sin, a hapless individual most charitably described as in over his head. Something of a "mama's boy," he portrayed himself as a beardless youth well into middle age, and the only attested name for his mother from his royal records is "Mommy." He surrounded himself with flatterers and other courtiers, and the imperial bureaucracy bloated under his rule.

His archives trace the anatomy of a dying empire. One by one, the royal archives trail off in the cities under Ur's dominion. Slowly but surely, Ibbi-Sin lost control of his empire, and ultimately turned to his field marshal, a man of Amorite descent named Ishbi-Irra. Ishbi-Irra was shrewd and ruthless, time and again letting affairs reach an impasse and then applying his considerable military talents only at the last moment in exchange for more power and prerogatives for himself. Thanks to Ishbi-Irra, Ibbi-Sin remained on the throne

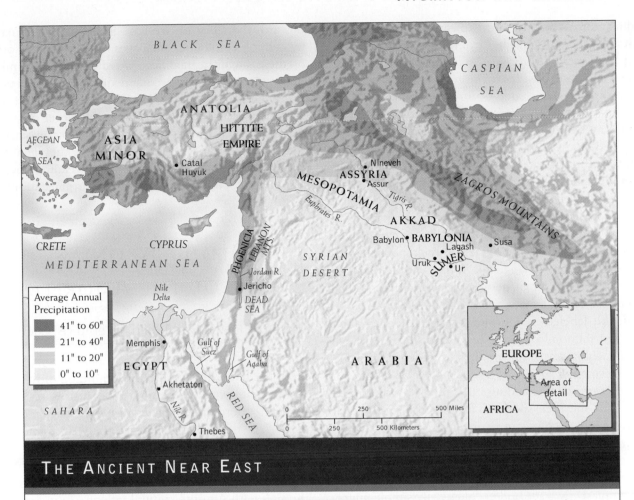

BLACK SEA

CASPIAN SEA

ANATOLIA

HITTITE EMPIRE

ASIA MINOR

AEGEAN SEA

• Catal Huyuk

• Nineveh

ASSYRIA

• Assur

MESOPOTAMIA

ZAGROS MOUNTAINS

Tigris R.

Euphrates R.

AKKAD

CRETE

CYPRUS

PHOENICIA

LEBANON MTS.

Babylon •

BABYLONIA

• Susa

Lagash

• Uruk

SUMER

• Ur

MEDITERRANEAN SEA

Jordan R.

SYRIAN DESERT

Nile Delta

• Jericho

DEAD SEA

Average Annual Precipitation

▮ 41" to 60"
▮ 21" to 40"
▮ 11" to 20"
▯ 0" to 10"

Memphis •

Gulf of Suez

Gulf of Aqaba

ARABIA

EUROPE

EGYPT

• Akhetaton

Area of detail

SAHARA

Nile R.

RED SEA

AFRICA

250   500 Miles
0
0   250   500 Kilometers

• Thebes

THE ANCIENT NEAR EAST

Notice the geographical relationship among the older centers of Sumer and Egypt, and among the newer civilizations such as Babylonia, Assyria, Phoenicia, and the Hittite empire of Anatolia. Which of the emerging cultures were most likely to show the strongest Sumerian influence, and why? Which cultures were more likely to become conduits for trade, and what was their role in spreading the Mesopotamian urban model? Also note where the major civilizations are located, and examine them in relation to the average rainfall displayed in the inset map. What does the comparison demonstrate regarding the relationship between urban activity and environmental factors such as climate?

for twenty-four years until an Elamite army sacked Ur. Only after the Elamites had carried Ibbi-Sin into captivity did Ishbi-Irra spring heroically into action, driving off the remaining invaders and claiming the kingship for himself. For the inhabitants of Mesopotamia, the memory of Ibbi-Sin resonated for centuries as the epitome of criminal stupidity and hopeless incompetence.

Ishbi-Irra was unable to reassert power over the whole of the shattered empire of Ur Dynasty III. The various cities of the realm had broken free for good, many of them now under the rule of ambitious and powerful Amorite chiefs. For the first two centuries of the second millenium, the geopolitical history of

Mesopotamia exhibits a pattern of warfare among a constellation of petty Amorite kingdoms based on the great urban centers of the Sumero-Akkadian past. Not until the eighteenth century B.C.E. would one of these Amorite-descended kings, the remarkable Hammurabi of Babylon, create a new unity in the region.

THE INDO-EUROPEANS

In 1786 Sir William Jones, a British judge serving in Calcutta, India, made a discovery that transformed knowledge about the world of prehistory and began the formal discipline of historical linguistics. Trained in "Oriental studies" before his legal education, Sir

William turned his spare time toward the study of Sanskrit, the ancient language from which the predominant languages of the South Asian subcontinent derive. In the course of his endeavor to master Sanskrit, he found that Sanskrit shared features of grammar and vocabulary with Latin and ancient Greek to an extent inexplicable by sheer coincidence. His interest piqued, Sir William examined the early Germanic tongue called Gothic, the ancient Celtic languages of Europe, and Old Persian. They likewise exhibited similar structure and shared extensive vocabularies with Sanskrit. He concluded that all of these languages must have come from a common source, probably long extinct by the time of Sanskrit and ancient Greek, and not preserved as any known language. Within another generation, the ancient language whose existence Jones had hypothesized, and the later languages derived from it, would be labeled as Indo-European, reflecting their wide distribution from India to Ireland.

Archaeologists, anthropologists, linguists, and ancient historians have done much since Jones to increase our understanding of the Indo-European languages and their speakers. But much of our knowledge remains highly controversial. Was there an original form of the language, Proto-Indo-European (PIE), spoken by a single population at some point in time? If so, when and where? How did Indo-European spread? By conquest? By trade and exchange? By simple migration and slow infiltration? Or by a "wave-of-advance" model, whereby PIE-speaking agriculturalists slowly spread their language(s) by seeking out new land to farm and establishing new settlements? Can their diffusion be traced archaeologically, by the presence of characteristic pottery types and burial practices, or are such things not be correlated at all with the patterns of linguistic change? We have no definitive answers to any of these questions.

It is certain, however, that Indo-European linguistic forms began to appear in the Near East and eastern Mediterranean shortly after 2000 B.C.E., when speakers of early forms of Persian and Sanskrit made their way into and through the Iranian Plateau, and the Hittites arrived in their historical homeland in central Anatolia. Around this same time, another group of Indo-European-speaking people began to move into the Aegean basin, combining the basic structure and much of their vocabulary with indigenous linguistic elements to produce an early form of Greek.

The impact that Semitic- and Indo-European-speaking peoples had on the history of the ancient world was tremendous. Indeed, from the second millennium onward, the story of Western antiquity is dominated by cultures employing languages from one or the other of these linguistic families. We should bear in mind, however, that these newcomers did not, at most times and in most places, constitute apocalyptic waves of destroyers who wiped the slate clean. However rude they may have been when they first came into contact with the older civilizations of the Near East, they generally accommodated themselves quickly, spreading and developing the pattern of urban life and organization.

THE OLD BABYLONIAN EMPIRE OF THE AMORITES

How did Hammurabi bind his empire together?

From the fall of Ibbi-Sin to the beginning of the eighteenth century B.C.E., Mesopotamian history resumed a familiar pattern under a new guise. Once again a cycle of warfare took place over water rights, arable land, trade routes, power, and prestige. Instead of being waged by independent Sumerian city-states, however, these wars were fought among small kingdoms shot through with Amorite cultural influence and governed by Amorite kings. Typically, these Amorite states are referred to as "petty," and indeed they are in comparison with the empires that preceded and followed them. A few of their kings made important contributions to the unfolding of the Western tradition, such as Lipit-Ishtar, king of Isin in the nineteenth century B.C.E. His "law code" advanced the notion of using precedent set in past cases to create general rules for future judicial problems. As we will see, this development had a profound influence on a later Amorite king of the region, Hammurabi.

THE RISE OF HAMMURABI OF BABYLON

In 1792 B.C.E. a young man named Hammurabi ascended the throne of Babylon, a weak kingdom in the middle of Mesopotamia based in an insignificant city of the same name. When Hammurabi came to power, Babylon was both fragile and precariously wedged between a number of other, more powerful Amorite kingdoms. Babylon's site on the Tigris and Euphrates was potentially of great economic and military significance; but it was also dangerous, because Babylon sat

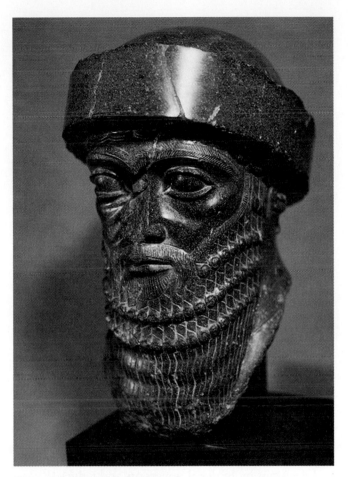

Mesopotamian Royal Head. A diorite head of a Mesopotamian king, conventionally identified as Hammurabi. Such headdresses were worn by the rulers of Mesopotamian cities between roughly 2100 and 1700 B.C.E. Hammurabi is shown wearing such a headdress on p. 52, but there is nothing else to identify this bust with Hammurabi.

much too late. He did not try to confront his mightier neighbors directly. Rather, with letters and embassies, double-dealing diplomacy, and general deceit, he induced his stronger counterparts to embroil themselves ever deeper in armed conflict with each other. While the other Amorite kingdoms exhausted themselves in costly and pointless wars, Hammurabi fanned their hatred for one another, skillfully and privately portraying himself as a friend to all sides. His role as a potential ally resulted often in his neighboring rulers' dispatching resources—material and military—to Hammurabi, in hopes that he might help them. Quietly he consolidated his kingdom, augmenting his own strength; when the time was right he fell on his depleted and weary neighbors. In so doing, he transformed his petty Amorite state into what historians describe as the Old Babylonian Empire.

Mesopotamia under Hammurabi's rule achieved an unprecedented degree of political integration. His realm ultimately stretched from the Persian Gulf into Assyria. The southern half of the region, formerly known as Sumer and Akkad, would for the rest of antiquity be known as Babylonia. Hammurabi introduced an innovation that affected religion and politics together. He elevated the otherwise little-known patron deity of Babylon, Marduk, to be the ruler-god of his entire empire. Although the king was careful to observe long-standing, traditional religious scruples by continuing to pay homage to the ancient gods of Sumer and Akkad, Marduk now sat atop the official pantheon. People could continue to worship the ancient patron deities of their cities if they wished; but all now owed allegiance to Marduk.

RELIGION AND LAW

The notion that political rule was tied to divine action and approval was nothing new, of course. Its foundations were readily discernible in the practices and beliefs of the Sumerians. What Hammurabi did was to utilize the rule of his god over a diverse people as a means of uniting them politically and conferring legitimacy on his rule over them all as king of Babylon, the city of Marduk. The precedent established by Hammurabi would become a hallmark of many Near Eastern civilizations thereafter. A number of peoples—among them the Assyrians and Hebrews—would launch wars of aggression in the name of their foremost god.

perilously amid mighty antagonists who were often tempted to "play through" the city on their way to other conquests.

Hammurabi may have been the first sovereign in world history to understand that power need not be based on brute force. He recognized that the application of intellect, political strategy, and ruthless cunning might accomplish what his army could not. A rich archive of tablets found at the city of Mari (which eventually fell under Hammurabi's rule) testifies to the cleverness and talent of this remarkable king.

The Babylonian king used writing as a weapon, but did so with such subtlety that his targets only noticed

> Hammurabi may have been the first sovereign in world history to understand that power need not be based on brute force.

Code of Hammurabi. The entire code of Hammurabi survives on an eight-foot column made of basalt. The top quarter of the column depicts the Babylonian king paying homage to the seated god of justice. Directly below one can make out the cuneiform inscriptions that are the law code's text.

between ritual intercourse and fertility. Temple prostitutes were highly respected, recruited from among both men and women. The Babylonians attached no stigma, as nearly as we can tell, to the practice of both heterosexual and homosexual relations with the sacred prostitutes. Temple prostitutes were of course busiest during times of high religious festivals, when people from around the empire came to worship Marduk. The Babylonians believed that sexual intercourse between worshipers and the temple prostitutes helped to inspire a mysterious and holy experience in the former.

Hammurabi did not rely entirely on religion to bind his empire together. Building on the precedents of centuries and rulers past, Hammurabi issued a collection of laws that more properly approached what we might consider a "code." Known from an impressive eight-foot stele (inscribed stone monument) discovered in southwestern Iran and now in the Louvre, the so-called Code of Hammurabi addressed a wide range of legal concerns. The code was not an attempt to prescribe remedies for all conceivable infractions that might occur in Babylonian society. Rather, the code represented actual rulings handed down by the king in particular cases. Hammurabi's innovation was to have his decisions published throughout his realm, expecting that they would serve as the foundation of future judicial decisions by his local governors and judges.

OLD BABYLONIAN SOCIETY

How did trade help spread urbanism in the kingdoms of the north?

Close associations continued to exist between political power and religious practice. The annual new year celebration of the Amorite Babylonians consisted of mock battles reenacting the victory of Marduk over the Sumerian god of chaos. It was because of this confrontation that Marduk had been able to claim his place astride heaven and earth as the chief god. Marduk's imposition of orderliness helped the predictability and controllability of the environment, the Babylonians believed, and thus helped fertility. Indeed, during the same new year festivities, as priests chanted the mythological stories recounting Marduk's ascent, the king would retire with a sacred prostitute inside the temple, and the two would have ritual sexual intercourse as a magical aid to the fertility of nature. The Babylonian king's importance was far from only political.

Babylonians believed strongly in the connections

Aside from the interesting cross-cultural influences embodied in the provisions of Hammurabi's code, as a source it reveals much about the structure of Amorite Babylonian society. Overall, the more complicated social arrangements of Sumerian civilization had been succeeded by a simpler but more oppressive system. An upper class of nobles—palace officials, temple priests, high-ranking military officers, and wealthy merchants—controlled large estates and staggering wealth. Beneath this small stratum was an enormous class of legally free individuals who in economic and political terms might best be described as "dependents" of the palace or the temple, or who leased land from the estates of the powerful. Among these dependents were laborers and artisans, small-time merchants,

THE CODE OF HAMMURABI

The laws of Hammurabi, published on the authority of the king and set up throughout the Babylonian empire, exhibit the influences both of the urban society on which they were imposed and the rough justice of Amorite tradition. While Hammurabi built on older, urban legal traditions, he sought to extend the authority of his law into more realms of life and provide sterner punishments for its violation. This sampling of his provisions illustrates the severity of his system for criminals, while providing protections in unusual circumstances.

If a man accuses a man, and charges him with murder, but cannot convict him, the accuser shall be put to death.

If a man steals an ox or sheep, ass or pig, or boat—if it belonged to the god or palace, he shall pay thirty fold; if it belonged to a common man, he shall restore ten fold. If the thief has nothing wherewith to pay, he shall be put to death.

If a fire breaks out in a man's house and a man who goes to extinguish it . . . takes the household property of the owner of the house, that man shall be thrown into the fire.

If a man aids a male or a female slave of the palace, or a male or female slave of a common man, to escape from the city, he shall be put to death.

If a man who is a tenant has paid the full amount of money for his rent for the year to the owner of the house, and he (the owner) says to him before "his days are full," "Vacate," the owner of the house, because he made the tenant move out of the house before "his days were full" shall lose the money which the tenant paid him.

If an agent should be careless and not take a receipt for the money which he has given to the merchant, the money not receipted for shall not be placed to his account.

If the wife of a man be taken in lying with another man, they shall bind them and throw them into the water.

If a woman hates her husband and says, "Thou shalt not have me," her past shall be inquired into for any deficiency of hers; and if she has been careful and without past sin and her husband has been going out and greatly belittling her, that woman has no blame. She shall take her dowry and go to her father's house.

If a man destroys the eye of another man, they shall destroy his eye. If a man knocks out the tooth of a man of his own rank, they shall knock out his tooth . . . if the tooth of a common man, he shall pay one-third mana of silver.

Sara Robbins, ed. *Law: A Treasury of Art and Literature.* (New York: Beaux Arts Editions), 1990, pp. 20–22 (slightly revised).

small-scale farmers, and the minor political and religious officials of the state.

At the bottom of Babylonian society were the slaves. Far more numerous in Babylonian than Sumerian culture, slaves at this time were also treated much more harshly. They were also readily identifiable as a separate group within Sumerian society. Both nobles and dependents wore long hair and beards, but slaves were shaven and branded. Babylonians acquired slaves by a number of means, including active importation through trade, a marked departure from Sumerian practice. Like previous Mesopotamian societies, the Babylonians also took prisoners of wars as slaves, and through debt and as punishment for certain offenses free citizens could fall into slavery. Restrictions were many, and treatment was harsh: slaves could accumulate property and borrow as a means of gaining freedom, but we have no way of knowing how often this occurred in practice.

Class had a significant influence on relationships in Babylonian society. As Hammurabi's code reveals, offenses committed against nobles carried far more severe penalties than did the same crime committed against a dependent or slave (although nobles were also punished more severely than were commoners for crimes they committed against other nobles). Marriage arrangements and customs also reflected class differences, with bride price and dowry depending on the status of the parties involved.

Hammurabi's code also provides evidence as to the status and treatment of women in Babylonian society. Women did enjoy certain protections under the law, especially with regard to the ability to divorce abusive, neglectful, or indigent husbands. Furthermore, a husband who chose to divorce a wife "without cause" was obligated to provide financial support for his wife and their children. It is important to bear in mind, however, that Babylonian law essentially regarded wives as the property of their husbands, and a wife who went around her city bad-mouthing or rumor-mongering about her spouse was subject to drowning; she would suffer the same fate, along with her lover, were she caught in the act of adultery. Husbands, however, enjoyed the legal right to significant sexual promiscuity.

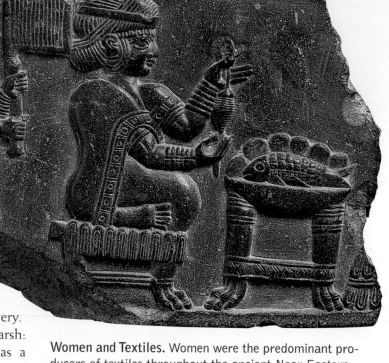

Women and Textiles. Women were the predominant producers of textiles throughout the ancient Near Eastern world. Even upper-class women spun thread and wove cloth for their households. Here, a servant fans an elegant lady spinning thread with a spindle.

HAMMURABI'S LEGACY

Hammurabi died around 1750 B.C.E. Although some contraction of the Old Babylonian empire followed under his successors, Hammurabi's efforts in establishing legal norms and consistent administration throughout his realm paid dividends. The Old Babylonian empire was no house of cards, dependent on the dynamism of talented kings to maintain viability. His administrative reforms, combined with his innovations in state religious worship around Marduk, created a durable and important state in Mesopotamia. For another two centuries the Old Babylonian empire played a significant role in the Near East, until invaders from the north sacked the capital and occupied it. Babylon itself remained the region's most famous city through the second and first millennia B.C.E.

Hammurabi's legacy extended well beyond the borders of his own kingdom. His success, and the flair and aplomb with which he achieved it, were instrumental in shaping the conception of kingship in the ancient Near East. After Hammurabi, religion would play an increasingly important role in the policies of Near

HOW DID TRADE HELP SPREAD URBANISM IN THE KINGDOMS OF THE NORTH?

OLD BABYLONIAN SOCIETY   55

Eastern kings. Hammurabi had also demonstrated the effectiveness and importance of writing as a political tool. Diplomacy, the keeping of extensive archives, international relations—all became characteristic concerns of subsequent Near Eastern rulers. So too did the claim of kings to be the protectors of the weak and the arbiters of justice within their realms. In this last accomplishment Hammurabi built on a long-standing tendency among Mesopotamian kings. His greatness, however, transformed law giving into an imperative for any ambitious ruler of a Near Eastern kingdom.

THE KINGDOMS OF THE NORTH

Beyond the northern reaches of Hammurabi's dominion important changes were taking shape during the first few centuries of the second millennium B.C.E. Through trade, the urban model had spread far and wide, making considerable inroads into Anatolia. At the same time, newcomers made their presence felt in dramatic ways, reshaping the face of the Near East and its history. They would establish powerful kingdoms and play an important role in the transmission of Near Eastern social and cultural patterns across the sea to the Aegean islands and the Greek mainland.

THE ASSYRIANS

The northern part of Mesopotamia was Assyria, homeland to another group of Semitic-speakers who played an influential role throughout Near Eastern history. The greatest phase of Assyrian civilization belonged to the first millennium B.C.E., and we will encounter these people in more detail in Chapter Three. But the Assyrians also played an important role in the second-millennium empires whose growth we are considering here.

The Assyrians were principally responsible for extending urbanism to the northwest, particularly into Anatolia. In antiquity, this mountainous region possessed astonishing natural wealth and played a vital role in the economic and political history of several empires well into the modern period. This bounty went untapped by the civilizations we have so far examined. It was the Assyrians who blazed economic trails into the region and accelerated the pace of urban life and society in Anatolia, especially in the central region known in classical times as Cappadocia.

The Assyrians were principally responsible for extending urbanism to the northwest, particularly into Anatolia.

Before 1900 B.C.E., the Assyrians began to organize extensive trade networks between Mesopotamia and Anatolia, as well as within Anatolia itself. Either because of their primary interest in commerce or the impracticality of conquest, the Assyrians did not seek military gains in the region. They were content to enter into understandings with the local Cappadocian rulers, who reigned from strongholds not dissimilar to the great villages of the late Neolithic. Assyrian merchants relied on the military protection of these local potentates, while they organized the trade that made the rulers of Cappadocia and other parts of Anatolia rich. The great Assyrian families organized themselves into boards of trade, determining prices, assigning trade routes and sharing out profits among themselves. Although they usually lived in the outlying districts of the great centers of Anatolian trade, Assyrians had a profound impact on Hattic (or "Cappadocian") culture. Assyrians served as advisors to kings, filling important posts and marrying into the important families of Hattic towns. In the process, they carried Mesopotamian civilization and its trappings into the region and into the districts lying between Assyria and Anatolia proper, such as northern Syria.

Mesopotamian civilization remained in many ways true to its Sumerian roots. Cuneiform remained the basic script in which many peoples of the Near East, including the Assyrians, wrote their language. Also, although Sumerian as a living, spoken language died out early in the second millenium, its legacy as a language of literature and education continued. Gilgamesh may have started as a Sumerian hero, but his fame and legend remained popular throughout Near Eastern history. Much like Latin during the Middle Ages, Sumerian was deemed a language worthy of study by educated people for many centuries after it had passed from daily usage. Therefore, the civilized tradition of Anatolia and the northern reaches of Syria was imbued with a substrate of the most revered traditions of the ancient Mesopotamian past. New peoples might move into the region, but they would accommodate themselves to the pattern of urban life established in Sumer centuries previously, absorb its heritage, and consider themselves fully a part of the Near Eastern synthesis, culturally as well as politically.

After 1800 B.C.E. the pace of direct commercial and cultural interaction between Assyria and Anatolia slackened. By the second quarter of the eighteenth century, the Assyrians had to dedicate their energies to fending off the ambitious Hammurabi to their south. At the same time, invaders were infiltrating Anatolia and northern Syria, disrupting the trade networks for a time as they overwhelmed the states of the Hattic peoples.

HURRIANS, HITTITES, AND KASSITES

In the wake of this Assyrian-assisted urbanization, new kingdoms and new population groups emerged throughout Anatolia, northern Syria, and Mesopotamia. One of these new kingdoms was established by the Hurrians. The Hurrians spoke a distinct language, neither Semitic nor Indo-European. Their exact origin and time of arrival are mysterious, but they probably entered eastern Anatolia and northern Syria from the north around the middle of the third millennium. By 1800 B.C.E. or so they had established a patchwork of Hurrian kingdoms that endured for two and a half centuries.

The Hurrians played a critical role in the transmission of Mesopotamian culture to the Hittites, an Indo-European-speaking people who penetrated Anatolia sometime around the turn of the second millennium. Hittite is but one of several closely related Indo-European languages whose speakers migrated and settled throughout Anatolia around this time, but over the course of several centuries the Hittites imposed themselves and their language on the peoples of the region as a ruling minority class. They established themselves within the growing cities of central Anatolia, particularly in Cappadocia, and remained politically independent of one another until about 1700 B.C.E. At that time the ruler of one of these city-states integrated the Hittites into a larger kingdom. About fifty years later, a ruler of this larger kingdom organized his warrior nobility into a more efficient military machine, expanded the frontiers of the kingdom, and captured a strategic mountain stronghold that dominated the area, named Hattusas. To reflect this new capital, the king changed his name to Hattusilis; he was the founder of the Hittite Old Kingdom.

Hittite culture was intensely militaristic. Partly as a result, the Hittites fielded some of the greatest armies of the Bronze Age. A great part of any Hittite king's energies was necessarily devoted to warfare and to maintaining control over his fractious and ambitious warrior nobility. Alongside this military tradition, the Hittites adopted enthusiastically the practices of those

they conquered. At some point, the Hittites adapted cuneiform to represent their own language. They seem to have begun fairly early the practice of writing down their laws, which reflect the influence of urban life on a previously nomadic culture.

Under Hattusilis I, the Hittites extended their power throughout the Anatolian plateau. Like the Assyrians, the Hittites were anxious to control trade routes throughout the region. Unlike the Assyrians, however, the Hittites also aimed at military conquest. For both reasons, the Hittites were particularly concerned to control the overland trade routes for copper and arsenic, the latter being one of the metals that can be alloyed with copper to produce bronze, the basic material of tools and weapons in the second millennium B.C.E. Combining plunder with trade, Hattusilis transformed his Hittite kingdom into an economic and military power.

Hattusilis's grandson and successor, Mursilis I (c. 1620–1590 B.C.E.) proved even more dynamic and ambitious. He sought to control the region of the upper Euphrates and to subjugate some of the small but powerful Hurrian kingdoms of northern Syria. In a brilliant campaign he drove southeastward into Mesopotamia, collecting booty and tribute until he found himself before the fabled gates of Babylon. Babylon was still the center of an Amorite kingdom, now ruled by a distant descendant of Hammurabi. Mursilis I captured and sacked Babylon in 1595 B.C.E., collecting for himself the accumulated riches of centuries. He then withdrew and abandoned the ruined city to its fate.

> The Hurrians played a critical role in the transmission of Mesopotamian culture to the West by preserving many of the literary and cultural ideas of the region.

What followed was something of a "dark age" in the history of the Near East, largely because our sources for the period are very poor. The next hundred years after the sack of Babylon seem to have been characterized by upheaval. A group known as the Kassites moved into the devastated city and seized control of the Old Babylonian Kingdom. The origins and language of the Kassites are highly debatable. Some scholars have claimed that certain Kassite names bear Indo-European traits, but the arguments are inconclusive. Like many invaders of Mesopotamia before them, the Kassites adapted themselves speedily to the older civilization they found there. Though they arrived as invaders, the Kassites ultimately presided over a largely peaceful and prosperous Babylonian realm for the next five hundred years.

The Hittites, however, brought no stability to the region. Mursilis achieved too much too soon; his growing

HOW DID TRADE HELP SPREAD URBANISM IN THE KINGDOMS OF THE NORTH?

OLD BABYLONIAN SOCIETY   57

THE NEAR EAST, C. 1400 B.C.E.

How has the spread of the urban model forced us to widen our geographical focus? Notice the proliferation of cities along the eastern shores of the Mediterranean; what does this tell us about the rise of the trade in this region of the Near East? Consider the centrality of this region in relation to the major empires of the time, as well as the emerging civilization of the Aegean basin. How crucial is trade becoming to the world of the Late Bronze Age?

strength alarmed the warrior nobility, not yet ready to cede so much prestige and authority to a centralized kingship. Mursilis may have been impelled to abandon Babylon so quickly because of trouble at home; shortly after his arrival back in his capital Hattusas, he fell victim to a palace conspiracy. After his assassination, Hittite power ebbed for the next century or so.

Mursilis left tremendous destruction in his wake. The Hurrians, who had the bad luck to lie between Mursilis and his ambitions, were overrun by the Hittite king, and the Hurrian kingdom was destroyed. When our sources once again become clearer after 1500

B.C.E., a new group had made their presence felt in northern Syria: the Mitannians.

THE KINGDOM OF MITANNI

Like the Hittites, the Mitannians were an Indo-European minority who imposed themselves on a native people as a ruling class. This warrior aristocracy penetrated northern Syria and assumed control of the Hurrian centers that Mursilis had undermined, knitting these petty Hurrian states into a single kingdom, the kingdom of Mitanni.

A Near Eastern War Chariot, here used for lion hunting by the Assyrian king Assurnasirpal II (883–859 B.C.E.).

Mitanni is significant for a variety of reasons. The appearance of the Mitannians in northern Syria may provide a clue regarding the movements of the Indo-European-speakers who would ultimately pass through the Iranian plateau and into the Indian subcontinent. The names of the rulers of this kingdom bear close similarity to those used by the later invaders of India, and they recognized gods familiar from northern India in later times: Mitrasil (the Aryan Mitra), Arunasil (Varuna), and Indar (Indra).

The Mitannians introduced a number of innovations into Near Eastern warfare, including a lighter, horse-drawn chariot, which they used to carry archers around the field and strike terror into their enemies. They were also masters of horse training and cavalry tactics. For a time, these inventions and skills allowed them to keep the Hittites in check to their west, while to their east they reduced the powerful Assyrians to the status of a vassal kingdom. But when the opponents of Mitanni began employing chariots themselves and using scale armor to protect both infantry and cavalry, the balance quickly turned.

The kingdom of Mitanni also played an important role in the diplomatic relations of the Late Bronze Age. The Egyptian pharaohs of the New Kingdom pursued an aggressive military and economic policy that brought them into competition with the New Hittite Kingdom. As a result, the Egyptians established an alliance with Mitanni as a counterpoise to Hittite power in the north. As a sign of this alli-ance, at least one Mitannian princess entered the harem of Pharaoh Thutmosis IV (1401–1391 B.C.E.). Weakened by a dynastic dispute in the middle of the fourteenth century, however, Mitanni finally collapsed in the face of renewed Hittite aggression. The Hittites allowed a rump kingdom of Mitanni to survive as a buffer state between themselves and Assyria. But the removal of the powerful Hurrian kingdom meant that the Egyptians and Hittites now embroiled themselves directly in military conflict, with enormous consequences for both.

CHRONOLOGY

TRANSFORMATIONS IN THE ANCIENT NEAR EAST

Semitic peoples invade Sumer	2000 B.C.E.
Indo-European peoples arrive in the Near East	2000 B.C.E.
Rise of Old Babylonian Empire	1800 B.C.E.
Assyrians organize trade networks	1900 B.C.E.
Creation of Hurrian, Hittite, Kassite, and Mittani kingdoms	1800–1400 B.C.E.

EGYPT IN THE SECOND MILLENNIUM B.C.E.

What distinctions characterize New Kingdom Egyptians?

Once the kingdom of Mitanni had been reduced by the Hittites, the way was open for the Egyptians and Hittites to compete directly for control of the Near East.

Compared with our description of Egypt in Chapter One, the notion of an imperialistic Egypt may seem odd. To explain this development, we must therefore shift our gaze away from the Asiatic Near East in the Late Bronze Age and return to Egypt at the end of the First Intermediate Period (2170–1983 B.C.E.).

MIDDLE KINGDOM EGYPT (1983–1795 B.C.E.)

The First Intermediate period was a time of political disunity and intense suffering for many Egyptians. The central authority of Memphis collapsed, and eventually a familiar pattern of Egyptian history reemerged: the consolidation of a northern center of power, opposed by a separate regime consolidating its power in the south. Based in the city of Herakleopolis in the north, men claiming to be pharaohs extended their sway over the northernmost part of Upper Egypt, but their control over Lower Egypt was tenuous at best. The delta region fell victim to incursions from Asiatic nomads from time to time, but curiously no native Lower Egyptian dynasty ever tried to assert itself in the power vacuum.

In the south, a competing dynasty arose around the city of Thebes, which refused to recognize the northern rulers as legitimate pharaohs. Likewise, the northerners at Herakleopolis scoffed at "the southern nomes" or "the head of the south." The close of the twenty-first century and the beginning of the twentieth century B.C.E. witnessed increasing warfare between the two dynasties until the Theban Mentuhotep II conquered the north and established himself as pharaoh of a united Egypt.

Mentuhotep is an intriguing figure. Although he clearly considered himself Egyptian, the location of Thebes in the deep south and the infiltration of Nubians during the First Intermediate gave the Eleventh Dynasty a slightly different cast and outlook, more akin in some respects to the cultures of sub-Saharan Africa than to the Old Kingdom. Mentuhotep's dynasty also exhibits a matriarchal element that may be linked with Nubian practice. After they became firmly established, however, Mentuhotep and his successors took pains to present themselves as traditional Egyptian rulers, and strove to be just as culturally "Egyptian" as their Old Kingdom counterparts.

With the reestablishment of unified government, now centered in the south at Thebes, Egypt entered the period of the Middle Kingdom. Soon after Mentuhotep II's death, a usurper, the vizier Amenemhet, established himself and his descendants as Egypt's brilliant Twelfth Dynasty. Amenemhet retained Thebes as a center of power but also built a new capital just south of Memphis (the name of which, Itj-towy, means "Amenemhet takes possession of the Two Lands"). Dynasty 12 remained in power for nearly two hundred years, producing a succession of remarkable pharaohs.

Under this dynasty, the Egyptians now began to exploit more thoroughly the potential for trade to the south. They mounted expeditions to the land of Punt (probably the coast of Somalia) and secured their border with Nubia. By the middle of the nineteenth century B.C.E., Nubia was firmly under Egypt's control, and the small states and principalities of Palestine and Syria were under heavy Egyptian political and economic influence. But despite Egypt's renewed strength, the Egyptians did not incorporate the lands to the northeast into their realm. Instead, Amenemhet I constructed the "Walls of the Prince" in Sinai to guard against incursions from Egypt's Asian neighbors.

The great fortifications built along Egypt's frontiers during Dynasty 12 demonstrate the great resourcefulness of these pharaohs, but they also betray a marked shift in the Egyptian outlook on the world. Long gone was the placid serenity epitomized by *ma'at*. Middle Kingdom Egyptians viewed the world beyond their borders with suspicion and fear. Egypt was not as yet an imperial power; pharaohs in the Middle Kingdom did not integrate their conquests into their kingdom in any meaningful way. But unlike their Old Kingdom counterparts, the Egyptians of the Middle Kingdom were now taking a direct interest in events beyond Egypt itself.

Pharaoh's position had also changed. None of the Middle Kingdom pharaohs portrayed themselves with the serene confidence of Old Kingdom depic-

C H R O N O L O G Y

EGYPTIAN PERIODS AND KINGDOMS IN THE SECOND MILLENNIUM

Middle Kingdom	1983–1795 B.C.E.
Second Intermediate Period	1795–1550 B.C.E.
New Kingdom	1550–1075 B.C.E.
Third Intermediate Period	1075–656 B.C.E.
Late Period	656–332 B.C.E.
Hellenistic Period	332–30 B.C.E.

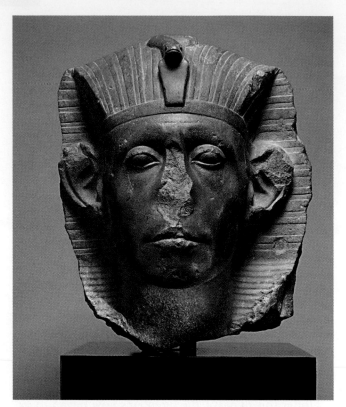

Sesostris III (1870–1831 B.C.E.). This powerful Twelfth-Dynasty pharaoh led military campaigns into Nubia, constructed massive, garrisoned fortresses along the Nile, and dug new waterways near Aswan. More than one hundred portrait busts of Sesostris survive, all with similar features. The overhanging brow, deep-set eyes, and drawn-down mouth are all intended to communicate the enormous burden of responsibility the pharaoh bore as the ruler of all Egypt.

tions. Pharaoh continued to enjoy a special position as god-king, but his authority did not derive from a vaunted, remote position as such. Rather, in the Middle Kingdom pharaohs represented themselves as—and were expected to be—good shepherds, tenders of their Egyptian flock. *Ma'at* could not help them in these duties; only by diligently protecting Egypt from a hostile outside world could pharaohs provide the peace, prosperity, and security desired by their subjects. Portraits of the great pharaohs of Dynasty 12 poignantly reflect the concern and anxiety with which they lived.

Egyptians had lost that vision of the Old Kingdom wherein the land was a perfect and inviolable paradise. The literature of the Middle Kingdom demonstrates the change in attitude. Among the most popular literary forms were "Instructions" to various kings, such as the *Instruction of King Merykare* or the *Instruction of*

Amenemhet. This literature is characterized by cynicism and resignation. A pharaoh must trust no one: not a brother, not a friend, not intimate companions. He must crush the ambitions of local nobles with ruthless ferocity, and he must always be on the lookout for potential trouble. In return for his exertions on behalf of his people, he should expect neither gratitude nor reward; he should expect only that each new year will bring new dangers and more pressing challenges.

Egyptian chauvinism nevertheless remained. Even at the zenith of Middle Kingdom power under Sesostris III, the Egyptians continued to produce execration texts, loaded with curses against foreign peoples and their rulers. Literary texts show the same attitudes. In the popular *Story of Sinuhe*, the title character of the tale—a royal courtier—is gripped by an irrational terror at the death of Amenemhet I and flees the country. He sojourns in Palestine, where he is rescued by Semitic nomads. Living as an exile among them, he rises to become a tribal leader. At the end of his life, however, hoping for a proper Egyptian burial, he returns to Egypt, where the pharaoh Sesostris I receives him and honors him. The story underscores that it was better to live and die as a subject of pharaoh in Egypt than to be a prince among "vile Asiatics"; at the same time, the *Story of Sinuhe* rhapsodizes on the theme of pharaoh's power, wisdom, and forgiveness.

Though the attitude of Middle Kingdom Egyptians may strike us as somewhat overwrought, their feelings of insecurity were justified. The Egyptians recognized that they had been slowly drawn into a much wider world, a world that underwent a series of upheavals during the course of the early second millennium. The first pharaohs of Dynasty 13 (c. 1786–1633 B.C.E.) were greatly alarmed by the growing power of Hammurabi and his imperial ambitions. Precisely because Egypt remained a highly distinct culture unto itself, the wider world beyond the frontiers of the Two Lands appeared all the more alien, frightening, and potentially dangerous to the Egyptians.

THE SECOND INTERMEDIATE PERIOD AND REUNIFICATION

Just how dangerous this world was became clear in the middle of the seventeenth century B.C.E., when a new group of invaders overran the country. Known as the Hyksos (a Greek version of the Egyptian *beka khaswt*, or "rulers of foreign lands"), these invaders—whose exact origins are unknown, but who may have been Amorites—carved out a kingdom in the eastern delta and projected their authority over most of Egypt.

The period of Hyksos domination lasted about a century and came to be regarded as the great shame of Egyptian national history. Never before had all Egypt fallen under the domination of foreigners. About the Hyksos themselves, however, we know little; and much of what we do know derives from later, highly propagandistic Egyptian accounts of them. Clearly, however, they took over the machinery of pharaonic government in the north, and took steps to legitimate their rule. Some Hyksos rulers even incorporated the name of Ra into their names, despite later Egyptian references to them as "those who ruled without Ra." But the Hyksos also retained much of their foreign material culture, while maintaining close economic and diplomatic ties with the Aegean world, Syria and Palestine. In southern Egypt, Hyksos control was less complete. A native regime maintained a tenuous independence in Thebes, although they too sometimes had to acknowledge the suzerainty of the foreigners in the north.

Despite later Egyptian characterizations of them, the Hyksos established themselves and Egypt as the most significant power in the Near East, especially after the eclipse of Hittite power following Mursilis's assassination. The Second Intermediate Period (1795–1550 B.C.E.) was a not a time of total anarchy and profound weakness for Egypt, as the First Intermediate had been. Nevertheless, the confusion created by the Hyksos conquest allowed the Nubians to break free and found an independent kingdom called Kush (a much greater threat to the native dynasty in the south than to the Hyksos in the north). Under pressure from all sides, the southern pharaohs began to play on nationalist sentiment, launching "wars of liberation" against the "hated" Hyksos in the north. The strategy succeeded. By the end of the sixteenth century B.C.E., the southern pharaoh Ahmose had driven out the invaders, establishing a new dynasty and a new era in Egyptian history.

THE NEW KINGDOM (1550–1075 B.C.E.)

During the Late Bronze Age, Egyptian civilization reached the zenith of its magnificence and power. This phase is termed the New Kingdom by historians, who date it from the foundation of the Eighteenth Dynasty by the pharaoh Ahmose around 1550 B.C.E. The New Kingdom is in many ways a radical departure in Egyptian history and culture, though many of the basic religious, economic, and political forms remained, and art and literature continued much in the tradition established in Egypt's "classical" period. However, the dynamism of the New Kingdom—particularly its focus on imperialism and militarism—changed the very fabric of Egyptian life.

PHARAONIC RULE IN DYNASTY 18

Easy characterizations of Dynasty 18 are impossible. The pharaohs of this regime ruled Egypt for more than two and a half centuries, and some striking developments, uncharacteristic even within Egyptian society, took place during the period. The dynasty was forged in battle, with Ahmose winning fame as the man who finally expelled the Hyksos from the country. During his reign and that of his successors, we witness the rise of a new type of nobility in the context of Egyptian society, an aristocracy of military commanders and leaders. These officers gained wealth through the spoils of pharaoh's wars—including slaves to work the crown lands granted them as rewards for their successful military service.

The earliest pharaohs of Dynasty 18 were not so outwardly aggressive or imperialistic as some of their successors, but certain exigencies necessitated conquest. After the reunification of Egypt proper, Ahmose and his immediate heirs directed their efforts to the south, toward Nubia. By the dawn of the fifteenth century, the entire Near East had more or less evolved a gold standard for commerce and finance, and if Egypt was to maintain its stature it needed to control the rich Nubian gold mines. Under Thutmosis I (c. 1504–1491 B.C.E.), the Egyptians also penetrated to the northeast, driving deep into Syria and Palestine. This great pharaoh claimed to rule the land from beyond the Fourth Cataract in the south to the banks of the Euphrates in the north; no pharaoh had ever held sway over so much territory. Nor was his success merely fleeting: the Egyptians would sustain a serious military presence in the Asiatic Near East for the remainder of the New Kingdom; more than a century after Thutmosis, pharaohs undertook massive temple- and statuary-building projects deep into the Sudan.

> During the Late Bronze Age, Egyptian civilization reached the zenith of its magnificence and power.

New Kingdom Egyptians embodied a new spirit and attitude, at once removed and yet also in touch with the brilliance of the Old Kingdom. The pharaohs of the Eighteenth Dynasty deliberately and consciously cultivated the heritage of Egypt's glorious past, encouraging the revival of certain artistic forms as well as the recording and archiving of historical records and literary monuments. Taking pride in the cultural and historical strength of Egyptian civilization, New Kingdom Egyptians resuscitated that sense of self-confident superiority that the Middle Kingdom, for all its achievements, had lacked.

The new Egyptian outlook also owed much to its Middle Kingdom predecessor. New Kingdom pharaohs —with one notable exception we shall soon meet—had no conception of Egypt as an isolated Nile kingdom detached from its surroundings. They understood, as did the pharaohs of the Twelfth Dynasty, that Egypt's success and survival depended in great measure on its involvement beyond its borders. Egyptian prosperity and security were ensured through active acquisition of resources—by trade and selective conquest—and by maintaining political and diplomatic contacts.

A major distinction characterized the New Kingdom, however. Whereas there was a certain defensiveness and paranoid concern during the Middle Kingdom, New Kingdom pharaohs pursued an ambitious strategy of defense through offense. The embarrassment of the Hyksos domination translated itself into a steely determination to prevent such an episode from occurring ever again. This was to be accomplished not by preparing for the day when more invaders might arrive, but by actively projecting Egyptian strength into regions from which danger might come. The Egyptians had also learned something about battle tactics from the Hyksos, employing the horse-drawn battle chariots the Hyksos had used against them to devastating effect against their new enemies.

The peak of military activity came during the fifteenth century, in the wake of what could have been a crisis for Dynasty 18. Thutmosis II died young (probably in 1479 B.C.E.), leaving a youth as his heir, the future Thutmosis III. In the course of Egyptian history, such incidents often led to instability and even changes of dynasty. On this occasion, however, family politics and a remarkable personality served as a force for cohesion and continuity. It was pharaonic practice

> Whereas there was a certain defensiveness and paranoid concern during the Middle Kingdom, New Kingdom pharaohs pursued an ambitious strategy of defense through offense.

in the New Kingdom (and perhaps earlier) that pharaoh—himself a manifestation of a god—could marry as his official "queen" only someone worthy of such a union. Put in baldest terms, this meant the daughter of a god, that is to say of the previous pharaoh, and thus a sister of the new pharaoh. Such brother-sister unions do not appear to have been the routine way to produce heirs: pharaoh also had a vast harem of subsidiary wives and concubines with whom to procreate. Such was the case with Thutmosis II, whose queen was his sister Hatshepsut, while his son and heir had been born to him by another wife.

QUEEN HATSHEPSUT

On the death of Thutmosis II, Hatshepsut assumed pharaonic authority along with her stepson-nephew Thutmosis III. She was not simply a regent, someone entrusted to rule until such time as a young monarch reaches his or her majority. While Thutmosis III was still a youth, Hatshepsut effectively pulled the strings of government. For her part, she was careful to mask her femininity from the majority of Egyptians. Her inscriptions typically utilize masculine pronouns, and many of her monumental statues portray her with the long, narrow beard of her male counterparts. Egyptian women had always enjoyed a relatively high status compared with that of women in other Near Eastern cultures, and a few had even ruled as queens. The Theban origin of this dynasty, with its strong Nubian attributes, may also have allowed for a certain matriarchal element and the accession of a woman as pharaoh, at least within court circles. However, in an increasingly militaristic society, Hatshepsut deemed it necessary, at the very least, not to flaunt the fact of her being a woman to her subjects.

Her dynamism and statecraft proved crucial to the continued vitality of the dynasty and of Egypt. As co-ruler with Thutmosis III, she reigned for twenty-two years, and several military campaigns are recorded under her leadership. She is best remembered for the spectacular mortuary temple she built for herself, which seems to have been the signature moment in a process by which the mortuary temple and the funerary-cult temple to the pharaoh became separate. (The famous "Valley of the Kings" near ancient Thebes was established in the New Kingdom, a remote location where—it was hoped—the locations of pharaonic tombs would remain secret and thus safe from robbery.

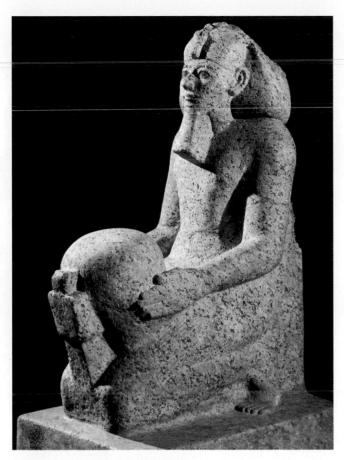

Hatshepsut as Pharaoh, c. 1460 B.C.E. Notice her masculine figure and ceremonial beard.

of the Syrian coast. Thutmosis's son, Amenhotep II (c. 1428–1397 B.C.E.), continued his father's conquests. He campaigned deep into Syria, crossing the Orontes River and capturing several important cities. His campaigns netted him seven Syrian princes, six of whom he sacrificed by hanging them upside down at Thebes (the seventh was similarly displayed at Napata, deep in the Sudan), and capturing some seventy-one thousand prisoners of war.

The Asian campaigns of Thutmosis III and Amenhotep II were intended not only to augment Egyptian strength, but also to undermine the economic and military might of the Hurrian kingdom of Mitanni. In this they were entirely successful, but to ironic effect. Mitanni was now so weakened that the Hittites were able to reassert themselves and their ambitions in Syria and Mesopotamia. The Assyrians also broke free of their vassalage to Mitanni, ultimately proving a far more aggressive foe to Egypt than the Mitanni had been. At the time, however, the long-term consequences of Mitanni's demise were not apparent, and the Eighteenth Dynasty basked in the glow of its military accomplishments.

In addition to the tremendous power and wealth Thutmosis III and Amenhotep II accrued, these rulers also established an Egyptian reputation for determination and ruthlessness. Amenhotep III (c. 1387–1350 B.C.E.), known as "the Magnificent," found therefore that he did not have to pursue military conquests equal to his grandfather's or his great-grandfather's. By and large, his task was to administer effectively the domains already gained for Egypt, and to exploit the economic and diplomatic advantages already won. This Amenhotep III did with skill and aplomb. The pharaoh received tribute from far and wide, including a land called Keftiu (usually identified with the Biblical Caphtor, and most likely the island of Crete). He concluded treaties with Mitanni and received at least two Mitannian princesses into his harem. So long as Amenhotep III remained vigilant with regard to his conquests and tended to his diplomatic interests, he had no need to do more than enjoy the benefits of his predecessors' endeavors.

Meanwhile, the actual cult rituals practiced in reverence to the pharaoh took place elsewhere.)

THUTMOSIS III

Thutmosis III enjoyed the tutelage and protection of his stepmother, who seems not to have begrudged him his position or to have schemed against him in any way. Once he reached adulthood, however, he began to chafe at sharing rule with her, and after a revolt in Palestine against Egyptian rule, she disappears from our records around 1458 B.C.E. From that date, Thutmosis III commenced the thirty-two years of his sole rule. Eventually he defaced many of Hatshepsut's monuments and removed her name from as many of her inscriptions as he could find, creating the impression that he had always ruled alone.

Despite his ingratitude, Thutmosis III was a great pharaoh. Launching a total of seventeen campaigns, he penetrated deep into Palestine, capturing the strategic town of Megiddo (Armageddon). He followed up this famous victory by seizing many of the vital port towns

RELIGIOUS CHANGE AND RELIGIOUS CHALLENGE

Another effect of the great conquests of Dynasty 18 was the mind-boggling amount of spoil brought back to Egypt. The wealth plundered from Nubia and the

Asian Near East seems to have left the pharaohs with a literal embarrassment of riches. Much of this wealth went to the personal glorification of the pharaoh, through grand temples, tombs, and other monuments, to say nothing of the ubiquitous royal stelae that provide us with so much historical information. Another significant portion of the booty went to the increasingly important officer class, the military aristocracy that made such conquests possible. But vast quantities of wealth still remained, and much of this went to propitiate the gods with thank offerings for Egypt's bountiful success. Temples throughout Egypt enjoyed the profits of conquest, and as the temples became wealthy, so too did the priests who administered those temples.

THE TEMPLE OF AMON

No temple complex made out quite so well as that dedicated to Amon in Thebes. Thebes was the hometown of the Eighteenth Dynasty, and the city's patron deity remained an important part of the dynasty's nomenclature, propaganda, worship, and general self-representation. The association between the pharaohs of this dynasty and Amon may have been crucial to their success within Egypt. Amon had grown in stature and popularity throughout the Middle Kingdom, and

increasingly the person of Amon was incorporated with that of the sun god Ra (thus the common New Kingdom formulation Amon-Ra). The Amon-Ra godhead became something of a national god, around whom Dynasties 17 and 18 had rallied as they reconquered and reunified Egypt.

The name *Amon* means "hidden": Amon was the unknowable god of the Old Kingdom, a powerful, transcendent, yet elusive deity. The theology of this god was most highly developed by the priests of the temples of Luxor and Karnak just outside Thebes, dedicated to Amon around the beginning of the New Kingdom. The priests had worked out a system that took advantage of Amon's invisible but mighty essence to elevate him above the other gods. All other gods became manifestations of Amon (thus facilitating identifi-

Tomb of Tutankhamon. Inside this solid gold coffin weighing twenty-five hundred pounds was the mummified body of "King Tut."

The Temple at Karnak. Most of this building has collapsed or been carried away, but the huge columns give an idea of the massiveness of Egyptian temples.

cations such as Amon-Ra). One Egyptian papyrus from the Nineteenth Dynasty states, "All the gods are three: Amon, Ra, and Ptah, without seconds; his identity is hidden as Amon, Ra is his face, Ptah his body." In other words, all gods were really just these three gods, and these three in turn were merely manifestations of a single godhead. This trinitarian conception of the Egyptian godhead represents the closest approach to monotheism yet seen in the ancient world and would remain an important part of Egyptian religious thought until Egypt became predominantly Christian in the second century C.E. As Egypt was an early center of Christian theological development, the impact of this ancient "trinity" on later Christian doctrines may have been substantial.

The favor shown to the priesthood of Amon at Thebes, coupled with the tremendous wealth deposited there, made the priests of Amon a formidable political and economic force. Indeed, by the end of Amenhotep the Magnificent's reign, the priesthood of Amon enjoyed political clout surpassing even that of the officer class, and the priests themselves had become influential persons within the court of pharaoh.

THE REIGN OF AKHENATEN

All these factors came to a fateful intersection in one of history's most intriguing figures. On the death of Amenhotep III in the middle of the fourteenth century, his son succeeded him as Amenhotep IV. Amenhotep IV showed early on a preference toward sun-god worship, as distinct from veneration of Amon: his earliest inscriptions exalt Ra not as an aspect of Amon, but as his own discrete divinity, visibly manifest in the light of the sun's rays. In his dedications to Ra the king laid aside the traditional depiction of a falcon (or a falcon-headed man), and replaced it with the *Aten*, the sun disk itself, its rays of light reaching toward earth. Before long, the new pharaoh had changed his name from Amenhotep ("Amon is pleased") to Akhenaten ("He is effective for the Aten"). As Akhenaten, he built a new capital halfway between Memphis in the north and Thebes in the south, calling it Akhetaten ("The place where the Aten becomes effective"), the modern site of el-Amarna. The short-lived but characteristic culture of Akhenaten's reign is therefore designated the Amarna Period.

Akhenaten introduced a variety of innovations into Egyptian religion and culture. The worship of Aten was more stringently monotheistic than the evolving, trinitarian view of Amon had been. Whereas Theban Amon theology recognized other gods as aspects of Amon, Akhenaten recognized only the life-giving power of light, embodied by the Aten. Unlike the ancient deities of Egyptian religion, Aten could not be captured or represented in art. The image of the Aten, a dominant feature of Amarna period art, is therefore an elaboration of the Egyptian hieroglyph for light.

Life and its affirmation seem to be central aspects of Akhenaten's religious revolution. The Aten was often depicted with hands at the end of each ray of light, holding in them the *ankh*, the Egyptian hieroglyph for "life." Akhenaten also had himself portrayed in curious fashion, although it is unclear whether the uniqueness of this representation was due to ideology or to features of his own anatomy. In a complete departure from the confident virility of his ancestors, Akhenaten is always shown with an elongated head and limbs, an exaggerated nose and exceptionally full lips. His eyes are catlike, and the pronounced protrusion in his belly is somewhat reminiscent of female fertility figurines. The overall effect is of a certain androgyny, the significance of which is unclear. Akhenaten was clearly a family man and had himself pictured as the most human of pharaohs, enjoying the company of his beautiful queen Nefertiti as they played with their children. Indeed, a palpable sense of humanity—an almost "common" touch compared with other pharaonic art—pervades the Amarna examples.

Beyond these observations, Akhenaten's theology is difficult to comprehend. It was clearly monotheistic, and the conception of Aten may have had an influence

Akhenaten, His Wife Nefertiti, and Their Children. The Aten is depicted here as a sundisk, raining down power on the royal family.

Nefertiti. The famous portrait bust executed in Akhenaten's studios at el-Amarna.

strenuous resistance to the pharaoh's religious innovations. To make matters worse, Akhenaten seems also to have been largely uninterested in military affairs. His exertions on behalf of his new god may even have encouraged him to neglect Egypt's interests abroad. The revolts that inevitably followed cost pharaoh the support of his officer class. Akhenaten's revolution failed.

His failure was the harbinger of the Eighteenth Dynasty's decline. He was ultimately succeeded by Tutankhaten, who changed his name to Tutankhamon (the famous "King Tut") to reflect his rejection of Akhenaten's heresies and the restoration of the god Amon and his priesthood. Akhetaten was abandoned as a capital and its memory cursed; its neglect thereafter is largely responsible for its high state of preservation today. Akhenaten, meanwhile, was remembered only as "Akhetaten's heretic." His monuments were destroyed throughout the land. But the damage had been done. Egypt's position in the wider world had eroded at an astonishing rate since the outset of Akhenaten's reign, and his heir was a sickly teenager. On the early death of the boy king, confusion ensued until an important military commander named Horemheb assumed the throne in 1319 B.C.E. Horemheb maintained stability for nearly three decades but had no heir. He passed his position to another general, who founded the next dynasty and restored Egypt to glory in the Near East.

well beyond New Kingdom Egypt. Great controversy still exists regarding Akhenaten's motives. Some believe him to be the world's first truly revolutionary intellectual, who applied imaginative force and exceptional insight to break the bonds of tradition and head in new directions. Others see him as a reactionary, troubled by the absorption of Ra into Amon, who chose to reassert the worship of the sun. Still further, one might argue for the evidence that he was a cagey politician who sought to undermine the disturbing influence of Amon's priests by shoving that god aside in favor of a new religious regime.

These various explanations are by no means mutually exclusive. As we have seen, politics and religion were inextricably intertwined in the ancient Near East, as they would be in Greece and Rome also. Akhenaten's religious revolution was by definition also a political coup of sorts, and he expended tremendous energy in trying to achieve it. Most of his fellow Egyptians were unimpressed, however, and did not follow pharaoh in his religious experiment. However bewildering and complex traditional Egyptian religion may seem to us, the average Egyptian apparently preferred it to a remote and impersonal god, however benevolent. The powerful priesthood of Amon also put up

Throne of "King Tut." Dating from about 1360 B.C.E., this relief in gold and silver is part of the back of the young pharaoh's throne. The relaxed lounging position of the pharaoh's right arm is typical of the stylistic informality of the period.

AKHENATEN, THE HEBREWS, AND MONOTHEISM

One of the great literary monuments of Akhenaten's religious revolution was his "Hymn to the Aten," extolling the life-affirming virtues of the god he sought to place atop the Egyptian religious system. Although Akhenaten's experiment failed in Egypt, it may have played a significant role in shaping the religious traditions of other societies throughout the Levant, including the ancient Hebrews.

HYMN TO THE ATEN

You appear beautifully on the horizon of the heavens, living Aten, the beginning of life! When you arise on the eastern horizon, you have filled every land with your beauty. You are gracious, great, glistening, and high over every land; your rays encompass the lands to the limit of all that you have made. . . . When you set in the western horizon, the land is in darkness, in the manner of death. They sleep in a room, with heads wrapped up, nor sees one eye the other. All their goods which are under their heads might be stolen, but they would not perceive it. . . .

Creator of seed in women, you who makes fluid into man, who maintains the son in the womb of his mother, who soothes him with that which stills his weeping, you nurse even in the womb, who gives breath to sustain all that he has made! . . . How manifold it is, that which you have made! They are hidden from the face of man. O sole god, like whom there is no other! You created the world according to your desire, while you were alone: all men, cattle, and wild beasts, whatever is on earth, going upon its feet, and what is on high, flying with its wings. . . .

The world came into being by your hand, according to how you have made them. When you have risen they live, when you set they die. You are lifetime itself, for one lives only through you.

Based on James B. Pritchard, ed. *Ancient Near Eastern Texts Relating to the Bible,* 3rd rev. ed. with supplement. (Princeton, N.J.: Princeton University Press, 1969), pp. 370–371.

PSALM 104

Bless the Lord, O my soul. . . . You are clothed with honor and majesty, wrapped in light as with a garment. You stretch out the heavens like a tent. . . . You set the earth on its foundations, so that it shall never be shaken. You cover it with the deep as with a garment; the waters stood above the mountains. At your rebuke they flee. . . . You cause the grass to grow for the cattle, and plants for people to use, to bring forth food from the earth, and wine to gladden the human heart. You make darkness, and it is night, when all the animals of the forest come creeping out. The young lions roar for their prey, seeking their food from God.

O Lord, how manifold are your works! In wisdom you have made them all; the earth is full of your creatures. . . . These all look to you to give them food in due season; when you give them to them, they gather it up; when you open your hand, they are filled with good things. When you hide your face, they are dismayed; when you take away your breath they die.

The New Oxford Annotated Bible. (Oxford: Oxford University Press, 1994).

THE INTERNATIONAL "SYSTEM" OF THE LATE BRONZE AGE

What factors facilitated the creation of the Late Bronze Age international system?

The fates of many nations after 1500 B.C.E., including Egypt, are intelligible only within the wider context of international relations. From the middle of the second millennium on, the destinies of the various Near Eastern kingdoms became increasingly interwoven, and an international system developed that stretched throughout the eastern and central Mediterranean.

The Late Bronze Age was an age of superpowers. As we have seen, the great pharaohs of the Eighteenth Dynasty had transformed Egypt into a conquering state, feared and respected throughout the Near East. But the pressure they applied to the kingdom of Mitanni allowed for the emergence of a revived Hittite empire after 1450 B.C.E. It was the Hittites who dealt Mitanni the most crushing blows, succeeding once again to the mantle of northern power in the region. The Assyrians also revived, and the Kassite kingdom of Babylonia remained a significant force in the economic and military relationships of the age. Between these imperial powers arose numerous smaller but important states, concentrated along the coasts and river valleys of Syria, but extending to Cyprus and the Aegean Sea.

INTERNATIONAL DIPLOMACY

Though warfare remained a characteristic feature of ancient international relations, the great states of the Late Bronze Age developed something of an equilibrium, a balance of power that helped to stabilize trade and diplomacy as the period progressed. Internationalism had existed in some form since the age of Hammurabi, who, as we have seen, employed diplomacy and intrigue to tip the scales in his own favor. But by the fourteenth century, an international standard had developed, within which many nations and their leaders came to understand the value of peace over war. This is not to say that war never occurred in the pursuit of political or economic advantage. However, many people at the time seem to have understood that security and stability helped trade to flourish, whereas war could prove disruptive and—in the long run—unprofitable.

The archives discovered by modern archaeologists at Akhenaten's accursed capital (present-day el-Amarna) provide us with a clear picture of this international diplomatic standard. Flurries of correspondence took place between the leaders of nations, sometimes over great matters, but often not. Maintaining lines of communication seems to have been an important end in and of itself. The most powerful kings developed a language of diplomatic rank, addressing one another as "brother," while the princes of lesser states showed their deference and respect to pharaoh, the Hittite king, or other powerful sovereigns by calling them "father." Breach of this protocol was cause for diplomatic offense. When an Assyrian king of the thirteenth century arrogated to himself the privilege of addressing the Hittite ruler Hattusilis III as "brother," he received a stern rebuke: "What is this you keep saying about 'brotherhood'? You and I were born of the same mother? Far from it; even as my father and grandfather were not in the habit of writing about 'brotherhood' to the King of Assyria, so stop writing to me about brotherhood and Great Kingship!"

Rulers of the period also exchanged lavish gifts and entered into marriage alliances with one another. After Akhenaten's death, his supporters even tried to gain the Hittite crown prince for the late pharaoh's daughter to shore up their failing power. Under more routine circumstances, groups of professional envoys journeyed back and forth between the centers of Near Eastern power, conveying valuable treasures as gifts and handling politically sensitive missions. In the case of Egypt, such emissaries were also often merchants, sent not only to handle matters of diplomacy but also to explore the possibility of trade opportunities for pharaoh.

INTERNATIONAL TRADE

Trade became an increasingly important aspect of international relations during the Late Bronze Age. Seaborne trade flourished up and down the coast of the eastern Mediterranean, allowing smaller, seaside centers such as Ugarit and Byblos to become powerful merchant city-states. The great coastal cities of the eastern Mediterranean became wealthy entrepots for the exchange of a bewildering variety of goods. A single merchant vessel's cargo might contain scores of distinct items originating anywhere from the interior of Africa to the Baltic Sea. At the same time, the great states of the region continued to exploit their control

WHAT FACTORS FACILITATED THE CREATION OF THE LATE BRONZE AGE INTERNATIONAL SYSTEM?

THE INTERNATIONAL "SYSTEM" OF THE LATE BRONZE AGE   69

of overland trade routes, relying more than ever on moving goods to an international market. Trade was rapidly becoming the lifeline of all these Late Bronze Age empires.

Busy and lucrative trade routes also served as a conduit for artistic motifs, literary and religious ideas, architectural forms, and ideas in tool making and weapon smithing. Whereas in the past such influences spread slowly and unintentionally, the societies of the Late Bronze Age were now developing a very self-conscious cosmopolitanism. Egyptians delighted in Canaanite glass; Bronze Age Greeks prized Egyptian amulets; and the merchants of Ugarit admired and desired Greek pottery and wool. Examples of such active longing for the products of other cultures could be endlessly multiplied.

In the great merchant towns such as Ugarit, this cosmopolitanism could have further repercussions. Ugarit was a meeting place of cultures, languages, and beliefs—not surprising, as the town had several "quarters," areas in which alien merchants and artisans plied their trades, worshiped their own gods, and took advantage of Ugarit's teeming commercial activity. Of course Ugaritic—a Semitic dialect and precursor to

later Phoenician—was spoken, as were Hurrian and Hittite, Assyrian, various dialects native to Cyprus and Crete, Egyptian, and probably the several Indo-European languages of western Anatolia. The swirl of commerce and the multiplicity of languages may have impelled the citizens of Ugarit to develop a simpler form of writing than the Sumero-Akkadian cuneiform system still current throughout the Near East. An Ugaritic alphabet appears at the end of the Bronze Age, a system of about thirty symbols representing consonants. Vowels had to be inferred, potentially sacrificing some clarity between reader and audience; but the elegant, less cumbersome alphabetic system was more easily mastered and more efficient for recording the heady pace of trade in the city's harbors.

The search for more markets, greater resources, and new trade routes heightened economic competition but promoted greater understanding between cultures. After a great battle between Egypt and the Hittites near Kadesh (c. 1286 B.C.E.), the magnificent Dynasty 19 pharaoh Ramses II realized that more was to be gained through peaceful relations with his northern neighbors than through pointless warfare. The treaty he established with the Hittites served as a pillar of

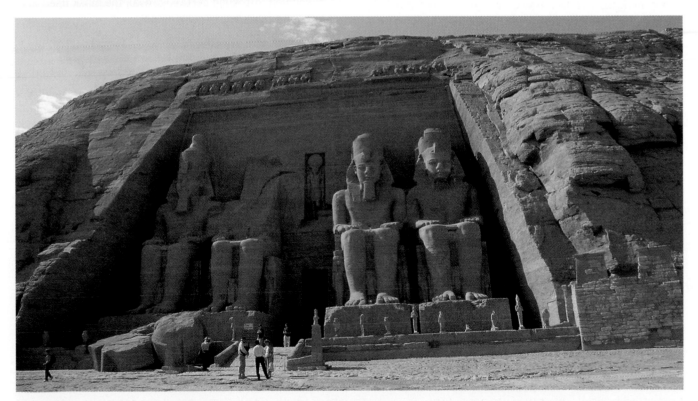

The Temple of Ramses II at Abu-Simbel. Each of these colossal figures stands sixty-six feet high. The smaller figures at Ramses' feet represent his wives and relatives. Ramses II lived to be more than ninety years old and fathered at least one hundred children.

geopolitical stability in the region and allowed even further economic integration to develop during the thirteenth century B.C.E. Greater integration also meant greater mutual dependence. If one economy suffered in this international system, the effects of that decline were sure to be felt elsewhere.

EXPANSION OF THE NEAR EASTERN SYNTHESIS

Heightened economic activity and the expansion of markets also introduced the Near Eastern synthesis to peoples beyond the Near Eastern heartland. In many cases, these new peoples adapted their societies to accommodate Near Eastern political and economic forms so as to trade more easily. The further the Near Eastern model of civilization spread from its roots in Mesopotamia and Egypt, however, the more superficial and potentially fragile it became. Furthermore, the new markets of the Late Bronze Age included societies whose own degree of "civilization," however enthusiastic they may have been, was questionable. Their rough, warlike spirit made them valuable mercenaries, especially for smaller states lacking the manpower resources to field large standing armies of their own. But these new trading partners and mercenaries could prove unreliable and may ultimately have helped to destroy the Near Eastern synthesis. We turn our attention now to their story.

AEGEAN CIVILIZATION: MINOANS AND MYCENAEANS

How did Minoan culture affect Mycenaean culture?

The ancient Greeks treasured many legends about a heroic and distant past, a golden age when great men mingled with the gods, and powerful kingdoms—larger and stronger than any known to the later world of classical Greece—contended for power and glory. For a very long time, scholars dismissed this picture of a "prehistoric" component of the Greek experience. Tales of the Trojan War, Theseus and the Minotaur, or

Mycenaean Death Mask, c. 1550–1500 B.C.E. When Schliemann discovered this gold mask in the shaft graves at Mycenae, he immediately declared it to be the mask of Agamemnon. Although certainly royal, the mask itself is too early to have been Agamemnon's.

the great adventure of Odysseus were regarded as myths—products of Greek imagination not at all reflective of any historical truth. For these scholars, Greek history began in 776 B.C.E., the date of the first recorded Olympic Games. The Bronze Age, it was believed, simply did not matter to the later, glorious history of classical Greece.

In the late nineteenth century, an amateur archaeologist named Heinrich Schliemann believed differently. He believed the epic poems of Homer, the *Iliad* and the *Odyssey*, were not merely stories. Using Homer as his guide, he discovered the site of the great city of Troy near the coast of northwest Anatolia. He then went on to discover a number of once-powerful citadels on the mainland of Greece, including Mycenae, the home of the legendary, powerful, and mythical king Agamemnon. Though Schliemann's work met with considerable skepticism, and many of his secondary conclusions have been demonstrated to be erroneous, his discoveries ultimately forced a reevaluation of Greek civilization and its roots. It is now no longer possible to dismiss Bronze Age Greece (or, as it is more

CHRONOLOGY

CIVILIZATIONS OF THE LATE BRONZE AGE NEAR EAST

New Kingdom Egypt	1550–1075 B.C.E.
Near Eastern international "system"	1550–1200 B.C.E.
Minoan civilization	1900–1500 B.C.E.
Mycenaean civilization	1600–1200 B.C.E.

often termed, Mycenaean Greece, after the mighty kingdom of Greek myth based at the site of Mycenae) as if it had nothing to do with the classical Greek civilization that succeeded it.

Schliemann's work stimulated further exploration, and at the turn of the twentieth century Sir Arthur Evans complicated our understanding even further. Excavating on the island of Crete, Evans found a great palace at Knossos that predated any of the major centers on the Greek mainland. A wealthy and magnificent culture had clearly thrived here in the Bronze Age, which Evans dubbed "Minoan" after King Minos, the powerful king whom the later Greeks believed had once ruled far and wide from Crete, dominating the Aegean Sea.

Both of these Aegean cultures, the Mycenaean and the Minoan, played an important role in the history of the Bronze Age Near East. Because of the nature of the evidence, there is much about them that remains mysterious. But their importance can no longer be denied.

THE MINOAN THALASSOCRACY

Thucydides, a fifth-century B.C.E. Athenian historian, wrote that King Minos had ruled a "thalassocracy," that is, a sea empire. Always careful about substantiating his claims—at least by ancient standards—Thucydides had deduced this statement from a variety of sources, including legend and the presence of many ancient towns around the Aegean basin named Minoa. Until the work of Arthur Evans, Thucydides' claim seemed mere fancy; afterward, more careful consideration became necessary.

Minoan civilization flourished from c. 1900 B.C.E. until the middle of the second millennium B.C.E., making it contemporary with Middle Kingdom Egypt, Hammurabi, and the Hittite Old Kingdom. It had a

much deeper prehistory and may have been a descendant of the Neolithic culture known as Cycladic that prevailed in the Aegean. The peoples of the Cycladic Aegean traded far and wide in a variety of goods, especially the volcanic glass obsidian, a highly prized commodity. The Minoans inherited the tradition of maritime commerce pioneered by these Stone Age inhabitants of the region.

As early as the middle of the third millennium we can see the outlines of a developing civilization on Crete. By 1900 B.C.E. this culture had developed a high degree of material and architectural sophistication; as a result, the period of Minoan civilization from 1900 to 1700 B.C.E. is sometimes referred to as the "Palace Age." Like its Near Eastern counterparts, the Minoan palace sat at the center of a redistributive economy, drawing in the resources under its control and then parceling them out as the palace bureaucracy saw fit. Several impressive complexes are to be found on Crete from this period, including the brilliant palace at Knossos, comprising several acres, hundreds of rooms, and winding hallways. It was obvious at once to excavators that such structures could have served as the inspiration for the famous story of the Labyrinth, in which the Greek hero Theseus slew the terrible Minotaur. The exact political relationship between these centers is unclear, but many scholars believe that by 1700 B.C.E. Knossos must have exerted some influence over the better part of the island.

Wall Painting from Thera. The volcanic eruption on the island of Thera preserved many splendid paintings. Here an elegant priestess is burning incense.

Scenes from the Bull Ring: Minoan Mural, c. 1500 B.C.E. Evident are the youth, skill, and agility of the Minoan athletes, the center one a male, the other two female. The body and horns of the bull are exaggerated, as are the slenderness of the athletes and their full-face eyes in profile heads. There is probably also some exaggeration in content: modern experts in bullfighting insist that it is impossible to somersault over the back of a charging bull.

The secret to Minoan success was certainly the control of overseas trade. An important site on the island of Santorini (ancient Thera), buried by a massive volcanic eruption in the middle of the second millennium, preserves evidence of the far-flung commercial and cultural influence of the Minoans. A thriving, cosmopolitan trading city existed there, exchanging a range of exotic goods. By 1700 B.C.E., the Minoans were trading regularly with Egypt, southwest Anatolia, and Cyprus. Through Cyprus, they also had indirect contacts with the Levant.

Wealth allowed the Minoans to build their magnificent palaces, palaces noteworthy for their lack of fortifications. Coupled with the playful, idyllic scenes depicted in surviving Minoan frescoes (frescoes are paintings executed in fresh plaster), the apparent serenity of the Minoans once led scholars to believe that they were a peace-loving people, interested only in the even-handed exchange of goods. Evidence of Minoan devotion to an obscure mother goddess, often portrayed with serpents in her hands as she tamed a wild beast at either side, was also seen as evidence of the peaceful nature of Minoan life, and as evidence for a strong matriarchal element in Minoan culture.

Such romanticism now appears misplaced. Crete's relative geographical isolation may have lessened the need for strong landward defenses; but the Minoans'

extensive trade networks and widespread cultural influence strongly suggest that they possessed a powerful navy, capable of stopping a hostile force before it reached Cretan shores. Evidence for a bull cult—a cult typically associated with patriarchal societies in the Near East—abounds within Minoan civilization, and there are strong arguments for human sacrifice as a regular part of Minoan religious life. Women were certainly important in Minoan culture, not least as producers of the famous Minoan textiles. But it seems unlikely, given current knowledge, that the Minoans were in any sense a matriarchal society.

Much about the Minoans remains unknown. They had a

Minoan Snake Goddess. A statuette in ivory and gold discovered near the palace of Knossos and dating from 1550 B.C.E.

Cretan Labyrinth Coin. According to legend, King Minos of Crete built a labyrinth to pen in the Minotaur, part man, part bull. This coin from about 300 B.C.E. shows the labyrinth as the emblem of Knossos.

written language, that Sir Arthur Evans dubbed Linear A to distinguish it from another script, similar but clearly distinct and far better represented, which he discovered and called Linear B. But although we can determine that the tongue enshrined in Linear A is non-Indo-European, the scanty Minoan records preserved in Linear A remain untranslatable. Scholars must rely instead on the distribution of pottery and other archaeological objects to determine how and when Minoan culture spread to the other islands and shores of the Aegean Sea.

One focus of Minoan commercial activity was clearly the mainland of Greece. The presence of a wide variety of objects there, including pottery, metalwork, and textiles, suggests the export of Minoan technologies, and perhaps even Minoan craftworkers, from Crete to the mainland. But the exact nature of the relationship between Minoan Crete and Mycenaean Greece remains controversial. There is no question that before 1600 B.C.E., the Minoans enjoyed a much higher level of sophistication than their mainland counterparts. As a result, they may have been able to dominate the inhabitants of Greece's rocky landscape, at least commercially and perhaps politically. The myth of Theseus and the Labyrinth claims that the hero went to Crete to free Athens from the heavy tribute laid on the city by King Minos. Might this story

perhaps preserve a memory of a time when Crete dominated the Greeks of the mainland?

Close contacts between the Minoans and the mainland led to a variety of developments in Mycenaean Greece. The quality of material culture improved, and the mainland was drawn more tightly into the network of international commercial and diplomatic relationships that characterized the Near East during these centuries. The inhabitants of the mainland learned how to build great fortified palaces, hybrids of the Minoan palaces and the imposing strongholds of the Hittites. The mainland Greeks also became prized throughout the Near East as valuable and dangerous mercenaries. They learned to write from the Minoans, taking Linear A and modifying it to suit their own language better. The resulting script is the one Sir Arthur Evans called Linear B—a script that captures the earliest written form of Greek.

THE MYCENAEANS

When Linear B was finally deciphered in the 1950s, it turned the world of Greek scholarship decisively toward a reckoning with the Bronze Age past. Until then, scholars could continue to wonder whether the impressive sites unearthed by Schliemann, Evans, and others had anything at all to do with the story of classical Greek civilization. That Linear B represented an ancient but unmistakably Greek dialect proved conclusively that Greek history stretched well back into the Bronze Age. But what role did the Mycenaean Greeks play in that story?

The question of the arrival of "Greeks" (or more accurately, peoples speaking a form of very primitive Greek) in the Aegean basin is a vexatious and contentious one. Greece was inhabited as early 6000 B.C.E., and a few scholars contend that these Neolithic villagers were already Indo-European-speakers and thus in some sense Greek. This, however, is a minority view. The ancient Greeks clearly believed that they

Linear B Tablet from Knossos.

were distinct from an earlier group, the Pelasgians, whose language was very different from their own. This belief has subsequently been confirmed by historical linguists who have pointed out the non-Indo-European endings on many Greek place names. Because geographical and topographical names tend to be preserved, even when one culture conquers another (witness the profusion of Native American place-names used in the United States), these endings must suggest that the Greeks dominated and absorbed an earlier, non-Indo-European-speaking people.

The arrival of early Greek speakers may coincide with the destruction of several important sites in Greece around the turn of the second millennium B.C.E. New or modified architectural types and the presence of a new pottery culture around this time may also testify to an invasion or immigration. But another significant displacement of peoples and material goods took place around 1600 B.C.E. Which one of these events represents "the coming of the Greeks"? The answer, as the eminent Mycenaean scholar John Chadwick has suggested, may be as simple as this: the Greeks were always in the process of "becoming" in the Middle and Late Bronze Age. Several groups of early Greek-speakers may have infiltrated the region over a period of several centuries, intermingling with and largely assimilating the native population in a process that may have continued over several further centuries.

Mycenaean civilization was the culmination of this process in Bronze Age Greece. By 1500 B.C.E., powerful citadels dotted the Greek landscape. The rulers of these early palaces were clearly warriors, who touted their martial prowess on their gravestones and had themselves buried with their implements of war. These early rulers no doubt based their authority on their ability to lead men successfully into battle and to reward their followers with plunder. The most effective leaders managed to gain control of strategic sites from which they could exploit the major passages through Greece while never straying too far from the sea, where they engaged in both trade and piracy. The line between trade and piracy was a fine one in the ancient world, and would remain so until the nineteenth century of the common era. Like many other maritime peoples, ancient and modern, the Mycenaeans raided where they could, and traded where they could not raid.

Over time, and perhaps under the influence of Mi-

> The line between trade and piracy was a fine one in the ancient world, and would remain so until the nineteenth century of the common era.

noan culture, the Mycenaean palace citadels developed into far more complex societies. By the thirteenth century B.C.E., the most powerful sites had carved out territorial kingdoms more extensive than anything the Greek world would see again for almost a millennium. The citadel served as a nerve center for the kingdom, functioning both as a place of government and as a warehouse for the storage of economic surpluses. The evidence of the Linear B tablets—of which there are thousands—suggests that the kings of the Myceanaean centers had gained control over a redistributive economy not unlike those we have seen operating in the Near East, Anatolia, and Crete. By the fourteenth and thirteenth centuries, a variety of such sites—Mycenae, Thebes, Athens, Iolkos, Pylos, and the Menelaion near the later site of Sparta—were flourishing. Some of these Mycenaean kingdoms had as many as a hundred thousand inhabitants, dwarfing the typical Greek urban centers of the Classical Period.

The Linear B tablets also reveal that the model of the Near Eastern palace center was not ideally suited to the Greek landscape. Archaeologists have pieced together evidence that reveals a high degree of inefficiency in a kingdom such as Pylos, and significant confusion as to who owed what to whom—between landowners, between farmer and palace, between palace and shrine, and so forth. In war also, Mycenaean imitation of Near Eastern examples had its limits. Although Mycenaean kings may have cherished the war chariot in imitation of their Near Eastern contemporaries, such chariots were highly impractical in Greece's rocky terrain.

Despite these and other differences between them, the Mycenaean Greeks played a very important role in the closing stages of the Near Eastern Bronze Age. We have already noted their commercial importance. They were no less important as soldiers. By c. 1400 B.C.E., they had subjugated the island of Crete, taking over Knossos and using it as a Mycenaean center; if the "Keftiu" mentioned by Amenhotep III is indeed Crete, it was most likely he treated with its Mycenaean conquerors. Their later, urban refinements notwithstanding, the Mycenaeans remained true to their martial roots and enjoyed great prestige in the Near East as warriors. At least one Mycenaean king exercised enough influence in western Anatolia to be addressed by a Hittite king as "my brother." Their combined activities as traders and raiders made it

MYCENAEAN GREECE

Note the mountainous landscape of Greece and how the peculiar shape of the region creates thousands of miles of coastline; consider that Greece is almost devoid of major rivers but that few places are far from the sight of the open sea. Notice that a map of "Greece" in antiquity always includes the western coast of Asia Minor as well as the islands of the Aegean. How would this dry, mountainous country surrounded by the sea potentially affect the nature of Greek civilization and its economic interests? Would the Near Eastern model be a good "fit" for Greece?

possible for the Mycenaeans to import food and other goods at levels far beyond what their land itself could support—with fateful consequences, as we shall see.

All of these features make the Mycenaeans more a part of the Near Eastern than the Greek story. The political and commercial arrangements of the Mycenaean world—a powerful palace, headed by a king who was also a war leader, a warrior aristocracy, a bureaucracy of local officials, state-mandated land holdings, a redistributive economy, large territorial kingdoms—distinguished the Mycenaeans fundamentally from the Greeks of the Classical Age. At the same time, however, we can trace certain fundamental features of later Greek civilization back to the Myce-

THE MYCENAEANS
AND THE NEAR EAST:
THE "TAWAGALAWAS LETTER"

Around 1260 B.C.E., the Hittite king Hattusilis III sent the following missive to the "King of Ahhiyawa," taken by most scholars to be the Hittite equivalent of one early Greek label for themselves, "Akhaiwoi," the Achaeans of Homer. In the letter we see the respect Hattusilis accorded this Greek king, as well as the adventures of one Greek warrior upsetting economic and political arrangements in the western Anatolian city of Millawanda (classical Miletus).

I have to complain of the insolent and treacherous conduct of one Tawagalawas. We came into contact in the land of Lukka [Lycia, in western Anatolia], and he offered to become a vassal of the Hittite Empire. I agreed, and sent an officer of most exalted rank to conduct him to my presence: he had the audacity to complain that the officer's rank was not exalted enough; he insulted my ambassador in public, and demanded that he be declared vassal-king there and then without the formality of interview. Very well: I order him, if he desires to become a vassal of mine, to make sure that no troops of his are found in Ijalanda when I arrive there. And what do I find when I arrive in Ijalanda?— the troops of Tawagalawas, fighting on the side of my enemies. I defeat them, take many prisoners . . . scrupulously leaving the fortress of Atrija intact out of respect for my treaty with you. Now a Hittite subject, Pijamaradus by name, steals my 7,000 prisoners, and makes off to your city of Millawanda. I command him to return to me: he disobeys. I write to you: you send a surly message unaccompanied by gift or greeting, to say that you have ordered your representative in Millawanda, a certain Atpas, to deliver Pijamaradus up. Nothing happens, so I go fetch him. I enter your city of Millawanda, for I have something to say to Pijamaradus, and it would be well that your subjects there should hear me say it. But my visit is not a success. I ask for Tawagalawas: he is not at home. I should like to see Pijamaradus: he has gone to sea. You refer me to your representative Atpas: I find that both he and his brother are married to daughters of Pijamaradus; they are not likely to give me satisfaction or to give you an unbiased account of these transactions. . . . Are you aware, and is it with your blessing, that Pijamaradus is going round saying that he intends to leave his wife and family, and incidentally my 7,000 prisoners, under your protections while he makes continual inroads on my dominion? . . . Do not let him use Ahhiyawa as a base for operations against me. You and I are friends. There has been no quarrel between us since we came to terms in the matter of Wilusa [very possibly the Greek Ilios, the territory of Troy]: the trouble there was my fault, and I promise it will not happen again. As for my military occupation of Millawanda, please regard it as a friendly visit. . . . [as for the problems between us], I suggest that the fault may not lie with ourselves but with our messengers; let us bring them to trial, cut off their heads, mutilate their bodies, and live henceforth in perfect friendship.

Denys Page, *History and the Homeric Iliad.* (Berkeley: University of California Press, 1959), pp. 11–12.

naeans, including the Greek language, as well as institutional and cultural continuities. The Linear B tablets speak of a group with considerable economic and political rights, the *damos*; this group would seem to be the precursor of the later *demos*, which later sought full political empowerment in many Greek cities. The tablets also preserve the names of several Greek gods familiar from the classical period, such as Zeus, Poseidon, Dionysos, and (possibly) Demeter; others, however, are absent, or their identities obscured behind completely different names. Finally, of whatever dubious use legends may be to the modern historian, for the classical Greeks the myths of their distant and heroic past were more than history—they were truth. The men and women who populated those stories were the same ones who built the massive stone walls that were still visible in the sixth, fifth and fourth centuries B.C.E., which the classical Greeks imagined to have been built by gods or monsters. However little the Greeks knew of their Mycenaean ancestors, the force on the Greek imagination of what they thought they knew about them was considerable.

Mycenaean civilization ended under a cloud of mystery on which the Linear B records, largely annual accounting books, shed very little light. Over the course of the thirteenth century B.C.E., some Mycenaean centers suffered violent destruction, whereas others prospered. This suggests a cycle of warfare within Greece that had the potential to destroy the entire culture. Mycenaean Knossos was already shattered before 1350 B.C.E.; Thebes followed shortly after 1300 B.C.E.; Pylos, around 1230 B.C.E.; Mycenae itself went through a period of conflagration and rebuilding until it succumbed in the twelfth century B.C.E.. And Troy, not perhaps properly Mycenaean but clearly a part of that world through trade and warfare, suffered its legendary destructions between roughly 1270 and 1180 B.C.E.

The Mycenaean world seems to have collapsed under its own weight around the end of the thirteenth century B.C.E. What triggered this collapse is impossible to say: natural disasters, drought, famine, disease, and social unrest have all been posited as causes. None of the theories can be proven or disproved in the current state of our knowledge. But the consequences of the Mycenaean collapse are clearer. Because it was such an integrated part of an intricate and fragile network of trade, military, and political relationships, the Mycenaean world could not implode without the reverberations of its collapse being felt across the entire Near East.

THE SEA PEOPLES AND THE END OF THE BRONZE AGE

Around the same time the Mycenaean world was in its death throes, a wave of destruction swept from north to south across the western portion of the Near East. The nature of this devastation is obscure, because it was the handiwork of a people so thorough that they utterly destroyed everything in their path until they reached Egypt. Were it not for the narrow victory of the Dynasty 20 pharaoh Ramses III in about 1179 B.C.E., we might know nothing at all of the invaders who so suddenly unraveled the Near Eastern synthesis.

In the commemorative inscription of his victory set up at Medinet Habu, Ramses III referred to the invaders as the "Sea Peoples" and named several of the groups within this coalition. The names he presented were familiar to the Egyptians. The Egyptians had employed many of them as mercenaries or had confronted them as mercenaries in the pay of other leaders. Ramses' description of these Sea Peoples marks certain of them out as clearly Aegean, from their battle gear and dress. Most notable of these were the Peleset, who, after their defeat by Egypt, withdrew to populate the coast of the region named after them, Palestine.

The arc of annihilation started in the north and may have helped to trigger the final collapse of Mycenaean Greece. Disruption of the northern trade networks must have had a profound effect on the Mycenaean kingdoms, which would have suddenly been faced with an apocalyptic combination of overpopulation, drastic food shortages, and incessant warfare. A wave of desperate refugees must have fled the Aegean basin. The undermining of commerce in the north would also have devastated the economy of the Hittites and the very underpinnings of their power. The Hittite New Kingdom collapsed with astonishing rapidity. We catch only a few glimpses in our sources of a desperate Hittite king fighting to save Hattusas against a myriad of enemies.

Down the coast of the Mediterranean we find other clues. The king of Ugarit had prepared a letter for his "brother," the king of Alashiya on Cyprus. Apparently, the invasions that overwhelmed him were as unexpected as they were terrifying. Taken completely off guard, Ugarit's ruler hoped to beseech his counterpart for immediate help. In a poignant note, however, we have his letter only because the clay tablet on which it was written was baked hard in the fire that destroyed the palace. The letter was never sent, and the Sea Peoples moved on.

On their arrival in Egypt, the picture of the Sea Peoples sharpens. These were not mindless marauders: they came with their families, their oxcarts, and their possessions. The Sea Peoples wanted land and food, but their search for it created more chaos and even more displacement. The invasion of the Sea Peoples began as a movement out of the Aegean; but it metastasized across the Near East, losing some groups who settled in the newly conquered lands. They gained desperate adherents longing to find a new place to settle, their previous homes and ways of life having been destroyed by the very force with which they now joined. Ramses III defeated them, killing many, driving others off. But the damage had been done; the world was a very different place by 1170 B.C.E. than it had been a generation or two before.

CONCLUSION

The eruption of the Sea Peoples destroyed much of civilization as the Mediterranean world had known it. The destruction was not total. Cities and kingdoms did not go away, and trade did not vanish. But the aftermath was nonetheless striking. The Hittite empire was gone, replaced by a bewildering variety of neo-Hittite principalities, possessed of little economic or military strength; they did not last long, for the most part. The great cosmopolitan cities of the eastern Mediterranean coast lay in ruins, and new groups—sometimes contingents of the Sea Peoples—populated the seaboard. Mycenaean Greece was no more. Depopulated by as much as 90 percent over the next century, the Greek mainland slipped into a "dark age," more or less isolated culturally and economically from the Near East for the next two and a half centuries. The Greeks would have to reinvent urbanism on terms more amenable to their unique environment.

Even where the Sea Peoples were defeated, they made their presence felt. Ramses III won the battle, but when the dust had settled his major trading partners had all been destroyed. Egypt went into a long decline; within a hundred years an Egyptian official would complain of his ill treatment at the hands of peoples who once feared Egypt (see p. 76). Assyria likewise suffered from the effects of the invasions. The next few centuries saw the Assyrians fighting for their very survival. To the south, the peaceful and prosperous rule of the Kassites also collapsed, along with Babylon's economy.

In the centuries immediately after the Sea Peoples, no great empires arose in the Near East. Economic and diplomatic internationalism, carefully elaborated over half a millennium, had disappeared. In the wake of all the destruction, however, new traditions and new cultural experiments began to emerge. With the international standard gone, new arrangements could now take its place. Fresh political and religious configurations could and did take shape, and a new metallurgical technology—based on iron—began to supplant the use of bronze. Out of the ashes of the Late Bronze Age, a more enduring, more integrated cultural synthesis arose, the culture of the Iron Age Near East.

SELECTED READINGS

Many of the works and source collections cited in the Selected Readings to Chapter 1 will also be of value for this chapter.

Aldred, Cyril. *Akhenaten.* London, 1988. An excellent overview of the reign, motivations, and cultural legacy of this enigmatic pharaoh. Compare with Redford's quite different account (below).

Beal, Richard H. *The Organization of the Hittite Military.* Heidelberg, 1992. A useful survey of the Hittite military that provides insight into the militaristic nature of Hittite society as a whole.

Bourriau, Janine. *Pharaohs and Mortals: Egyptian Art in the Middle Kingdom.* Cambridge, 1988. An enlightening examination of the material culture of the Middle Kingdom as a reflection of changing attitudes within Egyptian society and the world beyond Egypt.

Bryce, Trevor. *The Kingdom of the Hittites.* Oxford, 1998. The newest scholarly synthesis, with an emphasis on political and military history.

Budge, E. A. Wallis, ed. *The Egyptian Book of the Dead (The Papyrus of Ani): Egyptian Text, Transliteration and Translation.* New York, 1967. A reprinting of the original 1895 British Museum publication. An important if sometimes confusing text for understanding Egyptian funerary cult and belief.

Chadwick, John. *The Mycenaean World.* Cambridge, 1976. A fine, accessible introduction by the pioneering scholar who helped to decipher Linear B.

Dickinson, O. T. P. K. *The Aegean Bronze Age.* Cambridge, 1994. An excellent compendium of archaeological evidence and scholarly argument concerning the Minoan, Mycenaean and other cultures of the Bronze Age Aegean basin.

Drews, Robert. *The End of the Bronze Age: Changes in Warfare and the Catastrophe ca. 1200 B.C.* Princeton, 1993. A comprehensive but stimulating survey of the explanations that have been offered for the sudden collapse of Bronze Age civilization throughout the Near East, with excellent bibliographies.

————. *The Coming of the Greeks: Indo-European Conquests in the Aegean and the Near East*. Princeton, 1988. A courageous, lucidly written attempt to reconstruct the arrival of "Greeks" in the Aegean basin.

Gurney, O. R. *The Hittites*, rev. ed. London, 1990. Although a bit dated, Gurney's introduction remains an accessible starting point for discussion of the Hittites.

James, T. G. H., ed. *The Hekanakhte Papers and Other Early Middle Kingdom Documents*. New York, 1962. An extraordinary collection of domestic letters from an Egyptian father to his family, full of intimate details of family life.

Kemp, Barry. *Ancient Egypt: Anatomy of a Civilization*. London, 1989. A brilliant book, with an excellent treatment of el-Amarna.

Kitchen, K. A. *Pharaoh Triumphant: The Life and Times of Rameses II, King of Egypt*. Warminster, 1983. An elegant account of the long-lived pharaoh who reestablished Egypt as a superpower.

Kozloff, Arielle P., and Betsy M. Bryan, with Lawrence M. Berman. *Egypt's Dazzling Sun: Amenhotep III and His World*. Cleveland, 1992. A museum exhibition catalogue from an exhibit of treasures from the reign of this important New Kingdom pharaoh.

Lichteim, Miriam. *Ancient Egyptian Autobiographies, Chiefly of the Middle Kingdom*. Freiburg, 1988. A fine edition of some remarkable source material.

Macqueen, J. G. *The Hittites and their Contemporaries in Asia Minor*. London, 1986. A stimulating overview of Hittite culture that emphasizes the important intermediary role played by the Hittites in the ancient Near Eastern world.

McDowell, A. G. *Village Life in Ancient Egypt: Laundry Lists and Love Songs*. Oxford, 1999. A fascinating collection of translated texts recovered from an Egyptian peasant village, dating from 1539 to 1075 B.C.E.

Parkinson, Richard, ed. *Voices from Ancient Egypt*. London, 1991. Particularly strong on Middle Kingdom literature.

Potts, D. T. *The Archaeology of Elam*. Cambridge, 2000. A scholarly, demanding, but rewarding study of the territory that would later become Persia.

Redford, Donald. *Akhenaten: The Heretic King*. Princeton, 1984. Another influential treatment, quite different from Aldred (see above).

Renfrew, Colin. *Archaeology and Language: The Puzzle of Indo-European Origins*. Cambridge, 1987. A masterful but controversial work by one of the most creative archaeologists of the twentieth century.

Saggs, H. W. *The Greatness That Was Babylon: A Survey of the Ancient Civilizations of the Tigris-Euphrates Valley*, rev. ed. London, 1988. A useful and reliable introduction and reference work.

————. *Civilization before Greece and Rome*. New Haven, 1991. An excellent survey, focused mainly on the second millennium B.C.E.

Sandars, Nancy K. *The Sea Peoples: Warriors of the Ancient Mediterranean*, rev. ed. London, 1985. The essential starting point for all students interested in the subject.

Wilhelm, Gernot. *The Hurrians*. Trans. Jennifer Barnes. Warminster, 1989. A valuable introductory survey of this elusive but influential people that sets their history firmly in the context of the ancient Near East.

Wood, Michael. *In Search of the Trojan War*. New York, 1985. Aimed at a general audience, this carefully researched and engagingly written book is an excellent introduction to the late Bronze Age context of the Trojan War.

Chapter
THREE

GODS AND EMPIRES:
THE IRON AGE
NEAR EAST

THE SECOND-MILLENNIUM synthesis lay in tatters after 1200 B.C.E. For the peoples who lived through the invasions and the resulting chaos, the destruction the Sea Peoples left in their wake must have seemed a catastrophe. Certainly that is how it has appeared to modern scholars. Centuries-old centers of political, economic, and military power—not to mention great cultural achievement—had been wiped out. Mycenaean Greece, the Hittite kingdom, Kassite Babylonia, many of the great commercial kingdoms of the Eastern Mediterranean—by 1100 B.C.E. only the tattered remnants of these civilizations survived. Even those who weathered the storm were profoundly transformed by it. The Assyrians survived but would spend the next several centuries fighting for their lives, ultimately emerging as the most nakedly militaristic empire of the ancient world. Egypt endured also, but would not be a dominant power in the Mediterranean world again until the third century B.C.E., when descendants of one of Alexander the Great's generals returned it to prominence. Around the turn of the first millennium B.C.E., we thus enter a new world, organized along profoundly different lines from the great empires of the Near Eastern past.

At the heart of the great second-millennium empires of the Hittites and the Assyrians, for example, lay a very old model of organization—the Mesopotamian city-state. Even the Mycenaean Greeks drew heavily on this model. With the exception of Egypt, no Bronze Age empire came close to being an integrated, territorial state. The empires of the Bronze Age were ultimately collections of cities ruled by kings who claimed to rule through divine favor. Even in Egypt, where the accidents of geography encouraged greater territorial integration, the organization of political power and its religious trappings had remained surprisingly stable—almost static—through nearly two thousand years of Egyptian civilization. The only substantive attempt to reorganize political and religious governance in Egypt—the "revolution" initiated by Akhenaten—ended in utter failure.

The stagnation of the Late Bronze Age produced a precarious balance of power in the Mediterranean world. In an age of economic prosperity and military security,

• Why did Phoenician cities prosper during the Iron Age?

• How did David consolidate the Hebrew Kingdom?

• What were the bases for the structure of Assyrian government?

• Around what central ideas was Zoroastrianism formed?

• What developments marked the Hebrew transition from polytheism to monotheism?

few people at the time realized how fragile their world had become. By the turn of the first millennium B.C.E., however, that older world was gone. In the new age that was dawning, iron would slowly replace bronze as a primary ingredient for tools and weapons. New, larger, and more brutal empires would emerge, and new ideas about gods and their relationship to humanity would begin to displace older ones. In the Iron Age Near East, two of the world's most enduring religious traditions—Judaism and Zoroastrianism—were born, altering peoples' conceptions of religion, politics, ethics, and the relationship between humanity and the natural world. The Iron Age was a fateful historical crossroads for Western civilizations, as elements both old and new combined to reconfigure the ancient Near Eastern world.

> The Iron Age was a fateful historical crossroads for Western civilizations, as elements both old and new combined to reconfigure the ancient Near Eastern world.

gia, and the kingdom of Urartu. Similar developments were taking place in the Levant, the eastern Mediterranean coastal area that today comprises Israel, Lebanon, and parts of Syria. For centuries, this area had been under either Egyptian or Hittite control. With the collapse of both these empires, the resulting power vacuum in the region allowed new civilizations and petty states to emerge. As political and military powers, the small-scale states of the Early Iron Age were at best second rate. However, they had a profound impact on the intellectual and religious development of Western civilizations.

THE SMALL-SCALE STATES OF THE EARLY IRON AGE

Why did Phoenician cities prosper during the Iron Age?

With the destruction of the superpower balance of the Late Bronze Age, the geopolitical map of the Near East changed significantly. In Anatolia, a patchwork of small, largely Indo-European realms emerged from the collapse of the Hittite empire, including Lydia, Phry-

CHRONOLOGY

DEVELOPMENT OF IRON AGE EMPIRES

Phoenicians gain independence from Egypt	1200 B.C.E.
Philistine military dominance	1100–1000 B.C.E.
Consolidation of the kingdom of Israel	1000–973 B.C.E.
Revival of Assyrian power	883 B.C.E.
Persian defeat and annexation of Babylon	539 B.C.E.

THE PHOENICIANS

The coastal cities of present-day Lebanon were well positioned to recover from the onslaught of the Sea Peoples. Invasion and commercial disruption could not change basic facts of geography and climate. Although the Sea Peoples had destroyed the great city-state of Ugarit, the population centers of the coast survived and emerged from the chaos as some of the most famous cities of the ancient Mediterranean. Deep gorges divide the coast into naturally isolated and sheltered deep-water harbors, and many of the cities that flourished there during the Iron Age centered on the offshore islands opposite these great harbors. These cities thus enjoyed not only natural defenses from landward aggressors but still profited from the trade and commerce their ports attracted.

The group that succeeded to Ugaritic commercial success was the Phoenicians, related to the inhabitants of Ugarit by culture and language. The Phoenicians spoke a Semitic language closely related to Ugaritic, Hebrew, Amorite and other West Semitic dialects. They recognized themselves culturally and linguistically as Canaanites, "Phoenician" being the Greek designation for these residents of modern-day Lebanon and Israel. In political terms, however, the Phoenicians exhibited a familiar pattern of Near Eastern urbanism, almost a throwback to the days before the great empires of the Late Bronze Age. Phoenician cities were all independent of each other, and a Phoenician's first loyalty and identification would have been with his or her city, not to an abstract notion of being Canaanite or Phoenician. In the homeland of Phoenicia, the independent cities lived under hereditary royal governments, but in the overseas colonies a new type of

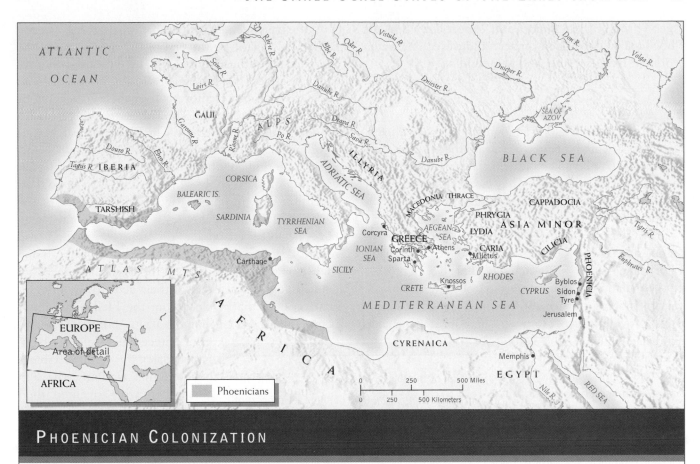

PHOENICIAN COLONIZATION

Examine the map and compare the more detailed one of Palestine on p. 86. Why would overseas colonization be of such crucial importance to Phoenician city-states? Consider in what ways the Phoenicians may have been partly driven by necessity. Notice that Phoenician colonization is concentrated in the western Mediterranean; then consider that the Phoenicians were the most active merchants of the eastern Mediterranean as well. What does their westward colonization imply about the Phoenicians' aims and the level of civilization in the West as compared with the East?

government ultimately emerged, perhaps spurred by the commercial interests of competing families. Aristocratic governments, wherein a sharing of power among a handful of elite families replaced royal authority, soon became the prevailing pattern in the overseas colonies.

Phoenicians had been active at the end of the Late Bronze Age, but most of their cities had lain under the control of the Egyptian Eighteenth and Nineteenth Dynasties. The erosion of Egyptian imperial power after 1200 B.C.E. gave rise to the possibility of independence once order was reestablished. The Phoenicians seized the opportunity, capitalizing on their natural commercial advantages and their reputation as great merchants going back to the Late Bronze Age. One Phoenician city, Gubla (the Greek name for

which was Byblos), had been a teeming center of trade under Egyptian rule, particularly as an entrepot for papyrus, the highly prized Egyptian writing material. So closely connected was Byblos with the trade in this commodity that the Greeks used their name for the city as the root of their word *biblion*, "book." All of the centers of Phoenician trade dealt in coveted luxury goods and building materials. The seabeds off the coast yielded the purple-reddish dye from the murex snail (hence the Greek name Phoenician, which essentially means "purple people"), and the finished textiles of Phoenician industry commanded a high price everywhere Phoenician merchants went. Also sought by trading partners were the Phoenicians' resources of tall timber (especially cedar), and the famous Canaanite glass that had also been traded in the Late Bronze

Age. Through their import and export activities, the Phoenicians developed expert industries in metal-working, ivory carving, and shipbuilding.

PHOENICIAN CITIES

Tucked as they were along a mountainous coast, Phoenician cities oriented themselves toward the sea. Throughout the first millennium, Phoenicians were famous as merchants and seafarers. They were also aggressive colonists; confronted by the dual pressure of commercial competition with each other and the limited carrying capacity of their surroundings, Phoenicians planted trading colonies across the Mediterranean. These colonies had a variety of purposes. First, they served as an outlet for excess population in the home city. Second, they were valuable trading partners for the cities of the Phoenician coast, providing access to new sources of raw materials and wealth. Third, the colonies acted as friendly ports for Phoenician merchant ventures and as bases from which to monopolize seaborne trade. By the end of the tenth century, Phoenicians were active from one end of the Mediterranean to the other. They probably sailed beyond as well. Evidence suggests that Phoenicians ventured as far away as Cornwall in Britain (a good source of tin), and the Greek historian Herodotus relates a credible story of how Phoenician merchant-explorers circumnavigated Africa. At the end of the ninth century, colonists from Tyre established Carthage in what is modern-day Tunisia. Carthage would ultimately rise to become the preeminent power in the western Mediterranean, bringing it into conflict with Rome centuries later.

CULTURAL INFLUENCES

The widespread colonial and mercantile efforts of the Phoenicians meant that they influenced cultures across the Mediterranean. Among their early overseas trading partners were the Greeks, and some scholars have made persuasive arguments that the Phoenicians played an important role in reintroducing urban life into the Greek world, as well as bringing a number of Near Eastern artistic and literary influences. Although the extent and nature of these borrowings are debatable, there is little question about the fundamental legacy of the Phoenicians to world history, via the Greeks: the alphabet.

> One of history's great ironies is that the Phoenicians, inventors of such an important and indispensable tool for record keeping, have left very little history of their own.

As we have seen, a "cuneiform alphabet" had already evolved at Ugarit by the end of the Bronze Age. The Phoenicians of the early twelfth and eleventh centuries further refined the system of writing to twenty-two characters, all representing consonants; vowel sounds had to be inferred from context, as is the case with modern Arabic and Hebrew. The Phoenicians had thus developed an even simpler, more efficient way of writing, which probably helped facilitate trade and the accounting of it. Precisely why they chose to share their invention with the previously illiterate Greeks of the eleventh and tenth centuries is uncertain; but it may have been to encourage the type of trading and record-keeping practices of the Phoenicians among their new partners. Whatever the case, the Greeks remained very much aware of their debt to the Phoenicians, a debt that is clear from the Hellenized letter names (alpha, beta, gamma, delta . . .) of their Phoenician antecedents (aleph, bayt, gimel, dalet . . .). The Greeks believed that Cadmus, the legendary hero who "invented" their alphabet, was a Phoenician who settled in Greece. Though we may doubt the details of the story, it betrays a consciousness on the part of the Greeks of this early borrowing.

One of history's great ironies is that the Phoenicians, inventors of such an important and indispensable tool for record keeping, have left very little history of their own. We know the Phoenicians largely through the accounts of other groups with whom they interacted—the Greeks, the Persians, and the Hebrews, the last of whom also referred to the Phoenicians as Canaanites. We can also infer a great deal from the rich documentary evidence from Ugarit, because the Phoenicians appear to have preserved many Ugaritic religious practices and beliefs.

Phoenician ritual exhibited a number of common Near Eastern features, and had a significant impact—both positive and negative—on other belief systems of the region. Death and fertility were preoccupations, and like the Babylonians many Phoenicians experienced the divine through temple prostitution. The chief god of the Phoenician pantheon was El. This primitive regional name for a divinity later manifested itself in Hebrew names and constructions (e.g., Israel, Gabriel, Michael, Samuel, and so on) as well. More crucial to the daily lives of Phoenicians however was the god Ba'al, who presented himself through various manifestations but was the primary

A Canaanite Deity. Thought to be an image of Baal, a god of storms and fertility, this statuette was discovered in a thirteenth-century B.C.E. temple in northern Palestine.

god of storms (important for the return of vegetation). His queen-consort was Ashtart, akin to the Mesopotamian Ishtar and better known by her Greek name (Astarte) and her biblical name (Ashtoreth). The goddess of war, sexual love and fertility, she enjoyed great veneration among the Phoenicians as well as many of their neighbors.

The cult practices of the Phoenicians, or Canaanites, were highly influential throughout the Levant. Worshiping at both elaborate temples and simple stone altars, the Phoenicians offered incense, various fruits, and wines to please the gods. Animal sacrifice, in which part of the animal would be burned on an altar, was a regular part of Phoenician worship. In times of crisis, the Phoenicians also practiced human sacrifice. Unlike most earlier Near East peoples, however, the Phoenicians were reluctant to represent their deities in corporeal form. Instead they used symbols such as cult stones and vacant thrones to represent their gods. Although stylized metal pendants depicting Ashtart as a fertility goddess or statues portraying Ba'al as a calf or a bull were known, these were symbols rather than portraits.

Phoenician ritual practice and Phoenician ideas about the unrepresentable qualities of the gods would exercise a profound influence on the neighboring Hebrews.

THE PHILISTINES

South along the Levantine coast from Phoenicia lay the Philistines. Few cultures have enjoyed historical reputations so bad as theirs. Regarded as villains of the Hebrew scriptural tradition, the uncouth, aggressive, and faithless Philistines have even suffered the ignominy of having their name used as an adjective in modern time to designate boorish, uncultured, and ignorant people. Their infamy stems from their unique position in the Levant at the beginning of the Iron Age, where as descendants of the Peleset—one of the Sea Peoples defeated by Ramses III—they settled, urbanized, and quickly gained the upper hand over their pastoralist neighbors in the region. One of those people was the Hebrews, for whom the Philistines were the great national enemy.

The Philistines retained a separate identity from the other peoples of the region for several generations; with each new archaeological discovery this identity becomes more and more rooted in an Aegean past. Although we know little about the Philistine language—few written materials survive, and they gradually adopted a Canaanite dialect—their material culture, behavior and organization all exhibit close affinities with the Mycenaean world. Scientific study of fossilized pollen and vegetation remains indicates that the Philistines also introduced the vine and the olive tree to the Levant from the Aegean basin. With the profits of their oil industry, they were able to create powerful armies that dominated the region in the twelfth and eleventh centuries B.C.E. They even established a monopoly over metalsmithing in the southern Levant, making it virtually impossible for their enemies to forge their own weapons.

Once they had settled themselves in the aftermath of the raid on Egypt, the Philistines established five great strongholds, the so-called Pentapolis. Less cities than citadels, the great Philistine centers—Gaza, Ashkelon and Ashdod on the coast, Ekron and Gath inland—exhibit striking similarities to the fortified palace centers of the Late Mycenaean world, and appear to have served many of the same functions. From the great citadels, each of the Philistine cities sought to dominate the surrounding countryside, organize agricultural production and control major trade routes, as well as provide strategic points from which

THE HEBREW KINGDOM, C. 900 B.C.E.

Notice the scale of the map and consider the comparatively small orbit of this world. Why did the Philistines and Phoenicians present such a perceived cultural challenge to the Hebrews? What advantages did the Philistines and Phoenicians possess, geographically and otherwise? What political and religious consequences might have resulted from the division of the kingdom of Israel after the death of King Solomon, especially the position of Jerusalem and the Temple in the south?

at an early date and have left behind virtually no written records. We know the Philistines primarily through the eyes of their enemies, the Hebrews, who at first feared them and later held them in contempt. Like other Near Eastern cultures, the Hebrew historical tradition was notorious for slandering its enemies, declaring, for example, that the Moabites and Ammonites were the descendants of Lot's incestuous union with his daughters, and decrying both Philistine and Canaanite cultural practices as "evil in the sight of the Lord." We should not be misled by such invective. The brutish arrogance of Goliath or the sexual treachery of Delilah, the two most infamous Philistines in the Hebrew Bible, is no basis for sweeping conclusions about the character of Philistine society. Unfortunately, however, we have little else on which to base our evaluations.

The Hebrews had good reason to fear the Philistines. By the end of the Late Bronze Age, these Aegean warriors were highly effective mercenaries; once they had established themselves in the Levant, they quickly turned toward the conquest and exploitation of their weaker, less organized neighbors. A Philistine prince of Ashkelon extended his control over the Phoenician city of Byblos for a short time, and felt confident in snubbing even Egyptian emissaries and court officials. If the Philistines could dominate the urbanized, wealthy, resourceful Phoenicians and hold their own against the Egyptians, however briefly, we can well imagine the challenges they presented to weaker, tribal societies such as the early Hebrews.

The picture we may glean from Hebrew texts such as the Books of Judges and Samuel makes the situation clear: at one point the southern tribes of Judah explain to Samson, the judge of the tribe of Dan, "You know the Philistines rule over us." Philistine pressure on the central Hebrew hill country of Ephraim was constant, threatening the holy sanctuary at Shiloh, the original resting place of the sacred Ark of the Covenant, which contained the original tablets of the law given by the Hebrew god Yahweh to Moses on Mount Sinai. In Hebrew tradition, the desperate tribes of Israel carried the Ark before them against the Philistines, only to lose it in battle and witness the destruction of Shiloh. The Philistines established garrisons throughout the land of the Hebrews and denied them access to metallurgical technology. Meanwhile, they exacted tribute and, according to the biblical account, engaged in the typical abuses of an occupying people.

to mount raids against neighbors while presenting virtually impregnable defenses against would-be attackers. An independent lord ruled over each Philistine citadel, and no doubt tensions and rivalries existed among them. But much like the heroes of Greek epic, the Philistines of the Bible could set aside their differences to confederate for the purpose of waging war.

Otherwise, it is difficult to know the Philistines on their own terms. Their history as an independent culture was brief. They abandoned their own language

THE REPORT OF WENAMUN

Around 1085 B.C.E. an official of the Theban temple to Amun-Re named Wenamun was sent to Lebanon to collect timber for a new ceremonial barge for the god. Egypt's power had declined, however, and the Philistine ruler of Byblos was not inclined to provide, unrewarded, the timber that Wenamun expected from him.

Wenamun of the Temple of Amun . . . [departed] to fetch timber for the great noble [river] bark of Amun-Re, King of Gods. . . . [Reaching the realm] of the prince of Byblos, [he]. . . sent to me saying: 'Leave my harbor!' I sent to him saying: "Where shall I go? If you have a ship to carry me, let me be taken back to Egypt!" I spent twenty-nine days in his harbor and he . . . [sent] to me daily to say: "Leave my harbor!". . . [Finally] I had found a ship headed for Egypt. I had loaded all my belongings into it and was watching for the darkness. . . . Then the harbor master came to me, saying: "Wait until morning, says the prince!"

When morning came, [the prince] sent for me. . . . I said to him: "Blessings of Amun!" He said to me: "How long is it . . . since you came from the place where Amun is?" I said to him: "Five whole months until now!" He said to me: ". . . where is the dispatch of Amun, which should be in your hand? Where is the letter of the High Priest of Amun, which should also be in your hand? . . . On what business have you come?" I said to him: "I have come in quest of timber for the great noble bark of Amun-Re, King of Gods. What your father did, what the father of your father did, you too will do it." . . . He said to me: "True they did it. If you pay me for doing it, I will do it. My relations carried out this business after Pharaoh had sent six ships laden with the goods of Egypt, and they had been unloaded into [my] storehouses. You, what have you brought for me?"

He said to me . . . "I am not your servant, nor am I the servant of him who sent you!" . . . I said to him: "Wrong! . . . There is no ship on the river that does not belong to Amun. His is the sea and his the Lebanon of which you say, 'It is mine.' . . . You too, you are the servant of Amun."

From Miriam Lichtheim, ed., *Ancient Egyptian Literature: Three Volumes*, Vol. 2, (Berkeley: University of California Press, 1976), pp. 224-229.

THE HEBREWS

How did David consolidate the Hebrew Kingdom?

We will have occasion at the end of this chapter to discuss the central feature of Hebrew cultural experience, the development of their monotheistic conception of divinity. In this section, we will focus our attention on the political development of Hebrew society within the Iron Age Levant. However, in any discussion of Hebrew society, religious conceptions and practices can never be far from the surface. Like all ancient cultures, the Hebrews initially made little distinction between politics and religion. What set them apart, however, was their unusual theology and the impact it had on their development as a people. Were it not for the resilience of their religious tradition, and the fundamental impact it has had on the subsequent development of Western civilizations, we would have little reason to discuss the early Hebrews at length. As it is, however, the Hebrews were one of the most important cultures in world history.

ORIGINS

We are blessed as historians by one of the unique achievements of the Hebrews: the Hebrew Bible, known to Christians as the Old Testament. The Bible is an unparalleled historical resource, full of extraordinary detail about cultural practices and historical events, as well as being a guide to the intellectual unfolding of the most important religious tradition of the Western world. It is not, however, a history as modern people would conceive of it. The Bible is a composite work, assembled over many centuries, mostly by unknown authors. Although it contains some ostensibly historical accounts, it is essentially a story of the relationship between a transcendent, unchanging, creator god and those whom he chose to be his special people; of the covenant that was forged between them; and of the trials by which that relationship was repeatedly tested and reaffirmed.

Most scholars regard with particular suspicion the historical accounts contained in the first five books of the Bible (these books are known to Christians as the Pentateuch, and to Jews as the Torah). Aside from the chronological difficulties posed by a series of impossibly long-lived patriarchs (Methusaleh, for example, is said to have lived for more than nine hundred years), much of this historical material appears to have been borrowed from other Near Eastern cultures. The creation and flood stories have Sumerian parallels; the laws and practices of the patriarchs have clear Hurrian antecedents; the tale of Moses' childhood is virtually a replica of Sargon's legend; and the story of the exodus from Egypt is fraught with problems from a historical standpoint. Although the Book of Joshua claims that the Hebrews who returned from Egypt conquered and expelled the Canaanites, many scholars now believe, on the basis of strong archaeological and linguistic evidence, that the Hebrews were essentially inland Canaanites who may have merged with scattered Hebrew refugees from Egypt in the aftermath of the Sea

> We are blessed as historians by one of the unique achievements of the Hebrews: the Hebrew Bible, known to Christians as the Old Testament.

Peoples, but who for the most part had been continuously resident in Canaan for centuries. Important religious and cultural developments clearly occurred among the Hebrews of the second millennium B.C.E., but the first five books of the Bible have the look and feel of retrospective extrapolation and justification, not secure historical record.

Once we move into the so-called historical books of the Bible, the information becomes more credible. In the Book of Judges, the Hebrews appear as a seminomadic people just beginning to settle down into seasonal occupation around the springs and valleys that provided sustenance in an otherwise arid landscape. The Hebrews had also organized themselves into twelve "tribes"—extended clan units in which families owed each other mutual aid and protection in times of war, cattle raiding, and judicial dispute. Each tribe was ruled over by a "judge" who exercised the typical functions of authority in a clan-based society: war leadership, high priesthood, and dispute settlement. By the middle of the twelfth century, these tribes had established some kind of rough territorial "turf," those in the south calling themselves Judah, and those in the north Israel.

HEBREWS AND PHILISTINES

These collective labels should not mislead us. Although they create an impression of greater cohesion, in fact the Hebrew tribes had few mechanisms for concerted action. The inherent weakness of their organization was laid bare by contact with the Philistines, who quickly conquered so much of the Levantine coastal region around 1050 B.C.E. that it became known as Palestine, meaning "the Philistine country." Faced with the threat of extinction, the Hebrews now put up desperate resistance from their bases in the hilly interior of the country. By the end of the eleventh century, however, the future of the Hebrews as a people was not promising. To their north, they felt the economic, religious and sometimes military pressure of the Phoenicians, with their dynamic and eclectic culture; to their west and south, they confronted the military might of the Philistines.

To meet the Philistine threat, a tighter, "national" form of government was needed. Accordingly, around 1025 B.C.E., Samuel, a tribal judge and holy man with the force of personality to gain adherence from all the

Hebrew tribes, selected for them a king who would make them, "like other nations," a united people. King Saul, however, quickly provoked the resentment of Samuel, who withdrew his support from the embattled king. Saul also proved an indifferent general. Although he succeeded in stopping Philistine penetration into the hill country, he was unable to oust the Philistines from the valleys or coastal plains. So Samuel threw his support behind a young warrior, David, a member of Saul's court who now schemed actively to draw popular support away from Saul. Waging his own military campaigns, David achieved one triumph over the Philistines after another. In contrast, the armies of Saul met frequent reverses, which the Biblical authors portrayed as divine retribution for Saul's own inadequacies. David, however, was not exactly a national patriot. When Saul finally drove him from his court, David first became an outlaw on the fringes of Hebrew and Philistine society before ultimately becoming a mercenary in Philistine service. It was as a Philistine mercenary that David fought against Saul in the climactic battle in which Saul was killed. Soon thereafter, David himself became king, first over Judah, his home territory, and later over Saul's home kingdom of Israel also.

> It was as a Philistine mercenary that David fought against Saul in the climactic battle in which Saul was killed.

CONSOLIDATION OF THE HEBREW KINGDOM

With David's ascension to the throne around 1000 B.C.E., the most glorious period in the political history of the ancient Hebrew kingdom began. David took advantage of a number of new developments and trends to extend his rule and the power of his kingdom. Egypt went into sharp decline at the very end of the eleventh century, and this may have had a significant impact upon the Philistine economy, disrupting Philistine society. At the same time, years of battle against the Philistines had hardened the Hebrew warriors and accustomed them to Philistine tactics. Through a combination of cunning, opportunism, and inspired leadership, David reduced the Philistines to an inconsequential strip of coastal land in the south. He also defeated the Moabites and Ammonites, extending his control east of the River Jordan and the Dead Sea. By David's death in 973 B.C.E., the united kingdom of Israel stretched from the middle Euphrates in the north to the Gulf of Aqaba in the south,

from the Mediterranean coast in the west into the Syrian deserts beyond the River Jordan. Israel was now a serious force in the politics of the Near East, its status increased by the temporary weakness of its imperial neighbors Egypt and Assyria.

Within his kingdom, David incorporated the native Canaanites to such a degree that during the next few generations they lost their separate identity and became fully merged with the Hebrew people. As this process of amalgamation progressed, the Hebrews increasingly put aside pastoralism and took up either farming or urban occupations. As David's power and prestige grew, he was able to impose on his subjects a highly unpopular system of taxation and forced labor. His goal was to build a glorious political and religious capital at Jerusalem, a Canaanite settlement that he transformed into the central city of his kingdom. It was a shrewd choice. As a newly conquered city, Jerusalem had no previous affiliation with any of Israel's twelve tribes, and so stood outside the ancient rivalries between them. Geographically, Jerusalem lay between the southern tribes of Judah (of which David was a member) and the northern tribes of Israel (from which Saul had come). David took steps to exalt the city as a religious center. He reorganized the priesthood of Yahweh; and by making Jerusalem the resting place of the sacred Ark of the Covenant, which contained the tablets of the religious law given by Yahweh to Moses on Mount Sinai, David made his new city the central place for the kingdom's unifying national cult of Yahweh. By so doing, he hoped to forge a new national identity, focused on the House of David, that would transcend the old divisions between Israel and Judah.

CHRONOLOGY

THE TRANSFORMATION OF HEBREW SOCIETY

Early efforts to form national government	1025 B.C.E.
David crowned king of Israel	1000 B.C.E.
Split between Israel and Judah	924 B.C.E.
Fall of Judah and start of Babylonian Captivity	586 B.C.E.

TWO ACCOUNTS OF SAUL'S ANOINTING

When the judge Samuel anointed Saul as the first king of the Hebrews, he opened a new chapter in the political history of Israel. Saul's kingship was not a success, however, and Samuel ultimately declared against him, throwing his support behind Saul's rival (and son-in-law) David. These two quite different accounts of Saul's elevation by Samuel may reflect the tensions that later arose between the supporters of Saul and of David. The first account also suggests the ambivalence some Hebrew scribes and prophets felt about having a human king at all.

1 SAMUEL 8:4–22, 10:20–25

All the elders of Israel gathered together and [said to Samuel]: "You are old and your sons do not follow in your ways; appoint for us, then, a king to govern us, like other nations." But the thing displeased Samuel [who] prayed to the Lord, and the Lord said to Samuel, "Listen to the voice of the people in all that they say to you; for they have not rejected you, but they have rejected me from being king over them. Just as they have done to me, from the day I brought them up out of Egypt to this day, forsaking me and serving other gods, so they are also doing to you. Now then, listen to their voice; only—you shall solemnly warn them, and show them the ways of the king who shall reign over them." So Samuel reported all the words of the Lord to the people who were asking for a king. "These will be the ways of the king who will reign over you: he will take sons and appoint them to his chariots . . . he will take your daughters to be perfumers and cooks and bakers . . . he will take one-tenth of your grain and your vineyards and give it to his officers and courtiers . . . and one-tenth of your flocks, and you shall be his slaves. But the people refused to listen, and Samuel said to the people, "Each of you return to his home."

Then Samuel brought all the tribes of Israel near, and the tribe of Benjamin was chosen by lot. He brought the tribe of Benjamin near by its families . . . and Saul the son of Kisk was chosen by lot. But when they sought him, he could not be found. So they inquired again of the Lord . . . and the Lord said, "See, he has hidden himself among the baggage." Then they ran and brought him from there. When he took his stand among the people, he was head and shoulders taller than any of them. Samuel said, "Do you see the one whom the Lord has chosen? There is no one like him among the people." And the people all shouted, "Long live the king!" Samuel told the people the rights and duties of the kingship; and he wrote them in a book and laid it up before the Lord.

1 SAMUEL 9:1—10:1

There was a man of Benjamin whose name was Kish . . . [who] had a son whose name was Saul, a handsome young man . . . he stood head and shoulders above everyone else. Now the donkeys of Kish had strayed. So Kish said to his son Saul, "Take one of the boys with you; go and look for the donkeys." . . . As they were entering [a] town, they saw Samuel coming out toward them on his way up to the shrine. Now the day before Saul came, the Lord revealed to Samuel, "Tomorrow about this time I will send you a man from the land of Benjamin, and you shall anoint him to be ruler over my people Israel. He shall save my people from the hand of the Philistines; for I have seen the suffering of my people, because their outcry has come to me." . . . Saul approached Samuel inside the gate and said, "Tell me please, where is the house of the seer?" Samuel answered Saul, "I am the seer, go up before me to the shrine. . . . As for your donkeys that were lost three days ago, give no further thought to them, for they have been found. And on whom is all Israel's desire fixed, if not on you and your ancestral house?" Saul answered, "I am only a Benjaminite, from the least of the tribes of Israel, and my family is the humblest of all the families of the tribe of Benjamin. Why then have you spoken of me this way?" . . . As they were going down to the outskirts of town, Samuel said to Saul, "Tell the boy to go on before us . . . that I may make known to you the word of God." Samuel took a vial of oil and poured it on [Saul's] head and kissed him; he said: "The Lord has anointed you ruler over his people Israel. You shall reign over the people of the Lord and you will save them from the hand of their enemies all around."

The New Oxford Annotated Bible. (Oxford: Oxford University Press, 1994), slightly adapted.

THE LEGEND OF KING DAVID

David was clearly a historical figure, and his successes are beyond doubt. But the legend of King David sits oddly nonetheless with the rest of the Hebrew Bible. David's exploits have the ring of another tradition, a heroizing element more in keeping with Greek epics such as the *Iliad* and *Odyssey*. David is presented as an adventurer, a singer of songs and a doer of deeds, who leaves a parade of lovers and a trail of decapitated victims in his wake. His individual military exploits are those of a Greek hero; while his relationship with Jonathan, the son of Saul, resembles the intimate friendship between Achilles and Patroclus in the *Iliad*. David is more Ajax than Ezra, more Agamemnon than Moses; and at its end, his life takes a turn typical of Greek tragedy, when his power and pride lead him to flout the laws of God against adultery and murder, and inevitable retribution falls on him and his house.

What, precisely, we ought to make of such parallels is unclear. Clearly, however, David's age was characterized by extensive cross-cultural influences. We know, for example, that the Philistines dominated the Hebrews during the early part of King David's life both militarily and culturally. The Philistines, with their epic traditions imported from the Aegean basin, may have had a profound impact on the way David was remembered among the Hebrews, as a figure more in keeping with early Greek than with Hebrew ideals. Nor should we discount the possibility that David himself modeled his own conduct in part on Aegean ideals of heroism he learned from his Philistine overlords. How much of what the Bible tells us about David is historical, and how much is literary and legendary, we have no way to determine. The earliest accounts of David's reign were not written down until at least the reign of his son Solomon; in their present form, these accounts may be as late as the fifth century B.C.E., five hundred years after David's death.

However much his life may be legendary, David succeeded in fashioning a patchwork of seminomadic tribes into a nation with a distinct religious identity. In creating a unified, centralized, vigorous nation, David transformed the Hebrews into the most fearsome power in the Levant. By instituting taxes, conscription, and custom duties on trade, David took full advantage of the region's limited natural resources. Furthermore, the Davidic episode founded the idea of Israel as a unified nation, a manifest fulfillment of the relationship the Hebrews believed they enjoyed with their god, Yahweh. This notion was to prove a powerful resource for the survival of Hebrew culture and identity when political and military events later turned against this people.

THE REIGN OF KING SOLOMON

Continuing his father's policies but on a much grander scale, King Solomon built a great temple complex at Jerusalem, wherein he housed the sacred Ark of the Covenant. Solomon's support of the Yahweh cult played particularly well with the writers of Hebrew scripture. His exaltation of Yahweh and the establishment of an official cult and a temple produced, in their eyes, a golden age for the Hebrews.

Despite his proverbial wisdom, however, Solomon

was a ruthless and often brutal ruler whose promotion of the Yahweh cult coincided with a program of despotic rule and royal self-aggrandizement. Solomon kept an enormous harem of some three hundred wives and seven hundred concubines, many of them drawn from subject or allied peoples. His palace complex—of which the temple was a part—allowed him to rule in the grand style of ancient Near Eastern potentates, and he instituted a variety of oppressive taxation and administrative schemes to finance his expensive tastes and programs. The king also profited from his kingdom's widening commercial contacts. With the help of Hiram, the Phoenician king of Tyre, Solomon constructed a commercial fleet based at the head of the Gulf of Aqaba. These ships plied the waters of the Red Sea and beyond, trading among other commodities the gold and copper mined by Solomon's slaves in the southern Negev. By the middle of the tenth century, widespread domestication of the camel had made long-distance caravans a regular feature of the Near Eastern landscape. Solomon imposed customs duties on the lucrative trade passing through his country, and wealth poured into Israel as never before.

> Their centuries-long fight for existence ultimately had a profound effect on the Assyrian world view.

But it was not enough. Solomon maintained a large standing army made up of conscripts from his own people, equipped with chariot and cavalry squadrons, and powered by horses purchased abroad. To undertake his ambitious building program, Solomon required many of his people, particularly from the agricultural north, to serve as forced labor four months out of every year. This level of oppression was too much for many Israelites. The north seethed with rebellion against the royal capital, and after Solomon's death, his son and successor was faced with revolt. Before long the united monarchy had split in two, the House of David ruling a southern kingdom still centered on Jerusalem (Judah), the ten northern tribes banding together into the kingdom of Israel with its capital at Shechem.

THE NORTHERN AND SOUTHERN KINGDOMS

The split not only weakened the Hebrews politically, but also had serious consequences religiously. The first king of the northern state of Israel, Jeroboam I, sought to establish worship and ritual independent from the temple in Jerusalem. He revived two ancient sanctuaries at Dan and Bethel and appealed to the popular but theologically taboo symbolism of Canaanite worship. Jeroboam and his successors hoped to stop the pilgrimages and dedications by the citizens of Israel at the temple in Judah, which drained the resources of the more populous northern kingdom. Jeroboam and his successors thus incurred the wrath of the temple-centered and pro-Judean scriptural tradition, but archaeology as well as the biblical account itself demonstrate that the cult of Yahweh was far from a monopoly in either the north or south. Foreign ritual and worship, particularly of the Canaanite deities Ba'al and Ashtart, remained a prominent feature of Hebrew religious life for several more centuries.

Although the two Hebrew kingdoms maintained an independent existence for several centuries—the north until 722 B.C.E., the south until 586 B.C.E.—the changing situation of the Near East made their divided state ever more vulnerable. Within a few generations of Solomon's death, the Hebrews and other nations of the Near East would find themselves menaced by the revived Mesopotamia-based empire of the Assyrians.

THE ASSYRIAN EMPIRE

What were the bases for the structure of the Assyrian government?

We have already encountered the Assyrians, a Semitic-speaking group with a rich past, centered in northern Mesopotamia. In Chapter Two, we learned how the Assyrians took advantage of their unique position along the upper Tigris and middle Euphrates to establish a network of caravan and trade routes. The Assyrians were also a crucial conduit for the spread of Mesopotamian urban society and organization into the Anatolian plateau. Although they were eclipsed temporarily by the rise of the Old Babylonian Empire, the Assyrians possessed a remarkably resilient identity and culture, which survived the power struggle between the Hittites and Egyptians and the catastrophe of the Sea Peoples. Their centuries-long fight for existence ultimately had a profound effect on the Assyrian world view; in the ninth century, they would extend their

WHAT WERE THE BASES FOR THE STRUCTURE OF THE ASSYRIAN GOVERNMENT?

THE ASSYRIAN EMPIRE   93

CHRONOLOGY

EVOLUTION OF ASSYRIA IN THE IRON AGE

Assyria begins to reestablish its influence	1362–883 B.C.E.
Assurnasirpal II founds neo-Assyrian empire	883–859 B.C.E.
Birth of the Sargonid dynasty	722 B.C.E.
Destruction of the Assyrian state	612–605 B.C.E.

power and influence by means of a terrible, brutal, long-lasting, and systematic victimization of their neighbors. Its terrors notwithstanding, their aggression helped to shape the religious and political traditions of their neighbors, spreading Near Eastern culture to the Aegean basin, synthesizing a new type of imperial organization, and imparting important lessons about what did and did not make for successful governance of a far-flung, international empire.

THE MIDDLE ASSYRIAN PERIOD (1362–859 B.C.E.)

The decline of the kingdom of Mitanni in the fourteenth century gave the Assyrians the opportunity to reestablish themselves as a great kingdom. As Hittite pressure from the west eroded the strength of the Hurro-Mitanni realm, Assyria extended its own influence and commercial control along its frontier with the kingdom of Mitanni, ultimately causing the collapse of what had become a Hittite puppet state. The first to take the title "king of Assyria" was a governor of the city of Assur (sometimes spelled Ashur), and thus the governor on earth of the city's patron deity of the same name. This man, Assur-uballit I (r. 1362–1327 B.C.E.), established the Assyrian kingship and sought to extend his power over northern Mesopotamia. He also fought against the Kassite kings of Babylonia. Assur-uballit and his successors possessed a very self-conscious sense of their history and identity. They regarded Babylonia as ancestral to their own culture and considered the Kassites interlopers. Assur-uballit's immediate successors evoked the distant, northern Mesopotamian past by arrogating to themselves the names of such Amorite kings as Shamshi-Adad. But despite their claim to be the heirs of Mesopotamian

culture, Assur-uballit and his immediate successors practiced great restraint in their policies, doing little to upset the delicate balance of the region.

With the accession of Tukulti-Ninurta I in 1244 B.C.E., the restraint was dropped. Tukulti-Ninurta was a conqueror of the first order, remembered in the Book of Genesis as Nimrud and in Greek tradition as Ninos. Tukulti-Ninurta sacked Babylon, carrying its Kassite king and the statues of the city's patron deity, Marduk, into captivity and claiming the prestigious kingship of Babylon for himself. To maintain his tenuous grip over Babylonia, however, Tukulti-Ninurta was forced to engage in constant campaigning; but endless warfare and his sacrilegious treatment of the Babylonian god alienated his own subjects, who murdered him in about 1208 B.C.E.

A century of Assyrian decline followed as its neighbors sought both vengeance and control over the vital trade routes that crisscrossed Assyrian territory. For nearly a century, the Assyrians once again fought for their survival. More than once, the Assyrians were almost destroyed; but the constant cycle of desperate fighting forged them into a highly militaristic people. A brief resurgence occurred during the reign of Tiglath-Pileser I (1115–1077 B.C.E.), who took the battle-hardened armies of Assyria on westward campaigns until his power reached the shores of the Mediterranean. But the Assyrians soon found themselves overextended and vulnerable to encroachments by other nations following Tiglath-Pileser's death.

The survivalist character of the Assyrian experience continued until the close of the Middle Assyrian period, when a brutal but brilliant ruler, Assurnasirpal II (883–859 B.C.E.), revived Assyrian strength and founded the neo-Assyrian empire. Under his ruthless leadership, the Assyrians conducted aggressive military campaigns on an annual basis. The targets of Assyrian might had to pay tribute or face the full onslaught of the Assyrian military machine, which under Assurnasirpal acquired a deserved reputation for savagery and viciousness. The great Near Eastern scholar A. H. Olmstead referred to Assurnasirpal's policy as one of "calculated frightfulness," a refined name for a strategy of military terror and the extraction of protection money through plunder.

THE NEO-ASSYRIAN EMPIRE

The conquests of Assurnasirpal and his son, Shalmeneser III, inspired stiff resistance to Assyrian expansion. The northern kingdom of Israel, along with a

THE ASSYRIAN EMPIRE, C. 700 B.C.E.

Compare this map with the one on p. 86. What do you find striking about the geography of the Assyrian empire? Why would the Assyrians concentrate their efforts in the river valleys and along the coast, leaving the Syrian interior largely alone? Notice the location of the Assyrian capitals of Nineveh and Assur; how was their situation in Mesopotamia likely to affect the Assyrians' sense of their own historical identity? Consider the position of Egypt. Why did the Assyrians find it difficult to subjugate Egypt permanently, despite the violence of their conquests?

variety of other states in the region of Syria-Palestine, formed an alliance to stop Shalmeneser III (853–827 B.C.E.). Shalmeneser had directed his father's terrifying military might against the west, dealing hammer blow after hammer blow to the petty states there. Ultimately the hostile coalition fought him to a standstill in the 850s; he had to settle for smaller victories against the Armenians to his northwest and the Medes to his northeast, until the "Great Revolt" of Assyrian elites ended his reign and nullified his western gains. In the aftermath of Assyrian aggression, new kingdoms such as Urartu to the north and the invigorated Medes to the northeast managed to hold their own and even extend suzerainty beyond their frontiers. The Aramaeans of Syria took advantage of Assyrian weakness to become the new bullies of the Levant, and Assyria found itself stalemated by the newfound strength of its opponents.

The respite proved brief for the Near East. A usurper who took the name Tiglath-Pileser III seized the Assyrian throne in 744 B.C.E. and immediately prepared a great western campaign. In his first year he demanded tribute from various western kingdoms that had not paid up for generations; many predictably refused, to their cost. The course of Tiglath-Pileser III's punitive western campaign was breathtaking. He destroyed the powerful Anatolian kingdom of Urartu, brought recalcirant Assyrian governors to heel, and

> The course of Tiglath-Pileser III's punitive western campaign was breathtaking.

WHAT WERE THE BASES FOR THE STRUCTURE OF THE ASSYRIAN GOVERNMENT?

THE ASSYRIAN EMPIRE   95

annexed the great Syrian principality of Carchemish—an important commercial center—along with several Phoenician cities. Menahem, the usurper king of Israel, paid tribute and hoped to enlist Assyrian support for his dynasty. When that support failed and an anti-Assyrian party came to power, Tiglath-Pileser pitilessly crushed the kingdom, destroying fortifications, detaching key regions from Israel, and reducing it to the status of a vassal state.

When Tiglath-Pileser III died in 727 B.C.E., the various states of western Asia apparently anticipated that the familiar pattern of Assyrian dynastic instability would repeat itself. Many of the newer acquisitions rebelled, only to find that Tiglath-Pileser's son, Shalmeneser V, proved a worthy successor, energetically crushing the rebellions. Though he died in battle, he was quickly and seamlessly replaced by one of his military commanders, Sargon II (722–705 B.C.E.). Typical of Assyrian historical consciousness, Sargon was thinking of Sargon of Akkad as the "first" Sargon; he was laying claim to be the successor to a great Near Eastern empire nearly fifteen hundred years in the past. The dynasty founded by Sargon II is called the Sargonid, and its century of rule proved the most magnificent and impressive in all of Assyrian history.

The Sargonids extended the frontiers of the Assyrian empire from the foothills of western Iran to the shores of the Mediterranean. Briefly, they even subjugated parts of Egypt. Sargon himself put an end to the kingdom of Israel on taking the throne, and scared the southern kingdom of Judah into remaining a loyal and quiet vassal. The ancient Elamite kingdom fell during the Sargonid period, and by the seventh century B.C.E. Assyria was the unrivaled power of the ancient Near East.

GOVERNMENT AND ADMINISTRATION

The neo-Assyrian empire was an armed state, based on the ability of its army to spread terror and oppress both enemies and subjects alike. At the head of the Assyrian government was the king, the earthly representative of the god Assur. As well as being its military leader, the king was also the empire's chief religious figure; when the army was not in the field the king's time was taken up with elaborate sacrifices and rituals to appease the "great god" Assur. Divination and the consultation of oracles were central features of Assyrian religion. The Assyrian king, as chief priest, had to be able to discern the will of Assur through the portents of nature.

The survivalist character of the Middle Assyrian period had encouraged the Assyrians to develop a very strong hereditary principle within their kingship. The crown prince underwent a thorough education and training for his future duties as king, and as he grew older assumed increasingly important functions of government at his father's side. Potential rivals within the royal family had to acknowledge and swear loyalty to the crown prince while the king lived. Although the position of women generally in Assyria did not differ much from that in other Mesopotamian societies, the prestige

Assyrian Winged Human-Headed Bull. This relief was found in the palace of King Sargon II (722–705 B.C.E.). It measures sixteen feet wide by sixteen feet high and weighs approximately forty tons.

and power of the queen were considerable. She enjoyed special deference as the wife of the king and mother of the crown prince, and if the king died while the crown prince was still young, the queen ruled as regent for her son until he came of age.

Around the central royal government was an extensive bureaucracy of governors, high priests and military commanders, professions by no means mutually exclusive in the Assyrian context. These administrators also formed the highest class in Assyrian society, exercising local authority on behalf of the king. As a people who ruled principally through military prowess, the Assyrians appreciated the importance of transportation and lines of communication. They constructed an extensive network of roads that would serve as the basis for travel and communication across the Near East for centuries. The Assyrians also deployed a system of messengers and spies to report to the royal court on the activities of subjects and provincial governors.

Provincial governors collected tribute, recruited for the army, maintained Assyrian control, and administered the king's law. Not surprisingly, the law of the Assyrians bore close resemblance to the code of Hammurabi, though many of its penalties were more severe. The Assyrians reserved the harshest punishments for practices deemed as detrimental to reproduction, and the penalties for homosexuality and abortion were barbaric and grisly. Assyrian law also demonstrates the subordinate position of women to men: only the husband had the power of divorce within his discretion, and for certain offenses he could inflict on his wife a variety of penalties, from corporal punishment through mutilation or even death.

THE ASSYRIAN MILITARY-RELIGIOUS ETHOS

Assyrian religious, political, and military ideas took shape in the centuries during which Assyria fought defensive wars to secure its survival. When the Assyrians gained the upper hand, however, this ethos became the foundation for their empire's relentless conquests.

The two fundamental characteristics of this Assyrian military-religious ethos were holy war and the exaction of tribute through terror. The Assyrians were convinced that their god Assur demanded that his worship be extended through military conquest. Even more than to the king, therefore, the Assyrian army belonged to Assur; and all who did not accept Assur's supremacy were, by that fact alone, enemies of Assur's people, the Assyrians. Ritual humiliation of a defeated

city's gods was therefore a regular feature of Assyrian conquests. Frequently the conquered gods would be carried off to the Assyrian capital, where they would live as hostages at the "court" of Assur. Meanwhile, an image of Assur himself (usually represented as a sun disk with the bust of an archer) would be installed in the defeated city, which the conquered people would now be required to worship. Worship of Assur did not necessarily mean that conquered peoples abandoned their previous gods altogether. But in Assyrian eyes, there was no question that Assur should be the supreme deity for all the peoples of their empire. As time went on, other gods gradually lost their defining characteristics, looking more and more like smaller versions of Assur, who became increasingly remote and aloof, the god of a state religion whom everyone in the Assyrian empire was expected to serve.

Tribute for the Assyrians initially meant the taking of

Assyrian Atrocities. These Judean captives are being impaled on stakes after their city has fallen to the Assyrian king Sennacherib (704–681 B.C.E.). This carving comes from the walls of Sennacherib's palace at Nineveh.

WHAT WERE THE BASES FOR THE STRUCTURE OF THE ASSYRIAN GOVERNMENT?

THE ASSYRIAN EMPIRE   97

Assyrian Relief Sculptures. These panels, representative of Assyrian "frightfulness," depict the emperor Assurbanipal on the hunt.

plunder. Rather than defeat their foes once and impose formal tribute thereafter, the Assyrians raided even their vanquished foes each year, extracting tribute by force. This strategy succeeded in terrifying Assyria's subjects and keeping the Assyrian military machine primed for battle. But it also entailed difficulties. Perpetual reconquests did little to inspire loyalty among subject peoples, who eventually reached a point of desperation at which they had little to lose through rebellion. Moreover, these annual Assyrian invasions not only sharpened the Assyrian army but also the forces of subjects, and by the end of the ninth century other nations of the region had become accomplished at the Assyrians' own game. It was not until Tiglath-Pileser III that the Assyrians abandoned the policy of collecting tribute by force each year, settling instead for more orthodox forms of payment.

Assyrian warfare was also notoriously savage. Ancient warfare was never pretty: mutilations of prisoners, decapitations, rape, and the mass deportations and/or enslavement of civilian populations were commonplace. The Assyrians, however, relished and celebrated such barbarities as did no other ancient empire. Their artwork and inscriptions revel in the butchering and torture of their enemies. Smiling Assyrian archers are shown shooting fleeing enemies in the back, while

> Rather than defeat their foes once and impose formal tribute thereafter, the Assyrians raided even their vanquished foes each year, extracting tribute by force.

remorseless soldiers fling the citizens of a captured Judean town from the walls, impaling them on stakes below. The most extreme barbarities were reserved for rebellious subjects whose rebellion was an offence not only against Assyria, but also against Assur.

The army itself had developed by the ninth century into a devastating force. Like many ancient societies, the Assyrians had originally employed a seasonal peasant army of part-time soldiers. But from the reign of Assurnasirpal II onward, the Assyrians recruited a massive standing army of over one hundred thousand soldiers. Furthermore, the Assyrians mastered large-scale iron-smelting techniques, and by the ninth century equipped their fighting men with high-quality steel weapons that overwhelmed opponents still reliant on bronze.

Assyrian strategy and tactics were the most highly sophisticated the world had yet seen, in great part due to the organization of the army. The core of the Assyrian army was heavily armed and armored shock troops, equipped with a variety of thrusting weapons and bearing tall shields for protection. These Assyrian storm troopers were the main force for crushing enemy infantry in the field and for routing the inhabitants of an enemy city once inside. To harass enemy infantry and break up their formations, the Assyrians deployed light skirmishers with slings and javelins. The Assyrians also combined archery and chariotry as never before. With a swift and efficient two-wheeled design, Assyrian chariots sped about the battlefield, carrying one to two archers and another couple of shield bearers. Thus chariots became highly mobile firing platforms, and from them the expert Assyrian archers could wreak havoc. Finally, the Assyrians during the course of their ascendancy managed to develop a true cavalry force, with individual warriors mounted on armored steeds and wielding bows and arrows or heavy lances.

In the open field the combined arms tactics of Assyrian warfare were too much for their opponents. The obvious answer was not to face the Assyrians in a stand-up fight, because the art of siege warfare was not highly evolved by the early first millennium. The warlike Assyrians trained a corps of combat engineers, however, highly skilled in sapping walls, building catapults, siege engines, battering rams, and battle towers. Thus the walls of most cities provided little refuge from Assyrian military onslaught. After a city fell, an even more extraordinary series of atrocities usually followed: in addition to the usual dismemberments and mutilations, captives might also be burned or skinned alive.

THE END OF ASSYRIA AND ITS LEGACY

The successors of Sargon II continued Assyrian military policies while at the same time devoting great energies to what we might broadly consider "culture." Sargon's immediate successor Sennacherib (704–681 B.C.E.) rebuilt the ancient Assyrian city of Nineveh, fortifying it with a double wall nine miles around. He constructed an enormous palace raised on a giant platform decorated with marble, ivory, and exotic woods. He also ordered the construction of a massive irrigation system, including an aqueduct that carried fresh water to the city from thirty miles away.

Sennacherib's son Esarhaddon (681–669 B.C.E.) sought to ease the tensions between Assyria and the city of Babylon, which had been brutally punished by his father. Esarhaddon also attempted to mollify the hard feelings caused by Assyria's religious imperialism, allowing for the conditional return of cult objects to conquered peoples. Esarhaddon rebuilt and glorified Babylon, and was a patron of the sciences and arts. None of this, however, changed the fact that he was at heart an Assyrian king. In 671 B.C.E. he invaded Egypt, chasing the Nubian pharaoh Taharqa from the throne. The expedition was largely punitive, Esarhaddon having tired of Taharqa's constant meddling with Assyria's vassal states. But Egypt was too far away for the Assyrians to maintain firm control, and Taharqa returned to power on Esarhaddon's departure. The conquest of Egypt was left to the next Assyrian king, Esarhaddon's son Assurbanipal.

Assurbanipal (669–627 B.C.E.) was perhaps the greatest of all the Assyrian kings. He maintained a strong military presence throughout the empire, and for a time ruled the entire Delta region of Egypt. After the Assyrian adventure in Egypt ultimately ended in failure, he turned his attention to a series of internal reforms, seeking ways to govern his empire other than through the traditional weapons of military terror and religious imperialism. Assur remained central—anything else would have been sacrilege. But following in his father's footsteps, Assurbanipal was something of an "enlightened" Assyrian king, hoping to knit the empire into something more permanent and stable than an armed camp in a perpetual state of warfare with its subjects and neighbors.

The study of the ancient Near East owes a tremendous debt to Assurbanipal. Like all Assyrian kings, he had a conscious sense of the rich traditions of Mesopotamian culture and history, and laid claim to these to justify Assyrian rule over the whole of the region. Assurbanipal went even further, however; at the great Assyrian capital of Nineveh, Assurbanipal ordered the construction of a magnificent library, where copies of all the great works of literature of the Mesopotamian past would be copied into Assyrian cuneiform and preserved. It also served as an important archive for the correspondence and official acts of the king. When the Englishman Austen Henry Layard and his assistant Hormuzd Rassam discovered Nineveh in the nineteenth century, they also unearthed this unexpected treasure trove of historical documentation. All modern editions of the Epic of Gilgamesh depend on the Assyrian versions from Nineveh.

When Assurbanipal died in 627 B.C.E., the Assyrian empire appeared to be at its zenith. Its borders were secure, the realm was largely at peace with its neighbors, and the most recent kings had adorned Assyrian

> Assurbanipal was something of an "enlightened" Assyrian king, hoping to knit the empire into something more permanent and stable than an armed camp in a perpetual state of warfare with its subjects and neighbors.

THE SENJIRLI STELE OF KING ESARHADDON

Set up in northern Syria by the Assyrian king Esarhaddon, this inscribed stone monument is one of the most important records of his reign. Accompanying the text (which proclaims his victories over Egypt and the Phoenician coast of Syria) was a depiction of Esarhaddon holding a cup in his right hand and a mace in his left. His left hand also grasped reins fastened to shackles holding a captured prince of Egypt and a Syrian ruler, both of whom begged for mercy. The inscription demonstrates Assyrian kingship's bombastic propaganda, its conscious connection to the Sumero-Akkadian past, and the cruelty which characterized Assyrian conquests. (Assur, Anu, Ba'al, Ea, and Ishtar were all gods or goddesses.)

To Assur, father of the gods, lover of my priesthood, Anu mighty and pre-eminent, who called me by name, Ba'al, the exalted lord, establisher of my dynasty, Ea, the wise, all-knowing . . . Ishtar, lady of battle and combat, who goes at my side . . . all of them who determine my destiny, who grant to the king, their favorite, power and might. . . . the king, the offering of whose sacrifices the great gods love . . . their unsparing weapons they have presented him as a royal gift . . . [he] who has brought all the lands in submission at his feet, who has imposed tribute and tax upon them; conqueror of his foes, destroyer of his enemies, the king, who as to his walk is a storm, and as to his deeds, a raging wolf; . . . the onset of his battle is powerful, he is a consuming flame, a fire that does not sink: son of Sennacherib, king of the universe, king of Assyria, grandson of Sargon, king of the universe, king of Assyria, viceroy of Babylon, king of Sumer and Akkad. . . . I am powerful, I am all powerful, I am a hero, I am gigantic, I am colossal, I am honored, I am magnified, I am without an equal among all kings, the chosen one of Assur . . . the great lord [who] in order to show to the peoples the immensity of my mighty deeds, made powerful my kingship over the four regions of the world and made my name great. . . . Of Tirhakah, king of Egypt and Kush, the accursed . . . without cessation I slew multitudes of his men, and him I smote five times with the point of my javelin, with wounds, no recovery. Memphis, his royal city, in half a day . . . I besieged, I captured, I destroyed, I devastated, I burned with fire . . . . The root of Kush I tore up out of Egypt and not one therein escaped to submit to me.

Daniel David Luckenbill, ed. *Ancient Records of Assyria and Babylonia*, Vol. 2. (Chicago: University of Chicago Press, 1926–1927), pp. 224–227.

capitals with culture and magnificent artwork that captured all the heritage of the ancient Near East. The end of Assyria is therefore all the more dramatic for its suddenness. Within fifteen years of the mighty Assurbanipal's reign, Nineveh lay in ruins; a few years later, the Assyrian state was no more, obliterated from the face of the earth with the same speed and violence by which it had established itself.

Despite the best efforts of Esarhaddon and Assurbanipal at reform, centuries of savagery had left deep scars on the psyche of the region, and hatred of the Assyrians was widespread by the end of the seventh

Assurbanipal Feasting with His Wife in a Garden. The head of his defeated enemy, the king of Elam, can be seen hanging from the pine tree on the left.

century. After the death of Assurbanipal, a coalition formed between the Indo-European-speaking Medes of northwestern Iran and the Chaldeans, a Semitic-speaking people who once controlled the southern half of Babylonia. In 626 B.C.E., the Assyrian governor of

Reconstruction of the Ishtar Gate. Visitors to the Near Eastern Museum in Berlin can see this impressive reconstruction of the gate built in Babylon by King Nebuchadnezzar around 575 B.C.E. rising to a height of fifty feet. About half of the reconstruction is original.

southern Babylonia, a Chaldean named Nabopolasser, revolted and enlisted the support of the powerful Median king Cyaxares. In one of history's many ironies, Cyaxares had grown mighty largely because the Assyrians had dismantled his principal rival for power, the ancient state of Elam.

The allies launched an attack on Nineveh in 612 B.C.E., taking the city and setting ablaze its great temples and palaces. By 605 B.C.E., the Chaldeans (also described as neo-Babylonians) had destroyed the last remnants of Assyrian culture and power on the upper Euphrates. The Medes retired to the Iranian Plateau and extended their suzerainty there; the Chaldeans inherited much of Assyria's power in Mesopotamia and the Levant. The Chaldeans proved little better than the hated Assyrians, however, earning the enmity of their subjects by exercising the same type of cruelty that had made the Assyrians infamous. They even continued the very practice that they themselves had found so detestable in the

Assyrians, the mass deportation of conquered foes. Whenever the Assyrians had wanted to hedge against future rebellion, they would remove thousands—sometimes tens of thousands—of the conquered inhabitants, sending them far away from their homelands and the places and symbols of their national cult. The Chaldeans were no different, the most famous example being when their ruthless king Nebuchadnezzar captured Jerusalem in 587/586 B.C.E., destroyed the Temple, and removed tens of thousands of Hebrews to Babylon, an exile known in Jewish history as the "Babylonian Captivity."

THE PERSIANS

Around what central ideas was Zoroastrianism formed?

Although they had succeeded to Assyrian power, a Chaldean empire based on plunder and fear would prove no more tenable than an Assyrian one. Furthermore, the Chaldeans possessed nothing like the great war machine of the Assyrian empire, nor did they exhibit the fervor of the Assyrian military-religious ethos. But in the power vacuum that existed after the fall of Assyria, the power of the Chaldeans went largely unchallenged. The other great powers of the Near East at the beginning of the sixth century were too distant or otherwise occupied to challenge Chaldean dominance. The Indo-European-speaking Lydians, one of the successor states to Hittite power, had carved out a wealthy kingdom in western Anatolia, but they tended to orient themselves west toward the Aegean and the Greeks. The Medes, meanwhile, sought to secure dominance over the various, closely related groups of the Iranian Plateau, effectively keeping themselves out of Mesopotamian and Levantine politics. One of the collection of tribes subject to the Medes, the Persians established themselves in the former area of the Elamites and would prove to be the deciding factor in breaking this stalemate and reuniting the ancient Near East.

THE ORIGINS OF THE PERSIAN EMPIRE

Almost nothing is known of the Persians before the middle of the sixth century B.C.E., except that they lived on the eastern shore of the Persian Gulf, spoke an Indo-European language, and were subject to the Medes. Out of this obscurity the Persians emerged suddenly into the spotlight of history under an extraordinary prince named Cyrus, who succeeded to the rule of a southern Persian tribe in 559 B.C.E. Shortly thereafter Cyrus made himself ruler of all the Persians, and around 549 B.C.E. he threw off the lordship of the Medes, taking over their domination of lands that stretched from the Persian Gulf to the Halys River in Asia Minor.

By occupying part of Asia Minor, Cyrus became a neighbor of the kingdom of Lydia, which then comprised the western half of Asia Minor up to the Halys. The Lydians by this time had attained great prosperity as a result of gold prospecting and acting as intermediaries for overland commerce between Mesopotamia and the Aegean Sea. They dominated the wealthy Greek cities of the western Anatolian coast and sat atop an abundance of natural resources themselves. In connection with their commercial and industrial enterprises the Lydians invented the use of metallic coinage as a medium of exchange for goods and services. When Cyrus reached their border, the reigning king of the Lydians was Croesus, a great admirer of the culture of the Greeks he ruled, and so rich that the expression "rich as Croesus" remains embedded in our language. Distrusting his new neighbor, Croesus decided in 546 B.C.E. to wage a preventive war in order to preserve his kingdom from conquest. According to Herodotus, Croesus consulted the oracle at Delphi in Greece whether he should attack immediately, and gained the reply that if he crossed the Halys he would destroy a great nation. He did, but the nation he de-

An Early Lydian Coin. Probably struck during the reign of Croesus.

THE RECEPTION OF PERSIAN RULE

After the centuries of Assyrian and Chaldean oppression, many peoples of the Near East viewed the Persians as liberators. So grateful were the Hebrews to Cyrus for allowing the Hebrews in exile to return from Babylon and rebuild the temple, that to many he seemed the messiah promised by the prophets, the one who would spread the cult of Yahweh among all nations. This selection from the Hebrew prophet Isaiah provides some sense of the initial glee with which the peoples of the Near East received Persian rule in the middle of the sixth century B.C.E.

Thus says the Lord to his anointed, to Cyrus, whose right hand I have grasped to subdue nations before him and strip kings of their robes, to open doors before him—and the gates shall not be closed: I will go before you and level the mountains. . . . I will give you the treasures of darkness and riches hidden in secret places, so that you may know that it is I, the Lord, the God of Israel, who calls you by your name. For the sake of my servant Jacob, and Israel my chosen, I call you by your name, I surname you, though you do not know me. . . . I have aroused Cyrus in righteousness, and I will make all his paths straight; he shall build my city and set my exiles free, not for price or reward says the Lord of hosts. Thus says the Lord: The wealth of Egypt and the merchandise of Kush, and Sabeans, tall of stature, shall come over to you and be yours, they shall follow you, they shall come over in chains and bow down to you. They will make supplication to you, saying "God is with you alone, and there is no other; there is no god besides him." . . . Israel is saved by the Lord with everlasting salvation.

Isaiah 45:1–4, 13–17, *The New Oxford Annotated Bible.* (Oxford: Oxford University Press, 1994).

stroyed was his own, as Cyrus defeated his forces and annexed his prosperous realm as a province of the Persian state.

Cyrus invaded Mesopotamia in 539 B.C.E., striking so quickly that he took Babylon without a fight. Once he was in Babylon the entire Chaldean Empire was his. Cyrus allowed the Hebrews captive in Babylon since the time of Nebuchadnezzar to return to Palestine and set up a semi-independent vassal state. Cyrus allowed other conquered peoples considerable self-determination as well, especially in terms of cult practices, making Persian rule a welcome change from that of the Assyrians and Chaldeans. Cyrus fell in bat-

tle in 529 from wounds he suffered while campaigning against barbarian tribes near the Aral Sea, to the north of his realms. He left behind the largest empire the world had yet seen. After his death, the trend of Persian expansion continued as his son and successor Cambyses conquered Egypt in 525 B.C.E.

THE CONSOLIDATION OF THE PERSIAN NEAR EAST

Cambyses was a brilliant general, a worthy successor to his father's military greatness. Difficulties abounded

THE PERSIAN EMPIRE UNDER DARIUS I, 521–486 B.C.E.

What accounts for the enormous extent of the Persian empire in comparison to earlier imperial realms? Why is the "royal road" especially noted on this map? Consider the location of the Persian heartland and the four administrative centers of Persepolis, Susa, Ecbatana, and Sardis. What purpose did such multiple "capitals" serve? Examine the northwest frontiers of the empire. Why would the Persians have an interest in continuing to expand in this direction?

during his reign, however, as both contemporaries and centuries of historians have argued over whether the young king was insane. In any event, he died young and without a son, throwing open the question of succession and leaving the Persian Empire a cumbersome and poorly organized collection of rapid conquests.

After a short period of civil war, the aristocratic inner circle that had served both Cyrus and his son settled on a collateral member of the royal family as the new king. Cambyses' successor, Darius I, ruled Persia from 521 to 486 B.C.E. and concentrated on consolidating his predecessors' military gains by improving the administration of the Persian state. Darius divided the empire into provinces called satrapies, each administered by a satrap. The satraps enjoyed extensive powers and considerable political latitude, but they owed fixed tributes and absolute loyalty to the central government, as did vassal states such as the technically autonomous Jewish kingdom.

Adhering to the tolerant policy of Cyrus, Darius allowed the various non-Persian peoples of the Persian Empire to retain most of their local institutions while enforcing a standardized currency and system of weights and measures. In Egypt, Darius's satrap restored ancient

> Darius divided the empire into provinces called satrapies, each administered by a satrap.

Egyptian temples and codified Egyptian laws in consultation with native priests. Throughout their empire the Persians established modest tribute payments; but otherwise, they were little interested in imposing onerous taxes, martial law, or their own religious practices on their subject peoples. After centuries of Assyrian and Chaldean tyranny, the light hand of Persian rule was welcomed throughout the Near East.

Darius was also a great builder. He erected a new royal residence and ceremonial capital, which the Greeks called Persepolis ("Persia City"). He ordered a canal dug from the Nile to the Red Sea to facilitate trade with the Egyptian interior, and installed irrigation systems on the Persian plateau and on the fringe of the Syrian desert to increase agricultural production. Darius also expanded the Assyrian road system to enhance trade and communications in his far-flung realms. The most famous was the "Royal Road" spanning sixteen hundred miles from Susa near the Persian Gulf to Sardis (the old Lydian capital) near the Aegean. Government couriers along this road were the first postal system, passing messages and goods in relay stages from one "post" to another. Each post was a day's horseback ride from the next: a fresh horse and rider would be ready at each post to carry what had been brought by the "postman" before him. The extensive spy network of the "great king" of Persia utilized this network to keep the crown informed of developments throughout the massive empire. The "intelligence service" founded by Darius was famed throughout Persian history as "the eyes and ears of the king."

An extraordinarily gifted administrator, Darius made an enormous mistake in military strategy when he attempted to extend Persian hegemony into Greece. After Cyrus' conquest of Lydia had made Persia the ruler of Greek-speaking cities on the western coast of Asia Minor, these cities disdained Persian toleration and yearned for the idealized freedom of other Greek city-states. Consequently, between 499 and 494 B.C.E. the Greeks on the Asian mainland waged a war for independence and briefly gained the support of troops from Athens, who joined the Asian Greeks in burning the important Persian regional administrative center at Sardis. After quelling the uprising in Asia, Darius sent a force across the Aegean to punish Athens and serve notice of his dominion to all European Greeks. At the battle of Marathon in 490, the Athenians dealt Darius the only major setback of his reign. In 480 his son and successor, Xerxes, attempted to avenge the humiliation by crushing Greece with a tremendous army, but heroic resistance by Athens and Sparta forced him to retreat and abandon his plans a year later. At that point the Persians realized that the limits of their expansion had been reached; they concentrated on their Asian possessions and settled for using money and diplomacy to meddle in Greek affairs.

In fact, from 479 B.C.E. until Alexander the Great's invasion of Asia Minor in 334 B.C.E., the Greeks were usually too embroiled in internal rivalries to pose any challenge to Persia. From the Persian perspective that was fortunate, for during this period the Persian empire was often beset by governmental instability caused by palace intrigues and provincial rebellions. Nevertheless, the cosmopolitan nature of Persian culture and the general toleration they exhibited served the Persians well in maintaining their immense realm. Unlike the Assyrians or the Chaldeans, the Persians could often count on the loyalty—sometimes even the affection—of their subjects. The recalcitrance of the Greeks should not blind us to the fact that the Persians successfully maintained a culturally and linguistically diverse empire for over two centuries and would have done so longer were it not for Alexander the Great's invasion in the later fourth century. The Persians established an imperial model based on the accommodation of local institutions and practices, steady and consistent administration through a trained bureaucracy, and rapid communications between center and periphery. It was a model from which both the Macedonians and the Romans would learn much in later centuries.

> The Persians successfully maintained a culturally and linguistically diverse empire for over two centuries.

ZOROASTRIANISM

Even more enduring than Persia's political legacy was its religious one, embodied in Zoroastrianism. This important world religion, along with Buddhism and Judaism, was one of the three major universal and personal religions known to the world before Christianity and Islam. The religion's founder was Zoroaster (the Greek form of the Persian name Zarathustra). Zoroaster, a Persian who lived shortly before 600 B.C.E., was the first real theologian in history, devising a fully developed system of religious belief. He seems to have conceived it as his mission to purify the traditional customs of the Persian tribes—to eradicate polytheism, animal sacrifice, and magic—and to establish worship on a more coherent and ethical plane.

Zoroastrianism was a universal religion insofar as Zoroaster taught that there was one supreme god in the universe, whom he called Ahura-Mazda, the "wise lord." Ahura-Mazda embodied the principles of light, truth, and righteousness; there was nothing wrathful or evil about him, and his light shone everywhere, not just on one tribe. Because sin and sorrow were inexplicable by reference to Ahura-Mazda, Zoroaster posited the existence of a counter-deity, Ahriman, treacherous and malignant, presiding over the forces of darkness and evil. Apparently in Zoroaster's own view Ahura-Mazda was vastly stronger than Ahriman, whom Ahura-Mazda allowed to exist almost by absentmindedness. Later, the priests of Zoroastrianism, the magi, emphasized the dualistic aspect of the founder's thought by insisting that Ahura-Mazda and Ahriman were evenly matched, engaged in a desperate struggle for supremacy. According to them, only on the last great day would "light" decisively triumph over "darkness," when Ahura-Mazda would overpower Ahriman and cast him into the abyss.

Zoroastrianism was a personal religion, making private, spiritual demands as opposed to public, cultic, and ritual ones. As a result, Zoroastrianism was quite different from traditional Near Eastern beliefs, in which politics and religion were necessarily indistinguishable. The fervor of the Persian dynasty for Zoroaster's teachings nevertheless made Zoroastrianism important to the conduct of Persian government, and helps to explain the general eclecticism and tolerance of Persian rule. Ahura-Mazda patronized neither tribes nor states but only individuals who served his cause of truth and justice. Humans possessed free will and could choose to sin or not to sin. Zoroastrianism urged people not to sin but to be truthful, to love and help one another to the best of their powers, to aid the poor, and to practice generous hospitality. Those who did so would be rewarded in an afterlife, for the religion posited the resurrection of the dead on "judgment day" and their consignment to a realm either of bliss or flames. In the scriptures of the Zoroastrian faith, known as the Avesta (a work compiled by accretion over the course of many centuries), the rewards for righteousness are explicit.

This recital of Zoroastrianism's tenets reveals numerous similarities to Judaism and Christianity. Zoroastrianism's ethical content resembles the teachings of the Hebrew prophets, and its heaven and hell resemble aspects of the afterlife teaching of Christianity. Even the existence of authoritative scriptures is reminiscent of the weight accorded by Jews (and later by Christians) to the Bible. As with so many other cultural phenomena in the Ancient Near East, central aspects of different religious and intellectual traditions took shape in a Near Eastern world characterized by cross-cultural influence. Cyrus and Darius—both convinced Zoroastrians—cast a considerable shadow across the cultural atmosphere of their times. Furthermore, entirely aside from likely Zoroastrian influence on Judaism and later Christian beliefs, the Persian faith exerted some influence on western Asia's later Greek conquerors, encouraging them to think of religion in ever more universalistic and personal terms.

Universalism also characterized Persia's cultural contribution to the unfolding story of Western civilizations. Unlike the Assyrians, the Chaldeans, or even the Egyptians, all of whom tried to impose their own customs on conquered peoples (when they did not simply enslave them), the Persians adopted a tolerant "one-world" policy. They conceived themselves to be the guiding force over an assemblage of nations. Whereas Mesopotamian potentates characteristically called themselves "true king," Persian rulers took the title "king of kings," implying that they recognized the continued existence of various peoples with native rulers under the canopy of Persian overlordship. The greatest Persian monarchs, such as Cyrus and Darius, also sought to learn whatever they could from the peoples they conquered. Among much else, they adopted metallic coinage from the Lydians, and learned to chart the night skies from Babylonian astronomers.

Persian eclecticism can also be observed in architecture. The Persians copied the terraced building style that had been standard in Babylonia, and they also imitated the winged bulls, the brilliantly colored glazed bricks, and other decorative motifs of Mesopotamian architecture. Yet in place of the Mesopotamian arch and vault they adopted the column and the colonnade from Egypt. Interior arrangements and the use of palm and lotus designs at the base of columns also show Egyptian influence. The fluting of columns and the scrolls beneath the capitals were not Egyptian, however, but Greek, adopted from the Greek cities of Asia Minor. But despite such evidence of cultural borrowing, relations between Persia

Zoroastrianism's tenets reveal numerous similarities to Judaism and Christianity.

Persian Gold Drinking Cup. Persian fondness for lions probably derived from the art of the Assyrians.

and Greece were hostile. As we will see in the next chapter, the Greeks and Persians held profoundly different values; this clash led to generations of warfare between these two great cultures.

THE DEVELOPMENT OF HEBREW MONOTHEISM

What developments marked the Hebrew transition from polytheism to monotheism?

Of all the cultural developments that took place in the Iron Age Near East, none was of greater significance to the civilizations of the West than was monotheism—the belief that there is but a single god, the creator and ruler of all things. This development is traditionally, and rightly, associated with the Hebrews. But even the Hebrews were not always monotheists. Those who argued for the exclusive worship of Yahweh—a group whom we shall refer to as the Yahwists—were often a minority within Hebrew society, albeit a vocal and as-

sertive one. That the Hebrews came ultimately to recognize Yahweh as the only divine being in the universe, and to root their identity as a people in such an exclusive religious outlook, is a development that can be explained only against the backdrop of the tumultuous and confusing world in which Hebrew society itself arose.

FROM MONOLATRY TO MONOTHEISM

The emergence of Hebrew monotheism took place in a world conditioned by polytheism. For those who later advocated the exclusive worship of Yahweh, the early history of the Hebrews was full of embarrassments. At every turn, the Hebrews of the twelfth through tenth centuries B.C.E. can be found worshiping gods other than Yahweh, and especially those of their Canaanite neighbors. Even Yahweh himself, in commanding that his people should "have no other gods before me," seemed implicitly to acknowledge that there were indeed other gods whom his people worshiped. In the Book of Judges, Yahweh is represented as more or less an equal of the Moabite god Chemosh. An older, polytheistic strain is visible also in Hebrew nature spirits such as Azazel, and in the popularity of the Canaanite god El, whose name is an important element in many Hebrew word constructions (for example, Bethel). Even Solomon included symbols of Ba'al and altars to Ashtart in the temple complex he built for Yahweh at Jerusalem. Such toleration of non-Yahwist cult practices continued among later Hebrew kings also, despite the protests of religious purists advocating the exclusive worship of Yahweh.

Despite lingering polytheism, however, by the beginning of the first millennium Hebrew religion had clearly moved into a new stage of national *monolatry*—the exclusive worship of one god, without denying utterly the existence of others. Precisely how this came about is unclear. Although Moses is often credited with the beginnings of the ascendancy of the cult of Yahweh, he is a figure too legendary and too distant to be fully understood. There is better evidence to suggest that the promotion of the Yahweh cult took place under the auspices of the Levites, a tribe whose unique claims to priestly authority made them a religious elite within Hebrew society. Advocating both the ritual and the prophetic elements of Yahweh worship, the Levites sought to enhance their

WHAT DEVELOPMENTS MARKED THE HEBREW TRANSITION FROM POLYTHEISM TO MONOTHEISM?

THE DEVELOPMENT OF HEBREW MONOTHEISM   107

own power and prestige by exalting Yahweh above the other gods traditionally revered in Hebrew and Canaanite society.

The Levites also enjoyed a higher degree of literacy than most of their fellow Hebrews. As a tool for shaping the traditions and consciousness of a society, the power of the written word is formidable. This was especially so in the ancient world, where writing enjoyed a sort of magical aura, and the authority surrounding texts was literally awe-inspiring. In an age of constant threats to Hebrew religious and political sovereignty, the literacy of the Levites thus helped to preserve and promote Yahweh worship. So too, of course, did the House of David, which by promoting the Yahweh cult and centralizing it in Jerusalem, helped to link the political and the religious identity of the Hebrews to the worship of Yahweh as the supreme (if not yet the only) god of the universe.

Nevertheless, the worship of other gods persisted, and there was a swell of popularity for Canaanite fertility cults in the eighth and seventh centuries, perhaps in reaction to the austere morality demanded and imposed by the Yahwists. Religious figures as late as Jeremiah (c. 637–587 B.C.E.) continued to rail against "foreign" cults, and to warn of the disastrous consequences that would arise if Yahweh's people did not remain faithful to Yahweh alone. Despite his supremacy over all other gods, however, Yahweh remained a somewhat limited god in the eighth and seventh centuries B.C.E., even in the eyes of the Yahwists. He was conceived as possessing a physical body and was sometimes capricious or irascible. Nor was Yahweh omnipotent, for his power was largely limited to the territory occupied by the Hebrews.

Despite these polytheistic holdovers, some of the Hebrews' most important contributions to subsequent Western religious thought had emerged by the middle of the eighth century B.C.E. One was their unique *transcendent theology*. In the eyes of his priests and prophets, Yahweh was not part of nature but entirely outside of it. He could therefore be understood in purely intellectual or abstract terms, entirely apart from the operations of the natural world he had created. Complementing this principle of divine transcendence was the belief that Yahweh had appointed humans to be the rulers of nature by divine mandate. The famous line from Genesis, in which Yahweh orders Adam and Eve to "be fruitful and multiply, and replenish the earth and subdue it, and have dominion over . . . every living thing," stands in striking contrast with Babylonian creation accounts, in which humans are created merely to serve the gods, "so that the gods might be at ease." Finally, although not fully developed, universalizing ethical considerations are also present in Hebrew religious thought during this period. According to the Babylonian flood story, a particularly petulant god decided to destroy humans on the grounds that their noise deprived him of sleep. In Genesis, by contrast, Yahweh sends a flood in response to human wickedness, but saves Noah and his family because "Noah was a just man."

The Hebrews honored Yahweh during the period of monolatry by subscribing to moral precepts, rituals, and taboos. The exact form of the Ten Commandments (as they became known from the seventh century B.C.E. onward, and as they appear in Exodus 20:3–17) may not have existed before the Babylonian captivity. But the Hebrews certainly observed some set of commandments, including ethical injunctions against murder, adultery, bearing false witness, and "coveting anything that is thy neighbor's." In addition they observed ritualistic demands, such as refraining from labor on the seventh day and not boiling a kid in its mother's milk. But the moral standards enjoined by Yahweh upon the Hebrew community were not necessarily binding when dealing with outsiders. Lending at interest, for example, was not acceptable between Hebrews, but was quite acceptable between a Hebrew and a non-Hebrew. Such distinctions applied also to more serious issues, such as the killing of civilians in battle. When the Hebrews conquered territories in Canaan, they took "all the spoil of the cities, and every man they smote with the sword . . . until they had destroyed them, neither left they any to breathe." Rather than having any doubts about such a brutal policy, the Yahwists believed it had been ordered by their Lord himself—indeed, that Yahweh had inspired the Canaanites to offer resistance so that there would be reason to slaughter them: "For it was of the Lord to harden their hearts, that they should come against Israel in battle, that He might destroy them utterly" (Joshua 11:20).

With the fragmentation of the united Hebrew kingdom after Solomon's death, however, important

> Some of the Hebrews' most important contributions to Western thought emerged by the middle of the eighth century B.C.E.

regional distinctions also arose within the Yahweh cult. The rulers of the northern kingdom discouraged their citizens from participating in cultic activities at Jerusalem, thereby earning the scorn of the Jerusalem-based Yahwists who shaped the biblical tradition. Disunity and the loss of Hebrew identity was accelerated by the appearance of the Assyrians, who under Sargon II absorbed the northern kingdom as a province and deported nearly twenty-eight thousand Hebrews to the interior of the Assyrian empire—the famous Ten Lost Tribes of Israel. The southern kingdom of Judah survived, but found it expedient to become an Assyrian vassal state. As we have seen, however, political collaboration with the Assyrians also meant acceptance of the Assyrian god Assur.

The Assyrian threat was the whetstone on which the Yahwist prophets sharpened their demands not for monolatry but for an exclusive monotheism. Prophets were political as much as religious figures, and most understood that military resistance to the Assyrians was futile. If the Hebrews were to survive as a people, then they had to exalt the one thing that separated them from everyone else in the region: the worship of Yahweh. The prophets' insistence, during the eighth and seventh centuries B.C.E., that Yahweh alone should be worshiped and that no other gods existed, was thus an aggressive reaction to the equally aggressive promotion of Assur by the Assyrians. Nor could there be any room for compromise in the Yahwists' demand for a thoroughgoing and exclusive monotheism. Only by worshiping Yahweh alone could the Hebrews combat the insinuating effects of Assyrian religious imperialism.

Although the word *prophet* has come to mean someone who predicts the future, its original meaning is closer to "preacher"—more exactly someone who has an urgent message to proclaim, because he or she believes that his or her message derives from divine inspiration. The foremost Hebrew prophets were Amos and Hosea, who preached in the kingdom of Israel before its fall to the Assyrians in 772 B.C.E.; Isaiah and Jeremiah, who prophesied in Judah before its fall in 586 B.C.E.; and Ezekiel and the second Isaiah (the Book of Isaiah was written by at least two and possibly three different authors), who prophesied "by the waters of Babylon" during the exile. Despite some differences in emphasis, the prophets' messages were sufficiently similar to each other to warrant treating them as if they formed a single coherent body of religious thought.

Three doctrines made up the core of the prophets' teachings: (1) absolute monotheism—Yahweh is the ruler of the universe; he even makes use of nations other than the Hebrews to accomplish his purposes; the gods of others are false gods; (2) Yahweh is exclusively a god of righteousness; he wills only the good, and evil in the world comes from humanity, not from him; (3) since Yahweh is righteous, he demands ethical behavior from his Hebrew people above all else; he cares less for ritual and sacrifice than that his followers should "seek justice, relieve the oppressed, protect the fatherless, and plead for the widow." The eighth-century B.C.E. prophet Amos summed up "the prophetic revolution" and marked one of the epoch-making moments in human cultural development when he expressed Yahweh's resounding warning in words that have echoed down to our own day (Amos 5:21–24):

> I hate, I despise your feasts, and I take no delight in
>   your solemn assemblies.
> Even though you offer me your burnt offerings and
>   cereal offerings,
> I will not accept them, and the peace offerings of your
>   fatted beasts I will not look upon.
> Take away from me the noise of your songs; to the
>   melody of your harps I will not listen.
> But let justice roll down like waters, and righteousness
>   like an ever-flowing stream.

THE COALESCENCE OF JUDAISM

Through their insistence that Yahwist monotheism was the cornerstone of the Hebrews' identity as a people, the Yahwists made it possible for the Hebrews to survive under Assyrian domination. As the Assyrian threat receded in the late seventh century B.C.E., the Yahwists triumphed religiously and politically. The new king of Judah, Josiah (621–609 B.C.E.), was a committed monotheist who employed prominent prophets at his court, including Jeremiah. With Assyrian power crumbling, Josiah found himself in a position where he could pursue a purification of cult practices. His efforts centered on redrafting and revising the "Law of Moses" and expelling corrupt priests

The Assyrian threat was the whetstone on which the Yahwist prophets sharpened their demands not for monolatry but for an exclusive monotheism.

WHAT DEVELOPMENTS MARKED THE HEBREW TRANSITION FROM POLYTHEISM TO MONOTHEISM?

THE DEVELOPMENT OF HEBREW MONOTHEISM 109

and "foreign" practices from holy places of worship. It was during his reign that the Book of Deuteronomy was discovered, purporting to be another book authored by Moses. As Deuteronomy is by far the most stridently monotheistic book of the Torah, it seems likely that it was authored during (or perhaps slightly before) the reign of Josiah to lend the weight and credibility of Moses' great name to the religious and political program Josiah pursued.

To the dismay of the Yahwists, Josiah died in battle while trying to prevent an Egyptian force from aiding the last remnants of Assyrian power. With his death, the monotheists fell hard from power. Jeremiah was placed under house arrest, denied the right to speak in public, and finally carried off into Egypt where he was murdered. All the while, he continued to denounce the corruption of the Hebrews, suggesting that they would fall before the Chaldeans just as they had before the Assyrians, in punishment for their disobedience to Yahweh.

Within a generation of King Josiah's death, Jeremiah's predictions were fulfilled. The Chaldeans under Nebuchadnezzar conquered Jerusalem, destroyed the Temple, and carried thousands of Hebrews off to Babylon. The Babylonian Captivity brought many challenges for the Hebrews living there, paramount among them being the maintenance of their religious and ethnic identity. The leading voices in defining that identity continued to be the patriotic Yahwists, the same people who would later spearhead the return to Palestine after Cyrus' capture of Babylon. Among the Yahwists, the prophetic tradition thus continued, even in a foreign land. The prophet Ezekiel stressed that salvation could be found only through religious purity, which meant ignoring all foreign gods and acknowledging Yahweh alone. States and empires and thrones did not matter in the long run, Ezekiel said. In this he made explicit the passing observations of predecessors such as Nahum and Jeremiah, who had also commented on the transitory nature of human power and existence. What mattered for the Hebrews living in exile was the creature God had created in his image—man—and the relationship between that Creator God, his chosen people, and his creation.

The disassociation of political identity from religious practice that triumphed during the Babylonian Captivity was an intensification of intellectual currents already discernible in the earlier prophetic tradi-

tion. The period of captivity was nevertheless decisive for the emergence of Judaism as a universalizing religion. In Babylon, Judaism became something more than simply the national cult of the Hebrews. No longer was Yahweh's worship tied to any particular political entity or dynasty, for after 586 B.C.E. neither a Hebrew state nor a Hebrew ruling dynasty existed. Nor was his worship tied to any specific place. In Babylon and in the Holy Land, Judaism survived despite the destruction of the Temple and the removal of the Jewish people from their land. In the ancient world, this was an unparalleled achievement. No other ancient people is known to have survived so long an exile from its central holy place.

After 538 B.C.E., when Cyrus permitted the Hebrews of Babylon to return to the Holy Land and re-

Within a generation of King Josiah's death, Jermiah's prophecies were fulfilled.

build the temple, Jerusalem became once again the central holy place of Jewish religious life. But the new developments that had arisen within Judaism during the Captivity would prove to be lasting ones, despite the religious conflicts that soon erupted between the returning exiles and those Hebrews who had managed to remain in the Holy Land, and so were untouched by the changes that had taken place within Judaism during the exile. These conflicts are a measure of the extent to which Judaism itself had been transformed in Babylon.

Increasingly, Jewish religious teachings would be presented in ethical and behavioral terms, as obligations owed by all human beings toward their creator, independent of place or political identity. Ritual requirements and religious taboos, by contrast, would remain the exclusive obligation of Jews, for whom they symbolized the special covenant that bound Yahweh to his people; and these would be rigorously reinforced by the late-fifth-century ruler Nehemiah. But the notion of a creator god who existed outside time, nature, place, and kingship became ever more powerful in Second Temple Judaism, and would be taken up later by Christianity and Islam. So too would the Hebrew claim that Yahweh was a jealous god, who would not permit his followers to worship any other divinity in any form. In the context of the ancient world, both remained peculiar ideas, which would not be fully absorbed for a millennium. But despite its peculiarity, the transcendental monotheism developed by the Hebrews would ultimately become a fundamental feature of the religious outlook of all Western civilizations.

CONCLUSION

Between 1200 and 1000 B.C.E., the devastation wrought by the Sea Peoples, combined with the declining power of Egypt, cleared the way for a number of new, small groups to emerge in the Near and Middle East. These included the Phoenicians, the Philistines, the Hebrews, and the Lydians. These small groups began and developed many of the crucial cultural and economic developments of the early Iron Age, including alphabetic writing, coinage, exclusive monotheism, and mercantile colonization. But the dominant states of the early Iron Age Mediterranean world continued to be the great land empires centered in Asia Minor: first Assyria, then Chaldean Babylonia, and finally Persia. On the surface, it may appear therefore as if nothing very dramatic had changed since the middle of the second millennium B.C.E. But such geographic continuities can be deceiving. The empires of the early Iron Age were quite different from the collections of quasi-independent city-states that had dominated Asia Minor a thousand years before. These new empires were much more highly unified than the earlier empires had been. They had capital cities, centrally managed systems of communication, sophisticated administrative structures, and imperial ideologies that justified their aggressive imperialism as a religious obligation imposed upon them by a single, all-powerful god. They commanded armies of unprecedented size, and they demanded from their subjects a degree of obedience impossible for any previous rulers to imagine. They were not all-powerful. As the Assyrian case reveals, a coalition of small states could still, on occasion, defeat them. But they were larger, more powerful, and more thoroughgoing in their claims to political and religious obedience than any previous western empires.

At the same time that these great land empires were declaring themselves to be the chosen instruments of their god's divine will, we also mark the emergence of more personalized monotheistic traditions in the early Iron Age. Cult and sacrifice were important religious obligations in both Zoroastrianism and Judaism, as they were to all ancient religions. Zoroastrianism in particular was fully compatible with an imperialist ideology. It was, indeed, the driving spiritual force that lay behind the expansion of the Persian empire. Judaism, by contrast, was forged in the struggle to resist the religious imperialism of Assyria and Chaldean Babylonia. But both Zoroastrianism and Judaism added an important new emphasis on personal ethical conduct as a fundamental element in religious life, and both pioneered the development of authoritative, written scriptures as a foundation for their religious teachings. These developments would exercise an enormous influence on Western religious life, and would provide the models on which Christianity and Islam would ultimately erect their own imperial traditions.

SELECTED READINGS

Aubet, Maria Eugenia. *Phoenicia and the West: Politics, Colonies, and Trade.* Trans. Mary Turton. Cambridge, 1993. An intelligent and thought-provoking examination of Phoenician civilization and its influence.

Boardman, John. *Assyrian and Babylonian Empires and Other States of the Near East from the Eighth to the Sixth Centuries B.C.* New York, 1991. Scholarly and authoritative.

———. *Persia and the West.* London, 2000. A great book by a distinguished classical scholar, with a particular focus on art and architecture as projections of Persian imperial ideologies.

Boyce, Mary. *Textual Sources for the Study of Zoroastrianism.* Totowa, N.J., 1984. An invaluable collection.

Brinkman, J. A. *Prelude to Empire: Babylonian Society and Politics, 747–626 B.C.* Philadelphia, 1984. A stimulating examination of the city and culture of Assyrian Babylon as a prelude to the later emergence of the neo-Babylonian (Chaldean) empire.

The Cambridge History of Iran, vols. 1–3. Cambridge, 1969–1983. The authoritative work, with chapters by expert contributors.

Curtis, John. *Ancient Persia.* Cambridge, Mass., 1990. Concise, solid, reliable.

Dothan, Trude, and Moshe Dothan. *People of the Sea: The Search for the Philistines.* New York, 1992. A wide-ranging examination of Philistine culture and its links to the late Bronze Age civilizations of the Aegean basin.

Finkelstein, Israel, and Nadav Na'aman, eds. *From Nomadism to Monarchy: Archaeological and Historical Aspects of Early Israel.* Jerusalem, 1994. A collection of scholarly articles on the Hebrews' transformation from pastoralists to a sedentary society focused on Yahweh worship.

Hallo, W. W., and K. L. Younger, eds. *The Context of Scripture: Canonical Compositions from the Biblical World.* 2 vols. Leiden, 1997. A fine collection of Egyptian, Sumerian, Babylonian, and Hittite texts (v. 1) and inscriptions (v. 2), with valuable introductions and notes.

Kamm, Antony. *The Israelites: An Introduction.* New York, 1999. A concise, accessible introduction covering the period up to 70 C.E. that balances biblical, archaeological, and historical sources.

Knapp, A. Bernard. *The History and Culture of Ancient Western Asia and Egypt.* Chicago, 1988. Although this book surveys the entire ancient period of ancient Near Eastern history, it is strongest on the period after 1200 B.C.E.

Kuhrt, Amélie. *The Ancient Near East, c. 3000–330 B.C.* 2 vols. London, 1995. An outstanding survey, intended for students, that includes Egypt and Israel as well as Mesopotamia, Babylonia, Assyria, and Persia. Excellent bibliographies.

Luckenbill, Daniel David, ed. and trans. *Ancient Records of Assyria and Babylonia.* 2 vols. Chicago, 1926–1927. Still one of the best and most readily accessible collections of primary sources on Assyrian attitudes and policies in war, religion, and politics.

Malandra, William W., ed. and trans. *An Introduction to Ancient Iranian Religion: Readings from the Avesta and Achaemenid Inscriptions.* Minneapolis, 1983. A helpful introduction to Zoroastrianism through the most important primary sources.

Mathews, Victor H., and D. C. Benjamin. *Social World of Ancient Israel, 1250–587 B.C.E.* Peabody, Mass., 1993. An examination of ancient Hebrew society from a variety of sources and perspectives.

Metzger, Bruce M., and Michael D. Coogan, eds. *The Oxford Companion to the Bible.* New York, 1993. An outstanding reference work, with contributions by leading authorities.

Niditch, Susan. *Ancient Israelite Religion.* New York, 1997. A short, suggestive introduction designed for students, emphasizing the diversity of Hebrew religious practice while remaining close to the biblical sources.

Redford, Donald B. *Egypt, Canaan, and Israel in Ancient Times.* Princeton, 1992. An up-to-date overview of the interactions between these peoples from around 1200 B.C.E. up to the beginning of the Common Era.

Saggs, H. W. F. *The Might That Was Assyria.* London, 1984. A lively narrative history of the Assyrian empire, with an analysis of the institutions that underlay its strength.

Tubb, Jonathan N., and Rupert L. Chapman. *Archaeology and the Bible.* London, 1990. A good starting point for students that illustrates clearly the difficulties in linking archaeological evidence to biblical accounts of early Hebrew history and society.

PART II
THE GREEK AND ROMAN WORLDS

THE CLASSICAL CIVILIZATIONS of Greece and Rome dominated the Mediterranean world from the sixth century B.C.E. until the sixth century C.E. Both drew heavily upon the traditions and achievements of the ancient Near East, but each represented a distinct departure from this earlier world. Together, however, Greece and Rome constituted the seedbed out of which all subsequent western civilizations would develop.

Beginning in the eighth century B.C.E., Greek civilization took shape in the warring, particularistic, and fiercely independent city-states that grew up around the Aegean and the Adriatic Seas. But it was not until the end of the fourth century B.C.E., when the conquests of Alexander the Great created an empire that stretched from Greece through Persia to India and Egypt, that Greek civilization became the common cultural currency of the Mediterranean and Near Eastern worlds.

In central Italy, the city of Rome was slowly extending its dominion over the Italian peninsula. In the last two centuries B.C.E., Rome extended its rule throughout the entire Mediterranean world and into western Europe. By the end of the first century C.E., Rome had built an empire larger even than Alexander's. In an extraordinary triumph of organization, discipline, and cultural adaptability, the Romans maintained that empire, substantially intact, for the next four hundred years.

	POLITICS	SOCIETY AND CULTURE	ECONOMY	INTERNATIONAL RELATIONS
B.C.E. 1150		The Dark Age of Greece (1150–800 B.C.E.)	Greek trade increases in Aegean Sea (1000–800 B.C.E.)	
	Birth of the Greek polis (800 B.C.E.)	Introduction of Phoenician alphabet into Greece (800 B.C.E.)		Carthage founded (800 B.C.E.)
		Archaic Greece (800–480 B.C.E.)		
		Homer's *Iliad* and *Odyssey* are written down (800 B.C.E.)		
		First Greek colonies appear (800–600 B.C.E.)		
		First Olympic games (776 B.C.E.)		Rome founded (753 B.C.E.)
	Spartans enslave Messenians (700–680 B.C.E.)			
	Kylon sent into exile for tyranny (632 B.C.E.)			
600	Hoplite tactics become military standard (600 B.C.E.)		Solon encourages cash-crop farming and urban industries (600–550 B.C.E.)	Miletus becomes colonial power (600–400 B.C.E.)
	Tarquin the Proud gains kingship over Rome (543 B.C.E.)			
500	Roman Republic (500-527 B.C.E.)		Athens becomes principal exporter of olive oil, wine, and pottery (500 B.C.E.)	
	Xerxes succeeds Darius the Great (486 B.C.E.)	Sophocles, author of *Oedipus*, (496–406 B.C.E.)		The Ionian Revolution (499–494 B.C.E.)
	Plebian rebellion leads to Law of the Twelve Tables (480 B.C.E.)	Emergence of Greek sculpture (490–480 B.C.E.)		Persians sack Eritrea (490 B.C.E.)
		Golden Age of Greek civilization (480–323 B.C.E.)		Hellenic League formed (480 B.C.E.)
		Socrates (469–399 B.C.E.)		Persian army defeated at battle of Salamis (480 B.C.E.)
	Pericles elected strategos of Athens (462–461 B.C.E.)	Thucydides (460–400 B.C.E.)		
		Sophists emerge (450 B.C.E.)		Athens gains control of Delian League (450s B.C.E.)
		Parthenon built in Athens (447–438 B.C.E.)		Peloponnesian War (431–404 B.C.E.)
		Plato, author of the *Republic*, (429–349 B.C.E.)		
		Aristotle, author of *Nicomachean Ethics*, (384–322 B.C.E.)		Corinthian War (394–387 B.C.E.)
	Reign of Philip II (359–336 B.C.E.)	Greek migrations into western Asia (325–225 B.C.E.)	Alexander's conquests open commercial routes between Greece and Asia (323 B.C.E.)	Philip II defeats Greek alliance and forms League of Corinth (338 B.C.E.)
	Reign of Alexander III, the Great (336–323 B.C.E.)	Euclid, *Elements of Geometry* (300 B.C.E.)		Reign of Alexander the Great (336–323 B.C.E.)
300				Ptolemy establishes dynasty in Egypt (332 B.C.E.)
				Alexander defeats the Persian army (331 B.C.E.)
				Seleucus establishes dynasty in Persia (281 B.C.E.)
			First standard coinage in Rome (269 B.C.E.)	Punic Wars (264–146 B.C.E.)
	Roman slave revolts (146–130 B.C.E.)			Carthage razed (146 B.C.E.)
100		Cicero (106–43 B.C.E.)	Roman commerce relies on one million slaves (100 B.C.E.)	
	Spartacus's revolt (73–71 B.C.E.)	Virgil, author of the *Aeneid*, (70–19 B.C.E.)		
		Horace (65–8 B.C.E.)		
	Caesar defeats Pompey (48 B.C.E.)	Livy, author of *History of Rome*, (59 B.C.E.–17 C.E.)		
	Octavian becomes emperor (27 B.C.E.)	Ovid, author of *Metamorphoses*, (43 B.C.E.–17 C.E.)		
	The Principate of early Roman empire (27 B.C.E.–180 C.E.)			

POLITICS	SOCIETY AND CULTURE	ECONOMY	INTERNATIONAL RELATIONS	
				C.E. 10
	Saul of Tarsus, or Paul the Apostle (10–67 C.E.)			
	Christians begin arriving in Rome (40 C.E.)		Claudius enters Britain (48 C.E.)	
	Gospel of Mark is written (70 C.E.)		Romans destroy the Temple of Jerusalem (70 C.E.)	
Pax Romana (96–180 C.E.)		Romans excel in engineering aqueducts and roads and develop new tax system under Trajan (98–117 C.E.)		100
			Romans destroy the city of Jerusalem (135 C.E.)	
The Third-Century Crisis in Roman empire (180–284 C.E.)				
	Growth of monasticism emerges (200s C.E.)	One-third of population of Roman empire dies as a result of disease, low birth rate, and war (180–284 C.E.)		
	Neoplatonism (200–300 C.E.)		Goths defeat Romans and cross the Danube (251 C.E.)	
The Dominate or later Roman empire (284–610 C.E.)		Currency is stabilized and new coinage introduced under Diocletian (284–305 C.E.)		
Diocletian, soldier-emperor (284–305 C.E.)				
	The Great Persecution of Christians (303–313 C.E.)			300
Reign of Constantine over Western Roman empire (312–324 C.E.)	Conversion of Constantine to Christianity (312 C.E.)			
Reign of Constantine over Roman empire from Constantinople (324–337 C.E.)	Saint Jerome (340–420 C.E.)		Council of Nicea condemns Arianism (325 C.E.)	
	Saint Ambrose (340–397 C.E.)		Visigoths defeat Romans (378 C.E.)	
	Saint Augustine, author of *Confessions* and *On the City of God*, (354–430 C.E.)			
	Christianity becomes official Roman religion (392 C.E.)		Visigoths sack Rome (410 C.E.)	400
	Saint Benedict (480–547 C.E.)			
			Vandals sack Rome from the sea (455 C.E.)	
Justinian rules as emperor in East (r. 527–565 C.E.)	Papacy of St. Gregory the Great (590–604 C.E.)		Justinian recaptures Italy from Ostrogoths (536 C.E.)	
Corpus Juris Civilus (532 C.E.)			The Lombards seize northern parts of Italy (568 C.E.)	
Tenure of Pope Gregory I (Saint Gregory the Great) (590–604 C.E.)				

CHAPTER FOUR

CHAPTER CONTENTS

THE GREEK
EXPERIMENT

THE IMAGE THAT COMES MOST OFTEN to mind when Americans or Europeans think of the ancient world is the Acropolis of Athens, its gleaming temples and shrines still impressive despite their age and ruined condition. The rationality, harmony, and repose of this symbol of Greek culture seem to many to bespeak something quintessentially "Western": the triumph of reason and freedom over the "superstition" and "despotism" of "Eastern" cultures such as Assyria or Persia.

Such easy and self-congratulatory contrasts tell us more about ourselves than they do about the ancient Greeks. Greek civilization developed under the heavy influence of the Near East from the Mycenaean period onward. The cross-cultural dialogue between the Greeks and their eastern neighbors has continued until the present day. The achievements of classical Greek civilization would have been impossible without the debt Greece owed to Phoenician, Assyrian, and Egyptian ideas and inventions.

Yet the florescence of Greek civilization during the first millennium B.C.E. is nonetheless a watershed in the development of Western civilizations. Building on their historical experiences after the Bronze Age collapse, the Greeks of the Iron Age came to cherish assumptions and values that differed greatly from those of their Near Eastern neighbors. Human dignity, individual liberty, participatory government, artistic innovation, scientific investigation, constitutional experimentation, confidence in the creative powers of the human mind—the Greeks espoused all of these values, although, as ever in human affairs, practice often fell short of their ideals.

What we mean by such terms as democracy, equality, justice, and freedom differs from what the Greeks would have meant by them. But there is nonetheless an intelligibility for the modern West in the institutions and beliefs of this tenacious, quarrelsome, and energetic people, whose small-scale societies started a cultural revolution and created a civilization distinctly different from any other before it. The democracies of the modern Western world are not the only heirs of this Greek experiment, but they are unimaginable without it.

• What cultural changes marked the end of the "Dark Age" of Greece?

• How did the emergence of hoplite tactics affect Greek political norms?

• What characteristics defined the Athenian, Spartan, and Milesian poleis?

 • How were the Greek armies able to defeat the much larger Persian forces?

• How was the fabric of society changed during the golden age of classical Greece?

• How did the Peloponnesian War influence Greek philosophy?

THE DARK AGE OF GREECE (1150–800 B.C.E.)

What cultural changes marked the end of the "Dark Age" of Greece?

By the end of the twelfth century the last remnants of Mycenaean civilization had vanished, and Greece entered on an undocumented Dark Age. Mainland Greece witnessed depopulation of up to 90 percent in the one hundred fifty years following 1200 B.C.E. Except at Athens, the great citadels were destroyed in the conflagrations at the end of the Bronze Age; and even in Athens, the population steadily declined. At Pylos, which in the thirteenth century B.C.E. had numbered one hundred thousand inhabitants, only scattered communities survived by the year 1000, containing at most one hundred households. Linguistic patterns suggest that many of the inhabitants of the mainland fled to the highlands of southern Greece and across the sea to Cyprus and the coast of Anatolia. In Greek legend and historical tradition, this flight was precipitated by the arrival of a related sub-group of Greeks from the north called Dorians. Many scholars now doubt the veracity of this tradition, seeing the Dorians at most as opportunists who migrated south when the palace centers collapsed. What is clear, however, is that tensions between the speakers of the Doric dialect and the "older," Attic-speaking peoples of Greece such as the Athenians would continue right on up until the end of the classical period of Greek history.

Pottery and burial remains suggest a world that remained static and backward, cut off from the centers of Near Eastern civilization, in which even Greek communities had little economic contact with each other.

Depopulation at the beginning of the Dark Age had severe effects on social organization, economy, and material culture in Greece. Settlements shrank in size and moved inland, away from vulnerable locations near the sea. Their residents were mainly pastoralists, producing little of the fine material culture of Mycenaean times. Dark Age pottery was

The Parthenon. The largest and most famous of Athenian temples, the Parthenon is considered the classic example of Doric architecture. Its columns were made more graceful by tapering them in a slight curve toward the top. Its friezes and pediments were decorated with lifelike sculptures of prancing horses, fighting giants, and confident deities.

WHAT CULTURAL CHANGES MARKED THE END OF THE "DARK AGE" OF GREECE?

THE DARK AGE OF GREECE (1150–800 B.C.E.)   119

functional and inelegant, but it did change in design over time, allowing archaeologists to construct at least a rough chronology of an illiterate people. Pottery and burial relics suggest a world that remained static and backward, cut off from the centers of Near Eastern civilization, in which even Greek communities had little economic contact with each other.

In the first centuries of the Dark Age, these small communities exhibited little social or political differentiation. Some villages may have had chiefs, but even a chief's home and material possessions differed little from those of his neighbors. Each household (*oikos*, from which the word "economy" is derived) was largely self-sufficient and substantially autonomous, with a fundamental social, political, and economic equality among the patriarchal heads of these households. This Dark Age background, with its presumptions of political and economic equality, had a profound effect on the later political assumptions of the classical Greeks.

In a world where survival was often precarious, the Greeks took a dim view of the gods. Religion and ritual remained interwoven in the fabric of Greek society, but the Greeks were very suspicious of their gods and did not necessarily see them as positive forces. The gods were capricious, possessing all the failings of any human being while wielding superhuman power and delighting in interfering in human affairs. For the Greeks, the gods were to be appeased and propitiated, but never trusted fully. Greeks relied far more on the power of the individual human spirit than on divine intervention, although the Greeks developed the idea of *hubris* (excessive pride) to discourage men from becoming too enamored of their own accomplishments. Being overly proud attracted the attention of the gods and threatened them, and they punished the hubristic man with relish. These notions were well developed in later, historical times, but have their roots in the Dark Age past.

HOMER AND THE HEROIC TRADITION

By the year 1000 B.C.E., the complete isolation of Greece was ending, and Greek society was becoming gradually more complex. In 1980, at Lefkandi on the island of Euboea, archaeologists unearthed an enormous house, apparently built as a tomb for one important individual, his stunning material possessions, and the other human members of his household. Dating to c. 1000 B.C.E., this tomb proves that the inhabitants of Euboea were once again trading for long-distance and luxury commodities, and that an economic and political elite had now reemerged.

Pottery also became more sophisticated from about the turn of the millennium. The production of finely made pottery with intricate geometric designs—soon to be prized across the eastern and central Mediterranean—must reflect an upswing in the material culture and prosperity of the Greek mainland. The villages that would ultimately become Corinth dominated this new pottery trade in its early years, but potters at other locales such as Athens would soon challenge Corinthian preeminence. The resulting competition fueled not only artistic but economic and political rivalries as well.

As trade became an increasingly important feature of the Dark Age Greek economy, wealth increased and social stratification became more pronounced. Because wealth acquired through trade did not derive directly from the local Greek community, it did not carry with it the same social obligations of gift giving and exchange that accompanied more traditional sources of wealth. Successful traders could therefore hoard their wealth or employ it to augment their own political and social standing. A small group of aristocrats thus began to emerge, who justified their preeminence as a reflection of their own superior qualities—the "best men." The late Dark Age remained a rough and tumble world, however. Although wealth might be acquired by trade, it was also to be had through warfare and plunder. Nor was wealth alone sufficient to establish one's aristocratic standing. A great man had also to be a singer of songs, a doer of deeds, a winner of battles, and above all favored by the gods. In short, he had to be a hero.

We know much about the heroic ideal of late Dark Age Greece through the *Iliad* and the *Odyssey*, epic poems ascribed to the authorship of Homer. Though these astonishing epics—among the finest examples of literature in the Western tradition—were not written down until after 800 B.C.E. and the introduction of the Phoenician alphabet, they were rooted in a much older oral tradition. The Greeks were aware of a deeper past—they could see the ruins of the Mycenaeans all around them. Homer's poems are set at the end of the

> Because wealth acquired through trade was not obligated to the rest of the community through ties of reciprocity and exchange, successful traders could hoard their wealth or employ it to augment their own political and social standing.

GREEK GUEST FRIENDSHIP AND HEROIC IDEALS

Before the reemergence of true state mechanisms in Greece, relations among communities depended largely on the personal and heritable connections made between the leading families of different villages and peoples. Often founded upon the exchange of gifts or hospitality, the bonds of guest friendship imposed serious obligations on those involved in such relationships. Honoring them was part and parcel of the heroic ideal, as this encounter in Homer's Iliad *between the Greek hero Diomedes and the Lycian Glaukos, fighting for Troy, illustrates. Hospitality remained an important value of Greek society throughout its ancient history.*

Glaukos son of Hippolochus and Tydeus' son Diomedes met in the no man's land between both armies: burning for battle, closing, squaring off and the lord of the war cry Diomedes opened up, "Who are you, my fine friend?—another born to die? I've never noticed you on the lines where we win glory, not till now. But here you come, charging out, in front of all the rest with such bravado—daring to face the flying shadow of my spear. Pity the ones whose sons stand up to me in war!"

The noble son of Hippolochus answered staunchly, "High-hearted son of Tydeus, why ask about my birth? . . . If you'd like to hear it, here's my story. . . . Brave Bellerophon [threatened by a jealous king] went off to Lycia, safe in the escort of the gods, and once he reached the highlands cut by the rushing Xanthus, the king of Lycia gave him a royal welcome . . . when the king could see the man's power at last, a true son of the gods, he pressed him hard to stay, he offered his own daughter's hand in marriage . . . his wife bore good Bellerophon three children: Isander,

Hippolochus, and Laodamia. . . . Hippolochus fathered me, I'm proud to say, and sent me off to Troy. . . . There you have my lineage. That is the blood I claim, my royal birth."

When he heard that, Diomedes' spirits lifted . . . and with winning words he called out to Glaukos, the young captain, "Splendid—you are my friend, my guest from the days of our grandfathers long ago! Noble Oeneus hosted your brave Bellerophon once . . . and they gave each other handsome gifts of friendship. . . . So now I am your host and friend in the heart of Argos, you are mine in Lycia when I visit your country. Come let us keep clear of each other's spears. . . . Plenty of Trojans for me to kill . . . and plenty of Argives [people of Argos] too—kill them if you can." Both agreed. Both fighters sprang from their chariots, clasped each other's hands and traded pacts of friendship.

Homer, *Iliad*, 6. 138–279. Translated by Robert Fagles. (New York: Penguin Classics, 1990), pp. 199–203.

Bronze Age, but over generations of retelling, only Bronze Age curiosities remained, while the social and political relationships portrayed in the poems changed to reflect the assumptions of each new generation. In other words, the great events and many of the material objects of Homeric epic are relics of the Bronze Age, but the society described in the epics is by and large the society of late Dark Age Greece.

WHAT CULTURAL CHANGES MARKED THE END OF THE "DARK AGE" OF GREECE?

THE DARK AGE OF GREECE (1150–800 B.C.E.)   121

Homer depicts a world in which competition and relative status are of paramount concern to the warrior elite. The aristocracy of one community would have had more in common with the aristocracy of another than with the commoners of their own village. Through the exchange of expensive gifts and hospitality, aristocrats created important ties of guest friendship with one another. In a stateless society, such ties often substituted for diplomacy among widely scattered communities. Competition between aristocratic households was constant, however, and ultimately gave rise to hero cults. An important family would claim that an impressive nearby Mycenaean tomb was that of their own famous ancestor and practice dutiful sacrifice and other observances at the tomb to strengthen the claim. This devotion could extend to their followers and dependents; sometimes an entire community could identify itself with such a famous local hero. The heroic ideal thus became a deeply ingrained feature of Greek society, which Homer's epics would preserve and propagate throughout the classical period and beyond.

FOREIGN CONTACTS AND THE RISE OF THE POLIS

The ninth century B.C.E. saw dramatic changes throughout the Aegean basin. Greeks had reestablished economic contact with the Phoenicians by the end of the eleventh century. During the ninth century, however, these contacts intensified. Most crucially, the Greeks adopted the Phoenician alphabet, improving it by converting unneeded consonantal symbols to represent vowels. A "vocalized" alphabet was thus created, capturing in script the sound of speech. The rolling melody and power of Homeric epic could now not only be heard but recorded and read. The Phoenicians also introduced many artistic and literary traditions of the Near East into Greece, which the Greeks incorporated and reshaped to their own purposes. Some famous Greek legends and myths may even have arisen to explain the strange and fascinating narrative scenes that appeared on pots imported into Greece from Phoenicia.

Phoenicians also pointed the way for a new activity among the Greeks—seafaring. Until the tenth century, most Greeks who engaged in trade were passive, al-

> These economic and cultural developments were accompanied by dramatic growth in the Greek population.

lowing the Phoenicians to come to them. By the end of the Dark Age, however, some Greeks had managed to copy Phoenician designs for merchant vessels, setting out on trading ventures of their own and engaging in piracy. The importance of these new activities and the wider awareness of the world the Greeks gained from them are reflected in the *Odyssey*. Greek commercial activity increased throughout the Aegean world during the tenth and ninth centuries B.C.E. Significant movements of Greeks among the homeland, the islands, and Anatolia also took place, foreshadowing the colonial explosion that issued from the Aegean in the eighth and seventh centuries.

These economic and cultural developments were accompanied by dramatic growth in the Greek population. Around Athens, the population may have quadrupled during the ninth and early eighth centuries. Such rapid population growth placed increased demands upon the resources of Greece, a mountainous country not blessed with copious amounts of good land. As smaller villages grew into towns, their territory and their requirements expanded, bringing increasing contact and rivalry with other settlements. The alternatives were conflict or cooperation, and there is evidence for both at the end of the Dark Age.

Warfare and conquest created obvious difficulties, but cooperation presented challenges also. While many religious rituals and customary practices were similar across different communities, they were not necessarily compatible with each other. Each local community had its own religious cults and its own aristocratic luminaries; each treasured its traditional

CHRONOLOGY

GREECE EMERGES FROM THE DARK AGE

Adoption and refinement of Phoenician alphabet	1000–900 B.C.E.
Sharp increase in Greek population	900–700 B.C.E.
Increase in commercial shipping throughout Aegean	1000–800 B.C.E.
Rise of the polis as major political unit	800 B.C.E.

autonomy and independence. As the population grew, some degree of economic, political, and social cooperation became necessary. But the heroic values of the Dark Age Greek world did not make such cooperation easy.

The Greek answer to these questions was the *polis*. The Greek polis was a unique blend of state and local practice. Many Greeks considered the polis not so much a state as a collectivity: ancient sources refer to "the Athenians," "the Spartans," or "the Thebans" more often than to *poleis* (the plural of *polis*) as such. Poleis differed widely, therefore, in size, institutions, importance, and means of livelihood. Structurally, however, each polis was organized around a political and social urban center known as the *asty*, the location of most markets and important meetings, where the basic business of the polis was conducted. Surrounding the asty was the *khora*, the "land." The khora of a larger polis might support several towns of significance besides the asty, as well as numerous villages. The vast majority of citizens were thus farmers, who came to the asty to participate in the affairs of their polis, but who did not reside in the urban center.

Synoikismos (the "bringing together of dwellings") was how Greeks described the process of early polis formation. Synoikismos—or synoecism—could be accomplished through conquest or absorption, and/or through the slow process of neighboring communities' working together and accommodating one another. What spurred synoecism is a matter of debate. The Greeks may have borrowed a Near Eastern (and particularly Phoenician) practice of orienting an urban center around a temple precinct; certainly the heightened frequency of temple building around and after 800 B.C.E. lends support to this theory. On the other hand, temple building and glorification of the gods may more often have been the result of polis formation rather than its cause, as elites competed with each other to exalt their polis and bring glory on themselves. The question remains troublesome and may not have a single answer. The developed polis typically did have a central temple site that served as the focus for the civic religion. But this site was not necessarily located within the city's walls. Athens, for example, had its temple to Athena and associated altars and temples to other gods located on the Acropolis, in the heart of the asty. Argos, by contrast, considered its principal shrine to be the massive temple to Hera located several miles away from any sizable settlement. As was typical of Greek life generally, there was probably no standard pattern by which the early Greek poleis took shape.

Athena. A relief dating from about 450 B.C.E., discovered in the ruins of ancient Athens. The mourning goddess is contemplating a list of citizens who died fighting for her city.

ARCHAIC GREECE (800–480 B.C.E.)

How did the emergence of hoplite tactics affect Greek political norms?

With the emergence of the polis and the return of writing and literacy, the Archaic Age begins. The name is misleading, coined at a time when modern research focused on the Classical Age (480–323 B.C.E.), to which the "archaic" period seemed a rude but necessary prelude. As our understanding of Greece has increased, so too has our appreciation of Archaic Greek culture. After languishing in obscurity for nearly four centuries, Greek civilization burst forth with a dynamism and energy that is breathtaking for all of its achievements,

HOW DID THE EMERGENCE OF HOPLITE TACTICS AFFECT GREEK POLITICAL NORMS?

ARCHAIC GREECE (800–480 B.C.E.)   123

and remarkable for its willingness to try new avenues in religion, society, and politics. Aptly, this period has been called the "Age of Experiment."

COLONIZATION AND PANHELLENISM

In the eighth and seventh centuries the physical and economic frontiers of the Greek world expanded considerably, as smaller-scale trading ventures and migrations across the Aegean developed into a full-fledged colonization effort. A colony was an independent foun-

dation with emotional and sentimental ties to its mother city, but no political obligations. By the end of the sixth century, Greeks had founded several hundred new colonies from the Black Sea to the western Mediterranean, permanently altering the cultural geography of the Mediterranean world. The western shores of Anatolia would remain a stronghold of Greek culture until the end of the Middle Ages; so many Greeks settled in southern Italy and Sicily that the Romans called the region Magna Graecia, "Greater Greece." By the fourth century B.C.E., more Greeks lived in Magna

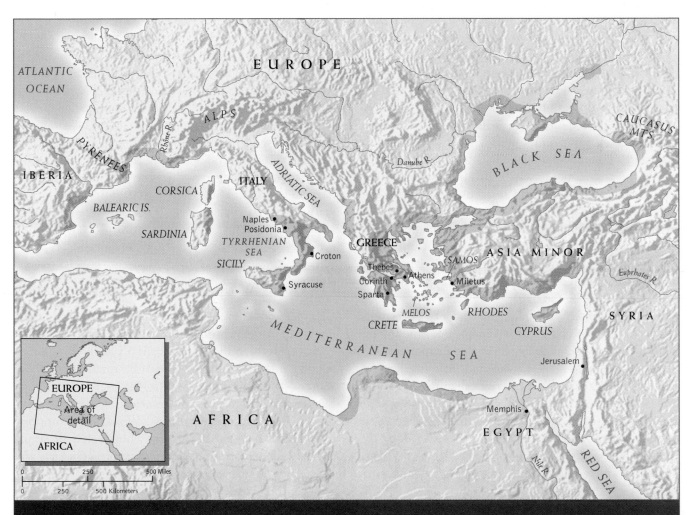

GREECE AND ITS SETTLEMENTS, 550 B.C.E.

Note the direction of Greek settlement, and compare this map with the one on p. 83. How did Greek colonization complement Phoenician expansion, and how did the position of some Greek colonies set up the potential for competition with Phoenician foundations in the West? Notice the major Greek settlements in southern Italy and Sicily. Why would the Greeks play an important role in the development of early Roman culture, and why did the Romans call the area to their south "Greater Greece"? How did small, land-starved communities in the Aegean homeland help to fuel the spread of Greek colonies in the Archaic Age?

Graecia than in Greece itself; and Greek colonies could be found even further westward, in North Africa and along the southern coast of France.

Motives for the colonization effort varied. Some of the emergent poleis, especially Corinth, had been blessed by geography but cursed by the agricultural poverty of its khora. Trade became especially important for Corinthian livelihood and survival, and so the ruling aristocratic clan of eighth-century Corinth undertook an ambitious colonization scheme, planting colonies up the coast of the Adriatic and in Sicily. Meanwhile, some Euboean poleis with older commercial traditions than most Greek cities also forged westward, founding colonies in southern Italy and nearby islands. Other poleis, confronted by population pressures and political turmoil, used colonization as an outlet for excess population and/or troublemakers.

Colonial expansion had important effects on the culture and outlook of the Greek mainland. Most obviously, it intensified Greek contacts with other cultures. The Greeks now encountered Egyptian art and culture firsthand, with profound effects upon archaic Greek art. At the same time, however, this intensified contact with cultures different from their own sharpened the Greeks' awareness of their own common identity and peculiarity as Hellenes (the Greeks' name for themselves). Whereas Dark Age Greeks noted differences among themselves, their contact with outsiders during the Archaic Period gave them a greater appreciation of what it meant to be Greek.

Such self-conscious "Hellenism" did not necessarily result in greater political cooperation among the fiercely independent poleis. Like the Sumerians, the Greeks were particularists, who had little use for permanent political associations larger than the individual polis. Apart from their political differences, they were also divided by linguistic distinctions. Athens, the Aegean Islands, and most of the Greek cities along the Anatolian coast spoke an Ionian dialect of Greek; Sparta, Corinth, Crete, and the southwestern coast of Anatolia spoke Dorian.

Hellenism did, however, encourage the growth and recognition of Panhellenic cult sites, such as the Oracle of Delphi. From all over the Greek world, people went to Delphi to ask questions of the priestess of Apollo (the Pythia), who sat over a vent in the earth munching on eucalyptus leaves. Her answer to a particular question would be unintelligible, spoken in an ecstatic state, but there were priests at hand to "translate" her answer into perfect verse. The fame of the Delphic oracle even spread to cultures beyond the frontiers of Hellenism.

Such oracular pronouncements played a large part in the historical thinking of the Greeks, who believed that divine will and intervention continued to be interwoven with human affairs. The answers of the Delphic priests were sufficiently vague that the oracle could rarely be proven wrong in hindsight.

Hellenism also encouraged the growth of Panhellenic festivals, in which the Greeks honored the gods through athletic competition. The competitive spirit was a constant feature of Greek culture, an important value outweighed perhaps only by victory—athletic, political, or military. The Greeks celebrated four great festivals, held in a quadrennial cycle. Of these, the Olympic Games were the most important, a festival to the king of the gods, Zeus, near the giant temple to him at Olympia. (Greek historians even dated events by "olympiads," four-year periods that began with the supposed date of the first games in 776 B.C.E.). The Greeks took great pride in these games. Only Greeks were permitted to participate in them; all wars among Greeks ceased while the competitions took place; a victory in the games could catapult the victor into a position of social and even political power within his polis. Although they did little to stop contentiousness and rivalry between the poleis, such Panhellenic events strengthened their cultural identification with each other.

HOPLITE WARFARE

Changes in warfare represent another hallmark of the Archaic Period. Through the late Dark and early Archaic ages, the military power of a Greek community resided with the elite, who had the time, material resources, and training (as well as the social impulse) to become "Homeric" warrior heroes. Common foot soldiers played a secondary role as followers and supporters of the aristocratic warriors who dueled in single combat. This monopoly on military prowess gave the aristocracy tremendous political and social leverage within the nascent poleis, which emerged with distinctly elite "constitutions," wherein aristocrats dominated magisterial offices and priesthoods as well as economic life. There was little the nonelite could do about it. Even a sizeable and angry rabble was still no match against a highly skilled, well-armed aristocratic warrior.

The introduction of hoplite tactics brought aristocratic military dominance to an end. Hoplites were foot soldiers armed with spears or short swords and protected by a large round shield (a *hopla*), a breast-

HOW DID THE EMERGENCE OF HOPLITE TACTICS AFFECT GREEK POLITICAL NORMS?

ARCHAIC GREECE (800–480 B.C.E.)   125

plate, a helmet, and sometimes wrist guards and leg guards (greaves). In battle, hoplites stood shoulder to shoulder in a close formation called a phalanx, several rows across and several lines deep, with each hoplite carrying his shield on the left arm to protect the unshielded right side of the man standing next to him. In the right hand each hoplite carried a thrusting weapon such as a spear or short sword, so that an approaching phalanx presented a nearly impenetrable wall of armor and weaponry to its opponents. If a man in the front rank fell, the one behind him stepped up to take his place; indeed, behind the front line was literally the weight of the entire phalanx, each soldier aiding the assault by leaning with his shield into the man in front of him. The tight formation and heavy armor (as much as seventy pounds including the shield) required but one skill: the ability to stay together. As long as the phalanx remained intact, it was a nearly unbeatable formation.

Where, when, and how hoplite tactics first came to Greece remains a mystery. They are first mentioned in the early seventh century B.C.E. when Pheidon, the king of Argos, employed a hoplite army to inflict crushing defeats on the surprised warrior champions of neighboring poleis. Pheidon (or one of his predecessors) may have learned these tactics from the Assyrians. The armor and large shield are reminiscent of Assyrian heavy infantry, and certainly the Assyrians had used tight infantry formations to great effect. But wherever they came from, once hoplite tactics were introduced into Greece, all the poleis rushed to adopt them. By the end of the seventh century, hoplite tactics (with their accompanying requirements for training in close-order drill) were a standard element in Greek warfare.

> By the end of the seventh century, hoplite tactics were a standard element in Greek warfare.

The result was a social and political revolution. Since every polis needed a hoplite force to protect its independence, those farmers who could afford the requisite armor soon became a recognizable political and social force within the archaic polis—a "hoplite class." But the sacrifices demanded by hoplite warfare were great, and the men who had now become indispensable to the polis's survival quickly grew restless without a share in its political decisions. Scholars once believed their disquiet was sufficient by itself to force a series of concessions by the aristocrats, including access to political decision making and the writing down of laws to guarantee "equal" justice. But while the hoplite class was indisputably an essential element in the growth of democracy in some poleis, the real impetus toward change and the rallying point for angry hoplites may in fact have come from disgruntled aristocrats.

Hoplite Infantry Advancing into Combat. This Corinthian vase, dating to around 650 B.C.E., is the earliest known depiction of hoplites.

ARISTOCRATIC CULTURE AND THE RISE OF TYRANNY

For the better part of the seventh and sixth centuries, aristocrats dominated the Greek poleis. But these aristocrats were not a monolithic, cohesive group. Struggles for influence between competing aristocratic families were commonplace; often enough, new laws and the dispatching of colonial expeditions were weapons by which aristocratic families sought to hamstring their enemies. Despite the aristocracy's internecine rivalries, however, serving as the magistrate of a polis was an unsalaried duty, which only the wealthy could afford. The aristocrats of a polis might not have a unified agenda, but they still held all of its official power.

The Greek aristocrats of the Archaic Age pursued not only wealth, power, and glory, but also a distinct culture and defining lifestyle. Holding office and participating in politics was part of this lifestyle; but so too was the symposium, an intimate gathering at which elite men would enjoy prodigious quantities of wine, the recitation of poetry (ranging from epics to bawdy drinking songs), dancing competitions, and female courtesans who provided musical accompaniment as well as sexual services. Respectable women were by definition excluded from such meetings, as they were excluded from all other aspects of political life. The symposium was thus far more than a social occasion. It was an essential feature of aristocratic male life within the polis.

Homosexuality was another important aspect of aristocratic culture in the archaic period. Appropriate aristocratic homosexual behavior was regulated by social custom. Typically, a man in his late twenties to late thirties and on the rise in political life took as a lover and protégé an aristocratic youth in his early to mid-teens. The two formed a close and intimate bond of friendship, in which sexual intercourse played an important role. The close personal bond between the man and the boy was believed to benefit the younger partner, as he learned the workings of government and society, and through his older lover made important political and social connections that would benefit him later in life. Indeed, Plato would argue that true love could only exist between two such male lovers, because only within such a relationship could a man find a partner worthy of his affections.

> The Greek aristocrats of the Archaic Age pursued not only wealth, power, and glory, but also a distinct culture and defining lifestyle.

A whole complex of values, ideas, practices, and assumptions thus informed aristocratic identity in the Archaic Period. As a result, it was impossible for those outside this elite world to participate fully in the political, economic, social, and cultural life of the polis. By the middle of the Archaic Age, however, the circle of the aristocratic elite was narrowing even further. A small number of aristocrats now dominated the higher magistracies, putting them in a position to control a wide swath of civic life at the expense of their one-time rivals. As the circle of aristocrats exercising real power narrowed, a significant number of elites were left on the outside of their own culture, looking in. For these men, the remedy to their problem was often close at hand—the hoplites, who had concerns and complaints of their own.

As the circles of political power narrowed during the seventh century, violence between aristocratic groups increased, ultimately giving rise to the emergence of tyranny as an alternative form of government. The word *tyrannos* was not originally Greek, but borrowed from Lydia, signifying someone who seized power and ruled outside the traditional constitutional framework. A tyrant in archaic Greece was thus not necessarily an abusive ruler. In fact, the fundamental features of Greek democracy—especially in Athens—could never

A bearded Greek male and his young lover. This illustration is from a red figure cup, c. 480 B.C.E.

HOW DID THE EMERGENCE OF HOPLITE TACTICS AFFECT GREEK POLITICAL NORMS?

ARCHAIC GREECE (800–480 B.C.E.)   127

Music and Poetry in Everyday Greek Life. The Greeks proudly used pottery design to depict their daily activities. Here a musician entertains a boy while a poet writes verses for another boy. The homoerotic implications of such scenes were intentional.

have succeeded without an episode of tyranny. Later Greek thinkers were fascinated and horrified by the unrestrained power of archaic tyrants, and Aristotle would condemn tyranny as a perversion of the "pure" form of monarchy, hereditary kingship. For many people in the Archaic Period, however, the tyrant led the way to greater political enfranchisement.

The Greek tyrant was usually an aristocrat who had tired of his exclusion from the elite or had become frustrated with the petty rows of aristocratic factions within the polis. Would-be tyrants appealed instead to the hoplite class, whose armed might could propel them to a position of sole power. To stay in power, however, the tyrant had then to redress the grievances of his hoplite supporters. In doing so, tyrants broadened rights of political participation, or gave hoplites new economic and judicial guarantees, while at the same time striving to retain the reins of power in their own hands. This was an inherently unstable state of affairs. As a result, on the Greek mainland tyranny rarely lasted more than two generations. Once the original tyrant and his heirs had fulfilled the wishes of the hop-

lites, the continuance of tyranny became an obstacle to even greater power for the people, the *demos*. After a second generation in power, tyrannical dynasties usually found the hoplite army more inclined to withdraw its support than lend it. Structurally, therefore, tyranny was often a way station on the road from aristocracy to democracy.

LYRIC POETRY

Characteristic of archaic Greek culture is lyric poetry, a new departure in literature that took place in the seventh century and continued as a strong tradition thereafter. The first monuments of Greek literature are the imposing epics of Homer, magnificent in scope and brimming with the heroic themes of Greek society. Hesiod (c. 700 B.C.E.), Homer's immediate successor in the epic tradition, composed shorter yet still impressive poems imbued with traditional outlooks. Hesiod's *Theogony* described the origins of the gods and the created cosmos. His *Works and Days*, a personal diatribe against his scheming brother and the elite of his home-

THRASYBOULOS ON HOW TO BE A TYRANT

The fifth-century historian Herodotus relates how Periander, tyrant of Corinth from 627 to 587 B.C.E., sought advice from his older contemporary, Thrasyboulos of Miletus, on how best to secure tyrannical power. The excerpt below describes Thrasyboulos' response to Periander's emissary, and the Corinthian's response to his strange reply. Although Herodotus' negative attitude toward tyranny is typical of later classical thought, Periander and his father before him had in fact been instrumental in breaking a narrow aristocratic regime and increasing Corinth's commercial prosperity.

At the beginning Periander was gentler than his father [Cypselus] had been. But afterwards, when he had dealt with Thrasyboulos, prince of Miletus, he became yet bloodier than Cypselus. . . . Thrasyboulos had led out Periander's messenger, outside the city, and with him entered a sown field; then he walked through the corn, questioning, and again questioning the herald, about his coming from Corinth. And ever and again as he saw one of the ears growing above the rest he would strike it down, and what he struck down he threw away, until by this means he had destroyed all the fairest and strongest of the corn. So he passed through the whole place and, having added no suggestions, sent the herald away. When the herald came back to Corinth, Periander was anxious to know what suggestion Thrasyboulos had made. But the man said that Thrasyboulos had made no suggestion at all, and indeed he wondered what sort of man this was he had been sent to, a madman and a destroyer of his own property. . . . But Periander understood the act of Thrasyboulos and grasped in his mind that what he was telling him was that he should murder the most eminent of the citizens. And so from this time forth he displayed every form of wickedness toward his fellow countrymen. Whatever Cypselus had spared of death and banishment, Periander completed.

Herodotus, v. 92. Translated by David Grene. (Chicago and London: University of Chicago Press, 1987), pp. 397–398 (somewhat revised).

town, quickly expands to such topics as the rewards of hard work, the place of justice in the polis, and the importance of treating one's neighbors well.

The next generations of poets were less ambitious in scope, but their work often has a greater appeal because of its highly personal nature. The poets of the lyric tradition avoided conventional motifs and concentrated on themes of more interest to themselves, often naming their authorship within the lines of the poem. In many instances, they flouted typical mores and values. Archilochus of Paros (c. 680–640 B.C.E.), commemorated his service as a mercenary by writing, "Some barbarian waves my shield, as I had to abandon it/ . . . but I escaped, so it matters not/ . . . I can get another just as good." So much for heroism and standing firm in battle! Archilochus happily threw away his equipment and fled to save himself. Archilochus also gave vent to his personal anger with a faithless lover and the best friend she ran off with, comparing her with a fig tree that feeds every raven and wishing that he would be taken as a slave to the wild country of Thrace.

Among the most famous and accomplished of the lyric poets was Sappho (c. 620–550 B.C.E.). Living in the polis of Mytilene on the island of Lesbos, Sappho witnessed political upheaval and factional strife in her homeland. She left the invective to an associate named Alcaeus, choosing for herself to write beautiful and poignant poetry on themes of romantic longing and sexual lust, sometimes about men, but more often about other women. Of a female lover she wrote, "Like the very gods in my sight is he who / sits where he can look in your eyes, who listens / close to you, to hear the soft voice, its sweetness murmur in love and / laughter, all for him. . . . Let me only glance where you are, the voice dies, I can say nothing, / but my lips are stricken to silence, under/neath my skin the tenuous flame suffuses . . ." She opened another poem with the following lines: "Some there are who say that the fairest thing seen / on the black earth is an array of horsemen; / some, men marching; some would say ships; but I say she whom one loves best is the loveliest."

Though some lyric poets did extol martial virtues and praise heroism, they did so in a new context, that of the collective hero, the hoplite phalanx. At Sparta, the poets Alcman and Tyrtaeus sang of the glory of those who fought for the polis, not those who fought for their own personal gain. Aside from these occasional civic-minded themes, the intimacy of lyric reveals to us something quite new in the history of the West: the individual who expresses his or her feelings, even when these are at odds with the dominant culture of the time.

THE ARCHAIC POLIS IN ACTION

What characteristics defined the Athenian, Spartan, and Milesian poleis?

Although some developments and trends were common across the Greek world, every Greek polis had a very conscious sense of its own history and culture. The variety of experience in the Archaic Age encouraged this outlook, and we will now examine the historical development of three different Greek poleis. Even these present a paradox, at once exemplary and excep-

tional: they illustrate the infinite possibilities for the expression of the Greek polis and stand as paradigms for the courses Greek political development might take, yet are also unique. We know a great deal about certain poleis, especially Athens. The vast majority of Greek poleis, however, remain quite obscure to us, and are likely to remain so.

ATHENS

The Athenians believed that they and their city had survived continuously since the Bronze Age, and that they were themselves an indigenous people. The patterns of linguistic distribution would indicate otherwise, but the Athenians promoted their Bronze Age origins as integral to their identity and their sense of self-importance within the larger Greek world. But although Attica (the area in which Athens was located) was one of the wealthiest and most populous regions in mainland Greece at the end of the Dark Age, Athens itself was not of any great significance. For much of the early Archaic Period, Corinth was the leading commercial city of Greece; Sparta was the preeminent military power; and the islands of the Aegean along with the central coast of Anatolia were the leading cultural centers.

Athens emerged from the Dark Age with a distinctly agricultural economy. Whatever gains the aristocracy had made from trade had been reinvested in the land, and by the early Archaic Age the Athenian elite believed commerce to be a disreputable means of earning a living. Nevertheless, their city's orientation toward the Aegean, the excellent harbors along the Attic coast, and the potential of the land were all inescapable legacies for Athens, which would become famous as a mercantile and seafaring polis.

The landed aristocracy of Athens was in an unassailable position of power until the sixth century. The central props of their power were the elected magistracies, which they monopolized, and the council of state, which was composed of former magistrates. By the early seventh century, aristocratic officials called *archons* wielded executive power in Athens; ultimately nine archons in all presided over the civil, military, judicial, and religious functions of the polis. The archons served a term of one year, after which they became lifetime members of the Areopagus Council, where much of the real power in Athens resided. Indeed, the Areopagus elected the archons, thus controlling its own future membership. The Areopagus served as a kind of "high court" for Athenian society, with tremendous influence over the judicial procedures of Athens.

Over the course of the seventh century, deep economic and social divisions developed in Athenian society, as a significant proportion of the population fell into debt slavery (the practice of securing a loan with one's person as collateral and, when unable to pay up, becoming indentured to the creditor). Add to this economic and social injustice a serious political rivalry between aristocratic political factions, and Athens by the last third of the seventh century was in upheaval. In 632 B.C.E. a prominent aristocrat named Kylon attempted to establish a tyranny, only to surrender under a pledge of safe conduct. Kylon's political rivals violated their promise of immunity, however, slaughtering his supporters and driving Kylon himself into exile. Hard feelings would endure for a generation.

It was a generation of momentous change, however. The endless cycle of revenge killing that followed Kylon's failed coup inspired the first attempt at written law in Athens. In 621 B.C.E., an aristocrat named Drakon was charged with "setting the laws," and his most famous dealt with the problem of homicide. His attempt at stabilizing Athens failed, and the work of reform was left to another, some three decades later when Athens was on the brink of civil war. Hoping to avoid this unthinkable state of affairs, aristocrats and hoplites alike settled on Solon as a compromise candidate for archon in 594 B.C.E. Solon was born an aristocrat but had made his name and fortune as a merchant; this led everyone in Athenian society to trust Solon, as he was not beholden to any single interest. The centerpiece of Solon's year as archon was a series of political and economic reforms essential to the later development of Athenian democracy.

Solon addressed a number of issues. He forbade the practice of debt slavery, and set up a fund to buy back Athenian debt slaves sold abroad. He encouraged the Athenians to cultivate olives and grapes, thus spurring cash-crop farming and the urban industries (such as pottery, oil production, and shipbuilding) necessary to making Athens a commercial power. Solon set up courts in which a broader range of citizens served as jurors, and to which any Athenian might appeal if he disliked a decision of the Areopagus. Crowning his program was a new political and social system that determined the level of political power and access of any Athenian citizen. Solon based eligibility for political office on property qualifications, thus making it possible for someone not born an aristocrat to gain access to power through the accumulation of wealth. He es-

tablished the *boule*, whose membership was drawn from a wider circle of the population and which served as a kind of steering committee for the policies and actions of the Athenian state. He also gave the citizen assembly, the *ekklesia*, a more prominent role in the political workings of the state. This was a significant step, since all free-born Athenian men over the age of eighteen would participate in that organ of government.

Despite the moderation of his reforms, Solon disappointed many Athenians. The aristocracy felt he had

Harmodius and Aristegiton were lovers who slew Peisistratos' son Hipparchus, and so helped bring the Peisistratid tyranny over Athens to an end. Athenians celebrated them as liberators. This statue is a Roman copy of an original carved around 500 B.C.E.

Ostracism. The system took its name from the potsherds (in Greek, *ostraka*) on which the names of unpopular citizens were scratched. Many of the "ballots" have survived. Here we see "Aristeides," "Kimon," and "Themistokles."

gone too far, the demos, not nearly far enough. Those in power resisted implementing Solon's laws, and three factions based on regional and economic rivalries within Attica vied for dominance. The aristocrat Peisistratos exploited this state of affairs and established himself as tyrant in 546 B.C.E. Peisistratos offered few original measures; he mainly insisted on observing Solon's laws, and allowed the organs of government to function as Solon intended. Behind it all, however, was the quiet but very present intimidation that Peisistratos practiced through the hiring of foreign mercenaries and the ruthlessness with which he crushed any dissent to his regime. By enforcing Solon's wishes, Peisistratos made the demos powerful, so much so that the later Athenian democracy tried to distance itself from him by heroizing the aristocrats who murdered one of Peisistratos' sons and successors and drove the other into exile.

In the aftermath of the Peisistratid overthrow in 510 B.C.E., there was a brief aristocratic counterrevolutionary regime supported by the Spartans. However, two generations of increasing access to power meant that the Athenian demos had no interest in returning to an elite oligarchy. For the first time in history, the populace at large spontaneously rose up and overthrew the government, preferring different leadership. They rallied behind Cleisthenes, also an aristocrat but a man who had served the Peisistratid government ably and who championed the cause of the demos after the fall of tyranny. Once voted in as archon in 508/507 B.C.E., Cleisthenes reformed the voting practices of the Athenians, reorganizing the countryside and the population into ten voting "tribes" that helped suppress natural economic and regional tension within Attica. He made the boule a more representative body and extended the machinery of democratic government to the local level throughout Attica. Cleisthenes also introduced the practice of ostracism, whereby the Athenians could decide each year whether they wanted to banish someone for ten years, and if so, whom. Cleisthenes believed that with this power, the demos could protect itself from the potential return of a tyrant and quell factional strife if it seemed civil war might result.

Over the course of the archaic period, men such as Solon, Peisistratos, and Cleisthenes helped transform the Athenian polis into one of the most powerful in all of Greece. By the end of the sixth century, Athens was the principal exporter of olive oils, wines, and pottery in the Greek world, surpassing even "wealthy Corinth." The history of Athenian political development culminated, in the age of Cleisthenes, in a far more democratic temper than any other Greek polis possessed. The Athenians of the fifth century came to view themselves as the guardian of all that was good in Greek culture, including their own, more inclusive brand of democracy.

CHRONOLOGY

THE CHANGING LANDSCAPE OF ARCHAIC GREECE

Panhellenic colonial expansion by Greek poleis	800–400 B.C.E.
Hoplite tactics become standard in Greek warfare	725–650 B.C.E.
Emergence of tyrannical governments	700–600 B.C.E.
Militarization of Sparta	600 B.C.E.
Solon's reforms	594 B.C.E.
Cleisthenes' reforms	508 B.C.E.

SPARTA

Located in the southern part of the Peloponnesus (the large peninsula that forms southern Greece), the Spartans represented for all of Greece everything that Athens was not. Athens was cultured, sophisticated, cosmopolitan; Sparta was basic, earthy, and traditional. Depending on one's point of view, either set of adjectives might serve as admiration or criticism.

Sparta underwent a synoikismos (see p. 118) when four villages (and ultimately a fifth) combined to form the polis of Sparta. Perhaps as a result of the unification process, Sparta retained a highly peculiar institution, a dual monarchy. Sparta had two royal families, with two lines of succession. Although seniority or capacity usually determined which of two ruling kings had more influence, neither was technically superior to the other, a situation that led to political intrigue within Sparta.

Greek historians believed—as did the Spartans—that a figure from the Heroic Age named Lycurgus had given Sparta its unique constitution and social system. "Lycurgus" was probably a person to whom the Spartans gave credit for achievements and developments spanning hundreds of years across the Dark and early Archaic Age. The Spartans believed Lycurgus promulgated the "Great Rhetra," a "document" that remained unwritten at a time when many Greek poleis were writing down their laws. The Great Rhetra, orally preserved (and no doubt altered as circumstances demanded) represented for the Spartans the constitutional wisdom of Lycurgus.

The "reforms of Lycurgus" militarized Sparta. By the end of the seventh century, everything in Sparta was oriented to the maintenance of Greece's most feared and respected hoplite army, a force so superior that the Spartans confidently left their city unfortified. The Spartan system made every full citizen, called a Spartiate (or, alternatively, an "equal"), a professional soldier of the phalanx. Whereas Athenian government was democratized to reflect the interests and outlook of her people, in Sparta the citizenry was in essence "aristocratized," making every citizen-soldier a warrior-champion of the hoplite phalanx.

The Spartan system depended on the conquest of Messenia, an agriculturally wealthy region west of Sparta. In the early seventh century, the Spartans subjugated the region and enslaved the population. These

helots (as the enslaved Messenians were now called) remained to work the land, which was now parceled out among the Spartiates. The result was that Spartiates did not have to engage in manual labor of any kind, freeing all their time for their military training.

Sparta was a society organized for war. At birth, every child was examined by the five *ephors,* Spartan officials who served as guardians of the Great Rhetra. They determined whether a child was healthy enough to bother raising; if not, the infant was exposed in the mountains. If deemed worthy of upbringing, a child was placed at age seven in the state-run Spartan educational system, the *agoge.* Boys and girls trained together until age twelve, participating in exercise, gymnastics, and other physical drills and competitions. At that age, boys went to live in the barracks, where their military training would commence in earnest, while girls continued an education in letters until they married (marriageable age being the onset of puberty). Barracks training was rigorous, designed to accustom the young Spartan male to physical hardships. At age eighteen, the young man would try to gain membership into a *syssition,* a communal mess tent as well as a kind of fighting brotherhood. Failure to gain admission to a syssition meant that the young man would not become a full Spartiate, falling to a lower status and losing his citizen rights.

Assuming the young man's career continued as anticipated, he remained in the barracks until he was thirty, although he could marry at twenty-one. By the time he could take up residence in his own home, he had thus spent eighteen years in the barracks. The homoerotic culture of the Spartan military—along with the limited opportunities for procreation afforded to a young married couple—may have been a significant contributing factor to the falling number of Spartiates over the course of sixth and fifth centuries. A Spartiate remained on active military duty until he was sixty years old, although after the age of forty-five he was unlikely to see phalanx combat.

All Spartiate males were members of the assembly, the *apella,* which voted yes or no on matters put to it by superior organs of government. The upper levels of government included the kings and the council of elders. Any Spartiate at the age of sixty could stand for election to this council, which included twenty-eight seats at large and two for the kings. The apella elected members to the council of elders for life, and the coun-

> Failure to gain admission to a syssition meant that the young man would not become a full Spartiate, falling to a lower status and losing his citizen rights.

cil served as the main policy maker of the polis. In addition, the five ephors ruled on whether certain proposals or courses of action were in keeping with the Great Rhetra. An ephor could even depose a king from command of the army while on campaign. The ephors, who usually served a term of one year, wielded tremendous power, further augmented by their supervision of the Spartan secret service, the *krypteia*. The ephors recruited agents for the krypteia from among the most promising young Spartiates. Although these agents spied on citizens suspected of unusual activities, their main job was to infiltrate the helot populations, identify potential troublemakers, and eliminate them.

Spartan policy often hinged on the precarious relationship between the helots and the Spartiates. The helots outnumbered the Spartiates ten to one, and Messenia routinely seethed with revolt. The Spartans took the helots on campaign with them as shield bearers, spear bearers, and baggage handlers. Remarkably, we know of no helot revolt on campaign. At home, however, the helots were prone to rebellion, one reason the Spartans disliked committing their army for long periods of time far from home, fearing that the prolonged absence of the fighting men might encourage an uprising. Every year the Spartans ritually declared war on the helots, as a reminder that they would not tolerate any attempt to break free. Although the existence of the helots made the might of Sparta possible, Sparta's reliance on a hostile population of slaves also proved a serious weakness.

Spartiates themselves could not engage in trades or commerce, and Lycurgus prohibited the use of coinage, instead prescribing the use of iron spits for currency, which were both cumbersome and worthless outside of Sparta. Lycurgus believed that the use of money and the ability to accumulate wealth would create serious economic and political divisions among Spartiates and distract them from the pursuit of martial virtue. Therefore economic activity in the Spartan state fell to the *perioikoi*, "those dwelling round about." The perioikoi were subjects of the Spartan state not reduced to helot status. The perioikoi enjoyed certain rights and protections within Spartan society and grew wealthy handling its business concerns. They were forever excluded from the exercise of any political rights within the Spartan state, however, and Sparta conducted their foreign

> Spartiates themselves could not engage in trades or commerce, and Lycurgus prohibited the use of coinage, instead prescribing the use of iron spits for currency, which were both cumbersome and worthless outside of Sparta.

policy for them. Spartiates who lost their rights of full participation also became perioikoi.

From the Archaic Period on, the Spartans professed little use for innovation or change. They styled themselves the protectors of the "traditional constitutions" of Greece, by which they meant older, aristocratic regimes. The Spartans often tried to prevent the establishment of tyrannies or overthrew them in neighboring states. In the late sixth century, the Spartan king Cleomenes even supported the aristocratic counter-revolution in Athens. Sparta's defense of tradition and its military-social system made it an object of admiration throughout the Greek world, though few Greeks had any desire to live that way themselves. And in certain respects, it was a system that was inherently flawed. There were many ways to fall from the status of Spartiate—such as criminal behavior or other unseemly conduct—but there was only one way to become one: by birth. As a result, the number of full Spartiates declined from perhaps as many as ten thousand in the sixth century to only a few thousand by the beginning of the fourth.

MILETUS

Across the Aegean from the Greek "homeland" lay the Greek poleis of Anatolia (an area also known as Asia Minor). During the archaic period, the city of Miletus was the foremost commercial, cultural, and military power of Ionia, a narrow coastal strip dominating the central part of the west coast of Anatolia. Miletus had long been a part of the Greek world. Archaeological evidence supports what the Milesians themselves claimed, that they had ties to both Minoan and Mycenaean civilization. But there must also have been a substantial influence from the indigenous peoples of the area, whom later Greek tradition claimed had been conquered by Ionian-speaking settlers from Athens.

Despite its diversity, Miletus' population was ultimately subsumed under a single, strongly Hellenic identity, but Near Eastern influences continued to shape Milesian culture. Ionia was the birthplace of Greek epic, and the proximity of Miletus to the Near East has occasioned scholarly debate over the extent to which Asian models influenced Greek epic. Certainly there was influence in other creative endeavors. Fantastic animals, a long-standing theme of Near Eastern decorative art, were frequently represented on Milesian pottery during the seventh and sixth centuries. The close though often difficult relationship between the Ionians of the coast and the interior kingdom of Lydia also led to extensive cross-cultural exchange. Through the Ionians, the Lydian invention of coinage was introduced to the Greek world, while the Ionians played a crucial role in hellenizing the interior of Asia Minor. Under the pressure of the Lydians—who sought the fabulous ports of the Aegean coast for themselves—the major cities of Ionia banded together to form the Ionian League, a political and religious confederation of independent poleis pledged to support one another in time of need. It was the first such organization known in the Greek world.

Milesians stood at the vanguard of the colonial movement, especially in and around the Black Sea. Miletus was also active in the Egyptian markets; the main Greek trading posts in Egypt were Milesian foundations. Their colonial efforts, combined with their advantageous position for trade with the rest of Asia Minor, brought Miletus great wealth. Miletus reached the peak of its power in the early sixth century, when its tyrant Thrasyboulos successfully warded off Lydian aggression and (probably) constructed a fleet to protect Milesian shipping interests. After his death, however, continuing Lydian pressure combined with competition from the Ionian island of Samos led to Miletus' slow decline over the course of the sixth century.

Miletus also became the center for Greek speculative thinking and philosophy. Beginning in the sixth century B.C.E., a series of thinkers known to historians as the "Pre-Socratics" (because they came before the great philosopher Socrates) raised serious questions about the relationship between the natural world (the *kosmos*), the gods, and humans. Oftentimes, their explanations moved divine agency to the margins or removed it altogether—and for that, everyday Greeks looked upon them with suspicion. The so-called Milesian School consisted of three successive thinkers. The first, Thales, was an accomplished astronomer, also concerned with questions about nature and the "first principle," a substance from which all other matter had been created. His intellectual successors, Anaximander and Anaximenes, posited theories about the heavens

and the first principle, and explored the problem of change, including the differentiation of animal species. All three built on older traditions of Near Eastern learning, such as Babylonian astronomy; but in typically Greek fashion, they turned those ideas on their heads. Calculating and observing the movements of the heavens, the thinkers of the Milesian School sought physical explanations for what they saw, refusing to presume that the heavenly bodies were gods. By making the observations of humans, not the will of the gods, the starting point for their thinking, the Milesian school began to formulate rational theories to explain the physical universe they observed.

> By making the observations of humans, not the will of the gods, the starting point for their thinking, the Milesian school began to formulate rational theories to explain the physical universe they observed.

Stimulated by the cosmopolitanism of their city, Milesian philosophers also began to rethink their place in the human world, inaugurating what has sometimes been called "the Ionian revolution in thought." Hecataeus of Miletus, the first Greek to attempt a map of the known world, wrote after extensive travels during which he studied other cultures and their gods: "Hecataeus of Miletus says this: the sayings of the Greeks are many and foolish." Xenophanes of Colophon observed that the Thracians (a barbarian people living to the north of the Greeks) believed the gods had blue eyes and red hair, whereas the Ethiopians portrayed their gods as dark skinned and curly haired. Xenophanes concluded from this that if oxen could speak and make objects, they would pray and fashion idols to gods who looked like oxen. For Xenophanes, men made gods in their image, not the other way around. Such relativism was new, but it would become a distinctive strand in the diversity of later Greek philosophy.

This fissure between religious belief and philosophical speculation was a crucial development in the history of Western thought. It was less complete, however, than is often imagined. Philosophy was a game for a few, not for the average Greek; and as philosophers turned their attention to humanity's relationship to the gods, citizens in even the most progressive of poleis were unnerved. The gods were too central a part of daily life for the average Greek not to feel threatened by such impious philosophizing.

The struggle between religion and philosophy would finally be fought out not in Miletus, but in Athens more than a hundred years after Xenophanes' bold proclamation. The Ionian revolution in thought

HOW WERE THE GREEK ARMIES ABLE TO DEFEAT THE MUCH LARGER PERSIAN FORCES?

THE PERSIAN WARS   135

slowed when Cyrus conquered Lydia in 546 and inherited Lydia's suzerainty over the Greek city-states of Asia Minor, including Miletus. Milesian independence was always in jeopardy under Persian rule. Although often autonomous, the city remained under the constant threat of Persian intervention. Ultimately, Miletus would trigger the greatest cultural clash the Greek world had yet known—war with the mighty Persian empire.

THE PERSIAN WARS

How were the Greek armies able to defeat the much larger Persian forces?

The Archaic Period of Greek history closed with dramatic struggles against Persia. When hostilities erupted between the Greeks and Persia, the latter was the mightiest state the world had ever seen, capable of mustering over a million armed men. The Greeks, in contrast, remained a collection of poleis, fiercely suspicious of one another and competitive to the bitter end. An exceptionally large polis, such as Athens or Sparta, might put ten thousand hoplites in the field; but the vast majority of Greek states could provide only a few hundred each. For two decades the threat of Persian conquest loomed on the Greek horizon. When finally the immediate danger to Greek freedom receded, the experience of war had changed the Greek world immeasurably.

THE IONIAN REVOLT (499–494 B.C.E.)

Our main source for the Persian Wars is Herodotus, the "father of history." His account reflects many of the intellectual currents of mid-fifth-century Athens, where he lived and worked. His account is idiosyncratic, anecdotal, sometimes dubious, but always entertaining. Though he was from Halicarnassus in Asia Minor, he was a keen judge of his Athenian audience, and so emphasized the role Athens itself played in the wars. With a kind of geographical and cultural determinism, he ascribed the war between Persia and Greece to the rekindling of an ancient hatred between Europe and Asia. But his own narrative shows that the immediate political cause of the war was a political conflict in Miletus.

By 501 B.C.E., Aristagoras—the Persians' puppet tyrant of Miletus—grew concerned that his days as a favorite of Darius the Great were numbered. To protect his political future, he turned from puppet to patriot, rousing the Milesians and the rest of Ionia to revolt against Persian rule. Because they had little hope of winning on their own, Aristagoras tried to enlist military support from the Greek mainland. The Spartans showed initial interest but opted out when Aristagoras showed them the Persian Empire on Hecataeus' map. He then approached Athens and the city of Eretria on Euboea, playing to their sympathies as fellow Ionians. The Athenians voted twenty ships and crews, the Eretrians five. With the help of this small expeditionary force, the Ionians managed to take the old Lydian capital of Sardis (now a Persian administrative center) by surprise. The Athenians and Eretrians burned the city and then sailed home, leaving the Ionians to their own devices. After five years of brave struggle, the rebels were finally overwhelmed by the vastly superior might of Persia in 494 B.C.E.

Darius realized, however, that so long as his Greek subjects in Asia Minor could cast a hopeful eye to their cousins across the Aegean, they would long for freedom. Darius therefore set out on a punitive expedition to teach Athens and Eretria a lesson. The king sent a force of twenty thousand soldiers under two of his finest generals on an island-hopping campaign across the Aegean. Landing on Euboea in the summer of 490, Persian forces captured Eretria, sacked and burned it, and then crossed the narrow strait to Attica, landing in the plain of Marathon.

MARATHON AND ITS AFTERMATH

Recognizing the danger they now faced, the Athenians sought help from the Spartans, who responded that they were unable to assist due to an ongoing religious festival. Only the small, nearby polis of Plataea offered the Athenians aid. The Athenians would have to engage the mighty Persians on their own.

Heavily outnumbered and without effective cavalry to counter the Persians, the Athenian phalanx took a position between two hills blocking the main road to the asty. After a standoff of several days, the Athenian general Miltiades received word that the Persians were watering their horses, and that the Persian infantry, numerically superior but poorly equipped compared with Athens' ten thousand hoplites, was vulnerable. Miltiades led a charge that smashed the Persian force and resulted in catastrophic losses for the Persians. Herodotus records that sixty-four hundred Persians fell,

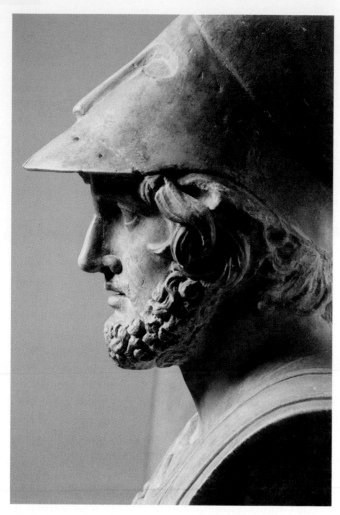

Bust of Themistocles. His leadership enabled Athens to defeat Persia and become the primary naval power in the Aegean Sea.

XERXES' EXPEDITION

Darius died in 486 B.C.E. and was succeeded by his son Xerxes. Xerxes spent the first several years of his reign quelling a revolt in Egypt, but he never forgot his father's desire to punish the Athenians. Indeed, Xerxes decided to go Darius one better. He planned an all-out, overland invasion of Greece to conquer the entire country. By the spring of 480, his grand army (probably numbering some three hundred fifty thousand troops) set out from Sardis, crossing the narrow strait separating Europe from Asia on pontoon bridges. Unlike his father, who had dispatched talented generals against Athens, Xerxes led this campaign himself.

Before his arrival in Greece, Xerxes had already received the submission of several important sites in northern and central Greece, including Thebes and Delphi. Athens, Sparta, and others refused to bow, however, and formed the Hellenic League to defeat the Persian menace. Under the military leadership of Sparta, the outnumbered Greek allies resolved to face Xerxes at the pass of Thermopylae in August of 480. For three days the Greeks held off the Persian multitude, while an allied Greek fleet engaged a Persian flotilla at nearby Artemisium. The Spartan-led defense at Thermopylae failed, but the naval engagement—though technically a draw—proved significant. The sacrifice at Thermopylae allowed the fleet, under Themistocles' guidance, to inflict heavy losses on the Persians and then withdraw safely to the south.

After the defeat at Thermopylae the road to Athens lay open. Realizing they could not defend their city, Themistocles persuaded his fellow Athenians to abandon the city and their possessions. They evacuated noncombatants to other locales and removed the core of Athenian military strength, including the fleet, to the island of Salamis off the coast of Attica. In early September, the Athenians watched the Persians put Athens to the torch, and Themistocles struggled to keep the allied fleet together as the Persians feigned an advance toward Corinth and Sparta.

Time, however, was on Themistocles' side. The massive size of his army meant Xerxes was dependent on his fleet for supplies. Bad weather made sailing the Aegean in autumn a risky business; the Persians were now desperate to force a decisive battle before the season turned against them. In late September, the numerically superior Persian fleet, believing the Greeks were about to flee Salamis, sailed into the Bay of Eleusis, only to find that Themistocles had the Greek fleet ready for combat. The Greeks smashed the Persian

compared with only 192 Athenians. The Persians withdrew.

The Athenians had defeated the world's greatest empire, and they had done it without Spartan help. It was a tremendous boost to Athenian confidence, and many exulted in their victory, a victory of the demos. The Athenian politician Themistocles believed, however, that Greece had not seen the last of the Persians, who would inevitably return in much greater force. Several years after Marathon, the Athenians discovered a rich silver vein in the Attic countryside. Themistocles persuaded them not to divide the windfall among themselves (the customary practice), but to build a fleet of two hundred triremes, state-of-the-art warships. Athens transformed itself into the preeminent naval power of the Greek world, just in time to confront a new Persian onslaught.

HOW WAS THE FABRIC OF SOCIETY CHANGED DURING THE GOLDEN AGE OF CLASSICAL GREECE?

THE GOLDEN AGE OF CLASSICAL GREECE   137

Greek Forces Defeat Persians. This detail from a fifth-century B.C.E. attic bowl depicts an Athenian soldier standing over a defeated Persian soldier from Xerxes' army.

fleet while Xerxes watched the disaster from a throne above the bay. The Persian king left behind a substantial army, but he himself withdrew to his empire; the battle of Salamis had effectively ended his campaign. The following year, the Greeks prevailed on land at the battle of Plataea, driving the Persians completely from mainland Greece. Against all odds, the small, fractious, outnumbered Greek poleis had defeated the mightiest empire of the Mediterranean world. It was a turning point in the history of Greece, ushering in the Classical (or "Golden") Age.

THE GOLDEN AGE OF CLASSICAL GREECE

How was the fabric of society changed during the golden age of classical Greece?

In the fifty years following the battle of Salamis, Athens enjoyed a meteoric rise in power and prestige, becoming the premier naval power of the eastern Mediterranean and a rival even to Sparta. When Spartan leadership failed after the war, those poleis who wished to continue the fight against the Persians formed an alliance on the island of Delos under the military leadership of Athens—the Delian League. Each member state contributed ships or money to the cause, and all vowed to fight until the Persians ceased to be a threat. As the leader of the league, Athens controlled the funds and resources of the alliance, a fact that allowed the Athenians to make their polis—in the words of their brilliant political leader Pericles—"the school of Hellas." The fifth century witnessed the greatest achievements of Greek culture and the fruition of the Athenian democracy. But both were fueled by the increasingly awkward relationship Athens enjoyed with its allies, who by the 430s had begun to look more like Athenian subjects than free allies.

PERICLEAN ATHENS

The reforms of Cleisthenes made possible further experiments in Greek democracy, including the election of major officers of the polis by lot. Only one major position was left open to traditional voting: the office of *strategos*, or general. A man could be elected strategos (unlike all other positions) year after year, and so this office became the focus for Athens' most talented and ambitious public figures. Themistocles had been a strategos, as had Cimon, who led the Delian League to stunning victories over Persia in the 470s and 460s. But Cimon also turned the league against members who tried to opt out, suppressing their "revolts" by force of arms, and turning the league more and more into an instrument of Athenian policy.

Cimon's military successes made him the most powerful politician in Athens. By the 460s, however, the political mood in Athens was changing, and new voices were calling for a greater role in government. Athens' power was a result not so much of its hoplite phalanx (mediocre by Greek standards) as its fleet. The enormous navy of triremes required nearly forty thousand rowers drawn from those Athenians too poor to afford hoplite equipment, the lowest of the four classes established by Solon. Since the beginning of the sixth century, these men had enjoyed very limited political power. For all of his magnanimity and generosity, Cimon was too conservative to consider shifting the balance of political power in the direction of the poorer mass of Athenian citizens, the *thetes*.

An unlikely champion emerged for their cause, an aristocrat from one of Athens' most prestigious noble

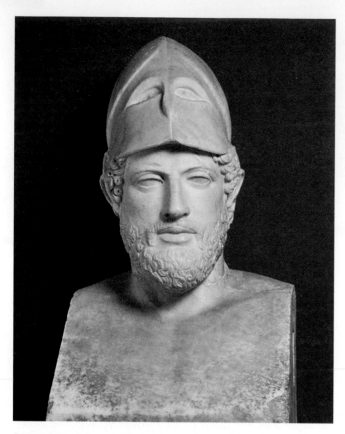

Bust of Pericles. A Roman copy, in marble, of a Greek original, made in bronze during Pericles' own lifetime. Like the tyrant Peisistratos, Pericles is said to have had a deformed head. Pericles wore a helmet to conceal this potentially provocative resemblance.

families—Pericles. A political rival of Cimon's, Pericles used a platform of greater enfranchisement of the thetes and an anti-Spartan foreign policy to defeat Cimon. Pericles was elected strategos for 462–461, and secured the ostracism of Cimon from Athens. He then pushed through reforms to make Athens more fully democratic. He gave every member of the assembly (that is, any Athenian citizen) the right to propose and amend legislation, not just vote yes or no. This shifted power away from the Areopagus—still made up of ex-archons and therefore wealthier citizens—and from the more deliberative boule. He also made it easier for any citizen to participate in the assembly and the great appeals courts of Athens by paying an average day's wage for attendance. This allowed Athens' poorer citizens to take part without losing income. They now became a significant force in politics, loyal to the man who had made it possible.

Along with these and other important political measures, Pericles glorified Athens' democracy with an am-bitious scheme of public building and lavish festivals to honor the gods, especially Athena. He was a great patron of the arts, sciences, and literature, attracting the best minds of the day to Athens. As a result of his populist political stance and his ability to inspire a sense of Athenian superiority, Pericles enjoyed an unprecedented run of success in politics. He was returned as strategos every year for three decades, and his guidance and vision have prompted historians to apply his name to this phase of Athenian history. Despite Pericles' often poor decisions regarding foreign policy, there is no question that Periclean Athens represents a dramatic and brilliant moment in the history of Western civilizations.

LITERATURE AND DRAMA

Although Athens was not the only city to produce great works of literature during the "golden age," our knowledge of classical Greek literature is dominated by the poetry and drama (both tragic and comedic) produced in fifth-century Athens. Epic and lyric poetry were already established Greek literary forms when the fifth century began. Drama, however, appears to have been an innovation that developed out of the choruses that chanted poetic odes to the god Dionysius at the great spring festival devoted to him. It was probably the tyrant Peisistratos who first organized the Great Dionysia, and Cleisthenes who converted it into a festival at which tragic dramas were presented. From the beginning, therefore, Athenian drama was closely connected to the political and religious life of the state, which sponsored it. Credit for transforming the Dionysian odes into a genuine drama with characters and a chorus belongs, however, to the great tragedian Aeschylus (525–456 B.C.E.), who by introducing a second (and later a third) character into the performance, made it possible to present conversation, and hence human conflict, on the stage for the first time. Staging remained very simple, however: two or three actors (all male) wearing masks, with a chorus of twelve to fifteen members chanting commentary on the action. Dialogue was in verse, and movements were slow, solemn, and formal, punctuated by music and dance; but the emotional impact of tragic drama could be overwhelming.

Efforts to define and explain the nature of tragedy began with Aristotle, who declared that the purpose of tragedy was to inspire pity and fear in the audience, and so to purge these emotions through a catharsis. Although enormously influential, this formulation is

HOW WAS THE FABRIC OF SOCIETY CHANGED DURING THE GOLDEN AGE OF CLASSICAL GREECE?

THE GOLDEN AGE OF CLASSICAL GREECE   139

probably too limiting to be helpful. The fundamental themes of tragedy—justice, law, and the conflicting demands of piety and obligation that drive a heroic man or woman to destruction—were derived from Homer. Although most tragedies told well-known tales from a legendary past—Agememnon's sacrifice of his daughter, his murder by his wife Clytemnestra, and the vengeance taken by his son Orestes; or the Oedipus story, about a king who unwittingly slays his father and marries his mother—tragedy could also have a decidedly contemporary aspect. In his *Persians*, Aeschylus told of the great Athenian victory at Salamis (in which Aeschylus himself may have participated) through the eyes of the Persian king Xerxes, who thus became its tragic hero. Sophocles' (496–406 B.C.E.) great masterpiece, *Oedipus at Colonus*, was presented in the midst of Athens' ultimately disastrous war with Sparta; Eu-

ripides' (485–406 B.C.E.) *Trojan Women* was presented in 415, the year of the expedition to Syracuse (see p. 141), and the turning point in the Athenians' march toward defeat. Tragedy dealt in absolutes, most memorably perhaps in Sophocles' *Antigone*, the story of a clash between justice and law, and the competing obligations of familial piety and civic necessity; but its context was inevitably the history of Athens in the period of its own greatest achievements and failures.

Comedy was even more directly a genre of direct political commentary. Comedy was crude, parodic, and outspoken, full of slapstick, absurdity, and vulgarity. Its themes were (in the scholar Peter Levi's words) "sex, life on the farm, the good old days, the nightmare of politics, the oddities of religion, the strange manners of the town." Aristophanes (c. 448–382 B.C.E.), the greatest of the Athenian comedic playwrights, ridiculed everything that offended or amused him: the philosophy of Socrates, the tragedies of Euripides, and especially the imperialistic warmongering of contemporary politicians such as Cleon. Some of his jokes were simply crude, as when he had Socrates explain thunder as "the farting of the clouds." In his timeless masterwork, *Lysistrata*, women of enemy cities bring an end to a stupid war by refusing to have sex with their husbands until a peace agreement is signed. Above all else, Aristophanes was a social critic, who routinely savaged the powerful political figures whom he believed (with justice) were leading Athens to its doom. He was repeatedly dragged into court to defend him-

Greek Theater in Epidauros. Greek dramas were invariably presented in the open air. The construction of this theater, which takes advantage of the slope of the hill, and the arrangement of the stage are of particular interest. The plan for the theater is shown above.

self against the politicians whom he had attacked. But despite their anger, the politicians never dared to shut down the comedic theater for long. It was too much a part of the spirit of democratic Athens.

Periclean Athens also proved fertile ground for the development of Greek prose. Through the sixth century, Greeks typically expressed philosophical or political ideas through poetry. In the fifth century, however, perhaps reflecting the increasing functional literacy of the Athenians, prose emerged as a distinct literary form. Herodotus found a ready market for his "inquiries" (*historiai*) in Athens. His younger contemporary Thucydides (c. 460–c. 400 B.C.E.) wrote a masterful history of the great war between Athens and Sparta at the end of the fifth century. Between them, these two historians developed a new approach to history, emphasizing among other things the reliability of their sources and looking for credible cause-and-effect relationships in historical events. The development and elaboration of prose would make possible in the fourth century even further literary achievements, such as the great philosophical treatises of Plato and Aristotle and the stirring political and legal speeches of the great Attic orators we will meet in the next chapter.

ART AND ARCHITECTURE

The Greeks of the golden age showed a similar range of genius in the visual arts as they did in their drama. Their comic gift—exuberance, cheerful sensuality, and coarse wit—can be seen especially in their pottery. In "black figure" vases and jugs done throughout the Greek world in the sixth and fifth centuries B.C.E., the characters often look like grinning rascals up to some sort of mischief, usually sexual. More dignified were the marble statuary and sculptured reliefs the Greeks made for temples and public places. Here too Athens was preeminent. Athenian sculptors took human greatness as their theme, depicting the beauty of the human form in statuary that was simultaneously naturalistic and idealizing.

Perhaps the most striking development in fifth-century sculpture was the relatively sudden appearance of the well-proportioned, naturalistic nude. This happened first in Athens in the years around 490 to 480 B.C.E., not coincidentally the time of the Greek victory over Persia. Nothing like it had ever been seen, and it is difficult not to conclude that the triumph of Greek ideals of human dignity and freedom in the Persian War had something to do with it. Convinced that all Persians bowed down to their rulers like slaves,

Greek Sculptor at Work. The Greeks were not prudish.

whereas they themselves enjoyed political and social equality, the Greeks expressed their idea of human greatness by commemorating the dignity of the unadorned human body in stone.

The Athenians also made exceptional contributions to architecture. The "classic" Greek temple was not an Athenian invention; it emerged gradually throughout the Greek world during the sixth century. All Greek temples sought to create an impression of harmony and repose; but of all the Greek temples ever built, the Parthenon of Athens, constructed between 447 and 438 B.C.E., and decorated with statuary and reliefs by the sculptor Phidias, is generally considered the finest. It was a stunning achievement, expensive and difficult, urged on the Athenians by their visionary leader Pericles. Once completed, the Parthenon became a symbol of the Athenians' devotion to their patron goddess and a triumphant celebration of their power and confidence.

WOMEN AND MEN IN THE DAILY LIFE OF ATHENS

Toward the end of his stirring Funeral Oration, Pericles briefly addressed the married women in his audience and urged them to do three things: to rear more children for the sake of Athens; to show no more weakness than was "natural to their sex," and to avoid gossip. His remarks reveal widely held male attitudes toward women in classical Greece.

HOW WAS THE FABRIC OF SOCIETY CHANGED DURING THE GOLDEN AGE OF CLASSICAL GREECE?

THE GOLDEN AGE OF CLASSICAL GREECE   141

Apollo of Tenea; Apollo of Piombino; "The Critian Boy." These three statues, dating from about 560, 500, and 480 B.C.E. respectively, display the progressive "unfreezing" of Greek statuary art. The first stiff and symmetrical statue is imitative of Egyptian sculpture (see statue of the pharaoh Menkaure, p. 41). Roughly half a century later it is succeeded by a figure that begins to display motion, as if awakening from a sleep of centuries in a fairy tale. The last figure introduces genuine naturalism in its delicate twists and depiction of the subject's weight resting on one leg.

Rather than leading to greater equality among the sexes, the growth of Greek democracy had the opposite result. In the aristocratic society of the Dark Age women were sometimes portrayed as possessing extraordinary traits of beauty, wisdom, or courage. The Trojan War was allegedly fought over Helen, the wise Andromache offered shrewd military advice to her husband, and Penelope exhibited heroic courage and fidelity waiting for Odysseus to return. Such women, while still clearly subordinate, did not exist entirely in the shadows.

But as aristocratic ideals gave way to more democratic ones throughout Greece, life in the shadows increasingly became women's lot. In Athens, an emphasis on the infantry and its spirit of equality encouraged training together and developing close relationships, often of a homosexual nature and perhaps reflective of the older, heroic ideal of the aristocratic age. In addition, the ostentation of individual aristocratic women was discouraged, and the rearing of children to supply the infantry became an imperative. Public spaces were located in towns for "male activities" such as athletics and political gatherings, and private spaces were delimited for female activities such as child rearing and weaving. "Respectable" women lived in seclusion.

Girls could be married at age fourteen—as soon as they were biologically ready for childbearing—to husbands twice their age (younger men were supposed to dedicate themselves more fully to war). A girl's father arranged her marriage without concern for his daugh-

Flute Player. An Athenian marble relief dating from about 470 B.C.E. The relaxed pose (reclining position, crossed legs) and naturalistic representation of the naked female form were unprecendented in human art before the classical age of the Greeks.

ter's preferences and provided her with a dowry that her husband was expected to use for her support. Legally, wives became the property of their husbands. Shortly after a wife entered her new home, a regular schedule of childbearing began. Typically the interval between births was between two and four years, meaning that the average young wife would have borne between four and six children before she died, usually around the age of thirty-five.

Women seldom went out of doors, because it was thought immodest for them to be seen by other men except at public festivals. At home, women were expected to prepare and weave cloth. Since the ideology of democratic Athens opposed excessive displays of wealth or leisure, women were not supposed to sit around idly; but since "women's work" was basically menial, men looked down on women for engaging in it. Available evidence suggests that husbands customarily had little emotional attachment to their wives, regarding them as natural inferiors. In a revealing passage Herodotus says of a certain Lydian king, "this

Candaules fell in love with his own wife, a fancy that had strange consequences. . . ." Athenian men of the fifth and fourth centuries B.C.E. tended to idealize male homosexual relationships, since men were considered superior to women. Athenian men did seek heterosexual physical pleasure also, but for sexual gratification a man could rely on household slaves or prostitutes. As an Athenian orator remarked, "prostitutes we have for pleasure, concubines for daily physical attendance, wives to bear us legitimate children and be our faithful housekeepers."

Athenian society was as dependent on slavery as the Spartans were on their helots. None of the extraordinary Athenian accomplishments in politics, thought, or art would have been possible had slaves not done the heavy labor while free men debated in assemblies or discussed the true and the beautiful at symposia. There is, indeed, a direct relationship between the rise of democratic government in Greece, especially in Athens, and the increasing prevalence of slavery in Greek society. The Athenian ideal of dividing and rotating governmental duties among all free men depended on the assumption that slaves would be widely available to work in fields, businesses, and homes while free men engaged in politics. In fact, the Athenian democratic system began to function fully only with the expansion of Athenian mining and commerce around 500 B.C.E. Whereas previously the supply of slaves had been limited to war captives, their new wealth now enabled the Athenians to buy slaves from the north and east in vastly larger numbers.

Although widespread, Athenian slavery was small in scale. The only exception was in the state-owned silver mines, where large numbers of slaves toiled in miserable conditions. Otherwise, slaves were distributed in small numbers among Athenian families, rather than working in large teams on plantations or in industries. Typically every family would own a slave or two to perform its hardest and most menial work, tilling the soil or doing the laundry. In such circumstances slaves seldom suffered cruel treatment, although their masters were free to inflict beatings. The very notion that slaves were not entirely human, made it easier for Athenian free men to assume that nature had chosen some for servile labor, and others, like themselves, for political life.

For the male citizen or resident alien, however, daily life in Periclean Athens had numerous attractions. Male citizens enjoyed considerable social and economic equality. Small-scale farming and commerce were the norms, and what little industry existed—pottery and

Women Processing in the Panathenaea, c. 447–438 B.C.E. This image shows a portion of a sculptural frieze from the Parthenon in Athens. Every four years, this annual religious procession in honor of Athena would be celebrated in a particularly elaborate manner. This procession was one of the few public occasions on which respectable Athenian women were permitted to appear in public.

armaments manufacture—was also limited in scale, being carried on in shops owned by individual artisans who produced their own wares. Factories employing large numbers of workers were rare but on the rise: one of the largest in fifth-century Athens, a shield factory, was staffed by 120 workers and owned by a resident alien. Some citizens were of course richer than others, but the richest were required to donate some of their wealth to support public festivals or equip the navy. Athens in the fifth century was an exciting, bustling, cosmopolitan center of commerce and culture.

LEAGUE BUILDING AND THE PELOPONNESIAN WAR

How did the Peloponnesian War influence Greek philosophy?

Athenians saw themselves as the freest of men, but their freedom rested on the servitude of others. Slaves performed much of the labor at home, while Athens' allies in the Delian League provided the resources that underlay Athenian greatness. During the 450s, the Athenians gained sole control over league policy and

the management of its funds, both of which the Athenian assembly determined under the guidance of Pericles. Without the surplus wealth flowing into Athens from the League, none of the projects which Pericles undertook—pay for political participation, the glorification of the Athenian democracy through great buildings (also, incidentally, an employment program for poorer citizens), the patronage of Athenian drama—would have been possible. All of this made Athens powerful and its democracy vibrant, and kept Pericles popular and in power. But Athens' democratic achievements rested upon her control over an alliance she had transformed into an empire.

Since the 470s, Athens had faced attempts by its allies to break away, and it had crushed those efforts ruthlessly. Through the 450s, such revolts were rare. But in the early 440s, Pericles determined on a more aggressive policy toward Sparta, by then Athens' only real rival for supremacy in the Greek world. To give himself a freer hand, he concluded a formal peace with Persia. After this peace, the purpose of the Delian League evaporated, and Athens had no justification for compelling its allies to remain within it. Many remained loyal nonetheless, paying their contributions and enjoying the economic benefits of warm relations with Athens. Others, however, did not, and Athens found itself increasingly forcing its allies back into line, often installing Athenian garrisons and planting

THRACE

BLACK SEA

MACEDONIA

SEA OF MARMORA

CHALCIDICE

SAMOTHRACE

THESSALY

THRACIAN

LEMNOS

Hellespont

CORCYRA

SEA

LESBOS

PERSIA

AETOLIA

Thermopylae ✕

AEGEAN

Delphi • BOEOTIA

EUBOEA

IONIAN

Thebes

SEA

Marathon

ACHAEA

SEA

✕

CHIOS

Plataea ✕ Athens ✕

SEA

Corinth •

✕ ATTICA

SAMOS

Salamis

Argos •

PELPONNESUS

DELOS

• Miletus

MESSENIA

• Sparta

MEDITERRANEAN

LACONIA

SEA

MELOS

RHODES

EUROPE

Area of detail

AFRICA

CRETE

	Sparta and allies
	Athens and allies
	Neutral Greek states
✕	Battle sites

GREECE DURING THE PELOPONNESIAN WAR

Consider that Macedonia and Thessaly were still rather backward by Greek standards, and then examine the pattern of Athenian and Spartan alliances. Why would Pericles have urged his fellow Athenians to abandon the land to Sparta and concentrate their own military efforts on the sea? How did the strength of Athens' navy present special problems for the Spartans? Consider that Athens relied for a great proportion of its grain supply on shipments from the Black Sea. How did the geography of the northeastern Aegean make Athens particularly vulnerable? What political consequences might there have been in Athens due to the great reliance placed on the lower-income rowers in the war fleet?

Athenian colonists—who retained their Athenian citizenship—to ensure future loyalty.

In the context of Greek culture, such behavior was disturbing. The Athenians had anchored the Delian League to preserve Greek independence against the Persians. Now many Greeks accused Athens of having become a tyrannical empire itself. Foremost among the accusers were the Corinthians, whose own economic standing was seriously threatened by Athenian dominance of the Aegean. The Corinthians were close allies of the Spartans, the central power of what historians call the "Peloponnesian League" (the Greeks called it simply "the Spartans and their allies"). When war finally erupted between Athens and Sparta, the great historian Thucydides ascribed it to the growing power of Athens, and the fear and envy this inspired in Sparta. No modern historian has improved upon Thucydides' formulation. For the Athenian democracy and its leader, there could be no question of relinquishing their empire, the cornerstone of their cultural and political ascendancy. By the 430s, however, Athens could not preserve that empire without threatening the interests of Sparta and her allies.

THE PELOPONNESIAN WAR ERUPTS

After a series of provocations, the Athenians and Spartans found themselves at war with one another in 431 B.C.E. Athens could not defeat Sparta on land; but neither Sparta nor her allies had a fleet capable of facing the Athenians on the seas. Pericles therefore developed a bold strategy: to pull the entire population of Attica within the walls of Athens and its harbor, abandoning the countryside to Sparta. In the meantime, the superior Athenian fleet would supply Athens from the sea and ravage the coasts of Spartan territory. As with many of history's pivotal contests, both sides believed a conclusion would come quickly. Instead, the war dragged on for twenty-seven years.

> Time appeared to be on Athens' side, but in 429 B.C.E. the crowded conditions of the besieged city gave rise to an epidemic that claimed over a third of the Athenian population, including Pericles.

The Spartans plundered the farms and pastures of Attica, frustrated that the Athenians would not send their hoplites out for a decisive battle. Meanwhile, the Athenians inflicted significant destruction on Spartan territory in a series of lightning raids, while at the same time successfully encouraging revolt among the helots. Time appeared to be on Athens' side, but in 429 B.C.E. the crowded conditions of the besieged city gave rise to an epidemic that claimed over a third of the Athenian population, including Pericles. Events after his death revealed that Pericles was the only man capable of managing the democratic political forces he had unleashed. His successors were mostly demagogues, ambitious men who played to the worst instincts of the demos in order to gain power for themselves. The most successful of these was a warmonger named Cleon, a particular target of Aristophanes' invective, who refused a Spartan offer of peace in 425 B.C.E. and continued the war until his own death in battle four years later.

A short-lived truce ensued, authored by an able Athenian leader named Nicias. But the Athenian demos was not in the mood for peace for very long, and ultimately fell under the spell of a charming but unscrupulous aristocrat named Alcibiades. A flamboyant adventurer and ne'er-do-well, Alcibiades convinced the Athenians in 415 B.C.E. to reopen hostilities with an ill-advised attack on the distant city of Syracuse in Sicily. Because of his own personal political problems, he did not lead the expedition; instead, the task fell to Nicias and Demosthenes, an accomplished general who, like Nicias, had opposed the venture. The expedition immediately ran into trouble and ultimately failed, with thousands of Athenians killed or falling into slavery.

News of the Syracusan disaster shattered the Athenian demos. Recriminations began immediately. Many politicians were driven from the polis, and in 411 B.C.E. the demos suffered a momentary but monumental lack of self-confidence. While many of the rowers in the fleet were away, the Athenians essentially voted the democracy out of existence, replacing it with a narrow oligarchy of four hundred citizens. The Athenian fleet, stationed in Samos, replied by reestablishing a democratic government in exile under the leadership of none other than Alcibiades. The oligarchy proved to be short lived, and democracy was restored to Athens by 409. But the fact that the war could force such desperation did not bode well for the future.

THE END OF THE WAR

The Spartans too despaired of bringing the war to an end. Despite Athens' problems, its fleet was still invincible. Sparta, a nation with no seafaring tradition to speak of and, thanks to its social system, notoriously short on cash, turned to the one power ready and willing to stir up trouble in the Greek world. The Persians supplied the gold and expertise necessary for the Spartans to take to the sea and try to beat the Athenians at their own game. By 407, a talented and ambitious Spartan commander, Lysander, was harrying the Athenians throughout the eastern Aegean.

Perhaps the most disturbing development of the closing years of the war was the self-destructive passion with which the Athenians now began to turn against each other. To take but one example: in 406, the Athenians won a key victory in the Aegean at Arginusae. After the engagement, a storm came up, preventing the Athenian commanders from rescuing those

A Modern Replica of an Athenian Trireme. These versatile warships were powered by both oars and sail.

sailors whose ships had been wrecked in the course of battle. When the sailors drowned, a firestorm of protest erupted in Athens, fanned by demagogues who secured through show trials the execution of those generals foolish enough to return to Athens. One of them was Pericles, the son of Pericles, who thus became a victim of the democracy his father had brought into being. Through such measures, the Athenians managed either to kill or drive into exile their most experienced and able commanders.

The result, in hindsight at least, was predictable. Lysander destroyed the poorly led Athenian fleet in 404 B.C.E. Without their fleet the Athenians could neither feed themselves nor defend their city. Lysander sailed around the Aegean unopposed, installing pro-Spartan oligarchies among the former allies of Athens. Finally, he besieged Athens itself. Facing the inevitable, the Athenians surrendered. Corinth and Thebes called for Athens' utter destruction. The Spartans declined, to their credit, but imposed harsh terms on the Athenians: the dismantling of their walls, the scrapping of their fleet, and the acceptance of an oligarchic government of thirty Athenians.

The war's postscript was grim, even for the victors. In Athens, the so-called Thirty Tyrants confiscated property and murdered over fifteen hundred of their political opponents in the roughly eighteen months of their rule. Their excesses drove committed demo-crats to desperate resistance; a bloodbath was averted only through the reasoned intervention of the Spartan king Pausanias. By the end of 401, Athens was once again a democracy, but more moderate in its behavior than during the war—although, as we will see, it still had one last act of brutality and shortsightedness to perform.

The Spartans now succeeded to the Athenians' unenviable role as the protector of the Greeks against the Persians. It was a thankless job, made worse by the losses Sparta itself had suffered during the war, and by the fact that the Spartans were far more heavy-handed in their control of the Aegean than the Athenians had been. The Spartans now found themselves in a position they had avoided throughout their history, as their far-flung imperial interests sapped their manpower and undermined their control over the helots. They also faced a reinvigorated Persian empire, which had benefited from the Greeks' fratricidal struggles. Within a decade of the Peloponnesian War's end, Sparta found itself opposed by four poleis whose ancient hatreds for each other were legendary—Athens, Argos, Thebes, and Corinth. Their cooperation speaks volumes about how unpopular Spartan preeminence had become in just a few short years.

For the Greeks, the Peloponnesian War was a disaster. From the long perspective of historical distance, we may view it as demonstrating the limitations of the

CHRONOLOGY

EVOLUTION OF PHILOSOPHICAL THOUGHT IN ARCHAIC
GREECE

Emergence of the "Milesian School" (pre-Socratics)	600–500 B.C.E.
Pythagoreans emerge in southern Italy	530 B.C.E.
Rise of the Sophists	450 B.C.E.
Death of Socrates	399 B.C.E.

polis system. The competitive ethos that characterized the Greek poleis had proved to be their tragic flaw. To the Greeks themselves, however, the war offered no such clear lessons. Instead, it brought demoralization and a questioning of all the old certainties. Democracies had collapsed, empires had crumbled, and aristocracies such as Sparta had proven themselves incapable of rising to the challenges they now confronted. Even the gods seemed to be in disarray. These were the circumstances in which the great Athenian philosopher Socrates (469–399 B.C.E.) attempted to refound ethical and political life on new and more certain foundations. To understand his accomplishments, however, we must trace briefly the history of philosophical speculation in the half century before his birth.

The competitive ethos that characterized the Greek poleis proved to be their tragic flaw.

THE PYTHAGOREANS AND THE SOPHISTS

After the Persian conquest of Asia Minor, many of the Milesian philosophers fled to Sicily and southern Italy. Philosophical speculation thus continued in the Greek "far west," but it was now tinged with a pessimism and religious coloration that reflected Greek distress over the loss of freedom. Typifying this reaction was Pythagoras, a thinker who migrated around 530 B.C.E. from the island of Samos to southern Italy, where he founded a sect—half philosophical, half mystical—in the city of Croton. Pythagoras and his followers regarded the speculative life as the highest good, but they believed that in order to pursue it, one must be purified of desires of the flesh. They believed that the

essence of things was not matter but number, and so they concentrated on the study of mathematics and musical theory, discovering harmonies and dividing numbers into categories such as odd and even. Pythagoreans also proved an old Babylonian assumption, preserved for us as the "Pythagorean theorem"—that the square of the hypotenuse of any right-angled triangle is equal to the sum of the squares of the other two sides. Thus, even though the Pythagoreans turned away from the material world, they still exhibited the characteristic Greek quest for regularity and predictability in that world.

Victory in the Persian War enabled the Greeks to overcome the failure of nerve exemplified by the Pythagoreans. Above all in Athens, the increasing power of the individual citizen motivated inquiry into how the individual might best act in the here and now. Around 450 B.C.E., to fulfill the demand to cultivate such worldly wisdom, teachers emerged who were called "Sophists," a term simply meaning "those who are wise." Unlike the Milesians or the Pythagoreans, the Sophists were professional teachers, the first in the history of the West who made a living from selling their knowledge. Because they were later opposed by Socrates and Plato, the term "Sophist" became one of abuse, meaning someone who deviously employs false reasoning, and their entire movement acquired a poor reputation. But modern research has shown that the Sophists were often impressive thinkers and educators.

The Sophists were not a coherent philosophical school. But their work displayed certain common threads, as shown by that of Protagoras, active in Athens from about 445 to 420 B.C.E. and the most prototypic of the intellectually ambitious Sophists. His famous dictum, "man is the measure of all things," meant that goodness, truth, and justice are relative to the needs and interests of human beings. In religious matters Protagoras was agnostic, declaring that he did not know whether the gods existed or what they did, "for there are many hindrances to such knowledge—the obscurity of the subject and the brevity of life." Since he knew nothing of the gods, he concluded that there could be no absolute truths or eternal standards of right. If sense perception was the only source of knowledge, there could be only particular truths valid for the individual knower.

Such teachings struck many Athenians as corrosive of social cohesion. Sophists were courageous in calling

TWO VIEWS OF SOPHISM

SOCRATES AS A SOPHIST

The image of Socrates held by most people is of the sage thinker who challenged the prevailing prejudices of his day and opposed the Sophists. During his own time, however, he was not so universally admired. In his comedy The Clouds, *Aristophanes' protagonist Strepsiades—ruined by the wastefulness of his son—goes to Socrates and his "Thought Shop" so that Socrates can make him and his son Pheidippides orators capable of winning lawsuits and thus enriching himself. Aristophanes implies throughout that Socrates is essentially just another Sophist, a man who teaches word games and logic tricks for hire.*

STREPSIADES: See that he [Pheidippides] learns your two Arguments, whatever you call them—oh yes, Right and Wrong—the one that takes a bad case and defeats Right with it. If he can't manage both, then at least Wrong—that will do—but that he must have.

SOCRATES: Well, I'll go and send the Arguments here in person, and they'll teach him themselves.

STREPSIADES: Don't forget, he's got to be able to argue against any kind of justified claim at all.

RIGHT: This way, Let the audience see you. . . .

WRONG: Sure, go wherever you like. The more of an audience we have, the more soundly I'll trounce you.

RIGHT: What sort of trick will you use?

WRONG: Oh, just a few new ideas.

RIGHT: Yes, they're in fashion now, aren't they, [to the audience] thanks to you idiots. . . . [to Pheiddipides] You don't want to be the sort of chap who's always in the agora telling stories about other people's sex lives, or in the courts arguing about some petty, filthy, little dispute. . . .

WRONG: People here at the Thought Shop call me Wrong, because I was the one who invented ways of proving anything wrong, laws, prosecutors, anything. Isn't that worth millions—to have a really bad case and yet win? . . . Suppose you fall in love with a married woman—have a bit of fun—and get caught in the act. As you are now, without a tongue in your head, you're done for. But if you come and learn from me, then you can do whatever you like and get away with it . . . and supposing you do get caught with someone's wife, you can say to him. . . . "What have I done wrong? Look at Zeus; wasn't he always a slave of his sexual passions? And do you expect a mere mortal like me to do any better than a god?" . . .

STREPSIADES [to Socrates]: I wonder if you'd accept a token of my appreciation? But my son, has he learned that Argument we were listening to a moment ago?

SOCRATES: Yes, he has.

STREPSIADES: Holy Fraud, how wonderful!

SOCRATES: Yes, you'll now be able to win any case at all.

STREPSIADES: Even if the witnesses were actually there when I was borrowing the money?

SOCRATES: Even if there were a thousand of them.

Aristophanes, *The Clouds,* based on the translation by Alan H. Sommerstein. (New York: Penguin, 1973), pp. 148–150, 154, 159–160.

Sophistry in Action: The Melian Dialogue

During the truce authored by the Athenian statesman Nicias in 421 B.C.E., both Athens and Sparta continued to pursue a "dirty war," living by the letter of their agreement but not its spirit, while preparing for the inevitable reopening of the conflict. The Aegean island of Melos—originally a Spartan colony—had so far maintained a policy of neutrality between Athens and Sparta. In 416, however, the Athenians insisted on their submission, and the Athenian envoys justified their position with a chillingly logical argument that "might makes right."

ATHENIANS: For ourselves, we will not trouble you with specious pretenses—either of how we have a right to our empire because we overthrew the Mede, or are now attacking you because of wrong that you have done us—and make a long speech which would not be believed; and in return we hope that you, instead of thinking to influence us by saying that you did not join the Spartans, although their colonists, or that you have done us no wrong, will aim at what is feasible, holding in view the real sentiments of us both; since you know as well as we do that right, as the world goes, is only in question between equals in power, while the strong do what they can and the weak suffer what they must. . . . We would desire to exercise empire over you without trouble, and see you preserved for the good of us both.

MELIANS: And how, pray, could it turn out as good for us to serve as for you to rule?

ATHENIANS: Because you would have the advantage of submitting before suffering the worst, and we should gain by not destroying you.

MELIANS: So you would not consent to our being neutral, friends instead of enemies, but allies of neither side?

ATHENIANS: No; for your hostility cannot so much hurt us as your friendship will be an argument to our subjects of our weakness, and your enmity of our power.

MELIANS: Is that your subjects' idea of equity, to put those who have nothing to do with you in the same category with peoples that are most of them your own colonists, and some conquered rebels?

ATHENIANS: As far as right goes they think one has as much of it as the other, and that if they maintain their independence it is because they are strong, and that if we do not molest them it is because we are afraid; so that besides extending our empire we should gain in security by your subjection. . . .

MELIANS: What is this but to make greater the enemies that you have already, and to force others to become so who would otherwise have never thought of it? . . . we know that the fortune of war is sometimes more impartial than the disproportion of numbers might lead one to suppose; to submit is to give ourselves over to despair, while action still preserves for us a hope that we may stand. . . .

ATHENIANS: Hope . . . may be indulged in by those who have abundant resources, if not without loss, at all events without ruin; but its nature is to be extravagant, and those who go so far as to stake their all upon the venture see it in its true colors only when they are ruined. . . . Let not this be the case with you, who are weak and hang on a single turn of the scale; nor be like the vulgar, who, when abandoning such security as human means may still afford, when visible hopes fail them in extremity, turn to the invisible, to prophecies and oracles, and other such inventions that delude men with hopes to their destruction. . . . When we come to your notion about the Spartans, which leads you to believe that shame will make them help you, here we bless your simplicity but do not envy your folly. . . . You do not adopt the view that expediency goes with security, while justice and honor cannot be followed without danger; and danger the Spartans generally court as little as possible. . . . Is it likely that while we are masters of the sea they will cross over to an island?

MELIANS: Should the Spartans miscarry in this, they would fall upon your land, and upon those left of your allies . . . and instead of places which are not yours, you will have to fight for your own country and your own confederacy.

ATHENIANS: Some diversion of the kind you speak of you may one day experience, only to learn, as others have done, that the Athenians never once yet withdrew from a siege for fear of any. . . . Think over the matter, therefore, and reflect once and again that it is for your country that you are consulting, and that upon this one deliberation depends its prosperity or ruin.

Thucydides, Book 5. *The Landmark Thucydides*, edited by Robert Strassler. (New York: Landmark Press, 1995), pp. 352–356.

Socrates. According to Plato, Socrates looked like a goat-man but spoke like a god.

THE LIFE AND THOUGHT OF SOCRATES

Socrates drew on sufficient income so that he never had to teach for a living. Having twice fought in the Athenian infantry, he was an ardent patriot who believed Athens was being corrupted by the shameful doctrines of the Sophists. Yet far from being an unthinking cherisher of slogans, he wished to submit every slogan to rigorous questioning in order to erect the life of the Athenian state on the firm basis of ethical certainties. It is bitterly ironic that such a dedicated idealist should have been put to death by his own countrymen. Shortly after the end of the Peloponnesian War, in 399 B.C.E., while Athens was recovering from the shock of defeat and violent internal upheavals, a democratic faction determined that Socrates was a threat to the state. A jury court agreed, condemning him to death on a charge of impiety and "corrupting the youth." Although his friends made arrangements for him to flee, Socrates decided to accept the popular judgment and abide by the laws of his polis. He died by calmly taking a cup of poison.

Because Socrates wrote nothing himself, it is difficult to determine exactly what he taught. Contemporary reports, however, especially by his student Plato, make a few points clear. First, Socrates wished to subject all inherited assumptions to reexamination. In his view the complacent people who thought they knew everything really knew nothing. Styling himself a "gadfly," he continually engaged such people in conversation and managed to show them by "Socratic" questioning that all their supposed certainties were nothing more than unthinking prejudices resting on false assumptions. According to Plato, an oracle once said that Socrates was the wisest person in the world and Socrates agreed: everyone else thought he knew something, but he was wiser because he knew he knew nothing. Second, he wished to base his philosophical speculations on sound definitions of words. Third, he wished to advance to a new system of truth by examining ethics rather than by studying the physical world. He shunned discussions of why things exist, why they grow, and why they perish, urging people instead to reflect on principles of conduct both for their own sake and for that of society. One should think of the meaning of one's life and actions at all times, for according to one of his most memorable

assumptions into doubt and encouraging Athenians to examine each new situation on its own terms and merits; everyday life became for the first time the subject of systematic discussion. Yet the relativism of Sophists such as Protagoras could easily degenerate into the doctrine that the wise man is the one who knows best how to manipulate others and gratify his own desires, and so could be used to rationalize monstrous acts of brutality. To some critics, such ideas were antidemocratic; to others, they smacked of atheism and anarchy. If there was no final truth, and if goodness and justice were merely relative to the whims of the individual, then religion, morality, the state, and society itself could not be maintained. This conviction led to the growth of a new philosophical movement grounded on the theory that truth is real and that absolute standards do exist. The initiator of this new trend was Socrates.

> Sophists were courageous in calling assumptions into doubt and encouraging Athenians to examine each new situation on its own terms and merits; everyday life became for the first time the subject of systematic discussion.

sayings, "the unexamined life is not worth living."

So far, Socrates might seem rather like a Sophist; indeed, he felt compelled at his trial to insist that he was not. Together with the Sophists, he was a "philosopher of the marketplace" who held tradition and cliché up to doubt, and like them he treated daily affairs in order to help people improve their lives. The overwhelming difference between Socrates and the Sophists lay in Socrates' belief in certainties—even if he avoided saying what they were—and in the standard of absolute good rather than expediency he applied to all aspects of life. To reestablish the polis, however, it would be necessary to go further and construct a system that offered a positive framework of truth and reality. This was the task that would be attempted in the next century

Socrates Gaining Wisdom from the Wise Woman Diotima. In Plato's *Symposium* Socrates learns the philosophical meaning of love from Diotima, an ethereal female being, wiser than he. In this sculptural representation of the scene the winged figure between Diotima and Socrates is probably a personification of love itself.

by Socrates' most brilliant student, Plato, in the wake of the disasters of the Peleponnesian War. In so doing, he would lay the groundwork for all Western philosophical thinking up to the present day.

CONCLUSION

Ever since the Renaissance, Western Europeans have liked to think of themselves as the heirs of the classical Greeks, and to imagine the Greeks as mirror images of themselves. Such uncritical admiration is misleading, both about the Greeks and ourselves. Despite the religious skepticism of a few intellectuals, the Greeks were neither secularists nor rationalists. Although they invented the concept of democracy, only a small percentage even of the male population of Athens was ever permitted to play a role in political affairs. The Spartans kept the mass of their population in serflike subjection, and the Athenians took slavery for granted, subjecting slaves who toiled in the mines to the most brutal treatment. Women throughout the

Greek world were exploited by what today would be called a "patriarchy"—a repressive system managed by fathers and husbands. Greek statecraft was characterized by imperialism and aggressive war. The Greeks made no great advances in economic enterprise, and they scorned commerce. Finally, not even the Athenians could be described as tolerant. Socrates was not the only man put to death merely for expressing his opinions.

And yet the profound significance of the Greek experiment for the history of the civilizations of the West is undeniable. This significance can be seen with particular clarity if we compare Greek cultural traits with those of Mesopotamia and ancient Egypt. Mesopotamian and Egyptian civilizations were dominated by autocracy, supernaturalism, and the subjection of the individual to the group. The typical political regime of the ancient Near Eastern world was that of an absolute monarch supported by a powerful priesthood. Culture served mainly as an instrument to enhance the prestige of rulers and priests, and economic life tended to be controlled by powerfully organized governmental and religious bodies.

In contrast, the civilization of Greece, notably in its Athenian form, was founded upon ideals of freedom, competition, individual achievement, and human glory. The Greek word for freedom—*eleutheria*—cannot be translated into any ancient Near Eastern language, not even Hebrew. The culture of the Greeks was the first in the West to be based on the primacy of the human intellect; there was no subject they feared to investigate. As Herodotus has a Greek (in this case a Spartan) say to a Persian, "You understand how to be a slave, but you know nothing of freedom. . . . If you had but tasted it you would counsel us to fight for it not only with spears but with axes."

Another way of appreciating the enduring importance of Greek civilization to the Western world is to recall some of the words that come to us from this civilization: politics, democracy, philosophy, metaphysics, history, tragedy. These are all ways of thinking and acting that have helped enrich human life immeasurably and that had hardly been known before the Greeks invented them. To a startling degree the Western concept of "humanity" itself—the exalted role within nature of the human race in general and the individual human in particular—comes to us from the Greeks. For the Greeks, the aim of existence was the fullest development of one's human potential: the work of becoming a person, called in Greek *paideia*, meant that every free man was supposed to be the sculptor of his or her own statue. When the Romans took up this ideal from the Greeks, they called it *humanitas*, from which we derive the English word "humanity." The Romans admitted their indebtedness when they remarked that "Greece was where humanity was invented." It is hard to doubt that they were right.

SELECTED READINGS

Penguin Classics and the Loeb Classical Library both offer reliable translations of Greek literary, philosophical, and historical texts.

Andrewes, Antony. *The Greek Tyrants*. London, 1974. Originally published in 1956, this work remains the standard treatment of its subject.

Boardman, John, Jaspar Griffin, and Oswyn Murray, eds. *Greece and the Hellenistic World*. Oxford, 1988. A reprint of the Greek and Hellenistic chapters from *The Oxford History of the Classical World*, originally published in 1986. Excellent, stimulating surveys, accessible to a general audience but provocative to specialists.

Brunschwig, Jacques, and Geoffrey E. R. Lloyd. *Greek Thought: A Guide to Classical Knowledge*. Trans. Catherine Porter. Cambridge, Mass., 2000. An outstanding, up-to-date work of reference.

Buckley, Terry, ed. *Aspects of Greek History, 750–323 B.C.: A Source-Based Approach*. London, 1999. An outstanding new collection of source materials.

Burkert, Walter. *Greek Religion*. Cambridge, Mass., 1985. Detailed and challenging, but fundamental for understanding the subject.

Cartledge, Paul A. *Sparta and Laconia: A Regional History, 1300–362 B.C.* London, 1979. The standard survey of Spartan history by the leading English-speaking authority.

Coldstream, J. N. *Geometric Greece*. New York, 1977. A thoroughgoing and illuminating discussion of Greek material culture in the late Dark Age.

Connor, W. Robert. *The New Politicians of Fifth-Century Athens*. Indianapolis, 1992. A ground-breaking discussion of how a new breed of politicians redefined Athenian democracy.

Donlan, Walter. *The Aristocratic Ideal and Selected Papers*. Wauconda, Ill., 1999. A reprint of Donlan's 1980 work, supplemented with a number of his scholarly articles, all emphasizing the central role played by elite status, power, and identity in Archaic Greece.

Dover, Kenneth J. *Greek Homosexuality*. Cambridge, Mass., 1978. The standard account of an important subject.

Fantham, Elaine, Helene Foley, Natalie Kampen, Sarah B. Pomeroy, and H. A. Shapiro. *Women in the Classical World: Image and Text*. Oxford, 1994. Wide-ranging analysis drawing on both visual and written sources, covering both the Greek and the Roman periods.

Finley, Moses I. *The World of Odysseus*. New York, 1979. A revised edition of the author's classic 1954 study, which forever changed the study of Dark Age Greece by demonstrating the historical nature of Homeric society.

Fornara, Charles W., and Loren J. Samons II. *Athens from Cleisthenes to Pericles*. Berkeley, 1991. An excellent narrative history of Athenian politics during the first half of the fifth century B.C.E.

Freeman, Charles. *The Greek Achievement: The Foundation of the Western World*. New York, 1999. An admiring survey written for a general audience.

Garlan, Yvon. *Slavery in Ancient Greece*. Ithaca, N.Y., 1988. Now the standard account.

Hanson, Victor Davis. *The Other Greeks: The Family Farm and the Agrarian Roots of Western Civilization*. New York, 1995. Occasionally polemical and idiosyncratic, but convincing in its emphasis on small-holding farmers as the backbone of Greek urban society.

Hodkinson, Stephen. *Property and Wealth in Classical Sparta*. London, 2001. A revisionist account that shows the Spartan economy to be much more like the economies of other Greek poleis than is often assumed.

Horden, Peregrine and Nicholas Purcell. *The Corrupting Sea: A Study of Mediterranean History*. Oxford, 2000. An immense and learned survey of the ecological history of the Mediterranean world from prehistory to the end of the Middle Ages.

Jones, Nicholas F. *Ancient Greece: State and Society*. Upper Saddle River, N.J., 1997. A concise survey from the Minoans up to the end of the classical period that emphasizes the connections between the social order and politics.

Levi, Peter. *Atlas of the Greek World*. New York, 1984. Excellent maps and illustrations supplement an outstanding text.

Morris, Ian, and Barry Powell, eds. *A New Companion to Homer*. Leiden, 1997. A collection of thirty specialist but accessible scholarly articles, encompassing the most recent research on Homer and Dark Age Greece.

Pomeroy, Sarah B., Stanley M. Burstein, Walter Donlan, and Jennifer Tolbert Roberts. *Ancient Greece: A Political, Social, and Cultural History*. Oxford, 1999. An outstanding new textbook: clear, lively, and up to date, with good bibliographies.

Price, Simon. *Religions of the Ancient Greeks*. Cambridge, 1999. Concise and authoritative, this survey extends from the archaic period up to the fifth century C.E.

Rowlandson, Jane, R. S. Bagnall, Alan Bowman, and Willy Clarysse, eds. *Women and Society in Greek and Roman Egypt: A Sourcebook*. Cambridge, 1999. A wide-ranging collection of sources from an extraordinarily well-documented area of the ancient world.

Snodgrass, Anthony. *The Dark Age of Greece: An Archaeological Survey of the Eleventh to the Eighth Centuries [B.C.E.]*. Edinburgh, 1971. Still a valuable starting point.

——. *Archaic Greece: The Age of Experiment*. Berkeley, 1980. A seminal work that thoroughly revised earlier views of the period.

Strassler, Robert B., ed. *The Landmark Thucydides*. New York, 1996. A reprinting of the classic Richard Crawley translation, with maps, commentary, notes, and appendices by leading scholars.

Tandy, David W. *Warriors into Traders: The Power of the Market in Early Greece*. Berkeley, 1997. A revisionist examination of the impact of economic change on the cultural and political outlook of Greeks in the eighth and seventh centuries B.C.E.

Thomas, Carol G. and Craig Conant. *Citadel to City-State: The Transformation of Greece, 1200–700 B.C.E.* Bloomington, 1999. A lucid and accessible study that examines developments at a number of representative Dark Age sites.

CHAPTER FIVE

THE EXPANSION OF GREECE

THE SUPREME TRAGEDY OF THE GREEKS was their failure to solve the problem of internecine political conflict. The fifth century in Greece had ended with a debilitating and destructive war of attrition between Athens and Sparta. The fourth century continued along much the same path, as the major poleis—Sparta, then Thebes, then Athens again—jockeyed for dominance within the Greek world. But the independent temper of Greek political life could not suffer such dominance for long; and so as each great polis appeared on the brink of realizing its goals, a coalition of age-old enemies would form to defeat it. Despite mounting calls for the Greeks to set aside their local differences and unite in a common cause, they could not escape their heritage of particularism.

Alongside the political difficulties, there were continuing social and economic problems. These stemmed from ideologically driven civil wars within the poleis as well as from the endemic warfare between them. Faith in the old ideals of equality decayed as a vast gulf opened up between the rich and the poor. Increasingly, the wealthy withdrew from politics altogether, while the number of free citizens declined as poverty-stricken freemen and freewomen descended into slavery. The result was despair and cynicism.

The age did not lack for creative energy. Philosophy, science, and literature blossomed in the fourth century, as men of talent shunned the vagaries of public life and devoted themselves instead to the life of the mind. As the polis system decayed, serious thinkers turned their attention to what the polis was, how and why it functioned, and how it might be improved. But even the greatest of these thinkers remained enclosed within the parochial world of the polis.

The unhappy equilibrium of the Greek world was shattered in the last half of the fourth century by the sudden emergence of the kingdom of Macedonia. The extraordinary conquests of Philip of Macedon unified Greece. Those of his son Alexander the Great extended Greek culture by force of arms from Egypt to Persia

FOCUS QUESTIONS

• What conditions led to the growing number of mercenaries in the fourth century B.C.E.?

• In his *Republic,* what prescriptions does Plato offer for the achievement of an ideal state?

• How did Philip II of Macedon strengthen his kingdom?

• What characteristics defined the three major Hellenistic kingdoms?

• Why was prosperity not more widespread in the Hellenistic economy?

• What was the relationship between Epicureanism and Stoicism?

• Why did Hellenistic architecture become grander?

• Why did science and medicine flourish in this period?

to the frontiers of India. Alexander's empire did not last. But the cosmopolitan, Greeklike (hence, *Hellenistic*, as opposed to *Hellenic*) culture to which it gave rise became the most powerful and pervasive cultural influence the Near Eastern world would know until the rise of Islam almost a thousand years later.

FAILURES OF THE FOURTH-CENTURY POLIS

What conditions led to the growing number of mercenaries in the fourth century B.C.E.?

There is little in the early fourth century B.C.E. to suggest that the greatest age of Greek cultural influence still lay ahead. The Peloponnesian War had left Sparta as the preeminent power in the Greek world, but the Spartans showed little talent for the position their unexpected victory had thrust upon them. At home, Spartan politicians remained deeply divided over the wisdom of committing Spartan force beyond their frontiers; while abroad, the Spartans showed even less restraint than had the Athenians in strong-arming their subject-allies. By 394, a significant portion of Greece had aligned itself against Sparta in the so-called Corinthian War (394–387 B.C.E.). The Spartans, for their part, could bring matters to a resolution only by forcing a peace on their fellow Greeks brokered from the outside—essentially composed and guaranteed by the Persians who had encouraged the conflict in the first place. This pattern was repeated time and again over the next fifty years, during which the advantage shifted steadily toward Persia.

THE STRUGGLE FOR HEGEMONY

The Spartans learned little from the resistance of their allies, hardly noticing that in the Corinthian War Athens had allied herself with one of Sparta's oldest allies (Corinth) and with one of her own ancient enemies (Thebes). After the Corinthian War, the Spartans did, however, occupy Thebes, placing a garrison there for four years. This was a grave and quite unjustified affront to the freedom of another great polis. After the

Thebans regained their autonomy, they elected as their leader Epaminondas, a fierce patriot and a military genius. For decades, Greeks had been experimenting with the basic form of the hoplite phalanx, adding light skirmishers and archers to enhance its effectiveness. Epaminondas now went further. In imitation of the Spartan system, he formed an elite hoplite unit known as the "Theban Sacred Band," made up of one hundred fifty homosexual couples. Epaminondas also developed lighter-armed troops. By the early 370s he was ready for a trial of strength with the Spartans.

The Theban and Spartan armies met at Leuctra in the Theban territory of Boeotia in 371. Epaminondas eschewed convention, placing his very best troops (the Sacred Band) not on the right-hand side of his formation, but on the left. He stacked the left-hand side of his phalanx fifty rows deep, a surprise he disguised with a flurry of arrow and javelin attacks. When the two sides met, the weight of the Theban left smashed the Spartan right, and with its best troops overrun, the Spartan phalanx collapsed. A Spartan king was left dead on the field, and Epaminondas followed his victory by marching through Messenia and freeing the helots. Spartan power—and in a sense Spartan society—was at an end. Overnight, Epaminondas had reduced Sparta to a merely local force.

As Theban power grew, so did the suspicions of others. Although in 371 Athens had supported Thebes, when the Thebans and Spartans squared off again in 362 at Mantinea in the northern Peloponnesus, the Athenians allied themselves with the Spartans. Although the Theban army carried the day, Epaminondas fell in battle, and the Theban hegemony died with him. Athens attempted to fill the vacuum by establishing a naval confederacy, organized more equitably than the Delian League. But the Athenians quickly reverted to abusing their allies, and the naval confederacy dissolved in rebellions. Greece thus remained a constellation of petty warring states, all greatly weakened by their struggles with each other over the course of a century.

Within the poleis themselves there was also great turmoil. Although Athens was spared the political revolutions many other cities had suffered (mostly because the Thirty Tyrants had discredited the cause of "oligarchy" there), strife between democrats and oligarchs continued throughout the Greek world. Argos suffered through civil war and brutal reprisals, as did many of the states of the Aegean islands and Thessaly,

> The Spartans learned little from the resistance of their allies.

IN HIS *REPUBLIC*, WHAT DOES PLATO PRESCRIBE FOR THE ACHIEVEMENT OF AN IDEAL STATE?

THE CULTURAL AND INTELLECTUAL RESPONSE   157

in northern Greece. An abortive coup attempt was even uncovered at Sparta, plotted by a disenfranchised Spartiate who had hoped to rally the disaffected elements of Spartan society.

SOCIAL AND ECONOMIC CRISES

The incessant warfare, combined with internal political struggles, profoundly affected society and economy throughout the Greek world. Even wealthy cities like Athens and Sparta had exhausted themselves through their war efforts. Many personal fortunes had been lost, and many ordinary people had been driven from their homes or reduced to slavery. Country towns had been ravaged, some repeatedly, as had farmlands throughout Greece. The destruction of orchards and vineyards was particularly devastating, because of the long time it takes to nourish olive trees and grape vines to a productive state; but even arable land was now less productive than it had been earlier. As a result, standards of living declined significantly during the fourth century. Although prices rose in general around 50 percent (and some staples tripled and quadrupled in cost), wages remained more or less the same. Taxes increased, and in Athens the wealthy were required to employ their personal wealth to underwrite the construction of public theaters and buildings, the maintenance of warships, and the presentation of festivals. Even so, state treasuries were never again as flush as they had been in the fifth century, and the kind of ambitious public spending undertaken by the tyrants or Pericles was unknown in the fourth-century polis.

Unemployment was widespread, and so many Greek men turned to the one profession where work was almost always available—mercenary service. The Greek states of Sicily and Italy hired mercenaries from the mainland, as did Sparta to supplement her own campaigns in Asia Minor. A pretender to the Persian throne even hired a mostly Greek mercenary army in an attempt to overthrow his older brother, the reigning king. These Greeks fought their way into the heart of the Persian empire, and when the pretender fell in battle, the ten thousand Greek mercenaries fought their way back out. It was a stunning demonstration of what even a smallish Greek army might accomplish on Persian soil. Long-term mercenary service abroad was disruptive to the household-based culture of many Greek poleis, and when mercenaries could not find work abroad, they were likely to terrorize the local Greek countryside. Such depredations only added to the disastrous cycle of destruction, inflation, and overpopulation caused by land failure.

THE CULTURAL AND INTELLECTUAL RESPONSE

In his *Republic,* what does Plato prescribe for the achievement of an ideal state?

The breakdown of polis society during the fourth century had a profound impact on philosophy, the arts, and political thought. These developments laid the groundwork for the even more stunningly creative departures of the Hellenistic era. In the past, scholars have sometimes described these fourth-century cultural developments as if they represented a decline from the great artistic and intellectual achievements of the fifth century B.C.E. But such a sweeping verdict on fourth-century B.C.E. culture is unjustified. It diminishes not only the continuities between fifth- and fourth-century Greek culture, but also the originality and creativity of these new, fourth-century developments.

ART AND LITERATURE

Sculptors, for example, were already attempting to achieve a heightened sense of realism, especially in portraiture, when the fourth century B.C.E. began. Realism had been a hallmark of fifth-century art, but in the fourth century artists tried increasingly to render objects as they actually looked, rather than portraying them in an idealized, dignified form. Artists also paid

CHRONOLOGY

DECLINE OF THE GREEK POLIS

Sparta becomes leading Greek polis	404 B.C.E.
Prices rise by 50 percent throughout Greece	400–350 B.C.E.
Corinthian War	394–387 B.C.E.
Epaminondas defeats Spartans at Leuctra	371 B.C.E.

Left: **Hellenistic Aphrodite.** This figure, dating from the fourth century B.C.E., displays the Hellenistic fascination with ungainly, "unnatural" postures.
Right: **French Bather.** This statuette done by Edgar Degas around 1890 shows some evident continuities between Hellenistic and modern art.

more attention to life and movement, particularly in the flow and fold of the drapery that clothed human figures. All these sculptural trends would continue and intensify in the breathtaking and evocative works of the Hellenistic period.

Drama changed even more dramatically during the fourth century than did sculpture, although here the verdict of "decline" may have more justification. No fourth-century authors emerged to match the great tragedians of the Athenian golden age. Even fourth-century audiences seem to have preferred the fifth-century tragedies of Sophocles, Aeschylus, and Euripedes to the works of their own fourth-century contemporaries. Nor did the comic genius of Aristophanes have any true fourth-century successors. Even in his own lifetime, however, Aristophanes' biting, satirical style was beginning to give way to a milder, less provocative drama that bears some resemblance to modern television comedies. It was this new style that laid the groundwork for the "New Comedy" of the fourth and third centuries B.C.E.

Perhaps the most striking development in fourth-century drama is the flight from social and political commentary. The new comedies of the fourth century offer none of the scathing indictments of society in general and of prominent individuals in particular that Aristophanes had pioneered. Fourth-century audiences looked to drama and literature for diversion and escape; they no longer cared for brutal critiques of their society. Comedic humor was now based on mistaken identities, tangled familial relationships, comic misunderstandings, and breaches of etiquette. Hellenistic novels (a new literary genre that emerges by the end of the fourth century) are broadly similar in tone to the new comedies. Lovers face extraordinary obstacles, but their affairs almost always end happily, with the lovers themselves reunited after perilous adventures and a long separation.

The most famous comic poet of the age was Menander (342 B.C.E.?–292 B.C.E.), most of whose work survives only in fragments. To some modern critics, his comedies can seem contrived and artificial. To his contemporaries, however, and also to the Romans (who based their own comedic tradition on the works of

IN HIS *REPUBLIC*, WHAT DOES PLATO PRESCRIBE FOR THE ACHIEVEMENT OF AN IDEAL STATE?

THE CULTURAL AND INTELLECTUAL RESPONSE   159

Menander and his contemporaries), these frothy, light-hearted comedies of daily life had great appeal.

PHILOSOPHY AND POLITICAL THOUGHT IN THE AGE OF PLATO AND ARISTOTLE

The intellectual shift begun by Socrates was carried on brilliantly by his most talented student, Plato. Born in Athens to an aristocratic family around 429 B.C.E., Plato joined Socrates' circle as a young man and soon saw his mentor condemned to death. This experience made such an indelible impression on Plato that from then until his own death around 349 B.C.E. he shunned direct political involvement, seeking instead to vindicate Socrates by constructing a philosophical system based on Socratic precepts. Plato taught this system in Athens in an informal school (no buildings, tuition, or set curriculum) called the Academy, and also by writing a series of *dialogues* (treatises expressed in

Plato was influenced by the two worlds in which he lived.

dramatic form) in which Socrates was the main speaker. The Platonic dialogues, among which some of the most important are the *Phaedo*, the *Symposium*, and the *Republic*, are enduring works of literature as well as the earliest surviving complete works of philosophy.

Plato was influenced by the two worlds in which he lived. As a young man, he had watched his teacher engage the relativism of the Sophists, and in his adult life he lived in a world of few apparent absolute truths and a remarkable amount of rapid and disturbing change. Plato understood that in order to combat skepticism and refute the Sophists he needed to provide a secure foundation for ethics. This he did by means of his doctrine of Ideas. He conceded that relativity and change are characteristics of the world we perceive with our senses, but he denied that this world is the entire universe. A higher, spiritual realm exists, composed of eternal forms or Ideas that only the mind can grasp. The Ideas are not mere abstractions but have a real existence. Each is the pattern of some class of objects, or relationships between objects, on earth. Thus there are Ideas of chair, tree, shape, color, proportion, beauty, and justice. Highest is the Idea of the Good, the cause and guiding principle of the universe. The things we perceive through our senses are merely imperfect copies of the supreme realities, the Ideas, and relate to them as shadows relate to material objects. By understanding and contemplating the Good, one might achieve the ultimate goal of fulfillment through virtue.

Understanding that a virtuous life would be difficult to attain in a society full of turbulence, Plato addressed himself to politics in his most famous dialogue, the *Republic*, the first systematic treatment of political philosophy ever written. Because Plato sought social harmony and order rather than liberty or equality, he argued for an elitist state in which most of the people—the farmers, artisans, and traders—would be governed by intellectually superior "guardians." The guardian class itself would be divided. All guardians would serve first as soldiers, living together without private property, but then those found to be the wisest would receive more education and ultimately become Plato's famous "philosopher-kings." In Plato's view neither wealth nor hereditary title equipped one properly to rule but only the greatest intelligence, enhanced by the best possible education. Once philosophers were in power they would always choose the wisest to succeed them and see to it that everyone in the state was subordinated to the Idea of the Good. Later commentators have usually

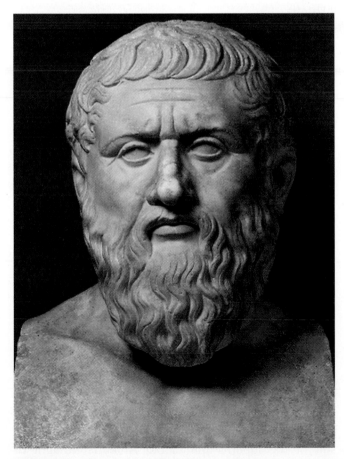

Plato.

found this ideal of rule by the wisest to be seductive, but they ask of Plato, "Who will guard the guardians?" Plato's system presumed that properly educated rulers would never be corrupted by power or wealth—a proposition that has yet to be sustained in practice.

ARISTOTELIAN THOUGHT

Such practical considerations were typical of the thought of Plato's own greatest student, Aristotle (384–322 B.C.E.). Aristotle was the son of a physician and learned from his father the importance of carefully observing natural phenomena. He accepted Plato's assumption that there are some things only the mind can grasp, but his own philosophical system was based on his confidence that the human mind could understand the universe through the rational ordering of sense experience. In contrast to Plato, who taught that everything we see and touch is but an untrustworthy reflection of some intangible truth, Aristotle believed in the objective reality of material objects and taught that systematic investigation of tangible things, combined with rational inquiry into how they function, could yield full comprehension of the natural order and of human beings' place within it.

Aristotle surveyed a wide variety of subjects in numerous separate but interrelated treatises on logic, metaphysics, ethics, poetics, and politics. He was the earliest formal logician known to human history, and probably the greatest. He established rules for the syllogism, a form of reasoning in which certain premises inevitably lead to a valid conclusion, and he established precise categories underpinning all philosophical and scientific analysis, such as substance, quantity, relation, and place. Aristotle's central belief was that all things in the universe consist of the imprint of form on matter. This was a compromise between Platonism, which tended to ignore matter, and the purest materialism, which saw no patterns in the universe other than the accidents of matter impinging on matter. For Aristotle, forms are the purposeful forces that shape the world of matter; thus the presence of the form of humanity molds and directs the human embryo until it ultimately becomes a human being. Since everything has a purposeful form, the universe for Aristotle is teleological—that is, every item and every class of items is inherently aiming toward its own particular end. Aristotle's universe is therefore in a constant state of motion, as everything within it moves toward its ultimate perfected form (known in Greek as its *telos*).

Aristotle's moral philosophy was expressed most

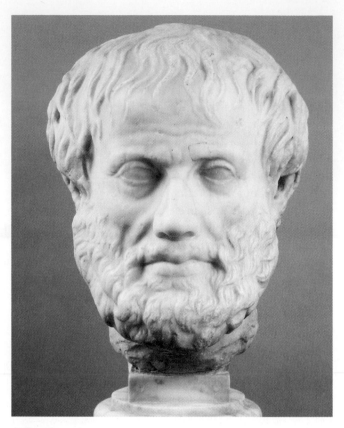

Aristotle.

fully in his *Nicomachean Ethics*, although important aspects of his ideas are also contained in his *Politics*. Aristotle taught that the highest good consists in the harmonious functioning of the individual human mind and body. Humans differ from the animals by virtue of their rational capacities, and so they find happiness by exercising these appropriately. For most people this will mean exercising reason in practical affairs. Good conduct is virtuous conduct, and virtue resides in aiming for the golden mean: courage rather than rashness or cowardice, temperance rather than excessive indulgence or ascetic denial. Better even than the practical life, however, is the contemplative life, for such a life allows those few men equipped by nature for it to exercise their rational capacities to the utmost. Aristotle believed therefore that philosophers were the happiest of men, but he understood that even they could not engage in contemplation without interruption. As a practical person, moreover, he deemed it necessary for them to intersperse their speculative activities with practical life in the real world. Whereas Plato conceived of politics as a means to an end, the orderly pursuit of the supernatural Good, Aristotle thought of politics as an end in itself, the collective exercise of the good life. But Aristotle also took it for granted that some people—"barbarians"—were not fully human and so were meant by nature to be slaves. He also excluded women from the life of the polis, and so from a full measure of humanity, since they could not share in the life of the state in which human rational faculties enjoyed their fullest exercise. All male citizens, on the other hand, were meant to share in it, for, as Aristotle proposed, "man is by nature a political animal" (or, to be more faithful to the Greek, "a creature of the polis"). This view did not mean that the best form of government was democracy, however; Aristotle saw that as a "debased" form of government. What he preferred was the polity, in which monarchical, aristocratic, and democratic elements were combined by means of checks and balances. Such a government would allow free men to realize their rational potential, showing themselves to be located in nature's hierarchy above the animals and right below the gods.

For all of their brilliance and originality, Plato and Aristotle could not "think outside the box" of their fourth-century world. Their answer to society's ills was not to restructure Greek political life, but to improve the life of the individual polis. Indeed, both men indicated that poleis such as Athens or Thebes were already too large to function as an ideal polis. Both imagined the perfect society as one made up of a few thousand households, largely engaged in agriculture and living in a face-to-face, participatory society. Although Greek civilization had begun in such a world, the realities of fourth-century political life were very different. The fact that Plato and Aristotle considered the problem at all is testament to their recognition that something was "wrong" with the polis; but for both men, the answer was a reorganization of the existing polity, not something new in its place.

XENOPHON AND ISOCRATES

Another product of the Socratic intellectual tradition was Xenophon, a contemporary of Plato. Xenophon had served in the mercenary army that fought its way out of Persia, and also fought for the Spartan king Agesilaus in Asia Minor. Disillusioned with what his fellow Athenians had done to his teacher Socrates, Xenophon lived most of his life as a comfortable exile in Spartan territory. There, Xenophon composed histories (including the tale of the ten thousand Greeks who fought their way out of Persia), biographies, his memories of Socrates, and treatises on ideal kingship, the Spartan constitution, household management (the

Oikonomikos, the root of our word *economics*), and on the raising of hunting dogs. Like most Greeks, Xenophon assumed that good government was to be sought through exemplars and moral paragons. This led him to embellish or omit facts that did not contribute toward moral uplift. Still, he was aware that the world had changed for the worse, a point driven home to him as he watched Epaminondas cripple the state Xenophon so admired, Sparta. So contemptuous was he of the Theban leader that in his "continuation" of Thucydides' history, Xenophon refused to record Epaminondas' name.

The Athenian orator Isocrates (436–338 B.C.E.) was also well aware that something had gone horribly awry. Again, his solution was not an overhaul of the Greek polis or the creation of greater forms of political organization. What he proposed was a great invasion of Persia led by a man of vision and ability, someone who could unite the Greek world behind his cause. Isocrates cast about most of his life for such a man, favoring at one point Agesilaus of Sparta, at other times powerful tyrants from the western and northern parts of the Greek world. Toward the end of his life, he began to think the man for the job was a man whom most Athenians considered no Greek at all: Philip II, the king of Macedon. Isocrates issued an open letter to Philip, detailing the ills of the Greek world, and declaring that masterful action was needed to rescue Greece from its endless cycle of self-destruction.

THE RISE OF MACEDON AND THE CONQUESTS OF ALEXANDER

How did Philip II of Macedon strengthen his kingdom?

By the middle of the fourth century, the Greeks had become so embroiled in political and socioeconomic turmoil that they at first barely noticed the growing power of Macedon, a kingdom on the northern fringes of the Greek world. There was little reason for them to do so; until the fourth century, Macedon had been a weak kingdom, ruled by a royal house barely strong enough to control its own nobility, and beset by intrigue and murderous ambition from within. As recently as the 360s, Macedon had teetered on collapse, surrounded by barbarian neighbors who nearly overran the kingdom. Most Greeks viewed the Macedonians as barbarians, despite the efforts of a few Macedonian kings to add a bit of Hellenic culture to their court (one late fifth-century king had successfully invited Euripides and Sophocles to Macedon; Socrates had refused a similar request). Therefore, when a young and energetic Macedonian king named Philip II consolidated the southern Balkans under his rule, many Greek patriots saw it as a development no less troubling than the approach of the Persian "barbarians" in the fifth century.

THE REIGN OF PHILIP II
(359–336 B.C.E.)

Philip came to the throne of Macedon after his older brother died fighting a barbarian invasion, leaving as his heir a small boy. Philip had himself made regent for the boy, but soon dispensed with that fiction and took the throne himself. By 356, he certainly considered himself king. That same year a son was born to him; Philip named the child Alexander, and marked him out as his successor.

Once he assumed the kingship, Philip's first problem was to stabilize his northern borders. Through a combination of warfare and diplomacy, Philip subdued the tribes of the southern Balkans and incorporated their territory into Macedonia. Philip's success had much to do with his reorganization of the Macedonian army. As a young boy, Philip had been a hostage at the court of Epaminondas; the observant youth may have learned something from watching the Theban general. In any event, Philip turned the Macedonian phalanx from an ill-organized peasant army into a highly drilled, well-

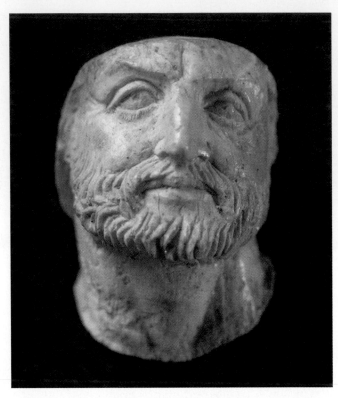

Philip II of Macedon. This tiny ivory head was discovered in the tomb of Philip of Macedon. The damaged right eye strongly suggests that it is a portrait of Philip himself, whose eye was damaged by a catapult bolt.

armed fighting machine. The mineral resources Philip captured early in his reign made him wealthy enough to establish what was in essence a professional army—just one of his gold mines produced as much in one year as the Delian League collected annually at its height. Philip also organized an elite cavalry squad—the Companions—who fought with and beside the king. These elite horsemen were drawn from the nobility; Philip hoped to inspire a greater esprit de corps

Macedonian Phalanx. Philip of Macedon's infantry—and Alexander the Great's thereafter—was armed with two-handed pikes and massed in squares sixteen rows deep and wide. Members of the phalanx were trained to wheel in step in any direction or to double their front by filing off in rows of eight.

TWO VIEWS OF PHILIP

Philip II of Macedon provoked strong reactions among the Athenians, through whose eyes we must evaluate him due to the nature of our sources. As these passages illustrate, we could interpret his actions very differently, depending on whether we see in him a savior of Greece or a would-be barbarian conqueror.

ISOCRATES, TO PHILIP

As I kept going over these questions [of war and peace] in my own thoughts, I found that . . . the greatest states of Hellas should resolve to put an end to their mutual quarrels and carry the war beyond our borders into Asia. . . . I am going to advise you to champion the cause of concord among the Hellenes and of a campaign against the barbarian. . . . I affirm that, without neglecting any of your own interests you ought to reconcile Argos and Lacedaemon [Sparta] and Thebes and Athens; for if you can bring these cities together, you will not find it hard to unite the others as well. . . . If you can persuade four cities only to take a sane view of things, you will deliver the others also from many evils. . . . No quarrel should ever have arisen between you and any one of them. But unfortunately we are all prone by nature to do wrong more often than right. . . . For the future you must be on your guard to prevent a like occurrence, and must consider what service you can render them which will make it manifest that you have acted in a manner worthy both of yourself and what these cities have done. . . . It is a good thing to have the appearance of conferring benefits upon the greatest states of Hellas and at the same time to profit yourself no less than them. . . . You see how utterly wretched these states have become because of their warfare . . . and now perhaps someone will venture to object to what I have proposed, saying that I am trying to persuade you to set yourself to an impossible task. . . . While I grant that no one else in the world could reconcile these cities, yet nothing of the sort is difficult for you; for I see that you have carried through to a successful end many undertakings which the rest of the world looked upon as hopeless and unthinkable.

George Norlin, trans. *Isocrates.* Vol. 1. (Cambridge, Mass.: Harvard University Press, 1928), pp. 251, 255, 263–271.

DEMOSTHENES, SECOND AND THIRD OLYNTHIACS

I do not choose, Athenians, to enumerate the resources of Philip and by such arguments to call on you to rise to the occasion. Because it seems to me that any dissertation on that topic is a tribute to his enterprise, but a record of our failure. For the higher he has raised himself above his proper level, the more he wins the admiration of the world; but the more you have failed to improve your opportunities, the greater is the discredit you have incurred. . . . Now to call a man perjured and faithless, without drawing attention to his acts, might justly be termed mere abuse. . . . I have two reasons for thinking the whole story worth telling: Philip shall appear as worthless as he really is, and those who stand against his apparent invincibility shall see that he has exhausted all the acts of chicanery on which his greatness was founded at the first, and that his career has now reached the extreme limit. . . . He has hoodwinked everyone that has had any dealings with him; he has played upon the folly of each party in turn and exploited their ignorance of his own character. This is how he has gained his power. . . . Never was there a crisis that demanded more careful handling than the present. . . . Quite apart from the disgrace that we should incur if we shirk our responsibilities [to out threatened allies], I see not a little danger . . . if there is nothing to hinder Philip, when he has crushed his present foe, from turning his arms against Attica.

J. H. Vince, ed. and trans. *Demosthenes*, Vol. 1. (Cambridge, Mass.: Harvard University Press, 1930), pp. 23–27, 43,47.

among them as well as a deeper loyalty to the royal house. Philip recruited future Companions (and gained valuable hostages) by bringing the most promising sons of the nobility to his capital at Pella, where they trained as pages with the crown prince, Alexander. Through a series of dynastic marriages, Philip also managed to gain the good will and alliance of many neighboring kingdoms.

His expansion and consolidation in the north, largely completed by 352 B.C.E., brought him into increasing conflict with Athenian commercial interests. Philip was slowly transforming Thessaly into a northern puppet state, and by the early 340s Thebes found its influence in the north all but gone. The growing power of Macedon alarmed some in the Greek world, most notably an Athenian orator named Demosthenes. Whereas some Greeks, like Isocrates, saw in Philip a potential answer to Greece's woes, Demosthenes and others believed that Philip was a half-barbarian aggressor whose ultimate aim was to end the independence of the poleis and subject Greece to his rule. There is no doubt of the threat that Philip now posed; nevertheless, Demosthenes and other Athenians seemed to have misunderstood Philip's ultimate policy aims. Athenian vanity simply could not accept that they were not Philip's final target.

There is no question that Philip was an aggressor, but his expansion in the north was designed to secure his frontiers and the resources necessary to support his real goal: an invasion of Asia Minor that would allow him to tap that land's fabulous wealth. From 348 on, he was keen to conciliate the major Greek poleis, especially Athens. At one point, he even asked for an alliance wherein the Athenians would provide the war fleet for his proposed invasion of the Persian Empire; in return he would support their claim to hegemony over Greece. The Athenians took Demosthenes' advice and refused to cooperate with Philip. This miscalculation would prove disastrous for Athens.

Although Demosthenes saw Philip's actions in the north as easing his entry into Greece, Philip was actually trying to prepare his exit from it. He wanted a secure and peaceful Greece behind him when he took on the might of Persia. But his inability to reach any understanding with Athens, despite strenuous diplomatic effort on Philip's part, ultimately led to war between the Macedonians on one side and Athens, Thebes, and a number of smaller poleis on the other (Sparta remained aloof). At the battle of Chaeronea in 338 B.C.E., the Macedonians won a narrow victory over the Athenians and their allies. In the aftermath, Philip called delegates from around mainland Greece to Corinth, where he established a new league. By and large, he left the independence of the major Greek poleis unaffected. The main purpose of the "League of Corinth" was to provide forces for the invasion of Asia Minor by electing Philip as their military commander. But the league also played some role in maintaining peace between the rival Greek poleis.

Philip's dream of invading Persian territory was never realized. At a festival in Macedon in 336 B.C.E., a disgruntled lover charged into the arena and assassinated Philip. The kingship now fell to the twenty-year-old young man who had led his father's cavalry at Chaeronea, Alexander III. To the Greeks he would be

CHRONOLOGY

MACEDONIAN CONQUEST

Philip II crowns himself king of Macedon	356 B.C.E.
Defeat of Athens and formation of the "League of Corinth"	338 B.C.E.
Alexander defeats the Persian army	331 B.C.E.
Death of Alexander	323 B.C.E.

known as Alexander Poliorcetes, the "Sacker of Cities." To the Romans, far more impressed by conquerors than were the Greeks, he was Alexander the Great.

THE CONQUESTS AND REIGN OF ALEXANDER (336–323 B.C.E.)

Alexander is a difficult figure for historians to understand, not least because in his own lifetime romantic legend had already built up around him and his achievements. Scholars have seen in Alexander a visionary, a genius, and a butcher; what he did was nothing less than transform the world, translating Greek culture from its parochial, small-scale homeland into a world culture, spreading it as far as the modern states of Afghanistan and Pakistan.

Alexander's military victories are well known. After first quelling revolts in Greece that erupted immediately on his father's death, by 334 he was ready to invade the Persian empire, then under the rule of Darius III. Persia had experienced internal weakness for over a decade. Darius III had been placed on the throne by a scheming vizier who sought to control the young nobleman, only to find that his puppet had designs of his own. Darius killed the kingmaker, and then ruled capably during the few years of peace he enjoyed until Alexander's appearance in Asia.

The Macedonian king won a series of startling victories, starting in northwest Asia Minor. At one point, Darius offered to cede his western possessions to

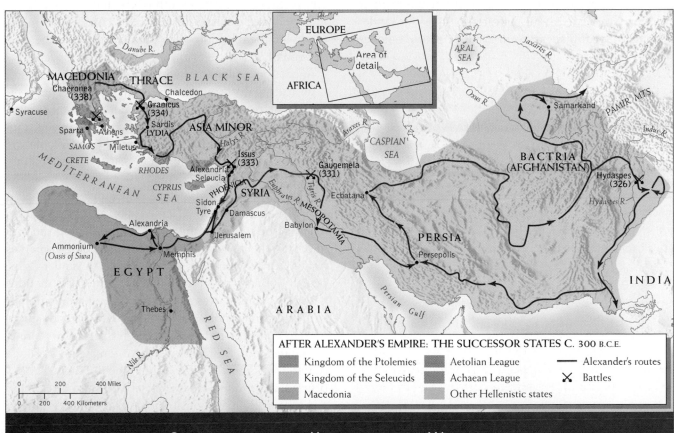

AFTER ALEXANDER'S EMPIRE: THE SUCCESSOR STATES C. 300 B.C.E.

- Kingdom of the Ptolemies
- Kingdom of the Seleucids
- Macedonia
- Aetolian League
- Achaean League
- Other Hellenistic states
- ⎯ Alexander's routes
- ✕ Battles

ALEXANDER THE GREAT AND THE HELLENISTIC WORLD

Why did Alexander continue eastward even after defeating Darius III at Gaugamela? Consider the vastness of his empire compared with the Aegean basin; how would the acquisition of so much territory profoundly reshape the Greek world? Note the position of the three successor kingdoms and how each one was based on one of three major axes of civilizations we have studied so far: Egyptian, Asian Near Eastern, and Aegean. What might the division of Alexander's empire along such "traditional" lines say about the durability of his empire even if he had lived?

Alexander in exchange for his family (whom Alexander had captured in battle) and a peace treaty. Alexander's field marshal, Parmenio, advised "I would accept it, if I were you." Alexander replied, "And I would too, if I were Parmenio." Within three years of his initial invasion, Alexander had subdued Anatolia, the Syria-Palestine coast, and had detached Egypt from the Persian empire. During his time in Egypt, Alexander appears to have reflected on what he had already achieved, and to have become increasingly convinced of his superhuman qualities. Indeed, to many Alexander had already achieved more than one might have expected out of the squabbling, petty gods of Mount Olympus, who seemed to grow smaller by comparison as Alexander and his talented staff of officers achieved ever more.

In September of 331 B.C.E., Darius mustered the remaining strength of his empire to face Alexander's Graeco-Macedonian army in what is today northern Iraq. At the battle of Gaugamela, Alexander destroyed the Persian army. Darius himself fled to the hills, where he was captured and slain by a chieftain hoping to ingratiate himself to Alexander. But as the new king of Persia, Alexander executed the chieftain for having killed his predecessor. The next spring, Alexander destroyed the Persian capital of Persepolis, lest it serve as a rallying point for Persian resistance.

Over the next few years, Alexander campaigned in the mountains of Bactria (modern Afghanistan), the hardest fighting of the campaign. He ultimately succeeded in conquering much of the region, but his grasp there was tenuous. Among the Bactrians he found the woman he would take as his queen, Roxane. From there he moved down the Indus Valley, meeting stiff resistance. At the mouth of the Indus, his soldiers mutinied and refused to press on. Alexander reluctantly led them back toward Babylon, arriving there by the end of 324 B.C.E.

What Alexander planned to do with his new empire is difficult to say. Some scholars see him merely as a pirate, bent on conquest and plunder in a self-serving quest for glory worthy of the Homeric heroes from whom he claimed descent. Others counter by pointing to his systematic foundation of Greek-style poleis along his campaign route. These new cities served not only as garrisons to control the local populations but also as foci of Greek culture. There is also the bizarre mass marriage he forced on his officers, compelling them to put aside their wives and take Persian noblewomen as brides. Once seen as a reflection of Alexander's supposed visionary desire to eliminate ethnic distinctions within his empire, this act is now viewed as an attempt to breed a new nobility, loyal not to Macedonian or Persian concerns but to him and his successors alone. Alexander took no realistic steps to create an administration for his new realm, although he did move various officers and groups of veterans about in an attempt to reshuffle certain responsibilities. Our sources hint at plans for further conquests, perhaps Arabia, perhaps toward Italy and Sicily in the west. Given what we know about Alexander, it is hard to imagine him ever being satisfied with what he had.

We will never know for certain. In late May 323, Alexander fell ill with malarial symptoms and, ignoring the advice of his doctors, continued to play the part of the Homeric king, drinking mightily and exerting himself incautiously. Alexander had often been wounded

> Given what we know now about Alexander, it is hard to imagine him ever being satisfied with what he had.

Marble Head of Alexander. Alexander the Great was reputed to have been very handsome, but all surviving representations doubtless make him more handsome still. This one dates from about 180 B.C.E. and is typical in showing Alexander with "lion's-mane hair."

in battle during the course of his career, and no doubt his body was the worse for wear. His condition declined until on June 10, 323 B.C.E., Alexander died, not yet thirty-three years old. His friends and officers had gathered around his deathbed, and asked to whom he wished to leave his empire. One source states that, just as he went unconscious, a wry smile adorned Alexander's face as he whispered "To the strongest." This might mean any of several talented and ambitious generals around him, who were second only to Alexander himself in prestige and martial skill.

THE HELLENISTIC KINGDOMS

What characteristics defined the three major Hellenistic kingdoms?

After Alexander's death, epic struggles unfolded among the men and women who wanted to keep the realm together, those who wished to mark out their own kingdoms, and among the latter, those who wanted the biggest possible share. The wars and intrigues that took place in the two generations after the death of the great conqueror are too involved to describe in detail. By 275 B.C.E., however, three separate axes of military and political power had emerged, each with a distinctive outlook despite their common background and their Graeco-Macedonian ruling class. One of the striking features of the period is the return to something old, especially in the Near East and Egypt, where the successors of Alexander the Great established sprawling cities and revived the concept of the god-king.

> Until the last Ptolemaic ruler, Cleopatra VII, no Ptolemaic ruler even bothered to learn Egyptian.

PTOLEMAIC EGYPT

Following Alexander's death in Babylon, his inner circle met to decide the fate of his empire. For the moment, the empire remained united, but Ptolemy asked to be made governor of Egypt. The rest of Alexander's generals seem to have been glad to let Ptolemy have the hot, sweltering land of Egypt, but Ptolemy himself recognized the country's vast potential and its virtual invulnerability to attack. As soon as he arrived,

Ptolemy set about making Egypt an independent kingdom under his rule. The dynasty he established would rule Egypt for the next three hundred years (332–30 B.C.E.). The male heirs of the line all took the name Ptolemy, hence Ptolemaic Egypt.

Ruling from Alexandria, the great coastal city founded by Alexander, the Ptolemies acted as Macedonian kings for the Greek and Macedonian subjects living in the thriving capital. Outside of Alexandria, however, they played the role of pharaohs, surrounding themselves with the trappings and symbols of Egypt's pharaonic heritage. The Ptolemies were by no means a political failure. The third century in particular was a time of prosperity and internal peace for Ptolemaic Egypt. But even in antiquity, people recognized the divide between the Macedonian kings and the ancient land they ruled. Geographers described Alexandria as "by" Egypt, not "of" it. No matter how well they aped the Egyptian rulers of the past, the Macedonian ruling class largely disdained their subjects. Until the last Ptolemaic ruler, Cleopatra VII, no Ptolemaic ruler even bothered to learn Egyptian.

For the Ptolemies as for the ancient pharaohs, all of Egypt was basically crown land, to be exploited for the benefit of the royal house. Alongside this Egyptian tradition, however, was the Macedonian idea that conquered land—land "won by the spear"—was plunder, to be used for personal enrichment and glorification. The Ptolemies attempted to squeeze every last drop of wealth from the Egyptian countryside. Most of this wealth ended up in Alexandria. The Ptolemies had little interest in improving the lot of the Egyptian peasantry; in the ancient world it was often assumed that what kept the poor complacent and dutiful was their desperate poverty. The Ptolemies, however, overdid it, and from the end of the third century they faced regular and dangerous revolts from the native peasantry.

Nevertheless, Ptolemaic Egypt proved the most durable of the Hellenistic kingdoms, and the dynasty used the wealth of the country to patronize science and the arts. Early in the dynasty the museum and library of Alexandria were established, and the city became a center of scholarship that attracted the greatest minds of the Hellenistic world, displacing even Athens, which had retained some importance as a sort of "university" town. Many breakthroughs in astronomy, applied sciences, and physics took place in Alexandria, and the study of medicine advanced greatly under Ptolemaic rule. Freed from the taboos of their homeland, Greek medical researchers in Egypt were permitted to perform autopsies on the bodies of dead criminals, making it possible for anatomy to become a scientific discipline in its own right. The Ptolemies were not selfless patrons. They were largely interested in the glory and prestige their patronage brought them, rather than the practical benefits that might arise from the research they sponsored. But whatever its motives, Alexandrine scholarship left a permanent mark on the Mediterranean world.

SELEUCID ASIA

The vast Asian possessions of Alexander the Great eventually fell to another Macedonian, Seleucus, by 281 B.C.E. Seleucus had not been a senior officer during Alexander's lifetime, but he had navigated the turmoil after Alexander's death successfully, exploiting the fears and suspicions among Alexander's more prominent successors.

Ruling such an expansive realm proved as much curse as blessing. The Persian dynasty founded by Seleucus, the Seleucids, struggled with the problem of secession throughout its history. Their hold on the easternmost provinces was especially tenuous—even during Alexander's lifetime that had been the case—as Seleucus recognized. He therefore ceded much of the Indus Valley to the great Indian warrior-king Chandragupta in exchange for peace and a squad of war elephants. By the middle of the third century, the Seleucids had also lost control of Bactria, where a series of Indo-Greek states were emerging with a unique cultural complex of their own. (One Bactrian Greek king, Menander, is remembered in Buddhist tradition and may have had Buddhist sympathies himself.) By the 260s, they had also lost control of the western half of Asia Minor. The Seleucid heartland now became Syria–Palestine, Mesopotamia, and the western half of Persia: still a great, wealthy kingdom, but far less than what Alexander had left.

Like the Ptolemies, the Seleucids offered two faces to their subjects, one rooted in ancient Near Eastern tradition for their Persian and Mesopotamian subjects, another decidedly more Greek for the heavily Hellenized populations of the coast. Seleucus' son, Antiochus I, proclaimed in terms reminiscent of a Sargon or a Hammurabi, "I am Antiochus, the Great King, the legitimate king . . . king of Babylon, king of all countries." Throughout their empire, the Seleucids encouraged the recognition of their divine status and the

Alexander the Great. Hellenistic rulers depicted Alexander on their coins in order to stress their connection with the revered hero. This dramatic profile was struck by Lysimachus of Thrace around 300 B.C.E.

Antiochus I, "Soter." A Hellenistic ruler of Syria (281–261 B.C.E.), whose chosen title of *soter* meant "savior." The faraway stare connotes supernatural inspiration.

divine honors owed to them. In the great urban centers of Seleucid Asia, shrines and temples were built for the cult of the living ruler.

Seleucid rulers continued the tradition of Alexander, planting new cities throughout their empire, cities that were fundamentally Greek in their assumptions but in many cases grew to be thriving commercial and industrial cities, such as Antioch. These cities attracted a great deal of professional and mercantile talent eastward, encouraging trade and manufactures that the Seleucids were expert at exploiting. While they controlled the land and agricultural production through the traditional Persian system of noble-held lands in return for loyalty and services to the king, the Seleucids employed a wide variety of taxes, tariffs, and levies to tap into the growing commercial wealth of their realm. Although their bureaucracy was less organized than that of the Ptolemies, in an empire of as many as 30 million inhabitants even haphazard tax col-

THE GREEK INFLUENCE ON ISRAEL

Greek culture was a powerfully intoxicating force throughout the Hellenistic world, even in a comparative cultural backwater like Israel. In the second century B.C.E., the Hellenized ways of the Jewish upper classes in Jerusalem finally occasioned a revolt by a native Hebrew dynasty known as the Maccabees, who decried the "debaucheries" Greek culture had introduced into Jewish life. In the passage that follows, note that even the high priest of the Temple bears the Greek name Jason.

In those days [the reign of Antiochus IV Epiphanes, 175–164 B.C.E.] certain renegades came out from Israel and misled many, saying, "Let us go and make a covenant with the Gentiles [Greeks] around us, for since we separated from them many disasters have come upon us." . . . Some of the people went to the king, who authorized them to observe the ordinances of the Gentiles. So they built a gymnasium in Jerusalem, according to Gentile custom, and removed the marks of circumcision, and abandoned the holy covenant. They joined with the Gentiles and sold themselves to do evil. . . . When Antiochus succeeded to the kingdom, Jason the brother of Onias obtained the high priesthood by corruption. . . . He at once shifted his compatriots over to the Greek way of life. . . . Despising the sanctuary and neglecting the sacrifices, they hurried to take part in the unlawful proceedings in the wrestling arena after the signal for the discus-throwing, disdaining the honors prized by their ancestors and putting the highest value upon Greek forms of prestige. . . . When the quadrennial games were being held at Tyre and the king was present, Jason sent envoys . . . to carry three hundred silver drachmas for the sacrifice to Heracles. . . . Harsh and utterly grievous was the onslaught of evil. For the Temple was filled with debauchery and reveling by the Gentiles, who dallied with prostitutes and had intercourse with women within the sacred precincts. . . . The altar was covered with abominable offerings that were forbidden by the laws.

1 Maccabees 2; 2 Maccabees 4–6. *The New Oxford Annotated Bible.* (Oxford: Oxford University Press, 1994).

---

lection could reap huge rewards. Like their Persian predecessors, however, the Seleucids did not reinvest their gains into what we would call capital improvements. Instead, they hoarded their wealth in great state treasuries. All the same, they had more than enough cash to provide for the smooth operation of their government and to defend their borders through the third century, a period of regular warfare with the Ptolemies. It was not until the second century, when Antiochus III lost a costly war with the Romans, that he had to plunder temples and private wealth in order to pay off his war indemnity.

ANTIGONID MACEDON AND GREECE

The Macedonian homeland did not possess the vast wealth of the new kingdoms carved from Alexander's conquests. It also remained highly unstable from the time of Alexander's death until 276 B.C.E., when a general named Antigonus was finally able to establish his rule over the area. Macedon drew its strength from considerable natural resources and its influence over Aegean trade, as well as its de facto overlordship of the Greek homeland. Furthermore, the Macedonians could still field the finest army of any of the successor states, and the Antigonid kings of Macedon held what many of the monarchs of the Hellenistic world desired, the kingship of the land once ruled by Philip and Alexander.

Antigonus was influenced by the Stoic outlook (see below) and viewed kingship as something of a noble servitude, an office to be suffered rather than enjoyed. This outlook, combined with his circumscribed resources, convinced him not to compete with the Seleucids and Ptolemies for dominance. Instead, Antigonid policy was to keep these other two powers at war and away from the Macedonian sphere of influence. Antigonus and his successors thus pursued a policy more reminiscent of Philip than of Alexander. They secured the northern frontiers, maintained a strong, standing military, and kept the fractious Greeks to the south at heel.

The Greeks, however, were restive under the Antigonids, and two emergent forces within the Greek world served as rallying points for cries of freedom and war against the "barbarian." These two forces, the Aetolian League and Achaean League, were a departure in Greek political organization. Unlike the defensive alliances of the classical period, these two leagues represented a real political unification, with some centralization of governmental functions. Under the Achaean League, for example, citizens of the member poleis participated in councils of state that dealt with foreign policy and military affairs, trials for treason, and the annual election of a league general (also the chief executive officer) and his second in command. New members were admitted on an equal footing with existing members, and all citizens of the various poleis enjoyed joint citizenship throughout the league. The same laws, weights and measures, coinage, and judicial procedures also applied throughout this federal system. So impressive was the degree of cooperation and unification that James Madison, John Jay, and Alexander Hamilton employed the Achaean League as one of their models in advocating federalism in the United States.

> Antigonus was influenced by the Stoic outlook and viewed kingship as something of a noble servitude, an office to be suffered rather than enjoyed.

THE GROWTH OF TRADE AND URBANIZATION

Why was prosperity not more widespread in the Hellenistic economy?

In regard to economics, the Hellenistic world was generally prosperous, owing to the growth of long-distance trade, finance, and cities. The growth of trade may be explained by several factors, first among which was the opening up of a vast trading area as the result of Alexander's conquests. Long before the time of Alexander, Greeks had been energetic long-distance traders, but they were hampered in trading with Persian realms and with areas east of Persia because Persian emperors and satraps preferred to act in their own economic interests rather than in Greek ones. But when Greek rulers became ensconced throughout Egypt and western Asia after 323 B.C.E., and when Greek-speaking communities dotted the terrain from Alexandria in Egypt, to another Alexandria in northern Syria, to yet another Alexandria at the head of the Persian Gulf, steady trading connections were facilitated from the eastern Mediterranean to central Asia. Moreover, with bases in Egypt, Asia Minor, Persia, and Bactria, Greek traders could fan out farther, venturing into sub-Saharan Africa, Russia, and India. Second, Alexander unwittingly stimulated a growth of intensive investment when he placed in circulation hoards of Persian gold and silver in the form of coins, jewelry, and luxury utensils. And third, manufacturing industries aimed at providing items for trade were now more consciously promoted by autocratic rulers as a means of increasing their revenues.

New trading ventures were particularly vigorous and lucrative in Ptolemaic Egypt and the area of western Asia ruled over by the Seleucid monarchs, the heartland of which was Syria. Every facility was provided by the Ptolemies and the Seleucids for the encouragement of trade. Harbors were improved, warships were sent out to police the seas, and roads and canals were built. Moreover, the Ptolemies employed geographers to discover new routes to distant lands and thereby open up valuable markets. As a result of such methods Egypt developed a flourishing commerce in the widest variety of products. Into the port of Alexandria came spices from Arabia, gold from Ethiopia and India, tin from Britain, elephants and ivory from Nubia, silver from Spain, fine carpets from Asia Minor, and even silk from China. Profits for the government and for some of the merchants were often as high as 20 or 30 percent.

Cities grew enormously during the Hellenistic Age, for a combination of reasons. Entirely aside from economic motives, Greek rulers imported Greek officials and especially Greek soldiers to maintain their control over non-Greek populations. Often this policy resulted in the creation of urban settlements from nothing. Alexander the Great himself had founded some seventy cities as outposts of Greek domination, and in the next two centuries his successors founded about two hundred more. Yet urbanization also increased because of the expansion of commerce and industry and the proliferation of governmental bureaus responsible for economic supervision. Hence the growth of populations in some urban centers was explosive. The population of Antioch in Syria quadrupled during a single century. Seleucia on the Tigris grew from nothing to a metropolis of several hundred thousand in less than two centuries. The largest and most famous of all the Hellenistic cities was Alexandria in Egypt, with about five hundred thousand inhabitants. Before imperial Rome, no other city in ancient times surpassed it in size or magnificence. Its streets were well paved and laid out in regular order. It had splendid public buildings and parks, a museum, and a library of half a million scrolls. The masses of its people, however, had no share in the brilliant and luxurious life around them, although it was paid for in part out of the fruits of their labor.

Although the Hellenistic economy was basically a dynamic one, throughout the Hellenistic period agriculture remained the major occupation and the primary source of wealth. (Only within the last century did trade and industry replace agriculture as the major source of wealth in western Europe and North America.) Furthermore, although industry advanced in Hellenistic Egypt and parts of western Asia, nowhere did a true "industrial revolution" based on any technological breakthrough occur. Rather, all industry was based on manual labor rather than being power driven.

Despite the overall growth and prosperity of the Hellenistic economy, prosperity was by no means en-

joyed by everyone. Quite to the contrary: for some people sudden wealth was followed by sudden penury, and for others poverty was a constant. Individual merchants and speculators were those most subject to drastic fluctuations in their fortunes, owing to the natural precariousness of mercantile endeavors. A trader who did very well selling a luxury cloth might decide to invest heavily in it, only to find that tastes had changed, or that a ship he had dispatched to convey his wares had sunk. Merchants were also particularly exposed to what economists now recognize as the "boom and bust" syndrome. A merchant, thinking he would make a fortune during an upward price spiral, might go into debt in order to take advantage of the upward trend, only to find that supply in the commodity he traded suddenly exceeded demand, leaving him nothing with which to pay back his creditors. Among those whose poverty remained unchanged were small-scale farmers who grew crops for sale in regional markets. (In Greece they may have become poorer because Greece suffered during the Hellenistic era from a negative balance of payments, having little to offer for long-distance trade except objects of art.) Those who emigrated to cities in most cases probably did not improve their economic status, and many of them became subject to badly overcrowded living conditions. All told, therefore, it seems clear that the economic landscape of the Hellenistic world was one of contrasting extremes, an image worth remembering as we move to a consideration of Hellenistic thought and culture.

> Although the Hellenistic economy was basically a dynamic one, throughout the Hellenistic period agriculture remained the major occupation and the primary source of wealth.

HELLENISTIC CULTURE: PHILOSOPHY AND RELIGION

What was the relationship between Epicureanism and Stoicism?

Hellenistic philosophy exhibited two trends that ran almost parallel throughout the civilization. The major trend, exemplified by Epicureanism and Stoicism, showed a fundamental regard for reason as the key to the solution of human problems. This trend was a manifestation of Greek influence, although philosophy and science, as combined by Aristotle, had now come to a parting of the ways. The minor trend, exemplified by the Skeptics and various cults, tended to reject reason, to deny the possibility of attaining truth, and in some cases to turn toward mysticism and reliance on faith. Despite the differences in their teachings, the philosophers and religious enthusiasts of the Hellenistic age generally agreed on one thing: the necessity of finding some release from the trials of human existence, for with the decline of free civic life as a means for the expression of human idealism, alternatives needed to be found to make life seem meaningful, or at least endurable.

EPICUREANISM AND STOICISM

Epicureanism and Stoicism both originated about 300 B.C.E. The founders were, respectively, Epicurus (c. 342–270 B.C.E.) and Zeno (fl. after 300 B.C.E.), both residents of Athens. The two philosophies had several features in common. Both were individualistic, concerned not with the welfare of society but with the good of the individual. Both were materialistic, denying the existence of any spiritual substances; even divine beings and the soul were declared to be formed of matter. Moreover, Stoicism and Epicureanism alike contained elements of universalism. Both taught that people are the same the world over and recognized no distinctions between Greeks and non-Greeks.

But in most ways the two systems were quite different. The Stoics believed that the cosmos is an ordered whole in which all contradictions are resolved for ultimate good. Evil is, therefore, relative; the particular misfortunes that befall human beings are but necessary incidents to the final perfection of the universe. Everything that happens is rigidly determined in accordance with rational purpose. No individual is master of his or her fate; human destiny is a link in an unbroken chain. People are free only in the sense that they can accept their fate or rebel against it. But whether they accept or rebel, they cannot overcome it. Their supreme duty is to submit to the order of the universe in the knowledge that this order is good. Through such an act of resignation the highest happiness will be attained, which consists of tranquility of mind. Those who are most truly happy are thus the ones who by the assertion of their

rational natures have accomplished a perfect adjustment of their lives to the cosmic purpose and purged their souls of all bitterness and whining protest against evil turns of fortune.

The Stoics' ethical and social theory grew from their general philosophy. Believing that the highest good is serenity of mind, they emphasized duty and self-discipline as cardinal virtues. Recognizing the prevalence of particular evils, they taught tolerance for and forgiveness of each other. They also urged participation in public affairs as a duty for those of rational mind. They condemned slavery and war, although they took no real actions against these evils since they believed that the results that might arise from violent measures of social change would be worse than the diseases they were meant to cure. With appropriate qualifications, the Stoic philosophy was one of the noblest products of the Hellenistic Age in teaching egalitarianism, pacifism, and humanitarianism.

The Epicureans based their philosophy on the materialistic "atomism" of an earlier Greek thinker named Democritus, who lived in the latter part of the fifth century B.C.E. According to this theory the ultimate constituents of the universe are atoms, infinite in number, indestructible, and indivisible. Every individual object or organism in the universe is the product of a fortuitous concourse of atoms. Taking this as given, Epicurus and his followers proposed that since there is no ultimate purpose in the universe, the highest good is pleasure—the moderate satisfaction of bodily appetites, the mental pleasure of contemplating excellence and satisfactions previously enjoyed, and above all, serenity of soul. The last end can be best achieved through the elimination of fear, especially fear of the supernatural, since that is the greatest source of mental pain. The individual must understand that the soul is material and therefore cannot survive the body, that the universe operates of itself, and that no gods intervene in human affairs. The Epicureans thus came by a different route to the same general conclusion as the Stoics—nothing is better than tranquility of mind.

The practical moral teachings and the politics of the Epicureans rested on utilitarianism. In contrast to the Stoics, they did not insist on virtue as an end in itself but taught that the only reason why one should be good is to increase one's own happiness. In like manner, they denied that there is any such thing as absolute justice: laws and institutions are just only insofar

> With appropriate qualifications, the Stoic philosophy was one of the noblest products of the Hellenistic Age in teaching egalitarianism, pacifism, and humanitarianism.

as they contribute to the welfare of the individual. Certain rules have been found necessary in every society for the maintenance of order. These rules should be obeyed solely because it is to each individual's advantage to do so. Epicurus considered the state as a mere convenience and taught that the wise man should take no active part in politics. He did not propose that civilization should be abandoned; yet his conception of the happiest life was essentially passive and defeatist. Epicurus taught that the thinking person will recognize that evils in the world cannot be eradicated by human effort; the individual will therefore withdraw to study philosophy and enjoy the fellowship of a few congenial friends.

SKEPTICISM

A more radically defeatist philosophy was that propounded by the Skeptics. Skepticism reached the zenith of its popularity about 200 B.C.E. under the influence of Carneades. The chief source of its inspiration was the teaching that all knowledge is derived from sense perception and therefore must be limited and relative. From this the Skeptics deduced that people cannot prove anything. Since the impressions of our senses deceive us, no truth can be certain. All we can say is that things appear to be such and such; we do not know what they really are. We have no definite knowledge of the supernatural, of the meaning of life, or even of right and wrong. It follows that the sensible course to pursue is suspension of judgment; this alone can lead to happiness. If we will abandon the fruitless quest for absolute truth and cease worrying about good and evil, we will attain peace of mind, which is the highest satisfaction that life affords. The Skeptics were even less concerned than the Epicureans with political and social problems. Their ideal was one of escape from a world neither reformable nor understandable.

According to the philosophy of Skepticism, people have no definite knowledge of the supernatural, of the meaning of life, or even of right and wrong.

RELIGION

Hellenistic religion similarly tended to offer vehicles of escape from collective political commitments. Although Greek religion in the age of the city-states had emphasized the worship of gods associated with given cities to advance the fortunes of those cities, such civic-oriented worship was now losing its vitality. Its place was taken for many of society's leaders by the philosophies of Stoicism, Epicureanism, and Skepticism. Most ordinary people, on the other hand, tended to embrace emotional personal religions offering elaborate ritual in this world and salvation in the next. In Greek-speaking communities, cults that stressed extreme ascetic atonement for sin, ecstatic mystical union with divinity, and otherworldly salvation attracted ever more followers. Among these mystery cults, so called because their membership was secret and their rites held in private, one of the most popular was the Orphic cult, based on the myth of the death and resurrection of the god Dionysius. Even today the word *dionysian* connotes dedication to ecstatic religious practices bordering on the orgiastic. In Persian communities Zoroastrianism became ever more extreme in its dualism, with Zoroastrian magi insisting that everything material was evil and demanding that believers practice austerities in order to ready their immaterial souls for ethereal joy in the afterlife. Finally, among Greeks and non-Greeks alike, an offshoot of Zoroastrianism known as Mithraism gained ever more popularity.

Exactly when Mithraism became an independent religion is unknown, but it was certainly not later than the fourth century B.C.E. The cult gained its name from Mithras, at first a minor deity in Zoroastrianism. Mithras gradually became recognized by many as the god most deserving of worship, probably because of his emotional appeal. He was believed to have lived an earthly existence involving great suffering and sacrifice. He performed miracles, giving bread and wine to humanity and ending a drought and also a disastrous flood. He proclaimed Sunday as the most sacred day of the week since the sun was the giver of light. He declared the twenty-fifth of December as the most sacred day of the year because, as the approximate date of the winter solstice, it was the "birthday" of the sun, when its life-giving powers began to increase for the benefit of humankind. Drawing its converts mostly from the lower classes of Hellenistic society, Mithraism offered them an elaborate ritual, contempt for life in this world, and a clearly defined doctrine of redemption through Mithras, a personal savior. Not surprisingly it outlasted the Hellenistic period, becoming after about 100 C.E. one of the most popular religions in the Roman Empire and exerting some influence on Christianity.

HELLENISTIC CULTURE: LITERATURE AND ART

Why did Hellenistic architecture become grander?

Both the literature and the art of the Hellenistic Age were characterized by a tendency to take aspects of earlier Greek accomplishments to extremes. It is difficult to be certain of the reasons for this tendency, but apparently writers and artists wished to demonstrate their purely formal skills in order to please their autocratic patrons. The greater uncertainties of existence in Hellenistic times may also have led consumers of art to seek gratification from more dramatic and less subtle forms of artistic expression. Whatever the case, rather than being an integral expression of civic activities, art during this period became more of a commodity. Artistic works became more numerous and more widely available: we know the names of at least eleven hundred Hellenistic authors. Many of these works are mediocre, but some are enduring masterpieces of art and literature.

PASTORAL LITERATURE

The most prominent Hellenistic verse form was the pastoral, a new genre depicting a make-believe world of shepherds and wood nymphs. The inventor of the genre was a Greek named Theocritus, who lived and wrote around 270 B.C.E. in the big-city environment of Alexandria. Theocritus was a merchant of escapism. In the midst of urban bustle, faced with despotic rulers, and within sight of overcrowded, slumlike conditions, he celebrated the charms of hazy country values and idealized the "simple pleasures" of rustic folk. One of his pastorals might start like this: "Begin my country song, sweet muses, begin, I am Thrysis from Etna, this is Thrysis's lovely voice." To many the falseness of such verse is alienating; how could shepherds talk this way? But other readers enjoy the poetic lushness. In creating the pastoral, Theocritus founded an enduring tradition that outlasted the Hellenistic world to be taken up by such masters as Virgil and Milton and that provided a wealth of themes for the visual arts. Even composers of modern concert music, such as Claude Debussy in his *Prelude to "The Afternoon of a Faun,"* owe a debt to the escapist poet from Alexandria.

PROSE

The field of Hellenistic prose literature was dominated by historians and biographers. By far the most profound of the writers of history was the mainland Greek Polybius, who lived during the second century B.C.E. According to Polybius, historical development proceeds in cycles, nations passing so inevitably through stages of growth and decay that it is possible to predict exactly where a nation is heading if one knows what has happened to it in the past. From the standpoint of historical method, Polybius deserves to be ranked second only to Thucydides among all the historians of ancient times, and he even surpassed Thucydides in his grasp of the importance of social and economic forces. Although most biographies of the time were light and gossipy, their popularity bears eloquent testimony to the literary tastes of the Hellenistic period.

Cupid and Psyche. Hellenistic tastes often inclined toward "dainty" representations of eroticism. Cupid's right hand conveys a studied sensuality held in check only by his fig leaf.

ARCHITECTURE

Consonant with the despotic style of rule, the main traits of Hellenistic architecture were grandeur and ornamentation. In place of the balance and restraint that had distinguished Greek architecture of the fifth and early fourth centuries B.C.E., Hellenistic public building drew on Greek elements but moved toward standards set by Persian monarchs and Egyptian pharaohs. Two examples (both of which unfortunately no longer survive) were the great lighthouse of Alex-

ESCAPE TO THE COUNTRYSIDE

The bewildering urban centers and social upheaval wrought by the Hellenistic Age encouraged some people to retreat into an imaginary world of simple country pleasures expressed in poetry and literature. Theocritus (born around 300 B.C.E. in Syracuse) was one of the poets who crafted such Arcadian fantasies of the simple life for an anxious urban audience looking for escape.

I finished my song, and with an ingenious laugh he gave me the (shepherd's) crook, a token of what we had shared. Then taking the road to the left which leads to Pyxa he parted from us. Eucritus and I turned off, with young Amyntas, for Phrasidemus's farm. There, happy in our welcome, we flung ourselves down on couches of fragrant reeds and freshcut vine-leaves. Above our heads a grove of elms and poplars stirred gently. We could hear the noise of water, a lively stream running from the cave of the Nymphs. Sunburnt cicadas, perched in the shadowy thickets, kept up their rasping chatter; a distant tree-frog muttered harshly as it picked its way among thorns; larks and linnets were singing, a dove made moan, and brown bees loitered, flitting about the springs. The tall air smelt of summer, it smelt of ripeness. We lay stretched out in plenty, pears at our feet, apples at our sides and plumtrees reaching down, branches pulled earthward by the weight of the fruit. The seal broken from the wine jars was four years old. Nymphs of Castalia, haunters of steep Parnassus, tell me, was Heracles given such wine to drink by ancient Chiron in Pholus's rocky cave? . . . May I set the winnowing fan in another year's heaped grain while the laughing goddess clutches her poppies and sheaves.

Robert Wells, trans. *The Idylls of Theocritus.* (Manchester and New York: Carcanet, 1988), pp. 86–87.

andria, which rose to a height of nearly four hundred feet with three diminishing stories and eight columns to support the light at the top, and the citadel of Alexandria, dedicated to the god Serapis and built of stone covered with blue-tinted plaster, and said by a contemporary to have "risen into mid-air." In Pergamon in Asia Minor an enormous altar to Zeus (transported in modern times to Berlin) and an enormous open-air theater looked out over a high hill. In Ephesus, not far away, the streets were paved with marble. The "signature" of Hellenistic architecture of whatever dimension was the Corinthian column, a form of column more ornate than the Doric and Ionic alternatives that had predominated in earlier Greek building.

SCULPTURE

In the final analysis, probably the most influential of all products of Hellenistic culture were works of sculpture. Whereas earlier Greek sculpture had sought to idealize humanity and to express Greek ideals of modesty by understated restraint, Hellenistic sculpture emphasized extreme naturalism and unashamed extravagance. In practice this meant that sculptors went to great lengths

The Marble Streets of Ephesus. Taken from the Persians by Alexander in 334 B.C.E., this cosmopolitan city on the west coast of Asia Minor was noted for its splendor.

to recreate facial furrows, muscular distensions, and complex folds of drapery. Awkward human postures were considered to offer the greatest challenges to the artist in stone, to the degree that sculptors might prefer to show people stretching themselves or balancing on one leg in ways that hardly ever occur in real life. Since most Hellenistic sculpture was executed for wealthy private patrons, it is clear that the goal was to create something unique in terms of its conception and craftsmanship—something a collector could show off as the only one of its type. Not surprisingly, therefore, complexity came to be admired for its own sake, and extreme naturalism sometimes teetered on the brink of dis-

Old Market Woman, second century B.C.E. Sculptures of this period often showed ordinary people engaged in ordinary activities. This realistic marble sculpture is of an old, tired woman who is carrying a basket of fruits and vegetables and chickens to market.

The Corinthian Order of Architecture. This characteristically Hellenistic style for constructing columns was much more ornate than its classical predecessors.

torted stylization. Yet when moderns see such works they frequently experience a shock of recognition, for the bizarre and exaggerated postures of Hellenistic sculptures exerted an enormous influence on Michelangelo and his followers, and later inspired some of the most "modern" sculptors of the nineteenth and twentieth centuries. Three of the most famous examples of Hellenistic sculpture, which reveal different aspects of Hellenistic aesthetic ideals, may be cited here: the *Dying Gaul*, done in Pergamon around 220 B.C.E., shows consummate skill in portraying a twisted human body; the *Winged Victory of Samothrace* of about 200 B.C.E. displays flowing drapery as if it were not stone but real cloth; and the *Laocoön* group, of the first century B.C.E., offers one of the most intensely emotional as well as complex compositions known in the entire history of sculptural art.

Dying Gaul Seen from Front and Back.
A famous example of Hellenistic realism and pathos, this statue was executed around 220 B.C.E. in the court of Pergamon in Asia Minor. (The original is lost; shown here is a faithful Roman copy.) The sculptor clearly wished to exhibit skill in depicting an unusual human posture and succeeded remarkably in evoking the thin line that separates human dignity from unappeasable loneliness and physical suffering.

Laocoön. In sharp contrast to the serenity of the *Winged Victory* is this famous sculpture group from the first century B.C.E., depicting the death of Laocoön. According to legend, Laocoön warned the Trojans not to touch the wooden horse sent by the Greeks and was punished by Poseidon, who sent two serpents to kill him and his sons. The intense emotionalism of this work later had a great influence on western European art from Michelangelo onward.

The Winged Victory of Samothrace. In this figure, done around 200 B.C.E., a Hellenistic sculptor preserved some of the calmness and devotion to grace and proportion characteristic of Hellenic art in the golden age.

SCIENCE AND MEDICINE

Why did science and medicine flourish in this period?

The most brilliant age in the history of science prior to the seventeenth century C.E. was the Hellenistic period. There are two major reasons for the impressive development of science in the centuries after Alexander's conquest of the Persian empire. One was the enormous stimulus given to intellectual inquiry by the fusion of Mesopotamian and Egyptian science with the learning and the curiosity of the Greeks. The other was that many Hellenistic rulers were generous patrons of scientific research, subsidizing scientists who belonged to their retinues just as they subsidized sculptors. It was once thought that the motives for such patronage were practical—that rulers believed the progress of science would enhance the growth of industry in their territories and would also improve their own material comforts. Yet students of Hellenistic civilization now doubt that any ruler was hoping for an "industrial revolution" in the sense of applying technology to save human labor, for labor was cheap and autocratic princes were completely indifferent to the sufferings of the laboring classes. As for the supposed connection between science and the enhancement of material comfort, Hellenistic rulers had adequate numbers of slaves to fan them and were not inclined to introduce mechanical devices that would have lessened the public grandeur of being tended by deferential subordinates. To be sure, practical aims motivated the patronage of science in some areas, above all in medicine and anything that might relate to military technology. Yet it has become clear that the autocrats who financed the scientific endeavors did so primarily for motives of prestige: sometimes a scientist might fashion a splendid gadget for a ruler that he could show off to visitors as he would show off his sculptures; and even if not, purely theoretical achievements were so much admired among the Greek-speaking leisured classes that a Hellenistic prince who subsidized a theoretical breakthrough would share the prestige for it in the way the mayor of an American city might bask in prestige today if his or her city's football team were to win the Super Bowl.

The most influential Hellenistic mathematician was Euclid, the master of geometry.

SCIENCE

The major Hellenistic sciences were astronomy, mathematics, geography, medicine, and physics. The most renowned of the earlier Hellenistic astronomers was Aristarchus of Samos (310–230 B.C.E.), sometimes called the "Hellenistic Copernicus." His primary accomplishment was his deduction that the earth and the other planets revolve around the sun. This view was not accepted by his successors because it conflicted with the teachings of Aristotle and with the conviction of the Greeks that humanity, and therefore the earth, must be at the center of the universe. Later the fame of Aristarchus was overshadowed by that of Ptolemy of Alexandria (second century C.E.). Although Ptolemy made few original discoveries, he systematized the work of others. His principal writing, the *Almagest*, based on the geocentric theory (the view that all heavenly bodies revolve around the earth), was handed down to medieval Europe as the classic summary of ancient astronomy.

Closely allied with astronomy were mathematics and geography. The most influential Hellenistic mathematician was Euclid, the master of geometry. Until the middle of the nineteenth century his *Elements of Geometry* (written around 300 B.C.E. as a synthesis of the work of others) remained the accepted basis for the study of that branch of mathematics. The most original of the Hellenistic mathematicians was probably Hipparchus (second century B.C.E.), who laid the foundations of both plane and spherical trigonometry. Hellenistic geography owed most of its development to Eratosthenes (c. 276–c. 196 B.C.E.), astronomer and librarian of Alexandria. By means of sundials placed some hundreds of miles apart, he calculated the circumference of the earth with an error of less than two hundred miles. Eratosthenes was also the first to suggest the possibility of reaching eastern Asia by sailing west. One of his successors divided the earth into the five climatic zones that are still recognized, and explained the ebb and flow of the tides as due to the influence of the moon.

MEDICINE

Other Hellenistic advances in science were in the field of medicine. Especially significant was the work of Herophilus of Chalcedon (c. 335–c. 280 B.C.E.), who conducted his research in Alexandria at about the beginning of the third century B.C.E. Herophilus was the greatest anatomist of antiquity and probably the first to practice human dissection. Among his achievements were a detailed description of the brain, with an insistence (against Aristotle) that the brain is the seat of human intelligence; the discovery of the significance of the pulse, and its use in diagnosing illness; and the discovery that the arteries contain blood alone (not a mixture of blood and air as Aristotle had taught), and that their function is to carry blood from the heart to all parts of the body. About the middle of the third century, Erasistratus of Alexandria gained much of his knowledge of bodily functions from vivisection. He discovered the valves of the heart and distinguished between motor and sensory nerves. In addition, he rejected Hippocrates' theory that the body consists of four "humors" and consequently criticized excessive bloodletting as a method of cure. Unfortunately the humoral theory and an emphasis on bloodletting were revived by Galen, the great encyclopedist of medicine who lived in the Roman empire in the second century C.E.

Prior to the third century B.C.E., physics had been a branch of philosophy. It was made a separate, experimental science by Archimedes of Syracuse (c. 287–212 B.C.E.), who discovered the law of floating bodies, or specific gravity, and formulated with scientific exactness the principles of the lever, the pulley, and the screw. Among his memorable inventions were the compound pulley and the screw propeller for ships. Although he has been considered the greatest technical genius of antiquity, in fact he placed no emphasis on his mechanical contraptions and preferred to devote his time instead to pure scientific research. Tradition relates that he discovered "Archimedes' principle" (specific gravity) while pondering possible theories in his bath: when he reached his stunning insight he dashed out naked into the street crying "Eureka" ("I have found it").

> Although the great decisions and events of history took place away from the traditional polis, some poleis—such as Rhodes and to a lesser extent Athens—continued to thrive as centers of trade.

CONCLUSION

The supremacy of the great Hellenistic kingdoms and the rise of new forms of political organization in the Greek world outside of monarchy might lead one to ask, What became of the polis, the foundation of Greek culture? Although the great decisions and events of history took place away from the traditional polis, some poleis—such as Rhodes and to a lesser extent Athens—continued to thrive as centers of trade. It is also important to remember that the great empires of the ancient Mediterranean were not so much modern-looking territorial concepts as they were collections of cities, and for the most part the Greco-Macedonian rulers of the Hellenistic era continued to carry the cultural and political baggage of the polis world.

Nevertheless, the Hellenistic polis—even when it had not grossly outgrown its heritage and become a sprawling megalopolis such as Alexandria or Antioch—was in many ways a fundamentally different place than its classical precursor. As we have already seen, the changes afoot in the fourth century were disrupting the traditional bonds of Greek social and political life. What Alexander achieved, apart from the conquest of western and central Asia, was a chance at escape for many of the Greeks in the fourth-century homeland. Alexander had created, perhaps unwittingly, a cosmopolitan world full of economic opportunity for a Greek-speaker, a common Greek-based culture that engulfed the eastern Mediterranean and western Asia, and a sense of "Greekness" that transcended political and geographical boundaries. Into this vast, exciting world, Greeks poured en masse, and the population of the Greek mainland declined by as much as one half in the century between 325 and 225 B.C.E. Many Greeks sought fortunes—financial and otherwise—in a "Greek" world of massive empires and bustling cosmopolitan cities simply unimaginable even in classical Athens.

CHRONOLOGY	
SCIENTIFIC LUMINARIES OF THE HELLENISTIC WORLD	
Herophilus of Chalcedon	c. 335–c. 280 B.C.E.
Euclid	330?–270? B.C.E.
Aristarchus of Samos	310–230 B.C.E.
Archimedes of Syracuse	c. 287–212 B.C.E.
Eratosthenes	c. 276–c. 196 B.C.E.

Such a transformation had serious effects on Greek culture and the polis. We need only think of the small-scale Dark Age communities and archaic poleis from which Greek cultural expression grew. In these societies everybody knew virtually everyone else, and innumerable social and political ties bound the citizens. Greek traditions of participation in government had led to a greater share in the franchise than any other culture had achieved in antiquity. Every citizen of the Greek world, to a lesser or greater extent, had some share, some stake in his society, its institutions, its gods, its army, and its cultural life.

If we transport the ingrained outlook inherited by the Greeks from this earlier pattern of life into the swirling cosmopolitanism of the Hellenistic city, we can well imagine the effects on the individual. All of those things that defined one's life as a person and a citizen were by and large gone. The intimate connection with the political life of the state, often even at the local level, had vanished. In place of the nexus of social and familial relationships prevalent in the Greek mainland, an average Greek in one of the Hellenistic kingdoms might have only his immediate family to rely on, if even that. What resulted was a traumatic separation between traditional values and assumptions and the social and political realities of the day.

Judged from the vantage point of classical Greece, Hellenistic civilization may at first seem no more than a degenerate phase of Greek civilization. The autocratic governments of the Hellenistic Age appear repugnant in contrast to Athenian democracy, and the Hellenistic penchant for extravagance may appear debased in contrast to the earlier Greek taste for chaste beauty. Even the best Hellenistic literary works lack the inspired majesty of the great Greek tragedies, and none of the Hellenistic philosophers matched the profundity of Plato and Aristotle. Yet Hellenistic civilization had its own achievements also, that the classical age could not match. Most Hellenistic cities offered a greater range of public facilities, such as museums and libraries, than earlier Greek cities did, and we have seen that numerous Hellenistic thinkers, writers, and artists left to posterity important new ideas, impressive new genres, and imaginative new styles. Above all, the fact that Hellenistic science was the most advanced in the Western world until the seventeenth century demonstrates the intellectual creativity that marked the Hellenistic world.

Probably the most important contribution of the

> Above all, the fact that Hellenistic science was the most advanced in the Western world until the seventeenth century demonstrates the intellectual creativity that marked the Hellenistic world.

Hellenistic era to subsequent historical development was the role it played as intermediary between Greece and Rome. In some cases the Hellenistic contribution was simply that of preservation. For example, most of the familiarity the ancient Romans had with classical Greek thought came to them by way of copies of Greek philosophical and literary texts preserved in Hellenistic libraries. In other areas, however, transfer involved transmutation. Hellenistic art, for example, evolved from earlier Greek art into something related but quite different, and it was this "Greek-like" art that exerted the greatest influence on the tastes and artistic accomplishments of the Romans. A similar case might be made for drama.

In conclusion, two particularly remarkable aspects of Hellenistic culture deserve special comment—Hellenistic cosmopolitanism and Hellenistic "modernity." Not only does the word "cosmopolitan" itself come from Greek cosmopolis, meaning "universal city," but it was the Greeks of the Hellenistic period who came the closest among Westerners to turning this ideal of cosmopolitanism into reality. Specifically, around 250 B.C.E. a leisure-class Greek could have traveled from Sicily to the borders of India, always meeting people who "spoke his language," both literally and in terms of shared ideals. Moreover, this same Greek would not have been a nationalist in the sense of professing any deep loyalty to a city-state or kingdom. Rather, he would have considered himself a "citizen of the world." Hellenistic cosmopolitanism was partly a product of the cosmopolitanism of Persia, and it helped in turn to create the cosmopolitanism of Rome, but in contrast to both it was not imperial—that is, it was entirely divorced from constraints imposed by a supranational state—although it was achieved through Greek exploitation of subject peoples. Finally, although cosmopolitanism is surely not an obvious condition of the present, other aspects of Hellenistic civilization must seem very familiar to observers today. Authoritarian governments, ruler worship, economic instability, extreme skepticism existing side by side with intense religiosity, rational science existing side by side with irrational superstition, flamboyant art and ostentatious art collecting: all these traits might make the thoughtful student of history wonder whether the Hellenistic Age is not one of the most relevant in the entire human record for comparison with our own.

SELECTED READINGS

Penguin Classics and the Loeb Classical Library both offer reliable translations of scores of literary and historical texts from this period. Particularly important are historical works by Arrian (*Anabasis of Alexander*) and Plutarch (*Lives*).

Adcock, F. E. *The Greek and Macedonian Art of War*. Berkeley, 1957. Still a valuable introduction to the guiding principles and assumptions of Greek and Macedonian warfare.

Austin, M. M. *The Hellenistic World from Alexander to the Roman Conquest: A Selection of Ancient Sources in Translation*. Cambridge, 1981.

Bagnall, R. S., and P. Derow. *Greek Historical Documents: The Hellenistic Period*. Chico, Calif., 1981.

Bosworth, A. B. *Conquest and Empire: The Reign of Alexander the Great*. Cambridge, 1988. A political and military analysis of Alexander's career that successfully strips away the romance, maintaining a clear vision of the ruthlessness and human cost of his conquests.

Borza, Eugene N. *In the Shadow of Olympus: The Emergence of Macedon*. Princeton, 1990. The standard account of the rise of Macedon up to the accession of Philip II.

Burstein, Stanley M., ed. and trans. *The Hellenistic Age from the Battle of Ipsos to the Death of Kleopatria VII*. Cambridge, 1985. An excellent collection, with sources not found elsewhere.

Cartledge, Paul A. *Agesilaus and the Crisis of Sparta*. Baltimore, 1987. A thorough but readable analysis of the social and political challenges besetting Sparta in the fourth century B.C.E.

Ellis, J. R. *Philip II and Macedonian Imperialism*. London, 1976. A densely written examination of Philip's actions that tries to strip away the biases of Athenian sources.

Green, Peter. *Alexander to Actium: The Historical Evolution of the Hellenistic Age*. Berkeley, 1990. An outstanding, comprehensive and wide-ranging history of the period; balanced and sensible.

———. *Alexander of Macedon, 356–323 B.C.* Berkeley, 1991. Revised edition of the author's 1972 biography; entertainingly written, and rich in detail and insight.

Hammond, Nicholas G. L. *The Genius of Alexander the Great*. Chapel Hill, 1998. A clear, authoritative, admiring account, distilling a lifetime of research on the subject.

Hansen, Mogens H. *The Athenian Democracy in the Age of Demosthenes*. Oxford, 1991. An intelligent examination of the political institutions of Athens in the fourth century B.C.E.

Ober, Josiah. *Mass and Elite in Democratic Athens: Rhetoric, Ideology, and the Power of the People*. Princeton, 1989. An excellent study of the ideology of democracy in Athens in the fourth century B.C.E. that borrows intelligently from modern social scientific insights.

Pollitt, Jerome J. *Art in the Hellenistic Age*. New York, 1986. The standard account, written from the perspective of cultural history as well as art history.

Sherwin-White, Susan, and Amélie Kuhrt. *From Samarkhand to Sardis: A New Approach to the Seleucid Empire*. London, 1993. A stimulating examination of the relationship between rulers and ruled in the vast expanses of the Seleucid empire.

Strauss, Barry. *Athens after the Peloponnesian War: Class, Faction, and Policy. 403–386 B.C.* London, 1986. A narrowly focused but highly informative analysis of the consequences of the Peloponnesian War for Athenian society.

Tritle, Lawrence A. ed. *The Greek World in the Fourth Century: From the Fall of the Athenian Empire to the Successors of Alexander*. New York, 1997. A wide-ranging collection of scholarly essays.

CHAPTER SIX

ROMAN
CIVILIZATION

WHILE THE GREEKS STRUGGLED against the Persians and then each other, a new civilization was emerging on the banks of the Tiber River in central Italy. By the end of the fourth century B.C.E. Rome was already the dominant power on the Italian peninsula. For five centuries thereafter Rome's power steadily increased. By the first century C.E., it ruled most of the Hellenistic world as well as most of western Europe. These conquests, together with Rome's destruction of the powerful North African city of Carthage, united the entire Mediterranean world and made the Mediterranean itself a "Roman lake." Rome's empire brought Greek institutions and ideas not only to the western half of the Mediterranean world, but also to Britain, France, Spain, and Romania. Rome was thus the builder of a great historical bridge that connected Europe to the cultural and political heritage of the ancient Near East. Without Rome, European civilization as we know it would not exist.

Rome was deeply influenced by Greek culture, but Rome was also a distinctive civilization in its own right. On the one hand, the Romans were much more tradition minded than were the Greeks. Rome revered its old agricultural traditions, its household gods, and its sternly military values. But as their empire grew, the Romans also came to see themselves as having a divinely ordained mission to civilize their world by teaching it the arts of law and government that were Rome's own peculiar genius. Virgil (70–19 B.C.E.), the great epic poet of Rome, expressed this self-conscious sense of Rome's historical mission in the *Aeneid*, which tells one of the several competing legends Romans treasured about the founding of their city. Here, Anchises of Troy speaks prophetically to his son Aeneas, who (in Virgil's account) would go on to become one of the founders of the city of Rome. Speaking about the Romans, Anchises tells his son of his people's future:

FOCUS QUESTIONS

• How did the Etruscans and Greeks influence early Roman society?

• In what ways did the early Roman Republic become more democratic?

• What economic and social changes resulted from Roman territorial expansion?

• What issues caused the social struggles of the Late Republic?

• How did Roman interaction with the Hellenistic world accelerate social changes?

• How did Rome control its far-flung territories?

• What role did upper-class women play in Roman society?

• What factors brought the Roman empire to the brink of ruin?

• Did Rome fall? Why or why not?

"Others will cast more tenderly in bronze
Their breathing figures, I can well believe,
And bring more lifelike portraits out of marble;
Argue more eloquently, use the pointer
To trace the paths of heaven accurately
And accurately foretell the rising stars.
Roman, remember by your strength to rule
Earth's peoples—for your arts are to be these:
To pacify, to impose the rule of law,
To spare the conquered, battle down the proud."

Virgil, *Aeneid*, Book VI, lines 848–857, trans. Robert Fitzgerald (New York: Random House, 1982) p. 190.

Not all the peoples whom Rome conquered welcomed the experience. But all were transformed by it.

EARLY ITALY AND THE ROMAN MONARCHY

How did the Etruscans and Greeks influence early Roman society?

The particular geography of the Italian peninsula had a decisive influence upon the course of Rome's development. Aside from excellent marble and small quantities of lead, tin, copper, iron (on the island of Elba), and silver, Italy has no mineral resources to speak of. Despite its extensive coastline, Italy has only a few good harbors, and most of these face toward the west, away from Greece and the Near East. Ancient Italy did have sizable forests and a considerably greater amount of fertile land than did Greece. But Italy was also more exposed to invasion. The Alps posed no effective barrier to the influx of peoples from central Europe, and the low-lying Italian coastline invited conquest by sea. The Romans were absorbed in military pursuits almost from the moment of their settlement on Italian soil because they were continuously forced to defend their own conquests against other invaders.

The particular geography of the Italian peninsula had a decisive influence upon the course of Rome's development.

THE ETRUSCANS

The dominant early settlers on the Italian peninsula were a non-Indo-European-speaking people known as the Etruscans. Our knowledge of the Etruscans is severely limited by the fact that their language, although written in a Greek alphabet, has not yet been fully deciphered. It appears, however, that Etruscan settlements go back to the late Bronze Age, and that they were in early and frequent contact with both Greece and Assyria. By the sixth century B.C.E., the Etruscans had established a confederation of cities that stretched over most of northern and central Italy. They were skilled metalworkers, artists, and architects, from whom the later Romans took their knowledge of the arch and the vault, among much else. In addition to their alphabet, the Etruscans also shared with the Greeks a religion based on the worship of gods in human (rather than animal or metereological) form.

In contrast with Greek practice, Etruscan women enjoyed a comparatively elevated place in society. Etruscan women participated in public life and sporting events; they attended dramatic performances and athletic competitions (which, because the participants were usually nude, were forbidden to Greek women); and they danced in ways that shocked both Greeks and Romans. Etruscan wives ate meals with their husbands, reclining together on the same banqueting couch; and after death, they were buried together in the same mortuary vaults. Some Etruscan families even traced their descent through the female line.

Early Roman society was deeply influenced by Etruscan example. Not only the Roman arch and vault, but also the cruel sport of gladiatorial combat and the practice of foretelling the future by studying the entrails of animals or the flight of birds went back to Etruscan beginnings. The Roman practice of centering urban life around massive stone temples with their attendant cults was probably adopted from an Etruscan example. Even the two most famous myths the Romans told about the founding of Rome itself they probably drew from the Etruscans: that involving Aeneas of Troy (noted above in connection with Virgil's *Aeneid*), and that involving the infant twins Romulus and Remus, who were raised by a female wolf after being abandoned by their parents.

The Romans also borrowed heavily from the Greek settlers of Italy. Large numbers of colonists from mainland Greece began to arrive in southern Italy and Sicily during the eighth century B.C.E. By the end of the seventh century B.C.E., Greek civilization in Magna Graecia (as southern Italy and Sicily were

HOW DID THE ETRUSCANS AND GREEKS INFLUENCE EARLY ROMAN SOCIETY?

EARLY ITALY AND THE ROMAN MONARCHY   185

Etruscan Sarcophagus.

across the Tiber River, making it a major land and river cross-roads. Rome therefore became an important and comparatively wealthy city in the region of Latium, sitting as it did along the frontier between that area and Etruria, the Etruscans' homeland.

The topography of Latium—a broad, flat plain with few natural obstacles—also influenced the way Rome dealt with neighboring communities. At an early date, the Romans established with the other Latin communities a series of common "rights," including *commercium* (all contracts between Latins were enforceable throughout Latium), *connubium* (Latins could intermarry with legal recognition in the community of both husband and wife), and *migratio* (a Latin of one town could migrate to another and, if he remained there for a year, transfer his citizenship). Together, these privileges were known as the "Latin Right," and stand in sharp contrast to the rigid particularism and jealous suspicion that divided the cities of Sumer or Greece.

known) was as advanced as it was in Greece itself. Such famous Greeks as Pythagorus, Archimedes, and even Plato for a time lived in Greek Italy, which also became a key battlefield in the Peleponnesian War between Athens and Sparta. From the Greeks, the Romans derived their alphabet, many of their religious concepts (it is difficult to disentangle Etruscan from Greek influence here), and much of their art and mythology. The high culture of Rome was thoroughly and pervasively Greek in inspiration and imitation.

THE RISE OF ROME

As for the Romans themselves, they descended from a cluster of peoples of the Indo-European language group who entered Italy by way of the Alps between 2000 and 1000 B.C.E. Recent archaeological research places the founding of the city of Rome by Latin-speaking people, thereafter known as Romans, quite near the traditional date of 753 B.C.E. Rome's strategic location along the Tiber brought it many advantages. Trading ships—but not large war fleets—could navigate the Tiber far up its course. Rome could thus serve as a port without being threatened by attack from the sea. Rome's famous hills increased the defensibility of the site. Rome also sat astride the first good ford

Romulus and Remus. A sixth-century B.C.E. Etruscan bronze statue known as the "Capitoline Wolf." Although the present statues of the twins were added during the fifteenth century C.E., there were probably comparable figures of Romulus and Remus in the same basic posture in the original statue.

The willingness of the Romans to extend the Latin Right to "outsiders" was a key fact in the success of their later expansion.

According to Roman legend, the government was initially a monarchy in which a patriarchal king exercised jurisdiction over his subjects comparable to what a male family head would exercise over the members of his household. A senate, or council of elders (*senex* is Latin for "old man"), was composed of the heads of the various clans that formed the community, but its function in this early period is unclear. It was probably an advisory body to Rome's kings.

The monarchy, however, did not last. Legend has it that in 534 B.C.E. an Etruscan tyrant, Tarquin the Proud, gained control of the kingship in Rome. This period of Etruscan overlordship was crucial in transforming Rome from a prosperous village into a true urban center, as Tarquin used Rome's strategic location to dominate Latium and the agriculturally wealthy district of Campania further south. But Tarquin lorded it over the Romans with extreme cruelty. The final indignity came in 510 B.C.E., when Tarquin's son raped a virtuous Roman wife, Lucretia. When Lucretia committed suicide rather than living on "in dishonor," the Romans rose up in revolt, overthrowing not only the Etruscan tyranny but the entire form of monarchical government itself.

The story of Lucretia is probably patriotic myth, but there was a change in government in Rome around 500 B.C.E. (whether gradual or sudden is unknown) that ended the kingship and replaced it with a republic. Thereafter, the Romans would cultivate the conviction that kingship itself was inherently dangerous; and they would come to hold the name of king (in Latin *rex*) in the same fear and contempt with which the Greeks ul-

timately held the name "tyrant." Whatever the truth of Lucretia's story, it does therefore tell us something important about early Roman attitudes toward government and the family.

THE EARLY REPUBLIC

In what ways did the early Roman Republic become more democratic?

The history of the early Roman Republic was one of almost constant warfare. At first the Romans were on the defensive because rival cities took advantage of the confusion accompanying the change of regime to invade Roman territory. After Rome managed to ward off these attacks, the city began to shift to the offensive. As time went on the Romans steadily conquered all the Etruscan territories and then took over the Greek cities of southern Italy, thus intensifying Roman contacts with Greek culture. The Romans did not usually impose heavy burdens on the cities they conquered. More often, they demanded instead that their defeated foes contribute soldiers to the Roman army. To many conquered cities, Rome also extended the Latin Right, giving them a further stake in Rome's continued political and military success. Thus Rome gained for itself nearly inexhaustible reserves of fighting men. By the middle of the third century B.C.E., Rome's army may have numbered as many as three hundred thousand men—a huge force by the standards of the ancient or the medieval worlds.

This long series of conflicts reinforced both the agrarian and the military character of the Roman nation. The acquisition of new lands made it possible for needy Roman citizens to maintain themselves as farmers in the new Roman colonies. By accommodating its increasing population in this way, Rome was thus able to remain a staunchly agricultural civilization for a surprisingly long time. As a result, it developed an interest in shipping and commerce fairly late, compared to the Greeks or Phoenicians. Continual warfare also confirmed among the Romans a steely military ideal. Many of the most familiar Roman legends of martial heroism date from the early Republican period. The brave Horatio, for example, with the help of two friends, held a key bridge against an entire army; the retired soldier Cincinnatus (with whom George Wash-

> The history of the early Roman Republic was one of almost constant warfare.

CHRONOLOGY

PERIODS OF ROMAN CIVILIZATION, 753 B.C.E.–610 C.E.

The rise of Rome	c. 753 B.C.E.
Roman Republic	c. 500–27 B.C.E.
Principate	27 B.C.E.–180 C.E.
Third-Century Crisis	180 C.E.–284 C.E.
Later Empire, or "Dominate"	284–610 C.E.

THE RAPE OF LUCRETIA

The Roman historian Livy compiled his history of Rome in the last half of the first century B.C.E., and most of what survives of his treatise involves the early history of Rome. The events he described surrounding Rome's beginnings are of dubious authenticity in historical terms, but nevertheless help to illustrate the archetypes and values that Romans had long held paramount in their society. The tale of Lucretia, her violation by an Etruscan prince, and the resulting revolution (traditionally dated to 509 B.C.E.) provide one such example.

The young princes spent most of their leisure enjoying themselves in entertainments on the most lavish scale. They were drinking one day in the quarters of Sextus Tarquinius—Collatinus was also present—when someone chanced to mention the subject of wives. Each of them extravagantly praised his own, until Collatinus cried, "Stop! What need is there of words, when in a few hours we can prove beyond doubt the incomparable superiority of my Lucretia? We are all young and strong: why shouldn't we ride to Rome and see with our own eyes what kind of women our wives are?". . .

They reached the city as dusk was falling; and there the wives of the royal princes were found enjoying themselves with a group of young friends at a dinner-party, in the greatest luxury. The riders then went on to Collatia, where they found Lucretia very differently employed: it was already late at night, but there, in the hall of her house, surrounded by her busy maid-servants, she was still hard at work by lamplight upon her spinning. Which wife had won the contest in womanly virtue was no longer in doubt. . . .

A few days later Sextus, without Collatinus's knowledge, returned where he was hospitably welcomed in Lucretia's house. . . . He waited till the house was asleep, and then, when all was quiet, he drew his sword and made his way to Lucretia's room. . . . Sextus urged his love, threatened . . . but not even the fear of death could bend her will. "If death will not move you," Sextus cried, "dishonor shall. I will kill you first, then cut the throat of a slave and lay his naked body by your side." . . . Even the most resolute chastity could not have stood against this dreadful threat. Lucretia yielded. Sextus enjoyed her and rode away, proud of his success.

[After Lucretia told her father and husband what had happened], she said, "What is due to [Sextus] is for you to decide. As for me I am innocent of fault, but I will take my punishment. Never shall Lucretia provide a precedent for unchaste women to escape what they deserve." With these words she drew a knife from under her robe, drove it into her heart and fell forward, dead.

Her father and husband were overwhelmed with grief. While they stood weeping helplessly, Brutus [her father] drew the bloody knife from Lucretia's body, and holding it before him cried: "By this girl's blood—none more chaste till a tyrant wronged her—and by the gods, I swear that with sword and fire, and whatever else can lend strength to my arm, I will pursue Lucius Tarquinius the Proud, his wicked wife, and all his children, and never again will I let them or any other man be King in Rome!"

Livy i.57–59. Based on A. de Selincourt, trans. *Livy: The Early History of Rome.* (New York: Penguin, 1960), pp. 97–99.

ROMAN EXPANSION TO 265 B.C.E.

Controlled by Rome in 485 B.C.E.
To 387 B.C.E.
To 334 B.C.E.
To 300 B.C.E.
To 290 B.C.E.
To 265 B.C.E.

ROMAN EXPANSION IN ITALY, 485–265 B.C.E.

Note the pattern of Roman expansion in central Italy, and that Latium (the area in red) was conquered early by the Romans. How did this early conquest help knit the Latins closely to the Romans? Why did the Romans conquer the Etruscans last, though they were just across the Tiber River? How did the Tiber River help the Romans solidify their control of central Italy? Consider whose interests Rome threatened after 265 B.C.E. by transforming itself into the dominant power of the Italian peninsula, and why.

IN WHAT WAYS DID THE EARLY ROMAN REPUBLIC BECOME MORE DEMOCRATIC?

THE EARLY REPUBLIC   189

ington would be frequently compared) left his farm at a moment's notice to fight for Rome on the battlefield.

THE GOVERNMENT OF THE EARLY REPUBLIC

Meanwhile, Rome underwent a very slow political evolution. Even the replacement of the monarchy was about as conservative a political change as it is possible for any political change to be. Its chief effect was to substitute for the king two elected officials called *consuls*, and to exalt the position of the Senate by granting it control over the public funds. Although the consuls were chosen by the *comitia centuriata* (literally, the Roman "people-in-arms"), this body differed greatly from the citizen assembly of ancient Athens because it met in groups. Each group in the Roman assembly had one vote, and since groups consisting of the wealthiest citizens voted first, a majority could be reached even before the votes of the poorer groups were cast. Consequently the consuls, who served annually, were usually senators who acted as the agents of aristocratic interests. Each consul was supposed to possess the full executive and judicial authority that had previously been wielded by the king, limited by the right each possessed to veto the action of the other. If a conflict arose between them, the Senate might be called on to decide; or in time of grave emergency, a dictator might be appointed for a term of not greater than six months.

After the establishment of the Republic the political dominance of the early aristocracy, known as the *patricians*, began to be challenged by the *plebeians*, who made up nearly 98 percent of the citizen population but who initially had no access to political power. The plebeians were a diverse group. Some had grown wealthy through trade or agriculture, but most were small-holding, prosperous farmers, merchants, or the urban poor. The grievances of the plebeians were numerous. Forced to serve in the army in time of war, they were nevertheless excluded from holding office. They frequently felt themselves the victims of discriminatory decisions in judicial trials. They did not even know what legal rights they were supposed to enjoy, for the laws were unwritten, and the patricians alone had the power to interpret them. Worst was the oppression that could stem from debt because a debtor could be sold into slavery outside Rome by his creditor.

These grievances prompted a plebeian rebellion in the early fifth century B.C.E. that forced the patricians to agree to the election of new officers known as *tribunes* who could protect the plebeians by vetoing unlawful patrician acts. This victory was followed by a successful demand for codification of the laws about 450 B.C.E. The result was the issuance of the famous Law of the Twelve Tables, so called because it was written on tablets ("tables") of wood. Although this law was later revered by the Romans as a kind of charter of the people's liberties, it was really nothing of the sort, for it mostly perpetuated ancient custom without even abolishing enslavement for debt. Nevertheless, at least there was now a clear definition of law. Roughly a generation later the plebeians won eligibility to positions as lesser magistrates, and about 367 B.C.E. the first plebeian consul was elected. Gradually, plebians also gained access to the Senate. The final plebeian victory came in 287 B.C.E. with the passage of a law stipulating that measures enacted by the *concilium plebis* (a more democratically organized assembly composed only of plebeians) would be binding on the Roman government whether the Senate approved them or not. It is from this citizen assembly that English derives its modern word *plebiscite*.

These reforms had several important consequences, although they took a very long time to manifest themselves, owing to the conservative outlook of the Romans and the constitutional safeguards of the Republic. Because successful plebeians could now work their way into the upper reaches of Roman society and compete for its honors, the Roman aristocracy gradually shifted (at least to some degree) from one of birth to one of wealth. At the same time, however, the social and economic standing of the poorer citizens was slowly being eroded. In an attempt to prevent

CHRONOLOGY

THE RISE OF ROME, 750–FIRST CENTURY B.C.E.

Legendary founding of the city of Rome	753 B.C.E.
Establishment of the Latin Right	493 B.C.E.
Roman Republic established	c. 500 B.C.E.
Plebeian rebellions	fifth century B.C.E.
Law of the Twelve Tables	c. 450 B.C.E.
Concillium plebis gains power	287 B.C.E.
Equestrian order established	third century B.C.E.

wealth from becoming too much of a factor in Roman political life, laws were passed barring senators from engaging directly in commerce. But this restriction only fueled the rise of the important "equestrian" order, men who had the wealth and influence of senators, but who chose a life of business rather than one in politics. Nor were the equestrians and the senators wholly distinct from each other. Often, some members of important families would stay "aloof" from politics by becoming equestrians, while underwriting the political careers of their brothers and cousins, who served as "silent partners" in the family's business concerns. Meanwhile, those few families who managed to win election generation after generation became increasingly prestigious and disproportionately influential. As a result, by the first century B.C.E. even powerful and aristocratic Romans were coming to feel excluded from real political influence within their city, styling themselves as the champions of a downtrodden public interest while pursuing their own private political agendas.

Scholars continue to debate how "democratic" Rome was in the fourth, third, and second centuries B.C.E. A republic differs from a monarchy insofar as supreme power resides in a body of citizens and is exercised by officers in some way responsible to those citizens. But a republic is not necessarily democratic, for it can devise systems for reserving power to an oligarchy or privileged group. The Roman constitution ensured oligarchical rule by the balance it struck between competing governmental institutions: the assembly, the Senate, and officeholders such as consuls, tribunes, judges, and administrators. In this system no single individual or family clique could become overwhelmingly strong, nor could direct expressions of the popular will unduly affect Roman policy. For the Greek historian Polybius, the Roman constitution was thus an ideal balance of monarchical, oligarchic, and democratic principles. It was, in his view, a perfect Aristotelian polity.

> For the Greek historian Polybius, the Roman constitution was an ideal balance of monarchical, oligarchic, and democratic principles. It was, in his view, a perfect Aristotelian polity.

CULTURE, RELIGION, AND MORALITY

Political changes in early republican Rome moved glacially. So too did intellectual and cultural ones. Although writing had been adopted as early as the sixth century B.C.E., the Romans made little use of it except for laws, treaties, and funerary inscriptions. Education was largely limited to instruction imparted by fathers to sons in manly sports, practical arts, and military virtues; as a result, literary culture long remained a minor part of Roman life, even among the aristocracy. War and agriculture continued to be the chief occupations for the bulk of the population. A few artisans could be found in the cities, and a minor development of trade had occurred. But the fact that the Republic had no standard system of coinage until 269 B.C.E. reflects the comparative insignificance of Roman commerce at this time.

During the period of the early Republic, religion assumed the character it retained through the greater part of Roman history. In several ways this religion resembled that of the Greeks—not surprising, since it was directly influenced by Roman knowledge of Greek beliefs. Thus major Roman deities performed the same functions as their Greek equivalents: Jupiter corresponded to Zeus as god of the skies, Neptune to Poseidon as god of the waves, Venus to Aphrodite as goddess of love. Like the Greeks, the Romans had no dogmas or sacraments, nor did they place great emphasis on rewards and punishments after death. But there were also significant differences between the two religions. One was that Romans literally revered their ancestors; their "household gods" included deceased members of a lineage who were worshiped in order to ensure a family's continued prosperity. Another difference was that Roman religion was even more closely tied up with political life. Since the Romans believed that their state could flourish only with divine support, they appointed committees of priests virtually as branches of government to tend to the cult of various gods, preside over public rites, and serve as guardians of sacred traditions. These priests were not full-time professionals, but rather prominent oligarchs who rotated in and out of priestly offices in addition to serving as leaders of the Roman state. This dual role made Roman religion an even more integral part of the fabric of public and political life.

The Romans looked to their gods to bestow on their households and their city the blessings of prosperity, victory, and fertility. Roman morality emphasized patriotism, duty, masculine self-control, and respect for authority and tradition. Its chief virtues were bravery, honor, self-discipline, and loyalty to country and family. A Roman's primary duty was to honor his ancestors

WHAT ECONOMIC AND SOCIAL CHANGES RESULTED FROM ROMAN TERRITORIAL EXPANSION?

THE FATEFUL WARS WITH CARTHAGE   191

Junius Brutus. A Roman noble of the first century B.C.E., Brutus is shown here holding the busts of two of his ancestors. Honoring one's ancestors was an important part of Roman social and religious life, especially among the aristocracy.

by his conduct, but the greatest honor attached to those who sacrificed themselves for Rome. For the good of the Republic, therefore, citizens had to be ready to sacrifice not only their own lives but, if necessary, those of their family and friends. The cold-bloodedness of certain consuls who put their sons to death for breaches of military discipline was to the Romans a matter of deep admiration bordering on awe.

THE FATEFUL WARS WITH CARTHAGE

What economic and social changes resulted from Roman territorial expansion?

By 265 B.C.E. the Romans had reduced the last vestiges of Etruscan resistance and thereby controlled three quarters of the Italian peninsula. Confident of their strength over Italy, the Romans were now free to engage in overseas ventures. Scholars disagree as to whether the Romans continually extended their rule as a matter of deliberate policy, or whether their conquests grew more accidentally, by a series of reactions to changes in the status quo that could be interpreted as a threat to Rome's security. Probably the truth lies between these extremes. Whatever the case, beginning in 264 B.C.E., a year after its final victory over the Etruscans, Rome became embroiled in a series of wars with overseas nations that decidedly altered the course of its history.

By far the most crucial was the struggle with Carthage, a great maritime empire that stretched along the northern coast of Africa from modern-day Tunisia to the Straits of Gibraltar, and that controlled parts of Sicily, Sardinia, and Corsica. Carthage had been founded about 800 B.C.E. as a Phoenician colony. In the sixth century it developed into a rich and powerful independent state. The prosperity of its upper classes was founded upon commerce and the exploitation of North African natural resources.

Carthaginian government was oligarchic. The real rulers were thirty merchant princes who constituted an inner council of the Senate. Carthaginian religion and culture remained true in many ways to its Canaanite roots, but by the third century B.C.E. its civilization had gained a material prosperity that would have baffled their Phoenician forebears. In naval might, commercial prowess, and control of crucial material resources, Carthage was far the superior of Rome.

The protracted struggles between Rome and Carthage are known collectively as the Punic Wars because the Romans called the Carthaginians Poeni, that is, "Phoenicians." The First Punic War began in 264 B.C.E., apparently because of Rome's genuine fear of potential Carthaginian expansion. Carthage already controlled most of Sicily and now was threatening to gain control of Messina, directly across from the Italian mainland. Unwilling to allow Carthage to become a menacing next-door neighbor, a Roman consul brought an army over the straits to defend Messina, against the objections of many prominent senators who wanted to avoid embroilment with the Carthaginians. Carthage took massive measures to counterattack and twenty-three years of bitter fighting ensued. Finally, by a peace agreement in 241, Carthage was forced to cede all of Sicily to Rome and to pay a large indemnity. As a result Sicily became Rome's first overseas province. Shortly after the war, a faction of Roman senators sought to renegotiate the terms, seizing Corsica and Sardinia in the process; hard feelings on the Carthaginian side understandably ran deep.

Because the Romans had fought so hard to defeat Carthage, they became determined not to let their enemy become dominant in other Mediterranean areas. Accordingly, in 218 the Romans interpreted Carthage's attempt to expand its rule in Spain as a threat to Roman interests and responded with a declaration of war. The renewed struggle, known as the Second Punic War, raged for sixteen years. At first Rome was entirely thrown off guard by the brilliant exploits of the famous Carthaginian commander Hannibal. Already commanding an army in Spain, Hannibal in a truly remarkable military feat brought this force, including war elephants, through southern France and then over the Alps into Italy. With Carthaginian troops on Italian soil, Rome escaped defeat by the narrowest of margins. Only "delaying tactics" ultimately saved the day, for time was on the side of those who could keep an invader short of supplies and worn down by harassment. No less decisive, however, was Hannibal's failure to win Rome's Latin allies over to his side. Rome's generous treatment had made them loyal and unshakable in their support of Rome. Deep reserves of Roman manpower and the discipline of Rome and her closest allies ultimately overcame Hannibal's military genius. From 212 B.C.E. onward, the Romans increasingly put the Carthaginians on the defensive, in Spain as well as in Italy and Sicily. The

Hannibal. A coin from Carthage representing Hannibal as a victorious general, with an elephant on the reverse.

architect of the Spanish offensive, Publius Cornelius Scipio, drove into North Africa and defeated Hannibal at Zama, near Carthage, in 202 B.C.E. His victory ended the Second Punic War, and Scipio was honored with the additional name "Africanus," as conqueror of Africa.

Carthage was now more completely humbled than before, being compelled to abandon all its possessions except the city of Carthage itself and its surrounding territory in Africa, and to pay an indemnity three times greater than that paid at the end of the First Punic War. Yet Roman suspicion of Carthage remained obsessive. About the middle of the second century B.C.E. Carthage had recovered some of its former prosperity—and this was enough to provoke the displeasure of the Romans. Nothing now would satisfy the most influential Roman senators but the total demolition of the Carthaginian state. In 150 B.C.E. the Roman war hawk

WHAT ECONOMIC AND SOCIAL CHANGES RESULTED FROM ROMAN TERRITORIAL EXPANSION?

THE FATEFUL WARS WITH CARTHAGE   193

Cato the Censor ended every speech he made in the Senate with the same words: "Carthage must be destroyed." The Senate agreed, and in the following year seized on a minor pretext to demand that the Carthaginians abandon their city and settle at least ten miles from the coast. Since this demand amounted to a death sentence for a nation dependent on commerce, it was refused—as the Romans probably realized it would be. The result was the Third Punic War, fought between 149 and 146 B.C.E. The final Roman assault was carried into the city of Carthage, and a frightful butchery took place. When the victorious Roman general—Scipio Aemilianus, the grandson of Africanus—saw Carthage going up in flames he said, "It is a glorious moment, but I have a strange feeling that some day the same fate will befall my own homeland." With the might of the Carthaginians completely broken, the fifty-five thousand that remained alive were sold into slavery, their once magnificent city was razed, and the site was accursed in Roman imagination. (The legend of the Romans sowing the land with salt was clearly an exaggeration, because a generation later a Roman politician proposed founding a Roman colony on the site.)

TERRITORIAL EXPANSION

The wars with Carthage had momentous effects on Rome's development. Most obvious was an enormous increase in Roman territory. The Roman victories over Carthage led to the creation of new overseas provinces in Sicily, North Africa, and Spain. This not only brought Rome great new wealth—above all Sicilian and African grain and Spanish silver—but was the be-

ginning of a policy of westward expansion that proved to be one of the great formative influences on the history of Europe.

The wars also brought Rome into conflict with eastern Mediterranean powers and thereby paved the way for still further conquests. During the Second Punic War, Philip V of Macedon had entered into an alliance with Carthage and was said to have designs on Egypt. Declaring a disinterested intention to forestall Philip's moves, Rome sent an army to the east. The result was the conquest of Greece and Asia Minor and the reduction of Egypt to a Roman sphere of influence. By 146 B.C.E., Greece and Macedon had become Roman provinces, Seleucid Asia had been deprived of most of its territories, and Ptolemaic Egypt was largely a pawn of Roman commercial and naval interests.

ECONOMIC AND SOCIAL CHANGE

As Roman tentacles stretched out over the Mediterranean, a host of fundamental economic and social changes ensued. One was a huge increase in slavery due to the capture and sale of prisoners of war. We have seen that fifty-five thousand Carthaginians were enslaved in 146 B.C.E.; not long before, one hundred fifty thousand Greeks had met the same fate. By the end of the second century about a million slaves toiled in Italy, mainly in the fields, making Rome one of the most slave-based economies known to history. Concomitant with this development was the decline of the small farmer as a result of the establishment of the plantation system based on slave labor and the influx of cheap grain from the provinces. Small farmers, in turn, took refuge in the cities, above all the city of Rome itself, creating a large new urban element; this dynamic was itself exacerbated by the great wealth empire brought to the aristocracy, who sought to reinvest their gains in land. Since many small farmers now served several years in the army away from home— whether in distant Spain or the Greek East—their farms declined, and the temptation to sell at above-market prices to a land-hungry elite was too much for their struggling families to resist. Inevitably this trend, along with the incorporation of overseas areas long oriented to trade, and the need for an administrative apparatus, expanded and strengthened the numbers and the political clout of the equestrians who, in addition to their private business activities, also held gov-

The wars with Carthage had momentous effects on Rome's development.

CHRONOLOGY

PUNIC WARS, 264–146 B.C.E.

First Punic War begins	264 B.C.E.
First Punic War ends	241 B.C.E.
Second Punic War begins	218 B.C.E.
Second Punic War ends	201 B.C.E.
Third Punic War begins	149 B.C.E.
Third Punic War ends	146 B.C.E.
City of Carthage destroyed	146 B.C.E.

THE EXPANSION OF ROME, 264–44 B.C.E.

Consider the position of the Mediterranean relative to Rome's possessions. Why would the Romans call it "our sea"? What challenges did Romans face politically and culturally in acquiring such a vast empire so quickly? Note the distribution of major cities on this map; how was the disparity between East and West in terms of urban development likely to affect Roman approaches to rule? What particular problems did Julius Caesar create by extending Roman rule into Gaul, well away from the Mediterranean basin?

ernment contracts to operate mines, build roads, or collect taxes. Yet the cities were also full of impoverished drifters because Rome never made a transition to industrialism; with slaves to do all the hard work, a great disincentive existed for the technological initiative that might have led to industrialism, and without large-scale manufacture the urban population remained underemployed. Thus a traveler to Italy around 150 B.C.E. would have found a countryside full

of slaves and cities full of disgruntled ex-farmers, living from hand to mouth.

FAMILY LIFE AND THE STATUS OF WOMEN

Yet another change that accompanied the acquisition of new territories was a change in the nature of family

WHAT ISSUES CAUSED THE SOCIAL STRUGGLES OF THE LATE REPUBLIC?

THE SOCIAL STRUGGLES OF THE LATE REPUBLIC   195

life and the status of women. In earlier times the Roman family was based on the husband's legal and financial authority, which gave him nearly absolute powers. The wife was subordinated and served as custodian of the home while the husband managed outside affairs and expected to be treated with reverence. In the second century B.C.E., however, two legal innovations greatly altered this pattern. One was the introduction of "free marriage," whereby the wife's share of her father's property remained her own instead of passing to her husband, and then reverted to her father or her father's heirs on her death. Together with "free marriage" came new rules for divorce, whereby either side, instead of just the man, could initiate proceedings. Apparently the motive of these changes was to prevent the transfer of property from one family to another, which would diminish the size of the large estates created with the influx of slaves. Yet both changes resulted in giving wives greater legal independence. In addition, the slave system itself gave wealthier women greater practical independence, for slaves could now take over tasks of child rearing and household maintenance. Upper-class Roman women began to spend more time away from the home and to engage in a range of social, intellectual, and artistic activities.

Cultivated upper-class life for both men and women had been made possible by a final change attendant on Roman expansion, the introduction of Greek ideas and customs. These flowed more easily to Rome with the conquest of the Hellenistic East and were adopted once upper-class Romans began to become really wealthy as a result of their conquests. In particular, children were given much more education, theater and literature increasingly were in fashion, and the creature comforts that Hellenistic Greeks had begun to prize in Syria and Egypt became equally prized in turn by the Roman conquerors of the Mediterranean world. Some conservative Roman males viewed such changes with repugnance. For them the "good old Roman ways" with emphasis on family life based on fatherly authority and sober military discipline were giving way to the collapse of the family and the debilitating lures of soft living. But whether they liked it or not, Rome had now become irreversibly transformed from a republic of farmers into a complex society with vast gaps between rich and poor and new habits, at least among the well-to-do, of greater personal autonomy.

> Rome had now become irreversibly transformed from a republic of farmers into a complex society with vast gaps between the rich and poor and new habits of greater personal autonomy.

THE SOCIAL STRUGGLES OF THE LATE REPUBLIC

What issues caused the social struggles of the Late Republic?

The period from the end of the Third Punic War in 146 to about 30 B.C.E. was one of enormous turbulence. Social conflicts, assassinations, struggles between rival dictators, wars, and insurrections were common occurrences of the time. Slave uprisings were also part of the general disorder. Some seventy thousand slaves defeated a Roman army in Sicily in 134 B.C.E. before this revolt was put down by further Roman reinforcements, with slaves again ravaging Sicily in 104. But the most threatening slave revolt of all was led by a slave named Spartacus from 73 to 71. Spartacus, who was being trained to become a gladiator (which meant certain death in the arena), escaped with a band of fugitives to Mount Vesuvius near Naples, there attracting a huge host of other fugitive slaves. For two years the escapees under his leadership held off Roman armies and overran much of southern Italy until they were finally defeated and Spartacus was slain in battle. Six thousand of those captured were left crucified along the length of a road from Capua to Rome (about one hundred fifty miles) to provide a terrible warning.

THE GRACCHI

Meanwhile, an extended conflict among elements of the Roman governing class began in 133 B.C.E. with the attempts at social and economic reform instituted by the two Gracchus brothers. Though of aristocratic lineage themselves, they proposed to alleviate social and economic stress by granting government lands to the landless. Although they and their senatorial allies stood to gain from the electoral loyalty of the many clients who would have received this land, Tiberius Gracchus also seems to have been motivated by genuine concern for the welfare of Rome's farmers and the attendant manpower shortage in the army. A man had to meet certain property qualifications to serve in the Roman army, and at a time when Rome's military commitments were expanding, the available pool of citizen soldiers was contracting. In 133 B.C.E. Tiberius Gracchus, as tribune, proposed a law that restricted the current renters or holders of state lands to a maximum of three hundred acres per citizen plus one hundred fifty acres for each child in the family. The excess was to be given to the poor in small plots. Conservative aristocrats bitterly opposed this proposal and engineered its veto by Octavius, Tiberius' fellow tribune. Tiberius removed Octavius from office, a highly irregular action, and when his own term expired attempted to stand for reelection. Both of these moves seemed to threaten a dictatorship and offered the conservative senators an excuse for resistance. Armed with clubs, they went on a rampage during the elections and murdered Tiberius and many of his followers.

Nine years later, Tiberius' younger brother, Gaius Gracchus, renewed the struggle. Though Tiberius' land law had finally been enacted by the Senate, Gaius believed that the campaign had to go further. Elected tribune in 123 B.C.E., and reelected in 122, he enacted several laws for the benefit of the less privileged. One provided for stabilizing the price of grain in Rome. For this purpose public granaries were built along the Tiber. Another exercised controls on governors suspected of exploiting the provinces for their own advantage, and gave the equestrian order a judicial role in checking the administrative abuses of the senatorial class. In an attempt to gain further support, he suggested the extension of full Roman citizenship to vast numbers of Italian allies, a move that would have completely altered the political landscape of Rome. These and similar measures provoked so much anger among the vested interests that they resolved to eliminate their enemy. The Roman Senate proclaimed Gaius Gracchus an outlaw and authorized the consuls to take all necessary steps for the defense of the Republic. In the ensuing conflict Gaius was killed, and about three thousand of his followers lost their lives in vengeful purges.

ARISTOCRATIC REACTION

After the downfall of the Gracchi, two military leaders who had won fame in foreign wars successively made themselves rulers of the state. The first was Marius, who was elevated to the consulship by the plebeian party in 107 B.C.E. and reelected six times. Unfortunately, Marius was no statesman and accomplished nothing for his followers beyond demonstrating the ease with which a general with an army behind him

could override opposition. Partly for party political motives, partly to meet the shortfall in manpower, Marius scrapped the property qualification for the army altogether. Thereafter, Rome's soldiers would come increasingly from the ranks of the urban poor and the landless country dwellers. The result was that gradually, Roman armies became more loyal to the individual interests of their commanders than they were to the Republic itself, because the political success of their generals could best guarantee rewards for the impoverished soldiers of the army.

Following Marius' death in 86 B.C.E., conservatives took a turn at governing through the army. Their champion was Sulla, another victorious commander. Appointed dictator in 82 B.C.E. for an unlimited term, Sulla ruthlessly proceeded to exterminate his opponents. He extended the powers of the Senate (whose ranks, depleted by civil war, he packed with men loyal to himself), and curtailed the authority of the tribunes. After three years of rule Sulla decided his job was done and retired to a life of luxury on his country estate.

POMPEY AND JULIUS CAESAR

Sulla's actions did not stand unchallenged after he relinquished his office, for the effect of his decrees was to give control to a selfish aristocracy. Several new leaders now emerged to espouse the cause of the people. The most prominent were Pompey (106–48 B.C.E.) and Julius Caesar (100–44 B.C.E.). For a time they cooperated in a plot to gain control of the government, but later they became rivals and sought to outdo each other in bidding for popular support. Both of them were men who, despite their successes, failed to gain complete acceptance from the established elite, but who in any event would have found the "rules" too much of an obstacle to their personal talents and ambitions. Pompey won fame as the conqueror of Syria and Palestine, while Caesar devoted his energies to a series of brilliant forays against the Gauls, adding to the Roman state the territory of modern Belgium, Germany west of the Rhine, and France. In 52 B.C.E., after protracted mob disorders in Rome, the Senate turned to Pompey and engineered his election as sole consul. Caesar, stationed in Gaul, was branded an enemy of the state, and Pompey conspired with the senatorial faction to deprive him of political power. The result was a deadly war between the two men. In 49 B.C.E. Caesar crossed the Rubicon River into Italy (ever since an image for a fateful decision) and marched on Rome. Pompey fled to the east in the hope of gathering an

THE INFLUENCE OF GREEK LUXURY

Lucius Licinius Lucullus (106?–57 B.C.E.) was a partisan of the dictator Sulla and a member of Rome's highest aristocracy. He commanded Roman forces admirably in the East, but his demands for discipline from the army and his intolerance of corruption among the equestrians and senatorial governors made him powerful enemies. His conquests made him quite wealthy and, once he tired of trying to preserve his political career against his foes, he retired from public life. This passage from Plutarch's biography of him demonstrates the effects Eastern luxury could have on the Roman elite, the staggering wealth they could acquire, and their enjoyment of it especially once they abandoned the public career for one of private pleasure.

And indeed, Lucullus' life, like the Old Comedy, presents us at the commencement with acts of policy and of war, at the end offering nothing but good eating and drinking, feastings, and revelings, and mere play. For I give no higher name to his sumptuous buildings, porticos, and baths, still less to his paintings and sculptures, and all his industry about these curiosities, which he collected with vast expense, lavishly bestowing all the wealth and treasure he got in the war upon them, insomuch that even now, with all the advance of luxury, the Lucullean gardens are counted the noblest the emperor has. Tubero the Stoic, when he saw his buildings at Naples, where he suspended the hills upon vast tunnels, brought in the sea for moats and fish-ponds round his house, and built pleasure-houses in the waters, called him Xerxes in a toga. He had also fine seats in Tusculum, belvederes, and large open balconies for men's apartments, and porticos to walk in, where Pompey, coming to see him, blamed him for making a house which would be pleasant in summer, but uninhabitable in winter; whom Lucullus answered with a smile, "You think me, then, less provident than cranes and storks, not to change my home with the season."

. . . Lucullus's daily entertainments were ostentatiously extravagant, not only with purple coverlets, and plate adorned with precious stones, and dancings, and interludes, but with the greatest diversity of dishes and the most elaborate cookery, for the vulgar to admire and envy. . . . Cato [the Younger] was his friend and connection, but, nevertheless, so hated his life and habits that when a young man made a long and tedious speech in praise of frugality and temperance, Cato got up and said, "How long do you mean to go on making money like Crassus, living like Lucullus, and talking like Cato?"

Plutarch, *Life of Lucullus*. Based on John Dryden, trans. *Plutarch's Lives*. (New York: Modern Library, 1992), pp. 621–622.

army large enough to regain control of Italy. In 48 B.C.E. the forces of the rivals met at Pharsalus in Greece. Pompey was defeated and soon afterward murdered by supporters of Caesar.

Caesar then intervened in Egyptian politics at the court of Cleopatra (whom he left pregnant). Then he conducted another military campaign in Asia Minor in which victory was so swift that he could report,

Julius Caesar.

some of the measures he took as dictator did have lasting effects. With the aid of a Greek astronomer he revised the calendar so as to make a 365-day year (with an extra day added every fourth year). This "Julian" calendar—adjusted by Pope Gregory XIII in 1582—is still with us. Appropriately, the seventh month is named after Julius as "July." By conferring citizenship on thousands of Spaniards and Gauls, Caesar took an important step toward eliminating the distinction between Italians and provincials. He also helped relieve economic inequities by settling many of his veterans and some of the urban poor on unused lands. Vastly more important than these reforms, however, was Caesar's farsighted resolve, made before he seized power, to invest his efforts in the West. Whereas Pompey, and before him Alexander, went to the East to gain fame

"I came, I saw, I conquered" (*Veni, vidi, vici*). After that Caesar returned to Rome. No one now dared challenge his power. With the aid of his veterans he cowed the Senate into granting his every desire. In 46 B.C.E. he became dictator for ten years, and two years later for life. In addition, he assumed nearly every other title that could augment his power. He obtained from the Senate full authority to make war and peace and to control the revenues of the state. For all practical purposes he was above the law, and rumors spread that he intended to make himself king. Such fears led to his assassination on the Ides of March (the 15th) in 44 B.C.E. by a group of conspirators under the leadership of Brutus and Cassius, who hoped to return Rome to republican government.

Although Caesar was once revered by historians as a superhuman hero, he is now often dismissed as insignificant. Both extremes of interpretation should be avoided. Certainly he did not "save Rome," nor was he the greatest statesman of all time. He treated the Republic with contempt and made the problem of governing more difficult for those who came after him. Yet

Ides of March Coin. This coin was struck by Brutus to commemorate the assassination of Julius Caesar. Brutus is depicted on the obverse; on the reverse is a liberty cap between two daggers and the Latin abbreviation for the Ides of March.

HOW DID ROMAN INTERACTION WITH THE HELLENISTIC WORLD ACCELERATE SOCIAL CHANGES?

LATE REPUBLICAN CULTURE AND SOCIETY   199

and fortune, Caesar was the first great leader to recognize the potential significance of northwestern Europe. By incorporating Gaul into the Roman world he brought Rome great agricultural wealth and helped bring urban life and culture to what was then the wild West. Western European civilization, later to be anchored in just those regions that Caesar conquered, might not have been the same without him.

LATE REPUBLICAN CULTURE AND SOCIETY

How did Roman interaction with the Hellenistic world accelerate social changes?

Between the end of the Punic Wars and the death of Julius Caesar, Rome came ever more under the influence of Hellenistic civilization. The result was a flowering of intellectual activity and the adoption of Hellenistic schools of thought, especially Epicureanism and Stoicism, by the upper classes of the western half of the empire.

EPICUREANISM AND STOICISM

The most renowned of the Roman exponents of Epicureanism was Lucretius (98–55 B.C.E.), the author of a book-length philosophical poem, *On the Nature of Things*. In writing this work Lucretius wished to explain the universe in such a way as to remove fear of the supernatural, which he regarded as the chief obstacle to peace of mind. Worlds and all things in them, he taught, are the result of fortuitous combinations of atoms. Though he admitted the existence of the gods, he conceived of them as living in eternal peace, neither creating nor governing the universe. Everything is a product of mechanical evolution, including human beings and their habits and beliefs. Since mind is indissolubly linked with matter, death means utter extinction; consequently, no part of the human personality can survive to be rewarded or punished in an afterlife. Lucretius' conception of the good life was simple: what one needs, he asserted, is not enjoyment but "peace and a pure heart." Whether one

It now became the fashion among the upper classes to learn Greek and to strive to reproduce in Latin some of the more popular forms of Greek literature.

agrees with Lucretius' philosophy or not, there is no doubt that he was an extraordinarily fine poet. In fact his musical cadences, sustained majesty of expression, and infectious enthusiasm earn him a rank among the greatest poets who ever lived.

Stoicism was introduced into Rome about 140 B.C.E. and soon came to include among its converts numerous influential leaders of public life. The greatest of these was Cicero (106–43 B.C.E.), the "father of Roman eloquence." Although Cicero adopted doctrines from a number of philosophers, including both Plato and Aristotle, he derived more of his ideas from the Stoics than from any other source. Cicero's ethical philosophy was based on the Stoic premises that virtue is sufficient for happiness and that tranquillity of mind is the highest good. He conceived of the ideal human being as one who has been guided by reason to an indifference toward sorrow and pain. Cicero diverged from the Greek Stoics in his greater approval of the active, political life. To this degree he still spoke for the older Roman tradition of service to the state. Cicero never claimed to be an original philosopher; rather his goal was to bring the best of Greek philosophy to the West. In this he was remarkably successful, for he wrote in a rich and elegant Latin prose style that has never been surpassed. Cicero's prose immediately became a standard for composition and has remained so until the present century. Thus even though not a truly great thinker, Cicero was the most influential Latin transmitter of ancient thought to the medieval and modern western European worlds.

Lucretius and Cicero were the two leading exponents of Greek thought but not the only fine writers of the later Roman Republic. It now became the fashion among the upper classes to learn Greek and to strive to reproduce in Latin some of the more popular forms of Greek literature. Some results of enduring literary merit were the ribald comedies of Plautus (257?–184 B.C.E.), the passionate love poems of Catullus (84?–54? B.C.E.), and the crisp military memoirs of Julius Caesar.

SOCIAL CHANGE DURING THE LATE REPUBLIC

In addition to its intellectual effects, Roman interaction with the Hellenistic world accelerated the process of social change, foremost of which was the cleavage between classes. The Italian people, numbering about 8 million on the death of Caesar, had come to be divided into four main social orders: the senatorial aristocracy, the equestrians, the common citizens, and the slaves. The senatorial aristocrats numbered three hundred citizens and their families (although the political maneuvers of the civil wars tended to bloat the Senate well beyond this number). Most of the aristocrats gained their living as officeholders and as owners of great landed estates. By the first century B.C.E., the equestrians had become the chief offenders in the exploitation of the poor and the provincials. As money-lenders they often charged exorbitant interest rates, and as tax farmers they squeezed the provinces for profit, often colluding with the senatorial governors in unconscionable corruption and abuse. By far the largest number of the citizens were mere commoners. Most of these were independent farmers, a few were industrial workers, and some were indigent city dwellers who lived by intermittent employment and public relief. When Julius Caesar became dictator, 320,000 citizens were receiving free grain from the state.

Roman slaves were scarcely considered people at all but instruments of production like cattle. Notwithstanding the fact that some of them were cultivated foreigners taken as prisoners of war, the standard policy of their owners was to get as much work out of them as possible during their prime until they died of exhaustion or were released to fend for themselves. The ready availability and cheapness of slaves, a consequence of Rome's conquests, made Roman slavery a far more impersonal and brutal operation than it had been among other ancient civilizations. Although domestic slaves might from time to time have been treated decently, and some slave artisans in the city of Rome were relatively free to run their own businesses, the general lot of the slave was horrendous. Slaves grew much of the food supply and did much of the work in the urban shops as well. Slaves were also employed in numerous nonproductive activities. A lucrative form of investment for the business classes was ownership of slaves trained as gladiators who could be slaughtered by each other or by wild animals for amusement. The growth of luxury also required the employment of thousands of slaves in domestic service. The man of great wealth insisted on having his doorkeepers, his litter-bearers, his couriers, his valets, and his tutors for his children. Some great households had special servants with no other duties than to rub

the master down after his bath or to care for his sandals. All such servants would have been slaves.

This extreme reliance on slave labor, combined with the relative cheapness of slaves, encouraged among the Romans a mindset that scorned the application of mechanical knowledge to improve industrial or agricultural productivity. Water mills and a crude steam engine, among many other labor-saving innovations, were known to the Romans during the course of their history, but they showed little interest in them. There was no need for labor-saving devices when the supply of cheap human labor seemed inexhaustible.

The religious beliefs of the Romans were altered in various ways in the last two centuries of the Republic—again mainly because of Rome's interaction with the Hellenistic world. Most pronounced was the spread of Eastern mystery cults, which satisfied the craving for a more emotional religion than traditional Roman worship and offered the reward of immortality to the wretched of the earth. From Egypt came the cult of Osiris (or Serapis, as the god was now more commonly called), while from Asia Minor was introduced the worship of the Great Mother, with her eunuch priests and ritualistic orgies. Most popular of all at the end of the period was the Persian cult of Mithraism (see Chapter Five), which offered awe-inspiring underground rites and a doctrine of the afterlife of the soul.

CHRONOLOGY

STRUGGLES OF THE LATE REPUBLIC, 146–27 B.C.E.

Third Punic War	149–146 B.C.E.
Slave revolts in Sicily	134–104 B.C.E.
Gracchian reforms	133–122 B.C.E.
Rule of Marius	107–86 B.C.E.
Sulla becomes dictator	82 B.C.E.
Slave revolt led by Spartacus	73–71 B.C.E.
Pompey becomes sole consul	52 B.C.E.
Caesar becomes sole consul	48 B.C.E.
Caesar becomes dictator	46 B.C.E.
Caesar assassinated	44 B.C.E.
Rule of Octavian, Mark Antony, and Lepidus	42–31 B.C.E.
Octavian becomes sole consul	31 B.C.E.
Octavian becomes emperor	27 B.C.E.

Roman Mystery Rites. The "Villa of the Mysteries" in Pompeii preserves an astonishing cycle of wall paintings done around 50 B.C.E. The exact meaning is debatable, but the most persuasive interpretation is that it shows a succession of cult rites. Here a young woman is being whipped, probably an initiation ceremony, while a cult member performs a solemn dance in the nude.

THE PRINCIPATE OR EARLY EMPIRE (27 B.C.E.–180 C.E.)

How did Rome control its far-flung territories?

In his will, Julius Caesar had adopted posthumously as his sole heir his grandnephew Octavian (63 B.C.E.–14 C.E.), then a young man of eighteen acting in his uncle's service in Illyria across the Adriatic Sea. On learning of Caesar's death, Octavian hastened to Rome to see if he could claim his inheritance. He soon found that he had to join forces with two of Caesar's powerful friends, Mark Antony and Lepidus. The following year the three formed an alliance to crush the political faction responsible for Caesar's murder, who had justified their actions as necessary to defend the Republic against a tyrant. The methods employed were not to the new leaders' credit. Prominent members of the opposition were hunted down and slain and their property confiscated. The most noted of the victims was Cicero, brutally slain by Mark Antony's thugs; though he had taken no part in the conspiracy against Caesar's life, Cicero had actively sought to undermine Antony during his term as consul and have him branded a public enemy. Caesar's real murderers, Brutus and Cassius, escaped and organized an army, but they were defeated by Antony and Octavian near Philippi in 42 B.C.E.

With the "republican" opposition effectively crushed, tensions mounted between the members of the alliance, inspired primarily by Antony's jealousy of Octavian. The subsequent struggle became a contest between East and West. Antony went to the East and made an alliance with Cleopatra, hoping to use the resources of the Egyptian kingdom in the power struggle with Octavian. Octavian, as the junior partner, established himself in Italy and the West. It was a risky move: Octavian had to deal with the problems of resettling veterans while maintaining his position in the roiling political environment in Rome. But Italy provided him with manpower and the opportunity to style himself as the protector of Rome and its heritage against Antony, whom he skillfully portrayed as in the clutches of a foreign, female potentate who intended to become queen over Rome. As in the earlier contest between Caesar and Pompey the victory again went to the West. In the naval battle of Actium (31 B.C.E.) Octavian's forces defeated those of Antony and Cleopatra, both of whom soon afterward committed suicide. Egypt's independent existence came to an end, and Rome reigned supreme throughout the Mediterranean world.

THE GOVERNMENT OF ROME UNDER AUGUSTUS

The victory at Actium ushered in a new period in Roman history, the most glorious and the most prosperous that Rome ever experienced. When Octavian returned to Rome he announced the restoration of complete peace. First he ruled for four years as consul, but in 27 B.C.E. he accepted from the Senate the honorific titles of *emperor* and *augustus,* a step that historians count as the beginning of the Roman empire. This periodization is somewhat arbitrary because Octavian was as strong before his title change as after; moreover, *emperor* at the time meant only "victorious general"; *augustus* signified "venerable" or "worthy of honor." But gradually, after his successors took the title of emperor as well, it became the primary designation for the ruler of the Roman state. Actually the title by which Octavian preferred to have his authority designated was the more modest *princeps,* or "first citizen." For this reason the period of his rule and that of his successors is properly called the Principate (or, alternatively, the early empire), to distinguish it from the periods of the Republic (sixth century–27 B.C.E.),

Octavian. When Octavian gained sole rule he became known as Augustus. Many statues of him survive, all of them idealized.

the "Third-Century Crisis" (180 C.E.–284 C.E.), and the later Empire or "Dominate" (284–610 C.E.).

Octavian, or Augustus as he was now called, was determined not to seem a dictator. In theory the Senate and the citizens were the supreme sovereigns, as they had always been. Hence most of the republican institutions were left in place even though their functioning had clearly become a charade. Augustus himself, in practical control of the army, freely determined all governmental policy. Fortunately he was a very gifted statesman. Among the measures he instituted were the establishment of a new coinage system for use throughout the Roman empire; the introduction within Rome itself of a range of public services, including police and fire fighting; and more self-government for cities and provinces than they had enjoyed before. He also abolished the old system of farming out the collection of financial dues. Whereas previously tax collectors were remunerated solely by being allowed to keep a percentage of their intake, a system that led inevitably to graft and extortion, Augustus now appointed his own representatives as tax collectors, paid them regular salaries, and kept them under strict supervision. Above all, Augustus instituted a program of incentives for colonization of the provinces in order to shift the excess free population out of Italy and thereby remove a major source of social tensions and political upheaval. All told, such measures did enhance local peace.

> Augustus instituted a program of incentives for colonization of the provinces in order to shift the excess free population out of Italy and thereby remove a major source of social tensions and political upheaval.

THE GROWTH OF THE ROMAN EMPIRE

From the time of Augustus until that of Trajan, the Roman empire continued to expand. Augustus gained more land for Rome than did any other Roman ruler. His generals advanced into central Europe, conquering the modern-day territories of Switzerland, Austria, and Bulgaria. Only in what is today central Germany did Roman troops meet defeat, a setback that convinced Augustus to hold the Roman borders at the Rhine and Danube. Subsequently, in 43 C.E., the Emperor Claudius began the conquest of Britain, and at the beginning of the next century Trajan pushed beyond the Danube to add Dacia (now Romania) to the empire's realms. Trajan also conquered territories in Mesopotamia, but in so doing aroused the enmity of the Persians. His successor Hadrian halted the conquests, and embarked on a defensive policy epitomized by the construction of

> Augustus' system of governance was so ingenious that even after his death Rome enjoyed nearly two centuries of peace, prosperity, and stability.

Hadrian's Wall in northern Britain. The Roman empire had now reached its territorial limits; in the third century these limits would begin to recede.

When Augustus died in 14 C.E. after four decades of rule, his remarkable experiments in statesmanship might have died with him. His system was so ingenious, however, that Rome enjoyed nearly two centuries of peace, prosperity, and stability as a result of his reforms. Aside from one brief period of civil war in 68 C.E., the transition of power was generally peaceful and the growing imperial bureaucracy managed affairs competently even when individual emperors proved to be vicious. Several talented men succeeded Augustus, but few of them had his panache for disguising the true power of the princeps. Many of his successors had difficult relationships with the Senate, and because members of the senatorial elite were almost invariably the historians of the time, several imperial reputations have suffered unfairly. Tiberius (14–37 C.E.) and Claudius (41–54 C.E.) were both skilled administrators, but their tensions with the Senate led them at times to extreme measures that angered the elite. Nero (54–68 C.E.) and Domitian (81–96 C.E.), both reviled by the senatorial aristocracy, were universally popular among the masses at Rome and in the provinces; indeed, Domitian's reforms of provincial government and his murderous disregard for senatorial privilege explains both the aristocracy's hostility and his subjects' adoration. The height of the Augustan system, however, came between 96 and 180 C.E., under the "Five Good Emperors." All five were capable administrators, and all proved worthy successors of Augustus, respecting the Senate and preserving republican forms while running an essentially autocratic government. Until 180, none had a son who survived him, and so each adopted a man deemed worthy of succeeding him; they thus avoided the difficulties of dynastic politics, one of the great horrors of first-century imperial life in the eyes of senatorial historians.

Rome's successful governance of such a vast empire from the time of Augustus to that of Marcus Aurelius (d. 180 C.E.) was certainly one of its greatest accom-

TWO VIEWS OF AUGUSTUS' RULE

AUGUSTUS SPEAKS FOR HIMSELF

The emperor Augustus was a master propagandist with an unrivaled capacity to present his own actions in the best possible light. This document was written by Augustus himself and was to be carved on two bronze pillars set up before his tomb, to tell the world what Augustus wanted remembered about his deeds.

Below is a copy of the accomplishments of the deified Augustus by which he brought the whole world under the empire of the Roman people, and of the moneys expended by him on the state and the Roman people. . . .

1. At the age of nineteen, on my own initiative and at my own expense, I raised an army by means of which I liberated the Republic, which was oppressed by the tyranny of a faction.

2. Those who assassinated my father I drove into exile, avenging their crime by due process of law.

3. I waged many wars throughout the whole world by land and by sea, both civil and foreign, . . .

5. The dictatorship offered to me . . . by the people and by the senate . . . I refused to accept. . . . The consulship, too, which was offered to me . . . as an annual office for life, I refused to accept.

6. [T]hough the Roman senate and people together agreed that I should be elected sole guardian of the laws and morals with supreme authority, I refused to accept any office offered me which was contrary to the traditions of our ancestors.

7. I have been ranking senator for forty years, . . . I have been *pontifex maximus,* augur, member of the college of fifteen for performing sacrifices, member of the college of seven for conducting religious banquets, member of the Arval Brotherhood, one of the Titii sodales, and a fetial [all priestly offices under the Republic].

9. The senate decreed that vows for my health should be offered up every fifth year by the consuls and priests. . . . the whole citizen body, with one accord, . . . prayed continuously for my health at all the shrines.

17. Four times I came to the assistance of the treasury with my own money. . . . providing bonuses for soldiers who had completed twenty or more years of service.

20. I repaired the Capitol and the theater of Pompey with enormous expenditures on both works, without having my name inscribed on them. I repaired . . . the aqueducts which were falling into ruin in many places . . . I repaired eighty-two temples . . . I reconstructed the Flaminian Way. . . .

34. [H]aving attained supreme power by universal consent, I transferred the state from my own power to the control of the Roman senate and people. . . . After that time I excelled all in authority, but I possessed no more power than the others who were my colleagues in each magistracy.

35. At the time I wrote this document I was in my seventy-sixth year.

"Res Gestae Divi Augusti," in *Roman Civilization, Sourcebook II: The Empire,* ed. Naphtali Lewis and Meyer Reinhold (New York: Harper and Row, 1966), pp. 9–19.

THE HISTORIAN TACITUS WEIGHS UP AUGUSTUS' REIGN

Writing in the first decades of the second century C.E., the senatorial historian Tacitus began his chronicle of imperial rule, the Annals, with the death of Augustus in 14 C.E. Tacitus placed the two contrasting evaluations that follow in the mouths of Augustus' contemporaries. Tacitus used this literary device often; but despite the appearance of even-handedness he thus creates, Tacitus' own views are rarely in doubt.

Intelligent people praised or criticized Augustus in varying terms. One opinion was as follows. Filial duty and a national emergency, in which there was no place for law-abiding conduct, had driven him to civil war—and this can be neither initiated nor maintained by decent methods. He had made many concessions to Antony and to Lepidus for the sake of vengeance on his father's murderers. When Lepidus grew old and lazy, and Antony's self-indulgence got the better of him, the only possible cure for the distracted country had been government by one man. However, Augustus had put the State in order not by making himself king or dictator but by creating the Principate. The empire's frontiers were on the ocean, or on distant rivers. Armies, provinces, fleets, the whole system was inter-related. Roman citizens were protected by the law. Provincials were decently treated. Rome itself had been lavishly beautified. Force had been sparingly used—merely to preserve peace for the majority.

The opposite view went like this. Filial duty and national crisis had been merely pretexts. In actual fact, the motive of Octavian, the future Augustus, was lust for power. Inspired by that, he had mobilized ex-army settlers by gifts of money, raised an army—while he was only a half-grown boy without any official status—won over a consul's brigade by bribery, pretended to support Sextus Pompeius [the son of Pompey], and by senatorial decree usurped the status and rank of a praetor. Soon both consuls . . . had met their deaths—by enemy action; or perhaps in the one case by the deliberate poisoning of his wound, and in the other at the hand of his own troops, instigated by Octavian. In any case, it was he who took over both their armies. Then he had forced the reluctant Senate to make him consul. But the forces given him to deal with Antony he used against the State. His judicial murders and land distributions were distasteful even to those who carried them out. True, Cassius and Brutus died because he had inherited a feud against them; nevertheless, personal enmities ought to be sacrificed to the public interest. Next he had cheated Sextus Pompeius by a spurious peace treaty, Lepidus by spurious friendship. Then Antony, enticed by treaties and his marriage with Octavian's sister, had paid the penalty of that delusive relationship with his life. After that, there had certainly been peace, but it was a bloodstained peace. . . . And gossip did not spare his personal affairs—how he had abducted [Livia] the wife of Tiberius Claudius Nero, and asked the priests the farcical question whether it was in order for her to marry while pregnant. Then there was the debauchery of his friend Publius Vedius Pollio. But Livia was a real catastrophe, to the nation, as a mother and to the house of the Caesars as a stepmother.

Tacitus, *Annals* i.9–10. Based on Michael Grant, trans. *Tacitus: The Annals of Imperial Rome.* (New York: Penguin, 1989), pp. 37–39.

---

plishments. During these two centuries, Rome had few external enemies. The Mediterranean was now under the control of a single military power and experienced the passage of centuries without a single naval battle; while on land, Roman officials ruled from the borders of Scotland to those of Persia. A contemporary orator justly boasted that "the whole civilized world lays down the arms which were its ancient burden, as if on holiday . . . all places are full of gymnasia, fountains, monumental approaches, temples, workshops, schools; one can say that the civilized world, which had been sick from the beginning . . . has been brought by right knowledge to a state of health."

ROMANIZATION AND ASSIMILATION

This "Roman Peace" (*Pax Romana*) was not universal. In Britain, the Roman army massacred tens of thousands of Britons in the aftermath of Queen Boudicca's revolt. In Judea, perhaps the most restive of all the Roman

THE ROMAN EMPIRE AT ITS GREATEST EXTENT, 97–117 C.E.

How had Roman expansion pushed well beyond the Mediterranean basin, and how does this expansion reveal the importance of water transport in the Roman world? Why did the Romans abandon their conquests toward the Elbe? What role did the wide rivers of the Rhine and Danube play in the defense of the European frontier? Why did the Romans cross that frontier to establish a province in Dacia?

provinces, a Roman army destroyed the Temple at Jerusalem in 70 C.E. in the wake of one rebellion, and in 135 C.E. destroyed the entire city of Jerusalem in the wake of another, massacring its inhabitants and scattering the survivors throughout the empire. Upwards of half a million people may have been killed in Judea during these years, and an equal number enslaved. Jerusalem, meanwhile, was refounded by the Emperor Hadrian as a pagan capital named Aelia Capitolina. For the next five hundred years, Jews would be forbidden to live there.

Rome controlled its far-flung territories by assimilating their residents into the common cultural and political life of Rome itself.

Such rebellions were not the norm, however, even in Palestine. Although the Roman empire rested on the backs of its armies, the empire was not really a military occupation. Rome controlled its far-flung territories by assimilating their residents into the common cultural and political life of Rome itself. Local gods became Roman gods and were adopted into the Roman pantheon of divinities. Cities were constructed, and the amenities of urban life introduced: baths, temples, amphitheaters, aqueducts, and paved roads. Rights of citizenship were extended, and able provincials could rise far in Roman service. Some, like Trajan and Hadrian, even rose to become emperors.

Even the frontier areas of the empire need to be understood in this light. Although for convenience' sake historians speak of the empire's "borders," in fact these borders were highly fluid and permeable. We ought, more properly, to speak not of "borders" but of "frontiers," and to see these frontiers as zones of particularly intensive cultural interaction between provincial Romans and the non-Roman peoples who lived beyond them. Roman influence thus reached far beyond the frontier areas, across the Rhine and the Danube into the heartland of Germany and the Gothic lands to the east. When, in the third century, frontier garrisons were withdrawn in order to take part in civil wars within the empire itself, many of these Romanized Germans and Goths moved into the empire, sometimes as plunderers, but often as settlers and aspiring Romans.

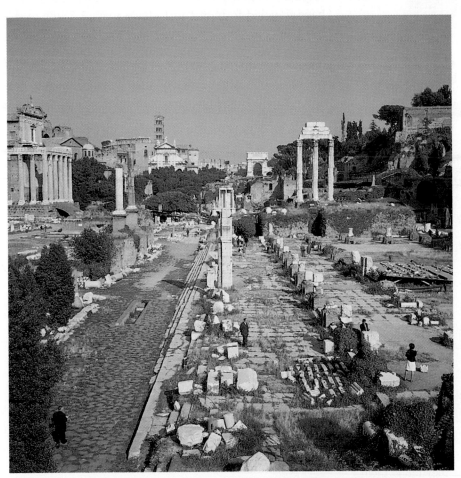

The Forum. The civic center of imperial Rome consisted of avenues, public squares, triumphal arches, temples, and government buildings. The arch of Titus, erected to celebrate Rome's final victory over Hebrew rebels, is in the background at the far right. Roman streets and buildings were arranged in rectilinear patterns to emphasize a sense of order and to facilitate triumphal processions.

CULTURE AND LIFE IN THE PERIOD OF THE PRINCIPATE

What role did upper-class women play in Roman society?

The intellectual and artistic achievements of the Principate outshone those of all other ages in the history of Rome. Three eminent exponents of Stoicism lived in Rome in the two centuries that followed the rule of Augustus: Seneca (4 B.C.E.–65 C.E.), wealthy adviser for a time to Nero; the slave Epictetus (60?–120 C.E.); and the emperor Marcus Aurelius (121–180 C.E.). All of them agreed that inner serenity is the ultimate human goal, that true happiness can be found only in surrender to the benevolent order of the universe. They preached the ideal of virtue for virtue's sake, deplored the sinfulness of human nature, and urged obedience to conscience. Seneca and Epictetus both expressed deep mystical yearnings as part of their philosophy, making it almost a religion. They worshiped the cosmos as divine, governed by an all-powerful Providence that ordained all that happened for ultimate good. The last of the Roman Stoics, Marcus Aurelius, was more fatalistic and less hopeful. Although he did not reject the concept of an ordered and rational universe, he did not believe that immortality would balance suffering on earth and was inclined to think of humans as creatures buffeted by evil fortune for which no distant perfection of the whole could fully compensate. He urged, nevertheless, that people should continue to live nobly, that they should not abandon themselves to either gross indulgence or angry protest, but that they should derive what contentment they could from dignified resignation to suffering and tranquil submission to death.

Marcus Aurelius. This equestrian statue is one of the few surviving from the ancient world: the Christians destroyed most Roman equestrian statues because they found them idolatrous, but they spared this one because they mistakenly believed that it represented Constantine, the first Christian Roman emperor. The statue stood outdoors in Rome from the second century until 1980, when it was taken into storage to protect it from air pollution.

LITERATURE OF THE GOLDEN AND SILVER AGES

Roman literature of the Principate is conventionally divided into two periods: works of the *golden age*, written during the reign of Augustus, and works of the *silver age*, written during the first and early second centuries C.E. Most of the literature of the golden age was vigorous, affirmative, and uplifting, and—it should be noted—much of it served the political and social propaganda programs of Augustus' government. The poetry of the greatest of all Roman poets, Virgil (70–19 B.C.E.), was prototypic. In a set of pastoral poems, the *Eclogues*, Virgil expressed an idealized vision of human life led in harmony with nature. The *Eclogues* also implicitly extolled Augustus as the bringer of peace and abundance. Virgil's masterpiece, the *Aeneid*, is an epic poem about a Trojan hero, Aeneas (whom the family of Caesar and Augustus claimed as an ancestor), who was reputed to have traveled to Italy and to have played a role in the formation of the Roman people (see p. 183). Written in elevated, yet sinewy and stirring metrical verse ("Arms and the man, I sing. . . ."), the *Aeneid* tells of the founding of a great state by means of warfare and toil and foretells Rome's glorious future.

Other major golden age writers were Horace (65–8 B.C.E.), Livy (59 B.C.E.–17 C.E.), and Ovid (43 B.C.E.–17 C.E.). Of these, Horace was the most philosophical. His *Odes* drew from the practical teachings of both the Epicureans and the Stoics, combining Epicurean justification of pleasure with Stoic passivity in the face of trouble. The chief claim to fame of Livy, a narrative historian, rests on his skill as a prose stylist. His *History of Rome*, starting "from the founding of the city," is often factually unreliable but replete with dramatic and picturesque narrative designed to appeal to patriotic emotions. Ovid was the least typical of the Latin golden age writers insofar as his outlook tended to be more satiric than heroically affirmative. His main poetic accomplishment was a highly sophisticated retelling of Greek myths in a long poem of fifteen books, the *Metamorphoses*, full of wit and eroticism. Whereas the emperor Augustus delighted in the *Aeneid*, he found the mocking and dissolute tone of Ovid's verses to be so repellent that he banished Ovid from his court. Augustus was trying to present himself as a stern moralist, whereas Ovid's verses treated such subjects as how to attract women at the race track and his adulterous affair with the wife of a Roman senator.

The literature of the silver age was typically less calm and balanced than that of the golden age. Its ef-

A SCATHING CRITIQUE OF ROMAN SOCIETY

Roman society, even at its height under the "Five Good Emperors," was not without its critics. Among the most incisive and resonant indictments were those of Juvenal, whose Satires *attacked everything from the general erosion of public morality to the effete tastes of the elite. His language is often bitter, and he did not shy away from lacing his intelligent and perceptive verses with a vulgarity still shocking across the centuries. Like those of Aristophanes, many of his references are highly topical, and their exact meaning is lost to us. No doubt his audience understood the allusions, making his public excoriations all the more personal and pointed. Contrast this portrayal of contemporary women with the model of the virtuous Lucretia.*

What conscience has Venus drunk? Our inebriated beauties can't tell head from tail at those midnight oyster suppers when the best wine's laced with perfume, and tossed down neat from a foaming conch-shell, while the dizzy ceiling spins round, and the tables dance, and each light shows double. Why, you may ask yourself, does the notorious Maura sniff at the air in that knowing, derisive way as she and her dear friend Tullia pass by the ancient altar of Chastity? And what is Tullia whispering to her? Here, at night, they stagger out of their litters and relieve themselves, pissing in long hard bursts all over the goddess's statue. Then, while the Moon looks down on their motions, they take turns to ride each other, and finally go home. So you, next morning, on your way to some great house, will splash through your wife's piddle. Notorious, too, are the ritual mysteries of the Good Goddess, when flute-music stirs the loins, and frenzied women, devotees of Priapus, sweep along in procession, howling, tossing their hair, wine-flown, horn-crazy, burning with the desire to get themselves laid. . . . So the ladies, with a display of talent to match their birth, win all the prizes. No make-believe here, no pretense, each act is performed in earnest, and guaranteed to warm the age-chilled balls of a Nestor or a Priam.

Juvenal, *Sixth Satire* 301–326. Based on Peter Green, trans. *Juvenal: The Sixteen Satires.* (New York: Penguin, 1974), pp. 138–139.

---

fects derived more often from self-conscious artifice. The tales of Petronius and Apuleius describe the more exotic and sometimes sordid aspects of Roman life. The aim of the authors is less to instruct or uplift than to tell an entertaining story or turn a witty phrase. An entirely different viewpoint is presented in the works of the other most important writers of this age: Juvenal the satirist (60?–140 C.E.) and Tacitus the historian (55?–117? C.E.). Juvenal wrote with savage indignation about what he took to be the moral degeneracy of his contemporaries. His taste for bitingly compressed rhetorical phrases has made him a favorite source for quotation. A similar attitude toward Roman society characterized the writing of Tacitus, who described the events of his age not with a view to dispassionate analysis but largely for the purpose of moral indictment. His description of the customs of the ancient Germans in his *Germania* heightened the contrast

Diana. A Roman painting depicting the goddess of the hunt. Roman art was often gentle and impressionistic, far from the military grandeur most often associated today with the Romans.

between the manly virtues of an unspoiled race and the effeminate vices of the decadent Romans. Whatever his failings as a historian, he was a master of ironic wit and brilliant aphorism. Referring to Roman conquests, he makes a barbarian chieftain say, "They create a wilderness and call it peace."

ART AND ARCHITECTURE

Roman art first assumed its distinctive character during the period of the Principate. Before this time what

passed for an art of Rome was really an importation from the Hellenistic East. Conquering armies brought back to Italy wagonloads of statues, reliefs, and marble columns as part of the plunder from Greece and Asia Minor. These became the property of the wealthy and were used to embellish their sumptuous mansions. As demand increased, hundreds of copies were made, with the result that by the end of the Republic Rome came to have a profusion of objects of art that had no more roots in the culture than the Picassos hanging on the walls of modern corporate offices.

The aura of national glory that surrounded the Principate, however, stimulated the growth of an art that was more indigenous; again Augustus led the way, encouraging and patronizing art that glorified the virtues of Rome, of which he saw himself as restorer. This art was more varied than is often assumed, running from the grandest public architecture to the most delicate wall paintings. In architecture Romans experimented with the dome and pioneered in the building of amphitheaters, public baths, and race courses. Public buildings were customarily of massive proportions and solid construction. Among the largest and most noted were the Pantheon, with its dome having a diameter of 142 feet, and the Colosseum, which could accommodate fifty thousand spectators at gladiatorial combats. Roman sculpture stayed close to the Greek, preferring ideals that were ever more naturalistic. This was particularly apparent on coins, since new coins with images of the current emperor were issued every year. Rather than being prettified, the rulers were usually depicted just as they looked: often one can trace on an annual basis a ruler's receding hairline or advancing double chin. But painting was the Romans' most original art. Wealthy Romans loved intense colors and surrounded themselves with wall paintings and mosaics—pictures produced by fitting together small pieces of colored glass or stone. These created a gamut of effects from fantastic seascapes to dreamy landscapes to introspective portraiture.

Closely related to achievements in architecture were Roman triumphs in engineering (although the Romans accomplished little in science). The imperial Romans built marvelous roads and bridges, many of which still survive. In the time of Trajan (98–117 C.E.) eleven aqueducts brought water into Rome from the nearby hills and provided the city with 300 million gallons daily for drinking and bathing as well as for flushing a well-designed sewage system. Water was cleverly funneled into the homes of the rich for their private gardens, fountains, and pools. The emperor Nero built a famous

The Pantheon in Rome. Built by the Emperor Hadrian, it boasted the largest dome without interior supports of the ancient world. The dome forms a perfect sphere, exactly as high as it is wide.

"Golden House" in the center of Rome with pipes fitted for sprinkling his guests with perfume, baths supplied with medicinal waters, and a pond "like a sea." In addition, a spherical ceiling in the banquet hall revolved day and night like the heavens, all contributing to Nero's deserved reputation as a voluptuary. (Supposedly, when Nero moved in he was heard to say, "At last I can live like a human being.")

ARISTOCRATIC WOMEN UNDER THE PRINCIPATE

One of the most striking aspects of Roman society under the Principate was the important role played by upper-class women.

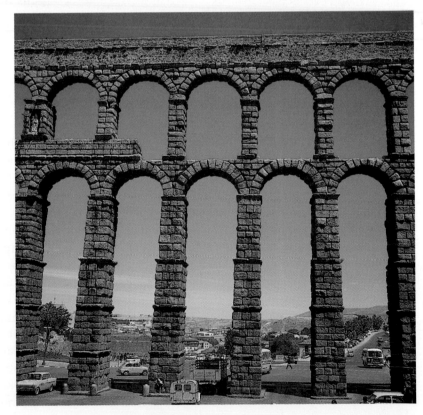

Roman Aqueduct at Segovia, Spain. Aqueducts conveyed water from mountains to the larger cities.

The Colosseum. Built by the Roman emperors between 75 and 80 C.E. as a place of entertainment, it was the scene of gladiatorial combats. The most common form of Greek secular architecture was the theater (see p. 135), but the most common Roman form was the amphitheater.

We have seen that under the Republic wealthier women were less confined to domesticity and obscurity than their counterparts in Athens, and this custom became even more pronounced in the early Empire. It is true that Roman women were assigned the names of their fathers with feminine endings—for example, Julia from Julius, Claudia from Claudius, Marcia from Marcus. Yet unlike women in most modern societies, they did not change their names when they were married. This was a reflection of the fact that wealthier Roman women had a status quite independent from that of their husbands. With numerous slaves to take care of their households and wealth of their own to draw on, upper-class Roman women customarily were educated in the liberal arts and were free to engage in intellectual and artistic pursuits. Some wrote poetry, others studied philosophy, and others presided over literary salons. Aristocratic Roman women often had their portraits painted or chiseled in stone, revealing their cultivation of physical elegance. The busts of several emperors' wives or daughters even appeared on the Roman coinage, partly because the emperors wished to proclaim the greatness of their families, and partly because some of these women really did play an influential role (albeit an informal one) in affairs of state. Of course, women wielded none of the power of men, yet by the standards of the ancient world they were relatively liberated. In less elevated circumstances, Roman women played an important role in the teeming shops and industries of the great cities, the wives of small-time shopkeepers more closely approximating partners than anything else.

GLADIATORIAL COMBATS

For most modern sensibilities, the most repellent aspect of Roman culture during the period of the Principate was cruelty. Whereas the Greeks entertained themselves with theater, the Romans more and more preferred "circuses," which were really exhibitions of human slaughter. During the Principate the spectacles became bloodier than ever. The Romans could no longer obtain a sufficient thrill from mere exhibitions of athletic prowess: pugilists were now required to have their hands wrapped with thongs of leather loaded with iron or lead. The most popular amusement of all was watching the gladiatorial combats in amphitheaters built for thousands of spectators. Fights between gladiators were nothing new, but they were now presented on a much more elaborate scale. Not only common people attended them, but also wealthy aristocrats, and frequently the head of the government himself. The gladiators fought to the accompaniment of savage cries and curses from the audience. When one went down with a disabling wound, the crowd was asked to decide whether his life should be spared or whether the weapon of his opponent should be plunged into his heart. One contest after another, often featuring the sacrifice of men to wild animals, was staged in the course of a single exhibition. Should the arena become too sodden with blood, it was covered over with a fresh layer of sand, and the revolting performance went on. Most of the gladiators were condemned criminals or slaves, but some were volunteers, even from the respectable classes. Commodus, the troubled and ineffectual son of Marcus Aurelius, entered the arena several times for the sake of the plaudits of the mob, and fancied himself a modern-day Hercules.

> The taste for blood and savagery may have been but one expression of a deeper psychological trend which sought not only outlets for its anxiety, but answers for it.

NEW RELIGIONS

The taste for blood and savagery may have been but one expression of a deeper psychological trend which sought not only outlets for its anxiety, but answers for it. The age of the Principate was characterized by an even deeper interest in salvationist religions than had prevailed under the Republic. Mithraism now gained adherents by the thousands, absorbing many of the followers of the cults of the Great Mother and of Serapis. About 40 C.E. the first Christians appeared in Rome. The new sect grew steadily and eventually displaced Mithraism as the most popular of the salvationist faiths, owing in part to its inclusion of women, at first on terms more or less equal to men.

THE ECONOMY OF THE PRINCIPATE

The establishment of stable government by Augustus ushered in a period of prosperity for Italy that lasted for more than two centuries. Trade was now extended to all parts of the known world, even to Arabia, India, and China. Manufacturing increased, especially in the production of pottery, textiles, and articles of metal and glass. In spite of all this, the economic order was far from healthy. Prosperity was not evenly distributed. Since the stigma attached to manual labor persisted as strongly as ever, production was bound to decline as the supply of slaves diminished. Perhaps worse was the fact that Italy had a decidedly unfavorable balance of trade. The meager industrial development was by no means sufficient to provide enough articles of export to meet the demand for luxuries imported from the provinces and from the outside world. As a consequence, Italy was gradually drained of its supply of precious metals. By the third century, the western Roman economy was beginning to collapse.

ROMAN LAW

There is general agreement that one of the most important legacies the Romans left to succeeding cultures was their system of law. The Roman legal system's gradual evolution began roughly with the publication of the Twelve Tables about 450 B.C.E. In the later centuries of the Republic, the Law of the Twelve Tables was transformed by the growth of new precedents and principles. These emanated from different sources: from changes in custom, from the teachings of the Stoics, from the decisions of judges, but especially from the edicts of the *praetors*, magistrates who had authority to define and interpret the law in particular suits and issue instructions to judges.

Roman law attained its highest stage of development under the Principate. This resulted in part from the extension of the law over a wider field of jurisdiction, over the lives and properties of aliens in strange environments as well as over the citizens of Italy. But the major reason was the fact that Augustus and his successors gave to certain eminent jurists the right to deliver opinions on the legal issues of cases under trial in the courts. The most prominent of the men thus designated from time to time were Gaius, Ulpian, Papinian, and Paulus. Although most of them held high judicial office, they had gained their reputations primarily as lawyers and writers on legal subjects. The responses of these jurists came to embody a science and philosophy of law unlike anything that had gone before, and were accepted as the basis of Roman jurisprudence.

The Roman law as it was developed under the influence of the jurists comprised three great branches or divisions: the civil law, the law of peoples, and the natural law. The civil law was the law of Rome and its citizens. As such it existed in both written and unwritten forms. It included the statutes of the Senate, the decrees of the emperor, the edicts of magistrates, and also certain ancient customs operating with the force of law. The law of peoples was the law held to be common to all people regardless of nationality, a sort of rudimentary "international law." This law authorized slavery and private ownership of property and defined the principles of purchase and sale, partnership, and contract. It was not superior to the civil law but supplemented it as especially applicable to the alien inhabitants of the Empire.

This development of the concept of abstract justice as a legal principle was one of the noblest achievements of the Roman civilization.

The most interesting and in many ways the most important branch of Roman law was the natural law, a product not of judicial practice, but of philosophy. The Stoics had developed the idea of a rational order of nature that is the embodiment of justice and right. They had affirmed that all men are by nature equal, and that they are entitled to certain basic rights that governments have no authority to transgress. The father of the law of nature as a legal principle, however, was not one of the Hellenistic Stoics, but Cicero. "True law," he declared, "is right reason consonant with nature, diffused among all men, constant, eternal. To make enactments infringing this law, religion forbids, neither may it be repealed even in part, nor have we power through Senate or people to free ourselves from it." This law existed prior to the state itself, and any ruler who defied it automatically became a tyrant. Most of the great jurists subscribed to conceptions of the law of nature very similar to those of the philosophers. Although the jurists did not regard this law as an automatic limitation upon the civil law, they

thought of it as an ideal to which the statutes and decrees of men ought to conform. This development of the concept of abstract justice as a legal principle was one of the noblest achievements of the Roman civilization.

THE CRISIS OF THE THIRD CENTURY (180–284 C.E.)

What factors brought the Roman empire to the brink of ruin?

With the death of Marcus Aurelius in 180 C.E. the period of beneficent imperial rule came to an end. One reason for the success of the "Five Good Emperors" was that the first four designated particularly promising young men, rather than sons or close relatives, for the succession. But Marcus Aurelius broke this pattern with unfortunate results. Although he was one of the most philosophic and thoughtful rulers who ever reigned, he was not wise enough to recognize that his son Commodus was a self-indulgent adolescent who lacked the discipline or the capacity to rule effectively. To some degree, Marcus Aurelius had his hands tied; it is likely that any attempt to make someone other than his natural son his heir would have met with stiff resistance from the army. Although history has been unkind to Commodus—not without reason—he did put an end to costly wars that profited Rome nothing, an eminently sensible step but one that made him unpopular with both the army and the Senate. He vacillated between trying to accommodate the Senate and terrifying its membership. When a policy proved unpopular among the senators, Commodus would attempt to placate them by executing one or more of his advisors. As a result, few talented people wanted to work for him. He treated the Senate with contempt, and he scorned the traditional expectations for aristocratic conduct, indulging his taste for perversities both public and private, and even appearing as a gladiator in the Colosseum. His erratic and frequently violent behavior resulted in a conspiracy originating inside his own palace: his wrestling coach finally strangled him in

Commodus. The self-deluded ruler encouraged artists to portray him as the equal of the superhuman Hercules.

brother and coemperor Gela. So desperate was Caracalla to raise revenues and pay bonuses to his increasingly covetous armies (especially to appease them after his assassination of his more popular brother), that he made everyone in the empire a Roman citizen. This was hardly an act of enlightenment, but rather was aimed at increasing the tax base of the Roman state. In the process, he cheapened Roman citizenship, once the prized glue that held the far-flung empire together. His successors in the Severan dynasty proved no better. Elagabalus tried to introduce an eastern sun cult as the official religion of Rome, and he flouted sexual and moral convention on the very floor of the Senate.

If not for a series of remarkable imperial women fighting to keep the dynasty and empire together, the results might have been disastrous. First Julia Domna, the wife of Septimius Severus, helped to manage the empire for her son Caracalla, and seems to have acted as the one restraint on his vicious personality; she took her own life when he fell victim to an assassin in 217 C.E. Her sister, Julia Maesa, was the grandmother of both Elagabalus and his successor, Severus Alexander. Her political influence was considerable (although probably somewhat exaggerated by the author Herodian), and she proved instrumental in Elagabalus's downfall when his abuses endangered the state. Finally, her daughter Julia Mamaea, mother of Severus Alexander, enjoyed unusual prominence and popularity during the reign of her young son (222–235 C.E.), and exercised an almost regentlike authority within his government. But they could not stem the tide started by the dynasty's founder, Septimius. The growing

192 C.E. Matters thereafter became worse. With no obvious successor to Commodus, the armies of the provinces raised their own candidates and civil war ensued. A provincial general, Septimius Severus (193–211 C.E.), emerged victorious, making it clear that provincial armies could now interfere in imperial politics at will.

THE SEVERAN DYNASTY

Severus and some of his successors aggravated the problem by eliminating even the theoretical rights of the Senate and ruling as military dictators. Severus dispensed with showing any deference at all to the Senate, and on his deathbed advised his two sons, "Enrich the soldiers, boys, and scorn the rest." His son Caracalla was little more than a thug who murdered his

Coin Depicting Emperor's Wife. This Roman coin, dating from about 200 C.E., bears the image of Julia Domna, wife of the emperor Septimius Severus.

prominence of the army made it increasingly uncontrollable. Once the role of brute force was openly revealed, any aspiring general could try his luck at seizing power. Severus Alexander and Julia Mamaea were murdered in 235 C.E. when the army turned against them. Fifty years of endemic civil war followed. From 235 to 284 C.E. there were no fewer than twenty-six "barracks emperors," of whom only one managed to escape a violent death.

THE HEIGHT OF THE THIRD-CENTURY CRISIS

The half century between 235 and 284 was certainly the worst for Rome since its rise to world power. In addition to political chaos, a number of other factors combined to bring the empire to the brink of ruin. The civil war had disastrous economic effects. Not only did constant warfare interfere with agriculture and trade, but the rivalry of aspirants to rule led them to drain the wealth of their territories in order to gain favor with their armies. Following the maxim of "enriching the soldiers and scorning the rest," they raised funds by debasing the coinage and by nearly confiscatory taxation of civilians. Landlords, small tenants, and manufacturers thus had little motive to produce at a time when production was most necessary. In human terms the poorest, as is usual in times of economic contraction, suffered the most. Often they were driven to the most abject destitution. In the wake of war and hunger, disease became rampant. Already during the reign of Marcus Aurelius a terrible plague had swept through the empire, decimating the army and the population at large. In the middle of the third century pestilence returned and struck at the population with its fearful scythe for fifteen years.

The resulting strain on human resources came at a time when Rome could least afford it, for still another threat to the empire in the middle of the third century was the advance of Rome's external enemies. With Roman ranks thinned by disease and Roman armies fighting each other, Germans in the West and Persians in the East broke through the old Roman defense lines. In 251 C.E. the Goths defeated and slew the emperor Decius, crossed the Danube, and marauded at will in the Balkans. An even more humiliating disaster came in 260 C.E. when the emperor Valerian was captured in battle by the Persians and made to kneel as a footstool for their ruler. When he died his body was stuffed and hung on exhibition. For a time, the western provinces

The Emperor Philip the Arab. An artistic legacy of the Roman "age of anxiety."

broke free as an independent empire in their own right, despairing of Rome's ability to help them, let alone actually provide lasting solutions. Clearly the days of Augustus were far in the past.

NEOPLATONISM

Understandably, the culture of the third century was marked by pervasive anxiety. One can even see expressions of worry in the surviving statuary, as in the bust of the Emperor Philip (244–249 C.E.), who appears almost to realize that he will soon be killed in battle. In response, the Neoplatonic philosophy of withdrawal from the world came to the fore. Neoplatonism (meaning "new Platonism") drew the spiritualist tendency of Plato's thought to extremes.

The first of its basic teachings was emanationism: everything that exists proceeds from the divine in a continuing stream of emanations. The initial stage in the process is the emanation of the world soul. From this come the divine Ideas or spiritual patterns, and then the souls of particular things. The final emanation is matter. But matter has no form or quality of its own; it is simply the residue that is left after the spiritual rays from the divine have burned themselves out. It follows that matter is to be despised as the symbol of evil and darkness.

Neoplatonism's second major doctrine was mysticism. The human soul was originally a part of God, but it has become separated from its divine source through its union with matter. The highest goal of life should be mystic reunion with the divine, which can be accomplished through contemplation and through emancipation of the soul from bondage to matter. Human beings should be ashamed of the fact that they possess a physical body and should seek to subjugate it in every way possible. Asceticism was therefore the third main teaching of this philosophy.

The real founder of Neoplatonism was Plotinus, who was born in Egypt about 204 C.E. In the later years of his life he taught in Rome and won many followers among the upper classes before he died in 270. His principal successors diluted the philosophy with more and more bizarre superstitions. In spite of its antirational viewpoint and its utter indifference to the state, Neoplatonism became so popular in Rome in the third and fourth centuries C.E. that it almost completely supplanted Stoicism. No fact could have expressed more eloquently the turn of Rome away from the realities of the here and now. At the same time, people turned increasingly to religions of redemption, of which Christianity was but one. The internal organization of the Christian churches gave them particular appeal and aided the spread of this particular cult, as we will see in the following chapter.

> More has been written on the fall of Rome than on the death of any other civilization.

ROMAN RULE IN THE WEST: A BALANCE SHEET

Did Rome fall? Why or why not?

As Rome was not built in a day, so it was not lost in one. As we will see in the next chapter, strong rule returned in 284 C.E. Thereafter the Roman empire endured in the West for two hundred years more and in the East for a millennium. But the restored Roman state differed greatly from the old one—so much so that it is proper to end the story of characteristically Roman civilization here and review the reasons for Rome's transformation into a distinctly different type of society, one that we will examine in detail in the next chapter.

EXPLAINING THE "FALL" OF ROME

More has been written on the fall of Rome than on the death of any other civilization. The theories offered to account for the decline have been many and varied. Perhaps the strangest recent one is that Rome fell from the effects of lead ingested from cooking utensils, but if this were true we would have to ask why Rome did so well for so long. Moralists have found the explanation for Rome's fall in the descriptions of lechery and gluttony presented in the writings of such authors as Juvenal and Petronius. Such an approach, however, overlooks the facts that much of this evidence is patently overdrawn, and that nearly all of it comes from the period of the early Principate: in the later centuries, when the empire was more obviously collapsing, morality became more austere through the influence of ascetic religions. One of the simplest explanations is that Rome fell only because of the severity of German attacks. But barbarians had always stood ready to attack Rome throughout its long history: German pressures did increase at certain times but German invasions would never have succeeded had they not come at moments when Rome was already weakened internally. Indeed, from the fourth century C.E. onward, increasing numbers of Germanic tribes were less interested in destroying Rome than in becoming a part of it. It was often the case that Roman bigotry, maladministration and abuse had more to do with violent outbursts from the Germans than any propensity for rape and pillage on the part of the "barbarians" themselves.

POLITICAL FAILURES

It is best then to concentrate on Rome's most serious internal problems. Some of these were political. The most obvious political failing of the Roman constitution under the Principate was the lack of a clear law of succession. Especially when a ruler died suddenly, there was no certainty about who was to follow him. In modern America the deaths of a Lincoln or Kennedy might shock the nation, but people at least knew what would happen next; in imperial Rome no one knew and civil war increasingly became the result. For all of Augustus' achievements, this was his system's greatest failure. Indeed, by disguising the reality of autocratic rule behind republican forms, there was little any emperor could do to provide for an orderly succession to an imperial position that did not officially exist. So long as prosperity and deference for the institutions of ancient Rome remained, transitions might be effected more or less smoothly. But from 235 to 284 C.E. warfare and instability fed on each other. Civil war was also nurtured by the lack of constitutional means for reform. If regimes became unpopular, as most did after 180 C.E., the only means to alter them was to overthrow them. But resorting to violence always bred more violence, especially as the soldiery became the arbiter of success or failure of an imperial regime.

> Rome's worst economic problems derived from its slave system and from labor shortages.

ECONOMIC CRISIS

The Roman empire also had its share of economic problems, though the lessons to be drawn from this remain unclear. Rome's worst economic problems derived from its slave system and from labor shortages. Roman civilization was based on cities, and Roman cities existed largely by virtue of an agricultural surplus produced by slaves. Slaves were worked so hard that they did not normally reproduce to fill their own ranks. Until the time of Trajan (98–117 C.E.), Roman conquests provided fresh supplies of slaves to keep the system going, but thereafter the economy began to run out of human fuel. Landlords could no longer be so profligate of human life, barracks slavery came to an end, and the countryside produced less of a surplus to feed the towns. The fact that no technological advance took up the slack may also be attributed to slavery. Later in Western history agricultural surpluses were produced by technological revolutions, but Roman landlords were indifferent to technology because interest in it was thought to be demeaning. As long as slaves were present to do the work, Romans had no interest in labor-saving devices, and attention to any sort of machinery was deemed a sign of slavishness. Landlords proved their nobility by their interest in "higher things," but while they were contemplating

> Ultimately, the decline of Rome was accompanied by lack of interest, and the Roman world slowly came to an end not so much with a bang as with a whimper.

these heights their agricultural surpluses gradually became depleted.

Labor shortages also aggravated Rome's economic problems, especially in the west. The end of foreign conquests and the decline of slavery meant a pressing need for people to stay on the farm, but barbarian pressures also meant a steady need for men to serve in the army. The plagues of the second and third centuries sharply reduced the population just at the worst time. It has been estimated that between the reign of Marcus Aurelius and the restoration of strong rule in 284 C.E. disease, warfare and a declining birthrate combined to reduce the population of the Roman empire by one third. The result was that there were neither sufficient farmers to work the land nor enough soldiers to fight Rome's enemies.

Despite all of this, it is important to remember that Rome was scarcely poverty stricken. Wealth still poured into Roman society, but in the western provinces especially it tended to concentrate itself in the hands of a very few families. These families gradually accrued to themselves such extensive privileges (to say nothing of their ability to hire, when necessary, private means of force) that they rarely contributed anything to the coffers of the Roman state. The burden for the upkeep of cities thus fell increasingly on a local elite that could not shoulder it; as these men were reduced to poverty or fled the cities altogether, the urban basis of classical Roman civilization and its commonly shared civic ideals was further undermined. Regional differences were also growing more pronounced, leading to a series of secessionist movements among the western provinces. Enormous dedication and exertion on the part of its citizenry might just possibly have saved the empire, but too few citizens were now willing to work hard for the public good. Ultimately, the decline of Rome was accompanied by lack of interest, and the Roman world slowly came to an end not so much with a bang as with a whimper.

ROMAN ACHIEVEMENTS

Focusing our attention on the dynamics of Rome's decline in the West should not cause us to overlook the many ways in which Roman society was a towering success. No state has ever encompassed so much territory, with such a large percentage of the world's population under its dominion, for so long a span of time. Roman rule maintained its vitality in the West from the Second Punic War to the end of the fourth century C.E. In the East, the Roman empire survived until 1453. Part of that success resulted from the Roman government's ability to create and maintain systems of communication, trade, and travel as no other state had done before, and as none would do again until modern times. Underlying these successes was the fundamental strength of the Roman economy. While much is made of the collapse of the Roman economy in the third century and its runaway inflation, the Romans had maintained a relatively stable currency and a prosperous international trade for four previous centuries without any of the mechanisms or safeguards of a modern market economy. This too remains an unparalleled achievement.

Most fundamentally, however, the Roman empire's survival was a political achievement. The Roman political system was inclusive to a degree no modern empire has ever matched. Through their willingness to extend the franchise to non-Romans, to allow even provincials to become senators and ultimately emperors, Rome gave a share of power to its population that no Near Eastern or Greek empire could have ever imagined. Although the Persians were tolerant of foreign cultic practice, and the Athenians generous with political rights among their own citizenry, extending real political power to "outsiders" was out of the question. For the Romans, extension of the franchise was key to their success, from the mechanism of the Latin Right in early Italy to the granting of citizenship to all the inhabitants of their empire under Caracalla. As a prominent historian of Rome once remarked, if the British empire had been as willing to extend its franchise as the Romans were to extend theirs, the American Revolution might never have occurred.

> No state has ever encompassed so much territory, with such a large percentage of the world's population under its dominion, for so long a span of time.

tiquity; and second, because Rome seems to bear such a close kinship to the modern temper. The resemblances between Roman history and the history of Great Britain or the United States in the nineteenth and twentieth centuries have often been noted. Like America's, the Roman economy evolved from a simple agrarianism to a complex urban system with problems of unemployment, gross disparities of wealth, and financial crises. Like the British empire, the Roman empire was founded on conquest. And like both the British and the American empires, the Roman empire justified its conquests by celebrating the peace those conquests allegedly brought to the world.

Ultimately, however, such parallels are superficial. Rome was an ancient, not a modern, society that differed profoundly from any of the societies of the modern Western world. As noted already, the Romans disdained industrial activities. Neither did they have any idea of the modern national state; ultimately their empire was a collection of cities, not an integrated territorial body politic. The Romans never developed an adequate representative government, and they never solved the problem of succession to imperial power. Nor were Roman social relations in any way comparable with those of more recent centuries. The Roman economy rested on slavery to a degree unmatched in any modern society. Technology was primitive; social stratification was extreme; and gender relations were profoundly unequal. Roman religion rested on the assumption that religious practice and political life were inseparable from one another, and Roman emperors were worshiped (especially in the East) as living gods.

Nevertheless, the civilization of Rome exerted a great influence on later cultures. Roman architectural forms survive to this day in the design of many of our government buildings, and Roman styles of dress continue to be worn by the clergy of the various Christian churches. Through the sixth-century code of the emperor Justinian (see Chapter 7), Roman law was handed down to the Middle Ages and on into modern times. American judges still cite legal maxims coined by Gaius or Ulpian; and third-century legal precedents continue to be valid in the legal systems of nearly all continental European countries and the American state of Louisiana. Roman sculpture provided the model on which virtually all modern sculpture rests, and Roman authors set the standards for prose composition in

CONCLUSION

It is tempting to believe that we today have many similarities to the Romans: first of all, because Rome is nearer to us in time than the other civilizations of an-

Europe and America until the end of the nineteenth century. Even the organization of the Catholic Church was adapted from the structure of the Roman state; today the pope bears the title of supreme pontiff (*pontifex maximus*), once born by the emperor in his role as head of the Roman civic religion.

But perhaps the most important of all Rome's contributions to the future was its role in transmitting Greek civilization throughout the length and breadth of its empire. When, finally, the united Roman empire did collapse, three different successor civilizations would emerge to occupy Rome's former territories: Byzantium, Islam, and western Europe. Each of these civilizations would be characterized by a distinctive religious tradition, and each would adopt and adapt different aspects of its Roman inheritance. What these three western civilizations shared, however, was a common cultural inheritance derived from Greece by way of Rome—an inheritance of urbanism, cosmopolitanism, imperialism, and learning that would forever mark the West as a unique experiment in human history.

This cultural inheritance would be Rome's epitaph; and in the mid-third century C.E., it must have seemed that an epitaph for the Roman empire was the only thing needed to bring the Roman empire to an end. In fact, the Roman empire did not collapse. It went on to enjoy another several centuries of life. Rome did not fall in the third century, or the fourth century, or even the fifth. But it was transformed, and in this transformed state the Roman inheritance would pass to the Western civilizations of the Middle Ages. It is to those transformations that we now turn.

SELECTED READINGS

Translations of Roman authors are available in the appropriate volumes of the Penguin Classics series and in the Loeb Classical Library.

Badian, Ernst. *Foreign Clientelae (264–70 B.C.).* Oxford, 1958. A seminal work demonstrating how the Roman aristocracy extended traditional bonds of personal obligation into conquered territories as a way to enhance their own power in Rome.

Beard, Mary, John North, and Simon Price. *Religions of Rome, Volume I: A History.* Cambridge, 1998. An authoritative account, full of new ideas.

———. *Religions of Rome, Volume II: A Sourcebook.* Cambridge, 1998. A definitive source collection that supplements *Volume I: A History.*

Boardman, John, Jasper Griffin, and Oswyn Murray. *The Oxford History of the Roman World.* Oxford, 1990. Reprint of relevant portions of the excellent *Oxford History of the Classical World* (1986). Stimulating, accessible topical chapters by British specialists.

Brunt, P. A. *Social Conflicts in the Roman Republic.* New York, 1971. An outstanding overview of the social and economic developments that undermined the republic.

Cornell, T. J. *The Beginnings of Rome: Italy and Rome from the Bronze Age to the Punic Wars (c. 1000–264 B.C.).* London, 1995. An expert, ambitious survey of the archaeological and historical evidence for early Rome.

Crawford, Michael. *The Roman Republic.* 2d ed. Cambridge, Mass., 1993. A lively, fast-paced survey of Republican Rome. An excellent place to start.

Gardner, Jane F. *Women in Roman Law and Society.* Bloomington, 1986. A monograph focused on Roman women's control over property.

Garnsey, Peter, and Richard Saller. *The Roman Empire: Economy, Society, and Culture.* Berkeley, 1987. A straightforward short survey.

Gruen, Erich S. *The Last Generation of the Roman Republic.* Berkeley, 1974. An important but controversial account of the personalities and dynamics that brought an end to the Roman Republic.

———. *The Hellenistic World and the Coming of Rome.* 2 vols. Berkeley, 1984. A massive survey, focused on the unpredictable rise of Rome to a position of dominance within the Mediterranean world.

Hallett, Judith. *Fathers and Daughters in Republican Rome: Women and the Elite Family.* Princeton, N.J., 1984. A detailed examination of the important role played by aristocratic women in shaping political relationships in the family-dominated world of Roman government.

Harris, William V. *War and Imperialism in Republican Rome, 327–70 B.C.* Oxford, 1979. A challenging study arguing that Rome's need for military conquest and imperial expansion was deeply embedded in the political and social fabric of Roman life.

Lancel, Serge. *Carthage: A History.* Trans. by Antonia Nevill. Oxford, 1995. An up-to-date account of Rome's great rival for control of the Mediterranean world.

Lewis, Naphtali, and M. Reinhold. *Roman Civilization: Selected Readings.* 2 volumes. New York, 1951–1955. The standard collection, especially for political and economic subjects. Volume I covers the Republic; Volume II, the empire.

MacMullen, Ramsay. *Roman Social Relations, 50 B.C.–A.D. 284.* New Haven, 1981. An excellent overview of the social structure of Rome from the end of the Republic to the end of the Principate.

Meier, Christian. *Caesar: A Biography.* New York, 1982. An entertaining but reliable biography of Julius Caesar, enlivened by sympathetic portraits of his foes as well as his friends.

Millar, Fergus G. B. *The Emperor in the Roman World, 31 B.C.–A.D. 337.* London, 1977. A classic work that showed (among much else) the importance of emperor worship to the religious outlook of the Roman empire.

———. *The Roman Near East, 31 B.C.–A.D. 337*. Cambridge, Mass., 1993. An exhaustive examination of Roman strategies of control and attitudes toward ethnicity under the Principate.

———. *The Crowd in Rome in the Late Republic*. Ann Arbor, 1999. A revisionist account that emphasizes the reality of Roman democracy in the late Republic, against those who would see the period's politics as entirely under the control of aristocratic families.

Ward, Allen M., Fritz Heichelheim, and Cedric A. Yeo. *A History of the Roman People*, 3d ed. Upper Saddle River, N.J., 1999. An informative, well organized textbook covering Roman history from its beginnings to the end of the sixth century C.E.

Wells, Colin. *The Roman Empire*, 2d ed. Cambridge, Mass., 1992. An easily readable survey from the reign of Augustus to the mid-third century C.E., particularly useful for its treatment of the relationship between the Roman central government and its Italian provinces.

CHRISTIANITY
AND THE
TRANSFORMATION
OF THE
ROMAN WORLD

THE ROMAN EMPIRE DECLINED after 180 C.E., but it did not collapse. In 284 C.E. the vigorous soldier-emperor Diocletian began a reorganization of the empire that gave it a new lease on life. Throughout the fourth century the Roman state continued to encompass the entire Mediterranean world. In the fifth century the western half of the empire did fall to foreign invasions, but many Roman institutions continued, and in the sixth century the empire reconquered a good part of the western Mediterranean shoreline. Only in the seventh century did it become fully evident that divisions between the eastern and western halves of the Roman empire would be permanent, and that the two regions would thereafter develop in fundamentally different ways. With this division, the world of classical antiquity came to an end.

Historians used to underestimate the longevity of Roman institutions and begin their discussions of medieval history in the third, fourth, or fifth century C.E. Since historical periodization is always approximate and depends largely on which aspects of development a historian wishes to emphasize, this approach cannot be dismissed. Certainly the transition from the ancient to the medieval world was gradual, with some "medieval" ways emerging in the West as early as the third century C.E. But it is now more customary to conceive of ancient history as continuing after 284 C.E. and lasting until the Roman empire lost control over the Mediterranean in the seventh century. The period from 284 to about 610 C.E., although transitional (as, of course, all ages are), has certain themes of its own and is best described as neither Roman nor medieval but as the age of late antiquity.

The major cultural trend of late antiquity was the spread and triumph of Christianity throughout the Roman world. At first Christianity was just one of many otherworldly religions that appealed to increasing numbers of people during the later empire. But in the fourth century it was adopted as the Roman state religion and thereafter became one of the greatest shaping forces in the development of Western civilizations.

FOCUS QUESTIONS

• How did Diocletian transform the Roman empire?

• What caused the substantial growth of Christianity in the third century?

• What major changes did Christianity undergo during the fourth century?

 • How did the Germanic tribes triumph over the western Roman empire?

• What was Augustine's conception of history?

• How was classical culture Christianized?

• What did Justinian's plan to reunite the Roman empire fail?

Outside Palestine, Christianity found its first adherents in the cities of the Roman empire, and spread only gradually from these urban centers into the surrounding countryside. Its extension, first from city to city, and then from city to countryside, was a vital element in an ongoing process of cultural assimilation that characterized the late antique Roman world. As cultural developments traveled from one part of the empire to another, however, they also became less sophisticated and less rooted in the local areas (such as Palestine) where they had originated. The result was an increasing cultural diffusion that brought with it a "watering down" of the high culture of the classical era—a process we shall call "vulgarization."

At the same time, cultural influences from outside the Mediterranean world were also having a growing impact, especially on the western parts of the empire. This process the Romans themselves called "barbarization," from the Greek word *barbaros*, meaning "foreigner." Barbarian culture was not necessarily primitive, but it was nonurban and non-Greek—and in the eyes of Mediterranean elites, these facts alone were enough to stigmatize it. But "barbarian" influence grew steadily nonetheless, first within the army, and then throughout society. None of these processes were cataclysmic; but by the end of the sixth century C.E., Christianization, vulgarization, and barbarization had combined to bring the ancient Mediterranean world to an end.

Diocletian. His short hair is in the Roman military style.

THE REORGANIZED EMPIRE

How did Diocletian transform the Roman empire?

The chaos of the mid-third century C.E. might well have destroyed the Roman empire. That it did not is largely due to the energetic work of a remarkable soldier named Diocletian, who ruled as emperor from 284 to 305 C.E. Well aware of the problems that had undone his predecessors, Diocletian embarked on a number of fundamental political and economic reforms. Recognizing that the dominance of the army in the life of the state had hitherto been too great, he introduced measures to separate military from civilian administrative chains of command. Aware that new pressures, both external and internal, had made it nearly impossible for one man to govern the entire Roman empire, he divided his realm in half, granting the western part to

a trusted colleague, Maximian, who recognized Diocletian as the senior ruler. The two then chose lieutenants, called caesars, to govern large subsections of their territories. This system (known as the Tetrarchy, "the rule of the four") was also meant to provide for an orderly succession, for the caesars were supposed to inherit the major rule of either East or West and then appoint new caesars in their stead.

THE REIGN OF DIOCLETIAN

In the economic sphere Diocletian stabilized the badly debased currency, introduced a new system of taxation, and issued legislation designed to keep agricultural workers and town dwellers at their jobs so that the basic work necessary to support the empire would continue to be done. To check inflation, he attempted (without much success) to fix prices and wages; to unite the empire, he sought to enforce observance of the rituals of the Roman imperial cult on dissident groups, such as Christians, who refused to participate in them. The result, between 303 and 313 C.E., was "the Great Persecution," in which hundreds of Christians perished throughout the empire.

Although Diocletian succeeded in restoring an empire that had been on the verge of expiring, he also transformed the empire by "orientalizing" it in three primary and lasting ways. Most literally, Diocletian began a geographical orientalization of the empire by shifting its administrative weight toward the East. Between 284 and 303 C.E. Diocletian ruled his empire not from Rome, but from Nicomedia, a city in modern-day Turkey, in a tacit recognition of the fact that the wealthier and more vital part of the empire now lay in the East. Second, as befitting one who turned his back on Rome, Diocletian adopted the titles and ceremonies of a Near Eastern potentate. Abandoning Augustus' policy of appearing to be a constitutional ruler, Diocletian presented himself as an undisguised autocrat. He took the title not of *princeps*, or "first citizen," but of *dominus*, or "lord." He wore a diadem and a purple gown of silk interwoven with gold, and he introduced Persian-style ceremony into his court. Those who gained an audience had to prostrate themselves before him; a privileged few were allowed to kiss his robe.

The third aspect of orientalization in Diocletian's policy was his growing reliance on an imperial bureaucracy. By separating civilian from military commands and legislating on a wide variety of economic and social matters, Diocletian created the need for many new officials. Not surprisingly, by the end of his reign subjects were complaining that "there were more tax collectors than taxpayers." These officials did keep the empire going, but the new bureaucracy was prone to graft and corruption; worse, the growing number of bureaucrats called for reservoirs of manpower and wealth at a time when the Roman empire no longer had large supplies of either. Taken together, the various aspects of Diocletian's easternizing made him seem more like a Hellenistic sacral monarch than a Roman ruler: it was almost as if the defeat of Antony and Cleopatra at Actium was now being avenged.

Diocletian's rigid regime left little room for spontaneity or individual freedom. The results can be seen most clearly in the architecture and art of the age. Dio-

Diocletian's Palace in Split. An artistic reconstruction.

Porphyry Sculptures of Diocletian and His Colleagues in Rule. Every effort is made to make the two senior rulers and their two junior colleagues look identical by means of stylization. Note also the emphasis on military strength.

Colossal Head of Constantine. In this head of Constantine the eyes are enlarged as if to emphasize the ruler's spiritual vision. The head is approximately seven times larger than life and weighs about nine tons.

THE REIGN OF CONSTANTINE

In 305 C.E. Diocletian decided to abdicate to raise cabbages—an unprecedented move for a late Roman ruler. At the same time he obliged his colleague Maximian to retire as well, and their two caesars moved peacefully up the ladder of succession. But the concord did not last. Civil war broke out among Diocletian's successors and continued until Constantine, the son of one of the original caesars, emerged victorious. From 312 until 324 Constantine ruled only in the West, but from 324 until his death in 337 C.E. he did away with power sharing and ruled over a reunited empire. Except for the fact that he favored Christianity, an epoch-making decision to be examined in the next section, Constantine continued to govern along the lines laid down by Diocletian. Bureaucracy proliferated and the state became so vigilant in keeping town dwellers and agricultural laborers at their posts that society began to harden into a caste system. In keeping with Constantine's grandiose conception of himself, he built a new capital in 330 C.E. and named it Constantinople. This new capital was the most visible manifestation yet of the continued shift in the "weight" of Roman civilization toward the East. Situated on the border of Europe and Asia, Constantinople had commanding advantages as a center for Eastern-oriented communications, trade, and defense. Surrounded on three sides by water and protected on land by walls, it was to prove nearly impregnable and would remain the center of "Roman" government for the next one thousand years.

Constantine also made succession to the imperial throne hereditary. By so doing he brought Rome back to the principle of dynastic monarchy that it had thrown off about eight hundred years earlier. But Constantine, who treated the empire as if it were his private property, did not pass on united rule to one son. Instead he divided his realm among three of them. Not surprisingly, his three sons started fighting each other after their father's death, a conflict exacerbated by religious differences. Warfare and dynastic squabbles continued on and off for most of the fourth century C.E., as did periodic challenges from aspiring usurpers of the imperial throne. But these disturbances were never so serious as the civil wars of the third century, and from time to time one or another contestant was able to reunite the empire for a period of years. The last to do so was Theodosius I (379–395 C.E.), who butchered thousands of innocent citizens of Thessalonica in retribution for the death of one of his officers, but whose energies in preserving the empire by holding off Ger-

cletian himself preferred a colossal, bombastic style of building that was meant to emphasize his own power. The baths he constructed in Rome, when he finally arrived there in 303 C.E., were the largest yet known, encompassing about thirty acres. When he retired in 305 Diocletian built a palace for himself in what is now Split (Croatia) that was laid out along a rectilinear grid like an army camp. A plan of this palace shows clearly how Diocletian favored regimentation in everything.

Roman portrait statuary, which had hitherto featured striking naturalism and individuality, also became impersonal and unexpressive during this period. Human faces were impassive and symmetrical rather than reflecting a free play of emotions. Porphyry, a particularly hard and dark stone that had to be imported from Egypt—another sign of easternization—often replaced marble for imperial busts. Sculpted in porphyry, groups of statues of Diocletian, Maximian, and their two caesars show the new hardness and symmetry at their fullest, for the figures were made to look so similar that they are indistinguishable from each other.

WHAT CAUSED THE SUBSTANTIAL GROWTH OF CHRISTIANITY IN THE THIRD CENTURY?

THE EMERGENCE AND TRIUMPH OF CHRISTIANITY   227

manic barbarians still gave him some claim to his title "the Great."

The period between Constantine and Theodosius saw the hardening of earlier tendencies. With Constantinople now the leading city of the empire, the center of commerce and administration was located clearly in the East. Regionalism too grew more pronounced: the Latin-speaking West was losing a sense of rapport and contact with the Greek-speaking East, and in both West and East local differences were becoming accentuated. In economic life the hallmark of the age was the growing gap between rich and poor. In the West large landowners were able to consolidate their holdings, and in the East some individuals became prosperous by rising through the bureaucracy and enriching themselves with graft, or by trading in luxury goods. But the taxation system initiated by Diocletian and maintained throughout the fourth century C.E. weighed heavily on the poor, forcing them to carry the burden of supporting the bureaucracy, the army, and the lavish imperial court or courts. The poor, moreover, had no chance to escape their poverty, for legislation demanded that they and their heirs stay at their unrewarding and heavily taxed jobs. Most people in the fourth century thus lived in desperate and unrelenting poverty against a backdrop of ostentatious wealth. The Roman empire may have been restored in the years from 284 to 395 C.E., but it was nonetheless a fertile breeding ground for a new religion of otherwordly salvation.

The Roman empire may been restored in the years from 284 to 395 C.E., but it was nonetheless a fertile breeding ground for a new religion of otherworldly salvation.

THE EMERGENCE AND TRIUMPH OF CHRISTIANITY

What caused the substantial growth of Christianity in the third century?

Christian beginnings of course go back several centuries before Constantine to the time of Jesus. Christianity was formed primarily by Jesus and Saint Paul and gained converts steadily thereafter. But the new religion became widespread only during the chaos of the third century C.E. and triumphed in the Roman empire only in the fourth century, after it became the favored religion of Constantine and his family. At the time of its humble beginnings no one could have predicted that Christianity would become the official religion of the Roman empire by the year 392 C.E.

THE CAREER OF JESUS

Jesus of Nazareth was born in Judea sometime near the beginning of the Common (or Christian) Era. He was not born exactly in the "year one"—we owe this mistake in our dating system to a sixth-century monk. When Jesus was born, the Roman conquest of Judea was not even a generation old. The atmosphere of the region was charged with religious division and political discontent. Banditry, sometimes tinged by nationalism, was commonplace in the countryside; in the cities and villages, the talk was of rebellion, and the hope for a messiah who would expel the idolatrous Romans from the holy land of Israel. Most extreme of those who sought hope in politics were the Zealots, who sought to overthrow the Romans by force of arms. Their activities eventually led to two disastrous revolts. The first, in 69–70 C.E., brought about the destruction of the Temple at Jerusalem; the second, in 132–135 C.E., caused the expulsion of the entire Jewish population of the city. Thereafter, Jews were forbidden to live there, and the shattered city itself was refounded as a pagan city, Aelia Capitolina.

For the career of Jesus, however, the religious divisions within Judaism matter most. In the centuries following the rebuilding of the Temple, Judaism had become an uncompromisingly monotheistic religion, built on the covenantal relationship between Yahweh and his chosen people, the Jews. Within Second Temple Judaism, however, important differences in the interpretation of that covenant soon emerged. By the fourth century B.C.E., the first five books of the Bible had assumed their present form. These books contain the written Torah—the laws and commandments binding on Jews as a result of their covenant with Yahweh. The guardians of these written traditions were the Temple priesthood and their aristocratic allies, a group known together as the Sadducees. As one would expect in the ancient world, the alliance between religious and political authorities in Judea was close. Before the Roman conquest, the high priest of the

Temple at Jerusalem had been appointed by the Hasmonean Jewish monarchs, who had secured their independence from the Seleucid rulers of Syria in the second century B.C.E. After the Roman conquest, however, the high priest was appointed by Rome. As a result, the Sadducees were inevitably tinged by suspicions of collaborationism, despite the central role they played in the religious observances of the Temple cult.

Their main rivals for the religious allegiance of the people were the Pharisees, a group of teachers and preachers of religious law who were in many ways the heirs of the prophetic tradition of the First Temple period. In contrast to the Sadducees, who considered most of the proscriptions of religious law to pertain only to the priesthood, the Pharisees insisted that all 613 of Yahweh's commandments were binding on all Jews. As interpreters of religious law, their authority rested on their claim that at Sinai, Yahweh had given Moses both a written and an oral Torah. The written Torah was contained in the Bible; but the oral Torah, which explained how the written Torah was to be applied to daily life, has been handed down by the spoken word, from teachers to students, across the generations from Moses to the present day. In addition to their rigorous legalism, the Pharisees also believed in a life after death characterized by individual rewards and punishments. They actively sought out converts through preaching; and they looked forward to the imminent arrival of the messiah whom God had promised to his people. In all these respects they differed from the more conservative and more traditional Sadducees. Even more radical, however, were various splinter groups such as the Essenes, a quasi-monastic group that hoped for spiritual deliverance through asceticism, repentance, and mystical union with God.

Although some scholars see Essene influence behind the career of Jesus of Nazareth, it seems clear that in most respects Jesus stood squarely within the Pharisaic tradition. As historians, we are handicapped, of course, in saying anything about Jesus' life by the fact that virtually the only sources of information about him are the Gospels, the first four books of the Christian New Testament, the earliest of which (the Gospel of Mark) was written some thirty years after Jesus' death. Inevitably, these sources are full of inaccuracies, in part because they were not eyewitness accounts, but primarily because they were never meant to be strictly factual reports—rather, they were intended as proclamations of supernatural faith. So far as we can know, however, when Jesus was about thirty years old he was acclaimed by a preacher of moral reform, John the

Baptist, as one "mightier than I, whose shoes I am not worthy to stoop down and unloose." For about three years thereafter Jesus' career was a continuous course of preaching, healing the sick, "casting out demons," and teaching humility by precepts, parables, and his own example.

Believing he had a mission to save humanity from sin, Jesus denounced greed and licentiousness and urged love of God and neighbor. Additionally, it seems reasonably clear that he taught the following: (1) the fatherhood of God and the brotherhood of humanity; (2) the Golden Rule ("do unto others as you would have others do unto you"); (3) forgiveness and love of one's enemies; (4) repayment of evil with good; (5) shunning of hypocrisy; (6) opposition to literalism in the application of Jewish religious law; (7) the imminent approach of the kingdom of God; and (8) the resurrection of the dead and the establishment of the kingdom of heaven. In so doing, Jesus crossed swords with both the Sadducees and many rival Pharisees. To the Pharisees, Jesus' willingness to bend religious law (for example, the prohibition against working on the Sabbath) in the name of ethical precepts threatened to undermine the obligatory nature of the law altogether; to the Sadducees, the turning point came at Passover, when Jesus entered Jerusalem in an openly messianic manner, and then proceeded to drive the merchants and moneychangers physically out of the Temple precincts, declaring that "It is written: my house shall be called a house of prayer, but you have made it a den of thieves."

The city's religious leaders quickly arrested him, tried him in their highest court for blasphemy, condemned him, and handed him over to Pontius Pilate, the Roman governor, for sentencing. As with any Roman governor, Pilate's principal interest lay in preserving peace during a volatile religious festival in a restive part of the empire. No doubt he was also anxious to maintain good relations with the religious authorities in Jerusalem, his capital city. He therefore condemned the troublemaker to death by crucifixion, a standard Roman criminal penalty for those judged guilty of sedition against Rome.

The crucifixion of Jesus marked a decisive moment in Christian history. At first Jesus' death was viewed by his followers as the end of their hopes. Yet after a few days their despair began to dissipate, for rumors began to spread that the Master was alive and had been seen by some of his disciples. In short order Jesus' followers became convinced that not only had Jesus risen from the dead but that he had walked on earth thereafter for

WHAT CAUSED THE SUBSTANTIAL GROWTH OF CHRISTIANITY IN THE THIRD CENTURY?

THE EMERGENCE AND TRIUMPH OF CHRISTIANITY   229

forty days; hence, he truly was a divine being. With their courage restored, they fanned out to preach the good news of Jesus' divinity and to testify in the name of their martyred leader. Soon belief in Jesus' godliness and resurrection became articles of faith for thousands: Jesus was the "Christ" (Greek for the "anointed one"), the divine Son of God who was sent to earth to suffer and die for the sins of humanity, and who, after three days in the tomb, had risen from the dead and ascended into heaven, whence he would come again to judge the world at the end of time.

THE PROPAGATION OF EARLY CHRISTIANITY

Christianity was broadened and invested with a more elaborate theology by Jesus' followers, above all by the Apostle Paul, originally known as Saul of Tarsus (c. 10–c. 67 C.E.). Paul was not a native of Palestine but a Jew born in the city of Tarsus in southeastern Asia Minor. A staunch Pharisee, Saul was initially a persecutor of Christians, but after a blinding conversion experience, he adopted Christianity, changed his name, and devoted his limitless energy to propagating the new faith throughout the Near East. It would be almost impossible to

> Christianity was broadened and invested with a more elaborate theology by Jesus' followers, above all by the Apostle Paul (c. 10–c. 67 C.E.).

overestimate the significance of his work. Denying that Jesus was sent merely as the redeemer of the Jews, Paul proclaimed Christianity to be a universal religion with a mission to the entire world. Furthermore, he placed major emphasis on the idea of Jesus as the Christ, as the anointed God-man whose death on the cross was an atonement for the sins of humanity. Declaring himself to be the Apostle to the Gentiles (non–Jews), Paul rejected the binding nature of Jewish religious law, declaring it to be irrelevant to salvation. Sinners by nature, human beings could be saved only by faith and by the grace of God "through the redemption that is in Christ Jesus." It follows, according to Paul, that salvation is almost entirely dependent on the will of God, for "has the potter no power over the clay, to make out of the same lump one vessel for beauty, and another for menial use?" (Romans 9:21). God has mercy "on whomever he wills, and he hardens the heart of whomever he wills" (Romans 9:18).

Despite the new faith's Jewish origins, Christianity drew relatively few converts from among the Jews of the Roman world. Most of the new converts were Gentiles, drawn perhaps from the groups of "god-fearers" who tended to gather around the Jewish communities scattered across the Roman world. But Christianity only began to attract substantial numbers of adherents in the third-century "age of anxiety." During a time of extreme political turbulence and economic hardship, people began to treat life on earth as an illusion and to place their hopes in a world beyond this one. The human body and the material world were more and more regarded as either evil or basically unreal. As the philosopher Plotinus wrote, "When I come to myself, I wonder how it is that I have a body. . . . by what deterioration did this happen?" Plotinus devised a philosophical system to answer this question, but his system was far too abstruse to have much meaning for large numbers of people. Instead, several religions that emphasized the dominance of spiritual forces in this world and the absolute preeminence of otherworldly salvation gained hold as never before.

At first Christianity was just one of these religions; Mithraism and the cult of Serapis were others. It is natural to ask, therefore, why Christianity gained converts in the third century at the expense of its rivals. A number of answers may be posited. Perhaps most strikingly, Christian preachers were unusually effective in "casting out demons." In a world that believed firmly in the ubiquity of demonic possession, this was no small recommendation for a new faith, and helped it to overcome the instinctive Roman hostility to religious novelties. More important ultimately, however, were the new religion's view of salvation, its social dimensions, and its organizational structure.

Although other religions also promised an afterlife, Christianity's doctrine on this subject was the most far reaching. In an age of fears, Christian warnings that nonbelievers would "liquefy in fierce fires" for eternity while believers would enjoy eternal blessedness understandably made many converts. Christians also drew converts from all classes. From its origins, Christianity had been a religion of the humble—carpenters, fishermen, and tentmakers—that promised the exaltation of the lowly. As the religion grew it gained a few wealthy patrons, but it continued to find its greatest strength among the lower and middle classes, who comprised the greatest numbers in the Roman empire. It may also have had a particular appeal to women, perhaps because it accorded women some role in worship at first

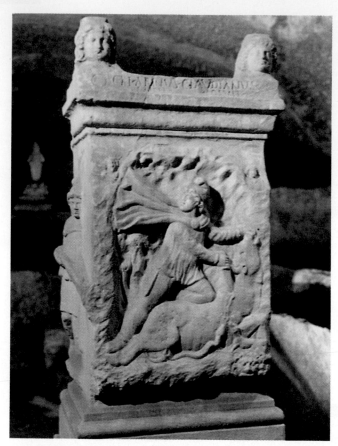

Altar of Mithras. Dating from the third century C.E., this altar used for Mithraic services in an underground chamber in the heart of Rome depicts Mithras slaying a bull. A century later, when Christianity triumphed in the Roman empire, a Christian church was built over the Mithraic sanctuary.

and an equal hope for salvation. This fact gave it an advantage over Mithraism, which excluded women from its cult entirely. In addition to all these considerations, a final reason for Christianity's success lay in its organization. Unlike the rival mystery religions, by the third century it had developed an organized hierarchy of priests to direct the life of the faith. More than that, Christian congregations were tightly knit communities that provided services to their members—such as nursing, support of the unprotected, and burial—that went beyond strictly religious concerns. Those who became Christians found human contacts and a sense of mission while the rest of the world seemed to be collapsing about them.

Christians were never so brutally persecuted by the

> Despite all that has been said, the triumph of Christianity in the Roman empire was by no means inevitable.

Roman state as used to be thought. In fact the attitude of Rome was usually one of indifference: Christians were customarily tolerated unless local magistrates chose to prosecute them for refusing to worship the official state gods. From time to time there were more concerted persecutions, but these were too intermittent and short lived to do irreparable damage; on the contrary, they served to give Christianity some helpful publicity. To this degree the blood of martyrs really was the seed of the church, but only because the blood did not flow too freely. One last great persecution took place toward the end of the reign of Diocletian and was continued by one of his immediate successors, a particularly bitter enemy of Christianity named Galerius. But by then the religion had gained too many converts to be wiped out by persecution, a fact that Galerius finally recognized by issuing an edict of toleration just before his death in 311 C.E..

Despite all that has been said, the triumph of Christianity in the Roman empire was by no means inevitable. Although exact statistics are impossible to come by, estimates of the number of Christians in the empire around 300 C.E. range from 1 percent to 5 percent of the total population. Even in the relatively more Christianized eastern part of the empire, Christians in the year 300 did not number more than 10 percent of the population, and were probably closer to 5 percent. It was only the conversion of the emperor Constantine in 312 C.E. that ensured the success of the new faith. Exactly why Constantine became a Christian will never be known; legend has it that he thought he saw a cross in the sky while preparing for battle and then switched allegiance to the new faith, hoping that it would yield him victory in a contest for political supremacy. As Constantine did in fact gain military victories and ultimately rose to become sole emperor, his commitment to Christianity became ever more pronounced. By the time of his death in 337 he had showered favors on the Christian clergy and patronized the building of churches throughout the empire. This was the turning point, for although Constantine did not yet prohibit paganism, his sons and emperors after them were raised as Christians and were ever less inclined to tolerate competing faiths. A brief exception was the reign from 360 to 363 C.E. of Julian "the Apostate," an emperor who attempted to launch a pagan revival. But after Julian was killed in battle with the Persians, his pro-pagan edicts were revoked, and by

PROSECUTING CHRISTIANS

THE LETTERS OF PLINY THE ELDER AND THE EMPEROR TRAJAN

Until the third century, the Roman imperial government rarely initiated the persecution of Christians. Local administrators, such as the elder Pliny, were anxious to follow proper legal procedures in dealing with the new sect, which they regarded as absurd but not particularly dangerous. But neither Pliny nor the emperor Trajan (98–117 C.E.) wanted to see the Roman state actively seek out Christians for punishment.

LETTER 97: PLINY TO TRAJAN

It is a rule, Sir, which I inviolably observe, to refer myself to you in all my doubts; for who is more capable of removing my scruples, or informing my ignorance? Having never been present at any trials concerning those who profess Christianity, I am unacquainted not only with the nature of their crimes, or the measure of their punishment, but how far it is proper to enter into an examination concerning them. . . .

The method I have observed towards those who have been brought before me as Christians, is this: I interrogated them whether they were Christians; if they confessed I repeated the question twice again, adding threats at the same time; when, if they still persevered, I ordered them to be immediately punished: for I was persuaded, whatever the nature of their opinions might be, a contumacious and inflexible obstinacy certainly deserved correction. . . .

But this crime spreading (as is usually the case) while it was actually under prosecution, several instances of the same nature occurred. An information was presented to me without any name subscribed, containing a charge against several persons, who upon examination denied they were Christians, or had ever been so.

They repeated after me an invocation to the gods, and offered religious rites with wine and frankincense before your statue (which for the purpose I had ordered to be brought together with those of the gods); and even reviled the name of Christ: whereas there is no forcing, it is said, those who are really Christians, into a compliance with any of these articles: I thought proper therefore to discharge them. . . .

I judged it . . . necessary to endeavor to extort the real truth [about Christian rites and beliefs] by putting two female slaves to the torture, who were said to administer in their religious functions: but I could discover nothing more than an absurd and excessive superstition. I thought proper therefore to adjourn all further proceedings in this affair, in order to consult with you. . . . For this contagious superstition is not confined to the cities only, but has spread its infection among the country villages. Nevertheless, it still seems possible to remedy this evil and restrain its progress. The temples, at least, which were once almost deserted, begin now to be frequented; and the sacred solemnities, after a long intermission, are again revived. . . . From hence it is easy to imagine, what numbers might be reclaimed from this error, if a pardon were granted to those who shall repent.

The method you have pursued, my dear Pliny, in the proceedings against those Christians which were brought before you, is extremely proper; as it is not possible to lay down any fixed plan by which to act in all cases of this nature. But I would not have you officiously enter into any enquiries concerning them. If indeed they should be brought before you, and the crime is proved, they must be punished; with the restriction, however, that where the party denies himself to be a Christian, and shall make it evident that he is not, by invoking our gods, let him (notwithstanding any former suspicion) be pardoned upon his repentence. Information without the accuser's name subscribed ought not to be received in prosecutions of any sort, as it is introducing a very dangerous precedent, and by no means agreeable to the equity of my government.

W. Melmoth, trans. *The Letters of Pliny the Consul, Vol. 2* (London: J. Dodsley, 1770), pp. 671–677. Reprinted in *Western Societies: A Documentary History*, Vol. 1, edited by Brian Tierney and Joan Scott (New York: Knopf, 1984), pp. 166–168.

the end of the century Theodosius the Great had completed Constantine's work by prohibiting pagan worship of any sort, public or private. Meanwhile most citizens of the Roman empire had converted to Christianity because of the environment of official support.

THE NEW CONTOURS OF FOURTH-CENTURY CHRISTIANITY

What major changes did Christianity undergo during the fourth century?

Once the new faith became dominant within the Roman empire it underwent some major changes in forms of thought, organization, and conduct. These changes all bore relationships to earlier tendencies, but the triumph of the faith greatly accelerated certain trends and altered the course of others. The result was that in many respects the Christianity of the late fourth century was a very different religion from that persecuted by Diocletian and Galerius.

DOCTRINAL QUARRELS

One consequence of Christianity's triumph was the flaring up of bitter doctrinal disputes. These brought great turmoil to the church but resulted in the hammering out of dogma and discipline. Before the conversion of Constantine there had of course been disagreements among Christians about doctrinal matters, but as long as Christianity was a minority religion it managed to control its internal divisions in order to present a united front against hostile outsiders. As soon as the new faith emerged victorious, however, sharp splits developed within its own ranks. These were due partly to the fact that there had always been a tension between the intellectual and emotional tendencies within the religion that could now come more fully into the open, and partly to the fact that different regions of the empire tried to preserve a sense of their separate identities by preferring different theological formulas.

The first of the bitter disputes was between the Arians and Athanasians over the nature of the Trinity. The Arians—not to be confused with Aryans (a racial term)—were followers of a priest named Arius. Under the influence of Greek philosophy they rejected the idea that Christ could be equal with God. Instead they maintained that the Son was created by the Father in time, and therefore was not coeternal with Him or formed of the same substance. The followers of Saint Athanasius held that even though Christ was the Son he was fully God: that Father, Son, and Holy Spirit were all absolutely equal and composed of an identical substance. After protracted struggles Athanasius' side won out and the Athanasian doctrine became the Christian doctrine of the Trinity, as it remains today.

The struggle between the Arians and Athanasians was followed by numerous other doctrinal quarrels during the next few centuries. The issues at stake were generally too abstruse to warrant explaining here, but the results were momentous. One was that the dogmas of the Catholic faith gradually became fixed. Granted, this was a slow development and many basic tenets of Catholicism were defined much later (for example, the theory of the Mass was not formally promulgated until

WHAT MAJOR CHANGES DID CHRISTIANITY UNDERGO DURING THE FOURTH CENTURY?

THE NEW CONTOURS OF FOURTH-CENTURY CHRISTIANITY   233

Jesus. Conception from a sixth-century mosaic in Ravenna.

1215; the doctrine of the Immaculate Conception of the Virgin Mary until 1854; and that of the bodily assumption of the Virgin into heaven until 1950). Nonetheless, the faith was beginning to take on a sharply defined form unprecedented in the history of earlier religions. Above all, this meant that anyone who differed from a certain formulation would be excluded from the community and often persecuted as a heretic. In the subsequent history of Christianity this concern for doctrinal uniformity was to result in both strengths and weaknesses for the church.

A second result of the doctrinal quarrels was that they aggravated regional hostilities. In the fourth century differences among Christians increased alienation between West and East and also worsened hostilities among regions within the East. Although the Roman empire was evolving toward regionalism for many different reasons, including economic and administrative

ones, and although regionalism was partly a cause of religious differences, the sharper and more frequent doctrinal quarrels became, the more they intensified regional antagonisms.

Finally, the doctrinal quarrels provoked the increasing involvement of the Roman state in the governance of the church. Because Constantine had hoped that Christianity would be a unifying rather than a divisive force in the empire, he was horrified by the Arian conflict and intervened in it by calling the Council of Nicea (325 C.E.), which condemned Arius. It is noteworthy that this council—the first general council of the church—was convened by a Roman emperor and that Constantine presided over it, assuming a role as Christ's representative on earth that would also be claimed by his successor emperors, especially in the East. There were two major reasons for this. First, religious disputes were more prevalent in the East than in the West, and quarreling parties often appealed to the emperor for support. Second, the weight of imperial government was generally heavier in the East, and after 476 C.E. there were no Roman emperors in the West at all. When Eastern emperors were not appealed to by quarreling parties they interfered in religious disputes themselves, as Constantine had done before them, in order to preserve unity. The result was that in the East the emperor assumed great religious authority and control, whereas in the West the future of relations between the state and the Church was more open.

GROWTH OF ECCLESIASTICAL ORGANIZATION

This fourth-century consolidation of religious with imperial authority was mirrored in the church's own internal organization. We have seen that some distinction between clergy and laity was recognized very early in the history of Christianity. The next step was the development of a hierarchical organization within the ranks of the clergy. Christian organization was centered in cities, and one bishop in each important city had become the authority to which all the clergy in the surrounding vicinity answered even before Constantine converted to Christianity. But as the number of congregations multiplied and as the influence of the church increased due to the adoption of Christianity as the official religion of Rome, distinctions of rank among the bishops themselves also began to appear. Those who had their headquarters in the larger cities came to be called metropolitans (today known in the West as archbishops), with authority over the clergy of an entire province. In the fourth century the still higher rank of patriarch was established to designate those bishops who ruled over the oldest and largest of Christian communities—such cities as Rome, Jerusalem, Constantinople, Antioch, and Alexandria, and their surrounding districts. Thus the Christian clergy by 400 C.E. had come to embrace a definite hierarchy of patriarchs, metropolitans, bishops, and priests.

The climax of all this development would be the growth of the primacy of the bishop of Rome, or the rise of the papacy. For several reasons the bishop of Rome claimed a preeminence over the other patriarchs of the Church. The city in which he ruled was venerated by the faithful as a scene of the missionary activities and eventual martyrdom of the Apostles Peter and Paul. The tradition was widely accepted that Peter had founded the bishopric of Rome, and that therefore all of his successors were heirs of his authority and prestige. This tradition was supplemented by the theory that Peter had been commissioned by Christ as his vicar on earth and had been given the keys of the kingdom of heaven with power to punish people for their sins and even to absolve them of guilt (Matthew 16:18–19). This theory, known as the doctrine of the Petrine Succession, has been used by popes ever since as a basis for their claims to authority over the Church. The bishops of Rome had an advantage also in the fact that after the transfer of the imperial capital to Constantinople, there was seldom an emperor with effective sovereignty in the West. Finally, in 445 C.E. the emperor Valentinian III issued a decree commanding all Western bishops to submit to the jurisdiction of the pope. It must not be supposed, however, that the church was by any means yet under a monarchical form of government. The patriarchs in the East regarded the extreme assertions of papal claims as brazen effrontery, and even many bishops in the West continued to ignore them.

The growth of ecclesiastical organization helped the church to conquer the Roman world in the fourth century and to minister to the needs of the faithful thereafter. The existence of an episcopal administrative structure was particularly influential in the West as the Roman empire decayed and finally collapsed in the fifth century C.E.. Since every city had a bishop trained to some degree in the arts of administration, the church in the West took over many of the functions of government and helped to preserve order amid the deepening chaos. But the new emphasis on administration also had its detrimental effects: as the church developed its own rationalized administrative structure, it inevitably became more worldly and distant in spirit from the simple faith of Jesus and the apostles.

> The growth of ecclesiastical organization helped the church to conquer the Roman world in the fourth century.

THE SPREAD OF MONASTICISM

The clearest reaction to this trend was expressed in the spread of monasticism. Today we are accustomed to thinking of monks as groups of priests who live communally in order to dedicate themselves primarily to lives of contemplation and prayer. In their origins, however, monks were not priests but laymen who al-

WHAT MAJOR CHANGES DID CHRISTIANITY UNDERGO DURING THE FOURTH CENTURY?

THE NEW CONTOURS OF FOURTH-CENTURY CHRISTIANITY   235

most always lived alone and who sought extremes of self-denial rather than ordered lives of spirituality. Monasticism began to emerge in the third century as a response to the anxieties of that age, but it became a dominant movement within Christianity only in the fourth century. Two obvious reasons for this fact stand out. First of all, the choice of extreme hermitlike asceticism was a substitute for martyrdom. With the conversion of Constantine and the abandonment of persecution, most chances of winning a crown of glory in heaven by undergoing death for the faith were eliminated. But the desire to prove one's religious ardor by self-abasement and suffering was still present. Second, as the fourth century progressed, the priesthood became more and more immersed in worldly concerns. Those who wished to avoid secular temptations fled to the deserts and woods to practice an asceticism that priests and bishops were forgetting. (Monks customarily became priests only later in history, during the late Middle Ages.) In this way even while Christianity was accommodating itself to practical needs, monasticism satisfied the inclinations of ascetic extremists.

Monasticism first emerged in the East, where for about one hundred years after Constantine's conversion it spread like a mania. Hermit monks of Egypt and Syria vied with each other in their pursuit of the most inhuman and humiliating excesses. Some grazed in the fields after the manner of cows, others penned themselves into small cages, and others hung heavy weights around their necks. A monk named Cyriacus stood for hours on one leg like a crane until he could bear it no more. The most extravagant of these monastic ascetics was Saint Simeon Stylites, who performed self-punishing exercises—such as touching his feet with his head 1,244 times in succession—on top of a high pillar for thirty-seven years, while crowds gathered below to worship "the worms that dropped from his body."

In time such ascetic hysteria subsided, and it became recognized that monasticism would be more enduring if monks lived in a community and did not concentrate on self-torture. The most successful architect of communal monasticism in the East was Saint Basil (c. 330–379), who started his monastic career as a hermit and ascetic extremist but came to prefer communal and more moderate forms of life. Basil expressed this preference in writings for monks that laid down the basic guidelines for Eastern monasticism

St. Simeon Stylites on his Pillar. The devil is shown as a huge snake. Admirers who wished to speak to the saint would climb the ladder shown on the left. This gold plaque dates from the sixth century.

down to the present. Rather than encouraging extremes of self-torture, Basil encouraged monks to discipline themselves by useful labor. Although his teachings were still extremely severe by modern standards, he prohibited monks from engaging in prolonged fasts or lacerating their flesh. Instead he urged them to submit to obligations of poverty and humility, and to spend many hours of the day in silent religious meditation. With the triumph of Saint Basil's ideas, Eastern monasticism became more organized and subdued, but even so Basilian monks preferred to live as far away from the "world" as they could and never had the same civilizing influence on the world outside the cloister as did their brothers in western Europe.

Monasticism did not at first spread quickly in the West because the appeal of asceticism was much weaker there. This situation changed only in the sixth century when Saint Benedict (c. 480–c. 547) drafted his famous Latin rule, which ultimately became the guide for nearly all Western monks. Modern scholarship has shown that Benedict copied much of his rule from an earlier and much harsher Latin text known as the "Rule of the Master." Benedict, however, produced a document notable for its brevity, flexibility, and moderation. The Benedictine rule imposed obligations similar to those laid down by Saint Basil: poverty, sexual chastity, obedience, labor, and religious devotion. Yet Benedict prescribed less austerity than Basil did: the monks were granted a sufficiency of simple food, clothing, and sleep; they were even allowed to drink a small amount of wine, although meat was granted only to the sick. The abbot's authority was absolute, and he was allowed to flog monks for disobedience. Yet Benedict urged him to try "to be loved rather than feared," and ordained that the abbot gather advice before making decisions "because the Lord often reveals to a younger member what is best." For such reasons the Benedictine monastery became a home of religious enrichment rather than a school for punishment.

We will continue the story of Benedictine monasticism in later chapters, but here we may point out in advance some of its greatest contributions to the development of Western European civilization. One was that Benedictine monks were committed from an early date to missionary work: they were primarily responsible for the conversion of England and later most of Germany. Such activities not only helped to spread the faith but also created a sense of cultural unity throughout western Europe. Another positive contribution lay in the attitude of the Benedictines toward work.

Whereas the highest goal for ancient philosophers and aristocrats was to have enough leisure time for unimpeded contemplation, Saint Benedict wanted his monks always to keep busy, for he believed that "idleness is an enemy of the soul." Therefore he prescribed that they should be occupied at certain times in manual labor, a prescription that would have horrified most thinkers of earlier times. Accordingly, early Benedictines worked hard themselves and spread the idea of the dignity of labor to others. With Benedictine support, this idea would become one of the most distinctive traits of Western culture. We read of Benedictines who gladly milked cows, threshed, plowed, and hammered: in so doing they increased the prosperity of their own monasteries and provided good examples for others. Benedictine monasteries became particularly successful in farming and later in the management of agricultural estates. Thus they often helped to advance the level of the western European economy and sometimes even to provide wealth that could be drawn on by emerging western European states.

CHANGING ATTITUDES TOWARD WOMEN AND MARRIAGE

Returning to our original subject—the changes that took place in Christian institutions and attitudes during the fourth century—a final fateful trend was the development of a negative attitude toward women. Compared with most other religions, Christianity was favorable to women. Female souls were regarded as equal to male souls in the eyes of God, and human nature was deemed to be complete only in both sexes. Saint Paul even went so far as to say that after baptism "there is neither male nor female" (Galatians 3:28), a spiritual egalitarianism that meant that women's salvation was no less important than men's. But Christians from earliest times shared the view of their contemporaries that in everyday life and in marriage women were to be strictly subject to men. Not only did early Christians believe that women should be excluded from positions of leadership or decision making, meaning that they should be "silent in Church" (1 Corinthians 14:34–35) and could never be priests, but they shared the standard classical view that women were more "fleshly" than men and therefore should be subjected to men as the flesh is subjected to the spirit (Ephesians 5:21–33).

With the growth of the ascetic movement in the third and fourth centuries, the denigration of women

WHAT MAJOR CHANGES DID CHRISTIANITY UNDERGO DURING THE FOURTH CENTURY?

THE NEW CONTOURS OF FOURTH-CENTURY CHRISTIANITY   237

An Early Christian Woman. A wall painting from the catacomb of Priscilla, Rome, third century C.E.

tion, and that those already married were obliged to live continently with their wives afterward.

Once virginity was accepted as the highest standard, marriage could be only second best. Saint Jerome expressed this view most earthily when he said that virginity was wheat, marriage barley, and fornication cow dung: since people should not eat cow dung he would permit them barley. The major purposes of marriage were to keep men from "burning" and to propagate the species. (Jerome went so far as to praise marriage above all because it brought more virgins into the world!) Thus Christianity reinforced the ancient view that woman's major earthly purpose was to serve as mother. Men and women were warned not to take pleasure even in marital intercourse but to indulge in it only for the purpose of procreation. Since they could not become priests and only a very few could become nuns (female monasticism was regarded as a very expensive luxury in the premodern world), almost all women were expected to become submissive wives and mothers. As wives they were not expected to have their own careers and were not meant to be educated or even literate. Hence even though they had full hopes for salvation, they were treated as inferiors in the everyday affairs of the world, a treatment that would endure until modern times.

as dangerously "fleshly" creatures became more and more pronounced. Since sexual abstinence lay at the heart of asceticism, the most perfect men were expected to shun women. Monks, of course, shunned women the most. This was a primary reason why they fled to deserts and forests. One Eastern ascetic was struck by the need for virginity in the midst of his marriage ceremony, ran off to a hermit's cell, and blocked the entrance; another monk who was forced to carry his aged mother across a stream swaddled her up as thoroughly as he could so that he would not catch any "fire" and no thoughts of other women would attack him. With monks taking such an uncompromising attitude, the call for continence was extended to the priesthood. Originally priests could be married, just as several of Jesus' apostles had been (1 Corinthians 9:5). But in the course of the fourth century the doctrine spread that priests could not be married after ordina-

CHRONOLOGY

THE GROWTH OF CHRISTIANITY, FIRST–FOURTH CENTURIES C.E.

Birth of Jesus	beginning of the Common Era
The apostles propagate Christianity	first century C.E.
Destruction of the Temple at Jerusalem	69–70 C.E.
Expulsion of the Jews from Jerusalem	132–135 C.E.
Emperor Constantine converts to Christianity	312–325 C.E.
Council of Nicea	325 C.E.
Christianity becomes official religion of Roman empire	392 C.E.
Era of "doctrinal quarrels"	fourth century C.E.
Growth of ecclesiastical organization	fourth–sixth centuries C.E.

CHANGING ATTITUDES TOWARD THE CELIBACY OF BISHOPS

Bishops had emerged as key figures in the organization of the early Christian church by the end of the first century C.E. By the mid-second century, a hierarchical structure of bishops, priests, deacons, and lesser officials was already in place. Until the fourth century, most of these officials were married, as were most socially respectable Roman men. By the end of the fourth century, however, efforts were being made, especially in the western parts of the empire, to require bishops and even priests to be celibate. This shift reflects an increasing admiration for asceticism as a mark of holiness that we find throughout the fourth-century world among both Christians and non-Christians, as shown in the following excerpt from an early third-century church manual and a papal letter.

THE DIDASCALIA

The shepherd who is appointed bishop and head among the presbyterate [that is, the priesthood] in the church in every congregation: "It is required of him that he shall be blameless, in nothing reproachable" [1 Timothy 3:2; Titus 1:7], one remote from all evil, a man not less than fifty years of age, who is now removed from the conduct of youth and from the lusts of the adversary, and from the slander and blasphemy of false brethren. . . . But if it is possible, let him be instructed and able to teach; but if he does not know letters, he shall be capable and skilful in the word; and let him be advanced in years.

And let him be vigilant and chaste and stable and orderly; and let him not be violent, and let him not be one who exceeds in wine; and let him not be malicious; but let him be quiet and not be contentious; and let him not be money-loving. And let him not be youthful in mind, lest he be lifted up and fall into the judgment of Satan, for everyone that exalts himself is humbled.

But it is required that the bishop shall be "a man that has taken one wife, and who has managed his house well" [1 Timothy 3:2, 4]. And thus let him be proved when he receives the imposition of hands to sit in the position of the episcopacy: whether he is chaste, and whether his wife also is a believer and chaste; and whether he has brought up his children in the fear of God, and admonished and taught them; and whether his household fear and reverence him and all of them obey him. For if his household in the flesh stands against him and does not obey him, how shall they who are without his house become his, and be subject to him?

Didascalia Apostolum Corpus Scriptorum Christianorum Orientalium, ed. Arthur Vööbus. (Louvain: Peeters, 1979). Reprinted in *After the New Testament: A Reader in Early Christianity*, ed. Bart D. Ehrman (Oxford and New York: Oxford University Press, 1999), pp. 333–334.

LETTER OF POPE DAMASUS I (366–384) ON PRIESTLY CELIBACY

This is what has been decided, about bishops in the first place, but also about priests and deacons, whose duty it is to take part in the divine sacrifice [of the Eucharist] and whose hands confer the grace of baptism and make present the body of Christ. It is not only us but divine Scripture that binds them to be perfectly chaste. . . . How could a bishop or priest dare to preach continence to a widow or virgin, or urge anyone to keep his bed pure, if he himself were more concerned to have children for this world than for God? Why did Paul say, "You are not in the flesh but in the spirit" and "Let those who have wives live as though they had none"? Would he, who so exhorted the people, complaisantly allow carnal activity to priests? — he who also said, "Make no provision for the flesh, to gratify its desires" and "I wish that all were as I myself am." One who is in the service of Christ, who sits in the chair of the master, can he not observe the rule of service. . . . Even idolaters, in order to celebrate their impious cult and sacrifice to demons, imposed continence on themselves as regards women and abstained from certain foods so as to remain pure. And you ask me if the priest of the living God, who is to offer spiritual sacrifices, should live always in a state of purity or if, wholly involved in the flesh he should give himself to the cares of the flesh. . . . Intercourse is defilement. . . . that is why the mystery of God may not be entrusted to men of that sort, defiled and faithless. . . . They doubtless know that "flesh and blood cannot inherit the kingdom of God, nor does the corrupt inherit the incorruptible"; shall a priest or deacon dare then to lower himself to act as the animals do?

Brian Tierney and Joan Scott, eds. *Western Societies: A Documentary History*, Vol. 1 (New York: Knopf, 1984), p. 174.

THE GERMANIC INVASIONS AND THE FALL OF THE ROMAN EMPIRE IN THE WEST

How did the Germanic tribes triumph over the western Roman empire?

While Christianity was conquering the Roman empire from within, another force, the Germanic barbarians, was threatening it from without. The Germans, who had already almost brought Rome to its knees in the third century, were held off from the time of Diocletian until shortly before the reign of Theodosius the Great. But thereafter they demolished western Roman resistance and, by the end of the fifth century, succeeded in conquering all of the Roman West. Germanic kingdoms then became the new form of government in territories once ruled over by Caesar and Augustus.

GERMANIC-ROMAN RELATIONS

It was once customary to think that the Germans were fierce and thoroughly uncouth savages who wantonly destroyed the western Roman empire out of sheer hatred for civilization. But that is a misunderstanding. The Germans were barbarians in Roman eyes because they did not live in cities and were illiterate, but they were not therefore savages. On the contrary, they often practiced settled agriculture—although they preferred hunting and grazing—and were adept in making iron tools and weapons as well as lavish jewelry. Physically they looked enough like Romans to intermarry without causing much comment, and their Indo-European language was related to Latin and Greek. Prolonged interaction with the Romans had a decisive civilizing influence on the Germans before they started their final conquests. Germans and Romans had shared common frontiers along the Rhine and the Danube for centuries, and had developed steady trading relations with each other. Even during times of war Romans were often allied with some German tribes while they fought others. By the fourth century, moreover, German tribes often served as auxiliaries of depleted Roman armies and were sometimes allowed to settle on borderlands of the empire where Roman farmers had given up trying to cultivate the land. Finally, many German tribes had been converted to Christianity in the fourth century, although the Christianity they accepted was of the heretical Arian version. All these interactions made the "barbarians" very familiar with Roman civilization and substantially favorable to it.

The Germans began their final push not to destroy Rome but to find more and better land. The first breakthrough occurred in 378 C.E. when the Visigoths, who had recently settled on some Roman lands in the Danube region, revolted against mistreatment by Roman officials and then defeated a punitive Roman army in the battle of Adrianople. The Visigoths did not immediately follow up this victory because Theodosius the Great cleverly bought them off and made them allies of the empire. But when Theodosius died in 395 C.E. he divided his realm between his two sons, neither of whom was as competent as he, and both halves of the empire were weakened by political intrigues. The Visigoths under their leader Alaric took advantage of this situation to wander through Roman realms almost at will, looking for the best land and provisions. In 410 they sacked Rome itself—a great shock to some contemporaries—and in the following years marched into southern Gaul. Meanwhile, in December of 406, a group of allied Germanic tribes led by the Vandals crossed the frozen Rhine and capitalized on Roman preoccupation with the Visigoths by streaming through Gaul into Spain. Later they were able to cross the straits of Gibraltar into northwest Africa, then one of the richest agricultural regions of the empire. From Africa they took control of the central Mediterranean, even sacking Rome from the sea in 455. By 476 C.E. the ineffectual western Roman emperor, a mere boy derisively nicknamed Augustulus ("little Augustus"), was easily deposed by a leader of a mixed band of Germans and Huns who then assumed the title of king of Rome. Accordingly, 476 is conventionally given as the date for the end of the western Roman empire. But it must be remembered that a Roman emperor, who maintained some claims to authority in the West, continued to rule in Constantinople.

THE SUCCESS AND IMPACT OF GERMAN INVASIONS

Two questions that historians of the German invasions customarily ask are, How did the Germans manage to triumph so easily? and Why was it that they were particularly successful in the West rather than the East? The ease of the German victories appears particularly striking when we recognize that the German armies were remarkably small: the Visigoths who won at Adrianople numbered no more than ten thousand men, and the total number of the Vandal "hordes" (including women and children) was about eighty thousand—about the same population as an average-sized American suburb. But the Roman armies themselves were depleted because of declining population and the need for manpower in other occupations, above all in the new bureaucracies. More than that, German armies often won by default (Adrianople was one of the few pitched battles in the history of their advance) because the Romans were no longer zealous about defending themselves. Germans were seldom regarded with horror—many German soldiers had even risen to positions of leadership within Roman ranks—and the coercive regime begun by Diocletian was not deemed worth fighting for by a great many of the empire's citizens, including its most prominent aristocrats.

The reasons that the Germans fared best in the West are complex—some having to do with personalities and mistakes of the moment, and others with geographical considerations. But the primary explanation why the eastern Roman empire survived while the western did not is that the East was simply richer. By the fifth century most western Roman cities had shrunk in terms of both population and space to a small fraction of their earlier size, and they were often little more than empty administrative shells or fortifications. The economy of the West was becoming more

CHRONOLOGY

GERMANIC INVASIONS OF THE ROMAN EMPIRE, FIFTH CENTURY C.E.

Visigoth victory at the battle of Adrianople	378 C.E.
Vandals invade Gaul, Spain, and North Africa	406 C.E.
Visigoths sack Rome	410 C.E.
Vandals sack Rome	455 C.E.
Germanic tribes depose last western Roman emperor	476 C.E.
Anglo-Saxon tribes invade England	c. 500 C.E.

HOW DID THE GERMANIC TRIBES TRIUMPH OVER THE WESTERN ROMAN EMPIRE?

THE GERMANIC INVASIONS AND THE FALL OF THE ROMAN EMPIRE   241

THE BARBARIAN INVASIONS OF THE ROMAN EMPIRE

Consider the extent of Christianity in relation to the territory of the Roman Empire. What might this suggest about the identification of imperial government with the church? What does the situation in Britain suggest about the nature and depth of Roman Christianity there? Notice the routes taken by the majority of the barbarian invaders. Why did so many bypass the wealthier, urbanized East in favor of targeting the West?

and more strictly agricultural, and agricultural produce served only to feed farm laborers and keep rich landlords in luxuries. In the East, on the other hand, cities like Constantinople, Antioch, and Alexandria remained teeming metropolises because of their trade and industry. Because the eastern part of the empire had greater reserves of wealth to tax, it was more vig-

orous. It could also afford to buy off the barbarians with tribute money, which it did with increasing regularity. So Constantinople was able to stay afloat while Rome floundered and sank.

A map of western Europe around the year 500 C.E. reveals the following major political divisions. Germanic tribes of Anglo-Saxons, who had crossed the

English Channel in the middle of the fifth century, were extending their rule on the island of Britain. In the northern part of Gaul, around Paris and east to the Rhine, the growing kingdom of the Franks was ruled by a crafty warrior named Clovis. South of the Franks stood the Visigoths, who ruled the southern half of Gaul and most of Spain. South of them were the Vandals, who ruled throughout previously Roman northwest Africa. In Italy the Ostrogoths, eastern relatives of the Visigoths, held sway under their impressive and highly Romanized king Theodoric; around the headwaters of the Rhone, the Burgundians ruled another wealthy and highly Romanized region of the western empire. Of these new barbarian realms, however, only that of the Franks would survive beyond the early eighth century as a unified kingdom; most of the rest would disappear within a century of their foundation.

The effects of the Germanic conquests in the West were not catastrophic. The greatest difference between the Germans and the Romans had been that the former did not live in cities, but since the western Roman cities were already in a state of decline, the invasions only accelerated a process of urban decay that was already well advanced. On the land Germans replaced Roman landlords without interrupting basic Roman agricultural patterns. Moreover, since the Germans were never very numerous, they usually took over no more than a part of Roman lands. Germans also tried to avail themselves of Roman administrative machinery, but administrations tended to decline gradually because of the decrease in wealth and literacy. The German invasions fractured the political unity of the empire, but they did not bring an end to Roman culture, or to the influence of Rome on the new immigrants. As Theodoric, the Ostrogothic conqueror of Italy, was fond of remarking: "An able Goth wishes to be like a Roman; but only a poor Roman would want to be like a Goth."

THE SHAPING OF WESTERN CHRISTIAN THOUGHT

What was Augustine's conception of history?

As the western Roman empire declined during the fourth and fifth centuries, a few Western Christian thinkers formulated an approach to the world and to God that was to guide the thought of the West for roughly the next eight hundred years. This concurrence of political decline and theological advance was not coincidental. With the empire falling and being replaced by barbarian kingdoms, it seemed clearer than ever to thinking Christians both that the classical inheritance had to be reexamined and that God had not intended the world to be anything more than a transitory testing place. The consequences of these assumptions accordingly became urgent questions. Between about 380 and 525 C.E., answers were worked out by Western Christian thinkers whose accomplishments were intimately interrelated. The towering figure among them was Saint Augustine, but others had great influence as well.

THE FIRST THREE GREAT FATHERS OF THE WESTERN LATIN CHURCH

Three contemporaries who knew and influenced each other—Saint Jerome (c. 340–420), Saint Ambrose (c. 340–397), and Saint Augustine (354–430)—count as three of the four greatest "Fathers" of the western, Latin Church. (The fourth, Saint Gregory the Great, came later and will be discussed in the next chapter.) Saint Jerome's greatest single contribution was his translation of the Bible from Hebrew and Greek into Latin. His version, known as the Vulgate (or "common" version), became the standard Latin Bible used throughout the Middle Ages; with minor variations it continued to be used long afterward by the Roman Catholic Church. Fortunately Jerome was one of the best writers of his day, and he endowed his translation with vigorous, often colloquial prose and, occasionally, fine poetry. Since the Vulgate was the most widely read work in Latin for centuries, Jerome's writing had as much influence on Latin style and thought as the King James Bible has had on English literature. Jerome, who was the least original thinker of the great Latin Fathers, also influenced western Christian thought by his contentious but eloquent formulations of contemporary views. Among the most important of these were the beliefs that much of the Bible was to be understood allegorically rather than literally, that classical learning could be valid for Christians if it was thoroughly subordinated to Christian aims, and that the most perfect Christians were rigorous ascetics. In keeping with the last position Jerome avidly supported monasticism. He also taught that women should not take baths so that they would not see their own bodies naked.

ROMANIZED BARBARIANS AND BARBARIANIZED ROMANS

These two letters from Sidonius Apollinaris (c. 430–c. 480) illustrate the ways in which cultural assimilation in the late-fifth-century western empire was rapidly blurring the boundaries between "Roman" and "barbarian." Sidonius himself was the descendant of an illustrious Roman provincial family in Gaul. He was one of the admired Latin stylists of his day, in both poetry and prose. Although he eventually became a bishop and was regarded locally as a saint after his death, his letter collection (from which these extracts are taken) tells us much more about the late Roman literary culture of Visigothic southern Gaul than it does about his Christianity. Arbogastes was the Frankish governor of Treves; Syagrius was from an ancient Gaulish Roman family.

LETTER 4:17: SIDONIUS TO HIS FRIEND ARBOGASTES

My honored Lord, your friend Eminentius has handed me a letter written by your own hand, a really literary letter, replete with the grace of a three-fold charm. The first of its merits is certainly the affection which prompted such condescension to my lowly condition, for if not a stranger I am in these days a man who courts obscurity; the second virtue is your modesty. . . . In the third place comes your urbanity which leads you to make a most amusing profession of clumsiness when as a matter of fact you have drunk deep from the spring of Roman eloquence and, dwelling by the Moselle, you speak the true Latin of the Tiber: you are intimate with the barbarians but are innocent of barbarisms, and are equal in tongue, as also in strength of arm, to the leaders of old, I mean those who were wont to handle the pen no less than the sword.

Thus the splendor of the Roman speech, if it still exists anywhere, has survived in you, though it has long been wiped out from the Belgian and Rhenic lands: with you and your eloquence surviving, even though Roman law has ceased at our border, the Roman speech does not falter. For this reason . . . I rejoice greatly that at any rate in your illustrious breast there have remained traces of our vanishing culture. If you extend these by constant reading you will discover for yourself as each day passes that the educated are no less superior to the unlettered than men are to beasts.

LETTER 5:5 SIDONIUS TO HIS FRIEND SYAGRIUS

You are the great-grandson of a consul, and in the male line too—although that has little to do with the case before us; I say, then, you are descended from a poet, to whom his literary glory would have brought statues had not his magisterial glories done so . . . and the culture of his successors has not declined one whit from his standard, particularly in this respect. I am therefore inexpressibly amazed that you have quickly acquired a knowledge of the German tongue with such ease.

And yet I remember that your boyhood had a good schooling in liberal studies and I know for certain that you often declaimed with spirit and eloquence before your professor of oratory. This being so, I should like you to tell me how you managed to absorb so swiftly into your inner being the exact sounds of an alien race, so that now after reading Virgil under the schoolmaster's cane and toiling and working the rich fluency of [Cicero] . . . you burst forth before my eyes like a young falcon from an old nest.

You have no idea what amusement it gives me, and others too, when I hear that in your presence the barbarian is afraid to perpetrate a barbarism in his own language. The bent elders of the Germans are astounded at you when you translate letters, and they adopt you as umpire and aribitrator in their mutual dealings. . . . And although these people are stiff and uncouth in body and mind alike, they welcome in you, and learn from you, their native speech combined with Roman wisdom.

Only one thing remains, most clever of men: continue with undiminished zeal, even in your hours of ease, to devote some attention to reading; and, like the man of refinement that you are, observe a just balance between the two languages: retain your grasp of Latin, lest you be laughed at, and practice the other, in order to have the laugh of them. Farewell.

W. B. Anderson, ed. *Sidonius, Poems and Letters*, Vol. 2 (Cambridge, Mass.: Harvard University Press, 1980), pp. 127–129, 181–183.

Unlike Jerome, who was primarily a scholar, Saint Ambrose was most active in the concerns of the world. As archbishop of Milan, the aristocratic Ambrose was the most influential church official in the West—more so even than the pope. Guided by practical concerns, he wrote an ethical work, *On the Duties of Ministers*, which followed closely Cicero's *On Duties* in title and form, and also drew heavily on Cicero's Stoic ethics. But Ambrose differed from Cicero and most of traditional classical thought on two major points. One was that the beginning and end of human conduct should be reverence for God rather than any self-concern or interest in social advancement. The other—Ambrose's most original contribution—was that God helps some Christians but not others in this pursuit by the gift of grace, a point that was to be greatly refined and amplified by Saint Augustine. Ambrose put his concern for proper conduct into action by his most famous act, his confrontation with the emperor Theodosius the Great over the massacre of innocent civilians. Ambrose argued that by violating divine commandments Theodosius had made himself subject to church discipline. Remarkably the archbishop succeeded in forcing the emperor to do penance. This famous incident symbolized the church's claim to preeminence in the sphere of morality, and epitomized the western church's developing sense of autonomy on religious matters, even when faced with the power of an emperor.

THE THOUGHT AND WRITINGS OF SAINT AUGUSTINE

Saint Ambrose's disciple, Saint Augustine, was the greatest of all the Latin Fathers; indeed he was one of the most powerful Christian intellects of all time. Augustine's influence on subsequent medieval thought was incalculable. Even after the Middle Ages his theology had a profound influence on the development of Protestantism; in the twentieth century many leading Christian thinkers called themselves neo-Augustinians. Augustine's Christianity may have been so searching because he began his career by searching for it. Although his mother was a Christian, he hesitated until the age of thirty-three to be baptized, passing from one system of thought to another without being able to find intellectual or spiritual satisfaction in any. Only increasing doubts about all other alternatives, the appeals of Saint Ambrose's teachings, and a mystical experience movingly described in his autobiographical *Confessions* led Augustine to embrace the faith wholeheartedly in 387. Thereafter he advanced rapidly in ecclesiastical positions, becoming bishop of the North African city of Hippo in 395. Although he led a most active life in this office, he still found time to write more than a hundred profound, complex, and powerful treatises in which he set forth his convictions concerning the most fundamental problems of Christian thought and action.

Saint Augustine's theology revolved around the principles of the profound sinfulness of humanity and divine omnipotence. Ever since Adam and Eve turned away from God in the Garden of Eden humans have remained basically sinful. One of Augustine's most vivid illustrations of human depravity appears in the *Confessions*, where he tells how he and some other boys once stole pears from a neighbor's garden, not because they were hungry or because the pears were beautiful, but simply for the sake of the evil itself. God would be purely just if He condemned all human beings to hell,

"The City of the Earth." A medieval illustration for Augustine's *On the City of God* showing Cain slaying Abel and Romulus slaying Remus. Its message is that all human society on earth is a product of sin.

the central guide to doing good was the doctrine of "charity," which meant leading a life devoted to loving God and loving one's neighbor for the sake of God, rather than a life of "cupidity," of loving earthly things for their own sake. Put in other terms, Augustine taught that humans should behave on earth as if they were travelers or "pilgrims," keeping their eyes at all times on their heavenly home and avoiding all materialistic concerns.

Augustine built an interpretation of history on this view in one of his major works, *On the City of God.* In this treatise, he argued that the entire human race from the Creation until the Last Judgment was and will be composed of two warring societies, those who "live according to man" and love themselves, and those who "live according to God." The former belong to the "City of Earth" and will be damned, whereas the blessed few who compose the "City of God" will on Judgment Day put on the garment of immortality. As for when the Last Judgment would come, Augustine argued vehemently that no human could know its exact date; nonetheless since the Judgment might come at any time, all mortals should devote their utmost efforts to preparing for it by leading lives of righteousness.

but since He is also merciful He has elected to save a few. Ultimately human will has nothing to do with this choice: although one has the power to choose between good and evil, one does not have the power to decide whether or not to be saved. God alone, from eternity, predestined a portion of the human race to salavation and sentenced the rest to be damned. In other words, God fixed for all time the number of human inhabitants of heaven. If this seems unfair, Augustine's answer is, first, that strict "fairness" would confine all to perdition; and second, that the basis for God's choice is a mystery shrouded in His omnipotence—far beyond the realm of human comprehension.

Even though it might seem to us that the practical consequences of this rigorous doctrine of predestination would be lethargy and fatalism, neither Augustine nor his later followers saw it that way at all. Humans themselves must do good, and if they are "chosen" they usually will do good; since no one knows who is chosen and who is not, all should try to do good in the hope that they are among the chosen. For Augustine

Although Saint Augustine formulated major new aspects of Christian theology, he believed that he was doing no more than drawing out truths found in the Bible. Indeed, he was convinced that the Bible alone contained all the wisdom worth knowing. But he also believed that much of the Bible was expressed obscurely, and that it was therefore necessary to have a certain amount of education in order to understand it thoroughly. This conviction led him to a modified acceptance of classical learning. The ancient world had already worked out an educational system based on the "liberal arts," or those subjects necessary for the worldly success and intellectual growth of free men. Augustine argued that privileged Christians could learn the fundamentals of these subjects, but only in a limited way and for a completely different end—study of the Bible. Since in his day nonreligious schools existed that taught these subjects, he permitted a Christian elite to attend them; later, when such schools died out, their place was taken by schools in monasteries and cathedrals. Thus Augustine's teaching laid the groundwork for some continuity of educational practice as well as for the theory behind the preservation of some classical treatises. But we must qualify this by remarking that Augustine intended liberal education only for an elite; all others were simply to be catechized, or drilled, in the faith. He also thought it far worse that anyone should become engaged in classical thought for its own sake than that someone might not know any classical thought at all. The true wisdom of mortals, he insisted, was piety.

BOETHIUS LINKS CLASSICAL AND MEDIEVAL THOUGHT

Augustine had many followers, of whom the most interesting and influential was Boethius, a Roman aristocrat who lived from about 480 to 524. Until recently, it was not customary to say that Boethius was a follower of Saint Augustine because some of Boethius' works do not make explicit mention of Christianity. Indeed, since Boethius was indisputably interested in ancient philosophy, wrote in a polished, almost Ciceronian style, and came from a noble Roman family, it has been customary to view him as the "last of the Romans." But in fact he intended the classics to serve Christian purposes, just as Augustine had prescribed, and his own teachings were basically Augustinian.

Because Boethius lived a century after Augustine he could see far more clearly that the ancient world was coming to an end. Therefore he made it his first goal to preserve as much of the best ancient learning as possible by a series of handbooks, translations, and commentaries. Accepting a contemporary division of the liberal arts into seven subjects—grammar, rhetoric, logic, arithmetic, geometry, astronomy, and music—he wrote handbooks on two: arithmetic and music. These summaries were meant to convey all the basic aspects of the subject matter that a Christian might need to know. Had Boethius lived longer he probably would have written similar treatments of the other liberal arts, but as it was he concentrated his efforts on his favorite subject: logic. In order to preserve the best of classical logic, he translated from Greek into Latin some of Aristotle's logical treatises as well as an introductory work on logic by Porphyry (another ancient philosopher). He also wrote his own explanatory commentaries on these works in order to help beginners. Since

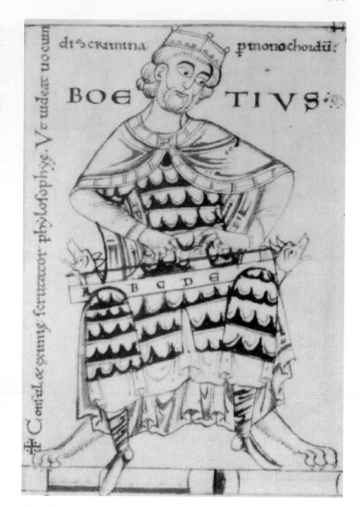

Boethius. A twelfth-century artist's conception of Boethius as a musician, a reputation he earned because of his treatise on music.

Latin writers had never been interested in logic, even in the most flourishing periods of Roman culture, Boethius' translations and commentaries became a crucial link between the thought of the Greeks and that of the Middle Ages. Boethius' works helped to endow the Latin language with a logical vocabulary, and when interest in logic was revived in the twelfth-century West it rested first on a Boethian basis.

Although Boethius was an exponent of Aristotle's logic, his world view was not Aristotelian but Augustinian. This can be seen both in his several orthodox treatises on Christian theology and above all in his masterpiece, *The Consolation of Philosophy*. Boethius wrote the *Consolation* at the end of his life, after he had been condemned to death for treason by Theodoric the Ostrogoth, whom he had served as an official. (Historians are unsure about the justice of the charges.) In it Boethius asks the age-old question of what is human

THE CHRISTIANIZATION OF CLASSICAL CULTURE IN THE WEST

❦ How was classical culture Christianized?

happiness and concludes that it is not found in earthly rewards such as riches or fame but only in the "highest good," which is God. Human life, then, should be spent in pursuit of God. Since Boethius speaks in the *Consolation* as a philosopher rather than a theologian, he does not refer to Christian revelation or to the role of divine grace in salvation. But his basically Augustinian message is unmistakable. *The Consolation of Philosophy* became one of the most popular books of the Middle Ages because it was extremely well written, because it showed how classical expression and some classical ideas could be appropriated and subordinated into a clearly Christian framework, and most of all, because it seemed to offer a real meaning to life. In times when all earthly things really did seem crude or fleeting it was genuinely consoling to be told eloquently and "philosophically" that life has purpose if led for the sake of God.

At a climactic moment in the *Consolation* Boethius retold in verse the myth of Orpheus in a way that might stand for the common position of the four writers just discussed: that is, how Christian thinkers were willing to accept and maintain some continuity with the classical tradition. But Boethius also made new sense of the story. According to Boethius, Orpheus' wife, Eurydice, symbolized hell, since Orpheus could not restrain from looking at her he was forced to die and was condemned to hell himself. In other words, Orpheus was too worldly and material; he should not have loved a woman but should have sought God. True Christians, on the other hand, know that "happy is he who can look into the shining spring of good [i.e., the divine vision]; happy is he who can break the heavy chains of earth."

As we have seen, none of the Christian intellectuals of late antiquity was prepared to throw out altogether the classical tradition of literature and philosophy they had inherited. For all of them, however, this tradition posed severe challenges. It was, in the first place, thoroughly pagan, and paganism remained a significant threat to Christianity until well into the fifth century. It was also associated with syncretism—that is to say, with the easy acceptance of both Christian and pagan beliefs simultaneously, which had been so marked a feature of aristocratic culture during the fourth century Constantinian Revolution. There was no denying the seductive lure of classical literature and philosophy, however. Jerome worried openly that on Judgment Day, God would find him less a follower of Christ than of Cicero; and Augustine spent years fighting to free himself from the attractions of pagan philosophical systems such as the Neoplatonism of Porphyry and Plotinus (see Chapter 6), or the dualistic doctrines of Manicheanism, which explained why there was evil in the world by positing the existence of two competing gods.

Moreover, these Christian thinkers were working within a world that still celebrated philosophers as purveyors of wisdom about the good life. Christian intellectuals—indeed, the Christian clergy generally—wanted desperately to be regarded as philosophers, so as to replace the doctrines of pagan philosophy with the doctrine of Christ. To do this, however, force alone

> None of the Christian intellectuals of late antiquity was prepared to throw out altogether the classical tradition of literature and philosophy they had inherited.

CHRONOLOGY

SHAPING OF WESTERN CHRISTIAN THOUGHT, FOURTH–SIXTH CENTURIES C.E.

Christianization of Classical Culture — Neoplatonism	fourth–sixth centuries C.E.
Writings of Saint Jerome	c. 340–420 C.E.
Translates Bible from Hebrew and Greek into Latin	
Writings of Saint Ambrose	c. 340–397 C.E.
Furthers the Church's autonomy on religious matters	
Writings of Saint Augustine	c. 354–430 C.E.
Confessions and *On the City of God*	
Writings of Boethius	480–524 C.E.
Provides link between classical and medieval thought	

would not be sufficient. What was needed was a way of Christianizing the classical inheritance, and conveying it to the Christian masses in an intellectually satisfying way. The political collapse of the western empire, and the growing barbarization of western Roman culture, further emphasized the urgency of the task. It was, therefore, to the preservation and reinterpretation of classical Latin culture for a mixed audience of vulgar Romans and aspiring barbarians that the Christian intellectuals of the fourth, fifth, and sixth centuries devoted themselves.

This process took two forms. The first was a gradual winnowing out of the classical texts that had been produced in Greece and Rome between the fifth century B.C. and the second century C.E. Much of this winnowing had been accomplished already. By and large, Roman readers of the third and fourth centuries had little taste for the scientific and mathematical works of the classical Greeks. They preferred bestiaries, with their entertaining tales of hyenas that changed their sex yearly, and of weasels who conceived through the ear. Nor did they have much interest in the philosophical works of Plato and Aristotle, or the literary works of the classical Greek dramatists. They preferred Neo-platonism, a quasi-mystical set of doctrines that posited a divine principle of some sort as lying behind the created world, and that saw creation and existence as part of a continuing process by which the material world emanated from this divinity, and gradually returned to it. In literature, their tastes ran toward come-dies and novels, of which Petronius' *Satyricon is* a ribald, but not atypical, example.

The second form of Christianizing classical culture was to arrive at an understanding of the purposes of classical culture for a Christian audience. The Chris-tian thinker Tertullian had raised this question in the second century C.E. by asking, "What has Athens (the symbol of classical learning) to do with Jerusalem (the symbol of Christian salvation)?" Tertullian's answer had been "Nothing", but this answer was not suitable to the changed circumstances of the Christian church from the fourth century on. Jerome and Augustine were more positive; but on the whole, the early monastic move-ment sided with Tertullian. Despite the later role Bene-dictine monasteries would play in the preservation of classical literary texts, Saint Benedict himself was no admirer of classical culture. Quite to the contrary, he wanted his monks to serve only Christ—not literature or philosophy. But unlike some of his monastic con-temporaries, he did assume that monks would have to read well enough to say their prayers and to read the

Bible. This meant that some teaching in the monaster-ies would be necessary, not least because boys were often given over from birth to the monastic profession, and would have no other way to learn their letters. For Benedict, however, preserving classical learning was no part of a monastery's proper duties.

CASSIODORUS AND THE BENEDICTINE TRADITION OF LEARNING

The impetus for the development of Benedictine mona-sticism's tradition of learning came not from Benedict himself, but from Cassiodorus (c. 490–c. 583), an offi-cial at the Ostrogothic court under Theodoric. Early in his career, Cassiodorus wrote a *History of the Goths* for his barbarian overlord. Cassiodorus showed the Goths to themselves in a Roman mirror, as a people whose history was a part of the history of Rome. He also composed (and eventually published) several volumes of his official correspondence, reflecting his training in the classical rhetorical tradition. During the last forty years of his life, however, Cassiodorus turned his at-tention to religion, composing commentaries on the Psalms and founding an important monastery at Vivar-ium in southern Italy. It was for his monks that Cas-siodorus composed his most influential work, the *Institutes.* Inspired by Saint Augustine, Cassiodorus be-lieved that study of classical literature was the essential preliminary to a proper understanding of the Bible and the church fathers. His *Institutes* were therefore a read-ing list at heart, comprising first the essential works of classical, pagan literature a monk should know before he moved on to the more difficult and demanding study of theology and the Bible. Through this work, Cassiodorus created a classical literary canon that would influence Christian educational practice until the end of the Middle Ages.

To provide his monks with books, Cassiodorus also encouraged the copying of manuscripts, arguing that such copying was in itself "manual labor" of the sort that Saint Benedict had demanded, and that it might even be more appropriate for monks than hard work in the fields. As Benedictines began to subscribe to these ideas, Benedictine monasteries emerged as the most important centers for the preservation and study of classical literature in the Latin-speaking West. They would have no serious rivals until the twelfth century. Hardly any of the works of classical Latin literature, in-cluding such "licentious" writings as the poems of Ca-tullus and Ovid, would survive today had they not been copied and preserved during the early Middle not only of aristocratic Christian bishops, but also of their barbarian overlords.

Boethius, whom we discussed earlier, and Cassiodorus both worked at the court of the most thoroughly Romanized ruler in the sixth-century barbarian world. Yet all their efforts to extend, preserve, and Christianize the classical cultural tradition bespeak their awareness that this world was passing away. Theodoric himself ruled Italy from 493 to 526 as the designated representative of the emperor at Constantinople. He was a great admirer of Roman civilization who tried to preserve it as best he could. He fostered agriculture and commerce, repaired public buildings and roads, patronized learning, and maintained a policy of religious toleration. In short, he provided Italy with a more enlightened government than it had known for several centuries. But none of this was sufficient to erase the palpable sense of distrust that in Theodoric's final years tore his kingdom apart. The problem was that for all their *romanitas* ("Romanness"), Theodoric and the Goths were Arian heretics, whereas the local bishops and landowners of Italy were orthodox Trinitarian Christians—and this fact made the Italian aristocrats the faithful subjects not of Theodoric, but of his imperial sponsor in Constantinople. When, in 523, the emperor issued an edict, valid also in Italy, forbidding Jews, pagans, and heretics (by whom he probably meant Arians) to hold public office, the storm broke. Although Cassiodorus remained loyal to Theodoric, Boethius was imprisoned, accused of conspiring to re-

Theodoric the Ostrogoth. The barbarian ruler is shown here in Roman dress, with an ornate Roman hairstyle and a Roman symbol of victory in his hand. The inscription reads REX THEODERICVS PIVS PRINCIS, Latin for "King Theodoric, pious prince."

Ages by Benedictine monks following the example of Cassiodorus.

Others too were active in trying to preserve and Christianize what remained of the classical literary tradition. At the request of Pope Symmachus (498–514), Priscian (c. 500) composed what would become the standard treatise of the Middle Ages on Latin grammar. At the request of another pope, the sixth-century scholar Dionysius Exiguus undertook to collect and codify the laws of the Roman church; yet another pope, Agapetus (535–536), assembled the greatest Christian library in Rome—a library from which his relative, Pope Gregory the Great (590–604), would draw most of his knowledge of Saint Augustine. To some degree, of course, all such efforts were aimed at an educated, aristocratic elite that was fast disappearing from the sixth-century Latin West. But this fact should not obscure the extent to which this Christianized classical culture was slowly becoming the common possession

Cassiodorus. This frontispiece of a Bible executed around 700 C.E. in an English Benedictine monastery depicts Cassiodorus as a copyist and preserver of books. (Since books were exceedingly rare until the invention of printing in the fifteenth century, they customarily were stored in cupboards, lying flat.)

turn Italy to direct imperial rule. Theodoric's last years were marked by his continuing persecution of Trinitarian Christians. When he died in 526, he left no son to succeed him, religious tensions continued to tear his kingdom apart. Ten years later, Theodoric's fears would be confirmed when a new emperor, Justinian, attempted to reconstitute the Roman empire of Augustus by reconquering Italy from the Ostrogoths.

EASTERN ROME AND THE WESTERN EMPIRE

❧ Why did Justinian's plan to reunite the Roman empire fail?

Boethius' execution by Theodoric in 524 was in many ways an important historical turning point. For one, Boethius was both the last noteworthy philosopher and last writer of cultivated Latin prose the West was to have for many hundreds of years. Then too Boethius was a layman, and for hundreds of years afterward almost all western European writers would be priests or monks. Boethius' execution was symptomatic in the political sphere as well because it was the harbinger of the collapse of the Ostrogothic kingdom in Italy. Whether or not he was justly condemned, Boethius' execution showed that Arian and Catholic Christians could not live in harmony anywhere in the barbarianized western empire. Soon afterward, the Ostrogoths were overthrown by the eastern Roman empire. That event in turn was to be a major factor in the ultimate divorce between East and West and the consequent final disintegration of the old Roman world.

JUSTINIAN'S REVIVAL OF THE ROMAN EMPIRE

The conquest of the Ostrogoths was part of a larger plan for Roman revival conceived and directed by the eastern Roman emperor Justinian (527–565). Eastern Rome, with its capital at Constantinople, had faced many external pressures from barbarians and internal religious dissensions since the time of Theodosius. But

throughout the fifth century it had managed to weather these crises, and by the time of Justinian's accession had regained much of its strength. Although the eastern Roman empire—which then encompassed the modern-day territories of Greece, Turkey, most of the Middle East, and Egypt—was largely Greek- and Syriac-speaking, Justinian himself came from a western province (modern-day Serbia) and spoke Latin. Not surprisingly, therefore, he concentrated his interests on the West. He saw himself as the heir of imperial Rome, whose ancient power and western territory he was resolved to restore. Aided by his astute and determined wife Theodora, who, unlike earlier imperial Roman consorts, played an influential role in his reign, Justinian took great strides toward this goal. But ultimately his policy of recovering the West proved unrealistic.

THE CODIFICATION OF ROMAN LAW

One of Justinian's most impressive and lasting accomplishments was his codification of Roman law. This project was part of his attempt to emphasize continuities with earlier imperial Rome and was also meant to enhance his own prestige and absolute power. Codification of the law was necessary because between the third and sixth centuries the volume of statutes had continued to grow, with the result that the vast body of enactments contained many contradictory or obsolete elements. Moreover, conditions had changed so radically that many of the old legal principles could no longer be applied. When Justinian came to the throne in 527, he immediately decided on a revision and codification of the existing law to bring it into harmony with the new conditions and to establish it as an authoritative basis for his rule. To carry out this work he appointed a commission of lawyers under the supervision of his minister, Tribonian. Within two years the commission published the first result of its labors. This was the Code, a systematic revision of all of the statutory laws that had been issued from the reign of Hadrian to the reign of Justinian. The Code was later supplemented by the Novels, which contained the legislation of Justinian and his immediate successors. By 532 the commission had completed the Digest, a summary of all of the writings of the great jurists. The final product of the work of revision was the Institutes, a textbook of the legal principles reflected in both the Digest and the Code.

> One of Justinian's most impressive and lasting accomplishments was his codification of Roman law.

Justinian and Theodora. Sixth-century mosaics from the Church of San Vitale, Ravenna. The emperor and empress are conceived here to have supernatural, almost priestly powers: they are advancing toward the altar, bringing the communion dish and chalice respectively. Both rulers are set off from their retinues by their haloes. The observant viewer is also meant to note the representation of the "three wise kings from the East" at the hem of Theodora's gown: just as the "three magi" once had supernatural knowledge of Christ, so now do their counterparts, Justinian and Theodora.

All four volumes together constitute the *Corpus Juris Civilis,* or the "body of civil law."

Justinian's *Corpus* was a brilliant achievement in its own terms: the Digest alone has been justly called "the most remarkable and important lawbook that the world has ever seen." In addition, the *Corpus* had an enormous influence on subsequent legal and governmental history. Revived and restudied in western Europe from the eleventh century on, Justinian's *Corpus* became the basis of all the law and jurisprudence of European states, exclusive of England (which followed its own "common law"). The nineteenth-century Napoleonic Code, which provided the basis for the laws of modern European countries and also those of Latin America, is fundamentally the Institutes of Justinian in modern dress.

Only a few of the more specific influences of Justinian's legal work can be enumerated here. One is that in its basic governmental theory the *Corpus* was a bastion of absolutism. Starting from the maxim that "what pleases the prince has the force of law," it granted unlimited powers to the imperial sovereign and therefore was adopted with alacrity by later European monarchs and autocrats. But the *Corpus* also provided some theoretical support for constitutionalism because it maintained that the sovereign originally obtained his powers from the people rather than from God. Since government came from the people it could in theory be given back to them. Perhaps most important and influential was the *Corpus'* view of the state as an abstract public and secular entity. In the Middle Ages rival views of the state as the private property of the ruler or as a supernatural creation meant to control sin often predominated. The modern conception of the state as a public entity concerned not with an afterlife but with everyday affairs gained strength toward the end of the Middle Ages in part because of the revival of assumptions found in Justinian's legal compilations.

JUSTINIAN'S MILITARY CONQUESTS

Justinian aimed to be a full Roman emperor in geographical practice as well as in legal theory. To this end he sent out armies to reconquer the West. At first they succeeded easily. In 533 Justinian's brilliant general Belisarius conquered the Vandal kingdom in Northwest Africa, and in 536 Belisarius seemed to have won all of Italy, where he was welcomed by the Trinitarian subjects of the Ostrogoths. But the first victories of the

Italian campaign were illusory. After their initial defeats the Ostrogoths put up stubborn resistance; the war dragged on for decades until the exhausted eastern Romans finally reduced the last Gothic outposts in 563. Shortly before he died, Justinian became master of all Italy as well as northwest Africa and the coastal parts of Spain that his troops had also managed to recapture. The Mediterranean was once more a "Roman" lake. But the cost of the endeavor was enormous and would soon call into question the very existence of the eastern Roman empire.

Justinian's Western campaigns were ill advised for two major reasons. One was that his realm really could not afford them. Belisarius seldom had enough troops to do his job properly; he began his Italian campaign with only eight thousand men. Later, when Justinian did grant his generals enough troops, it was only at the cost of oppressive taxation. But additional troops would probably have been insufficient to hold the new lines in the West because the empire

> Justinian's *Corpus Juris Civilis* was a brilliant achievement in its own terms.

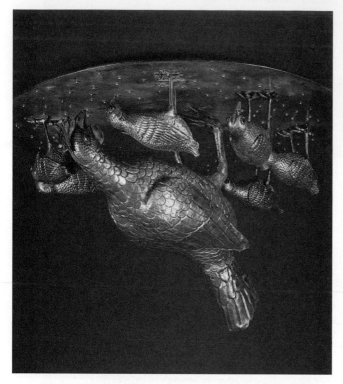

Hen and Chicks. North Italian small figures from the sixth century made from silver overlaid with gold. The purpose of this luxurious and seemingly humorous work dating from a time of economic decline and grave political crisis is unknown; there are as many theories offered for it as there are chicks.

had greater interests, as well as enemies, to the East. While the eastern Roman empire was exhausting itself in Italy, the Persians were gathering strength. Justinian's successors had to pull away from the West in order to meet the threat of a revived Persia. Even so, by the beginning of the seventh century it seemed as if the Persians would be able to march all the way to the waters that faced Constantinople. Only a heroic reorganization of the empire after 610 avoided that fate, but this reorganization helped eastern Rome from the West and helped the West begin to lead a life of its own.

Justinian's wars left most of Italy in a shambles. The protracted fighting had wrought much devastation. Around Rome aqueducts were cut and parts of the countryside returned to marshes not drained until the twentieth century. In 568, only three years after Justinian's death, another, much more primitive Germanic tribe, the Lombards, invaded Italy and took much of it away from the eastern Romans. They met little resistance because the latter were now paying more attention to the East, but the Lombards were still too weak to conquer the whole Italian peninsula. Instead, Italy became divided between Lombard, Eastern Roman, and papal territories. The actors would change, but this division between northern, central and southern

THE MEDITERRANEAN WORLD UNDER JUSTINIAN, 527–565

Note the extent of the Mediterranean world under Justinian. What areas had been permanently lost to imperial control? Consider that the territories in North Africa, Spain, and Italy were added during Justinian's reign; also note the position of the Byzantine capital, Constantinople. In what direction—east or west—were imperial interests most likely to be focused under normal circumstances? How permanent were Justinian's conquests to be, and what burdens did they place on imperial resources?

Italy would continue to characterize Italian political life until the nineteenth century.

Eastern Roman control over North Africa lasted only a few generations longer than it did in Italy. Weakened by religious dissension and heavy taxation, this area fell during the seventh century to the invading armies of Islam, along with Egypt and the rest of Roman North Africa. At this time, Christianity in north Africa largely disappeared.

Further north, the Visigothic kingdom of Spain continued to control the interior portions of the country, despite Justinian's conquest of the Mediterranean coast. After the Roman armies departed, the Visigoths resumed such control as they had ever exercised over these coastal regions. But tensions between the Arian Visigoths and their Trinitarian subjects continued until 582, when the Visigothic king Reccared finally converted to orthodox Christianity. By then, however, a pattern of hostility between the Visigothic kings, their bishops, and the Romanized population of the Mediterranean coast had been established that would last until the end of the Visigothic kingdom. Despite the Visigothic kings' efforts to pattern their rule on the Byzantine example, their kingdom quickly collapsed in the early eighth century when Muslim armies crossed the Strait of Gibraltar. By the end of the century, the Christian rulers of Spain controlled only the northern-most parts of Iberian peninsula, along with the area around Barcelona. For the next three hundred years, Spain would be an important part of the Muslim world.

CHRONOLOGY

THE ROMAN REVIVAL OF JUSTINIAN, 527–568 C.E.

Reign of Justinian	527–565 C.E.
Publication of the *Corpus Juris Civilis*	529–532 C.E.
Justinian conquers the Vandal kingdom of northwest Africa	533 C.E.
Justinian reconquers Italian peninsula	536 C.E.
Justinian Defeats last Gothic outposts	563 C.E.
Justinian rules over Mediterranean world	563–565 C.E.
Death of Justinian	565 C.E.
Germanic Lombards conquer Italian peninsula	568 C.E.

CONCLUSION

From its earliest days, Roman culture had been characterized by its remarkable capacity to assimilate the disparate cultures of the lands Rome conquered. In this process, both Rome and its empire were steadily transformed. The pace of these transformations accelerated markedly, however, from the mid-third century on—so much so that historians now commonly refer to the period from the mid-third century to the early seventh century as "Late Antiquity" to distinguish it from the classical Roman world that preceded it. During these centuries, larger numbers of immigrants entered the Roman empire than ever before, drawn by a combination of land hunger, opportunity, and the desire to participate in the material and cultural benefits of Roman life. In the western empire especially, the number of these new immigrants became so large during the late fourth and fifth centuries that the frontier areas of the empire ceased to be distinguishable from the more "Romanized" areas of the interior.

At the same time, two internal cultural processes were transforming what it meant to be Roman. The learned culture of the Greek and Roman world was being steadily extended to larger numbers of people; but in the process, learned culture itself was increasingly vulgarized. And finally, the empire itself became Christian, first by persuasion, as Constantine and his successors made it attractive for individuals to convert to the new religion, and later by coercion, as Christianity became the official religion of the entire Roman empire. As a result, a new fusion of Christian culture and late Roman governance began to evolve, not only around the imperial court at Constantinople, but also in the provinces.

What did not change, however, was the Mediterranean focus of this evolving Late Antique world. Despite the emergence of new political units in the western Roman empire, Roman civilization in the fifth and sixth centuries remained firmly centered upon the Mediterranean Sea. That too was soon to change. The seventh century would witness the final fracturing of this unified Mediterranean world, and the emergence in its place of three quite different Western civilizations: Byzantium, Western Europe, and Islam. This development marks the end of the classical world and the beginning of the Middle Ages. It is to this development that we now turn.

SELECTED READINGS

Saint Augustine. *The City of God*. Trans. by Henry Bettenson. Baltimore, 1972.

———. *Confessions*. Trans. by Henry M. Chadwick. Oxford, 1991.

———. *The Enchiridion on Faith, Hope and Love*. Ed. by H. Paolucci. Chicago, 1961.

———. *On Christian Doctrine*. Trans. by D. W. Robertson, Jr. New York, 1958.

Boethius. *The Consolation of Philosophy*. Trans. by R. Green. Indianapolis, 1962.

Brown, Peter. *Augustine of Hippo*. Berkeley, 1967. A great biography, by the greatest living scholar of late antiquity.

———. *The World of Late Antiquity*. New York, 1971. Still the best short survey of the period, with excellent illustrations.

———. *The Body and Society: Men, Women and Sexual Renunciation in Early Christianity*. New York, 1988. A revealing study of one of the fundamental transformations Christianity brought to the late antique world.

———. *Power and Persuasion in Late Antiquity: Toward a Christian Empire*. Madison, 1992. An important revisionist account of the impact of Christianization on the political culture of the later Roman empire.

———. *The Rise of Western Christendom: Triumph and Diversity, 200–1000*. Oxford, 1996. Evocatively written picture of the diverse forms Christianity took as it spread east and north from the Mediterranean world.

Bowersock, G. W., Peter Brown, and Oleg Grabar. *Late Antiquity: A Guide to the Postclassical World*. Cambridge, Mass., 1999. An authoritative compilation. The first half is devoted to essays on the cultural features of the period, the second half is organized as an encyclopedia.

Cameron, Averil. *The Later Roman Empire, A.D. 284–430*. London, 1993. Now the standard account of its period, with an emphasis on imperial politics.

———. *The Mediterranean World in Late Antiquity, A.D. 395–600*. London, 1993. Masterful, with excellent, succinct bibliographical essays.

Cassiodorus. *An Introduction to Divine and Human Readings*. Trans. by L. W. Jones. New York, 1946.

Chadwick, Henry M. *Boethius*. Oxford, 1981. The best intellectual biography of this important thinker.

———. *Augustine*. Oxford, 1986. The best short introduction to Augustine's thought.

Clark, Gillian. *Women in Late Antiquity*. Oxford, 1993. A clear, compact account of an important subject.

Ehrman, Bart D., ed. *After the New Testament: A Reader in Early Christianity*. Oxford, 1999.

Eusebius. *The History of the Church*. Trans. by G. A. Williamson. Baltimore, 1965.

———. *Life of Constantine*. Trans. by Averil Cameron and Stuart Hall. Oxford, 1999.

Fowden, Garth. *Empire to Commonwealth: Consequences of Monotheism in Late Antiquity*. Princeton, 1993. Argues for connections between the universalism of monotheisms and empires during this period.

Jones, A. H. M. *The Later Roman Empire, 284–602: A Social, Economic, and Administrative Survey*. 2 volumes. London, 1964. An immense, detailed analysis, difficult to read but packed with information.

Lane Fox, Robin. *Pagans and Christians*. New York, 1987. A subtle, perceptive, lengthy, but highly readable exploration of the pagan world within which Christianity grew up.

Lawrence, Clifford Hugh. *Medieval Monasticism*. 3d ed. London, 2000. Concise, intelligent, perceptive survey of monasticism from its beginnings to the end of the Middle Ages.

MacMullen, Ramsay. *Corruption and the Decline of Rome*. New Haven, 1988. Argues for the corrosive effects on the empire of Roman efforts to privatize governmental responsibilities.

Markus, R. A. *The End of Ancient Christianity*. New York, 1990. An expert synthetic study of Christianity in the Western Roman empire between 350 and 600 C.E.

Moorhead, John. *Justinian*. New York, 1994. An up-to-date survey of the emperor and his times.

Pelikan, Jaroslav. *The Christian Tradition, Volume 1: The Emergence of the Catholic Tradition*. Chicago, 1971. A history of Christian doctrine that is one of the tours de force of twentieth-century scholarship. Synthetic, clear, and objective.

Procopius. *The Secret History*. Trans. by G. A. Williamson. Baltimore, 1966.

O'Donnell, James J. *Cassiodorus*. Berkeley, 1979. Difficult but rewarding.

Shanks, Hershel, ed. *Christianity and Rabbinic Judaism: A Parallel History of Their Origins and Early Development*. Washington, D.C., 1992. Accessible chapters, written by top authorities, that cover the period from the first to the sixth centuries C.E.

Wallace-Hadrill, John Michael. *The Barbarian West*, 3d ed. London, 1966. Still the most interesting and suggestive analysis of the Romano-Germanic world created by the invasions of the fifth century C.E.

Whittaker, C. R. *Frontiers of the Roman Empire: A Social and Economic Study*. Baltimore, 1994. A convincing picture of the frontiers of the Roman empire as zones of intensive cultural interaction.

Williams, Stephen. *Diocletian and the Roman Recovery*. New York, 1997. A recent account that modifies, but does not replace, A. H. M. Jones (see above).

Wolfram, Herwig. *The Roman Empire and Its Germanic Peoples*. Berkeley, 1997. The best recent survey of its subject.

PART III

THE MIDDLE AGES

THE TERM "MIDDLE AGES" was coined by Europeans in the seventeenth century to express their view that a long and dismal period of interruption extended between the glorious accomplishments of Greece and Rome and their own "modern age." Because the term became so widespread, it is now an ineradicable part of our historical vocabulary; but no serious scholar today uses it with the sense of contempt it once invoked. To the contrary, most scholars would now argue that it was during the Middle Ages—roughly the years between 600 and 1500—that the cultural, political, and religious foundations of all three western civilizations were established. Whether we speak of Byzantium, the Islamic world, or Europe, the Middle Ages were a formative and creative period in the history of western civilizations.

Only with respect to Europe, however, do the years between 600 and 1500 constitute a true "middle age." For the Islamic world, these centuries witnessed the birth, expansion, and maturation of a new civilization that drew heavily upon its classical past, but fused that past with a sweeping new religious vision. For Byzantium, the so-called Middle Ages ended in 1453 with the conquest of the Byzantine empire by the Ottoman Turks. Even for Europe, the metaphor of a middle age is to some extent misleading. Like Islamic civilization, European civilization began to take shape from the seventh century on, but it was not until the twelfth century that a truly distinctive European tradition with respect to politics, religion, and art emerged.

	POLITICS	SOCIETY AND CULTURE	ECONOMY	INTERNATIONAL RELATIONS
570	Muhammad, founder of Islam, born (570) Pope Gregory I (Saint Gregory the Great) (590–604) Umayyad family governs Islamic world (661–750)	Growth of monasteries (600–700) The Hijrah (622)	Economic unity of Mediterranean world ends (650)	Arabs, under Abu-Bakr, rout Byzantium army in Syria (636) Arabs take Antioch, Damascus, and Jerusalem (637) Attempts by Muslims to take Constantinople (677, 717) Arabs take Visigothic Spain (717)
700	Abbasid family governs Islamic world (750–1258) Charlemagne crowned Holy Roman Emperor (800) Capetian dynasty (987–1328)	Iconoclast Contoversy begins (717) Islamic civilization's "middle period" (900–1250) Rise of Romanesque architecture (900s)	Agricultural revolution (700–1300) Invention of iron horseshoe (900) Rus establish principality near Kiev (900s)	Rus sack Constantinople (860) Otto I defeats Hungarians at Lechfield (955)
1000	Split between Roman and Byzantium Churches (1054) Saxon civil war begins (1073) Investiture Conflict (1075) Concordat of Worms distinguishes temporal power of kings from spiritual power of clergy (1122) Reign of Frederick I, Barbarossa, as Holy Roman emperor (1152–1190)	European population triples (1000–1300) *Song of Roland* (1050) Taking of monastic orders increases tenfold (1066–1200) Cisterian order flourishes (1090–1153) Catharism in southern France (1150–1300) Rise of chivalry (1150) Troubadour poets travel Europe (1150–1300) Chretien de Troyes, author of Arthurian legends (1165–1190) Rome decrees all cathedrals must support one schoolteacher (1179) Saint Francis of Assisi (1182–1226)	Invention of tandem harness for plowing (1050) Water mill becomes widely used in Europe (1050) Manorial lords begin trading serfs' freedom for cash (1100s)	Battle of Hastings, England falls to the Normans (1066) Battle of Manzikert, Turks take Anatolia (1071) The First Crusade (1095–1099)
1200	Magna Carta (1215) Fourth Lateran Council (1215) Emergence of English Parliament (1272–1307) Formation of French Estates General (1285–1314)	Theater appears outside of church (1200) *The Cid* and Norse sagas are written down (1200s) Saint Thomas Aquinas, author of *Summa Theologica*, (1225–1274) Dante Alighieri, author of *The Divine Comedy*, (1265–1321) Giotto of Florence, painter (1267–1337) William of Ockham, founder of nominalism (1285–1349)		Crusaders sack Constantinople (1204) England ousted from Normandy, Anjou, and Brittany (1204) Mongols conquer eastern Slavic region (1200s) Mongols take Kiev (1240) Mongols dispose of Abbasid caliphate (1258) Jews expelled from southern Italy, England, and France (1288–1306)

THE MIDDLE AGES

	POLITICS	SOCIETY AND CULTURE	ECONOMY	INTERNATIONAL RELATIONS
1300	Babylonian Captivity of the Church (1305–1378)	Giovanni Boccaccio (1313–1375) Over a tenth of Europe dies during the Great Famine (1316–1322) John Wyclif, Oxford theologian (1330–1384) Geoffrey Chaucer (1340–1400) Onset of the Black Death, from which over half of Europe dies (1347)	Development of mechanical clocks and compasses (1300) Severe flooding ruins crops, breeds pestilence (1315) Heavy cannons first employed (1330)	Explorers reach Azores and Cape Verde (1300s) Hundred Year's War (1337–1453)
	Jacquerie rebellion in France (1358) The Great Schism, ended by Council of Constance (1378–1417)	University of Heidelberg founded (1385)		
1400	English Peasants' Revolt (1381) Florentine Ciompi uprising (1378)	Jan van Eyck (1380–1441)	Medici family, originators of modern banking, flourishes (1397–1494)	Poland and Lithuania united (1386)
	The Italian territorial papacy (1417–1517)		Invention of movable type (1450)	Rise of Grand Duchy of Moscow (1400s)
	Edward, duke of York dethrones Henry VI after War of the Roses (1461) Reign of Ivan III, the Great, tsar of all Russias (1462–1505) Ferdinand of Aragon marries Isabella of Castile, forming modern Spain (1469)		Explorers round the Cape of Good Hope (1487) West Indies reached (1492) India reached by sea (1498)	Turks conquer Constantinople (1453) England loses Bordeaux (1453) French monarchy absorbs Burgundy (1477) Christian monarchs expel Muslims and Jews from Spain (1492)

CHAPTER EIGHT

CHAPTER CONTENTS

ROME'S THREE HEIRS: THE BYZANTINE, ISLAMIC, AND EARLY MEDIEVAL WORLDS

- How did the Byzantine state survive for nearly a millennium?
- How was Islam able to spread so rapidly?
- What forces combined to undermine the political unity of the Islamic empire?
- What caused economic and social change in seventh-century western Europe?
- How did Charlemagne redefine the relationship between Christianity and kingship?

A NEW PERIOD in the history of Western civilizations began in the seventh century. In the year 600, it was still possible for the rulers of the Roman empire living in Constantinople to imagine their empire as uniting the entire Mediterranean world. By the end of the seventh century, however, three different successor civilizations to the Greco-Roman world of antiquity had emerged: the Byzantine, the Islamic, and the western European, each with its own language and distinctive ways of life. The history of Western civilizations from the seventh to the eleventh centuries is largely a story of the rivalries and interactions among these three emerging worlds, each of which preserved and extended different aspects of the late-antique inheritance they shared.

Like the provinces of the eastern Roman empire over which it ruled, Byzantine civilization after 610 was Greek-speaking. It combined the bureaucratic and imperial traditions of late Roman governance with an intense pursuit of the Christian faith. This fusion had been pioneered in the fourth century by Constantine and his successors, and was continuously elaborated in the eastern Roman empire thereafter. Islamic civilization, in contrast, was Arabic-speaking. It was the most cosmopolitan and wide ranging (both geographically and culturally) of the three successor civilizations. The Islamic world was the heir both to the Roman ideal of an expansive empire itself, and to Roman ideals of cultural and religious assimilation as essential attributes of imperial rule. By combining the philosophical and scientific interests of the Hellenistic world with the literary and artistic culture of Persia, Islam created the most dynamic cultural amalgam of the early Middle Ages.

Western Christian civilization in the early Middle Ages was rooted in Latin, but with important cultural influences from Germanic, Celtic, and Latin-derived vernacular languages. In contrast to Byzantium and Islam, it owed relatively little to Roman ideals of empire, except briefly under the Carolingians. It was, however, profoundly influenced by Roman ideals of law and local government, which carried with them a continuing influence from the republican traditions of ancient Rome. For western Europe in the early Middle Ages, law and Latin Christianity represented the pinnacles of Roman cultural achievement. They were, indeed, the very essence of what it meant to be Roman, and to be Roman remained an almost universal aspiration in the early medieval West. If we measure civilizations by their highest philosophical and literary accomplishments, western Europe in the early Middle Ages was a laggard in comparison with Byzantium and Islam. It was also the least economically advanced of these three successor states, and faced the greatest or-ganizational weaknesses in both government and reli-gion. By the end of the eleventh century, however, Latin Christian civilization was no longer on the defen-sive against its rivals in military, economic, or religious terms. Rather, it stood on the verge of an extraordinary period of expansion and conquest that would bring it ultimately to a dominant position in world affairs dur-ing the early modern and modern eras.

THE BYZANTINE EMPIRE AND ITS CULTURE

How did the Byzantine state survive for nearly a millennium?

It is impossible to date the beginning of Byzantine his-tory with any precision because the Byzantine empire was the uninterrupted successor of the Roman state. For this reason different historians prefer different be-ginnings. Some argue that "Byzantine" characteristics had already emerged in Roman history as a result of the eastern-izing policy of Diocletian; others assert that Byzantine history began when Constantine moved his capital from Rome to Con-stantinople, the city that subse-quently became the center of the Byzantine world. (The old name for the site on which Con-stantinople was built was "Byzan-tium," from which we get the adjective "Byzantine"; it would be more accurate but cumbersome to say con-stantinopolitine.) Diocletian and Constantine, how-ever, continued to rule a united Roman empire. As we have seen, as late as the sixth century, after the western part of the empire had fallen to the Germans, the east-ern Roman emperor Justinian thought of himself as an

heir to Augustus and fought hard to win back the West. Justinian's reign was clearly an important turning point in the direction of Byzantine civilization because it saw the crystallization of new forms of thought and art that can be considered more "Byzantine" than "Roman." But this still remains a matter of subjective emphasis: some scholars emphasize these newer forms, whereas others respond that Justinian continued to speak Latin and dreamed of restoring old Rome. Only after 610 did a new dynasty emerge that came from the East, spoke Greek, and maintained a fully Eastern or "Byzantine" orientation. Hence, although good argu-ments can be made for beginning Byzantine history with Diocletian, Constantine, or Justinian, we will begin here with the accession in 610 of the Emperor Heraclius.

It is also convenient to begin in 610 because from then until 1071 the main lines of Byzantine military and political history were determined by resistance against successive waves of invasion from the East. When Heraclius came to the throne the very exis-tence of the Byzantine empire was being challenged by the Persians, who had conquered almost all of the empire's Asian territories. As a symbol of their triumph the Persians in 614 even carried off from Jerusalem the relic believed to be part of the original cross on which Jesus had been crucified. This relic had been discov-ered by Helena, the mother of the emperor Con-stantine, in one of the earliest archaeological "digs" in the Holy Land, and had become a potent symbol of the Christian legitimacy of the eastern Roman emper-ors. By enormous effort Heraclius rallied Byzantine strength and turned the tide, routing the Persians, re-capturing Jerusalem, and retriev-ing the cross in 627. Persia was then reduced to subordination and Heraclius reigned in glory until 641. But in his last years new armies began to invade Byzantine territory, swarming out of hitherto placid Arabia. In-spired by the new religion of Islam and profiting from Byzan-tine exhaustion after the struggle with Persia, the Arabs made astonishingly rapid gains. By 650 they had taken most of the Byzantine territo-ries that the Persians had occupied briefly in the early seventh century, including Jerusalem, which became a holy site for Muslims no less than for Christians and Jews. Arab armies also conquered Persia itself, and rapidly made their way westward across North Africa,

> Justinian's reign was clearly an important turning point in the direction of Byzantine civilization because it saw the crystalliza-tion of new forms of thought and art that can be considered more "Byzantine" than "Roman."

HOW DID THE BYZANTINE STATE SURVIVE FOR NEARLY A MILLENNIUM?

THE BYZANTINE EMPIRE AND ITS CULTURE   263

where Byzantine control had long been resented. Having become a Mediterranean power, the Arabs also took to the sea. In 677 they tried to conquer Constantinople with a fleet. Failing that, they attempted to take the city again in 717 by means of a concerted land and sea operation.

The Arab threat to Constantinople in 717 marked a new low in Byzantine fortunes, but the threat was countered by the emperor Leo the Isaurian (717–741) with as much resolution as Heraclius had shown in meeting the Persian threat a century before. With the help of a secret incendiary device known as "Greek fire" (a mixture of sulphur, naphtha, and quicklime aimed at the enemy from the prows of ships) and great military ability, Leo was able to defeat the Arab forces on sea and land. Leo's relief of Constantinople in 717 was one of the most significant battles in European history. Had the Islamic armies taken Constantinople there would have been little to stop them from sweeping through the rest of Europe. Over the next few decades, however, the Byzantines reconquered most of Asia Minor, which became the heartland of their empire for the next three hundred years. A stalemate with the Islamic forces prevailed until the Byzantines were able to take the offensive against a decaying Islamic power in the second half of the tenth century. In that period—the greatest in Byzantine history—Byzantine

troops reconquered most of Syria. But in the eleventh century a different Islamic people, the Seljuk Turks, canceled out all the prior Byzantine gains. In 1071 the Seljuks annihilated a Byzantine army at Manzikert in Asia Minor, a stunning victory that allowed them to overrun the remaining Byzantine eastern provinces. Constantinople was now thrown back on itself more or less as it had been in the days of Heraclius and Leo. By

CHRONOLOGY

THE BYZANTINE EMPIRE, 610–1095 C.E.

610	Ascension of the emperor Heraclius
c. 650	Arabs seize most of Byzantine territory
717	Constantinople nearly falls to the Arabs
717–750	Byzantines reconquer most of Asia Minor
750–950	Stalemate between Arabs and Byzantines
c. 950–1000	Byzantines reconquer most of Syria
1071	Seljuk Turks overrun eastern Byzantine provinces
1095	First Crusade

Greek Fire.

and large, it would remain on the defensive for the next four hundred years until the last remnants of the Byzantine empire fell to the Ottoman Turks in 1453. Turks continue to rule in Constantinople—which they renamed Istanbul—to the present day.

SOURCES OF STABILITY

That Constantinople was finally taken was no surprise. What is a cause for wonder is that the Byzantine state survived for so many centuries in the face of so many different hostile forces. This wonder becomes all the greater when we recognize that the internal political history of the empire was exceedingly tumultuous. Because Byzantine power was so completely focused upon the imperial court at Constantinople, and because rulers followed their late Roman predecessors in claiming the powers of divinely appointed absolute monarchs, there was no way of opposing them other than by intrigue and violence. Hence Byzantine history was marked by repeated palace revolts, mutilations, murders, and blindings were almost commonplace. Byzantine politics became so famous for their behind-the-scenes complexity that we still use the word "byzantine" to refer to highly complex and devious backstage machinations. Fortunately for the empire, some very able rulers did emerge from time to time to wield their unrestrained powers with efficiency. Even more fortunately, a bureaucratic machinery continued to function during times of palace upheaval.

Efficient bureaucratic government indeed was one of the major elements of Byzantine success and longevity. The Byzantines could count on having an adequate labor supply for their bureaucracy because Byzantine civilization preserved and encouraged the practice of education for the laity. This was one of the major differences between the Byzantine East and the early Latin West: from about 600 to about 1200 lay literacy in Western Christendom was very limited, whereas in the Byzantine East widespread lay literacy was the basis of governmental accomplishment. Literate Byzantine bureaucrats supervised education and religion and presided over all forms of economic endeavor. Imperial officials in Constantinople regulated prices and wages, maintained systems of licensing, controlled exports, and enforced the observance of the Sabbath. Even chariot racing fell under strict governmental supervision, with the populace of Constantinople being assigned by governmental command to root for particular teams. Bureaucratic methods also helped regulate the army and navy, the courts, and the diplomatic ser-

The Emperor John I (969-976) Being Crowned by Christ. Byzantine rulers characteristically used coins as objects of propaganda designed to show that their powers came to them supernaturally.

vice, endowing these agencies with organizational strengths incomparable for their age.

Another explanation for Byzantine endurance was the comparatively sound economic base of the state until the eleventh century. As the historian Sir Steven Runciman has said, "if Byzantium owed her strength and security to the efficiency of her Services, it was her trade that enabled her to pay for them." Commerce and cities continued to flourish in the Byzantine East, as they had done in the late-antique period. Above all, in the ninth and tenth centuries Constantinople was a vital trade emporium for Far Eastern luxury goods and Western raw materials. The empire also nurtured and protected its own industries, most notably that of silk making, and it was renowned until the eleventh century for its stable gold and silver coinage. Constantinople, which at times may have had a population of close to a million, was not its only great urban center. During certain periods Antioch, and up until the end of Byzantine history the bustling cities of Thessalonica and Trebizond, were also large and prosperous.

Historians emphasize Byzantine trade and industry because these were so advanced for the time and provided most of the surplus wealth that supported the state. But agriculture really was at the heart of the Byzantine economy as it was of all premodern ones. The story of Byzantine agricultural history consists mainly of the struggle by independent peasant farmers to stay free of the encroachments of large estates owned by wealthy aristocrats and monasteries. Until the eleventh century the free peasantry managed to

HOW DID THE BYZANTINE STATE SURVIVE FOR NEARLY A MILLENNIUM?

THE BYZANTINE EMPIRE AND ITS CULTURE 265

maintain its existence with the help of state legislation, but after 1025 the aristocracy gained power in the gov- ernment and began to transform the peasants into im- poverished tenants. This had many unfortunate results, not the least of which was that the peasants became less interested in resisting the enemy. The defeat at Manzikert in 1071 was in part the result of the gov- ernment's short-sighted acquiescence to aristocratic ambitions.

BYZANTINE RELIGION

So far we have spoken about military campaigns, gov- ernment, and economics as if they were at the center of Byzantine survival. Seen from hindsight they were, but what the Byzantines themselves cared about most was the religious orthodoxy of their empire. Remarkable as it might seem, Byzantines battled over abstruse religious questions as vehemently as we today might argue about politics and sports— indeed they struggled more ve- hemently, because they were often willing to fight and even die over words in a religious creed. The intense preoccupation with questions of doctrine is well illus- trated by the report of an early Byzantine writer who said that when he asked a baker for the price of bread, the answer came back, "the Father is greater than the Son," and when he asked whether his bath was ready, was told that "the Son proceeds from nothing." Such zealotry could cause great harm during times of reli- gious dissension, but it also endowed the Byzantine state with a powerful sense of confidence and mission during times of religious concord.

Byzantine religious dissensions were greatly compli- cated by the fact that the emperors took an active role in them. Because the emperors carried great power in the life of the church—emperors were sometimes deemed by churchmen to be "similar to God"—they exerted great influence in religious debates. None- theless, especially in the face of provincial separatism, rulers could never force all their subjects to believe the same doctrine they themselves did. Even Byzantine governmental authority did not stretch that far. Only after the loss of many eastern provinces and the refine- ment of doctrinal formulae did religious peace seem near in the eighth century. But then it was shattered for still another century by what is known as the Icono- clastic Controversy.

The Iconoclasts were those who wished to prohibit

> What the Byzantines themselves cared most about was the religious orthodoxy of their empire.

the worship of icons—that is, images of Christ and the saints. Since the Iconoclastic movement was initiated by the Emperor Leo the Isaurian, and subsequently di- rected with even greater energy by his son Con- stantine V (740–775), historians have discerned in it different motives. One was certainly theological. The worship of images seemed to the Iconoclasts to smack of paganism. They believed that nothing made by human beings should be worshiped by them, that Christ was so divine that he could not be conceived of in terms of human art, and that the prohibition of wor- shiping "graven images" in the Ten Commandments (Exodus 20.4) placed the matter beyond dispute.

In addition to these theological points, there were probably other considerations. Since Leo the Isaurian was the emperor who saved Constantinople from the onslaught of Islam, and since Muslims zealously shunned im- ages on the grounds that they were "the work of Satan" (Qur'an, V. 92), Leo's Iconoclas- tic policy may have been an at- tempt to answer one of Islam's greatest criticisms of Christianity and thereby deprive Islam of some of its appeal. There may also have been certain internal political and financial motives. By pro- claiming a radical new religious movement the emper- ors may have wished to reassert their control over the church and combat the growing strength of monaster- ies. As events turned out, the monasteries did rally be- hind the cause of images, and as a result, they were bitterly persecuted by Constantine V, who took the opportunity to confiscate much monastic wealth.

The Iconoclastic Controversy was resolved in the ninth century by a return to the status quo, namely the worship of images, but the century of turmoil over the issue had some profound results. One was the de- struction by imperial order of a large amount of reli- gious art. Pre-eighth-century Byzantine religious art that survives today comes mostly from places such as Italy or Palestine, which were beyond the easy reach of the Iconoclastic emperors. A second consequence of the controversy was the opening of a serious religious breach between East and West. The pope, who until the eighth century had usually been a close ally of the Byzantines, strongly opposed Iconoclasm. This was not least because Iconoclasm tended to question the cult of saints, and the claims of papal primacy were based on an assumed descent from Saint Peter. Papal opposition to Iconoclasm during the eighth century led to worsening relations between East and West that culminated with the crowning of the Frankish leader Charlemagne as the new Roman emperor in the West on Christmas Day 800.

The ultimate defeat of Iconoclasm led to the reassertion of some major traits of Byzantine religiosity, which from the ninth century until the end of Byzantine history remained predominant. One of these traits was a renewed emphasis on the traditional, Orthodox faith of the empire as the key to its political unity and military success. Religious tradition became the touchstone of doctrinal correctness and political legitimacy. As one opponent of Iconoclasm said, "If an angel or an emperor announces to you a gospel other than the one you have received, close your ears." This view strengthened Byzantine religion by ending controversy and heresy, and it helped the religion gain new adherents in the ninth and tenth centuries. But it also reinforced the hegemony of Constantinople's own religious traditions within the empire, thus marginalizing even further the differing religious traditions of Syrian and Armenian Christianity. The fear of heresy also tended to inhibit free speculation, not just in religion but also in related intellectual matters. Although the Byzantine emperors founded and supported a uni-

Christ as Ruler of the Universe. A twelfth-century Byzantine mosaic from the Cathedral of Cefalù in Sicily. Although the Byzantines did not rule in Sicily in the twelfth century, the Norman rulers employed Byzantine workmen. Note the use of Greek—the Byzantine language—on the left-hand Bible page and Latin—the Norman language—on the right.

versity in Constantinople, they never permitted it to exercise any significant degree of intellectual freedom, in marked contrast with the freewheeling intellectual atmosphere of the growing universities of twelfth- and thirteenth-century western Europe.

BYZANTINE CULTURE

Religion dominated Byzantine life, but commitment to Christianity by no means inhibited the Byzantines from revering and preserving their ancient Greek heritage. Byzantine schools based their instruction on classical Greek literature, and especially Homer, to an astonishing degree. Educated people around the Byzantine court could quote but a single line of Homer, and expect that their audience would know immediately the entire passage from which it came. In the English-speaking world, only the King James Bible has ever achieved a degree of cultural saturation comparable with Homer in Byzantium. Like the seventeenth-century Bible, Homer for the Byzantines was simultaneously a literary model, an instructional text-book, and a guide to personal morality and wisdom.

Byzantine scholars also studied intensively the philosophy of Plato and the historical prose of Thucydides. Aristotle's works were also known but were regarded with less interest. By and large, the Greek scientific and mathematical tradition was neglected by the Byzantines, and even philosophy was considerably restricted. Justinian, for example, shut down the Athenian philosophical academies that had existed since Plato's day, declaring that everything worth knowing was already known. Inventiveness was prized in Byzantine culture, but original discoveries and interpretations were not the goal toward which Byzantine intellectual life was directed. Preservation rather than innovation was the hallmark of Byzantine classicism. Nevertheless, such dedicated classicism enriched Byzantine intellectual and literary life and helped preserve the Greek classics for later ages. The bulk of classical Greek

Byzantine achievements in the realms of architecture and art are more familiar. The finest example of Byzantine architecture was the church of Santa Sophia (Holy Wisdom) in Constantinople, constructed at enormous cost by the emperor Justinian in the sixth century. Although built before the date taken here as the beginning of Byzantine history, it was typically Byzantine in both its style and subsequent influence. It was designed by architects of Hellenic descent, but was vastly different from any Greek temple. Its purpose was not to express pride in human accomplishment, but rather to symbolize the inward and spiritual character of the Christian religion. For this reason the architects gave little attention to the

literature that we have today survives only because it was copied by Byzantine scribes.

Byzantine classicism was a product of an educational system for the laity that extended to women as well as to men. Given attitudes and practices in the contemporary Christian West and in Islam, Byzantine commitment to female education was truly unusual. Girls from aristocratic or prosperous families did not go to schools but were relatively well educated at home by private tutors. In the Byzantine world of the ninth, tenth, and eleventh centuries, learned women were praised for being able to discourse like Plato or Pythagoras. The most famous of these Byzantine female intellectuals was the princess Anna Comnena, who described the deeds of her father Alexius in an urbane biography in which she copiously cited Homer and Euripides. But in addition to such literary figures

there were also female physicians in the Byzantine empire, a fact of note given their scarcity in Western society until recent times.

> Given attitudes and practices in the contemporary Christian West and in Islam, Byzantine commitment to female education was truly unusual.

BYZANTINE CLASSICISM

This poem, by an eleventh-century Byzantine scholar, illustrates the sense of continuity learned Byzantines felt between their own Christian world and the world of the ancient Greek philosophers and authors.

May Christ Save Plato and Plutarch from Eternal Damnation

I f perchance you wish to exempt certain pagans from punishment, my Christ,
May you spare for my sake Plato and Plutarch,
For both were very close to your laws in both teaching and way of life.
Even if they were unaware that you as God reign over all,
In this matter only your charity is needed,
Through which you are willing to save all men while asking nothing in return.

Deno John Geanokoplos, ed. and trans. *Byzantium: Church, Society, and Civilization Seen through Contemporary Eyes.* (Chicago: University of Chicago Press, 1984), p. 395.

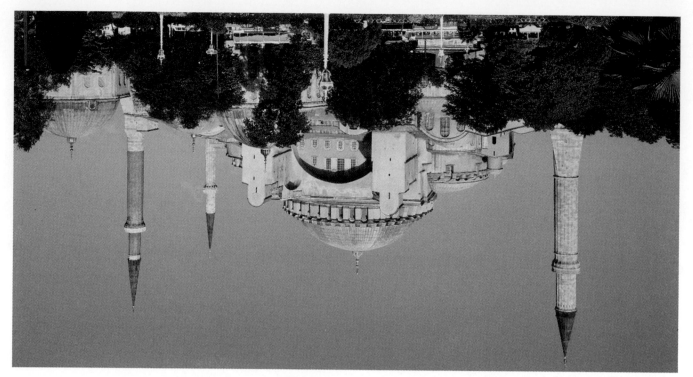

external appearance of the building. Nothing but plain brick covered with plaster was used for the exterior walls; there were no marble facings, graceful columns, or sculptured friezes. The interior, however, was decorated with richly colored mosaics, gold leaf, colored marble columns, and bits of tinted glass set on edge to refract the rays of sunlight after the fashion of sparkling gems. To emphasize a sense of the miraculous, the building was constructed in such a way that light appeared not to come from the outside at all, but to be generated within.

The structural design of Santa Sophia was something altogether new in the history of architecture. Its central feature was the application of the dome principle to a building of square shape. The church was designed in the form of a cross with a magnificent dome over its central square. The main problem was how to fit the circumference of the dome to the square area it was supposed to cover. The solution was to have four great arches spring from the four corners of the square. The rim of the dome was then made to rest on the keystones of the arches, with the curved triangular spaces between the arches filled in with masonry.

The interior of Justinian's church of Santa Sophia in modern Istanbul, looking from east to west and showing the great dome. Since 1453 the church has been in use as a mosque, as shown in this 1852 drawing.

Santa Sophia. The greatest monument of Byzantine architecture. The four minarets were added after the fall of the Byzantine Empire, when the Turks turned the church into a mosque.

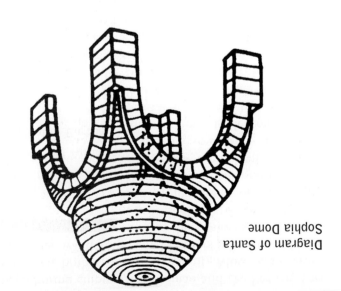

Diagram of Santa Sophia Dome

The result was an architectural framework of marvelous strength, which at the same time made possible a style of imposing grandeur and even some delicacy of treatment. The great dome of Santa Sophia has a diameter of 107 feet and rises to a height of nearly 180 feet from the floor. So many windows are placed around its rim that the dome appears to have no support at all but to be suspended in midair.

BYZANTIUM AND THE WESTERN CHRISTIAN WORLD

After the skirmishes of the Iconoclastic period relations between eastern and western Christians remained tense, partly because Constantinople resented Western claims (initiated by Charlemagne in 800) to rule a rival Roman empire, but most of all because religious differences between the two continued to grow. From the Byzantine point of view westerners were uncouth and ignorant, incapable of understanding the Greek language, in which all serious theologians worked, whereas to western European eyes, the Byzantines were arrogant, effeminate, and prone to heresy. In 1054, papal claims to primacy over the eastern church provoked a religious schism that has never healed. Thereafter the Crusades drove home the dividing wedge.

After the sack of Constantinople in 1204 by crusaders, Byzantine hatred of westerners became intense. "Between us and them," one Byzantine wrote, "there is now a deep chasm: we do not have a single thought in common." Westerners called easterners "the dregs of the dregs . . . unworthy of the sun's light." Easterners called westerners the children of darkness, alluding to the fact that the sun sets in the west. The beneficiaries of this hatred were the Turks, who conquered Constantinople in 1453, and soon thereafter conquered most of southeastern Europe up to Vienna.

In view of this long history of hostility (which we will discuss more fully in the next chapter), it is best to end our treatment of Byzantine civilization here by recalling how much the modern Western world owes to it. In simple physical terms the Byzantine empire acted as a bulwark against Islam from the seventh to the eleventh centuries, thus helping to preserve an independent and Christian West. Western Europeans also owe an enormous cultural debt to Byzantine scholars, who preserved much of the classical Greek literary tradition during centuries when these texts were entirely unknown outside the Byzantine empire itself. Byzantine art has also exerted a great and continuing influence on the art of western Europe. Saint Mark's Basilica in Venice was built in close imitation of the Byzantine style, and the art of such great Western painters as Giotto and El Greco owes much in different ways to Byzantine influences. Nor should we stop at listing influences because the great surviving monuments of Byzantine culture retain their imposing appeal in and of themselves. Travelers who view Byzantine mosaics in such cities as Ravenna and Palermo are continually awestruck, others who make their way to Istanbul still find Santa Sophia to be a marvel. In such jeweled beauty, then, the light from the Byzantine East, which once glowed so brightly, continues to shimmer.

THE GROWTH OF ISLAM

How was Islam able to spread so rapidly?

In contrast to Byzantine history, which has no clearly datable beginning but a definite end in 1453, the history of Islamic civilization has a clear point of origin, beginning with the career of Muhammad in the seventh century, but no end. Believers in Islam, known as Muslims, currently comprise about one-seventh of the global population in their greatest concentrations they extend from Africa through the Middle East and the states of the former Soviet Union to South Asia and Indonesia. All Muslims subscribe both to a common religion and a common way of life, for Islam has always demanded from its followers not just adherence to common forms of worship but also adherence to certain social and cultural norms. Indeed, more than Judaism or Christianity, Islam has been a great experiment in trying to build a worldwide society based on the fullest harmony between religious requirements and precepts for everyday existence. In this section we will trace the early history of the Islamic experiment, with primary emphasis on its orientation toward the West. Nonetheless we must remember that Islam expanded in many directions and that it ultimately had as much influence on the history of Africa and South Asia as it did on that of Europe or western Asia.

We must remember that Islam expanded in many directions and that it ultimately had as much influence on the history of Africa and South Asia as it did on that of Europe or western Asia.

The Kabah. It contains the black stone which was supposed to have been miraculously sent down from heaven, and rests in the courtyard of the great mosque in Mecca.

THE RISE OF ISLAM

Islam was born in Arabia, a desert land and so backward before the founding of Islam that the two dominant neighboring empires, the Roman and the Persian, had not even bothered to conquer it. Most Arabs were Bedouins, wandering camel herders who lived off the milk of their animals and the produce, such as dates, that was grown in desert oases. In the second half of the sixth century Arabia saw a quickening of economic life owing to a shift in long-distance trade routes. The protracted wars between the Byzantine and Persian empires made Arabia a safer transit route than other alternatives for caravans going between Africa and Asia. Some towns grew to direct and take advantage of this growth of trade. The most prominent of these was Mecca, which not only lay on the junction of major trade routes, but also had long been a local religious center. In Mecca was located the Kabah, a pilgrimage shrine that served as a central place of worship for many different Arabian clans and tribes. (Within the Kabah was the Black Stone, a meteorite worshiped as a miraculous relic by adherents of many different divinities.) The men who controlled this shrine and also directed the economic life of the Meccan area belonged to the tribe of Quraish, an aristocracy of traders and entrepreneurs who provided the area with whatever little government it knew.

Muhammad, the founder of Islam, was born in Mecca to a family of Quraish about 570. Orphaned early in life, he entered the service of a rich widow whom he later married, thereby attaining financial security. Until middle age he lived as a prosperous trader little different from his fellow townsmen, but around 610 he underwent a religious experience that changed the course of his life and ultimately that of a good part of the world. Although most Arabs until then had been polytheists who recognized at most the vague superiority of a more powerful god they called Allah, Muhammad in 610 heard a voice from heaven tell him that there was no god but Allah alone. In other words, as the result of a conversion experi-once he became an uncompromising monotheist. Thereafter he received further messages that became the basis for a new religion and that commanded him to accept the calling of "Prophet" to proclaim the monotheistic faith to the Quraish. At first he was not very successful in gaining converts beyond a limited circle, perhaps because the leading Quraish tribesmen believed that establishment of a new religion would deprive the Kabah, and therewith Mecca, of its central place in local worship. The town of Yathrib to the north, however, had no such concerns, and its representatives invited Muhammad to emigrate there so that he could serve as a neutral arbiter of local rivalries. In 622 Muhammad and his followers accepted the invitation. Because their migration—called in Arabic the Hijrah (or Hegira)—saw the beginning of an advance in Muhammad's fortunes, Muslims regard it as marking the beginning of their era: as Christians begin their era with the birth of Christ, so Muslims begin their dating system with the Hijrah of 622.

Muhammad changed the name of Yathrib to Medina (the "city of the Prophet") and quickly established himself as ruler of the town. In the course of doing this he consciously began to organize his converts into a political as well as a religious community. But he still needed to find some means of support for his original Meccan followers, and he also desired to wreak vengeance on the Quraish for not heeding his calls for conversion. Accordingly, he started leading his followers in raids on Quraish caravans traveling beyond Mecca. The Quraish endeavored to defend themselves, but after a few years Muhammad's band, fired by religious enthusiasm, succeeded in defeating them. In 630, after several desert battles, Muhammad entered Mecca in triumph. The Quraish thereupon submitted to the new faith and the Kabah was not only preserved but made the main shrine of Islam, as it remains today. With the taking of Mecca other tribes throughout Arabia in turn accepted the new faith. Thus, although Muhammad died in 632, he lived long enough to see the religion he had founded become a success.

THE RELIGIOUS TEACHINGS OF ISLAM

The doctrines of Islam are straightforward. The word *islam* itself means "submission," and the faith of Islam calls for absolute submission to God. Although the Arabic name for the one God is Allah, it is mistaken to believe that Muslims worship a god like Zeus or Jupiter who is merely the first among many; Allah for Muslims means the Creator, God Almighty—the same omnipotent deity worshiped by Christians and Jews. Instead of saying, then, that Muslims believe "there is no god but Allah," it is more correct to say they believe that "there is no divinity but God." In keeping with this, Muslims believe that Muhammad himself was God's last and greatest prophet, but not that he was God himself. In addition to strict monotheism Muhammad taught above all that men and women must surrender themselves entirely to God because divine judgment is imminent. Mortals must make a fundamental choice about whether to begin a new life of divine service: if they decide in favor of this, God will guide them to blessedness, but if they do not, God will turn away from them and they will become irredeemably wicked. On Judgment Day the pious will be granted eternal life in a paradise of delights, but the damned will be sent to a realm of eternal fire and torture. The practical steps the believer can take are found in the Qur'an, the compilation of the revelations sent by God to Muhammad, and hence the definitive Islamic scripture. These steps include thorough dedication to moral rectitude and compassion, and fidelity to set religious observances—a regimen of prayers and fasts, pilgrimage to Mecca, and frequent recitation of parts of the Qur'an.

The fact that much in the religion of Islam resembles Judaism and Christianity is not coincidental; Muhammad was definitely influenced by the two earlier religions. (There were many Jews in Mecca and Medina, Christian thought was also known to Muhammad, although more indirectly.) Islam most resembles Judaism and Christianity in its strict monotheism, its emphasis on personal morality and compassion, and its reliance on written, revealed scripture. Muhammad proclaimed the Qur'an as the ultimate source of religious authority but accepted both the Hebrew Bible and the Christian New Testament as divinely inspired. From Christianity Muhammad seems to have derived his doctrines of the Last Judgment and the resurrection of the body with subsequent rewards and punishments, and his belief in angels (he reported that God's first message to him had been sent by the angel Gabriel). But although Muhammad accepted Jesus Christ as one of the greatest of a long line of prophets, he did not believe in Christ's divinity and

The fact that much in the religion of Islam resembles Judaism and Christianity is not coincidental; Muhammad was definitely influenced by the two earlier religions.

THE ISLAMIC CONQUESTS

This move toward world influence began immediately on Muhammad's death. Since he had made no provision for the future, and since the Arabs had no clear concept of political succession, it was unclear whether Muhammad's community would survive at all. But his closest followers, led by his father-in-law, Abu-Bakr, and a zealous early convert named Umar, quickly took the initiative by naming Abu-Bakr *caliph*, meaning "deputy of the Prophet," and so the supreme religious and political leader of all Muslims. Immediately after becoming caliph Abu-Bakr began a military campaign to subdue various Arab tribes that had followed Muhammad but were not willing to accept his successor's authority. In the course of this successful military action Abu-Bakr's forces began to spill northward over the borders of Arabia. Probably to their surprise they found that they met minimal resistance from Byzantine and Persian forces.

Abu-Bakr died two years after his accession but was succeeded as caliph by Umar, who continued to direct the Arabian invasions of the neighboring empires. In the following years Arab triumphs were virtually uninterrupted. In 636 the Arabs routed a Byzantine army in

laid claim to no miracles himself other than the writing of the Qur'an. He also preached a religion without sacraments or priests. Every Muslim believer has direct responsibility for living the life of the faith without intermediaries, instead of priests there are only religious scholars who comment on problems of Islamic faith and law, and who may act as judges in disputes. Muslims are expected to pray together in mosques, but there is no such thing as a Muslim mass. The absence of clergy makes Islam more like Judaism, a similarity that is enhanced by Islamic stress on the inextricable connection among the religious, social, and political life of the divinely inspired community. But unlike Judaism, Islam played a unique role in uniting the world as it started to spread far beyond the confines of Arabia.

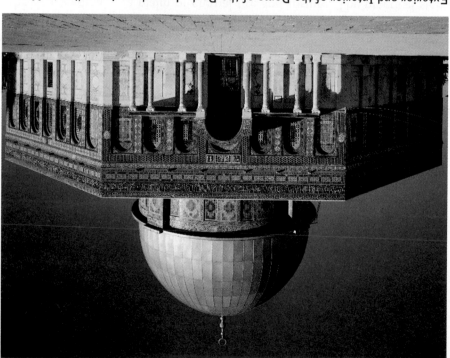

Exterior and Interior of the Dome of the Rock, Jerusalem. According to Muslim tradition, Muhammad made a miraculous journey to Jerusalem before his death and left a footprint in a rock. The mosque that was erected over the site in the seventh century is, after the Kabah, Islam's second-holiest shrine.

THE EXPANSION OF ISLAM TO 750

This map shows the steady advance of Islam from the time of Muhammad to the height of Muslim expansion in the middle of the eighth century. Note the rapid expansion in the generation after Muhammad's death. What about Islam's organization and fervor helped contribute to the spread of Muslim armies? What does the rapid advance suggest about the preparedness of their initial foes, such as Byzantium and Persia? Why were these foes not better able to resist? Why was the capture of Constantinople so crucial to successive Muslim rulers even after Islam had spread well beyond the eastern Mediterranean?

Legend

- At the death of Muhammad, 632
- After the conquests of the first four caliphs, 661
- After the conquests of the Umayyad caliphs, 750
- - - - Outer limits of the Byzantine Empire

Map labels: EUROPE; AFRICA; Area of detail; ATLANTIC OCEAN; FRANKS; Tours; PYRENEES; SPAIN; Toledo; Cordoba; Barcelona; CORSICA; SARDINIA; Rome; LOMBARDS; Ravenna; AVARS; BULGARIANS; BLACK SEA; Constantinople; BYZANTINE EMPIRE; CRETE; SICILY; Tunis; Tripoli; BERBERS; MEDITERRANEAN SEA; CYPRUS; Alexandria; Cairo; EGYPT; Nile R.; RED SEA; Mecca; Medina; ARABIA; ARABIAN SEA; Persian Gulf; Jerusalem; Damascus; SYRIA; Antioch; Baghdad; Euphrates R.; Tigris R.; PERSIA; ARMENIA; CASPIAN SEA

Scale: 0 250 500 Miles / 0 250 500 Kilometers

Syria and then quickly swept over the entire area, occupying the leading cities of Antioch, Damascus, and Jerusalem. In 637 they destroyed the main army of the Persians and marched into the Persian capital of Ctesiphon. Once the Persian administrative center was taken, the highly centralized Persian empire offered little resistance. By 651 the Arabian conquest of the entire Persian realm was complete. The Islamic forces now turned west toward North Africa, capturing Byzantine Egypt by 646 and extending their control throughout the rest of North Africa during the following decades. Attempts in 677 and 717 to capture Constantinople failed, but in 711 the Arabs crossed from North Africa into Visigothic Spain and quickly took almost all of that area too. Thus within less than a century the forces of Islam had conquered all of ancient Persia and much of the late Roman world.

How can we explain this prodigious expansion? The best approach is to see first what impelled the conquerors and then to see what circumstances helped to ease their way. Contrary to widespread belief, the early spread of Islam was not achieved through a religious crusade. At first the Arabs were not at all interested in converting other peoples; instead, they hoped that conquered populations would not convert so that they could maintain their own identity as a community of rulers and tax gatherers. But although their motives for expansion were not religious, religious enthusiasm played a crucial role in making the hitherto unruly Arabs take orders from the caliph and in instilling a sense that they were carrying out the will of God. What really moved the Arabs out of the desert was the search for richer territory and booty, and what kept them moving ever farther was the ease of acquiring new wealth as they progressed.

The Arabs' inspiration by Islam also coincided with a period of weakness in their principal enemies. The Byzantines and Persians had become so exhausted by their long wars with each other and with the "barbar-ians" that they could hardly rally for a new effort. Moreover, many of the local populations of Egypt, North Africa, and Asia Minor were already fed up with

THE "PACT OF UMAR"

When the caliph Umar (d. 644) conquered the city of Jerusalem, he issued a charter of protection to the people of the city, defining the relationship that should exist in the future between the Muslim conquerors and their Christian subjects. In its surviving form, the "Pact of Umar" contains provisions that were probably not in Umar's original document. Nonetheless, the "Pact" does describe accurately the rules that governed Christians and Jews living under Muslim rule during the early middle ages.

T his letter is addressed to Allah's servant Umar, the Commander of the Faithful, by the Christians of such-and-such a city. When you advanced against us, we asked you for a guarantee of protection for our per-sons, our offspring, our property, and the people of our sect, and we have taken upon ourselves the following obligations toward you, namely:

We shall not build in our cities or in the vicinity any new monasteries, churches, hermitages, or monks' cells. We shall not restore . . . any of them that have fallen into ruin or which are located in the Muslims' quarters.

We shall keep our gates wide open for passersby and travelers. We shall provide three days' food and lodging to any Muslims who pass our way. . . .

We shall not teach our children the Koran. We shall not hold public religious ceremonies. We shall not seek to proselytize anyone. We shall not pre-vent any of our kin from embracing Islam if they so desire.

We shall show deference to the Muslims and shall rise from our seats when they wish to sit down. We shall not attempt to resemble the Muslims in any way. . . .

We shall not ride on saddles. We shall not wear swords or bear weapons of any kind, or ever carry them with us. . . .

We shall not display our crosses or our books anywhere in the Muslims' thorough-fares or in their marketplaces. We shall only beat our clappers in our churches very qui-etly. We shall not raise our voices when recit-ing the service in our churches, nor when in the presence of Muslims. Neither shall we raise our voices in our funeral processions. . . .

We shall not build our homes higher than theirs. . . .

Norman A. Stillman, ed. and trans. *The Jews of Arab Lands: A History and Source Book.* (Philadelphia: Jewish Publication Society, 1979), pp. 157–58.

pires. To them, Islamic conquest brought deliverance not only from oppressive taxation, but also from the persecuting religious orthodoxy of Constantinople, which had sought systematically to suppress "hereti-cal" Christian groups in all these areas. Because the Arabs did not demand conversion and exacted fewer taxes than the Byzantines and the Persians, they were often preferred to the old rulers. One Christian writer in Syria went so far as to say, "the God of vengeance delivered us out of the hands of the Romans [that is, the Byzantine empire] by means of the Arabs." For all these reasons Islam quickly spread over the territory between Egypt and Iran, and has been rooted there ever since.

THE SHIITE-SUNNI SCHISM

While the Arabs were extending their conquests they ran into their first serious political divisions. In 644 the caliph Umar died, he was replaced by Uthman, a weak ruler who had the added drawback for many of be-longing to the Umayyad family, a wealthy clan from Mecca that had not at first accepted Muhammad's call. Those dissatisfied with Uthman rallied around the Prophet's cousin and son-in-law Ali, whose blood, background, and warrior spirit made him seem a more appropriate leader of the cause. When Uthman was murdered in 656 by mutineers, Ali's partisans raised him up as caliph. But Uthman's powerful family and supporters were unwilling to accept Ali. In subsequent disturbances Ali was murdered and Uthman's party emerged triumphant. In 661 a member of the Umay-yad family took over as caliph, and that house ruled the Islamic world until 750. Even then, however, Ali's followers did not accept defeat. As time went on they hardened into a minority religious party known as Shiites (shi'a is Arabic for "party" or "faction"); this group insisted that only descen-dants of Ali could be caliphs or have any authority over the Mus-lim community. Those who stood instead for the ac-tual historical development of the caliphate and became committed to its customs were called Sunnites (sunna is Arabic for "religious custom"). The cleft be-tween the two parties has been a lasting one in Islamic history. Often persecuted, Shiites developed great mil-itancy and a deep sense of being the only true pre-servers of the faith. From time to time they were able

> For some peoples, Islamic conquest brought deliverance not only from oppressive taxa-tion, but also from the persecuting religious orthodoxy of Constantinople.

to seize power in one or another area, but they never succeeded in converting the majority of Muslims. Today they rule in Iran and are very numerous in Iraq but make up only about one tenth of the worldwide population of Islam.

UMAYYADS AND ABBASIDS

The triumph of the Umayyads in 661 began a more settled period in the history of the caliphate that would last until the tenth century. During these cen-turies there were two major governing orientations: the westward-looking one represented by the Umay-yads, and the eastward-looking orientation of their successors, the Abbasids. The Umayyad capital was Damascus in the old Byzantine territory of Syria, and in many ways the Umayyad caliphate functioned as a Byzantine successor state, continuing even to employ formerly Byzantine bureaucrats. The Umayyads con-centrated their energies on dominating the Mediter-ranean and conquering Constantinople. When their most massive attack on the Byzantine capital failed in 717, Umayyad strength was seriously weakened, it was only a matter of time before a new orientation would develop.

This new perspective came with the takeover by a new family, the Abbasids, in 750. Their rule stressed Persian more than Byzantine elements. Characteristic of this change was a shift in capitals, for the second Abbasid caliph built his new capital of Baghdad in Iraq, near the ruins of the old Persian capital, and even ap-propriated stones from the ruins. The Abbasids devel-oped their own Muslim administration and imitated Persian absolutism. Abbasid caliphs ruthlessly cut down their enemies, surrounded themselves with elab-orate court ceremonies, and lav-ishly patronized sophisticated literature. This is the world de-scribed in the Arabian Nights, a collection of stories of dazzling splendor written in Baghdad under the Abbasids. The domi-nating presence in those stories, Harun al-Rashid, reigned as caliph from 786 to 809 and behaved as extravagantly as he was described, tossing coins in the streets, passing out sumptuous gifts to his favorites and severe punishments to his enemies. In Spain, however, an Umayyad dynasty continued to rule. Not wishing to be outdone by their Abbasid ri-vals, the Umayyad rulers of Spain were equally lavish in their literary and cultural patronage. One Umayyad

For the Christians of Byzantium and western Europe, the Abbasid caliphate was significant not only for its cultural achievements, but also because its eastern orientation took a certain amount of military pressure off the Mediterranean West. The Byzantine state, accordingly, was able to recover somewhat after a century of military pressure from the Umayyads. Farther west, the Franks of Gaul also benefited from the advent of the Abbasids. Because an Umayyad dynasty continued to control Spain, the great Frankish ruler Charlemagne (800–814) maintained diplomatic and trade relations with the Abbasid caliphate of Harun al-Rashid against their common Umayyad enemy. The most famous symbol of this connection was the elephant that Harun al-Rashid sent to Charlemagne. More important, however, was the flow of silver that found its way from the Abbasid empire north through Russia and the Baltic and into the Rhineland in exchange for Frankish exports of furs, slaves, wax, honey, and leather. Jewels, silks, spices, and other luxury goods from India and the Far East also flowed north and west into the Frankish world through the Abbasid empire. These trading links with the Abbasid world helped to fund the extraordinary cultural achievements of the Carolingian Renaissance which we will describe in the next section of this chapter.

CHRONOLOGY

THE SPREAD OF ISLAM, 622–750 C.E.

Expulsion of Muhammad from Mecca (Hijrah)	622
Muhammad returns to Mecca	630
Muhammad dies	632
Abu-Bakr becomes caliph	632
Umar becomes caliph	634
Arabs occupy Antioch, Damascus, Jerusalem	636
Arabs occupy Persian capital	637
Arabs invade Egypt	646
Arabs conquer Persian empire	651
Shiite-Sunni schism	661
Arabs conquer North Africa	646–711
Umayyad reign	661–750
Arabs invade Spain	711
Beginning of Abbasid reign	750

ter of learning.

ruler of the ninth-century went to enormous lengths to recruit to his court a famous Persian musician, astronomer, and geographer, who became a kind of arbiter of elegance to Spanish high society, introducing to the eager Umayyad court a new eastern hairstyle, a taste for asparagus, and a fashion for wearing underarm deodorant. But the rival Muslim rulers also competed with each other in intellectual pursuits. The caliph Al-Hakem II of Cordoba (961–976), for example, amassed a library of more than four hundred thousand volumes—the catalogue of titles alone ran to forty-four volumes—at a time when, in western Europe, a monastery with one hundred books qualified as a center of learning.

Carolingian Trade Routes. This sixth or seventh century statue of the Buddha, originally made in northern India, was bought to Helgö, an island off the North Sea coast of Germany, probably in the late eighth century. It was originally one of a pair; its mate is now in a private collection in Kashmir. This object illustrates the enormous geographical extent of Carolingian trade connections.

WHAT FORCES COMBINED TO UNDERMINE THE POLITICAL UNITY OF THE ISLAMIC EMPIRE?

THE CHANGING ISLAMIC WORLD 277

THE CHANGING ISLAMIC WORLD

What forces combined to undermine the political unity of the Islamic empire?

During the ninth and tenth centuries, however, the power of the Abbasid dynasty rapidly declined. An extended period of decentralization followed that was mirrored during the eleventh century in Umayyad Spain. The major cause for the Abbasid collapse was the gradual impoverishment of the economic base—the agricultural wealth of the Tigris-Euphrates basin—resulting from ecological crises and a devastating revolt by the enslaved African work force that farmed the southern Iraqi marshlands. Tax revenues from the Abbasid empire were also declining, as provincial rulers in North Africa, Egypt, and Syria retained larger and larger portions of these revenues for themselves. As their revenues declined, the Abbasids found themselves unable to support either their large civil service or the new-style mercenary army they had built up. This new army was manned largely by slaves whose loyalties lay not with the caliphate itself, but with the individual caliphs who employed them. To defend its interests, the army soon became a dominant force in making and murdering caliphs. Massively expensive building projects, including the refoundation of the Abbasid capital of Baghdad, further exacerbated the fiscal, military, and political crisis.

Behind the Abbasid crisis lay two fundamental developments of great significance for the future of the Islamic world: the growth of regionalism and the increasing religious divisions between Sunnis and Shiites and among the Shiites themselves. In 909 regional and religious hostilities came together when a local Shiite dynasty known as the Fatimids seized control of the Abbasid province of North Africa. In 969, the Fatimids succeeded in conquering Egypt also. Meanwhile, another Shiite group, rivals of both the Fatimids and the Abbasids, attacked Baghdad in 927 and Mecca in 930, seizing the sacred Black Stone, the Kabah. Thereafter, the effective power of the Abbasids over their empire collapsed entirely. Although an Abbasid caliphate continued to exist in Baghdad until 1258, when invading Mongol armies finally disposed of its last remnants, in practice the Abbasid empire had disappeared by the 930s. In its place a new order began to emerge in the eastern Muslim world that was centered around the rise of an independent Egyptian kingdom and a new Muslim state based in Persia.

In Spain, Umayyad weakness was more directly a consequence of political failures and succession disputes than of economic collapse. Muslim Spain in the ninth and tenth centuries was an enormously wealthy agricultural and commercial region. But from the mid-ninth century on, renewed military pressure from the reviving Christian kingdoms of northern and eastern Spain exacerbated the internal political difficulties of the Umayyad caliphate. In the opening years of the eleventh century, the united Umayyad caliphate in Spain finally dissolved, to be replaced by a host of local, small-scale *taifa* kingdoms, some of which were now paying tribute to the Christian rulers of the north. In 1085, the great city of Toledo fell to the Christian king Alfonso of León. Alarmed, a new group of North African Islamic purists known as the Almoravids invaded Muslim Spain, checking the Christian advance and amalgamating Islamic Spain with their North African empire. Another such group, the Almohades, repeated this pattern during the twelfth century. But neither the Almoravids nor the Almohades succeeded in reuniting the warring petty kingdoms of Islamic Spain. One by one, these local kingdoms fell gradually victim to the advancing forces of the Christian kings of Spain. Although the last Muslim kingdom, the principality of Granada, would not fall to the Christians until 1492, the Christian reconquest of Spain was essentially complete by the middle of the thirteenth century.

Extravagance and incompetence by the Muslim rulers of eleventh-century Spain certainly played a role in the Umayyad caliphate's collapse. But there were larger factors at work in breaking up the unity of the Islamic world that transcended the failures of particular caliphs. Although Islamic society was religiously tolerant, at least with respect to Jews and Christians (who, as "dhimmis," "peoples of the book" were permitted to retain their religions by paying a special tax to their Muslim rulers, pagans, however, were forced to convert to Islam), ethnic tensions within the Islamic world were rampant and grew more divisive as the early idealism of the initial conquests faded with time. These ethnic tensions among Arabs, Turks, Berbers, sub-Saharan Africans, and Persians additionally complicated the deep regional divisions that had characterized this area of the world for centuries before the Islamic conquests began. Adding further to the political instability of the Muslim world was the uncompromising monotheism and religious egalitarianism of Islam itself. Muslim rulers (such as some of the Abbasids) who took on Persian styles of semidivine rulership were frequently murdered as blasphemers. Tensions between the universality of Islamic belief and the realities of regional particularism, ethnic hostility, and religious conflict between Sunnis and Shiites thus combined to undermine the political unity of the Islamic empire.

MUSLIM SOCIETY AND CULTURE, 900–1250

The political decentralization of the Muslim world did not automatically bring cultural decay, however. In fact, Islamic civilization prospered greatly in the "middle period," above all from about 900 to about 1250. During these centuries Islamic rule expanded into modern-day Turkey and India despite the collapse of the caliphates. Islamic history is certainly not a story of steady decline from the time of Harun al-Rashid. On the contrary, Islam's most creative cultural period was only beginning as the ninth century came to an end.

Islamic culture and society were extraordinarily cosmopolitan and dynamic from their earliest days. Muhammad himself was not a desert Arab but a town-dwelling trader imbued with advanced ideals. Subsequently, Muslim culture became highly cosmopolitan for several reasons: it inherited the sophistication of Byzantium and Persia, it remained centered at the crossroads of long-distance trade between the Far East and West, and the prosperous town life in most Muslim territories counterbalanced agriculture. The importance of trade meant much geographical mobility. Muhammad's teachings furthermore encouraged social mobility because the Qur'an stressed the equality of all Muslims. The result was that at the courts of Baghdad and Córdoba, and later at those of the Muslim states that succeeded them, careers were open to those with talent. Since literacy was remarkably widespread—a rough estimate for around the year 1000 is that 20 percent of all Muslim males could read the Arabic of the Qur'an—many could rise through education. Offices were seldom regarded as hereditary, and "new men" could arrive at the top by enterprise and skill.

There was one major exception to this rule of Muslim egalitarianism: the treatment of women. Perhaps because social status was so fluid, successful men were extremely anxious to preserve and enhance their posi-

tions and their "honor." They could accomplish this by maintaining or expanding their worldly possessions, which included women. For a man's females to be most "valuable" to his status, their inviolability had to be assured. The Qur'an allowed a man to marry four wives, so women were at a premium, and married ones were segregated from other men. A wealthy man would also have a number of female servants and concubines, whom he kept in a part of his residence called the harem, where they were guarded by eunuchs, that is, castrated men. Within these enclaves women vied with each other for preeminence and engaged in intrigues to advance the fortunes of their children. Although large harems could be kept only by the wealthy, the system was imitated as far as possible by all classes. Based on the principle that women were chattel property, these practices did much to debase women and to emphasize attitudes of domination in sexual life. Although male homosexual relations were tolerated in upper-class society, these relationships too were based on patterns of domination, usually of a powerful adult over an adolescent boy, much as they had been in the ancient Greek world.

Two major avenues were open to men wishing to devote themselves to Islamic religious life. One was that of the ulama, learned men whose job was to study and offer advice on all aspects of religion and religious law. Not surprisingly these men usually stood for tradition and rigorous maintenance of the faith, often they exerted great influence on the conduct of public life. Complementary to them were the sufis, religious mystics who might be equated with Christian monks were it not for the fact that they were not committed to celibacy and seldom withdrew from the life of the community. Sufis stressed contemplation and ecstasy as the ulama stressed religious law; they had no common program and in practice behaved very differently. Some Sufis were "whirling dervishes," so known in the West because of their dances, others were faqirs, associated in the West with snake charming in marketplaces, and others were quiet, meditative men who practiced no exotic rites. Sufis were usually organized into "brotherhoods" that did much to convert outlying areas such as Africa and India. Throughout the Islamic world Sufism provided a channel for the most intense religious impulses. The ability of the ulama and the Sufis to coexist is testimony to the cultural pluralism of the Islamic world. But the absence of any avenues for religious women comparable with the convents of the Christian world is a reminder of the limits imposed by gender on that pluralism.

WHAT FORCES COMBINED TO UNDERMINE THE POLITICAL UNITY OF THE ISLAMIC EMPIRE?

THE CHANGING ISLAMIC WORLD 279

MUSLIM PHILOSOPHY, SCIENCE, AND MEDICINE

More remarkable still is the fact that the *ulama* and the Sufis often coexisted with representatives of yet another world view, students and practitioners of philosophy and science. Islamic philosophers were called *faylasufs* in Arabic because they were dedicated to the cultivation of what the Greeks had called *philosophia*. Islamic philosophy was based on the study of earlier Greek thought, above all the Aristotelian and Neo-platonic strains. Around the time when the philosophical schools were closed in Athens by order of the emperor Justinian, Greek philosophers migrated east, and the works of Aristotle and others were translated into Syriac, a Semitic dialect. From that point of transmission Greek philosophy gradually entered the life of Islam and became cultivated by the class of faylasufs, who believed that the universe is rational and that a philosophical approach to life was the highest God-given calling. The faylasufs' profound knowledge of Aristotle can be seen, for example, in the fact that Avicenna (d. 1037), one of the greatest faylasufs, read practically all of Aristotle's works in the remote town of Bukhara before he reached the age of eighteen.

The most serious problem faced by the faylasufs was that of reconciling Greek philosophy with Islamic religion. The faylasufs followed their Greek sources in believing—in opposition to Islamic doctrine—that the world is eternal and that there is no immortality for the individual soul. Different faylasufs reacted to this problem in different ways. Of the three greatest, Al-Farabi (d. 950), who lived mainly in Baghdad, was least concerned by it; he taught that an enlightened elite could philosophize without being distracted by the common religious beliefs of the masses. Even so, he never attacked those beliefs, considering them necessary to hold society together.

Unlike Al-Farabi, Avicenna (980–1037), who was active farther east, taught a less rationalistic philosophy that came close in many points to Sufi mysticism. (A later story held that Avicenna said of a Sufi, "All I know, he sees," while the Sufi replied, "All I see, he knows.") Finally, Averroës (1126–1198) of Córdoba, Spain, was a thoroughgoing Aristotelian who led two lives, one in private as an extreme rationalist and the other in public as a believer in the official faith, indeed even as an official censor. Averroës was the last really important Islamic philosopher: after him rationalism either blended into Sufism, the direction pointed to by Avicenna, or became too constrained by religious orthodoxy to lead an independent existence. But in its heyday between about 850 and 1200, Islamic philosophy was far more advanced and sophisticated than anything found in either the Byzantine or Western Christian realms.

Before their decline Islamic faylasufs were as distinguished in studying natural science as they were in philosophical speculation. Usually the same men were both philosophers and scientists, because they could not make a living by commenting on Aristotle (there were no universities in which to teach), they could rise to positions of wealth and power by practicing astrology and medicine. As it was throughout the ancient and medieval world, astrology among the Muslims was an "applied science" intimately related to accurate astronomical observation. After an Islamic astrologer carefully studied and foretold the courses of the heavenly bodies, he would endeavor to apply his knowledge to the course of human events, particularly the fortunes of wealthy patrons. To account for heavenly motion, some Muslims considered the possibilities that the earth rotates on its axis and revolves around the sun, but these theories were not accepted because they did not fit in with ancient preconceptions such as the assumption of circular planetary orbits. It was therefore not in these suggestions that Muslim astrologers later influenced the West, but rather in their extremely advanced observations and predictive tables that often went beyond the most careful work of the Greeks.

Islamic accomplishments in medicine were equally remarkable. Faylasufs serving as physicians appropriated the knowledge contained in the medical writings of the Hellenistic age but were rarely content with that. Avicenna discovered the contagious nature of tuberculosis, described pleurisy and several varieties of nervous ailments, and pointed out that disease can be spread through contamination of water and soil. His chief medical writing, the *Canon of Medicine*, was accepted in Europe as authoritative until late in the seventeenth century. Avicenna's older contemporary Rhazes (865–925) was the greatest clinical physician of the medieval world. His major achievement was the discovery of the difference between measles and small-pox. Other Islamic physicians discovered the value of

> The most serious problem faced by the faylasufs was that of reconciling Greek philosophy with Islamic religion.

cauterization and of styptic agents, diagnosed cancer of the stomach, prescribed antidotes for cases of poisoning, and made notable progress in treating diseases of the eyes. In addition, they recognized the infectious character of bubonic plague, pointing out that it could be transmitted by clothes. Finally, the Muslims excelled in the organization of hospitals and in the control of medical practice. At least thirty-four great hospitals were located in the principal cities of Persia, Syria, and Egypt, and appear to have been organized in a strikingly modern fashion. Each had wards for particular cases, a dispensary for giving out medicine, and a library. The chief physicians and surgeons lectured to the students and graduates, examined them, and issued licenses to practice. Even the owners of leeches (used for bloodletting, a standard medical practice of the day) had to submit them for inspection at regular intervals.

Other great Islamic scientific achievements came in optics, chemistry, and mathematics. Islamic physicists founded the science of optics and drew a number of significant conclusions regarding the theory of magnifying lenses and the velocity, transmission, and refraction of light. Islamic chemistry was an outgrowth of alchemy, an invention of the Hellenistic Greeks, the system of belief that was based on the principle that all metals were the same in essence, and that baser metals could therefore be transmuted into gold if only the right instrument, the philosopher's stone, could be found. But the efforts of scientists in this field were by no means confined to this fruitless quest; some even denied the whole theory of transmutation of metals. As a result of experiments by Muslim scientists, various new substances and compounds were discovered, among them carbonate of soda, alum, borax, nitrate of silver, saltpeter, and nitric and sulphuric acids. In addition, Islamic scientists were the first to describe the chemical processes of distillation, filtration, and sublimation. In mathematics Islam's greatest accomplishment was to unite the geometry of the Greeks with the number science of the Hindus. Borrowing what Westerners know as "Arabic numerals," including the zero, from the Hindus, Islamic mathematicians developed an arithmetic based on the decimal system and made advances in algebra (itself an Arabic word). Building on Greek geometry with reference to heavenly motions, they also made great progress in spherical trigonometry. Thus they brought together and advanced all the

> Islam brought together and advanced all the areas of mathematical knowledge that would later be developed in the Christian West.

areas of mathematical knowledge that would later be developed in the Christian West.

LITERATURE AND ART

In addition to its philosophers and scientists, medieval Islamic culture was distinguished by its poets. Even before their conversion to Islam, Arabs had excelled in writing poetry. Afterward, literary accomplishment quickly became recognized as a way to distinguish oneself at the Umayyad and Abbasid courts. Probably the greatest of Islamic poets were the Persians (who wrote in their own language more often than in Arabic), of whom the best known in the West is Umar Khayyam (d. 1123), whose Rubaiyat was turned into a popular English poem by the Victorian Edward Fitzgerald. Although Fitzgerald's translation distorts much, the hedonism of Umar's poem ("a jug of wine, a loaf of bread—and thou") faithfully reflects a common theme in much Islamic and Jewish poetry of the period. Similarly sensuous lyric poetry was cultivated in the courts of Muslim Spain. Such poetry too was by no means inhibited, as can be seen from lines like "such was my kissing, such my sucking of his mouth / that he was almost made toothless." As these lines will suggest, much of this work was frankly homosexual, a fact which seems to have occasioned no concern amongst the elite court circles within which this poetry was composed and performed.

Jews too participated in this new literary world, especially in Spain, where they wrote sensuous and playful poems, in both Hebrew and Arabic verse, praising wine, sexuality, and song. Muslim Spain also saw a great flowering of Jewish religious culture. The greatest of the Jewish scholars who flourished during this period was Moses Maimonides (1135–1204), a physician as well as a profound religious thinker, who is sometimes called "the second Moses" for his work in synthesizing the teachings of Jewish law in his famous *Mishneh Torah*. Scores of other Jewish scholars—grammarians, biblical commentators, and legal authorities—preceded Maimonides. But few followed him, at least in Spain. Maimonides himself was driven into exile by the Almohades, first to North Africa and ultimately to Egypt, where he became physician to the Muslim ruler of Cairo. His story is a reminder of the reactionary religious winds blowing through the Islamic world during the twelfth century, and that would ultimately bring this Islamic cultural efflorescence to an end, first in Spain but ultimately throughout the Islamic Mediterranean world.

In their artistic endeavors Muslims were highly eclectic. Their main sources of inspiration came from the art of Byzantium and Persia. The former contributed many of the structural features of Islamic architecture, especially the dome, the column, and the arch. Persian influence was probably responsible for the intricate, nonnaturalistic designs that were used as decorative motifs in practically all of the arts. From both Persia and Byzantium came the tendency to subordinate form to rich and sensuous color. Architecture was the most important of the Islamic arts, the development of both painting and sculpture was inhibited by religious prejudice against representation of the human form. By no means were all of the examples of this architecture mosques, many were palaces, schools, libraries, private dwellings, and hospitals. Among the principal elements of Islamic architecture were bulbous domes, minarets, horseshoe arches, and twisted columns, together with the use of tracery in stone, alternating stripes of black and white, mosaics, and Arabic script as decorative devices. As in the Byzantine style, comparatively little attention was given to exterior ornamentation. The so-called minor arts of the Muslims included the weaving of gorgeous pile carpets and rugs, magnificent leather tooling, and the making of brocaded silks and tapestries, inlaid metalwork, enameled glassware, and painted pottery. Most of the products of these arts were embellished with complicated patterns of interlacing geometric designs, plants and fruits and flowers, Arabic script, and fantastic animal figures. In general, art laid particular emphasis on pure visual design. Separated from any role in religious teaching, it became highly abstract and nonrepresenta-tional.

A HEBREW POEM IN PRAISE OF WINE, BY SAMUEL THE NAGID

In the courts of tenth- and eleventh-century Muslim Spain, Jewish poets and courtiers began to write a new style of Hebrew verse, closely modeled on contemporary Arabic examples. Samuel the Nagid was perhaps the most remarkable of this group of poets. He became the military leader of the Muslim kingdom of Granada as well as the head of the Jewish community there. In addition to his three volumes of poetry, he also wrote treatises on Hebrew grammar and on Jewish religious law.

Your debt to God is righteously to live,
And His to you, your recompense to give.
Do not wear out your days in serving God;
Some time devote to Him, some to yourself.
To Him give half your day, to work the rest,
But give the jug no rest throughout the night.

Put out your lamps! Use crystal cups for light.
Away with singers! Bottles are better than lutes.
No song, nor wine, nor friend beneath the sward—
These three, O fools, are all of life's reward.

Raymond P. Scheindlin, ed. and trans. *Wine, Women, and Death: Medieval Hebrew Poems on the Good Life.* (Philadelphia: The Jewish Publication Society, 1986), p. 47.

tional. For these reasons Islamic art often seems more "modern" than any other art of premodern times.

TRADE AND INDUSTRY

The economic life of the Islamic world varied greatly according to time and place, but underdevelopment was certainly not one of its primary characteristics. On the contrary, in the central areas of Islamic civilization from the first Arab conquests until about the fourteenth century, mercantile life was extraordinarily advanced. The principal reason for this was that the Arabs inherited in Syria and Persia an area that was already marked by an enterprising urban culture and that lay at the crossroads of the Mediterranean world, linking together the major trade routes between Africa, Europe, India, and China. Islamic traders built venturesomely on these earlier foundations. Muslim merchants penetrated into southern Russia and equatorial Africa, caravans of thousands of camels traveled to the gates of India and China. Ships from the Muslim world established new routes across the Indian Ocean, the Persian Gulf, and the Caspian Sea. For periods of time Islamic ships also dominated parts of the Mediterranean. Indeed, one reason for the eventual decline of medieval Islamic civilization was that Western Christians took hold of the Mediterranean in the tenth and eleventh centuries and seized control of the Indian Ocean in the sixteenth century.

The great Islamic expansion of commerce would scarcely have been possible without a corresponding development of industry. It was the ability of the people of one region to turn their natural resources into finished products for sale to other regions that provided a basis for a large part of the trade. Nearly every one of the great cities specialized in some particular

The Great Mosque of Córdoba, in Spain, was built in stages between 784 and 990. Its striped, horseshoe-shaped arches are characteristic of Islamic architecture at this time, visible in the right-hand background. A Christian cathedral, was later constructed within a small portion of this enormous building.

WHAT CAUSED ECONOMIC AND SOCIAL CHANGE IN SEVENTH-CENTURY WESTERN EUROPE?

WESTERN CHRISTIAN CIVILIZATION IN THE EARLY MIDDLE AGES 283

variety of manufacture. Mosul, in Syria, was a center of the manufacture of cotton cloth; Baghdad specialized in glassware, jewelry, pottery, and silks; Damascus was famous for its fine steel and for its "damask," or woven-figured silk; Morocco was noted for the manufacture of leather; and Toledo, in Spain, for its excellent swords. The products of these cities did not exhaust the list of manufactures. Drugs, perfumes, carpets, tapestries, brocades, woolens, satins, metal items, and a host of other products were turned out by the craftsmen of many cities. From the Chinese the Muslims learned the art of papermaking, and the products of that industry were in great demand, not only within the empire itself but in Europe as well.

CONTRIBUTIONS OF EARLY ISLAMIC CIVILIZATIONS

In all the areas we have reviewed, Islamic civilization so overshadowed that of the Christian West until the twelfth century that there can be no comparison. When the West did move forward it was able to do so partly because of what it learned from Islam. In the economic sphere westerners absorbed many accomplishments of Islamic technology, such as irrigation techniques, the raising of new crops, papermaking, and the distilling of alcohol. Islamic economic influence is also reflected in the large number of common English words that were originally of Arabic or Persian origin. Among these are traffic, tariff, magazine, alcohol, muslin, orange, lemon, alfalfa, saffron, sugar, syrup, and musk. The word "admiral" also comes from Arabic—in this case deriving from the title of emir.

Western Europe was equally indebted to Islam in intellectual and scientific life. Here too, borrowed words tell some of the story: algebra, cipher, zero, nadir, amalgam, alembic, alchemy, alkali, soda, almanac, and names of many stars such as Aldebaran and Betelgeuse all derive from Arabic originals. Islamic civilization preserved and expanded Greek philosophical and scientific knowledge when such knowledge was almost entirely forgotten in the West. All the important Greek scientific works surviving from ancient times were translated into Arabic; during the twelfth and thirteenth centuries, most were in turn translated from Arabic into Latin through the combined efforts of

Muslim, Jewish, and western Christian scholars. Above all, the preservation and interpretation of the works of Aristotle was one of Islam's most enduring accomplishments. About two-thirds of Aristotle's works were reacquired in the West by means of Latin translations from Arabic texts. Aristotle's ideas were also interpreted with Islamic help, above all that of Averroës, whose prestige was so great that he was simply called "the Commentator" by medieval Western writers.

Arabic numerals, adopted from India by Muslim mathematicians, are another tremendously important intellectual legacy, as anyone will discover by trying to balance a checkbook with Roman ones.

Aside from these specific contributions, the civilization of Islam arguably had its greatest influence on the West merely by standing as a powerful rival and spur to the imagination. Byzantine civilization was at once too closely related to the Christian West and, from the eleventh century on, too weak to serve this function. Westerners in the high and late Middle Ages usually looked down on the Byzantine Greeks, but they respected and feared the Muslims. And they were right to do so, for Islamic civilization at its zenith (to use another Arabic word) was surely one of the world's greatest. Though loosely organized, it brought Arabs, Persians, Turks, Africans, and Indians together into a common cultural and religious world, creating a diverse society and a splendid legacy of original discoveries and achievements.

WESTERN CHRISTIAN CIVILIZATION IN THE EARLY MIDDLE AGES

What caused economic and social change in seventh-century western Europe?

In western Europe also, the seventh century marked the transition between the late antique and the early medieval worlds. At the end of the sixth century, the Frankish chronicler Gregory of Tours still saw himself as living in a discernibly Roman world of cities, trade,

> Islamic civilization so overshadowed that of the Christian West until the twelfth century that there can be no comparison. When the West did move forward it was able to do so partly because of what it learned from Islam.

taxation, and local administration. Gregory was proud of his family's status as Roman senators, and took it for granted that he and his male relatives should be bishops who ruled, by right of birth and status, over their episcopal cities and the surrounding countryside. Like others of his class, Gregory still spoke and wrote Latin—a quite different Latin, to be sure, from the polished prose of Cicero six hundred years before, but a Latin that was nonetheless the same language, and that had certainly changed less since Cicero's day than English has changed since the time of Chaucer. Gregory was of course aware that the western Roman empire was now in the hands of Frankish, Visigothic, Ostrogothic, and Lombard kings. But he saw those kings as Romans nonetheless, because they ruled in accordance with Roman models and, in the case of the Franks, because they ruled with the approval of the Roman emperor in Constantinople. It was also a source of satisfaction to Gregory that in recent years, all these barbarian kings had converted to orthodox, Catholic Christianity. This too, for Gregory, reinforced their *romanitas* ("Roman-ness"), and thus lent legitimacy, both earthly and heavenly, to their rule.

Two hundred years later, however, when Charlemagne, the greatest of all the Frankish rulers, was crowned as the new Roman emperor in the West, the sense of direct continuity that Gregory of Tours had had with the Roman world was gone. When Charlemagne set out to reform the cultural, religious, and political life of his empire, his goal was to revive a Roman empire from which he and his contemporaries now saw themselves as estranged. Charlemagne sought a *renovatio Romanorum imperii*—a renewal of the empire of the Romans—thus conceding in his very motto that he sought to revive an empire that had fallen. Somewhere between Gregory of Tours and Charlemagne a rupture occurred in western Europeans' relationship to their Roman past. Cultured Europeans ceased to see themselves as living in a continuing Roman empire and began to dream of reconstructing it. This awareness of a break with the Roman past developed during the seventh century. It was the consequence of profound economic, religious, and cultural changes; and it marks the beginning of a new era in the history of western European civilization.

> This awareness of a break with the Roman past developed during the seventh century. It was the consequence of profound economic, religious, and cultural changes; and it marks the beginning of a new era in the history of western European civilization.

ECONOMIC DISINTEGRATION AND POLITICAL INSTABILITY

As we have seen, the economy of the western Roman empire was becoming increasingly regionalized from the third century C.E. onward. The Mediterranean world, however, remained a reasonably well-integrated economic unit until the late sixth century. In the year 550, a gold coinage still circulated in both the eastern and the western Roman empire, a luxury trade in silks, spices, swords, and jewelry continued to move west; and slaves, wine, grain, and leatherwork still moved east from North Africa, Gaul, and Spain toward Constantinople, Egypt, and Syria. By 650, however, the economic unity of the Mediterranean world had broken down. This breakdown resulted partly from the destructiveness of Justinian's efforts to reconquer the western empire. Partly it was a consequence of ruinous Byzantine taxation of agricultural land, especially in Egypt and North Africa, where the resentments of overtaxed peasant farmers prepared the way for the Islamic conquests. Piracy by Muslim raiders also played a role in undermining the economy of the seventh-century Mediterranean world—although Muslims quickly became important maritime traders, and in the long run Muslim conquests did more to reconstruct than to destroy the patterns of Mediterranean commerce.

For western Europe, however, the most important causes of these seventh-century economic changes were internal. The cities of Italy, Gaul, and Spain continued to decline. Although bishops still ruled from cities, and so continued to provide a market for certain kinds of luxury goods, the kings and nobles of western Europe were moving to the countryside during the seventh century, living as much as possible from the produce of their own estates rather than purchasing their supplies in the marketplace. At the same time, agricultural land was passing out of cultivation, especially on the larger estates, whose owners were finding it too costly to maintain the gangs of field slaves that had been the backbone of late Roman commercial agriculture. As trade declined, so too did the revenues lords took from tolls. The late Roman system of land taxes was also collapsing, not least because free-born Franks and Goths were claiming exemptions from it, leaving only the Roman population and the servile peasantry

WHAT CAUSED ECONOMIC AND SOCIAL CHANGE IN SEVENTH-CENTURY WESTERN EUROPE?

WESTERN CHRISTIAN CIVILIZATION IN THE EARLY MIDDLE AGES 285

and meat into the weapons, jewelry, and silks that brought prestige in seventh-century aristocratic society. In a world in which the power of lords depended on their ability to give such high-prestige gifts to their military followers, the inability to convert peasant renders into cash was a serious handicap. It meant that for great men to give weapons and jewelry to their followers, they first had to acquire these items either through traders and artisans, or else through plunder and tribute. Either way, the processes by which such gifts were acquired were likely to be destabilizing.

Some rulers attempted to solve this problem by establishing and controlling special ports, known as *emporia*, where foreign merchants and craft workers would gather at specific seasons of the year to exchange their goods. Emporia offered a degree of security to merchants and provided the rulers who controlled them with an important source of power and influence. Control over these emporia was therefore a frequent source of conflict. Far more disruptive, however, were the incessant wars and raids fought among the various kings and lords of seventh-century Europe. The causes of these wars were almost infinitely various, but behind them lay the fundamental importance of plunder and tribute to the dynamics of power in the early medieval world.

The successful rulers of the seventh, eighth, and ninth centuries tended to be those whose territories adjoined wealthy but poorly defended territories that could be easily and profitably attacked. Such "soft frontiers" provided rulers with land and wealth they could distribute to their followers. Successes of this sort would bring more followers to a lord's service; so long as more conquests then followed, the process of amassing power and wealth would continue. But power acquired through plunder and conquest was inherently unstable. A few defeats might speedily reverse the entire process.

Another factor contributing to the instability of power in this world was the difficulty all the royal dynasties of the early middle ages experienced in trying to regulate the succession to their thrones. The kings who established themselves during the invasion period of the fifth and sixth centuries did not come from the traditional royal families of their peoples. Moreover, the barbarian armies who took over the western Roman empire during these years were rarely if ever composed of a single people anyway. They were usually made up of many different peoples, including a sizable number of disaffected Romans. Such unity as they possessed was largely the creation of the charis-

to pay these taxes. The coinage systems of western Europe were also breaking down. From the 630s on, the Islamic conquests seriously reduced the supply of gold available in western Europe; but gold coins were already too valuable to be useful in local marketing anyway. From the 660s on, western European rulers shifted from a gold to a silver coinage. Europe would remain a silver-based economy for the next one thousand years.

During the seventh century, western Europe thus became a basically two-tier economy. Gold, silver, and luxury goods circulated among the wealthy, but the peasantry relied mainly on barter and various currency substitutes to facilitate their transactions. Lords collected rents from their peasants in foodstuffs but found it difficult to convert these payments of grain, wine,

Book Cover The cover of a gospel book encrusted with jewels and ivory cameos presented by Pope Gregory the Great to a Lombard queen around the year 600.

matic warrior-kings who led them, and this charisma was not easily passed on by inheritance.

Of all the barbarian groups that established kingdoms in the western empire during the fifth and sixth centuries, only the Franks succeeded in establishing a single royal dynasty from which the future kings of the Franks would be drawn for the next two hundred fifty years. This dynasty was established by Clovis (d. 511), the great warrior-king of the Franks, who by converting to orthodox, Catholic Christianity also established an alliance between his dynasty and the powerful Roman bishops of Gaul. But the dynasty itself came to be known as the Merovingians, after Clovis' legendary grandfather Merovech, who was a sea dragon. We need not take this claim seriously, but it is, at the very least, a telling indication of how short was Clovis' known genealogy, that no one could be quite sure who his grandfather actually was.

Even in Gaul, however, the Merovingians were not the only noble family with a plausible claim to be kings; and in Visigothic Spain, Anglo-Saxon England, and Lombard Italy, the numbers of such rival royal families were even greater. Nor was the right of succession limited to the eldest male claimant of each competing royal family. Early medieval Europe was a world in which all the sons of a king (and frequently all his cousins and nephews too) could stake a plausible claim to the throne. In Visigothic Spain, the bloody succession disputes that resulted when a reigning king died so horrified the resident Roman population that they spoke of this inability to regulate the succession as a kind of a sickness: the *morbus Gothorum*, the "sickness of the Goths." In Gaul, the Franks were more successful in restricting claims to kingship to descendants of the Merovingian dynasty, but the Merovingians' custom of dividing the kingdom up into its constituent, regional parts, and installing a different king over each part, guaranteed plenty of civil strife in Merovingian Gaul also.

MONASTICISM AND CONVERSION

The brutal conflicts between these rival Merovingian kings, together with the blackening of their reputations by their Carolingian rivals and successors, can easily obscure the real strength and sophistication of Merovingian governance. Many elements of late Roman local administration survived throughout the Merovingian period. Literacy remained an important element in Merovingian administration, providing a foundation on which the Carolingians would build. Even the cultural

renaissance associated with the reign of Charlemagne really began in the late seventh century, with the production of deluxe biblical and other manuscripts at Merovingian monasteries such as Luxeuil.

Monasteries grew remarkably under the Merovingians, especially during the seventh century, reflecting the great wealth of the country. Of the approximately five hundred fifty monasteries that existed in Gaul by the year 700, more than three hundred had been established in the preceding century. The Frankish bishoprics also prospered greatly under the Merovingians, amassing approximately three quarters of their total landed possessions by the end of the seventh century. This massive redistribution of wealth reflected a fundamental shift in the economic gravity of the Frankish kingdom. In the year 600, the wealth of Gaul was still concentrated in the south, where it had been throughout the late Roman period. By the year 750, however, the economic center of the kingdom lay north of the Loire, in the territories that extended from the Rhineland westward to the North Sea. It was here that most of the new monastic foundations of seventh-century Gaul were established.

Behind this shift in wealth from south to north lay a long and successful effort to bring under cultivation the rich, heavy soils of northern France. This effort was assisted by the development of heavy-wheeled plows capable of cutting and turning grassland sod and heavy clay, and by increasingly efficient devices for harnessing animals (particularly oxen, but sometimes horses) to pull these plows. Gradually warming weather improved the fertility of these wet, northern soils, lengthening the growing season and so making possible more efficient crop-rotation systems. The population began to expand as food became more plentiful. Northern France remained a land of scattered settlements separated by heavy forest, but it was a much more densely populated region by 750 than it had been in 600. All these developments would continue during the Carolingian period and beyond. But although the Carolingians would enjoy the fruits of this gradually increasing northern agricultural prosperity, the developments that made it possible began during the seventh century under their Merovingian predecessors.

THE SPREAD OF MONASTICISM

Momentous developments also took place in religious life during the seventh century, especially in the monasteries. Throughout Christian Europe, the seventh century witnessed a rapid increase in the founda-

WHAT CAUSED ECONOMIC AND SOCIAL CHANGE IN SEVENTH-CENTURY WESTERN EUROPE?

WESTERN CHRISTIAN CIVILIZATION IN THE EARLY MIDDLE AGES 287

tion of monastic houses. Monasteries had existed in Gaul, Italy, and Spain since the fourth century, but most were located in the highly Romanized cities of southern Spain, Gaul, and northern Italy. In Gaul, where the Merovingian kings were Catholic, kings had begun to forge ties with monasteries during the sixth century. In Spain, Italy, and England, whose rulers had previously been Arian heretics (Spain and Italy) or pagans (England), ties between monasticism and monarchy arose only in the seventh century, after the royal dynasties of these areas had converted to Catholic Christianity. Even in Gaul, however, relations between the Merovingian kings and the Frankish monasteries became markedly closer from the late sixth century on, as the royal dynasty and the principal noble families embarked on a massive campaign of new monastic foundations that permanently altered the spiritual geography of western Europe.

Most of the new monastic foundations of the seventh century were deliberately located in rural areas, where they played an important role in the continuing struggle to Christianize the countryside. Often they were granted special privileges known as immunities, which by freeing them from the control of local bishops cemented their dependence on their founders. Frequently these new foundations were either double monasteries (in which a house of religious men was joined to a house of religious women), or convents, established for women only. Either way, they were usually ruled over by abbesses drawn from among the women of the royal family: dowager queens, royal princesses, or sometimes even a reigning queen herself.

Monastic life had great appeal to the royal and noble women of the early Middle Ages. It provided them with a socially sanctioned arena within which they could exercise a degree of power over their lives denied them outside the cloister. It gave them an honorable position in society from which they could influence the affairs of their families, while protecting them from abduction, rape, or forced marriages arranged to promote their families' diplomatic or dynastic interests. And it also guaranteed them salvation, at a time when salvation outside the cloister seemed a perilously uncertain prospect. But convents and double monasteries served the interests of the male members of these royal dynasties also—one reason, of course, why they founded and supported them. Convents provided a dignified place of retirement for inconvenient but potentially powerful women, such as dowager queens. The prayers of holy women were regarded as particularly effective in securing divine support for the kingdom. And by limiting the number of royal women who could reproduce, convents also helped to reduce the number of potential claimants to the throne. Establishing royal women in convents was thus an important way of controlling the succession disputes that so regularly tore these early medieval kingdoms apart.

Many of these new monastic establishments also played an important role in the new round of missionary activity that characterized the seventh-century world. The most famous example of such monastic missionary activity is the conversion of Anglo-Saxon England. In northern England, the work of Christianization began in the late sixth century, led by missionary monks from Ireland. The decisive moment came in 597, however, when a group of forty Benedictine monks, sent by Pope Gregory I (590–604) and led by Saint Augustine of Canterbury (not to be confused with Saint Augustine of Hippo), brought the traditions of Roman Christianity to the kingdom of Kent in southeastern England. Despite some initial setbacks, by the end of the seventh century all of England had been brought firmly within the boundaries of the Roman, Christian world, and English monks had begun their own missionary campaigns in Frisia and Saxony. Frankish missionaries were also active in these areas, as they were in the Low Countries and the Basque lands of the southwest also. But it was the particular loyalty the English monks felt toward the papacy that was to have the most momentous consequences, not only for the papacy, but also for Gaul.

THE REIGN OF POPE GREGORY I

The architect of this new alliance between the Roman papacy and Benedictine monasticism was Pope Gregory I, known as Saint Gregory the Great. Until his time the Roman popes were generally subordinate to the emperors in Constantinople and to the greater religious prestige of the Christian East. Byzantine power in Italy was declining, however, and although Gregory worked hard to prevent a breach with Constantinople; he also sought to create a more autonomous, Western-oriented Latin Church. As a theologian—the fourth great "Latin father" of the church—he built on the work of Saint

Many of the new monastic establishments also played an important role in the new round of missionary activity that characterized the seventh-century world.

Jerome, Saint Ambrose, and especially Saint Augustine of Hippo, in articulating a theology with distinctively Western elements. Among these were an emphasis on the necessity of penance for the forgiveness of sins, and the concept of purgatory as a place where the soul was purified before it was admitted into heaven. (Western belief in purgatory was thereafter to become one of the major differences in the teachings of the eastern and western churches.) Gregory emphasized the importance of pastoral care by bishops toward the laity, writing an influential book on the subject in a deliberately simplified Latin prose style that made it one of the most accessible and influential books of the early Middle Ages. A powerful liturgical chant with unaccompanied vocal music in Latin has become known as "Gregorian chant," although Gregory's role in creating this music is conjectural and debatable. All these innovations helped to make the Christian West religiously and culturally more independent of the Greek-speaking East than it had ever been before.

Gregory was also a statesman and ruler in the model of his Roman forebears. Within Italy he ensured the survival of the papacy against the barbarian Lombards by clever diplomacy and expert management of the papacy's estates and revenues. He maintained good relations with Byzantium while asserting his authority as pope over the other bishops of the Western church. Above all, he patronized the order of Benedictine monks. Gregory's patronage helped the Rule of Saint Benedict become the predominant monastic rule in the

Pope Gregory the Great. In this tenth-century German ivory panel the pope is receiving inspiration from the Holy Spirit in the form of a dove.

West, through his encouragement, Benedictine monks emerged as the most important missionary group of the early Middle Ages. Among these Benedictine missionaries, Englishmen such as Saint Boniface and Saint Willibrord deserve pride of place. Their missionary work in Frisia and Germany brought both regions into the western Catholic Church, and laid the groundwork for an alliance between the papacy and the Frankish monarchy that would transform early medieval Europe. Gregory did not live to see this alliance, but his policy of invigorating the Western church contributed greatly to bringing it about.

THE RISE OF THE CAROLINGIANS

How did Charlemagne redefine the relationship between Christianity and kingship?

In Gaul, the weaknesses of the Merovingian dynasty were steadily becoming more apparent as the seventh century drew to a close. Tensions among noble families in the Merovingian heartland of Neustria and those in the border region of Austrasia were increasing. The Austrasian nobles had profited from their steady push into the "soft frontier" areas east of the Rhine, acquiring wealth and military power in the process. The Merovingians, based in Neustria, had no such easy conquests at their disposal. Moreover, a considerable portion of the land they did hold had been given to the church in the course of the seventh century. A succession of short-lived Merovingian kings complicated matters further, producing a series of civil wars between Austrasians and Neustrians. Briefly, in 687, the leader of the Austrasian nobility, Pepin of Herstal, succeeded in forcing his way into office as "mayor of the palace," seeking thereby to control both Austrasia and Neustria. But not until 717, when Pepin's illegitimate son Charles Martel ("the Hammer") finally triumphed over his opponents in both territories, was Pepin's family secure in its control over the Merovingian court. Thereafter, however, the Merovingian kings were largely figureheads in a kingdom ruled by Charles Martel and his sons.

Charles Martel is sometimes considered the second founder (after Clovis) of the Frankish state. His claim to this title is twofold. First, in 733 or 734 (the tradi-

HOW DID CHARLEMAGNE REDEFINE THE RELATIONSHIP BETWEEN CHRISTIANITY AND KINGSHIP?

THE RISE OF THE CAROLINGIANS 289

tional date of 732 is erroneous), he turned back a Muslim force from Spain at the battle of Tours (not Poitiers), some one hundred fifty miles from the Merovingian capital of Paris. Although the Muslim contingent was a raiding party rather than a full-scale army, the incursion was nonetheless the high-water mark of Umayyad progress toward northwestern Europe, and Charles's victory won him great prestige. Equally important, Charles began to develop an alliance with the English Benedictine missionaries who were attempting to convert Frisia and central Germany to Christianity. Charles's family had long been active in the drive to conquer and settle these areas, and he understood clearly how missionary work and Frankish expansion could go hand in hand. Charles readily assisted Saint Boniface and his followers in their conversion efforts. In return, the English Benedictines brought Martel and his descendants into contact with the papacy and assisted him in his efforts to reform (and so control) the Frankish church.

Charles Martel died in 741. Although Charles never sought to become king himself, during the last years of his life he was so clearly the effective ruler of Gaul that he did not even bother to arrange for a new king to be selected when, in 737, the reigning Merovingian king died. In 743, however, Martel's sons, Carloman and Pepin, bowed to the forces of legitimism, and a new Merovingian king took the throne. By 750, however, Carloman had withdrawn from public life to a monastery, and Pepin had decided to seize the throne for himself. To effect such a change in dynasties, Pepin needed the support of the Frankish church. It was highly unlikely, however, that the bishops of Merovingian Gaul would support such a usurpation without papal approval. This did not deter Pepin. Through his family's support for Saint Boniface, Pepin was already well regarded in Rome. And the papacy, locked in a bitter fight with the Byzantine emperors over Iconoclasm and with the Lombard kings for control over central Italy, proved only too happy to cooperate in Pepin's elevation, hoping that a powerful new Frankish ruler would take over from the Byzantines the responsibility for protecting papal interests in Italy against the Lombards.

In 751 Saint Boniface, acting as papal emissary, anointed Pepin as king of the Franks. The idea of anointing a newly created king with holy oil was bor-

rowed from the Bible, in which the Hebrew prophet Samuel had anointed Saul as the first king of Israel. The power of these Old Testament associations would grow under Pepin's son Charles the Great (who thus became David) and his grandson Louis the Pious (who became Solomon). In 751, however, they mainly underscored the novelty and uncertainty of the process by which the last Merovingian king was deposed and sent to a monastery, and a new king, who had not a drop of Merovingian blood, was raised to the Frankish throne for the first time in almost three centuries. In 756, Pepin repaid his debt to the pope by launching a military expedition against the Lombards in Italy; but when the expedition went badly, Pepin abandoned it and returned home. Pepin's coronation symbolized the integration of the new Frankish monarchy into the papal-Benedictine orbit. For the moment, however, Pepin had his hands full simply trying to control his new kingdom.

THE REIGN OF CHARLEMAGNE

The real consolidation of this new pattern of papal-Frankish-Benedictine relations took place during the reign of Pepin's son, Charlemagne, from whom the new dynasty takes its name of Carolingian (from "Carolus," the Latin form of "Charles"). When Charlemagne came to the throne in 768, it seemed possible that the Frankish kingdom would break up into its hostile regional parts of Austrasia, Neustria, and Aquitaine. But in an astonishing series of military campaigns, Charlemagne united the Franks by leading them on a series of conquests that annexed the Lombard kingdom of Italy, the greater part of Germany including Saxony, portions of central Europe, and Catalunya. These conquests set a seal of divine approval on the new Carolingian dynasty. They also provided the plunder, booty, and new lands that enabled Charlemagne to promote his Frankish followers to dizzying heights of wealth and grandeur. Many of the peoples whom Charlemagne conquered were already Christians. In Saxony, however, Charlemagne's armies campaigned for twenty years before finally subduing the pagan Saxons and forcing their conversion to Christianity. Germany was thus forcibly integrated into the Frankish realm. Equally momentous was the connection Charlemagne's conquest of Saxony forged between conquest

> Charlemagne's conquest of Saxony forged the connection between conquest and conversion, which would characterize western Christian thinking for the next one thousand years.

THE EMPIRE OF CHARLEMAGNE, 814

Note the extent of Charlemagne's empire in 814. Could he legitimately claim to be renewing the Roman Empire? How did his possession of Rome strengthen such a claim, and how might it complicate the strong alliance between his house and the papal court? What economic and religious benefits did Charlemagne's exploitation of his large, eastern, "soft frontier" on a national level bring to his reign? Note the inset in the upper left: what does this map suggest about the power of tradition and custom in a world as supposedly "sophisticated" as the one wrought by Charlemagne?

Legend:
- The empire of Charlemagne, 814
- Tributary peoples
- Byzantine empire

Inset: The Division of the Carolingian Empire under Charlemagne's Grandsons

and conversion, which would characterize western Christian thinking for the next one thousand years.

To rule the vast empire he had conquered, Charlemagne appointed Frankish aristocrats called counts (in Latin, *comites*, meaning "followers") to supervise local administration within their territories. Among the counts' many duties were the administration of justice and the raising of armies. Charlemagne also established a network of other local administrators to supervise courts, collect tolls, administer crown lands, and extract taxation. Charlemagne also created a new coinage system, based on a division of the silver pound

into two hundred forty pennies, which would last in France until the French Revolution and in Great Britain until the 1970s, when it was finally replaced by a decimal-based currency. As we have seen, much of the silver for this new coinage originated in the Abbasid empire. Scandinavian traders carried it north through Russia and the Baltic Sea, and then into the Rhineland, where they exchanged it for furs, cloth, and slaves captured in Charlemagne's wars against the Saxons, which they then transported to Baghdad.

Like Carolingian administration generally, this new monetary system depended on the regular use of writ-

THE RISE OF THE CAROLINGIANS 291

HOW DID CHARLEMAGNE REDEFINE THE RELATIONSHIP BETWEEN CHRISTIANITY AND KINGSHIP?

Charlemagne. A silver penny struck between 804 and 814 in Mainz (as indicated by the letter M at the bottom) showing Charlemagne in a highly stylized fasion as emperor with Roman military cloak and laurel. The inscription reads KAROLVS IMP AVG (Charles, Emperor, Augustus). Charlemagne's portrait is closely modeled upon the imperial portraits on Hellenistic and Roman coins.

ten records and instructions. But Charlemagne did not rely on the written word alone to make his will felt. Periodically he sent special representatives from his court (known as *missi*) on tours through the countryside to relay his instructions personally and check up on local administrators. Charlemagne himself also journeyed regularly around his kingdom from his capital city at Aachen, leading armies, supervising administrators, and listening to the complaints of his subjects. Charlemagne's governmental system was far from perfect. Local officials abused their positions, nobles sought to turn free peasants into unfree serfs; justice in local courts was more often denied than done. But Charlemagne's system produced nonetheless the best government Europe had seen since the Romans, and it became the model on which Western rulers would base their own administrations for the next three hundred years.

CHRISTIANITY AND KINGSHIP

Throughout his reign, Charlemagne took seriously his responsibilities as a Christian king. As his empire expanded, however, he came to see himself not only as the ruler of the Franks, but as the leader of a unified Christian society, Christendom, which he was obliged to defend both militarily and spiritually against its enemies. The Carolingian world did not make the distinc-

tions between the religious and the political realms that would characterize European life from the twelfth century on, any more than did Byzantium or Islam. Especially among churchmen, kingship in early medieval Europe was regarded as a sacred office created by God to protect the church, defend the Christian people, and promote their salvation. Religious reforms were therefore no less central to proper kingship than were justice and defense. In some ways, indeed, a king's responsibilities for his kingdom's religious life were even more important than his other responsibilities: for surely no kingdom could prosper if the lives of its subjects were displeasing to God.

These ideas about the spiritual responsibilities of kingship were not new in the late eighth century, but they took on a new importance as a result of the extraordinary power Charlemagne wielded over his empire. Like other early medieval kings, Charlemagne appointed and deposed bishops and abbots, just as he did his counts and other officials. But he also changed the liturgy of the Frankish church, reformed rules of worship in Frankish monasteries, declared changes in basic statements of Christian belief, prohibited pagan observances, enforced tithes on the Frankish peasantry (a tithe was a tenth of peasants' produce, owed to the church), and imposed basic Christian observances, including baptism, on the conquered peoples of Saxony. To Charlemagne, such measures were clearly required if God's new Israel, the Franks, were to avoid the fate that befell biblical Israel whenever its people turned away from their obedience to God.

As the dominant political power in central Italy, Charlemagne was also the protector of the papacy. Although carefully acknowledging the pope's role as the spiritual leader of western Christianity, Charlemagne dealt with the pope much as he did with the other bishops of the Frankish empire. He supervised and approved papal elections, while protecting the pope against his enemies. In 796, just after the election of Pope Leo III, Charlemagne explained the relationship between his authority and that of the pope in the following words: "It is for us," wrote Charlemagne to Leo, "in accordance with the help of divine goodness, outwardly to defend by force of arms the Holy Church of Christ in all places from the incursions of pagans and the ravages of infidels, and inwardly to fortify her with our confession of the Catholic faith. It is for you, most holy father . . . to aid our armies, to the end that with you as intercessor and with God as guide and giver, our Christian people may in all places have the victory over the enemies of its holy name, and that the name of Our Lord Jesus Christ may be renowned throughout all the world."

THE CAROLINGIAN RENAISSANCE

Similar ideals lay behind the Carolingian Renaissance, a cultural and intellectual flowering that took place around the Carolingian royal court. Like their biblical exemplars, the Hebrew kings David and Solomon, Charlemagne and Louis the Pious took seriously their role as patrons of poetry and learning. In so doing, they created an ideal of the court as an intellectual and culture center that would profoundly influence Western European cultural life until the end of the nineteenth century. What lay behind the Carolingians' support for scholarship, however, was their conviction that classical learning was the foundation on which Christian wisdom rested, and that such wisdom was essential to the salvation of God's people. Supporting scholarship was therefore a paramount obligation for a Christian king.

To promote classical learning and Christian wisdom, Charlemagne recruited scholars from throughout Europe to his court, including the English Benedictine monk Alcuin, whose command of classical Latin grammar established him as the intellectual leader of Charlemagne's court school. Carolingian scholars produced a good deal of original Latin poetry and an impressive number of theological and pastoral tracts. Under Alcuin, however, their primary efforts were devoted to collating, correcting and recopying classical Latin texts, including, most important, the text of the Latin Bible, which had become corrupted by generations of copyists' mistakes. To detect and correct these errors, Alcuin and his associates gathered as many different versions of the biblical text as they could find and compared them word by word. After determining the correct version among all the variants, they made a new, corrected copy and destroyed the other versions. They also developed a new style of hand-writing, with simplified letter forms and spaces inserted between words, that further reduced the likelihood that subsequent copyists would misread the corrected texts. Although modified again by Italian Renaissance scholars in the fifteenth century, this new style of handwriting, known as Carolingian minuscule, is the foundation for the typefaces in which almost all European books, including this one, are still printed.

CHARLEMAGNE AND THE REVIVAL OF THE WESTERN ROMAN EMPIRE

The climax of Charlemagne's career came in Rome on Christmas Day 800, when he was crowned as the new Roman emperor in the West by Pope Leo III. Centuries later, popes would cite their role in this event as precedent for the political superiority they claimed over the Holy Roman emperor (a title that became common only in the twelfth century, but that can be used for convenience to designate the Western emperors from Charlemagne on). In the year 800, however, Pope Leo was entirely under Charlemagne's thumb. Although Charlemagne said later that he would never have gone to church that day had he known Leo's plans to crown him, it is highly unlikely Pope Leo would have mounted such a coronation ceremony with-

> Incipit Liber VI de simus Tertius.

Carolingian Handwriting. Even the untrained reader has little difficulty in reading this excerpt from a Carolingian manuscript. For example, the first two words in the heading read "Incipit Liber," and the two words below them "Haec Hannibal."

Historians do not know. What is clear, however, is the symbolic significance of the action. Until 800 only the Roman emperor who ruled in Constantinople could lay claim to being the direct heir of Caesar Augustus. Although the Byzantines had lost most of their influence in the West, they continued to regard it

out Charlemagne's knowledge or consent, not least because it was certain to anger the Byzantines, with whom Charlemagne already had strained relations. Nor did the imperial title add much to Charlemagne's position as king of the Franks. Why, then, did he accept it, and in 813 transfer it to his son, Louis the Pious?

CHARLEMAGNE ON THE IMPORTANCE OF MONKS STUDYING CLASSICAL LITERATURE

To Charlemagne and his contemporaries, a Christian king bore total responsibility for the salvation of his people. To this end, Charlemagne believed it essential to encourage the study of both classical and Christian literature within his kingdom. Copies of this letter were probably sent to most of the monasteries in the Frankish kingdom.

We, Charles, by the grace of God King of the Franks and Lombards and patrician of the Romans, to Abbot Baugulf and all your congregation. . . . Be it known to your devotion . . . that we, along with our faithful advisers, have deemed it useful that the bishoprics and monasteries, which through the favor of Christ have been entrusted to us to govern should, in addition to the way of life prescribed by their rule and their practice of holy religion, devote their efforts to the study of literature and to the teaching of it . . . so that those who seek to please God by living aright may not fail to please him also by righteousness in their speaking. . . . For . . . letters have often been sent to us in these last years from certain monasteries . . . and we found that in most of these writings their sentiments were sound but their speech uncouth. . . . And so . . . we began to fear that their lack of knowledge of writing might be matched by a more serious lack of wisdom in the understanding of holy scripture. We all know well that, dangerous as are the errors of words, yet much more dangerous are the errors of

doctrine. Wherefore we urge you, not merely to avoid the neglect of the study of literature, but . . . to strive to learn it, so that you may be able more easily and more rightly to penetrate the mysteries of the holy scriptures. For since there are figures of speech, metaphors and the like to be found on the sacred pages, there can be no doubt that each man who reads them will understand their spiritual meaning more quickly if he is first of all given full instruction in the study of literature. . . . For we want you, as befits the soldiers of the Church, to be inwardly devout and outwardly learned, pure in good living and scholarly in speech, so that whoever comes to see you in the name of God and for the inspiration of your holy converse, just as he is strengthened by the sight of you, so he may be instructed also by your wisdom, both in reading and chanting, and return rejoicing, giving thanks to Almighty God.

H. R. Loyn and J. Percival, eds. *The Reign of Charlemagne. Documents of Medieval History 2.* (London: Edward Arnold, 1975), pp. 63–64.

THE COLLAPSE OF THE CAROLINGIAN EMPIRE

When Charlemagne died in 814, his empire descended intact to his only surviving son, Louis the Pious. Under Louis, however, the empire rapidly began to disintegrate. When Louis died in 843, the empire was divided between his three sons. Western Francia, which became France, went to Charles the Bald; Eastern Francia, which became Germany, went to Louis the German; and the so-called Middle Kingdom, stretching from the Rhineland to Rome, went to Lothair, along with the imperial title. When Lothair's line died out in 856, a civil war erupted between the East Franks and the West Franks for control over Lothair's former

THE RISE OF THE CAROLINGIAN EMPIRE, 717–814 C.E.

717	Charles Martel becomes mayor of the palace
	The Carolingians (Charles, Pepin, and Carloman) share power with
717–751	the Merovingian kings
751	Pepin becomes king of the Franks
768	Charlemagne succeeds Pepin
800	Charlemagne is crowned Holy Roman emperor
813	Louis the Pious becomes emperor
814	Charlemagne dies

territories and the imperial mantle. Lotharingia (or, in French, Alsace-Lorraine) would remain a flashpoint for hostilities between France and Germany until the end of the Second World War.

The collapse of the Carolingian empire is often blamed on Louis the Pious' incapacity as a ruler; but this is much too simple. Louis was not an incompetent ruler, but he faced an almost impossible task in trying to hold together the empire his father had created. Charlemagne's empire had been built on successful conquest. By 814, however, Charlemagne had pushed the borders of his empire as far as they could reasonably go. To the west, he now faced the Umayyad rulers of Spain, to the north, the Vikings, in the east, his armies were too preoccupied with settling the German territories they had already conquered to push far into the Slavic lands that lay beyond them. The pressures that had driven the Frankish conquests, however—the need for booty, land, and plunder with which to reward and promote one's followers—had become even more pronounced as a result of Charlemagne's successes. Under Charlemagne, the number of counts in the Frankish empire had tripled, from approximately one hundred to three hundred. Louis the Pious could not possibly turn three hundred counts into nine hundred. The resources to do so simply did not exist.

Frustrated by their emperors' inability to reward them, Frankish nobles turned on each other. Civil wars erupted among Louis' quarrelsome and difficult sons; regional hostilities between Austrasians, Neustrians, and Aquitanians flared up again. As central imperial authority broke down, free peasants, a critical group in the eighth-century Carolingian world, found themselves increasingly under the thumb of powerful local nobles who treated them as if they were unfree serfs, bound to the soil and forbidden to leave it. At the same time, internal troubles in the Abbasid empire caused a breakdown in the foreign trade routes through which Viking traders brought Abbasid silver into Carolingian domains. The Vikings then turned to destructive raiding along the coasts and up the river systems. Under these combined pressures the Carolingian empire fell apart completely, and a new political map of Europe began to emerge.

THE LEGACY OF THE CAROLINGIANS

Just the Carolingian period was crucial for marking the beginnings of a common North Atlantic, western European civilization, so the tenth century was crucial for marking the beginnings of the major modern Euro-

vaguely as an outlying province of their empire. Charlemagne's assumption of the imperial title was a clear slap in the face to the Byzantines, who were already suspicious of Charlemagne's relationship with Byzantium's enemy Harun al-Rashid, the Abbasid caliph in Baghdad. In the West, however, it was a declaration of self-confidence and independence that was never forgotten. With only occasional interruptions, western Europeans would continue to crown Roman emperors until the nineteenth century, when Napoleon retired the title. Whatever his specific motives may have been, Charlemagne's revival of the western Roman empire proved to be a major step in the developing self-consciousness of western European civilization.

kings of England, the Saxon kings of Germany modeled their kingship closely on Carolingian example. They drew, however, on different aspects of their common Carolingian inheritance. Tenth-century England became a highly effective administrative monarchy, with a centralized monetary and judicial system and extensive control over towns and trade. In Germany, by contrast, royal power in the tenth century rested much more on the profits of successful conquest than it did on the profits of trade and administration. In the eighth century, the Carolingians had built their power on successful conquests in Saxony. In the tenth century, the Ottonian kings of Germany, based in Saxony, built their authority on successful conquests into the Slavic lands that lay on their "soft" eastern frontier. They were also careful to nurture their image as Christian kings on the Carolingian model. In 955, Otto I defeated the pagan Hungarians in a decisive battle while carrying a sacred lance that had once belonged to Charlemagne. This victory established Otto as the dominant power in central Europe and as a man worthy to inherit Charlemagne's imperial throne. In 962 Otto went to Rome to be crowned western emperor by the pope, a thoroughly dissolute young man named John XII, who hoped to use Otto in his own factional squabbles in Rome. Otto, however, refused to go home when Pope John had no further use for him. Scandalized by John's behavior as pope, Otto instead deposed John, and selected a new pope to replace him.

By becoming emperor, Otto hoped to strengthen his control over the church in Germany and to claim a variety of dormant but potentially lucrative imperial rights in northern Italy and Burgundy, parts of the "Middle Kingdom" once held by the emperor Lothair. Protecting the papacy was, of course, Otto's responsibility as a Carolingian-style emperor, but Otto also needed papal support to achieve these other, more concrete, objectives. In Italy, however, Otto quickly discovered that unless he was prepared to remain there full time, he could not even control the papacy, much less the rapidly growing and highly independent towns of northern Italy. If he remained in Italy too long, however, his authority in Saxony would break down, as local lords began to lead and profit from the continuing conquests in the Slavic east. Balancing their local concerns in Saxony with their imperial concerns in Italy presented a dilemma neither Otto I nor his son (Otto II, 973–983) nor his grandson (Otto III, 983–1002) were able to solve. The result was a gradually increasing alienation of the Saxon nobility from their emperor. This alienation accelerated dramatically

pean political entities. England, which never had been part of Charlemagne's empire, and which hitherto had been divided among smaller warring Anglo-Saxon states, became unified in the late ninth and the tenth century owing to the work of King Alfred the Great (871–899) and his successors. Alfred and his heirs reorganized the army, infused new vigor into local government, founded new towns, and codified English laws. In addition, Alfred established a court school and fostered an interest in Anglo-Saxon writing and other elements of a national culture. In all these respects, Alfred modeled himself closely on Carolingian example. His success in defending his own West Saxon kingdom from Viking attacks, combined with the destruction of every other competing Anglo-Saxon royal dynasty by the Vikings, allowed Alfred and his successors to claim for themselves the mantle of a single, united English monarchy. The increasing prosperity of the country, largely a product of the wool trade, also brought increasing power to the monarchy. By the year 1000, Anglo-Saxon England had become the most administratively sophisticated state in western Christian Europe.

On the Continent, the most powerful monarchs of the tenth century were the dukes of Saxony, who became kings of Germany (East Francia) in 917, after the Carolingian line of kings expired. Like the West Saxon

Viking Dragon Head. Wooden carvings like these on the stemposts of Viking ships were calculated to inspire terror.

The Crown of the Tenth-Century Holy Roman Emperors.

after 1024, when the German throne passed to a new dynasty, the Salians, centered not in Saxony but in Franconia. It was not until the 1070s that the Salian king Henry IV finally attempted to reassert his control over the formerly royal lands in Saxony and the Slavic east. When he did so, he touched off a civil war between himself and the Saxon nobility that was to have momentous repercussions not only for Germany, but for the entirety of western Europe. The consequences of this great Saxon war are discussed more fully in Chapter Ten.

Aspects of the Carolingian inheritance also survived in the tenth-century Mediterranean world. In Catalunya, counts descended from Carolingian appointees continued to administer public, territorial law through a system of public courts throughout the tenth century. Free peasants prospered as they settled new lands. Classical and Christian learning flourished in reformed Benedictine abbeys and cathedrals. The counts drew their revenues from public fiscal lands and from tolls on a rapidly expanding trade; and the city of Barcelona grew rapidly as both a long-distance and a regional market under the protection of the Catalunyan counts. In Aquitaine also, the counts of Poitiers and Toulouse continued to rest their authority on Carolingian foun-

dations until the eleventh century, when in both Aquitaine and Catalunya these Carolingian traditions of public authority finally collapsed.

The tenth century also witnessed a remarkable growth of towns and cities in western Europe, particularly in areas where rulers patterned themselves on Carolingian example. In Anglo-Saxon England, the West Saxon kings established new towns and encouraged the growth of marketing, not least by insisting that the taxation they collected be paid in coin. They tightly regulated coinage and encouraged existing ones. By 1066, when England fell to the invading Normans, at least 10 percent of the English population lived in towns, making it the most highly urbanized country in eleventh-century Europe. Cities also grew rapidly in the Low Countries and the Rhineland, fueled by long-distance trade (especially in wool and wool cloth) and by the discovery of silver deposits in the mountains of Saxony. In Catalunya, the growth of Barcelona was beginning to transform the political and social life of the country, while in Aquitaine, both Poitiers and Toulouse prospered from their location along the overland trade route that connected Mediterranean with Atlantic Europe.

In tenth- and eleventh-century Italy, urban growth occurred in the absence of an effective Carolingian-style ruler. Instead, the prosperity of tenth-century Italian cities depended on the success of the Byzantine emperors in suppressing Muslim piracy in the eastern Mediterranean. The most prosperous cities in tenth-century Italy lay in the Byzantine-controlled areas of the peninsula: Venice in the north, Amalfi, Naples, and Palermo in the south. Their prosperity rested upon their role in the carrying trade that brought silks, spices, and other luxury goods from the Byzantine and Muslim worlds into western Europe. In the eleventh century, however, Norman invasions of southern Italy disrupted this trade, as Turkish invasions of Asia Minor turned Byzantine attentions eastward. By the end of the eleventh century, it would be the north Italian cities whose navies would control the eastern Mediterranean, and which would profit from their role as middlemen in the lucrative traffic between Byzantium, the Muslim world, and western Europe.

On the Carolingian heartland, however, these developments had little influence. Here, Carolingian-style kingship disintegrated during the tenth century under the combined weight of Viking raids, economic collapse, and the growing power of local lords. In some areas, a few Carolingian institutions, such as public courts and a centrally minted coinage, survived in

HOW DID CHARLEMAGNE REDEFINE THE RELATIONSHIP BETWEEN CHRISTIANITY AND KINGSHIP?

THE RISE OF THE CAROLINGIANS 297

the lands of counts and dukes who utilized them in building up new, essentially autonomous territorial principalities in Anjou, Flanders, and Aquitaine. Elsewhere in France, even this modicum of con-

tinuity with the Carolingian world disappeared. France still had a king who continued to be recognized as the ruler of the western part of Charlemagne's former territories. After 987, however, the kings of France were no

EUROPE IN THE ELEVENTH CENTURY

This map shows the alignment of geopolitical power that had emerged by 1050, a few generations after the final collapse of Carolingian rule. What states appeared to be the most dominant ones in this world? What recent successes could a resurgent Byzantium claim? What advantages did the German rulers of the empire possess in terms of resources and their strategic position in northern and central Italy? Note the position of Kievan Russia. In what ways was its development affected by the West, and in what respects was it isolated from the Western experience? What disadvantages or challenges did these various powers face?

This spectacle of Carolingian collapse may suggest that little had changed in western Europe between 750 and 1000. Any such impression would, however, be seriously misleading. It is certainly true that compared with Byzantium or the Muslim world, western Europe remained an intellectual and cultural backwater, more so perhaps by the year 1000 than it had been two centuries before. Politically, no western European ruler in the year 1000 could approach the power of the Byzantine emperor or the Umayyad caliph of Córdoba. Economically also, western Europe was a dependency of Byzantium and Islam, importing finished and luxury goods, and exporting furs, leather, and slaves. Beneath the surface, however, western European society was becoming steadily more formidable. Urbanization was proceeding rapidly on the margins of the collapsing Carolingian world. Long-distance trade was also growing. Italian traders were active in Constantinople, and Muslim traders were common in the south Italian ports. Anglo-Saxon merchants were regular visitors to Italy, the Low Countries and the Rhineland. Jewish merchants in the Rhineland were carrying on an active trade with the Jewish communities of Muslim Egypt, while Viking traders had reopened the trade routes from the Baltic through Russia to the Black Sea and were busily founding cities from Novgorod to Dublin. Western Europe's borders were also expanding. By the year 1000, its boundaries extended from the Baltic to the Mediterranean Sea, and from the Pyrenees to Poland. Within this vast territory, moreover, every ruler was, or would soon be, Christian. The Christian church was as yet highly localized, but the emergence of new confederations of reformed Benedictine monasteries under papal protection (to be discussed in more detail in Chapter Ten) was beginning to point the way toward a more unified and centralized Latin Christian church. Political omens were less promising. But out of the chaos of tenth-century western Europe, effective

CONCLUSION

power in France upon new foundations.

predecessors, and begin again to rebuild monarchical begin to reverse the trends that had destroyed their century before the Capetian kings of France could that city against the Vikings. But it would be another lished their reputation as Counts of Paris by defending Capetians, had taken the throne, after having established longer Carolingians. Instead, a new dynasty, the

territorial principalities and kingdoms were beginning to emerge. During the early Middle Ages, Europe had become a society mobilized for war to a degree unmatched in either Byzantium or Islam. This was, to be sure, a mixed blessing. In the centuries to come, however, the militarization of western European society was to prove a decisive factor in the steadily shifting balance of power between Europe, Byzantium and the Muslim world.

SELECTED READINGS

Arberry, Arthur John. *The Koran Interpreted.* 2 volumes. London, 1955.

Bede. *A History of the English Church and People.* Trans. by Leo Sherley-Price. Baltimore, 1955. A fascinating account by the greatest historian of eighth-century Europe.

Brand, Charles M., ed. *Icon and Minaret: Sources of Byzantine and Islamic Civilization.* Englewood Cliffs, N.J., 1969.

Campbell, James, ed. *The Anglo-Saxons.* Oxford, 1982. The best and most interesting treatment of its subject, splendidly illustrated.

Collins, Roger. *Early Medieval Europe, 300–1000.* 2d ed. New York, 1999. Dry and detailed, but a useful textbook nonetheless.

———. *Early Medieval Spain: Unity in Diversity 400–1000.* New York, 1983. An excellent introduction, written for students, that gives equal attention to Visigothic and Umayyad Spain.

Donner, Fred. *The Early Islamic Conquests.* Princeton, 1981. A scholarly but readable narrative and analysis.

Einhard and Notker the Stammerer. *Two Lives of Charlemagne.* Trans. by Lewis Thorpe. Baltimore, 1969. Lively and entertaining.

Fletcher, Richard A. *The Barbarian Conversion: From Paganism to Christianity.* Berkeley, 1999. Slow paced but informative, perceptive, and enjoyable to read.

———. *Moorish Spain.* Berkeley, 1993. The best short survey in English.

Geanakoplos, Deno John, ed. *Byzantium: Church, Society and Civilization Seen through Contemporary Eyes.* Chicago, 1984. An outstanding source book, with a great deal of fresh material.

Geary, Patrick J. *Before France and Germany: The Origins and Transformation of the Merovingian World.* New York, 1988. Accessible introduction to recent scholarship, much of it otherwise unavailable in English.

Gibb, H. A. R. *Arabic Literature: An Introduction.* 2d ed. Oxford, 1974. An excellent survey.

Godman, Peter, and Roger Collins. *Charlemagne's Heir: New Perspectives on the Reign of Louis the Pious (814–840).* Oxford, 1990. A massive collection of revisionist essays by almost all of the top scholars in the field.

Gregory of Tours. *History of the Franks.* Trans. by Lewis Thorpe.

Baltimore, 1974. Difficult to follow, but by far the most revealing single source on Merovingian kingship.

Herrin, Judith. *The Formation of Christendom.* Princeton, 1987. A synthetic history of the Christian civilizations of Byzantium and western Europe from 500 to 800 C.E., written by a prominent Byzantinist.

Hodges, Richard. *Dark Age Economics: The Origins of Towns and Trade, A.D. 600–1000.* London, 1982. Emphasizes the importance of trade connections between early medieval Europe and the Islamic world.

Hodges, Richard, and David Whitehouse. *Mohammed, Charlemagne and the Origins of Europe.* London, 1983. An analysis and recasting of the "Pirenne thesis," which claimed (wrongly, as this book shows) that the advent of Islam disrupted the economic unity of the Mediterranean world.

Hourani, Albert. *A History of the Arab Peoples.* New York, 1992. A sympathetic, clear, and intelligent survey written for nonspecialists.

Hussey, Joan M. *The Byzantine World.* 4th ed. London, 1970. A useful short introduction that combines narrative with topical chapters.

———. *The Orthodox Church in the Byzantine Empire.* Oxford, 1986. A broad but deep and sophisticated survey.

Kazhdan, Alexander P., ed. *The Oxford Dictionary of Byzantium.* 3 volumes. Oxford, 1991. An authoritative reference work.

Kennedy, Hugh. *The Early Abbasid Caliphate: A Political History.* Totowa, N.J., 1981. A standard account.

———. *The Prophet and the Age of the Caliphates.* London, 1986. A lucid introduction to the political history of Islam from the sixth through the eleventh centuries.

Krautheimer, Richard. *Early Christian and Byzantine Architecture.* 4th ed. New York, 1986. A classic work by one of the greatest Byzantine art historians of the twentieth century.

Leyser, Karl. *Rule and Conflict in an Early Medieval Society: Ottonian Saxony.* Oxford, 1979. A concise, challenging, brilliant account of the dynamics of rule in tenth-century Saxony, that pays special attention to the importance of royal women.

Loyn, Henry R., and John Percival, eds. and trans. *The Reign of Charlemagne.* London, 1975. An excellent collection of sources, not easy to find, but worth the trouble.

Mango, Cyril. *Art of the Byzantine Empire, 312–1453.* Englewood Cliffs, N.J., 1972. A standard survey.

———. *Byzantium: The Empire of New Rome.* London, 1980. A traditional but still valuable picture of Byzantine civilization.

McKitterick, Rosamond. *The Frankish Kingdoms Under the Carolingians, 751–987.* New York, 1983. An authoritative account of politics and intellectual developments.

———, ed. *The Uses of Literacy in Early Medieval Europe.* New York, 1990. A superb collection of essays representing some of the freshest recent thinking on this subject.

McNamara, Jo Ann, and John E. Halborg, eds. *Sainted Women of the Dark Ages.* Durham, N.C., 1992. Translated saints' lives from Merovingian and Carolingian Europe.

Obolensky, Dimitri. *Byzantium and the Slavs.* Crestwood, N.Y., 1994. The classic survey of the Byzantine empire's relations with the Balkans.

Ostrogorsky, George. *History of the Byzantine State.* rev. ed. New Brunswick, N.J., 1969. A classic political history.

Pelikan, Jaroslav. *The Christian Tradition, Volume II: The Spirit of Eastern Christendom.* Chicago, 1974. An outstanding synthetic treatment of the doctrines of Byzantine Christianity.

Peters, F. E. *Aristotle and the Arabs.* New York, 1968. Well written and engaging.

Reuter, Timothy. *Germany in the Early Middle Ages, 800–1056.* New York, 1991. The best and most up-to-date survey in English.

Saint Boniface. *Letters of Saint Boniface.* Trans. by Ephraim Emerton. New York, 1972.

Sawyer, Peter, ed. *The Oxford Illustrated History of the Vikings.* Oxford, 1997. The best one-volume account, lavishly illustrated.

Stillman, Norman A. *The Jews of Arab Lands: A History and Source Book.* Philadelphia, 1979. An essential resource.

Todd, Malcolm. *The Early Germans.* Oxford, 1992. A reliable survey, particularly strong in its use of archaeological evidence.

Treadgold, Warren. *A History of the Byzantine State and Society.* Stanford, 1997. A massive, encyclopedic narrative of the political, economic, and military history of Byzantium from 284 until 1461.

Wallace-Hadrill, John Michael. *The Barbarian West, 400–1000.* 3d ed. London, 1967. More a set of interpretive essays than a conventional textbook, this book remains the most stimulating introduction to its subject.

———. *Early Germanic Kingship in England and on the Continent.* Oxford, 1971. A remarkably interesting analysis of changing ideas about the nature and responsibilities of kingship in early medieval Europe, emphasizing the links between Anglo-Saxon and Carolingian theories of kingship.

———. *The Frankish Church.* Oxford, 1983. A masterful account that links together the Merovingian and the Carolingian churches.

Watt, W. Montgomery. *Islamic Philosophy and Theology,* 2d ed. Edinburgh, 1985. The standard English account.

Wemple, Suzanne Fonay. *Women in Frankish Society: Marriage and the Cloister, 500–900.* Philadelphia, 1981. An influential account of changing attitudes toward marriage among the early Franks.

Whittow, Mark. *The Making of Orthodox Byzantium, 600–1025.* London, 1996. Emphasizes the centrality of orthodoxy in shaping Byzantine history. Particularly good on Byzantine relations with the peoples outside the empire.

Wood, Ian. *The Merovingian Kingdoms, 450–751.* New York, 1994. Full of the latest thinking, but detailed and difficult for beginners.

CHAPTER NINE

THE EXPANSION OF EUROPE: ECONOMY, SOCIETY, AND POLITICS IN THE HIGH MIDDLE AGES, 1000–1300

B
ETWEEN 1000 AND 1300, the balance of power between western Europe, Byzantium, and the Islamic world shifted profoundly. In the year 1000, Europe remained politically fractured and militarily threatened by Viking, Magyar, and Muslim attacks. Although towns in western Europe were beginning to grow, none could compare in size or sophistication with the ancient Mediterranean cities of Byzantium and the Islamic world. Economically, western Europe continued to depend on Byzantine and Islamic traders for its cotton, silk, spices, and precious metals. With respect to literature and learning, the imbalances were even greater. Europeans knew only a small portion of the cultural and intellectual riches Byzantium and Islam had inherited from the classical world. Outside Sicily, Venice, and the Muslim-controlled areas of Spain, western Europeans knew no Arabic and virtually no Greek. Even Latin, the language of western learning for more than a thousand years, was increasingly a foreign tongue. King Alfred (871–899) complained that in his day hardly anyone in England knew enough Latin to perform correctly the services of the Christian church. A century later, Latin learning in England and Germany was somewhat better. In France and Italy it was probably worse.

By the year 1300, however, Europe was the dominant military, economic, and political power among the three western successor civilizations to Greece and Rome. Hungary, Poland, and Bohemia were now thoroughly integrated parts of a Catholic, European world. Combining conquest with conversion, European Christians had forcefully pushed their borders eastward into Prussia, Livonia, Lithuania, and the Balkans. They had conquered Spain from the Muslims and Constantinople from the Byzantines. They had also established (and in 1300, just lost) a Latin kingdom in the Middle East, with its capital at Jerusalem. European navies controlled the Mediterranean Sea and had outposts on the Black Sea and the Caspian Sea, allowing

FOCUS QUESTIONS

• What impact did the first agricultural revolution have on the lives of Europeans?
• What were the major causes of urban growth during the High Middle Ages?
• How did the First Crusade alter the balance of power between Europe and Byzantium?

• What was the relationship between chivalry and the cult of "courtly love"?
• How did government and politics change in the High Middle Ages?
• What was the relationship between feudalism and the rise of national monarchies?

European traders to dominate the long-distance trade routes that brought eastern luxury goods into western Europe. European missionaries and traders were beginning to follow these trade routes back through Central Asia, opening up connections with Mongolia and China, to the west, Italian merchants had initiated a seaborne trade route through the Strait of Gibraltar, thus connecting the Mediterranean and the north Atlantic world.

This expansion of European commerce, both local and long distance, was accompanied by significant urbanization. By 1300, Europe could claim at least a dozen cities with populations between fifty thousand and one hundred thousand people, with hundreds of smaller towns and cities scattered across the landscape. The growth of cities mirrored the general growth in the European population which, on a rough estimate, tripled between 1000 and 1300. The economy grew even more rapidly, however, leading to increased per capita wealth and a rising standard of living. By no means, however, were these economic gains distributed equally among the entire population. Governments grew more powerful, and social stratification increased. New wealth increased the demand for luxury goods among social elites, but it also freed up huge sums of money for investment in agriculture, commerce, and construction. It fueled remarkable new religious, cultural, and intellectual developments, which will be discussed in the next chapter.

Not all of this growth proved sustainable. By 1300, living standards for many Europeans were falling as western Europe began to approach the demographic limits of its natural resources. More powerful governments kept better internal peace, but they also claimed a larger proportion of their subjects' wealth, which they used to support bigger armies and grander campaigns of conquest and domination. In the fourteenth century, famine, war, and plague reduced the European population by at least a third, fundamentally transforming the economic, political, and social order of the High Middle Ages. Despite these setbacks, however, the predominance western Europe established over Byzantium and the Islamic world during the High Middle Ages would endure, providing the foundation on which the European world empires of the modern era would be built.

THE FIRST AGRICULTURAL REVOLUTION

What impact did the first agricultural revolution have on the lives of Europeans?

Like all premodern economies, the western European economy in the Middle Ages rested on agriculture. Change in agricultural practices tends to be slow; even so, it may seem absurd to speak of agricultural changes that took place across six hundred years as constituting a "revolution." In western Europe, however, the agricultural changes that took place between 700 and 1300 were so sweeping, and their consequences so profound, that comparisons with the more famous agricultural revolution of the early eighteenth century seem justified. Technological innovations, combined with an improved climate, new crop rotation systems, and increased investment in tools, livestock, and mills, increased the productivity of European agriculture dramatically. As agricultural productivity increased, so too did the marketing of agricultural surpluses, leading to increased specialization of production with resulting efficiencies of scale. Without these changes, western Europe could never have supported the tripling of its overall population, or the massive investments in buildings, ships, books, armies, and art that shaped the high medieval world.

TECHNOLOGICAL ADVANCES

The basic technological advances that made possible the increasing productivity of high medieval agriculture were developed in the early Middle Ages. The heavy-wheeled plow, fitted with an iron-tipped coulter and dragged by a team of oxen, could cut and turn the rich, wet soil of northern Europe to a depth impossible for the Mediterranean scratch plow to reach, thus aerating the soil and providing excellent drainage for water-logged territories. The new plow also saved labor, allowing more frequent plowing and better control of weeds. Related improvements in collars and harnesses increased the efficiency of plow oxen, and made

The agricultural changes that took place in western Europe between 700 and 1300 were so sweeping, and their consequences so profound, that comparisons with the more famous agricultural revolution of the early eighteenth century seem justified.

WHAT IMPACT DID THE FIRST AGRICULTURAL REVOLUTION HAVE ON THE LIVES OF EUROPEANS?

THE FIRST AGRICULTURAL REVOLUTION 303

it possible for the first time for horses to pull heavy loads without choking themselves. Oxen remained the most commonly used plow animals in Europe until at least the fourteenth century. They were cheaper, more powerful, and less prone to disease than were horses, and when they died they could be eaten. Horses, however, were faster and more efficient cart animals, especially after the development of iron horseshoes (around 900) and tandem harnessing (around 1050), which allowed horses to pull behind each other. As marketing of agricultural produce increased during the twelfth and thirteenth centuries, so too, therefore, did the prevalence of horses in the European countryside.

Other labor-saving devices further increased the productivity of high medieval agriculture. Despite the advent of the heavy-wheeled plow, most of the work of raising crops continued to be done by individual peasant farmers using hand tools. As iron became more

Light Plow and Heavy Plow. Note that the peasant using the light plow (above) had to press his foot on it to give it added weight. The major innovation of the heavy plow (often wheeled, as shown below) was the long moldboard, which turned over the ground after the plowshare cut into it. The picture below depicts a second crucial medieval invention as well—the padded horse collar, which allowed horses to throw their full weight into pulling.

Medieval Windmill. The peasant on the left is bringing his grain in a sack to be ground into flour. Note that the mill is built on a pivot so that it can rotate in the direction of any prevailing wind.

common during the High Middle Ages, the quality of these hand tools steadily improved. Iron-tipped hoes, forks, and shovels were much more effective than the wooden implements with which most eighth-century farmers had had to make do; the increasing number of iron sickles and scythes permitted speedier and more efficient harvesting of hay and grain, especially by women, whose field labor was critically important, particularly during harvesttime. Wheelbarrows were another homely but important technological innovation. So too was the harrow, a tool drawn over the field after the plow to level the earth and mix in the seed.

Technology also had an impact on cooking techniques, and hence on nutrition. Iron pots allowed food to be boiled rather than just warmed, reducing the chances of contamination; communal ovens preserved a larger share of the nutrients in food than did boiling. Mills represented another major technological innovation in food processing. The Romans had known about water mills but hardly used them, relying instead upon human- and animal-powered wheels to grind grain into flour. Starting around 1050, however, there was a veritable craze in northern Europe for building water mills of steadily increasing efficiency. One French area saw a growth from fourteen water mills in the eleventh century to sixty in the twelfth; in another part of France about forty mills were built between 850 and 1080, forty more between 1080 and 1125, and 245 between 1126 and 1175. Once Europeans had mas-

tered the complex technology of building water mills, they turned their attention to windmills, which proliferated rapidly from the 1170s on, especially in flat lands such as Holland that had no swiftly flowing streams. Although the major use of mills was to grind grain, they could be adapted to drive saws, process cloth, press oil, provide power for iron forges, and crush pulp for manufacturing paper. The importance of such mills cannot be overstated. They would remain the world's only source of mechanical power for manufacturing until the nineteenth-century invention of the steam engine.

With the exception of the windmill and tandem harnessing, most of the technological innovations that lay behind the medieval agricultural revolution were already known to the Carolingians. Only from the mid-eleventh century, however, did these innovations become sufficiently widespread as to have a decisive effect on European agricultural production. Various explanations for this delay have been offered. Climatic change must have played some role, but although the warming climate benefited northern Europe by drying the soil and lengthening the growing season, it hurt Mediterranean agriculture in equal measure. Greater physical security also played a role. Viking, Magyar, and Muslim attacks were decreasing, and more powerful governments kept better domestic peace than they had been able to do a century before. The fundamental change, however, lay in the growing confidence of en-

WHAT IMPACT DID THE FIRST AGRICULTURAL REVOLUTION HAVE ON THE LIVES OF EUROPEANS?

THE FIRST AGRICULTURAL REVOLUTION 305

repreneurial peasants and lords that if they invested labor and money in agricultural improvements, they would profit from the resulting surpluses. More than anything else, it was the expanding demand for agricultural produce that encouraged peasants and landlords to make productive investments in the land. Behind the growing demand for foodstuffs lay the two fundamental economic factors that drove the high medieval economy forward: a rapidly increasing European population, and an increasingly efficient market for goods.

MANORIALISM, SERFDOM, AND AGRICULTURAL PRODUCTIVITY

In England, northern France, and western Germany, increasing use of the heavy-wheeled plow between 800 and 1050 coincided with a fundamental change in patterns of peasant settlement. During the early

Diagram of a Manor.

Middle Ages, most free peasant farmers lived on individual plots of land that they farmed with their own resources, and for which they paid their landlord some kind of customary rent. Starting in the ninth century, however, many of these individual peasant holdings began to be consolidated into large, common fields that were farmed communally by peasants living in villages. The resulting complex of rents, renders, dues, fines, and fields is sometimes called a "manor."

In some areas, the impetus for these changes in settlement patterns may have come from the peasants themselves. Large fields could be farmed more efficiently than small fields. Investment costs were lower: a single plow and a dozen oxen might suffice for an entire village, obviating the need for every farmer to maintain his own plow and plow beasts. Common fields were potentially more productive also, allowing the villagers to experiment with new crops and new crop-rotation systems and to support larger numbers of animals on common pastures. Peasants living together in a village might be able to support a parish church, a communal oven, a blacksmith, a mill, and a tavern. They could also converse and socialize, celebrate and mourn with their neighbors. In a difficult and demanding natural environment, these were not negligible considerations.

Despite the potential advantages the manorial system offered to peasants, lords played the dominant role in forcing its creation, and it was they who took the greatest benefits from it. It was easier for lords to control and exploit peasants living in villages than peasants living on scattered individual farms. Manorialism also allowed lords to claim a larger share of their peasants' agricultural production. On many manors, the common fields were divided into narrow strips assigned in alternating fashion to individual peasants, for which each peasant landholder paid rent to the lord, but from which each peasant took the profits. In addition to their rents, however, most lords also claimed a third to a half of the total acreage in the common fields as their own demesne (pronounced "demean") land, from which they took all the produce for their own use. To farm this demesne land, manorial lords imposed or increased labor services on peasant farmers, reducing many formerly free peasants to the status of serfs.

Serfs had existed in Europe for centuries, even in areas where the manorial system never took hold. There is no doubt, however, that the development of manorialism considerably increased the incidence of serfdom in northern Europe as compared with Spain, northern Italy, southern France, and central Germany. Unlike free peasants, serfs could not leave their land or their lord without his permission (although in practice, many did so, especially to become town dwellers). Serfs worked for their lords regularly without pay, paid humiliating fines to their lord when they fornicated illicitly, married, or died, and were subject to the jurisdiction of their lord's manorial court. Like slaves, their servile status was heritable; but unlike slaves, their obligations to their lord were fixed by custom, and they were not supposed to be sold apart from the lands they held.

NEW CROP ROTATION SYSTEMS

From the standpoint of agrarian productivity, the greatest advantage of the manorial system was the fact that it made possible the adoption of new, more efficient crop-rotation systems. For centuries, farmers had known that if they sowed the same crop on the same land year after year, they would eventually exhaust the soil. The traditional solution to this difficulty was to divide one's land, planting half in the fall to harvest in the spring, and leaving the other half to lie fallow. In the dry, thin soils of the Mediterranean, this remained the most common cropping pattern throughout the Middle Ages. In the wet, fertile soils of northern Europe, however, farmers slowly discovered that a three-field crop-rotation system could pro

Sowing Seed. When the peasant sows his seed broadcast, the crows are not far off to help themselves. Here, one is bold enough to peck at the sack while another is momentarily chased off by a dog.

> The new crop-rotation system immediately increased, from 50 percent to 67 percent, the amount of land under cultivation in any given year.

duce a sustainable increase in overall agricultural production. Under this system, one third of the land would lie fallow, often being used for pasturage, so that the animals' droppings would fertilize the soil; one third would be planted with winter wheat or rye, which was sown in the fall and harvested in the early summer; and one third would be planted with another crop (usually oats or barley, but sometimes legumes or fodder crops such as alfalfa, clover, or vetch) that could be sewn in the spring and harvested in the fall. The fields were then rotated over a three-year cycle.

This system immediately increased, from 50 percent to 67 percent, the amount of land under cultivation in any given year. No less important, it also produced higher yields per acre of wheat and rye, particularly if legumes or fodder crops (which replace the nitrogen that wheat and rye leach out of the soil) were a regular part of the crop-rotation pattern. With two separate growing seasons, the system provided some insurance against loss from natural disasters. It also produced new types of food. Oats could be consumed by both humans and horses, while legumes provided a source of protein to balance the major intake of cereal carbohydrates from bread and beer, the two main staples of the peasant diet. Additional fodder made it possible to support more and healthier animals, increasing the efficiency of plow beasts, diversifying the economy of the manor, and providing an additional source of protein in the human diet through meat and milk. The new crop-rotation system also helped to spread labor more evenly over the course of the year, allowing more careful attention to weed control, liming, and fertilizing of the common fields.

With all these advantages, it may seem surprising that the three-field system was not adopted more widely and more quickly than it was on the great manors of northern Europe. Some of the resistance was cultural. Northern Europeans thought of oats and legumes primarily as food for animals, to be

WHAT IMPACT DID THE FIRST AGRICULTURAL REVOLUTION HAVE ON THE LIVES OF EUROPEANS?

THE FIRST AGRICULTURAL REVOLUTION 307

nant form for European agriculture. By and large, the manorial system was limited to England, northern France, and western Germany. Even in these areas, moreover, it was beginning to break down by the end of the twelfth century, as lords began to commute labor services into cash payments, to free their serfs (again in return for cash payments), and to live from rents rather than from the direct agricultural revenues of their estates.

The reasons for the decline of serfdom during the thirteenth century are complex and did not affect all areas of Europe equally. As the European economy became increasingly monetarized, many lords simply found it more convenient to collect their revenues directly from their peasants in cash, rather than taking the risks associated with marketing agricultural produce directly. This strategy also had its dangers, however. In the inflationary circumstances of the thirteenth century, lords who could not increase the rents their peasants paid them suffered marked declines in their real incomes, sending many knights and lesser lords into economic crisis. In England and Catalunya, by contrast, which had two of the most thoroughly commercialized agricultural economies in medieval Europe, serfdom lasted longer than almost anywhere else in western Europe. In Austria and Poland, which were far less monetized, serfdom also actually increased during the thirteenth century, as it did in northern Spain also. There is thus no simple correlation between commercialization and the decline of serfdom. In most of Europe, however, the generalization holds: serfs and free peasants became increasingly indistinguishable during the thirteenth century as lords enfranchised serfs in return for cash. Even in France, however, some servile obligations would continue to exist as nagging indignities right down to the French Revolution in 1789. And in central and eastern Europe and Russia, serfdom underwent a resurgence during the later Middle Ages that would carry it into the eighteenth and nineteenth centuries.

TRANSFORMATIONS OF THE FIRST AGRICULTURAL REVOLUTION

Between 1050 and 1300, the growing European population made use of improved technology and new crop-rotation systems to produce a remarkable intensification of European agriculture. Crop yields on existing lands increased, and new lands were opened up to cultivation. Forests were cleared, wetlands drained, and

SERFDOM AND THE LIMITS OF MANORIALISM

It is important to remember that "classic" manorialism of the high medieval type, with servile peasants laboring on lordly demesne lands, was never the predominant labor of unfree peasants.

heavily on the unpaid labor of unfree peasants.

Lesser knights and not on manors, which depended most enthusiastically on the medium-sized (twenty- to fifty-acre) farms owned by free peasant proprietors and lesser knights, and not on manors, which depended new crop-rotation patterns seem to have been adopted the great estates lasted into the fifteenth century, the therefore, that in England, where peasant servility on ductivity of their lords' lands. It may be significant, stood to gain little personally from improving the pro- been political, the mute protest of servile peasants who tance to the new crop-rotation systems may also have growing barley, oats, or legumes. But some of the resis- favor wheat cultivation, even on lands better suited to pean agriculture, both lords and peasants tended to was the most important "cash crop" in northern Euro- Some of the obstacles were economic. Because wheat eaten by humans only when nothing else was available.

Medieval Peasants Slaughtering a Pig. Deep in winter, probably around Christmas, it is finally time to slaughter the household pig. But nothing can be wasted, so even the blood is caught in a pan to make blood pudding.

wastelands turned into arable or pasture, sometimes through the self-directed efforts of peasant communities, sometimes at the command of entrepreneurial lords. New lands were opened up between existing settlements, and new peasant communities were established in the "frontier" areas of eastern Germany, Holland, northern England, and Castile. As agricultural production increased, it also became more specialized. No longer was it necessary or even desirable for individual peasant communities to produce for themselves the wide variety of crops and goods they needed to consume over the course of a year. As towns grew and local and regional markets expanded, it became possible for individual manors and even entire regions to produce only those crops best suited to their own soil and climate. Gascony became a region of vineyards, Sicily a region of grainfields, northern England a region of sheep. Further increases in productivity resulted as European agriculturalists benefited from the resulting efficiencies of specialization and scale.

THE GROWTH OF TOWNS AND COMMERCE

What were the major causes of urban growth during the High Middle Ages?

This agricultural revolution was the foundation on which the commercial revolution of the High Middle Ages rested. Here too, the groundwork for new developments had been laid in the ninth and tenth centuries. By the year 1000, silver from the Harz Mountains in Saxony was already fueling a triangular trade among England, Flanders, and the expanding cities of the Rhineland that brought raw wool from England to Flanders and wool cloth from Flanders to the Rhineland, whose merchants then distributed it as far away as Italy and Byzantium. Millions of silver pennies were in circulation around the North Sea, where an integrated system of exchange among English, Scandinavian, and Rhenish currencies had developed. English merchants were active in Constantinople and northern Spain, exchanging northern silver for Byzantine silks, Islamic spices, and African gold. Scandinavian merchants and warriors ranged even more widely, establishing cities in Ireland, principalities in Normandy and southern Italy, and trading outposts

Medieval Tollbooth. Whoever made use of a medieval road for transporting merchandise had to pay tolls to finance its upkeep.

such as Novgorod and Kiev along the Russian trade routes that ran from the Baltic to the Black Sea (and thence to Constantinople) and to the Caspian Sea (and on into the Abbasid empire).

COMMERCE

During the eleventh and twelfth centuries, however, the greatest developments in long-distance commerce took place in the burgeoning cities of northern Italy. A series of victories by Venetian, Pisan, and Genoese naval forces gave these cities control over the carrying trade between Constantinople, Alexandria, and the West. The growing prosperity of western European nobles and churchmen created an expanding market for eastern luxury goods, while the improved domestic security of high medieval Europe made it possible for merchants to provide such goods with at least a modicum of security and safety. In the twelfth century, an organized system of fairs emerged in the central French region of Champagne, where Flemish mer-

WHAT WERE THE MAJOR CAUSES OF URBAN GROWTH DURING THE HIGH MIDDLE AGES?

THE GROWTH OF TOWNS AND COMMERCE   309

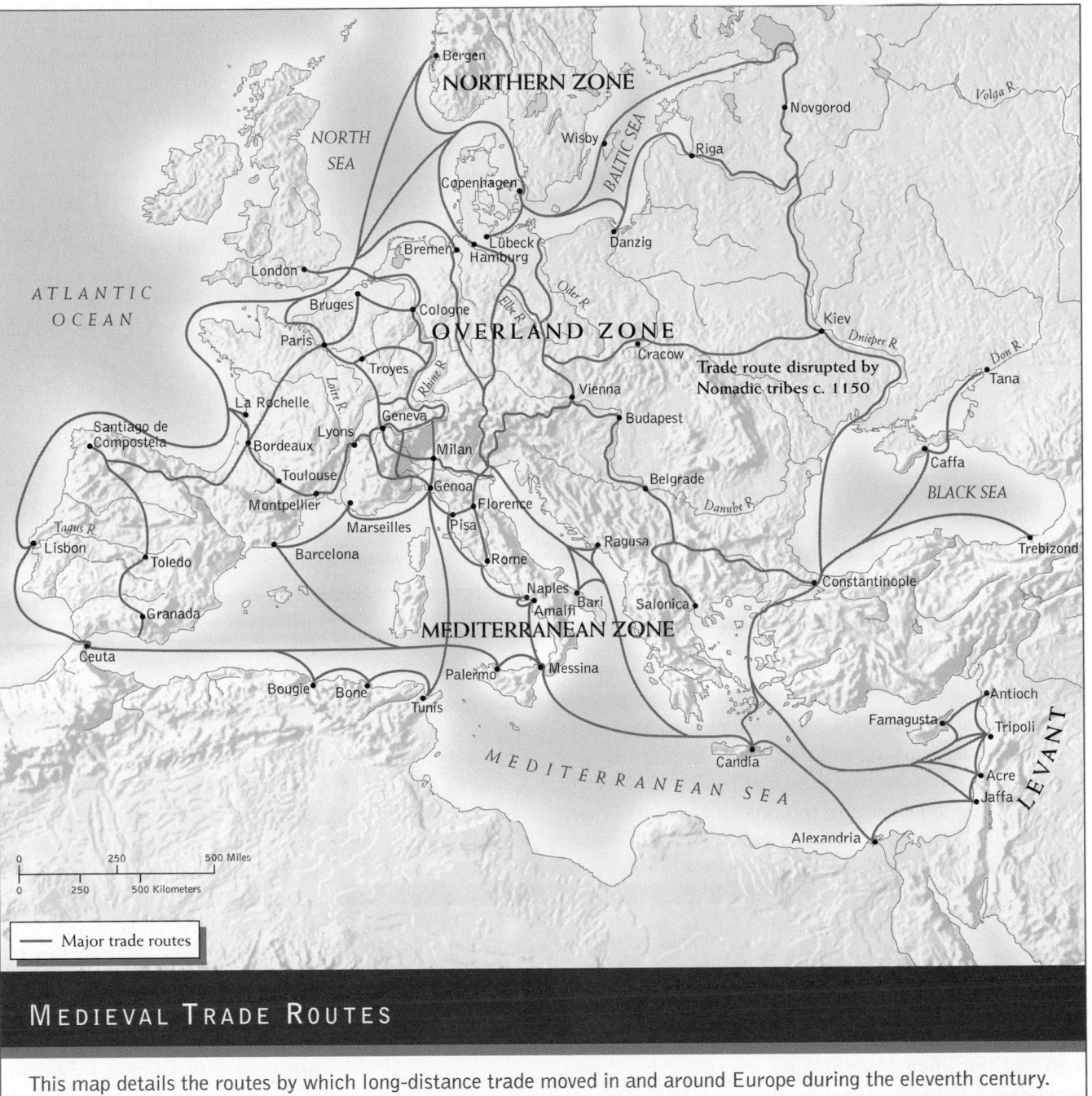

MEDIEVAL TRADE ROUTES

This map details the routes by which long-distance trade moved in and around Europe during the eleventh century. What was the relationship between trade routes and rivers, and why? Why was the agricultural revolution and the revival of trade crucial to the extension of major trade routes in the west? What factors led to the intense proliferation of trade routes between England, Bruges, and the Rhine Valley?

chants sold cloth to Italians, and Italian merchants sold Muslim spices and Byzantine silks to Flemings, French, and Germans. By 1300, however, these fairs were beginning to decline as Italian merchants succeeded in opening up a direct route by sea between Italy and the Atlantic ports of northern Europe. It now became practical to import raw wool directly from England to

northern Italy, where towns like Florence could produce and finish wool cloth themselves. As the Italian cloth industry grew, the Flemish cloth industry declined, yet another sign of the increasing extent to which Europe was becoming a unified economy.

Long-distance trade was a risky enterprise. Fortunes could be lost as easily as they could be made. Piracy

View of Paris. The city looked this way at the end of the Middle Ages, around 1480. Note the prominence of the Cathedral of Notre Dame in the center and the large number of other church spires; note, too, how closely all the buildings are packed behind the walls.

was commonplace, and the Mediterranean Sea was notoriously dangerous to sailors and their ships. Merchants were often disdained by the landed aristocracy because they could claim no ancient lineages and because they were too obviously concerned with pecuniary gain. Their courage, however, was undeniable; even in battle, the citizen armies of Milan or Florence often got the better of their aristocratic opponents. Above all, however, Italian success in opening up the new trade routes of the High Middle Ages depended on the willingness of both merchants and nobles to invest substantial sums of money in ships, cargoes, and pack animals. To facilitate such investment, Italian merchants developed new forms of commercial partnership contracts, new methods of accounting (including double-entry bookkeeping), and new credit mechanisms, some of which they borrowed from Byzantine and Muslim examples. Some of these new credit arrangements ran afoul of the western Christian church, which condemned almost all forms of moneylending as usury. But the demand for capital to fuel the new commercial economy was irresistible, and slowly attitudes began to change.

Although the medieval church never formally abandoned its prohibition of moneylending, it did come to approve making profits on commercial risks, which was often close to the same thing. From the thirteenth century on, leading churchmen also began to speak more favorably of merchants. Saint Bonaventura, a thirteenth-century Italian Franciscan, argued, for example, that in Old Testament times, God had shown special favor to shepherds such as King David; in New Testament times, he had favored fishermen such as Saint Peter; but in modern times, God's favor now went out to merchants such as Saint Francis of Assisi.

It would be misleading, however, to think of the commercial revolution or the urban revolution of the High Middle Ages as principally the result of long-distance trade. Some towns did receive great stimulus from such trade, and the growth of such major cities as Venice (about one hundred thousand people in 1300) and Genoa (eighty thousand) would have been impossible without it. But the prosperity of most towns, including such enormous cities as Paris (with a population of two hundred thousand people in 1300), Florence (one hun-

> Italian success in opening up the new trade routes of the High Middle Ages depended on the willingness of both merchants and nobles to invest substantial sums of money in ships, cargoes, and pack animals.

WHAT WERE THE MAJOR CAUSES OF URBAN GROWTH DURING THE HIGH MIDDLE AGES?

THE GROWTH OF TOWNS AND COMMERCE 311

dred thousand), Milan (eighty thousand to one hundred thousand), and London (sixty thousand to eighty thousand), depended primarily on the wealth of their surrounding hinterlands, from which they drew their food supplies, their raw materials, and the bulk of their population. The quickening of economic life in general was the major cause of urban growth during the High Middle Ages. Long-distance trade was but one aspect of this larger economic and commercial transformation of European life.

TOWNS

Towns, both large and small, existed in a symbiotic relationship with the countryside around them, providing markets and manufactured goods while living off the rural food surplus and expanding through the constant immigration of free peasants and escaped serfs in search of a better life. (Escaped serfs were guaranteed their freedom if they stayed in a town a year and a day.) Once towns started to flourish, many of them began to specialize in certain enterprises. Paris and Bologna gained considerable wealth by becoming the homes of leading universities; Venice, Genoa, Cologne, and London became centers of long-distance trade; Milan, Florence, Ghent, and Bruges specialized in manufactures. The most important urban industries were those devoted to the making and finishing of wool (and in Venice, cotton) cloth. Some cloth manufacturers developed techniques of large-scale production and investment that are ancestors of the modern factory system and industrial capitalism. Nonetheless, large industrial enterprises of this sort were not typical of medieval economic life as a whole. Most urban manufacturing continued to be done by individual artisans in small, privately owned workshops whose production was regulated by professional associations known as "guilds."

Usually only master artisans, who were experts at their trade and ran their own shops, were allowed to be fully fledged, voting members of a craft guild. As a result, guilds generally promoted the interests of their richest and most successful members by trying to preserve monopolies and limit competition. To these ends, terms of employment were strictly regulated. If an apprentice or a journeyman (from the French *journée*, meaning "day," or by extension "day's work": that is, someone who had completed his apprenticeship but still worked

> Guilds generally promoted the interests of their richest and most successful members by trying to preserve monopolies and limit competition.

for a master craftsman) wished to become a master, he often had to produce a "masterpiece" for judging by the masters of the guild. If the market was judged too weak to support additional master craftsmen, even a masterpiece would not secure a craftsman the coveted right to set up his own shop, yet without such status, some towns even forbade journeymen to marry. Craft guilds also controlled prices and wages, prohibited after-hours work, and formulated detailed regulations governing methods of production and the quality of materials to be used by their members. They also served important social functions as religious associations, benevolent societies, and drinking clubs, looking after their members in times of trouble and supporting his dependents when a master craftsman died.

Merchants established guilds also, which in some towns became so powerful that membership in a merchant guild became a prerequisite for service in town government. Like the more numerous but less powerful craft guilds, merchant guilds sought to maintain a monopoly of the local market for their members by restricting competition and enforcing uniform pricing. Often they also controlled admissions to citizenship in the city. By their nature, guilds were exclusionary organizations. Because they were explicitly Christian, they were almost invariably closed to Jews and Muslims. They also significantly restricted the economic opportunities available to ordinary wage earners, and especially to women. Women were not automatically excluded from most guilds, and a few craft guilds were specifically female. Despite the important role women played as urban wage earners, however, the male-dominated guilds ensured that women would have no influence over the terms and conditions under which they worked, or the wages they would be paid for their labor.

To modern eyes, most medieval towns and cities would still have seemed half rural even in 1300. Streets were often unpaved, houses had gardens for raising vegetables, and farm animals were everywhere. In the early twelfth century, the heir to the throne of France was killed when his horse tripped over a pig running loose in the streets of Paris. Sanitary conditions were poor and the air must have reeked of excrement, both animal and human. One fourteenth-century Londoner channeled his sewage for months into the basement of his neighbor's house, only when the basement

BYZANTIUM, ISLAM, AND THE CRUSADES

How did the First Crusade alter the balance of power between Europe and Byzantium?

As the power of the Abbasid caliphate declined during the ninth and tenth centuries, the Byzantine empire expanded in its military, religious, and cultural aspects. In the mid-ninth century, Byzantium's position was still precarious. A Muslim fleet had recently captured Sicily and Crete; pagan Slav immigration into the Balkans was rapidly undermining Byzantine control of that region; Muslim pressure on the eastern borders of the empire continued unabated, although the borders themselves remained pretty much where they had been since the early eighth century, and a new enemy had emerged in the Viking raiders and traders (known locally as the Rus, for their reddish complexions) who had established themselves along the Russian river systems (in particular, the Volga and the Dnieper) that fed into the Black and the Caspian Sea. The Rus's most important trading connections were with the Abbasids, with whom they exchanged slaves, honey, wax, and furs for Abbasid silver, Indian spices, and Chinese silks. But the Rus knew their way to Constantinople also. In 860, when the Byzantine emperor and his army were busy on the eastern frontier with the Muslims, a Rus fleet sailed into the Black Sea and sacked Constantinople itself.

THE BYZANTINE REVIVAL

By 1025, however, Byzantium's position had been transformed. After several centuries of missionary inactivity, ninth-century Byzantine missionaries, most famously Saints Cyril and Methodius, converted the Balkan Slavs to Orthodox Christianity, devising for them a written language known as Old Church Slavonic and creating the Cyrillic alphabet which is

A City on Fire. Once a fire began to spread in a medieval city, women, children, and priests were swiftly evacuated and servants of the rich would start carrying out their masters' possessions. Here the Swiss city of Bern is shown in flames; although a "bucket brigade" tried desperately to extinguish the fire with water taken from the town moat, chronicles report that the city was leveled by flames in less than half an hour.

filled and the sewage began to flood the public street was his offense detected. In such a world, disease ran rampant, especially in the overcrowded neighborhoods where the poorest urban dwellers lived. At every level of urban society, however, fertility rates were low and infant mortality high. Most cities sustained their population only through continuing immigration from the countryside. Fire was an omnipresent danger, and economic tensions and family rivalries could lead to bloody riots. Yet for all this, urban folk took great pride in their new cities and ways of life. A famous paean to London, for example, written by a twelfth-century denizen of the city, boasted of its prosperity, piety, and perfect climate (i), and claimed that except for frequent fires, London's only nuisance was "the immoderate drinking of fools." His pride was echoed in scores of other European cities as their citizens increasingly asserted their distinctive local identities and their communal privileges as merchants, artisans, and self-governing corporations.

HOW DID THE FIRST CRUSADE ALTER THE BALANCE OF POWER BETWEEN EUROPE AND BYZANTIUM?

BYZANTIUM, ISLAM, AND THE CRUSADES   313

still used today in Bulgaria, Serbia, and Russia. Military conquest quickly followed. By 1025, when Emperor Basil II ("the Bulgar-slayer") died, the Byzantines had firmly annexed Greece, Bulgaria, and modern-day Serbia to their empire. They had also established a military and commercial alliance with the western Rus

THE BYZANTINE EMPIRE, C. 1025

What challenges faced the Byzantine Empire in the eleventh century? Note the land controlled by the Muslims and the emerging power of Kievan Russia. How was the long-standing influence of the Muslims in the Near East likely to affect the character of Byzantine culture? How did the domain of Kievan Russia potentially create additional economic and military pressure on Byzantium, directly as well as indirectly?

kingdom centered around Kiev, decisively reorienting the Rus toward Constantinople and away from Islam. In 911, seven hundred Rus served with the Byzantine fleet in an attack on Muslim Crete. In 945 a commercial treaty was established. In 957, a Kievan Christian princess named Olga was lavishly entertained on a state visit to Constantinople. And in 989, the emperor Basil II turned to Vladimir, prince of Kiev, for the troops he needed to win a civil war against his imperial rival, Bardas Phokas, a member of the increasingly powerful nobility from the eastern borders of the empire. In return for Vladimir's help, Basil gave his sister, Anna, in marriage to Vladimir, and Vladimir, along with his people, accepted baptism into the Orthodox church. Russia has remained an Orthodox bastion until the present day.

Between the 930s and the 970s, the Byzantines also launched a series of successful campaigns along their eastern and southeastern frontiers with the Abbasids, reconquering territories that had not been in Byzantine hands since the seventh century. Paradoxically, however, the consequences of these campaigns ultimately undermined the survival of the Byzantine empire itself by fueling the forces of regional separatism. As ever in Byzantium, a good part of the difficulty was religious. Although most of the peoples of the reconquered territories had remained Christian through three centuries of Islamic rule, the Armenians and the Syrians in particular had their own distinctive Christian traditions that were at odds, both doctrinally and linguistically, with the Greek-speaking church at Constantinople. For an empire that had defined itself for centuries on the basis of its orthodoxy (the word itself means "correct belief"), incorporating such "heretics" threatened the foundations on which the unity of the empire rested.

Even more important, however, the eastern conquests greatly increased the power of the local noble families who led them and profited from them, creating for the first time a center of power within the empire that lay outside the imperial capital at Constantinople. Tensions and rivalries between these eastern noble families and the imperial officials at the capital disturbed Byzantine politics for most of the tenth century. After an attempted coup by the head of one such family, the emperor Basil II (976–1025) savagely suppressed the leading eastern magnate families, building up his own imperial lands in the east and promoting new families, among them the Comneni. He also reoriented Byzantine military power westward toward Bulgaria, which he conquered with the assistance

of a naval force supplied by the Venetians. But this check on the eastern magnates' ambitions proved only temporary. After Basil's death, the imperial throne passed to a series of aged and incompetent relations. In the resulting power vacuum, noble military families came more and more to dominate the countryside, while at court, tax revenues decreased as imperial expenditures rose. To pay the bills, the emperors debased the Byzantine gold coinage, reducing its value by 50 percent between 1040 and 1080 and undermining Byzantine commerce precisely when Venice, Genoa, and Pisa were consolidating their control over the eastern Mediterranean trade routes. By 1081, when the eastern magnate families triumphed by placing Alexius Comnenus on the imperial throne, the Byzantine empire had been crippled as a Mediterranean power.

THE INVASION OF THE TURKS

By the late eleventh century, Byzantium faced new threats from several quarters. Viking adventurers from Normandy, already established in Sicily and southern Italy, were beginning to eye Constantinople itself as a target for conquest. Venice, Genoa, and Pisa had emerged as the dominant naval powers in the eastern Mediterranean and had to a considerable extent taken over the lucrative trade between Islamic North Africa (including Egypt) and the west. The growing power of

Venetian Coin. The patron saint of Venice, Saint Mark, grants a banner symbolizing worldly rule to the Venetian doge. The Venetians consciously imitated Byzantine coinage (see p. 264) as part of a successful effort to replace the Byzantine Empire as the dominant trading power in the Mediterranean basin.

ADVICE TO THE BYZANTINE EMPEROR, ELEVENTH CENTURY

This anonymous work was addressed to one of the eleventh-century Byzantine emperors. It reflects the author's concern with the indolence of the emperor and the growing power of the nobility on the eastern frontiers of the empire. The problems the author addresses here would culminate in 1081 with the ascension of one of these eastern nobles, Alexius Comnenus, to the imperial throne.

Holy Lord, God has elevated you to the imperial authority and has made you by his grace, as you are called, a god on earth, to do and to act as you will. Let then your acts and your deeds be full of understanding and truth, and may justice dwell in your heart. Look, therefore, and act toward all—toward those who are in a position of authority and toward all others—with an equal eye. And do not evilly coerce some while bestowing benefits on others. . . . But let there be equality for all. . . .

The emperor is the model and example for all, and all men look up to him and imitate his conduct. And if his ways are good, men are eager to follow them quickly, but if they are bad and worthy of blame, men will do the same. Therefore, I beg you, take hold of and adopt the four virtues: courage (I mean that of the soul), and justice, temperance, and wisdom. . . .

I know, Your Majesty, that by nature man is desirous of relaxation. But there has come into fashion a custom not helpful but rather damaging, that the emperor not go abroad into the countries under his rule, both in the East and in the West, but that he spend his time in Constantinople, as if in prison there. If someone had indeed restricted you to a single city, in that case you would have to make an effort to leave that area. But the fact is that you have done this to yourself. What, then, is to be said? Go out into the countries under your rule and into your provinces and see for yourself what injustices the poor suffer and what the tax collectors, whom you dispatch, are doing. Ascertain whether the poor have been wronged, and correct all wrong things. Thus both the provinces of the Byzantines and the lands of the peoples under your rule will know that they have an emperor and lord who rules them. Then you yourself will know the strength of each province and fortress and land, how each is situated, and what damage it suffers and what benefits accrue to it. Then there will arise no rebellion or revolt against your agents, but all the areas under your rule will be at peace.

I realize that your ministers . . . will admonish you that this advice is not sound, they will tell you that, as you advance through your countries and provinces with your army and imperial entourage, you will oppress them. They may even say that, if you leave Byzantium, another will seize the imperial throne in your place. When I have thought of this, I have laughed. For the one left by you in the palace, charged with the direction of affairs will, if he is energetic and adequate, be entirely effective, and he will be ever vigilant and will do whatever should be done.

Deno John Geanakoplos, ed. and trans. *Byzantium: Church, Society and Civilization Seen through Contemporary Eyes.* (Chicago: University of Chicago Press, 1984), pp. 20–21.

Fatimid Egypt was beginning to roll back Byzantine gains along the empire's southeastern frontier with Syria. But most disastrously of all, a new Sunni Muslim power, the Seljuk Turks, had emerged in central Asia and had begun to move into Asia Minor, the very heartland of the Byzantine empire. When the Turks captured Armenia, the emperor tried to eject them, but the eastern noble families refused their support, and in the decisive battle of Manzikert (1071), the imperial army was annihilated. The way now lay open for the Turks to seize all of Anatolia, at a blow, the wealthiest and most productive part of the Byzantine empire now fell into Turkish hands. In the same year, another Turkish band captured Jerusalem from the Shi'ite Fatimids, restoring the Holy City to Sunni control. Within five years, almost all of Syria and Asia Minor lay in Turkish hands. In the west, a rebellion by the Balkan Slavs also erupted around this time, further reducing the already severely depleted treasury of the Byzantine empire.

By the 1090s, however, Alexius Comnenus had rebuilt the treasury, repulsed an attempted Norman invasion from southern Italy, restored Byzantine control over the Balkans, and was beginning to plan a campaign against the Turks. For more than a century, the Byzantine army had utilized western mercenaries in its armies. During the eleventh century, however, western knights had emerged as the most effective heavily armored cavalry troops in the world. Alexius had confronted such knights in 1085, when he repelled a Norman invasion of Greece. He was anxious to make use of them, however, against the mounted but lightly armored Turks. To recruit a force of heavy cavalry, Alexius sent a request to Pope Urban II, hoping for a contingent of a few thousand troops with which he

---

C H R O N O L O G Y

BYZANTINE EMPIRE, 1025–1204

Annexation of Greece, Bulgaria, and Serbia	1025
Successful campaigns against the Abbasid rulers	930–970
Russia converts to orthodoxy	911–989
Turkish invasions (defeat of Manzikert)	1071
Reign of Alexius Comnenus	1081–1118
First Crusade	1095–1099
Fourth Crusade, Capture of Constantinople	1204

---

might be able to roll back Turkish gains in Anatolia. Within a year, however, the pope had set in motion a vast crusading army of one hundred thousand Westerners to retake the Holy City of Jerusalem for Christendom.

THE FIRST CRUSADE

The reasons that Urban's summons met with such a massive response are complex. Urban himself probably saw the crusade as a means for achieving at least four ends. One was to bring the Orthodox church back into communion with the papacy. Relations between the two churches had been ruptured in 1054, when a papal emissary and the Orthodox patriarch of Constantinople had each excommunicated the other. In 1095, Alexius himself had hinted that some accommodation might be possible between the churches. If Urban could succeed in uniting the two churches, he would gain a great victory for the Gregorian program of papal monarchy, one of whose goals was to establish the primacy of the papacy over all other bishops and churches. A second motive was to embarrass Urban's greatest enemy, the German emperor Henry IV. Henry and the papacy had been at war for more than twenty years over their respective claims to supremacy within Christendom. By calling a mighty crusade to retake Jerusalem, Urban probably hoped to establish his own claims as pope to be the rightful leader of western Christian society. Third, by sending off a large contingent of fighters, Urban hoped to achieve peace at home. Earlier in the century, a number of French bishops and abbots had supported a "peace movement" that prohibited attacks on noncombatants (the "Peace of God") and prohibited fighting on certain holy days (the "Truce of God"). At the 1095 ecclesiastical council at Clermont where he announced the First Crusade, Urban also promulgated the first full papal approval of this peace movement. In effect, Urban told the assembled knights that if they wished to fight, they could do so justly for a Christian cause overseas. Finally, the goal of Jerusalem itself genuinely inspired Urban. Jerusalem was regarded by medieval geographers as the center of the earth as well as being the most sacred shrine of the Christian religion because it was Jesus' homeland. To the untutored knights of western Europe, as perhaps to Urban himself (whose family came from the knighthood of southern France), it seemed only right that Christian knights should assist their Lord Christ to recover his own land from the Muslims who had seized it from him.

THE SPURIOUS LETTER OF ALEXIUS COMNENUS TO COUNT ROBERT, SEEKING HIS AID AGAINST THE TURKS

This letter to Count Robert of Flanders is a forgery from around the time of the First Crusade. It reflects the kind of propa- ganda that helped to spur enthusiasm for the crusade against the Turks. With its focus on the sexual sins of the Turks and the riches to be had in Constantinople, the letter offers quite different reasons for going on crusade from those advanced by Pope Urban II at Clermont. There is no evidence that any of the charges against the Turks contained in this letter were true.

O incomparable Count, great defender of the faith, it is my desire to bring to your attention the extent to which the most holy empire of the Christian Greeks is fiercely beset every day by the Patzinaks and Turks . . . and how massacres and unspeakable murders and out- rages against Christians are perpetrated. . . .

For they circumcise Christian boys and youths over the baptismal fonts of Christian [churches] and spill the blood of circumcision right into the bap- tismal fonts and compel them to urinate over them, afterward leading them violently around the church and forcing them to blas- pheme the name of the Holy Trinity. Those who are unwilling they torture in various ways and finally murder. When they cap- ture noble women and their daughters, they abuse them sexually in turns, like animals. Some, while they are wickedly defiling the maidens, place the mothers facing, constraining them to sing evil and lewd songs while they work their evil. . . .

But what next? We pass on to worse yet. They have degraded by sodomizing them men of every age and rank—boys, adolescents, young men, old men, nobles, servants, and, what is worse and more wicked, clerics and monks, and even—alas and for shame! Something which from the beginning of time has never been spo- ken or heard of—bishops! They have already killed one bishop with this nefarious sin.

They have polluted and ruined the holy places in in- numerable ways and threaten even worse things. In the face of all this, who would not weep—Who would not be moved? Who would not shudder? Who would not pray? Nearly the entire territory from Jerusalem to Greece, and all of Greece with its upper regions . . . have all been invaded by them, and hardly anything remains except Constantinople, which they threaten soon to take from us unless we are speedily relieved by the help of God and the faithful Latin Christians. . . . For the sake of the name of God and the piety of all those who uphold the Christian faith, we therefore im- plore you to lead us and all Greek Chris- tians, every faithful soldier of Christ you can obtain in your lands, great, small or middling, that they might struggle for the salvation of their souls to free the kingdom of the Greeks, just as in past years they have liber- ated, to some extent, Galicia and other western kingdoms from the yoke of the un- believers. For although I am emperor, no remedy remains to me . . . and I am reduced to waiting in a single city for the imminent ar- rival of the Turks. And since I prefer to be subject to you, the Latins, rather than have Constantinople taken by the Turks, you should fight courageously and with all your strength so that you might receive in bliss a glorious and indescribable reward in heaven.

[The letter then goes on to describe the many Christian relics in Constantinople, and the wealth of the city, urging Robert to prevent all this from falling into the hands of the Turks.]

Act therefore while you have time, lest you lose the kingdom of the Christians and, what is worse, the sep- ulcher of the Lord, and so that you may earn a reward rather than a punishment hereafter. Amen.

John E. Boswell, ed. and trans. *Christianity, Social Tolerance and Homosex- uality.* (Chicago: University of Chicago Press, 1980), pp. 367–369.

The response to Urban's call exceeded all expecta-tions. Within a year of the pope's summons, an army of a hundred thousand men, women, and children, drawn from all over western Europe, was on the march to-ward Constantinople, where they intended to gather before departing for Jerusalem. As with any large en-terprise, the participants' motives for joining the cru-sade varied. Some hoped to win lands or establish principalities for themselves in the east. Others were drawn simply by the prospect of adventure. Many were dependents of greater men, accompanying their lords because it was their duty to do so. A few may have been motivated by obscure prophecies and apoc-alyptic fervor. Most probably had no idea how long a journey would be involved, or even what direction they would be traveling.

But the dominant motive for going on the First Cru-sade was religious. Except for a few of the greatest lords—and they mostly Normans from southern Italy—the prospect of winning new lands in the east was both unlikely and undesired. Indeed, one of the greatest chal-lenges facing the Latin (Crusader) kingdom of Jerusalem after 1099 was precisely the fact that crusaders so rarely wanted to stay on in the east. After fulfilling their vows, the vast majority of crusaders went home. The risks of dying on such a journey were high, the costs of embarking on it were enormous. Crusading knights needed a minimum of two years' revenues in hand to finance their journey. To raise such sums, most were forced to mortgage lands and borrow heavily from family, friends, monasteries, and merchants. They then had to find some way to pay back these loans if and when they returned home. On any rational judgment of financial advantage, the crusade was a fool's errand. But it did offer solace to the Christian soul. For centuries pil-grimages had been the most popular type of Christ-ian penance, and the pilgrimage to Jerusalem was considered to be the most sacred and efficacious one of all. Urban II made this point explicit at Clermont, promising that crusaders would be freed from all other penances imposed by the church. Some cru-sade preachers went even further by promising what became known as a plenary indulgence: that cru-saders would be entirely freed from otherworldly punishments in purgatory for all the sins they had committed up to that point in their lives, and that the souls of those who died on crusade would go straight to heaven. The plenary indulgence was a

> The dominant motive for going on the First Crusade was religious.

truly extraordinary offer, and crowds flocked to take advantage of it.

Crusade preaching emphasized the vengeance that Christ's soldiers should exact on his enemies in the East. But to some crusaders, it seemed absurd to wait until they arrived in Jerusalem to undertake this aspect of their obligations. Muslims might hold Jesus' prop-erty at Jerusalem, but Christian theology held Jews responsible for the death of Jesus himself. During the course of the eleventh century, Jewish communities had grown up in most of the larger cities of the Rhineland and in many of the smaller towns and cities of northern France. Assaults by bands of crusaders against Jewish communities began in northern France in the spring of 1096 and quickly spread to the Rhineland as the crusaders moved east. Hundreds of Jews were killed in Mainz, Worms, Speyer, and Cologne, and hundreds more were forcibly baptized as the price for escaping death at the hands of crusading knights. Despite the efforts of church authorities to prevent them, at-tacks on Jews would remain a regular and predictable feature of Christian crusading until the thirteenth century.

Surprised by the nature and scale of the western re-sponse to his appeal, Alexius Comnenus did his best to move the crusaders quickly through Constantinople and into Asia Minor. Differences in outlook between the western crusaders and the Byzantine emperor quickly became apparent, however. Alexius had little interest in an expedition to Jerusalem, but insisted that the crusaders promise to restore to the empire any ter-ritory they captured from the Muslims. To the cru-saders, this seemed like treachery—an impression that heightened into certainty when supplies they expected from Constantinople on their journey failed to materi-alize. From Alexius' standpoint, the crusader army was a threat, not least because it contained within it several of the Norman leaders who had attempted to conquer his empire only ten years earlier. The crusaders, how-ever, saw themselves as on a mission from God. They did not understand the Byzantine emperor's willing-ness to make alliances with some Muslim rulers against other Muslim rulers, and they speedily concluded that the Byzantines were in fact working to undermine the crusading effort, perhaps even supporting the Muslims against them. Such suspicions were unfounded, but they contributed to a growing western conviction that the Byzantine empire itself was an obstacle to the suc-cessful recovery of Jerusalem for Christendom.

Against great odds the First Crusade succeeded. In 1098 the crusaders captured Antioch and with it most of Syria. At the end of 1099, they took Jerusalem, mercilessly slaughtering Muslim, Jewish, and Christian inhabitants alike. Their success stemmed mainly from the fact that the crusaders' Muslim opponents were at that moment internally divided. The Fatimids had recaptured Jerusalem from the Turks just months before the crusaders arrived, and the Turks themselves were at war with each other. But western military tactics, in particular the dominance in the open field of the heav-ily armored knights, also played an important role in the crusaders' success.

Equally critical was the naval support the First Crusade received from Genoa and Pisa, which hoped that a successful crusade would allow them to control the Indian spice trade that passed through the Red Sea and on to Alexandria in Egypt. Venice, which had its own connections to this trade through Constantinople, remained largely neutral during the First Crusade, but moved quickly to establish itself in the new crusader kingdom after 1099. In this respect, the

THE ROUTES OF THE CRUSADERS, 1096–1204

What factors led to the First Crusade? What was the object of the first three crusades? Why did the Fourth Crusade go no farther than Constantinople? What do the Crusades reveal about the differences in outlook between Eastern and Western Christians? Why was the First Crusade a military success, whereas the others met with mixed results at best?

Boundaries shown are those at time of First Crusade

Population predominantly Christian

Population predominantly Muslim

→ First Crusade

→ Second Crusade

→ Third Crusade

→ Fourth Crusade

THE EXPANSION OF EUROPE

First Crusade contributed to the further decline of Byzantine commerce, which was already suffering both from Italian competition in the Mediterranean and from the disruptive impact of the Turkish invasions on the trade routes that had previously connected Constantinople with Baghdad and the Central Asian silk route to China. All these trends were underway before the First Crusade began, but the establishment of the Latin kingdom accelerated them. To that extent, the First Crusade contributed significantly to the changing balance of power between Byzantium and the West.

THE LATER CRUSADES

The First Crusade had much less of an impact on the balance of power between Islam and the West. The crusader kingdom was never more than an underpopulated, narrow strip of colonies along the coastline of Syria and Palestine. So long as the crusaders did not control the Red Sea, the main routes of Islamic commerce with India and the Far East were unaffected by the change in Jerusalem's religious allegiance. Nor, for that matter, did the crusaders in any way wish to interfere with the overland caravan routes that led through their new territories. For the Muslims, the loss of Jerusalem was a religious affront much more than an economic one, and it was for religious reasons that they began to plan its recovery. By 1144, most of the crusader principalities in Syria had been recaptured. When Christian warriors led by the king of France and the emperor of Germany came east in the Second Crusade, they were too internally divided to recoup the losses. Not long afterward, Syria and Egypt were united under the great Muslim leader Saladin, who finally recaptured Jerusalem in 1187. In response, the Third Crusade was launched, led by the German emperor Frederick Barbarossa, the French king Philip Augustus, and the English king Richard the Lionheart. This campaign also failed. Barbarossa drowned in Asia Minor on the way to Jerusalem, and Philip Augustus soon went home. Richard the Lionheart's heroic efforts enabled the Latin kingdom to survive for another century; but even he could not recapture Jerusalem.

The dream, however, did not die. When Innocent III became pope in 1198, his main ambition was to win back Jerusalem. He summoned the Fourth Crusade to

> The First Crusade contributed significantly to the changing balance of power between Byzantium and the West, but had much less of an impact on the balance of power between Islam and the West.

CHRONOLOGY

THE CRUSADES

First Crusade (recapture of Jerusalem)	1095–1099
Second Crusade (defeated by Seljuk Turks)	1145–1149
Third Crusade (Frederick Barbarossa and Richard "the Lionheart")	1187–1192
Fourth Crusade (sack of Constantinople)	1201–1204
Fifth Crusade (capture of Damietta)	1217–1221
Peace treaty regains Jerusalem	1228–1229
Sixth Crusade (defeat of Louis IX of France)	1248–1254
Seventh Crusade (death of Louis IX of France)	1270

that end, but it proved a disaster. Civil war in Germany, combined with war between England and France, severely reduced the number of knights willing to participate; and when the Venetians, who had contracted to transport the crusader army to the Holy Land, discovered that only half the predicted crusaders would arrive and that they would therefore not be properly paid, they diverted the crusade toward a successful attack on Constantinople itself in 1204. The result was an enormous commercial windfall for Venice, but the effective destruction of the Byzantine empire, which for the next sixty years was divided into Latin-ruled and Greek-ruled provinces. In 1261 the Venetians' rivals, the Genoese, helped a new imperial claimant, Michael VIII Palaeologus, to recover the Byzantine throne and, with it, control over Constantinople. But the Byzantine empire was now reduced to little more than the city itself, leaving both Asia Minor and the Balkans open to their eventual conquest by the Ottoman Turks.

Despite the debacle of the Fourth Crusade, western efforts to recover Jerusalem continued throughout the thirteenth century. Only in 1229, however, when the western Roman emperor Frederick II negotiated a treaty with the Egyptian sultan that returned Jerusalem to Christian control for a period of ten years, did any

PREPARING TO DEPART ON CRUSADE

Before crusaders departed for the Holy Land, they were obliged to remedy all injustices they might have committed, and to put their affairs in order. This was a religious requirement for anyone setting out on a penitential pilgrimage, but it was also a practical recognition that many crusaders would die on their journey. The human emotions that accompanied such departures are clearly expressed in Jean de Joinville's account of his preparations to depart with King Louis IX of France on the Sixth Crusade (1248–1254).

At Easter, in the year of our Lord 1248, I summoned my men, and all who held fiefs from me, to Joinville. On Easter Eve, when all the people I had summoned had arrived, my son, Jean . . . was born to me by my first wife. . . . We feasted and danced the whole of that week. . . .

On the Friday I said to them: "My friends, I'm soon going overseas and I don't know whether I shall ever return. So will any of you who have a claim to make against me come forward. If I have done you any wrong I will make it good, to each of you in turn, as I have been used to do in the case of those who had any demand to make of me or my people." I dealt with each claim in the way the men on my lands considered right; and in order not to influence their decision I withdrew from the discussion, and afterwards agreed without demur to whatever they recommended.

Since I did not wish to take away with me a single penny to which I had no right, I went to Metz in Lorraine, and mortgaged the greater part of my land. I can assure you that, on the day I left our country to go to the Holy Land, I had in my possession, since my lady mother was still alive, an income of no more than a thousand *livres* from my estates. All the same I went, and took with me nine knights, and two knights-banneret besides myself. I bring these things to your notice so that you may understand that if God, who has never failed me, had not come to my help, I should scarcely have been able to hold out for so long a time as the six years that I remained in the Holy Land. . . .

On the day I left Joinville I sent for the Abbot of Cheminon, who was said to be the wisest and worthiest monk of the Cistercian Order. . . . This same abbot . . . gave me my pilgrim's staff and wallet. I left Joinville immediately after—never to enter my castle again until my return from oversea— on foot, with my legs bare, and in my shirt. Thus attired I went to Blécourt and Saint-Urbain, and to other places where there are holy relics. And all the way . . . I never once let my eyes turn back towards Joinville, for fear my heart might be filled with longing at the thought of my lovely castle and the two children I had left behind.

M. R. B. Shaw, ed. and trans. *Chronicles of the Crusades.* (Baltimore: Penguin Classics, 1963), pp. 192, 195.

western leader attempt to achieve this objective directly. Instead, thirteenth-century crusades were directed mainly toward Egypt (1217–1219, 1248–1254), and, in 1270, Tunis. The crusaders' strategic goal was to cut the economic lifelines that supported Muslim control of the Holy Land. In explaining these later crusades, however, it becomes increasingly difficult to disentangle crusade-motivated calculations toward recapturing Jerusalem (which was, in any event, a shattered city with no walls and a tiny population) from the aspirations of Italian merchants to control the Far Eastern trade that ran through Egypt, and the gold trade from sub-Saharan Africa that ran through Tunis. The great mercantile city of the thirteenth century Latin kingdom was Acre, not Jerusalem. Its fall in 1291 marked the end of any further western expeditions (though not of plans for such expeditions) to recover the Holy Land from Islam.

THE CONSEQUENCES OF THE CRUSADES

For Byzantium, the impact of the crusading movement was disastrous. The crusades coincided with, and to some extent caused, a decisive shift in the balance of economic and military power between Western Europe and the faltering Bzyantine empire. On the Islamic world, by contrast, the impact of the crusades was much more modest. Trade between Islam and the West continued despite periodic interruptions caused by crusader attacks on Syria, Egypt, and North Africa. The greatest economic gains went to the Italian maritime republics of Venice and Genoa; but Islamic merchants too came to depend increasingly upon western markets for their goods. Both sides also gained in military terms: westerners learned new technques of fortification, and Muslims learned new methods of siege warfare and new respect for the uses of heavy cavalry. Finally, the crusades also helped to crystallize both Christian and Islamic doctrines of holy war against the infidel. Neither Christian holy war nor Muslim *jihad* drew much doctrinally from the other. The collision between them, however, deepened the mutual hostility that already separated the Islamic world and Christian Europe.

The impact of the crusades on western Europe is more difficult to assess. From one standpoint, the crusades were an ultimately unsuccessful chapter in a generally successful story of western expansionism during the High Middle Ages. In the Middle East, however, as they did in Greenland and North America, western Europeans overreached themselves. They could not maintain the colonies they established, and they were ultimately forced to withdraw. Nor did the crusades "open up" Europeans to a wider world of which they had previously known nothing. That wider world already existed in 1095, and Europeans were already part of it. The economic and cultural horizons of Europeans certainly broadened during the twelfth and thirteenth centuries. But the driving force here was the expansion of the European economy, along with the entrepreneurial enterprise of western merchants. To these developments, the crusades had only a peripheral relevance. Trade with the Islamic world, and beyond it with India and the Far East, did bring enormous prosperity to the Italian maritime republics, especially Genoa and Venice. But these trading links had existed before the crusades and continued after they ended. It is arguable, indeed, that crusading diminished, rather than increased, the economic and cultural exchange between western Europe and the Islamic world that might otherwise have taken place.

It would be wrong, however, to end our discussion of the crusades on such a minor note. A drive by western merchants, backed by western military force, to control the trade in spices, silks, and gold by "cutting out the Islamic middleman" is clearly visible in thirteenth-century crusading. This impulse would continue, and would eventually lead to the creation of worldwide European mercantile and colonial empires from the sixteenth century on. Nor should we ignore or diminish the lasting influence of the crusading ideal on Europeans' image of themselves. Crusading had dramatic successes in Spain, where between 1100 and 1250 the kings of Castile and Portugal and the crown of Aragon led the reconquest of the Iberian peninsula from Islam. In Iberia particularly, crusading retained its ideological significance until the end of the sixteenth century, providing an important motivation behind the Portuguese and Spanish voyages of discovery during the fifteenth century, and the conquest of the Americas during the sixteenth century. Crusading would also continue to color European relations with Islam, and

> It is arguable that crusading diminished, rather than increased, the economic and cultural exchange between western Europe and the Islamic world that might otherwise have taken place.

WHAT WAS THE RELATIONSHIP BETWEEN CHIVALRY AND THE CULT OF "COURTLY LOVE"?

SOCIAL MOBILITY AND SOCIAL INEQUALITY IN HIGH MEDIEVAL EUROPE   323

especially with the Ottoman Turks, whose conquests would eventually lead them to the gates of Vienna and the borders of Italy. Even Napoleon, the last of the western Roman emperors, was not immune to the crusading ideal. He too would lead a successful, but short-lived, reconquest of Jerusalem.

SOCIAL MOBILITY AND SOCIAL INEQUALITY IN HIGH MEDIEVAL EUROPE

What was the relationship between chivalry and the cult of "courtly love"?

The increasing wealth of high medieval Europe also transformed the social structure of European society. In the tenth century, it was still possible to describe European society as being divided among "those who worked, those who prayed, and those who fought." By 1300, however, such functional descriptions no longer bore even a tangential relationship to reality. New commercial and professional elites had emerged in the burgeoning cities of western Europe. By 1300, the wealthiest members of European society were merchants and bankers, not nobles. The greatest noble families affected a disdain for commerce, but nobles too found themselves drawn increasingly into the world of trade, despite their contempt for such "calculators." Nobles still fought, of course; but so too did knights, urban crossbowmen, peasant longbowmen, citizen militias, and peasant levies. Even work had become more complex. By 1300, more than half the peasants in England farmed plots of land too small to support their families. They survived, and sometimes even prospered, on a shifting combination of farming, wage labor, hunting, gathering, and charity. Such lines as existed between town and countryside were easily crossed. Rural people moved to towns and townspeople moved back to the countryside with regularity and ease. Schools of all sorts had emerged, and the products of those schools—lawyers, doctors, estate administrators, clerks, and government officials—comprised a new and growing professional class that further complicated efforts to describe European society in terms of "three orders" of workers, prayers, and fighters.

Increasing wealth made European society more complex. Society also became more fluid. The image of "fortune's wheel," whose ceaseless turning raised the unimportant to greatness while reducing the great to poverty, was a favorite image during the High Middle Ages, and for good reason. A shipwreck, a stolen cargo, a bad investment, or a political miscalculation could ruin even the wealthiest and most powerful families. At the same time, however, poor people with ability and luck could sometimes rise to extraordinary heights. Careers in the church were particularly open to men of talent. Robert Grosseteste, the son of an English peasant family, rose to become bishop of Lincoln and one of the greatest intellectuals of the thirteenth century. Royal service was another route to social advancement. William the Marshal, the fourth son of a minor English baronial family, made a name for himself on the twelfth-century knightly tournament circuit. Recruited into the household of King Henry II of England, Marshal rose to become (through marriage) one of the greatest earls in the land and, at his death, regent of England for the child king Henry III. But fortune's wheel also brought men down. William Cade, the wealthiest Flemish wool merchant of the twelfth century, had his entire fortune confiscated by King Henry II. Dante Alighieri, a rising man in the government of his native city of Florence, in 1301 was exiled from Florence for life. He wrote his greatest poetry in exile, "tasting the bitter crumbs of other men's bread."

> In the tenth century, it was still possible to describe European society as being divided among "those who worked, those who prayed, and those who fought." By 1300, such functional descriptions no longer bore even a tangential relationship to reality.

NOBLES AND KNIGHTS

New wealth brought social mobility, but it also created a more highly stratified society. We have noted already the hierarchies of status and wealth that characterized the guild system. With the rise of serfdom, new distinctions between free and unfree families also emerged within peasant society. Nowhere, however, is the growing stratification of European society more evident than among the nobility. In the Carolingian period, the nobility comprised a relatively small number of ancient families of approximately equal social rank who married endogamously (that is, among themselves). During the tenth and eleventh centuries, however, new families began to establish themselves as territorial lords, rivaling and sometimes surpassing the old Carolingian noble families in power and wealth. Some of these new families were descended from Carolingian officeholders who had taken advantage of the Carolingians' collapse to establish their independence. Others were simply freebooters whose power rested on their control over castles, knights, and manors. Until the twelfth century, the old Carolingian noble families attempted to resist the claims of these new families to noble rank and status. By the end of the thirteenth century, however, a new nobility had emerged in western Europe that included these new families of counts, castle holders, and knights, but that also made a series of careful distinctions in rank among dukes, counts, castellans (castle holders), and knights.

Knights were not necessarily nobles in the eleventh century. Knighthood was instead a social "order" consisting of men of widely varying social rank. Some eleventh-century knights were the sons of great nobles, but others were little more than peasants mounted on horseback and armed with a sword. Some knights were "lords," living from the payments of dependent peasants attached to manors. But most knights were landless hirelings, living in the households of greater men (mostly rural, but some urban) who relied on them to prosecute their quarrels and intimidate their enemies. As a specialized warrior group, knights associated with the nobility. A degree of social prestige rubbed off on them from this fact. But the key developments that raised the knights into the ranks of the nobility took place during the twelfth and thirteenth centuries and were directly connected with the growing wealth of medieval European society. As the costs of knightly equipment rose, the number of men who could afford the heavier horses, stronger swords, and improved armor that mid-thirteenth-century knights required declined dramatically. The style of domestic life expected of knights also became more elaborate and expensive. In 1100, a knight could get by with a woolen surcoat,

Aristocratic Table Manners. There are knives but no forks or napkins on the table. The large stars mark these nobles as members of a chivalric order.

two horses, and a groom. By 1250, a knight required a string of horses, silk clothing, and a retinue of servants, squires, and grooms. To support such an extravagant lifestyle, a knight needed either a sizable annual fee from his lord or else large estates, a minimum of twelve hundred acres. At four pence per acre in rent, twelve hundred acres would produce an annual income of twenty pounds per year, the minimum income considered necessary in thirteenth-century England to sustain a man as a knight. By way of comparison, a common laborer, working for wages of around two pence per day, might hope to earn one to two pounds per year.

CHIVALRY AND COURTLY LOVE

As the costs of knighthood increased, so too did its social prestige. From the mid-twelfth century on, the kings and nobles of Europe began to embrace and encourage the knightly code of values known as "chivalry," which stressed bravery, loyalty, generosity, skill with weapons, and proper manners as constituent elements in true nobility. Chivalry literally means "horsemanship," and mounted combat (whether on the battlefield or in tournaments) would for long remain the defining element in the European nobility's image of itself. First and foremost, however, chivalry was a social ideology that appealed to the knights and nobles of western Europe because it gave them a way of distinguishing themselves from all those other groups in high medieval society—merchants, lawyers, artisans, and prosperous free farmers—who were their ri-

WHAT WAS THE RELATIONSHIP BETWEEN CHIVALRY AND THE CULT OF "COURTLY LOVE"?

SOCIAL MOBILITY AND SOCIAL INEQUALITY IN HIGH MEDIEVAL EUROPE   325

vals in wealth and sometimes in political influence. Although traditionally the nobility had stressed descent from noble ancestors as the key element in social rank, in the socially mobile world of the High Middle Ages many families who lived nobly did not in fact have prestigious ancestors, whereas other families who did have such ancestors no longer had the wealth to maintain an appropriately noble style of life. Of what, then, did nobility consist? Was noble status a matter of birth, or was it a result of an individual's own achievements? The amalgamation between knighthood and nobility fostered by chivalry offered something to both sides. To the old noble families, it assured them that virtue inhered in their blood, and that chivalric values were most often to be found in those born to noble parents. To the knights, however, as to the merchants and lawyers who sometimes adopted its language and customs, chivalry offered a way of legitimizing the social positions they had attained through their own loyalty, bravery, and skill.

Chivalry began as the value system of a socially diverse knightly order. By the end of the thirteenth century, however, it had become the ideology of a social class, functioning to demarcate those who were (or aspired to be) noble from those who were (or did) not. These lines of social demarcation were particularly clear on the battlefield, where the chivalric code pertained exclusively to knights. Chivalry obliged a knight to treat a knightly opponent with courtesy and respect, capturing him for ransom rather than killing him, and trusting in his prisoner's word (his *parole*) that his ransom would be paid. No such compunctions applied, however, to common soldiers, urban militias, and archers. Under the laws of chivalric war, they could be slaughtered at will by the knights, without any prospect of being captured for ransom.

Closely linked to the ideology of chivalry was the so-called cult of courtly love, which made noble women into objects of veneration for their knightly admirers. Here too, there was an important element of social class. Courtly love was "refined" love, the "courteous" love appropriate to a royal or noble court. But the exponents of courtly love distinguished sharply between noble women, who alone were capable of "refined" love (and who should therefore be wooed and won through proper manners, poetry, and valiant deeds) and peasant women, on whom such "courtliness" would be wasted. Noble women were to be courted; but peasant women could be taken by force, if they would not yield willingly to the desires of a nobleman.

To what extent did the new doctrines of courtly love (which will be discussed in more detail in the next chapter) actually affect the attitudes of noblemen toward noblewomen? The question remains controversial for two reasons. One is that most of our evidence about courtly love comes from literature, and historians differ as to how accurately literature actually reflects life. The other is that putting women on a pedestal is itself another, albeit gentler, way of constraining women's choices. There can be no question, however, that the material quality of noble life improved for both men and women during the High Middle Ages. Wooden castles gave way to stone during the twelfth century. By 1300, most castles were equipped with chimneys and mantled fireplaces, which meant that instead of having one large fire in a central great hall, individual rooms could be heated and individuals gained some privacy. Some thirteenth-century castles even had glass windows, making their private rooms both warmer and lighter. Nor is there any doubt that there was a revolution in some verbalized attitudes toward the female sex. Until the twelfth century, aside from a few female saints, women were virtually ignored in literature. The typical French epic, such as *The Song of Roland*, told of bloody, warlike deeds that either made no mention of women at all, or portrayed them only in passing as subservient wives and mothers. But within a few decades after 1100, noblewomen were suddenly turned into objects of elaborate veneration by lyric poets and writers of romances.

Although the literature of courtly love was extremely idealistic and somewhat artificial, it surely expressed the values of a gentler noble culture wherein upper-class women were in practice more respected than before. Moreover, certain royal women in the twelfth and thirteenth centuries actually did rule their states on various occasions when their husbands or sons were unable to do so or dead. From 1109 until her death in 1126, Queen Urraca ruled the combined kingdom of León-Castile in Spain. The indomitable Eleanor of Aquitaine (1122?–1204), wife of Henry II, played a crucial role in the government of England when her son Richard I (the Lionheart) went on crusade from 1190 to 1194. The strong-willed Blanche of Castile ruled France extremely well twice in the thirteenth century, once during the minority of her son Louis IX and again when he was off crusading. Queens are not, of course, typical women, and from a modern perspective, high medieval noblewomen were still very constrained. But from the point of view of the past, the High Middle Ages was a time of progress for the women of the upper classes. The most striking symbol of this change comes from the history of the game of chess. Before the twelfth century chess was played in the Islamic world, but there the equivalent of the queen was a male figure, the king's chief minister, who could move only diagonally, one square at a time. In twelfth-century Europe, however, this piece was turned into a queen, and sometime before the end of the Middle Ages she began to move all over the board.

POLITICS AND GOVERNMENT

How did government and politics change in the High Middle Ages?

The profound social and economic changes of the High Middle Ages also gave rise to new forms of government and political life. In the early Middle Ages, monarchy was virtually the only form of government western Europeans knew. Towns were small and usually ruled by their bishops or kings. Kingdoms too were small and were thought of as pertaining to a particular people such as the Lombards, the Visigoths, the West Saxons, or the Salian Franks. During the eighth and ninth centuries, most of these ethnic kingdoms disappeared as larger, more powerful, territorially based kingdoms emerged in England and in the Carolingian empire. In England, the West Saxon monarchy survived the

> During the eighth and ninth centuries, most of these ethnic kingdoms disappeared as larger, more powerful, territorially based kingdoms emerged in England and the Carolingian empire.

ninth-century Viking invasions to become the sole rulers of a united English kingdom. In Germany also, a single royal dynasty, the Ottonians, emerged during the tenth century as the undisputed kings of the East Frankish realm. In France, Catalunya, and northern Italy, however, the Carolingians' collapse came near to erasing monarchical power altogether. In the resulting power vacuum, two new structures of political authority slowly emerged in the heartland of the former Carolingian empire: feudal principalities and self-governing cities.

URBAN GOVERNMENT

Early medieval kings were well aware of the value of towns, and where strong monarchies survived (as, for

example, in England and Germany), tenth-century kings were active founders of new towns and cities. In Flanders, Catalunya, and northern Italy, however, where kingship collapsed during the late ninth and tenth centuries, self-governing cities developed during the tenth and eleventh centuries without any close monarchical control. We have spoken already of the general economic factors that led to the growth of cities during the High Middle Ages: the increasing agricultural wealth of the countryside, growing population, and developing networks of local and long-distance trade. These factors brought large numbers of immigrants into the cities. They also attracted the local nobility, many of whom became involved in the burgeoning economic and political life of the city, especially as cities began to extend their control over the surrounding countryside. In northern Italy especially, nobles moved to the cities, where they lived in fortified urban towers surrounded by their knightly retainers, their servants, and their urban supporters just as they would have done in a castle in the countryside. Their presence lent a distinctly aristocratic cast to political life in the towns, but it also introduced a violent culture of honor and vendetta into urban life. Attempts to control noble violence in Italian cities led, in the thirteenth century, to efforts in some towns (such as Florence) to ban nobles from holding governmental office altogether. But the destabilizing effects of such feuds continued, ultimately undermining traditions of urban republican government and paving the way for the emergence, during the later Middle Ages, of such great princely families as the Visconti of Milan and the Medici of Florence, whose dynastic rule made a mockery of the democratic forms of urban political life.

Considering how large the great cities of western Europe became during the twelfth and thirteenth centuries, it is astonishing to realize how informal, even ad hoc, their governmental arrangements were. Where kings or powerful feudal lords continued to rule, towns and cities often received special charters of liberty that defined their jurisdictional rights and established the basic structures of urban self-government. In northern Europe, these usually involved a mayor and a council elected from among the leading citizens of the town. Elsewhere, for example in Rome, powerful rulers such as the pope resisted all efforts to establish independent city governments. In northern Italy, however, only a few powerful lords—mostly bishops—remained to sup-

WHAT WAS THE RELATIONSHIP BETWEEN FEUDALISM AND THE RISE OF NATIONAL MONARCHIES?

FEUDALISM AND THE EMERGENCE OF NATIONAL MONARCHIES   327

port or to resist demands for urban self-government. Urban dwellers in Italy therefore had to work out their governmental arrangements for themselves.

In the twelfth century, many north Italian cities entrusted their governments formally to "consuls," drawn from among the leading magnates of the city. Often, however, an informal association of citizens known as "the commune" undertook a wide variety of governmental functions side by side with the consuls. In the later twelfth century, as consular governments collapsed under the demands of war, the communes emerged as the only effective government many cities had. Even the communes, however, were distinctly oligarchical in character. As social stratification increased during the thirteenth century, many cities found themselves split between a ruling class of "magnates" and a popular party that felt itself excluded from the interlocking structures of power that controlled city government and the guilds. These tensions were heightened by magnates who sought to mobilize the *populares* against their own factional enemies. To control the resulting violence, cities sometimes turned to an outsider, known as a *podestá*, usually a noble with legal training, who ruled as a virtual dictator for a strictly limited term of office. Others cities adopted the model of Venice and became more formally oligarchical, casting off even the pretence of being a popular republic. By 1300, however, even cities that remained republics in principle were becoming increasingly oligarchical in practice. Terms of office were getting longer; the jurisdictional claims of urban governments were expanding; and traditions of dynastic succession to office were beginning that would lead to the urban principalities of the later Middle Ages.

FEUDALISM AND THE EMERGENCE OF NATIONAL MONARCHIES

What was the relationship between feudalism and the rise of national monarchies?

In theory, of course, Europe remained a continent of kingdoms even during the tenth and eleventh centuries, when monarchical power in France and Italy was at its lowest ebb. In France, the Capetian dynasty succeeded the Carolingians without interruption in 987, keeping alive the memory that all France had once owed allegiance to a single king. In northern Italy, a number of local rulers vied with each other to claim the Carolingians' fallen mantle of royalty for themselves until their claims were finally trumped, after 962, by the newly crowned Ottonian emperors of Germany. In practice, however, neither the Ottonians in Italy nor the Capetians in France were able to control the territories over which they claimed to rule. By the year 1000, effective political and military power in France lay in the hands of lesser men—dukes, counts, castellans, and knights—whose power rested on their capacity to channel the increasing wealth of the countryside into their own hands. The symbol of their authority was the castle, often little more than a wooden tower set on a hill with a wooden palisade around it. But when manned by a sufficient force of mounted knights, even a wooden castle could be a formidable fortification, certainly sufficient to overawe the peasant farmers of an area, and frequently capable of withstanding the attacks of rival lords. From their castles, these counts, castellans, and knights constructed "lordships": self-contained territories within which they exercised not only the property rights of landlords over peasants, but also the public rights to mint money, judge legal cases, raise troops, wage war, collect taxes, and impose tolls. By the year 1000, France had thus become a patchwork kingdom composed of essentially independent territorial principalities ruled by counts or dukes, which were in turn divided into smaller lordships ruled by castellans and knights.

THE PROBLEM OF FEUDALISM

This highly decentralized political system, in which "public" powers of minting, justice, taxation and defense were vested in the hands of private lords, is conventionally referred to as *feudalism*. As a term, "feudalism" is in many ways unsatisfactory, not least because it has been used by historians to mean so many different things. Marxist historians use it to describe an economic system—in Marxist terms, a "mode of production"—in which wealth is overwhelmingly agricultural and cities have not yet formed. Social historians see "feudal society" as characterized by an aristocratic social order bound together by mutual ties of land holding and supported by the labor of serfs attached to manors. Legal historians speak of feudalism as a system of land tenure in which lesser men held land from greater men in return for services of various kinds, whereas military historians see feudalism as a method of raising troops, a system whereby kings, dukes, and counts granted land to lesser lords in return for specified quotas of knightly military service. Reflecting on this plethora of meanings, some recent historians have suggested we should abandon the term "feudalism" altogether, arguing that because economic, social, and political relations differed so greatly from one area of medieval Europe to another it is misleading to speak of feudalism as any kind of "system" at all.

> Some recent historians have suggested we should abandon the term "feudalism" altogether.

If, however, we define feudalism as a political system in which public powers are exercised by private lords, then there is general agreement that feudalism took shape first and most fully in tenth- and eleventh-century France, after the Carolingian empire had disintegrated. As we have seen, this was also the era during which manorialism was expanding, with a consequent loss of freedom for many peasant families. It is the coincidence of rapid political decentralization with the growth of manorialism that gives northern European feudalism during the tenth and eleventh centuries its particular character. From France, the language and customs of feudalism spread to other areas of Europe, changing as they were adapted to the particular social, economic, and political circumstances of different regions and countries. Finally, in the twelfth and thirteenth centuries, feudalism developed into an ideology justifying a hierarchical legal and political order that subordinated knights to counts and counts to kings. In this modified form, feudalism gave rise to powerful feudal monarchies and helped to lay the groundwork for the emergence of European nation-states.

What then was feudalism? At its simplest level, a "fee" or "fief" (rhymes with "reef"; in Latin, *feudum*) was a kind of contract, in which someone granted something of value—often land, but sometimes revenues from tolls or mills, or an annual grant of money—to someone else in return for service of some kind. Frequently there was a degree of inequality in such contracts, particularly if land was involved, because land was regarded as the most valuable gift one person could give to another. In a gift-giving society, such inequalities had direct implications for the social status of the two parties involved in the exchange. When a man accepted land from another in return for promises of service, a degree of subordination by the recipient toward the giver was usually implied. In some areas, the recipient of a fief might therefore become the "vassal" (from a Celtic word meaning "boy") of the gift giver, who thereby became his "lord"; and their new relationship might be solemnized by an act of "homage," whereby the vassal became "the man" (in French, *l'homme*) of his lord in return for his fief. Elsewhere, however, fiefs existed without vassalage, and vassalage existed without homage. The terms themselves matter less than the relationship that arose when one individual held land from another in return for service. It was this relationship that lay at the heart of feudalism as it emerged in the chaos of tenth-century France.

In a world in which central governmental authority had collapsed, these essentially personal relationships of service in return for land holding became an important element in ordering social and political relations between counts, castellans, and knights. At the same time, however, these relationships were entirely unsystematic. Even in France, where feudalism pervaded aristocratic life, many castellans and knights held their lands freely, owing no service whatsoever to the count or duke within whose territories their lands lay. Nor were feudal relationships necessarily hierarchical. Counts sometimes held lands from knights; knights frequently held lands from each other, and many landholders held fiefs from a number of different lords. Feudalism in the tenth and eleventh centuries created no "feudal pyramids," in which knights held from counts, and counts held from kings in an orderly, hierarchical system of land holding and loyalty. Feudalism of this sort emerged only in the twelfth and thirteenth centuries, when powerful kings began to insist that feudalism *should* be structured in such an orderly way, with kings at the apex of a political and social pyramid.

THE NORMAN CONQUEST OF ENGLAND

Feudalism first emerged as an ordered, hierarchical system of landholding and military service in England, in the peculiar circumstances resulting from the Norman Conquest of 1066. During the tenth and eleventh centuries, England was the wealthiest, most highly centralized, and administratively sophisticated kingdom in western Europe. In 1066, however, Duke William of Normandy, the descendant of Vikings (known as "Northmen," hence "Normans") who had settled this northwestern corner of France during the tenth cen-

WHAT WAS THE RELATIONSHIP BETWEEN FEUDALISM AND THE RISE OF NATIONAL MONARCHIES?

FEUDALISM AND THE EMERGENCE OF NATIONAL MONARCHIES   329

The Bayeux Tapestry. Embroidered shortly after the Battle of Hastings, the Bayeux Tapestry is a 231-foot document of the battle and the events leading up to it. Here the Saxons have sighted a shooting star (Halley's comet, actually) and, taking it for an omen, report it to King Harold.

tury, laid claim to the English crown and crossed the Channel to conquer what he had claimed. Fortunately for him the newly installed English king, Harold, had just warded off a Viking attack in the north and thus could not offer resistance at full strength. At the battle of Hastings Harold and his English troops fought bravely, but ultimately could not withstand the on-slaught of the fresher Norman troops. As the day waned Harold fell, mortally wounded by a random arrow; his forces dispersed, and the Normans took the field—and with it, the kingdom of England. Duke William now became King William the Conqueror and set about to exploit his new prize.

William rewarded his Norman followers with exten-sive grants of English land. As the kingdom's con-queror, however, William could claim with some justice that all the land of England belonged ultimately to him, and therefore that all the land in England must be held from him in return for feudal service of some sort. For the new Norman lords, the feudal service they owed their new king was mainly military. Even the bishops and abbots of England were assigned fixed knight-service quotas for the lands they held. The Norman lords were already accustomed to feudalism in Normandy. In England, however, feudalism after 1066 was much more highly centralized than it had ever been in Normandy, because in England William could draw on the administrative authority of the English state to enforce his claims to be the feudal lord of the entire country.

As king of England, William also exercised a variety of public rights that did not derive from feudalism at all. In England, only the king could coin money, and only the king's money was allowed to circulate. Like their Anglo-Saxon predecessors, William and his sons also collected a national land tax, supervised justice in public courts, and had the sole authority to summon the population of England to arms. The Norman kings also retained the Anglo-Saxon officer of local govern-ment known as the sheriff to help them administer and enforce their rights. William was also able to insist that all the landholders in England owed loyalty ultimately to the king—even if they did not hold a scrap of land directly from him. William's kingship thus represented a powerful fusion of Carolingian-style traditions of public power with the new feudal structures of power and land holding that had grown up in northern France in the tenth and eleventh centuries.

FEUDAL MONARCHY IN ENGLAND

The history of English government in the two cen-turies after William is primarily a story of kings tight-ening up the feudal system to their advantage until they superseded it and created a strong national monarchy. The first to take steps in this direction was the Conqueror's energetic son Henry I (1100–1135). One of his most important accomplishments was to start a process of specialization at the royal court whereby certain officials began to take full professional responsibility for supervising financial accounts; these officials became known as clerks of the Exchequer. Another accomplishment was to institute a system of traveling circuit judges to administer justice as direct royal representatives in various parts of the realm.

THE REIGN OF HENRY II

After an intervening period of civil war Henry I was succeeded by his grandson Henry II (1154–1189), who was very much in his grandfather's activist mold.

Martyrdom of Thomas Becket. From a thirteenth-century English psalter. One of the knights has struck Becket so mightily that he has broken his sword.

Henry II's reign was certainly one of the most momentous in all of English history. One reason was that it saw a great struggle between the king and the flamboyant archbishop of Canterbury, Thomas Becket, over the status of church courts and church law. In Henry's time priests and other clerics were tried for any crimes in church courts under the rules of canon law. Punishment in these courts was notoriously lax. Even murderers were seldom sentenced to more than penance and loss of their clerical status. Also, decisions handed down in English church courts could be appealed to the papal curia (court) in Rome. Henry, who wished to have royal law prevail as far as possible and maintain judicial standards for all subjects in his realm, tried to limit these practices by the Constitutions of Clarendon of 1164. On the matter of clerics accused of crimes he was willing to compromise by allowing them to be judged in church courts but then have them sentenced in royal courts. Becket, however, resisted all attempts at change with great determination. The quarrel between king and archbishop was made more bitter by the fact that the two had earlier been close friends. It reached a tragic climax when Becket was murdered in Canterbury Cathedral by four of Henry's knights, after the king, in an outburst of anger, had rebuked them for doing nothing to rid him of his antagonist. The crime so shocked the English public that Becket was quickly revered as a martyr and became the most famous English saint. Even King Henry was compelled to appear as a penitent, barefoot and dressed only in a shirt, before Becket's tomb to ask the saint's forgiveness for the rash words that had provoked his murder. He was also forced to surrender several of the claims, including the right to try criminal clerics in royal courts, that had provoked his dispute with Becket.

Despite this setback, Henry II made enormous governmental gains in other areas, so much so that some historians maintain that he was the greatest king that England has ever known. His most important contributions were judicial. He greatly expanded the use of the itinerant judges instituted by Henry I and began the practice of commanding sheriffs to bring before these judges groups of men who were familiar with local conditions. These men were required to report under oath every case of murder, arson, robbery, or other major crimes known to them to have occurred since the judges' last visit. This was the origin of the grand jury. Henry also for the first time allowed parties in civil disputes regular access to royal justice through standardized procedures. In the most prevalent type of case, someone who claimed to have been recently dis-

WHAT WAS THE RELATIONSHIP BETWEEN FEUDALISM AND THE RISE OF NATIONAL MONARCHIES?

FEUDALISM AND THE EMERGENCE OF NATIONAL MONARCHIES   331

possessed of his land could obtain a writ from the crown, which would order the sheriff to bring twelve men who were assumed to know the facts before a judge. The twelve were then asked under oath if the plaintiff's claim was true, and the judge rendered his decision in accordance with their answers. Out of such practices grew the institution of the trial jury, although the trial jury was not used in criminal cases until the thirteenth century.

Henry II's legal innovations benefited both the crown and the country in several ways. Most obviously, they made justice more uniform and equitable throughout the realm. They also thereby made royal justice sought after and popular. Particularly in disputes over land—the most important and frequent disputes of the day—the weaker party was no longer automatically at the mercy of a strong-arming neighbor. Even free peasants could sometimes win a legal case against their lords. Only serfs remained entirely at the mercy of their lords, and even they were protected by the criminal jurisdiction of the royal courts. The widespread use of juries in Henry's reign brought more and more people into actual participation in royal government, strengthening their sense of attachment to it. Since these people served without pay, Henry brilliantly managed to expand the competence and popularity of his government at very little cost.

The most concrete proof of Henry II's success is that after his death his government worked so well that it more or less ran on its own. Henry's son, the swashbuckling Richard I, the "Lionheart," ruled for ten years, from 1189 to 1199, but in that time he stayed in England for only six months because he was otherwise engaged in crusading or defending his possessions on the Continent. Throughout the time of Richard's absence governmental administration actually became more efficient, owing to the work of capable ministers. The country also raised two huge sums for Richard by taxation: one to pay for his crusade to the Holy Land and the other to pay his ransom when he was captured by an enemy on his return. But later when a new king needed still more money, most Englishmen were disinclined to pay it.

THE REIGN OF JOHN AND THE MAGNA CARTA

The new king was Richard's brother John (1199–1216), who has the reputation of being a villain but was also a victim of circumstances. Ever since the time of William the Conqueror, the Norman kings had continued to rule their French homeland of Normandy as well as England. When Henry II married Eleanor of Aquitaine, however, her vast estates brought more than half of modern-day France under the control of the English crown. When King Philip Augustus came to the French throne in 1181, he was determined to recover these territories for France. Against Richard, who was the ablest military leader of his day, Philip suffered a series of reverses. Against John, Philip had much greater success. In 1204, he succeeded in ousting John from Normandy, Anjou, and Brittany, leaving only Aquitaine still in English hands.

John devoted the rest of his reign to raising the money he would need to recover his lost French territories. To do so, he pressed his feudal rights to their limits, forcing massive fines from his nobility and imposing heavy taxes upon the country. When John's 1214 military expedition to France met with another crushing defeat at the hands of Philip Augustus, the exasperated magnates of England rebelled. In 1215 they forced John to renounce his extortionate fiscal practices in a great charter of liberties known to posterity as Magna Carta. Because John had relied so heavily on his feudal powers, most of Magna Carta's provisions dealt directly with such matters, insisting that the king must in future respect the traditional rights of his vassals. But it did also enunciate in writing some important general principles: that taxation could not be raised by the crown without consent given by the barons in a common council, and that no free man could be punished by the crown except by the judgment of his equals and by the law of the land. It is in these respects that Magna Carta has sometimes been compared, a bit misleadingly, to the American Bill of Rights. Above all, however, Magna Carta was important as an expression of the principle of limited government and of the idea that the king is bound by the law.

As the American medievalist J. R. Strayer has said, "Magna Carta made arbitrary government difficult, but it did not make centralized government impossible." In the century following its issuance, the progress of centralized government continued apace. In the reign of John's son, Henry III (1216–1272), the barons vied with the king for control of the government but did so on the assumption that centralized government itself was a good thing. Throughout Henry's reign, adminis-

> Magna Carta was important as an expression of the principle of limited government and of the idea that the king is bound by the law.

Legend

- Angevin Empire under Henry II, about 1180
- French Royal Domain, 1180
- Boundary of France, 1180
- ✕ Battle sites

France at the Death of Philip Augustus 1223

- Royal domain
- Under English rule

ATLANTIC OCEAN

Campostela

Bay of Biscay

ENGLAND

Paris

FRANCE

LÉON

0   100   200   300 Miles
0   300 Kilometers

SCOTLAND
Bannockburn ✕ Edinburgh

IRELAND
Dublin

Carlisle   Durham

York   Stamford Bridge

WALES   Bosworth Field

Hereford   ENGLAND   Ely

Gloucester   Cambridge

Oxford   London

Runnymede

Southampton   Winchester   Canterbury

Hastings ✕

English Channel

Calais   Bruges   Antwerp
Ypres   Brussels
Agincourt ✕ FLANDERS Lille   *Scheldt R.*   *Meuse R.*
Arras   Bouvines ✕

Amiens

Beauvais   VERMANDOIS   HOLY

Rouen   *Seine R.*   Rheims   Verdun   *Mosel R.*

Bayeux   St. Denis   ROMAN

Caen   Paris   CHAMPAGNE   LORRAINE

NORMANDY   ISLE DE FRANCE   *Marne R.*

Mont-St. Michel

BRITTANY   Chartres   EMPIRE

MAINE   Brétigny   Troyes

ANJOU   BURGUNDY

Nantes   *Loire R.*

TOURAINE   Bourges

Poitiers   Autun   Dijon

POITOU   *Saône R.*

ATLANTIC OCEAN

Bay of Biscay

AQUITAINE   Geneva

Lyon

Bordeaux   Angoulême   *Rhône R.*

Garonne R.   Périgueux

PROVENCE

GASCONY   Avignon

Albi   Montpellier

NAVARRE   TOULOUSE   Aigues-Mortes   Marseilles

LANGUEDOC   Narbonne

ARAGON   *MEDITERRANEAN SEA*   CORSICA

CATALUNYA

EUROPE
Area of detail
AFRICA

0   100   200 Miles
0   100   200 Kilometers

FRANCE AND ENGLAND, 1180–1223

Consider the vast geographical expanse of the Angevin empire in 1180. What were the primary requirements for holding this empire together? What advantages did the kings of France enjoy in their struggles with the Angevins? What did it mean to be "French" in such a world? Would the wars between the Angevins and the Capetians have encouraged the emergence of national identities within their kingdoms?

WHAT WAS THE RELATIONSHIP BETWEEN FEUDALISM AND THE RISE OF NATIONAL MONARCHIES?

FEUDALISM AND THE EMERGENCE OF NATIONAL MONARCHIES   333

trators continued to perfect more efficient legal and administrative institutions, including a system of central and local courts, and a taxation system that assessed both nobles and commoners in proportion to their wealth.

The last and most famous branch of the medieval English governmental system was Parliament. This gradually emerged as a separate branch of government in the decades before and after 1300, above all owing to the wishes of Henry III's son, Edward I (1272–1307). Although Parliament later became a check against royal absolutism, in its origins Parliament was very much a royal institution, summoned because kings found it useful to consult with their nobles, knights, and burgesses in a single assembly. Edward I called Parliaments frequently to raise money to finance his wars in Wales, Scotland, and France. Magna Carta had demanded that no taxation be imposed without the common consent of the realm. Parliament provided an efficient way to secure such consent, as well as to inform those present (principally the nobility, but frequently including knightly representatives from the counties and the major towns) why such taxation was necessary. Edward also used Parliaments to take advice about pressing concerns; to hear judicial cases involving great men; and to review local administration, hear complaints from the countryside, and promulgate new laws in response to those complaints. Parliaments were thus political institutions no less than financial and judicial ones. They played an essential role in English government from the fourteenth century on.

Edward I's reign also saw the development of a strongly nationalistic monarchy. As a political concept, "Englishness" dates back to King Alfred. Under Edward I, however, Englishness was emerging as not only a political but also a social and cultural force. Edward himself spurred the development of such nationalistic feelings by his aggressive wars of conquest in Wales and Scotland. He also played on such feelings in rallying support for his defensive wars in France against King Philip IV. During the unpopular reign of his father, Henry III, popular and baronial resentments against the "insufferable French" helped provoke a rebellion against the king himself, who was accused of favoring too much his foreign, French relatives. Edward I, however, was able to harness this sense of English national identity and use it to support his own wars of conquest in Wales and Scotland. By the end of his reign, patience was growing thin with the king's arbitrary and imperious style of kingship, and a reaction would follow against the incompetent rule of his son,

CHRONOLOGY	
NOTEWORTHY NORMAN AND ANGEVIN KINGS, 1066–1327	
William I (the Conqueror)	1066–1087
Henry I	1100–1135
Henry II	1154–1189
Richard I (the Lionheart)	1189–1199
John	1199–1216
Henry III	1216–1272
Edward I	1272–1307
Edward II	1307–1327

Edward II. But the link Edward I forged between English nationalism and foreign conquests would endure for centuries to come.

FEUDAL MONARCHY IN FRANCE

While the process of governmental centralization was making impressive strides in England, it developed more slowly in France. But by around 1300 it had come close to reaching the same point of completion. French governmental unification proceeded more slowly because France in the eleventh century was more decentralized than England and faced greater problems. The last of the weak Carolingian monarchs was replaced in 987 by Hugh Capet, the count of Paris, but the new Capetian dynasty—which was to rule without interruption until 1328—was at first no stronger than the old Carolingian one. Even through most of the twelfth century the kings of France ruled directly only in a small area around Paris known as the Île-de-France, roughly the size of Vermont. Beyond that territory the kings had shadowy claims to being the feudal overlords of numerous counts and dukes throughout much of the area of modern France, but for practical purposes those counts and dukes were almost entirely independent. Thus, whereas William the Conqueror inherited in England a country that had long been unified, the French kings of the High Middle Ages had to unify their country from scratch, with only a vague reminiscence of Carolingian unity to build on.

In many respects, however, luck was on their side. First of all, they were fortunate for hundreds of years in having direct male heirs to succeed them. Consequently, there were no deadly quarrels over the right of succession. In the second place, most of the French kings lived to an advanced age, the average period of rule being about thirty years. That meant that sons were already mature men when they came to the throne and therefore few regencies to squander the royal power during the minority of a prince. More than that, the kings of France were always highly visible, if sometimes not very imposing, when there were power struggles elsewhere, so people in neighboring areas became accustomed to thinking of the kingship as a force for stability in an unstable world. A third favorable circumstance for the French kings was the growth of agricultural prosperity and trade in their home region; this provided them with important sources of revenue. A fourth fortuitous development was that the kings were able to gain the support of the popes because the latter usually needed allies in their incessant struggles with the German emperors. The popes lent the French kings prestige, as they earlier had done for the Carolingians, and they also allowed them much direct power over the local church, thereby bringing the kings further income and influence from patronage. A fifth factor in the French kings' favor was the growth in the twelfth and thirteenth centuries of the University of Paris as the leading European center of studies, and the prestige this lent to the monarchy. Finally, and by no means least of all, great credit must be given to the shrewdness and vigor of several of the French kings themselves.

THE CAPETIAN KINGS

The first noteworthy Capetian king was Louis VI, "the Fat" (1108–1137). Although accomplishing nothing startling, Louis at least managed to pacify his home base, the Île-de-France, by driving out or subduing its turbulent "robber barons." Once this was accomplished, agriculture and trade could prosper and the intellectual life of Paris could start to flourish. But the really startling additions to the realm were made by Louis's grandson Philip Augustus (1180–1223). Philip was wily enough to know how to take advantage of his feudal rights over the counts and dukes of France, including King John of England, who was forced to acknowledge Philip's feudal supremacy over Normandy, Anjou, Brittany, and Aquitaine in 1199. Philip was also decisive enough to defend his gains in battle—at least against King John, who was known to his detractors as "soft sword." Most impressive of all, Philip worked out an excellent formula for governing his new acquisitions. Since these increased his original

King Philip the Fair of France. An author is presenting a copy of his book to the mighty king, enthroned on a pedestal.

lands close to fourfold, and since each new area had its own highly distinct local customs, it would have been hopeless to try to enforce strict governmental standardization by means of what was then a very rudimentary administrative system. Instead, Philip allowed his new provinces to maintain most of their indigenous governmental practices but superimposed on them new royal officials known as *baillis*. These officials were entirely loyal to Philip because they never came from the regions in which they served and were paid impressive salaries for the day. They had full judicial, administrative, and military authority in their bailiwicks: on royal orders they tolerated regional diversities but guided them to the king's advantage. Thus there were no revolts in the conquered territories and royal power was enhanced. This pattern of

WHAT WAS THE RELATIONSHIP BETWEEN FEUDALISM AND THE RISE OF NATIONAL MONARCHIES?

FEUDALISM AND THE EMERGENCE OF NATIONAL MONARCHIES   335

CHRONOLOGY

NOTEWORTHY CAPETIAN KINGS, 987–1328

Hugh Capet	987–996
Louis VI	1108–1137
Philip Augustus	1180–1223
Louis VIII	1223–1226
Louis IX	1226–1270
Philip IV	1285–1314

local diversity balanced against bureaucratic centralization was to remain the basic pattern of French government. Thus Philip Augustus can be seen as an important founder of the modern French state.

In the brief reign of Philip's son, Louis VIII (1223–1226), almost all of southern France was added to the crown in the name of intervention against religious heresy. Once incorporated, this territory was governed largely on the same principles laid down by Philip. The next king, Louis IX (1226–1270), was so pious that he was later canonized by the church and is commonly referred to as Saint Louis. He ruled strongly and justly (except for great intolerance of Jews and heretics), and brought France a long, golden period of internal peace. Because he was so well loved, the monarchy lived off his prestige for many years afterward.

That prestige, however, came close to being squandered by Saint Louis's ruthless grandson Philip IV, "the Fair" (1285–1314). Philip fought many battles at once, seeking to round out French territories in the northeast and southwest and to gain full control over the French church instead of sharing it with the pope in Rome. All these activities forced him to accelerate the process of governmental centralization, especially with the aim of trying to raise money. Thus his reign saw the quick formulation of many administrative institutions that came close to completing the development of medieval French government, as the contemporary reign of Edward I did in England. Philip's reign also saw the calling of assemblies that were roughly equivalent to the English Parliaments, but these—later called Estates-General—never played a central role in the French governmental system. Philip the Fair was successful in most of his ventures; above all, as we will later see, in reducing the pope to the level of a virtual French figurehead. After his death there would be an antimonar-

chical reaction, as there was at the same time in England, but by his reign France was unquestionably the strongest power in Europe.

ENGLAND AND FRANCE: COMPARISONS AND CONTRASTS

Although England and France followed certain similar processes of monarchical centralization and nation building, they were also marked by basic differences that are worth describing because they typified differences in development for centuries after. England, a far smaller country than France, was much better unified. Aside from Wales and Scotland, no regions in Britain had such different languages or traditions that they thought of themselves as separate territories. Consequently, no aristocrats could move toward separatism by drawing on regional resentments. This meant that England never really had to face the threat of internal division and could develop strong institutions of united national government such as Parliament. It also meant that the English kings, starting primarily with

Images of Aristocracy. This early fifteenth-century illustration, from the *Très Riches Heures* commissioned by Jean, Duke of Berry, depicts the leisurely elegance that became such an important feature of medieval aristocratic life.

Henry II, could rely on numerous local dignitaries, above all, the knights, to do much work of local government without pay. The obvious advantage was that local government was cheap, but the hidden implication of the system was that government also had to be popular, or else much of the voluntary work would grind to a halt. This doubtless was the main reason that English kings went out of their way to seek formal consent for their actions. When they did not they could barely rule, so wise kings learned the lesson and as time went on England became more and more clearly a limited monarchy. The French kings, in contrast, ruled a richer and larger country, which gave them—at least in times of peace—sufficient wealth to pay for a more bureaucratic, salaried administration at both the central and local levels. French kings relied less, therefore, on the direct consent of the people over whom they ruled. At the same time, however, they were continually faced with serious threats of regional separatism. Different regions continued to cherish their own traditions and often veered toward separatism in league with the upper aristocracy. So French kings often had to struggle with attempts at regional breakaways and take various measures to subdue their aristocrats. Up to around 1700 the monarchy had to fight a steady battle against regionalism, but it had the resources to win consistently and thereby managed to grow from strength to strength.

GERMANY

Germany in the High Middle Ages followed a very different pattern. In the year 1050, Germany appeared to be the strongest monarchy in western Europe. Although the country was divided into a number of quasi-autonomous duchies, the German emperors had constructed a powerful monarchy on Carolingian-style foundations: a close alliance with the church, a tradition of sacral kingship, and profitable conquests in the Slavic lands to the east. To rule their wide territories—which included Switzerland, eastern France, and most of the Low Countries, as well as claims to northern Italy—the emperors relied heavily on cooperation with the church. The leading royal administrators were archbishops and bishops whom the German emperors appointed and installed in their sacred offices, just as their Carolingian predecessors had done. Even the pope was frequently an imperial appointee. Often, these leading churchmen were members of the imperial family itself, who could counterbalance the strength of the regional dukes. Germany was not so

administratively sophisticated as was eleventh-century England, but there was no question about the effectiveness of monarchical authority. It simply rested on other foundations.

THE CONFLICT WITH THE PAPACY

In 1056, however, the emperor Henry III died, leaving as his heir a small boy, the future Henry IV. From this point on, the strength of the monarchy began to unravel. Henry III had installed a new group of reforming clergy at the papal court, whose policies will be discussed more fully in the next chapter. Conflicts between the regents for the boy king Henry IV and the papal reformers began almost immediately. Conflicts also erupted between the regents (who came from central and southern Germany) and the nobility of Saxony. When Henry IV began to rule on his own, the Saxon conflicts escalated. In 1073, these hostilities erupted into a disastrous and destructive civil war.

Just as the Saxon war ended, however, a new conflict broke out with the papal reformers at Rome. For reasons that will be discussed in the next chapter, the newly elected pope Gregory VII (1073–1085) became convinced that to reform the spiritual life of the church, it was necessary first to free the church from the control of laymen, including the emperor. Henry refused to accept Gregory's attempts to prohibit him from selecting and installing in office his own bishops and abbots, and began to plot to remove Gregory from the papacy. Gregory, in turn, allied himself with the Saxon nobility, reigniting the civil war from which Germany had not yet recovered. This time, the war went against Henry, and the dissident nobles, supported by Gregory, began to plot Henry's own deposition. There then followed one of the most dramatic scenes of the Middle Ages. In the depths of winter in 1077 Henry hurried across the Alps to abase himself before Pope Gregory in the north Italian castle of Canossa. As Gregory described the scene in a letter to the German princes, "There on three successive days, standing before the castle gate, laying aside all royal insignia, barefooted and in coarse attire, Henry ceased not with many tears to beseech the apostolic help and comfort." No German ruler, much less a Roman emperor, had ever been so humiliated. The memory would remain etched in German historical consciousness for centuries to come.

The events at Canossa forestalled Henry's deposition, but they did not resolve the war. The struggle between pope and emperor continued until 1122, when

WHAT WAS THE RELATIONSHIP BETWEEN FEUDALISM AND THE RISE OF NATIONAL MONARCHIES?

FEUDALISM AND THE EMERGENCE OF NATIONAL MONARCHIES   337

THE HOLY ROMAN EMPIRE, C. 1200

How does the political geography of Germany present challenges to feudal organization? Why would the German king (and often emperor) rely heavily on the power of church officials as a counterweight to the dukes? Note the position of the papal states and the German dominance of northern Italy. Why was a single heir to the German and Sicilian thrones such a threat to the papacy? Were the fears of successive popes well founded? Why or why not?

Henry's son Henry V finally reached a compromise with the papacy. By then, however, the German nobility had won far more practical independence from the crown than they had had before. After fifty years of nearly constant war, they had also become far more militarized and dangerous. In 1125, when Henry V died childless, they gained further authority by making good on their claims to elect a new ruler regardless of hereditary succession—a principle that would thereafter often lead them to choose the weakest successors or to embroil the country in civil war. The pope's right to crown any new Roman emperor gave him a stake in the selection process also. For obvious reasons, the papacy feared an overly powerful German monarch. Although the popes valued the German emperors as counterweights to the Normans in southern Italy, they feared them in equal measure. Should the German emperors succeed in ruling northern and central Italy directly, the papacy—on whose spiritual independence the salvation of all Christians depended—risked becoming their puppet. This fear propelled the next century of papal-imperial conflict.

FREDERICK BARBAROSSA AND HENRY VI

A major attempt to stem the tide running against the German monarchy was made by Frederick I (1152–1190), who came from the family of Staufen (or Hohenstaufen, meaning "high Staufen"). Frederick, called "Barbarossa" ("red beard"), reasserted the independent dignity of the empire by calling his realm the "Holy Roman Empire," on the theory that it was a universal empire descending from Rome and blessed by God. To make good this claim, Frederick added his own laws directly to those of the sixth-century Roman emperor Justinian and tried to enforce Roman law throughout his empire. At the same time, however, he also tried to rule in cooperation with the German princes, supporting their efforts to bring their own territorial nobles to heel, and trusting that the princes would in turn support his attempts to reassert imperial control over the wealthy but increasingly independent cities of northern Italy.

By and large, Frederick made this system work, but at the cost of a lengthy war in Italy and destructive conflict with the papacy. Led by Milan and supported by the papacy, the north Italian cities formed an urban coalition, the Lombard League, to resist Frederick's claims to rule in Italy. Meanwhile, the princes in Germany were continuing to gather strength, especially by colonizing the rich agricultural lands east of the Elbe. Ultimately, however, Frederick achieved a compromise with both the Lombard League and the papacy, which guaranteed the political independence of the towns in return for large cash payments they would make to the emperor. His 1184 imperial court at Mainz was one of the most splendid occasions of the twelfth century. He secured the princes' approval for his son Henry to succeed him as king and emperor, and he arranged a marriage between Henry and the sister of the Norman king of Sicily. Finally, in 1189, he departed on the Third Crusade and died on his way to the Holy Land.

Barbarossa's careful planning bore fruit in the reign of his son Henry VI. Henry succeeded to his father's throne without difficulty. He enjoyed a huge income from the north Italian towns, and when his wife's brother died suddenly without heirs, he became the king of Sicily also. This was the nightmare the papacy had always feared, for now a single, enormously powerful ruler controlled both northern and southern Italy, leaving the papal lands in central Italy surrounded on all sides. Fortunately for the papacy, however, Henry VI died in 1197 at the age of thirty-two, leaving as his heir a three-year-old son, the future Frederick II. The new pope, Innocent III (1198–1216), threw all his energy into an attempt to break the links that Barbarossa and Henry VI had forged among Germany, northern Italy, and the kingdom of Sicily. When a civil war erupted in Germany over the succession to the throne, Innocent threw his support back and forth between the two main claimants, hoping to secure some kind of promise from the successful claimant that would return Sicily to the papacy, which claimed to have granted it to the Normans as a fief. When Otto IV, the non-Staufen claimant to the throne, finally appeared to have won a decisive victory, Innocent played his last card. He sent the sixteen-year-old Frederick II north with a small army, never imagining that so small a force, led by so young a man, could ever triumph. Otto, however, threw in his lot with his cousin, King John of England; and when Otto's forces were routed at the battle of Bouvines by King Philip Augustus of France, Frederick II wound up as the new, and undisputed, king of Germany.

FREDERICK II

Frederick II (1216–1250) was one of the most fascinating of all medieval rulers. Having grown up in Sicily, Frederick spoke Arabic as well as Latin, German, French, and Italian. He was a patron of learning who composed a famous treatise on falconry that holds an

WHAT WAS THE RELATIONSHIP BETWEEN FEUDALISM AND THE RISE OF NATIONAL MONARCHIES?

FEUDALISM AND THE EMERGENCE OF NATIONAL MONARCHIES 339

honored place in the early history of Western observational science. He maintained a menagerie of exotic animals, a troop of Muslim archers, and a harem of veiled and secluded women, all of which traveled with him on his journeys. When Frederick entered a town, the effect was electrifying. But despite this appearance of exoticism, he was also a very conventional medieval ruler who sought to pursue his grandfather's policies of supporting the territorial princes in Germany while enforcing imperial rights in Italy. Much had changed, however, in the two decades of anarchy that had followed the death of the emperor Henry VI. In Germany, the princes had already become so entirely autonomous that there was little Frederick could do except to recognize their privileges. This he proceeded to do; but in exchange, he got them to elect his sons (first Henry, and then Conrad) to succeed him as kings of Germany. Frederick's biggest problems lay in Italy. In northern Italy, the cities of the Lombard League had once again shaken off their obligations to pay taxes to the empire; while in Sicily, the enormously powerful and administratively sophisticated kingdom created by the Normans had fallen into chaos.

Frederick tackled these problems in order. From 1212 until 1220, Frederick was in Germany, solidifying his relationship with the German nobility and recovering as much Staufen land as he could after twenty years of war. From 1220 until 1226 he was in Sicily and northern Italy, reestablishing his authority there. From 1227 until 1229 he was on crusade, where he succeeded in recovering Jerusalem through negotiations with the Muslim ruler of Egypt, with whom Frederick spoke Arabic and shared a love of falconry. From 1230 to 1235 he was again in Sicily, restoring his authority after an abortive papal invasion of the territory. From 1235 to 1237 he was in Germany, arguably the high point of his reign. In 1237, however, he overreached himself by asserting his rights as emperor to rule the north Italian cities directly, bypassing their own governmental structures. The result was another Lombard League, and another lengthy war, which continued until Frederick's death in 1250. The papacy was a key player in this war, going so far as to excommunicate Frederick from the church, and after his death forbidding any of his descendants to ever again occupy the thrones of Germany or Sicily. We will never know whether the papacy could have made this claim effective, for in 1254, Frederick's last surviving legitimate son died. With him went the last prospect for the continuation of effective monarchical rule in Germany. Emperors would continue to be elected, but in prac-

The Emperor Frederick II. He is shown holding a *fleur de lis,* as a symbol of rule, with a falcon, his favorite bird, at his side. Frederick was the author of a notable book on falconry.

tice, monarchical authority in Germany had effectively collapsed. Power in Germany would henceforth be divided among several hundred territorial princes whose rivalries would embroil German politics until the end of the nineteenth century.

THE "FAILURE" OF MEDIEVAL GERMANY?

Since most other areas of Europe were gaining stronger rule in the twelfth and thirteenth centuries, the decline of monarchical authority in Germany during this period is an intriguing historical problem. It is also a problem of fundamental importance, not least because Germany's "belated" emergence as a European nation state under Bismarck (and the exaggerated nationalism that accompanied this emergence) has been frequently cited to explain German involvement in the disastrous world wars of the twentieth century. Such a "long" view has difficulties, however. If we see the nation-state as the proper historical culmination of European political development, then it makes sense to ask, What went wrong

FREDERICK II CHANGES THE HEIGHT OF THE HEAVENS

As a result of the propaganda war that erupted between Frederick II and the papacy during the 1240s, a series of stories began to circulate about Frederick's "exotic" intellectual and scientific interests: that he had ordered infants to be raised in isolation, to discover what language they would naturally speak; that he had had men disemboweled before him, in order to study the processes of digestion; and that he sealed a man up in a cask to die, to prove that the soul perished with the body. None of these stories has any basis in fact, but all illustrate the impact the image of Frederick had on his contemporaries.

The following story concerns Frederick's court astrologer, Michael Scot (d. 1236), an influential scholar who translated a number of Aristotelian and astronomical works and commentaries from Arabic to Latin. It is taken from the chronicle of Salimbene de Adam, a Franciscan supporter of the pope in the struggle against Frederick.

The seventh example [of Frederick's idiosyncracies] was that he once asked Michael Scot to tell him the distance of his palace from heaven. And after Michael gave the answer that seemed correct to him, the Emperor took him away for a few months as if merely on a pleasure trip, commanding his architects and stone masons in the meantime to lower that room of his palace in such a way that no one could detect it. This was done, and when the Emperor returned to his palace with the astrologer, he asked him again how far distant the palace was from heaven. And after he had completed his calculations, Michael Scot answered that either the heavens had risen or the earth had sunk. Then the emperor know that he was a true astrologer.

I have heard and know many other idiosyncrasies of Frederick, but I keep quiet for the sake of brevity, and because reporting so many of the Emperor's foolish notions is tedious to me.

Joseph Baird, Giuseppe Baglivi, and John Robert Kane, eds. and trans. *The Chronicle of Salimbene de Adam*, v. 40 of Medieval and Renaissance Texts and Studies (Series). (Binghamton, N.Y.: Medieval and Renaissance Texts and Studies, 1986), pp. 355–356.

---

with Germany? If, however, the nation-state itself should prove to be a passing historical phase—a view that becomes more plausible as the European Community becomes more and more powerful—then the history of medieval Germany may come to appear not as a story of failure, but rather as a story about the deep regional divisions that have characterized the history of Europe throughout its recorded history, lasting until the present day. As so often in history, what we see depends greatly upon the perspective from which we look.

IBERIA

The Iberian peninsula was even more regionalized than was Germany. In contrast to Germany, however, Spain would emerge from the Middle Ages with the most powerful monarchy in Europe. The key to the strength of the Spanish monarchies of the High Middle Ages lay in their successful reconquest of the peninsula from the Muslims, and in the lands, booty, and plunder these conquests provided. During the High Middle Ages

WHAT WAS THE RELATIONSHIP BETWEEN FEUDALISM AND THE RISE OF NATIONAL MONARCHIES?

FEUDALISM AND THE EMERGENCE OF NATIONAL MONARCHIES   341

THE RECONQUEST OF IBERIA, 900–1250

Note the position of the Christian kingdoms circa 900, and the progress of the reassertion of Christian control over the subsequent few centuries. What factors helped to shelter and sustain the small Christian kingdoms that survived Islam's initial push? Why did Castile become the largest of the Christian kingdoms as the reconquest progressed? Why did the smaller Aragon and Catalunya maintain important positions as wealthy and significant powers? How did the struggles and successes of Christians in Iberia influence the crusader movement?

Iberia contained four major Christian kingdoms: the northern mountain state of Navarre, which would always remain comparatively insignificant; Portugal in the west; the combined kingdom of Aragon and Catalunya in the southeast, and Castile in the center. Throughout the twelfth century, Christian armies steadily advanced, culminating in the year 1212 in a major victory by a combined Aragonese-Castilian army over the Muslims at Las Navas de Tolosa. The rest was mostly mopping up. By the end of the thirteenth century all that remained of earlier Muslim domination was the small state of Granada in the extreme south, and Granada existed mostly because it was willing to pay tribute to the Christians. Castile became by far the largest Spanish kingdom in area, but it was balanced in wealth by the more urban and trade-oriented kingdom of Aragon and Catalunya. Wars between these two rivals weakened both kingdoms during the later Middle Ages; but when the marriage of Ferdinand of Aragon and Isabella of Castile joined these two ancient enemies, a united Spanish monarchy was born. In 1492, the Catholic monarchs (as Ferdinand and Isabella were known) captured Granada, the last remaining Muslim territory in Spain. A few months later, Isabella commissioned an Italian adventurer named Christopher Columbus to sail to India by heading west across the Atlantic Ocean. Columbus failed. But his accidental encounter with the American continents made sixteenth century Spain the most powerful kingdom in Europe.

CONCLUSION

Until the emergence of national monarchies during the High Middle Ages, there had been two basic patterns of government in Europe: city-states and empires. City-states had the advantage of drawing heavily on citizen participation and loyalty and thus were able to make highly efficient use of their human potential. But they were often divided by economic rivalries, and they were not sufficiently large or militarily strong to defend themselves against imperial forces. The empires, on the other hand, could win battles and often had the resources to support an efficient bureaucratic administrative apparatus, but they drew on little voluntary participation and were too far flung or rapacious to inspire any deep loyalties. The new national monarchies were to prove the "golden mean" between these extremes. They were large enough to have adequate military strength, and they developed administrative techniques that would rival and eventually surpass those of the Roman or Byzantine empires. More than that, building at first on the basis of feudalism, they commanded sufficient citizen participation and loyalty to help support them in times of stress when empires would have foundered. By about 1300 the monarchies of England, France, and the Iberian peninsula had gained the primary loyalties of their subjects, superseding loyalties to communities, regions, or to the government of the church. For all these reasons they brought much internal peace and stability to large parts of Europe where there had been little stability before. Thus they contributed greatly to making life fruitful. The medieval national monarchies were also

the ancestors of the modern nation-states—the most effective and equitable governments of our day (the former Soviet Union was more like an empire). In short, they were one of the Middle Ages' most beneficial bequests to modern times.

SELECTED READINGS

Abulafia, David. *Frederick II: A Medieval Emperor*, London and New York, 1988. The only reliable biography of Frederick II; it strips away much of the legend that has hitherto surrounded this monarch.

Abulafia, David, ed. *The New Cambridge Medieval History. Volume 5: c. 119–c. 1300*. Cambridge, 1999. An up-to-date survey, with contributions by more than thirty specialists. Excellent bibliographies.

Amt, Emily, ed. *Women's Lives in Medieval Europe: A Sourcebook*. New York, 1993. An excellent source collection.

Arnold, Benjamin. *Princes and Territories in Medieval Germany*. Cambridge and New York, 1991. The best English-language survey; it correctly avoids portraying the political history of medieval Germany as a story of failure.

Baldwin, John W. *The Government of Philip Augustus*. Berkeley and Los Angeles, 1986. A landmark scholarly account, detailed but readable.

Bartlett, Robert. *The Making of Europe: Conquest, Colonization and Cultural Change, 950–1350*. Princeton, N.J., 1993. A wide-ranging examination of the economic, social, and religious expansion of Europe, full of stimulating ideas and insights.

———. *England under the Norman and Angevin Kings, 1075–1225*. Oxford and New York, 2000. An outstanding new synthesis, part of the New Oxford History of England series.

Dunbabin, Jean. *France in the Making, 843–1180*, 2d ed. Oxford and New York, 2000. An authoritative survey of the disparate territories that came to make up the medieval French kingdom.

Fuhrmann, Horst. *Germany in the High Middle Ages, c. 1050–1200*. Cambridge, 1986. A useful, short account in English of the history of twelfth-century Germany.

Gillingham, John. *The Angevin Empire*, 2d ed. Oxford and New York, 2001. The best treatment by far of its subject, brief but full of ideas.

Hallam, Elizabeth, and Judith Everard. *Capetian France, 987–1328*, 2d ed. New York, 2001. An excellent textbook; a bit dry, but clear and well organized.

Herlihy, David, ed. *The History of Feudalism*. New York, 1970. Collects the texts on which scholarly discussion continues to focus.

———. *Medieval Households*. Cambridge, Mass., 1985. Covers family history from late antiquity until the end of the Middle Ages.

Holt, Richard. *The Mills of Medieval England*. Oxford and New

York, 1988. An authoritative account by an historian of medieval agricultural technology.

Hyde, J. Kenneth. *Society and Politics in Medieval Italy*. New York, 1973. A survey that sets the political history of the Italian city-states in its social context.

Jones, P. J. *The Italian City-State: From Commune to Signoria*. Oxford and New York, 1997. A fundamental reinterpretation, with important revisions to the standard accounts of Hyde and Waley.

Kaeuper, Richard W. *Chivalry and Violence in Medieval Europe*. Oxford and New York, 1999. A darker view of chivalry than Keen's (see below).

Keen, Maurice. *Chivalry*. New Haven, 1984. Masterful treatment of chivalry from its origins to the sixteenth century, engagingly written.

Lambert of Ardres. *The History of the Counts of Guines and Lords of Ardres*. Translated by Leah Shopkow. Philadelphia, 2000. A tremendously informative and important chronicle of an important Flemish family, now available for the first time in English.

Leyser, Henrietta. *Medieval Women: A Social History of Women in England, 440–1500*. New York, 1995. Although limited to one country, this is the best of the recent surveys treating medieval women.

Lopez, Robert S., and Irving W. Raymond, eds. *Medieval Trade in the Mediterranean World*. New York, 1990. A pathbreaking collection of source material on Italian medieval trade.

Moore, Robert I. *The First European Revolution, c. 970–1215*. Oxford and Cambridge, Mass., 2000. A remarkable description of the ways in which European society was fundamentally reshaped during the eleventh and twelfth centuries.

Mortimer, Richard. *Angevin England, 1154–1258*. Oxford and Cambridge, Mass., 1994. An expert treatment of politics and society, organized topically.

Otto, Bishop of Freising. *The Deeds of Frederick Barbarossa*. Translated by C. C. Mierow. New York, 1953. A contemporary chronicle interesting enough to read from start to finish.

Poly, Jean-Pierre, and Eric Bournazel. *The Feudal Transformation, 900–1200*. Translated by Caroline Higgitt. New York and London, 1991. A synthesis of recent work by French historians, building on the works of Marc Bloch and Georges Duby.

Pounds, N. J. G. *An Economic History of Medieval Europe*, 2d ed. London and New York, 1994. An excellent textbook, the second edition integrates English economic history into its analysis.

Reilly, Bernard F. *The Medieval Spains*. New York, 1993. A succinct account that covers the entire Iberian peninsula from 500 to 1500.

Reynolds, Susan. *Fiefs and Vassals: The Medieval Evidence Reinterpreted*. Oxford and New York, 1994. A detailed revisionist account that sees feudalism as the invention of high and late medieval legal thinkers rather than as a description of tenth and eleventh century realities.

Richard, Jean. Saint Louis: *Crusader King of France*. Cambridge, 1992. An abridged version of Richard's standard biography of King Louis IX, originally published in French.

Southern, Richard W. *The Making of the Middle Ages*. New Haven, 1992. A classic work, first published in 1951 but still fresh and exciting.

Stow, Kenneth R. *Alienated Minority: The Jews of Medieval Latin Europe*. Cambridge, Mass., 1992. An excellent survey of a neglected topic.

Suger, Abbot of Saint Denis. *The Deeds of Louis the Fat*. Translated by R. Cusimano and J. Moorhead. Washington, D. C., 1992. A revealing picture of the challenges that faced the early twelfth-century kings of France as they fought to subdue the local nobility of the Île-de-France.

Waley, Daniel. *The Italian City-Republics*. New York, 1969. A classic introduction to the subject.

THE HIGH MIDDLE
AGES: RELIGIOUS
AND INTELLECTUAL
DEVELOPMENTS,
1000–1300

THE RELIGIOUS AND INTELLECTUAL CHANGES of the High Middle Ages altered European life profoundly. Indeed, it is not too much to say that the fundamental character of European civilization was permanently transformed by the developments that occurred during these crucial centuries. With respect to religious life, the period witnessed both the emergence of the papacy as the dominant organizational force in western Christianity and a remarkable effort on the part of the church to extend and deepen the influence of Christianity among the laity. Parish churches mushroomed across the landscape, and new monastic and religious orders developed, many of which took as their primary mission the task of ministering to the world outside the monastic cloister. For the first time since the late Roman period, preaching, confession, pilgrimages, and private prayer became central elements in the religious life of European Christians. At the same time, however, these new patterns of Christian piety emphasized the religious and social distinctions between Christians and their non-Christian neighbors. The result was a marked increase in the persecution of minority groups within European society, and the creation of what some historians have called "a persecuting society" in which the identification and oppression of heretics, Jews, gay people, lepers, and Muslims became an essential element in the growing power of both church and state.

The High Middle Ages also witnessed a remarkable revival of intellectual and cultural life. From the mid-twelfth century on, hundreds of new works of classical literature and philosophy, including the entirety of the surviving works of Aristotle, poured into western Europe from the Islamic world and, to a lesser degree, from Byzantium. Even before the stimulus of these new texts, however, European intellectuals had begun to think in new, more rigorous ways about fundamental problems in theology, philosophy, and law. Fueling this intellectual revolution (which is sometimes referred to as the "Renaissance of the Twelfth Century") was the emergence and rapid growth of universities, accompanied by an even more widespread expansion of primary schooling. New literary forms also began to emerge: vernacular lyric poetry, extended allegories, and above all romances. For the first time in centuries it began to be possible to speak of a European reading public.

FOCUS QUESTIONS

- How was the Latin Church reformed?
- How did the Latin Church control popular heresy?

- How did the recovery of classical learning affect medieval intellectual life?
- What constituted the "Renaissance of the Twelfth Century"?

C H R O N O L O G Y

POLITICAL DEVELOPMENTS OF THE HIGH MIDDLE AGES, 1000–c. 1250

Capetian dynasty in France	987–1328
Norman Conquest of England	1066
First four crusades	1095–1204
Reign of Frederick Barbarossa	1152–1190
Magna Carta	1215
Reconquest of Spain	c. 1000–c. 1250

In education, thought, and the arts, early medieval Europe had been a backwater, especially in comparison with Byzantium and Islam. By 1300, however, Europe had become the intellectual and artistic leader among these three western civilizations. Westerners boasted that learning and the arts had come to them from Egypt, Greece, and Rome; and that although they were pygmies who sat on the shoulders of giants, they nonetheless saw farther and more clearly than had the intellectual giants of antiquity on whose shoulders they sat. Such boasts were largely justified. In the High Middle Ages, Europeans built their intellectual and artistic accomplishments on ancient foundations, but they also began to make major contributions of their own.

In the High Middle Ages, Europeans built their intellectual and artistic accomplishments on ancient foundations, but they also began to make major contributions of their own.

THE REFORM OF THE CHURCH

How was the Latin Church reformed?

The combined effects of Carolingian collapse, Viking, Muslim, and Magyar attacks, and the growing power of local noble families were disastrous for the religious life of ninth- and tenth-century Europe. For several centuries, church reformers had sought to improve the religious lives of the laity by strengthening the control that powerful bishops exercised over the local clergy within their dioceses. By the middle of the tenth century, however, that strategy lay in ruins. Many parish churches had been abandoned or destroyed, while those that survived were often regarded as the personal possession of some powerful local family, whose responsibility for protecting these churches easily became a license to oppress them. In these circumstances, a parish church frequently became simply a manorial appurtenance, like the lord's mill or oven or forge, which his peasants were obliged to use and from which he took the profits. Even bishoprics fell into the hands of noble families, who appointed relatives to them and or sold them as if they were pieces of family property. Monasteries underwent a similar process of "privatization." Some became dumping grounds for aristocratic younger sons who might live in the monastery without ever taking monastic vows. Other monasteries had troops of knights thrust on them. Some even had lay abbots. It was all very distant from what Saint Benedict had outlined in his *Rule for Monasteries.*

In the absence of effective kingship, bishops were helpless against such entrenched local power. Nor could the papacy correct the situation. Indeed, as the bishops of Rome, the popes themselves were among the worst examples of the negative impact too much local influence could have on the spiritual standards of the clergy. Most of the tenth-century popes were incompetent or corrupt, the sons or tools of powerful Roman families who sought to control the papacy in order to rule the city of Rome itself. Some were astonishingly debauched. The worst of them, John XII, became pope in 955 at the age of eighteen through the influence of his family, which had ruled Rome for half a century. Pope John was nearly illiterate and thoroughly licentious. His critics claimed that female pilgrims would not even enter the Lateran Palace for fear that the pope would molest them; and he is reported to have died in the midst of yet another carnal act, either from sheer amorous exertion or else by the sword of a jealous husband who found the pope in bed with his wife. As the guardian of the tombs of Saints Peter and Paul and the spiritual head of western Christendom, the papacy remained a respected institution, even in its tenth-century nadir. But the popes who occupied Saint Peter's chair left a great deal to be desired as moral and spiritual leaders of Western society.

MONASTIC REFORM, 900–1050

The first stirrings of reform emerged in the monasteries of tenth-century Europe, beginning with that of Cluny in Burgundy. Founded in 910 by a pious nobleman, Cluny was a Benedictine house, but with two important constitutional innovations. One was that in order to keep it free from domination by local noble families or the local bishop, Cluny was placed directly under the protection of the papacy. The second was that it undertook the reform or foundation of a large number of "daughter monasteries." Whereas formerly all Benedictine houses had been independent and equal, Cluny established a network of dependent Cluniac houses across Europe, all of which remained subordinate to the mother house at Cluny. By 1049, there were sixty-seven such Cluniac priories (as the daughter monasteries were called), each one performing the same elaborate round of prayer and worship for which Cluny became famous, and each entirely free from the control of local secular or ecclesiastical powers. Under the rule of a series of pious and remarkably long-lived abbots, Cluny became famous for its high spiritual standards and its carefully ordered liturgical life. In the eyes of the Cluniacs, however, their success depended on their absolute freedom from outside interference in their religious life. When Cluny reformed a monastery, therefore, it insisted on two things: first, that the Benedictine vows of poverty, chastity, and obedience be strictly enforced on all monks; and second, that the selection of new abbots and priors be accomplished by a free election of the monks, without any buying or selling of the office (a sin known as "simony," after Simon Magus, a magician in the New Testament who tried to buy the power of the Holy Spirit from Jesus' disciples).

Cluniac influence was strongest in France and Italy, where the virtual absence of effective kingship made royally sponsored monastic reforms impossible. Here, and also in Lotharingia, pious nobles usually took the lead in promoting monastic reforms. In Germany and England, by contrast, monastic reform emerged during the tenth and eleventh centuries as an essential responsibility of a Christian king. Following Cluniac example, these kings insisted on the strict observance of poverty, chastity, and obedience within the monastery, and instituted elaborate rounds of group liturgical prayer. In contrast to Cluny, however, it was the kings themselves who guaranteed the reformed monasteries' freedom from outside interference, and it was they who appointed the abbots, just as they also appointed the bishops of their kingdom.

As a result of these parallel movements for monastic reform, monasticism became the dominant spiritual model for tenth- and eleventh-century Latin Christianity. The peaceful, orderly round of the monks' daily worship was seen as mirroring the perfect harmony of heaven; their prayers were regarded as uniquely effective in preserving a sinful world from the destruction a just God might otherwise wreak on it; and monks themselves were seen as "angelic men," whose personal poverty, chastity, and perfect obedience faithfully reflected the virtues of heaven itself. But monasteries also had an important influence on patterns of piety outside the cloister. For centuries, monasteries had been the repositories and guardians for the relics of departed saints, whose powers were believed to protect the monasteries that housed their earthly bodies. From the tenth century on, however, monasteries increasingly attracted the attentions of pious laypeople, who came seeking miraculous cures from the saint (or saints) whose relics were housed there. The vast majority of such pilgrimages were to local shrines. But regular long-distance pilgrimage routes also began to develop, to such places as Santiago de Compostela in Spain and the Church of Saint Faith in southern France. Traffic also increased to such traditional pilgrimage sites as Rome and Jerusalem. Pilgrimage was one of the important ways in which the new patterns of Christian piety developed in monasteries began to spread to the laity outside the monastic walls.

THE PAPAL REFORM MOVEMENT

From the monasteries, the reform movement began to affect the bishops also. In England, kings appointed a number of reformed monks to bishoprics. In Germany, kings retained nonmonastic bishops but enforced strict requirements of personal holiness on the bishops and abbots whom they appointed to office. With royal encouragement, bishops also began to rebuild and expand their cathedral churches to make them more suitable reflections of divine majesty, in accordance with Cluniac example. The Cluniacs themselves, however, went further, and began to lobby for the reform of the entire church, including bishops, unreformed monasteries, and even the parish clergy. They centered their attacks upon simony—the buying and selling of church offices—but they also demanded that personal poverty and celibacy be enforced on all monks and priests. This last demand was in some ways the most radical. Although a series of

A MIRACLE OF SAINT FAITH

Although pilgrimages and relics cults had been a part of Christian religious practice for centuries, they became much more central elements in popular piety from the tenth century on. To the monasteries that housed miracle-working relics, pilgrims brought money and spiritual prestige, resulting in competition between monastic houses that sometimes led one house to steal the relics of another. But some critics worried that these newly popular pilgrimage shrines were encouraging idolatry. The author of this account, Bernard of Angers, was one such critic, but in this case he was quickly won over by the evidence of Saint Faith's miracles.

The relics of Saint Faith, a fourth-century martyr, were stolen by the monks of Conques (in southern France) during the ninth century, and became famous during the tenth century for their miraculous healing powers. They were housed in the reliquary shown in the accompanying illustration. Bernard's description of his visit to her shrine is a very revealing account of the initially negative impression this ornate reliquary made on him.

It is an ancient custom in all of Auvergne, Rodez, Toulouse and the neighboring regions that the local saint has a statue of gold, silver, or some other metal . . . [that] serves as a reliquary for the head of the saint or for a part of his body. The learned might see in this a superstition and a vestige of the cult of demons, and I myself . . . had the same impression the first time I saw the statue of Saint Gerard . . . resplendent with gold and stones, with an expression so human that the simple people . . . pretend that it winks at pilgrims whose prayers it answers. I admit to my shame that turning to my friend Bernerius and laughing I whispered to him in Latin, "What do you think of the idol? Wouldn't Jupiter or Mars be happy with it?" . . .

Three days later we arrived at St. Faith. . . . We approached [the reliquary] but the crowd was such that we could not prostrate ourselves like so many others already lying on the floor. Unhappy, I remained standing, fixing my view on the image and murmuring this prayer, "St. Faith, you whose relics rest in this sham, come to my assistance on the day of judgment." And this time I looked at my companion . . . because I found it outrageous that all of these rational beings should be praying to a mute and inanimate object. . . .

Later I greatly regretted to have acted so stupidly toward the saint of God. This was because among other miracles Don Adalgerius, at that time dean and later . . . abbot [of Conques] told me a remarkable account of a cleric named Oldaric. One day when the venerable image had to be taken to another place, . . . he restrained the crowd from bringing offerings and he insulted and belittled the image of the saint. . . . The next night, a lady of imposing severity appeared to him: "You," she said, "how dare you insult my image?" Having said this, she flogged her enemy with a staff. . . . He survived only long enough to tell the vision in the morning.

Thus there is no place left for arguing whether the effigy of St. Faith ought to be venerated since it is clear that he who reproached the holy martyr nevertheless retracted his reproach. Nor is it a spurious idol where nefarious rites of sacrifice or of divination are conducted, but rather a pious memorial of a holy virgin, before which great numbers of faithful people decently and eloquently implore her efficacious intercession for their sins.

Bernard of Angers, *The Book of the Miracles of St. Faith*, chapter 28. Slightly modified from *Readings in Medieval History*, 2d edition, edited and translated by Patrick J. Geary. (Petersborough, Ont.: Broadview Press, 1997), p. 317.

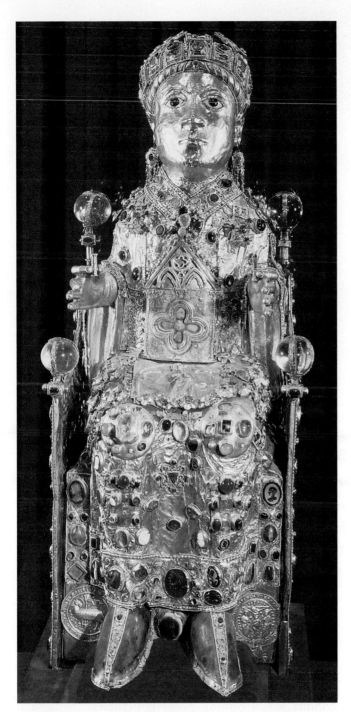

The Reliquary of Saint Faith, early tenth century.

fourth- and fifth-century church councils had declared that priests should be celibate, this requirement had been largely ignored thereafter. In the year 1000, the vast majority of the parish priests across Europe were married. Married bishops were rarer, but not unknown. In Brittany, the archbishop of Dol and his wife publicly celebrated the marriage of their daughters, endowing them with lands belonging to the bish-

opric; in Milan, the archbishops flatly rejected reformers' calls for celibacy, declaring that their patron saint, Bishop Ambrose of Milan, had been married, and that he had granted his diocese permission to have a married priesthood forever.

In Rome, however, the papacy remained resolutely unreformed until 1046, when the German emperor Henry III came to Rome, deposed all three of the local Roman nobles who claimed to be pope, and appointed in their place his own relative, a German monastic reformer who took the name Pope Leo IX (1049–1054). Leo and his supporters (mostly German, but some Italian) quickly took control over the papal court and began to promulgate decrees against simony, clerical marriage, and immorality of all sorts throughout the church. To enforce these decrees, Leo and his entourage traveled through France, Italy, Germany, and Hungary, disciplining and deposing clerics who had purchased their positions or who refused to give up their wives (whom the reformers insisted on calling "concubines"). Implicit in Leo's reforming efforts was thus a new vision of the church itself as a hierarchical organization in which priests obeyed bishops and bishops obeyed the pope not only as the spiritual and doctrinal leader of western Christendom, but as the legal and jurisdictional ruler of the entire Christian church.

Leo and the reform popes were able to enforce their decrees only in those areas of Europe where they could count on the support of secular rulers. Among these secular supporters, the most important was of course the emperor Henry III, whose protection insulated the papal reformers from the Roman noble families who would otherwise have deposed them. In 1056, however, Henry III died, leaving a young child as his heir, the future Henry IV. Without their imperial protector, the reformers were now at the mercy of the Roman political factions. When the reigning reform pope died in 1058, the Roman nobles seized their opportunity to install as pope one of their own lackeys. Briefly, it looked as if the entire reform program might be lost. But the reformers rallied outside Rome, and elected their own pope (who took the name Nicholas II). Allying themselves militarily with the Norman rulers of central and southern Italy, they drove the nonreformed pope out of Rome.

In 1059, Pope Nicholas II issued a new decree on papal elections, vesting the right to elect a pope solely with the cardinals, but "saving the rights of the Emperor." The decree is significant for two quite different reasons. First, it represents a milestone in the evolution of the College of Cardinals as a special body within the

Church. Ever since the tenth century a number of bishops and clerics drawn from churches in and near Rome had taken on an important role as advisers and administrative assistants of the popes. This decree was the first time, however, that the cardinals' powers had been clearly recognized. Thereafter the College of Cardinals took on an increasingly well-defined identity, becoming an important force in creating continuity of papal policy, especially when there was a quick succession of pontiffs. The cardinals still elect the pope today.

The decree was also significant, however, because it opened up a breach between the reform party in Rome and the German imperial court. In the circumstances of 1059, the Electoral Decree was intended to justify the reformers' actions of the previous year and to protect future papal elections from the influence of the Roman aristocracy. But although the decree obviously drew on Cluniac ideals about free elections as an essential element in a reformed church, it was not intended to deprive the German emperor of his traditional role as papal protector. The simple fact was, however, that in 1059 there was no emperor who could play this role; and if the alternative was the return of the Roman nobility and the destruction of the entire reform effort, then even an alliance with the brutal and unreliable Normans seemed preferable. Nonetheless, the electoral decree greatly offended the advisors of the young king Henry IV, who saw it as a challenge to the emperors' rights to nominate new popes, and who also bitterly resented the reformers' alliance with the Normans, whose designs on imperial territories in central Italy were well known. The resulting hostility between the young king's regents and the papal court poisoned the atmosphere in which King Henry IV grew to maturity.

THE INVESTITURE CONFLICT

A new and momentous phase in the history of the reform movement began in 1073 with the election of Pope Gregory VII (1073–1085). Gregory was a Roman whose election was violently supported by a mob of Roman citizens. Gregory was already a well-known reformer with long experience at the papal court. It is likely that he would have been elected by the cardinals anyway, even without the interference of the Roman mob. But the circumstances of his election clearly vio-

lated the terms of the 1059 Electoral Decree, and this fact weakened Gregory in his first few years as pope. Henry IV was also anxious for a reconciliation with Rome, not least because between 1073 and 1075 he was involved in a major civil war with his own nobility in Saxony. Both Gregory and Henry began, therefore, by treating one another with great deference. Henry blamed the advisors of his youth for the troubles that had arisen between his own court and Rome, and promised to make amends. Gregory, in turn, spoke of pope and emperor as the two eyes of a single, Christian body, and promised to leave the church in Henry's care if he, Gregory, should lead (as he briefly hoped to do) a military expedition eastward against Islam. On the surface, it appeared that the harmonious relations between papacy and empire that had existed under Henry's father had been fully restored.

By the end of 1075, however, relations between the two men were at a breaking point. For the next half century, western Europe would be riven by conflict between the papacy and the empire—a conflict that would permanently alter the relationship between spiritual and temporal authority in western Christendom. Superficially, the issue that divided Gregory and Henry was whether Henry or any other layman could appoint a bishop or abbot and then dress him with the symbols of his spiritual office, a practice known as "lay investiture." In fact, however, the "Investiture Conflict" raised fundamental issues about the nature of Christian kingship, the relationship between political and religious authority, and the control that popes and kings should exercise over the clergy. Not all these issues were fully resolved by 1122, when a compromise known as the Concordat of Worms finally ended the Investiture Conflict. But the conflict was a turning point nonetheless, because it brought to a permanent end the old Carolingian traditions of sacred kingship and established once and for all the independent jurisdictional authority of the church versus all lay rulers.

Gregory was a devoted church reformer whose goals were the traditional ones of ending simony and clerical marriage. Unlike previous papal reformers, however, Gregory became convinced that these goals could not be achieved until the Cluniac goal of ensuring free elections to all church offices had first been realized. Gregory therefore proceeded to prohibit all cler-

The "Investiture Conflict" raised fundamental issues about the nature of Christian kingship, the relationship between political and religious authority, and the control that popes and kings should exercise over the clergy.

Henry IV and Gregory VII. In the top panel, King Henry appoints Wibert, Archbishop of Milan, to be the new pope, and drives Pope Gregory from Rome. In the lower panel, Pope Gregory is received by the bishops of the Norman kingdom of southern Italy, and then dies in exile. From a twelfth-century German manuscript.

election had violated the terms of the 1059 Electoral Decree, and calling on him to resign. Gregory responded by excommunicating Henry, along with a large number of German and Italian bishops who were supporting Henry.

In itself, the excommunication of a king was not terribly unusual. As we have seen, in the fourth century, Saint Ambrose had even excommunicated the Roman emperor Theodosius the Great. Gregory, however, went much further by equating excommunication with deposition, declaring that since Henry was no longer a faithful son of the church, he was therefore no longer the king of Germany. Gregory now called on Henry's subjects to rebel, prompting the Saxon nobility to renew the civil war that had ended only a few months before. In January 1077, Henry was forced to make a humiliating public submission to Pope Gregory at Canossa in the Italian Alps; but when the pope absolved him of his excommunication, Henry used the opportunity to rally his forces, crush his Saxon opponents, and drive Gregory himself from Rome. In 1085, the aged pope died in exile at Salerno, a virtual prisoner of his Norman allies. His last words were reportedly, "I have loved justice and hated iniquity; that is why I die in exile."

By instinct, Pope Gregory was a radical whose confidence in his own rectitude knew no bounds. Early in his career he had been part of the delegation that provoked the 1054 schism with the Byzantine church by demanding that the patriarch of Constantinople acknowledge the primacy of the papacy. As pope, Gregory was convinced that he spoke with Saint Peter's voice and so could not err. When told that his ideas were novel, he replied "The Lord did not say 'I am custom'; the Lord said 'I am truth.'" When it was suggested to him that his policies had brought war, not peace, he replied by citing Scripture: "Cursed be he that shall withhold his sword from blood." His calls for the people of Germany to rise up against their errant king and his sinful bishops were nothing short of revolutionary. Even his admirers referred to him as a "Holy Satan," recalling the rebellious angel whose pride had caused his downfall.

ics from accepting any church office from a layman, declaring this prohibition to be "a truth . . . necessary for salvation." Henry IV flatly refused to accept this decree, not only because it infringed on his own traditional rights as a Carolingian-style king and emperor, but also because the bishops and abbots of Germany and northern Italy were critically important to his own ability to rule his kingdoms. Henry proceeded, therefore, to appoint and invest a new archbishop in Milan in defiance of Gregory's prohibition. Gregory responded by reminding Henry that he, Gregory, occupied Saint Peter's chair, and that Henry therefore owed to Gregory the same obedience he owed to Saint Peter, who was the gatekeeper to heaven. To drive the point home, Gregory excommunicated a number of Henry's advisors, including several of the north Italian bishops who had participated in the investiture of the new archbishop of Milan. Henry thereupon renounced his obedience to Gregory, reminding the pope that his

Gregory's radical instincts must not obscure, however, his profoundly traditional vision of Christendom. Although the ultimate solution to the Investiture Conflict was to distinguish between "church" and "state" by reserving the symbols of spiritual office to the clergy while permitting laymen to award the symbols of temporal rule, such a distinction was no part of Gregory's own world view. Indeed, it was precisely because neither Henry nor Gregory could conceive of Christendom as anything other than a thoroughly unified religious and political society that the conflict between them was so intractable. Both Henry and Gregory shared the standard Carolingian presumption that it was the responsibility of earthly rulers to lead their subjects to heaven. They disagreed only about whether the supreme ruler within this unified Christian society should be the emperor or the pope. To borrow Gregory's own metaphor, both Gregory and Henry agreed that Christendom was a single body with two eyes. The issue between them was whether pope or emperor should be the lead eye, and so determine the direction in which the Christian body would walk. Neither could imagine a world in which a bishop's spiritual office could be separated from the lands and military forces he controlled, or in which there could be two entirely separate systems of courts, one dealing with religious matters and controlled by the papacy, the other dealing with secular matters and controlled by kings. Without such a division between the spiritual and the temporal, however, the Investiture Conflict was irresolvable. Neither pope nor emperor was powerful enough to defeat the other; and on some level, all Europe was agreed that both spiritual and temporal authorities were necessary. For had not Jesus himself declared that two swords (both of course borne by Peter, as papal champions were quick to point out) were sufficient for the days of trouble that lay ahead?

The consequences of the Investiture Conflict were thus quite different from what Pope Gregory or King Henry had imagined. On the immediate issue of lay investiture, the Concordat of Worms was a compromise. The German emperor was forbidden to invest prelates with the religious symbols of their office, but was allowed to invest them with the symbols of their rights as temporal rulers because the emperor was recognized as their temporal overlord. In practice, the German emperors, like the other kings of western Europe, thus managed to retain a great deal of influence over appointments to bishoprics and abbeys despite allowing the appearance of free elections.

In a larger sense, however, the ultimate consequence of the Investiture Conflict was to create a lasting conceptual distinction between religion and politics in western Europe, and to identify the church with religious authority and the state with political authority. Both ideas had been largely absent from western Europe since the fourth century Constantinian revolution. When the Investiture Conflict began, Henry's principal supporters were his bishops. Gregory's supporters were, for the most part, the Saxon nobility and the other disaffected German princes. In no sense, therefore, did the Investiture Conflict begin as a "church-state" conflict. By 1122, however, that is what it had become. The Concordat of Worms resolved the papal-imperial conflict by distinguishing between the temporal power of kings and the spiritual power of the clergy. It also firmly identified the bishops as a part of a hierarchical clerical order headed by the pope. The boundaries between temporal and spiritual authority would continue to be subject to controversy in medieval Europe. Should kings or clerics judge clergy who committed secular crimes? Who should rule on the validity of marriages when rights to inherit property were at issue? But these were jurisdictional conflicts that sought to define the boundaries between religion and politics. These conflicts did not challenge the fundamental presumption that such a distinction existed. Therefore, these conflicts were resolvable through law—one reason that the elaboration of legal systems, both ecclesiastical and secular, became such a preoccupation for twelfth- and thirteenth-century western Europe. In this respect also, the Investiture Conflict marks a watershed in European history.

> The ultimate consequence of the Investiture Conflict was to create a lasting conceptual distinction between religion and politics in western Europe.

THE CONSOLIDATION OF THE PAPAL MONARCHY

The Concordat of Worms was a compromise, but the Investiture Conflict as a whole was a victory for the papacy. The conflict helped rally the Western clergy behind the pope, strengthening the papacy's claim to jurisdictional supremacy over the entire clerical hierarchy. The dramatic struggle also galvanized the European populace. As one contemporary reported, nothing else was talked about "even in the women's spinning rooms and the artisans' workshops." Pope Gregory and his successors had urged the common people of Europe to reject the authority of simoniac bishops and married priests. Thousands had responded, sometimes with violence. The result was a vastly greater popular interest in religious matters, which the church thereafter would struggle to contain within the bounds of religious orthodoxy.

Like Gregory VII, the popes of the twelfth and thirteenth century were fully committed to establishing the monarchical authority of the papacy over the church. But they were far less impetuous than Gregory had been, choosing instead to pursue their aims by carefully building up the governmental apparatus of the church. The papal writing office (known as the Chancery) was already the most sophisticated in Europe, producing thousands of letters annually on a huge variety of subjects. Specially commissioned papal officials ("legates") were also sent out from Rome to convey and enforce papal commands. Many of these commands arose from the hundreds (and eventually thousands) of legal cases that poured into Rome from litigants seeking justice from the pope. In turn, this growing mass of litigation encouraged the development of an authoritative body of church law by which such cases could be resolved. The key step in this development was taken around 1140 in Bologna by a law teacher named Gratian, whose massive compilation and codification of the decrees of previous popes and church councils (known as the *Decretum* or, more descriptively, as *The Concord of Discordant Canons*) quickly became the standard collection of church ("canon") law.

Gratian's *Decretum* claimed ecclesiastical jurisdiction for all sorts of cases pertaining not only to the clergy but also to the laity, including such matters as marriage, inheritance, and wills. Although all such cases were supposed to be heard first in local church courts, the popes insisted that they alone could issue dispensations from the strict letter of the law and that the papal consistory—the pope and the cardinals—should be the final court of appeals for all canon-law cases. As the power of the papacy and the prestige of the church mounted, cases in canon-law courts and appeals to Rome rapidly increased. By the mid-twelfth century legal expertise had become so important that almost all popes were trained canon lawyers, whereas previously they had usually been monks. Purists decried this de-

> By the mid-twelfth century legal expertise had become so important that almost all popes were trained canon lawyers, whereas previously they had usually been monks.

velopment, but it was an inevitable consequence of the growing power and sophistication of the papal monarchy itself.

THE REIGN OF INNOCENT III

By common consent the most capable and successful of all the high medieval popes was Innocent III (1198–1216). Innocent, who was elected at the age of thirty-seven, was one of the youngest and most vigorous individuals ever to be raised to the papacy; more than that, he was expertly trained in theology and had also studied canon law. His major goal was to unify all Christendom under papal hegemony and thereby to bring about the "right order in the world" so fervently desired by Pope Gregory VII. Unlike Gregory, Innocent never questioned the right of kings and princes to rule directly in the secular sphere. But Innocent believed nonetheless that as pope he was obliged to discipline kings whenever they sinned. Needless to say, this opened a wide arena for papal involvement in temporal affairs. And he was no less insistent on the obligation of every Christian to obey Saint Peter's representative than Gregory VII had been. As Innocent himself remarked, just "as every knee is bowed to Jesus . . . so all men should obey His Vicar [i.e., the pope]."

Innocent sought to implement his goals in many different ways. In order to place papal independence on a solid territorial foundation, Innocent consolidated and

CHRONOLOGY

REFORM OF THE CHURCH, 900–1215

Monastic reform	900–1050
Cluniac priories	910–1050
Papal reform movement	1049–1122
Pope Leo IX	1049–1054
Pope Gregory VII	1073–1085
Investiture Conflict	1075–1122
Concordat of Worms	1122
Consolidation of the Papal monarchy	1100–1216
Concord of Discordant Canons	1140
Reign of Innocent III	1198–1216
Fourth Lateran Council	1215

Pope Innocent III. A thirteenth-century fresco from the lower church of Sacro Speco, Subiaco, in Italy.

expanded the papacy's territories in central Italy. For this reason Innocent is often regarded as the founder of the Papal States, of which Vatican City is the last surviving modern remnant. Innocent's policies in central Italy bear some resemblance to those pursued by the twelfth-century kings of France in the Île-de-France; but he was never able to subject the independent urban communities of central Italy to effective papal control. In other projects he was more completely successful. In Germany, he engineered the triumph of his own candidate for the imperial office, the emperor Frederick II —a triumph his papal successors would live to regret. Innocent disciplined the French king Philip Augustus for his marital misconduct, and forced King John of England to accept Stephen Langton, the pope's own choice, as archbishop of Canterbury. Innocent also compelled John to grant England to the papacy as a fief; and he claimed, with varying degrees of success, a comparable feudal overlordship of Aragon, Sicily, and

Hungary. When southern France was threatened by the spread of the Albigensian heresy (to be discussed later), the pope called a crusade to extinguish it by force. He also levied the first income tax on the clergy to support a crusade to the Holy Land. The crowning achievement of Innocent's pontificate, however, was the summoning of the Fourth Lateran Council to Rome in 1215. This representative assembly of the entire western Church defined central dogmas of the faith and made the leadership of the papacy within Christendom more apparent than ever. The pope was now clearly both disciplining kings and ruling over the church without hindrance.

POPES OF THE THIRTEENTH CENTURY

Innocent's reign was certainly the zenith of the papal monarchy, but it also sowed some of the seeds of future ruin. Innocent himself could administer the Papal

States and seek new sources of income without seeming to compromise the spiritual dignity of his office. But future popes who followed his policies had less of his stature and thus began to appear more like ordinary, acquisitive rulers. Moreover, because the Papal States bordered on the kingdom of Sicily, Innocent's successors quickly came into conflict with the neighboring ruler, who was none other than Innocent's protégé Frederick II. Innocent had raised up Frederick, but he did not suppose that Frederick would later become an inveterate opponent of papal power in Italy.

At first these and other problems were not fully apparent. The popes of the thirteenth century continued to enhance their powers and centralize the government of the church. They gradually asserted the right to name candidates for ecclesiastical positions, both high and low, and they asserted control over the curriculum and doctrine taught at the University of Paris. But they also became involved in a protracted political struggle

Charles of Anjou. One of the earliest known medieval statues that may have been done from life.

that led to their own demise as temporal powers. This struggle began with the attempt of the popes to destroy Frederick II. To some degree they were acting in self-defense because Frederick threatened their own rule in central Italy. But in combating him they overemployed their spiritual weapons. Instead of merely excommunicating and deposing Frederick, they also called a crusade against him—the first time a crusade was called on a large scale for blatantly political purposes.

After Frederick's death in 1250 a succession of popes made a still worse mistake by renewing and maintaining their crusade against all of the emperor's heirs, whom they called the "viper brood." In order to implement this crusade they became preoccupied with raising funds, and they sought and won as their military champion a younger son from the French royal house, Charles of Anjou. But Charles helped the popes only for the purely political motive of acquiring the kingdom of Sicily for himself. Charles won Sicily in 1268 by defeating the last of Frederick II's male heirs. But he then taxed the realm so excessively that the Sicilians revolted in the "Sicilian Vespers" of 1282 and offered their crown to the king of Aragon, who had married Frederick II's granddaughter. The king of Aragon accordingly entered the Italian arena and came close to winning Frederick's former kingdom for himself. To prevent such an event Charles of Anjou and the reigning pope prevailed on the king of France—then Philip III (1270–1285)—to embark on a crusade against Aragon. This crusade was a terrible failure, and Philip III died on it. In the wake of these events Philip's son, Philip IV, resolved to alter the traditional French propapal policy. By that time France had become so strong that such a decision was fateful. More than that, by misusing the institution of the crusade and trying to raise increasingly large sums of money to support it, the popes lost much of their spiritual prestige. In 1291 the last crusader outpost in the Holy Land fell without any papal help being offered. Instead, the popes were still trying to salvage their losing crusade against Aragon. Pope Boniface VIII's papal jubilee of 1300, which offered a full crusader's indulgence to anyone who made a pilgrimage to Rome, was a tacit recognition that the Eternal City and not the Holy Land would henceforth be the central goal of Christian pilgrimage.

DECLINE OF THE PAPAL MONARCHY

The temporal might of the papal monarchy finally collapsed in the reign of Boniface VIII (1294–1303). Not all Boniface's troubles were of his own making.

Pope Boniface VIII (1294–1303) commissioned dozens of statues of himself which he distributed throughout the papal states. Despite its idealized features, this statue—from the Museo Civico in Bologna—does also suggest something of the pope's pugnacious obstinacy.

His greatest obstacle was that the national monarchies had gained more of their subjects' loyalties than the papacy could draw on because of the steady growth of royal power and the erosion of papal prestige. Boniface also had the misfortune to succeed a particularly pious, although inept, pope who resigned his office within a year. Since Boniface was entirely lacking in conventional piety or humility, the contrast turned many Christian observers against him. Some even maintained—incorrectly—that Boniface had convinced his predecessor to resign and had murdered him shortly afterward. Boniface ruled assertively and presided over the first papal "jubilee" in Rome in 1300.

This was an apparent, but, as events would show, hollow demonstration of papal might.

Two disputes with the kings of England and France proved to be Boniface's undoing. The first concerned the clerical taxation that had been initiated by Innocent III. Although Innocent had levied this tax to support a crusade and had collected it himself, during the course of the thirteenth century the kings of England and France had begun to levy and collect clerical taxes on the pretext that they would use the funds to help the popes on future crusades to the Holy Land or aid in papal crusades against the Hohenstaufens. Then, at the end of the century, the kings started to levy their own war taxes on the clergy without any pretexts at all. Boniface understandably tried to prohibit this step, but quickly found that he had lost the support of the English and French clergy. Thus when the kings offered resistance, he had to back down.

Boniface's second dispute was with King Philip IV of France, who deliberately challenged the pope by preparing to try a French bishop for treason, in violation of canon-law protections for the clergy. As in the earlier struggle between Gregory VII and Henry IV of Germany, a bitter propaganda war ensued, but now hardly anyone listened to the pope. Instead, Philip pressed absurd charges of heresy against Boniface and sent his minions to arrest the pope to stand trial. At the papal residence of Anagni in 1303 Boniface, who was in his seventies, was captured and mistreated by Philip's forces. Although the pope was finally rescued by the local citizens, the shock of these events was too much for the old man's strength, and he died a month later. But still Philip pressed his advantage. He forced the new pope, Clement V, not only to justify his attack on Boniface, but to thank him publically for his zealous defence of the Catholic faith. Thereafter, any shred of papal independence in regard to the interests of the French monarchy was gone. For the next seventy years, the popes would reside not in Rome, but in Avignon, on the borders of the kingdom of France; and the papacy would come to be regarded as a virtual pawn of French diplomatic interests.

The humiliating defeat of Pope Boniface VIII at the hands of King Philip of France illustrates the enormous gap that had opened up by 1300 between the rhetoric and the reality of papal power. Although Boniface continued to lay claim to a universal spiritual and temporal authority over Christendom, declaring that kings ruled only through the "will and sufferance" of the church, in fact the papal monarchy now exercised its authority only through the will and sufferance of kings. The growth of nationalism, combined with the increasing sophistication of royal justice, royal taxation, and royal propaganda, had shifted the balance of power in Europe decisively toward the state and away from the church. Europeans were not less religious than they had been before, quite the opposite. But from the later thirteenth century on, pious Christians would look increasingly toward the state, and not toward the papacy, to spearhead campaigns of moral and spiritual improvement within their territories. After one hundred fifty years during which the religious nature of royal authority had been steadily undermined, the kings of the later thirteenth century were beginning to restore their sacred luster. This trend would continue throughout the later Middle Ages. It would be shattered, finally, only in the seventeenth century, at the end of a century of religious wars brought on by the Protestant Reformation. Only then would the distinctions between religion and politics established by the Investiture Conflict be fully and firmly established as fundamental principles of European life.

THE OUTBURST OF RELIGIOUS VITALITY

How did the Latin Church control popular heresy?

The papal reform movement spearheaded by Pope Gregory stimulated a European religious revival for two reasons. One was that the campaign to cleanse the Church actually achieved a large measure of success: the laity could now respect the clergy more, and many were inspired to join the clergy themselves. According to a reliable estimate, the number of people who joined monastic orders in England increased tenfold between 1066 and 1200, a statistic that does not include the increase in priests. The other reason that the work of Gregory VII in particular helped inspire a revival was that Gregory explicitly called on the laity to help discipline their priests. In letters of great propagandistic power he denounced the sins of "fornicating priests" (by which he really meant just married ones) and urged the laity to drive them from their pulpits or boycott their services. Not surprisingly, he touched off something close to a vigilante movement in many parts of Europe. This excitement, taken together with the

fact that the papal struggle with Henry IV was really the first European event of universal interest, increased religious commitment immensely. Until about 1050, most western Europeans were Christians in name, but after the Gregorian period Christianity was becoming an ideal and a practice that really began to direct human lives.

CISTERCIANS AND CARTHUSIANS

One of the most visible manifestations of the new piety was the spread of the Cistercian movement in the twelfth century. By around 1100 no form of Benedictine monasticism seemed fully satisfactory to aspirants to holiness who sought great asceticism and, above all, intense "interiority"—unrelenting self-examination and meditative striving toward knowledge of God. The result was the founding of new orders to provide for the fullest expression of monastic idealism. One was the Carthusian order, whose monks were required to live in separate cells, abstain from meat, and fast three days each week on bread, water, and salt. The Carthusians never sought to attract great numbers and therefore remained a small group. But the same was by no means true of the Cistercians. The latter were monks who were first organized around 1100 and who sought to follow the Benedictine rule in the purest and most austere way possible. In order to avoid worldly temptations, they founded new monasteries in forests and wastelands as far away from civilization as possible. They shunned all unnecessary church decoration and ostentatious utensils, abandoned the Cluniac stress on an elaborate liturgy in favor of more contemplation and private prayer, and seriously committed themselves to hard manual labor. Under the charismatic leadership of Saint Bernard of Clairvaux (1090–1153), a spellbinding preacher, brilliant writer, and the most influential European religious personality of his age, the Cistercian order grew exponentially. There were only five houses in 1115 but no less than 343 at the time of Bernard's death in 1153. This growth not only meant that many more men were becoming monks, but also that many pious lay people were donating funds and lands to support the new monasteries.

At the same time that more people were entering or patronizing new monasteries, the very nature of religious belief and devotion was also changing. One of many examples was a shift away from the cult of saints to emphasis on the worship of Jesus and veneration of the Virgin Mary. Older Benedictine monasteries encouraged the veneration of the relics of local saints that

The Mystery of the Mass. In this illustration by the twelfth-century visionary Hildegard of Bingen, the Church (shown as a crowned queen, and associated by Hildegard with the Virgin Mary, the Queen of Heaven) receives the blood of Christ in a communion chalice, while below, the bread and wine of the Mass, which have now become the body and blood of Christ, rest on the altar.

they housed in order to attract pilgrims and donations. But the Cluniac and Cistercian orders were both centralized congregations that allowed only one saintly patron for all their houses: respectively, Saint Peter (to honor the founder of the papacy) and the Virgin. Since these monasteries contained few relics (the Virgin was thought to have been taken bodily into heaven, so there were no bodily relics of her at all) they deemphasized the cult. The veneration of relics was replaced by a concentration on the Eucharist, or sacrament of the Lord's Supper. Of course celebration of the Eucharist had always been an important part of the Christian faith, but only in the twelfth century was it made really central, for only then did theologians fully work out the doctrine of transubstantiation. According to this doctrine, the priest during mass cooperates with God in the performance of a miracle whereby the bread and wine on the altar are changed or "transubstantiated" into the body and blood of Christ. Popular reverence for the Eucharist became so great in the twelfth century that for the first time the practice of elevating the consecrated bread, or host, was initiated so that the whole congregation could see it. The new theology of the Eucharist greatly enhanced the dignity of the priest and also encouraged the faithful to meditate on the sufferings of Christ. As a result many developed an intense sense of identification with Christ and tried to imitate his life in different ways.

THE CULT OF THE VIRGIN MARY

Coming a very close second to the renewed worship of Christ in the twelfth century was veneration of the Virgin Mary. This development was more unprecedented because until then the Virgin had been only negligibly honored in the Western church. Exactly why veneration of the Virgin became so pronounced in the twelfth century is not fully clear, but whatever the explanation, in the twelfth century the cult of Mary blossomed throughout all of western Europe. The Cistercians made her their patron saint, Saint Bernard constantly taught about her life and virtues, and practically all the magnificent new cathedrals of the age were dedicated to her: there was Notre Dame ("Our Lady") of Paris, and also a "Notre Dame" in Chartres, Rheims, Amiens, Rouen, Laon, and many other places. Mary's theological role was that of intercessor with her son for the salvation of human souls. It was held that Mary was the mother of all, an infinite repository of mercy who urged the salvation even of sinners so long as they were loving and ultimately

Mary and Eve. The "correct" medieval theological view of women. On the left (Latin: *sinister*) side of the naked Adam the naked Eve takes the apple of sin from the serpent and feeds it to erring mortals while a skeleton waits to carry them to hell. On Adam's right Mary counteracts Eve by feeding a different "fruit"—the Eucharistic wafer—to the devout.

HILDEGARD OF BINGEN

Not only did a woman, Mary, gain a particularly prominent role in the religious cult of the twelfth century, but a few living women gained great religious authority. By far the most famous and influential was the German nun and visionary Hildegard of Bingen (1098–1179). Hildegard's descriptions of her religious visions, dictated in freshly original Latin prose, were so compelling that contemporaries had no difficulty in believing that she was directly inspired by God. Consequently when the pope visited Germany he gave her his blessing, and religious and secular leaders sought her advice. Hildegard wrote on a variety of other subjects such as pharmacology and women's medicine. She also composed religious songs whose beauty has been rediscovered in recent times. Visionary though she was, she probably would be surprised to see people today looking for her works in racks of compact discs, where she is often alphabetized as "Bingen" between Beethoven and Brahms.

THE CHALLENGE OF POPULAR HERESY

Sometimes the great religious enthusiasm of the twelfth century went beyond the bounds approved by the church. After Gregory VII had called on the laity to help discipline their clergy it was difficult to control lay enthusiasm. As the twelfth century progressed and the papal monarchy concentrated on strengthening its legal and financial administration, some people began to wonder whether the church, which had once been so inspiring, had not begun to lose sight of its idealistic goals. Another difficulty was that the growing emphasis on the miraculous powers of priests tended to inhibit the religious role of the laity and place it in a distinct position of spiritual inferiority. The result was that in the second half of the twelfth century large-scale movements of popular heresy swept over western Europe for the first time in its history.

The two major twelfth-century heresies were Catharism and Waldensianism. The Cathars, who were strongest in northern Italy and southern France, believed that all matter was created by an evil principle and that holiness required extreme ascetic practices. Some Cathars even argued that there were two gods, one good, the other evil; that the created world was entirely in the power of the evil god; and that spiritual people must seek to escape it. Although such teachings were at variance with Christianity, most Cathar followers believed themselves nonetheless to be Christians.

contrite. Numerous stories circulated about seeming reprobates who were saved because they venerated Mary, who then spoke for them at the hour of death.

The significance of the new cult was manifold. For the first time a woman was given a central and honored place in the Christian religion. Theologians still taught that sin had entered the world through Eve, the first woman; but they now counterbalanced this by explaining how the triumph over sin had come through Mary, who gave birth to Christ, the second Adam. Artists and writers who portrayed Mary were also able to concentrate on femininity and scenes of human tenderness and family life. This contributed greatly to a general softening of artistic and literary style. But perhaps most important of all, the rise of the cult of Mary was closely associated with a general rise of hopefulness and optimism in the twelfth-century West.

THE CONVERSION OF PETER WALDO

The founder of the Waldensian heresy was a layman, Peter Waldo, who was moved to take up a life of preaching and poverty after hearing the story of Saint Alexis, who had abandoned his family and his wealth to pursue a religious life. Waldo's story bears remarkable similarities to the story of Saint Francis of Assisi a generation or so later. But whereas Saint Francis succeeded in getting his movement recognized by the church, Waldo and his followers were ultimately declared heretical because they refused to accept the church's authority to prohibit them from preaching. Waldo's story illustrates the new spiritual impulses that were influencing lay people in twelfth-century Europe.

At about this time, in 1173, there was a citizen of Lyons named Peter Waldo, who had made a great deal of money by the evil means of usury. One Sunday he lingered by a crowd that had gathered round a traveling story-teller, and was much struck by his words. He took him home with him, and listened carefully to his story of how St. Alexis had died a holy death in his father's house. Next morning Waldo hastened to the schools of theology to seek advice about his soul. When he had been told of the many ways of coming to God he asked the master whether any of them was more sure and reliable than the rest. The master quoted to him the words of the Lord, "If thou wilt be perfect go sell what thou hast and give it to the poor and thou shalt have treasure in heaven. And come follow me."

Waldo returned to his wife and gave her the choice between having all his movable wealth or his property in land. . . . She was very upset at having to do this and chose the property. From his movable wealth he returned what he had acquired wrongly, conferred a large portion on his two daughters, whom he placed in the order of Fontevrault without his wife's knowledge, and gave a still larger amount to the poor.

At this time a terrible famine was raging through Gaul and Germany. . . . from May 27 until August 1, Waldo generously distributed bread, soup and meat to anyone who came to him. On the Assumption of the Virgin [August 15] he scattered money among the poor in the streets saying, "You cannot serve two masters, God and Mammon." The people around thought he had gone out of his senses. Then he stood up on a piece of high ground and said, "Friends and fellow-citizens, I am not mad as you think. . . . I know that many of you disapprove of my having acted so publicly. I have done so both for my own sake and for yours: for my sake, because anybody who sees me with money in future will be able to say that I am mad; for your sake, so that you may learn to place your hopes in God and not in wealth.". . .

1177   Waldo, the citizen of Lyons whom we have already mentioned, who had vowed to God that he would possess neither gold nor silver, and take no thought for the morrow, began to make converts to his opinions. Following his example they gave all they had to the poor, and willingly devoted themselves to poverty. Gradually, both in public and in private they began to inveigh against both their own sins and those of others. . . .

1178   Pope Alexander III held a council at the Lateran palace. . . . The council condemned heresy and all those who fostered and defended heretics. The pope embraced Waldo, and applauded the vows of voluntary poverty which he had taken, but forbade him and his companion to assume the office of preaching except at the request of the priests. They obeyed this instruction for a time, but later they disobeyed, and affronted many, bringing ruin on themselves.

Robert I. Moore, ed. and trans. *The Birth of Popular Heresy*. (London: Edward Arnold Publishers, 1975), pp. 111–113 (slightly modified).

They were attracted to the heresy mainly because it challenged the authority of insufficiently zealous Catholic priests and provided an outlet for intense lay spirituality. Noblewomen in southern France played a particularly important role in the spread of Catharism, sheltering the sect's wandering preachers and converting their households to the new faith.

More typical of twelfth-century religious dissent was Waldensianism, a movement that originated in the French city of Lyons and spread to much of southern France, northern Italy, and Germany. Waldensians were lay folk who wished to imitate the life of Christ and the apostles to the fullest. They therefore translated and studied the Gospels and dedicated themselves to lives of poverty and preaching. Since the earliest Waldensians did not attack any Catholic doctrines, the church hierarchy did not at first interfere with them. Indeed, the Waldensians may have seen themselves initially as a countermovement to Catharism. But the papacy forbade the Waldensians to preach without authorization and condemned them for heresy when they refused to obey. At that point they became more radical and started to create an alternative church, which they maintained offered the only route to salvation.

When Innocent III became pope in 1198 he was faced with a very serious challenge from growing heresies. His response was characteristically decisive and fateful for the future of the church. Simply stated it was two pronged. On the one hand, Innocent resolved to crush all disobedience to papal authority, but on the other, he decided to patronize whatever idealistic religious groups he could find that were willing to acknowledge obedience. Papal monarchy could thus be protected without frustrating all dynamic spirituality within the church. Innocent not only launched a full-scale crusade against the Cathars, he also encouraged the use against heresy of judicial procedures that included ruthless techniques of religious "inquisition." In 1252 the papacy first approved the use of torture in inquisitorial trials, and burning at the stake became the prevalent punishment for religious disobedience. Neither the crusade nor the inquisitorial procedures were fully successful in uprooting the Catharian heresy in Innocent's own lifetime, but the extension of such measures did result in destroying the heresy by fire and sword after about the middle of the thirteenth century. Waldensians, like Cathars, were hunted down by inquisitors and their numbers reduced, but scattered Waldensian groups did manage to survive until modern times.

Another aspect of Innocent's program was to pronounce formally the new religious doctrines that enhanced the special status of priests and the ecclesiastical hierarchy. Thus at the Fourth Lateran Council of 1215 he reaffirmed the doctrine that the sacraments administered by the church were the indispensable means of procuring God's grace, and that no one could be saved without them. The decrees of the Lateran Council emphasized two sacraments: the Eucharist and penance. The doctrine of transubstantiation was formally defined. All Catholics were required—as they still are—to confess their sins to a priest and then receive the Eucharist at least once a year. The council also promulgated other doctrinal definitions and disciplinary measures that served both to oppose heresy and to assert the unique dignity of the clergy.

FRANCISCANS AND DOMINICANS

As stated above, the other side of Innocent's policy was to support obedient idealistic movements within the church. The most important of these were the new orders of friars—the Dominicans and the Franciscans. Friars resembled monks in vowing to follow a rule, but they differed greatly from monks in their actual conduct. Above all, they did not withdraw from society into monasteries. Assuming that the way of life originally followed by Christ and the apostles was the most holy, they wandered through the countryside and especially the towns, preaching and offering spiritual guidance. They also accepted voluntary poverty and begged for their subsistence. In these respects they resembled the Waldensian heretics, but they professed unquestioning obedience to the pope and sought to fight heresy themselves.

The Dominican order, founded by the Spaniard Saint Dominic (1170–1221) and approved by Innocent III in 1216, was particularly dedicated to the fight against heresy and also to the conversion of Jews and Muslims. At first the Dominicans hoped to achieve these ends by preaching and public debate. Hence they became intellectually oriented. Many members of the order gained teaching positions in the infant European universities and contributed much to the development of philosophy and theology. The most influential thinker of the thirteenth century, Saint Thomas Aquinas, was a Dominican who addressed one of his major theological works to converting the "gentiles" (that is, all non-Christians). The Dominicans always retained their reputation for learning, but they also came to believe that stubborn heretics were best controlled by legal procedures. Accordingly, they became the leading medieval administrators of inquisitorial trials.

In its origins the Franciscan order was quite different from the Dominican, being characterized less by a commitment to doctrine and discipline and more by a sense of emotional fervor. Whereas Saint Dominic and his earliest followers had been ordained priests who were licensed to preach by their office, the founder of the Franciscans, the Italian Saint Francis of Assisi (1182–1226), was a layman who behaved at first remarkably like a social rebel and a heretic. The son of a rich merchant, he became dissatisfied with the materialistic values of his father and determined to become a servant of the poor. Giving away all his property, he threw off his clothes in public, put on the tattered garb of a beggar, and began without official approval to preach salvation in town squares and minister to outcasts in the darkest corners of Italian cities. He rigorously imitated the life of Christ and displayed indifference to doctrine, form, and ceremony, except for reverencing the sacrament of the Eucharist. But he did wish to gain the support of the pope. One day in 1209 he appeared in Rome with a small ragged band to request that Innocent III approve a primitive "rule" that was little more than a collection of Gospel precepts. Some other pope might have rejected the layman Francis as a hopelessly unworldly religious anarchist. But Francis was thoroughly willing to profess obedience, and Innocent had the genius to approve Francis's rule and grant him permission to preach. With papal support, the Franciscan order spread, and though it gradually became more "civilized," conceding the importance of administrative stability and doctrinal training for all its members, it continued to specialize in revivalistic outdoor preaching and in offering a model for "apostolic living" within an orthodox framework. Thus Innocent managed to harness a vital new force that would help maintain a sense of religious enthusiasm within the Church.

Until the end of the thirteenth century both the Franciscans and Dominicans worked closely together with the papal monarchy in a mutually supportive relationship. The popes helped the friars establish themselves throughout Europe and often allowed them to infringe on the duties of parish priests. On their side, the friars combated heresy, helped preach papal crusades, were active in missionary work, and otherwise undertook special missions for the popes. Above all, by the power of their examples and by their vigorous preaching, the friars helped maintain religious intensity throughout the thirteenth century.

The Earliest Known Portrait of St. Francis. Dating from the year 1228, this fresco shows the saint without the "stigmata," the wounds of Christ's crucifixion he was believed to have received miraculously toward the end of his life.

CHRONOLOGY

EUROPEAN RELIGIOUS REVIVAL, 1100–1300

Cistercian order established	1098
Cult of the Virgin Mary	c. 1100
Catharist heresy emerges	c. 1140
Waldensian heresy emerges	c. 1180
New theology of the Eucharist	c. 1150–1215
Franciscan order established	1209
Fourth Lateran Council	1215
Dominican order established	1216

HOW DID THE RECOVERY OF CLASSICAL LEARNING AFFECT MEDIEVAL INTELLECTUAL LIFE?

THE MEDIEVAL INTELLECTUAL REVIVAL 363

The success of the Franciscans and the Dominicans in combating the appeal of heretical movements represented a great victory for the church, but this success was not sufficient to make the church feel secure in its hold on the people of Europe. Quite the opposite: despite its victories over the Cathars and the Waldensians, the church's inquisitorial processes ground on, discovering heretics even where none in fact existed.

JEWS AND CHRISTIANS

The church also became more and more concerned by the threat it believed that Jews posed to the faith of Christians, despite the fact that persecution and ex-

Burning of Jews. From a late medieval German manuscript. After the persecutions of the First Crusade, treatment of Jews in western Europe became worse and worse. These Jews were set upon by the populace because they were suspected of poisoning wells.

ploitative taxation had made most Jewish communities both smaller and weaker by 1300 than they had been in 1150. Although the church never officially endorsed the wilder flights of popular anti-Semitism, it did little to combat such attitudes either. As a result, by 1300 many ordinary Christians had come to believe that the Jews who lived among them were nothing less than agents of Satan, who routinely crucified Christian children, consumed Christian blood, and profaned the body of Christ in the Eucharist. The failures of organized campaigns to convert Jews to Christianity added to the sense among Christians that there was something demonic about the continuing Jewish presence in Christian society. Fanciful stories of Jewish wealth added an economic element to the developing anti-Semitism of European society, as did the fact that across much of thirteenth-century Europe, many Jews made their living as moneylenders.

Throughout the thirteenth century, the church had cooperated with kings in imposing more and more severe restrictions on Jewish life. Starting in the late 1280s, however, kings began to expel their Jewish subjects from their kingdoms altogether: in 1288 from southern Italy, in 1290 from England, and in 1306 from France. Further expulsions followed during the fourteenth century in the Rhineland, and in 1492 from Spain. By 1500, only Italy and Poland still retained any substantial Jewish populations, where they would survive until the Nazi Holocaust during the Second World War.

THE MEDIEVAL INTELLECTUAL REVIVAL

How did the recovery of classical learning affect medieval intellectual life?

The major intellectual accomplishments of the High Middle Ages were of four related but different sorts: the spread of primary education and literacy; the origin and spread of universities; the acquisition of classical and Muslim knowledge; and the actual progress in thought made by westerners. Any one of these accomplishments would have earned the High Middle Ages a signal place in the history of Western learning; taken together they began the era of Western intellectual predominance that became a hallmark of modern times.

Two Medieval Conceptions of Elementary Education. On the left, an illumination from a fourteenth-century manuscript depicts a master of grammar who simultaneously points to the day's lesson and keeps order with a cudgel. Grammar school education is portrayed more gently on the right, a late medieval scene in which a woman personifying the alphabet leads a willing boy into a tower of learning wherein the stories ascend from grammar through logic and rhetoric to the heights of theology.

THE GROWTH OF SCHOOLS

Around 800 Charlemagne ordered that primary schools be established in every bishopric and monastery in his realm. Although it is doubtful that this command was carried out to the letter, many schools were certainly founded during the Carolingian period. But their continued existence was later endangered by the Viking invasions. Primary education in some monasteries and cathedral towns managed to survive, but until around 1050 the extent and quality of basic education in the European West were meager. Thereafter, however, there was a blossoming that paralleled the efflorescence we have seen in other human activities. Even contemporaries were struck by the rapidity with which schools sprang up all over Europe. One French monk writing in 1115 stated that when he was growing up around 1075 there was "such a scarcity of teachers that there were almost none in the villages and hardly any in the cities," but that by his maturity there was "a great number of

schools," and the study of grammar was "flourishing far and wide." Similarly, a Flemish chronicle referred to an extraordinary new passion for the study and practice of rhetoric around 1120. Clearly, the economic revival, the growth of towns, and the emergence of strong government allowed Europeans to dedicate themselves to basic education as never before.

The high medieval educational boom was more than merely a growth of schools, for the nature of the schools changed, and as time went on so did the curriculum and the clientele. The first basic mutation was that monasteries in the twelfth century abandoned their practice of educating outsiders. Earlier, monasteries had taught a few privileged nonmonastic students how to read because there were no other schools for such pupils. But by the twelfth century sufficient alternatives existed. The main centers of European education became the cathedral schools located in the growing towns. The papal monarchy energetically supported this development by ordering in 1179 that all

HOW DID THE RECOVERY OF CLASSICAL LEARNING AFFECT MEDIEVAL INTELLECTUAL LIFE?

THE MEDIEVAL INTELLECTUAL REVIVAL   365

cathedrals should set aside income for one school-teacher, who could then instruct all who wished, rich or poor, without fee. The papacy believed correctly that this measure would enlarge the number of well-trained clerics and potential administrators.

At first the cathedral schools existed almost exclusively for the basic training of priests, with a curriculum designed to teach only such literacy as was necessary for performing the basic services of the church. But soon after 1100 the curriculum was broadened, for the growth of both ecclesiastical and secular governments created a growing demand for trained officials who had to know more than how to read a few prayers. The revived reliance on law especially made it imperative to improve the quality of primary education in order to train future lawyers. Above all, a thorough knowledge of Latin grammar and composition began to be inculcated, often by studying some of the Roman classics such as the works of Cicero and Virgil. The revived interest in these texts, and attempts to imitate them, have led scholars to refer to a "renaissance of the twelfth century."

Until about 1200 the students in the urban schools remained predominantly clerical. Even those who hoped to become lawyers or administrators rather than mere priests usually found it advantageous to take church orders. But afterward more pupils entering schools were not in the clergy and never intended to be. Some were children of the upper classes who began to regard literacy as a badge of status. Others were future notaries (men who drew up official documents), estate officials, or merchants who needed some literacy and/or computational skills to advance their own careers. Customarily, the latter groups would not go to cathedral schools but to alternate ones that were more practically oriented. Such schools grew rapidly in the course of the thirteenth century and became completely independent of ecclesiastical control. Not only were their students recruited from the laity, their teachers were usually laymen as well. As time went on instruction ceased to be in Latin, as had hitherto been the case, and was offered in the European vernacular languages instead. But the schools continued to be restricted to males. Some laywomen did become highly educated, but they were taught at home by private tutors.

The rise of lay education was an enormously important development in western European history for two related reasons. The first was that the church lost its monopoly over education for the first time in almost a millennium. Learning and resultant attitudes could now become more secular, and they did just that increasingly over the course of time. Laymen could not only evaluate and criticize the ideas of priests, they could also pursue entirely secular lines of inquiry. Western culture therefore ultimately became more independent of religion, and of the traditionalism associated with religion, than any other culture in the world. Second, the growth of lay schools, taken together with the growth of church schools that trained the laity, led to an enormous growth of lay literacy: by 1340 roughly 40 percent of the Florentine population could read; by the later fifteenth century about 40 percent of the total population of England was literate as well. (These figures include women, who were usually taught to read by paid tutors or by female family members at home rather than in schools.) When we consider that literacy around 1050 was almost entirely limited to the clergy and that the literate comprised less than 1 percent of the population of western Europe, we can appreciate that an astonishing revolution had taken place. Without it, many of Europe's other accomplishments would have been inconceivable.

The growth of lay and church schools that trained the laity led to an enormous growth of lay literacy.

THE RISE OF UNIVERSITIES

The emergence of universities was part of the same high medieval educational boom. Originally, universities were institutions that offered instruction in advanced studies that could not be pursued in average cathedral schools: advanced liberal arts and the professional studies of law, medicine, and theology. The earliest Italian university was that of Bologna, an institution that took shape during the course of the twelfth century. Although liberal arts were taught at Bologna, the institution's greatest prominence from the time of its twelfth-century origins until the end of the Middle Ages was as Europe's leading center for the study of law. North of the Alps, the earliest and most prestigious university was that of Paris. The University of Paris started out as a cathedral school like many others, but in the twelfth century it began to become a recognized center of northern intellectual life. One reason for this was that scholars there found the necessary conditions of peace and stability provided by the increasingly strong French kingship; another was that

SCOTLAND
Aberdeen
St. Andrews
Glasgow

NORTH
SEA

NORWAY
SWEDEN
Uppsala

DENMARK
Copenhagen

BALTIC SEA

ENGLAND
Cambridge
Oxford

Greifswald
Rostock
Elbe R.

Frankfurt
Wittenburg
Leipzig

Vistula R.
Warsaw

POLAND

ATLANTIC
OCEAN

Louvain
Cologne

Erfurt

HOLY ROMAN EMPIRE

Prague

Cracow

Caen
Seine R.
Paris

Trier
Mainz
Würzburg

Heidelberg
Ingolstadt
Tübingen

Vienna
Pressburg
Buda

Angers
Orléans

Rhine R.

Freibourg

AUSTRIA

HUNGARY

Nantes

Bourges
Poitiers

Loire R.

Besançon
Dôle

Basel

SWITZERLAND

Danube R.

Fünfkirchen

FRANCE

Lyons

Vercelli

Treviso

Bordeaux

Cahors

Grenoble
Valence
Orange
Avignon

Turin
Rhône R.

Padua
Pavia
Piacenza
Reggio
Bologna

Ferrara

VENETIAN EMPIRE

ADRIATIC SEA

Toulouse
Montpellier
Aix

Perpignan

Florence
Siena

PAPAL
STATES
Arezzo
Perugia

PORTUGAL

Palencia
Valladolid

Huesca
Lérida

CORSICA

Rome

Coimbra

Salamanca
Avila

Siguenza
Toledo

Saragossa

Barcelona

SARDINIA

Naples
Salerno

Lisbon

Tagus R.
SPAIN

Valencia

Palma
BALEARIC ISLANDS

KINGDOM
OF TWO
SICILIES

Seville

MEDITERRANEAN
SEA

Palermo
Catania

CENTURY UNIVERSITY FOUNDED

- ■ 12th Century
- ■ 13th Century
- ■ 14th Century
- ■ 15th Century
- — Boundaries c. 1500

0   100   200   300 Miles
0 100 200 300 Kilometers

THE RISE OF THE MEDIEVAL UNIVERSITY

This map shows the distribution and dates of origin of the major universities of medieval Europe. Why were the twelfth- and thirteenth-century universities founded primarily in France, England, and northern Italy? Notice the number and geographical distribution of universities founded in the fourteenth and fifteenth centuries. How would you explain the pattern of these later foundations?

HOW DID THE RECOVERY OF CLASSICAL LEARNING AFFECT MEDIEVAL INTELLECTUAL LIFE?

THE MEDIEVAL INTELLECTUAL REVIVAL   367

food was plentiful because the area was rich in agricultural produce; third was that the cathedral school of Paris in the first half of the twelfth century boasted the most charismatic and controversial teacher of the day, Peter Abelard (1079–1142). Abelard, whose intellectual accomplishments we will discuss later, attracted students from all over Europe in droves. According to an apocryphal story told at the time, he was such an exciting teacher that when he was forbidden to teach in French lands because of his controversial views, he climbed a tree and students flocked under it to hear him lecture; when he was then forbidden to teach from the air he started lecturing from a boat and students massed to hear him from the banks. As a result of his reputation many other teachers settled in Paris and began to offer much more varied and advanced instruction than anything offered in other French cathedral schools. By 1200 the Paris school was evolving into a university that specialized in liberal arts and theology. Around that time Innocent III, who had studied in Paris himself, called the school "the oven that bakes the bread for the entire world."

It should be emphasized that the institution of the university was really a medieval invention. Of course advanced schools existed in the ancient world, but they did not have fixed curricula or organized faculties, and they did not award degrees. At first, medieval universities themselves were not so much places as groups of scholars. The term "university" originally meant a corporation or guild. In fact, all of the medieval universities were corporations, either of teachers or students, organized like other guilds to protect their interests and rights. But gradually the word "university" came to mean an educational institution with a school of liberal arts and one or more faculties in law, medicine, and theology. After about 1200 Bologna and Paris were regarded as the prototypical universities. During the thirteenth century such famous institutions as Oxford, Cambridge, Montpellier, Salamanca, and Naples were founded or granted formal recognition. In Germany there were no universities until the fourteenth century—a reflection of the disorganized condition of that area—but in 1385 the first university on German soil was founded in Heidelberg, and many others quickly followed.

Every university in medieval Europe was patterned after one or the other of two different models. Throughout Italy, Spain, and southern France the standard was generally the University of Bologna, in which the students themselves constituted the corporation. They hired the teachers, paid their salaries, and fined or discharged them for neglect of duty or inefficient instruction. The universities of northern Europe were modeled after Paris, which was a guild not of students but of teachers. It included four faculties—arts, theology, law, and medicine—each headed by a dean. In the great majority of the northern universities arts and theology were the leading branches of study. Before the end of the thirteenth century separate colleges came to be established within the University of Paris. The original college was nothing more than an endowed home for poor students, but eventually the colleges became centers of instruction as well as residences. Although most of these types of colleges have disappeared from the Continent, the universities of Oxford and Cambridge still retain the pattern of federal organization copied from Paris. The colleges of which they are composed are semi-independent educational units.

Most of our modern degrees as well as our modern university organization derive from the medieval system, but actual courses of study have been greatly altered. No curriculum in the Middle Ages included history or anything like the modern social sciences. The medieval student was assumed to know Latin grammar thoroughly before entrance into a university—this he learned in the primary, or "grammar," schools. On admission—limited to males—he was required to spend about four years studying the basic liberal arts, which meant doing advanced work in Latin grammar and rhetoric and mastering the rules of logic. If he passed his examinations he received the preliminary degree of bachelor of arts (the prototype of our B.A.), which conferred no unusual distinction. To assure himself a place in professional life he then usually had to devote additional years to the pursuit of an advanced degree, such as master of arts (M.A.), or doctor of laws, medicine, or theology. The M.A. degree required three or four years given to the study of mathematics, natural science, and philosophy. This was accomplished by reading and commenting on standard ancient works, such as those of Euclid and especially Aristotle. Abstract analysis was emphasized; laboratory science did not exist. The requirements for the doctor's degrees included more specialized training. Those for the doctorate in theology were particularly arduous: by the end of the Middle Ages the course for the doctorate in theology at the University of Paris had been extended to twelve or thirteen years after the roughly eight years taken for the M.A.! Continuous residence was not required, and accordingly few men became doctors of theology before the age of forty; statutes in fact forbade awarding the degree to anyone under thirty-five. Strictly speaking, doctor's degrees, including even that

A Lecture Class in a Medieval University. Some interesting similarities and contrasts may be observed between this scene and a modern classroom.

in medicine, conferred only the right to teach. But in practice university degrees of all grades were recognized as standards of attainment and became pathways to nonacademic careers.

Student life in medieval universities was often rowdy. Many students were very immature because it was customary to begin university studies between the ages of twelve and fifteen. Moreover, all university students believed that they comprised an independent and privileged community, apart from that of the local townspeople. Since the latter tried to reap financial profits from the students and the students were naturally boisterous, riots and sometimes pitched battles were frequent between "town" and "gown." But actual study was very intense. Because the greatest emphasis was placed on the value of authority and also because

books were prohibitively expensive (they were handwritten on rare parchment), there was an enormous amount of rote memorization. As students advanced in their disciplines they were also expected to develop their own skills in formal, public disputations. Advanced disputations could become extremely complex and abstract; sometimes they might last for days. The most important fact pertaining to medieval university students was that, after about 1250, there were so many of them. The University of Paris in the thirteenth century numbered about seven thousand students, and Oxford somewhere around two thousand in any given year. This means that an appreciable proportion of male Europeans who were more than peasants or artisans were gaining at least some education at the higher levels.

HOW DID THE RECOVERY OF CLASSICAL LEARNING AFFECT MEDIEVAL INTELLECTUAL LIFE?

THE MEDIEVAL INTELLECTUAL REVIVAL   369

THE RECOVERY OF CLASSICAL LEARNING

As the numbers of those educated at all levels vastly increased during the High Middle Ages, so did the quality of learning. This was owing first and foremost to the reacquisition of Greek knowledge and to the absorption of intellectual advances made by the Muslims. Since practically no western Europeans knew Greek or Arabic, works in those languages had to be transmitted by means of Latin translations. But there were very few of these before about 1140: of all the many works of Aristotle only a few logical treatises were available in Latin translations before the middle of the twelfth century. But suddenly an enormous burst of translating activity made almost all of ancient Greek and Arabic scientific knowledge accessible to western Europeans. This activity occurred in Spain and Sicily because Christians there lived in close proximity with Arabic speakers, or Jews who knew Latin and Arabic, either of whom could aid them in their tasks. Greek works were first translated into Latin from earlier Arabic translations; then many were retranslated directly from the Greek by a few westerners who had managed to learn that language, usually by traveling in Greek-speaking territories. The result was that by about 1260 almost the entire Aristotelian corpus that is known today was made available in Latin. So also were basic works of such important Greek scientific thinkers as Euclid, Galen, and Ptolemy. Plato's works were still unknown in Europe, as were the works of the classical Greek poets and dramatists. For the most part, these remained the jealously guarded cultural preserve of Byzantium. But in addition to the thought of the Greeks, Western scholars also became familiar with the accomplishments of the major Islamic philosophers and scientists such as Avicenna and Averroës.

> Having acquired the best of Greek and Arabic scientific and speculative thought, the West was able to build on it and make its own advances.

Having acquired the best of Greek and Arabic scientific and speculative thought, the West was able to build on it and make its own advances. This progress came in different ways. In natural science, westerners could build without much difficulty on this new learning, because it seldom conflicted with the principles of Christianity. One of the most advanced thirteenth-century scientists was the Englishman Robert Grosseteste (c. 1168–1253), who was not only a great thinker but was also very active in public life as bishop of Lincoln. Grosseteste became so proficient at Greek that he translated all of Aristotle's *Ethics*. He also made very significant theoretical advances in mathematics, astronomy, and optics. He formulated a sophisticated scientific explanation of the rainbow, and he posited the use of lenses for magnification. Grosseteste's leading disciple was Roger Bacon (c. 1214–1294), who is today more famous than his teacher because he seems to have predicted automobiles and flying machines. Bacon in fact had no real interest in machinery, but he did follow up on Grosseteste's work in optics, discussing, for example, further properties of lenses, the rapid speed of light, and the nature of human vision. Grosseteste, Bacon, and some of their followers at the University of Oxford argued that natural knowledge was more certain when it was based on sensory evidence than when it rested on abstract reason. To this degree they can be seen as early forerunners of modern sci-

Averroës and Porphyry in Conversation. From a late-thirteenth-century Christian manuscript.

ence. But the important qualification remains that they did not perform any real laboratory experiments.

SCHOLASTICISM

The story of the high medieval encounter between Greek and Arabic philosophy and Christian faith is basically the story of the emergence of Scholasticism. This word can be, and has been, defined in many ways. In its root meaning Scholasticism was simply the method of teaching and learning followed in the medieval schools. That meant that it was highly systematic and also that it was highly respectful of authority. Yet Scholasticism was not only a method of study: it was a world view. As such, it taught that there was a fundamental compatibility between the knowledge humans can obtain naturally—that is, by experience or reason—and the teachings imparted by divine revelation. Since medieval scholars believed that the Greeks were the masters of natural knowledge and that all revelation was in the Bible, Scholasticism consequently was the theory and practice of reconciling classical philosophy with Christian faith.

PETER ABELARD

One of the most important thinkers who paved the way for Scholasticism without yet being fully a Scholastic himself was the stormy Peter Abelard, who was active in and around Paris in the first half of the twelfth century. Probably the first western European who consciously sought to forge a career as an intellectual (rather than being merely a cleric who taught on the side or a schoolteacher who had no goal of adding to knowledge), Abelard was so adept at logic and theology that even as a student he easily outshone the experts of his day who had the misfortune to be his teachers. Others might have been tactful about such superiority, but Abelard gloried in openly humiliating his elders in public debate, thereby making himself many enemies. To complicate matters, in 1118 he seduced a brilliant seventeen-year-old girl, Heloise, who had been taking private lessons with him. When Heloise became pregnant, Abelard married her (against Heloise's own wishes), but the two decided to keep the marriage secret for the sake of his career. This, however, enraged Heloise's uncle because he thought that Abelard was planning to abandon Heloise; therefore he took revenge for his family's honor by having Abelard castrated. Seeking refuge as a monk, Abelard soon witnessed his enemies engineer his first conviction for heresy. Still restless and cantan-

kerous, he found no spiritual solace in monasticism and after quarreling and breaking with the monks of two different communities he returned to life in the world by setting himself up as a teacher in Paris from about 1132 to 1141. This was the peak of his career. But in 1141 he again was charged with heresy, now by the highly influential Saint Bernard, and condemned by a church council. Not long afterward the persecuted thinker abjured, and in 1142 he died in retirement.

Abelard told of many of these trials in a letter called *The Story of My Calamities*, one of the first autobiographical accounts written in the West since Saint Augustine's *Confessions*. On first reading, this work appears atypically modern because the author seems to defy the medieval Christian virtue of humility by constantly boasting about himself. But Abelard did not write about his calamities in order to boast. Rather, his main intention was to moralize about how he had been justly punished for his "lechery" by the loss of those parts which had "offended" and for his intellectual pride by the burning of his writings after his first condemnation. Since Abelard urged intense self-examination and analysis of human motives in an ethical treatise programmatically entitled *Know Thyself*, it seems wisest to conclude that he never intended to recommend egotism but rather was one of several prominent twelfth-century thinkers (ironically including his mortal enemy Saint Bernard) who sought to take stock of the human personality by means of personal introspection.

Abelard's greatest contributions to the development of Scholasticism were made in his *Sic et Non* ("Yes and No") and in a number of original theological works. In the *Sic et Non* Abelard prepared the way for the Scholastic method by gathering a collection of statements from the church fathers that spoke for both sides of one hundred fifty theological questions. It was once thought that the brash Abelard did this in order to embarrass authority, but the contrary is true. What Abelard really hoped to do was begin a process of careful study whereby it could be shown that the Bible was infallible and that other authorities, despite any appearances to the contrary, really agreed with each other. Later Scholastics would follow his method of studying theology by raising fundamental questions and arraying the answers that had been put forth in authoritative texts. Abelard did not propose any solutions of his own in the *Sic et Non*, but he did start to do this in his original theological writings. In these he proposed to treat theology like a science by studying it as comprehensively as possible and by applying to it

HOW DID THE RECOVERY OF CLASSICAL LEARNING AFFECT MEDIEVAL INTELLECTUAL LIFE?

THE MEDIEVAL INTELLECTUAL REVIVAL   371

the tools of logic, of which he was a master. He did not even shrink from applying logic to the mystery of the Trinity (see p. 232), one of the excesses for which he was condemned. Peter Abelard was one of the first to try to harmonize religion with rationalism and was in this capacity a herald of the Scholastic outlook.

THE TRIUMPH OF SCHOLASTICISM

Immediately after Abelard's death two further steps were taken to prepare for mature Scholasticism. One was the writing of the *Book of Sentences* between 1155 and 1157 by Abelard's student Peter Lombard. This raised all the most fundamental theological questions in rigorously consequential order, adduced answers from the Bible and Christian authorities on both sides of each question, and then proposed judgments on every case. By the thirteenth century Peter Lombard's work had become a standard text. Once formal schools of theology were established in the universities, all aspirants to the doctorate were required to study and comment on it; not surprisingly, theologians also followed its organizational procedures in their own writings. Thus the full Scholastic method was born.

> Peter Abelard was one of the first to try to harmonize religion with rationalism and was in this capacity a herald of the Scholastic outlook.

The other basic step in the development of Scholasticism was the reacquisition of classical philosophy that occurred after about 1140. Abelard would probably have been glad to have drawn on the thought of the Greeks, but he could not because few Greek works were yet available in translation. Later theologians, however, could avail themselves fully of the Greeks' knowledge, above all, the works of Aristotle and his Arabic commentators. By around 1250 Aristotle's authority in purely philosophical matters became so great that he was referred to simply as "the Philosopher." Scholastics of the mid-thirteenth century accordingly adhered to Peter Lombard's organizational method, but considered Greek and Arabic philosophical authorities as well as purely Christian theological ones. In doing this they tried to construct systems of understanding the entire universe that most fully harmonized the earlier separate realms of faith and natural knowledge.

THE WRITINGS OF SAINT THOMAS AQUINAS

By far the greatest accomplishments in this endeavor were made by Saint Thomas Aquinas (1225–1274), the leading Scholastic theologian of the University of Paris. As a member of the Dominican order, Saint Thomas was committed to the principle that faith could be defended by reason. More important, he believed that natural knowledge and the study of the created universe were legitimate ways of approaching theological wisdom because "nature" complements "grace." By this he meant to say that because God created the natural world, he can be approached through its terms even though ultimate certainty about the highest truths can only be obtained through the supernatural revelation of the Bible. Imbued with a deep confidence in the value of human reason and human experience, as well as in his own ability to harmonize Greek philosophy with Christian theology, Thomas was the most serene of saints. In a long career of teaching at the University of Paris and elsewhere he indulged in few controversies and worked quietly on his two great Summaries of theology: the *Summa Contra Gentiles* ("Summary against Non-Christians") and the much larger *Summa Theologica* ("Summary of Theology"). In these he hoped to set down all that could be said about the faith on the firmest of foundations.

Most experts think that Saint Thomas came extremely close to fulfilling this extraordinarily ambitious goal. His vast Summaries are awesome for their rigorous orderliness and intellectual penetration. He admits in them that there are certain "mysteries of the faith," such as the doctrines of the Trinity and the Incarnation of God in Christ, that cannot be approached by the unaided human intellect; otherwise, he subjects all theological questions to philosophical inquiry. In this, Thomas relied heavily on the work of Aristotle, but he was by no means merely "Aristotle baptized." Instead, he fully subordinated Aristotelianism to basic Christian principles and thereby created his own original philosophical and theological system. Scholars disagree about how far this system diverges from the earlier Christian thought of Saint Augustine, but there seems little doubt that Aquinas placed a higher value on human reason, on human life in this world, and on the abilities of humans to participate in their own salvation. Not long after his death Thomas was canonized, for his intellectual accomplishments seemed like miracles. His influence lives on today insofar as he helped to inspire confidence in rationalism and human experience. More directly, philosophy in the modern Roman Catholic Church is supposed to be taught according to the Thomistic method, doctrine, and principles.

THE PINNACLE OF WESTERN MEDIEVAL THOUGHT

With the achievements of Saint Thomas Aquinas in the mid-thirteenth century, Western medieval thought reached its pinnacle. Not coincidentally, other aspects of medieval civilization were reaching their pinnacles at the same time. France was enjoying its ripest period of peace and prosperity under the rule of (Saint) Louis IX, the University of Paris was defining its basic organizational forms, and the greatest French Gothic cathedrals were being built. Some ardent admirers of medieval culture have fixed on these accomplishments to call the thirteenth the "greatest of centuries." Such a judgment, of course, is a matter of taste, and many might respond that life was still too harsh and requirements for religious orthodoxy too restrictive to justify this extreme celebration of the lost past. Whatever our individual judgments, it seems wise to end this section by correcting some false impressions about medieval intellectual life.

It is often thought that medieval thinkers were excessively conservative, but in fact the greatest thinkers of the High Middle Ages were astonishingly receptive to new ideas. As committed Christians they could not allow doubts to be cast on the principles of their faith, but otherwise they were glad to incorporate whatever they could from the Greeks and Arabs. Considering that Aristotelian thought differed radically from anything accepted earlier in its emphasis on rationalism and the fundamental goodness and purposefulness of nature, its rapid acceptance by the Scholastics was a philosophical revolution. Another false impression is that Scholastic thinkers were greatly constrained by authority. Certainly they revered authority more than we do today, but such Scholastics as Saint Thomas did not regard the mere citation of texts—except biblical revelation concerning the mysteries of the faith—as being sufficient to clinch an argument. Rather, the authorities were brought forth to outline the possibilities, but reason and experience then demonstrated the truth. Finally, it is often believed that Scholastic thinkers were "antihumanistic," but modern scholars are coming to the opposite conclusion. Scholastics unquestionably gave primacy to

the soul over the body and to otherworldly salvation over life in the here and now. But they also exalted the dignity of human nature because they viewed it as a glorious divine creation, and they believed in the possibility of a working alliance between themselves and God. Moreover, they had extraordinary faith in the powers of human reason—probably more than we do today.

THE BLOSSOMING OF LITERATURE, ART, AND MUSIC

What constituted the "Renaissance of the Twelfth Century"?

The literature of the High Middle Ages was varied, lively, and impressive. The revival of grammatical studies in the cathedral schools and universities led to the production of some excellent Latin poetry. The best examples were secular lyrics, especially those written in the twelfth century by a group of poets known as the Goliards. How these poets got their name is uncertain, but it possibly meant "followers of the devil." That would have been appropriate because the Goliards were riotous poets who wrote parodies of the liturgy and burlesques of the Gospels. Their lyrics celebrated the beauties of the changing seasons, the carefree life of the open road, the pleasures of drinking and sport, and especially the joys of love. The authors of these rollicking and satirical songs were mainly wandering students, although some were men of more advanced years. The names of most are unknown. Their poetry is particularly significant both for its robust vitality and for being the first clear counterstatement to the ascetic ideal of Christianity.

VERNACULAR LITERATURE

In addition to Latin, the vernacular languages of French, German, Spanish, and Italian became increasingly popular as media of literary expression. At first, most of the literature in the vernacular languages was

> With the achievements of Saint Thomas Aquinas in the mid-thirteenth century, Western medieval thought reached its pinnacle.

A GOLIARDIC PARODY OF THE GOSPEL OF MARK, SATIRIZING THE PAPAL COURT

This selection is typical of the parodies of the liturgy and the Bible written by the freewheeling Latin poets of the twelfth century. This particular poem is written in mock biblical verse, and puns on the Christian Gospel of Mark—a mark being a sum of money equal to two thirds of a pound of silver. Like all parodies, it was meant to be humorous, but its accusations—that bribery around the papal court perverted justice—were widespread in twelfth- and thirteenth-century Europe.

Here beginneth the Holy Gospel according to the marks of silver. In those days the Holy Father said unto the Romans: "When the Son of Man shall come unto the seat of our Majesty, first say unto Him: 'Friend, why art Thou come?' but if he continue knocking and give you nothing, then cast Him forth into outer darkness."

And it came to pass that a certain poor priest came to the court of the Lord Pope and cried out, saying, "Do ye at least have pity on me, servants of the Pope, for the hand of poverty hath afflicted me. Verily I am poor and have nothing. I beseech you, therefore, have mercy upon me and pity me." They, however, hearing this were sorely wroth and said unto him, "Friend, may thy poverty go with thee to hell. Get thee behind us, Satan; thou savorest not of money. Amen, Amen we say to thee: thou shalt not enter into the blessings of thy Lord until thou hast given thy last penny."

The poor man went therefore and sold his cloak and his coat and all that he had, and gave unto the cardinals and the treasurers and the papal flunkies. But they said unto him, "And this, what is this among so many?"

And they cast him out utterly, and going forth he wept bitterly and would not be comforted.

After this there came to the court a rich priest, exceedingly wealthy, anointed with grease and great with wealth, who had committed murder for the sake of gain. He first gave unto the treasurer, then he gave unto the flunky, and then he gave unto the cardinals. But they reasoned among themselves, thinking they would receive more. Therefore when the Lord Pope heard that the cardinals and his servants had received many gifts from a priest he was sick, even unto death. But the rich man sent unto him a pallet of gold and silver, and immediately he was made whole.

The Lord Pope called unto him the cardinals and ministers and spake unto them saying: "Beware, brethren, lest any deceive you with vain words. For I have given you an example, so that as I have grasped, so should you grasp also."

Carmina Burana, 21, trans. by Helen Waddell, in *The Wandering Scholars*, 7th ed. (London: Constable, 1934), pp. 150–151, as revised by John E. Boswell.

Charlemagne Weeping for His Knights. A scene from the *Song of Roland*.

written in the form of the heroic epic. Among the leading examples were the French *Song of Roland*, the Norse eddas and sagas, the German *Song of the Nibelungs*, and the Spanish *Poem of the Cid*. Practically all of these works were originally composed between 1050 and 1150, although some (such as the *Cid* and the Norse sagas) were not written down until the thirteenth century. These epics portrayed a virile but unpolished warrior society. Blood flowed freely, skulls were cleaved by battle axes, and heroic warfare, honor, and loyalty were the major themes. If women were mentioned at all, they were subordinate to men. Brides were expected to die for their beloveds, but husbands were free to beat their wives. In one French epic a queen who tried to influence her husband met with a blow to the nose; even though blood flowed she replied, "Many thanks, when it pleases you, you may do it again." Although we find such passages repugnant, the best of the vernacular epics have great literary power despite their unrelentingly masculine focus.

TROUBADOUR POETRY AND COURTLY ROMANCES

In comparison to the epics, an enormous change in both subject matter and style was introduced in twelfth-century France by the troubadour poets and the writers of courtly romances. The troubadours were courtier poets who came from southern France and wrote in a language related to French known as Provençal. The origin of their inspiration is debated, but there can be no doubt that they initiated a movement of profound importance for all subsequent Western literature. Their style was far more finely wrought and sophisticated than that of the epic poets, and the most eloquent of their lyrics, which were meant to be sung to music, originated the theme of romantic love. The troubadours idealized women as marvelous beings who could grant intense spiritual and sensual gratification. Whatever greatness the poets found in themselves they usually attributed to the inspiration they found in love. But they also assumed that their love would lose its magic if it were too easily or frequently gratified. Therefore, they wrote more often of longing than of romantic fulfillment.

In addition to their love lyrics, the troubadours wrote several other kinds of short poems. Some were simply bawdy. In these, love is not mentioned at all, but the poet revels in thoughts of carnality, comparing, for example, riding his horse to "riding" his mistress. Other troubadour poems treat feats of arms, others comment on contemporary political events, and a few even meditate on matters of religion. But whatever the subject matter, the best troubadour poems were always cleverly and innovatively expressed. The literary tradition originated by the southern French troubadours was continued by the trouvères in northern France and by the minnesingers in Germany. Thereafter many of their innovations were developed by later lyric poets in all Western languages. Some of their poetic devices were consciously revived in the twentieth century by such literary modernists as Ezra Pound.

An equally important twelfth-century French innovation was the composition of longer narrative poems known as romances, so called because there were written in vernacular, Romance (that is, deriving from Latin) languages. Romances told engaging stories; they often excelled in portraying character, and their subject matter was usually love and adventure. Some romances elaborated on classical Greek themes, but the most famous and best were "Arthurian." These took their material from the legendary exploits of the

British hero King Arthur and his many chivalrous knights. The first great writer of Arthurian romances was the northern Frenchman Chrétien de Troyes, who was active between about 1165 and 1190. Chrétien did much to help create and shape the new form, and he also introduced innovations in subject matter and attitudes. Whereas the troubadours exalted extramarital love, Chrétien was the first to hold forth the ideal of romantic love within marriage. He also described not only the deeds but the thoughts and emotions of his characters.

A generation later, Chrétien's work was continued by the great German poets Wolfram von Eschenbach and Gottfried von Strassburg, who are recognized as the greatest writers in the German language before the eighteenth century. Wolfram's *Parzival*, a story of love and the search for the Holy Grail, is more subtle, complex, and greater in scope than any other high medieval literary work except Dante's *Divine Comedy*. Like Chrétien, Wolfram believed that true love could be fulfilled only in marriage, and in Parzival, for the first time in Western literature since the Greeks, one can see a full psychological development of the hero. Gottfried von Strassburg's *Tristan* is a more somber work that tells of the tragic, adulterous love between Tristan and Isolde. Indeed, it might almost be regarded as the prototype of modern tragic romanticism. Gottfried was one of the first to develop fully the idea of individual suffering as a literary theme and to point out the in-

distinct line that separates pleasure from pain. For him, to love is to yearn, and suffering and unfulfilled gratification are integral chapters of the book of life. Unlike the troubadours, he could see complete fulfillment of love only in death. *Parzival* and *Tristan* have become most famous today in the form of their operatic reconceptions by the nineteenth-century German composer Richard Wagner.

Not all high medieval narratives were so elevated as the romances in either form or substance. A very different new narrative form was the *fabliau*, or verse fable. Although *fabliaux* derived from the moral animal tales of Aesop, they quickly evolved into short stories that were written less to edify or instruct than to amuse. Often they were very coarse, and sometimes they dealt with sexual relations in a broadly humorous and thoroughly unromantic manner. Many were also strongly anticlerical, making monks and priests the butts of their jokes. Because the *fabliaux* are so "uncourtly" it was once thought that they were written solely for the new urban classes. But there is now little doubt that they were addressed at least equally to the "refined" aristocracy, who liked to have their laughs too. They are significant as expressions of growing worldliness and as the first manifestations of the robust realism that was later to be perfected by Boccaccio and Chaucer.

Completely different in form but similar as an illustration of growing worldliness was the sprawling *Romance of the Rose*. As its title indicates, this was begun as a romance, specifically around 1230 by the courtly Frenchman William de Lorris. But William left his rather flowery, romantic work unfinished, and it was completed around 1270 by another Frenchman, Jean de Meung. The latter changed its nature greatly, inserting long, biting digressions in which he skewered religious hypocrisy. Jean's major theme was the need for procreation. Not love, but the service of "Dame Nature" in sexual fecundity is urged in numerous witty but extremely earthy images and metaphors. At the climax the originally dreamy hero seizes his mistress, who is allegorically depicted as a rose, and rapes her. The work became

Rabbit on the Hunt. Marginal illustrations in medieval manuscripts (this one dates from about 1340) often exhibit ironic humor.

enormously popular, but then as now it provoked strong reactions, including a sweeping condemnation of its treatment of women by the fourteenth-century writer Christine de Pisan.

THE DIVINE COMEDY

In a class by itself as the greatest work of medieval literature is Dante Alighieri's *Divine Comedy*. Dante (1265–1321) was active during the early part of his career in the political affairs of his native city of Florence, and remained throughout his life intensely connected to his native city. Despite his engagement in politics and the fact that he was a layman, he managed to acquire an awesome mastery of the religious, philosophic, and literary knowledge of his time. He not only knew the Bible and the church fathers, but—most unusual for a layman—he also absorbed the most recent Scholastic theology. In addition, he was thoroughly familiar with Virgil, Cicero, Boethius, and numerous other classical writers, and was fully conversant with the poems of the troubadours and the Italian poetry of his own day. In 1301 he was expelled from Florence after a political upheaval and was forced to live the rest of his life in exile. The *Divine Comedy*, his major work, was written during this final period.

> In a class by itself as the greatest work of medieval literature is Dante Alighieri's *Divine Comedy*.

Dante's *Divine Comedy* is a monumental narrative in powerful rhyming Italian verse, which describes the poet's journey through hell, purgatory, and paradise. At the start Dante tells of finding himself in a "dark wood," his metaphor for a deep personal midlife crisis in which he had wandered away from his Christian faith. He is led out of this forest of despair by the Roman poet Virgil, who represents the heights of classical reason and philosophy. Virgil guides Dante on a trip through hell and purgatory; then Dante's deceased beloved, Beatrice, who symbolizes Christian wisdom and blessedness, takes over and guides him through paradise. In the course of this progress from hell to heaven Dante meets both historical personages and his own contemporaries; he is instructed by them and his guides as to why they met their several fates. As the poem progresses Dante grows in wisdom and understanding, until finally he returns with new confidence and certainty to his own lost Christian faith.

Every reader finds a different combination of wonder and satisfaction in Dante's magnificent work. Some—especially those who know Italian—marvel at the vigor and inventiveness of Dante's language and images. Others are awed by his subtle complexity and poetic symmetry; others by his array of learning; others by the vitality of his characters and individual sto-

The Poet Dante Driven into Exile. On the left Dante is expelled from Florence; on the right he begins work on his great poem, the *Divine Comedy*. From a mid-fifteenth-century Florentine manuscript. (The nearly completed dome of Florence's cathedral can be seen at the far left.)

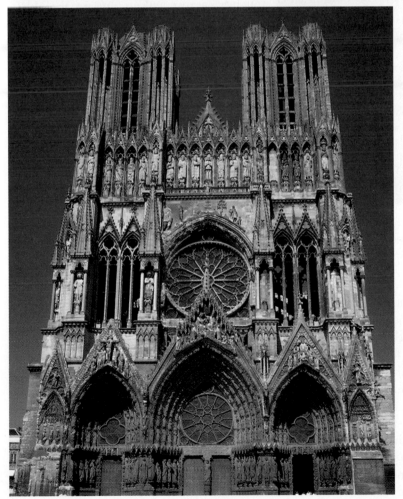

ries; and still others by his soaring imagination. The historian finds it particularly remarkable that Dante could sum up the best of medieval learning in such an artistically satisfying manner. Dante stressed the precedence of salvation, but he viewed earth as existing for human benefit. He allowed humans free will to choose good and avoid evil, and accepted Greek philosophy as authoritative in its own sphere; for example, he called Aristotle "the master of them that know." Above all, his sense of hope and his ultimate faith in humanity—remarkable for a defeated exile—most powerfully expresses the dominant mood of the High Middle Ages and makes Dante one of the two or three most stirringly affirmative writers who ever lived.

ART AND ARCHITECTURE

The closest architectural equivalents of the *Divine Comedy* are the great high medieval Gothic cathedrals, for they too have qualities of vast scope, balance of intricate detail with careful symmetry, soaring height, and affirmative religious grandeur. But before we approach the Gothic style, it is best to introduce it by means of its high medieval predecessor, the style of architecture and art known as the Romanesque. This style had its origins in the tenth century, but became fully formed in the eleventh and the first half of the twelfth centuries, when the religious reform movement sparked the building of many new monasteries and large churches. The Romanesque style aimed to manifest the majesty of God in stone by rigorously subordinating all architectural details to a uniform

Romanesque and Gothic. Top: West front of the Church of Notre Dame la Grande, Poitiers. Constructed between 1135 and 1145, this typical example of Romanesque architecture emphasizes the repetition of rounded arches and horizontal lines. Bottom: Rheims Cathedral. Built between 1220 and 1299, this High Gothic cathedral places great stress on vertical elements. The gabled portals, pointed arches, and multitude of pinnacles all accentuate the height of this structure.

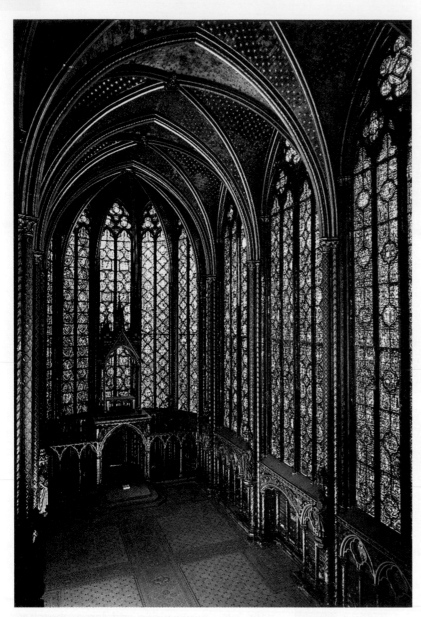

The Upper Chapel of the Sainte-Chapelle, Paris. High Gothic is here carried to its extreme. Slender columns, tracery, and stained-glass windows take the place of walls.

much evocative power and represent the first manifestations of a revived interest in sculpting the human form.

In the course of the twelfth and thirteenth centuries the Romanesque style was supplanted throughout most of Europe by the Gothic. Although trained art historians can see how certain traits of the one style led to the development of the other, the actual appearance of the two styles is distinctively different. In fact, the two seem as different as the epic is different from the romance, an appropriate analogy because the Gothic style emerged in France in the mid-twelfth century exactly when the romance did, and because it was far more sophisticated, graceful, and elegant than its predecessor, in the same way that the romance compared with the epic. The rapid development and acceptance of the Gothic is yet another example of the experimental and dynamic character of twelfth-century culture. When the abbey church of Saint Denis, venerated as the shrine of the French patron saint and burial place of French kings, was torn down in 1144 in order to make room for a much larger one in the strikingly new Gothic style, it was as if the president of the United States were to tear down the White House and replace it with a Mies van der Rohe or Helmut Jahn edifice. Such an act today would be highly improbable, or at least would create an enormous uproar. But in the twelfth century the equivalent actually happened and was taken in stride.

Gothic architecture was one of the most intricate of building styles. Its basic elements were the pointed arch, groined and ribbed vaulting, and the flying buttress. These devices made possible a much lighter and loftier construction than could ever have been achieved with the round arch and the engaged pier of the Romanesque. In fact, the Gothic cathedral could be described as a skeletal framework of stone enclosed by enormous windows. Other features included lofty spires, rose windows, delicate tracery in stone, elaborately sculpted facades, multiple columns, and the more frequent use of gargoyles, or representations of mythical monsters, as decorative devices. Ornamentation was generally concentrated on the exterior. But the inside of the

system. The essential features of the Romanesque style were the rounded arch, massive stone walls, enormous piers (support columns), small windows, and the predominance of horizontal lines. Together, these features gave Romanesque architecture a sense of stability and permanence. Interiors were plain, but sometimes relieved by mosaics or frescoes in bright colors and—a very important innovation for Christian art—the introduction of sculptural decoration, both within and without. For the first time, full-length human figures appeared on facades. These are usually grave and elongated far beyond natural dimensions, but they have

Gothic cathedral was never somber or gloomy. The stained-glass windows served not to exclude the light but to glorify it, to catch the rays of sunlight and suffuse them with a richness and warmth of color that nature itself could hardly duplicate even in its happiest moods.

Many people still think of the Gothic cathedral as the expression of purely ascetic otherworldliness, but this estimation is highly inaccurate. Certainly all churches are dedicated to the glory of God and hope for life everlasting, but Gothic ones sometimes included stained-glass scenes of daily life that had no overt religious significance at all. More important, Gothic sculptures of religious figures such as Jesus, the Virgin, and the saints were becoming far more naturalistic than anything hitherto created in the medieval West. So also was the sculptural representation of plant and animal life, which rose to extraordinary levels of botanical and zoological accuracy. Moreover, Gothic architecture was also an expression of the medieval intellectual genius. Each cathedral, with its many symbolic figures, was a kind of encyclopedia of medieval knowledge carved in stone. Finally, Gothic cathedrals were manifestations of urban pride. Always located in the growing medieval cities, they were meant to be both centers of community life and expressions of a town's greatness. When a new cathedral went up the people of the entire community participated in erecting it, and rightfully regarded it as almost their own property. Many of the Gothic cathedrals were the products of urban rivalries. Each city or town sought to overawe its neighbor with ever bigger or taller buildings, to the degree that ambitions sometimes got out of bounds and many of the cathedrals were left unfinished. But most of the finished ones are still vast enough. Built to last into eternity, they provide the most striking visual manifestation of the soaring exuberance of their age.

DRAMA AND MUSIC

Surveys of high medieval accomplishments should not omit drama and music. Our own modern drama descends at least as much from the medieval form as from the classical one. Throughout the medieval period some Latin classical plays were known in manuscript but were never performed. Instead drama was born all over again within the church. In the early Middle Ages

> Many people still think of the Gothic cathedral as the expression of purely ascetic otherworldliness, but this estimation is highly inaccurate.

certain passages in the liturgy began to be acted out. Then, in the twelfth century, primarily in Paris, these were superseded by short religious plays in Latin, performed inside a church. Rapidly thereafter, the Latin plays were supplemented or supplanted by ones in the vernacular so that the whole congregation could understand them. Around 1200, these started to be performed outside, in front of the church, so that they would not take time away from the services. As soon as that happened, drama entered the everyday world: nonreligious stories were introduced, character portrayal was expanded, and the way was prepared for the Elizabethans and Shakespeare.

As the drama grew out of developments within the liturgy and then moved far beyond them, so did characteristically Western music. Until the High Middle Ages Western music was homophonic, as is much non-Western music even today. That is, it developed only one melody at a time without any harmonic background. The great high medieval invention was polyphony, the playing or singing of two or more harmonious melodies together. Some experiments along these lines may have been made in the West as early as the tenth century, but the most fundamental breakthrough was achieved at the cathedral of Paris around 1170, when the mass was first sung by two voices weaving together two different melodies in "counterpoint." Roughly concurrently, systems of musical notation were invented and perfected. Because performers no longer had to rely on memory, music could become more complex. All the greatness of Western music followed from these first steps.

 CONCLUSION

For almost one hundred years, scholars have spoken of the sweeping intellectual, religious, and cultural changes of the High Middle Ages as constituting the "Renaissance of the Twelfth Century." This categorization still seems apt. Like those of the more famous Italian Renaissance of the fourteenth and fifteenth centuries, the intellectual changes of the High Middle Ages were profoundly influenced by the recovery and intensive study of classical texts. But in both periods, the use made of these classical texts was distinctive and unique. Neither of these movements were mere revivals; rather, both were creative adaptations of classical ideas to a new and distinctively Christian culture.

Even more so than the Italian Renaissance, however, the twelfth-century renaissance marks the origin of a set of characteristic attitudes and ideas that have characterized western European civilization ever since. Our modern conceptions of love and friendship; our understanding of human motivation and intention; indeed, our very interest in psychology itself, all derive from twelfth-century developments. So too does our emphasis on the essential interiority of Christian piety; our vision that "true religion" ought to be expressed in practical works of charity in the world; and our presumption that religion and politics are separable spheres of human endeavor and concern. Even our modern impulse to define and persecute minority groups has roots in twelfth- and thirteenth-century efforts to suppress Jews, heretics, and sexual minorities.

Many of the people who made such important contributions to learning, thought, literature, architecture, drama, and music must have intermingled with each other in the Paris of the High Middle Ages. Some of them no doubt prayed together in the cathedral of Notre Dame. The names of the leading scholars are remembered, but the names of most of the others are unknown. Yet taken together they did as much for the civilization of Europe, and created as many enduring monuments, as did their counterparts in ancient Athens. Their names may be forgotten, but their achievements live on still.

SELECTED READINGS

Baldwin, John W. *The Scholastic Culture of the Middle Ages: 1000–1300* Lexington, Mass., 1971. A fine introduction.

Blumenthal, Uta-Renate *The Investiture Controversy.* Philadelphia, 1988. A clear review of a complicated subject.

Boswell, John E. *Christianity, Social Tolerance, and Homosexuality: Gay People in Western Europe from the Beginning of the Christian Era to the Fourteenth Century.* Chicago, 1980. A pioneering account, particularly good on twelfth-century poetry.

Chrétien de Troyes. *Arthurian Romances.* Translated by W. W. Kibler. New York, 1991.

Clanchy, Michael T. *Abelard: A Medieval Life.* Oxford and Cambridge, Mass., 1997. A great biography, which now needs to be supplemented by Mews (see below).

Cobban, Alan B. *The Medieval Universities.* London, 1975. The best short treatment in English.

Colish, Marcia. *Medieval Foundations of the Western Intellectual Tradi-*

tion, 400–1400. New Haven, 1997. An encyclopedic and exhaustive work, best used as a reference.

Dante Alighieri. *The Divine Comedy.* Translated by Mark Musa. 3 vols. Baltimore, 1984–1986.

Dronke, Peter. *Women Writers of the Middle Ages.* New York, 1984. A rich literary study.

Gilson, Etienne. *Reason and Revelation in the Middle Ages.* New York, 1938. Somewhat dated, but still a useful introduction for students to the intellectual world of scholasticism.

Goldin, F., ed. *Lyrics of the Troubadours and Trouvères.* Garden City, N.Y., 1973.

Gottfried von Strassburg. *Tristan.* Translated by A. T. Hatto. Baltimore, 1960.

Grundmann, Herbert. *Religious Movements in the Middle Ages.* Notre Dame, Ind., 1995. A classic work, now translated into English, that shows how much of high medieval religious vitality, orthodox and heretical, originated from the search for the "apostolic life."

Knowles, David. *The Evolution of Medieval Thought,* 2d ed. London, 1988. An authoritative survey, thoroughly revised in the second edition.

Lambert, Malcolm. *Medieval Heresy,* 2d ed. Oxford and Cambridge, 1992. The standard synthesis; deeply learned and fully annotated.

Lawrence, Clifford Hugh. *The Friars: The Impact of the Early Mendicant Movement on Western Society.* London and New York, 1994. The best short introduction to the early history of the Franciscans and the Dominicans.

———. *Medieval Monasticism: Forms of Religious Life in Western Europe in the Middle Ages,* 3d ed. London and New York, 2000. This new edition includes material on the friars drawn from his 1994 book.

Leclercq, Jean. *Bernard of Clairvaux and the Cistercian Spirit.* Kalamazoo, Mich., 1976. An empathetic account by the greatest twentieth-century scholar of Cistercianism.

———. *The Love of Learning and the Desire for God,* 3d ed. New York, 1982. A beautiful account of twelfth-century monastic culture, seen from the perspective of Saint Bernard of Clairvaux.

The Letters of Abelard and Heloise. Translated by Betty Radice. London and New York, 1974. Includes Abelard's autobiographical *Story of My Misfortunes.*

Mews, Constant J. *The Lost Love Letters of Heloise and Abelard.* New York, 1999. A recently identified treasure trove of correspondence between the lovers, written before they were detected and separated.

Morris, Colin. *The Papal Monarchy: The Western Church from 1050 to 1250.* Oxford, 1989. An excellent scholarly survey; part of the Oxford History of the Christian Church series.

Newman, Barbara. *Sister of Wisdom: St. Hildegard's Theology of the Feminine.* Berkeley and Los Angeles, 1980. A pioneering work; the 1989 edition includes a discography of Hildegard's music.

———, ed. *Voice of the Living Light: Hildegard of Bingen and Her World.* Berkeley and Los Angeles, 1998. The best introduction to Hildegard's life and work; discusses her roles as abbess, religious thinker, prophet, correspondent, artist, medical writer, composer, dramatist, and poet.

Peters, Edward, ed., *The First Crusade: The Chronicle of Fulcher of Chartres and Other Source Materials*, 2d ed. Philadelphia, 1998. The second edition contains a great deal of new material not available in the first edition.

———. *The Crusades: A Short History*, New Haven, 1987. A reliable account that contains a very useful list of primary sources.

Riley-Smith, Jonathan. *The First Crusade and the Idea of Crusading.* Philadelphia, 1986. A clear and accessible account by an acknowledged expert.

———, ed. *The Oxford Illustrated History of the Crusades*, Oxford and New York, 1995. The most engaging introduction to the subject; first-class text, splendidly illustrated.

Sheingorn, Pamela, trans. *The Book of Sainte Foy.* Philadelphia, 1995.

Smalley, Beryl. *The Study of the Bible in the Middle Ages*, 3d ed. Oxford, 1983. The standard work, gracefully written yet immensely learned.

Southern, Richard W. *Western Society and the Church in the Middle Ages.* Baltimore, 1970. An extremely insightful interpretation of the interplay between society and religion, engagingly written by one of the greatest historians of the twentieth century.

———. *Scholastic Humanism and the Unification of Europe.* Vol. 1: *Foundations.* Oxford and Cambridge, Mass., 1995. A major reinterpretation of scholasticism and humanism by the foremost historian of both traditions.

Swanson, R. N. *The Twelfth-Century Renaissance.* Manchester, Eng., 1999. The most accessible and up-to-date survey of the intellectual developments of the twelfth century.

Tierney, Brian. *The Crisis of Church and State, 1050–1300.* Toronto, 1988. An indispensable collection for both teachers and students.

Wakefield, Walter, and Austin P. Evans, eds. and trans. *Heresies of the High Middle Ages.* New York, 1969, 1991. A comprehensive collection of sources, best used in conjunction with Lambert (see above).

Wilhelm, James J., ed. and trans. *Medieval Song: An Anthology of Hymns and Lyrics.* New York, 1971. An excellent collection of sacred and secular poetry that illustrates the connections between them.

Wolfram von Eschenbach. *Parzival.* Translated by H. M. Mustard and C. E. Passage. New York, 1961.

CHAPTER ELEVEN

THE LATER MIDDLE AGES, 1300–1500

I F THE HIGH MIDDLE AGES were "times of feasts," then the late Middle Ages were "times of famine." From about 1300 until the middle or latter part of the fifteenth century calamities struck throughout western Europe with appalling severity and dismaying persistence. Famine first prevailed because agriculture was impeded by soil exhaustion, colder weather, and torrential rainfalls. Then, on top of those "acts of God," came the most terrible natural disaster of all: the dreadful plague known as the "Black Death," which cut broad swaths of mortality throughout western Europe. As if all that were not enough, incessant warfare continually brought hardship and desolation. Common people suffered most because they were most exposed to raping, stabbing, looting, and burning by soldiers and organized bands of freebooters. After an army passed through a region one might see miles of smoldering ruins littered with putrefying corpses; in many places the desolation was so great that wolves roamed the countryside and even entered the outskirts of the cities. In short, if the serene Virgin symbolized the High Middle Ages, the grinning death's-head symbolized the succeeding period. But despite the hardships they faced, Europeans displayed a tenacious perseverance in the face of adversity. Instead of abandoning themselves to apathy, they resolutely sought to adjust to changed circumstances. Thus civilization did not collapse, but rather a period of creativity and innovation preserved and extended the most enduring features of high medieval European life.

FOCUS QUESTIONS

• How did famine and plague transform economic life in late medieval Europe?

• What were the causes of the popular rebellions from 1300 to 1450?

• What were the main forms of late medieval popular piety?

• What caused the rise of national monarchies?

 • Why was medieval Russia so unlike any other European state?

• What trends led to the rise of vernacular literature?

• How did technological advances affect everyday life?

ECONOMIC DEPRESSION AND THE EMERGENCE OF A NEW EQUILIBRIUM

How did famine and plague transform economic life in late medieval Europe?

By around 1300 the agricultural expansion of the High Middle Ages had reached its limits. Thereafter yields and areas under cultivation began to decline, causing a downturn in the whole European economy that was accelerated by the disruptive effects of war. Accordingly, the first half of the fourteenth century was a time of growing economic depression in both town and countryside. The coming of the Black Death in 1347 made this depression particularly acute because it completely disrupted the affairs of daily life. Recurrences of the plague and protracted warfare continued to depress most of the European economy until deep into the fifteenth century. But between roughly 1350 and 1450 Europeans learned how to adjust to the new economic circumstances and succeeded in placing their economy on a sounder basis. Wages rose while grain prices fell. Although this hurt large-scale grain producers, it benefited smaller farmers (who could more easily diversify their agricultural production) and wage earners. The resulting prosperity was reflected in better diets and housing among European laborers and farmers, and a gradual recovery in overall population. Although the total size of the European economy almost certainly shrank in the century after the Black Death, by 1450 Europe was wealthier per capita than it had been in 1300, and its wealth was more evenly distributed among its people. All told, therefore, Europe emerged in the later fifteenth century with a healthier economy than it had known earlier.

> The first half of the fourteenth century was a time of growing economic depression in both town and countryside.

CLIMATE CHANGE AND AGRICULTURAL FAILURE

The checks on agricultural expansion reached around 1300 were natural ones. There was a limit to the amount of land that could be cleared and a limit to the amount of crops that could be raised without the introduction of scientific farming. In fact, Europeans had gone further in clearing and cultivating than they should have: in the enthusiasm of the high medieval colonization movement, marginal lands had been cleared that were not rich enough to sustain intense cultivation. In addition, even the best plots were becoming overworked. To make matters worse, after around 1300 the weather deteriorated. Whereas western Europe had been favored with a drying and warming trend in the eleventh and twelfth centuries, in the fourteenth century the climate became colder and wetter. Although the average decline in temperature over the course of the century was only about one degree Centigrade, this was sufficient to curtail wine production in many northern areas such as England. Cereal farming too became increasingly impractical in far northern regions because the growing season became too short: in Greenland and parts of Scandinavia, agricultural settlements were abandoned entirely. Increased rainfall also took its toll. Terrible floods deluged all of northwestern Europe in 1315, ruining crops and causing a prolonged, deadly famine that was made worse by epidemic diseases that swept through sheep flocks and cattle herds. For three years peasants were so driven by hunger that they ate their seed grain, ruining their chances for a full recovery in the following season. In desperation they also ate cats, dogs, and rats. Many peasants were so exposed to unsanitary conditions and weakened by malnutrition that they became highly susceptible to disease. The death rate was appalling. In one Flemish city a tenth of the population was buried within a six-month period of 1316 alone. Between 1316 and 1322, 10 percent to 15 percent of the entire European population may have perished in this "Great Famine." Relatively settled farming conditions returned after 1322, but in many parts of Europe heavy rains or other climatic disasters came again. In Italy, floods swept away Florentine bridges in 1333; a tidal wave destroyed the port of Amalfi in 1343. With nature so recurrently capricious, economic life could only suffer.

Although ruinous wars combined with famine to kill off many, Europe remained overpopulated relative to its food supplies until the middle of the fourteenth century. Despite the high mortality rate, this imbalance between population and resources probably worsened after 1300. As cereal production declined, grain prices soared and the poor throughout Europe paid the

HOW DID FAMINE AND PLAGUE TRANSFORM ECONOMIC LIFE IN LATE MEDIEVAL EUROPE?

ECONOMIC DEPRESSION AND THE EMERGENCE OF A NEW EQUILIBRIUM   385

penalty in hunger. Then a disaster struck that was so horrifying that it seemed to many to presage the end of the world.

THE BLACK DEATH

The Black Death was a combined onslaught of bubonic and pneumonic plague that first swept through Europe from 1347 to 1350, returning at periodic intervals for the next three hundred years. This epidemic originated in the Gobi Desert of Mongolia, where the plague bacillus is endemic among the rodents of the area and among the fleas that live on the rodents. Both are capable of carrying the plague; we have no way of knowing which initially carried the disease out of Mongolia during the late 1330s and into China, northern India, and the Crimea. The rapid spread of the disease was an unfortunate consequence of the increasing commercial integration between these areas that the Mongol conquests of the thirteenth century had created. By 1346 the plague had reached the ports along the Black Sea, and from there, in 1347, Genoese galleys brought it, inadvertantly, to Sicily and northern Italy. From Italy it spread throughout western Europe along the trade routes, first striking the seaports, then moving inland.

This calamity was fully comparable—in terms of the death, dislocation, and horror it wrought—with the two world wars of the twentieth century. The clinical effects of the plague were hideous. Once infected with bubonic plague by a flea bite, the diseased person would develop enormous swellings in the groin or armpits, black spots might appear on the arms and legs, diarrhea would ensue, and the victim would die between the fourth and seventh days. If the infection came in the pneumonic form (caused by inhalation) there would be coughing of blood instead of swellings, and death would follow within three days. Some people went to bed healthy and were dead the next morning after a night of agony; ships with dead crews floated aimlessly on the seas. Although the successive epidemics left a few localities unscathed, the overall demographic effects of the plague were devastating. In England, the total population of the country declined by at least 40 percent between 1347 and 1381. The total population of eastern Normandy fell by 30 percent between 1347 and 1357, and again by 30 percent before 1380; in the rural area around Pistoia in Italy a population depletion of about 60 percent occurred between 1340 and 1404. Altogether, the combined effects of famine, war, and, above all, plague reduced the total population of western Europe by at least one half

and perhaps as much as two thirds between 1300 and 1450.

At first, the Black Death caused great hardships for most of the survivors. Since panic-stricken people wished to avoid contagion, many fled from their jobs to seek isolation. Town dwellers fled to the country, and country dwellers fled from each other. Even the pope retreated to the interior of his palace and allowed no one entrance. With large numbers dead and others away from their posts, harvests were left rotting, manufacturing was disrupted, and trade collapsed. Basic commodities became scarcer and prices rose. For these

Bubonic Plague. This representation from a late-fifteenth-century French painting shows a man in the throes of death from the plague. The swelling on his neck is a *bubo*, a form of lymphatic swelling that gave the bubonic plague its name.

THE PROGRESS OF THE BLACK DEATH, FOURTEENTH CENTURY

Where did the Black Death come from, and where did it enter Europe, generally speaking? Why was the onslaught of the disease so devastating, and what agricultural, economic, and demographic factors helped to make Europeans around 1350 so vulnerable to the disease? Note the rapid spread of the Black Death. Would such a rapid advance have been likely during the early Middle Ages, or even in the ancient world? How did the growth of towns, trade, and travel contribute to the spread of the Black Death?

HOW DID FAMINE AND PLAGUE TRANSFORM ECONOMIC LIFE IN LATE MEDIEVAL EUROPE?

ECONOMIC DEPRESSION AND THE EMERGENCE OF A NEW EQUILIBRIUM   387

reasons the onslaught of the plague greatly intensified Europe's economic crisis.

By 1400, however, the new demographic realities began to turn prices around and alter basic economic patterns. In particular, the prices of staple foodstuffs (for example, grains) began to decline because production gradually returned to normal and there were fewer mouths to feed. Recurrences of the plague or natural disasters sometimes caused prices to fluctuate greatly in certain years, but overall prices of basic commodities throughout most of the fifteenth century went down or remained stable. This trend led to new agricultural specialization. Since cereals were cheaper, people could afford to spend a greater percentage of their income on comparative luxuries such as dairy products, meat, and wine. Hitherto farmers all over Europe had concentrated on growing cereals, but now it was wisest, particularly in areas of poorer soil or unpropitious climate, to shift to specialized production. Depending upon whatever seemed most feasible, land might be used for the raising of livestock for milk, grapes for wine, or malt for beer. Specialized regional economies resulted: parts of England were given over to sheep raising or beer production, parts of France concentrated on wine, and Sweden traded butter for cheap German grain. Most areas of Europe turned to what they could do best, and reciprocal trade of basic commodities over long distances created a sound new commercial equilibrium.

THE IMPACT ON TOWNS

Towns were particularly sensitive barometers of the changing economic climate of the later Middle Ages. After reaching their demographic peak around 1300, many towns were already experiencing declining populations and economic crises even before the Black Death struck. The plague, however, made the existing situation infinitely worse. Overcrowding, combined with the generally unsanitary conditions of medieval urban life, made Europe's cities particularly vulnerable to the plague. In some cities, mortality rates from the plague may have exceeded 60 percent. In northern Italy, southern France, and parts of Spain, however, warfare was even more destructive of urban life than was the plague. Toulouse, for example, weathered the onset of the plague relatively well. Between 1355 and 1385, its population declined only about 15 percent,

from approximately thirty thousand to twenty-six thousand. By 1430, however, after several decades of war, Toulouse's population had dropped to around eight thousand. By 1450, however, as a century of warfare came to an end and visitations of the plague became less frequent and less devastating (presumably because Europeans were beginning to develop some resistance to the plague bacillus), urban life was well on the road to recovery. By 1500, a larger percentage of Europe's people lived in towns, and towns themselves played a larger role in the European economy, than had been the case two centuries before.

Certain urban centers, especially those in northern Germany and northern Italy, profited the most from the new economic circumstances. In Germany a group of cities and towns under the leadership of Lübeck and Bremen allied in the so-called Hanseatic League to control long-distance trade in the Baltic and North seas. Their fleets transported German grain to Scandinavia and brought back dairy products, fish, and furs. The enhanced European per capita ability to buy luxury goods brought new wealth to the northern Italian trading cities of Genoa and, especially, Venice because these cities controlled the importation of spices from the East. Greater expenditures on luxury also aided the economies of Florence, Venice, Milan, and other neighboring cities because those cities concentrated on the manufacture of silks and linens, light woolens, and other fine cloths. Milan, in addition, prospered from its armaments industry, which kept the warring European states supplied with armor and weapons. Because of varying local conditions, some cities and towns, above all those of Flanders, became economically depressed, but altogether European urban centers profited remarkably well from the new economic circumstances and emphasis on specialization.

The changed circumstances also helped stimulate the development of sophisticated business, accounting, and banking techniques. Because sharp fluctuations in prices made investments precarious, new forms of partnerships were created to minimize risks. Insurance contracts were also invented to take some of the risk out of shipping. Europe's most useful accounting invention, double-entry bookkeeping, was first put into use in Italy in the mid-fourteenth century and spread rapidly thereafter north of the Alps. This method allowed for quick discovery of computational errors and easy overview of profits and losses, credits and debits. Large-

> Certain urban centers, especially those in northern Germany and northern Italy, profited the most from the new economic circumstances.

The Banker and His Wife, by Quentin Massys.

THE NEW EQUILIBRIUM

In surveying the two centuries of late medieval economic history, we must emphasize both the role of nature and that of human beings. Bad weather and disease may come at any time, but when humans are already suffering from hunger and conditions of overcrowding, the results of natural disasters will be particularly devastating. That certainly is what happened in the fourteenth century. Nature intervened cruelly in human affairs, but no matter how cruel the immediate effects, the results were ultimately beneficial. By 1450 a far smaller population had a higher average standard of living than the population of 1300. In this result humans too played their part. Because people were determined to make the best of the new circumstances and avoid a recurrence of economic depression, they managed to reorganize their economic life and place it on a sounder footing. The gross European product of about 1450 was probably lower than it was in 1300, but this is not surprising given the much smaller population. In fact, per capita output had risen with per capita income, and the European economy was ready to move on to new conquests.

scale banking had already become common after the middle of the thirteenth century, but the economic crises of the later Middle Ages encouraged banks to alter some of their ways of doing business. Most important was the development of prudent branch-banking techniques, especially by the Florentine house of the Medici. Earlier banks had built branches, but the Medici bankers, who flourished from 1397 to 1494, organized theirs along the lines of a modern holding company. The Medici branches, located in London, Bruges, and Avignon, as well as several Italian cities, were dominated by senior partners from the Medici family who followed common policies. However, each branch was a separate, formal partnership that did not carry any other branch down with it if it collapsed. Other Italian banks experimented with advanced credit techniques. Some even allowed their clients to transfer funds between each other without any real money changing hands. Such "book transfers" were at first executed only by oral command, but around 1400 they started to be carried out by written orders. These were the earliest ancestors of the modern check.

SOCIAL AND EMOTIONAL DISLOCATION

What were the causes of the popular rebellions from 1300 to 1450?

Before the healthy new equilibrium was reached, the economic crises of the later Middle Ages contributed from about 1300 to 1450 to provoking a rash of lower-class rural and urban insurrections more numerous than Europe had ever known before. It was once thought that these were all caused by extreme deprivation, but as we will see, often that was not the case.

WHAT WERE THE CAUSES OF THE POPULAR REBELLIONS FROM 1300 TO 1450?

SOCIAL AND EMOTIONAL DISLOCATION   389

THE JACQUERIE

The one large-scale rural uprising that was most clearly caused by economic hardship was the northern French "Jacquerie" of 1358. This took its name from the proto-typical French peasant, "Jacques Bonhomme," who had suffered more than he could endure. In 1348 and 1349 the Black Death had brought its terror and wreaked havoc with the economy. Then a flare-up of war between England and France had spread great desolation over the countryside. The peasants, as usual in late medieval warfare, suffered most from the pillaging and burning carried out by the rapacious soldiers. To make matters even less endurable, after the English decisively defeated the French in 1356 at the battle of Poitiers the French king, John II, and numerous aristocrats had to be ransomed. As always in such cases, the peasants were asked to bear the heaviest share of the burden, but by 1358 they had enough and rose up with astounding ferocity. Without any clear program they burned down castles, murdered their lords, and raped their lords' wives. Undoubtedly their intense economic resentments were the major cause for the uprising, but two qualifications remain in order. The first is that the peasants who participated in the Jacquerie were, comparatively speaking, among the richest in France: apparently those who suffered most abjectly were entirely unable to organize themselves for revolt. The other qualification is that political factors surely help account for the Jacquerie as well as economic ones. While the king was in captivity in England, groups of townsmen were trying to reform the governmental system by limiting monarchical powers, and aristocratic factions were plotting to seize power. Since nobody quite knew which element was going to rule where, the peasants seem to have sensed an opportunity to take advantage of France's political confusion. But in fact the opportunity was not so great as they may have thought: within a month the privileged powers closed ranks, massacred the rebels, and quickly restored order.

THE ENGLISH PEASANTS' REVOLT

The English Peasants' Revolt of 1381—the most serious lower-class rebellion in English history—is frequently bracketed with the Jacquerie, but its causes were very different. Instead of being a revolt of desperation, it arose from a combination of rising economic expectations combined with political grievances associated with English defeats in the war with France. By 1381 the effects of the Black Death should have been working in favor of the peasants. Above all, a shortage of labor should have placed their services in demand. In fact, the incidence of the plague did help to increase manumissions (freeings) of serfs and to raise salaries or lower rents of free farm laborers. But aristocratic landlords fought back to preserve their own incomes. They succeeded in passing legislation that aimed to keep wages at preplague levels and force free laborers to work at the lower rates. Aristocrats also tried to exact all their old dues and unpaid services from the serfs that remained under their control. Because the peasants were unwilling to be pushed down into their previous poverty and subservience, a collision was inevitable.

The spark that ignited the great revolt of 1381 was an attempt to collect a new type of national tax to pay for the failing war with France. Traditionally, English taxes had been assessed village by village in rough proportion to wealth. In 1377 and 1379, however, the government imposed a much less graduated head tax instead of the traditional income tax. These two taxes were collected without resistance, but when agents tried to collect a third, much heavier such tax in 1381, the peasants, artisans, and town dwellers of eastern England rose up to resist. First they burned local records and sacked the dwellings of those they considered their exploiters; then they marched into London, where they executed the lord chancellor and treasurer of England, whose fiscal mismanagement they blamed for recent English defeats in the French war. Recognizing the gravity of the situation, the fourteen-year-old king, Richard II, went out to meet the peasants and won their confidence by promising to abolish serfdom and keep rents low; meanwhile, during negotiations the peasant leader, Wat Tyler, was murdered in a squabble with the king's escort. Lacking leadership, the peasants, who mistakenly thought they had achieved their aims, rapidly dispersed. But once the boy king was no longer in danger of his life he kept none of his promises. Instead, the scattered peasant forces were quickly hunted down and a few alleged troublemakers were executed without any mass reprisals. The revolt itself therefore did not accomplish its objectives. It did, however, frighten the English nobility profoundly. No further head taxes were at-

The incidence of the plague did help to increase manumissions of serfs and raise salaries or lower rents of free farm laborers.

FROISSART ON THE ENGLISH PEASANTS' REVOLT, 1381

Jean Froissart (1337?–1410?) is best known as the author of a lengthy history of the Hundred Years' War. He began his career in the service of the queen of England, but spent much of his later life in the Netherlands and in France. He was not an eyewitness to the events of the Peasants' Revolt, but he had excellent English connections from whom he presumably derived his information. Froissart's perspective is entirely that of the aristocrats whom he served and with whom he associated. This fact makes his modest sympathy for the rebels of 1381 all the more interesting, particularly compared with his earlier, entirely negative portrayal of the 1358 Jacquerie rebels in France.

While these negotiations and discussions were going on, there occurred in England great disasters and uprisings of the common people, on account of which the country was almost ruined beyond recovery. Never was any land or realm in such great danger as England at that time. It was because of the abundance and prosperity in which the common people then lived that this rebellion broke out, just as in earlier days the Jack Goodmans rose in France and committed many excesses, by which the noble land of France suffered grave injury. . . .

It is the custom in England, as in several other countries, for the nobles to have strong powers over their men and to hold them in serfdom: that is, that by right and custom they have to till the lands of the gentry, reap the [grain] . . . , thresh and winnow it; mow the hay . . . , cut logs . . . , and all such forced tasks; all this the men must do by way of serfage to their masters. In England there is a much greater number than elsewhere of such men who are obliged to serve the prelates and the nobles. . . .

These bad people . . . began to rebel because, they said, they were held too much in subjection, and when the world began there had been no serfs and could not be, unless they had rebelled against their Lord, as Lucifer did against God; but they were not of that stature, being neither angels nor spirits, but men formed in the image of their masters, and they were treated as ani-mals. This was a thing they could no longer endure, wishing rather to be all one and the same; and, if they worked for their masters, they wanted to have wages for it. In these machinations they had been greatly encouraged originally by a crack-brained priest of Kent called John Ball . . . who had the habit on Sundays after mass, when everyone was coming out of church, of going to the cloisters or the graveyard, assembling the people round him and preaching thus:

"Good people, things cannot go right in England and never will, until goods are held in common and there are no more serfs and gentlefolk, but we are all one and the same. In what way are those whom we call lords greater masters than ourselves? How have they deserved it? Why do they hold us in bondage? If we all spring from a single father and mother, Adam and Eve, how can they claim or prove that they are lords more than us, ex-cept by making us produce and grow the wealth which they spend? They are clad in vel-vet and camlet lined with squirrel and ermine, while we go dressed in coarse cloth. They have the wines, the spices, and the good bread: we have the rye, the husks and the straw, and we drink water. They have shelter and ease in their fine manors, and we have hardship and toil, the wind and the rain in the fields. And from us must come, from our labor, the things which keep them in luxury. We are called serfs and beaten if we are slow in our service to them, yet we have no sovereign lord we can complain to, none to hear us and do us justice. Let us go to the King—he is young—and show him how we are oppressed, and tell him that we want things to be changed, or else we will change them ourselves. If we go in good earnest and all together, very many people who are called serfs and are held in subjection will follow us to get their freedom. And when the King sees and hears us, he will remedy the evil, either willingly or otherwise."

These were the kind of things which John Ball usually preached in the villages on Sundays . . . and many of the common people agreed with him.

Geoffrey Brereton, ed. and trans. *Froissart: Chronicles.* (London and New York: Penguin Books, 1968), pp. 211–213.

tempted, and enforcement of wage controls on peasant labor came to an end. Within a few decades the natural play of economic forces considerably improved the lot of small- to medium-scale farmers and rural wage laborers, and within a century had brought about the effective disappearance of serfdom in England. The result was a kind of mid-fifteenth-century "golden age" for the English peasantry.

URBAN REBELLIONS

Other rural revolts took place in other parts of Europe, but we may now look at some urban ones. The urban revolts of the later Middle Ages are conventionally viewed as uprisings of exploited workers who were more oppressed than ever because of the effects of economic depression. But this is probably too great a simplification because each case differed and complex forces were always at work. For example, an uprising in the north German town of Brunswick in 1374 was much less a movement of the poor against the rich than a political upheaval in which one political alliance replaced another. A different north German uprising, in Lübeck in 1408, has been aptly described as a "taxpayer's" revolt. This again was less a confrontation of the poor versus the rich than an attempt by a faction that was out of power to initiate less costly government.

The nearest thing to a real proletarian revolt was the uprising in 1378 of the Florentine Ciompi (pronounced "cheeompi"). The *ciompi* were wool combers who had the misfortune to be engaged in an industry that had become particularly depressed. Some of them had lost their jobs; others were frequently cheated or underpaid by the masters of the woolen industry. The latter wielded great political power in Florence, and thus could pass economic legislation in their own favor. This fact in itself meant that if there were to be economic reforms, they would have to go together with political changes. As events turned out, it was a political crisis that called the Ciompi into direct action. In 1378 Florence had become exhausted by three years of war with the papacy. Certain patrician leaders overthrew the old regime in order to alter the war policy and gain their own political advantage. Circumstances led them to seek the support of the lower classes and, once stirred up, the Ciompi became emboldened after a few months to launch their own far more radical rebellion. This rebellion was inspired primarily by economic hardship and grievances, but personal hatreds also played a role. The Ciompi held power for six weeks, during which they tried to institute tax relief, fuller employment, and representation of themselves and other workers' groups in the Florentine government. But they could not maintain their hold on power and a new oligarchical government revoked all their reforms.

If we try to draw any general conclusions about these various uprisings, we can certainly say that few if any of them would have occurred had there not been an economic crisis. But political considerations always had some influence, and the rebels in some uprisings were more prosperous than in others. It is noteworthy that all the genuinely lower-class uprisings of economically desperate groups quickly failed. This was certainly because the upper classes were more accustomed to wielding power and giving orders; even more important, they had access to the money and troops necessary to quell revolts. Sometimes elements within the lower classes might fight among themselves, whereas the privileged always managed to form a united front when faced by a lower-class threat to their domination. In addition, lower-class rebels were usually more intent on redressing immediate grievances than on developing coherent long-term governmental programs; inspiring ideals for cohesive action were generally lacking. The case of the Hussite Revolution in Bohemia—to be treated later—shows that religion in the later Middle Ages was a more effective rallying force for large numbers of people than political, economic, and social demands.

A Party of Late Medieval Aristocrats. Notice the pointed shoes and the women's pointed hats, twice as high as their heads.

ARISTOCRATIC INSECURITIES

Although the upper classes succeeded in overcoming popular uprisings, they perceived the economic and emotional insecurities of the later Middle Ages and the possibility of revolt as constant threats, and became obsessed with maintaining their privileged social status. Late medieval aristocrats were in a precarious economic position because most of their income came from land. In times when grain prices and rents were falling and wages rising, landowners were obviously in economic trouble. Aristocrats also felt threatened by the rapid rise of merchants and financiers who could

make quick killings because of sharp market fluctuations. In practice, really wealthy merchants bought land and were absorbed into the aristocracy, while many land-owning aristocrats were able to stave off economic threats by expert estate management. But most aristocrats still felt more exposed to social and economic insecurities than before. The result was that they tried to set up social and cultural barriers by which to separate themselves from other classes.

Two of the most striking examples of this separation were the aristocratic emphasis on luxury and the formation of exclusive chivalric orders. The later Middle Ages were the period par excellence of aristocratic os-

WHAT WERE THE CAUSES OF THE POPULAR REBELLIONS FROM 1300 TO 1450?

SOCIAL AND EMOTIONAL DISLOCATION   393

The Crucifixion, by Matthias Grünewald from the *Insenheim Altarpiece.*

gant or boisterous diversions just as often went to the other emotional extreme when faced with the psychic stress caused by the troubles of the age, and abandoned themselves to sorrow. Throughout the period grown men and women shed tears in abundance. The queen mother of France wept in public when she first viewed her newborn grandson; the great preacher Vincent Ferrer had to interrupt his sermons on Christ's Passion and the Last Judgment because he and his audience were sobbing too convulsively; and the English king Edward II supposedly wept so much when imprisoned that he gushed forth enough hot water for his own shave. The last story taxes the imagination, but it does illustrate well what contemporaries thought was possible. We know for certain that the church encouraged crying because of the survival of statuettes of weeping Saint Johns, which were obviously designed to call forth tears from their viewers.

People also were encouraged by preachers to brood on the Passion of Christ and on their own mortality. Fearsome crucifixes abounded, and the figure of the Virgin Mary was less a smiling madonna than a sorrowing mother: now she was most frequently depicted

tentation. While famine or disease raged, aristocrats entertained themselves with lavish banquets and magnificent pageants. At one feast in Flanders in 1468, a table decoration was forty-six feet high. Aristocratic clothing too was extremely ostentatious: men wore long, pointed shoes, and women ornately festooned headdresses. Throughout history rich people have always enjoyed dressing up, but the aristocrats of the later Middle Ages seem to have done so obsessively. They even imposed special sumptuary laws that defined the type of clothing that each rank in society could wear. This aristocratic insistence on maintaining a sharply defined social hierarchy also accounts for the late medieval proliferation of chivalric orders, such as those of the knights of the Garter or the Golden Fleece. By joining together in exclusive orders that prescribed special conduct and boasted special insignia of membership, aristocrats tried to set themselves off from others, in effect, by putting up a sign that read "for members only."

EMOTIONAL EXTREMES

We must not think, however, that late medieval Europeans gave themselves over to riotous living without interruption. In fact, the same people who sought ele-

CHRONOLOGY

FAMINE, PLAGUES, REBELLION, AND WARFARE,
1300–1450

"Great Famine"	1315–1322
Black Death	1347–1350
"Jacquerie" rebellion	1358
Ciompi revolt	1378
English peasant rebellion	1381
Hundred Years' War	1337–1453
Venice, Milan, and Florence consolidate their territories	1400–1454

A Dead Man Before His Judge. A late medieval reminder of human mortality.

played figures of grinning Death with his scythe, carrying off elegant and healthy men and women, or sadistic devils roasting pain-wracked humans in hell. Because people who painted or brooded on such pictures might the next day indulge in excessive revels, late medieval culture often seems to border on the manic depressive. But apparently such extreme reactions were necessary to help people cope with their fears.

TRIALS FOR THE CHURCH AND HUNGER FOR THE DIVINE

What were the main forms of late medieval popular piety?

The intense concentration on the meaning of death was also a manifestation of a very deep and pervasive religiosity. The religious enthusiasm of the High Middle Ages by no means flagged after 1300; if anything, it became more intense. But religious enthusiasm took on new forms of expression because of the institutional difficulties of the church and the turmoils of the age.

THE LATE MEDIEVAL PAPACY

After the humiliation and death of Pope Boniface VIII in 1303 (see p. 356), the church experienced a period of institutional crisis that was as severe and prolonged as the contemporary economic crisis. We may distinguish three phases: the so-called Babylonian Captivity of the papacy, 1305–1378; the Great Schism, 1378–1417; and the period of the Italian territorial papacy, 1417–1517. During the "Babylonian Captivity" the papacy was located in Avignon instead of Rome and was generally subservient to the interests of the French crown. There were several reasons for this: the most obvious was that since the test of strength between Philip the Fair and Boniface VIII had resulted in a clear victory for the French king, subsequent popes were unwilling to risk French royal ire. In fact, once the popes realized that they could not give orders to the French kings, they found that they could gain certain advantages from currying their favor. One was a safe home in southern France, away from the tumult of Italy. Cen-

slumping with grief at the foot of the cross, or holding the dead Christ in her lap. The late medieval obsession with mortality can also still be seen in sculptures, frescoes, and book illustrations that reminded viewers of the brevity of life and the torments of hell. The characteristic tombs of the High Middle Ages were surmounted by sculptures that either showed the deceased in some action that had been typical of his or her accomplishments in life, or else in a state of repose that showed death to be nothing more than peaceful sleep. But in the late fourteenth century, tombs appeared that displayed the physical ravages of death in the most gruesome ways imaginable: emaciated corpses were displayed with protruding intestines or covered with snakes or toads. Some tombs bore inscriptions stating that the viewer would soon be "a fetid cadaver, food for worms"; some warned chillingly, "What you are, I was; what I am, you will be." Omnipresent illustrations dis-

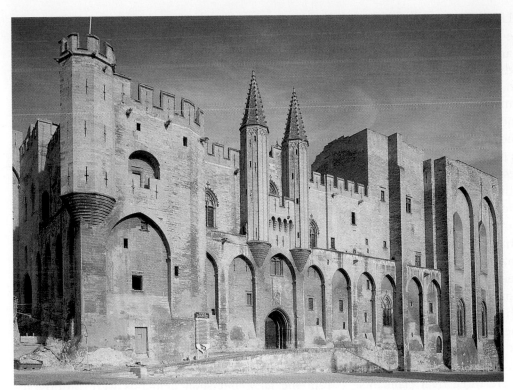

Papal Palace at Avignon. This great palace was begun in 1339 and symbolizes the apparent permanence of the papal residence in Avignon.

tral Italy and the city of Rome in the fourteenth century had become so politically turbulent and rebellious that the pope could not even count on finding personal safety there, let alone sufficiently peaceful conditions to maintain orderly ecclesiastical administration. But no such danger existed in Avignon. Even though Avignon was not then part of the French kingdom—it was the major city of a small papal territory—French military might was close enough to guarantee the pope much-needed security. Another advantage of papal subservience to French power was help from the French in pursuing mutually advantageous policies in Germany and southern Italy. Perhaps most important was a working agreement whereby the French king would propose his own candidates to become bishops and the pope would then name them in return for sizable monetary payments. Although most of the Avignon popes tried hard to maintain their independence, in practice the balance of power rested clearly with the French king.

At Avignon the popes were more successful than ever in pursuing their policy of centralizing the government of the church. For the first time they worked out a sound system of papal finance, based on the systematization of dues collected from the clergy throughout

Europe. The papacy also succeeded in appointing more candidates to vacant church positions than before (in practice often naming candidates proposed by the French and English kings), and they proceeded against heresy with great determination, indeed with ruthlessness. But whatever the popes achieved in power they lost in respect and loyalty. The clergy became alienated as a result of being asked to pay so much money, and many lay people were horrified by the corruption and unbridled luxury displayed at the papal court: there the cardinals lived more splendidly than lords, dining off peacocks, pheasants, grouse, and swans, and drinking from elaborately sculptured fountains that spouted the finest wines. Most of the Avignonese popes themselves were personally upright and abstemious, but one, Clement VI (1342–1352), was worse than his cardinals. Clement was ready to offer any spiritual benefit for money, boasted that he would appoint even a jackass as bishop if political circumstances warranted, and defended his incessant sexual transgressions by insisting that he fornicated on doctors' orders.

As time went on the pressures of informed public opinion forced the popes to promise that they would return to Rome. After one abortive attempt by Urban V in 1367, Pope Gregory XI finally did return to the Holy City in 1377. But he died a year later, and then disaster struck. The college of cardinals, surrounded in Rome by clamoring Italians, yielded to local sentiment by naming an Italian pope who took the title of Urban VI. But most of the cardinals were Frenchmen and quickly regretted their decision, especially because Urban VI immediately began quarreling with them and revealing what were probably paranoid tendencies. Therefore, after only a few months, the cardinals met again, declared the previous election void, and replaced Urban with one of their own number, who called himself Clement VII.

Unfortunately, however, Urban VI did not meekly resign. On the contrary, he named an entirely new Italian college of cardinals and remained entrenched in Rome. Clement VII quickly retreated with his own party to Avignon, and the so-called Great Schism ensued. France and other countries in the French political orbit—such as Scotland, Castile, and Aragon—recognized Clement, while the rest of Europe recognized Urban as the true pope. For three decades Christians looked on helplessly while the rival pontiffs hurled curses at each other and the international monastic orders became divided into Roman and Avignonese camps. The death of one or the other pope did not end the schism; each camp had its own set of cardinals, which promptly named either a French or Italian successor. The desperateness of the situation led a council of prelates from both camps to meet in Pisa in 1409 to depose both popes and name a new one instead. But neither the Italian nor the French pope accepted the council's decision, and both had enough political support to command some obedience. So after 1409 there were three rival claimants hurling curses instead of two.

The Great Schism was finally ended in 1417 by the Council of Constance, the largest ecclesiastical gathering in medieval history. This time the assembled prelates made certain to gain the crucial support of secular powers and also to eliminate all the prior claimants before naming a new pope. After the council's election of Martin V in 1417, European ecclesiastical unity was finally restored. But a struggle over the nature of church government followed immediately. The members of the Council of Constance challenged the prevailing medieval theory of papal monarchy by calling for balanced, "conciliar" government. In two momentous decrees they stated that a general council of prelates was superior in authority to the pope, and that such councils should meet regularly to govern the Church. Not surprisingly, subsequent popes—who had now returned to Rome—sought to nullify these decrees. When a new council met in Basel in 1431, in accordance with the principles laid down at Constance, the reigning pope did all he could to sabotage its activities. Ultimately he was successful: after a protracted struggle the Council of Basel dissolved in 1449 in abject failure, and the attempt to institute constitutional government in the Church was defeated.

But the papacy won this victory over conciliarism only by gaining the support of the rulers of the European states. In separate concordats with kings and princes the popes granted the secular rulers much authority over the various local churches. The popes thus became assured of theoretical supremacy at the cost of surrendering much real power. To compensate for this they concentrated on consolidating their own direct rule in central Italy. Most of the fifteenth-century popes ruled very much like any other princes, leading armies, jockeying for alliances, and building magnificent palaces. Hence, although they did succeed for the first time in creating a viable political state, their reputation for piety remained low.

POPULAR PIETY AND POPULAR HERESY

While the papacy was enduring these vicissitudes, the local clergy throughout Europe was also losing prestige. One reason was that the pope's greater financial demands forced the clergy to demand more from the laity, but such demands were bitterly resented, especially during times of prevailing economic crisis. Then too during outbreaks of plague the clergy sometimes fled their posts just like everyone else, but in so doing they lost whatever claim they had to moral superiority.

Probably the single greatest reason for growing dissatisfaction with the clergy was the increase in lay literacy. The continued proliferation of schools and the decline in the cost of books—a subject we will treat later—made it possible for large numbers of lay people to learn how to read. Once that happened, the laity could start reading parts of the Bible, or, more frequently, popular religious primers. This reading made it clear that their local priests were not living according to the standards set by Jesus and the apostles. In the meantime, the upheavals and horrors of the age drove people to seek religious solace more than ever. Where lay people found the conventional channels of church attendance, confession, and submission to clerical authority insufficient, they sought supplementary or alternate routes to piety. These differed greatly from each other, but they all aimed to satisfy an immense hunger for the divine.

The most widely traveled route was to perform repeated acts of external devotion in the hope that they

> Where lay people found the conventional channels of church attendance, confession, and submission to clerical authority insufficient, they sought supplementary or alternate routes to piety.

THE CONCILIARIST CONTROVERSY

The Great Schism produced a fundamental and far-reaching debate about the nature of authority within the church. Arguments for papal supremacy rested upon the traditional claims that the popes were the successors of Saint Peter, to whom Jesus Christ had delegated his own authority over the church. Arguments for the supremacy of a general council had been advanced around the University of Paris throughout much of the fourteenth century, but it was only in the circumstances of the Schism that these arguments found a wide audience. The documents below trace the history of the controversy, from the declaration of conciliar supremacy at the Council of Constance (Haec Sancta, 1415), to the Council's efforts to guarantee regular meetings of general councils thereafter (Frequens, 1417), to the papal condemnation of appeals to future general councils issued in 1460 (Execrabilis). Note, however, the limitations on Execrabilis. Even this condemnation does not go so far as to actually contradict Haec Sancta. It merely condemns appeals from papal judgment to future general councils that have no specified meeting date. The conciliar ideal was still powerful at the end of the fifteenth century, and in the sixteenth and seventeenth centuries, it would have a profound impact on European political thought about kings.

HAEC SANCTA SYNODUS (1415)

This holy synod of Constance . . . declares that being lawfully assembled in the Holy Spirit, constituting a general council and representing the Catholic Church Militant, it has its power directly from Christ, and that all persons of whatever rank or dignity, even a Pope, are bound to obey it in matters relating to faith and the end of the Schism and the general reformation of the church of God in head and members.

Further, it declares that any person of whatever position, rank, or dignity, even a Pope, who contumaciously refuses to obey the mandates, statutes, ordinances, or regulations enacted or to be enacted by this holy synod, or by any other general council lawfully assembled, relating to the matters aforesaid or to other matters involved with them, shall, unless he repents, be . . . duly punished. . . .

FREQUENS (1417)

The frequent holding of general councils is the best method of cultivating the field of the Lord, for they root out the briars, thorns, and thistles of heresies, errors, and schisms, correct abuses, make crooked things straight, and prepare the Lord's vineyard for fruitfulness and rich fertility. Neglect of general councils sows the seeds of these evils and encourages their growth. This truth is borne in upon us as we recall times past and survey the present.

Therefore by perpetual edict we . . . ordain that henceforth general councils shall be held as follows: the first within the five years immediately following the end of the present council, the second within seven years from the end of the council next after this, and subsequently every ten years forever. . . . Thus there will always be a certain continuity. Either a council will be in session or one will be expected at the end of a fixed period. . . .

EXECRABILIS (1460)

An execrable abuse, unheard of in earlier times, has sprung up in our period. Some men, imbued with a spirit of rebellion and moved not by a desire for sound decisions but rather by a desire to escape the punishment for sin, suppose that they can appeal from the Pope, Vicar of Jesus Christ; from the Pope, to whom in the person of blessed Peter it was said, "Feed my sheep" and "whatever you bind on earth will be bound in heaven"—from this Pope to a future council. How harmful this is to the Christian republic, as well as how contrary to canon law, anyone who is not ignorant of the law can understand. For . . . who would not consider it ridiculous to appeal to something which does not now exist anywhere nor does anyone know when it will exist? The poor are heavily oppressed by the powerful, offenses remain unpunished, rebellion against the Holy See is encouraged, license for sin is granted, and all ecclesiastical discipline and hierarchical ranking of the Church are turned upside down.

Wishing therefore to expel this deadly poison from the Church of Christ, and concerned with the salvation of the sheep committed to us . . . with the counsel and assent of our venerable brothers, the Cardinals of the Holy Roman Church, together with the counsel and assent of all those prelates who have been trained in canon and civil law who follow our Court, and with our own certain knowledge, we condemn appeals of this kind, reject them as erroneous and abominable, and declare them to be completely null and void. And we lay down that from now on, no one should dare . . . to make such an appeal from our decisions, be they legal or theological, or from any commands at all from us or our successors. . . .

Haec Sancta and *Frequens* from *The Council of Constance*, L. R. Loomis, ed. and trans. (New York: Columbia University Press, 1961), pp. 229, 246–247; *Execrabilis: Defensorum Obedientiae Apostolicae et alia Documenta*, Heiko A. Oberman, Daniel E. Zerfoss, and William J. Courtenay, eds. and trans. (Cambridge, Mass: Harvard Univ. Press, 1968), pp. 224–227, with modifications by R. C. Stacey.

A German Flagellant Procession. These penitents hoped they could ward off the Black Death by their mutually inflicted tortures.

would gain the devotee divine favor on earth and salvation in the hereafter. People flocked to go on pilgrimages as never before and participated regularly in barefoot religious processions: the latter were often held twice a month and occasionally as often as once a week. Men and women also eagerly paid for thousands of masses to be said by full-time "Mass priests" for the souls of their dead relatives, and left legacies for the reading of numerous requiem masses to save their own souls after death. Obsession with repeating prayers reached a peak when some pious individuals tried to compute the number of drops of blood that Christ shed on the cross so that they could say the same number of Our Fathers. The most dramatic form of religious ritual in the later Middle Ages was flagellation. Some women who lived in communal houses beat themselves with the roughest animal hides, chains, and knotted thongs. A young girl who entered such a community in Poland in 1331 suffered extreme internal injuries and became completely disfigured within eleven months. Flailings were not usually performed in public, but during the first onslaught of the Black Death in 1348 and 1349, whole bands of lay people marched through northern Europe chanting and beating each other with metal-tipped scourges in the hope of appeasing the apparent divine wrath.

MYSTICISM

An opposite route to godliness was the inward path of mysticism. Throughout the European continent, but particularly in Germany and England, male and female mystics, both clerical and lay, sought union with God by means of "detachment," contemplation, or spiritual exercises. The most original and eloquent late medieval mystical theorist was Master Eckhart (c. 1260–1327), a German Dominican who taught that there was a power or "spark" deep within every human soul that was really the dwelling place of God. By renouncing all sense of selfhood one could retreat into one's innermost recesses and there find divinity. Eckhart did not recommend ceasing attendance at church—he hardly could have because he preached in churches—but he made it clear that outward rituals were of comparatively little importance in reaching God. He also gave the impression to his lay audiences that they might attain godliness largely on their own volition. Thus ecclesiastical authorities charged him with inciting "ignorant and undisciplined people to wild and dangerous excesses." Although Eckhart pleaded his own doctrinal orthodoxy, some of his teachings were condemned by the papacy.

That Eckhart's critics were not entirely mistaken in their worries is shown by the fact that some lay people in Germany who were influenced by him did fall into the heresy of believing that they could become fully united with God on earth without any priestly intermediaries. But these so-called heretics of the Free Spirit were few in number. Much more numerous were later orthodox mystics, sometimes influenced by Eckhart and sometimes not, who placed greater emphasis on the divine initiative in the meeting of the soul with God and made certain to insist that the ministrations of the church were a necessary contribution to the mystic way. Even they, however, believed that "churches make no man holy, but men make churches holy." Most of the great teachers and practitioners of mysticism in the fourteenth century were clerics, nuns, or hermits, but in the fifteenth century a modified form of mystical belief spread among lay people. This "practical mysticism" did not aim for full ecstatic union with God, but rather for an ongoing sense of some divine presence during the conduct of daily life. The most popular manual that pointed the way to this goal was the *Imitation of Christ*, written around 1427, probably by the north German canon Thomas à Kempis. Because this book was written in a simple but forceful style and taught how to be a pious Christian while still living ac-

tively in the world, it was particularly attractive to lay readers. Thus it quickly became translated into the leading European vernaculars. From then until today it has been more widely read by Christians than any other religious work except the Bible. The *Imitation* urges its readers to participate in one religious ceremony—the sacrament of the Eucharist—but otherwise it emphasizes inward piety. According to its teachings, the individual Christian is best able to become the "partner" of Jesus Christ both by receiving communion and by engaging in biblical meditation and leading a simple, moral life.

LOLLARDS AND HUSSITES

A third distinct form of late medieval piety was outright religious protest or heresy. In England and Bohemia especially, heretical movements became serious threats to the church. The initiator of heresy in late medieval England was an Oxford theologian named John Wyclif (c. 1330–1384). Wyclif's rigorous adherence to the theology of Saint Augustine led him to believe that a certain number of humans were predestined to be saved while the rest were irrevocably damned. He thought the predestined would naturally live simply, according to the standards of the New Testament, but in fact he found most members of the church hierarchy indulging in splendid extravagances. Hence he concluded that most church officials were damned. For him the only solution was to have secular rulers appropriate ecclesiastical wealth and reform the church by replacing corrupt priests and bishops with men who would live according to apostolic standards. Wyclif's position was obviously attractive to the aristocracy of England, who may have looked forward to enriching themselves with church spoils and at least saw nothing wrong with using Wyclif as a bulldog to frighten the pope and the local clergy. Thus Wyclif at first received influential aristocratic support. But toward the end of his life he moved from merely calling for reform to attacking some of the most basic institutions of the church, above all the sacrament of the Eucharist. This radicalism frightened off his influential protectors, and Wyclif probably would have been formally condemned for heresy had he lived longer. His death brought no respite for the church, however, because he had attracted numerous lay followers—called Lollards—who zealously continued to propagate some of his most radical ideas. Above all, the Lollards taught that pious Christians should not entrust their salvation to the sacraments of a corrupt church, but should instead study the Bible (which Lollards speedily translated into English) and Lollard religious tracts. Lollardy gained many adherents in the last two decades of the fourteenth century, but after the introduction in England of the death penalty for heresy in 1401 and the failure of a Lollard uprising in 1414, the heretical wave greatly receded. Nonetheless, Lollards survived until the sixteenth century, when they merged into the new religious movements set loose by the Protestant Reformation.

Much greater was the influence of Wyclifism in Bohemia. Around 1400, Czech students who had studied in Oxford brought back Wyclif's ideas to the Bohemian capital of Prague. There Wyclifism was enthusiastically adopted by an eloquent preacher named Jan Hus (c. 1373–1415), who had already been inveighing in well-attended sermons against "the world, the flesh, and the devil." Hus employed Wyclifite theories to back up his own calls for an end to ecclesiastical corruption, rallying many Bohemians to the cause of reform in the years between 1408 and 1415. In contrast to the Lollards, however, whose heretical views on the Eucharist cost them much support, Hus emphasized the centrality of the Eucharist to Christian piety by demanding that the laity too should receive not only the consecrated bread of the Mass, but also the consecrated wine, which the late medieval Church reserved solely for priests. This demand, known as Utraquism, gained broad popular support among the Bohemian laity and became a rallying symbol for the Hussite movement. Influential aristocrats supported Hus partly out of national pride, but partly too in the hope that Hus' reforms might allow them to recover the revenues they had lost to the orthodox Catholic clergy over the previous century. Influenced by the politics of the Great Schism, even the king of Bohemia lent Hus his protection. Above all, however, Hus gained a mass following because of his eloquence and concern for social justice. Accordingly, most of Bohemia was behind him when Hus in 1415 agreed to travel to the Council of Constance to defend his views and try to convince the assembled prelates that only thoroughgoing reform could save the Church. But although Hus had been guaranteed his personal safety, this assurance was revoked as soon as he arrived at the Council: rather than being given a fair hearing, the betrayed idealist was tried for heresy and burned.

Hus' supporters in Bohemia were justifiably out-

> The Hussite declaration of religious independence was a foretaste of what was to come one hundred years later with Protestantism.

raged and quickly raised the banner of open revolt. The aristocracy took advantage of the situation to seize church lands, and poorer priests, artisans, and peasants rallied together in the hope of achieving Hus' goals of religious reform and social justice. Between 1420 and 1424 armies of radical Hussites known as Taborites, led by a brilliant blind general, Jan Zizka, resoundingly defeated several invading forces of well-armed crusading knights from Germany sent against them by the papacy. These victories increased the radicalism of the Taborites, inspiring them to heights of apocalyptic fervor. Finally, in 1434 more conservative, aristocratically dominated Hussites overcame the radicals and negotiated a settlement with the Church that permitted Utraquism in the Bohemian church alongside Catholic orthodoxy. Bohemia did not return fully to the Catholic fold until the seventeenth century. The Hussite declaration of religious independence was both a foretaste of what was to come one hundred years later with Protestantism and the most successful late medieval expression of dissatisfaction with the government of the church.

POLITICAL CRISIS AND RECOVERY

What caused the rise of national monarchies?

The story of late medieval politics at first seems very dreary because throughout most of the period there was incessant strife. Almost everywhere neighbors fought neighbors and states fought states. But closer inspection makes it clear that despite the turmoil there was ultimate improvement in almost all the governments of Europe. In the course of the fifteenth century peace returned to most of the Continent, the national monarchies in particular became stronger, and the period ended on a new note of political as well as economic strength.

ITALY

In southern Italy, the kingdom of Naples remained mired in endemic warfare and maladministration throughout the fourteenth and fifteenth centuries. The fourteenth century was also a time of troubles for the Papal States in central Italy, because forces representing the absent or divided papacy were seldom able to overcome the resistance of refractory towns and rival leaders of marauding military bands. But after the end of the Great Schism in 1417 the popes consolidated their Italian territories and became the effective rulers of most of the middle part of the peninsula. Farther north some of the leading city-states—such as Florence, Venice, Siena, and Genoa—had experienced at least occasional and more often prolonged social warfare during the fourteenth century because of the economic pressures of the age. But sooner or later the most powerful families or interest groups overcame internal resistance. By around 1400 the three leading cities of the north—Venice, Milan, and Florence—had fixed definitively on their own different forms of government: Venice was ruled by a merchant oligarchy, Milan by a dynastic despotism, and Florence by a complex, supposedly republican system that was actually controlled by the rich. (After 1434 the Florentine republic was in practice dominated by the Medici banking family.)

Having settled their internal problems, Venice, Milan, and Florence proceeded from about 1400 to 1454 to expand territorially, conquering almost all the other northern Italian cities and towns except Genoa, which remained prosperous and independent but gained no new territory. Thus, by the middle of the fifteenth century Italy was divided into five major parts: the states of Venice, Milan, and Florence in the north; the Papal States in the middle; and the kingdom of Naples in the south. A treaty of 1454 initiated a half century of peace between these states: whenever one threatened to upset the "balance of power," the others usually allied against it before serious warfare could break out. Accordingly, the last half of the fifteenth century was a fortunate age for Italy. But in 1494 a French invasion initiated a period of renewed warfare in which the French attempt to dominate Italy was successfully countered by Spain.

GERMANY

North of the Alps political turmoil prevailed throughout the fourteenth century and lasted longer into the fifteenth. Probably the worst instability was experienced in Germany. There the virtually independent princes continually warred with the greatly weakened emperors, or else they warred with each other. Between about 1350 and 1450 near anarchy prevailed,

because while the princes were warring and subdividing their inheritances into smaller states, petty powers such as free cities and knights who owned one or two castles were striving to shake off the rule of the princes. Throughout most of the German west these attempts met with enough success to fragment political authority more than ever, but in the east after about 1450 certain stronger German princes managed to assert their authority over divisive forces. After they did so, they started to rule firmly over middle-sized states on the model of the larger national monarchies of England and France. The strongest princes were those in eastern territories such as Bavaria, Austria, and Brandenburg, because there towns were fewer and smaller and the princes had been able to take advantage of imperial weakness to preside over the colonization of large tracts of land. Especially the Habsburg princes of Austria and the Hohenzollern princes of Brandenburg—a territory joined in the sixteenth century with the easternmost lands of Prussia—would be the most influential powers in Germany's future.

FRANCE

France too was torn by strife for much of the period, primarily in the form of the Hundred Years' War between France and England. The Hundred Years' War was actually a series of conflicts that lasted from 1337 to 1453 and whose roots reached back into the 1290s. Of the several different causes for this prolonged struggle, the major one was the longstanding problem of French territory held by the English kings. At the beginning of the fourteenth century the English kings, as vassals of the French crown, still ruled much of the rich southern French lands of Gascony and Aquitaine. The French, who since the reign of Philip Augustus had been expanding and consolidating their rule, obviously hoped to expel the English, making war inevitable. Another cause for strife was that English economic interests in the woolen trade with Flanders led England to support the frequent attempts of Flemish burghers to rebel against French rule. Finally, the war involved a succession dispute over the French crown itself. In 1328, the last of King Philip IV's three sons died without leaving a son to succeed him. A new dynasty, the Valois, thereupon replaced the Capetians on the throne of France. Only by prohibiting inheritance through women, however, could the Valois kings claim to be the closest heirs to the Capetians. Otherwise, the rightful heir to the throne of France was King Edward III of England, whose mother was the daughter

1328
Under English influence

1360
Under English influence

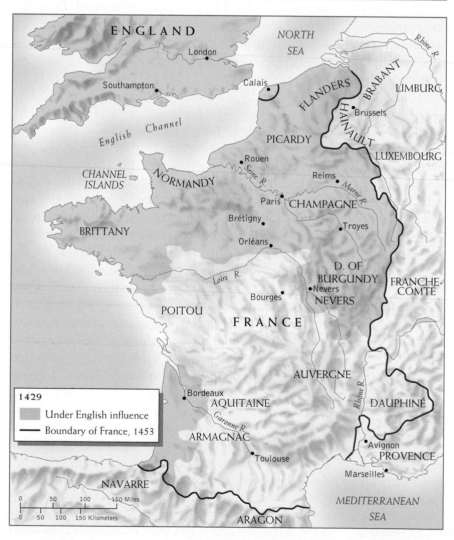

1429
Under English influence
Boundary of France, 1453

FRANCE DURING THE HUNDRED YEARS' WAR

This map shows three snapshots of the political geography of France during the Hundred Years' War between France and England. How did the long-standing lord and vassal relationship between the French and English crowns regarding lands in France help to precipitate the war? How did the change of dynasty in France create additional difficulties for the French war effort? How were the English able to exploit the deep feudal tensions within France to further complicate the situation for the French? How were the French kings ultimately able to strengthen the central, royal government as a result of the war?

of Philip IV of France. In 1328, Edward was only fifteen years of age, and he did not protest the succession of his Valois cousins. In 1337, however, when hostilities erupted between France and England, Edward responded by claiming to be the rightful king of France—a claim that all subsequent English kings would uphold until the eighteenth century.

France should have had no difficulty in defeating England at the start: it was the richest country in Europe and outnumbered England in population by at least three to one. Nonetheless, until the 1430s the English won most of the pitched battles. One reason for this was that the English had learned superior military tactics in their earlier battles with the Welsh and the Scots, and so could use well-disciplined archers to fend off and scatter the heavily armored mounted French knights. In the three greatest battles of the long conflict—Crécy (1346), Poitiers (1356), and Agincourt (1415)—the outnumbered English relied on a tightly disciplined professional army and effective use of the longbow to inflict crushing defeats on the French. Another reason for English success was that the war was always fought on French soil. That being the case, English soldiers were eager to fight because they could look forward to rich plunder, while their own homeland suffered none of the disasters of war. Worst of all for the French was the fact that they often were badly divided. The French crown always had to fear provincial attempts to assert autonomy: during the long period of warfare, many aristocratic provincial leaders took advantage of the confusion to ally with the enemy and seek their own advantage. The most dramatic and fateful instance was the breaking away of Burgundy, whose dukes from 1419 to 1435 allied with the English, an act that called the very existence of an independent French crown into question.

It was in this dark period that the heroic figure of Joan of Arc came forth to rally the French. In 1429 Joan, an illiterate but extremely devout peasant girl, sought out the uncrowned French ruler, Charles VII, to announce that she had been divinely commissioned to drive the English out of France. Charles was persuaded to let her take command of his troops, and her piety and sincerity made such a favorable impression on the soldiers that their morale was raised immensely. Within a few months Joan inflicted several defeats on English forces in central France and had brought Charles to Rheims, where he was crowned

CHRONOLOGY

HUNDRED YEARS' WAR, 1337–1453

Valois dynasty begins	1328
Edward III claims French throne	1337
Battle of Crécy	1346
Battle of Poitiers	1356
Battle of Agincourt	1415
French Burgundy allies with English	1419–1435
Joan of Arc commands French troops	1429–1430
Capture of Bordeaux ends war	1453

king. But in May 1430 she was captured by the Burgundians and handed over to the English, who accused her of being a witch and tried her for heresy. Condemned in 1431 after a show trial, she was publicly burned to death in the market square at Rouen. Nonetheless, the French, fired by their initial victories, continued to move on the offensive. When Burgundy withdrew from the English alliance in 1435, and the English king Henry VI proved to be totally incompetent, there followed an uninterrupted series of triumphs for the French side. In 1453 the capture of Bordeaux, the last of the English strongholds in the southwest, finally brought the long war to an end. The English now held no land in France except for the Channel port of Calais, which they ultimately lost in 1558.

More than merely expelling the English from French territory, the Hundred Years' War resulted in greatly strengthening the powers of the French crown. Although several French kings during the long war were ineffective personalities— one, Charles VI (1380–1422), suffered periodic bouts of insanity—the monarchy demonstrated remarkable staying power. And under competent leadership, warfare emergencies allowed the Valois kings to gather new powers, above all, the rights to collect national taxes and maintain a standing army. Hence after Charles VII succeeded in defeating the English, the crown was able to renew the high medieval royal tradition of ruling the country assertively. In the reigns of Charles's successors, Louis XI (1461–1483) and Louis XII (1498–1515), the monarchy became ever stronger. Its greatest single achievement was the destruction of the power of Burgundy in 1477

> More than merely expelling the English from French territory, the Hundred Years' War resulted in greatly strengthening the powers of the French crown.

THE CONDEMNATION OF JOAN OF ARC BY THE UNIVERSITY OF PARIS, 1431

After Joan's capture by the Burgundians, she was handed over to the English, who put her on trial for heresy. Paris was at this date in English hands, so the verdict of the Parisian masters should not be considered unbiased. On the other hand, there is no evidence that it was extracted by force. Learned theologians were not inclined to approve of peasant women who claimed to hear the voices of angels, who dressed in men's clothes, and who led aristocrats into battle. Joan was condemned for heresy and burned at the stake.

You, Joan, have said that, since the age of thirteen, you have experienced revelations and the appearance of angels, of St Catherine and St Margaret, and that you have very often seen them with your bodily eyes, and that they have spoken to you. As for the first point, the clerks of the University of Paris have considered the manner of the said revelations and appearances. . . . Having considered all . . . they have declared that all the things mentioned above are lies, falsenesses, misleading and pernicious things and that such revelations are superstitions, proceeding from wicked and diabolical spirits.

Item: You have said that your king had a sign by which he knew that you were sent by God, for St Michael, accompanied by several angels, some of which having wings, the others crowns, with St Catherine and St Margaret, came to you at the chateau of Chinon. All the company ascended through the floors of the castle until they came to the room of your king, before whom the angel bearing the crown bowed. . . . As for this matter, the clerks say that it is not in the least probable, but it is rather a presumptuous lie, misleading and pernicious, a false statement, derogatory of the dignity of the Church and of the angels. . . .

Item: you have said that, at God's command, you have continually worn men's clothes, and that you have put on a short robe, doublet, shoes attached by points; also that you have had short hair, cut around above the ears, without retaining anything on your person which shows that you are a woman; and that several times you have received the body of Our Lord dressed in this fashion, despite having been admonished to give it up several times, the which you would not do. You have said that you would rather die than abandon the said clothing, if it were not at God's command, and that if you were wearing those clothes and were with the king, and those of your party, it would be one of the greatest benefits for the kingdom of France. You have also said that not for anything would you swear an oath not to wear the said clothing and carry arms any longer. And all these things you say you have done for the good and at the command of God. As for these things, the clerics say that you blaspheme God and hold him in contempt in his sacraments; you transgress Divine Law, Holy Scripture and canon law. You err in the faith. You boast in vanity. You are suspected of idolatry and you have condemned yourself in not wishing to wear clothing suitable to your sex, but you follow the custom of Gentiles and Saracens.

Carolyne Larrington, ed. and trans. *Women and Writing in Medieval Europe.* (New York and London: Routledge, 1995), pp. 183–184.

when the Burgundian duke Charles the Bold fell in battle at the hands of the Swiss, whom Charles had been trying to dominate. Since Charles died without a male heir, Louis XI of France was able to march into Burgundy and reabsorb the breakaway duchy. Later, when Louis XII gained Brittany by marriage, the French kings ruled powerfully over almost all of what is today included in the borders of France.

ENGLAND

Although the Hundred Years' War was fought on French soil rather than English, the war produced great political instability in England also. When English armies in France were successful—as by and large they were during the reigns of Edward III (1327–1377) and Henry V (1413–1422)—the crown rode a crest of popularity and the country prospered from military spoils and the ransoms of captured French prisoners. When the tide of battle turned against the English, however, as it did under Richard II (1377–1399) and Henry VI (1422–1461), the exasperated taxpayers of England held their monarchs responsible for these costly and shameful military failures. Defeat abroad thus quickly undermined a king's political and fiscal support at home, making it politically impossible to withdraw from the French war despite its mounting costs. To make matters worse, England in the later Middle Ages was ruled by an unusually large number of dangerous or incompetent kings. Of the nine English kings who came to the throne between 1307 and 1485, no fewer than five were deposed and murdered by their subjects.

The particular propensity of the English for murdering their monarchs (a subject of comment across Europe) was a consequence of England's peculiar political system. As we have seen, England was the most tightly governed kingdom in Europe, but its political system depended on a monarch's ability to mobilize popular support for his policies through Parliament while maintaining the support of his nobility through successful wars in Wales, Scotland, and France. As a result, incompetent or tyrannical kingship was even more destabilizing and dangerous in England than it was elsewhere in Europe, because of the complexity and power of the English state itself. In France, nobles could endure the insanity of Charles VI because his government was not powerful enough to threaten them. In England, however, the inanity and ultimate insanity of Henry VI (1422–1461) provoked an aristocratic rebellion against him known as the Wars of the Roses, so called (by the nineteenth-century novelist

Sir Walter Scott) from the emblems of the two competing factions: the red rose of Henry's family of Lancaster, and the white rose of Henry's cousin, the rival Duke of York. In 1461, after a six-year struggle, Edward, Duke of York finally succeeded in ousting Henry VI and ruled successfully until his death in 1483. But when Edward's brother Richard seized the throne from Edward's own young sons, political stability in England collapsed once again. In 1485, Richard III was in turn defeated and killed in the battle of Bosworth Field by the last surviving Lancastrian claimant, Henry Tudor, who resolved the feud between Lancaster and York by marrying Elizabeth of York. Henry VII systematically elimated rival claimants to the throne, avoided expensive foreign wars, built up a financial surplus through careful management of his estates, and reasserted royal control over the aristocracy. When he died in 1509 the new Tudor dynasty was securely established on the English throne, and English royal power was fully restored. His son Henry VIII (1509–1547) would build on the foundations his father had restored, dissolving the English monasteries and declaring his country religiously independent of Rome.

Despite the turmoil caused by war and rebellion, late medieval English political life had an essential stability. Local institutions continued to function; Parliament became increasingly important as a point of contact between crown, aristocracy, and local communities; and the political community itself became steadily larger as prosperity brought new social groups into prominence. Most important of all, there was never any fundamental challenge to the power of the English state itself. Even aristocratic rebels always sought to control the central government rather than destroy or break away from it. Thus when Henry VII came to the throne, he did not have to win back any English territories as Louis XI of France had to win back Burgundy. More than that, the antagonisms of the Hundred Years' War had the ultimately beneficial effect of strengthening English national identity. From the Norman Conquest until the fourteenth century, French was the preferred language of the English crown and aristocracy, but mounting anti-French sentiment contributed to the triumph of English as the national language by around 1400. The loss of lands in France was also ultimately beneficial. England became an island nation, without significant territorial interests on the European mainland. This fact gave England more diplomatic maneuverability in sixteenth-century European politics and later helped strengthen England's ability to invest its energies in overseas expansion in America and elsewhere.

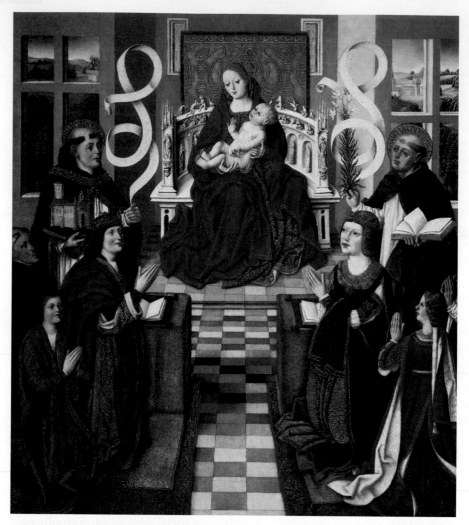

Ferdinand and Isabella Worshiping the Virgin. A contemporary Spanish painting in which the royal pair are shown with two of their children in the company of saints from the Dominican order.

new country was able to embark on united policies. Isabella and Ferdinand, ruling respectively until 1504 and 1516, subdued their aristocracies, and, in the same year (1492), annexed Granada, the last Muslim state in the peninsula, and expelled all of Spain's Jews. Some historians believe that the expulsion of the Jews was motivated by religious bigotry, others that it was a cruel but dispassionate act of state that aimed to keep Spanish *conversos* (Jews who had previously converted to Christianity) from backsliding. Either way, the forced Jewish exodus led Ferdinand and Isabella to suppose that they had eliminated an internal threat to cohesive nationhood and emboldened them to initiate an ambitious foreign policy: not only did they turn to overseas expansion, most famously in their support of Christopher Columbus, but they also entered decisively into the arena of Italian politics. Enriched by the influx of American gold and silver after the conquest of Mexico and Peru, and nearly invincible on the battlefields, Spain quickly became Europe's most powerful state in the sixteenth century.

SPAIN

While Louis XI of France and Henry VII of England were reasserting royal power in their respective countries, the Spanish monarchs, Ferdinand and Isabella, were doing the same on the Iberian peninsula. The latter area had also seen incessant strife in the Later Middle Ages; Aragon and Castile had often fought each other, and aristocratic factions within those kingdoms had continually fought the crown. But in 1469 Ferdinand, the heir of Aragon, married Isabella, the heiress of Castile, thereby creating a union that laid the basis for modern Spain.

Although Spain did not become a fully united nation until 1716 because Aragon and Castile retained their separate institutions, at least warfare between the two previously independent kingdoms ended, and the

THE TRIUMPH OF NATIONAL MONARCHIES

Ultimately the clearest result of political developments throughout Europe in the late Middle Ages was the preservation of basic high medieval patterns. The areas of Italy and Germany that had been politically divided before 1300 remained politically divided thereafter. The emergence of middle-sized states in both of these areas in the fifteenth century brought more stability than had existed before, but events would show that Italy and Germany would still be the prey of the western powers. The latter were clearly much stronger because they were consolidated around stronger national monarchies. The events of the later Middle Ages put the existence of these monarchies to the test, but after

1450 they emerged stronger than ever. The clearest illustration of their superiority is shown by the history of Italy in the years immediately following 1494. Until then the Italian states appeared to be relatively well governed and prosperous. They experimented with advanced techniques of administration and diplomacy. But when France and Spain invaded the peninsula the Italian states fell over like houses of cards. The national monarchies could simply draw on greater resources and thus inherited the future of Europe.

KIEVAN RUS AND THE RISE OF MUSCOVY

Why was medieval Russia so unlike any other European state?

Just as the later fifteenth century witnessed the consolidation of the power of the western European national monarchies, so too it saw the consolidation of the state that would become the dominant power in the European east—Russia. But Russia was not at all like a Western nation-state; rather, by about 1500 Russia had taken the first decisive steps on its way to becoming Europe's leading Eastern-style empire.

Had it not been for a combination of late medieval circumstances, one or several east Slavic states might well have developed along typical Western lines. As we saw in Chapter Nine, the founders of the first political entity located in the territories of modern-day Russia, Ukraine, and Belarus were themselves Westerners— Swedish Vikings (known as Rus) who in the tenth century established a principality at Kiev along the trade routes that led from Scandinavia to Constantinople. Because the Kievan state they founded lay on the westernmost extremity of the Russian plain (today it is the capital of Ukraine), it was natural for Kiev to maintain diplomatic and trading relations with western Europe as well as with Byzantium. For example, in the eleventh century King Henry I of France was married to a Kievan princess, Anne; their son was consequently given the Kievan name of Philip, a christening that marked the introduction of this hitherto foreign first name into the West. Aside from such direct links with Western cul-

> By about 1500 Russia had taken the first decisive steps on its way to becoming Europe's leading Eastern-style empire.

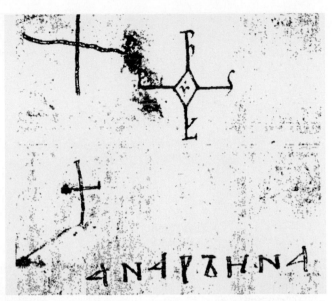

Signature of Anne of Kiev. The Kievan princess who became queen of France must have learned how to write her name in her native land, for the letters at the bottom of this document dating from 1063 spell out "Queen Anne" in the Russian (Cyrillic) alphabet. Her son Philip, however, could only make his "sign," as indicated at the top.

ture, Kievan government also bore some similarity to Western monarchical patterns inasmuch as the ruling power of the Kievan princes was limited by the institution of the *veche*, or popular assembly.

THE MONGOL INVASIONS

But after 1200 four epoch-making developments conspired to separate Russia from western Europe. The first was the conquest of most of the eastern Slavic states by the Mongols in the thirteenth century. As early as the eleventh century Kiev had been buffeted by the incursions of an Asian tribe known as the Polovtsy, but Kiev and the other loosely federated Russian principalities ultimately managed to hold the Polovtsy at bay. The Mongols, who invaded Russia in 1237, were quite another matter. Commanded by Batu, a grandson of the great Chingiz (Genghis) Khan, the Mongols cut such swaths of devastation as they advanced westward that, according to one contemporary, "no eye remained open to weep for the dead." In 1240 the Mongols overran Kiev, and two years later they created their own state on the lower Volga River—the khanate of the Golden

Moscow c. 1300
Expansion to 1389
Expansion to 1462
Expansion to 1505

THE EXPANSION OF MUSCOVITE RUSSIA TO 1505

This map shows the expansion of the Grand Duchy of Moscow, the heart of what would soon become the Russian empire. How did the relative isolation of Moscow compared with Kiev allow for the growth of Muscovite power on the one hand, and Moscow's distinctively non-Western culture on the other? Why did the Muscovite Russians identify so closely with the Byzantines, and why did they reserve such pronounced hostility for the West and Latin Christianity? What role did the Kingdom of Poland-Lithuania play in the development of this Russian attitude? How did the natural direction of the expansion of Muscovite power until 1505 help encourage attitudes often at odds with those of western European civilization?

Horde—that exerted suzerainty over almost all of Russia for the following hundred and fifty years. In the thirteenth century, the Mongol rulers of Russia carried out direct censuses, installed their own administrative officials, and required the native Russian princes to travel to Mongolia to secure permission from the great khan to rule their territories. After around 1300, however, the Mongols changed course. Rather than attempting to rule Russia directly, they instead tolerated the existence of several native Slavic states, from which they demanded obedience and regular tribute payments. Kiev, however, never recovered the dominant position it had enjoyed before the Mongol invasions.

THE RISE OF MUSCOVY

The native principality that finally emerged to defeat the Mongols and unify much of Russia was the grand duchy of Moscow. Moscow rose to power in the early fourteenth century as a tribute-collecting center for the Mongol khanate. Moscow's alliance with the Mongols did not necessarily protect it from Mongol attacks: the city was destroyed at the time of the Mongol invasions, and again in 1382. But despite these setbacks, Moscow was able, with Mongol support, to absorb the territory of the grand principality of Vladimir, and so gradually to become the dominant political power in northeastern Russia.

Moscow also had the advantage of being very far away from the Mongol power base on the lower Volga. This remote location made Moscow a particularly valuable ally for the Mongol khanate, while allowing the grand dukes to consolidate their strength without attracting too much attention from the khans. Despite Moscow's remote location (it lay about six hundred miles farther away from France or Italy than did Kiev), the grand duchy maintained some trade contacts with both the Baltic and the Black Sea regions. What really distanced Moscow from western Europe was the enormous religious hostility that existed between the eastern Orthodox churches (of which Moscow was one) and the western church headed by the papacy. As we have seen, the hostility between these two great branches of Christianity had deep historical roots. In the late Middle Ages, however, what particularly excited the religious animosity of Moscow toward western European Christians was the growing strength of the kingdom of Poland and the circumstances that led to the fall of Constantinople to the Ottoman Turks in 1453.

THE RIVALRY WITH POLAND

Throughout most of the Middle Ages the Kingdom of Poland had been a second-rate power, usually on the defensive against German encroachments. But in the fourteenth century that situation changed dramatically, partly because German strength had by then become a ghost of its former self, and above all because

the marriage in 1386 of Poland's reigning queen, Jadwiga, to Jagiello, grand duke of Lithuania, more than doubled Poland's size and enabled it to become a major expansionist state. Even before 1386 the grand duchy of Lithuania had begun to carve out an extensive territory for itself, not just on the shores of the Baltic where the present territory of Lithuania lies, but in Belarus and the Ukraine. Lithuania's expansionist momentum increased after the union with Poland. In 1410 combined Polish-Lithuanian forces in the battle of Tannenberg inflicted a stunning defeat on the German military order of Teutonic knights who ruled neighboring Prussia. In the early fifteenth century, Poland-Lithuania extended its borders so far east that the new power seemed on the verge of conquering all of Russia. Although many of the Lithuanian nobility were eastern Orthodox, Poland subscribed to Roman Catholicism, and the established church in Lithuania was also Roman Catholic. Thus when Moscow took the offensive against Poland-Lithuania in the late fifteenth century, it was able to appeal to religious as well as national sentiments. Prolonged warfare ensued, greatly exacerbating antagonisms toward Poland and toward the Latin Christian tradition it represented in the eyes of Muscovites.

MOSCOW AND BYZANTIUM

The growing alienation between Moscow and western Europe was further increased by events leading up to the fall of Constantinople to the Turks in 1453. Connections between Byzantium and the Rus went back to the tenth century, when missionaries from the Byzantine empire had converted the Kievan Slavs to Orthodox Christianity. Relations between the eastern and western churches had been tense ever since 1054, when the two churches split over papal primacy and the wording of the Nicene Creed. But embittered hatred is the only expression to describe Byzantine attitudes toward Rome after 1204 when the Fourth Crusade sacked Constantinople. Eastern Orthodox Russians sympathized with their Byzantine mentors, and felt all the more that they had extraordinarily good reason to shun the "Roman infection" after the debacle of 1453. This was because in 1438 the Byzantines in Constantinople, sensing correctly that a mighty Turkish onslaught was in the offing, agreed to submit to papal authority and unite with the western church, in the hope that these promises might earn them Western military support for their last stand. But despite this submission, no Western help was forthcoming and Constantinople fell to the Turks in 1453 without a single Roman Catholic knight lifting a hand.

The Orthodox hierarchy of Moscow had refused to follow Byzantium in its religious submission, regarding it as a betrayal of Christian orthodoxy. After Constantinople fell, therefore, the Muscovites concluded that the Turkish victory was a divine punishment for the Byzantines' religious perfidy. The Muscovite state thus became the center of a particularly zealous anti-Roman ideology, as Moscow began to see itself as the divinely appointed successor to Byzantium. The Russian ruler took the title of *tsar*—which simply means "caesar"—and Russians asserted that Moscow was both "a second Jerusalem" and "the third Rome": "Two Romes have fallen," said a Russian spokesman, "the third is still standing, and a fourth there shall not be." This Byzantine-derived ideology underlay both the later growth of Russian imperialism, and the sacred position ascribed to the rulers of the Muscovite (and later Russian) state.

THE REIGN OF IVAN THE GREAT (1462–1505)

Behind such imperial self-confidence lay the steadily growing power of the grand dukes of Moscow. Moscow itself had been effectively independent of the Mongols since the end of the fourteenth century, when a rival Mongol ruler named Timur the Lame (Tamurlane) had destroyed the Mongol khanate of the Golden Horde. But it was Ivan III, customarily known as Ivan the Great, who did the most to transform the grand duchy of Moscow into a true imperial power. Declaring himself to be the White Tsar (and thus the legitimate successor to the Mongol Golden Horde as the emperor of the West), Ivan launched a series of conquests between 1468 and 1485 that annexed, one by one, all the independent Russian principalities that lay between Moscow and the Poland-Lithuania border. After two successive invasions of Lithuania in 1492 and 1501, Ivan also succeeded in bringing parts of Belarus and Ukraine under his control. Battles between Russia and Poland-Lithuania would continue for several centuries thereafter, but by 1505, when Ivan died, he had established Muscovy as a power to be reckoned with on the European scene.

Under Ivan III, Muscovy was evolving in the direction of political autocracy and imperialism. Ivan's assumption of the imperial title meant that he was claiming to be the successor not only of the Mongol khans, but also of the defunct Byzantine emperors, who

CHRONOLOGY

THE RISE OF MUSCOVY, c. 1200–1505

Mongols conquer east Slavic States	1237–1241
Ivan III annexes western principalities	1468–1485
Ivan III declares himself White Tsar	1480
Invasions of Lithuania	1492 and 1501

themselves had been heirs of the Roman caesars. In 1452, Ivan married the niece of the last Byzantine ruler; later he adopted as his insignia the double-headed eagle and rebuilt Moscow's fortified princely residence, the Kremlin, in magnificent Italian Renaissance style to display his imperial splendor. As tsar, Ivan conceived of himself as the autocratic potentate not just of the Russians of Moscow but of all Russians, and even, potentially, of Belarussians and Ukrainians. In the sixteenth century, Russian expansionism was principally directed toward the south and east, against the small successor states to the Mongol Golden Horde. From the mid-seventeenth century on, however, Muscovite pressure against Ukraine would escalate, leading on to the enormous land empire Peter the Great would construct in the early eighteenth century. We cannot draw a direct line from Ivan III to Peter the Great. But the foundations Ivan laid would be appealed to as justification for Peter's claims to incorporate both Russians and a wide variety of non-Russian peoples into what would become Europe's largest empire.

THOUGHT, LITERATURE, AND ART

What trends led to the rise of vernacular literature?

Although we might guess that the extreme hardships of the later Middle Ages in western Europe should have led to the decline or stagnation of intellectual and artistic endeavors, in fact the period was an extremely fruitful one in the realms of thought, literature, and art.

In this section we will postpone treatment of certain developments most closely related to the early history of the Italian Renaissance, but will discuss some of western Europe's other important late medieval intellectual and artistic accomplishments.

THEOLOGY AND PHILOSOPHY

Theology and philosophy after about 1300 faced a crisis of doubt. This doubt did not concern the existence of God and his supernatural powers, but was rather doubt about human ability to comprehend the supernatural. Saint Thomas Aquinas and other Scholastics in the High Middle Ages had serenely delimited the number of "mysteries of the faith" and believed that everything else, both in heaven and earth, could be thoroughly understood by humans. But the floods, frosts, wars, and plagues of the fourteenth century helped undermine such confidence in the powers of human understanding. Once human beings experienced the universe as arbitrary and unpredictable, fourteenth-century thinkers began to wonder whether there was not far more in heaven and earth than could be understood by their philosophies. The result was a thoroughgoing reevaluation of the prior theological and philosophical outlook.

The leading late medieval abstract thinker was the English Franciscan William of Ockham, who was born around 1285 and died in 1349, apparently of the Black Death. Traditionally, Franciscans had always had greater doubts than Dominicans such as Saint Thomas Aquinas concerning the abilities of human reason to comprehend the supernatural; Ockham, convinced by the events of his age, expressed these doubts most formidably. He denied that the existence of God and numerous other theological matters could be demonstrated apart from scriptural revelation, and he emphasized God's freedom and absolute power to do anything. In the realm of human knowledge per se, Ockham's searching intellect drove him to look for absolute certainties instead of mere theories. In investigating earthly matters he developed the position, known as *nominalism*, that only individual things, not collectivities, are real, and that one thing therefore cannot be understood by means of another: to know a chair one has to see and touch it rather than just know what several other chairs are like. The formal logical system Ockham developed from this fundamental principle became

the most influential philosophical system of the later Middle Ages.

Ockham's outlook, which gained widespread adherence in late medieval universities, today often seems overly methodological and verging on the arid, but it had several important effects on the development of Western thought. Ockham's concern about what God might do led his followers to raise some of the seemingly absurd questions for which medieval theology has been mocked: for example, asking whether God can undo the past, or whether an infinite number of pure spirits can simultaneously inhabit the same place (the nearest medieval thinkers actually came to asking how many angels can dance on the head of a pin). Nonetheless, Ockham's emphasis on preserving God's autonomy led to a stress on divine omnipotence that became one of the basic presuppositions of sixteenth-century Protestantism. Further, Ockham's determination to find certainties in the realm of human knowledge ultimately helped make it possible to discuss human affairs and natural science without reference to supernatural explanations—one of the most important foundations of the modern scientific method. Finally, Ockham's opposition to studying collectivities and his refusal to apply logic to abstract categories helped encourage empiricism, or the belief that knowledge of the world should rest on sense experience rather than abstract reason. This too is a presupposition for scientific progress: thus it is probably not coincidental that some of Ockham's fourteenth-century followers made significant advances in the study of optics and physics.

VERNACULAR LITERATURE

Ockham's search for reliable truths finds certain parallels in the realm of late medieval literature, although Ockham surely had no direct influence in that field. The major trait of the best late medieval literature was *naturalism*, or the attempt to describe things the way they really are. This was more a development from high medieval precedents—such as the explorations of human conduct pursued by Chrétien de Troyes, Wolfram von Eschenbach, and Dante—than a reaction against them. Furthermore, the steady growth of a lay reading public encouraged authors to avoid theological and philosophical abstractions and seek more to entertain by portraying people realistically with all their strengths and foibles. Another main characteristic of

> Theology and philosophy after 1300 faced a crisis of doubt about the human ability to comprehend the supernatural.

late medieval literature, the predominance of composition in the European vernaculars instead of Latin, also developed out of high medieval precedents but gained great momentum in the later Middle Ages for two reasons. One was that international tensions and hostilities, including the numerous wars of the age and the trials of the universal papacy, led more and more people to identify themselves in national terms, and to regard vernacular tongues as a key element in their national identity. Another even more important was the fact that the continuing spread of education for the laity greatly increased the number of people who could read in a given vernacular language but not in Latin. Hence although much poetry had been composed in the vernacular during the High Middle Ages, in the later Middle Ages use of the vernacular was widely extended to prose. Moreover, countries such as Italy and England, which had just begun to cultivate their own vernacular literatures around 1300, subsequently began to employ their native tongues to impressive literary effect.

BOCCACCIO

The greatest writer of vernacular prose fiction of the later Middle Ages was the Italian Giovanni Boccaccio (1313–1375). Although Boccaccio would have taken an honored place in literary history for some of his lesser works, which included courtly romances, pastoral poems, and learned treatises, by far the most impressive of his writings is the *Decameron*, written between 1348 and 1351. This is a collection of one hundred stories, mostly about love and sex, adventure, and clever trickery, supposedly told by a sophisticated party of seven young ladies and three men who are sojourning in a country villa outside Florence in order to escape the ravages of the Black Death. Boccaccio by no means invented all one hundred plots, but even when he borrowed the outlines of his tales from earlier sources he retold the stories in his own characteristically exuberant, masterful, and extremely witty fashion.

For many reasons, the *Decameron* must be counted as epoch making from a historical point of view. The first is that it was the earliest ambitious and successful work of vernacular creative literature ever written in western Europe in narrative prose. Boccaccio's prose is "modern" in the sense that it is brisk, for unlike the medieval authors of flowery romances, Boccaccio purposely wrote in an unaffected, colloquial style. Simply stated, in the *Decameron* he was less interested in being "elevated" or elegant than in being unpretentiously entertaining. From the point of view of content, Boccaccio wished to portray men and women as they really are rather than as they ought to be. Thus when he wrote about the clergy he showed them to be as susceptible to human appetites and failings as other mortals. His women are not pallid playthings, distant goddesses, or steadfast virgins, but flesh-and-blood creatures with intellects; they interact more comfortably and naturally with men and with each other than any women in Western literature had ever done before. Boccaccio's treatment of sexual relations is often graphic, but never demeaning. In his world the natural desires of both women and men are not meant to be thwarted. For all these reasons the *Decameron* is a robust and delightful appreciation of what it means to be human.

CHAUCER

Similar in many ways to Boccaccio as a creator of robust, naturalistic vernacular literature was the Englishman Geoffrey Chaucer (c. 1340–1400). Chaucer was the first major writer whose English can still be read today with relatively little effort. Remarkably, he was both a founding father of England's mighty literary tradition and one of the four or five greatest contributors to it: most critics rank him just behind Shakespeare and in a class with Milton, Wordsworth, and Dickens.

Chaucer wrote several highly impressive works, but his masterpiece is unquestionably the *Canterbury Tales*, dating from the end of his career. Like the *Decameron*, this is a collection of stories held together by a frame, in Chaucer's case the device of having a group of people tell stories while on a pilgrimage from London to Canterbury. But there are also differences between the *Decameron* and the *Canterbury Tales*. Chaucer's stories are told in sparkling verse instead of prose, and they are recounted by people of all different classes—from a chivalric knight to a dedicated university student to a thieving miller with a wart on his nose. Lively women are also represented, most memorably the gap-toothed, oft-married "Wife of Bath," who knows all "the remedies of love." Each character tells a story that is particularly illustrative of his or her own occupation and outlook on the world. By this device Chaucer was able to create a highly diverse "human comedy." His range is greater than Boccaccio's, and although he is no less witty, frank, and lusty as the Italian, he is sometimes more profound.

CHRISTINE DE PISAN

The later Middle Ages also saw the emergence of professional authors who made their living with their pen.

Christine de Pisan. A leading writer of late-medieval vernacular prose literature, Christine de Pisan (1365–c. 1430) was intent on upholding the dignity of women. She is shown here writing about a gigantic Amazon warrior who could defeat men effortlessly in armed combat.

Significantly, one of the first of these professional *litterati* was a woman, Christine de Pisan. Although she herself was born in Italy, Christine spent her adult life in France, where her husband was a member of the king's household. When he died, the widowed Christine turned to writing to support herself and her children. She wrote in a wide variety of literary genres, including treatises on chivalry and on the art of warfare that she dedicated to her patron, King Charles VI of France. But she also wrote for a larger and more popular audience. Her imaginative tract *The City of Ladies* is an extended defense of the character, nature, and capacities of women against their male detractors, written in the form of an allegory. She also took part in a vigorous pamphlet literature that debated the misogynistic claims made against

women in the *Romance of the Rose* (see Chapter 10). This debate continued for several hundred years, and became so famous that it was given a name: the *querelle des femmes*, "the debate over women." Christine was by no means the first female writer of the Middle Ages, but she was the first lay woman to earn a living by her writing.

> Christine de Pisan was by no means the first female writer of the Middle Ages, but she was the first lay woman to earn a living by her writing.

SCULPTURE AND PAINTING

As naturalism was a dominant trait of late medieval literature, so it was of late medieval art. Already by the thirteenth century Gothic sculptors were paying far more attention than their Romanesque predecessors had to the way plants, animals, and human beings really looked. Whereas earlier medieval art had empha-

The Meeting of Joachim and Anna at the Golden Gate, a fresco by Giotto (c. 1267–1337). Note how the haloes merge: this old and barren couple will soon miraculously have a child, none other than Mary, the mother of Jesus.

to be cultivated in the Middle Ages and long afterward, especially in the form of *frescoes,* or paintings done on wet plaster. But in addition to frescoes, Italian artists in the thirteenth century first started painting pictures on pieces of wood or canvas. These were first done in tempera (pigments mixed with water and natural gums or egg whites), but around 1400 painting in oils was introduced in the European north. These new technical developments created new artistic opportunities. Artists were now able to paint religious scenes on altarpieces for churches and for private devotions practiced by the wealthier laity at home. Artists also painted the first Western portraits, which were meant to gratify the self-esteem of monarchs and aristocrats. The earliest surviving example of a naturalistic, painted portrait is one of a French king, John the Good, executed around 1360. Others followed quickly, so that within a short time the art of portraiture from life was highly developed. Visitors to art museums will notice that some of the most realistic and sensitive portraits of all time date from the fifteenth century.

sized abstract design, the stress was now increasingly on realism: thirteenth-century carvings of leaves and flowers must have been made from direct observation and are clearly recognizable to modern botanists as distinct species. Statues of humans also gradually became more naturally proportioned and realistic in their portrayals of facial expressions and bodily proportions. By around 1290 the concern for realism had become so great that a sculptor working on a tomb portrait of the German emperor Rudolf of Habsburg allegedly made a hurried return trip to view Rudolf in person, because he had heard that a new wrinkle had appeared on the emperor's face.

In the next two centuries the trend toward naturalism continued in sculpture and was extended to manuscript illumination and painting. The latter was in certain basic respects a new art. Ever since the Ice Age, people had painted on walls, but walls of course were not easily movable. The art of wall painting continued

The most pioneering and important painter of the later Middle Ages was the Florentine Giotto (c. 1267–1337). He did not engage in individual portraiture, but he brought deep humanity to his religious images painted on both walls and movable panels. Giotto was preeminently a naturalist, that is, an imitator of nature. Not only do his human beings and animals look more natural than those of his predecessors, they seem to do more natural things. When Christ enters Jerusalem on Palm Sunday, boys climb trees to get a better view; when St. Francis is laid out in death, one onlooker takes the opportunity to see whether the saint had really received Christ's wounds; and when the Virgin's parents, Joachim and Anna, meet after a long separation, they actually embrace and kiss—perhaps the first deeply tender kiss in Western art. It was certainly not true, as one fanciful storyteller later reported, that an onlooker found a fly Giotto had painted so real that he attempted to brush it away with his hand, but Giotto in fact accomplished something more. Specifically, he was the first to conceive of the painted space in fully three-dimensional terms: as one art historian has put it, Giotto's frescoes were the first to "knock a hole into the wall." After Giotto's death a reaction in Italian painting set in. Mid-fourteenth century artists briefly moved away from naturalism and painted stern, forbidding religious figures who seemed to float in space. But by around 1400 artists came back down to earth and started to build on Giotto's influence in ways that led to the great Italian renaissance in painting.

In the north of Europe painting did not advance impressively beyond manuscript illumination until the early fifteenth century, but then it suddenly came very much into its own. The leading northern European

Man with a Red Hat, by Hans Memling (c. 1430–1494).

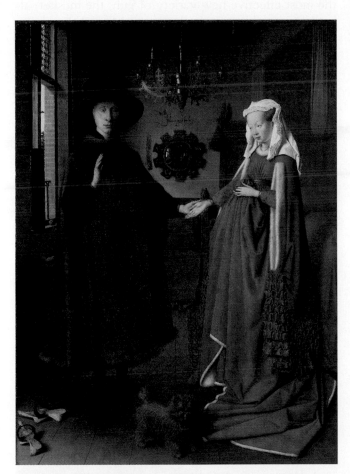

The Arnolfini Betrothal, by Jan van Eyck. A characteristic synthesis of everyday life and religious devotion. Scenes from Christ's Passion surround the mirror. The artist himself appears reflected in the mirror as if to indicate that he is a witness to the betrothal. In addition, he wrote (above the mirror) "Johannes de eyck fuit hic" (Jan van Eyck was here).

painters were Flemish, first and foremost Jan van Eyck (c. 1380–1441), Roger van der Weyden (c. 1400–1464), and Hans Memling (c. 1430–1494). These three were the greatest early practitioners of painting in oil, a medium that allowed them to engage in brilliant coloring and sharp-focused realism. Van Eyck and van der Weyden excelled most at two things: communicating a sense of deep religious piety and portraying minute details of familiar everyday experience. These may at first seem incompatible, but it should be remembered that contemporary manuals of practical mysticism such as the *Imitation of Christ* also sought to link deep piety with everyday existence. Thus it was by no means blasphemous when a Flemish painter would portray behind a tender Virgin and Child a vista of contemporary life with people going about their usual business and a man even urinating against a wall. This union of the sacred and the profane tended to fall apart in the work of Memling, who excelled in either straightforward religious pictures or secular portraits, but it would return in the work of the greatest painters of the Low Countries, Brueghel and Rembrandt.

ADVANCES IN TECHNOLOGY

How did technological advances affect everyday life?

No account of enduring late medieval accomplishments would be complete without mention of certain epoch-making technological advances. Sadly, but probably not unexpectedly, treatment of this subject has to begin with reference to the invention of artillery and firearms. The prevalence of warfare stimulated the development of new weaponry. Gunpowder itself was a Chinese invention, but it was first put to devastating military uses in the late medieval West. Heavy cannons, which made terrible noises "as though all the dyvels of hell had been in the way," were first employed around 1330. The earliest cannons were so primitive that it often was more dangerous to stand be-hind than in front of them, but by the middle of the fifteenth century they were greatly improved and began to revolutionize the nature of warfare. In one year, 1453, heavy artillery played a leading role in determining the outcome of two crucial conflicts: the Ottoman Turks used German and Hungarian cannons to breach the defenses of Constantinople—hitherto the most impregnable in Europe—and the French used heavy artillery to take the city of Bordeaux, thereby ending the Hundred Years' War. Cannons thereafter made it difficult for rebellious aristocrats to hole up in their stone castles, and thus they aided in the consolidation of the national monarchies. Placed aboard ships, cannons enabled European vessels to dominate foreign waters in the subsequent age of overseas expansion. Hand-held firearms, also invented in the fourteenth century, were gradually perfected. Shortly after 1500 the most effective new variety of gun, the musket, allowed foot soldiers to end once and for all the earlier military dominance of heavily armored mounted knights. Once lance-bearing cavalries became outmoded and fighting could more easily be carried on by

A Fifteenth-Century Siege with Cannon.

Devil with Eyeglasses. Once spectacles became common even devils in hell sported them.

all, the monarchical states that could turn out the largest armies completely subdued internal resistance and dominated the battlefields of Europe.

Other late medieval technological developments were more life enhancing. Eyeglasses, first invented in the 1280s, were perfected in the fourteenth century. These allowed older people to keep on reading when farsightedness would otherwise have stopped them. For example, the great fourteenth-century scholar Petrarch, who boasted excellent sight in his youth, wore spectacles after his sixtieth year and was thus enabled to complete some of his most important works. Around 1300 the use of the magnetic compass helped ships to sail farther away from land and venture out into the Atlantic. One immediate result was the opening of direct sea commerce between Italy and the north. Subsequently, numerous improvements in shipbuilding, map making, and navigational devices enabled Europe to start expanding overseas. In the fourteenth century the Azores and Cape Verde Islands were reached; then, after a long pause caused by Europe's plagues and wars, the African Cape of Good Hope was rounded in 1487, the West Indies reached in 1492, India reached by the sea route in 1498, and Brazil sighted in 1500. Partly as a result of technology, the world was thus suddenly made much smaller.

Among the most familiar implements of our modern

Horloge de Sapience (Lady Wisdom with Clocks). This miniature, from a French manuscript of about 1450, reflects the growing fascination with machines of all sorts and clocks in particular.

life that were invented by Europeans in the later Middle Ages were clocks and printed books. Mechanical clocks were invented shortly before 1300 and proliferated in the years immediately thereafter. The earliest clocks were too expensive for private purchase, but towns quickly vied with each other to install the most elaborate clocks in their prominent public buildings. These clocks not only told the time but showed the courses of sun, moon, and planets, and performed mechanical tricks on the striking of the hours. The new invention ultimately had two profound effects. One was the further stimulation of European interest in complex machinery of all sorts. This interest had already been awakened by the high medieval proliferation of mills, but clocks ultimately became even more omnipresent than mills because after about 1650 they became quite cheap and were brought into practically every European home. Household clocks served as models of marvelous machines. Equally if not more significant was the fact that clocks began to rationalize the course of European daily affairs. Until the advent of clocks in the later Middle Ages time was flexible. Men and women had only a rough idea of how late in the day it was and rose and retired more or less with the sun. People who lived in the country in particular performed different jobs at different rates according to the rhythm of the seasons. Even when hours were counted, they were measured at different lengths according to the amount of light in the different seasons of the year. In the fourteenth century, however, clocks first started relentlessly striking equal hours through the day and night. Thus they began to regulate work with new precision. People were expected to start and end work "on time" and many came to believe that "time is money." This emphasis on timekeeping brought new efficiencies but also new tensions: Lewis Carroll's white rabbit, who is always looking at his pocket watch and muttering "how late it's getting," is a telling caricature of time-obsessed Western humanity.

As soon as books became easily accessible, literacy increased even more and book culture became a basic part of the European way of life.

The invention of printing with movable type was equally momentous. The major stimulus for this invention was the replacement of parchment by paper as Europe's primary writing material between 1200 and 1400. Parchment, made from the skins of sheep or calves, was extremely expensive: since it was possible to get only about four good parchment leaves from one animal, it was necessary to slaughter between two to three hundred sheep or calves to gain enough parchment for a Bible! Paper, made from rags turned into pulp by mills, brought prices down dramatically. Late medieval records show that paper sold at one sixth the price of parchment. Accordingly, it became cheaper to learn how to read and write. With literacy becoming ever more widespread, there was a growing market for still cheaper books, and the invention of printing with movable type around 1450 fully met this demand. By greatly saving labor, the invention made printed books about one fifth as expensive as handwritten ones within about two decades.

As soon as books became easily accessible, literacy increased even more and book culture became a basic part of the European way of life. After about 1500, Europeans could afford to read and buy books of all sorts—not just religious tracts, but instructional manuals, light entertainment, and, by the eighteenth century, newspapers. Printing ensured that ideas would spread quickly and reliably; moreover, revolutionary ideas could no longer be easily extinguished once they were

Paper Making at a Paper Mill.

A Printing Press. From a title page of a Parisian printer, 1520.

set down in hundreds of copies of books. Thus the greatest religious reformer of the sixteenth century, Martin Luther, gained an immediate following throughout Germany by employing the printing press to run off pamphlets: had printing not been available to him, Luther might have died as Hus did. The spread of books also helped stimulate the growth of cultural nationalism. Before printing, regional dialects in most European countries were often so diverse that people who supposedly spoke the same language often could barely understand each other. Such a situation hindered governmental centralization because a royal servant might be entirely unable to communicate with inhabitants of the provinces. Shortly after the invention of printing, however, each European country began to develop its own linguistic standards, which were disseminated uniformly by books. The "king's English" was what was printed in London and carried to Yorkshire or Wales. Thus communications were enhanced and governments were able to operate ever more efficiently.

CONCLUSION

Despite economic dislocation and demographic collapse, the later Middle Ages were one of the most creative and inventive periods in the history of western Europe. Why this was so will always remain something of a mystery, until and unless future scholars should unlock the secrets of human creativity itself. What we can see behind the artistic, philosophical, literary, and technological developments of the period, however, is a consistent drive to understand, control, and replicate the workings of the natural world. This fact may offer some clues toward explaining the sources of these developments.

Perhaps most fundamentally, in the later Middle Ages intellectuals broke with the traditional, Neoplatonic vision of nature as a book in which one could read the mind of God. Instead, they came to see the natural world as operating according to its own laws, which were empirically verifiable but which could tell human beings nothing about the God who lay behind them. The resulting sense of the contingency and independence of the natural world was an essential step toward the emergence of a scientific world view. It also encouraged Europeans to believe that nature itself could be manipulated and directed toward human ends.

Powerful economic and political factors also encouraged the technological inventiveness of the period. Despite the disruptive impact of plague and war, the market for goods was not destroyed. Instead, the resulting labor shortages encouraged European entrepreneurs to experiment with labor-saving technologies and new crops. Incessant warfare in particular encouraged a remarkable burst of military inventiveness. It also enabled more powerful governments to extract a larger percentage of their subjects' wealth through taxation, which they proceeded to invest in ships, cannons, muskets, and the standing armies that the new weaponry made possible. Increasing per capita wealth produced the capital necessary to invest in mills, factories, clocks, books, and compasses. It also made possible a remarkable increase in the educational level of the European population. Between 1300 and 1500 hundreds and perhaps thousands of new grammar schools were established, and scores of new universities emerged, because parents saw such schools as a reliable route to social advancement for their sons. Women were still excluded from the schools, but increasing numbers of girls were being taught at home, making women an extremely important (perhaps even the dominant) part of the "reading public" that was emerging in later medieval Europe.

Finally, it may be that dislocation itself promotes innovation, so long as it does not destroy people's confidence in the ultimate improvability of their lives. Europeans suffered enormously from war, plague, and economic crises during the later Middle Ages. But those who survived seized the opportunities their new world presented to them. The confidence they had developed in the High Middle Ages was not destroyed by the travails of the later Middle Ages. By 1500, most Europeans lived more secure lives than their ancestors had two hundred years before; and they stood on the verge of an extraordinary new period of expansion and conquest that would take European armies, merchants and settlers around the globe.

SELECTED READINGS

Allmand, Christopher T., ed. *Society at War: The Experience of England and France During the Hundred Years' War.* Edinburgh, 1973. An outstanding collection of documents.

———. *The Hundred Years' War: England and France at War, c. 1300–c. 1450.* Cambridge and New York, 1988. Still the best analytic account of the war; after a short narrative, the book is organized topically.

Boccaccio, Giovanni. *The Decameron.* Translated by Mark Musa and P. E. Bondanella. New York, 1977.

Bynum, Caroline Walker. *Holy Feast and Holy Fast: The Religious Significance of Food to Medieval Women.* Berkeley and Los Angeles, 1987. A pathbreaking study of the patterns of female piety in the later middle ages.

Campbell, Bruce M. S. *English Seignorial Agriculture, 1250–1450.* Cambridge and New York, 2000. A definitive, up-to-date, and comprehensive account.

Chaucer, Geoffrey. *The Canterbury Tales.* Translated by Nevill Coghill. New York, 1951. A modern English verse translation, lightly annotated.

Cole, Bruce. *Giotto and Florentine Painting, 1280–1375.* New York, 1976. A clear and stimulating introduction.

Crummey, Robert O. *The Formation of Muscovy, 1304–1613.* New York, 1987. The standard account.

Dobson, R. Barrie. *The Peasants' Revolt of 1381,* 2d ed. London, 1983. A comprehensive source collection, with excellent introductions to the documents and an illuminating discussion of the revolt.

Duffy, Eamon. *The Stripping of the Altars: Traditional Religion in England, 1400–1580.* New Haven, 1992. The fullest study anywhere of the patterns of fifteenth-century piety at the parish level.

Dyer, Christopher. *Standards of Living in the Later Middle Ages: Social Change in England, c. 1200–1520.* Cambridge and New York, 1989. Detailed but highly rewarding.

Froissart, Jean. *Chronicles.* Translated by Geoffrey Brereton. Baltimore, 1968. A selection from the most famous contemporary account of the Hundred Years' War to c. 1400.

Hilton, Rodney H., and Trevor Aston, eds. *The English Rising of 1381.* Cambridge and New York, 1984. An excellent collection of articles that also includes chapters on the *Jacquerie* and the *Ciompi* rebellions.

Horrox, Rosemary, ed. *The Black Death.* New York, 1994. A fine collection of documents reflecting the impact of the Black Death, especially in England.

Hudson, Anne. *The Premature Reformation: Wycliffite Texts and Lollard History.* Oxford and New York, 1988. Despite its misleading title, this is the fullest and best account of Lollardy, written by the premier modern historian of the subject.

Huizinga, Johan. *The Waning of the Middle Ages: A Study of the Forms of Life, Thought, and Art in France and the Netherlands in the Dawn of the Renaissance,* New York, 1924. A classic picture of the "expiring" Middle Ages; a book from whose influence historians are still struggling to escape. Frequently republished, the most recent translation of this work is entitled *The Autumn of the Middle Ages.* Translated by Rodney J. Payton and Ulrich Mammitzsch. Chicago, 1996.

John Hus at the Council of Constance. Translated by M. Spinka, New York, 1965. The translation of a Czech chronicle with an expert introduction and appended documents.

Jordan, William Chester. *The Great Famine: Northern Europe in the Early Fourteenth Century.* Princeton, 1996. An outstanding social and economic study of the disastrous famines that swept northern Europe between 1315 and 1322.

Keen, Maurice, ed. *Medieval Warfare: A History.* Oxford and New York, 1999. The most attractive introduction to this crucially important subject. Lively and well illustrated.

Kempe, Margery. *The Book of Margery Kempe.* Translated by Barry Windeatt. New York, 1985. A fascinating autobiography by an early fifteenth-century Englishwoman who hoped she might be a saint.

Lerner, Robert E. *The Age of Adversity: The Fourteenth Century.* Ithaca, N.Y., 1968. A short, evocative account.

———. *The Heresy of the Free Spirit in the Later Middle Ages,* 2d ed. Notre Dame, Ind., 1991. A revealing study of a heretical movement that terrified contemporaries, yet hardly existed at all.

Lewis, Peter S. *Later Medieval France: The Polity.* London, 1968. Still fresh and suggestive after almost thirty-five years. A masterwork.

McFarlane, K. Bruce. *The Nobility of Later Medieval England.* Oxford, 1980. A pioneering collection of essays by one of the most influential historians of the mid-twentieth century.

Memoirs of a Renaissance Pope: The Commentaries of Pius II, abridged ed. Translated by F. A. Gragg, New York, 1959. Remarkable insights into the mind of a particularly well-educated mid-fifteenth-century pope.

Nicholas, David. *The Transformation of Europe, 1300–1600.* Oxford and New York, 1999. The best textbook presently available.

Oakley, Francis C. *The Western Church in the Later Middle Ages.* Ithaca, N.Y., 1979. The best book by far on the history of conciliarism, the late medieval papacy, Hussitism, and the efforts at institutional reform during this period. On popular piety, see Swanson (below).

Panofsky, Erwin. *Early Netherlandish Painting.* 2 vols. Cambridge, Mass., 1953. A brilliant specialized history by a master art historian.

Pernoud, Régine, ed. *Joan of Arc, by Herself and Her Witnesses.* New York, 1966. A collection of contemporary writings about Joan, including the transcripts of her trial.

Shirley, Janet, trans. *A Parisian Journal, 1405–1449.* Oxford, 1968. A marvelous panorama of Parisian life recorded by an eyewitness.

Swanson, R. N. *Religion and Devotion in Europe, c. 1215–c. 1515.* Cambridge and New York, 1995. An excellent study of late medieval popular piety; an excellent complement to Oakley (see above).

Sumption, Jonathan. *The Hundred Years' War.* Vol. 1, *Trial by Battle;* Vol. 2, *Trial by Fire.* Philadelphia, 1999. The first two volumes of a massive narrative history of the war take the story up to 1369.

Vaughan, Richard. *Valois Burgundy.* London, 1975. A summation of the author's four-volume study of the Burgundian dukes.

Ziegler, Philip. *The Black Death.* New York, 1969. A popular account, but reliable and engrossing.

PART IV

FROM MEDIEVAL TO MODERN

FOR MOST OF THE TWENTIETH CENTURY, historians portrayed the Italian Renaissance and the Protestant Reformation as marking a dramatic break in European history, which brought the Middle Ages to an end and ushered in the modern world. To be sure, the sixteenth and seventeenth centuries saw decisive transformations in European life. For the first time, European sailors, soldiers, and merchants forged worldwide trading networks that brought the mineral and agricultural riches of the western hemisphere into their Atlantic ports. The Protestant Reformation brought an end to the religious unity of Europe, and a century of religious wars served only to cement those divisions. Meanwhile, new trends in cultural and intellectual life, many of which had begun in fourteenth- and fifteenth-century Italy, began to spread widely throughout the rest of Europe.

It is increasingly clear, however, that most of the new developments of the sixteenth and seventeenth centuries had deep roots in the later Middle Ages. The voyages that took sixteenth century Europeans around the globe began in the thirteenth century with the conquest of the "Atlantic Mediterranean." The intensive study of classical Roman and Greek literature that characterized the "humanism" of the Italian Renaissance, developed from the classical revival in the twelfth and thirteenth centuries. Even the theological doctrines of the Protestant reformers had roots in the theological controversies of the later Middle Ages. And all these developments took place in the context of continuing cultural and economic exchange between Europe, the Islamic world, and Byzantium.

	POLITICS	SOCIETY AND CULTURE	ECONOMY	INTERNATIONAL RELATIONS
1200	(Ghengis) Khan rules over Mongol clans (1206–1227)		"Silk Road" connects Europe with India, China, and Indonesia (1200s) Polo brothers travel to China (1200s)	Mongols conquer southern Russia (1237–1240) Mongols annihilate Hungarian army at River Sajo (1241) Mongol forces withdraw from Europe (1241)
1300	Yuan dynasty in China (1279–1368) Rise of Ottoman dynasty (1300) Ming dynasty in China (1368–1644)	Civic humanism begins in Italy (1300s) Francesco Petrarch (1304–1374) Mongols transmit bubonic plague at siege of Caffa (1346) Leonardo Bruni (1370–1444)	Silver shortage begins in Europe (1340s)	
1400			Portugal establishes Atlantic colonies (late 1400–1460)	Ottomans defeat Serbian empire at battle of Kosovo (1389)
		Giovanni Aurispa returns with classical manuscripts (1423) Sandro Botticelli (1445–1510) Neoplatonism in Italy (1450–1600) Leonardo da Vinci (1452–1519) Desiderius Erasmus (1469–1536) Niccolò Machiavelli, author of *The Prince* (1469–1527) Albrecht Dürer (1471–1528) Sir Thomas More (1478–1535) Raphael (1483–1520) The High Renaissance begins (1490) The Catholic Reformation begins (1490)	Dias rounds southern tip of Africa (1488) Portugal founds slave-based plantation in St. Thomas (1490) Columbus lands in West Indies (1492) Disease kills much of Native American population (1492–1538) Vasco da Gama reaches India (1498)	Mehmet II conquers Constantinople (1453)
1500	Reign of Charles V, Holy Roman Emperor (1506–1556)	Roman Inquisition begins (1500) Saint Peter's Basilica erected in Rome (1500–1520) Papacy of Julius II (1503–1513) Saint Francis Xavier, missionary in Asia, (1506–1552) Andrea Palladio (1508–1580) John Calvin (1509–1564) Papacy of Leo X, son of Lorenzo de Medici (1513–1521) Luther posts Ninety-Five Theses (1517) Emergence of Zwinglianism, Anabaptism, and Calvinism (1520–1550) Edict of Worms (1521) Peter Brueghel, painter of *Harvesters* and *Massacre of the Innocents* (1525–1569) Baldassare Castiglione's *The Book of the Courtier* (1528)	Grain prices in Europe increase fivefold (1500–1650) Portuguese ships reach Spice Islands and China (1515)	Cortes conquers Aztec empire (1519–1522) Ottomans conquer Syria, Egypt, and the Balkans (1520–1540) Charles V, Holy Roman Emperor, sacks Rome (1527)

POLITICS	SOCIETY AND CULTURE	ECONOMY	INTERNATIONAL RELATIONS	
	Michel de Montaigne (1533–1592) Henry VIII becomes head of the Church of England (1533–1534) Calvin's *Institutes of the Christian Religion* (1536) St. Ignatius Loyola publishes *The Spiritual Exercises* (1541) El Greco, painter of *View of Toledo,* (1541–1614) Council of Trent (1545)	Rapid inflation marks the Price Revolution (1540s) Silver found in Mexico and Bolivia (1543–1548)	Francisco Pizarro topples Incas (1533)	1533
Reign of Philip II of Spain (1556–1598) Reign of Elizabeth I of England (1558–1603)	Edmund Spenser, author of *The Faerie Queen,* (1552–1599)		Peace of Augsburg (1555)	
	First *Roman Index of Prohibited Books* established (1564) William Shakespeare (1564–1616) Papacy of Pius V (1566–1572) St. Bartholomew's Day massacre (1572)		Ottomans defeated by Hapsburgs and Venetians at Lepanto (1571) Philip II annexes Portugal (1580)	
English navy defeats the Spanish Armada (1588) Reign of Henry IV, first of the Bourbon dynasty in France (1589–1610) Edict of Nantes (1598) Reign of James I, first of the Stuart dynasty (1603–1625) Cardinal Richelieu, first minister of France (1624–1642) Reign of Charles I of England (1625–1649) English Civil War (1642–1649) The Fronde, a series of French aristocratic revolts (1648–1653) Oliver Cromwell rules during the Commonwealth (1649–1658) Louis XIV of France comes of age (1651) Charles II and the Restoration (1660–1685)	John Milton (1608–1674) Blaise Pascal (1623–1662) Thomas Hobbes' *Leviathan* (1651)	New World silver production peaks at 10 million ounces (1590s) Spanish economy collapses when silver imports drop (1620–1640)	Thirty Year's War (1618–1648) Gustavus Adolphus of Sweden enters Thirty Years' War (1630) Peace of Westphalia (1648)	1600

COMMERCE,
CONQUEST, AND
COLONIZATION,
1300–1600

B Y 1300, THE GREAT EUROPEAN expansion of the High Middle Ages was coming to an end. In Iberia, there would be no further conquests of Muslim territory until 1492, when Granada fell to King Ferdinand and Queen Isabella. In the east, the Crusader kingdoms of Constantinople and Acre collapsed, in 1261 and 1291 respectively. Only the German drive into eastern Europe continued; but by the mid-fourteenth century, it too had been slowed by the rise of a new Baltic state in Lithuania. Internal expansion was also slowing, as Europe reached the ecological limits of its resources. Thereafter, the pressure on resources was eased only by the dramatic population losses that resulted during the fourteenth century from the combined effects of famine, plague, and war.

But despite these checks, Europeans in the late Middle Ages did not turn inward on themselves. Although land-based conquests slowed, new, sea-based empires emerged in the Mediterranean world during the fourteenth and fifteenth centuries with colonies that extended from the Black Sea to the Canary Islands. New maritime trade routes were opened up through the Strait of Gibraltar, resulting in greater economic integration between the Mediterranean and Atlantic economies and increasing the demand in northwestern Europe for Asian spices and African gold. By the late fifteenth century, Mediterranean mariners and colonists had extended their domination out into the Atlantic, from the Azores in the north to the Canary Islands in the south. Portuguese navigators were also pushing down the west coast of Africa. In 1498 one such expedition would sail all the way around the Cape of Good Hope to India.

The fifteenth-century conquest of the "Atlantic Mediterranean" was the essential preliminary to the dramatic events that began in 1492 with Columbus's attempt to reach China by sailing westward across the Atlantic Ocean and that led, by 1600, to the Spanish and Portuguese conquests of the Americas. Because these events are so familiar, we can easily underestimate their importance. For the native peoples and empires of the Americas, the results of European contact were cataclysmic. By 1600, somewhere between 50 and 90 percent of the indigenous peoples of the

FOCUS QUESTIONS

- How did the Mongols affect trade along the Silk Road?

- Why were slaves important to Ottoman society?

 • How were the Portuguese able to control Indian Ocean trade?

- What was the impact of New World silver on the European economy?

Americas had perished from disease, massacre, and enslavement. For Europeans, the results of their conquests were far less fatal, but no less far reaching. By 1300, Europe had eclipsed both Byzantium and the empire of Islam as a Mediterranean power, but outside the Mediterranean and the north Atlantic European power was negligible. By 1600, however, Europe had emerged as the first truly global power in world history, capable of pursuing its imperial ambitions and commercial interests wherever its ships could sail and its guns could reach. European control over the interiors of the African, Asian, and American land masses would not be fully achieved until the end of the nineteenth century, and would last thereafter for less than a century. By 1600, however, European navies ruled the seas and the world's resources were increasingly being channeled through European hands—patterns that have continued until the present day.

THE MONGOLS

How did the Mongols affect trade along the Silk Road?

Trade between the Mediterranean world and the Far East dated back to antiquity, but it was not until the late thirteenth century that Europeans began to establish direct trading connections with India, China, and the "Spice Islands" of the Indonesian archipelago. For Europeans, these connections would prove profoundly important, although less for their economic significance than for their impact upon the European imagination. For the peoples of Asia, however, the appearance of European traders on the "Silk Road" between Central Asia and China was merely a curiosity. The really consequential event was the rise of the Mongol empire that made such connections possible.

For the peoples of Asia, the appearance of European traders on the "Silk Road" was merely a curiosity. It was the rise of the Mongol empire that made such connections possible.

THE RISE OF THE MONGOL EMPIRE

The Mongols were one of a number of nomadic peoples inhabiting the steppes of central Asia. Although closely connected with various Turkish-speaking peoples with whom they frequently intermarried, the Mongols spoke their own distinctive language and had their own homeland to the north of the Gobi Desert in present-day Mongolia. Sheep provided them with shelter (in the form of wool tents), clothing, milk, and meat. Horses made possible their seasonal movements across the steppes, and also provided them with their national drink, an intoxicating fermented mare's milk called *qumis*. Like many nomadic peoples throughout history, the Mongols were highly accomplished cavalry soldiers who supplemented their own pastoralism and craft production by raiding the sedentary peoples to their south. (It was in part to control such raiding from Mongolia that, many centuries before, the Chinese had built the famous Great Wall.) Primarily, however, China defended itself by attempting to ensure that the Mongols remained internally divided, and so turned their martial energies most often against each other.

In the late twelfth century, however, a Mongol chief named Temüjin began to unite the various Mongol tribes under his rule. By incorporating the army of each defeated tribe into his own army, Temüjin quickly built up a large military force. In 1206, his supremacy was formally acknowledged by all the Mongols, and he took the title Chingiz (Genghis) Khan—"the oceanic (possibly meaning universal) ruler." Chingiz now turned his enormous army against his non-Mongol neighbors. China at this time was divided into three hostile states. In 1209, Chingiz launched an attack on northwestern China; in 1211 he invaded the Chin empire in north China. At first these attacks were probably looting expeditions rather than deliberate attempts at conquest, but by the 1230s a full-scale Mongol conquest of northern and western China was under way, culminating in 1234 with the fall of the Chin. In 1279, Chingiz's grandson Qubilai (Kublai) Khan completed the conquest of southern (Sung) China, thus reuniting China for the first time in centuries. The Yuan dynasty Qubilai established ruled China until 1368, when it was overthrown by a native Chinese dynasty known as the Ming.

Meanwhile, Chingiz turned his forces westward, conquering much of Central Asia and incorporating the important commercial cities of Tashkent, Samarkand, and Bukhara into his expanding empire. When Chingiz died in 1227, he was succeeded by his third son Ögedei, who completed the conquest of the Chin, con-

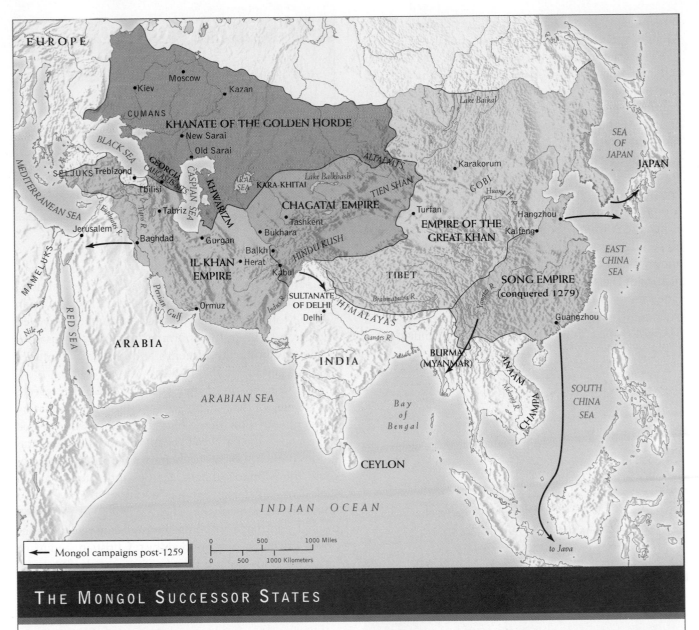

THE MONGOL SUCCESSOR STATES

Consider the breakup of Chingiz Khan's empire after 1259, and the passing similarities its fracture might possess to the disintegration of Alexander's empire, also conquered swiftly and encompassing vast swaths of Europe and Asia. Why did Chingiz Khan's empire splinter? How did the Mongol onslaught against and occupation of major sections of the Arab Muslim world possibly aid the expansion of European civilization and trade into the Mediterranean? At the same time, how did it complicate the situation for the crusader efforts in the Holy Land?

quered the lands between the Oxus River and the Caspian Sea, and then laid plans for a massive invasion toward the west. Between 1237 and 1240, the Mongol horde (so called from the Turkish word *ordu*, meaning "tent" or "encampment") conquered southern Russia, and then launched a two-pronged assault farther west. The smaller of the two Mongol armies swept through Poland toward eastern Germany; the larger army went

southwest toward Hungary. In April 1241 the smaller Mongol force met a hastily assembled army of Germans and Poles at the battle of Liegnitz, where the two sides fought to a bloody standstill. Two days later, the larger Mongol army annihilated the Hungarian army at the River Sajo.

How much farther west the Mongol armies might have pushed will forever remain in doubt, for in

December 1241 the Great Khan Ögedei died, and the Mongol forces withdrew from eastern Europe. It took five years before a new great khan could establish himself, and when he died in 1248, the resulting interregnum lasted for three more years. Mongol conquests continued in Persia, the Middle East, and China, but after 1241 the Mongols never resumed their attacks on Europe. After 1260, when the Mamluk sultanate of Egypt stopped the Mongols' advance toward the southwest, the Mongol empire split into competing and frequently hostile parts. By 1300, the period of Mongol expansion had come to an end.

But the Mongol threat did not suddenly disappear. Descendants of Chingiz Khan continued to rule this enormous land empire (the largest such empire in the history of the world) until the mid-fourteenth century. Later, under the leadership of Timur the Lame (known as Tamerlane to Europeans) it looked briefly as if the Mongol empire might be reunited. But Timur died in

The Head of Timur the Lame. A forensic reconstruction based on his exhumed skull.

1405 on his way to invade China; thereafter the various parts of the Mongol empire fell into the hands of local rulers, including (in Asia Minor) the Ottoman Turks. Mongol cultural influence continued, however, and can be seen in the enormously impressive artwork produced during the fifteenth and sixteenth centuries in Persia and in Mughal India.

The Mongols owed their success to the size, speed, and training of their mounted armies; to the intimidating savagery with which they butchered those who resisted them; and to their ability to adapt the administrative traditions of their subjects to their own purposes. Partly because the Mongols themselves put little store even in their own shamanistic religious traditions, they were also unusually tolerant of the religious beliefs of others—a distinct advantage in controlling an empire that comprised a dizzying array of Buddhist, Christian, and Muslim sects. However, little was distinctively "Mongol" about the way they governed their empire. Except in China, where the Yuan dynasty inherited and maintained a complex administrative bureaucracy, the Mongols' rule was relatively unsophisticated, being chiefly directed at securing the steady payment of tribute from their subjects.

EUROPE, THE MONGOLS, AND THE FAR EAST

The Mongols had a keen eye for the commercial advantages their empire could offer them. They took steps to control the caravan routes that led from China through Central Asia to the Black Sea. They also encouraged commercial contacts with European traders, especially through the Iranian city of Tabriz, from which both land and sea routes led on to China. Until the Mongol conquests, the "Silk Road" to China

MARCO POLO'S DESCRIPTION OF JAVA

The Venetian merchants Niccolo and Maffeo Polo traveled overland from Constantinople to the court of Qubilai Khan between 1260 and 1269. When they returned a few years later, they brought with them Niccolo's son Marco. A gifted linguist, Marco would remain at the Mongol court until the early 1290s, when he returned to Europe after a journey through Southeast Asia, the Spice Islands, and the Indian Ocean. Marco's account of his Travels *would shape European images of the Far East for centuries.*

Departing from Ziamba, and steering between south and south-east, fifteen hundred miles, you reach an island of very great size, named Java. According to the reports of some well-informed navigators, it is the greatest in the world, and has a compass above three thousand miles. It is under the dominion of one king only, nor do the inhabitants pay tribute to any other power. They are worshipers of idols.

The country abounds with rich commodities. Pepper, nutmegs, spikenard, galangal, cubebs, cloves and all the other valuable spices and drugs, are the produce of the island; which occasion it to be visited by many ships laden with merchandise, that yields to the owners considerable profit.

The quantity of gold collected there exceeds all calculation and belief. From thence it is that . . . merchants . . . have imported, and to this day import, that metal to a great amount, and from thence also is obtained the greatest part of the spices that are distributed throughout the world. That the Great Khan [Qubilai] has not brought the island under subjection to him, must be attributed to the length of the voyage and the dangers of the navigation.

The Travels of Marco Polo, revised and edited by Manuel Komroff. (New York: Random House), 1926, pp. 267–268.

---

had been closed to Western merchants and travelers. But almost as soon as the Mongol empire was established, we find Europeans venturing on these routes. The first such travelers were Franciscan missionaries such as William de Rubruck, sent by King Louis IX of France in 1253 as his ambassador to the Mongol court. But Western merchants quickly followed. The most famous of these early merchants were three Venetians: Niccolo, Maffeo, and Marco Polo. Marco Polo's account of his twenty-year sojourn in China in the service of Qubilai Khan, and of his journey home through the Spice Islands, India, and Iran, is one of

the most famous travel accounts of all time. Its effect upon the imagination of his contemporaries was enormous. For the next two centuries, most of what Europeans knew about the Far East they learned from Marco Polo's *Travels*. Christopher Columbus's copy of this book still survives.

European connections with the western end of the Silk Road would continue until the mid-fourteenth century. The Genoese were especially active in this trade, not least because their rivals, the Venetians, already dominated the Mediterranean trade with Alexandria and Beirut, through which the bulk of Europe's Far Eastern luxury goods continued to pass. But the Mongols of Iran become progressively more hostile to Westerners as the fourteenth century progressed. By 1344, the Genoese had abandoned Tabriz after attacks on Westerners had made their position there untenable. In 1346, the Mongols of the Golden Horde besieged the Genoese colony at Caffa on the Black Sea. Apart from crippling Genoese commerce in the Black Sea, this siege is memorable chiefly because during it the Black Death was passed from the Mongol army (which had inadvertently brought it from the Gobi Desert, where the disease was endemic) to the Genoese defenders, who returned with it to western Europe, where it proceeded to kill approximately one-third of the entire European population.

The "window of opportunity" that made Marco Polo's travels possible was thus relatively short. By the middle of the fourteenth century, hostilities between the various parts of the Mongol empire were already making travel along the Silk Road perilous. After 1368, when the Mongol (Yuan) dynasty was overthrown, Westerners were excluded from China altogether, and Mongols were restricted to cavalry service in the Ming imperial armies. The overland trade routes from China to the Black Sea continued to operate; Europeans, however, were no longer able to travel along them. But the new, more integrated commercial world the Mongols created had a lasting impact upon Europe, despite the relatively short time during which Europeans themselves were able to participate directly in it. European memories of the Far East would be preserved, and the dream of reestablishing direct connections between Europe and China would survive to influence a new round of European commercial and imperial expansion from the late fifteenth century onward.

THE RISE OF THE OTTOMAN EMPIRE

Why were slaves important to Ottoman society?

Like the Mongols, the Ottoman Turks were initially a nomadic people whose economy continued to depend on raiding even after they had conquered an extensive empire. The peoples who would become the Ottomans were already established in northwestern Anatolia when the Mongols arrived, and were already at least nominally Muslims. But unlike the established Muslim powers in the region, whom the Mongols destroyed, the Ottoman Turks were among the principal beneficiaries of the Mongol conquest. By toppling the Seljuk sultanate and the Abbasid caliphate of Baghdad, the Mongols eliminated the two traditional authorities that had previously kept Turkish border chieftains like the Ottomans in check. Now the Ottomans were free to raid along their soft frontiers with Byzantium unhindered. At the same time, however, they remained far enough away from the centers of Mongol authority to avoid being destroyed themselves.

THE CONQUEST OF CONSTANTINOPLE

By the end of the thirteenth century, the Ottoman dynasty had established itself as the leading family among the Anatolian border lords. By the mid-fourteenth century, it had solidified its preeminence by capturing a number of important cities. These successes brought the Ottomans to the attention of the Byzantine emperor, who in 1345 hired a contingent of Ottomans as mercenaries. Thus introduced into Europe, the Ottomans quickly made themselves at home. By 1370, they had extended their control all the way to the Danube. In 1389 Ottoman forces defeated the powerful Serbian empire at the battle of Kosovo, enabling them to consolidate their control over Greece, Bulgaria, and the Balkans.

In 1396 the Ottomans attacked Constantinople, but were forced to withdraw in order to repel a Western crusading force that had been sent against them. In 1402, they attacked Constantinople again, but once more they were forced to withdraw, this time to confront Timur the Lame's invasion of Anatolia. Ottoman pressure on Constantinople continued after Timur's death in 1405, producing a steady stream of refugees fleeing to Italy, who brought with them the surviving masterworks of classical Greek literature. But it was not until 1451 that a new sultan, Mehmet II, turned his full attention to the conquest of the imperial city. In 1453, after a brilliantly executed siege, Mehmet succeeded in breaching the city's walls. The Byzantine emperor was killed in the assault, and the city itself was thoroughly plundered. The Ottomans then settled down to rule their new imperial capital in a style reminiscent of their Byzantine predecessors.

The Ottoman conquest of Constantinople was an enormous psychological shock to Christian Europe, but its economic impact on western Europe was minor. Ot-

Sultan Mehmet II, "The Conqueror" (1451–1481), by the Ottoman artist Siblizade Ahmed. The sultan's pose and handkerchief are Central Asian conventions in portraiture, but the subdued color and three-quarter profile show the influence of Italian Renaissance portraits. The sultan wears the white turban of a scholar, but also wears the thumb ring of an archer, neatly reflecting his combination of scholarly and military attainments.

between Europe and India, it was their efforts to exclude Muslims from the Indian Ocean spice trade that helped spur the Ottoman conquests of Syria, Egypt, and the Balkans during the 1520s and 1530s. To be sure, these Ottoman conquests had other motives also, including the desire to control the Egyptian grain trade. But by eliminating the merchants who had traditionally dominated the overland spice trade through Beirut and Alexandria, the Ottomans may also have hoped to redirect this trade through Constantinople, and then up the Danube into western Europe.

The effects of the Ottoman conquest of Constantinople on western Europe were modest. Upon the Ottomans themselves, however, their conquest was transformative. Vast new wealth poured into Ottoman society, which the Ottomans further increased by carefully tending to the industrial and commercial interests of their new capital city. Trade routes were redirected to feed the capital, and the Ottomans became a naval power in the eastern Mediterranean and the Black Sea. As a result, Constantinople's population grew from less than one hundred thousand in 1453 to more than five hundred thousand in 1600, making it the largest city in the world outside China.

WAR, SLAVERY, AND SOCIAL ADVANCEMENT

Despite the Ottomans' careful attention to commerce, their empire and its capital city could only be sustained through continuous raiding and conquest. Until the end of the sixteenth century, the Ottoman empire was therefore on an almost constant war footing. The result, however, was a kind of vicious cycle. To continue its conquests, the size of the Ottoman

toman control over the former Byzantine empire did reduce European access to the Black Sea, but the bulk of the Far Eastern luxury trade with Europe had never passed through the Black Sea ports in the first place. Europeans got most of their spices and silks through Venice, which imported them from Alexandria and Beirut. These two cities did not fall to the Ottomans until the 1520s. In no sense, therefore, can the Ottomans be seen as the spur that propelled Portuguese efforts during the late fifteenth century to establish a direct sea route between Europe, India, and the Spice Islands of the Far East. If anything, the opposite is the case. After the Portuguese established a direct sea route

CHRONOLOGY

RISE OF THE OTTOMAN EMPIRE, 1300–1571

Ottomans become leading Anatolian family	1300
Byzantine emperor hires Ottoman mercenaries	1345
Ottomans enter Europe	1350s
Ottomans defeat Serbian empire	1389
Ottomans conquer Constantinople	1453
Ottomans conquer Syria, Egypt, Balkans	1520s
Battle of Lepanto	1571

The Turkish Slave Girl, by the early sixteenth-century Italian artist Parmigianino. This portrait illustrates the expensive clothes and jewels worn by some Ottoman slaves. It also reflects the sensuality and exoticism that many Europeans saw in the Ottoman Turks.

more than twenty thousand slave attendants, not including his bodyguard and his elite infantry units, both of which were also composed of slaves.

The result was an almost insatiable demand for slaves, especially in Constantinople itself. Many of these slaves were captured in war. Many others were taken from Poland and Ukraine in raids by Crimean slave merchants, who then shipped their captives to the slave markets of Constantinople. But slaves were also recruited (some willingly, some by coercion) from rural areas of the Ottoman empire itself. Because the vast majority of Ottoman slaves were household servants and administrators rather than laborers, some people willingly accepted enslavement, believing that they would be better off as slaves in Constantinople than as impoverished peasants in the countryside. In the Balkans especially, many people were enslaved as children, handed over by their families to pay the infamous "child tax" the Ottomans imposed on rural areas too poor to pay a monetary tribute. Although unquestionably a wrenching experience for families, this practice did open up opportunities for social advancement. Special academies were created at Constantinople to train the most able of these enslaved children to act as administrators and soldiers, and some rose to become powerful figures in the Ottoman empire. Slavery therefore carried relatively little social stigma. Even the sultan himself was most often the son of an enslaved woman.

Because Muslims were not permitted to enslave other Muslims, the vast majority of Ottoman slaves were Christians (although many converted to Islam later in life). But because so many of the elite positions within Ottoman government were held by slaves, the paradoxical result of this reliance on slave administrators was that Muslims, including Turks, were effectively excluded from the main avenues of social and political advancement in Ottoman society. Nor was Ottoman society characterized by a powerful, hereditary nobility of the sort that dominated contemporary European society. As a result, power in the fifteenth- and sixteenth-century Ottoman empire was remarkably, perhaps even uniquely, open to men of ability and talent, provided that such men were slaves and so were not Muslims by birth.

Nor was this pattern of Muslim exclusion limited to government and the army. Commerce and business also remained largely in the hands of non-Muslims, most frequently Greeks, Syrians, and Jews. Jews in particular found in the Ottoman empire a

army and administration grew exponentially. But this growth drew more and more manpower from the empire. Because the Ottoman army and administration were largely composed of slaves, the demand for more soldiers and administrators could best be met through further conquests that would capture yet more slaves. Further conquests, however, required a still larger army and an even more extensive bureaucracy; and so the cycle continued.

Slaves were the backbone of the Ottoman army and administration, as they had for long been in Mamluk Egypt also. But slaves were also critical to the lives of the Ottoman upper class. One of the important measures of status in Ottoman society was the number of slaves in one's household. After 1453, new wealth permitted some Ottoman notables to maintain households in which thousands of slaves attended to their masters' whims. In the sixteenth century, the sultan's household alone numbered

> Slaves were the backbone of the Ottoman army and administration.

OTTOMAN JANISSARIES

The following account is from a memoir written by a Christian Serb who was captured as a youth by Sultan Mehmet II the Conqueror, converted to Islam, and who then served eight years in the Ottoman janissary corps. In 1463, however, the fortress he was defending for the Sultan was captured by the Hungarians, and the author thereupon returned to Christianity.

Whenever the Turks invade foreign lands and capture their people an imperial scribe follows immediately behind them, and whatever boys there are, he takes them all into the Janissaries and gives five gold pieces for each one and sends them across the sea [to Anatolia]. There are about two thousand of these boys. If, however, the number of them from enemy peoples does not suffice, then he takes from the Christians in every village in his land who have boys, having established what is the most every village can give so that the quota will always be full. And the boys whom he takes in his own land are called *cilik*. Each one of them can leave his property to whomever he wants after his death. And those whom he takes among the enemies are called *pendik*. These latter after their deaths can leave nothing; rather, it goes to the emperor, except that if someone comports himself well and is so deserving that he be freed, he may leave it to whomever he wants. And on the boys who are across the sea the emperor spends nothing; rather, those to whom they are entrusted must maintain them and send them where he orders. Then they take those who are suited for it on ships and there they study and train to skirmish in battle. There the emperor already provides for them and gives them a wage. From there he chooses for his own court those who are trained and then raises their wages.

Konstantin Mihailovic, *Memoirs of a Janissary*, trans. Benjamin Stolz. Michigan Slavic Translations no. 3. (Ann Arbor: Michigan Slavic Publications, 1975), pp. 157–159.

welcome refuge from the persecutions and expulsions that had characterized Jewish life in late medieval Europe. After their 1492 expulsion from Spain, more than a hundred thousand Spanish (Sephardic) Jews ultimately immigrated into the Ottoman empire.

RELIGIOUS CONFLICTS

The Ottomans themselves were relentlessly orthodox Sunni Muslims, who lent staunch support to the religious and legal pronouncements of the Islamic scholarly schools. Ottoman emphasis on their religious orthodoxy began in the fourteenth century and increased steadily thereafter. In 1516, the Ottomans captured the cities of Medina and Mecca, thus becoming the defenders of the holy sites. Soon after, they captured Jerusalem and Cairo, putting an end to the Mamluk sultanate of Egypt. In 1538 the Ottoman ruler formally adopted the title of caliph, thereby declaring himself to be the legitimate successor of the Prophet Muhammad.

In keeping with Sunni traditions, the Ottomans were also religiously tolerant toward non-Muslims, especially during the fifteenth and sixteenth centuries.

THE GROWTH OF THE OTTOMAN EMPIRE

What factors led to the successful expansion of the Ottoman empire? What challenges did the steady conquest of such a large and diverse area pose, and how did the Ottomans meet those challenges? Why did they succeed in taking Constantinople where so many other would-be conquerors had failed? How did their encroachment in the Balkans affect European attitudes toward the Ottoman conquest? Why did European states allow the East to fall to the Ottoman Turks? How did the Ottoman domination of western Asia encourage economic enterprise in the European states?

They organized the major religious groups of their empire into legally recognized units known as *millets*, permitting them considerable rights of religious self-government. After 1453, however, the Ottomans were particularly careful to protect and promote the authority of the Greek Orthodox patriarch of Constantinople over the Orthodox Christians of their empire. As a result, the Ottomans enjoyed staunch support from their Orthodox Christian subjects during their sixteenth century wars with the Latin Christians of western Europe. Despite the religious diversity of their empire, the Ottomans' principal religious conflicts were therefore not with their own subjects, but with the Shi'ite Muslim dynasty that ruled neighboring Persia. Time and again during the sixteenth century, Ottoman expeditions against western Europe had to be abandoned when hostilities erupted with the Persians.

THE OTTOMANS AND EUROPE

During the sixteenth century, the Habsburg rulers of Spain, Germany, and Austria were similarly distracted by their own conflicts with the Catholic kings of France (with whom the Ottomans made an alliance) and with the Protestant princes of Germany, the Netherlands, and England. As a result, the contest between the Ottoman empire and the Western powers never really lived up to the rhetoric of "holy war" that both sides employed in their propaganda. In 1396, a Western crusader army was annihilated by the Ottomans at the battle of Nicopolis. In the sixteenth and seventeenth centuries, Ottoman armies several times besieged Vienna. But despite these dramatic moments, such conflicts as there were between the Ottomans and the rulers of western Europe were fought out mainly through pirate raids and naval battles in the Mediterranean. The main result of this contest was thus a steady escalation in the scale and cost of navies. In 1571, when a combined Habsburg and Venetian force defeated the Ottoman fleet at Lepanto, more than four hundred ships took part, with both sides deploying naval forces ten times larger than they had possessed half a century before.

Although undeniably a victory for the Habsburgs and their Venetian allies, the battle of Lepanto was far less decisive than is often suggested. The Ottoman

Ottoman Orthodoxy. This Ottoman genealogical chart shows the descent of Sultan Mehmet III (1595–1603) from the Prophet Muhammad (shown veiled).

The Battle of Lepanto. The victory of Spain, Venice, and the papacy over the Ottomans at Lepanto in 1571 became a favorite subject for propagandistic paintings by European artists.

navy was speedily rebuilt; by no means did Lepanto put an end to Ottoman influence over the eastern Mediterranean Sea. Nevertheless, after 1571 both Ottoman and Habsburg interests shifted away from their conflict with each other. The Ottomans embarked upon a long and costly war with Persia, while the Spanish Habsburgs turned their attention toward their new empire in the Atlantic. By the mid-seventeenth century, when a new round of Ottoman-European conflicts began, the strength of the Ottoman empire had been sapped by a series of indolent, pleasure-loving sultans and by the tensions that arose within the Ottoman empire itself as it ceased to expand. The Ottoman empire would last until 1918; but from the mid-seventeenth century on, it was no longer a serious rival to the global hegemony the European powers were beginning to achieve.

MEDITERRANEAN COLONIALISM

How were the Portuguese able to control Indian Ocean trade?

During the fifteenth century, European colonial and commercial ambitions came to be focused more and more on the western Mediterranean and the Atlantic world. Although historians have sometimes argued the contrary, this reorientation was not a result of the rising power of the Ottoman empire. Instead, this westward orientation was the product of two related developments: the growing importance to late medieval Europe of the African gold trade; and the growth of European colonial empires in the western Mediterranean Sea.

SILVER SHORTAGES AND THE SEARCH FOR AFRICAN GOLD

Europeans had been trading for African gold for centuries, mainly through Muslim middlemen who transported this precious metal in caravans from the Niger River area where it was produced to the North African ports of Algiers and Tunis. From the thirteenth century on, Catalan and Genoese merchants both maintained merchant colonies in Tunis, where

they traded woolen cloth for North African grain and sub-Saharan gold.

What accelerated the late medieval demand for gold, however, was a serious silver shortage that affected the entire European economy during the fourteenth and fifteenth centuries. Silver production in Europe fell markedly during the 1340s and remained at a low level thereafter, as Europeans reached the limits of their technological capacity to extract silver ore from deep mines. The resulting shortage of coin had a seriously deflationary effect on the European economy. It was not until the 1470s that new mining techniques, combined with discoveries of new silver deposits, began to alleviate this shortage.

This shortfall in silver production was compounded during the fifteenth century by a serious balance-of-payments problem: more European silver was flowing east in the spice trade than could be replaced using existing mining techniques on known silver deposits. Gold currencies represented an obvious alternative for large transactions, and from the thirteenth century on European rulers with access to gold were minting gold coins. But Europe itself had few natural gold reserves. To maintain and expand these gold coinages, new and larger supplies of gold were needed. The most obvious source for this gold was Africa.

MEDITERRANEAN EMPIRES: CATALUNYA, VENICE, AND GENOA

The growing European interest in the African gold trade coincided with the creation of sea-based Mediterranean empires by the Catalans, the Venetians, and the Genoese. During the thirteenth century, the Catalans conquered and colonized a series of western Mediterranean islands, including Majorca, Ibiza, Minorca, Sicily, and Sardinia. Except in Sicily, the pattern of Catalan exploitation was largely the same on all these islands: expropriation or extermination of the native (usually Muslim) population; economic concessions to attract new settlers; and a heavy reliance on slave labor to produce foodstuffs and raw materials for export.

Unlike Catalan colonization efforts, which were mainly carried on by private individuals operating under a crown charter, Venetian colonization was directed by the city's rulers, and was focused mainly on the eastern Mediterranean, where the Venetians dominated the trade in spices and silks. The Genoese, by contrast, had more extensive interests in the western Mediterranean world, where their trade focused on bulk goods such as cloth, hides, grain, timber, and sugar. Genoese colonies tended to be more informal and family based than Venetian or Catalan colonies, constituting more of a network than an extension of a sovereign empire. They were also more closely integrated into the native societies of North Africa, Spain, and the Black Sea than were the Venetian or the Catalan colonies. In particular, the Genoese pioneered the production of sugar and sweet "Madeira" wines in the western Mediterranean, first in Sicily and later in the Atlantic islands off the west coast of Africa. To transport such bulky goods, the Genoese moved away from the oared galleys favored by the Venetians toward larger, fuller-bodied sailing ships that could carry greater volumes of cargo. With further modifications to accommodate the rougher sailing conditions of the Atlantic Ocean, these were the ships that would carry sixteenth-century Europeans around the globe.

FROM THE MEDITERRANEAN TO THE ATLANTIC

Until the late thirteenth century, European maritime commerce had been divided between a Mediterranean and a north Atlantic world. Starting around 1270, however, Italian merchants began to sail through the Strait of Gibraltar and on to the wool-producing regions of England and the Netherlands. This was the essential first step in the extension of Mediterranean patterns of commerce and colonization into the Atlantic Ocean. The second step was the discovery (or possibly rediscovery), during the fourteenth century, of the Atlantic island chains known as the Canaries and the Azores by Genoese sailors. Efforts to colonize the Canary Islands, and to convert and enslave their inhabitants, began almost immediately. But an effective conquest of the Canary Islands did not really begin until the fifteenth century, when it was undertaken by Portugal and completed by Castile. The Canaries, in turn, became the base from which further Portuguese voyages down the west coast of Africa proceeded. They were also the "jumping-off point" from which Christopher Columbus would sail westward across the Atlantic Ocean in hopes of reaching Asia.

Italian merchants sailing through the Strait of Gibraltar was the essential first step in the extension of Mediterranean patterns of commerce and colonization into the Atlantic Ocean.

THE TECHNOLOGY OF SHIPS AND NAVIGATION

The European empires of the fifteenth and sixteenth centuries rested on a mastery of the oceans. This mastery was partly the product of long experience in Atlantic waters. For example, the Portuguese caravel—the workhorse ship of the fifteenth-century voyages to Africa—was based on ship and sail designs that had been in use among Portuguese fishermen since the thirteenth century. Starting in the 1440s, however, Portuguese shipwrights began building larger caravels of about fifty tons displacement, with two masts each carrying a triangular (lateen) sail. Such ships were capable of sailing against the wind much more effectively than were the older, square-rigged vessels. They also required much smaller crews than did the multi-oared galleys that were still commonly used in the Mediterranean. By the end of the fifteenth century, even larger caravels of around two hundred tons were being constructed, with a third mast and a combination of square and lateen rigging. Columbus's *Niña* was of this design, having been refitted with two square sails in the Canary Islands to enable it to sail more efficiently before the wind during the Atlantic crossing.

Europeans were also making significant advances in navigation during the fifteenth and sixteenth centuries. Quadrants, which calculated latitude in the Northern Hemisphere by the height above the horizon of the North Star, were in widespread use by the 1450s. As sailors approached the equator, however, the quadrant became less and less useful, and they were forced instead to make use of astrolabes, which reckoned latitude by the height of the sun. Like quadrants, astrolabes had been known in western Europe for centuries. In the twelfth century, Abelard and Heloise had even named their son Astrolabe. But it was not until the 1480s that the astrolabe became a really useful instrument for seaborne navigation, with the preparation of standard tables sponsored by the Portuguese crown. Compasses too were also coming into more widespread use during the fifteenth century. Longitude, however, remained impossible to calculate accurately until the eighteenth century, when the invention of the marine chronometer finally made it possible to keep accurate time at sea. In the sixteenth century, Europeans sailing

OVERSEAS EXPLORATION IN THE FIFTEENTH AND SIXTEENTH CENTURIES

This map shows the routes taken by major European explorers of the fifteenth and sixteenth centuries, as well as the distribution of outposts established by the Portuguese and Spanish. Why were the Portuguese and Spanish the first Europeans to underwrite and encourage such adventures? What economic and cultural factors precipitated such efforts? What were the motives for such voyages? How did the establishment of economic outposts in Africa, America, and the East Indies radically alter the balance of power in the "Old World," and why? Might the Americas have had to wait even longer for European "discovery" had da Gama found the route around Africa sooner?

Legend:

EXPLORERS

— Columbus: first voyage
— Columbus: next three voyages
— Bartholomew Diaz
— Vasco Da Gama
— Amerigo Vespucci
— Magellan and Magellan's ship

CONQUISTADORES

····· Cortes
······ Pizzarro

OUTPOSTS AND SETTLEMENTS

■ Portuguese
■ Spanish

east or west across the oceans generally had to rely on their skill at dead reckoning to determine where they were on the globe.

European sailors also benefited from a new interest in maps and navigational charts. Especially important to Atlantic sailors were books known as *rutters* or *routiers.* These contained detailed sailing instructions and descriptions of the coastal landmarks a pilot could expect to encounter on route to a variety of destinations. Mediterranean sailors had had similar books, known as *portolani,* since at least the fourteenth century. In the fifteenth century, however, this tradition was extended to the Atlantic Ocean; by the end of the sixteenth century, rutters spanned the globe.

<table>
<tr><td colspan="2">C H R O N O L O G Y</td></tr>
<tr><td colspan="2">PORTUGUESE MARITIME EXPANSION, 1420s–1515</td></tr>
<tr><td>Colonization of Madeira and
    Canary Islands</td><td>1420s</td></tr>
<tr><td>Colonization of the Azores</td><td>1430s</td></tr>
<tr><td>Dias rounds the Cape of Good Hope</td><td>1488</td></tr>
<tr><td>Da Gama reaches India</td><td>1497–1498</td></tr>
<tr><td>Portuguese reach Malacca in
    Southeast Asia</td><td>1511</td></tr>
<tr><td>Portuguese reach Spice Islands</td><td>1515</td></tr>
</table>

PORTUGAL, AFRICA, AND THE SEA ROUTE TO INDIA

It was among the Portuguese that these dual interests—in the African gold trade and in Atlantic colonization—first came together. In 1415, a Portuguese expedition captured the north African port of Ceuta. During the 1420s the Portuguese colonized both the island of Madeira and the Canary Islands. During the 1430s, they extended these colonization efforts to the Azores. By the 1440s they had reached the Cape Verde Islands. In 1444 Portuguese explorers first landed in the area between the Senegal and the Gambia river mouths on the African mainland, where they began to collect cargoes of gold and slaves for export back to Portugal. By the 1470s, Portuguese sailors had rounded the African "bulge" and were exploring the Gulf of Guinea. In 1483 they reached the mouth of the Congo River. In 1488 the Portuguese captain Bartholomeu Dias rounded the southern tip of Africa. Blown around it accidentally by a gale, Dias named the point "Cape of Storms," but the king of Portugal took a more optimistic view of Dias's achievement. He renamed it the Cape of Good Hope and began planning a naval expedition to India. Finally in 1497–1498, Vasco de Gama rounded the cape, and then, with the help of a Muslim navigator named Ibn Majid, crossed the Indian Ocean to Calicutt on the southwestern coast of India, opening up for the first time a direct sea route between Europe and the Far Eastern spice trade. Although de Gama lost half his fleet and one-third of his men on his two-year voyage, his cargo of spices was so valuable that his losses were deemed insignificant. His heroism became legendary, and his story became the basis for the Portuguese national epic, the *Lusiads.*

Now master of the quickest route to riches in the world, the king of Portugal swiftly capitalized on de Gama's accomplishment. After 1500, Portuguese trading fleets sailed regularly to India. In 1509, the Portuguese defeated an Ottoman fleet and then blockaded the mouth of the Red Sea, attempting to cut off one of the traditional routes by which spices had traveled to Alexandria and Beirut. By 1510 Portuguese military forces had established a series of forts along the western Indian coastline, including their headquarters at Goa. In 1511 Portuguese ships seized Malacca, a center of the spice trade on the Malay peninsula. By 1515 they had reached the Spice Islands and the coast of China. So completely did the Portuguese now dominate the spice trade that by the 1520s even the Venetians were forced to buy their pepper in the Portuguese capital of Lisbon.

ARTILLERY AND EMPIRE

Larger, more maneuverable ships and improved navigational aids made it possible for the Portuguese and other European mariners to reach Africa, Asia, and the Americas by sea. But fundamentally, these sixteenth-century European commercial empires were a military achievement. As such, they reflected what Europeans had learned in their wars against each other during the fourteenth and fifteenth centuries. Perhaps the most critical military advance of the late Middle Ages was the increasing sophistication of artillery, a devel-

Fundamentally these sixteenth-century European commercial empires were a military achievement.

opment made possible not only by gunpowder, but also by improved metallurgical techniques for casting cannon barrels. By the middle of the fifteenth century, the use of artillery pieces had rendered the stone walls of medieval castles and towns obsolete, a fact brought home in 1453 by the successful French siege of Bordeaux (which brought to an end the Hundred Years' War), and by the Ottoman siege of Constantinople (which brought to an end the Byzantine empire).

One of the reasons the new ship designs (first caravels, and later the even larger galleons) were so important was that their larger size made it possible to mount more effective artillery pieces on them. Increasingly during the sixteenth century, European naval vessels were conceived as floating artillery platforms, with scores of guns mounted in fixed positions along their sides and swivel guns mounted fore and aft. These guns were vastly expensive, as were the ships that carried them; but for those rulers who could afford to possess them, such ships made it possible to project military power around the world. In 1498, Vasco de Gama became the first Portuguese captain to sail into the Indian Ocean; but the Portuguese did not gain control of that ocean until 1509, when they defeated a combined Ottoman and Indian naval force at the battle of Div. Portuguese trading outposts in Africa and Asia were fortifications, built to guard not only against the attacks of native peoples, but also to ward off assaults from other Europeans. Without this essential military component, the European maritime empires of the sixteenth century would not have existed.

> Increasingly, European naval vessels were conceived as floating artillery platforms, with scores of guns mounted along the sides.

PRINCE HENRY THE NAVIGATOR

Because we know that these fifteenth-century Portuguese expeditions down the African coast did ultimately open up a sea route to India and the Far East, it is tempting to presume that this was their goal from the beginning. It was not. The traditional narrative of these events, which presents exploration as their mission, India as their goal, and Prince Henry the Navigator as the guiding genius behind them, no longer commands the confidence of most historians. Only from the 1480s did India clearly become the goal toward which these voyages were directed. Prior to the 1480s, Portuguese involvement in Africa was driven instead by much more traditional goals: crusading ambitions against the Muslims of North Africa; the desire to establish direct links with the sources of African gold production south of the Sahara Desert; the desire to colonize the Atlantic islands; the burgeoning market for slaves in Europe and in the Ottoman empire; and the hope that somewhere in Africa they might find the legendary Prester John, a mythical Christian king whom Europeans believed would be their ally against the Muslims if only they could locate him. In the twelfth and thirteenth centuries, they had sought him in Asia. But from the 1340s on, he was believed to reside in Ethiopia, an expansive term that to most Europeans seems to have meant "somewhere in Africa."

Nor does Prince Henry (whose title, "the Navigator," was not assigned to him until the seventeenth century) seem so central a figure in Portuguese exploration as he was once thought to be. In fact, he directed only eight of the thirty-five Portuguese voyages to Africa between 1419 and his death in 1460; and the stories about his gathering a school of navigators and cartographers on the Atlantic coast of Portugal, about his role in designing improved ships and navigational instruments, and about his encouragement for scientific learning generally, have all been shown to be false. Henry did play an important role in organizing Portuguese

A Turkish Brass Cannon of the Fifteenth Century. This eighteen-ton gun fired balls twenty-five inches in diameter.

THE LEGEND OF PRESTER JOHN

THE TRAVELS OF SIR JOHN MANDEVILLE is an almost entirely fictional account of the wonders of the East, written by an English expatriate during the first half of the fourteenth century. Despite the fact that "Mandeville" (almost certainly a pseudonym) knew almost nothing about the lands he describes, his book became a primary source for European ideas about South and East Asia. Although Mandeville locates the legendary Prester John in Persia, India, or China (his geography is fuzzy, to say the least), by the fifteenth century Europeans were searching for Prester John in Africa.

This emperor Prester John has great lands and has many noble cities and good towns in his realm and many great, large islands. For all the country of India is separated into islands by the great floods that come from Paradise, that divide the land into many parts. And also in the sea he has many islands. . . .

This Prester John has under him many kings and many islands and many varied people of various conditions. And this land is full good and rich, but not so rich as is the land of the Great Khan. For the merchants do not come there so commonly to buy merchandise as they do in the land of the Great Khan, for it is too far to travel to. . . .

[Mandeville then goes on to describe the difficulties of reaching Prester John's lands by sea.]

This emperor Prester John always takes as his wife the daughter of the Great Khan, and the Great Khan in the same way takes to wife the daughter of Prester John. For these two are the greatest lords under the heavens.

In the land of Prester John there are many diverse things, and many precious stones so great and so large that men make them into vessels such as platters, dishes, and cups. And there are many other marvels there that it would be too cumbrous and too long to put into the writing of books. But of the principal islands and of his estate and of his law I shall tell you some part.

This emperor Prester John is Christian and a great part of his country is Christian also, although they do not hold to all the articles of our faith as we do. . . .

And he has under him 72 provinces, and in every province there is a king. And these kings have kings under them, and all are tributaries to Prester John.

And he has in his lordships many great marvels. For in his country is the sea that men call the Gravelly Sea, that is all gravel and sand without any drop of water. And it ebbs and flows in great waves as other seas do, and it is never still. . . . And a three-day journey from that sea there are great mountains out of which flows a great flood that comes out of Paradise. And it is full of precious stones without any drop of water. . . .

He dwells usually in the city of Susa [in Persia]. And there is his principal palace, which is so rich and so noble that no one will believe the report unless he has seen it. And above the chief tower of the palace there are two round pommels of gold and in each of them are two great, large rubies that shine full brightly upon the night. And the principal gates of his palace are of a precious stone that men call sardonyxes [a type of onyx], and the frames and the bars are made of ivory. And the windows of the halls and chambers are of crystal. And the tables upon which men eat, some are made of emeralds, some of amethyst, and some of gold full of precious stones. And the legs that hold up the tables are made of the same precious stones. . . .

Mandeville's Travels, edited by M. C. Seymour. (Oxford: Clarendon Press, 1967), pp. 195–199 (language modernized from Middle English by R. C. Stacey).

Prince Henry the Navigator, by a fifteenth-century Portuguese painter. This portrait is taken from a group portrait of the Portuguese royal family. Although thought to depict Henry, the identification is not certain.

The Tower of Belem. The Tower of Belem, a fifteenth-century fort, stands at the beach where Vasco da Gama departed in 1497 to sail beyond the Cape of Good Hope to India.

colonization of Madeira, the Canary Islands and the Azores, and he also pioneered the Portuguese slave trade, first on the Canaries (whose Stone-Age population was almost entirely enslaved) and then along the Sene-Gambian coast of Africa. His main goal, however, was to outflank the cross-Saharan African gold trade by intercepting this trade at its source. To this end, he built a series of forts along the African coastline, most famously at Arguim, to which he hoped to divert the cross-Saharan gold caravans. This was also his main goal in colonizing the Canary Islands, which he saw as a staging ground for expeditions into the African interior. There is no evidence that he ever dreamed of reaching India by sailing around Africa. Indeed, quite the opposite seems to be the case. Portuguese progress toward the Cape of Good Hope proceeded much more rapidly in the years after Henry's death than it had during his lifetime. Henry himself was a crusader against Islam; a prince in search

of a kingdom; a lord seeking resources to support his followers; and an aspiring merchant who hoped to make a killing in the gold trade but found his main profits in slaving. He was, in all these respects, a man of his time, which is to say, of the fifteenth century. He was not the architect, or even the visionary, of Portugal's sixteenth-century maritime empire.

ATLANTIC COLONIZATION AND THE GROWTH OF SLAVERY

The profits Prince Henry had hoped would come from the African gold trade did not materialize during his lifetime. He therefore had to make his expeditions pay by other means. One of those means was the slave trade. Although slavery in most of western Europe had effectively disappeared by the early twelfth century, slavery continued in Iberia (and to a lesser extent in

WHAT WAS THE IMPACT OF NEW WORLD SILVER ON THE EUROPEAN ECONOMY?

EUROPE ENCOUNTERS A NEW WORLD   445

Italy) throughout the high and late Middle Ages. Until the mid-fifteenth century, however, slavery on the Iberian mainland and in Italy remained very small in scale. The major Mediterranean slave markets of the fourteenth and early fifteenth centuries lay in Muslim lands, and especially in the Ottoman empire. Relatively few of the slaves who passed through these markets were Africans. Most were European Christians, predominantly Poles, Ukrainians, Greeks, and Bulgarians. Thus the patterns of slavery were not racialized in the late medieval Mediterranean world, except insofar as "primitive" peoples such as the natives of the Canary Islands or of Sardinia were more likely to be regarded as targets for enslavement.

From the mid-fifteenth century on, however, Lisbon began to emerge as a significant market for enslaved Africans. Something on the order of fifteen to twenty thousand Africans were sold in Lisbon during Prince Henry's lifetime, most of them between 1440 and 1460. In the half century after his death, the numbers grew, amounting to perhaps one hundred fifty thousand African slaves imported into Europe by 1505. For the most part, these slaves were regarded as status symbols—one reason they were so frequently depicted in paintings of the period. Even in the Atlantic colonies—Madeira, the Canaries, and the Azores—the land was worked mainly by European settlers and sharecroppers. Slave labor, if it was employed at all, was generally used only in sugar mills. This meant that on the Azores, which remained a wheat-producing colony, slavery found no real foothold. On Madeira and the Canaries, where sugar became the predominant cash crop during the last quarter of the fifteenth century, some slaves were introduced. But even sugar production did not lead to the widespread introduction of slavery on these islands.

A new style of slave-based sugar plantations began to emerge in Portugal's Atlantic colonies only in the 1460s, starting on the Cape Verde Islands and then extending southward into the Gulf of Guinea. These islands were not populated when the Portuguese began to settle them, and their climate was such as to discourage any large number of Europeans from settling there. They were ideally located, however, to purchase laborers from the slave traders along the nearby West African coast. No comparable system of large-scale, slave-based plantation production had been seen in Europe or Africa since the Roman period. But it was this model of sugar plantations staffed by enslaved Africans that would be exported to the Caribbean islands of the Americas by their Spanish conquerors, with incalculable consequences for Africa, the Americas, and Europe.

EUROPE ENCOUNTERS A NEW WORLD

What was the impact of New World silver on the European economy?

The decision by Spain's rulers to underwrite Columbus's famous voyage was an outgrowth of the progress of these Portuguese ventures. After 1488, when Dias successfully rounded the Cape of Good Hope, it was clear that Portugal would soon dominate the sea lanes leading eastward to Asia. The only alternative for Portugal's Spanish rivals was to finance someone bold enough to try to reach Asia by sailing west. The popular image of Christopher Columbus (1451–1506) as a visionary who struggled to convince hardened ignoramuses that the world was round does not bear up under scrutiny. In fact, the sphericity of the earth had been widely known throughout European society since at least the twelfth century. What made Columbus's scheme seem plausible to King Ferdinand and Queen Isabella was, first, the discovery and colonization of the Canary Islands and the Azores, which had reinforced a view of the Atlantic as being dotted with islands all the way to Japan; and second, the Genoese mariner's own astonishing miscalculation of the actual size of the earth, which convinced him that he could reach Japan and China in about a month's clear sailing westward from the Canary Islands. America was actually rediscovered by Europeans at the end of the fifteenth century as the result of a colossal error in reckoning. Columbus himself never realized his mistake. When he reached the Bahamas and the island of Hispaniola in 1492 after only a month's sailing, he returned to Spain to report that he had indeed reached the outer islands of Asia.

THE DISCOVERY OF A NEW WORLD

Columbus was not the first European to set foot on the American continents. Viking sailors had reached and briefly settled present-day Newfoundland, Labrador, and perhaps New England around the year 1000. But knowledge of these Viking landings had been forgotten or ignored throughout Europe for hundreds of years. In the fifteenth century, even the Scandinavian settlements in Greenland had been abandoned. It would be perverse, therefore, to deny Columbus credit for his accomplishments. Although Columbus himself

The realization that this was indeed a new world was at first a disappointment to the Spanish, for with a major land mass lying between Europe and Asia, Spain could not hope to beat Portugal in the race for Asian spices. Any remaining doubt that not one, but two vast oceans separated Europe from Asia was completely removed in 1513, when Vasco Núñez de Balboa first viewed the Pacific Ocean from the Isthmus of Panama. Not entirely admitting defeat, Ferdinand and Isabella's grandson, the Holy Roman emperor Charles V, accepted Ferdinand Magellan's offer in 1519 to see whether a route to Asia could be found by sailing around South America. But Magellan's voyage demonstrated beyond question that the globe was simply too large for any such plan to be feasible. Of the five ships that left Spain under Magellan's command, only one returned three years later, having been forced to circumnavigate the globe. Out of a crew of 265 sailors, only eighteen survived. Most had died from scurvy or starvation; Magellan himself had been killed in a skirmish with native peoples in the Philippines. This fiasco brought to an end all hope of discovering an easy "southwest passage" to Asia. The dream of a "northwest passage" survived, however, and continued to motivate European explorers of North America until the nineteenth century.

The Creator as Architect. This scene from a late-thirteenth-century French Bible shows God working on Creation with a draftsman's compass. Note that the artist understood clearly that the world was round.

never accepted the reality of what he had discovered, those who followed him soon did, and busily set out to exploit this new world.

Understandably, Columbus brought back no Asian spices from his voyages. He did, however, return with some small samples of gold and a few indigenous people, whose existence gave promise of entire tribes that might be "saved" (by conversion to Christianity) and enslaved by Europeans. This provided sufficient incentive for the Spanish monarchs to finance three more expeditions by Columbus and many more by others. Soon the mainland was discovered as well as further islands, and the conclusion quickly became inescapable that a new world had indeed been found. Awareness of this new world was most widely publicized by the Italian geographer Amerigo Vespucci. Though he may not have deserved this honor, the continents of the Western Hemisphere became known thereafter as "America" after Vespucci's first name.

A Spaniard Kicking an Indian. As this sixteenth-century drawing makes clear, Spanish treatment of the indigenous American population was often brutal.

WHAT WAS THE IMPACT OF NEW WORLD SILVER ON THE EUROPEAN ECONOMY?

EUROPE ENCOUNTERS A NEW WORLD   447

THE SPANISH CONQUEST OF AMERICA

Although the discovery of this new continent was initially a disappointment to the Spanish, it quickly became clear that the New World had great wealth of its own. From the start, Columbus's gold samples, in themselves rather paltry, had nurtured hopes that somewhere in America gold might lie piled in ingots, ready to enrich whatever European adventurer discovered them. Rumor fed rumor, until a few freelance Spanish soldiers really did strike it rich beyond their most avaricious imaginings. Between 1519 and 1521, the *conquistador* (Spanish for "conqueror") Hernando Cortés, with a force of six hundred Europeans but with the assistance of thousands of the Aztecs' unhappy subjects, overthrew the Aztec empire of Mexico and carried off its rulers' fabulous wealth. Then in 1533 another conquistador, Francisco Pizarro, this time with only one hundred eighty men, toppled the highly centralized South American empire of the Incas, and carried off its great stores of gold and silver. Cortés and Pizarro had the advantage of some cannons and a few horses (both unknown to the native peoples of the Americas), but they achieved their victories primarily by sheer audacity, courage, and treachery. They were aided also by the unwillingness of the indigenous peoples whom the Aztecs and the Incas had subjected to fight on behalf of their oppressors. Little did the Spaniards' erstwhile allies know how much worse their new conquerors would soon prove to be.

THE PROFITS OF EMPIRE IN THE NEW WORLD

Cortés and Pizarro were plunderers who captured in one fell swoop hoards of gold and silver that had been accumulated for centuries by the native civilizations of Mexico and Peru. Already, however, a search had begun for the sources of these precious metals. The first gold deposits were discovered in Hispaniola, where surface mines were speedily established utilizing native laborers who died in appalling numbers from disease, brutality, and overwork. Of the approximately one million native people who lived on Hispaniola in 1492, only one hundred thousand survived by 1510.

By 1538, their numbers were down to five hundred. With the loss of so many workers, the Hispaniola mines became uneconomical to operate, and the European colonists turned instead to cattle raising and sugar production. Modelling their sugar cane plantations on those of the Cape Verde Islands and St. Thomas, they imported African slaves to labor in the new industry. Sugar production was by its nature a highly capital-intensive undertaking. The need to import slave labor added further to its costs, guaranteeing that control over the sugar industry would fall into the hands of a few extremely wealthy planters and financiers.

Despite the importance of sugar production on the Caribbean islands and of cattle ranching on the Mexican mainland, it was mining that shaped the Spanish colonies of Central and South America most fundamentally. Gold was the lure that had initially drawn the Spanish conquerors to the New World, but it was silver that became their most lucrative export. Between 1543 and 1548, vast silver deposits were discovered north of Mexico City and at Potosí in Bolivia. Even before the discovery of these deposits, the Spanish crown had taken steps to assume direct governmental control over its Central and South American colonies. It was therefore to the Spanish crown that the profits from these astonishingly productive mines accrued. Potosí quickly became the most important mining town in the world. By 1570, it numbered one hundred twenty thousand inhabitants, despite being located at an altitude of fifteen thousand feet where the temperature never climbs above 59 degrees Fahrenheit. As in Hispaniola, enslaved native laborers died by the tens of thousands in these mines and in the disease-infested boom towns that surrounded them.

New developments in mining techniques (in particular, the mercury-amalgamation process, introduced into Mexico in 1555 and Potosí in 1571) made it possible to produce even greater quantities of silver, at the cost of even greater mortality among the native laborers. Between 1571 and 1586, silver production at Potosí quadrupled, reaching a peak in the 1590s, when ten million ounces of silver per year were arriving in Spain from the Americas. In the 1540s, the corresponding figure was only one and one half million ounces. In the peak years of domestic European silver production, between 1525 and 1535, only about three million ounces of silver per year were being produced, and this figure

Mining shaped the Spanish colonies of Central and South America most fundamentally.

ENSLAVED NATIVE
LABORERS AT POTOSÍ

Since the Spanish crown received one fifth of all the revenues from mines (as well as maintaining a monopoly over the mercury used to refine the silver ore into silver), it had an important stake in ensuring the productivity of the mines. To this end, the Crown granted colonial mine owners the right to conscript native peoples to work in the mines. This account from about 1620 describes the conditions under which these forced native laborers worked. Not surprisingly, mortality rates among such laborers were horrendous.

According to His Majesty's warrant, the mine owners on this massive range [at Potosí] have a right to the conscripted labor of 13,300 Indians in the working and exploitation of the mines, both those which have been discovered, those now discovered, and those which shall be discovered. It is the duty of the *Corregidor* (municipal governor) of Potosí to have them rounded up and to see that they come in from all the provinces between Cuzco . . . and as far as the frontiers of Tarija and Tomina. . . .

The conscripted Indians go up every Monday morning to the . . . foot of the range; the *Corregidor* arrives with all the provincial captains or chiefs who have charge of the Indians assigned him for his miner or smelter; that keeps him busy till 1 P.M., by which time the Indians are already turned over to these mine and smelter owners.

After each has eaten his ration, they climb up the hill, each to his mine, and go in, staying there from that hour until Saturday evening without coming out of the mine; their wives bring them food, but they stay constantly underground, excavating and carrying out the ore from which they get the silver. They all have tallow candles, lighted day and night; that is the light they work with, for as they are underground, they have need for it all the time. . . .

These Indians have different functions in the handling of the silver ore; some break it up with bar or pick, and dig down in, following the vein in the mine; others bring it up; others up above keep separating the good and the poor in piles; others are occupied in taking it down from the range to the mills on herds of llamas; every day they bring up more than 8,000 of these native beasts of burden for this task. These teamsters who carry the metal are not conscripted, but are hired.

Antonio Vázquez de Espinosa, *Compendium and Description of the West Indies,* trans. Charles Upson Clark. (Washington, D.C.: Smithsonian Institution Press, 1968), p. 62.

dropped steadily from about 1550 on. Europe's silver shortage came triumphantly to an end during the sixteenth century, but the silver that now circulated there came almost entirely from the New World.

This massive infusion of silver into the European economy exacerbated an inflation that had begun already in the later fifteenth century and had accelerated during the sixteenth century. Initially, this inflation was driven by the renewed growth of the European population, an expanding economy, and a relatively fixed supply of food. From the 1540s on, however, the accelerating inflation was largely the product of the greatly

The Silver Mines of Spanish America. An engraving of 1602. Some of the miners work naked because of the heat.

After 1600, lessening quantities of New World silver entered the European economy, but prices continued to rise until at least mid-century. By 1650, the price of grain within Europe had risen to five or six times its level in 1500, producing social dislocation and widespread misery for many of Europe's poorest inhabitants. In England, the period between about 1590 and 1610 was probably the most desperate the country had experienced for 300 years. As population rose and wages fell, living standards dropped dramatically. If we compute living standards by dividing the price of an average basket of food by the average daily wage of a building laborer, then standards of living were lower in England in 1600 than they had been even in the terrible years of the early fourteenth century. It is no wonder, then, that so many Europeans found emigration to the Americas a tempting prospect. We may wonder, indeed, what might have happened in seventeenth-century Europe had the new world of the Americas not existed as an outlet for Europe's growing population.

increased supply of silver that was now entering the European economy. The result was what historians have termed "the Price Revolution." Although the effects of this inflation were felt throughout the European continent, Spain was affected with particular severity. Between 1500 and 1560, Spanish prices doubled; between 1560 and 1600, they doubled again. Such exceptionally high prices in turn undermined the competitiveness of Spanish industries. When the flow of New World silver to Spain slowed dramatically during the 1620s and 1630s, the Spanish economy collapsed.

CHRONOLOGY

ENCOUNTERING THE NEW WORLD, 1000–1545

Vikings settle Newfoundland	c. 1000
Columbus reaches Hispaniola	1492
Balboa reaches Pacific Ocean	1513
Magellan's fleet sails around the world	1519–1522
Cortés conquers the Aztecs	1521
Pizarro conquers the Incas	1533
Potosí silver mines opened	1545

CONCLUSION

By 1600, colonization and overseas conquest had produced profoundly important changes within Europe and on the wider world. The emergence during the sixteenth century of Portugal and Spain as Europe's leading long-distance traders permanently moved the center of gravity of European economic power away from Italy and the Mediterranean toward the Atlantic. Deprived of its role as the principal conduit for the spice trade, Venice gradually declined. The Genoese moved increasingly into the world of finance, backing the commercial ventures of others, and particularly of Spain. By contrast, the Atlantic ports of sixteenth-century Spain and Portugal bustled with vessels and shone with wealth. By the mid-seventeenth century, however, economic predominance was passing to the north Atlantic states of England, Holland, and France. Spain and Portugal would retain their American colonies until the nineteenth century. But from the seventeenth century on, it would be the Dutch, the French, and especially the English who would establish new European empires in North America, Asia, Africa, and Australia. By and large, these new empires would last until the Second World War.

SELECTED READINGS

Abu-Lughod, Janet L. *Before European Hegemony: The World System A.D. 1250–1350*. Oxford and New York, 1989. A study of the trading links between Europe, the Middle East, India, and China, with special attention to the role of the Mongol empire; extensive bibliography.

Allsen, Thomas T. *Mongol Imperialism: The Policies of the Grand Qan Möngke in China, Russia, and the Islamic Lands, 1251–1259*. Berkeley and Los Angeles, 1987. A pioneering study of how the Mongols ruled their empire.

———. *Commodity and Exchange in the Mongol Empire: A Cultural History of Islamic Textiles*. Cambridge and New York, 1997. A scholarly monograph that emphasizes the sophistication and importance of Mongol involvement in Eurasian trade.

Amitai-Preiss, Reuven, and David O. Morgan, eds. *The Mongol Empire and Its Legacy*. Leiden, 1999. A collection of essays that represents the newest work in Mongol studies.

The Book of Prophecies, Edited by Christopher Columbus. Translated by Blair Sullivan. Edited by Roberto Rusconi. Berkeley and Los Angeles, 1996. After his third voyage, from which Columbus was returned to Spain in chains, he compiled a book of quotations from various sources, selected to emphasize the millenarian implications of his discoveries; a fascinating insight into the mind of the explorer.

Christian, David. *A History of Russia, Central Asia and Mongolia*. Volume 1: *Inner Eurasia from Prehistory to the Mongol Empire*. Oxford, 1998. The first volume of what will surely become the authoritative English-language work on the subject.

Coles, Paul. *The Ottoman Impact on Europe*. London, 1968. An excellent introductory text, still valuable despite its age.

Fernández-Armesto, Felipe. *Before Columbus: Exploration and Colonisation from the Mediterranean to the Atlantic, 1229–1492*. London, 1987. An indispensible study of the medieval background to the sixteenth-century European colonial empires.

———. *Columbus*. Oxford and New York, 1991. An excellent biography that stresses the millenarian ideas that underlay Columbus' thinking. A good book to read after the Phillips' book (see below).

Fleet, Kate. *European and Islamic Trade in the Early Ottoman State: The Merchants of Genoa and Turkey*. Cambridge and New York, 2000. A scholarly monograph that discusses the fifteenth-century rise and decline of Italian (and particularly Genoese) trade with the Ottoman empire.

Flint, Valerie I. J. *The Imaginative Landscape of Christopher Columbus*. Princeton, N.J., 1992. A short, suggestive analysis of the intellectual influences that shaped Columbus's geographical ideas.

The Four Voyages: Christopher Columbus. Translated by J. M. Cohen. New York, 1992. Columbus's own self-serving account of his four voyages to the "Indies."

Goodwin, Jason. *Lords of the Horizons: A History of the Ottoman Empire*. London: Chatto and Windus, 1998. Colorful and engaging popular account; not the most reliable place to look up facts.

Halperin, C. J. *Russia and the Golden Horde: The Mongol Impact on Medieval Russian History*. Bloomington, 1985. The standard authority.

The History and the Life of Chinggis Khan: The Secret History of the Mongols. Translated by Urgunge Onon. Leiden, 1997. A newer version of *The Secret History* (see below), likely to become the standard English version of this important Mongol source.

Inalcik, Halil. *The Ottoman Empire: The Classical Age, 1300–1600*. London, 1973. The standard history by the dean of Turkish historians.

———, ed. *An Economic and Social History of the Ottoman Empire, 1300–1914*. Cambridge, 1994. An important collection of essays, spanning the full range of Ottoman history.

———. *Essays in Ottoman History*. Istanbul, 1998. A collection of Inalcik's own essays; although some are too specialized for students, a number are quite accessible.

Larner, John. *Marco Polo and the Discovery of the World*. New Haven, 1999. A study of the influence of Marco Polo's *Travels* on Europeans by an excellent historian of medieval Italy.

Morgan, David. *The Mongols*. Oxford, 1986. The most accessible introduction to Mongol history and its sources, written by a noted expert on medieval Persia.

Parker, Geoffrey. *The Military Revolution: Military Innovation and the Rise of the West (1500–1800)*, 2d ed. Cambridge and New York, 1996. A work of fundamental importance for understanding the global dominance achieved by early modern Europeans.

Phillips, J. R. S. *The Medieval Expansion of Europe*, 2d ed. Oxford, 1998. An outstanding study of the thirteenth- and fourteenth-century background to the fifteenth-century expansion of Europe. Important synthetic treatment of European relations with the Mongols, China, Africa, and North America. The second edition includes a new introduction and a bibliographical essay; the text is the same as in the first edition (1988).

Phillips, William D., Jr., and Carla R. Phillips. *The Worlds of Christopher Columbus*. Cambridge and New York, 1991. The first book to read on Columbus: accessible, engaging, and scholarly. Then read Fernández-Armesto's biography (above).

Ratchnevsky, Paul. *Genghis Khan: His Life and Legacy*. Translated by Thomas Nivison Haining. Oxford, 1991. An English translation and abridgment of a book first published in

German in 1983. The author was one of the greatest Mongol historians of his generation.

Rossabi, M. *Khubilai Khan: His Life and Times.* Berkeley, 1988. The standard English biography.

Russell, Peter. *Prince Henry "The Navigator": A Life.* New Haven, 2000. A masterly biography by a great historian who has spent a lifetime on the subject. The only book one now needs to read on Prince Henry.

Saunders, J. J. *The History of the Mongol Conquests.* London, 1971. Still the standard English-language introduction; somewhat more positive about the Mongols' accomplishments than is Morgan.

Scammell, Geoffrey V. *The First Imperial Age: European Overseas Expansion, 1400–1715.* London, 1989. A useful introductory survey, with a particular focus on English and French colonization.

The Secret History of the Mongols. Translated by F. W. Cleaves. Cambridge, Mass., 1982.

The Secret History of the Mongols and Other Pieces. Translated by Arthur Waley. London, 1963. The later Chinese abridgment of the Mongol original.

The Travels of Marco Polo, trans. R. E. Latham. Baltimore, 1958. The most accessible edition of this remarkably interesting work.

The Civilization of the Renaissance, c. 1350–1550

THE PREVALENT MODERN NOTION that a "Renaissance period" followed western Europe's Middle Ages was first expressed by numerous Italian writers who lived between 1350 and 1550. According to them, one thousand years of unrelieved darkness had intervened between the Roman era and their own times. During these "Dark Ages" the muses of art and literature had fled Europe before the onslaught of barbarism and ignorance. Almost miraculously, however, in the fourteenth century the muses suddenly returned, and Italians happily collaborated with them to bring forth a glorious "renaissance of the arts."

Ever since this periodization was advanced, historians have taken for granted the existence of some sort of "renaissance" intervening between medieval and modern times. Indeed, from the late eighteenth to the early twentieth centuries many scholars went so far as to argue that the Renaissance was not just an epoch in the history of learning and culture but that a unique "Renaissance spirit" transformed all aspects of European life—political, economic, and religious, as well as intellectual and artistic. Today, however, most experts no longer accept this characterization because they find it impossible to locate any truly distinctive "Renaissance" politics, economics, or religion. Instead, most scholars reserve the term "Renaissance" to describe certain trends in thought, literature, and the arts that emerged in Italy from roughly 1350 to 1550 and then spread to northern Europe during the first half of the sixteenth century. That is the approach that we will follow here: accordingly, when we refer to a "Renaissance" period in this chapter we mean to limit ourselves to an epoch in intellectual and cultural history.

THE RENAISSANCE AND THE MIDDLE AGES

What was distinctive about the Renaissance?

Granted this restriction, some further qualifications are still necessary. Since the word *renaissance* literally means "rebirth," it is sometimes thought that after about 1350 certain Italians who were newly cognizant of Greek and Roman cultural accomplishments initiated a rebirth of classical culture after a long period during which that culture had been essentially dead. In fact, however, the High Middle Ages witnessed no "death" of classical learning. Saint Thomas Aquinas considered Aristotle to be "the Philosopher"; Dante revered Virgil. Similar examples could be cited almost without limit. It would be equally false to contrast an imaginary "Renaissance paganism" with a medieval "age of faith" because however much most Renaissance personalities loved the classics, none saw their classicism as superseding their Christianity. And finally, all discussions of the Renaissance must be qualified by the fact that there was no single Renaissance position on anything. Renaissance thinkers and artists were enormously diverse in their attitudes, achievements, and approaches. As we assess their accomplishments, we need to beware not to force them into too narrow a mold.

> The High Middle Ages witnessed no "death" of classical learning. Aquinas considered Aristotle to be "the Philosopher" and Dante revered Virgil.

RENAISSANCE CLASSICISM

Nonetheless, in the realms of thought, literature, and the arts, we can certainly find distinguishing traits that make the concept of a "Renaissance" meaningful for intellectual and cultural history. First, regarding knowledge of the classics, there was a significant quantitative difference between the learning of the Middle Ages and that of the Renaissance. Medieval scholars knew many Roman authors, such as Virgil, Ovid, and Cicero, but during the Renaissance the works of others such as Livy, Tacitus, and Lucretius were rediscovered and made familiar. Equally if not more important was the Renaissance recovery of the literature of classical Greece from Byzantium. In the twelfth and thirteenth centuries Greek scientific and philosophical treatises were made available to Westerners in Latin translations through Islam, but none of the great Greek literary masterpieces and practically none of the major works of Plato were yet known. Nor could more than a handful of medieval Westerners read the Greek language. During the Renaissance, on the other hand, large numbers of Western scholars learned Greek and mastered almost the entire Greek literary heritage that is known today.

Second, Renaissance thinkers not only knew many more classical texts than their medieval counterparts, but they used them in new ways. Whereas medieval writers presumed that their ancient sources would complement and confirm their own Christian assumptions, Renaissance writers were more aware of the conceptual and chronological gap that separated their own world from that of their classical sources. At the same time, however, the structural similarities between the ancient city-states and those of Renaissance Italy encouraged Italian thinkers in particular to find in these ancient sources models of thought and action directly applicable to their own day. This firm determination to learn from classical antiquity was even more pronounced in the realms of architecture and art, areas in which classical models contributed most strikingly to the creation of fully distinct "Renaissance" styles.

Third, although Renaissance culture was by no means pagan, it was more worldly and overtly materialistic in its orientation than was the culture of the twelfth and thirteenth centuries. The evolution of the Italian city-states created a supportive environment for attitudes that stressed the importance of the urban political arena and of living well in this world. Such ideals helped to create a culture that was increasingly nonecclesiastical. The relative weakness of the church in Italy also contributed to the more secular culture that emerged there. Italian bishoprics were small, and for the most part poorly endowed. Italian universities were also largely independent of ecclesiastical supervision and control. Even the papacy was severely limited in its ability to intervene in the cultural life of the Italian city-states, not least because the papacy's own role as a political rival in central Italy compromised its moral authority as an arbiter of cultural and religious values. All these factors helped to create a space within which the worldly, materialistic culture of the Renaissance could emerge effectively untrammelled by ecclesiastical opposition.

RENAISSANCE HUMANISM

One word above all comes closest to summing up the most common and basic Renaissance intellectual ideals, namely *humanism*. Renaissance humanism was a program of studies that aimed to replace the thirteenth and fourteenth century scholastic emphasis on logic and metaphysics with the study of language, literature, rhetoric, history, and ethics. The humanists always preferred ancient literature; although some (notably Francesco Petrarch and Leon Batista Alberti) wrote in both Latin and the vernacular, most humanists regarded vernacular literature as at best a diversion for the uneducated. Serious scholarship and literature could only be written in Latin or Greek. That Latin, moreover, had to be the Latin of Cicero and Virgil. Renaissance humanists were self-conscious elitists, who condemned the living Latin of their scholastic contemporaries as a barbarous departure from ancient (and therefore correct) standards of Latin style. Despite their belief that they were thereby reviving the study of the classics, the humanists' position was thus inherently ironic. By insisting on ancient standards of Latin grammar, syntax, and word choice, the humanists of the Renaissance succeeded ultimately in turning Latin into a fossilized language that thereafter ceased to evolve. They thus contributed, quite unwittingly, to the ultimate triumph of the European vernaculars as the primary languages of intellectual and cultural life.

Humanists were convinced that their own educational program—which placed the study of Latin language and literature at the core of the curriculum and then encouraged students to go on to Greek—was the best way to produce virtuous citizens and able public officials. Their elitism was to this extent intensely practical, and directly connected to the political life of the city-states in which they lived. Because women were excluded from Italian political life, the education of women was therefore of little concern to most humanists, although some aristocratic women were given humanist training to make them appear more polished and attractive to men. As more and more fifteenth century city-states fell into the hands of princes, however, the humanist educational curriculum lost its immediate connection to the republican ideals of Italian political life. Nevertheless, humanists never lost their conviction that the study of the "humanities" (as the humanist curriculum came to be known) was the best way to produce leaders for European society. This faith has continued to animate higher education in Europe ever since.

The humanists' faith in the moral value of their curriculum, and in the spiritual and intellectual capacities of properly educated men, led some of them to emphasize the dignity of man as the most excellent of all God's creatures below the angels. Some humanists argued that man was excellent because he alone of earthly creatures could obtain knowledge of God—a standard scholastic position that the humanists were too graceless to acknowledge having borrowed from their opponents. Others saw humanity's excellence as lying in our ability to master our fate and live happily in the world through our own attainments. Either way, many Renaissance humanists, especially in the fifteenth century, had a firm belief in the nobility and possibilities of the human race. Today, such faith in the nobility of human beings' natural capacities is sometimes referred to as "humanism"—or even "secular humanism." For our purposes, however, it is important to remember that Renaissance humanism was first and foremost an educational program securely rooted in Catholic Christian orthodoxy, and that it gave rise only incidentally to a more general outlook that stressed the potential of human beings to shape and improve their world unaided by divine intervention.

One word above all comes closest to summing up the Renaissance intellectual ideals, namely *humanism.*

THE RENAISSANCE IN ITALY

Why did the Renaissance occur in Italy?

Although the Renaissance eventually became a Europe-wide intellectual and artistic movement, it developed first and most distinctively in fourteenth- and fifteenth-century Italy. Understanding why this was so is important not only to explaining the origins of this movement, but also to understanding its fundamental characteristics.

THE ORIGINS OF THE ITALIAN RENAISSANCE

The Renaissance originated in Italy for several reasons. The most fundamental reason was that Italy in the later

THE HUMANISTS' EDUCATIONAL PROGRAM

These three selections illustrate the confidence of civic humanists such as Vergerius, Bruni, and Alberti that their elite educational program would be of supreme value to the state as well as to the individual students who pursued it. Not everyone agreed with the humanists' claims, however, and a good deal of self-promotion lies behind them..

VERGERIUS ON LITERAL STUDIES

We call those studies *liberal* which are worthy of a free man; those studies by which we attain and practice virtue and wisdom; that education which calls forth, trains, and develops those highest gifts of body and of mind which ennoble men, and which are rightly judged to rank next in dignity to virtue only. . . . It is, then, of the highest importance that even from infancy this aim, this effort, should constantly be kept alive in growing minds. For . . . we shall not have attained wisdom in our later years unless in our earliest we have sincerely entered on its search. [P. P. Vergerius (1370–1444), *"Concerning Excellent Traits"*]

ALBERTI ON THE IMPORTANCE OF LITERATURE

Letters are indeed so important that without them one would be considered nothing but a rustic, no matter how much a gentlemen [he may be by birth]. I'd much rather see a young nobleman with a book than with a falcon in his hand. . . .

Be diligent, then, you young people, in your studies. Do all you can to learn about the events of the past that are worthy of memory. Try to understand all the useful things that have been passed on to you. Feed your minds on good maxims. Learn the delights of embellishing your souls with good morals. Strive to be kind and considerate [of others] when conducting civil business. Get to know those things human and divine that have been put at your disposal in books for good reason. Nowhere [else] will you find . . . the elegance of a verse of Homer, or Virgil, or of some other excellent poet. You will find no field so delightful or flowering as in one of the orations of Demosthenes, Cicero, Livy, Xenophon, and other such pleasant and perfect orators. No effort is more fully compensated . . . as the constant reading and rereading of good things. From such reading you will rise rich in good maxims and good arguments, strong in your ability to persuade others and get them to listen to you; among the citizens you will willingly be heard, admired, praised, and loved. [Leon Battista Alberti (1404–1472), *"On the Family"*]

BRUNI ON THE HUMANIST CURRICULUM

The foundations of all true learning must be laid in the sound and thorough knowledge of Latin: which implies study marked by a broad spirit, accurate scholarship, and careful attention to details. Unless this solid basis be secured it is useless to attempt to rear an enduring edifice. Without it the great monuments of literature are unintelligible, and the art of composition impossible. To attain this essential knowledge we must never relax our careful attention to the grammar of the language, but perpetually confirm and extend our acquaintance with it until it is thoroughly our own. . . .

But the wider question now confronts us, that of the subject matter of our studies, that which I have already called the realities of fact and principle, as distinct from literary form. . . . First among such studies I place History: a subject which must not on any account be neglected by one who aspires to true cultivation. . . . For the careful study of the past enlarges our foresight in contemporary affairs and affords to citizens and to monarchs lessons . . . in the ordering of public policy. From History, also, we draw our store of examples of moral precepts. . . .

The great Orators of antiquity must by all means be included. Nowhere do we find the virtues more warmly extolled, the vices so fiercely decried. From them we may learn, also, how to express consolation, encouragement, dissuasion or advice. . . .

Familiarity with the great poets of antiquity is essential to any claim to true education. For in their writings we find deep speculations upon Nature, and upon the Causes and Origins of things, which must carry weight with us both from their antiquity and from their authorship. . . .

Proficiency in literary form, not accompanied by broad acquaintance with facts and truths, is a barren attainment; whilst information, however vast, which lacks all grace of expression would seem to be put under a bushel or partly thrown away. . . . Where, however, this double capacity exists—breadth of learning and grace of style—we allow the highest title to distinction and to abiding fame. . . . [Leonardo Bruni (1369–1444), *"Concerning the Study of Literature"*]

Vergerius and Bruni: William Harrison Woodward, ed., *Vittorino da Feltre and Other Humanist Educators*. (London: Cambridge University Press, 1897), pp. 96–110, 124–129, 132–133. Alberti: Eric Cochrane and Julius Kirshner, eds. *University of Chicago Readings in Western Civilization*, Vol. 5: *The Renaissance*. (Chicago: University of Chicago Press, 1986), pp. 81–82.

Middle Ages encompassed the most advanced urban society in all of Europe. Unlike aristocrats north of the Alps, Italian aristocrats customarily lived in urban centers rather than in rural castles and consequently became fully involved in urban public affairs. Moreover, since the Italian aristocracy built its palaces in the cities, the aristocratic class was less sharply set off from the class of rich merchants than in the north. Hence whereas in France or Germany most aristocrats lived on the income from their landed estates while rich town dwellers (*bourgeois*) gained their living from trade, in Italy so many town-dwelling aristocrats engaged in banking or mercantile enterprises and so many rich mercantile families imitated the manners of the aristocracy that by the fourteenth and fifteenth centuries the aristocracy and upper bourgeoisie were becoming virtually indistinguishable. The noted Florentine family of the Medici, for example, emerged as a family of physicians (as the name suggests), made its fortune in banking and commerce, and rose into the aristocracy in the fifteenth century. The results of these developments for the history of education are obvious: not only was there a great demand for education in the skills of reading and counting necessary to become a successful merchant, but the richest and most prominent families sought above all to find teachers who would impart to their offspring the knowledge and skills necessary to argue well in the public arena. Consequently, Italy produced a large number of lay educators, many of whom not only taught students but also demonstrated their learned attainments in the production of political and ethical treatises and works of literature. Italian schools created the best-educated upper-class public in all of Europe, along with a considerable number of wealthy patrons who were ready to invest in the cultivation of new ideas and new forms of literary and artistic expression.

A second reason why late medieval Italy was the birthplace of an intellectual and artistic renaissance lay in the fact that it had a far greater sense of rapport with the classical past than any other territory in western Europe. Given the Italian commitment to an educational curriculum that stressed success in urban politics, the best teachers understandably sought inspiration from ancient Latin and Greek texts because politics and political rhetoric were classical rather than medieval arts. Elsewhere, resort to classical knowledge and classical literary style might have seemed antiquarian and artificial, but in Italy the classical past appeared most "relevant" because ancient Roman monuments were omnipresent throughout the peninsula, and ancient Latin literature referred to cities and sites that Renaissance Italians

Pope Julius II, by Raphael. The acorns at the top of the throne posts are visual puns for the pope's family name, "della Rovere" (of the oak).

recognized as their own. Moreover, Italians became particularly intent on reappropriating their classical heritage in the fourteenth and fifteenth centuries because Italians then were seeking to establish an independent cultural identity in opposition to a scholasticism most closely associated with France. Not only did the removal of the papacy to Avignon for most of the fourteenth century and then the Great Schism from 1378 to 1417 heighten antagonisms between Italy and France, but during the fourteenth century an intellectual reaction against scholasticism on all fronts encouraged Italians to prefer the intellectual alternatives offered by classical literary sources. Once Roman literature and learning became particularly favored in Italy, so too did Roman art and architecture, for Roman models could help Italians create a splendid artistic alternative to French Gothicism just as Roman learning offered an intellectual alternative to French scholasticism.

Finally, the Italian Renaissance could not have occurred without the underpinning of Italian wealth. The Italian economy as a whole was probably more prosperous in the thirteenth century than it was in the fourteenth and fifteenth. But late medieval Italy was wealthier in comparison with the rest of Europe than it had been before, a fact that meant that Italian writers and artists were more likely to stay at home than to seek employment abroad. Moreover, in late medieval Italy unusually intensive investment in culture arose from an intensification of urban pride and the concentration of per capita wealth. Although these two trends overlapped somewhat, most scholars tend to agree that a phase of predominantly public urban support for culture came first in Italy from roughly 1250 to about 1400 or 1450, depending on place, with the private sector taking over thereafter. In the first phase the richest cities vied with each other in building the most splendid public monuments and in supporting writers whose role was to glorify the urban republics in letters and speeches as full of magniloquent Ciceronian prose as possible. But in the course of the fifteenth century, when most Italian city-states succumbed to the hereditary rule of princely families, patronage was monopolized by the princely aristocracy. It was then that the great princes—the Visconti and Sforza in Milan, the Medici in Florence, the Este in Ferrara, and the Gonzaga in Mantua—patronized art and literature in their courts to glorify themselves, while lesser aristocratic families imitated those princes on a smaller scale. Not least of the great princes in Italy from about 1450 to about 1550 were the popes in Rome, who were dedicated to a policy of basing their strength on temporal control of the Papal States. Hence the most worldly of the Renaissance popes—Alexander VI (1492–1503); Julius II (1503–1513); and Leo X (1513–1521), son of the Florentine ruler Lorenzo de' Medici—obtained the services of the greatest artists of the day and for a few decades made Rome the unrivaled artistic capial of the Western world.

THE ITALIAN RENAISSANCE: LITERATURE AND THOUGHT

In surveying the greatest accomplishments of Italian Renaissance scholars and writers it is natural to begin with the work of Petrarch (Francesco Petrarca, 1304–1374), the most famous of the early Renaissance humanists. Petrarch was a deeply committed Catholic who believed that scholasticism was entirely misguided because it concentrated on abstract speculation rather than on teaching people how to live virtuously and attain salvation. Petrarch thought that the Christian writer must above all cultivate literary eloquence so that he could inspire people to do good. For him the best models of eloquence were to be found in the ancient literary classics, which he thought repaid study doubly inasmuch as they were filled with ethical wisdom. So Petrarch dedicated himself to searching for undiscovered ancient Latin texts and writing his own moral treatises in which he imitated classical style and quoted classical phrases. Thereby he initiated a program of "humanist" studies that was to be influential for centuries to come. Petrarch also has a place in purely literary history because of his poetry. Although he prized his own Latin poetry over the poems he wrote in the Italian vernacular, only the latter have proved enduring. Above all, the Italian sonnets—later called Petrarchan sonnets—that he wrote for his beloved Laura in the chivalrous style of the troubadours were widely imitated in form and content throughout the Renaissance period.

> Civic humanists had great success in opening up the field of classical Greek studies.

Because he was a very traditional Christian, Petrarch's ultimate ideal for human conduct was the solitary life of contemplation and asceticism. But from about 1400 to 1450, subsequent Italian thinkers and scholars, located mainly in Florence, developed the alternative of what is customarily called civic humanism. Civic humanists such as the Florentines Leonardo Bruni (c. 1370–1444) and Leon Battista Alberti (1404–1472) agreed with Petrarch on the need for eloquence and the study of classical literature, but they also taught that man's nature equipped him for action, for usefulness to his family and society, and for serving the state—ideally a republican city-state after the classical or contemporary Florentine model. In their view ambition and the quest for glory were noble impulses that ought to be encouraged. They refused to condemn the striving for material possessions, for they argued that the history of human progress is inseparable from mankind's success in gaining mastery over the earth and its resources. Perhaps the most vivid of the civic humanists' writings is Alberti's *On the Family* (1443), in which he argued that the nuclear family was instituted by nature for the well-being of humanity. Within this framework, however, Alberti consigned women to purely domestic roles, asserting that "man [is] by nature more energetic and industrious," and that woman was created "to increase and continue generations, and to nourish and preserve those already born." Although such dismissals of women's intellectual abilities were fiercely resisted by a few notable women humanists, for the most part Italian Renaissance humanism was characterized by a pervasive denigration of women—a denigration expressed

also in the works of classical literature that the humanists so much admired.

THE EMERGENCE OF TEXTUAL SCHOLARSHIP

In addition to differing with Petrarch in their preference for the active over the solitary or contemplative life, the civic humanists went far beyond him in their study of the ancient literary heritage. Some discovered important new Latin texts, but more important was their success in opening up the field of classical Greek studies. In this they were aided by a number of Byzantine scholars who had migrated to Italy in the first half of the fifteenth century and gave instruction in the Greek language. Italian scholars also traveled to Constantinople and other Eastern cities in search of Greek masterpieces hitherto unknown in the West. In 1423 one Italian, Giovanni Aurispa, alone brought back 238 manuscript books, including works of Sophocles, Euripides, and Thucydides. Soon followed the work of translation into Latin, not word for word, but sense for sense in order to preserve the literary force of the original. In this way most of the Greek classics, particularly the writings of Plato, the dramatists, and the historians, were first made available to western Europe.

Related in his textual interests to the civic humanists, but by no means a full adherent of their movement, was the atypical yet highly influential Renaissance thinker Lorenzo Valla (1407–1457). Born in Rome and active primarily as a secretary in the service of the king of Naples, Valla had no inclination to espouse the ideas of republican political engagement as the Florentine civic humanists did. Instead, he preferred to advertise his skills as an expert in grammar, rhetoric, and the painstaking analysis of Greek and Latin texts by showing how the thorough study of language could discredit old verities. Most decisive in this regard was Valla's brilliant demonstration that the so-called Donation of Constantine was a medieval forgery. Whereas papal propagandists had argued that the papacy possessed rights to temporal rule in western Europe on the grounds of a charter purportedly granted by the emperor Constantine in the fourth century, Valla proved beyond dispute that the document in question was full of nonclassical Latin usages and anachronistic terms. Hence he concluded that the "Donation" was the work of a medieval forger whose "monstrous impudence"

SOME RENAISSANCE ATTITUDES TOWARD WOMEN

Italian society in the fourteenth and fifteenth centuries was characterized by marriage patterns in which men in their late twenties or thirties customarily married women in their mid to late teens. This demographic fact probably contributed to the widely shared belief in this period that wives were essentially children, who could not be trusted with important matters, and who were best trained by being beaten. Renaissance humanism did little to change such attitudes. In some cases, it even reinforced them.

After my wife had been settled in my house a few days, and after her first pangs of longing for her mother and family had begun to fade, I took her by the hand and showed her around the whole house. I explained that the loft was the place for grain and that the stores of wine and wood were kept in the cellar. I showed her where things needed for the table were kept, and so on, through the whole house. At the end there were no household goods of which my wife had not learned both the place and the purpose. . . .

Only my books and records and those of my ancestors did I determine to keep well sealed. . . . These my wife not only could not read, she could not even lay hands on them. I kept my records at all times . . . locked up and arranged in order in my study, almost like sacred and religious objects. I never gave my wife permission to enter that place, with me or alone. . . .

[Husbands] who take counsel with their wives . . . are madmen if they think true prudence or good counsel lies in the female brain. . . . For this very reason I have always tried carefully not to let any secret of mine be known to a woman. I did not doubt that my wife was most loving, and more discreet and modest in her ways than any, but I still considered it safer to have her unable, and not merely unwilling, to harm me. . . . Furthermore, I made it a rule never to speak with her of anything but household matters or questions of conduct, or of the children.

Leon Batista Alberti, "On the Family," in *The Family in Renaissance Florence*, translated and edited by Renée N. Watkins. (Columbia: University of South Carolina Press, 1969), pp. 208–213, as abridged in *Not in God's Image: Women in History from the Greeks to the Victorians*, edited by Julia O'Faolain and Lauro Martines. (New York: Harper & Row, 1973), pp. 187–188.

was exposed by the "stupidity of his language." This demonstration not only discredited a prize specimen of "medieval ignorance," but, more important, introduced the concept of anachronism into all subsequent textual study and historical thought. Valla also employed his skills in linguistic analysis and rhetorical argumentation to challenge a wide variety of philosophical positions, but his ultimate goals were by no means purely destructive,

for he revered the literal teachings of the Epistles of Saint Paul. Accordingly, in his *Notes on the New Testament* he applied his expert knowledge of Greek to elucidating the true meaning of Saint Paul's words, which he believed had been obscured by Saint Jerome's Latin Vulgate translation. This work was to prove an important link between Italian Renaissance scholarship and the subsequent Christian humanism of the north.

RENAISSANCE NEOPLATONISM

From about 1450 until about 1600 dominance in the world of Italian thought was assumed by a school of Neoplatonists, who sought to blend the thought of Plato, Plotinus, and various strands of ancient mysticism with Christianity. Foremost among these were Marsilio Ficino (1433–1499) and Giovanni Pico della Mirandola (1463–1494), both of whom were members of the Platonic Academy founded by Cosimo de' Medici in Florence. The academy was a loosely organized society of scholars who met to hear readings and lectures. Their hero was Plato: sometimes they celebrated Plato's birthday by holding a banquet in his honor, after which everybody gave speeches as if they were characters in a Platonic dialogue. From the standpoint of posterity, Ficino's greatest achievement was the translation of Plato's works into Latin, thereby making them widely available to western Europeans for the first time. Ficino himself, however, regarded his *Hermetic Corpus*, a collection of passages drawn from a

Pico della Mirandola. When the young nobleman Pico arrived in Florence at age nineteen he was said to have been "of beauteous feature and shape." This contemporary portrait may have been done by the great Florentine painter Botticelli.

variety of ancient mystical writings including the Hebrew Kabbalah, as his greatest contribution to learning. It is debatable whether Ficino's own philosophy should be called humanist because he moved away from ethics to metaphysics and taught that the individual should look primarily to the hereafter. In Ficino's opinion, "the immortal soul is always miserable in its mortal body." The same issue arises with respect to Ficino's disciple Giovanni Pico della Mirandola. Pico was certainly not a civic humanist, since he saw little worth in mundane public affairs. He also fully shared his teacher's penchant for extracting and combining snippets taken out of context from ancient mystical tracts. But he did also believe—and so argued in his famous *Oration on the Dignity of Man*—that there is "nothing more wonderful than man" because he believed that man is endowed with the capacity to achieve union with God if he so wills.

MACHIAVELLI

Hardly any of the Italian thinkers between Petrarch and Pico were really original: their greatness lay mostly in their manner of expression, their accomplishments in technical scholarship, and their popularization of different themes of ancient thought. The same, however, cannot be said of Renaissance Italy's greatest political philosopher, the Florentine Niccolò Machiavelli (1469–1527). Machiavelli's writings reflect the unstable condition of Italy in his time. At the end of the fifteenth century Italy had become the cockpit of international struggles. Both France and Spain had invaded the peninsula and were competing for the allegiance of the Italian city-states, which in many cases were torn by internal dissension, making them easy prey for foreign conquerors. In 1498 Machiavelli became a prominent official in the government of the Florentine republic, set up four years earlier when the French invasion had led to the expulsion of the Medici. His duties largely involved diplomatic missions to other Italian city-states. While in Rome he became fascinated with the achievements of Cesare Borgia, son of Pope Alexander VI, in cementing a solidified state out of scattered elements. He noted with approval Cesare's combination of ruthlessness with shrewdness and his complete subordination of personal morality to political ends. In 1512 the Medici returned to overthrow the republic of Florence, and Machiavelli was deprived of his position. Disappointed and embittered, he spent the remainder of his life at his country estate, devoting his time primarily to writing.

Machiavelli remains a controversial figure even today. Some modern scholars see him as an amoral theorist of *realpolitik*, disdainful of morality and Christian piety, caring nothing about the proper purposes of political life, but interested solely in the acquisition and exercise of power as an end in itself. Others see him as an Italian patriot, who viewed princely tyranny as the only way to liberate Italy from its foreign conquerors. Still others see him as a follower of Saint Augustine of Hippo, who understood that in a fallen world populated by sinful people, a ruler's good intentions do not guarantee that his policies will have good results. Instead, Machiavelli insisted that a prince's actions must be judged by their consequences and not by their intrinsic moral quality. Human beings, Machiavelli argued, "are ungrateful, fickle, and deceitful, eager to avoid dangers, and avid for gain." This being so, "the necessity of preserving the state will often compel a prince to take actions which are opposed to loyalty, charity, humanity, and religion. . . . So far as he is able, a prince should stick to the path of good but, if the necessity arises, he should know how to follow evil."

The puzzle is heightened by the fact that, on the surface, Machiavelli's two great works of political analysis appear to contradict each other. In his *Discourses on Livy* he praised the ancient Roman republic as a model for his own contemporaries, lauding constitutional government, equality among the citizens of a republic, political independence on the part of city-states, and the subordination of religion to the service of the state. There is little doubt, therefore, that Machiavelli was a committed republican, who believed in the free city-state as the ideal form of human government. But Machiavelli also wrote *The Prince*, "a handbook for tyrants" in the eyes of his critics, and he dedicated this work to Lorenzo, son of Piero de Medici, whose family had overthrown the Florentine republic that Machiavelli himself had served.

Because *The Prince* has been so much more widey read than the *Discourses*, interpretations of Machiavelli's political thought have often mistaken the admiration he expressed in *The Prince* for Cesare Borgia as an endorsement of princely tyranny for its own sake. Machiavelli's real position was quite different. In the political chaos of early sixteenth-century Italy, Machiavelli saw a ruthless prince such as Borgia as the only hope for revitalizing the spirit of independence among his con-

temporaries, and so making them fit, once again, for republican self-rule. However dark his vision of human nature, Machiavelli never ceased to hope that his Italian contemporaries would rise up, expel their French and Spanish conquerors, and restore their ancient traditions of republican liberty and equality. Princes such as Borgia were necessary steps toward that end, but they did not represent, for Machiavelli, the ideal form of government for humankind. In Italy's sunken political situation, however, a princely state such as Borgia's was the best form of government toward which Machiavelli's downtrodden contemporaries could aspire.

THE IDEAL OF THE COURTIER

Far more congenial to contemporary tastes than the shocking political theories of Machiavelli were the guidelines for proper aristocratic conduct offered in *The Book of the Courtier* (1528) by the diplomat and count Baldassare Castiglione. This cleverly written forerunner of modern handbooks of etiquette stands in sharp contrast to the earlier civic humanist treatises of Bruni and Alberti, for whereas they taught the sober "republican" virtues of strenuous service in behalf of city-state and family, Castiglione, writing in an Italy dominated by magnificent princely courts, taught how to attain the elegant and seemingly effortless qualities necessary for acting like a "true gentleman." More than anyone else, Castiglione popularized the ideal of the "Renaissance man": one who is accomplished in many different pursuits and is also brave, witty, and "courteous," meaning civilized and learned. Unlike Alberti, Castiglione said nothing about women's role in "hearth and home," but stressed instead the ways in which court ladies could be "gracious entertainers." Widely read throughout Europe for over a century after its publication, Castiglione's *Courtier* spread Italian ideals of "civility" to princely courts north of the Alps, resulting in the ever-greater patronage of art and literature by the European aristocracy.

Had Castiglione's ideal courtier wished to show off his knowledge of contemporary Italian literature, he would have had many works from which to choose, for sixteenth-century Italians were highly accomplished creators of imaginative prose and verse. Among the many impressive writers who might be mentioned, Machiavelli himself wrote a delightful short story, "Belfagor," and an engagingly bawdy play, *Mandragola;*

> Machiavelli never ceased to hope that his Italian contemporaries would restore their ancient traditions of republican liberty and equality.

MACHIAVELLI'S ITALIAN PATRIOTISM

These passages are from the concluding chapter to Machiavelli's treatise The Prince. *Like the book itself, they are addressed to Lorenzo, the son of Piero de' Medici.*

Reflecting on the matters set forth above and considering within myself whether the times were propitious in Italy at present to honor a new prince and whether there is at hand the matter suitable for a prudent and virtuous leader to mold in a new form, giving honor to himself and benefit to the citizens of the country, I have arrived at the opinion that all circumstances now favor such a prince, and I cannot think of a time more propitious for him than the present. If, as I said, it was necessary in order to make apparent the virtue of Moses, that the people of Israel should be enslaved in Egypt, and that the Persians should be oppressed by the Medes to provide an opportunity to illustrate the greatness and the spirit of Cyrus, and that the Athenians should be scattered in order to show the excellence of Theseus, thus at the present time, in order to reveal the valor of an Italian spirit it was essential that Italy should fall to her present low estate, more enslaved than the Hebrews, more servile than the Persians, more disunited than the Athenians, leaderless and lawless, beaten, despoiled, lacerated, overrun and crushed under every kind of misfortune. . . . So Italy now, left almost lifeless, awaits the coming of one who will heal her wounds, putting an end to the sacking and looting in Lombardy and the spoliation and extortions in the Realm of Naples and Tuscany, and cleanse her sores that have been so long festering. Behold how she prays God to send her some one to redeem her from the cruelty and insolence of the barbarians. See how she is ready and willing to follow any banner so long as there be some one to take it up. Nor has she at present any hope of finding her redeemer save only in your illustrious house [the Medici] which has been so highly exalted both by its own merits and by fortune and which has been favored by God and the church, of which it is now ruler. . . .

This opportunity, therefore, should not be allowed to pass, and Italy, after such a long wait, must be allowed to behold her redeemer. I cannot describe the joy with which he will be received in all these provinces which have suffered so much from the foreign deluge, nor with what thirst for vengeance, nor with what firm devotion, what solemn delight, what tears! What gates could be closed to him, what people could deny him obedience, what envy could withstand him, what Italian could withhold allegiance from him? THIS BARBARIAN OCCUPATION STINKS IN THE NOSTRILS OF ALL OF US. Let your illustrious house then take up this cause with the spirit and the hope with which one undertakes a truly just enterprise. . . .

Niccolò Machiavelli, *The Prince*, translated and edited by Thomas G. Bergin. (Arlington Heights, Ill.: AHM Publishing Corporation, 1947), pp. 75–76, 78.

the great artist Michelangelo wrote many moving sonnets; and Ludovico Ariosto (1474–1533), the most eminent of sixteenth-century Italian epic poets, wrote a lengthy verse narrative called *Orlando Furioso* (*The Madness of Roland*). Although woven substantially from materials taken from the medieval Charlemagne cycle, this work differed radically from any of the medieval epics because it introduced elements of lyrical fantasy and above all because it was totally devoid of heroic idealism. Ariosto wrote to make readers laugh and to charm them with felicitous descriptions of the quiet splendor of nature and the passions of love. His work embodies the disillusionment of the late Renaissance, the loss of hope and faith, and the tendency to seek consolation in the pursuit of pleasure and aesthetic delight.

painting in oil, probably from Flanders, also characterized fifteenth-century painting. The use of the new technique doubtless had much to do with the artistic advance of this period. Since oil does not dry so quickly as fresco pigment, the painter could now work more slowly, taking time with the more difficult parts of the picture and making corrections if necessary as he went along.

RENAISSANCE PAINTING IN FLORENCE

The majority of the great painters of the fifteenth century were Florentines. First among them was the precocious Masaccio (1401–1428), known to his contemporaries as "Giotto reborn." Although he died at the

THE ITALIAN RENAISSANCE: PAINTING, SCULPTURE, AND ARCHITECTURE

Why did Italian art become fully mature around 1500?

Despite numerous intellectual and literary advances, the longest-lived achievements of the Italian Renaissance were made in the realm of art. Of all the arts, painting was undoubtedly supreme. We have already seen the artistic genius of Giotto around 1300, but it was not until the fifteenth century that Italian painting began to come fully of age. One reason for this was that in the early fifteenth century the laws of linear perspective were discovered and first employed to give the fullest sense of three dimensions. Fifteenth-century artists also experimented with effects of light and shade (*chiaroscuro*) and for the first time carefully studied the anatomy and proportions of the human body. By the fifteenth century, too, increasing private wealth and the growth of lay patronage had opened the domain of art to a variety of nonreligious themes and subjects. Even subject matter from biblical history was now frequently infused with nonreligious themes. Artists sought to paint portraits that revealed the hidden mysteries of the soul. Paintings intended to appeal primarily to the intellect were paralleled by others whose main purpose was to delight the eye with gorgeous color and beauty of form. The introduction of

The Impact of Perspective. Masaccio's painting *The Trinity with the Virgin* illustrates the startling sense of depth made possible by the rules of perspective.

The Birth of Venus, by Botticelli. Botticelli was a mystic as well as a lover of beauty, and the painting is most often interpreted as a Neoplatonic allegory.

age of twenty-seven, Masaccio inspired the work of Italian painters for a hundred years. Masaccio's greatness as a painter is based on his success in "imitating nature," which became a primary value in Renaissance painting. To achieve this effect he employed perspective, perhaps most dramatically in his fresco of the Trinity; he also used chiaroscuro with originality, leading to a dramatic and moving outcome.

The best known of the painters who directly followed the tradition represented by Masaccio was the Florentine Sandro Botticelli (1445–1510), who depicted both classical and Christian subjects. Botticelli's work excels in linear rhythms and sensuous depiction of natural detail. He is most famous for paintings that strike the eye as purely pagan because they portray figures from classical mythology without any overt sign of a Christian frame of reference. His *Allegory of Spring* and *Birth of Venus* employ a style greatly indebted to Roman depictions of gods, goddesses, zephyrs, and muses moving gracefully in natural settings. Consequently these works were once understood as the expression of "Renaissance paganism" at its fullest, a celebration of

earthly delights breaking sharply with Christian asceticism. More recently, however, scholars have preferred to view them as allegories fully compatible with Christian teachings. According to this interpretation, Botticelli was addressing himself to learned aristocratic viewers, well versed in the Neoplatonic theories of Ficino that considered ancient gods and goddesses to represent various Christian virtues. Venus, for example, might have stood for a species of chaste love. Although Botticelli's great "classical" works remain cryptic, two points remain certain: any viewer is free to enjoy them on their naturalistic sensuous level, and Botticelli had surely not broken with Christianity, since he painted frescoes for the pope in Rome at just the same time.

LEONARDO DA VINCI

Perhaps the greatest of the Florentine artists was Leonardo da Vinci (1452–1519), one of the most versatile geniuses who ever lived. Leonardo was practically the personification of the "Renaissance man": he was a painter, architect, musician, mathematician,

Ginevra da Benci, by Leonardo da Vinci.

The Virgin of the Rocks, by Leonardo da Vinci.
This painting reveals not only Leonardo's
interest in human physiognomy, but also his
absorption in the atmosphere of natural settings.

The Last Supper, by Leonardo da Vinci.

engineer, and inventor. The illegitimate son of a lawyer and a peasant woman, Leonardo set up an artist's shop in Florence by the time he was twenty-five and gained the patronage of the Medici ruler of the city, Lorenzo the Magnificent. But if Leonardo had any weakness, it was his slowness in working and difficulty in finishing anything. This naturally displeased Lorenzo and other Florentine patrons, who thought an artist was little more than an artisan, commissioned to produce a certain piece of work of a certain size for a certain price on a certain date. Leonardo, however, strongly objected to this view because he considered himself to be no menial craftsman but an inspired creator. Therefore in 1482 he left Florence for the Sforza court of Milan where he was given freer rein in structuring his time and work. He remained there until the French invaded Milan in 1499; after that he wandered about Italy, finally accepting the patronage of the French king, Francis I, under whose auspices Leonardo lived and worked in France until his death.

The paintings of Leonardo da Vinci began what is known as the High Renaissance in Italy. His approach to painting was that it should be the most accurate possible imitation of nature. Leonardo was like a naturalist, basing his work on his own detailed observations of a blade of grass, the wing of a bird, a waterfall. He obtained human corpses for dissection and reconstructed in drawing the minutest features of anatomy, which knowledge he carried over to his paintings. Leonardo worshiped nature, and was convinced of the essential divinity in all living things. It is not surprising, therefore, that he was a vegetarian, and that he went to the marketplace to buy caged birds, which he released to their native habitat.

It is generally agreed that Leonardo's masterpieces are the *Virgin of the Rocks* (which exists in two versions), the *Last Supper*, and his portraits of the Mona Lisa and Ginevra da Benci. *The Virgin of the Rocks* typifies not only his marvelous technical skill but also his passion for science and his belief in the universe as a well-ordered place. The figures are arranged geometrically, with every rock and plant depicted in accurate detail. The *Last Supper*, painted on the walls of

the refectory of Santa Maria delle Grazie in Milan, is a study of psychological reactions. A serene Christ, resigned to his terrible fate, has just announced to his disciples that one of them will betray him. The artist succeeds in portraying the mingled emotions of surprise, horror, and guilt in the faces of the disciples as they gradually perceive the meaning of their master's statement. The third and fourth of Leonardo's major triumphs, the *Mona Lisa* and *Ginevra da Benci*, reflect a similar interest in the varied moods of the human soul.

THE VENETIAN SCHOOL

The beginning of the High Renaissance around 1490 also witnessed the rise of the so-called Venetian school, the major members of which were Giovanni Bellini (c. 1430–1516), Giorgione (1478–1510), and Titian (c. 1490–1576). The work of all these men

Portait of Doge Francesco Venier (1555), by Titian. Titian served as the official painter of the Venetian Republic for sixty years. This superb portrait of Venice's ruler shows Titian's mastery of light and color.

reflected the luxurious life and the pleasure-loving interests of the thriving commercial city of Venice. Most Venetian painters had little of the concern of the Florentine school with philosophical and psychological interests. Their aim was to appeal primarily to the senses rather than to the mind. They delighted in painting idyllic landscapes and gorgeous symphonies of color. For their subject matter they chose not merely the natural beauty of Venetian sunsets and the shimmering silver of lagoons in the moonlight but also the artificial splendor of sparkling jewels, richly colored satins and velvets, and gorgeous palaces. Their portraits were invariably likenesses of the rich and the powerful. In the subordination of form and meaning to color and elegance they mirrored the sumptuous tastes of the wealthy merchants for whom they were created.

The Madonna of the Dawn ("Alba Madonna"), by Raphael (1483–1520). Raphael's art was distinguished by warmth, serenity, and tenderness. Here, the artist emphasizes the humility of the Virgin Mary by having her seated on the ground. The fact that the child John the Baptist and the child Christ are holding a cross reminds the viewer of the Crucifixion to come.

PAINTING IN ROME

The remaining great painters of the High Renaissance all accomplished their most important work in the first half of the sixteenth century when Renaissance Italian art reached its peak. Rome was now the major artistic center of the Italian peninsula, although the traditions of the Florentine school still exerted a potent influence.

RAPHAEL

Among the eminent painters of this period at least two must be given more than passing attention. One was Raphael (1483–1520), a native of Urbino, and perhaps the most beloved artist of the entire Renaissance. The lasting appeal of his style is due primarily to his ennobling portrayals of human beings as temperate, wise, and dignified creatures. Although Raphael was influenced by Leonardo and copied many features of his work, he cultivated a much more symbolical or allegorical approach. His *Disputà* symbolized the dialectical relationship between the church in heaven and the church on earth. In a worldly setting against a brilliant sky, theologians debate the meaning of the Eucharist, while in the clouds above, saints and the Trinity repose in the possession of a holy mystery. Raphael's *School of Athens* depicts harmony between the Platonist and Aristotelian philosophies. Plato (painted as a portrait of Leonardo) is shown pointing upward to emphasize the

spiritual basis of his world of Ideas, while Aristotle stretches a hand forward to exemplify his claim that the created world embodies these same principles in physical form. Raphael is noted also for his portraits and Madonnas. To the latter, especially, he gave a softness and warmth that seemed to endow them with a sweetness and piety quite different from Leonardo's enigmatic and somewhat distant Madonnas.

MICHELANGELO

The last towering figure of the High Renaissance was Michelangelo (1475–1564), a native of Florence. If Leonardo was a naturalist, Michelangelo was an idealist; where the former sought to recapture and interpret fleeting natural phenomena, Michelangelo, who embraced Neoplatonism as a philosophy, was more con-

The School of Athens, by Raphael.

cerned with expressing enduring, abstract truths. Michelangelo was a painter, sculptor, architect, and poet—and he expressed himself in all these forms with a similar power and in a similar manner. At the center of all of his paintings is the male figure, which is always powerful, colossal, magnificent. If humanity, embodied in the male body, lay at the center of Italian Renaissance culture, then Michelangelo, who depicted the male figure without cease, is the supreme Renaissance artist.

Michelangelo's greatest achievements in painting appear in a single location—the Sistine Chapel in Rome—yet they are products of two different periods in the artist's life and consequently exemplify two different artistic styles and outlooks on the human condition. More famous are the sublime frescoes Michelangelo painted on the ceiling of the Sistine Chapel from 1508 to 1512, depicting scenes from the book of Genesis. All the panels in this series, including *God Dividing the Light from Darkness*, *The Creation of Adam*, and *The Flood*, exemplify the young artist's commitment to classical Greek aesthetic principles of harmony, solidity, and dignified restraint. Correspondingly, all exude a sense of sublime affirmation regarding the Creation and the heroic qualities of mankind. But a quarter of a century later, when Michelangelo returned to work in the Sistine Chapel, both his style and mood had changed dramatically. In the enormous *Last Judgment*, a fresco done for the Sistine Chapel's altar wall in 1536, Michelangelo repudiated classical restraint and substituted a style that emphasized tension and distortion in order to communicate the older man's pessimistic conception of a humanity wracked by fear and bowed by guilt.

SCULPTURE

In the realm of sculpture the Italian Renaissance took a great step forward by creating statues that were no longer carved as parts of columns or doorways on church buildings or as effigies on tombs. Instead, Italian sculptors for the first time since antiquity carved

The Creation of Adam, by Michelangelo (1475–1564). One of a series of frescoes on the ceiling of the Sistine Chapel in Rome. Inquiring into the nature of humanity, it represents Renaissance affirmativeness at its height.

free-standing statues "in the round." These freed sculpture from its bondage to architecture and established its status as a separate art frequently devoted to secular purposes.

DONATELLO

The first great master of Renaissance sculpture was Donatello (c. 1386–1466). He emancipated his art from Gothic mannerisms and introduced a new vigorous note of individualism. His bronze statue of David triumphant over the head of the slain Goliath, the first free-standing nude since antiquity, established a precedent of glorifying the life-size nude. Donatello's

David, moreover, was a first step in the direction of imitating classical sculpture, not just in the depiction of a nude body, but also in the subject's posture of resting his weight on one leg. Yet this David is clearly a lithe adolescent rather than a muscular Greek athlete. Later in his career, Donatello more consciously imitated ancient statuary in his commanding portrayal of the proud warrior Gattamelata—the first monumental equestrian statue in bronze executed in the West since the time of the Romans. Here, in addition to drawing very heavily on the legacy of antiquity, the sculptor most clearly expressed his dedication to immortalizing the earthly accomplishments of a contemporary secular hero.

David, by Donatello (c. 1386–1466). The first free-standing nude statue executed in the West since antiquity.

MICHELANGELO

Certainly the greatest sculptor of the Italian Renaissance—indeed, probably the greatest sculptor of all time—was Michelangelo. Believing with Leonardo that the artist was an inspired creator, Michelangelo pursued this belief to the conclusion that sculpture was the most exalted of the arts because it allowed the artist to imitate God most fully in recreating human forms. Furthermore, in Michelangelo's view the most God-like sculptor disdained slavish naturalism, for anyone could make a plaster cast of a human figure,

but only an inspired creative genius could endow his sculpted figures with a sense of life. Accordingly, Michelangelo subordinated naturalism to the force of his imagination and sought restlessly to express his ideals in ever more arresting forms.

Like his painting, Michelangelo's sculpture followed a course from classicism to mannerism, that is, from harmonious modeling to dramatic distortion. The sculptor's most distinguished early work, his *David*, executed in 1501, is surely his most perfect classical statue. Choosing, like Donatello, to depict a male nude, Michelangelo nonetheless conceived of his own

David, by Michelangelo. Over thirteen feet high, this serenely self-confident affirmation of the beauty of the human form was placed prominently by the Florentine government in front of Florence's city hall to proclaim the city's humanistic values.

Descent from the Cross, by Michelangelo. This portrayal of tragedy was made by the sculptor for his own tomb. Note the distortion for effect exemplified by the elongated body and left arm of the figure of Christ. The figure in the rear is Nicodemus, but was probably intended to represent Michelangelo himself.

anatomical distortion to create effects of emotional intensity—in this case, the biblical prophet's righteous rage. While such statues remained awesomely heroic, as Michelangelo's life drew to a close he experimented more and more with exaggerated stylistic mannerisms for the purpose of communicating moods of brooding pensiveness or outright pathos. The culmination of this trend in Michelangelo's statuary is his unfinished but intensely moving *Descent from the Cross,* a depiction of an old man resembling the sculptor himself grieving over the distended, slumping body of the dead Christ.

ARCHITECTURE

To a much greater extent than either sculpture or painting, Renaissance architecture had its roots in the past. The new building style was a compound of elements derived from the Middle Ages and from antiquity. It was not the Gothic, however, a style that had never found a congenial soil in Italy, but the Italian Romanesque that provided the medieval basis for the architecture of the Italian Renaissance. The great architects of the Renaissance generally adopted their building plans from Romanesque churches, some of which they believed, mistakenly, to be Roman rather than medieval. They also copied their decorative devices from the ruins of ancient Rome. The result was an architecture based on the cruciform floor plan of transept and nave and embodying the decorative features of the column and arch, or the column and lintel, the colonnade, and frequently the dome. Horizontal lines predominated. Renaissance architecture also emphasized geometrical proportion because Italian builders, under the influence of Neoplatonism, con-

David as a public expression of Florentine civic ideals, and hence as heroic rather than merely graceful. To this end he worked in marble—the "noblest" sculptural medium—and created a figure twice as large as life. Above all he employed classical style to depict a serenely confident young man at the peak of physical fitness, thereby representing the Florentine republic's own "fortitude" in resisting tyrants and upholding ideals of civic justice. The serenity seen in *David* is no longer prominent in the works of Michelangelo's middle period; rather, in a work such as his *Moses* of about 1515, the sculptor has begun to explore the use of

CHRONOLOGY	
LIVES OF ITALIAN RENAISSANCE SCHOLARS AND ARTISTS	
Petrarch	1304–1374
Leon Battista Alberti	1404–1472
Giovanni Pico della Mirandola	1463–1494
Niccolò Machiavelli	1469–1527
Leonardo da Vinci	1452–1519
Titian	c. 1490–1576
Raphael	1483–1520
Michelangelo	1475–1564

The Villa Rotonda, by Palladio. A highly influential Renaissance private dwelling near Vicenza.

cluded that certain mathematical ratios reflect the harmony of the universe. A fine example of Renaissance architecture is St. Peter's Basilica in Rome, built under the patronage of popes Julius II and Leo X and designed by some of the most celebrated architects of the time, including Donato Bramante (c. 1444–1514) and Michelangelo. Equally impressive are the artfully proportioned aristocratic country houses designed by the northern Italian architect Andrea Palladio (1508–1580), who created secular miniatures of ancient temples such as the Roman Pantheon to glorify the aristocrats who dwelled within them.

THE WANING OF THE ITALIAN RENAISSANCE

Why did the Renaissance decline around 1550?

Around 1550 the Renaissance in Italy began to decline. The causes of this decline were varied. The French invasion of 1494 and the incessant warfare that ensued was one of the major factors. The French king Charles

VIII viewed Italy as an attractive target for his expansive dynastic ambitions. In 1494 he led an army of thirty thousand well-trained troops across the Alps to press his claims to the Duchy of Milan and the Kingdom of Naples. Florence swiftly capitulated; within less than a year the French had promenaded down the peninsula and conquered Naples. By so doing, however, they aroused the suspicions of the rulers of Spain, who feared an attack on their own territory of Sicily. An alliance among Spain, the Papal States, the Holy Roman empire, Milan, and Venice finally forced Charles to withdraw from Italy. But the respite was brief. Charles's successor, Louis XII, launched a second invasion, and from 1499 until 1529 warfare in Italy was virtually uninterrupted. Alliances and counteralliances followed each other in bewildering succession, but they managed only to prolong the hostilities. The French won a great victory at Marignano in 1515, but they were decisively defeated by the Spanish at Pavia in 1525. The worst disaster came in 1527 when rampaging troops under the command of the Spanish ruler and Holy Roman emperor Charles V sacked the city of Rome, causing enormous destruction. Only in 1529 did Charles V finally manage to gain control over most of the Italian peninsula, putting an end to the fighting for a time. Once triumphant, Charles retained two of the largest portions of Italy for Spain—the Duchy of

THE STATES OF ITALY DURING THE RENAISSANCE, C. 1494

How had the troubles of the papacy in the late fourteenth and early fifteenth centuries helped allow for the growth of aggressive and vibrant states that challenged the papacy within Italy? Why was the kingdom of Naples, despite its more extensive and consolidated territory, at a disadvantage compared with some of its rivals? What event made it possible for the papal states to reassert their influence after 1417? On what economic and political bases did the smaller states of northern Italy grow so powerful? How were these rival states able to maintain equilibrium and prosperity for much of the fifteenth century? How did the Italian "system" leave all of them potentially vulnerable?

Milan and the Kingdom of Naples—and installed favored princes as the rulers of almost all the other Italian political entities except for Venice and the Papal States. These protégés of the Spanish crown continued to preside over their own courts, to patronize the arts, and to adorn their cities with luxurious buildings, but

HOW DID THE NORTHERN AND ITALIAN RENAISSANCES DIFFER FROM ONE ANOTHER?

THE RENAISSANCE IN THE NORTH   475

they were puppets of a foreign power and unable to inspire their retinues with a sense of vigorous cultural independence.

To the Italian political disasters was added a waning of Italian prosperity. Whereas Italy's virtual monopoly of trade with Asia in the fifteenth century had been one of the chief economic supports for Italian Renaissance culture, the gradual shifting of trade routes from the Mediterranean to the Atlantic region, following the overseas discoveries of around 1500, slowly but surely cost Italy its supremacy as the center of world trade. Since the incessant warfare of the sixteenth century also contributed to Italy's economic hardships, as did Spanish financial exactions in Milan and Naples, there was gradually less and less of a surplus to support artistic endeavors.

A final cause of the decline of the Italian Renaissance was the Counter-Reformation. During the sixteenth century the Roman church sought increasingly to exercise firm control over thought and art as part of a campaign to combat worldliness and the spread of Protestantism. In 1542 the Roman Inquisition was established; in 1564 the first Roman Index of Prohibited Books was published. The extent of ecclesiastical interference in cultural life was enormous. For example, Michelangelo's great *Last Judgment* in the Sistine Chapel was criticized by some straitlaced fanatics for looking like a bordello because it showed too many naked bodies. Therefore, Pope Paul IV ordered a second-rate artist to paint in clothing wherever possible. (The unfortunate artist was afterward known as the "underwear maker.") Although this incident may appear merely grotesquely humorous, the determination of ecclesiastical censors to enforce doctrinal uniformity could lead to death, as in the case of the unfortunate Neoplatonic philosopher Giordano Bruno, whose insistence that there may be more than one world (in contravention of the biblical book of Genesis) resulted in his being burned at the stake by the Roman Inquisition in 1600.

The most notorious example of inquisitorial censorship of intellectual speculation was the disciplining of the great scientist Galileo, whose achievements we will discuss in more detail in Chapter 18. In 1616 the Holy Office in Rome condemned the new astronomical theory that the earth moves around the sun as "foolish, absurd, philosophically false, and formally heretical." When Galileo published a brilliant defense of the heliocentric system in 1632 the Inquisition ordered Galileo to recant his "errors" and sentenced him to house arrest for the duration of his life. Galileo was not willing to die for his beliefs, but after he publicly retracted his view that the earth revolves around the sun he supposedly whispered, "despite everything, it still moves." Not surprisingly, the great astronomical discoveries of the next generation were made in northern Europe, not in Italy.

Cultural and artistic achievement was by no means extinguished in Italy after the middle of the sixteenth century. On the contrary, impressive new artistic styles were cultivated between about 1540 and 1600 by painters who drew on traits found in the later work of Raphael and Michelangelo. In the seventeenth century came the dazzling Baroque style, which was born in Rome under ecclesiastical auspices. Similarly, Italian music registered enormous accomplishments virtually without interruption from the sixteenth to the twentieth century. But as Renaissance culture spread from Italy to the rest of Europe, the cultural dominance of the Italians began to wane, and the focus of European high culture shifted toward the princely courts of Spain, France, England, Germany, and Poland.

THE RENAISSANCE IN THE NORTH

How did the northern and Italian Renaissances differ from one another?

Throughout the fifteenth century a continuous procession of northern European students went to Italy to study in Italian universities such as Bologna or Padua, and an occasional Italian writer or artist traveled briefly north of the Alps. Such interchanges helped spread ideas, but only after around 1500 did most of northern Europe once again become sufficiently prosperous and politically stable as to provide a truly congenial environment for the widespread cultivation of art and literature. Intellectual interchanges also became much more extensive after 1494, when France and Spain started fighting on Italian battlefields. The result of this development was that more and more northern Europeans began to learn what the Italians had been accomplishing. Leading Italian thinkers and artists, such as Leonardo, also began to enter the retinues of northern kings or aristocrats. Accordingly, the Renaissance became an international movement and continued to be vigorous in the north even as it started to wane on its native ground.

CHRISTIAN HUMANISM AND THE NORTHERN RENAISSANCE

The Renaissance outside Italy was by no means identical to the Renaissance within Italy. Above all, the northern European Renaissance was more explicitly Christian in its outlook and orientation. The main explanation for this difference lies in the different social and cultural traditions that had evolved in Italy and northern Europe during the High Middle Ages. As we have seen, the vigorous urban society of medieval Italy fostered a lay educational system that led, in union with a revival of classicism, to the evolution of new, more secular forms of expression from the thirteenth century on. Northern Europe, in contrast, had a less mercantile and urban-oriented economy than did Italy. City-states on the Italian model did not emerge there. Instead, political power coalesced around the nation-states (or in Germany the princedoms), whose rulers were willing until about 1500 to acknowledge the educational and cultural hegemony of the clergy. This was especially the case with respect to northern universities, which tended to specialize in theological studies and which remained, therefore, under the closer supervision of the church. As a result, the Italian tradition of urban-based lay intellectual and cultural elites simply did not exist in the north. Nor did the northern European universities, dominated as they were by scholasticism, provide a hospitable environment for the new humanist learning emerging out of Italy. Instead, the northern European Renaissance was principally promoted by scholars working outside the university system under the patronage of kings and princes.

The northern Renaissance was the product of the grafting of certain Italian Renaissance ideals onto pre-existing northern traditions. This can be seen very clearly in the case of the most prominent northern Renaissance intellectual movement, Christian humanism. Although agreeing with Italian humanists that medieval scholasticism was too ensnarled in logical hair splitting to have any value for the practical conduct of life, northern Christian humanists more often looked for practical guidance from biblical and religious precepts rather than from Cicero or Virgil. Like their Italian counterparts, they sought wisdom from antiquity, but the antiquity they had in mind was Christian rather than classical—the antiquity, that is, of the

> The northern European Renaissance was more explicitly Christian in its outlook and orientation.

New Testament and the early Christian fathers. Similarly, northern Renaissance artists were moved by the accomplishments of Italian Renaissance masters to turn their backs on medieval Gothic artistic styles and to learn instead how to employ classical techniques. Yet these same artists depicted classical subject matter far less frequently than did the Italians, and virtually never ventured to portray completely undressed human figures.

DESIDERIUS ERASMUS

Any discussion of northern Renaissance accomplishments in the realm of thought and literary expression must begin with the career of Desiderius Erasmus (c. 1469–1536), the "prince of the Christian humanists." The illegitimate son of a priest, Erasmus was born near Rotterdam in Holland, but later, as a result of his wide travels, became in effect a citizen of all northern Europe. Forced into a monastery against his will when he was a teenager, the young Erasmus found there little religion or formal instruction of any kind but plenty of freedom to read what he liked. He devoured all the classics he could get his hands on and the writings of many of the Church fathers. When he was about thirty years of age, he obtained permission to leave the monastery and enroll in the University of Paris, where he completed the requirements for the degree of bachelor of divinity. But Erasmus subsequently rebelled against what he considered the arid learning of Parisian scholasticism. In one of his later writings he reported the following exchange: "Q. Where do you come from? A. The College of Montaigu. Q. Ah, then you must be bowed down with learning. A. No, with lice." Erasmus also never entered into the active duties of a priest, choosing instead to make his living from teaching, writing, and the proceeds of various ecclesiastical offices that required no spiritual duties of him. Ever on the lookout for new patrons, he changed his residence at frequent intervals, traveling often to England, staying once for three years in Italy, and residing in several different cities in Germany and the Netherlands before settling finally toward the end of his life in Basel, Switzerland. By means of a voluminous correspondence that he kept up with learned friends he made wherever he went, Erasmus became the leader of a northern European humanist coterie. And by means of the popularity of

HOW DID THE NORTHERN AND ITALIAN RENAISSANCES DIFFER FROM ONE ANOTHER?

THE RENAISSANCE IN THE NORTH   477

his numerous publications, he became the arbiter of "advanced" northern European cultural tastes during the first quarter of the sixteenth century.

Erasmus' many-sided intellectual activity may best be appraised from two different points of view: the literary and the doctrinal. As a Latin prose stylist, Erasmus was unequaled since the days of Cicero. Extraordinarily learned and witty, he reveled in tailoring his mode of discourse to fit his subject, creating dazzling verbal effects and coining puns that took on added meaning if the reader knew Greek as well as Latin. Above all, Erasmus excelled in the deft use of irony, poking fun at all and sundry, including himself. For example, in his *Colloquies* (from the Latin for "discussions") he had a fictional character lament the evil signs of the times thus: "kings make war, priests strive to line their pockets, theologians invent syllogisms, monks roam outside their cloisters, the commons riot, and Erasmus writes colloquies."

But although Erasmus' urbane Latin style and wit

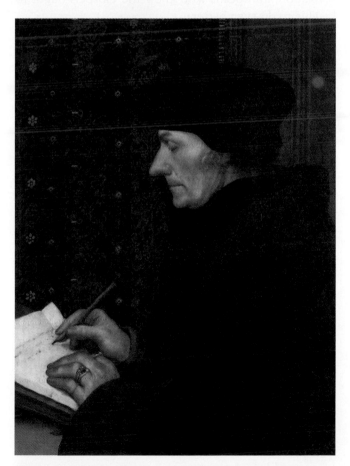

Erasmus, by Hans Holbein the Younger (1497–1543). This portrait is generally regarded as the most telling visual characterization of "the prince of the Christian humanists."

earned him a wide audience for purely literary reasons, he by no means thought of himself as a mere entertainer. Rather, he intended everything he wrote to propagate in one form or another what he called the "philosophy of Christ." The essence of Erasmus' Christian humanist convictions was his belief that the entire society of his day was caught up in corruption and immorality as a result of having lost sight of the simple teachings of the Gospels. Accordingly, he offered to his contemporaries three different categories of publication: clever satires meant to show people the error of their ways, serious moral treatises meant to offer guidance toward proper Christian behavior, and scholarly editions of basic Christian texts.

In the first category belong the works of Erasmus that are still most widely read today—*The Praise of Folly* (1509), in which he pilloried scholastic pedantry and dogmatism as well as the ignorance and superstitious credulity of the masses; and the *Colloquies* (1518), in which he held up contemporary religious practices for examination in a more serious but still pervasively ironic tone. In such works Erasmus let fictional characters do the talking; hence his own views can be determined only by inference. But in his second mode Erasmus did not hesitate to speak clearly in his own voice. The most prominent treatises in this second genre are the quietly eloquent *Handbook of the Christian Knight* (1503), which urged the laity to pursue lives of serene inward piety, and the *Complaint of Peace* (1517), which pleaded movingly for Christian pacifism. Erasmus' pacifism was one of his most deeply held values, and he returned to it again and again in his published works.

Despite this highly impressive literary production, Erasmus probably considered his textual scholarship his single greatest achievement. Revering the authority of the early Latin fathers Augustine, Jerome, and Ambrose, he brought out reliable editions of all their works. He also applied his extraordinary skills as a student of Latin and Greek to producing a more accurate edition of the New Testament. After reading Lorenzo Valla's *Notes on the New Testament* in 1504, Erasmus became convinced that nothing was more imperative than divesting the New Testament of the myriad errors in transcription and translation that had piled up during the Middle Ages, for no one could be a good Christian without being certain of exactly what Christ's message really was. Hence he spent ten years studying and comparing all the best early Greek biblical manuscripts he could find in order to establish an authoritative text. Finally appearing in 1516, Erasmus'

Greek New Testament, published together with explanatory notes and his own new Latin translation, was one of the most important landmarks of biblical scholarship of all time. In the hands of Martin Luther, it would play a critical role in the early stages of the Protestant Reformation.

SIR THOMAS MORE

One of Erasmus' closest friends, and a close second to him in distinction among the ranks of the Christian humanists, was the Englishman Sir Thomas More (1478–1535). Following a successful career as a lawyer and as speaker of the House of Commons, in 1529 More was appointed lord chancellor of England. He was not long in this position, however, before he incurred the wrath of his royal master, King Henry VIII. More, who was loyal to Catholic universalism, opposed the king's design to establish a national church under subjection to the state. Finally, in 1534, when More refused to take an oath acknowledging Henry as head of the Church of England, he was thrown into the Tower of London, and a year later met his death on the scaffold as a Catholic martyr. Much earlier, however, in 1516, long before More had any inkling of how his life

Sir Thomas More, by Hans Holbein the Younger.

was to end, he published the one work for which he will ever be best remembered, *Utopia*. Creating the subsequently popular genre of "utopian fiction," More's *Utopia* expressed an Erasmian critique of contemporary society. Purporting to describe an ideal community on an imaginary island, the book is really an indictment of the glaring abuses of the time—of poverty undeserved and wealth unearned, of drastic punishments, religious persecution, and the senseless slaughter of war. The inhabitants of Utopia hold all their goods in common, work only six hours a day so that all may have leisure for intellectual pursuits, and practice the natural virtues of wisdom, moderation, fortitude, and justice. Iron is the precious metal "because it is useful," war and monasticism do not exist, and toleration is granted to all who recognize the existence of God and the immortality of the soul. Although More advanced no explicit arguments in his *Utopia* in favor of Christianity, he clearly meant to imply that if the "Utopians" could manage their society so well without the benefit of Christian revelation, Europeans who knew the Gospels ought to be able to do even better.

ULRICH VON HUTTEN

Whereas Erasmus and More were basically conciliatory in their temperaments and preferred to express themselves by means of wry understatements, a third representative of the Christian humanist movement, Erasmus' German disciple Ulrich von Hutten (1488–1523), was of a much more combative disposition. Dedicated to the cause of German cultural nationalism, von Hutten spoke up truculently to defend the "proud and free" German people against foreigners. But his chief claim to fame was his collaboration with another German humanist, Crotus Rubianus, in the authorship of the *Letters of Obscure Men* (1515), one of the most stinging satires in the history of literature. This was written as part of a propaganda war in favor of a scholar named Johann Reuchlin who wished to pursue his study of Hebrew writings, above all, the Talmud. When scholastic theologians and the German inquisitor general tried to have all Hebrew books in Germany destroyed, Reuchlin and his party strongly opposed the move. After a while it became apparent that direct argument was accomplishing nothing, so Reuchlin's supporters resorted to ridicule. Von Hutten and Rubianus published a series of letters, written in intentionally bad Latin, purportedly by some of Reuchlin's scholastic opponents from the University of Cologne. These opponents, given such ridiculous names as

HOW DID THE NORTHERN AND ITALIAN RENAISSANCES DIFFER FROM ONE ANOTHER?

THE RENAISSANCE IN THE NORTH   479

Goatmilker, Baldpate, and Dungspreader, were shown to be learned fools who paraded absurd religious literalism or grotesque erudition. Heinrich Sheep's-mouth, for example, the supposed writer of one of the letters, professed to be worried that he had sinned grievously by eating on Friday an egg that contained the embryo of a chick. The author of another boasted of his "brilliant discovery" that Julius Caesar could not have written Latin histories because he was too busy with his military exploits ever to have learned Latin. Although immediately banned by the church, the letters circulated nonetheless and were widely read, giving ever more currency to the Erasmian proposition that scholastic theology and Catholic religious observances had to be set aside in favor of the most earnest dedication to the simple teachings of the Gospels.

THE DECLINE OF CHRISTIAN HUMANISM

With Erasmus, More, and von Hutten the list of energetic and eloquent Christian humanists is by no means exhausted, for the Englishman John Colet (c. 1467–1519), the Frenchman Jacques Lefèvre d'Étaples (c. 1455–1536), and the Spaniards Cardinal Francisco Ximénez de Cisneros (1436–1517) and Juan Luís Víves (1492–1540) all made signal contributions to the collective enterprise of editing biblical and early Christian texts and expounding Gospel morality. But despite a host of achievements, the Christian humanist movement, which possessed such an extraordinary degree of international solidarity and vigor from about 1500 to 1525, was thrown into disarray by the rise of Protestantism and subsequently lost its momentum. The irony here is obvious, for the Christian humanists' emphasis on the literal truth of the Gospels and their devastating criticisms of clerical corruption and excessive religious ceremonialism certainly helped pave the way for the Protestant Reformation initiated by Martin Luther in 1517. But, as we will see in Chapter 14, very few of the older generation of Christian humanists were willing to go the whole route with Luther in rejecting the most fundamental principles on which Catholicism was based, and the few who did became such ardent Protestants that they lost the sense of quiet irony that earlier had been a hallmark of Christian humanist expression. Most Christian humanists tried to remain within the Catholic fold while still espousing their ideal of non-ritualistic inward piety. But as time went on, the leaders of Catholicism had less and less tolerance for them because lines were hardening in the war with Protestantism. Hence, any internal criticism of Catholic religious practices seemed like giving covert aid to the "enemy." Erasmus himself, who remained a Catholic, died early enough to escape opprobrium, but several of his less fortunate followers lived on to suffer as victims of the Inquisition.

LITERATURE, ART, AND MUSIC IN THE NORTHERN RENAISSANCE

Yet if Christian humanism faded rapidly after about 1525, the northern Renaissance continued to flourish throughout the sixteenth century in literature and art. In France, the highly accomplished poets Pierre de Ronsard (c. 1524–1585) and Joachim du Bellay (c. 1522–1560) wrote elegant sonnets in the style of Petrarch, and in England the poets Sir Philip Sidney (1554–1586) and Edmund Spenser (c. 1552–1599) drew impressively on Italian literary innovations. Indeed, Spenser's *Faerie Queene*, a long chivalric romance written in the manner of Ariosto's *Orlando Furioso*, communicates as well as any Italian work the gorgeous sensuousness typical of Italian Renaissance culture.

RABELAIS

More intrinsically original than any of the aforementioned poets was the French prose satirist François Rabelais (c. 1494–1553), probably the best loved of all the great European creative writers of the sixteenth century. Like Erasmus, whom he greatly admired, Rabelais began his career in the clergy, but soon after taking holy orders he left his cloister to study medicine. Becoming thereafter a practicing physician in Lyons, Rabelais interspersed his professional activities with literary endeavors of one sort or another. He wrote almanacs, satires against quacks and astrologers, and burlesques of popular superstitions. But by far his most enduring literary legacy consists of his five volumes of "chronicles" published under the collective title of *Gargantua and Pantagruel*.

Rabelais' account of the adventures of Gargantua and Pantagruel, originally the names of legendary medieval giants noted for their fabulous size and gross appetites, served as a vehicle for his lusty humor and his penchant for exuberant narrative as well as for the expression of his philosophy of naturalism. To some degree, Rabelais drew on the precedents of Christian humanism. Thus, like Erasmus, he satirized religious ceremonialism, ridiculed scholasticism, scoffed at superstitions, and pilloried every form of bigotry. But unlike Erasmus, who wrote in a highly cultivated classical Latin style comprehensible to only the most learned readers, Rabelais chose to address a far wider audience by writing in an extremely down-to-earth French loaded with the crudest vulgarities. Likewise, Rabelais wanted to avoid seeming in any way "preachy" and therefore eschewed all suggestions of moralism in favor of giving the impression that he wished merely to offer his readers some rollicking good fun. Yet, aside from the critical satire in *Gargantua and Pantagruel*, there runs through all five volumes a common theme of glorifying the human and the natural. For Rabelais, whose robust giants were really life-loving human beings writ very large, every instinct of humanity was healthy, provided it was not directed toward tyranny over others. Thus in his ideal community, the utopian "abbey of Thélème," there was no repressiveness whatsoever, but only a congenial environment for the pursuit of life-affirming, natural human attainments, guided by the single rule of "do what thou wouldst."

ARCHITECTURE

Were we to imagine what Rabelais' fictional abbey of Thélème might have looked like, we would do best to picture it as resembling one of the famous sixteenth-century French Renaissance châteaux built along the River Loire, for the northern European Renaissance had its own distinctive architecture that often corresponded in certain essentials to its literature. Thus, just as Rabelais recounted stories of medieval giants in order to express an affirmation of Renaissance values, so French architects who constructed such splendid Loire châteaux as Amboise, Chenonceaux, and Chambord combined elements of the late medieval French flamboyant Gothic style with an up-to-date emphasis on classical horizontality to produce some of the most impressively distinctive architectural landmarks ever constructed in France. Yet much closer architectural imitation of Italian models occurred in France as well, for just as Ronsard and du Bellay modeled their poetic style very closely on Petrarch, so Pierre Lescot, the French architect who began work on the new royal palace of the Louvre in Paris in 1546, hewed closely to the classicism of Italian Renaissance masters in constructing a facade that emphasized classical pilasters and pediments.

PAINTING

Northern Renaissance painting is another realm in which links between thought and art can be discerned. Certainly the most moving visual embodiments of the ideals of Christian humanism were conceived by the foremost of northern Renaissance artists, the German Albrecht Dürer (1471–1528). From the purely technical and stylistic points of view, Dürer's greatest signifi-

Chambord. Built in the early sixteenth century by an Italian architect in the service of King Francis I of France, this magnificent Loire Valley château combines Gothic and Renaissance architectural traits.

HOW DID THE NORTHERN AND ITALIAN RENAISSANCES DIFFER FROM ONE ANOTHER?

THE RENAISSANCE IN THE NORTH   481

The West Side of the Square Court on the Louvre, by Pierre Lescot. The enlargement of the Louvre, begun by Lescot in 1546, took more than a century to complete. In it, he achieved a synthesis of the traditional château and the Renaissance palace.

cance lies in the fact that, returning to his native Nuremberg after a trip to Venice in 1494, he became the first northerner to master Italian Renaissance techniques of proportion, perspective, and modeling. Dürer also shared with contemporary Italians a fascination with reproducing the manifold works of nature down to the minutest details and a penchant for displaying various postures of the human nude. But whereas Michelangelo portrayed his naked *David* or *Adam* entirely without covering, Dürer's nudes are seldom lacking their fig leaves, in deference to more restrained northern traditions. Moreover, Dürer consistently refrained from abandoning himself to the pure classicism and sumptuousness of much Italian Renaissance art because he was inspired primarily by the more traditionally Christian ideals of Erasmus. Thus Dürer's serenely radiant engraving of Saint Jerome expresses the sense of accomplishment that Erasmus or any other contemporary Christian humanist may have had while working quietly in his study; and his *Four Apostles* intones a solemn hymn to the dignity and penetrating insight of Dürer's favorite New Testament authors, Saints Paul, John, Peter, and Mark.

Dürer would have loved nothing more than to have immortalized Erasmus in a major painted portrait, but circumstances prevented him from doing this because the paths of the two men crossed only once, and after Dürer started sketching his hero on that occasion his work was interrupted by Erasmus' press of business.

Saint Jerome in His Study, by Dürer. Saint Jerome, a hero for both Dürer and Erasmus, represents inspired Christian scholarship. Note how the scene exudes contentment, even down to the sleeping lion, which seems rather like an overgrown tabby cat.

Instead, the accomplishment of capturing Erasmus' pensive spirit in oils was left to another great northern Renaissance artist, the German Hans Holbein the Younger (1497–1543; see p. 477). As good fortune would have it, during a stay in England Holbein also painted an extraordinarily acute portrait of Erasmus' friend and kindred spirit Sir Thomas More, which enables us to see clearly why a contemporary called More "a man of . . . sad gravity; a man for all seasons" (see p. 478). These two portraits in and of themselves point up a major difference between medieval and Renaissance culture. Whereas the Middle Ages produced no convincing naturalistic likenesses of any leading intellectual figures, Renaissance culture's greater commitment to capturing the essence of human individuality created the environment in which Holbein was able to make Erasmus and More come to life.

Music

Music in western Europe in the fifteenth and sixteenth centuries reached such a high point of development that it constitutes, together with painting and sculpture, one of the most brilliant aspects of Renaissance endeavor. The musical theory of the Renaissance was driven largely by the humanist-inspired but largely fruitless effort to recover and imitate classical musical forms and modes. Musical practice, however, showed much more continuity with medieval musical traditions of number and proportion. At the same time, however, a new expressiveness emerges in Renaissance music, along with a new emphasis on coloration and emotional quality. New musical instruments were also developed, including the lute, the viol, the violin, and a variety of woodwind and keyboard instruments including the harpsichord. New musical forms also emerged: madrigals, motets, and, at the end of the sixteenth century, a new Italian form, the opera. As earlier, musical leadership came from men trained in the service of the church. But the distinction between sacred and profane music was becoming less sharp, and most composers did not restrict their activities to a single field. Music was no longer regarded merely as a diversion or an adjunct to worship, but came into its own as a serious independent art.

Different areas of Europe vied with one another for musical leadership. As with the other arts, advances were related to the generous patronage afforded by the prosperous cities of Italy and the northern European princely courts. During the fourteenth century a pre- or early Renaissance musical movement called *ars nova*

Renaissance Singers. A relief by Luca della Robbia.

("new art") flourished in Italy and France. Its outstanding composers were Francesco Landini (c. 1325–1397) and Guillaume de Machaut (c. 1300–1377). The madrigals, ballads, and other songs composed by the *ars nova* musicians testify to a rich fourteenth-century tradition of secular music, but the greatest achievement of the period was a highly complicated yet delicate contrapuntal style adapted for ecclesiastical motets. Machaut, moreover, was the first known composer to provide a polyphonic version of the major sections of the Mass.

The fifteenth century ushered in a synthesis of French, Flemish, and Italian elements in the ducal court of Burgundy. This music was melodious and gentle, but in the second half of the century it hardened a little as northern Flemish elements gained in importance. As the sixteenth century opened, Franco-Flemish composers appeared in every important court and cathedral all over Europe, gradually establishing regional-national schools, usually in attractive combinations of Flemish with German, Spanish, and Italian musical cultures. The various genres thus created show a close affinity with Renaissance art and poetry. In the second half of the sixteenth century the leaders of the nationalized Franco-Flemish style were the Fleming Roland de Lassus (1532–1594), the most versatile composer of the age, and the Italian Giovanni Pierluigi da Palestrina (c. 1525–1594), who specialized in highly intricate polyphonic choral music written for Catholic church services under the patronage of the popes in Rome. Music also flourished in sixteenth-century England, where the Tudor monarchs Henry VIII and Elizabeth I were active patrons of the arts. Not only did the Italian madrigal, imported toward the end of the sixteenth century, take on remarkable new life in England, but songs and instrumental music of an original cast anticipated future developments on the Continent. In William Byrd (1543–1623) English music produced a master fully the equal of the great Flemish and Italian composers of the Renaissance period. The general level of musical proficiency seems to have been higher in Queen Elizabeth's day than in ours: the singing of part-songs was a popular pastime in homes and at informal social gatherings, and the ability to read a part at sight was expected of the educated elite.

Although accomplishments in counterpoint were already very advanced in the Renaissance period, our modern harmonic system was still in its infancy, and thus there remained much room for experimentation. At the same time we should realize that the music of the Renaissance constitutes not merely a stage in evolution but a magnificent achievement in itself, with

masters who rank among the greatest of all time. The composers Lassus, Palestrina, and Byrd are as truly representative of the artistic triumph of the Renaissance as are the painters Leonardo, Raphael, and Michelangelo. Their heritage, long neglected, has within recent years begun to be appreciated, and is now gaining in popularity as interested groups of musicians devote themselves to its revival.

CONCLUSION

The contrasts between the Italian and the northern Renaissance are real, but they must not be exaggerated. The intellectuals of Renaissance Italy were formed in a more secular and a more urban educational environment than were the northerners, but they were no less fervent in their Christianity. Petrarch's criticism of scholasticism was not that it was too Christian, but rather that it was not Christian enough. Petrarch opposed the emotional aridity and stylistic inelegance of scholasticism because he believed they threatened the salvation of Christians. Much the same point might be made about Lorenzo Valla. His critique of the temporal claims of the papacy sprang not only from the conclusions of his textual scholarship, but also from a firm Christian piety. The Platonic Academy might honor Plato as if he were a saint of the church, but these men approached Plato's works in the same spirit with which thirteenth century scholastic theologians had approached the works of Aristotle. As committed Christians, they were convinced that the conclusions reached by the greatest philosophical minds of classical antiquity must be compatible with Christian truth. It was the task of Christian intellectuals to reveal this compatibility, and by so doing, to strengthen the one true faith.

In considering the contrasts between "civic" and "Christian" humanism, we must keep in mind the enormous diversity of Renaissance thought. Machiavelli is no more "typical" an Italian Renaissance thinker than is Ficino, Alberti, or Bruno. In comparing Italian thinkers with northern thinkers, we must therefore be careful to compare "like" with "like." Too often, scholars overdraw the contrasts between Renaissance thought in Italy and northern Europe by choosing Machiavelli, for example, to represent all of Italian humanism and Erasmus to represent northern humanism. Two more different figures can hardly be imagined; but their differences have much more to do with their contrasting

CHRONOLOGY

LIVES OF NORTHERN RENAISSANCE SCHOLARS AND ARTISTS

Erasmus	c. 1469–1536
Thomas More	1478–1535
Ulrich von Hutten	1488–1523
Edmund Spenser	c. 1552–1599
François Rabelais	c. 1494–1553
Albrecht Dürer	1471–1528
Hans Holbein the Younger	1497–1543

presuppositions about human nature than they do with their "allegiances" to Italian or northern humanism. A very different picture emerges if we compare, for example, John Colet as a representative of northern humanism with Marsilio Ficino as a representative of Italian humanism, or compare Petrarch with Sir Thomas More.

Nor should we overdraw the contrasts between the Renaissance and the High Middle Ages. Both Italian and northern humanists shared an optimistic view of human nature as improvable despite the consequences of Adam and Eve's disobedience; but none were more optimistic on this score than was Saint Thomas Aquinas. Both groups emphasized the importance of personal introspection and self-examination; but none took this injunction more seriously than did the Cistercian thinkers of the twelfth century. And finally, both groups shared a belief that the exhortations of intellectuals would lift everyone's morals and conduct them to new heights of virtue. In this regard, High Renaissance intellectual life has a kind of naïve optimism that contrasts sharply with the darker, more psychologically complex world of the Middle Ages, and with the Reformation era that was about to begin.

SELECTED READINGS

Alberti, Leon Battista. *The Family in Renaissance Florence (Della Famiglia)*. Translated by Renée Neu Watkins. Columbia, S.C., 1969.

Baron, Hans. *The Crisis of the Early Italian Renaissance*. Princeton, 1966. A highly influential account of "civic humanism."

Baxandall, Michael. *Painting and Experience in Fifteenth Century Italy*. Oxford, 1972. A classic study of the perceptual world of the Renaissance.

Brucker, Gene. *Florence, the Golden Age, 1138–1737*. Berkeley and Los Angeles, 1998. The standard account by a master historian.

———. *The Society of Renaissance Florence: A Documentary Study*. New York, 1971. A revealing portrait of Florentine society and social mores through original documents.

Bruni, Leonardo. *The Humanism of Leonardo Bruni: Selected Texts*. Translated by Gordon Griffiths, James Hankins, and David Thompson. Binghamton, N.Y., 1987. Excellent translations, with introductions, to the Latin works of a key Renaissance humanist.

Burke, Peter. *The Renaissance*. New York, 1997. A brief introduction by an influential modern historian.

———. *Culture and Society in Renaissance Italy*, 2d ed. Princeton, N.J., 1999. A revision and restatement of arguments first advanced in 1972.

Burkhardt, Jacob. *The Civilization of the Renaissance in Italy*. Many editions. The nineteenth-century work that first crystallized an image of the Italian Renaissance with which scholars have been wrestling ever since.

Cassirer, Ernst, et al., eds. *The Renaissance Philosophy of Man*. Chicago, 1948. Important original works by Petrarch, Ficino, and Pico della Mirandola, among others.

Castiglione, Baldassare. *The Book of the Courtier*. Many editions. The translations by C. S. Singleton (New York, 1959) and by George Bull (New York, 1967) are both excellent.

Cellini, Benvenuto. *Autobiography*. Translated by George Bull. Baltimore, 1956. The autobiography of a Florentine goldsmith (1500–1571); the source for many of the most famous stories about the artists of the Florentine Renaissance.

Cochrane, Eric, and Julius Kirshner, eds. *The Renaissance*. Chicago, 1986. An outstanding collection, from the University of Chicago Readings in Western Civilization series.

Erasmus, Desiderius. *The Praise of Folly*. Translated by J. Wilson. Ann Arbor, Mich., 1958.

Fox, Alistair. *Thomas More: History and Providence*. Oxford, 1982. A balanced account of a man too easily idealized.

Grafton, Anthony, and Lisa Jardine. *From Humanism to the Humanities: Education and the Liberal Arts in Fifteenth- and Sixteenth-Century Europe*. London, 1986. An influential recent account that presents Renaissance humanism as the elitist cultural program of a self-interested group of pedagogues.

Grendler, Paul, ed. *Encyclopedia of the Renaissance*. New York, 1999. A valuable reference work.

Hale, John R. *The Civilization of Europe in the Renaissance*. New York, 1993. A synthetic volume summarizing the life's work of a major Renaissance historian.

Hankins, James. *Plato in the Italian Renaissance*. Leiden and New York, 1990. A definitive study of the reception and influence of Plato on Renaissance intellectuals.

———, ed. *Renaissance Civic Humanism: Reappraisals and Reflections*. Cambridge and New York, 2000. An excellent collection of scholarly essays reassessing republicanism in the Renaissance.

Jardine, Lisa. *Worldly Goods*. London, 1996. A revisionist account that emphasizes the acquisitive materialism of Italian Renaissance society and culture.

Kanter, Laurence, Hilliard T. Goldfarb, and James Hankins. *Botticelli's Witness: Changing Style in a Changing Florence*. Boston, 1997. This catalogue, for an exhibit of Botticelli's works at the Gardner Museum in Boston, offers an excellent introduction to the painter and his world.

King, Margaret L. *Women of the Renaissance*. Chicago, 1991. Deals with women in all walks of life and in a variety of roles.

Kristeller, Paul O. *Renaissance Thought: The Classic, Scholastic, and Humanistic Strains*. New York, 1961. Very helpful in defining the main trends of Renaissance thought.

———. *Eight Philosophers of the Italian Renaissance*. Stanford, 1964. An admirably clear and accurate account that fully appreciates the connections between medieval and Renaissance thought.

Lane, Frederic C. *Venice: A Maritime Republic*. Baltimore, 1973. An authoritative account.

Machiavelli, Niccolò. *The Discourses* and *The Prince*. Many editions. These two books must be read together if one is to understand Machiavelli's political ideas properly.

Martines, Lauro. *Power and Imagination: City-States in Renaissance Italy*. New York, 1979. Insightful account of the connections between politics, society, culture, and art.

More, Thomas. *Utopia*. Many editions.

Muir, Edward. *Mad Blood Stirring: Vendetta and Factions in Friuli during the Renaissance*. Baltimore, 1993. A revealing local study of one of the primary challenges to the political and social order of Renaissance cities.

Murray, Linda. *High Renaissance and Mannerism*. London, 1985. The place to start for fifteenth- and sixteenth-century Italian art.

Olson, Roberta, *Italian Renaissance Sculpture*, New York, 1992. The most accessible introduction to the subject.

Perkins, Leeman L. *Music in the Age of the Renaissance*. New York, 1999. A massive new study that nonetheless needs to be read in conjunction with Reese (see below).

Rabelais, François. *Gargantua and Pantagruel*. Translated by J. M. Cohen. Baltimore, 1955. A robust modern translation.

Reese, Gustave. *Music in the Renaissance*, rev. ed. New York, 1959. A great book; still authoritative, despite the more recent work by Perkins (see above), which supplements but does not replace it.

Rice, Eugene F., Jr., and Anthony Grafton. *The Foundations of Early Modern Europe, 1460–1559*, 2d ed. New York, 1994. The best textbook account of its period.

Rocke, Michael. *Forbidden Friendships: Homosexuality and Male Culture in Renaissance Florence*. New York, 1996. A remarkable quantitative study of efforts by the civic authorities of fifteenth-century Florence to suppress same-gender sexual activity among Florentine men; opens up an important subject to detailed examination.

Rowland, Ingrid D. *The Culture of the High Renaissance: Ancients and Moderns in Sixteenth-Century Rome*. Cambridge and New York, 2000. Beautifully written examination of the social, intellectual, and economic foundations of the Renaissance in Rome.

CHAPTER FOURTEEN

THE PROTESTANT
REFORMATION

AFTER TWO CENTURIES of economic, social, and political turmoil, Europe in the year 1500 was well on the road to recovery. The population was increasing, the economy was expanding, cities were growing, and the national monarchies of France, England, Spain, and Poland were all securely established. Throughout Europe, governments at every level were extending and deepening their control over their subjects' lives. After a late-fourteenth-century hiatus, Europe had also resumed its commercial and colonial expansion. Even Catholic Christianity appeared to be going from strength to strength as the sixteenth century dawned. Although the papacy remained mired in territorial wars in Italy, the church itself had weathered the storms that had beset it during the fifteenth century. The Lollards had been suppressed and the Hussites reincorporated into the church. In the struggle over conciliarism, the Papacy had successfully won the support of all the major European rulers, reducing the conciliarists to academic isolation at the University of Paris. Meanwhile, at the parish level, the devotion of ordinary Christians to their faith had probably never been higher. To be sure, there were also problems. Although the educational standards of the parish clergy were higher than they had ever been, reformers were quick to note that too many priests were still absent, ignorant, or neglectful of their spiritual duties. Monasticism, by and large, seemed to have lost its spiritual fire; while among the populace, religious enthusiasm sometimes led the faithful into gross superstition and doctrinal error. But these were manageable problems. On the whole, the "prospect of Europe" had not looked brighter for several centuries.

No one in 1500 could have predicted that within fifty years Europe's religious unity would be irreparably shattered by a new and powerful Protestant reform movement—or that in the century thereafter an appallingly destructive series of religious wars would shake to their core the foundations of European political life. Remarkably, these extraordinary events began with a single German monk named Martin Luther (1483–1546), whose personal quest for a more certain understanding of sin, grace, and Christian salvation set off a chain reaction throughout Europe, resulting in the secession of millions of Europeans from the Roman Catholic Church and affecting the religious practices of nearly every Christian in Europe, whether

FOCUS QUESTIONS

- What were the theological premises of Lutheranism?

- How did the teachings of Calvin and Luther differ?

 • How did notions of family and marriage change during the Reformation?

- What caused the Catholic Reformation?

Catholic or Protestant. The religious movement that Luther touched off was much larger than the man himself; nor should Martin Luther's own spiritual journey be seen as an epitome for all of Protestantism. But that said, there is no doubt that the Reformation movement began with Martin Luther—and so must we if we are to understand the extraordinary upheaval this new religious movement brought about.

THE LUTHERAN UPHEAVAL

What were the theological premises of Lutheranism?

In searching for the causes of the Lutheran revolt in Germany, three main questions arise: (1) why Martin Luther instigated a break with Rome; (2) why large numbers of Germans rallied to his cause; and (3) why a number of German princes decided to put the Lutheran Reformation into effect within their territories. Reduced to the barest essentials, the answers to these questions are that Luther broke with Rome because of his doctrine of justification by faith, that the German masses followed him in a surge of religious nationalism, and that the princes were moved to institute Lutheranism particularly because of their quest for governmental sovereignty. Within a decade preachers, the populace, and many of the German princes would all sing the same stirring Lutheran hymn, "A Mighty Fortress Is Our God," in the same church, but they arrived there by rather different paths.

LUTHER AND LATE MEDIEVAL CATHOLICISM

Many people think that Luther rebelled against Rome because he was disgusted with contemporary religious abuses—superstitions, frauds, and the offer of salvation for money—but that is only part of the story. Certainly abuses in Luther's day were grave and intensely upsetting to religious idealists. In a world beset by disease and disaster, frail mortals clutched at supernatural straws to seek health on earth and salvation in the hereafter. Some superstitious men and women, for ex-

ample, believed that viewing the consecrated host during Mass in the morning would guard them from death throughout the day, and others neglected to swallow the consecrated wafer so that they could use it later as a charm to ward off evil, an application to cure the sick, or a powder to fertilize their crops. Similarly, belief in the miraculous curative powers of saints was hard to distinguish from belief in magic. Every saint had his or her specialty: "for botches and biles, Cosmas and Damian; Saint Clare for the eyes, Saint Apolline for teeth, Saint Job for pox. And for sore breasts, Saint Agatha." Because relics of Christ and the saints were believed to radiate marvelous healing effects, traffic in relics boomed. Luther's patron, the elector Frederick the Wise of Saxony, had a collection in his castle church at Wittenberg of seventeen thousand relics, including a supposed remnant of Moses' burning bush, pieces of the holy cradle, shreds from Christ's swaddling clothes, and thirty-three fragments of the True Cross. In Florence, the Medici family's relic collection was even larger. The authenticity of many of these relics was highly doubtful, but the demand for them seemed to be insatiable.

Superstitions and gross credulity were offensive enough to religious idealists of Luther's stamp, but worse still were the granting of dispensations and the promises of spiritual benefits for money. If a man wished to marry his first cousin, for example, for a fee he could usually receive an official religious dispensation allowing the marriage. Annulments of marriage—divorce being prohibited—similarly came for a price. Most malodorous to many, however, was the sale of indulgences. In Catholic theology, an indulgence is a remission by papal authority of all or part of the temporal punishment due for sin—that is, of the punishment in this life and in purgatory—after the guilt of sin itself is absolved by sacramental confession. As we have seen, the practice of granting indulgences began at the end of the eleventh century as an incentive for encouraging men and women to become crusaders. Once it became accepted that the pope could dispense grace from a "Treasury of Merits" (that is, a storehouse of surplus good works piled up by Christ and the saints), it was taken for granted that the pope could promise people time off in purgatory as well. But indulgences originally granted for extraordinary deeds gradually came to be sold for money; by the fourteenth century, popes started granting indulgences to raise money for

> By the fourteenth century, popes started granting indulgences to raise money for any worthy cause whatsoever.

any worthy cause whatsoever, such as the building of cathedrals or hospitals; and finally, in 1476 Pope Sixtus IV (the patron of the Sistine Chapel) took the extreme step of declaring that the benefits of indulgences could be extended to the dead already in purgatory as well as to the living. Money, then, could not only save an individual from works of penance but could save his dearest relatives from eons of agonizing torments after death.

Certainly Luther was horrified by the traffic in relics and the sale of indulgences; indeed, the latter provided the immediate grounds for his revolt against Rome. But it was less the abuses of the late medieval Church than it was medieval Catholic theology itself that Luther ultimately came to reject. To this degree the term "Lutheran Reformation" is misleading, for Luther was no mere "reformer" who wanted to cleanse the current religious system of its impurities. Many Christian humanists of Luther's day were reformers in just that sense, but they shrank from breaking with Rome because they had no objections to the basic principles of medieval Catholicism. Luther, on the other hand, would not have been satisfied with the mere abolition of abuses because it was the entire Catholic "religion of works" that appalled him.

Simply stated, Luther preferred a rigorously Augustinian system of theology to a medieval Thomistic one. As we have seen, around the year 400 Saint Augustine of Hippo had formulated an uncompromising doctrine of predestination, maintaining that God alone determined human salvation and that his decisions concerning whom to save and whom to damn were made from eternity, without any regard to merits that given humans might show while sojourning on earth. This extreme view, however, left so little room for human freedom and responsibility that it was modified greatly in the course of the Middle Ages. Above all, during the twelfth and thirteenth centuries theologians such as Peter Lombard and Saint Thomas Aquinas (hence the term "Thomistic") set forth an alternative belief system that rested on two assumptions: (1) since God's saving grace is not irresistible, humans can freely reject God's advances and encompass their own doom; and (2) since the sacramental ministrations of the church communicate ongoing grace, they help human sinners improve their chances of salvation. In Luther's opinion, however, all of this amounted to saying that humans could be saved by the performance of "good works," and it was

> It was less the abuses of the late medieval Church than it was medieval Catholic theology itself that Luther ultimately came to reject.

this theology of works that he became prepared to resist even unto death.

LUTHER'S QUEST FOR RELIGIOUS CERTAINTY

Martin Luther may ultimately have been a source of inspiration for millions, but at first he was a terrible disappointment to his father. The elder Luther, who had risen from Thuringian German peasant stock and gained prosperity by leasing some mines, wanted his son Martin to rise still further. The father therefore sent young Luther to the University of Erfurt to study law, but while there in 1505, Martin shattered his father's ambitions for him by instead becoming a monk of the Augustinian order. In some sense, however, Luther always remained faithful to his father's humble roots. Even after he became famous, Martin Luther always lived simply and expressed himself in the vigorous, earthy vernacular of the German peasantry.

Martin Luther. A portrait by Lucas Cranach.

Like many great figures in the history of religion, Luther arrived at what he conceived to be the truth by a dramatic conversion experience. As a monk, young Martin zealously pursued all the traditional means for achieving his own salvation. Not only did he fast and pray continuously, but he confessed so often that his exhausted confessor would sometimes jokingly say that his sins were actually trifling and that if he really wanted to have a rousing confession he should go out and do something dramatic like committing adultery. Yet, try as he might, Luther could find no spiritual peace because he feared that he could never perform enough good deeds to deserve so great a gift as salvation. But in 1513 he hit upon an insight that granted him relief and changed the course of his life.

Luther's guiding insight pertained to the problem of the justice of God. For years he had worried that God seemed unjust in issuing commandments that he knew human beings could not observe and then in punishing them with eternal damnation for not observing them. But after becoming a professor of biblical theology at the University of Wittenberg (many members of his monastic order were expected to teach), Luther was led by the Bible to a new understanding of the problem. Specifically, while meditating on the words in the Psalms "deliver me in thy justice," it suddenly struck him that God's justice had nothing to do with his disciplinary power but rather with his mercy in saving sinful mortals through faith. As Luther later wrote, "At last, by the mercy of God, I began to understand the justice of God as that by which God makes us just in his mercy and through faith . . . and at this I felt as though I had been born again, and had gone through open gates into paradise." Since the fateful moment of truth came to Luther in the tower room of his monastery, it is customarily called his "tower experience."

After that, everything seemed to fall into place. Lecturing on the Pauline Epistles in Wittenberg in the years immediately following 1513, Luther dwelled on the text of Saint Paul to the Romans (1:17): "the just shall live by faith" to reach his central doctrine of "justification by faith alone." By this he meant that God's justice does not demand endless good works and religious ceremonies, for no one can hope to be saved by his or her own works. Rather, humans are "justified"—that is, granted salvation—by God's saving grace alone, offered as an utterly unmerited gift to those predestined for salvation. Since this grace is manifested in

> Like many great figures in the history of religion, Luther arrived at what he conceived to be the truth by a dramatic conversion experience.

humans through the gift of faith, men and women are justified from the human perspective by faith alone. In Luther's view those who had faith would do good works anyway, but it was the faith that came first. Although the essence of this doctrine was not original but harked back to the predestinarianism of Saint Augustine, it was new for Luther and the early sixteenth century, and if followed to its conclusions could only mean the dismantling of much of the contemporary Catholic religious structure.

THE REFORMATION BEGINS

At first Luther remained merely an academic lecturer, teaching within the realm of theory, but in 1517 he was goaded into attacking some of the actual practices of the church by a provocation that was too much for him to bear. The story of the indulgence campaign of 1517 in Germany is colorful but unsavory. The worldly Albert of Hohenzollern, youngest brother of the elector of Brandenburg, had sunk himself into enormous debt for several discreditable reasons. In 1513 he had to pay large sums for gaining dispensations from the papacy to hold the bishoprics of Magdeburg and Halberstadt concurrently, and for assuming these offices even though at twenty-three he was not old enough to be a bishop at all. Not satisfied, when the see of Mainz fell vacant in the next year, Albert gained election to that too, even though he knew full well that the costs of becoming archbishop of Mainz meant still larger payments to Rome. Obtaining the necessary funds by loans from the German banking firm of the Fuggers, he then struck a bargain with Pope Leo X (1513–1521): Leo proclaimed an indulgence in Albert's ecclesiastical territories on the understanding that half of the income raised would go to Rome for the building of St. Peter's Basilica, with the other half going to Albert so that he could repay the Fuggers. Luther did not know the sordid details of Albert's bargain, but he did know that a Dominican friar named Tetzel soon was hawking indulgences throughout much of northern Germany with Fugger banking agents in his train, and that Tetzel was deliberately giving people the impression that the purchase of an indulgence regardless of contrition in penance was an immediate ticket to heaven for oneself and one's dear departed in purgatory. For Luther this was more than enough because Tetzel's advertising campaign flagrantly violated his own conviction that people are saved by faith, not works. So on October 31, 1517, the earnest theologian offered to his university colleagues a list of ninety-five theses objecting to Catholic indulgence doctrine, an act by which the Protestant Reformation is conventionally thought to have begun.

In circulating his theses within the University of Wittenberg, Luther by no means intended to bring his criticism of Tetzel to the public. Quite to the contrary, he wrote his objections in Latin, not German, and meant them only for academic dispute. But some unknown person translated and published Luther's theses, an event that immediately gained the hitherto obscure monk wide notoriety. Since Tetzel and his allies outside the university did not mean to let the matter rest, Luther was called upon to withdraw his theses or defend himself. At that point, far from backing down, he became ever bolder in his attacks on the government of the church. In 1519 in public disputation before throngs in Leipzig, Luther defiantly maintained that the pope and all clerics were merely fallible men and that the highest authority for an individual's conscience was the truth of Scripture. Thereupon Pope Leo X responded by charging the monk with heresy, and after that Luther had no alternative but to break with the Catholic faith entirely.

Luther's year of greatest creative activity came in 1520 when, in the midst of the crisis caused by his defiance, he composed three seminal pamphlets formulating the outlines of what was soon to become the new Lutheran religion. In these writings he put forth his three theological premises: justification by faith, the primacy of Scripture, and "the priesthood of all believers." We have already examined the meaning of the first. By the second he simply meant that the literal meaning of Scripture was always to be preferred to the accretions of tradition, and that all beliefs (such as purgatory) or practices (such as prayers to saints) not explicitly grounded in Scripture were to be rejected. As for "the priesthood of all believers," that meant that the true spiritual estate was the congregation of all the faithful rather than a society of ordained priests.

> Luther's year of greatest creative activity came in 1520 when he put forth his three theological premises of justification by faith, the primacy of Scripture, and "the priesthood of all believers."

From these premises a host of practical consequences followed. Since works themselves had no intrinsic value for salvation, Luther discarded such formalized practices as fasts, pilgrimages, and the veneration of relics. He also called for the dissolution of monasteries and convents. Far more fundamentally, he recognized only baptism and the Eucharist as sacraments (in 1520 he also included penance, but he later changed his mind on this), denying that even these had any supernatural effect in bringing down grace from heaven. For Luther, Christ was really present in the consecrated elements of the Lord's Supper, but there was no grace in the sacrament as such; rather, faith was essential to render the Eucharist effective as a means for aiding the believer along the road to eternal life. To make the meaning of the ceremony clear to all, Luther proposed the substitution of German for Latin in church services, and, to emphasize that those who presided in churches had no supernatural authority, he insisted on calling them merely ministers or pastors rather than priests. On the same grounds there was to be no ecclesiastical hierarchy since neither the pope nor anyone else was a custodian of the keys to heaven, and monasticism was to be abolished since it served no purpose whatsoever. Finally, firm in the belief that no

Pope Leo X. Raphael's highly realistic portrait shows the pope with two of his nephews.

enced different people to rally behind Luther, but the uproar in Germany on Luther's behalf was above all a national religious revolt against Rome.

Ever since the High Middle Ages many people throughout Europe had resented the centralization of church government because it meant the interference of a foreign papacy in local ecclesiastical affairs and the siphoning off of large sums of money to the papal court. But certain concrete circumstances made Germany in the early sixteenth century particularly ripe for religious revolt. Perhaps greatest among these was the fact that the papacy of that time had clearly lost the slightest hint of apostolic calling but was demanding as much, if not more, money from German coffers as before. Although great patrons of the arts, successive popes of Luther's day were worldly scoundrels or sybarites. As Luther was growing up, the Borgia pope, Alexander VI (1492–1503), bribed the cardinals to gain the papacy, used the money raised from the jubilee of 1500 to support the military campaigns of his son Cesare, and was so lascivious in office that he was suspected of seeking the sexual favors of his own daughter Lucrezia. Alexander's scandals could hardly have been outdone, but his successor, Julius II (1503–1513), was interested only in enlarging the papal states by military means (a contemporary remarked that he would have gained the greatest glory had he been a secular prince), and Leo X, the pope obliged to deal with Luther's defiance, was a self-indulgent esthete who, in the words of a modern Catholic historian, "would not have been deemed fit to be a doorkeeper in the house of the Lord had he lived in the days of the apostles." Under such circumstances it was bad enough for Germans to know that fees sent to Rome were being used to finance papal politics and the upkeep of luxurious courts, but worse still to pay money in the realization that Germany had no influence in Italian papal affairs, for Germans, unlike the French or Spaniards, were seldom represented in the College of Cardinals and practically never gained employment in the papal bureaucracy.

In this overheated atmosphere, reformist criticisms voiced by both traditional clerical moralists and the new breed of Christian humanists exacerbated resentments. Ever since about 1400 prominent German critics of the papacy had been saying that the entire church needed to be reformed "in head and members," and as the fifteenth century progressed, anonymous prophecies mounted to the effect, for example, that a future heroic emperor would reform the church by removing the papacy from Rome to the Rhineland. Then in the early years of the sixteenth century, Christian human-

Luther and his wife, Katherine von Bora. Portraits done by Cranach for the couple's wedding in 1525.

sacramental distinction existed between clergy and laity, Luther argued that ministers could marry, and in 1525 he took a wife himself.

THE BREAK WITH ROME

Widely disseminated by means of the printing press, Luther's pamphlets of 1520 electrified much of Germany, gaining him broad and enthusiastic popular support. Because this response played a crucial role in determining the future success of the Lutheran movement—emboldening Luther to persevere in his defiance of Rome and soon encouraging some ruling princes to convert to Lutheranism themselves—it is appropriate before continuing to inquire into its causes. Of course, different combinations of motives influ-

Two specimens of Lutheran visual propaganda concerning "true" and "false" spiritual insight. Left: **Luther with Dove and Halo.** While Luther was still a monk (before the end of 1522), the artist Hans Baldung Grien portrayed him as a saint whose insight into Scripture was sent by the Holy Spirit in the form of a dove. Right: **The Pope as a Donkey Playing Bagpipes.** This 1545 woodcut depicts Luther's view that "the pope can interpret Holy Scripture just as well as he can play the bagpipes."

ists began to chime in with their own brand of satirical propaganda. Most eloquent of these humanists, of course, was Erasmus, who lampooned the religious abuses of his day with no mercy for Rome. Thus in *The Praise of Folly*, first published in 1511 and frequently reprinted, Erasmus stated that if popes were ever forced to lead Christlike lives, no one would be more disconsolate than themselves, and in his more daring pamphlet called *Julius Excluded*, published anonymously in Basel in 1517, the clever satirist imagined a dialogue held before the pearly gates in which Pope Julius II was locked out of heaven by Saint Peter because the saint refused to believe that the armored, vainglorious figure who stood before him could possibly be his successor.

In addition to the objective reality of a corrupt Rome and the circulation of anti-Roman propaganda, a final factor that made Germany ready for revolt in Luther's time was the belated growth of universities.

All revolts need to have some general headquarters; universities were the most natural centers for late medieval religious revolts because assembled there were groups of enthusiastic, educated young people accustomed to working together, who could formulate doctrinal positions with assurance, and who could turn out militant manifestos at a moment's notice. There had hardly been any universities on German soil until a spate of new foundations between 1450 and 1517 provided many spawning grounds for cultural nationalism and religious resistance to Rome. Luther's own University of Wittenberg was founded as late as 1502, but soon enough it became the cradle of the Lutheran Reformation, offering immediate support to its embattled hero.

Still, of course, there would have been no Lutheran Reformation without Luther himself, and the daring monk did the most to enflame Germany's dry kindling

Pope Alexander VI: "Appearance and Reality." Even before Luther initiated the German Reformation, anonymous critics of the dissolute Alexander VI surreptitiously spread propaganda showing him to be a devil. By lifting a flap one can see Alexander transformed into a monster who proclaims "I am the pope."

of resentment in his pamphlets of 1520, above all in one entitled *To the Christian Nobility of the German Nation.* Here, in highly intemperate colloquial German, Luther stated that "if the pope's court were reduced ninety-nine percent it would still be large enough to give decisions on matters of faith"; that "the cardinals have sucked Italy dry and now turn to Germany"; and that, given Rome's corruption, "the reign of Antichrist could not be worse." Needless to say, once this savage indictment was lodged, everyone wanted to read it. Whereas the average press run of a printed book before 1520 had been one thousand copies, the first run of *To the Christian Nobility* was four thousand, and these copies were sold out in a few days, with many more thousands following.

THE DIET OF WORMS

Meanwhile, even as Luther's pamphlets were selling so rapidly, his personal drama riveted all onlookers. Late in 1520 the German rebel responded to Pope Leo X's edict ordering his recantation by casting not only the bull but all of church law as well onto a roaring bonfire in front of a huge crowd. With the lines so drawn,

events moved with great swiftness. Since in the eyes of the church Luther was now a stubborn heretic, he was formally "released" to his lay overlord, the elector Frederick the Wise, for proper punishment. Normally this would have meant certain death at the stake, but in this case Frederick was loath to silence the pope's antagonist. Instead, claiming that Luther had not yet received a fair hearing, he brought him early in 1521 to be examined by a "diet" (that is, a formal assembly) of the princes of the Holy Roman empire convening in the city of Worms.

At Worms the initiative lay with the presiding officer, the newly elected Holy Roman emperor, Charles V. Charles was not a German; rather, as a member of the Habsburg family by his paternal descent, he had been born and bred in his ancestral holding of the Netherlands. Since he additionally held Austria, and as grandson of Ferdinand and Isabella by his maternal descent, all of Spain, including extensive Spanish possessions in Italy and America, the emperor had primarily international rather than national interests and surely thought of Catholicism as a sort of glue necessary to hold together all his far-flung territories. Thus from the start Charles had no sympathy for Luther, and

HUMANISM, NATIONALISM, AND THE GERMAN UNIVERSITIES

Conrad Celtis (1459–1508) mastered a humanist curriculum in Italy, then returned to Germany to push forward this new approach to learning in his native land. This oration, delivered in Latin to the faculty of the University of Ingolstadt in 1492, exemplifies the way in which humanism, despite its Italian origins, could fuel anti-Italian feelings of nationalism in German universities.

But I now direct my speech to you, distinguished men and well-born youths, to whom by virtue of the courage of your ancestors and the unconquerable strength of Germany the Italian empire has passed. . . . I urge you to direct your studies to those things first and foremost which will ripen and improve the mind and call you away from the habits of the common herd to devote yourselves to higher pursuits. Keep before your eyes true nobility of spirit, considering that you bring not honor but dishonor to our empire if you neglect the study of literature only to rear horses and dogs and pursue ecclesiastical preferment. . . .

Emulate, noble men, the ancient nobility of Rome, which, after taking over the empire of the Greeks assimilated all their wisdom and eloquence. . . . In the same way you who have taken over the empire of the Italians should cast off repulsive barbarism and seek to acquire Roman culture. Do away with that old disrepute of the Germans in Greek, Latin and Hebrew writers, who ascribe to us drunkenness, cruelty, savagery and every other vice bordering on bestiality and excess. . . .

Assume, O men of Germany, that ancient spirit of yours, with which you so often confounded and terrified the Romans, and turn your eyes to the frontiers of Germany; collect together her torn and broken territories. Let us be ashamed, ashamed I say, to have placed upon our nation the yoke of slavery, and to be paying tributes and taxes to foreign and barbarian kings. O free and powerful people, O noble and valiant race, plainly worthy of the Roman empire, our famous harbor is held by the Pole and the gateway of our ocean by the Dane! In the east also powerful peoples live in slavery, the Bohemians, the Moravians, the Slovaks and the Silesians, who all live as it were separated from the body of our Germany. And I may add the Transylvanian Saxons who also use our racial culture and speak our native language. . . .

But from the south we are oppressed by a sort of distinguished slavery, and under the impulse of greed . . . new commercial ventures are continually established by which our country is drained of its wonderful natural wealth while we pay to others what we need for ourselves. So persistent is fortune or destiny in persecuting and wiping out the Germans, the last survivors of the Roman empire. . . . To such an extent are we corrupted by Italian sensuality and by fierce cruelty in exacting filthy lucre. . . .

And I will assign no other cause for the ever-flourishing condition of Italy than the fact that her people surpass us in no blessing other than the love of literature and its cultivation. By this they overawe other nations as if by force of arms, and win their admiration for their genius and industry. . . .

Leonard Forster, ed. *Selections from Conrad Celtis.* (Cambridge: Cambridge University Press, 1948), pp. 43–47, 53.

The Emperor Charles V. Two views by the Venetian painter Titian depict the emperor in a grandiose military pose, and as a sage ruler.

since Luther fearlessly refused to back down before the emperor, declaring instead "Here I stand," it soon became clear that Luther would be condemned by the power of state as well as by the church. But just then Frederick the Wise once more intervened, this time by arranging a "kidnapping" whereby Luther was spirited off to the elector's castle of the Wartburg and kept out of harm's way for a year.

Thereafter Luther was never again to be in danger of his life. Although the Diet of Worms did issue an edict shortly after his disappearance proclaiming him an outlaw, the Edict of Worms was never properly enforced because, with Luther in hiding, Charles V soon left Germany to conduct a war with France. In 1522 Luther returned in triumph from the Wartburg to Wittenberg to find that all the changes in ecclesiastical government and ceremonial he had called for had spontaneously been put into practice by his university cohorts. Then, in rapid succession, several German

princes formally converted to Lutheranism, bringing their territories with them. Thus by around 1530 a considerable part of Germany had been brought over to the new faith.

THE GERMAN PRINCES AND THE LUTHERAN REFORMATION

At this point the last of the three major questions regarding the early history of Lutheranism arises: why did German princes, secure in their own powers, heed Luther's call by establishing Lutheran religious practices within their territories? We should by no means underestimate the importance of this question, because no matter how much intense admiration Luther may have gained from the German populace, his cause surely would have failed had it not been for the decisive intervention and support of constituted political authorities. There had been heretics aplenty in Europe before, but most of them had died at the stake, as Luther would have without the intervention of Frederick the Wise. And even if Luther had not been executed, spontaneous popular expressions of support alone would not have succeeded in instituting Lutheranism because they could easily have been put down by the power of the state. In fact, although in the early years of Luther's revolt he was more or less equally popular throughout Germany, only in those territories where rulers formally established Lutheranism (mostly in the north) did the new religion prevail, whereas in the others Luther's sympathizers were forced to flee, face death, or conform to Catholicism. In short, the word of the prince in religious matters was law.

The distinction between populace and princes should not obscure the fact that the motivations of both for turning to Lutheranism were similar, with the emphasis on the princely side being the search for sovereignty. As little as common people liked the idea

of money being pumped off to Rome, princes liked it less: German princes assembled at the Diet of Augsburg in 1500, for example, went so far as to demand the return of some of the ecclesiastical dues sent to Rome on the grounds that Germany was being drained of its coin. Since such demands fell on deaf ears, many princes were quick to perceive that if they adopted Lutheranism, they would not have to send ecclesiastical dues to support unloved foreigners, and much of the savings would directly or indirectly wind up in their own treasuries.

Yet the matter of taxation was only part of the larger issue of the search for absolute governmental sovereignty. Throughout Europe the major political trend in the years around 1500 was toward making the state dominant in all areas of life, religious as well as secular. Hence rulers sought to control the appointments of church officials in their own realms and to limit or curtail the independent jurisdictions of church courts. Because the papacy in this period had to fight off the attacks of internal clerical critics who wanted recogni-

The Seven-Headed Papal Beast. Around 1530 a Lutheran cartoon was circulated in Germany that turned the papacy into the "seven-headed beast" of the Book of Revelation. The papacy's "seven heads" consist of pope, cardinals, bishops, and priests; the sign on the cross reads "for money, a sack full of indulgences"; and a devil is seen emerging from an indulgence treasure chest below.

The Seven-Headed Martin Luther. In response, a German Catholic propagandist showed Luther as Revelation's "beast." In the Catholic conception Luther's seven heads show him by turn to be a hypocrite, a fanatic, and "Barabbas"—the thief who should have been crucified instead of Jesus.

tion of the "conciliarist" principle that general councils of prelates rather than popes should rule the church (see Chapter 11), many popes found it advantageous to sign concordats with the most powerful rulers in the West—primarily the kings of France and Spain—whereby they granted the rulers much of the sovereignty they wanted in return for support against conciliarism. Thus in 1482 Sixtus IV conceded to the Spanish monarchs Ferdinand and Isabella the right to name candidates for all major church offices. In 1487 Innocent VIII consented to the establishment of a Spanish Inquisition controlled by the crown, giving the rulers extraordinary powers in dictating religious policies. And in 1516, by the Concordat of Bologna, Leo X granted the choice of bishops and abbots in France to the French king, Francis I, in return for Francis's support against the conciliarists who had gathered at the Fifth Lateran Council (1512–1517). In Germany, however, primarily because there was no political unity, princes were not strong enough to gain such concessions. Hence what they could not achieve by concordats some decided to wrest by force.

In this determination they were fully abetted by Luther. Certainly as early as 1520 the fiery reformer recognized that he could never hope to institute new religious practices without the strong arm of the princes behind him, so he implicitly encouraged them to expropriate the wealth of the Catholic Church as an incentive for creating a new order. At first the princes bided their time, but when they realized that Luther had enormous public support and that Charles V would not act swiftly to defend the Catholic faith, several moved to introduce Lutheranism into their territories. Motives of personal piety surely played a role in individual cases, but political and economic considerations were more generally decisive. By instituting Lutheranism within their territories, Protestant princes could consolidate their authority by naming pastors, cutting off fees to Rome and curtailing the jurisdiction of church courts. They could also guarantee that the political and religious boundaries of their territories would now coincide. No longer, therefore, would an ecclesiastical prince be able to use his position as a bishop to undermine a rival secular prince's sovereignty over his territory. Given the added fact that under Lutheranism monasteries could be shut down and their wealth simply pocketed by the princes, the practical advantages of establishing the new faith were overwhelming, quite apart from any considerations of religious zeal.

Once safely ensconced in Wittenberg as the protégé of princes, Luther began to express ever more vehemently his own profound conservatism in political and social matters. In a treatise of 1523, *On Temporal Authority*, he insisted that "godly" rulers must be obeyed in all things and that even ungodly ones should never be actively resisted, since tyranny "is not to be resisted but endured." Then, in 1525, when peasants throughout Germany rose up in economic revolt against their landlords—in some places encouraged by the religious radical Thomas Müntzer (c. 1490–1525), who urged the use of fire and sword against "ungodly" powers—Luther responded with intense hostility. In his vituperative pamphlet of 1525, *Against the Thievish, Murderous Hordes of Peasants*, he went so far as to urge all who could to hunt the rebels down like mad dogs, to "strike, strangle, stab secretly or in public, and remember that nothing can be more poisonous than a man in rebellion." Once the princes had ruthlessly put down the Peasants' Revolt of 1525, the firm alliance of Lutheranism with the powers of the state helped ensure social peace. In fact, after the bloody punishment of the peasant rebels there would never again be a mass lower-class uprising in Germany.

As for Luther himself, he concentrated in his last years on debating with younger, more radical religious reformers and on offering spiritual counsel to all who sought it. Never tiring in his amazingly prolific literary activity, he wrote an average of one treatise every two weeks for twenty-five years. To the end Luther was unswerving in his new faith: on his deathbed in 1546 he responded to the question "Will you stand firm in Christ and the doctrine which you have preached?" with a resolute "Yes."

THE SPREAD OF PROTESTANTISM

How did the teachings of Calvin and Luther differ?

Originating as a term applied to Lutherans who "protested" an action of the German Imperial Diet of 1529, the word "Protestant" has come to mean any non-Catholic, non–Eastern Orthodox Christian. In fact, it was soon applied to non-Lutherans after 1529 because the particular form of Protestantism that Luther developed did not prove to be popular much beyond its na-

CHRONOLOGY

ORIGINS OF THE REFORMATION, 1450–1529

Christian humanists call for reforms	fifteenth–sixteenth centuries
Growth of German Universities	1450–1517
Luther posts the Ninety-Five Theses	1517
Luther charged with heresy	1519
Publication of Lutheran theological premises	1520
Diet of Worms declares Luther an outlaw	1521
Peasant Revolt defeated	1525
Luther's break with Zwingli	1529

tive environment of Germany. To be sure, Lutheranism was instituted as the state religion of Denmark, Norway, and Sweden by official decrees of rulers made during the 1520s, and remains the religion of most Scandinavians today. But elsewhere early Protestantism spread in different forms. In England a break with Rome was introduced from above, just as in Germany and Scandinavia, but since Lutheranism appeared too radical for the reigning English monarch, a compromise variety of religious belief and practice, subsequently known as Anglicanism (in America, Episcopalianism), was worked out. At the other extreme, Protestantism spread more spontaneously in several cities of Switzerland where it took on forms that were more radical than Lutheranism.

THE ENGLISH REFORMATION

Although the original blow against the Roman Church in England was struck by the head of the government, King Henry VIII (1509–1547), in breaking with Rome the English monarch had the support of most of his subjects. For this there were at least three reasons. First, in England, as in Germany, many people in the early sixteenth century had come to resent Rome's corruption and the siphoning off of the country's wealth to pay for the worldly pursuits of foreign popes. Second, England had already been the scene of protests against religious abuses voiced by John Wyclif's heretical followers, known as Lollards. The Lollards had indeed been driven underground in the course of the fifteenth century, but numbers of them survived in pockets throughout England, where they

promulgated their anticlerical ideas whenever they could. The Lollards enthusiastically welcomed Henry VIII's revolt from Rome when it occurred. Finally, soon after the outbreak of the Reformation in Germany, Lutheran ideas were brought into England by travelers and by the circulation of printed tracts. As early as 1520 a Lutheran group was meeting at the University of Cambridge, and Lutheranism began to gain more and more clandestine strength as the decade progressed.

HENRY VIII AND THE BREAK WITH ROME

Despite all this, England would not have broken with Rome had Henry VIII not commanded it because of his marital difficulties. By 1527 the imperious Henry had been married for eighteen years to Ferdinand and Isabella's daughter, Catherine of Aragon, yet all the offspring of this union had died in infancy, save only Princess Mary. Since Henry needed a male heir to preserve the succession of his Tudor dynasty, and since Catherine was now past childbearing age, Henry had good reasons of state to break his marriage bonds, and in 1527 an immediate incentive arose when he became

Henry VIII, by Hans Holbein the Younger.

infatuated with the dark-eyed lady-in-waiting Anne Boleyn, who would not give in to his advances out of wedlock. The king hence appealed to Rome to allow the severance of his marriage to Catherine so that he could make Anne his queen. Although the law of the Church did not sanction divorce, it did provide that a marriage might be annulled if proof could be given that conditions existing at the time of the wedding had made it unlawful. Accordingly, the king's representatives, recalling that Queen Catherine had previously been married to Henry's older brother, who had died shortly after the ceremony was performed, rested their case on a passage from the Bible that pronounced it "an unclean thing" for a man to take his brother's wife and cursed such a marriage with childlessness (Leviticus 20:31).

Henry's suit put the reigning pope, Clement VII (1523–1534), in a quandary. If he rejected the king's appeal, England would probably be lost to Catholicism, for Henry was indeed firmly convinced that the scriptural curse had blighted his chances of perpetuating his dynasty. On the other hand, if the pope granted the annulment he would provoke the wrath of the Emperor Charles V, Catherine of Aragon's nephew, for Charles was then on a military campaign in Italy and threatening the pope with a loss of his temporal power. There seemed nothing for Clement to do but procrastinate. At first he made a pretense of having the question settled in England, empowering his officials to hold a court of inquiry to determine whether the marriage to Catherine had been legal. Then, after a long delay, he suddenly transferred the case to Rome. Meanwhile Henry had lost patience and resolved to take matters into his own hands. In 1531 the king obliged an assembly of English clergy to recognize him as "the supreme head" of the English Church. Next he induced Parliament to enact a series of laws abolishing all payments to Rome and proclaiming the English church an independent, national unit, subject only to royal authority. With the passage of the parliamentary Act of Supremacy (1534), declaring "the King's highness to be supreme head of the Church of England [having] the authority to redress all errors, heresies, and abuses," the last bonds uniting the English church to Rome had been cut.

Yet these enactments did not yet make England a Protestant country. Quite to the contrary, although the break with Rome was followed by the dissolution of all of England's monasteries, with their lands and wealth being sold to many of the king's loyal supporters, the system of church government by bishops (episco-

palianism) was retained, and the English church remained Catholic in doctrine. The Six Articles promulgated by Parliament in 1539 at Henry VIII's behest left no room for doubt as to official orthodoxy: oral confession to priests, masses for the dead, and clerical celibacy were all confirmed; moreover, the Catholic doctrine of the Eucharist was not only confirmed but its denial was made punishable by death.

EDWARD VI

Nonetheless, the influence of Protestantism in England was growing, and during the reign of Henry's son, Edward VI (1547–1553), Protestantism gained the ascendancy. Since the new king (born from Henry's union with his third wife, Jane Seymour) was only nine years old when he inherited the crown, the religious policies of his government were dictated by Thomas Cranmer, archbishop of Canterbury, and the dukes of Somerset and Northumberland, who dominated the regency government. Inasmuch as all three of these men had strong Protestant leanings (as too did the young king himself), the creeds and ceremonies of the Church of England were soon drastically altered. Priests were permitted to marry; English was substituted for Latin in the services; the veneration of images was abolished; and new articles of belief were drawn up repudiating all sacraments except baptism and communion and affirming the Lutheran doctrine of justification by faith alone. Thus when the youthful Edward died in 1553 it seemed as if England had definitely entered the Protestant camp.

MARY TUDOR AND THE RESTORATION OF CATHOLICISM

But Edward's pious Catholic successor, Mary (1553–1558), Henry VIII's daughter by Catherine of Aragon, thought otherwise. Mary associated the revolt against Rome with her mother's humiliations and her own removal from direct succession. On coming to the throne she attempted to return England to Catholicism. Not only did she restore the celebration of the mass and the rule of clerical celibacy, but she prevailed on Parliament to vote a return to papal allegiance.

Yet Mary's policies ended in failure for several reasons. Many of the leading families that had profited from Henry VIII's dissolution of the monasteries had become particularly committed to Protestantism because a restoration of Catholic monasticism would have meant the loss of their newly acquired wealth.

THE SIX ARTICLES

Although Henry VIII withdrew the Church of England from obedience to the papacy, he continued to lean more toward Catholic than Protestant theology. Some of his advisors, most notably Thomas Cromwell, were committed Protestants; and the king allowed his son and heir, Edward VI, to be raised as a Protestant. But after several years of rapid (and mostly Protestant) change in the English church, in 1539 the king reasserted a set of traditional Catholic doctrines in the Six Articles. These would remain binding on the Church of England until the king's death in 1547.

First, that in the most blessed sacrament of the altar, by the strength and efficacy of Christ's mighty word, it being spoken by the priest, is present really, under the form of bread and wine, the natural body and blood of our Savior Jesus Christ, conceived of the Virgin Mary, and that after the consecration there remains no substance of bread or wine, nor any other substance but the substance of Christ, God and man;

Secondly, that communion in both kinds is not necessary for salvation, by the law of God, to all persons, and that it is to be believed and not doubted . . . that in the flesh, under the form of bread, is the very blood, and with the blood, under the form of wine, is the very flesh, as well apart as though they were both together;

Thirdly, that priests, after the order of priesthood received as afore, may not marry by the law of God;

Fourthly, that vows of chastity or widowhood by man or woman made to God advisedly ought to be observed by the law of God. . . .

Fifthly, that it is right and necessary that private masses be continued and admitted in this the king's English Church and congregation . . . whereby good Christian people . . . do receive both godly and goodly consolations and benefits; and it is agreeable also to God's law;

Sixthly, that oral, private confession is expedient and necessary to be retained and continued, used and frequented in the church of God. . . .

Statutes of the Realm, Vol. 3 (London: Her Majesty's Stationery Office, 1810–1828), p. 739, modernized.

Mary also erred by ordering the burning of Cranmer and a few hundred Protestant extremists. These executions were insufficient to wipe out religious resistance—instead, Protestant propaganda about "Bloody Mary" and the "fires of Smithfield" hardened resistance to Mary's rule, making her seem like a vengeful persecutor. But perhaps the most serious cause of Mary's failure was her marriage to Philip, Charles V's son and heir to the Spanish throne. Although the marriage treaty stipulated that in the event of Mary's death Philip could not succeed her, patriotic Englanders never trusted him. Hence when the queen allowed herself to be drawn by Philip into a war with France on Spain's behalf, in which England lost Calais, its last foothold on the European continent, many English people became highly disaffected. No one knows what might have happened next because death soon after ended Mary's troubled reign.

L. Receiue my spirit.

Friar John.

The Burning of Archbishop Cranmer. In this Protestant conception an ugly Catholic, "Friar John," directs the proceedings, while the martyred Cranmer repeats Christ's words, "Lord, receive my spirit." John Foxe's *Book of Martyrs* (1563), in which this engraving first appeared, was an extraordinarily successful piece of English Protestant propaganda.

THE ELIZABETHAN COMPROMISE

The question of whether England was to be Catholic or Protestant was thereupon settled definitively in favor of Protestantism by Elizabeth I (1558–1603). Daughter of Anne Boleyn and one of the most capable and popular monarchs ever to sit on the English throne, Elizabeth was predisposed in favor of Protestantism by the circumstances of her parents' marriage as well as by her upbringing. But Elizabeth was no zealot, and wisely recognized that supporting radical Protestantism in England posed the danger of provoking bitter sectarian strife. Accordingly, she presided over what is customarily known as "the Elizabethan compromise." By a new Act of Supremacy (1559), Elizabeth repealed all of Mary's Catholic legislation, prohibited the exercise of any authority by foreign religious powers, and made herself "supreme governor" of the English church—a more Protestant title than Henry VIII's "supreme head" insofar as most Protestants be-

> As a result of the Elizabethan compromise, the Church of England today is broad enough to include such diverse elements as the "Anglo-Catholics" and the "low-church" Anglicans.

lieved that Christ alone was the head of the Church. At the same time she accepted most of the Protestant ceremonial reforms instituted during the reign of her brother Edward. On the other hand, she retained church government by bishops and left the definitions of some controversial articles of the faith, especially the meaning of the Eucharist, vague enough so that all but the most extreme Catholics and Protestants could accept them. Long after Elizabeth's death this settlement remained in effect. Indeed, as a result of the Elizabethan compromise, the Church of England today is broad enough to include such diverse elements as the "Anglo-Catholics," who differ from Roman Catholics only in rejecting papal supremacy, and the "low-church" Anglicans, who are as thoroughgoing in their Protestant practices as members of most other modern Protestant denominations.

THE REFORMATION IN SWITZERLAND

If the Elizabethan compromise came about through royal decision making, in Switzerland more spontaneous movements to establish Protestantism resulted in the victory of greater radicalism. In the early sixteenth century Switzerland was neither ruled by kings nor dominated by all-powerful territorial princes; instead, prosperous Swiss cities were either independent or on the verge of becoming so. Hence when the leading citizens of a Swiss municipality decided to adopt Protestant reforms no one could stop them, and Protestantism in Switzerland could usually take its own course. Although religious arrangements tended at first to vary in detail from city to city, the three main forms of Protestantism that emerged in Switzerland from about 1520 to 1550 were Zwing-

RELIGIOUS SITUATION IN EUROPE, C. 1560

This map shows the complicated religious boundaries of Europe in the generation after the protest begun by Martin Luther. Why did the Lutheran movement take such strong hold in Germany and Scandinavia? What political as well as spiritual factors played a role in the success of religious uprising there? What were the central beliefs of John Calvin and similarly inspired religious movements? Why did this movement enjoy the influence it did in Switzerland, Scotland, and along the river valleys of central France? What consequences were there for the Calvinists (Huguenots) in France under a regime that remained Roman Catholic? What relationships can you discern among religious movements and national identities in this map?

lianism, Anabaptism, and, most fateful for Europe's future, Calvinism.

ULRICH ZWINGLI

Zwinglianism, founded by Ulrich Zwingli (1484–1531) in Zürich, was the most moderate form of the three. Although Zwingli was at first a somewhat indifferent Catholic priest, around 1516 he was led by close study of the Bible to conclude that contemporary Catholic theology and religious observances conflicted with the Gospels. But he did not speak out until Luther set the precedent. In 1522, Zwingli started attacking the authority of the Catholic Church in Zürich, and soon all Zürich and much of northern Switzerland had accepted his leadership in instituting reforms that closely resembled those of the Lutherans in Germany. Zwingli differed from Luther, however, concerning the theology of the Eucharist: whereas Luther believed in the real presence of Christ's body, for Zwingli Christ was present merely in spirit. Thus for him the sacrament conferred no grace at all and was to be retained merely as a memorial service. This fundamental disagreement prevented Lutherans and Zwinglians from uniting in a common Protestant front. Fighting independently, Zwingli fell in battle against Catholic forces in 1531, whereupon his successors in Zürich lost their leadership over Swiss Protestantism, and the Zwinglian movement was soon after absorbed by the far more radical Protestantism of John Calvin.

The name Anabaptism means "rebaptism," and stemmed from the Anabaptists' conviction that baptism should be administered only to adults.

ANABAPTISM

Before Calvinism prevailed, however, the phenomenon of Anabaptism briefly flared up in Switzerland and also Germany. The first Anabaptists were members of Zwingli's circle in Zürich, but they quickly broke with him around 1525 on the issues of infant baptism and their conception of an exclusive church of true believers. The name Anabaptism means "rebaptism," and stemmed from the Anabatists' conviction that baptism should be administered only to adults because infants have no understanding of the meaning of the service. Yet this was only one manifestation of the Anabaptists' main belief that men and women were not born into any church. Although Luther and Zwingli alike taught the "priesthood of all believers," they still insisted that everyone, believer or not, should attend services and be part of one and the same officially instituted religious community. But the Anabaptists were separatists, firm in the conviction that joining the true church should be the product of an individual's inspired decision. For them, one had to follow the guidance of one's own "inner light" in opting for church membership, and the rest of the world could go its own way. Since this was a hopelessly apolitical doctrine in an age when almost everyone assumed that church and state were inextricably connected, Anabaptism was bound to be anathema to the established powers, both Protestant and Catholic. Yet in its first few years the movement did gain numerous adherents in Switzerland and Germany, above all because it appealed to sincere religious piety in calling for extreme simplicity of worship, pacifism, and strict biblical morality.

Unhappily for the fortunes of Anabaptism, an unrepresentative group of Anabaptist extremists managed to gain control of the German city of Münster in 1534. These zealots combined sectarianism with millennarianism, or the belief that God wished to institute a completely new order of justice and spirituality throughout the world before the end of time. Determined to help God bring about this goal, the extremists attempted to turn Münster into a new Jerusalem. A former tailor named John of Leyden assumed the title of "King of the New Temple," proclaiming himself the successor of David. Under his leadership Anabaptist religious practices were made obligatory, private property was abolished, the sharing of goods was introduced, and even polygamy was instituted on the grounds of Old Testament precedents. Nonetheless, Münster succumbed to a siege by Catholic forces little more than a year after the Anabaptist takeover, and the new David, together with two of his lieutenants, was put to death by excruciating tortures. Given that Anabaptism had already been proscribed by many governments, this episode thoroughly discredited the movement, and its adherents were subjected to ruthless persecution throughout Germany, Switzerland, and wherever else they could be found. Among the few who survived were some who banded together in the Mennonite sect, named for its founder, the Dutchman Menno Simons (c. 1496–1561). This sect, dedicated to the pacifism and simple "religion of the heart" of original Anabaptism, has continued to exist until the present. Various An-

The Anabaptists' Cages, Then and Now. After the three Anabaptist leaders who had reigned in Münster for a year were executed in 1535, their corpses were prominently displayed in cages hung from a tower of the marketplace church. As can be seen from the photo on the right, the bones are now gone but the iron cages remain to this very day as a grisly reminder of the horrors of sixteenth-century religious strife.

abaptist tenets were also revived later by religious groups such as the Quakers and different Baptist and Pentecostal sects.

JOHN CALVIN

A year after events in Münster sealed the fate of Anabaptism, a twenty-six-year-old French Protestant named John Calvin (1509–1564), who had fled to the Swiss city of Basel to escape religious persecution, published the first version of his *Institutes of the Christian Religion*, a work that was soon to prove the most influential systematic formulation of Protestant theology ever written. Born in Noyon in northern France, Calvin originally had been trained for the law and around 1533 was studying the Greek and Latin classics while living off the income from a church benefice. But then, as he later wrote, while he was "obstinately devoted to the superstitions of Popery," a stroke of light made him feel that God was extricating him from "an abyss of filth," and he thereupon opted for becoming a Protestant theologian and propagandist. Though some of these details resemble the early career of Luther, there was one essential differ-

> Calvin's *Institutes of the Christian Religion* became the most theologically authoritative statement of basic Protestant beliefs.

ence: namely, whereas Luther was always a highly volatile personality, Calvin remained a cool legalist through and through. Thus, whereas Luther never wrote systematic theology but only responded to given problems as they arose or as the impulse struck him, Calvin resolved in his *Institutes* to set forth all the principles of Protestantism comprehensively, logically, and consistently. Accordingly, after several revisions and enlargements (the definitive edition appeared in 1559), Calvin's *Institutes of the Christian Religion* became the most theologically authoritative statement of basic Protestant beliefs and the nearest Protestant equivalent of Saint Thomas Aquinas's *Summa Theologica*.

The hallmark of Calvin's rigorous theology in the *Institutes* is that he started with the omnipotence of God and worked downward. For Calvin the entire universe is utterly dependent on the will of the Almighty, who created all things for his greater glory. Because of the original fall from grace, all human beings are sinners by nature, bound hand and foot to an evil inheritance they cannot escape. Nevertheless, the Lord for reasons of his own has predestined some for eternal salvation and damned all the rest to the torments of hell. Nothing that human

John Calvin. A recently discovered anonymous portrait.

Although Calvin always acknowledged a great theological debt to Luther, his religious teachings differed from those of the Wittenberg reformer in several essentials. First of all, Luther's attitude toward proper Christian conduct in the world was much more passive than Calvin's: for the former, the good Christian should merely endure the trials of this life in suffering, whereas for the latter the world was to be mastered in unceasing labor for God's sake. Second, Calvin's religion was more legalistic and more nearly an Old Testament faith than Luther's. This can be illustrated in the attitude of the two men toward Sabbath observance. Luther's conception of Sunday was similar to that which prevails among most Christians today. He insisted, of course, that his followers attend church, but he did not demand that during the remainder of the day they refrain from all pleasure or work. Calvin, on the other hand, revived the Jewish Sabbath with its strict taboos against anything faintly resembling worldliness. Finally, the two men differed explicitly on basic matters of church government and ritual. Although Luther broke with the Catholic system of a gradated ecclesiastical hierarchy, Lutheran district superintendents were not unlike bishops, and Luther also retained a good many features of Catholic worship such as altars and vestments (special clothing for the clergy). In contrast, Calvin rejected everything that smacked to him of "popery." Thus he argued for the elimination of all traces of the hierarchical system, instead having congregational election of ministers and assemblies of ministers and "elders" (laymen responsible for maintaining proper religious conduct among the faithful) governing the entire church. Further, he

beings may do can alter their fate; their souls are stamped with God's blessing or curse before they are born. But this does not mean, in Calvin's opinion, that Christians should be indifferent to their conduct on earth. If they are among the elect, God will implant in them the desire to live rightly. Upright conduct is a sign, though not an infallible one, that whoever practices it has been chosen to sit at the throne of glory. Public profession of faith and participation in the services of the reformed church are also presumptive signs of election to be saved. But most of all, Calvin required an active life of piety and morality as a solemn obligation for members of the Christian commonwealth. For him, good Christians should conceive of themselves as chosen instruments of God with a mission to help in the fulfillment of his purposes on earth, striving not for their souls' salvation but for the glory of God. In other words, Calvin clearly did not encourage his readers to sit with folded hands, serene in the knowledge that their fate was sealed.

Services in a Calvinist Church. "Four bare walls and a sermon."

insisted on the barest simplicity in church services, prohibiting all ritual, vestments, instrumental music, images, and stained-glass windows. When these teachings were put into practice, Calvinist services became little more than "four bare walls and a sermon."

CALVINISM IN GENEVA

Not content with mere theory, Calvin was intent upon putting his teachings into practice. Sensing an opportunity to influence the course of events in the French-speaking Swiss city of Geneva, then in the throes of combined political and religious upheaval, he moved there late in 1536 and began preaching and organizing immediately. In 1538 his activities caused him to be expelled, but in 1541 he returned, with the city eventually coming completely under his sway. Under Calvin's guidance Geneva's government became theocratic. Supreme authority in the city was vested in a "Consistory," made up of twelve lay elders and five ministers. (Although Calvin himself was seldom the presiding officer, he usually dominated the Consistory's decisions until his death in 1564.) In addition to passing on legislation submitted to it by a congregation of ministers, the Consistory had as its main function the supervision of morals. This activity was carried out not merely by the punishment of antisocial conduct but by a persistent snooping into the private life of every individual. Geneva was divided into districts, and a committee of the Consistory could visit any household without warning to check on the habits of its members. Even the mildest forms of self-indulgence were strictly prohibited. Dancing, card playing, attending the theater, working or playing on the Sabbath—all were outlawed as works of the devil. Innkeepers were forbidden to allow anyone to consume food or drink without first saying grace, or to permit any patron to stay up after nine o'clock. Needless to say, penalties were severe. Not only were murder and treason classified as capital crimes, but also adultery, "witchcraft," blasphemy, and heresy. During the first four years after Calvin gained control in Geneva, no fewer than fifty-eight people were executed out of a total population of only sixteen thousand.

As reprehensible as such interference in the private sphere may seem today, in the middle of the sixteenth century Calvin's Geneva appeared as a beacon of thoroughgoing Protestantism to thousands throughout Europe. Calvin's disciple John Knox, for example, who brought Calvinism to Scotland, declared that Geneva under Calvin was "the most perfect school of Christ that ever was on earth since the days of the Apostles." Accordingly, many foreigners flocked to the "perfect school" for refuge or instruction, and usually returned home to become ardent proselytizers of Calvinism. Moreover, since Calvin himself thought of Geneva as a staging point for bringing Calvinism to France and the rest of the world, he encouraged the dispatching of missionaries and propaganda into hostile territories,

Left: **Calvin as seen by His Friends.** An idealized contemporary portrait of Calvin as a pensive scholar.

Right: **Calvin as Seen by His Enemies.** A Catholic caricature in which Calvin's face is a composite made from fish, a toad, and a chicken drumstick.

CHRONOLOGY

SPREAD OF PROTESTANTISM, 1520–1560

Lutheranism becomes state religion in Denmark, Norway, and Sweden	1520s
England breaks with Rome	1534
Geneva adopts theocratic government based on Calvinism	1541
Calvinism spreads to Scotland, England, Netherlands, and France	1540–1560s
Elizabethan Compromise	1559

with the result that from about the middle of the sixteenth century Geneva became the center of a concerted and militant attempt to spread the new faith far and wide. Soon Calvinists became a majority in Scotland, where they were known as Presbyterians; a majority in Holland, where they founded the Dutch Reformed Church; a substantial minority in France, where they were called Huguenots; and a substantial minority in England, where they were called Puritans. In addition, Calvinist preachers zealously made converts in many other parts of Europe, including Hungary, Lithuania and Poland. But just as the Calvinists were fanning out through Europe, the forces of Catholicism were hardening in their determination to head off any further Protestant advances. The result, as we will see in the next chapter, was a bloody series of religious wars that would wrack Europe for the next one hundred years.

THE DOMESTICATION OF THE REFORMATION, 1525–1560

How did notions of family and marriage change during the Reformation?

Protestantism had begun as a revolutionary doctrine whose radical claims for the spiritual equality of all true Christian believers had the potential to undermine the social, religious, political and even gender hierarchies on which European society rested. Luther himself seems not to have anticipated that his ideas about the priesthood of all believers might have such implications, and he was genuinely shocked and appalled when he realized that the rebellious German peasants and the religious millennarianists at Münster were interpreting his ideas in this way. But Luther was by no means solely responsible for the increasing conservatism of Protestant social ideology after 1525. Outside the ranks of the Anabaptists, none of the early Protestant leaders was a social or political radical. To spread their reform message, moreover, Protestant reformers depended on the support of existing social and political leaders: the princes of course, but no less important, the ruling elites of the German and Swiss towns. As a result, the Reformation movement was speedily "domesticated" in two senses. Not only was the revolutionary potential of Protestantism curbed (Luther rarely spoke about the priesthood of all believers after 1525); but there was also an increasing emphasis within all branches of the burgeoning Protestant movement on the patriarchal family as the central institution of reformed life.

PROTESTANTISM AND THE FAMILY

The domestication of the Reformation in this second sense took place principally in the free towns of Germany and Switzerland ("free" in the sense that they were self-governing, and not controlled by a territorial prince). Here, Protestant attacks on monasticism and clerical celibacy found a receptive audience among townsmen who resented the immunity of monastic houses from taxation, and regarded clerical celibacy as a subterfuge for the seduction of their wives and daughters. The Protestant insistence on the depravity of the human will, and the consequent need for that will to be trained and disciplined by godly authority, also resonated powerfully with guilds and town governments, which were anxious to maintain and increase the control that town elites (mainly merchants and master craftsmen) exercised over the apprentices and journeymen who made up the majority of the town's male population. By eliminating the competing jurisdictional authority of the Catholic Church, Protestantism also allowed town governments to consolidate all authority within the city into their own hands.

Protestantism also offered a powerful reinforcement to the control of individual craftsmen over their wives and children, their servants, and the apprentices who

HOW DID NOTIONS OF FAMILY AND MARRIAGE CHANGE DURING THE REFORMATION?

THE DOMESTICATION OF THE REFORMATION, 1525–1560   509

lived within their households. Protestantism brought a new importance to the family as a "school of godliness" in which an all-powerful father figure was expected to assume responsibility for instructing and disciplining his household in accordance with the precepts of reformed religion. At the same time, Protestantism also introduced a new religious ideal for women. No longer was the celibate nun the exemplar of female holiness; in her place now stood the married and obedient Protestant "goodwife." To this extent, Protestantism resolved the tensions between piety and sexuality that had characterized late medieval Catholicism by declaring firmly in favor of the holiness of marital sexuality.

This did not reflect a newly elevated view of women's spiritual potential, however—quite the contrary. Luther, like his medieval predecessors, continued to regard women as more sexually driven than men and less capable of controlling their sexual desires (although, to be fair, Luther had only a slightly higher view of men's capacity for celibacy). His opposition to convents rested on his belief that, except in extraordinary circumstances, it was impossible for women to remain celibate, so convents simply made illicit sexual behavior inevitable. To control women and prevent sin, it was therefore necessary that all women should be married, preferably at a young age, and so placed under the governance of a godly husband.

For the most part, Protestant town governments were happy to cooperate in shutting down convents. The convent's property went to the town, and most of the nuns were from aristocratic families anyway. But conflicts did arise between Protestant reformers and town fathers over marriage and sexuality, especially over the reformers' insistence that both men and women should marry young as a check on sin. Many German towns were like Augsburg, where men were expected to delay marriage until they had achieved the status of a master craftsmen—a requirement that had become increasingly difficult to enforce as guilds sought to restrict the number of journeymen permitted to become masters. In theory, however, apprentices and journeymen were not supposed to marry. Instead, they were expected to frequent the brothels and taverns, a legally recognized world of non-marital sexuality that town fathers saw as necessary to protect their own wives and daughters from seduction or rape, but that Protestant reformers found morally abhorrent and demanded be abolished.

Towns responded in a variety of ways to these opposing pressures. Some instituted special committees to police public morals, of the sort we have seen already in Calvin's Geneva. Some abandoned Protestantism altogether. Others, like Augsburg, flipflopped back and forth between Protestantism and Catholicism for several decades, before finally settling on one religion or the other. But regardless of a town's final choice of religious allegiance, by the end of the sixteenth century a revolution had taken place with respect to town governments' attitudes toward public morality. In their competition with each other, neither Catholics nor Protestants wished to be seen as "soft on sin." The result, by 1600, was the abolition of publicly recognized brothels throughout Europe, the criminalization of prostitution, and far stricter governmental supervision of many other aspects of private life in both Catholic and Protestant urban communities.

PROTESTANTISM AND CONTROL OVER MARRIAGE

Protestantism also increased parental control over their children's choice of marital partners. The medieval Catholic Church defined marriage as a sacrament that did not require the involvement of a priest. The mutual free consent of the two parties, even if given without witnesses or parental approval, was enough to constitute a legally valid marriage in the eyes of the church; at the same time, however, the church would annul a marriage if either of the parties could prove that he or she had not freely consented to it. Opposition to this doctrine came from many quarters, but especially from parents and other relatives. Because marriage involved rights of inheritance to property, most families regarded it as far too important a matter to be left to the free choice of their children. Instead, parents wanted the power to prevent unsuitable matches, and ideally, to force their children to accept the marriage arrangements that their families might negotiate on their behalf. Protestantism offered an opportunity to achieve such control. Luther had declared marriage to be a purely secular matter, not a sacrament at all, that could be regulated however the governing authorities thought best. Calvin largely followed suit, although Calvinist theocracy drew less of a distinction than did Lutheranism between the powers of church and state. Even Catholicism was eventually forced to give way. Although it never entirely abandoned its insistence that both members of the couple must freely consent to their marriage, by the end of the sixteenth century the

LUTHER ON CELIBACY AND WOMEN

Luther urged the dissolution of monasteries and convents on both theological and practical grounds. In theological terms, he argued that such institutions contributed nothing to the world, aside from (perhaps) the salvation of their inmates. But as the extracts below reveal, he also considered their demands for celibacy to be impossible for most men and women to meet. The result was therefore to increase, rather than decrease, sin.

Listen! In all my days I have not heard the confession of a nun, but in the light of Scripture I shall hit upon how matters fare with her and know I shall not be lying. If a girl is not sustained by great and exceptional grace, she can live without a man as little as she can without eating, drinking, sleeping, and other natural necessities. Nor, on the other hand, can a man dispense with a wife. The reason for this is that procreating children is an urge planted as deeply in human nature as eating and drinking. That is why God has given and put into the body the organs, arteries, fluxes, and everything that serves it. Therefore what is he doing who would check this process and keep nature from running its desired and intended course? He is attempting to keep nature from being nature, fire from burning, water from wetting, and a man from eating, drinking, and sleeping.

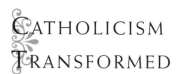

E.M. Plass, ed., *What Luther Says* (St. Louis: Concordia Publishing House, 1959), vol. II, pp. 888–889.

Catholic Church required formal public notice of intent to marry, and insisted on the presence of a priest at the actual wedding ceremony. Both were efforts to prevent elopements, allowing families time to intervene before an unsuitable marriage was concluded. Individual Catholic countries sometimes went even further in trying to reassert parental control over their children's choice of marital partners. In France, for example, although couples might still marry without parental consent, those who did so now forfeited all of their rights to inherit their families' property. In somewhat different ways, however, both Protestantism and Catholicism thus moved to strengthen the control that parents could exercise over their children—and, in the case of Protestantism, that husbands could exercise over their wives.

CATHOLICISM TRANSFORMED

What caused the Catholic Reformation?

The historical novelty of Protestantism in the sixteenth century inevitably tends to cast the spotlight on such religious reformers as Luther and Calvin, but a powerful internal reform movement within the Catholic Church also exercised as profound an effect on the course of European history as did Protestantism. Historians differ about whether to call this movement the "Catholic Reformation" or the "Counter-Reformation." Some prefer the former term because it emphasizes that significant efforts to reform the Catholic Church from within antedated the posting of Luther's theses and that Catholic reform in the sixteenth century was thus not merely a response to Protestantism. Others, however, insist quite properly that most sixteenth-century Catholic reformers were indeed inspired primarily by the urgency of resisting what they regarded as heresy and schism. Fortunately the two interpretations are by no means irreconcilable, for they allude to two complementary phases: a Catholic Reformation that came before Luther and a Counter-Reformation that followed.

> The Council of Trent reaffirmed without exception all the tenets challenged by the Protestant reformers.

THE CATHOLIC REFORMATION

The Catholic Reformation, beginning around 1490, was primarily a movement for moral and institutional reform inspired by principles of Christian humanism and carried on with practically no help from the dissolute Renaissance papacy. In Spain around the turn of the fifteenth century, reform activities directed by Cardinal Francisco Ximénes de Cisneros (1436–1517) with the cooperation of the monarchy led to the imposition of strict rules of behavior for Franciscan friars and the elimination of abuses prevalent among the diocesan clergy. Although Ximénes aimed primarily at strengthening the church in its warfare with the Muslims, his work had some effect in regenerating Spanish Christian spiritual life. Italy had no similarly centralized reform movement, but a number of earnest clerics in the early sixteenth century labored on their own to make the Italian church more worthy of its calling. The task was a difficult one on account of the entrenchment of abuses and the example of profligacy set by the papal court, but despite these obstacles, the Italian reformers did manage to establish some new religious orders dedicated to high ideals of piety and social service. Finally, it cannot be forgotten that such leading Christian humanists as Erasmus and Thomas More were in their own way Catholic reformers, for in criticizing abuses and editing sacred texts, such men helped to enhance spirituality.

Once Protestantism began to sweep over Europe, however, Catholic reform of the earlier variety clearly became inadequate to defend the church, let alone turn the tide of revolt. Thus a second, more aggressive phase of reform under a new style of vigorous papal leadership gained momentum during the middle and the latter half of the sixteenth century. The leading Counter-Reformation popes—Paul III (1534–1549), Paul IV (1555–1559), Saint Pius V (1566–1572), and Sixtus V (1585–1590)—were collectively the most zealous crusaders for reform to preside over the papacy since the High Middle Ages. All led upright personal lives. Indeed, some were so grimly ascetic that contemporaries were unsure whether they were not too holy: as a Spanish councilor wrote in 1567, "We should like it even better if the present Holy Father were no longer with us, however great, inexpressible, unparalleled, and extraordinary His Holiness may be." But in the face of the Protestant onslaught, a pope's reputation for excessive asceticism was vastly preferable to a reputation for profligacy. More than that, becoming fully dedicated to activist revitalization of the church, the Counter-Reformation popes reorganized their finances and filled ecclesiastical offices with bishops and abbots as renowned for austerity as themselves. These appointees in turn set high standards for their own priests and monks.

These papal activities were supplemented by the actions of the Council of Trent, convoked by Paul III in 1545 and meeting at intervals thereafter until 1563. This general council was one of the most important in the history of the church. After early debates about possible grounds for compromise, the Council of Trent reaffirmed without exception all the tenets challenged by the Protestant reformers. Good works were held to be necessary for salvation. The doctrine of the sacraments as indispensable means of grace was upheld. Likewise, transubstantiation, the apostolic succession of the priesthood, the belief in purgatory, the invocation of saints, and the rule of celibacy for the clergy were all confirmed as essential elements in the Catholic system. The Bible and the traditions of apostolic teaching were held to be of equal authority as sources of Christian truth. Papal supremacy over every bishop and priest was expressly maintained, and the supremacy of the pope over any church council was taken for granted. The Council of Trent even reaffirmed the doctrine of indulgences that had touched off the Lutheran revolt, although it did condemn the worst scandals connected with the selling of indulgences.

The legislation of Trent was not confined to matters of doctrine. It also included provisions for the elimination of abuses and for reinforcing the discipline of the mained in the faith. A commission was appointed to draw up a list of writings that ought not to be read by faithful Catholics. The publication of this list in 1564 resulted in the formal establishment of the Index of Prohibited Books as a part of the machinery of the church. Later, a permanent agency known as the Congregation of the Index was set up to revise the list from time to time. Altogether more than forty such revisions have been made. The majority of the books condemned have been theological treatises, and probably the effect in retarding the progress of learning has been slight. Nonetheless, the establishment of the Index must be viewed as a symptom of the intolerance that characterized sixteenth-century Christianity, both Catholic and Protestant.

SAINT IGNATIUS LOYOLA AND THE SOCIETY OF JESUS

In addition to the independent activities of popes and the legislation of the Council of Trent, a third main force propelling the Counter-Reformation was the foundation of the Society of Jesus, commonly known as the Jesuit order, by Saint Ignatius Loyola (1491–1556). In the midst of a youthful career as a worldly soldier, the Spanish nobleman Loyola was wounded in battle in 1521 (the same year in which Luther defied Charles V at Worms); while recuperating, he decided to change his ways and become a spiritual soldier of Christ. Shortly afterward he lived as a hermit in a cave near the Spanish town of Manresa for ten months, during which time, instead of reading the Bible as Luther or Calvin might have done, he experienced ecstatic visions and worked out the principles of his subsequent meditational guide, *The Spiritual Exercises.* This manual, completed in 1535 and first published in 1541, offered practical advice on how to master one's will and serve God by a systematic program of meditations on sin and the life of Christ. Soon made a basic handbook for all Jesuits and widely studied by numerous Catholic lay people as well, Loyola's *Spiritual Exercises* had an influence second only to Calvin's *Institutes* among all the religious writings of the sixteenth century.

Nonetheless, Saint Ignatius's founding of the Jesuit order itself was certainly his greatest single accomplishment. Originating as a group of six disciples who gathered around Loyola in Paris in 1534 to serve God in poverty, chastity, and missionary work, Loyola's Society of Jesus was formally constituted as an order of

The Inspiration of Saint Jerome, by Guido Reni. In 1546 the Council of Trent declared Saint Jerome's Latin translation of the Bible, known as the Vulgate, to be the official version of the Catholic Church; then, in 1592, Pope Clement VIII chose one edition of the Vulgate to be authoritative above all others. Since Biblical scholars had known since the early sixteenth century that Saint Jerome's translation contained numerous mistakes, Counter-Reformation defenders of the Vulgate insisted that even his mistakes had been divinely inspired and thus were somehow preferable to the original meaning of Scripture. The point is made visually in Guido Reni's painting of 1635.

church over its members. To improve pastoral care of the laity, bishops and priests were forbidden to hold more than one benefice. To address the problem of an ignorant priesthood, it was provided that a theological seminary must be established in every diocese. The council also took steps to suppress a variety of local religious practices and saints cults, replacing them with officially approved and centrally directed observances from Rome. Toward the end of its deliberations the council also decided to censor books, to prevent heretical ideas from corrupting those who still re-

OBEDIENCE AS A JESUIT HALLMARK

The necessity of obedience in the spiritual formation of monks and nuns had been a central theme in Catholic religious thought since the Rule of Saint Benedict. By focusing its demands for obedience specifically on the papacy, however, the Society of Jesus brought a new militancy to this old ideal.

RULES FOR THINKING WITH THE CHURCH

1. Always to be ready to obey with mind and heart, setting aside all judgment of one's own, the true spouse of Jesus Christ, our holy mother, our infallible and orthodox mistress, the Catholic Church, whose authority is exercised over us by the hierarchy.
2. To commend the confession of sins to a priest as it is practised in the Church; the reception of the Holy Eucharist once a year, or better still every week, or at least every month, with the necessary preparation. . . .
4. To have a great esteem for the religious orders, and to give the preference to celibacy or virginity over the married state. . . .
6. To praise relics, the veneration and invocation of Saints: also the stations, and pious pilgrimages, indulgences, jubilees, the custom of lighting candles in the churches, and other such aids to piety and devotion. . . .
9. To uphold especially all the precepts of the Church, and not censure them in any manner; but, on the contrary, to defend them promptly, with reasons drawn from all sources, against those who criticize them.
10. To be eager to commend the decrees, mandates, traditions, rites and customs of the Fathers in the Faith or our superiors. . . .
13. That we may be altogether of the same mind and in conformity with the Church herself, if she shall have defined anything to be black which to our eyes appears to be white, we ought in like manner to pronounce it to be black. For we must undoubtingly believe, that the Spirit of our Lord Jesus Christ, and the Spirit of the Orthodox church His Spouse, by which Spirit we are governed and directed to salvation, is the same. . . .

FROM THE CONSTITUTIONS OF THE JESUIT ORDER

Let us with the utmost pains strain every nerve of our strength to exhibit this virtue of obedience, firstly to the Highest Pontiff, then to the Superiors of the Society; so that in all things . . . we may be most ready to obey his voice, just as if it issued from Christ our Lord . . . leaving any work, even a letter, that we have begun and have not yet finished; by directing to this goal all our strength and intention in the Lord, that holy obedience may be made perfect in us in every respect, in performance, in will, in intellect; by submitting to whatever may be enjoined on us with great readiness, with spiritual joy and perseverance; by persuading ourselves that all things [commanded] are just; by rejecting with a kind of blind obedience all opposing opinion or judgment of our own. . . .

Henry Bettenson, ed. *Documents of the Christian Church,* 2d ed. (Oxford: Oxford University Press, 1967), pp. 259–261.

the church by Pope Paul III in 1540; by the time of its founder's death it already numbered fifteen hundred members. The Society of Jesus was by far the most militant of the religious orders fostered by the Catholic reform movements of the sixteenth century. It was not merely a monastic society but a company of soldiers sworn to defend the faith. Their weapons were not to be bullets and spears but eloquence, persuasion, instruction in correct doctrines, and if necessary, more worldly methods of exerting influence. The organization was patterned after that of a military company, with a general as commander-in-chief and iron discipline enforced for all members. Individuality was suppressed, and a soldierlike obedience to the general was exacted of the rank and file. The Jesuit general, sometimes known as the "black pope" (from the color of the order's habit), was elected for life and was not bound to take advice offered by any other member. But he did have one clear superior, namely the Roman pope himself, for in addition to the three monastic vows of poverty, chastity, and obedience, all senior Jesuits took a "fourth vow" of strict obedience to the Vicar of Christ and were held to be at the pope's disposal at all times.

The activities of the Jesuits consisted primarily of proselytizing Christians and non-Christians, and establishing schools. Originally founded to engage in missionary work abroad, the early Jesuits preached to non-Christians in India, China, and Spanish America. For example, one of Saint Ignatius's closest early associates, Saint Francis Xavier (1506–1552), baptized thousands of native people and covered thousands of miles missionizing in South and East Asia. Yet, although Loyola had not at first conceived of his society as comprising shock troops against Protestantism, that is what it primarily became as the Counter-Reformation mounted in intensity. Through preaching and diplomacy—sometimes at the risk of their lives—Jesuits in the second half of the sixteenth century fanned out through Europe in direct confrontation with Calvinists. In many places the Jesuits succeeded in keeping rulers and their subjects loyal to Catholicism, in others they met martyrdom, and in some others—notably Poland and parts of Germany and France—they succeeded in regaining territory temporarily lost to Protestantism. Wherever they were allowed to settle, the Jesuits set up schools and colleges, for they firmly believed that a vigorous Catholicism depended on widespread literacy and education. Their schools were often so well regarded that, after the fires of religious hatred began to subside, upper-class Protestants sometimes sent their sons to receive a Jesuit education.

COUNTER-REFORMATION CHRISTIANITY

From the foregoing it should be self-evident that there is a "Counter-Reformation heritage" every bit as much as there is a Protestant one. Needless to say, for committed Catholics, the greatest achievement of sixteenth-century Catholic reform was the defense and revitalization of the faith. Without question, Catholicism would not have swept over the globe and reemerged in Europe as the vigorous spiritual force it remains today had it not been for the determined efforts of the sixteenth-century reformers. But other results stemmed from the Counter-Reformation as well. One was the spread of literacy in Catholic countries due to the educational activities of the Jesuits, and another was the growth of intense concern for acts of charity. Since Counter-Reformation Catholicism continued to emphasize good works as well as faith, charitable activities took on an extremely important role in the revitalized religion. Spiritual leaders of the Counter-Reformation such as Saint Francis de Sales (1567–1622) and Saint Vincent de Paul (1581–1660) urged almsgiving in their sermons and writings, and a wave of founding of orphanages and houses for the poor swept over Catholic Europe.

Two other areas in which the Counter-Reformation had less dramatic but still noteworthy effects were in the realm of women's history and intellectual developments. Whereas Protestantism encouraged female literacy so that women could read the Bible, reinvigorated Catholicism pursued a different course. Catholicism did not exalt marriage as a route to holiness for women to the same degree as did Protestantism, but Catholicism did foster a distinctive role for a female religious elite—countenancing the mysticism of Saint Teresa of Avila (1515–1582), and allowing the foundation of new orders of nuns such as the Ursulines and the Sisters of Charity that had no parallel under Protestantism. Both Protestants and Catholics continued to exclude women

> Although Loyola had not at first conceived of his society as comprising shock troops against Protestantism, that is what it primarily became as the Counter Reformation mounted in intensity.

CHRONOLOGY

THE COUNTER-REFORMATION, 1534–1564

Counter-Reformation popes	1534–1590
Saint Ignatius Loyola founds the Jesuits	1534
Council of Trent convenes	1545–1563
Index of Prohibited Books	1564

from the ministry or priesthood, but under Catholicism celibate women were permitted to pursue religious lives with at least some degree of independence.

The Counter-Reformation did not perpetuate the tolerant Christianity of Erasmus. Instead, Christian humanists lost favor with Counter-Reformation popes, and all of Erasmus's writings were immediately placed on the Index of Prohibited Books. But sixteenth-century Protestantism was just as intolerant as sixteenth-century Catholicism, and far more hostile to the cause of rationalism. Indeed, because Counter-Reformation theologians returned for guidance to the scholasticism of Saint Thomas Aquinas, they were much more committed to acknowledging the dignity of human reason than were their Protestant counterparts, who emphasized scriptural authority and unquestioning faith. Thus although a hallmark of the subsequent seventeenth-century scientific revolution was the divorce between spirituality of any variety and strict scientific work, it does not seem entirely coincidental that René Descartes, one of the founders of the scientific revolution, who coined the famous phrase "I think, therefore I am," was trained as a youth by the Jesuits.

CONCLUSION: THE HERITAGE OF THE REFORMATION

Inasmuch as Luther's revolt from Rome and the spread of Protestantism occurred after the height of the civilization of the Renaissance and before some particularly fundamental advances in modern European political, economic, and social development, it is tempting to think of historical events unfolding in an inevitably cumulative way, from the Renaissance to the

Reformation to the "Triumph of the Modern World." But history is seldom as neat as that. Although scholars continue to disagree on points of detail, most agree that the Protestant Reformation drew relatively little from the civilization of the Renaissance, that indeed in certain basic respects Protestant principles were completely at odds with the major assumptions of most Renaissance humanists.

In considering the relationship between the Renaissance and the origins of the Protestant Reformation, it would admittedly be false to say that the one had absolutely nothing to do with the other. Certainly, criticisms of religious abuses by Christian humanists helped prepare Germany for the Lutheran revolt. Furthermore, close humanistic textual study of the Bible led to the publication of new, reliable biblical editions used by the Protestant reformers. In this regard a direct line ran from the Italian humanist Lorenzo Valla to Erasmus to Luther, insofar as Valla's *Notes on the New Testament* inspired Erasmus to produce his own Greek edition and accompanying Latin translation of the New Testament in 1516, and that in turn enabled Luther in 1518 to reach some crucial conclusions concerning the literal biblical meaning of penance. For these and related reasons, Luther addressed Erasmus in 1519 as "our ornament and our hope."

But in fact Erasmus quickly showed that he had no sympathy whatsoever with Luther's first principles, and most other Christian humanists shunned Protestantism as soon as it became clear to them what Luther and other Protestant reformers actually were teaching. The reasons for this were that most humanists believed in free will whereas Protestants believed in predestination; that humanists tended to think of human nature as basically good whereas Protestants found it unspeakably corrupt; and that most humanists favored urbanity and tolerance whereas the followers of Luther and Calvin emphasized obedience and conformity.

Although the Protestant Reformation was not the natural outgrowth of the civilization of the Renaissance, it did contribute to certain traits most characteristic of modern European historical development. Foremost among these was the rise of the untrammeled powers of the sovereign state. As we have seen, those German princes who converted to Protestantism were moved to do so primarily by the search for sovereignty. The kings of Denmark, Sweden, and England followed suit for much the same reasons. Since Protestant leaders—Calvin as well as Luther—preached absolute obedience to "godly" rulers, and since the state in Protestant countries assumed direct control of the church, the spread of Protestantism definitely resulted in the growth of state power. But, as we have also seen, the power of the state was growing already, and it continued to grow also in such Catholic countries as France and Spain, where kings had already been granted, by 1500, most of the same rights over the church that were forcibly seized by Lutheran German princes and Henry VIII in the course of their own Reformations.

As for the growth of nationalism, a sense of national pride was already present in sixteenth-century Germany that Luther played on in his appeals of 1520. But Luther himself did much to foster German cultural nationalism by translating the entire Bible into a vigorous German idiom. Up until then Germans from some regions spoke a language so different from that of Germans from other areas that they could not understand each other, but the form of German given currency by Luther's Bible soon became the linguistic standard for the entire nation. Religion did not help to unite the German nation politically because the non-German Charles V opposed Lutheranism, and as a result Germany soon became politically divided into Protestant and Catholic camps. But elsewhere, as in Holland, where Protestants fought successfully against a foreign, Catholic overlord, Protestantism enhanced a sense of national identity. Perhaps the most familiar case of all is that of England, where a sense of nationhood existed before the advent of Protestantism, but where the new faith lent to that nationalism a new confidence that England was indeed a nation peculiarly favored by God.

Finally, we come to the subject of Protestantism's effects on social relationships, specifically those between the sexes. No consensus among historians exists on this subject. What does seem clear, however, is that Protestant men as individuals could be just as ambivalent about women as their medieval Catholic predecessors had been. John Knox, for example, inveighed against the Catholic regent of Scotland, Mary Stuart, in a treatise called *The First Blast of the Trumpet Against the Monstrous Regiment of Women*, yet maintained deeply respectful relationships with women of his own faith. But if we ask how Protestantism as a belief system affected women's lot, the answer appears to be that it enabled women to become just a shade more equal to men, albeit still clearly within a framework of subjection. Above all, since Protestantism, with its stress on the primacy of Scripture and the priesthood of all believers, called on women as well as men to undertake serious Bible study, it sponsored primary schooling for both sexes and thus enhanced female as well as male literacy. But Protestant male leaders still insisted that

women were naturally inferior to men and thus should always defer to men in arguments. As Calvin himself said, "let the woman be satisfied with her state of subjection and not take it ill that she is made inferior to the more distinguished sex." Both Luther and Calvin appear to have been happily married, but clearly that meant being happily married on their own terms.

SELECTED READINGS

Bainton, Roland. *Here I Stand: A Life of Martin Luther.* Nashville, Tenn., 1950. The best introductory biography in English; although old, and obviously biased in Luther's favor, it remains absorbing and dramatic.

————. *Erasmus of Christendom.* New York, 1969. Still the best biography in English of the Dutch reformer and intellectual.

Bossy, John. *Christianity in the West, 1400–1700.* Oxford and New York, 1985. A brilliant, challenging picture of the changes that took place in Christian piety and practice as a result of the sixteenth-century reformations.

Bouwsma, William J. *John Calvin: A Sixteenth-Century Portrait.* Oxford and New York, 1988. Still the best biography of the magisterial reformer.

Cameron, Euan. *The European Reformation.* Oxford and New York, 1991. An excellent survey, judicious and fair toward all the competing parties.

Collinson, Patrick. *The Religion of Protestants: The Church in English Society, 1559–1625.* Oxford, 1982. A great book by the best contemporary historian of early English Protestantism.

Dillenberger, John, ed. *Martin Luther: Selections from His Writings.* Garden City, N.Y., 1961. The standard selection, especially good on Luther's theological ideas.

————. *John Calvin: Selections from His Writings.* Garden City, N.Y., 1971. An excellent selection.

Dixon, C. Scott, ed. *The German Reformation: The Essential Readings.* Oxford, 1999. A collection of important recent articles.

Duffy, Eamon. *The Stripping of the Altars: Traditional Religion in England, c. 1400–c. 1550.* By far the best study of the hesitant way in which England eventually became a Protestant country.

Eire, Carlos M. N. *From Madrid to Purgatory: The Art and Craft of Dying in Sixteenth-Century Spain.* Cambridge and New York, 1995. A powerful picture of the religious culture of Spanish Catholicism.

Hillerbrand, Hans J., ed. *The Protestant Reformation.* New York, 1967. Selections are particularly good for illuminating the political consequences of Reformation theological ideas.

Loyola, Ignatius. *Personal Writings.* Translated by Joseph A. Munitiz and Philip Endean. London and New York, 1996. An excellent collection that includes Loyola's autobiography, his spiritual diary, and some of his letters, as well as his *Spiritual Exercises.*

Luebke, David, ed. *The Counter-Reformation: The Essential Readings.* Oxford, 1999. A collection of nine important recent essays.

McGrath, Alister E. *Reformation Thought: An Introduction.* Oxford, 1993. A useful explanation, accessible to non-Christians, of the theological ideas of the major Protestant reformers.

Monter, E. William. *Calvin's Geneva.* New York, 1967. The standard English work.

Mullett, Michael A. *The Catholic Reformation.* London, 2000. A sympathetic survey of Catholicism from the mid-sixteenth to the eighteenth century that presents the mid-sixteenth-century Council of Trent not as a response to Protestantism, but as a continuation of a series of reform efforts dating from the fifteenth century.

Oberman, Heiko A. *Luther: Man Between God and the Devil.* Translated by Eileen Walliser-Schwarzbart. New Haven, 1989. The best recent biography of Luther, stressing his preoccupations with sin, death, and the devil.

O'Malley, John W. *The First Jesuits.* Cambridge, Mass., 1993. A scholarly account of the origins and early years of the Society of Jesus.

Ozment, Steven. *Protestants: The Birth of a Revolution.* New York, 1992. A stirring introduction to the ideas of an influential modern historian of the Protestant Reformation.

Pettegree, Andrew, Alastair Duke, and Gillian Lewis, eds. *Calvinism in Europe, 1540–1620.* Cambridge and New York, 1994. A collection of articles dealing with Calvinism across Europe, mostly from the context of local history.

Pettegree, Andrew, ed. *The Reformation World.* New York, 2000. An exhaustive compendium of articles representing the most recent thinking about the Reformation.

Pelikan, Jaroslav. *Reformation of Church and Dogma, 1300–1700.* Volume 4: *A History of Christian Dogma.* Chicago, 1984. A masterful synthesis of Reformation theology in its late medieval context.

Roper, Lyndal. *The Holy Household: Women and Morals in Reformation Augsburg.* Oxford, 1989. A pathbreaking study of how Protestantism was adopted and adapted by the town councillors of Augsburg, with special attention to its impact on attitudes toward women, the family, and marriage.

Scribner, Robert W. *The German Reformation.* Atlantic Heights, N.J., 1986. A brief survey of work on the social and cultural context for the Reformation. Includes superb bibliographies.

Tracy, James D. *Europe's Reformations, 1450–1650.* Lanham, Md., 1999. An outstanding survey, especially strong on Dutch and Swiss developments, but excellent throughout.

Williams, George H. *The Radical Reformation,* 3d ed. Kirksville, Mo., 1992. Originally published in 1962, this is still the best book on Anabaptism and its offshoots.

RELIGIOUS WARS
AND
STATE BUILDING,
1540–1660

STRANGE AS IT MAY SEEM in retrospect, Martin Luther never intended to fracture the religious unity of Europe. He sincerely believed that once the Bible was available to everyone in an accurate, vernacular translation, then everyone who read the Bible would interpret it in exactly the same way as did he himself. The result, of course, was quite different, as Luther quickly discovered in his bitter disputes with Zwingli and Calvin. Nor did Catholicism crumble in the face of reformed teachings as Luther had believed that it would. Instead, Europe's religious divisions multiplied, speedily crystallizing along political lines. By Luther's death in 1546, a clear pattern had already emerged. With only rare exceptions, Protestantism triumphed in those areas where political authorities supported the reformers. Where rulers remained Catholic, so too did their territories.

This was not the result Martin Luther had intended, but it did faithfully reflect the most basic presumptions of sixteenth-century European life. Anabaptists apart, neither Protestant nor Catholic reformers set out to challenge the standard medieval beliefs about the mutual interdependence of religion and politics—quite the contrary. Sixteenth-century Europeans continued to believe that the proper role of the state was to enforce true religion on its subjects, and sixteenth-century rulers remained convinced that religious pluralism would bring disunion and disloyalty to any state that embraced it. Ultimately, both Catholics and Protestants believed that western Europe had to return to a single religious faith enforced by properly constituted political authorities. What they could not agree on was, "Which faith?" and "Which authorities?"

The result was a brutal series of religious wars between 1540 and 1660 whose reverberations would continue to be felt until the eighteenth century. Vastly expensive and enormously destructive, these wars affected everyone in Europe from peasants to princes. They did not arise solely from conflicts over religion. Regionalism, dynasticism, and nationalism were also potent contributors to the chaos into which Europe now plunged. Together, however, these forces of division and disorder brought into question the very survival of the European political order that had emerged since the thirteenth century. Faced with the prospect of political collapse,

FOCUS QUESTIONS

• Why was the period 1540 to 1660 one of the most turbulent in European history?

• What caused the decline of Spain in the seventeenth century?

 • What was Hobbes's solution to the search for authority?

• What was the relationship between the Baroque school and the Counter-Reformation?

Europeans by 1660 were forced to embrace, gradually and grudgingly, a notion that in 1540 had seemed impossible to conceive: that religious toleration, however limited in scope, might be the only way to preserve the political, social, and economic order of the European world.

ECONOMIC, RELIGIOUS, AND POLITICAL TESTS

Why was the period 1540 to 1660 one of the most turbulent in European history?

The troubles that engulfed Europe during the traumatic century between 1540 and 1660 crept up on contemporaries unawares. From the mid-fifteenth century on, most of Europe had enjoyed steady economic growth, and the discovery of the New World seemed the basis of greater prosperity to come. Political trends too seemed auspicious, since most western European governments were becoming ever more efficient and providing more internal peace for their subjects. By the middle of the sixteenth century, however, thunderclouds were gathering that would soon burst into terrible storms.

THE PRICE REVOLUTION

Although the causes of these storms were interrelated, we can examine each separately, starting with the great price inflation. Nothing like the upward price trend that affected western Europe in the second half of the sixteenth century had ever happened before. The cost of a measure of wheat in Flanders, for example, tripled between 1550 and 1600, grain prices in Paris quadrupled, and the overall cost of living in England more than doubled during the same period. The twentieth century would see much more dizzying inflations than this, but since the skyrocketing of prices in the later sixteenth century was a novelty, most historians agree on calling it a "price revolution."

Two developments in particular underlay the soaring prices. The first is demographic. Starting in the later fifteenth century, Europe's population began to mount again after the plague-induced falloff: roughly estimated, there were about 50 million people in Europe around 1450 and 90 million around 1600. Since Eu-

rope's food supply remained more or less constant owing to the lack of any noteworthy breakthrough in agricultural technology, food prices were driven sharply higher by greater demand. At the same time, wages stagnated or even declined. As a result, workers around 1600 were paying a higher percentage of their wages to buy food than ever before, even though their basic nutritional levels were declining.

Population trends explain much, but since Europe's population did not increase nearly so rapidly in the second half of the sixteenth century as did prices, other explanations for the great inflation are necessary. Foremost among these is the enormous influx of bullion from Spanish America. Whereas in the five years from 1556 to 1560 roughly 10 million ducats worth of silver passed through the Spanish entry point of Seville, between 1576 and 1580 that figure had doubled, and between 1591 and 1595 it had more than quadrupled. Because most of this silver was used by the Spanish crown to pay its foreign creditors and its armies abroad, or by private individuals to pay for imports from other countries, this Spanish bullion quickly circulated throughout Europe, where much of it was minted into coins. This dramatic increase in the volume of money in circulation further fueled the spiral of rising prices. "I learned a proverb here," said a French traveler in Spain in 1603, "everything costs much here except silver."

Aggressive entrepreneurs and landlords profited most from the changed economic circumstances, while the masses of laboring people were hurt the worst. Merchants in possession of sought-after goods were able to raise prices at will. Landlords profited directly from the rising prices of agricultural produce; or, if they did not farm their own lands, they could always raise rents. But laborers were caught in a squeeze because wages rose far more slowly than prices, owing to the presence of a more than adequate labor supply. Moreover, because the cost of food staples rose at a sharper rate than the cost of most other items of consumption, poor people had to spend an ever greater percentage of their paltry incomes on necessities. When disasters such as wars or poor harvests drove grain prices out of reach, some of the poor literally starved to death. The picture that thus emerges is one of the rich getting richer and the poor getting poorer—splendid feasts enjoyed amid the most appalling suffering.

In addition to these direct economic effects, the price inflation of the later sixteenth century had significant political effects as well because higher prices

WHY WAS THE PERIOD 1540 TO 1660 ONE OF THE MOST TURBULENT IN EUROPEAN HISTORY?

ECONOMIC, RELIGIOUS, AND POLITICAL TESTS   521

placed new pressures on the sovereign states of Europe. The reasons for this were simple. Since the inflation depressed the real value of money, fixed incomes from taxes and tolls in effect yielded less and less. Thus merely to keep their incomes constant governments would have been forced to raise taxes. But to compound this problem, most states needed much more real income than previously because they were undertaking more wars, and warfare, as always, was becoming increasingly expensive. The only recourse, then, was to raise taxes precipitously, but such draconian measures aroused great resentment on the part of their subjects—especially the very poor who were already suffering from the effects of the inflation. Hence governments faced continuous threats of defiance and potential armed resistance.

On the whole, the period from 1600 to 1660 was one of economic stagnation.

After 1600 prices stabilized, as population growth slowed and the flood of silver from America began to abate. On the whole, however, the period from 1600 to 1660 was one of economic stagnation rather than growth, even though a few areas—notably Holland—bucked the trend. The rich were usually able to hold their own, but the poor as a group made no advances, since the relationship of prices to wages remained fixed to their disadvantage. Indeed, if anything, the lot of the poor in many places deteriorated because the mid-seventeenth century saw some particularly expensive and destructive wars, causing helpless civilians to be plundered by rapacious tax collectors or looting soldiers, or sometimes both. The Black Death also returned, wreaking havoc in London and elsewhere during the 1660s.

Until religious passions began to cool toward the end of the period, most Catholics and Protestants viewed each other as minions of Satan who could not be allowed to live.

RELIGIOUS CONFLICTS

It goes without saying that most people would have been far better off had there been fewer wars during this difficult century, but given prevalent attitudes, newly arisen religious rivalries made wars inevitable. Simply stated, until religious passions began to cool toward the end of the period, most Catholics and Protestants viewed each other as minions of Satan who could not be allowed to live. Worse, sovereign states attempted to enforce religious uniformity on the grounds that "crown and altar" offered each other mutual support and in the belief that governments would totter where diversity of faith prevailed. Rulers on both sides felt certain that religious minorities, if allowed to survive in their realms, would inevitably engage in sedition; nor were they far wrong, since militant Calvinists and Jesuits were indeed dedicated to subverting constituted powers in areas where their party had not yet triumphed. Thus states tried to extirpate all potential religious resistance, but in the process sometimes provoked civil wars in which each side tended to assume there could be no victory until the other was exterminated. And of course civil wars might become international in scope when one or more foreign powers resolved to aid embattled religious allies elsewhere.

POLITICAL INSTABILITY

Compounding the foregoing problems were the inherent weaknesses of the major European kingdoms. Most of the major states of early modern Europe had built themselves up during the later Middle Ages by absorbing smaller, traditionally autonomous territories, sometimes by conquest, but more often through marriage alliances or inheritance arrangements between their respective ruling families (a policy known as "dynasticism"). At first some degree of provincial autonomy was usually preserved in these newly absorbed territories. But between 1540 and 1660, when governments were making ever greater financial claims on all their subjects or trying to enforce religious uniformity, rulers often rode roughshod over the rights of these traditionally autonomous provinces. The result, once again, was civil war, in which regionalism, economic grievances, and religious animosities were compounded into a volatile and destructive mixture. Nor was that all, since most governments seeking money and/or religious uniformity tried to rule with a firmer hand than before, and thus sometimes provoked armed resistance from subjects seeking to preserve their traditional constitutional liberties. Given this bewildering variety of motives for revolt, it is by no means surprising that the long century between 1540 and 1660 was one of the most turbulent in all of European history.

A CENTURY OF RELIGIOUS WARS

What caused the decline of Spain in the seventeenth century?

The greatest single cause of warfare during this period was religious conflict. The wars themselves divide into four phases: a series of German wars from the 1540s to 1555; the French wars of religion from 1562 until 1598; the Dutch wars with Spain between 1566 and 1609; and the Thirty Years' War in Germany between 1618 and 1648.

THE GERMAN WARS OF RELIGION TO 1555

Wars between Catholics and Protestants in Germany began in the 1540s when the Holy Roman emperor Charles V, a devout Catholic, tried to reestablish Catholic unity in Germany by launching a military campaign against several German princes who had instituted Lutheran worship in their territories. Despite several notable victories, Charles's efforts to defeat the Protestant princes failed. Partly this was because he was simultaneously involved in wars against France, and so could not devote his entire attention to German affairs. Primarily, however, Charles failed because the Catholic princes of Germany feared that if Charles succeeded in defeating the Protestant princes, he might then suppress their own independence also. As a result, the Catholic princes' support for the foreign-born Charles was only lukewarm; at times, they even joined with the Protestant princes in battle against the emperor. Accordingly, religious warfare sputtered on and off until a compromise settlement was reached in the Religious Peace of Augsburg (1555). This rested on the principle of *cuius regio, eius religio* ("as the ruler, so the religion"), which meant that in those principalities where Lutheran princes ruled, Lutheranism would be the sole state religion; where Catholic princes ruled, their territories would be Catholic also. Although the Peace of Augsburg was a historical milestone inasmuch as Catholic rulers for the first time acknowledged the legality of Protestantism, it boded ill for the future in assuming that no sovereign state larger than a free city (for which it made exceptions) could tolerate religious diversity. Moreover, in excluding Calvinism entirely, it ensured that the German Calvinists would become aggressive opponents of the status quo.

> The Peace of Augsburg boded ill for the future in assuming that no sovereign state could tolerate religious diversity.

THE FRENCH WARS OF RELIGION

From the 1560s on, Europe's religious wars became far more brutal, partly because the combatants had become more intransigent (Calvinists and Jesuits customarily took the lead on their respective sides), and partly because the later religious wars were aggravated by regional, political, and dynastic hostilities. Since Geneva bordered on France, and since Calvin himself was a Frenchman who longed to convert his mother country, the next act in the tragedy of Europe's confessional warfare was played out on French soil. Calvinist missionaries made considerable headway in France between 1541 (when Calvin took power in Geneva) and the outbreak of religious warfare in 1562. By 1562, Calvinists comprised between 10 and 20 percent of France's population, with their numbers swelling daily. Greatly assisting the Calvinist (Huguenot) cause in France was the conversion of many aristocratic French women to Calvinism because such women often won over their husbands, who in turn maintained large private armies. The foremost example is that of Jeanne d'Albret, queen of the tiny Pyrenean kingdom of Navarre, who brought over to Calvinism her husband, the prominent French aristocrat Antoine de Bourbon, and her brother-in-law, the prince de Condé. Condé took command of the French Huguenot party when civil war broke out in 1562, and was later succeeded in this capacity by Jeanne's son, Henry of Navarre, who came to rule all of France at the end of the century as King Henry IV. But Calvinism in France was also nourished by long-standing regional hostilities within the French kingdom, especially in southern France, where the animosities aroused by the thirteenth-century Albigensian crusade continued to fester.

Until 1562, an uneasy peace continued between the Catholic and the Calvinist forces in France. In 1562, however, the French king died unexpectedly, leaving a young child as his heir. A struggle immediately broke out between the Huguenot Condé and the ultra-Catholic duke of Guise for control of the regency gov-

WHAT CAUSED THE DECLINE OF SPAIN IN THE SEVENTEENTH CENTURY?

A CENTURY OF RELIGIOUS WARS   523

ernment. And since both Catholics and Protestants assumed that France could have only a single *roi, foi,* and *loi* (king, faith, and law), this political struggle immediately took on a religious aspect. Soon all France was aflame. Rampaging mobs, often incited by members of the clergy, ransacked churches and settled local scores. Although the Huguenots were not strong or numerous enough to gain victory, they were too strong to be defeated, especially in their southern French territorial stronghold. Hence, despite intermittent truces, warfare dragged on at great cost of life until 1572, when a truce was arranged by which the Protestant leader, Henry of Navarre, was to marry the Catholic sister of the reigning French king. At this point, however, the cultivated queen mother Catherine de Medici, normally a woman who favored compromise, panicked. Instead of honoring the truce, she plotted with members of the Catholic Guise faction to kill all the Huguenot leaders while they were assembled in Paris for her daugher's wedding to Henry of Navarre. In the early morning of St. Bartholomew's Day (August 24) most of the Huguenot chiefs were murdered in bed and two to three thousand other Protestants were slaughtered in the streets or drowned in the Seine by Catholic mobs. When word of the Parisian massacre spread to the provinces, some ten thousand more Huguenots were killed in a frenzy of blood lust that swept through France. Henry of Navarre escaped, along with his new bride; but after 1572, the conflict entered a new and even more bitter phase.

Only when the politically astute Henry of Navarre succeeded to the French throne as Henry IV (1589–1610), initiating the Bourbon dynasty that would rule until 1792, did the civil war finally come to an end. In 1593 Henry abjured his Protestantism in order to placate France's Catholic majority, declaring as he did so that "Paris is worth a mass." In 1598, however, he offered limited religious freedom to the Huguenots by the Edict of Nantes. Although the Edict recognized Catholicism as the official religion of the kingdom, guaranteeing Catholics the right to practice their religion everywhere in the kingdom, Huguenot nobles were now allowed to hold Protestant services privately in their castles; other Huguenots were allowed to worship at specified places (excluding Paris and all cities where bishops and archbishops resided); and the Huguenot party was permitted to fortify some towns, especially in the south and west, for their own

military defense. Huguenots were also guaranteed the right to serve in all public offices, and to enter the universities and hospitals without hindrance.

Although the Edict of Nantes did not countenance absolute freedom of worship, it nevertheless represented a major stride in the direction of toleration. But despite its efforts to create one kingdom with two faiths, the effect of the Edict was to divide the French kingdom into separate religious enclaves. In southern and western France, Huguenots came to have their own law courts, staffed by their own judges. They also received substantial powers of self-government, because it was presumed on all sides that the members of one religious group could not be ruled equitably by the adherents of a competing religion. Because of its regional character, Nantes also represented a concession to the long-standing traditions of provincial autonomy within the kingdom of France. In some ways, indeed, the Huguenot areas became "a state within a state," thus raising again the perpetual fear in Paris that the kingdom of which it was the capital might once again fly apart into its constituent parts, as had happened during the Hundred Years' War. On its own terms, however, the Edict of Nantes was a success. With religious peace established, France quickly began to recover from decades of devastation, even though Henry IV himself was cut down by the dagger of a Catholic fanatic in 1610.

> Although the Edict of Nantes did not countenance absolute freedom of worship, it nevertheless represented a major stride in the direction of toleration.

THE REVOLT OF THE NETHERLANDS

Bitter warfare also broke out between Catholics and Protestants in the Netherlands, where national resentments exacerbated the predictable religious hatreds. For almost a century the Netherlands (or Low Countries), comprising modern-day Holland in the north and Belgium in the south, had been ruled by the Habsburg family of Holy Roman emperors. Particularly the southern part of the Netherlands prospered greatly from trade and manufacture: southern Netherlanders had the greatest per capita wealth of all Europe, and their metropolis of Antwerp was northern Europe's leading commercial and financial center. Moreover, the half-century-long rule of the Habsburg emperor Charles V (1506–1556) had been popular because Charles, who had been born in the Belgian city of Ghent, felt a sense of rapport with his subjects, and allowed them a large degree of local self-government.

EUROPE, C. 1560

This map details the political situation in Europe around the year 1560. Despite the fact that the Habsburgs were Catholic, many Catholic nations such as France routinely opposed them; why? How did the rise of nationalism and the emergence of the state further complicate the religious conflicts of the sixteenth century? Note the situation of the Netherlands at this moment in history. Why did the leaders for independence from the Habsburgs convert to Protestantism to achieve their ends? What might this suggest about the use of religion for political ends during the mid-sixteenth century?

Map legend:

— Boundary of the Holy Roman Empire

Possessions of Charles V, 1526 (Spanish Habsburgs)

Added by Ferdinand I, 1556 (Austrian Habsburgs)

WHAT CAUSED THE DECLINE OF SPAIN IN THE SEVENTEENTH CENTURY?

A CENTURY OF RELIGIOUS WARS   525

But around 1560 the good fortune of the Netherlands began to ebb. When Charles V retired to a monastery in 1556 (dying two years later) he ceded all his vast territories outside of the Holy Roman empire and Hungary—not only the Netherlands, but Spain, Spanish America, and close to half of Italy—to his son Philip II (1556–1598). Unlike Charles, Philip had been born in Spain, and thinking of himself as a Spaniard, made Spain his residence and the focus of his policy. Thus he viewed the Netherlands primarily as a potentially rich source of income necessary for pursuing Spanish affairs. But in order to tap the wealth of the Netherlands Philip had to rule it more directly than his father had, and such attempts were naturally resented by the local magnates who until then had dominated the government. To make matters worse, a religious storm also was brewing, for after a treaty of 1559 ended a long war be-

Protestants Ransacking a Catholic Church in the Netherlands. The "Protestant fury" of 1566 was responsible for the large-scale destruction of religious art and statuary in the Low Countries, provoking the stern repression of Phillip II.

tween France and Spain, French Calvinists had begun to stream over the Netherlandish border, making converts wherever they went. Soon there were more Calvinists in Antwerp than in Geneva, a situation that Philip II could not tolerate because he was an ardent Catholic who subscribed wholeheartedly to the goals of the Counter-Reformation. Indeed, as he wrote to Rome on the eve of conflict, "rather than suffer the slightest harm to the true religion and service of God, I would lose all my states and even my life a hundred times over because I am not and will not be the ruler of heretics."

There is much evidence of the complexity of the Netherlandish situation. For example, the leader of resistance to Philip, William "the Silent," was at first not a Calvinist; also, the territories that ultimately succeeded in breaking away from Spanish rule were at first the most Catholic in the Low Countries. William the Silent, a prominent nobleman with large landholdings in the Netherlands, was actually very talkative. He received his nickname from his ability to hide his true religious and political feelings when the need arose. In 1566, while still a Catholic, he and other local nobles not formally committed to Protestantism appealed to Philip to allow toleration for Calvinists. But while Philip momentarily temporized, radical Protestant

mobs proved to be their own worst enemy—ransacking Catholic churches throughout the country, methodically desecrating hosts, smashing statuary, and shattering stained-glass windows. Though local troops soon had the situation under control, Philip II nonetheless decided to dispatch an army of ten thousand commanded by the steely Spanish duke of Alva to wipe out Protestantism in the Low Countries forever. Alva's tribunal, the "Council of Blood," soon examined some twelve thousand persons on charges of heresy or sedition, of whom nine thousand were convicted and one thousand executed. William the Silent fled the country, and all hope for a free Netherlands seemed lost.

But the tide turned quickly for two related reasons. First, instead of giving up, William the Silent converted to Protestantism, sought help from Protestants in France, Germany, and England, and organized bands of sea rovers to harass Spanish shipping on the Netherlandish coast. And second, Alva's tyranny helped William's cause, especially when the hated Spanish governor attempted to levy a 10 percent sales tax. With internal disaffection growing, in 1572 William, for tactical military reasons, was able to seize the northern Netherlands even though the north until then had been predominantly Catholic. Thereafter geography played a major role in determining the outcome of the conflict.

Spanish armies repeatedly attempted to win back the north, but they were stopped by a combination of impassable rivers and dikes that could be opened to flood out the invaders. Although William the Silent was assassinated by a Catholic in 1584, his son continued to lead the resistance until the Spanish crown finally agreed by a truce in 1609 to stop fighting and thus implicitly recognized the independence of the northern Dutch Republic. Meanwhile, the pressures of war and persecution had made the whole north Calvinistic, whereas the south—which remained under Spanish control—returned to uniform Catholicism.

ENGLAND AND THE DEFEAT OF THE SPANISH ARMADA

Religious strife could thus take the form of civil war, as in France, or war for national liberation, as in the Netherlands. But it could also take the form of warfare between sovereign states, as in the late-sixteenth-century struggle between England and Spain. After narrowly escaping domination by the Catholic queen Mary and her Spanish husband Philip II, English Protestants rejoiced in the rule of Queen Elizabeth I (1558–1603) and naturally harbored great antipathy toward Philip II and the Counter-Reformation. Furthermore, English economic interests were directly opposed to those of the Spanish. A seafaring and trading people, the English in the later sixteenth century were steadily making inroads into Spanish naval and commercial domination, and were also determined to resist any Spanish attempt to block England's lucrative trade with the Low Countries. But the greatest source of antagonism lay in naval contests in the Atlantic, where English privateers, with the tacit consent of Queen Elizabeth, could not resist raiding silver-laden Spanish treasure ships. Beginning around 1570, and taking as an excuse the Spanish oppression of Protestants in the Netherlands, English admirals or pirates (the terms were really interchangeable) such as Sir Francis Drake and Sir John Hawkins began plundering Spanish vessels on the high seas. In a particularly dramatic sailing exploit lasting from 1577 to 1580, lust for treasure and prevailing winds propelled Drake all the way around the world, to return with stolen Spanish treasure worth twice as much as Queen Elizabeth's annual revenue.

All this would have been sufficient provocation for Philip II to retaliate against England, but because he had his hands full in the Netherlands he resolved to invade the island only after the English openly allied with the Dutch rebels in 1585. And even then Philip did not act without extensive planning and a sense of assurance that nothing could go wrong. Finally, in 1588 he dispatched an enormous fleet, confidently called the "Invincible Armada," to invade insolent Britannia. After an initial standoff in the English Channel, however, the smaller, longer-gunned English warships outmaneuvered the Spanish fleet, while English fireships set some Spanish galleons ablaze and forced the rest to break formation. "Protestant gales" did the rest. After a disastrous circumnavigation of the British Isles and Ireland, the shattered flotilla limped home with almost half its ships lost.

The defeat of the Spanish Armada was one of the most decisive battles of Western history. Had Spain conquered England it is quite likely that the Spanish would have gone on to crush Holland and perhaps even to destroy Protestantism elsewhere in Europe. But, as it was, the Protestant day was saved, and not long afterward Spanish power began to decline, with English and Dutch ships taking ever greater command of the seas. In England, patriotic Protestant fervor became especially intense. Popular even before then, "Good Queen Bess" was virtually revered by her subjects until her death in 1603, and England embarked on its golden "Elizabethan Age" of literary endeavor. War with Spain dragged on inconclusively until 1604, but the fighting never brought England any serious harm and was just lively enough to keep the English people deeply committed to the cause of their queen, their country, and the Protestant religion, which they increasingly saw as identical.

THE THIRTY YEARS' WAR

With the promulgation of the Edict of Nantes in 1598, the peace between England and Spain of 1604, and the truce between Spain and Holland of 1609, religious warfare in northwestern Europe came briefly to an end in the early seventeenth century. But in 1618 a major new war broke out, this time in Germany. Since this struggle raged more or less unceasingly until 1648 it is known as the Thirty Years' War. Far from returning to enduring peace, Spain and France now became engaged in the conflict in Germany and in war with one another. Internal resentments in Spain, France, and England flared up in the decade of the 1640s in concurrent outbreaks of civil war. As an English preacher said in 1643, "these are days of shaking, and this shaking is universal."

WHAT CAUSED THE DECLINE OF SPAIN IN THE SEVENTEENTH CENTURY?

A CENTURY OF RELIGIOUS WARS   527

The Thirty Years' War began in a welter of religious passions as a war between Catholics and Protestants, but it quickly raised basic German constitutional issues and ended as an international struggle in which the initial religious dimension was almost entirely forgotten. Between the Peace of Augsburg in 1555 and the outbreak of war in 1618, Calvinists had replaced Lutherans in a few German territories, but the overall balance between Protestants and Catholics within the Holy Roman Empire had remained undisturbed. In 1618, however, war broke out after Ferdinand, the Catholic Habsburg prince of Poland, Austria, and Hungary, was elected king of the Protestant territory of Bohemia (not a German territory, yet part of the Holy Roman Empire). The staunchly Protestant Bohemian nobility had opposed Ferdinand's election, and when Ferdinand began to suppress Protestantism in Bohemia, they rebelled. German Catholic forces ruthlessly counterattacked, first in Bohemia and then in Germany proper, now led by Ferdinand, who in 1619 became Holy Roman emperor also. Within a decade, a German Catholic league seemed close to extirpating Protestantism throughout Germany.

Ferdinand's success, however, raised once again the prospect that an overly powerful Holy Roman emperor might threaten the political autonomy of the German princes, Catholic and Protestant alike. Thus when the Lutheran king of Sweden, Gustavus Adolphus, the "Lion of the North," marched into Germany in 1630 to champion the Protestant cause, he was welcomed by several German Catholic princes who preferred to see the former religious balance restored rather than risk surrendering their sovereignty to Ferdinand II. To make matters still more ironic, Gustavus' Protestant army was secretly subsidized by Catholic France, whose policy was then dictated by a cardinal of the church, Cardinal Richelieu. This was because Habsburg Spain had been fighting in Germany on the side of Habsburg Austria, and Richelieu was determined to resist any possibility of France being surrounded by a strong Habsburg alliance on the north, east, and south. In any event, the military genius Gustavus Adolphus started routing the Habsburgs, but when he fell in battle in 1632, Cardinal Richelieu had little choice but to send ever greater support to the remaining Swedish troops in Germany, until in 1635 French armies entered the war directly on Sweden's side. From then until 1648 the struggle was really one of France and Sweden against Austria and Spain, with most of Germany a helpless battleground.

The result was that Germany suffered more from warfare in the terrible years between 1618 and 1648 than it ever did before or after until the twentieth century. Several German cities were besieged and sacked nine or ten times over, and soldiers from all nations, who often had to sustain themselves by plunder, gave no quarter to defenseless civilians. With plague and disease adding to the toll of outright butchery, some parts of Germany lost more than half their populations, although others went relatively unscathed. Most horrifying was the loss of life in the final four years, when the carnage continued unabated even while peace negotiators had already arrived at broad areas of agreement and were dickering over subsidiary clauses.

Nor did the Peace of Westphalia, which finally ended the Thirty Years' War in 1648, do much to vindicate anyone's death, even though it did establish some abiding landmarks in European history. Above all, from the international perspective, the Peace of Westphalia marked the emergence of France as the predominant power on the continental European scene, replacing Spain. France would hold this position for the next two centuries. The greatest losers in the conflict (aside, of course, from the German people themselves) were the Austrian Habsburgs, who were forced to surrender all the territory they had gained in Germany and to abandon their hopes of using the office of Holy Roman emperor to dominate central Europe. Otherwise, something very close to the German status quo of 1618 was reestablished, with Protestant principalities in the north balancing Catholic ones in the south, and Germany so hopelessly divided that it could play no united role in European history until the nineteenth century.

> The Thirty Years' War began as a war between Catholics and Protestants and ended as an international struggle in which the religious dimension was almost entirely forgotten.

CHRONOLOGY

RELIGIOUS WARS, 1540s–1648

German wars	1540s–1555
French wars of religion	1562–1598
Dutch wars with Spain	1566–1609
Thirty Years' War	1618–1648

THE DESTRUCTIVENESS OF THE THIRTY YEARS' WAR

Hans Jakob Christoph von Grimmelshausen (1621–1676) lived through the horrors of the Thirty Years' War. His parents were killed, probably when he was thirteen years of age, and he himself was kidnapped the following year. By age fifteen, he was himself a soldier. His comic masterpiece, Simplicissimus, *from which this extract is taken, drew heavily upon these wartime experiences. Although technically "fiction," it portrays with brutal accuracy the cruelty and destructiveness of this war, especially for its peasant victims.*

Although it was not my intention to take the peaceloving reader with these troopers to my dad's house and farm, seeing that matters will go ill therein, yet the course of my history demands that I should leave to kind posterity an account of what manner of cruelties were now and again practised in this our German war: yes, and moreover testify by my own example that such evils must often have been sent to us by the goodness of Almighty God for our profit. For, gentle reader, who would ever have taught me that there was a God in Heaven if these soldiers had not destroyed my dad's house, and by such a deed driven me out among folk who gave me all fitting instruction thereupon? . . .

The first thing these troopers did was, that they stabled their horses: thereafter each fell to his appointed task: which task was neither more nor less than ruin and destruction. For though some began to slaughter and to boil and to roast so that it looked as if there should be a merry banquet forward, yet others there were who did but storm through the house above and below stairs. Others stowed together great parcels of cloth and apparel and all manner of household stuff, as if they would set up a frippery market. All that they had no mind to take with them they cut in pieces. Some thrust their swords through the hay and straw as if they had not enough sheep and swine to slaughter: and some shook the feathers out of the beds and in their stead stuffed in bacon and other dried meat and provisions as if such were better and softer to sleep upon. Others broke the stove and the windows as if they had a never-ending summer to promise. Houseware of copper and tin they beat flat, and packed such vessels, all bent and spoiled, in with the rest. Bedsteads, tables, chairs, and benches they burned, though there lay many cords of dry wood in the yard. Pots and pipkins must all go to pieces, either because they would eat none but roast flesh, or because their purpose was to make there but a single meal.

Our maid was so handled in the stable that she could not come out; which is a shame to tell of. Our man they laid bound upon the ground, thrust a gag into his mouth, and poured a pailful of filthy water into his body: and by this, which they called a Swedish draught, they forced him to lead a party of them to another place where they captured men and beasts, and brought them back to our farm, in which company were my dad, my mother, and our Ursula.

And now they began: first to take the flints out of their pistols and in place of them to jam the peasants' thumbs in and so to torture the poor rogues as if they had been about the burning of witches: for one of them they had taken they thrust into the baking oven and there lit a fire under him, although he had as yet confessed no crime: as for another, they put a cord round his head and so twisted it tight with a piece of wood that the blood gushed from his mouth and nose and ears. In a word each had his own device to torture the peasants, and each peasant his several tortures.

Hans Jakob Christoph von Grimmelshausen, *Simplicissimus*, translated by S. Goodrich (New York: Daedalus, 1995), pp. 1–3, 8–10, 32–35.

RUSSIA

BLACK SEA

CYPRUS
(to Ottoman Empire)

SWEDEN

TEUTONIC ORDER

POLAND

• Kiev

OTTOMAN EMPIRE

• Constantinople

AEGEAN SEA

MEDITERRANEAN SEA

CRETE
(to Venice)

Stockholm •

BALTIC SEA

EAST PRUSSIA

Danzig

Vistula R.

Warsaw •

HUNGARY

Budapest •

Danube R.

(to Venice)

(to Venice)

CRETE
(to Venice)

Christiana •

DENMARK

Copenhagen •

MECKLEN-BURG

BRANDENBURG

Berlin •

SAXONY

HOLY
ROMAN
EMPIRE

Elbe R.

AUSTRIA

Vienna •

Zara

Ragussa

Cattaro

ADRIATIC SEA

KINGDOM
OF THE
TWO SICILIES

NETHERLANDS

Amsterdam •

HANOVER

Hamburg •

HESSE

BAVARIA

WÜRTTEM-BERG

PARMA

PAPAL
STATES

ITALY

VENICE

MILAN

Naples •

NORTH SEA

SCOTLAND

Edinburgh •

Liverpool •

ENGLAND

London •

English Channel

Rhine R.

SPANISH NETH.

LORRAINE

FRANCHE COMTÉ

SWITZ.

SAVOY

GENOA

MODENA

TUSCANY

CORSICA
(to Genoa)

Rome •

SARDINIA
(to Spain)

Seine R.

Paris •

FRANCE

Loire R.

Bordeaux •

Garonne R.

Rhone R.

Marseilles •

AVIGNON

PIEDMONT

BALEARIC
ISLANDS

IRELAND

Dublin •

ATLANTIC OCEAN

ARAGON

CASTILE

Madrid •

SPAIN

Tagus R.

Strait of Gibraltar

PORTUGAL

Lisbon •

500 Miles

500 Kilometers

250

250

The Church
Spain
Austria
Brandenburg–Prussia
Boundary of the
Holy Roman Empire

EUROPE
AFRICA
Area of detail

EUROPE AT THE END OF THE THIRTY YEARS' WAR

What was at issue in the Thirty Years' War? Why did Catholic France ally with Lutheran Sweden against German and Austrian Catholics? Why did this war, which began as a religious one, soon encompass issues regarding the constitutional government of Germany? How much longer did the Holy Roman empire play an effective role within Europe given the internal upheavals in England, Holland and elsewhere? Why?

DIVERGENT PATHS: SPAIN, FRANCE, AND ENGLAND, 1600–1660

The long century of war between 1540 and 1660 decisively altered the balance of power among the major kingdoms of western Europe. Germany emerged from the Thirty Years' War a devastated and exhausted nation. But after 1600, Spain too was crippled by its unremitting military commitments and exertions. The French monarchy, by contrast, steadily increased its authority over France. By 1660 France had become the most powerful country on the European mainland, decisively eclipsing Spain. In England, meanwhile, a bloody civil war broke out between the king and his critics in Parliament; but after a short-lived experiment in republican rule, England in 1660 returned to its constitutional status as a "mixed" monarchy in which power was shared between king and Parliament.

THE DECLINE OF SPAIN

The story of seventeeth-century Spain's fall from grandeur is almost like a Greek tragedy in its relentless unfolding. Despite the defeat of the "Invincible Armada" in 1588, in 1600 the Spanish empire—comprising all of the Iberian Peninsula (including Portugal, which had been annexed by Phillip II in 1580), half of Italy, half of the Netherlands, all of Central and South America, and the Phillipine Islands in the Pacific Ocean—was still the mightiest power not just in Europe but in the world. Yet a bare half century later this empire on which the sun never set had come close to falling apart

Spain's greatest underlying weakness was economic. At first this may seem like a very odd statement considering that in 1600, as in the three or four previous decades, huge amounts of American silver were being unloaded on the docks of Seville. Yet as contemporaries themselves recognized, "the new world that Spain had conquered was conquering Spain in turn." Lacking either rich agricultural or mineral resources, Spain desperately needed to develop industries and a balanced trading pattern as its rivals England and France were doing. But the dominant Spanish nobility had prized ideals of chivalry over practical business ever since the medieval days when Spanish nobles were engaged in reconquering Christian territory from the Muslims. Thus the Span-

The new world that Spain had conquered was conquering Spain in turn.

ish governing class was only too glad to use American silver to buy manufactured goods from other parts of Europe in order to live in splendor and dedicate itself to military exploits. Thus bullion left the country as soon as it entered, virtually no industry was established, and when the influx of silver began to decline after 1600 the Spanish economy remained with nothing except increasing debts.

Nonetheless, the crown, dedicated to supporting the Counter-Reformation and maintaining Spain's international dominance, would not cease fighting abroad. Indeed, the entire Spanish budget remained on such a war footing that even in the relatively peaceful year of 1608 four million out of a total revenue of seven million ducats were paid for military expenditures. Thus when Spain became engaged in fighting France during the Thirty Years' War it overextended itself. The clearest visible sign of this was that in 1643 French troops at Rocroi inflicted a stunning defeat on the famed Spanish infantry, the first time that a Spanish army had been overcome in battle since the reign of Ferdinand and Isabella. Worse still was the fact that by then two territories belonging to Spain's European empire were in open revolt.

In order to understand the causes of these revolts, we must recognize that in the seventeenth century the governing power of Spain lay entirely in Castile. After the marriage of Isabella of Castile and Ferdinand of Aragon in 1469, Castile had emerged as the dominant partner in the Spanish union, becoming even more dominant when it took over Portugal in 1580. In the absence of any great financial hardships, semi-autonomous Catalunya (the most fiercely independent part of Aragon) endured Castilian hegemony. But in 1640, when the strains of warfare induced Castile to limit Catalan liberties in order to raise more money and men for combat, Catalunya revolted and drove out its Castilian governors. Immediately afterward the Portuguese learned of the Catalan uprising and revolted as well, followed by southern Italians who revolted against Castilian viceroys in Naples and Sicily in 1647. At that point only the momentary inability of Spain's greatest external enemies, France and England, to take advantage of its plight saved the Spanish Empire from utter collapse. Nothing if not determined, the Castilian government quickly put down the Italian revolts and by 1652 also brought Catalunya to heel. But Portugal retained its independence, and by the Peace of the Pyre-

WHAT CAUSED THE DECLINE OF SPAIN IN THE SEVENTEENTH CENTURY?

A CENTURY OF RELIGIOUS WARS   531

nees, signed with France in 1659, Spain in effect abandoned its ambition of dominating Europe.

THE GROWING POWER OF FRANCE

A comparison of the fortunes of Spain and France in the first half of the seventeenth century is highly instructive. Some striking similarities existed between the two countries, but in the end their differences turned out to be most decisive. Spain and France were of almost identical territorial extent, and both countries had been created by the same process of accretion. Just as the Castilian crown had gained Aragon in the north, Granada in the south, and then Portugal, so the kingdom of France had grown by adding on such diverse territories as Languedoc, Dauphiné, Provence, Burgundy, and Brittany. Since the inhabitants of all these territories cherished traditions of local independence as much as the Catalans or Portuguese, and since the rulers of France, like those of Spain, were determined to govern their provinces ever more firmly—especially when the financial stringencies of the Thirty Years' War made ruthless tax collecting urgently necessary—a direct confrontation between the central government and the provinces in France became inevitable, just as in Spain. But France weathered the storm whereas Spain did not, a result largely attributable to France's greater wealth and the greater prestige of the French crown.

In good times most French people, including those from the outlying provinces, tended to revere their king. Certainly they had excellent reason to do so during the reign of Henry IV. Having established religious peace in 1598 by the Edict of Nantes, the affable Henry, who declared that there should be a chicken in every French family's pot each Sunday, set out to restore the prosperity of a country devastated by four decades of civil war. Fortunately France had enormous economic resiliency, owing primarily to its extremely rich and varied agricultural resources. Unlike Spain, which had to import food, France normally was able to feed itself, and Henry's finance minister, the duke of Sully, quickly saw to it that France could feed itself once more. Among other things, Sully distributed throughout the country free copies of a guide to recommended farming techniques and financed the rebuilding or new construction of roads, bridges, and canals to facilitate the flow of goods. In addition, Henry IV was not content to see France rest its economic development on agricultural wealth alone; instead he ordered the construction of royal factories to manufacture luxury goods such as crystal, glass, and tapestries, and he also supported the growth of silk, linen, and woolen cloth industries in many different parts of the country. Moreover, Henry's patronage allowed the explorer Samuel de Champlain to claim parts of Canada as France's first foothold in the New World. Thus Henry IV's reign certainly must be counted as one of the most benevolent in all French history.

CARDINAL RICHELIEU

Far less benevolent was Henry's de facto successor as ruler of France, Cardinal Richelieu (1585–1642). The cardinal, of course, was never the real king of France—the actual title was held from 1610 to 1643 by Henry IV's ineffectual son Louis XIII. But as first minister from 1624 to his death in 1642 Richelieu governed as he wished, and what he wished most of all was to enhance centralized royal power at home and expand French influence in the larger theater of Europe. Accordingly, when Huguenots rebelled against restrictions placed on them by the Edict of Nantes, Richelieu put them down with an iron fist and amended the Edict in 1629 by depriving them of all their political and military rights. Since his armed campaigns against the Huguenots had been very costly, the cardinal then moved to gain more income for the crown by abolishing the semi-autonomy of Burgundy, Dauphiné, and Provence so that he could introduce direct royal taxation in all three areas. Later, to make sure all taxes levied were efficiently collected, Richelieu instituted a new system of local government by royal officials known as intendants, who were expressly commissioned to ride roughshod over any provincial resistance. By these and related methods Richelieu made French government more centralized than ever and managed to double the crown's income during his rule. But since he also engaged in an ambitious foreign policy directed against the Habsburgs of Austria and Spain, resulting in France's costly involvement in the Thirty Years' War, internal pressures mounted in the years after Richelieu's death.

THE FRONDE

A reaction against French governmental centralization manifested itself in a series of revolts between 1648 and 1653 collectively known as "the slingshot tumults," or in French, the *Fronde*. By this time Louis XIII had been succeeded by his son Louis XIV, but because the latter

CARDINAL RICHELIEU ON THE COMMON PEOPLE OF FRANCE

Armand Jean du Plessis, duke of Richelieu and cardinal of the Roman Catholic church was the effective ruler of France from 1624 until his death in 1642. His Political Testament was assembled after his death from historical sketches and memoranda of advice he prepared for King Louis XIII, the ineffectual monarch whom he served. Although the book itself was not published until 1688, there is now little doubt that the writings it contains are indeed Richelieu's own thoughts.

All students of politics agree that when the common people are too well off it is impossible to keep them peaceable. The explanation for this is that they are less well informed than the members of the other orders in the state, who are much more cultivated and enlightened, and so if not preoccupied with the search for the necessities of existence, find it difficult to remain within the limits imposed by both common sense and the law.

It would not be sound to relieve them of all taxation and similar charges, since in such a case they would lose the mark of their subjection and consequently the awareness of their station. Thus being free from paying tribute, they would consider themselves exempted from obedience. One should compare them with mules, which being accustomed to work, suffer more when long idle than when kept busy. But just as this work should be reasonable, with the bur-dens placed upon these animals proportionate to their strength, so it is likewise with the burdens placed upon the people. If they are not moderate, even when put to good public use, they are certainly unjust. I realize that when a king undertakes a program of public works it is correct to say that what the people gain from it is returned by paying the *taille* [the most important tax paid to the crown by the French peasantry]. In the same fashion it can be maintained that what a king takes from the people returns to them, and that they advance it to him only to draw upon it for the enjoyment of their leisure and their investments, which would be impossible if they did not contribute to the support of the state.

The Political Testament of Cardinal Richelieu, translated by Henry Bertram Hill (Madison: University of Wisconsin Press, 1961), pp. 31–32.

was still a boy, France was governed by a regency consisting of Louis' mother, Anne of Austria, and her paramour Cardinal Mazarin. Considering that both were foreigners (Anne was a Habsburg and Mazarin originally an Italian adventurer named Giulio Mazarini), it is not surprising that many of their subjects, including some extremely powerful nobles, hated them. Popular resentments were greater still because the costs of war and several consecutive years of bad harvests had brought France temporarily into a grave economic plight. Thus when cliques of nobles expressed their disgust with Mazarin for primarily self-interested reasons, they found much support throughout the country, and uncoordinated revolts against the regency government flared on and off for several years.

France, however, did not come close to falling apart. Above all, the French crown itself, which retained great reservoirs of prestige owing to a well-established

WHAT CAUSED THE DECLINE OF SPAIN IN THE SEVENTEENTH CENTURY?

A CENTURY OF RELIGIOUS WARS   533

national tradition and the undoubted achievements of Henry IV and Richelieu, was by no means under attack. On the contrary, neither the aristocratic leaders of the Fronde nor the commoners from all ranks who joined them in revolt claimed to be resisting the young king but only the alleged corruption and mismanagement of Mazarin. Some of the rebels, it is true, insisted that part of Mazarin's fault lay in his pursuit of Richelieu's centralizing, antiprovincial policy. But since most of the aristocrats who led the Fronde were merely "outs" who wanted to be "in," they often squabbled among themselves—sometimes even arranging agreements of convenience with the regency or striking alliances with France's enemy, Spain, for momentary gain—and proved completely unable to rally any unified support behind a common program. Thus when Louis XIV began to rule in his own name in 1651 and pretexts for revolting against "corrupt ministers" no longer existed, all opposition was soon silenced. As so often happens, the idealists and poor people paid the greatest price for revolt: in 1653 a defeated leader of popular resistance in Bordeaux was broken on the wheel, and not long afterward a massive new round of taxation was proclaimed. Remembering the turbulence of the Fronde for the rest of his life, Louis XIV resolved never to let his aristocracy or his provinces get out of hand again and ruled as the most effective royal absolutist in all of French history.

THE ENGLISH CIVIL WAR

Compared with the civil disturbances of the 1640s in Spain and France, those in England proved the most momentous in their results for the history of limited government. Whereas the revolts against Castile accomplished only the achievement of Portuguese independence and the crippling of an empire that was already in decline, and all that happened in France was a momentary interruption of the steady advance of royal power, in England a king was executed and enduring barriers were erected against royal absolutism.

England around 1600 was caught up in a trend toward the growth of centralized royal authority characteristic of all western Europe. Not only had Henry VIII and Elizabeth I brought the English church fully under royal control, but both monarchs also employed so called prerogative courts wherein they could proceed against subjects in disregard of traditional English legal safeguards for the rights of the accused. Furthermore, although Parliament met regularly during both reigns, members of Parliament were far less independent than they had been in the fifteenth century: any parliamentary representative who might have stood up to Henry VIII would have lost his head, and almost all parliamentarians admired Elizabeth enough to abide by her policies. Thus when the Stuart dynasty succeeded Elizabeth, the last of the Tudors, it was only natural that the Stuarts would try to increase royal power still more. And indeed they might have succeeded had it not been for their ineptness and an extraordinary combination of forces ranged against them.

JAMES I

Lines of contention were drawn immediately at the accession of Elizabeth's nearest relative, her cousin James VI of Scotland, who in 1603 retained his Scottish crown but also became king of England as James I (1603–1625). Homely but vain, addled but erudite, James fittingly was called by Henry IV of France "the wisest fool in Christendom," and presented the starkest contrast to his predecessor. Whereas Elizabeth knew how to gain her way with Parliament without making a fuss about it, the schoolmasterish foreigner insisted on lecturing parliamentarians that he was semidivine and would brook no resistance: "As it is atheism and blasphemy to dispute what God can do, so it is presumption and high contempt in a subject to dispute what a king can do." Carrying these sentiments further, in a speech to Parliament of 1609 he proclaimed that "kings are not only God's lieutenants on earth . . . but even by God Himself they are called gods."

That such extreme pretensions to divine authority would arouse strong opposition was a result even James should have been able to foresee, for the English ruling groups were still intensely committed to the theory of parliamentary controls on the crown. Yet not just theory was at stake, for the specific policies of the new king antagonized large numbers of his subjects. For example, James insisted on supplementing his income by modes of money raising that had never been sanctioned by Parliament; when the leaders of that body objected, he angrily tore up their protests and dissolved their sessions. Worse, he interfered with the freedom of business by granting monopolies and

England around 1600 was caught up in a trend toward the growth of centralized royal authority characteristic of all western Europe.

James I. "The wisest fool in Christendom."

Charles I. This portrait by Anthony Van Dyck vividly captures the ill-fated monarch's arrogance.

lucrative privileges to favored companies. And, worst of all in the eyes of most patriotic Englishmen, James quickly put an end to the long war with Spain and refused thereafter to become involved in any foreign military entanglements. Today many of us might think that James's commitment to peace was his greatest virtue; certainly his pacifism was justifiable financially since it spared the crown enormous debts. But in his own age James was hated particularly for his peace policy because it made him seem far too friendly with England's traditional enemy, Spain, and because "appeasement" meant leaving the embattled Protestants of Holland and Germany in the lurch.

Although almost all English people (except for a small minority of clandestine Catholics) objected to James I's pacific foreign policy, those who hated it most were a group destined to play the greatest role in overthrowing the Stuarts, namely, the Puritans. Extreme Calvinist Protestants, the Puritans believed that Elizabeth I's religious compromises had not broken fully enough with the forms and doctrines of Roman Catholicism. Called Puritans from their desire to "purify" the English church of all traces of Catholic ritual and observance, they vehemently opposed the English "episcopal system" of church government by bishops. But James I was as committed to retaining episcopalianism as the Puritans were intent on abolishing it because he viewed royally appointed bishops as one of the pillars of a strong monarchy: "No bishop, no king." Since the Puritans were a powerful influence in the House of Commons and many Puritans were also prosperous merchants who opposed James's monopolistic policies and money-raising expediencies, throughout his reign James remained at loggerheads with an extremely powerful group of his subjects for a combination of religious, constitutional, and economic reasons.

CHARLES I

Nonetheless, James survived to die peacefully in bed in 1625, and had it not been for mistakes made by his son Charles I (1625–1649), England might have gone the way of absolutist France. Charles held even more inflated notions of royal power while lacking altogether the "wise pliancy" that had characterized his father. Consequently, Charles was quickly at odds with the leaders of Parliament. Soon after his accession to the throne Charles became involved in a war with France and needed revenue desperately. When Parliament refused to make more than the customary grants, he resorted to forced loans from his subjects, punishing

WHAT CAUSED THE DECLINE OF SPAIN IN THE SEVENTEENTH CENTURY?

A CENTURY OF RELIGIOUS WARS   535

those who failed to comply by quartering soldiers in their homes or throwing them into prison without a trial. In reaction to these practices, Parliament forced the Petition of Right on the king in 1628. This document declared all taxes not voted by Parliament illegal, condemned the quartering of soldiers in private houses, and prohibited arbitrary imprisonment and the establishment of martial law in time of peace.

Angered rather than chastened by the Petition of Right, Charles I soon resolved to rule entirely without Parliament—and nearly succeeded. From 1629 to 1640 no Parliaments were called. During this "eleven years' tyranny," Charles's government lived off a variety of makeshift dues and levies. For example, the crown sold monopolies at exorbitant rates, revived highly antiquated medieval financial claims, and admonished judges to collect the stiffest of fines. Though technically not illegal, all of these expedients were deeply resented. Most controversial was the collection of "ship money," a levy taken on the pretext of a medieval obligation of English seaboard towns to provide ships (or their worth in money) for the royal navy. Extending the payment of ship money from coastal towns to the whole country, Charles threatened to make it a regular tax in contravention of the Petition of Right, and was upheld in a legal challenge of 1637 brought against him on these grounds by the Puritan squire John Hampden.

By such means the king managed to make ends meet without the aid of taxes granted by Parliament. But he became ever more hated by most of his subjects, above all the Puritans, not just because of his constitutional and financial policies but also because he and his intensely unpopular archbishop of Canterbury, William Laud, seemed to be pursuing a course in religion that came much closer to Catholicism than to Calvinism. It was in Scotland, however, not England, that the storm suddenly broke. Like his father, Charles believed in the adage "no bishop, no king" and hence decided, foolhardily, to introduce church government through bishops into staunchly Presbyterian Scotland. The result was an armed rebellion by the Scots, and the first steps toward civil war in England.

To obtain the funds necessary to put down the Scots, Charles had no other choice but to summon Parliament and soon found himself the target of pent-up resentments. Knowing full well that the king was helpless without money, the leaders of the House of Commons determined to take England's government into their own hands. Accordingly, they not only executed the king's first minister, the earl of Strafford, but

they abolished ship money and the prerogative courts that ever since the reign of Henry VIII had served as instruments of arbitrary rule. Most significant, they enacted a law forbidding the crown to dissolve Parliament and requiring the convening of sessions at least once every three years. After some indecision, early in 1642 Charles replied to these acts with a show of force. He marched with his guard into the House of Commons and attempted to arrest five of its leaders. All of them escaped, but an open conflict between crown and Parliament could no longer be avoided. Both parties collected troops and prepared for an appeal to the sword.

CIVIL WAR AND COMMONWEALTH

These events initiated the English civil war, a conflict at once political and religious, which lasted from 1642 to 1649. Arrayed on the royal side were most of England's most prominent aristocrats and largest landowners, who were almost all loyal to the established Church of England, despite their opposition to some of Charles's own religious innovations. Opposed to them, the followers of Parliament included smaller landholders, tradesmen, and manufacturers, the majority of whom were Puritans. The members of the king's party were commonly known by the aristocratic name of Cavaliers. Their opponents, who cut their hair short in contempt for the fashionable custom of wearing curls, were derisively called Roundheads. At first the royalists, having obvious advantages of military experience, won most of the victories. In 1644, however, the parliamentary army was reorganized, and soon afterward the fortunes of battle shifted. The Cavalier forces were badly beaten, and in 1646 the king was compelled to surrender. Soon thereafter, the episcopate was abolished and a Presbyterian church was established throughout England.

The struggle would now have ended had not a quarrel developed within the parliamentary party. The majority of its members, who had allied with the Presbyterian Scots, were ready to restore Charles to the throne as a limited monarch under an arrangement whereby a uniform Calvinistic Presbyterian faith would be imposed on both Scotland and England as the state religion. But a radical minority of Puritans, commonly known as Independents, distrusted Charles and insisted on religious toleration for themselves and all other non-Presbyterian Protestants. Their leader was Oliver Cromwell (1599–1658), who had risen to command the Roundhead army. Taking advantage of the dissension within the ranks of his opponents, Charles renewed the war in 1648, but after a brief campaign was forced to surrender. Cromwell now resolved to end the life of "that man of blood," and, ejecting all the Presbyterians from Parliament by force of arms, obliged the "Rump" Parliament that remained to vote an end to the monarchy. On January 30, 1649 Charles I was beheaded; a short time later the hereditary House of Lords was abolished, and England became a republic.

But founding a republic was far easier than maintaining one, and the new form of government, officially called a Commonwealth, did not last long. Technically the Rump Parliament continued as the legislative body, but Cromwell, with the army at his command, possessed the real power and soon became exasperated by the attempts of the legislators to perpetuate themselves in office and to profit by confiscating the wealth of their opponents. Accordingly, in 1653 he marched a detachment of troops into the Rump Parliament. Saying "Come, I will put an end to your prating," he ordered the members to disperse. Thereby the Commonwealth ceased to exist and was soon followed by the "Protectorate," a virtual dictatorship established under a constitution drafted by officers of the army. Called the *Instrument of Government*, this text was the nearest approximation to a written constitution England has ever had. Extensive powers were given to Cromwell as "lord protector" for life, and his office was made hereditary. At first a Parliament exercised limited authority in making laws and levying taxes, but in 1655 Cromwell abruptly dismissed its members. Thereafter the government became a thinly disguised autocracy, with Cromwell now wielding a sovereignty more absolute than any Stuart monarch ever dreamed of claiming.

THE RESTORATION OF THE MONARCHY

Given the choice between a Puritan military dictatorship and the old royalist regime, when the occasion arose England unhesitatingly opted for the latter. Years of unpopular Calvinist austerities such as the prohibition of any public recreation on Sundays had discredited the Puritans, making most people long for the milder style of the original Elizabethan church. Thus not long after Cromwell's death in 1658, one of his generals seized power and called for elections for a new Parliament, which met in the spring of 1660 and proclaimed as king Charles I's exiled son, Charles II. With the reign of Charles II (1660–1685) an episcopal Church of England was restored, but the same was not true for unrestrained monarchical power. Rather, stat-

CHRONOLOGY

ORIGINS OF THE ENGLISH CIVIL WAR, 1603–1660

Reign of the Stuarts begins	1603
Reign of Charles I	1625–1649
Rule without Parliament	1629–1640
English civil war	1642–1649
Charles I beheaded	1649
Commonwealth	1649–1652
Protectorate	1653–1658
Restoration of the monarchy	1660

ing with characteristic good humor that he did not wish to "resume his travels," Charles agreed to respect Parliament and observe the Petition of Right. Of greatest constitutional significance was the fact that all the legislation passed by Parliament immediately before the outbreak of the civil war, including the requirement to hold Parliaments at least once every three years, remained as law. Thus in striking contrast to absolutist France, England became a limited monarchy. After one further test in the late seventeenth century, the realm of England would soon live up to the poet Milton's prediction of "a noble and puissant nation rousing herself like a strong man after sleep."

THE PROBLEM OF DOUBT AND THE QUEST FOR CERTAINTY

What was Hobbes's solution to the search for authority?

Between 1540 and 1660, Europeans were forced to confront a world in which all that they had once taken for granted was suddenly cast into doubt. An entirely new world had been discovered in the Americas, populated by millions of people whose very existence compelled Europeans to rethink some of their most basic ideas about humanity and human nature. Equally disorienting, the religious uniformity of Europe, although never absolute, had been shattered to an unprecedented extent by the Reformation and the religious wars that arose from it. In 1540, it was still possible to imagine that these religious divisions might be temporary. By 1660, it was clear they would be permanent. No longer, therefore, could Europeans regard revealed religious faith as an adequate foundation for universal philosophical conclusions, for even Christians now disagreed about the fundamental truths of the faith. Political allegiances were similarly under threat, as intellectuals and common people alike began to assert a right to resist princes with whom they disagreed on matters of religion. Even morality and custom were beginning to seem arbitrary and detached from the natural ordering of the world.

> The religious uniformity of Europe had been shattered to an unprecedented extent by the Reformation and the religious wars that arose from it.

Europeans responded to this pervasive climate of doubt in a variety of ways, ranging from radical skepticism to authoritarian assertions of religious fideism and political absolutism. What united their responses, however, was a sometimes desperate search for new foundations upon which to reconstruct some measure of certainty in the face of Europe's new intellectual, religious, and political challenges.

WITCHCRAFT ACCUSATIONS AND THE POWER OF THE STATE

Adding to the fears of Europeans was their conviction that witchcraft was a mortal and increasing threat to their world. Although most people in the Middle Ages believed that certain persons, usually women, could heal or harm through the practice of magic, it was not until the fifteenth century that learned authorities began to insist that such powers could only derive from some kind of "pact" made by the "witch" with the devil. Once this belief became accepted, judicial officers became much more active in seeking out suspected witches for prosecution. In 1484 Pope Innocent VIII ordered papal inquisitors to use all the means at their disposal to detect and eliminate witchcraft, including torture of suspected witches. Predictably, torture increased the number of accused witches who confessed to their alleged crimes; and as more accused witches confessed, more and more witches were "discovered," accused, and executed, even in areas (such as England) where torture was not employed and where the Inquisition did not operate.

In considering the rash of witchcraft persecution that swept early modern Europe, two facts need to be kept in mind. First of all, the witchcraft trials were by no means limited to Catholic countries. Protestant reformers believed in the insidious powers of Satan just as much as Catholics did. Both Luther and Calvin urged that persons accused as witches be tried more peremptorily and sentenced with less leniency than ordinary criminals, a recommendation their followers were only too happy to follow. Second, it was only when the efforts of religious authorities to detect witchcraft were backed up by the coercive powers of secular governments to execute them that the fear of witchcraft became truly murderous. Between 1580 and about 1660, however, enthusiasm for catching and killing "witches" became something like a mania across much of Europe, claiming tens of thousands of victims, of whom at least three quarters were women. The final death toll will never be known, but in the 1620s there was an average of one hundred burnings a year in the German cities of Würzburg and Bamberg; around the

Supposed Witches Worshiping the Devil in the form of a Billy Goat. In the background other "witches" ride bareback on flying demons. This is one of the earliest visual conceptions of witchcraft, dating from around 1460.

same time it was said that the town square of Wolfen-büttel "looked like a little forest, so crowded were the stakes." After 1660, accusations of witchcraft gradually diminished, but isolated incidents, such as the one at Salem, Massachusetts, continued to crop up for another half century.

This witch mania reflects the fears that early modern Europeans held not only about the devil, but also about the adequacy of traditional remedies (such as prayers, amulets, and holy water) to combat the evils of their world. But it also reflects their growing conviction that only the state, and not the church, had the power to protect them. One of the most striking features of the mania for hunting down "witches" is the extent to which these prosecutions, in both Catholic and Protestant countries, were state-sponsored affairs, carried out by secular authorities claiming to act as the protectors of society against the spiritual and temporal evils that assailed it. Even in Catholic countries, where witchcraft prosecutions were sometimes begun in church courts, these cases would be transferred to the state's courts for final judgment and punishment, because church courts were forbidden to impose capital penalties. In Protestant countries, where church courts had been abolished (only England retained church courts), the entire process of detecting, prosecuting, and punishing suspected witches was carried out under the supervision of the state. In both Catholic and Protestant countries, the result of these witchcraft trials was thus a considerable increase in the scope of the state's powers and responsibilities to regulate the lives of its subjects.

> The result of these witchcraft trials was a considerable increase in the scope of the state's powers and responsibilities to regulate the lives of its subjects.

THE SEARCH FOR AUTHORITY

The crisis of Europe's iron century (as even contemporaries sometimes called it) was fundamentally a crisis of authority. Attempts to reestablish some foundation for agreed authority took many forms. For the French nobleman Michel de Montaigne (1533–1592), who wrote during the height of the French wars of religion, the result was a searching skepticism about the possibilities of any certain knowledge whatsoever. The son of a Catholic father and a Huguenot mother of Jewish ancestry, the well-to-do Montaigne retired from a legal career at the age of thirty-eight to devote himself to a life of leisured reflection. The Essays that resulted were a new literary form originally conceived as "experi-

ments" in writing (the French essai simply means "trial"). Because they are extraordinarily well written as well as searchingly reflective, Montaigne's Essays are among the most enduring classics of French literature and thought.

Although the range of subjects of the Essays is wide, two main themes are dominant. One is a pervasive skepticism. Making his motto Que sais-je? ("What do I know?"), Montaigne decided that he knew very little for certain. According to him, "it is folly to measure truth and error by our own capacities" because our capacities are severely limited. Thus, as he maintained in one of his most famous essays, "On Cannibals," what may seem indisputably true and proper to one nation may seem absolutely false to another because "everyone gives the title of barbarism to everything that is not of his usage." From this Montaigne's second main principle followed—the need for moderation. Since all people think they know the perfect religion and the perfect government, yet few agree on what that perfection might be, Montaigne concluded that no religion or government is really perfect and consequently no belief is worth fighting for to the death. Instead, people should accept the teachings of religion on faith, and obey the governments constituted to rule over them, without resorting to fanaticism in either sphere.

Although Montaigne can sound surprisingly modern, he was very much a man of the sixteenth century, believing that "reason does nothing but go astray in everything," and that intellectual curiosity "which prompts us to thrust our noses into everything" is a "scourge of the soul." Montaigne was also a fatalist who thought that in a world governed by unpredictable fortune the best human strategy was to face the good and the bad with steadfastness and dignity. Lest people begin to think too highly of their own abilities, he reminded them that "sit we upon the highest throne in the world, yet we do sit upon our own behinds." And he urged a deliberate attitude of detachment toward the struggles of the day: "To compose our character is our duty, not to compose books, and to win, not battles and provinces, but order and tranquillity in our conduct. Our great and glorious masterpiece is to live appropriately. All other things, ruling, hoarding, building, are only little appendages and props, at most." Nonetheless, despite his unheroic and highly personal tone, the wide circulation of Montaigne's Essays did

MONTAIGNE ON
SKEPTICISM AND FAITH

Michel de Montaigne's Essays *reflect the curious contradictions of his thought, which in turn mirror the tortured combination of uncertainty and faith that characterized the century in which he lived. Although he begins here by asserting the limits on human knowledge, he ends by concluding that these limits impose on human beings an obligation to accept completely every aspect of the church's religious teachings.*

Perhaps it is not without reason that we attribute facility in belief and conviction to simplicity and ignorance; for . . . the more a mind is empty and without counterpoise, the more easily it gives beneath the weight of the first persuasive argument. That is why children, common people, women, and sick people are most subject to being led by the ears. But then, on the other hand, it is foolish presumption to go around disdaining and condemning as false whatever does not seem likely to us; which is an ordinary vice in those who think they have more than common ability. I used to do so once. . . . But reason has taught me that to condemn a thing thus, dogmatically, as false and impossible, is to assume the advantage of knowing the bounds and limits of God's will and of the power of our mother Nature; and that there is no more notable folly in the world than to reduce these things to the measure of our capacity and competence. . . .

It is a dangerous and fateful presumption, besides the absurd temerity that it implies, to disdain what we do not comprehend. For after you have established, according to your fine understanding, the limits of truth and falsehood, and it turns out that you must necessarily believe things even stranger than those you deny, you are obliged from then on to abandon these limits. Now what seems to me to bring as much disorder into our consciences as anything, in these religious troubles that we are in, is this partial surrender of their beliefs by Catholics. It seems to them that they are being very moderate and understanding when they yield to their opponents some of the articles in dispute. But, besides the fact that they do not see what an advantage it is to a man charging you for you to begin to give ground and withdraw, and how much that encourages him to pursue his point, those articles which they select as the most trivial are sometimes very important. We must either submit completely to the authority of our ecclesiastical government, or do without it completely. It is not for us to decide what portion of obedience we owe it.

Montaigne: Selections from the Essays, translated and edited by Donald M. Frame (Arlington Heights, Ill.: AHM Publishing Corporation, 1971), pp. 34–38.

help combat fanaticism and religious intolerance in his own and subsequent ages.

Montaigne sought refuge from the trials of his age in skepticism, distance, and resigned dignity. His contemporary, the French lawyer Jean Bodin (1530–1596), looked instead to resolve the disorders of the day by reestablishing the powers of the state on new and more secure foundations. Like Montaigne, Bodin was particularly troubled by the upheavals caused by the religious wars in France—he had even witnessed the frightful St. Bartholomew's Day Massacre of 1572 in Paris. But instead of shrugging his shoulders about the bloodshed, he resolved to offer a political plan to make sure turbulence would cease. This he did in his monumental *Six Books of the Commonwealth* (1576), the earliest fully developed statement of absolute governmental sovereignty in Western political thought. According to Bodin, the state arises from the needs of collections of families, but once constituted should brook no opposition, for maintaining order is its paramount duty. Whereas previous writers on law and politics had groped toward a theory of governmental sovereignty, Bodin was the first to offer a succinct definition; for him, sovereignty was "the most high, absolute, and perpetual power over all subjects," consisting principally in the power "to give laws to subjects without their consent." Although Bodin acknowledged the theoretical possibility of government by aristocracy or democracy, he assumed that the nation-states of his day would be ruled by monarchs and insisted that such monarchs could in no way be limited, either by legislative or judicial bodies, or even by laws made by their predecessors or themselves. Expressing the sharpest opposition to contemporary Huguenots who were saying (in contravention of the original teachings of Luther and Calvin) that subjects had a right to resist "ungodly princes," Bodin maintained that every subject must trust in the ruler's "mere and frank good will." Even if the ruler proved a tyrant, Bodin insisted that the subject had no warrant to resist, for any resistance would open the door "to a licentious anarchy which is worse than the harshest tyranny in the world."

The case for resisting unrestrained state power was expressed most eloquently by the great English Puritan poet John Milton, who enunciated a stirring defense of freedom of the press in his *Areopagitica* (1644). Similarly bold critics of the unlimited power of monarchs were a party of Milton's Puritan contemporaries known as Levellers, the first exponents of popular democracy in the West since the ancient Greeks. Organizing themselves as a pressure group within Cromwell's army, the Levellers—who derived their name from their advocacy of equal political rights for all classes—agitated in favor of a parliamentary republic based on nearly universal male suffrage. But since Oliver Cromwell, who believed that the only grounds for suffrage was sufficient property, would have none of this, once Cromwell assumed power the Leveller party disintegrated. No widespread extension of the right to vote in England would occur until the nineteenth century.

Far to the other extreme from the Levellers was the political philosopher Thomas Hobbes (1588–1679), whose reactions to the English civil war led him to become the most forceful advocate of unrestrained state power of all time. Like Bodin, who was moved by the events of St. Bartholomew's Day to formulate a doctrine of political absolutism, Hobbes was moved by the turmoil of the English civil war to do the same in his classic of political theory, *Leviathan* (1651). Yet Hobbes differed from Bodin in several respects. For one, whereas Bodin assumed that the absolute sovereign power would be a royal monarch, Hobbes made no such assumption. Any form of government capable of protecting its subjects' lives and property might act as a sovereign (and hence all-powerful) Leviathan. Then too, whereas Bodin defined his state as "the lawful government of families" and hence did not believe that the state could abridge private property rights because families could not exist without property, Hobbes's state existed to rule over atomistic individuals and thus was licensed to trample over both liberty and property if the government's own survival was at stake.

But the most fundamental difference between Bodin and Hobbes lay in the latter's uncompromisingly pessimistic view of human nature. Hobbes posited that the "state of nature" that existed before civil government came into being was a condition of "war of all against all." Since man naturally behaves as "a wolf" toward other men, human life without government is necessarily "solitary, poor, nasty, brutish, and short." To escape such consequences, people therefore surrendered their liberties to a sovereign ruler in exchange for his agreement to keep the peace. Having granted away their liberties, subjects have no right whatsoever to seek them back, and the sovereign could therefore tyrannize as he likes—free to oppress his charges in any way other than to kill them, an act that would negate the very purpose of his rule, which is to preserve his subjects' lives.

Hobbes's views were vastly unpopular—proponents of constitutional liberties detested his conclusions, and royalists detested his premises. Although he buttressed his conclusions in the (rarely read) third and fourth books of *Leviathan* by citing biblical passages, he developed his arguments in the first two books like a geometric proof, starting with the observable facts of individual sense perception, and then reasoning upwards to the political principles that must flow from these facts. Hobbes was contemptuous of dynastic

DEMOCRACY AND THE ENGLISH CIVIL WAR

The English civil war raised fundamental issues about the political rights and responsibilities of Englishmen. Many of these issues were addressed in a lengthy debate held within the General Council of Cromwell's New Model Army at Putney in October 1647. Interestingly none of the participants in these debates seems to have recognized the implications their arguments might have for the political rights of women. Only King Charles, speaking moments before his execution in 1649, saw the radical implications of the constitutional experiment on which the Parliamentary forces had embarked—but ironically, it was his own radical assertions of monarchical authority that prompted the rebellion that overthrew him.

THE ARMY DEBATES, 1647

Colonel Rainsborough: Really, I think that the poorest man that is in England has a life to live as the greatest man; and therefore truly, sir, I think it's clear, that every man that is to live under a government ought first by his own consent to put himself under that government; and I do think that the poorest man in England is not at all bound in a strict sense to that government that he has not had a voice to put himself under . . . insomuch that I should doubt whether I was an Englishman or not, that should doubt of these things.

General Ireton: Give me leave to tell you, that if you make this the rule, I think you must fly for refuge to an absolute natural right, and you must deny all civil right; and I am sure it will come to that in the consequence. . . . For my part, I think it is no right at all. I think that no person has a right to an interest or share in the disposing of the affairs of the kingdom, and in determining or choosing those that shall determine what laws we shall be ruled by here, no person has a right to this that has not a permanent fixed interest in this kingdom, and those persons together are properly the represented of this kingdom who, taken together, and consequently are to make up the representers of this kingdom. . . .

We talk of birthright. Truly, birthright there is. . . . [M]en may justly have by birthright, by their very being born in England, that we should not seclude them out of England. That we should not refuse to give them air and place and ground, and the freedom of the highways and other things, to live amongst us, not any man that is born here, though he in birth or by his birth there come nothing at all that is part of the permanent interest of this kingdom to him. That I think is due to a man by birth. But that by a man's being born here he shall have a share in that power that shall dispose of the lands here, and of all things here, I do not think it is a sufficient ground.

Divine Right and Democracy: An Anthology of Political Writing in Stuart England, edited by David Wootton (New York: Viking Penguin, 1986), pp. 286–287 (language modernized).

CHARLES I ON THE SCAFFOLD, 1649

I think it is my duty, to God first, and to my country, for to clear myself both as an honest man, a good king, and a good Christian.

I shall begin first with my innocence. In truth I think it not very needful for me to insist long upon this, for all the world knows that I never did begin a war with the two Houses of Parliament; and I call God to witness, to whom I must shortly make an account, that I never did intend to incroach upon their privileges. . . .

As for the people—truly I desire their liberty and freedom as much as anybody whatsoever. But I must tell you that their liberty and freedom consists in having of government those laws by which their lives and goods may be most their own. It is not for having share in government. That is nothing pertaining to them. A subject and a sovereign are clean different things, and therefore, until they do that—I mean that

you do put the people in that liberty as I say—certainly they will never enjoy themselves.

Sirs, it was for this that now I am come here. If I would have given way to an arbitrary way, for to have all laws changed according to the power of the sword, I needed not to have come here. And therefore I tell you (and I pray God it be not laid to your charge) that I am the martyr of the people.

Great Issues in Western Civilization, edited by Brian Tierney, Donald Kagan, and L. Pearce Williams (New York: Random House, 1967), pp. 46–47.

claims based on blood lineage, and had seen at first hand that the "divine right of kings" was no deterrent to rebellion and anarchy. He sought therefore to establish a new science of politics that would ground political obligation not on tradition or divine delegation, but instead on empirical observation, reason, and the effective use of force to preserve order. In his attempt to resolve the seventeenth-century crisis of authority, what is most revealing about Hobbes is therefore not his conclusions, but the reasoning by which he arrives at them.

Perhaps the most moving attempt to respond to the problem of doubt in seventeenth-century culture was offered by the French moral and religious philosopher Blaise Pascal (1623–1662). Pascal began his career as a mathematician and scientific rationalist. A modern computer language has been named for him because he constructed the first calculating machine. (He did this when he was nineteen years old.) But at age thirty Pascal abandoned science as the result of a conversion experience and became a firm adherent of Jansenism, a puritanical faction within French Catholicism. From then until his death he worked on a highly ambitious philosophical-religious project meant to persuade

doubters of the truth of Christianity by appealing simultaneously to their intellects and their emotions. Because of his premature death all that came of this effort was his *Pensées* ("Thoughts"), a collection of fragments and short informal pieces about religion written with great literary power. In these he argued that faith alone could show the way to salvation and that "the heart has its reasons of which reason itself knows nothing." Pascal's *Pensées* express the author's own terror, anguish, and awe in the face of evil and eternity, but present that awe itself as evidence for the existence of God. Pascal's hope was that on this foundation, some measure of hopefulness about humanity and its capacity for self-knowledge could be re-erected that would avoid both the dogmatism and the extreme skepticism that were so prominent in seventeenth-century society.

LITERATURE AND THE ARTS

What was the relationship between the Baroque school and the Counter-Reformation?

Doubt and the uncertainty of human knowledge were also primary themes in the profusion of literature and art produced during western Europe's iron century. Of course not every poem, play, or painting of the era expressed the same message. During a hundred twenty years of extraordinary literary and artistic creativity, works of all genres and sentiments were produced, ranging from the frothiest farces to the darkest tragedies, from the serenest still lifes to the most violent scenes of religious martyrdom. The greatest writ-

CHRONOLOGY

THE SEARCH FOR AUTHORITY, 1572–1670

Montaigne's *Essays*	1572–1580
Bodin's *Six Books of the Commonwealth*	1576
Milton's *Areopagatica*	1644
Hobbes's *Leviathan*	1651
Pascal's *Pensées*	1670

WHAT WAS THE RELATIONSHIP BETWEEN THE BAROQUE SCHOOL AND THE COUNTER-REFORMATION?

LITERATURE AND THE ARTS   543

ers and painters of the period all were moved by a realization of the ambiguities and ironies of human existence not unlike that expressed in different ways by Montaigne and Pascal. They all were fully aware of the horrors of war and human suffering so rampant in their day, but they also sought some measure of redemption for human beings caught up in a world that treated them so cruelly. Out of this tragic balance came some of the greatest works in the entire history of European literature and art.

MIGUEL DE CERVANTES (1547–1616)

Cervantes' masterpiece, the satirical romance *Don Quixote*, recounts the adventures of a Spanish gentleman, Don Quixote of La Mancha, who becomes slightly unbalanced by his constant reading of chivalric epics. His mind filled with all kinds of fantastic adventures, he sets out at the age of fifty on the slippery road of knight-errantry, imagining windmills to be glowering giants and flocks of sheep to be armies of infidels whom it is his duty to rout with his spear. In his distorted fancy he mistakes inns for castles and serving girls for courtly ladies on fire with love. Set off in contrast to the "knight-errant" is the figure of his faithful squire, Sancho Panza. The latter represents the ideal of the practical man, with his feet on the ground and content with the modest but substantial pleasures of eating, drinking, and sleeping. Yet Cervantes clearly does not wish to say that the realism of a Sancho Panza is categorically preferable to the "quixotic" idealism of his master. Rather, the two men represent different facets of human nature. Without any doubt, *Don Quixote* is a devastating satire on the anachronistic chivalric mentality that was already hastening Spain's decline. But for all that, the reader's sympathies remain with the protagonist, the man from La Mancha who dares to "dream the impossible dream."

ELIZABETHAN AND JACOBEAN DRAMA

Writing after England's victory over the Spanish Armada, when national pride was at a peak, the dramatists of the so-called English Renaissance exhibited great exuberance without descending into a facile optimism. In fact a strain of reflective seriousness pervades all their best works, and a few, such as the tragedian John Webster (c. 1580–c. 1625), who "saw the skull beneath the skin," were if anything morbid pessimists. Among a bevy of great Elizabethan and Jacobean playwrights, however, the most outstanding were Christopher Marlowe (1564–1593), Ben Jonson (c. 1572–1637), and William Shakespeare (1564–1616). Of the three, the fiery Marlowe, whose life was cut short in a tavern brawl before he reached the age of thirty, was the most popular in his own day. In plays such as *Tamburlaine* and *Doctor Faustus* Marlowe created larger-than-life heroes who seek and come close to conquering everything in their path and feeling every possible sensation. But they meet unhappy ends because, for Marlowe, there are limits on human striving, and wretchedness as well as greatness lies in the human lot. Thus although Faustus asks a reincarnated Helen of Troy, conjured up by Satan, to make him "immortal with a kiss," he dies and is damned in the end because immortality is not awarded by the devil or to be found in earthly kisses.

In contrast to the heroic tragedies of Marlowe, Ben Jonson wrote corrosive comedies that expose human vices and foibles. In the particularly bleak *Volpone* Jonson shows people behaving like deceitful and lustful animals, but in the later *Alchemist* he balances an attack on quackery and gullibility with admiration for resourceful lower-class characters who cleverly take advantage of their supposed betters.

The greatest of the Elizabethan dramatists, William Shakespeare was born into the family of a tradesman in the provincial town of Stratford-on-Avon. Little is known about his early life. He left his native village, having gained a modest education, when he was about twenty, and went to London where he found employment in the theater. How he eventually became an actor and still later a writer of plays is uncertain, but by the age of twenty-eight he had definitely acquired a reputation as an author sufficient to excite the jealousy of his rivals. Before he retired to his native Stratford about 1610 to spend the rest of his days in ease, he had written or collaborated in writing nearly forty plays, over and above one hundred fifty sonnets, and two long narrative poems.

Since their author's death, Shakespeare's plays have become a kind of secular Bible wherever the English language is spoken. The reasons lie in the author's unrivaled gift of expression, in his scintillating wit, and most of all in his profound analysis of human character seized by passion and tried by fate. Shakespeare's dramas fall thematically into three groups. Those written during the playwright's early years are characterized by a sense of confidence that, despite human foolishness, the world is fundamentally orderly and just. These include a number of the history plays, which recount England's struggles and glories leading up to the triumph of the Tudor dynasty; the lyrical romantic tragedy *Romeo and Juliet;* and a number of comedies including the magical *Midsummer Night's Dream, Twelfth Night, As You Like It,* and *Much Ado about Nothing.* Despite the last-named title, few even of the plays of Shakespeare's early, lightest period are "much ado about nothing." Rather, most explore fundamental problems of psychological identity, honor and ambition, love and friendship. Occasionally they also contain touches of deep seriousness, as in *As You Like It,* when Shakespeare has a character pause to reflect that "all the world's a stage, and all the men and women merely players" who pass through seven "acts" or stages of life.

The plays from Shakespeare's second period are far darker in mood, being characterized by bitterness, pathos, and a troubled searching into the mysteries and meaning of human existence. The series begins with the tragedy of indecisive idealism represented by *Hamlet,* goes on to the cynicism of *Measure for Measure* and *All's Well That Ends Well,* and culminates in the searing tragedies of *Macbeth* and *King Lear,* wherein characters assert that "life's but a walking shadow . . . a tale told by an idiot, full of sound and fury signifying nothing," and that "as flies to wanton boys are we to the gods; they kill us for their sport." Despite their gloom, however, the plays of Shakespeare's second period contain some of the dramatist's greatest flights of poetic grandeur.

Shakespeare ended his dramatic career, however, with a third period characterized by a profound spirit of reconciliation and peace. Of the three plays (all idyllic romances) written during this final period, the last, *The Tempest,* is the widest ranging in its reflections on human nature and the power of art. Ancient animosities are buried and wrongs are righted by a combination of natural and supernatural means, and a wide-eyed, youthful heroine rejoices on first seeing men with the words "O brave new world, that has such people in it!" Here, then, Shakespeare seems to be saying that despite humanity's trials, life is not so bitter after all, and the divine plan of the universe is ultimately benevolent and just.

Though less versatile than Shakespeare, not far behind him in eloquent grandeur stands the Puritan poet John Milton (1608–1674). The leading publicist of Oliver Cromwell's regime, Milton wrote the official defense of the beheading of Charles I as well as a number of treatises justifying Puritan positions in contemporary affairs. But he also loved the Greek and Latin classics at least as much as the Bible, and wrote a perfect pastoral elegy, *Lycidas,* mourning the loss of a dear friend in purely classical terms. Later, when forced into

retirement by the accession of Charles II, Milton, though now blind, embarked on writing a classical epic, *Paradise Lost,* out of material found in Genesis concerning the creation of the world and the fall of man. Setting out to "justify the ways of God to man," Milton in *Paradise Lost* first plays "devil's advocate" by creating the compelling character of Satan, who defies God with boldness and subtlety. But Satan is more than counterbalanced in the end by the real "epic hero" of *Paradise Lost,* Adam, who learns to accept the human lot of moral responsibility and suffering, and is last seen leaving Paradise with Eve, the world "all before them."

MANNERISM

The ironies and tensions inherent in human existence were also portrayed with eloquence and profundity by several immortal masters of the visual arts who flour-

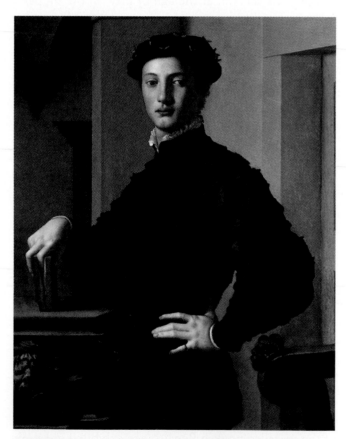

Portrait of a Young Man, by Bronzino (1503–1572). Bronzino was a Florentine Mannerist painter who preferred the "objective" representation of oddities. Notice the carefully chiseled grotesques at the bottom and the young man's wandering left eye. The numerous contrasts between light and shade and the large number of vertical surfaces in the background contribute to a sense of surrealism.

WHAT WAS THE RELATIONSHIP BETWEEN THE BAROQUE SCHOOL AND THE COUNTER-REFORMATION?

LITERATURE AND THE ARTS   545

View of Toledo, by El Greco. Light breaks where no sun shines. One of the most awesomely mysterious paintings in the entire Western tradition.

indebted to Michelangelo but went much farther than he did in emphasizing shadowy contrasts, restlessness, and distortion. Of this second group, the two most outstanding were the Venetian Tintoretto (1518–1594) and the Spaniard El Greco (c. 1541–1614). Combining aspects of Michelangelo's style with the traditionally Venetian taste for rich color, Tintoretto produced an enormous number of monumentally large canvases devoted to religious subjects that still inspire awe with their broodingly shimmering light and gripping drama. More emotional still is the work of Tintoretto's disciple, El Greco. Born Domenikos Theotokopoulos on the Greek island of Crete, this extraordinary artist absorbed some of the stylized elongation characteristic of Greco-Byzantine icon painting before traveling to Italy to learn color and drama from Tintoretto. Finally he settled in Spain, where he was called "El Greco"—"the Greek." El Greco's paintings were too strange to be greatly appreciated in his own age, and even now they appear so unbalanced as to seem the work of one almost deranged. Yet such a view slights El Greco's deeply mystical Catholic fervor as well as his technical achievements. Best known today is his transfigured landscape, the *View of Toledo*, with its somber but awesome light breaking where no sun shines. But equally inspiring are his swirling religious scenes and several of his stunning portraits in which gaunt, dignified Spaniards radiate a rare blend of austerity and spiritual insight.

ished during this tumultuous century. The dominant goal in Italian and Spanish painting during the first half of this period, the years between about 1540 and 1600, was to fascinate the viewer with special effects. This goal, however, was achieved by means of two entirely different styles. (Confusingly, both styles are sometimes referred to as "Mannerism.") The first was based on the style of the Renaissance master Raphael, but moved from that painter's gracefulness to a highly self-conscious elegance bordering on the bizarre and surreal. Representatives of this approach were the Florentines Pontormo (1494–1557) and Bronzino (1503–1572). Their sharp-focused portraits are flat and cold, yet strangely riveting.

The other extreme was theatrical in a more conventional sense—highly dramatic and emotionally compelling. Painters who followed this approach were

BAROQUE ART AND ARCHITECTURE

The dominant artistic school of southern Europe from about 1600 until the early 1700s was that of the Baroque, a school not only of painting but of sculpture and architecture. The Baroque style retained aspects of the dramatic and the irregular, but it avoided seeming bizarre or overheated and aimed above all to instill a

David, by Bernini (1598–1680). Whereas the earlier conceptions of David by the Renaissance sculptors Donatello and Michelangelo were reposeful (see p. 471), the Baroque Sculptor Bernini chose to portray his young hero at the peak of physical exertion.

sense of the affirmative. Originating in Rome as an expression of the ideals of the Counter-Reformation papacy and the Jesuit order, Baroque architecture in particular aimed to gain adherence for a specifically Catholic world view. Similarly, Baroque painting often was done in the service of the Counter-Reformation church, which at its high tide around 1620 seemed everywhere to be on the offensive. When Baroque painters were not celebrating Counter-Reformation ideals, most of them worked in the service of monarchs who sought their own glorification.

The most imaginative and influential figure of the Roman Baroque was the architect and sculptor Gianlorenzo Bernini (1598–1680), a frequent employee of the papacy who created a magnificent celebration of papal grandeur in the sweeping colonnades leading up to St. Peter's Basilica. Breaking with the serene Renaissance classicism of Palladio, Bernini's architecture retained such classical elements as columns and domes, but combined them in ways meant to express both aggressive restlessness and great power. Bernini was also one of the first to experiment with church facades built "in depth"—building frontages not conceived as continuous surfaces but that jutted out at odd angles and

The Maids of Honor, by Diego Velázquez. The artist himself is at work on a double portrait of the king and queen of Spain (who can be seen in the rear mirror), but reality is more obvious in the foreground in the persons of the delicately impish princess, her two maids, and a misshapen dwarf. The twentieth-century Spanish artist Picasso gained great inspiration from this work.

WHAT WAS THE RELATIONSHIP BETWEEN THE BAROQUE SCHOOL AND THE COUNTER-REFORMATION?

LITERATURE AND THE ARTS   547

seemed to invade the open space in front of them. If the purpose of these innovations was to draw the viewer emotionally into the work of art, the same may be said for Bernini's aims in sculpture. Harking back to the restless motion of Hellenistic statuary —particularly the Laocoön group— and building on tendencies already present in the later sculpture of Michelangelo, Bernini's statuary emphasizes drama and incites the viewer to respond to it rather than serenely to observe.

Since most Italian Baroque painters lacked Bernini's artistic genius, to view the very greatest masterpieces of southern European Baroque painting one must look to Spain and the work of Diego

The Harvesters, by Brueghel. Brueghel chose to depict both the hard work and the recreation of the peasantry.

Velázquez (1599–1660). Unlike Bernini, Velázquez, a court painter in Madrid just when Spain hung on the brink of ruin, was not an entirely typical exponent of the Baroque style. Certainly many of his canvases display a characteristically Baroque delight in motion, drama, and power, but Velázquez's best work is characterized by a more restrained thoughtfulness than is usually found in the Baroque. Thus his famous *Surrender of Breda* shows muscular horses and splendid Spanish grandees on the one hand, but un-Baroque sympathy for defeated, disarrayed troops on the other. Velázquez's single greatest painting, *The Maids of Honor*, done around 1656 after Spain's collapse, is one of the most thoughtful and probing artistic examinations of illusion and reality ever executed.

DUTCH PAINTING IN THE GOLDEN AGE

Southern Europe's main northern rival for artistic laurels was the Netherlands, where three extremely dissimilar painters all explored the theme of the greatness and wretchedness of man to the fullest. The earliest, Peter Brueghel (c. 1525–1569), worked in a vein related to earlier Netherlandish realism. But unlike his predecessors, who favored quiet urban scenes,

Brueghel exulted in portraying the busy, elemental life of the peasantry. Most famous in this respect are his rollicking *Peasant Wedding* and *Peasant Wedding Dance,* and his spacious *Harvesters,* in which guzzling and snoring field hands are taking a well-deserved break from their heavy labors under the noon sun. Such vistas give the impression of uninterrupted rhythms of life, but late in his career Brueghel became appalled by the intolerance and bloodshed he witnessed during the Calvinist riots and the Spanish repression in the Netherlands and expressed his criticism in an understated yet searing manner. In *The Blind Leading the Blind,* for example, we see what happens when ignorant fanatics start showing the way to each other. More powerful still is Brueghel's *Massacre of the Innocents,* which from a distance looks like a snug scene of a Flemish village buried in snow. In fact, however, heartless soldiers are methodically breaking into homes and slaughtering babies, the simple peasant folk are fully at their mercy, and the artist—alluding to a Gospel forgotten by warring Catholics and Protestants alike—seems to be saying "as it happened in the time of Christ, so it happens now."

Vastly different from Brueghel was the Netherlandish Baroque painter Peter Paul Rubens (1577–1640). Since the Baroque was an international movement closely linked to the spread of the Counter-

The Massacre of the Innocents, by Brueghel (c. 1525–1569). This painting shows how effectively art can be used as a means of social commentary. Many art historians believe that Brueghel was tacitly depicting the suffering of the Netherlands at the hands of the Spanish in his own day.

The Horrors of War, by Rubens (1577–1640). The war god Mars here casts aside his mistress Venus and threatens humanity with death and destruction. In his old age Rubens took a far more critical view of war than he did for most of his earlier career.

Reformation, it should offer no surprise that Baroque style was extremely well represented in just that part of the Netherlands which, after long warfare, had been retained by Spain. In fact, Rubens of Antwerp was a far more typical Baroque artist than Velázquez of Madrid, painting literally thousands of robust canvases that glorified resurgent Catholicism or exalted second-rate aristocrats by portraying them as epic heroes dressed in bearskins. Even when Rubens's intent was not overtly propagandistic he customarily reveled in the sumptuous extravagance of the Baroque manner, being perhaps most famous today for the pink and rounded flesh of his well-nourished nudes. But unlike a host of lesser Baroque artists, Rubens was not lacking in subtlety and was a man of many moods. His gentle portrait of his son Nicholas catches unaffected childhood in a moment of repose, and though throughout most of his career Rubens had celebrated martial valor, his late *Horrors of War* movingly portrays what he himself called "the grief of unfortunate Europe, which, for so many years now, has suffered plunder, outrage, and misery."

Aristotle Contemplating the Bust of Homer, by Rembrandt (1606–1669). The artist brilliantly captures the philosopher as he appears to be mesmerized by the aura of one of the greatest poets.

In some ways a blend of Brueghel and Rubens, the greatest of all Netherlandish painters, Rembrandt van Rijn (1606–1669), defies all attempts at facile characterization. Living across the border from the Spanish Netherlands in staunchly Calvinistic Holland, Rembrandt belonged to a society that was too austere to tolerate the unbuckled realism of a Brueghel or the fleshy Baroque pomposity of a Rubens. Yet Rembrandt managed to put both realistic and Baroque traits to new uses. In his early career he gained fame and fortune as a painter of biblical scenes that lacked the Baroque's fleshiness but retained its grandeur in their swirling forms and stunning experiments with light. Rembrandt was also active as a portrait painter who knew how to flatter his subjects by emphasizing their Calvinistic steadfastness, to the great advantage of his purse. But gradually his prosperity faded, apparently in part because he grew tired of flattering and definitely because he made some bad investments. As personal tragedies mounted in the painter's middle and declining years, his art became more pensive and sombre, but it gained

in dignity, subtle lyricism, and awesome mystery. Thus his later portraits, including several self-portraits, are imbued with introspective qualities and a suggestion that only half the story is being told. Equally moving are explicitly philosophical paintings such as *Aristotle Contemplating the Bust of Homer,* in which the philosopher seems spellbound by the radiance of the epic poet, and *The Polish Rider,* in which realistic and Baroque elements merge into a higher synthesis portraying a pensive young man setting out fearlessly into a perilous world. Like Shakespeare, Rembrandt knew that life's journey is full of perils, but his most mature paintings suggest that these can be mastered with a courageous awareness of one's human shortcomings.

CONCLUSION

Between 1540 and 1660, Europe was racked by a combination of religious war, political rebellions, and economic crises that undermined confidence in traditional

Self-Portraits. Self-portraits became common during the sixteenth and seventeenth centuries, reflecting the intense introspectiveness of the period. Left: Rembrandt painted more than sixty self-portraits; this one, dating from around 1660, captures the artist's creativity, theatricality (note the costume), and the honesty of his self-examination. Right: Judith Leyster (1609–1660) was a Dutch contemporary of Rembrandt who pursued a successful career as an artist during her early twenties, before she married. Respected in her own day, she was all but forgotten for centuries thereafter.

structures of social, religious, and political authority. The result was fear, skepticism, and a search for new, more certain foundations on which to rebuild the social, political, and religious order of Europe. For artists and intellectuals, the period proved to be one of the most creative epochs in the history of Europe. But for common people, the century was one of extraordinary suffering.

After a hundred years of destructive efforts to restore the religious unity of Europe through war, a de facto religious toleration between states was beginning to emerge by 1660 as the only way to preserve the European political order. Within states, toleration was still very limited when this terrible century ended. But in territories where religious rivalries ran too deep to be overcome, rulers were beginning to discover that loyalty to the state was a value that could override even the religious divisions among their subjects. The end result of this century of crises was thus to strengthen Europeans' confidence in the powers of the state to heal their wounds and right their wrongs, with religion relegated more and more to the private sphere of individual conscience. In the following centuries, this new confidence in the state as an autonomous moral agent that acts in accordance with its own "reasons of state," and for its own purposes, would prove a powerful challenge to the traditions of limited consensual government that had emerged out of the Middle Ages.

SELECTED READINGS

Bonney, Richard. *The European Dynastic States, 1494–1660.* Oxford and New York, 1991. An excellent recent survey of continental Europe during the "long" sixteenth century.

Briggs, Robin. *Witches and Neighbors: The Social and Cultural Context of European Witchcraft.* New York, 1996. An influential recent account of continental witchcraft.

———. *Early Modern France, 1560–1715,* 2d ed. Oxford and New York, 1997. Updated and authoritative, with new bibliographies.

Cervantes, Miguel de. *Don Quixote.* Translated by Walter Starkie. New York, 1957.

Clarke, Stuart. *Thinking with Demons: The Idea of Witchcraft in Early*

Modern Europe. Oxford and New York, 1999. By placing demonology into the context of sixteenth- and seventeenth-century intellectual history, Clarke makes sense of it in new and exciting ways.

Cochrane, Eric, Charles M. Gray, and Mark A. Kishlansky. *Early Modern Europe: Crisis of Authority.* Chicago, 1987. An outstanding source collection from the University of Chicago Readings in Western Civilization series.

Dunn, Richard S. *The Age of Religious Wars, 1559–1715,* 2d ed. New York, 1979. Still the best textbook on this period.

Guy, John A. *Tudor England.* Oxford and New York, 1988. An excellent textbook account of a highly controversial subject.

Haigh, Christopher. *Elizabeth I.* 1988. A reliable scholarly biography of this much-studied queen, stressing her political acumen.

Held, Julius S., and Donald Posner. *Seventeenth- and Eighteenth-Century Art: Baroque Painting, Sculpture, Architecture.* New York, 1971. The most complete and best-organized introductory review of the subject in English.

Hibbard, Howard. *Bernini.* Baltimore, 1965. The basic study in English of this central figure of Baroque artistic activity.

Hirst, Derek. *England in Conflict, 1603–1660: Kingdom, Community, Commonwealth.* Oxford and New York, 1999. A complete revision of the author's *Authority and Conflict* (1986), this is an up-to-date and balanced account of a period that has been a historical battleground over the past twenty years.

Hobbes, Thomas. *Leviathan.* Edited by C. B. Macpherson. New York, 1968. Macpherson's introduction is dated, but the text is as Hobbes wrote it and contains the entirety of *Leviathan,* not just the first two parts.

Holt, Mack P. *The French Wars of Religion, 1562–1629.* Cambridge and New York, 1995. The most recent and best account.

Kors, Alan Charles, and Edward Peters. *Witchcraft in Europe, 400–1700: A Documentary History,* 2d ed. Philadelphia, 2000. A superb collection of documents, significantly expanded in the second edition, with up-to-date commentary.

Israel, Jonathan I. *The Dutch Republic and the Hispanic World, 1606–1661.* Oxford and New York, 1982. Particularly good on the economic implications of the Dutch revolt.

Kingdon, Robert. *Myths about the St. Bartholomew's Day Massacres, 1572–1576.* Cambridge, Mass., 1988. The most recent detailed account in English of this pivotal moment in the history of France.

Levack, Brian P. *The Witch-Hunt in Early Modern Europe,* 2d ed. London and New York, 1995. The best account of the persecution of suspected witches; coverage extends from Europe in 1450 to America in 1750.

Levin, Carole. *The Heart and Stomach of a King: Elizabeth I and the Politics of Sex and Power.* Philadelphia, 1994. A provocative argument for the importance of Elizabeth's gender if one wishes to understand her reign.

Limm, Peter, ed. *The Thirty Years' War.* London, 1984. An outstanding short survey, followed by a selection of primary source documents.

Lynch, John. *Spain, 1516–1598: From Nation-State to World Empire.* Oxford and Cambridge, Mass., 1991. The best book in English on Spain at the pinnacle of its sixteenth-century power.

MacCaffrey, Wallace. *Elizabeth I.* New York, 1993. An outstanding traditional biography by an excellent scholar.

Martin, Colin, and Geoffrey Parker. *The Spanish Armada.* London, 1988. Incorporates recent discoveries from undersea archaeology with more traditional historical sources.

Martin, John Rupert. *Baroque.* New York, 1977. A thought-provoking, thematic treatment, less a survey than an essay on the painting, sculpture, and architecture of the period.

Mattingly, Garrett. *The Armada.* Boston, 1959. A great narrative history that reads like a novel; for the latest work, however, see Martin and Parker (above).

Montaigne, Michel de. *Essays.* Translated by J. M. Cohen. Baltimore, 1958.

Parker, Geoffrey. *Philip II.* Boston, 1978. A fine biography by an expert in both the Spanish and the Dutch sources.

———, ed. *The Thirty Years' War,* rev. ed. London and New York, 1987. A wide-ranging collection of essays by scholarly experts.

———. *The Dutch Revolt,* 2d ed. Ithaca, N.Y., 1989. The standard survey in English on the revolt of the Netherlands.

Pascal, Blaise. *Pensées* (French-English edition). Edited by H. F. Stewart. London, 1950.

Quint, David. *Montaigne and the Quality of Mercy: Ethical and Political Themes in the "Essais."* Princeton, N.J., 1999. A fine treatment that presents Montaigne's thought as a response to the French wars of religion.

Roberts, Michael. *Gustavus Adolphus and the Rise of Sweden.* London, 1973. Still the authoritative English-language account.

Russell, Conrad. *The Causes of the English Civil War.* Oxford, 1990. A penetrating and provocative analysis by one of the leading "revisionist" historians of the period.

Sprenger, Jakob, and H. Kramer. *Malleus Maleficarum,* 2d ed. Translated by Montague Summers. London, 1948. The *Hammer of Witches* is the most famous of the handbooks written for early modern witch-hunters. Summers' translation is unreliable but has the great merit of existing.

Thomas, Keith. *Religion and the Decline of Magic.* London, 1971. An extremely influential account that sees the rise of witchcraft allegations in England as linked to the particularities of Protestant religious practice.

Tracy, James D. *Holland under Habsburg Rule, 1506–1566: The Formation of a Body Politic.* Berkeley and Los Angeles, 1990. A political history and analysis of the formative years of the Dutch state.

Van Gelderen, Martin. *Political Theory of the Dutch Revolt.* Cambridge, 1995. A fine book on a subject whose importance is too easily overlooked.

PART V
EARLY MODERN EUROPE

SEVENTEENTH- AND EIGHTEENTH-CENTURY European life was shaped by the combined effects of commerce, war, and a steadily growing population. A commercial revolution spurred the development of overseas colonies and trade, while opening up new markets for European industry. Agricultural productivity increased, making it possible for Europe to feed a population that had now reached unprecedented levels. Population growth in turn enabled European governments to wage more frequent wars, and to employ larger and larger armies.

Although monarchs continued to meet with opposition from the various estates within their realms, they increasingly asserted their power as absolute rulers. Warfare remained the chief instrument of European foreign policy; but slowly the notion of a diplomatic and military "balance of power" began to displace the pursuit of unrestrained aggrandizement as the primary goal of European state relations.

Profound changes were also occurring in European intellectual life during these centuries. Using new instruments and applying new mathematical techniques, astronomers proved beyond question that the earth was not the center of the universe. Biologists and physicians pioneered a more sophisticated understanding of the nature and processes by which life was created and sustained, and physicists such as Sir Isaac Newton established for the first time a true science of mechanics. During the eighteenth century, these discoveries gave rise to a new confidence in the capacity of human reason alone to understand nature and so to improve human life—a confidence those who held to it declared to be a sign of Enlightenment.

	POLITICS	SOCIETY AND CULTURE	ECONOMY	INTERNATIONAL RELATIONS
1500		Copernicus's *On the Revolutions of the Heavenly Spheres* (1543) Claudio Monteverdi, father of opera (1567–1643) Johannes Kepler (1571–1630) William Harvey (1578–1657)	Enclosure movement (1500–1700s) Demand for sugar escalates in Europe (late 1500s) Widespread crop failure in France (1597–1694)	Sir Francis Drake leads attack on Spanish fleet at Cadiz (1587)
1600		Literacy increases across Europe (1600–1800) Increased urbanization (1600–1750) Smoking spreads in Europe (early 1600s) Over 80,000 leave England for the New World (1607–1650) Galileo's *The Starry Messenger* (1610) Bacon's *New Instruments* (1620)	Mechanically powered saws and calico-printing from the Far East (1600s) Dutch East India Company founded (1602)	A total of 6 million Africans forcibly shipped across the middle passage (1600–1800) English colonists establish Jamestown (1607) *Mayflower* lands in the New World (1620)
	Jean Baptiste Colbert, French finance minister (1619–1683)	Galileo charged with heresy (1632) John Locke (1632–1704) Descartes's *Discourse on Method* (1637)	French government introduces head tax (c. 1645)	
	Reign of Louis XIV, the Sun King, (1643–1715) England promulgates Navigation Acts (1651, 1660) The Restoration and return of Charles II (1660)	Plague outbreaks (1649–1665) Edmond Halley (1656–1742) Founding of the Royal Society of London and the French Academy of Sciences (1660) Daniel Defoe, author of *Robinson Crusoe*, (1660–1731) The "great fire" in London (1666)	Coffee consumption escalates in Europe (1650s) Bank of Sweden founded (1657)	Dutch surrender New Amsterdam to England (1667) Austrian Habsburgs repulse Turks' assault on Vienna (1683)
	Louis XIV revokes the Edict of Nantes (1685)	Johann Sebastian Bach (1685–1750) George Frideric Handel (1685–1759) Newton's *Principia Mathematica* (1687) Locke's *Treatise of Civil Government* and *Essay Concerning Human Understanding* (1690)		Peace of Augsburg (1686) Portugal regains independence from Spain (1688) William of Orange rules England and Holland (1688) War of the League of Augsburg (1688–1697) Battle of the Boyne, English solidify control of Ireland (1690)
	Glorious Revolution in England (1689) Reign of Peter the Great of Russia (1689–1725)		Bank of England founded (1694)	
1700		Maize and the potato are introduced in Europe (1700s) Proliferation of salons and coffee-houses (1700s) First daily newspaper in England (1702) Rousseau's *Social Contract* (1712–1778)	Fly-shuttle for weaving loom invented (early 1700s) Physiocrats promote concept of *laissez-faire* (1700s) West India replaces the Spice Islands as largest supplier of European sugar (1700s)	War of Spanish Succession (1702–1713) England and Scotland unite to form Great Britain (1707)
	Reign of Charles VI, emperor of Holy Roman Empire (1711–1740) Treaty of Utrecht (1713) Reign of George I, first of Hanoverian dynasty in England (1714–1727) Louis XV (1715–1774) Robert Walpole serves as England's first prime minister (1720–1742)			

POLITICS	SOCIETY AND CULTURE	ECONOMY	INTERNATIONAL RELATIONS	
		German imperial law prohibits journeyman associations (1731) France establishes the Road and Bridge Corps of Engineering (1747)		1731
Reign of Frederick the Great, the "enlightened despot" (1740–1786)	Voltaire's *The Philosophical Letters* (1734) Montesquieu's *The Spirit of Laws* (1748) Steady increase in population begins (1750) *The Encyclopedia* published by Diderot and d'Alembert (1751–1772) Wolfgang Amadeus Mozart (1756–1791) Beccaria's *On Crimes and Punishment* (1764)			
		Antislavery movements emerge in Europe (1760s)	Seven Years' War/ French and Indian War (1756–1763)	
Reign of George III of England (1760–1820) Reign of Catherine the Great of Russia (1762–1796) Maria Theresa and Joseph II of Austria rule jointly (1765–1780)		James Cook explores Pacific (1768–1779) Abbe Raynal's *Philosophical History of Europeans in the Two Indies* (1770)	Treaty of Paris: France concedes Canada and India to England (1763) French East India Co. dissolves (1769) Russo-Turkish War (1769–1792) American Revolution (1774–1782)	
Reign of Louis XVI of France (1774–1792) The French Revolution breaks out (1789)	Kant's "What Is Enlightenment?" (1784) Wollstonecraft's *A Vindication of the Rights of Woman* (1792) Austen's *Pride and Prejudice* (1813–1817)	Smith's *Inquiry into the Nature and Causes of the Wealth of Nations* (1776)	Russia, Austria, and Prussia fully partition Poland (1795)	1800

THE ECONOMY
AND SOCIETY OF
EARLY MODERN
EUROPE

BETWEEN 1600 AND 1800, the European economy underwent sweeping transformations. The freebooting overseas expansionism of the sixteenth century brought Europe into the center of a vast system of worldwide trade. In the seventeenth and eighteenth centuries, European governments took deliberate steps to maximize their profits from the new commercial empires they had acquired. Employing an economic theory known as mercantilism, governments attempted to monopolize international trade with their colonies while building up their own domestic industries through protective regulations.

Despite being widely practiced, however, mercantilism was only modestly successful. The true engine of economic development during these centuries was not mercantilism but capitalism, a new economic system that rested on the entrepreneurial ambitions of thousands of individuals willing to invest their own money (capital) in the hope of gain. New institutions developed to facilitate such investment, including banks and joint-stock companies, and these gradually took over the financing of international commercial ventures. As these new financial institutions became larger and more sophisticated, their leaders became influential figures in the halls of government. Trade and governance thus became more and more closely intertwined.

European society changed much more slowly. Europeans remained committed to ideas of social order and hierarchy that had originated in the Middle Ages. Landlords still dominated peasants, and nobles continued to see themselves as entitled, by rank and birth, to rule in consultation with kings. Although vast fortunes were sometimes made in overseas trade, famine, disease, and poverty remained ubiquitous features of seventeenth-century European society. Only in the late eighteenth century, after a series of changes had greatly increased the productivity of European agriculture, did Europe finally break out of the traditional limitations imposed on population growth by epidemic disease and an inadequate food supply. From the mid-eighteenth century onward, however, the European population increased rapidly. Capital cities in particular exploded in size, largely through immigration from the swelling population of the countryside. A new, urban middle class began to emerge with its

FOCUS QUESTIONS

• What factors affected early modern population growth?

• What were the advantages of the putting-out system?

• What factors facilitated the commercial revolution?

• What was the "triangular trade"?

• How did the lives of eastern and western European peasants differ?

own distinctive social, economic, and cultural outlook. For the majority of Europeans, however, the availability of work did not keep pace with the number of laborers looking for employment, and this imbalance was being made worse by the introduction of new, labor-saving technological inventions. As the eighteenth century drew to a close, the tensions and disjunctions between the economy and the social order were approaching a crisis.

LIFE AND DEATH: PATTERNS OF POPULATION

What factors affected early modern population growth?

No facts better illustrate the degree to which the two hundred years of European history between 1600 and 1800 were subject to chance and change than those having to do with life and death—patterns of population—as they imprinted themselves across the early modern period.

FAMINE, DISEASE, AND THE BIRTH RATE

The pattern of life for most Europeans centered on the struggle to stay alive. In most instances their enemy was not an invading army, but famine; it is not surprising that one's well-being was measured simply by one's girth. At least once a decade, climatic conditions—usually a long period of summer rainfall—would produce a devastatingly bad harvest, which in turn would result in widespread malnutrition, often leading to serious illness and death. A family might survive for a time by eating less, but eventually, with its meager stocks exhausted and the cost of grain high, the human costs would mount. In the absence of grain, peasants sometimes ate grass, nuts, and tree bark, but they starved nonetheless.

The patterns of marriages, births, and deaths revealed in local parish registers indicate that the populations of individual communities rose and fell dramatically in rhythm with the fortunes of the harvest. Widespread crop failures occurred at fairly regular intervals—the worst in France, for example, about every thirty years (1597, 1630, 1662, 1694). They helped to cause the series of population crises that are the outstanding feature

Left: **A Plague Hospital in Vienna.** The efforts to contain outbreaks of plague by gathering the sick in establishments such as this and burying the dead on the site proved unsuccessful. Right: **A Physician's Mask.** This German device containing smelling salts in its curved beak was designed to combat the plague, which physicians incorrectly believed was spread by poisonous vapors.

A DESCRIPTION OF THE IMPOVERISHED PEASANTRY OF RURAL FRANCE

The author of this passage, Marshall Vauban, lived in the region around Vézélay that he is here describing. This account, dated January 1696, must therefore be regarded as that of an eyewitness.

All the so-called *bas peuple* ["little people"] live on nothing but bread of mixed barley and oats, from which they do not even remove the bran, which means that bread can sometimes be lifted by the straw sticking out of it. They also eat poor fruits, mainly wild, and a few vegetables from their gardens, boiled up with a little rape- or nut-oil sometimes, but more often not, or with a pinch of salt. Only the most prosperous eat bread made of rye mixed with barley and wheat. . . .

The general run of people seldom drink [wine], eat meat not three times a year, and use little salt. . . . So it is no cause for surprise if people who are so ill-nourished have so little energy. Add to this what they suffer from exposure: winter and summer, three fourths of them are dressed in nothing but halfrotting tattered linen, and are shod throughout the year with *sabots* [wooden clogs], and no other covering for the foot. If one of them does have shoes he only wears them on saints' days and Sundays: the extreme poverty to which they are reduced, owning as they do not one inch of land, rebounds against the more prosperous town and country bourgeois, and against the nobility and the clergy. . . .

The poor people are ground down in another manner by the loans of grain and money they take from the wealthy in emergencies, by means of which a high rate of usury is enforced, under the guise of presents which must be made after the debts fall due, so as to avoid imprisonment. After the term has been extended by only three or four months, either another present must be produced when the time is up, or they face the *sergent* [bailiff] who is sure to strip the house bare. Many others of these poor people's afflictions remain at my quill's tip so as not to offend anybody.

Since hardship can hardly go much further, its normal effects are a matter of course: firstly, it makes people weak and unhealthy, especially the children, many of whom die for want of good food; secondly, the men become idle and apathetic, being persuaded that only the least and worst part of the fruit of their labors will turn to their own profit; thirdly, there are liars, robbers, men of bad faith, always willing to perjure themselves provided that it pays, and to get drunk as soon as they lay hands on the wherewithal. . . .

Pierre Goubert. *The Ancien Regime: French Society, 1600-1750*, translated by Steve Cox (London: Weidenfeld and Nicolson, 1973), pp. 118–119.

of early modern demographic history. Poor harvests and the high grain prices that resulted meant not only undernourishment and possible starvation, but increasing unemployment: with fewer crops to be harvested, more money was spent on food and, consequently, less on manufactured goods. The despair such conditions bred would in turn contribute to a postponement of marriage and of births, and thus to a population decline.

An undernourished population is also particularly susceptible to disease. Bubonic plague ravaged seventeenth-century Europe. Severe outbreaks occurred in Seville in 1649, in Amsterdam in 1664, and in London

"Summer Amusement: Bugg Hunting." In this joking treatment of one of the facts of everyday life, the bedbugs meet sudden death in a full chamber pot.

the following year. By 1700 it had all but vanished; it last appeared in western Europe in a small area of southern France in 1720, though Moscow suffered an outbreak as late as 1771. Epidemics of dysentery, smallpox, and typhus also occurred with savage regularity. As late as 1779, more than one hundred thousand people died of dysentery in the French province of Brittany. Water supplies were contaminated by heedless disposal of human waste and by all manner of garbage and filth. Bathing, feared at one time as a method of spreading disease, was by no means a weekly habit even for the upper classes. Samuel Pepys, a royal official in seventeenth-century London, is typical of the standards of hygiene customary among prosperous urban dwellers. In his diary, Pepys reports that his housemaid regularly picked the lice from his scalp; that he took his first bath only after his wife introduced him to the pleasures of cleanliness; and that he thought nothing of using the fireplace in his bedroom as a toilet when the maid failed to provide him with a chamberpot. Standards of cleanliness among the lower classes were even worse.

The precariousness of life helped encourage most men and women in early-modern Europe to postpone marriage until their mid- to late twenties, by which time they hoped not only to have survived but also to have accumulated sufficient resources to establish a household. Young couples lived on their own, and not, as in societies elsewhere, as part of "extended" families of three generations. Since a son could not inherit until his father died, he was compelled to establish himself independently, and to postpone starting his own family until he had done so. Though historians have failed to find a clear explanation for this pattern of later marriages, it may have resulted from a growing desire on the part of younger men and women for a higher standard of living. Late marriage helped to control the birth rate. Once married, however, a couple generally produced their first child within a year. Although subsequent children appeared with annual or biennial regularity, long periods of breastfeeding, which tends to reduce the mother's fertility, and near poverty went some way toward limiting childbirth.

POPULATION GROWTH

Until the middle of the eighteenth century, populations continued to wax and wane according to the outbreak of warfare, famine, and disease. From about 1750 on, however, there was a steady and significant population increase, with almost all countries experiencing major growth. In Russia, where territorial expansion added further to the increases, the population may have tripled in the second half of the eighteenth century. Gains elsewhere, though not usually so spectacular, were nevertheless significant. The population of Prussia doubled; Hungary's more than tripled; and England's population, which was about 5.5 million in 1700, reached 9 million in 1800. France, already in 1700 the most populous country in Europe (about 20 million), added another 6 million before 1790. Spaniards multiplied from 7.6 million in 1717 to 10.5 million in 1797. Although reasons for the population increase remain something of a mystery, historians believe that it was the cumulative result of a decrease in infant mortality, earlier age at marriage, and a very gradual decline in the death rate, all due in large measure to a gradual increase in the food supply. Partly this increase in the food supply was the result of new agricultural methods and new crops, which we will describe in the following section. Partly it was the result of a change in the weather: it appears that whereas the climate of seventeenth-century Europe was abnormally bad, that of the succeeding hundred years was on the whole favorable. But partly too, Europe's population was better fed because transportation improvements made it possible to distribute existing food supplies more efficiently.

Population increase brought with it new problems and new attitudes. In France, it meant pressure on the land, as more peasants attempted to wring survival from an overpopulated countryside. The consequence was migration from the country to the city. The decline in the death rate among infants—along with an apparent increase in illegitimacy at the end of the eighteenth century—created a growing population of unwanted babies among the poor. Some desperate women resorted to infanticide, though since children murdered at birth died without benefit of baptism, the crime was regarded with particular horror. More often, babies were abandoned at the doors of foundling hospitals. In Paris during the 1780s from seven to eight thousand children were abandoned yearly out of a total of thirty thousand new births. As a British benefactor of several such institutions, Jonas Hanway, remarked in 1766, "it is much less difficult to the human heart and the dictates of self-preservation to drop a child than to kill it." But the distinction between child abandonment and infanticide was less absolute in practice than Hanway's statement might lead us to presume. Mortality rates in the foundling hospitals were horrendous, running as high as 80 or even 90 percent.

URBANISM

Although the vast majority of the population lived in small rural communities, towns and cities were coming to play an increasingly important role in the life of early modern Europe. We must speak of the "rise" of towns and cities with caution, however, since the pace of urbanization varied greatly across the Continent. Russia remained almost entirely rural: only 2.5 percent of its population lived in towns in 1630, and that percentage had risen by only 0.5 percent by 1774. In Holland, on the other hand, 59 percent of the population was urban in 1627 and 65 percent in 1795.

The total number of urban dwellers did not vary markedly after the end of the sixteenth century, when approximately two hundred cities in Europe had a population of over ten thousand. What did change between 1600 and 1800 was, first, the way in which those cities were distributed across the map, concentrated increasingly in the north and west; and second, the growing proportion of very large cities to the whole. Patterns of trade and commerce had much to do with these shifts. Cities such as Hamburg in Ger-

many, Liverpool in England, Toulon in France, and Cadíz in Spain grew by about 250 percent between 1600 and 1750. Amsterdam, the hub of early modern international commerce, increased from 30,000 in 1530 to 115,000 in 1630 and 200,000 by 1800. Naples, the busy Mediterranean port, went from a population of 300,000 in 1600 to nearly half a million by the late eighteenth century. Where goods were traded, processed, and manufactured, fleets built and provisioned, people flocked to work. An eighteenth-century commentator noted that the laborers in Paris were "almost all foreigners"—that is, men and women born outside the city: carpenters from Savoy, water carriers from Auvergne, porters from Lyons, stonecutters from Normandy, wigmakers from Gascony, shoemakers from Lorraine.

The most spectacular urban population growth occurred, however, in the administrative capitals of the increasingly centralized nations of Europe. By the middle of the eighteenth century, Madrid, Berlin, and St. Petersburg all had populations of over 100,000. London grew from 674,000 in 1700 to 860,000 a century later. Paris, a city of approximately 180,000 in 1600, increased to over half a million by 1800. Berlin grew from a population of 6,500 in 1661, to 60,000 in 1721, to 140,000 in 1783. Its increase was due in part to the fact that successive Prussian rulers undertook to improve its position as a trade center by the construction of canals that linked it with Breslau and Hamburg. Its population rose as well, however, because of the marked increase in Prussian army and bureaucratic personnel based in the capital city. Of the 140,000 citizens of Berlin in 1783, approximately 65,000 were state employees or members of their families.

THE DYNAMICS OF AGRICULTURE AND INDUSTRY

What were the advantages of the putting-out system?

The dramatic shifts in population we have been tracing were in some cases the cause, in others the effect, of equally important changes occurring in agriculture and industry. Throughout most of the two-hundred-year period under review, agricultural production was generally carried on according to traditional techniques that kept the volume of production low. By the end of the eighteenth century, however, agricultural productivity in some areas was increasing rapidly as tradition gave way to innovation. This in turn made it possible to feed a population which was larger, by 1800, than any that had ever lived in Europe before.

ENCLOSING THE COMMON FIELDS

One of the obstacles to more efficient agricultural practices was the medieval tradition of open, or "common-field" farming. Under this system, the holdings of individual peasants and their lords were scattered throughout the village's fields, usually (at least in the north) in long, narrow strips. The fields themselves were farmed communally, with livestock grazing together on common pastureland. This system "spread the risk" of localized crop failures, and guaranteed that the most productive lands would not be monopolized by a few peasant families. But it also acted as a serious check on agricultural experimentation and on the introduction of new crops, since it required the agreement of the entire village community before any such innovations could be introduced.

Once landlords, particularly in England and Holland, began to compete for markets as capitalist agricultural entrepreneurs, however, they looked for ways to overcome these inefficiencies, so as to improve the yield on their lands. The most drastic of these methods was the enclosure of open fields to allow for more systematic and therefore more productive farming. "Enclosure" was the term for land reorganization within a traditional village community. The earliest enclosures in England took place in the fifteenth and sixteenth centuries. Because of the great profits from wool, some landlords converted common pastures that hitherto had supported peasant livestock into their own preserves for sheep raising, thus threatening the livelihood of entire peasant communities. The really dramatic enclosure movement in England took place during the eighteenth century, however, when many landlords took steps to abolish the common-field system altogether on their estates, shifting instead toward a system of "scientific farming." Key to this new system was a reduction in the amount of land (traditionally a

third, or in some cases even a half) that lay fallow in any given year. By introducing new farming methods and new crops, "scientific farmers" discovered that they could keep a much higher percentage of their arable land under continuous cultivation. The most important new crops with which landowners experimented were clover, alfalfa, and turnips, which helped to restore the fertility of soil whose nitrogen content had been depleted by grain growing.

Clover, alfalfa, and turnips not only helped landlords do away with fallow lands; they also provided excellent winter food for animals, thereby aiding the production of more and better livestock. More livestock also meant more manure. Accordingly, intensive manuring became another way in which scientific farmers could eliminate the need for fallow land. Other improvements in farming methods introduced in the period were more intensive hoeing and weeding (made possible by the surplus of cheap labor in the countryside), and the use of the seed drill for planting grain. The seed drill in particular eliminated the old wasteful method of broadcast sowing grain by hand, much of it remaining on top of the soil to be eaten by birds.

The enclosure of open fields allowed for more systematic and therefore more productive farming.

All these improvements were most easily accomplished on enclosed fields under the direct management of a single, "improving" landlord. The impact of such improvements on agricultural productivity could be enormous. For villagers, however, the social and economic costs of enclosure were high. Common land afforded the poor not only a place to tether a cow, to fish, or to gather firewood, but to breathe at least a bit of the air of social freedom. Enclosure cost villagers their modest liberties, as well as the traditional right to help determine how the community's subsistence economy was to be managed. Cottagers (very small landholders) and squatters, who had over generations established a customary right to the use of common lands, were reduced to the rank of landless laborers.

Enclosure was more easily accomplished in those countries—England most notably—where there was a system of absolute property rights and wage labor. Where the tradition of "common" rights to grazing and foraging was strong, as in France, landlords found it far more difficult to impose a new economic order. In France, also, a large peasantry owned small plots of land outright, adding up to approximately one-third of all agricultural land. These peasants had neither an interest in nor the financial capacity for change. In France, monarchs also tended to oppose enclosure, because the monarchy needed an economically stable peasantry to support its expanding tax programs. It therefore worked to secure peasants in the customary tenure of their farms. Thus defended, French peasants were better able to resist effectively attempts at enclosure launched by large landholders. English property owners were more fortunate, taking advantage of the absence of royal opposition during the Cromwellian period to enclose on a broad scale.

On the Continent, except for Holland, there was nothing comparable to the English advance in scientific farming. Nor, with the notable exception of Spain, was there a pronounced enclosure movement as in England and the Low Countries. Yet despite that fact, European food production became increasingly capitalistic in the seventeenth and eighteenth centuries. Landlords leased farms to tenants and reaped profits as rent. Often they allowed tenants to pay rent in the form of half their crops. This system of sharecropping was most prevalent in France, Italy, and Spain. Farther east, in Prussia, Poland, Hungary, and Russia, landowners continued to rely on unpaid serfs to till the land. But wherever the scale of production and marketing was altered to increase profits, it brought change in its wake.

NEW WORLD CROPS: MAIZE AND POTATOES

The eighteenth century saw the introduction of two crops from the New World, maize (Indian corn) and the potato, which eventually resulted in the provision of a more adequate diet for the poor. Since maize can be grown only in areas with substantial periods of sunny and dry weather, its cultivation spread through Italy and the southeastern part of the Continent. Whereas an average ear of grain would yield only about four seeds for every one planted, an ear of maize would yield about seventy or eighty. That made it a "miracle" crop, filling granaries that had been almost empty before. The potato was an equally miraculous innovation for the European north. Its advantages were numerous: potatoes could be grown on the poorest, sandiest, or wettest of lands where nothing else could be raised; they could be fitted into the smallest of patches. Raising potatoes even in small patches was profitable because the yield of potatoes was extraordinarily abundant. Finally, the potato provided an inexpensive means of improving the human diet. It is rich in calories and contains many vitamins and minerals. Northern European peasants initially resisted growing and eating potatoes. Clergymen taught them to fear the plant because it is not mentioned in the Bible. Some claimed that it transmitted leprosy. Still others insisted that it was a cause of flatulence, a property acknowledged by a French authority on diet in 1765, although the writer added, "What is a little wind to the vigorous organs of the peasants and workers?" Yet in the course of the eighteenth century the poor grew accustomed to the potato, although sometimes after considerable pressure. Frederick the Great compelled Prussian peasants to cultivate potatoes until the crop achieved acceptance and became a staple throughout much of northern Germany. By about 1800 the average north German peasant family ate potatoes as a main course at least once a day.

RURAL MANUFACTURING

Agriculture was not the only commercial enterprise in early modern rural Europe. Increasingly, manufactured goods—particularly textiles—were being produced in the countryside, as entrepreneurs battled to circumvent artisanal and guild restrictions that limited production in urban manufacturing centers. Unfettered rural industry was a response to the constantly growing demand of new markets created by the increase in regional, national, and international commerce. Entrepreneurs made use of the so-called putting-out system to address this demand and to reap large profits. Unhampered by guild regulations, which in medieval times had restricted the production and distribution of textiles to maintain price levels, merchants would buy up a stock of raw material, most often wool or flax, which they would then "put out," or supply, to rural workers for carding (combing the fibers) and spinning. Once spun, the merchant collected the yarn or thread and passed it to rural weavers, who wove it into cloth. Collected once more, the material was processed by other workers at bleaching or dyeing shops and collected a final time by the entrepreneur, who then sold it either to a wholesaler or directly to retail customers.

> Entrepreneurs made use of the so-called putting-out system to address the growing demand of new markets and to reap large profits.

"Rustic Courtship." This detail from an etching (1785) by the English satirist Thomas Rowlandson suggests the advantages of doorstep domestic industry: natural lighting, improved ventilation, and a chance to converse with visitors. Work under these self-paced conditions, though usually long and hard, was carried on to a personal rhythm.

Artisan and Family, by Gerard ter Borch. This seventeenth-century wheelwright, though a skilled artisan, is nevertheless depicted as living in a house whose condition suggests near-poverty. Sickness, a bad harvest, unemployment—any of these might easily drive him and his family over the edge.

Although the putting-out phenomenon—or, as it is often referred to, the process of protoindustrialization—occurred throughout Europe, it was usually concentrated regionally. Most industrial areas specialized in the production of particular commodities, depending on the availability of raw materials. Flanders was a producer of linens; Verviers (in present-day Belgium) of woolens; Silesia of linens. As markets—regional, national, and international—developed, these rural manufacturing areas grew accordingly. Industries employed home workers by the thousands. A major mid-eighteenth-century textile firm in Abbeville, France, provided work to eighteen hundred in central workshops but to ten thousand in their own homes. One of the largest woolen manufacturers in Linz, Austria, in 1786 was employing thirty-five thousand, of whom more than twenty-nine thousand were domestic spinners.

Rural workers accepted this system of manufacture as a means of staving off poverty or possible starvation in years of particularly bad harvests. Domestic textile production involved the entire family. Even the youngest children could participate in the process of cleaning the raw wool. Older children carded. Wives and husbands spun or wove. Spinning, until the invention of the jenny at the end of the eighteenth century (see p. 727), was a far more time-consuming process than weaving, which had been speeded considerably by the Englishman John Kay's early-eighteenth-century invention of the fly shuttle, a mechanical device that automatically returned the shuttle to its starting place after it had been "thrown" across the loom.

In addition to providing extra income, the putting-out system brought other advantages to rural home workers. They could regulate the pace of their labor to some degree, and could abandon it altogether when farm work was available during the planting and harvest seasons. Their ability to work at home was a mixed blessing, however, for conditions in cottages that were wretchedly built and poorly ventilated were often exceedingly cramped and unpleasant, especially when workers were compelled to accommodate a bulky loom within their already crowded living quarters. But domestic labor, however unpleasant, was preferable to working away from home in a shop, where conditions might be even more oppressive under the watchful eye of an unsympathetic master. There were also advantages for the merchant-entrepreneur, who benefited not only from the absence of guild restrictions, but from the fact that none of his capital was tied up in expensive equipment. (Spinners usually owned their spinning wheels; weavers either owned or rented their looms.) Governments appreciated the advantages of the system too, viewing it as one way to alleviate the ever-present problem of rural poverty. The French abolished the traditional privileges of urban manufacturers in 1762, acknowledging by law what economic demand had long since established: the widespread practice of unrestricted rural domestic production. By that time, proto-industrialization prevailed not only in northern France, but in the east and northeast of England, in Flanders, and in much of northern Germany—all areas where a mixed agricultural and manufacturing economy made economic sense to those engaged in it as entrepreneurs and producers.

Later generations, looking back nostalgically on the putting-out system, often compared it favorably to the factory system that displaced it. Life within the system's "family economy" was hard, however. Although workers could set their own pace to some extent, they remained subject to the demands of small, often inexperienced entrepreneurs who, misjudging their markets, might overload spinners and weavers with work at one moment, then abandon them for lack of orders the next. Though it often kept families from starvation, the system did little to mitigate the monotony and harshness of their lives. Its pressures are crudely if eloquently expressed in an English ballad in which the weaver husband responds to his wife's complaint that she has no time to sit at the "bobbin wheel," what with the washing and baking and milking she must do. No matter, the husband replies. She must "stir about and get things done. / For all things must aside be laid, / when we want help about our trade."

Textiles were not the only manufactured goods produced in the countryside. In France, for example, metalworking was as much a rural as an urban occupation, with migrant laborers providing a work force for small, self-contained shops. In various parts of Germany, the same sort of unregulated domestic manufacturing base prevailed: in the Black Forest for clock making, in Thuringia for toys. English production of iron grew fivefold from the mid-sixteenth to the late seventeenth century. The phenomenon of protoindustrialization

increased demand for raw materials. Pressure on timber reserves for fuel led to widespread deforestation, with a resulting exploitation of coal reserves, particularly in the Rhineland, England, and the south Netherlands. In 1550 the English mined two hundred thousand tons of coal. By 1800 that figure had risen to 3 million.

TRANSPORTATION

Rural industry flourished despite the fact that for most of the early modern period transportation systems remained rudimentary. In all but a very few cases, roads were little more than ill-defined tracks, full of holes as much as four feet deep, and all but impassable in the rain, when carts and carriages might stay mired in deep ruts for days. One of the few paved roads ran from Paris to Orléans, the main river port of France, but that was a notable exception. In general, no one could travel more than twelve miles an hour—"post haste" at a gallop on horseback—and speed such as that could be achieved only at the expense of fresh horses at each stage of the ride. In the late seventeenth century, a journey of sixty miles over good roads could be accomplished in twentyfour hours, provided that the weather was fair. To travel by coach from Paris to Lyons, a distance of approximately two hundred fifty miles, took ten days. Merchants ran great risks when they shipped perishable goods. Breakables were not expected to survive for more than fifteen miles. Transportation of goods by boat along coastal routes was far more reliable than shipment overland, though in both cases the obstacle of excessive tolls was frequently inhibiting. In 1675, English merchants calculated that it was cheaper to ship coal three hundred miles by water than to send it fifteen miles overland, so impassable were the roads to heavy transport. Madrid, without a river, relied upon mules and carts for its supplies. By the mid-eighteenth century, the city required the services of over half a million mules and one hundred fifty thousand carts, all forced to labor their way into town over rugged terrain. In 1698, a bronze statue of Louis XIV was sent on its way from the river port of Auxerre, southeast of Paris, to the town of Dijon. The cart in which it was dispatched was soon stuck in the mud, however, and the statue remained marooned in a wayside shed for twenty-one years, until the road was improved to the point that it could continue its belated journey.

Gradually during the eighteenth century transportation improved. The French established a Road and Bridge Corps of civil engineers, with its own training

Outside an Inn, by Thomas Rowlandson. Coaching inns brought the outside world into the lives of isolated villagers. Note the absence of any clearly defined roadway.

school, in 1747. Work began in the 1670s on a series of canals that eventually linked the English Channel to the Mediterranean. In England, private investors constructed a network of waterways and turnpikes tying provincial towns to each other and to London. With improved roads came stagecoaches, feared at first for their speed and recklessness much as automobiles were feared in the early twentieth century. People objected to being crowded into narrow carriages designed to reduce the load pulled by the team of horses. "If by chance a traveller with a big stomach or wide shoulders appears," an unhappy passenger lamented, "one has to groan or desert." But improvements such as stagecoaches and canals, much as they might increase the profits or change the pattern of life for the wealthy, meant little to the average European. Barges plied the waterways from the north to the south of France, but most men and women traveled no farther than the nearest market town, on footpaths or on rutted cart tracks eight feet wide, which had served their ancestors in much the same way.

URBAN MANUFACTURING

That industry flourished to the extent it did, despite the hazards and inefficiencies of transport, is a measure of the strength of Europe's ever-increasing commercial impulse. Rural protoindustrialization did not prevent the growth of important urban manufacturing centers. In northern France, many of the million or so men and women employed in the textile trade lived and worked in cities such as Amiens, Lille, and Rheims. The eighteenth-century rulers of Prussia made it their policy to develop Berlin as a manufacturing center, taking advantage of an influx of French Protestants to establish the silk-weaving industry there. Even in cities, however, work was likely to be carried out in small shops, where anywhere from five to twenty journeymen labored under the supervision of a master to manufacture the particular products of their craft. Despite the fact that manufacturing was centered in homes and workshops, by 1700 these industries were increasing significantly in scale as many workshops grouped together to form a single manufacturing district. Textile industries led this trend, but it was true as well of brewing, distilling, soap and candle making, tanning, and the manufacturing of various chemical substances for the bleaching and dyeing of cloth. These and other industries might often employ several thousand men and women congregated together into towns—or larger communities of several towns—all dedicated to the same occupation and production.

Techniques in some crafts remained much as they had been for centuries. In others, however, inventions changed the pattern of work as well as the nature of the product. Knitting frames, simple devices to speed the manufacture of textile goods, made their appearance in England and Holland. Wire-drawing machines and slitting mills, the latter enabling nail makers to convert iron bars into rods, spread from Germany into England. Mechanically powered saws were introduced into shipyards and elsewhere across Europe in the seventeenth century. The technique of calico printing, the application of colored designs directly to textiles, was imported from the Far East. New and more efficient printing presses appeared, first in Holland and then elsewhere. The Dutch invented a machine called a "camel," by which the hulls of ships could be raised in the water so that they could be more easily repaired.

Innovations of this kind were not readily accepted by workers. Labor-saving machines such as mechanical saws threw men out of work. Artisans, especially those organized into guilds, were by nature conservative, anxious to protect not only their restrictive "rights" but also the secrets of their trade. Often, too, the state would intervene to block the widespread use of machines if they threatened to increase unemployment. The Dutch and some German states, for example, prohibited the use of what was described as a "devilish invention," a ribbon loom capable of weaving sixteen or more ribbons at the same time. Sometimes the spread of new techniques was curtailed by states in order to protect the livelihood of powerful commercial interest groups. On behalf of both domestic textile manufacturers and importers of Indian goods, calico printing was for a time outlawed in both France and England. The cities of Paris and Lyons and several German states banned the use of indigo dyes because they were manufactured abroad.

THE HUMAN IMPLICATIONS OF CHANGE

Changes that occurred in trade, commerce, agriculture, and industry, though large-scale phenomena, nevertheless touched individual men and women directly. Enclosure stripped away customary rights. A British cottager by 1780 might well have lost his family's age-old right to tether a cow on the common, which was now an enclosed and "scientifically" manured cornfield. Markets developed to receive and transmit goods from around the world altered the lives of those whose work now responded to their rhythms. A linen weaver in rural Holland in 1700, whose peasant father had eked out a meager living from his subsistence farm, now supplemented his income by working for an Amsterdam entrepreneur, and paid progressively less for his food as a result of the cheap grain imported to the Low Countries across the Baltic Sea from eastern Europe. A carpenter in an early eighteenth-century Toulon shipyard lost his job when his employer purchased a mechanical saw that did the work of five men. A sailor on one of the ships built in that Toulon shipyard died at sea off the French colony of Martinique, an island of which he had never heard, at a distance so far from home as to be inconceivable to those who mourned his death when they learned of it months later. Meanwhile, in vast areas of southern and eastern Europe, men and women led lives that followed the same patterns they had for centuries, all but untouched by the changes taking place elsewhere. They clung to the life they knew, a life that, if harsh, was at least predictable.

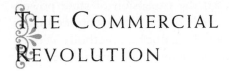

THE COMMERCIAL REVOLUTION

What factors facilitated the commercial revolution?

Hand in hand with changes in agriculture and industry came an alteration in the manner in which commerce was organized and trade conducted. So extensive were changes in these areas over the course of two hundred years that it is accurate to speak of them as comprising a commercial revolution.

CAPITALISM AND MERCANTILISM

The early modern world of commerce and industry grew increasingly to be governed by the assumptions of capitalism and mercantilism. Reduced to its simplest terms, capitalism is a system of production, distribution, and exchange, in which accumulated wealth is invested by private owners for the sake of gain. Its essential features are private enterprise, competition for markets, and business for profit. Generally it involves the wage system as a method of payment of workers—that is, a mode of payment based not on the amount of wealth workers create, but rather on their willingness to compete with each other for jobs. The capitalist system encouraged commercial expansion on a national and international scale. Activity on this wider scale demanded the resources and expertise of wealthy and experienced entrepreneurs. Capitalists studied patterns of international trade. They knew where markets were and how to manipulate them to their advantage.

The capitalist system was designed to reward the individual. In contrast, mercantilist doctrine emphasized direct governmental intervention in economic policy to enhance the general prosperity of the state and to increase political authority. Mercantilism was by no means a new idea. It was a variation on the medieval notion that the economic well-being of communities depended on the willingness of their populace to work at whatever task God or their rulers assigned them to benefit the community as a whole. The mercantilism of the seventeenth and eighteenth centuries translated this earlier concept of community as a privileged, but regimented, economic unit from the level of towns to the level of the entire state. The theory and practice of mercantilism reflected the expansion of state power. Responding to the needs of war, rulers enforced mercantilist policies, often by autocratic methods, certain that the needs of the state must take precedence over those of individuals.

Mercantilist theory held that a state's power depended on its actual, calculable wealth. The degree to which a state could remain self-sufficient, importing as little as necessary while exporting as much as possible, was the clearest gauge not only of its economic prosperity but of its power. This doctrine had profound effects on state policy. First, it led to the establishment and development of overseas colonies. Colonies, mercantilists reasoned, would, as part of the national community, provide it with raw materials, including precious metals in some instances, which would otherwise have to be obtained outside the community. Second, the doctrine of mercantilism inspired state governments to encourage industrial production and trade, both sources of revenue that would increase the state's income. Third, it led to the presumption that trade and industry were a "zero sum" game. Since the quantity of world trade and production was presumed to be fixed, the goal of a mercantilist state was to reduce the volume of trade and industrial production among its rivals, while increasing its own.

Although most western European statesmen were prepared to endorse mercantilist goals in principle, the degree to which their policies reflected those goals varied according to national circumstance. Spain, despite its insistence on closed colonial markets and its determination to amass a fortune in bullion, never succeeded in attaining the economic self-sufficiency that mercantilist theory demanded. But mercantilism, which appealed at least in theory to the rulers in Madrid, had little attraction for the merchants of Amsterdam. The Dutch recognized that the United Provinces were too small to permit them to achieve economic self-sufficiency. Throughout the seventeenth and eighteenth centuries the Dutch remained dedicated in principle and practice to free trade, often investing, contrary to mercantilist doctrine, in the commercial enterprises of other countries and promoting national prosperity by encouraging the rest of Europe to rely upon Amsterdam as a hub of international finance and trade.

Capitalism and mercantilism produced important consequences for individuals as well as for nations and regions. Laboring men and women frequently found themselves the victims of the policies and programs of those who managed and controlled dynamic, expansionist national economies. For example, capitalists could afford to invest in large quantities of manufactured goods, and if necessary, hold them unsold until they could command a high price, favorable to them but damaging to the budget of humbler consumers. Mercantilism persuaded policy makers to discourage domestic consumption, since goods purchased on the home market reduced the goods available for export. Government policy was thus to keep wages low, so that laborers would not have more money to spend than it took to provide them with basic food and shelter.

THE GROWTH OF INTERNATIONAL TRADE AND BUSINESS

Together, governments and entrepreneurs designed new institutions that facilitated the expansion of global commerce during the seventeenth and eighteenth centuries to effect the commercial revolution of early modern Europe. While local and regional markets continued to flourish, international centers such as Antwerp, Amsterdam, and London became hubs for a flourishing and complex system of international trade. An increasing number of European men and women grew dependent on the commerce that brought both necessities and luxuries into their lives. The eighteenth-century essayist Joseph Addison sang the praises of beneficent merchant princes: "There are not more useful members in the Commonwealth," he wrote. "They distribute the gifts of nature, find work for the poor, and wealth to the rich, and magnificence to the great."

Enterprise on this new scale depended on the availability of capital for investment. And that capital was generated primarily by a long-term, gradual increase in agricultural prices throughout much of the period. Had that increase been sharp, it would probably have produced enough hunger and suffering to retard rather than stimulate economic growth. Had there been no increase, however, the resulting stagnation produced by marginal profits would have proved equally detrimental to expansion. Agricultural entrepreneurs had surplus capital to invest in trade; bankers put that surplus to use to expand their commercial enterprises. Together, capitalist investors and merchants profited.

Banks played a vital role in the history of this expansion. Strong religious and moral disapproval of lending money at interest meant that banking had enjoyed a dubious reputation during the Middle Ages. Because the church did come to allow profit making on com-

TWO VIEWS OF MERCANTILISM

Giovanni Botero (1544–1617) was a Jesuit educator and author, who is best known for his book entitled The Reason of State, *from which the following extract is taken. The connections Botero emphasizes between agriculture, industry and trade make it one of the most illuminating early expositions of mercantilist doctrines.*

The population and the power of the state are augmented in two ways: by increasing your own, and by attracting others' to you. You can increase your own through agriculture and the arts, by encouraging the education of children, and with colonies. You can attract others' by absorbing your enemies, destroying nearby cities, bestowing citizenship [on foreigners], concluding alliances, raising armies, establishing marriage bonds, and doing other similar things such as we will explain briefly one by one.

Agriculture is the foundation of population growth. . . .Thus the prince must favor and promote agriculture and show that he values people who improve the fertility of their lands and whose farms are exceptionally well cultivated. It will be his duty to initiate and direct everything that belongs to the public good of his land: drying up swamps, uprooting useless or excess forests and thus reducing the land to cultivation, and helping and encouraging those who undertake such works. . . .

It is up to the prince, then, to make provision for such inconveniences and, finally, to support all means for making sure that his country abounds and is fecund in all things he knows it to be capable of producing. If plants or seeds are not to be found in his state, it is his duty to see that they are brought in from elsewhere. . . .

Over and above these things, the prince must do his best to prevent money from leaving his state needlessly. Even if things that are needed are expensive within the state, the money spent on them will still remain within the country or return to the treasury in the long run in customs charges and taxes. Once the money leaves the state, however, both it and the profits it would have earned are lost. . . .

There is nothing more important for enlarging a state and for assuring it a multitude of population and of all kinds of goods than the industry of its people and the quantity of its trades. . . . They attract money, and they attract the people who make or traffic in manufactured goods, who provide materials to the workers, and who buy, sell, or transport the products of man's hands and ingenuity from one place to another. . . . Some may ask whether fertile soil or man's industry is more important for enlarging and populating an area. Industry, undoubtedly. . . . The things produced by a man's skilled hand are far superior in quantity and value than things generated by nature. . . . Moreover, many more people live from industry than from rents. Many cities in Italy can attest to this, but principally Venice, Florence, Genoa, and Milan, whose size and magnificence we need not dwell on, and where almost two thirds of the inhabitants live by the silk and the wool trades. . . .

Eric Cochrane and Julius Kirshner, eds. *The Renaissance: University of Chicago Readings in Western Civilization*, vol. 5. (Chicago: University of Chicago Press, 1985), pp. 244–247 (translated by Lydia Cochrane).

In the following selection, taken from a memorandum by King Louis XIV's great finance minister Jean Baptiste Colbert (1619–1683), we see clearly the mercantilist assumption that the total amount of trade is fixed and cannot be increased. Therefore, if France is to grow richer, this can only be at the expense of other countries, which must grow poorer.

The commerce of all Europe is carried on by ships of every size to the number of 20,000, and it is perfectly clear that this number cannot be increased, since the number of people in all the states remains the same and consumption likewise remains the same. . . .

It must be added that commerce causes a perpetual combat in peace and war among the nations of Europe, as to who shall win the most of it. . . . Each nation works incessantly to have its legitimate share of commerce or to gain an advantage over another nation. The Dutch fight at present, in this war with 15,000 to 16,000 ships, a government of merchants, all of whose maxims and power are directed solely toward the preservation and increase of their commerce, and much more care, energy, and thrift than any other nation.

The English with 3,000 to 4,000 ships, less energy and care, and more expenditures than the Dutch.

The French with 500 to 600.

Those two last cannot improve their commerce save by increasing the number of their vessels, and cannot increase this number save from the 20,000 which carry all the commerce and consequently by making inroads on the 15,000 to 16,000 of the Dutch.

J. H. Robinson. *Readings in European History*, vol. 2. (New York: Ginn and Company, 1934), pp. 279–280.

mercial risks, however, banks in Italy and Germany were organized during the fourteenth and fifteenth centuries, most notably by the Medici family in Florence and the Fugger family in Augsburg. The rise of these private financial houses was followed by the establishment of government banks, reflecting the mercantilist goal of serving the monetary needs of the state. The first such institution, the Bank of Sweden, was founded in 1657. The Bank of England was established in 1694, at a time when England's emergence as a world commercial power guaranteed that institution a leading role in international finance. The growth of banking was necessarily accompanied by the adoption of various aids to financial transactions on a large scale, further evidence of a commercial revolution. Credit facilities were extended and payment by check introduced, thereby encouraging an increase in the volume of trade, since the credit resources of the banks could now be expanded far beyond the actual amounts of cash in their vaults.

International commercial expansion called forth larger units of business organization. The prevailing unit of production and trade in the Middle Ages was the workshop or store owned by an individual or a family. Partnerships were also quite common, even though each partner was liable for the debts of the entire firm. Obviously neither the workshop or the partnership was well adapted to business involving heavy risks and a huge investment of capital. The attempt to devise a more suitable business organization resulted in the formation of regulated companies, which were associations of merchants banded together for a common venture. Members did not pool their resources but agreed merely to cooperate for their mutual advantage and to abide by certain definite regulations.

The commercial revolution was facilitated during the seventeenth century when regulated companies were largely superseded by a new type of organization at once more compact and broader in scope. This was the joint-stock company, formed through the issuance of shares of capital to a considerable number of investors. Those who purchased the shares might or might not take part in the work of the company. Whether they did or not, they were joint owners of the business and therefore entitled to share in its profits in proportion with the amount they had invested. The joint-stock company of the early modern period is best understood not so much as a conscious precursor of capitalist endeavor but as a pragmatic attempt at commercial expansion by both individuals and the state. A joint-stock company's structure was dictated by present opportunity and circumstance. Initially, for example, the Dutch United East India Company, one of the earliest joint-stock ventures, had expected to pay off its investors ten years after its founding in 1602, much as regulated companies had. Yet when that time came, the directors recognized the impossibility of the plan. By 1612, the company's assets were scattered—as ships, wharves,

A Square in Seventeenth-Century Amsterdam. This contemporary painting emphasizes the central role independent merchants, consumers, and trade played in Dutch city life.

The Lyons Stock Exchange. Built in 1749, the stylish and impressive facade of the structure bespeaks the prominent role of commerce in French society.

operation of their enterprise and, in the process, establishing a practice of continuous financing that was soon to become common.

Most of the early joint-stock companies were founded for commercial ventures, but later some were organized in industry. A number of the outstanding trading combinations were also chartered companies. They held charters from the government granting a monopoly of the trade in a certain locality and conferring extensive authority over the inhabitants, and were thus an example of the way capitalist and mercantilist interests might coincide. Through a charter of this kind, the British East India Company undertook the exploitation of vast territories on the Indian subcontinent, and remained the virtual ruler there until the end of the eighteenth century.

In most European countries, and particularly in France, government and commerce generally worked to promote each other's interests. The exception was the Netherlands. The Dutch almost exclusively put their capital to work not for the state but for the rest of Europe. In time of war, governments called upon commercial capitalists to assist in the financing of their campaigns. When England went to war against France in 1689, for example, the government had no long-range borrowing mechanism available to it; during the next quarter century the merchant community, through the Bank of England, assisted the government in raising over £170 million and in stabilizing the national debt at £40 million. In return, trading companies used the war to increase long-distance commercial traffic at the expense of their French enemy,

warehouses, and cargoes—around the globe. As a result, the directors urged those anxious to realize their profits to sell their shares on the Amsterdam exchange to other eager investors, thereby ensuring the sustained and exerted powerful pressure on the government to secure treaties that would work to their advantage.

A final important feature of the commercial revolution was the development of a more efficient money economy. Money had been used widely since the early Middle Ages, but the growth of trade and industry in the commercial revolution accentuated the need for more stable and uniform monetary systems at the national level. The problem was solved when every important state adopted a standard system of money to be used for all transactions within its borders. Much time elapsed, however, before the reform was complete.

The economic institutions just described never remained static, but rather existed in a continuously volatile state of development. This volatility, in turn, had a direct effect on the lives of individual men and women. One major result of overseas expansion, for example, was the severe inflation caused by the increase in the supply of silver that plagued Europe at the end of the sixteenth century. Price fluctuations, in turn, produced further economic instability. Businessmen were tempted to expand their enterprises too rapidly; bankers extended credit so liberally that their principal borrowers, especially noblemen, often defaulted on loans. In both Spain and Italy, wages failed to keep pace with rising prices, which brought severe and continuing hardships to the lower classes. Impoverishment was rife in the cities, and bandits flourished in the rural areas.

Speculative greed could, and sometimes did, threaten to bring a nation to its knees. Though feverish speculation characterized the early modern period as a whole, the most notorious bouts of that particular economic disease occurred in the early eighteenth century. The so-called South Sea Bubble was the result of deliberate inflation of the value of stock of the South Sea Company in Britain, whose offer to assume the national debt led to unwarranted confidence in the company's future. When buoyant hopes gave way to fears, investors made frantic attempts to dispose of their shares for whatever they would bring. The crash that came in 1720 was the inevitable result.

During the years when the South Sea Bubble was being inflated in Britain, the French were engaged in a similar wave of speculative madness. In 1715 a Scotsman by the name of John Law persuaded the regent of France to adopt his scheme for paying off the national debt through the issuance of paper money and to grant him the privilege of organizing the Mississippi Company for the colonization and exploitation of Louisiana. As happened in Britain, stock prices soared in response to this alluring but basically unrealistic scheme. Stories were told of butchers and tailors who made fortunes from their few initial shares. Ultimately, however, panic set in, and in 1720 the Mississippi Bubble burst in a wild panic.

COLONIZATION AND OVERSEAS TRADE

What was the "triangular trade"?

Despite the existence of increasingly profitable European commercial routes and centers, the most visible evidence of the economic expansionism of early modern Europe were the overseas colonies and trading posts developed and exploited during the seventeenth and eighteenth centuries.

SPANISH COLONIALISM

Following the exploits of the conquistadors, the Spanish established colonial governments in Peru and in Mexico, which they controlled from Madrid in proper mercantilist fashion by a Council of the Indies. The governments of Philip II and his successors were determined to defend their monopoly in the New World. They issued trading licenses only to Spanish merchants; exports and imports passed only through the port of Seville (later the more navigable port of Cadíz), where they were registered at the government-operated Casa de Contratación, or customs house. In their heyday, Spanish traders circled the globe. The lucrative market for silver in East Asia made it profitable even to establish an outpost in far-off Manila in the Philippines, where Asian silk was exchanged for South American bullion. The silk was then shipped back to Spain by way of the Mexican ports of Acapulco and Veracruz. The search for gold and silver was accompanied by the establishment of permanent colonies in Central and South America and on the east and west coasts of North America in what are now the states of Florida and California.

Spain's predominance did not deter other countries

> The lucrative market for silver in East Asia made it profitable even to establish an outpost in the far-off Philippines, where Asian silk was exchanged for South American bullion.

THE ATLANTIC WORLD

Why were European governments so concerned with closely controlling the means by which certain products traveled from the colonies to European ports? How and why did the financial institutions of the late medieval period thrive on and encourage the economic policies of colonial powers? Why are the trade routes carrying slaves so prominently marked on this map? What does this suggest about the importance of unfree labor to the economic achievements of Europeans in the New World?

from attempting to win a share of the treasure for themselves. Probably the boldest challengers were the English. Their leading buccaneer was the "sea dog" Sir Francis Drake, who three times raided the east and west coasts of Spanish America. In 1587, the year before the Armada set sail on its ill-fated voyage north, Drake "singed the beard of the Spanish king" by attacking the Spanish fleet at its anchorage in Cadíz harbor. Yet despite dashing heroics of that sort, the English could do no more than dent the Spanish trade.

ENGLISH COLONIALISM

English colonists sought profits elsewhere by establishing agricultural settlements in North America and the Caribbean basin. Their first permanent (though ultimately unsuccessful) colony was Jamestown in Virginia, founded in 1607. Over the next forty years, eighty thousand English emigrants sailed to over twenty autonomous settlements in the New World. In this instance, however, religious freedom, as well as economic gain, was often the motive of the settlers. The renowned band of "Pilgrim fathers" that landed on the New England shores in 1620 was but one of a large number of dissident groups, both Protestant and Catholic, that sought to escape attempts to impose religious conformity. Religion also played a role in the efforts of the Spanish to colonize Central and South America, and of the French to penetrate the hinterlands of North America. Roman Catholic Jesuit missionaries, intent on converting Native Americans to Christianity, joined fur traders in journeys across the continent to the Great Lakes and the Mississippi.

Both England and France were quick to extract profit from their expanding colonial empires. England's agricultural colonies were producing crops in high demand throughout Europe. The success of colonial planters encouraged the governments of both Oliver Cromwell and Charles II to intervene in the management of their overseas economy. Navigation acts, passed in 1651 and 1660, and rigorously enforced thereafter, decreed that all exports from English colonies to the mother country be carried in English ships, and forbade the direct exporting of certain "enumerated" products directly from the colonies to Continental ports.

The most valuable of those products were sugar and tobacco. Sugar, virtually unknown in Christian Europe prior to the fifteenth century, became a popular luxury during the sixteenth century. Where once it had been considered a rarity or even a medicine, one observer now noted that the wealthy were "devouring it out of

gluttony." As we saw in Chapter 12, Europeans had first begun to produce sugar in their Mediterranean and African island colonies during the fifteenth century. Only in the New World, however, did sugar production reach such volumes as to create a mass market for the product. By the middle of the seventeenth century, however, demand for sugar had reached enormous proportions. In the eighteenth century, the value of the sugar that Britain imported from its small West Indian colonies exceeded the total value of its imports from the vast subcontinents of China and India.

Sugar, however, could only be grown in a fairly limited geographical and climatic area. Tobacco was much more adaptable. Although the tobacco plant was imported into Europe by the Spaniards about fifty years after the discovery of America, another half century passed before Europeans took up the habit of smoking. At first the plant was believed to possess miraculous healing powers and was referred to as "divine tobacco" and "our holy herb nicotian." (The word *nicotine* derives from the name of the French ambassador to Portugal, Jean Nicot, who brought the tobacco plant to France.) The practice of smoking was popularized by English explorers, especially by Sir Walter Raleigh, who had learned to smoke while living among the Native Americans of Virginia. It spread rapidly through all classes of European society. Governments at first joined the church in condemning the use of tobacco because of its socially and spiritually harmful effects, but by the end of the seventeenth century, having realized the profits to be made from its production, they encouraged its use.

FRENCH COLONIALISM

French colonial policy matured during the administration of Louis XIV's mercantilist finance minister, Jean Baptiste Colbert (1619–1683), who regarded overseas expansion as an integral part of state economic policy. He organized joint-stock companies to compete with those of the English. He encouraged the development of lucrative sugar-producing colonies in the West Indies, the largest of which was St. Domingue (present-day Haiti). France also dominated the interior of the North American continent. Frenchmen traded furs and preached Christianity to the native peoples in a vast territory that stretched from Acadia and the St. Lawrence River in the northeast to Louisiana in the west. Yet the financial returns from these lands were hardly commensurate with their size. Furs, fish, and tobacco were exported to home markets, but not in sufficient amounts to match the profits from the sugar colonies of the Caribbean or from the trading posts the French maintained in India.

DUTCH COLONIALISM

The Dutch were even more successful than the English and the French in establishing a flourishing commercial empire in the seventeenth century. They succeeded in establishing a colony on the southern tip of Africa at the Cape of Good Hope. Far more important, however, were their commercial adventurings in Southeast Asia. Their joint-stock East India Company, founded in 1602, rivaled its English counterpart in Asia, gaining firm control of Sumatra, Borneo, and the Moluccas, or Spice Islands, and driving Portuguese traders from an area where they had heretofore enjoyed an undisturbed commercial dominion. The result was a Dutch monopoly in

The Dutch East India Company Warehouse and Timber Wharf at Amsterdam. The substantial warehouse, the stockpiles of lumber, and the company ship under construction in the foreground illustrate the degree to which overseas commerce could stimulate the economy of the mother country.

pepper, cinnamon, nutmeg, mace, and cloves. The Dutch also secured an exclusive right to trade with the Japanese, and maintained outposts in China and India as well. In the Western Hemisphere, their achievements were less spectacular. Following a series of trade wars with England, they formally surrendered their North American colony of New Amsterdam (subsequently renamed New York) in 1667, retaining Surinam, off the northern coast of South America, as well as the islands of Curaçao and Tobago in the West Indies in compensation.

CONTRASTING PATTERNS OF COLONIAL SETTLEMENT

Differences in the commercial relationships European countries established with their New World colonies reflected important differences in settlement patterns between the colonies. In Central and South America, a relatively small number of Spaniards had conquered complex, highly populous Native American societies. To rule these new territories, the Spanish quickly replaced native elites with Spanish administrators and churchmen. But by and large they did not attempt to uproot or eliminate existing native cultures. Instead, Spain focused its efforts on controlling and exploiting native labor, so as to extract the maximum possible profit for the crown from the colonies' mineral resources. The native peoples of Spanish America already lived, for the most part, in large, well-organized villages and towns. Spanish colonial policy was to collect tribute from such communities and to convert them to Catholicism, but to do so without fundamentally disrupting their existing patterns of life.

The result was widespread cultural assimilation between the Spanish colonizers and the native populace, combined with a relatively high degree of intermarriage between them. Out of this reality emerged a complex and distinctive system of racial and social castes, with "pure-blooded" Spaniards at the top, peoples of mixed descent in the middle (native, Spanish, and African, in various combinations), and nontribal "Indians" at the bottom. In theory, these racial categories corresponded with class distinctions, but in practice race and class did not always coincide, and race itself was often a social fiction. Mixed race individuals who prospered economically often found ways to establish their "pure" Spanish ancestry by adopting the social practices that characterized elite (that is,

Spanish) status. Spaniards, however, always remained at the top of the social hierarchy of honor and status, even when they fell into poverty.

Like the Spanish colonies, the French colonies were established and administered as direct crown enterprises. The French colonies, however, were dependent almost entirely on the fur trade and on fishing; and the fur trade in particular depended in turn upon cooperative relationships with the native peoples of the New World. French colonial settlements were conceived mainly as military outposts and trading centers; as a result, they were overwhelmingly populated by men. The elite members of French colonial society were the military officers and administrators sent out from Paris. But below their narrow ranks, there was a broad community of interest among the fishermen, fur traders, small farmers, and common soldiers who constituted the bulk of the French settlers of North America. A mutual economic interdependence quickly grew up between these French colonies and the native peoples of the surrounding region, and intermarriage between French fur traders and native women was common. But most of these French colonies remained dependent upon the wages and supplies sent to them from the mother country. Only rarely did they become truly self-sustaining economic enterprises.

The English colonies along the Atlantic seaboard followed a very different model. English colonies did not begin as crown enterprises. Instead they were established either by joint-stock companies (as in Virginia and the Massachusetts Bay colony) or as private, proprietary colonies (such as Maryland and Pennsylvania). Building on their experience in Ireland, English colonists established planned settlements (known as plantations), in which they attempted to replicate as many features of English life as possible. Geography too contributed to the resulting concentration of English settlement patterns. The rivers and bays of eastern North America provided the first footholds for English colonists in the New World, and the Atlantic Ocean helped to tie these separated settlements together. But aside from the Hudson, there were no great rivers to lead colonists very far inland. Instead, the English colonies clung to the seacoast, and so to each other.

Like the French colonies, the early English colonies relied on fishing and the fur trade. But primarily, English colonies were agricultural communities, populated by small- and medium-scale landholders for whom control over land was the key to wealth. Partly this was a reflection of the kinds of people whom these privately owned colonial enterprises could persuade to immigrate to the New World. But this focus on agriculture was also the result of the demographic catastrophe that had struck the native populations of the Atlantic seaboard during the last half of the sixteenth century. European diseases, brought by the Spanish and by the French, English, and Portuguese fishermen who frequented the rich fishing banks off the New England coast, had already decimated the native peoples of eastern North America even before the first colonists set foot there. By the early seventeenth century, a great deal of rich agricultural land had been abandoned, simply because there were no longer enough native farmers to till it—one reason that many native groups initially welcomed the new arrivals.

Unlike the Spanish, English colonists along the Atlantic seaboard therefore had neither the need nor the opportunity to control a large native labor force. What they wanted, rather, was complete and exclusive control over native lands. To this end, the English colonists soon set out to eliminate, through expulsion and massacre, the native peoples of their colonies. To be sure, there were exceptions. In the Quaker colony of Pennsylvania, colonists and Native Americans maintained friendly relations for more than half a century. In the Carolinas, by contrast, enslavement of the native people was widespread, either for sale to the West Indies or, from the 1690s, to work on the rice plantations. Elsewhere, however, attempts to enslave native people failed. When English planters looked for bond laborers, they therefore either recruited indentured servants from England (who would be freed after a specified period of service) or else they purchased Africans (who by and large would be enslaved for life).

Social relations between the English colonists and native peoples also differed from the patterns we find elsewhere in the New World. In contrast to the Spanish and French colonies, intermarriage between English colonists and natives was rare. Instead, a rigid racial division emerged that distinguished all Europeans, regardless of class, from all Native Americans and Africans. Nor did the English make any significant effort to convert native peoples to Christianity. Intermarriage between natives and Africans was relatively common, but between the English and the non-European peoples of their colonies there remained an unbridgeable gulf.

COLONIAL RIVALRIES

The fortunes of these European colonial empires rose and fell over the course of the seventeenth and eigh-

The Rewards of Commercial Exploitation. An English employee of the East India Company enjoying his ease and his opium, as depicted by an eighteenth-century Indian artist.

ilar preferential treatment for Portuguese wines. (The notorious affection of the English upper class for port wine dates from the signing of the Treaty of 1703.) British trade with the mother country led in time to British trade with the Portuguese colony of Brazil, and indeed to the opening of commercial offices in Rio de Janeiro.

During the eighteenth century, however, a growing Anglo-French rivalry in India stole the commercial spotlight from the Dutch spice monopoly in the Far East. The French and British East India Companies employed mercenaries to establish and expand trading areas such as Madras, Bombay, and Pondichéry. By exploiting indigenous industries, European capitalists continued to increase the flow of fine cotton textiles, tea, and spices, which passed through these commercial depots on their way to Europe. The struggle for worldwide economic dominance reached a peak in the mid-eighteenth century (see pp. 623–24). At that time the Anglo-French rivalry in India was resolved in Britain's favor. As a sign of France's defeat, in 1769 the French East India Company was dissolved.

teenth centuries. The Spanish, mired in persistent economic stagnation and embroiled in a succession of expensive wars and domestic rebellions, were powerless to prevent losses to their empire. Their merchant marine, once a match for cunning pirate-admirals such as Drake, was by the middle of the seventeenth century unable to protect itself from attack by its commercial rivals. In a war with Spain in the 1650s, the English captured not only the island of Jamaica but treasure ships lying off the Spanish harbor of Cadíz. Further profit was obtained by bribing Spanish customs officials on a grand scale. During the second half of the century, two thirds of the imported goods sold in Spanish colonies were smuggled in by Dutch, English, and French traders. By 1700, though Spain still possessed a colonial empire, that empire now lay at the mercy of its more dynamic rivals. A brief revival of its fortunes under more enlightened leadership in the mid-eighteenth century did nothing to prevent its ultimate eclipse.

Portugal, too, found it impossible to prevent foreign penetration of its colonial economies. The British worked diligently and successfully to win commercial advantages. They obtained concessions to export woolens duty free into Portugal itself in return for sim-

THE TRIANGULAR TRADE IN SUGAR AND SLAVES

Despite the commercial importance of India, however, patterns of world trade came increasingly to be dominated by western routes that had developed in response to the lucrative West Indian sugar industry, and to the demand for slaves from Africa to work the plantations in the Caribbean. Here Britain again eventually assumed the lead. Typically, a ship might begin its voyage from New England with a consignment of rum and sail to Africa, where the rum would be exchanged for a cargo of slaves. From the west coast of Africa the ship would then cross the South Atlantic to the sugar colonies of Jamaica or Barbados, where slaves would be traded for molasses, which would make the final leg of the journey to New England, where it would be made into rum. A variant triangle might see cheap manufactured goods move from Britain to Africa, where they would be traded for slaves. Those slaves would then be shipped to Virginia and exchanged for tobacco, which would be shipped to Britain and processed there for sale in Continental markets. Other eighteenth-century trade routes were more direct: the Spanish, French, Portuguese, and Dutch all engaged in the slave trade between Africa and Central and South America; the Spanish attempted, in vain, to retain a mercantilist monopoly on direct trade between Cadíz and their South American colonies; others sailed from Britain, France, or North America to the Caribbean and back again. And of course trade continued to flourish between Europe and the Near and Far East. But the triangular western routes, dictated by the grim economic symbiosis of sugar and slaves, remained dominant.

> The triangular western routes, dictated by the grim economic symbiosis of sugar and slaves, remained dominant.

The cultivation of sugar and tobacco depended on slave labor, and as demand for those products increased, so did the traffic in black slaves, without whose labor those products could not be raised or harvested. At the height of the Atlantic slave trade in the eighteenth century, somewhere between seventy-five thousand and ninety thousand Africans were shipped across the Atlantic yearly: at least 6 million during the eighteenth century, out of a total of over 11 million for the entire history of the trade. About 35 percent went to British and French Caribbean plantations, 5 percent (roughly five hundred thousand) to North America, and the rest to the Portuguese colony of Brazil and to Spanish colonies in South America. Although run as a monopoly by various governments in the sixteenth and early seventeenth centuries, in its heyday the slave trade was open to private entrepreneurs who operated ports on the West African coast. Traders exchanged cheap Indian cloth, metal goods, rum, and firearms with African slave merchants in return for their human cargo. Already disoriented and degraded by their capture at the hands of rival tribes, men, women, and children were packed by the hundreds into the holds of slave ships for the gruesome "middle passage" across the Atlantic (so called to distinguish it from the ship's voyage from Europe to Africa, and from the slave colony back to Europe again). Shackled to the decks, without sanitary

How Slaves Were Stowed Aboard Ship during the Middle Passage. Men were "housed" on the right; women on the left; children in the middle. The human cargo was jammed onto platforms six feet wide without sufficient headroom to permit an adult to sit up. This diagram is from evidence gathered by English abolitionists and depicts conditions on the Liverpool slave ship *Brookes.*

CONDITIONS ON BOARD A SLAVE SHIP

Olaudah Equiano (1745–1797) was born in West Africa. At the age of eleven, he was kidnapped by African slavers; after being bought and sold several times, he wound up on a slave ship to the West Indies. His account of conditions on the "middle passage" between Africa and the Americas is drawn from the memoir he wrote of his life many years later, after he was freed and had become a successful merchant in England.

When I looked round the ship too and saw a large furnace or copper boiling, and a multitude of black people of every description chained together, every one of their countenances expressing dejection and sorrow, I no longer doubted of my fate; and, quite over-powered with horror and anguish, I fell motionless on the deck and fainted. . . .

I was not long suffered to indulge my grief; I was soon put down under the decks, and there I received such a salutation in my nostrils as I had never experienced in my life: so that, with the loathsomeness of the stench, and crying together, I became so sick and low that I was not able to eat, nor had I the least desire to taste any thing. I now wished for the last friend, death, to relieve me; but soon, to my grief, two of the white men offered me eatables; and, on my refusing to eat . . . flogged me severely. . . .Could I have got over the nettings, I would have jumped over the side, but I could not. . . .

At last, when the ship we were in had got in all her cargo, they made ready with many fearful noises, and we were all put under deck. . . . The stench of the hold while we were on the coast was so intolerably loath-

some, that it was dangerous to remain there for any time, and some of us had been permitted to stay on the deck for the fresh air; but now that the whole ship's cargo were confined together, it became absolutely pestilential. The closeness of the place, and the heat of the climate, added to the number in the ship, which was so crowded that each had scarcely room to turn himself, almost suffocated us. This produced copious perspirations, so that the air soon became unfit for respiration . . . and brought on a sickness among the slaves, of which many died, thus falling victims to the improvident avarice, as I may call it, of their purchasers. This wretched situation was again aggravated by the galling of the chains, now become unsupportable; and the filth of the necessary tubs [latrines], into which the children often fell, and were almost suffocated. The shrieks of the women, and the groans of the dying, rendered the whole a scene of horror almost inconceivable.

Olaudah Equiano. *The Interesting Narrative of the Life of Olaudah Equiano, or Gustavus Vassa, The African, Written by Himself,* edited by Werner Sollors. (New York: W.W. Norton and Company, 2001), pp. 39–41.

facilities, the human "cargo" suffered horribly; the mortality rate, however, remained at about 10 or 11 percent, not much higher than the rate for a normal sea voyage of one hundred days or more. Since traders had to invest as much as £10 per slave in their enterprise, they ensured that their consignment would reach its destination in good enough shape to be sold for a profit.

CHAPTER

The slave trade was risky, dependent on good wind and fair weather, and competition was increasing. Yet profits could run high, occasionally as much as 300 percent. Demand for slaves remained constant throughout the eighteenth century. By the 1780s, there were more than five hundred thousand slaves on the largest French plantation island, St.- Domingue, and two hundred thousand or more on the British counterpart, Jamaica. Those numbers reflected the expanding world market for slave-grown crops. As long as there was a market for the crops cultivated by slaves—as long as the economy relied to the extent it did on slave labor—governments would remain unwilling to halt the system that, as one Briton wrote in 1749, provided "an unexhaustible fund of wealth to this nation."

Apologists for the slave trade argued that though there was reason to rejoice that slavery had been banished from the continent of Europe (forgetting, apparently, the extent to which it continued to exist east of the Elbe in the form of serfdom), it remained a necessity in other parts of the world. Not until the very end of the eighteenth century did Europeans begin to protest the ghastly traffic. Public pressure, first from Quakers and then from others motivated by either religious or humanitarian zeal, helped put an end to the trade in Britain in 1807, and to slavery itself in British colonies in 1833. Slavery in French colonies was abolished in 1793, but only after slaves had risen in massive revolt on St.-Domingue. Elsewhere, in Latin and North America, slavery lasted well into the nineteenth century—in the United States, until the Civil War of 1861–1865. The racism it promoted has lasted until the present day.

Social ranks were demarcated by rights and privileges.

The slave trade was an integral part of the history of the dramatic rise of British and French commerce during the eighteenth century. French colonial trade, valued at 25 million livres in 1716, rose to 263 million livres in 1789. In Britain, during roughly the same period, foreign trade increased in value from £10 million to £40 million, the latter amount more than twice that for France. These figures suggest the degree to which statecraft and private enterprise were bound to each other. If merchants depended on their government to provide a navy to protect and defend their overseas investments, governments depended equally on entrepreneurship, not only to generate money to build ships, but to sustain the trade on which national power had come to rely so heavily.

LIFE WITHIN A SOCIETY OF ORDERS

How did the lives of eastern and western European peasants differ?

Despite the economic and demographic shifts that were occurring in early modern Europe, society remained divided into traditional orders, or ranks. The economic changes we have been describing occurred against the continuity of long-accepted social divisions based on birth and occupation. As circumstances altered, the fluid patterns of economic reorganization clashed with older, rigid assumptions about the place of men and women within a preordained—to many, a divinely ordained—social hierarchy. Jean Bodin, the French philosopher, wrote in 1570 that the division of the citizenry into "the three orders of nobles, clergy and people" was no more than natural. "There never was a commonwealth, real or imaginary, where citizens were in truth equal in all rights and privileges. Some always have more, some less than the rest." And some had none.

Most Europeans would have recognized subtle subdivisions among and between the three orders Bodin specified. Ranks were demarcated by rights and privileges. "Freedom" was understood as one such privilege, as a benefit, bestowed not on all men and women but on special groups whose position "freed" them to do certain things others could not do, or freed them from the burden of doing certain things that were required of others. A British landowner was, because of the position his property conferred upon him, privileged, and therefore "free" to participate directly in the election of his government. A French nobleman was privileged, and therefore "free" of the heavy burden of taxation levied upon the unprivileged orders. A German tailor who had served out his seven-year apprenticeship was free to set up his own shop for profit, something an unapprenticed man was not traditionally "at liberty" to do, no matter what his degree of skill with needle and thread. The master tailor's position conferred his freedom, just as the position of aristocrat and property owner conferred theirs.

HOW DID THE LIVES OF EASTERN AND WESTERN EUROPEAN PEASANTS DIFFER?

LIFE WITHIN A SOCIETY OF ORDERS   581

DISPLAYS OF RANK

The members of the higher orders attempted at all times to live their lives in a particular style that accorded with their rank. The nobility was taught from birth to consider itself above and apart from the rest of society. Merchants and manufacturers were just as insistent upon maintaining the traditional marks of privilege that separated them from artisans and peasants. Sumptuary laws decreed what could be worn and by whom. An edict promulgated in the German principality of Brunswick in 1738, for example, forbade servant girls to wear silk dresses, gold or silver ornaments, or anything but plain black shoes. A similar seventeenth-century law in the Polish city of Posen prohibited the wives of burghers from wearing capes or long hair. Style was not simply a matter of current whim. It was a badge of status, carefully adhered to. An aristocratic lady powdered her hair and rouged her cheeks as a sign that she was an aristocrat. Life within a society of orders demanded a certain degree of theatricality, especially from those at the top of the social hierarchy. Aristocrats "acted" their part in a calculatedly self-conscious way. Their manner of speech, their dress, the ceremonial swords noblemen were privileged to wear, the titles by which they were addressed—these were the props of a performance that constantly emphasized the distinctions between those above and those below. Noble families lived in castles, chateaux, or country houses whose size and antiquity were a fur-

ther proclamation of superiority. When they built new mansions, as did the *nouveau riche* capitalist British gentry during the eighteenth century, they made certain their elaborate houses and spacious private parks declared their newfound power. The English politician Robert Walpole had an entire village moved to improve the view from his grand new residence.

THE NOBILITY

The vast majority of men and women defined and understood social hierarchy in terms of the rural communities in which they lived. At the head of those communities, in all likelihood, stood a representative of the noble elite. The nobility probably numbered about 3 percent of the total population of Europe. The percentage was higher in Poland, Hungary, and Spain; lower in Russia, Germany, France, and Britain. Ownership of a landed estate was proof of one's elevated rank. Generally speaking, the more land one possessed, the higher one stood within the social hierarchy. In Hungary, five noble families owned about 14 percent of the entire country; the greatest of these nobles, Prince Esterházy, controlled the lives of more than half a million peasants. Most noblemen were not nearly so rich and powerful. Some, indeed, could rely on little more than inherited privilege to distinguish themselves from peasants.

Tradition had it that noble service meant military service; yet, as we shall see, that tradition was increasingly breached during the early modern period. Noble title was granted by a monarch, in theory for service to the state. But such service was more and more frequently defined as nonmilitary—as support, financial and political, for the expanding apparatus of local and central government. The pattern of noble life varied considerably from country to country. In Britain and Prussia, nobles tended to reside on their estates; in south and west Germany, and in France, they were more likely to leave the management of their estates to stewards and to live at the royal

Middle-Class Fashion. In this seventeenth-century portrait of a Dutch burgomaster and his family, the patriarch and his wife are wearing the costume of an earlier generation, while the children are clothed in the current style. All display the opulence characteristic of their prosperous class.

Gala Dinner at Schoenbrunn Palace in Vienna. Given on the occasion of Joseph II's wedding, this banquet was an example of the extravagance this Habsburg monarch believed suitable to the occasion.

through the purchase of expensive offices from the crown. Membership could be purchased in the legal nobility of the "robe," headed by members of the thirteen provincial parlements whose function it was to record, and thereby sanction, the laws of the kingdom, and to adjudicate cases appealed from lower courts.

THE PEASANTRY

Land ownership brought the nobility into direct relationship with the peasants and laborers who worked the land and over whose lives their masters exercised dominion. The status of the peasantry varied greatly across the face of rural Europe. In the east—Russia, Poland, Hungary, and in parts of Germany beyond the Elbe—the desire for profit in agriculture and the collusion of the state with the nobility led to the growth of a "second serfdom," a serf system much stronger than that which had existed during the Middle Ages. In East Prussia, serfs often had to work from three to six days a week for their lord, and some had only late evening or night hours to cultivate their own lands.

Peasants throughout eastern Europe found their destinies controlled in almost all respects by their masters. Noble landlords dispensed justice in manorial courts and even ruled in cases to which they were themselves interested parties. These men were a combination of sheriff, chief magistrate, and police force in one, able to sentence their "subjects" to corporal punishment, imprisonment, exile, or even death, without right of appeal. Peasants could not leave their land, marry, or learn a trade unless permitted to do so by their lord. In Russia, where half the land was owned by the state, peasants were bound to work in mines or workshops if their masters so ordered, and could be sold to private owners. Although Russian peasant serfs were said to possess a "legal personality"

court or in cities. Despite the traditional assumption that noblemen should not soil their aristocratic reputation by commercial dealing, by the end of the eighteenth century they were involving themselves in increasing numbers in a variety of entrepreneurial enterprises. Some exploited mineral deposits on their estates; others invested in overseas trade. In France, two of the four largest coal mines were owned and operated by noblemen, while the duke of Orléans was an important investor in the newly established chemical dye industry. In eastern Europe, where there were few middle-class merchants, noblemen frequently undertook to market their agricultural produce themselves.

In no country was the nobility a completely closed order. Men who proved useful to the crown as administrators or lawyers, men who amassed large fortunes as a consequence of judicious—and often legally questionable—financial transactions, moved into the ranks of the nobility with increasing frequency during the late seventeenth and eighteenth centuries. Joseph II of Austria was making financiers into noblemen by the dozen during the late eighteenth century. In France, it was possible to attain nobility

> In no country was the nobility a completely closed order.

HOW DID THE LIVES OF EASTERN AND WESTERN EUROPEAN PEASANTS DIFFER?

LIFE WITHIN A SOCIETY OF ORDERS   583

that distinguished them from slaves, the distinction was obscured in practice. They lived as bound to their masters as had their great-grandfathers.

In western Europe, the position of the peasantry reflected the fact that serfdom had all but disappeared by the sixteenth century. Peasants might theoretically own land, although the vast majority were either tenants or laborers. Hereditary tenure was in general more secure than in the east; peasants could dispose of their land and had legal claim to farm buildings and implements. Although far freer than their eastern European counterparts, the peasants of western Europe still lived to a great degree under the domination of landowners. They were in many cases responsible for the payment of various dues and fees: an annual rent paid to landlords by those who might otherwise own their land outright; a special tax on re-

> Although far freer than their eastern European counterparts, the peasants of western Europe still lived to a great degree under the domination of landowners.

cently cleared land; a fee, often as much as one sixth of the assessed value of the land, collected by the manorial lord whenever peasant property changed hands; and charges for the use of the lord's mill, bakery, or wine press. In France, peasants were compelled to submit to the corvée, a requirement that they labor for several weeks a year maintaining local roads. Even access to the often questionable justice meted out in the manorial courts, which endured throughout the early-modern period in almost all of western Europe, was encumbered with fees and commissions. To many peasants, however, the most galling badge of their inferiority was their inability to hunt within the jurisdiction of their landlord's manor. The slaughter of game was a privilege reserved to the nobility, a circumstance generating sustained resentment on the part of a population that looked on deer and pheasant not as a symbol of aristocratic status but as a necessary supplement to a meager diet. Noble landlords rarely missed an opportunity to extract all the money they could from their peasants while constantly reminding them of the degree to which their destiny was controlled by the lord of the manor.

Despite their traditional subservience, however, western European peasants found themselves caught up directly in the process of economic change. The growth of centralized monarchies intensified the states' need for income, with the result that peasants were more burdened than ever with taxes and required services. They responded by accepting a new role as wage earners in an expanding market economy, some as agricultural day laborers on enclosed estates, others as part of the work force in expanding rural industries. A few were genuinely independent, literate, influential members of the communities where they lived, owning not only land but considerable livestock. In France, some acted as intermediaries between their landlords, from whom they leased several large farms, and the sharecroppers who actually worked the land. Most, however, were far less fortunate. Those with claim to a small piece of property usually worked it into infertility in the course of one or two generations as they scrambled to make it produce as much as possible.

Poor peasants often lived, contrary to the biblical injunction, by bread alone—two pounds a day if they were lucky, the dark dough a mixture of wheat and rye flour. According to region, bread was supplemented by peas and beans, beer, wine, or, far less often, skimmed

A French Peasant. Tattered and overworked, this peasant farmer is shown feeding his livestock as the tax collector at his door relieves him of all of his profits.

milk. Peasant houses usually contained no more than one or two rooms, and were constructed of wood, plastered with mud or clay. Roofs were most often thatched with straw, which was used as fertilizer when replaced, and provided fodder for animals in times of scarcity. Furnishings seldom consisted of more than a table, benches, pallets for sleeping, a few earthenware plates, and simple tools—an axe, a wooden spade, a knife.

Peasant women tended livestock and vegetables and managed the dairy, if there was one. Women went out as field workers, or worked at home knitting, spinning, or weaving in order to augment the family income. A popular seventeenth-century poem has a laborer's wife lamenting her lot with a refrain that has echoed down the ages: "My labor is hard, / And all my pleasures are debarr'd; / Both morning, evening, night and noon, / I am sure a woman's work is never done."

URBAN SOCIETY

The spread of protoindustrialization broke down the demarcations between town and country, between the life lived inside a city's medieval walls and that lived outside. Suburbs merged urban and rural existence. In some suburbs, textile workers labored. In others, families of fashion took their ease, creating an environment "where the want of London smoke is supplied by the smoke of Virginia tobacco," as one Briton remarked wryly. Houses in areas inhabited by the wealthy were increasingly built of brick and stone, which replaced the wood, lath, and plaster of the Middle Ages. This change was a response to the constant danger of fire. The great fire of London in 1666, which destroyed three quarters of the town—twelve thousand houses—was the largest of the conflagrations that swept cities with devastating regularity. Urban dwellings of the laboring poor remained firetraps. Workers' quarters were badly overcrowded; entire families lived in one-room accommodations in basements and attics that were infested with bugs and fleas.

Urban society was, like its rural counterpart, a society of orders. In national capitals, noble families occupied the highest social position, as they did in the countryside, living a parasitic life of conspicuous consumption. The majority of cities and towns were dominated by a nonnoble bourgeoisie. That French term

In national capitals, noble families occupied the highest social position, as they did in the countryside, living a parasitic life of conspicuous consumption.

originally designated a burgher or townsman who was a long-term, resident property owner or leaseholder and taxpayer. By the eighteenth century it had come to mean a townsman of some means who aspired to be recognized as a person of local importance and evinced a willingness to work hard, whether at countinghouse or government office, and a desire to live a comfortable, if by no means extravagant, existence. A bourgeois might derive his income from rents; or he might be an industrialist, banker, merchant, lawyer, or physician. If he served in the central bureaucracy, he would consider himself the social superior of those provincials whose affairs he administered. Yet he would himself be looked down on by the aristocracy, many of whom enjoyed thinking of the bourgeoisie as a class of vulgar social climbers, often conveniently forgetting their own commercial origins a generation or two previously. The French playwright Molière's comedy *The Bourgeois Gentleman* (1670) reflected this attitude, ridiculing the manners of those who were trying to ape their betters. "Bourgeois," another French writer observed, "is the insult given by noblemen to anybody they deem slow-witted or out of touch with the court." The bourgeoisie usually constituted about 20 to 25 percent of a town's population. As its economic elite, these men were almost always its governing elite as well.

Throughout the early modern period, there was considerable movement into and out of the urban bourgeoisie. Prosperous tradesmen and successful small-time commercial entrepreneurs might see their offspring rise in station, particularly if they married well. At the same time, those who made their money in trade could purchase land, and by paying fees to their king, gain the right to an ennobling office. In seventeenth-century Amiens, a major French textile center, the upper bourgeoisie deserted trade and derived the majority of its income from land or bonds. Where the bourgeoisie thrived, it more often than not did so as the result of a burgeoning state or regional bureaucracy.

Next within the urban hierarchy was a vast middle range of shopkeepers and artisans. Many of the latter continued to learn and then to practice their crafts as members of guilds, which in turn contained their own particular ascending order of apprentice, journeyman, and master, thus preserving the pervasive principle of hierarchy. Throughout the early modern period, however, commercial expansion threatened the rigid hierar-

HOW DID THE LIVES OF EASTERN AND WESTERN EUROPEAN PEASANTS DIFFER?

LIFE WITHIN A SOCIETY OF ORDERS   585

The "Bon Ton." This English cartoon mocks the rage for French fashion and illustrates the affluence of a middle class able to afford the changing dictates of fashion.

chy of the guild structure. The expense and curtailed output resulting from restrictive guild practices met with serious opposition in big cities such as Paris and London, and in the industrial hinterlands of France and Germany, where expanding markets called for cheaper and more readily available goods. Journeymen tailors and shoemakers in increasing numbers set up shops without benefit of mastership and produced cheaper coats and shoes in defiance of guild regulations. In the silk workshops of Lyons, both masters and journeymen were compelled to labor without distinction of status for piece rates (wages paid per finished article, rather than per hour) set by merchandising middlemen and far below an equitable level in the opinion of the silk workers. Artisans like these, compelled to work for low wages at the behest of profiteering middlemen, grew increasingly restive. In France and Germany, journeymen's associations had originated as social and mutual-aid organizations for young men engaged in "tramping" the country to gain experience in their trade. In some instances, however, these associations fostered the development of a trade consciousness that led to strikes and boycotts against masters and middlemen over wages and working conditions. An imperial law passed in Germany in 1731 deprived the associations of their right to organize, and required journeymen to carry a certificate of identification as testimony of their respectability during their travels.

At the bottom of urban society was a mass of semi-skilled and unskilled workers: carters and porters; stevedores and dockers; water carriers and sweepers; seamstresses, laundresses, cleaners, and domestic servants. These men and women, like their rural counterparts, lived on the margins of life, constantly battling the trade cycles, seasonal unemployment, and epidemics that threatened their ability to survive. A number existed in shanties on the edges of towns and cities. In Genoa, the homeless poor were sold as galley slaves each winter. In Venice, the poor lived on decrepit barges under the city's bridges. A French ordinance of 1669 ordered the destruction of all houses "built on poles by vagabonds and useless members of society." Deprived of the certainty of steady work, these people were prey not only to economic fluctuations and malevolent "acts of God," but to a social system that left them without any "privilege" or "freedom" whatsoever.

THE PROBLEM OF POVERTY

Attitudes toward poverty varied from country to country. Most localities extended the concept of orders to include the poor: the "deserving"—usually orphans, the insane, the aged, the infirm; and the "undeserving"—able-bodied men and women who were out of work or who, even though employed, could not support themselves and their families. The authorities tended to assume in the latter case that poverty was the result of personal failings; few made a connection between general economic circumstances and the plight of the individual poor. For the deserving, private charitable organizations, such as those in France founded by the order of Saint Vincent de Paul and by the Sisters of Charity, provided assistance. For the undeserving, there was harsh treatment at the hands of the state whose concern to alleviate extreme deprivation arose more from a desire to avert public disorder than from motives of human charity. Food riots were common occurrences. In times of scarcity the French government frequently intervened to reduce the price of grain, hoping thereby to prevent an outbreak of rioting. Nevertheless, riots occurred. When property damage resulted, the ringleaders were generally severely punished, usually by hanging. The remainder of

Hanging Thieves. This seventeenth-century engraving is designed to teach a lesson. Troops stand by and priests bless the condemned criminals as they are executed by the dozen. "At last," the engraver's caption reads, "these infamous lost souls are hung like unhappy fruit."

the crowd was often left untouched by the law, a fact suggesting the degree to which governments were prepared to tolerate rioting itself as a means of dealing with the chronic consequences of poverty.

Poverty remained a central and intractable problem for the governments of all European countries. Poor vagrants were perceived as a serious threat to social tranquillity. They were therefore frequently rounded up at harvesttime to keep them from plundering the fields. Vagrants and other chronically unemployed persons were placed in poorhouses, where conditions were little better than those in prisons. Often the very young, the very old, the sick, and the insane were housed together with hardened criminals. Poor relief in England was administered parish by parish in accordance with a law passed in 1601. Relief was tied to a "law of settlement," which stipulated that paupers might receive aid only if still residing in the parish of their birth. An unemployed weaver who had migrated fifty miles in search of work could thus expect assistance only if he returned home again. In the late eighteenth century, several European countries established modest public works programs in an attempt to relieve poverty by reducing unemployment. France, for example, undertook road-building projects in the 1770s under the auspices of its progressive finance minister, Turgot. But generally speaking, indigence was perceived not as a social ill for which a remedy might be sought, but as an indelible stigma demarking those at the bottom of society.

EDUCATION AND LITERACY

European social institutions reflected the patterns of hierarchy. Nowhere was this more apparent than in the field of education. One barrier—a knowledge of Latin—separated nobles and a fair number of scholars and professionals from the commercial middle ranks; a second—the ability to read and write—separated the middle from the rest. Noblemen were generally educated by private tutors; though they might attend university for a time, they did so not in preparation for a profession but to receive further educational "finishing." Indeed, during the late seventeenth and eighteenth centuries, universities more or less surrendered intellectual leadership to various academies established with royal patronage by European monarchs to enhance their own reputations as well as to encourage the advancement of science and the arts: the Royal Society of London, founded by Charles II in 1660; the French Academy of Sciences, a project on which Louis XIV lavished a good deal of ostentatious attention; and the Berlin Royal Academy of Science and Letters, patronized by Frederick the Great of Prussia in the eighteenth century. Few noblemen had the interest or the education to participate in the activities of these august organizations, which were not, in any case, teaching institutions. Far better suited to their needs and inclinations was "the grand tour," often of many months' duration, which led the young nobleman through the capitals of Europe, and during which he

HOW DID THE LIVES OF EASTERN AND WESTERN EUROPEAN PEASANTS DIFFER?

LIFE WITHIN A SOCIETY OF ORDERS 587

was expected to acquire a kind of international politesse. One observer, commenting on the habits of young British noblemen abroad, remarked, "they game; purchase pictures, mutilated statues, and mistresses to the astonishment of all beholders."

Endowed, fee-charging institutions for the training of a governmental elite existed in France (the *collège*) and Spain (the *colegio mayor*) and in Germany and Austria (the *gymnasium*). Here the emphasis was by no means on "practical" subjects such as modern language or mathematics, but on the mastery of Greek and Latin translation and composition, the intellectual badge of the educated elite. An exception was the Prussian University of Halle, designed to teach a professional elite; a contemporary described that institution as teaching only what was "rational, useful, and practical."

Boys from the middle orders destined to enter the family business or profession as a rule attended small private academies where the curriculum included the sort of "useful" instruction ignored in the collèges and gymnasia. Girls, from both the upper and the middle orders, were almost invariably educated at home, receiving little more than rudimentary instruction in gentlewomanly subjects such as modern language, literature, and music, if from the noble ranks; and a similar, if slightly more practical training, if from the bourgeoisie.

No European country undertook the task of providing primary education to all its citizens until the middle of the eighteenth century, when Frederick the Great in Prussia and the Habsburg monarchs Maria Theresa and her son Joseph II in Austria instituted systems of compulsory attendance. Available evidence suggests that their results fell far short of expectation. An early nineteenth century survey from the relatively enlightened Prussian province of Cleves revealed dilapidated schools, poorly attended classes, and an incompetent corps of teachers. Educational conditions were undoubtedly worse in most other European communities.

Though modern scholars can make no more than educated guesses, it appears certain that literacy rates increased considerably in the seventeenth and eighteenth centuries; in England, from one in four males in 1600 to one in two by 1800; in France, from 29 percent of the male population in 1686 to 47 percent in 1786. Literacy among women grew as well, though their rate of increase generally lagged behind that of men: only 27 percent of the female population in France was literate in 1786. Naturally, such rates varied according to particular localities and circumstances, and from country to country. Literacy was higher in urban areas that contained a large proportion of artisans. In rural eastern Europe, literacy remained extremely low (20 to 30 percent) well into the nineteenth century. Notwithstanding state-directed efforts in Prussia and Austria, the rise in literacy was largely the result of a growing determination on the part of religiously minded reformers to teach the poor to read and write as a means of encouraging obedience to divine and secular authority. A Sunday-school movement in eighteenth-century Britain and similar activities among the Christian Brotherhood in France are clear evidence of this trend.

POPULAR CULTURE

Though the majority of the common people were probably no more than barely literate, they possessed a flourishing culture of their own. Village life, particularly in Roman Catholic countries, centered about the church, to which men and women would go on Sundays not only to worship but to socialize. Much of the remainder of their day of rest would be devoted to participation in village games. Religion provided the opportunity for association and for a welcome break from the daily work routines. Pilgrimages to a nearby shrine, for example, would include a procession of villagers led by one of their number carrying an image of the village's patron saint and accompanied by drinking, dancing, and picnicking. In towns, Catholics joined organizations called "confraternities" in France, Italy, Austria, and the Netherlands, which provided mutual aid and a set of common rituals and traditions centered around a patron saint. Religious community was expressed as well in popular Protestant movements that arose in the eighteenth century: Pietism on the Continent and Methodism in England. Both emphasized the importance of personal salvation through faith and the potential worth of every human soul regardless of station. Both therefore appealed particularly to people whose position within the community had heretofore been presumed to be without any value. Though Methodism's founder, John Wesley (1703–1791), preached obedience to earthly authority,

> The rise in literacy was largely the result of a growing determination on the part of religiously minded reformers to teach the poor to read and write as a means of encouraging obedience to divine and secular authority.

OPPOSITION TO THE EDUCATION OF THE LOWER CLASSES

During the eighteenth century, education began to appeal more and more to the laboring classes as a route to social advancement. Not everyone welcomed this development, however. Some, like the two authors cited here, argued that education would simply make such persons dissatisfied with their "natural" station in life.

L. R. CARADEUC DE LA CHALOTAIS, *Essay on National Education* [France, 1763]

Today, even the lower classes want to study. Laborers and artisans send their children to boarding schools in the small towns where living is cheap, and when they have received a wretched education, which has taught them merely to despise their fathers' trades, they fling themselves into the monasteries, become priests or officers of justice, and frequently turn out to be a danger to society. . . . The good of society requires that the lower classes' knowledge should go no further than their occupations. No man who can see beyond his depressing trade will ply it with patience and courage. The lower classes scarcely need to know how to read or write except for those members of it who live by these skills or are helped by them to make their living. . . . [France, 1763]

SARAH TRIMMER, *Reflections upon the Education of Children in Charity Schools* [Britain, 1792]

However desirable it may be to rescue the lower kinds of people from ignorance . . . it cannot be right to train them all in a way which will probably raise their ideas above the very lowest occupations of life and disqualify them for those servile offices which must be filled by some members of the community, and in which they may be equally happy with the highest, if they will do their duty. . . . The children of the poor should not be educated in such a manner as to set them above the occupations of humble life, or so as to make them uncomfortable among their equals. [Britain, 1792]

Julia O'Faolain and Lauro Martines, eds. *Not in God's Image: Women in History from the Greeks to the Victorians* (New York: Harper and Row, 1973), pp. 245–246.

---

his willingness to rely on working men and women as preachers and organizers gave them a new sense of personal importance.

Popular culture often combined in one event traditions that were part religious, part secular, and, indeed, part pagan. One such occasion was Carnival, that vibrant pre-Lenten celebration indigenous not only to Mediterranean Europe but to Germany and Austria as well. Carnival represented an opportunity for common folk to cast aside the burdens and restraints imposed upon their order by secular authority. Performances and processions celebrated a "world turned upside down." Popular throughout much of Europe since the later Middle Ages, this theme appealed to commoners for a variety of ambiguous psychological reasons, but in large part, certainly, as a way of avenging symbolically the economic and social oppression under which they lived. For a few days, the oppressed played the

HOW DID THE LIVES OF EASTERN AND WESTERN EUROPEAN PEASANTS DIFFER?

LIFE WITHIN A SOCIETY OF ORDERS   589

French Tavern. Often located outside the city limits so as to avoid the payment of municipal taxes, taverns such as this provided a gathering place for workers to drink, gossip, and relax after the day's labors. The tavern also served as a convenient place for public readings and for airing common grievances.

role of the oppressor and rulers were made to look like fools and knaves. In parades, men dressed as kings walked barefoot while peasants rode on horseback or in carriages; the poor threw pretend money to the rich. These occasions, although emphasizing social divisions, bound communities to a common cultural center, since, through most of the early modern period, both rich and poor celebrated together, as they did on major religious holidays. Annual harvest festivals, once sponsored by the church, became increasingly secular celebrations of release from backbreaking labor, punctuated by feasting, drinking, sporting, and lovemaking. Fairs and traveling circuses brought something of distant places and people into lives bound to one spot. The drudgery of everyday life was also relieved by horse races, cockfights, and bear baiting. Taverns played an even more constant role in the daily life of the village, providing a place for men to gather over tobacco and drink and indulge in gossip and gambling.

Laboring men and women depended on an oral tradition of myth, legend, and superstition to steady their lives and give them point and purpose. Stories in books sold at fairs by peddlers were passed on by those who could read. They told of heroes and saints, and of kings such as Charlemagne whose paternal concern for his common subjects led him into battle against his selfish nobility. Belief in villains matched belief in heroes. Witchcraft, as we have seen, was a reality for much of the period. So was Satan. So was any supernatural force, whether for good or evil, that could help people make sense of a world in which they, more than any, were victims of events beyond their control.

Though increasingly secularized, popular customs, celebrations, and beliefs remained a stabilizing force in early modern Europe. They were the cultural expression of that social order to which the vast majority of Europeans belonged. Popular culture in the main tended to reinforce the traditions and assumptions of order and hierarchy. Peasants and urban workers worshiped saints and venerated heroic rulers, thereby accepting the authority of the established, ordered society of which they were a part. They were seldom satisfied with their lot, yet they were as seldom willing to question the social structure they saw as a bulwark against the swift changes so often surrounding them. Popular culture helped to bind men and women to what civilization had been, as capitalism and mercantilism impelled them in the direction of what it would become.

CONCLUSION

Between 1600 and 1800, the European economy grew steadily larger and more complex. Powered by the profits of overseas colonial empires and fueled by enslaved African labor, European trade expanded enormously despite the efforts of mercantilist governments to restrict or channel it toward the direct support of political rulers. New institutions, including banks and joint stock companies, emerged to meet the capital needs of this expanding commercial economy. Industrial production also grew rapidly, in part as a result of investments in new, more efficient machines, but in part because wages for industrial workers remained low.

From the mid-eighteenth century on, economic growth was also driven by the rapidly increasing European population. Behind this population growth lay changes in agrarian organization and in crop rotation systems that vastly increased the productivity of European agriculture, albeit at the cost of considerable social and cultural dislocation among traditional peasant farmers. Throughout European society, the economic changes of the seventeenth and eighteenth centuries were undermining the rigidly hierarchical presumptions of a social order whose structures and categories had changed little since the Middle Ages. In western Europe, a new, urban-based middle class was emerging whose values and outlook differed both from the nobility and from the rural peasantry. In eastern Europe, by contrast, these same economic changes actually strengthened the traditional control that nobles exercised over their serfs. For the moment, Europeans in both east and west continued to believe that their social order was divinely ordained and immutable. But storm clouds were gathering that would soon wash away this entire early modern world in the tumult of the French Revolution.

SELECTED READINGS

Berlin, Ira. *Many Thousands Gone: The First Two Centuries of Slavery in North America.* Cambridge, Mass., 1998. An excellent new synthesis, which tells the story from the perspective of the enslaved.

Burke, Peter. *Popular Culture in Early Modern Europe.* London, 1978. An influential account; somewhat dated, but colorful and full of interesting detail.

Bush, M. L., ed. *Social Orders and Social Classes in Europe since 1500.* New York, 1992. Essays on a broad range of subjects, including the church, tenant rights, and the concept of class.

Cameron, Euan, ed. *Early Modern Europe: An Oxford History.* Oxford and New York, 1999. A wide-ranging and stimulating multiauthor survey, topically arranged, that spans the entire period from the Renaissance to the French Revolution.

Canny, Nicholas, ed. *The Oxford History of the British Empire.* Volume I: *The Origins of Empire: British Overseas Enterprise to the Close of the Seventeenth Century.* Oxford and New York, 1998. A definitive, multiauthor account.

Cressy, David. *Birth, Marriage, and Death: Ritual, Religion, and the Life Cycle in Tudor and Stuart England.* Oxford and New York, 1997. A huge, wonderful book, full of arresting detail and riveting stories about daily life in early modern England.

Davis, Natalie Zemon. *Society and Culture in Early Modern France.* Stanford, 1975. Eight scintillating essays by a pioneer in the use of anthropological methods for the study of early modern European history.

———. *Women on the Margins: Three Seventeenth-Century Lives.* Cambridge, Mass., 1995. Artful biographical accounts by a master historian.

De Vries, Jan. *The Economy of Europe in an Age of Crisis, 1600–1750.* Cambridge and New York, 1976. Still the best survey of the economic history of the period.

Doyle, William. *The Old European Order, 1660–1800.* Oxford and New York, 1992. The best recent account of European society during the *ancien régime*, with chapters on population, trade, social orders, and public affairs.

Goubert, Pierre. *The Ancien Régime: French Society, 1600–1750.* London, 1973. A discussion with plentiful extracts from primary sources; particularly strong in its descriptions of rural life.

Hufton, Olwen. *The Prospect Before Her: A History of Women in Western Europe, 1500–1800.* New York, 1996. A great book by an important social historian; extensive bibliographies.

Israel, Jonathan I. *Dutch Primacy in World Trade, 1585–1740.* Oxford and New York, 1989. An account of the rise and fall of the Dutch trading empire by the preeminent English-language authority.

———. *The Dutch Republic: Its Rise, Greatness, and Fall, 1477–1806.* Oxford and New York, 1995. The standard English-language account.

———. *European Jewry in the Age of Mercantilism, 1550–1750,* 3d ed. Portland, Ore., 1998. The best account of the economic and political context of early modern Jewish history.

Klein, Herbert S. *The Atlantic Slave Trade.* Cambridge and New York, 1999. An excellent and accessible introductory survey by a leading quantitative historian.

McManners, John. *Church and Society in Eighteenth-Century France.* 2 vols. Oxford and New York, 1998. A great book, both comprehensive and wise.

Ménétra, Jacques Louis. *Journal of My Life.* Translated by Arthur Goldhammer. Introduction by Daniel Roche. New York, 1986. The autobiography of a Parisian glazier who played checkers with Rousseau and was an eyewitness to the French Revolution.

Merrick, Jeffrey, and Bryant Ragan, eds. *Homosexuality in Early Modern France: A Documentary Collection.* Oxford and New York, 2000. An outstanding and scholarly collection of original sources, most previously unknown.

Mintz, Sidney. *Sweetness and Power.* New York, 1985. Anthropological investigation of the impact of sugar on Western societies.

Muir, Edward. *Ritual in Early Modern Europe.* Cambridge and New York, 1997. A sophisticated study of one of the central features of early modern life.

Northrup, David, ed. *The Atlantic Slave Trade.* Lexington, Mass., 1994. A judicious collection of primary and secondary sources that examines the entire sweep of the trade, from beginnings to the fight for abolition.

Overton, Mark. *Agricultural Revolution in England: The Transformation of the Agrarian Economy, 1500–1850.* Cambridge and New York, 1996. Authoritative and wide ranging.

Sabean, David. *Power in the Blood: Popular Culture and Village Discourse in Early Modern Germany.* New York, 1984. Anthropologically influenced investigation of peasant life in a single German village.

Schama, Simon. *The Embarrassment of Riches: An Interpretation of Dutch Culture in the Golden Age.* New York, 1988. A controversial account that describes the social and psychological tensions produced by the growing wealth of seventeenth-century Holland.

Thomas, Hugh. *The Slave Trade: The History of the Atlantic Slave Trade, 1440–1870.* London and New York, 1997. A survey notable for its breadth and depth of coverage, as well as for its attractive prose style.

Tracy, James D. *The Rise of Merchant Empires: Long-Distance Trade in the Early Modern World, 1350–1750.* Cambridge and New York, 1993. Important collection of essays by leading authorities.

Underdown, David. *Fire from Heaven: The Life of an English Town in the Seventeenth Century.* New York, 1992. A superb local study of the impact of Puritanism on an English town.

Wiesner, Merry E. *Women and Gender in Early Modern Europe,* 2d ed. Cambridge and New York, 2000. A thorough revision of a pathbreaking book

Wrigley, Edward Anthony. *People, Cities, and Wealth: The Transformation of Traditional Society.* Oxford and New York, 1987. Assesses the demographic impact of urbanization on European society since the sixteenth century.

——. *English Population History from Family Reconstitution, 1580–1837.* Cambridge and New York, 1997. The life's work of a pioneering historical demographer.

Young, Arthur. *Travels in France during the Years 1787, 1788, 1789.* London, various editions. Vivid observations by an English traveler.

CHAPTER SEVENTEEN

THE AGE
OF ABSOLUTISM,
1660–1789

THE PERIOD FROM AROUND 1660 (when the English monarchy was restored, and Louis XIV of France began his personal rule) to 1789 (when the French Revolution erupted) is traditionally known as the age of absolutism. *Absolutism* was a political theory that encouraged rulers to claim complete sovereignty within their territories. To seventeenth- and eighteenth-century absolutists, complete sovereignty meant that a ruler could make law, do justice, direct a complex administrative bureaucracy, declare war, and levy taxation without needing the formal approval of churchmen, parliaments, assemblies, or local authorities for his or her policies. Absolutism therefore involved subordinating or eliminating the independence of all other governing authorities, such as towns, representative assemblies, or ecclesiastical councils, that might stand between the will of the sovereign ruler and the obedience of his or her subjects. Frequently, assertions of absolute authority were buttressed by claims that rulers exercised their authority over their kingdoms or territories by the same divine right that established a father's absolute authority over his household. After the chaos of the previous century, many Europeans came to believe that only by exalting the sovereignty of such absolute, "patriarchal" rulers over their families and their kingdoms could order be restored to European life.

Like all such labels, the "age of absolutism" is useful only so long as we acknowledge its limitations. In the first place, this label narrows our attention to politics, diplomacy, and economic policy. Although these are the primary subjects of this chapter, they are not the only important areas in which change was occuring during the age of absolutism. The social, demographic, agricultural, and economic developments of this period have already been described in Chapter 16. Intellectural, cultural, and religious changes will be discussed in Chapter 18. We have divided these changes in order to present them clearly; but we must remember that to the people of the later seventeenth and eighteenth centuries, they were a connected whole.

FOCUS QUESTIONS

- What were the aims of absolutist rulers?
- How did Louis XIV try to strengthen his control over France?
- What was the main challenge for most absolutist rulers?
- How was Russian absolutism unique?

- What was political power according to Locke?
- What was the "balance of power"?
- How did seventeenth- and eighteenth-century forms of absolutism differ?
- How did the balance of power shift in the eighteenth century?

Nor was absolutism the only political theory according to which European governments sought to rule during this period. In England, Scotland, the Dutch Republic, Switzerland, Venice, Sweden, and Poland-Lithuania, limited monarchies or republics continued to operate effectively; whereas in Russia, an autocratic tradition was emerging that envisioned the tsar as the absolute owner of his empire and as the unrestricted arbiter of his subjects' lives.

Finally, we must acknowledge the practical limitations of absolutism itself, even in such prototypically "abolutist" monarchies as that of King Louis XIV of France. Although absolutist rulers might claim the authority to make law by their own will, all acknowledged that they must nonetheless act in accordance with the rule of law. Law continued to have an authority independent of the will of any particular prince; and the traditional privileges of the social orders in European society (the nobility, the clergy, and even the common people) were still regarded as having a legal force that even an absolute monarch was obliged to acknowledge and respect. Nor, in fact, was the "intermediate" authority of representative assemblies, towns, and ecclesiastical councils so inconsequential as absolutist theory declared that it should be. In practice, even the most absolute rulers of seventeenth- and eighteenth-century western Europe could rule effectively only so long as their subjects were prepared, at least tacitly, to consent to their policies. When opposition erupted, even absolutists were forced to back down. And when, in 1789, an outright political revolution occurred, the entire structure of absolutism came crashing to the ground.

THE APPEAL AND JUSTIFICATION OF ABSOLUTISM

What were the aims of absolutist rulers?

Absolutism appealed to Europeans for the same reasons that mercantilism did. Just as mercantilists maintained that economic regimentation would produce prosperity, so absolutists contended that social and political harmony would result when subjects obeyed their divinely sanctioned rulers in all matters. Abso-

lutist monarchs insisted, in turn, on *their* duty to teach their subjects how to order their domestic affairs. As the eighteenth-century ruler of the German principality of Baden expressed it: "We must make them, whether they like it or not, into free, opulent and law-abiding citizens."

Absolutism's promise of stability, prosperity, and order was an appealing alternative to the disorder of the iron century that preceded it. This was especially the case for the quintessential absolutist monarch, Louis XIV of France. The political disturbances of his minority (known collectively as the *Fronde*) left a life-long impression on the young king. When marauding Parisians entered the bedchamber of the eight-year-old king one night in 1651, Louis saw the intrusion as a horrid affront not only to his own person, but to the majesty of the French state he personified. Squabbles among the nobility and criticisms of royal policy by the Paris *Parlement* during his minority convinced him that he must exercise his powers and prerogatives assertively and without limitation if France was to survive and prosper as a great European state.

To accomplish these objectives, such absolutist monarchs as Louis XIV sought to gather into their own hands command of the state's armed forces, control over its legal system, and the right to collect and spend the state's financial resources at will. These goals in turn required an efficient bureaucracy that owed its allegiance directly to the monarchy itself, and not to the towns, provinces, or privileged social groups over which that bureaucracy ruled. Creating such a centralized bureaucracy was expensive, but it was essential to the larger absolutist goal of restricting or even destroying the privileged "special interests" that had hindered the free exercise of royal power in the past. The legally privileged estates of nobility and clergy, the political authority of semi-autonomous regions, and the pretensions of independent-minded representative assemblies such as parliaments, diets, or estates general, were all obstacles in the eyes of absolutists to the achievement of strong, centralized monarchical government. The history of absolutism is, as much as anything, a history of attempts by aspiring absolutists to bring these institutions to heel.

In most Protestant countries, the independent power of the church had already been subordinated to the interests of the state when the age of absolutism began. In France, Spain, and Austria, by contrast, where Roman Catholicism remained the state religion, during the late seventeenth and eighteenth centuries monarchs devoted concerted attention to "nationaliz-

HOW DID LOUIS XIV TRY TO STRENGTHEN HIS CONTROL OVER FRANCE?

THE ABSOLUTISM OF LOUIS XIV   595

ing" the church and its clergy within their territories. These efforts built on the concordats that the French and Spanish monarchies had extracted from the papacy during the fifteenth and sixteenth centuries, but they went even further in consolidating authority over the church into the hands of the monarchy. Even Charles III, the devout Spanish king who ruled from 1759 to 1788, pressed successfully for a papal concordat granting the Spanish monarchy control over ecclesiastical appointments and establishing his right to sanction (or prevent) the proclamation of papal bulls affecting Spain.

The most important potential opponents of royal absolutism were not churchmen, however, but nobles. Monarchs dealt with this threat in various ways. Louis XIV attempted to control the French aristocrats by depriving them of political power while increasing their social prestige by associating them directly with his own lavish court at Versailles. Peter the Great, the talented but erratic tsar of early eighteenth-century Russia, required noblemen to enter government service. Later in the century, Catherine II struck a bargain whereby in return for vast estates and a variety of social and economic privileges including exemption from taxation, the Russian nobility virtually surrendered the administrative and political power of the state into the empress's hands. In Prussia, under Frederick the Great, the army was staffed by nobles, as was generally the case in Spain, France, and England. But in eighteenth-century Austria, the emperor Joseph II adopted a policy of confrontation rather than accommodation, denying the nobility exemption from taxation and deliberately blurring the distinctions between nobles and commoners.

Struggles between monarchs and nobles frequently had implications for the additional struggle between local and central government. Absolutists in France waged a constant but never entirely successful war against the autonomy of provincial institutions, often headed by nobles, just as the Spanish monarchy, centered in Castile, battled independent-minded nobles in Aragon and Catalunya. Prussian rulers intruded into the governance of formerly "free" cities, assuming policing and revenue powers over their inhabitants. And in Austria, the Habsburg emperors tried to suppress the largely autonomous nobility of Hungary. Rarely, however, was confrontation between crown and nobility successful in the long run. The most successful absolutist monarchies of the eighteenth century succeeded in establishing a political and social order in which nobles came to see their own interests as tied to

the those of the monarchy. For this reason, cooperation more often characterized the relations between kings and nobles during the eighteenth century than did conflict.

THE ABSOLUTISM OF LOUIS XIV

How did Louis XIV try to strengthen his control over France?

Examine a portrait of Louis XIV (1643–1715) in court robes; it is all but impossible to discern the human being behind the façade of the absolute monarch. That façade was carefully and artfully constructed by Louis,

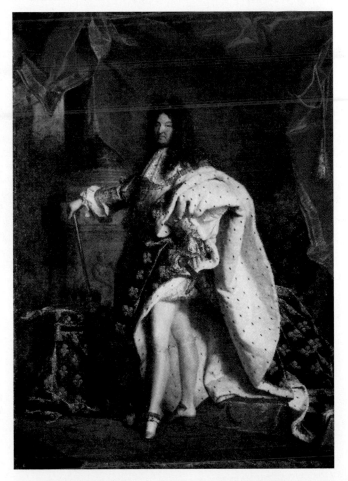

Louis XIV, the Sun King. This portrait by Hyacinthe Rigaud illustrates the degree to which absolute monarchy was defined in terms of studied performance.

ABSOLUTISM AND PATRIARCHY

These selections show how two political theorists justified royal absolutism by deriving it from the absolute authority of a father over his household. Bishop Jacques-Benigne Bossuet (1627–1704) was a famous French preacher who served as tutor to the son of King Louis XIV of France before becoming bishop of Meaux. Sir Robert Filmer (1588–1653) was an English political theorist. Filmer's works attracted particular attention in the 1680s, when John Locke directed the first of his Two Treatises of Government to refuting Filmer's views on the patriarchal nature of royal authority.

BOSSUET ON THE NATURE OF MONARCHICAL AUTHORITY

There are four characteristics or qualities essential to royal authority. First, royal authority is sacred; Secondly, it is paternal; Thirdly, it is absolute; Fourthly, it is subject to reason. . . . All power comes from God. . . . Thus princes act as ministers of God, and his lieutenants on earth. It is through them that he exercises his empire. . . . In this way . . . the royal throne is not the throne of a man, but the throne of God himself. . . .

We have seen that kings hold the place of God, who is the true Father of the human race. We have also seen that the first idea of power that there was among men, is that of paternal power; and that kings were fashioned on the model of fathers. Moreover, all the world agrees that obedience, which is due to public power, is only found . . . in the precept which obliges one to honor his parents. From all this it appears that the name "king" is a father's name, and that goodness is the most natural quality in kings. . . .

Royal authority is absolute. In order to make this term odious and insupportable, many pretend to con-fuse absolute government and arbitrary government. But nothing is more distinct, as we shall make clear when we speak of justice. . . . The prince need account to no one for what he ordains. . . . Without this absolute authority, he can neither do good nor suppress evil: his power must be such that no one can hope to escape him. . . . [T]he sole defense of individuals against the public power must be their innocence. . . .

One must, then, obey princes as if they were justice itself, without which there is neither order nor justice in affairs. They are gods, and share in some way in divine independence. . . . It follows from this that he who does not want to obey the prince . . . is condemned irremissibly to death as an enemy of public peace and of human society. . . . The prince can correct himself when he knows that he has done badly; but against his authority there can be no remedy. . . .

Jacques-Benigne Bossuet. *Politics Drawn from the Very Words of Holy Scripture,* translated by Patrick Riley. (Cambridge: Cambridge University Press, 1990), pp. 46–69 and 81–83.

FILMER ON THE PATRIARCHAL ORIGINS OF ROYAL AUTHORITY

The first government in the world was monarchical, in the father of all flesh, Adam being commanded to multiply, and people the earth, and to subdue it, and having dominion given him over all creatures, was thereby the monarch of the whole world; none of his posterity had any right to possess anything, but by his grant or permission, or by succession from him. . . . Adam was the father, king and lord over his family: a son, a subject, and a servant or a slave were one and the same thing at first. . . .

I cannot find any one place or text in the Bible where any power . . . is given to a people either to govern themselves, or to choose themselves governors, or to alter the manner of government at their pleasure. The power of government is settled and fixed by the commandment of "honour thy father"; if there were a higher power than the fatherly, then this commandment could not stand and be observed. . . .

All power on earth is either derived or usurped from the fatherly power, there being no other original to be found of any power whatsoever. For if there should be granted two sorts of power without any subordination of one to the other, they would be in perpetual strife which should be the supreme, for two supremes cannot agree. If the fatherly power be supreme, then the power of the people must be subordinate and depend on it. If the power of the people be supreme, then the fatherly power must submit to it, and cannot be exercised without the licence of the people, which must quite destroy the frame and course of nature. Even the power which God himself exercises over mankind is by right of fatherhood: he is both the king and father of us all. As God has exalted the dignity of earthly kings . . . by saying they are gods, so . . . he has been pleased. . . . [t]o humble himself by assuming the title of a king to express his power, and not the title of any popular government.

Robert Filmer, *Observations upon Aristotle's Politiques* (1652) in *Divine Right and Democracy: An Anthology of Political Writing in Stuart England*, edited by David Wootton. (Harmondsworth: Penguin Books, 1986), pp. 110–118.

who recognized, perhaps more fully than any other early modern ruler, the importance of theater as a means of establishing his authority. Louis and his successors deliberately staged theatrical demonstrations of their sovereignty to enhance their position as rulers endowed with godlike powers and far removed from common humanity.

PERFORMING ROYALTY AT VERSAILLES

Louis's exhibitions of his sovereignty were performed most elaborately at his palace at Versailles, the town outside of Paris to which he moved his court. The palace and its grounds became a stage on which Louis attempted to mesmerize the aristocracy into obedience by his performance of the daily rituals and demonstrations of royalty. The main façade of the palace was a third of a mile in length. Inside, tapestries and paintings celebrated French military victories and royal triumphs, while mirrors reflected shimmering light throughout the building. In the vast gardens outside, statues of the Greek sun god Apollo recalled Louis's claim to be the "Sun King" of France. Noblemen vied to attend him when he arose from bed, ate his meals (usually stone cold, having traveled the distance of several city blocks from royal kitchen to royal table), strolled in his gardens (even the way the king walked was choreographed by the royal dancing master), or rode to the hunt. As Louis called himself the Sun King, so his court was the epicenter of his glittering royal resplendence. Louis required France's leading nobles to reside with him at Versailles for a portion of the year; the splendor of Louis's court was deliberately calculated to blind them to the possibility of disobedience, while raising their prestige by associating them directly with the king. Instead of plotting some minor treason on his estate, a marquis enjoyed the pleasure of knowing that on the morrow he would be privileged to engage the king in two or three minutes of vapid conversation as the royal party made its stately progress through the vast palace halls, whose smells were evidence of the absence of sanitation facilities and of the seamy side of absolutist grandeur. At the same time, however, the elaborate, almost impossibly detailed rules of etiquette around the court left these same privileged nobles in a state of constant suspense, forever fearful of offending the king by committing some trivial violation of proper manners.

Louis understood such theatricality as part of his duty as sovereign, a duty that he took with utmost seriousness. Though far from brilliant, he was hardworking and conscientious. Whether or not he actually re-

The Château of Versailles. Dramatically expanded by Louis XIV in the 1660s from a hunting lodge to the principal royal residence and the seat of government, the château became a monument to the international power and prestige of the Grand Monarch.

marked *"L'état, c'est moi"* ("I am the State"), he clearly saw himself as serving the interests of the State. As such, he also saw himself as personally responsible for the well-being of his subjects. "The deference and the respect that we receive from our subjects," he wrote in a memoir he prepared for his son on the art of ruling, "are not a free gift from them but payment for the justice and the protection that they expect from us. Just as they must honor us, we must protect and defend them."

ADMINISTRATION AND CENTRALIZATION

Louis defined his responsibility in absolutist terms: to concentrate royal power so as to produce domestic tranquillity. While coopting the nobility into his own theater of royalty, he conciliated the upper bourgeoisie by enlisting its members to assist him in the task of administration. He appointed them as *intendants*, responsible for administering and taxing the thirty-six *generalités*

into which France was divided. Intendants usually served outside the region where they were born, and were thus unconnected with the local elites over which they exercised authority. They held office at the king's pleasure, and were clearly "his" men. Other administrators, often from families newly ennobled as a reward for their administrative service, assisted in directing affairs of state from Versailles. These men were not actors in the theater of Louis the Sun King; rather, they were the hardworking assistants of Louis the royal custodian of his country's welfare.

Louis's bureaucrats devoted much of their time and energy to collecting the taxes necessary to finance the large standing army on which the king's aggressive and highly personal foreign policy depended. These personal elements of early modern absolutism are important to remark. Despite its pretensions to represent a political theory, absolutism was fundamentally a mechanism designed to assist ambitious monarchs in their determination to increase their own power through conquest and display. As such, it was enormously ex-

HOW DID LOUIS XIV TRY TO STRENGTHEN HIS CONTROL OVER FRANCE?

THE ABSOLUTISM OF LOUIS XIV   599

pensive. In addition to the *taille*, or land tax, which increased throughout the seventeenth century and on which a surtax was levied as well, Louis's government introduced a *capitation* (head tax) payable by all, and pressed successfully for the collection of indirect taxes on salt (the *gabelle*), wine, tobacco, and other products. Since the nobility was exempt from the *taille*, its burden fell most heavily on the peasantry, whose periodic local revolts Louis easily crushed.

Regional opposition—indeed, regionalism generally—was curtailed, but by no means eliminated, during Louis's reign. Although intendants and lesser administrators came from afar, did not speak the local dialect, and ignored local custom, they were generally obeyed. The semi-autonomous outer provinces of Brittany, Languedoc, and Franche-Comté (several of the territories known collectively as the *pays d'états*) suffered the crippling of their provincial Estates. To put an end to the power of regional *parlements*, Louis decreed that members of those bodies that refused to register his laws would be summarily exiled. The Estates General, the national French representative assembly last summoned in 1614 during the troubled regency that followed the death of Henry IV, did not meet again until 1789.

LOUIS XIV'S RELIGIOUS POLICIES

Louis was equally determined, both for reasons of state and of personal conscience, to impose religious unity upon the French. That task proved to be difficult and time consuming. The Huguenots were not the only source of religious heterodoxy in France. Quietists and Jansenists—both claiming to represent the "true" Roman faith—battled for adherents to their particular brand of Catholicism. Quietists preached retreat into personal mysticism, emphasizing a direct relationship between God and the individual human heart. Such doctrine, dispensing as it did with the intermediary services of the church and of the orthodox authority those services represented, was suspect in the eyes of absolutists wedded to the doctrine of *un roi, une loi, une foi* (one king, one law, one faith). Jansenism—a movement named for its founder Cornelius Jansen, a seventeenth-century bishop of Yprés—challenged the authority of the state church with an unorthodox doctrine of predestination, proclaiming the salvation of no more than an elected few.

> The state extracted a profit from every office it created and from every privilege it controlled, demonstrating the way in which economy and politics were inextricably intertwined.

Louis vigorously persecuted Quietists and Jansenists, offering them the choice of recanting or prison and exile.

Against the Huguenots, however, he waged an even sterner war. Protestant churches and schools were destroyed; Protestant families were forced to convert. In 1685, Louis revoked the Edict of Nantes, the legal foundation of the toleration Huguenots had enjoyed since 1598. French Protestants were thereafter denied civil rights, and their clerics were exiled. As a result, two hundred thousand religious refugees fled France for England, Holland, the Protestant states of Germany, and America, where their professional and artisanal skills made a significant contribution to economic prosperity. Among many other examples, the silk industries of Berlin and of Spitalfields, an urban quarter of London, were established by Huguenots fleeing Louis XIV's persecution.

COLBERT AND ROYAL FINANCE

Louis's drive for unification and centralization was assisted by his ability to rely on increased revenues. These revenues were largely the result of policies and programs initiated by Jean Baptiste Colbert (1619–1683), the country's finance minister from 1664 until his death. Colbert was an energetic and committed mercantilist who believed that until France could put its fiscal house in order, it could not achieve economic or political greatness. He tightened the process of tax collection, and he eliminated wherever possible the practice of tax farming, whereby collection agents were permitted to withhold a certain percentage of what they gathered for themselves. When Colbert assumed office, only about 25 percent of the taxes collected throughout the kingdom reached the treasury. By the time he died, that figure had risen to 80 percent.

Colbert's efforts were not limited to managing the public debt and ridding the tax system of inefficiencies. Under his direction, the state also sold public offices, including judgeships and mayoralities, on an increasing scale. Guilds purchased the right to enforce trade regulations. The state extracted a profit from every office it created and from every privilege it controlled, demonstrating once again the way in which economy and politics were inextricably intertwined.

Jean Baptiste Colbert.

As a mercantilist, Colbert did all he could to increase the nation's income by means of protection and regimentation. Tariffs he imposed in 1667 and 1668 were designed to discourage the importation of foreign goods into France. He invested in the improvement of France's roads and waterways. And he used state money to promote the growth of national industry, in particular the manufacture of goods such as silk, lace, tapestries, and glass, which had long been imported.

Yet Colbert's efforts to achieve national economic stability and self-sufficiency could not withstand the insatiable demands of Louis XIV's wars. Indeed, by the end of Louis's reign, the limitations of his absolutist ambitions were strikingly evident. His aggressive foreign policy lay in ruins, and the country's finances had been shattered by the increasing costs of war. Colbert himself foresaw Louis's ultimate failure when he lectured him in 1680, "Trade is the source of public finance and public finance is the vital nerve of war. . . . I beg your Majesty to permit me only to say to him that in war as in peace he has never consulted the amount of money available in determining his expenditures."

ABSOLUTISM IN CENTRAL AND EASTERN EUROPE, 1660–1720

What was the main challenge for most absolutist rulers?

The success Louis XIV enjoyed as an absolute monarch was due in part to his own abilities, and in part to the efforts of his advisors and administrators. But it rested also on the fact that he could claim to stand as the supreme embodiment of the nation of France. Despite its internal divisions, France was already a unified kingdom with a sense of national identity long before Louis XIV ascended its throne. In this respect, France differed profoundly from the empires, kingdoms, and principalities to its east. In central and eastern Europe, rulers faced a much more formidable task than did Louis as they attempted to weld their disparately constructed monarchies into united, centralized, absolutist states.

THE HOLY ROMAN EMPIRE

The Thirty Years' War delivered a final, fatal blow to the power of the Holy Roman empire—memorably described by the eighteenth-century French philosopher Voltaire as being "neither holy, nor Roman, nor an empire." Instead, power now lay in the hands of over three hundred princes, bishops, and magistrates, who would continue to govern the assorted states of Germany until the nineteenth century.

Despite the small size of their territories, many of these local rulers attempted nonetheless to establish themselves as absolutists, building lesser versions of Louis XIV's Versailles and remodeling their capital cities to serve as explicit expressions of their authority. Broad avenues led to monumental squares and eventually to the grand palace of the ruler. Whereas the crowded, twisted streets and passageways of medieval cities had tended to mask the inequalities of the social order by forcing different social classes to live together in close physical proximity, absolutist capital cities celebrated inequality, their planning and architecture deliberately emphasizing the vast distance that separated their rulers from those over whom they ruled.

Aspiring German absolutists also followed the

MERCANTILISM AND WAR

Jean-Baptiste Colbert (1619–1683) served as Louis XIV's finance minister from 1664 until his death. He worked assiduously to promote commerce, build up French industry, and increase exports. However much Colbert himself may have seen his economic policies as ends in themselves, to Louis they were always means to the end of waging war. Ultimately, Louis's wars undermined the prosperity that Colbert tried so hard to create. This memorandum, written to Louis in 1670, illustrates clearly the mercantlist presumptions of self-sufficiency on which Colbert operated: every item needed to build up the French navy must ultimately be produced in France, even if it could be acquired at less cost from elsewhere.

And since Your Majesty has wanted to work diligently at reestablishing his naval forces, and since afore that it has been necessary to make very great expenditures, since all merchandise, munitions and manufactured items formerly came from Holland and the countries of the North, it has been absolutely necessary to be especially concerned with finding within the realm, or with establishing in it, everything which might be necessary for this great plan.

To this end, the manufacture of tar was established in Médoc, Auvergne, Dauphiné, and Provence; iron cannons, in Burgundy, Nivernois, Saintonge and Périgord; large anchors in Dauphiné, Nivernois, Brittany, and Rochefort; sailcloth for the Levant, in Dauphiné; coarse muslin, in Auvergne; all the implements for pilots and others, at Dieppe and La Rochelle; the cutting of wood suitable for vessels, in Burgundy, Dauphiné, Brittany, Normandy, Poitou, Saintonge, Provence, Guyenne, and the Pyrenees; masts, of a sort once unknown in this realm, have been found in Provence, Languedoc, Auvergne, Dauphiné, and in the Pyrenees. Iron, which was obtained from Sweden and Biscay, is currently manufactured in the realm. Fine hemp for ropes, which came from Prussia and from Piedmont, is currently obtained in Burgundy, Mâconnais, Bresse, Dauphiné; and markets for it have since been established in Berry and in Auvergne, which always provides money in these provinces and keeps it within the realm.

In a word, everything serving for the construction of vessels is currently established in the realm, so that Your Majesty can get along without foreigners for the navy and will even, in a short time, be able to supply them and gain their money in this fashion. And it is with this same objective of having everything necessary to provide abundantly for his navy and that of his subjects that he is working at the general reform of all the forests in his realm, which, being as carefully preserved as they are at present, will abundantly produce all the wood necessary for this.

Charles W. Cole, *Colbert and a Century of French Mercantilism*, 2 vols. (New York: Columbia University Press, 1939), p. 320.

French example by maintaining standing armies and and imposing local tariffs and tolls that severely hampered economic development within the region as a whole. Such rulers often prided themselves on their independence from imperial control, but many were in fact the political clients of France. A sizable portion of the money Louis devoted to the conduct of foreign affairs went into the pockets of these German princelings, who were happy to form alliances against their own emperor.

BRANDENBURG-PRUSSIA

Most notable among these middle-sized German states was Brandenburg-Prussia, whose emergence as a power of consequence during this period was the result of the single-minded determination of its rulers. Foremost among these was Frederick William, elector of Brandenburg from 1640 to 1688, whose abilities have earned him the title of the "Great Elector." The rise of Brandenburg-Prussia from initial insignificance, poverty, and devastation in the wake of the Thirty Years' War resulted from three basic achievements that can be credited to the Great Elector. First, he pursued an adroit foreign policy that enabled him to establish effective sovereignty over the widely dispersed and underdeveloped territories under his rule: Brandenburg, a large but not particularly productive territory in north-central Germany; Prussia, a duchy to the east that was dangerously exposed on three sides to Poland; and a sprinkling of tiny states—Cleves, Mark, and Ravensberg—to the west. By siding with Poland in a war against Sweden in the late 1650s, the Great Elector obtained the Polish

king's surrender of nominal overlordship in East Prussia. And by some crafty diplomatic shuffling during the 1670s, he secured his western provinces from French interference by returning Pomerania, captured in a recent war, to France's Swedish allies.

Frederick William's second achievement was to create a large standing army, which became the primary instrument of his diplomatic successes. By 1688, Brandenburg-Prussia had thirty thousand troops permanently under arms. The Elector's ability to sustain an army of this size in a state with comparatively limited resources was a measure of the degree to which the army more than repaid its costs. Beyond its diplomatic and military value, the army ensured for the elector and his successors absolute political control by fostering obedience among the populace—an obedience they were prepared to observe if their lands might be spared the devastation of another Thirty Years' War.

The third factor contributing to the emergence of Brandenburg-Prussia as an international power was the Elector's imposition of an effective system of taxation and his creation of a bureaucracy to administer it. Here he struck an important bargain with the powerful and privileged landlords (*Junkers*) without whose cooperation his programs would have had no chance of success. In return for an agreement that allowed them to reduce their peasant underlings to the status of serfs, the Junkers gave away their right to oppose a permanent tax system—provided, of course, that they were made immune from the payment of taxes themselves. As in most European countries, taxes in absolutist Prussia thus fell most heavily on the peasantry.

Henceforth, the political privileges of the landlord class diminished. Secure in their right to manage their own estates as they wished, the Junkers were content to surrender management of the Prussian state to a centralized bureaucracy. Its most important department was a military commissariat, whose functions included not only the dispensing of army pay

Prussians Swearing Allegiance to the Great Elector at Königsberg, 1663. The occasion upon which the Prussian estates first acknowledged the overlordship of their ruler. This ceremony marked the beginning of the centralization of the Prussian state.

and matériel, but the development of industries to manufacture military equipment. Frederick William's success was due primarily to his ability to gain the active cooperation of the Junker class. Without their support, he could never have hammered together a state from the disparate territories that were his political raw material. To obtain that support, he used the army not only to maintain order, but as a way of enlisting Junker participation in the Prussian state. The highest honor that could befall a Brandenburg squire was a commission and promotion as a military officer in Frederick William's army.

THE AUSTRO-HUNGARIAN EMPIRE

Like the Prussian rulers, the Habsburg monarchs of Austria were confronted with the task of transforming four different regions into a cohesive state. In Austria, however, this effort was complicated by the ethnic and linguistic diversity of the empire's four main regions: the southern, German-speaking lands that roughly make up the present-day country of Austria; the northern Czech- (Slavic-) speaking provinces of Bohemia and Moravia; German-speaking Silesia, inherited in 1527; and Hungary (where the Magyar population spoke a non-Slavic, Finno-Ugric language), also acquired in 1527 but largely lost to Turkish invasion just a few years afterward. For the next one hundred fifty years the Habsburgs and the Ottoman Turks vied for control of Hungary. Until 1683 the Ottomans ruled three-fourths of the Magyar kingdom, extending their control to within eighty miles of the Habsburg capital of Vienna. In 1683 the Turks beseiged Vienna itself but were repulsed by the Austrians, assisted by a mixed German and Polish army under the command of King John Sobieski of Poland. This victory was a prelude to the Habsburg reconquest of virtually all of Hungary by the end of the century.

The task of constructing an absolutist state from these extraordinarily varied territories was tackled with limited success during the seventeenth century by the emperors Ferdinand III (1637–1657) and Leopold I (1658–1705). Most of their efforts were devoted to establishing productive agricultural estates in Bohemia and Moravia, and to dealing with the independent-minded nobility of these territories and of Hungary. Landlords were encouraged to farm for export and were supported in this effort by a government decree that compelled peasants to provide three days of unpaid work service per week to the lords. In return for this support, Bohemian and Moravian landed elites surrendered the political independence that had in the past expressed itself in the activities of their territorial legislative Estates.

Habsburg rulers tried to strike this same sort of bargain in Hungary as well. But there the tradition of independence was stronger and died harder. Hungarian (or Magyar) nobles in the west claimed the right to elect their king, a right they eventually surrendered to Leopold in 1687. But the imperial government's attempts to reduce the country further by administering it through the army, by granting large tracts of land to German aristocrats and settlers, and by persecuting non-Catholics were an almost total failure. The result was a powerful nobility that remained fiercely determined to retain its traditional constitutional and religious "liberties." The Habsburg emperors could boast that they too, like absolutists elsewhere, possessed a large standing army and an educated (in this case, German-speaking) bureaucracy. But the exigencies imposed by geography and ethnicity prevented them from achieving the absolutist goal of a unified, centrally controlled and administered state.

AUTOCRACY IN RUSSIA

How was Russian absolutism unique?

Undoubtedly the most dramatic episode in the history of early modern absolutism was the dynamic reign of Tsar Peter I of Russia (1689–1725). Peter's accomplishments alone would have earned him his history-book title, Peter the Great. But his imposing height—he was nearly seven feet tall—as well as his mercurial personality—jesting one moment, raging the next—certainly added to the outsized impression he made on his contemporaries. Peter is best remembered as the tsar whose policies brought Russia into direct contact with the western European world. Previously the country's rulers had set their faces firmly against the West, disdaining a civilization at odds with the Eastern Orthodox culture that was their heritage, while laboring to keep the various ethnic groups that comprised their empire—Russians, Ukrainians, and a wide variety of nomadic tribes—from destroying not only each other but the tsarist state itself. As a young man, however, Peter traveled to several western European capitals, and returned to Russia determined to remodel his country's institutions along western lines.

Peter the Great. An eighteenth-century mosaic.

THE BACKGROUND OF PETER'S REIGN

Since 1613 Russia had been ruled by members of the Romanov dynasty, who had attempted with some success to restore political stability following the chaotic "time of troubles" that occurred after the death of the bloodthirsty, half-mad Tsar Ivan IV (the Terrible) in 1584. Tsar Alexis I (1645–1676) took a significant step toward unifying his empire in 1654 when he secured an agreement with the Ukrainians to incorporate that portion of Ukraine lying east of the Dneiper River into the Muscovite state. But the early Romanovs were faced with a severe threat to their rule between 1667 and 1671, when a Cossack leader (the Russian Cossacks were semi-autonomous bands of peasant cavalrymen) named Stenka Razin led much of southeastern Russia into rebellion. This uprising found widespread support, not only from serfs who had been oppressed by their masters, but also from non-Russian tribes in the lower Volga area who longed to cast off Muscovite domination. But ultimately Tsar Alexis and the Russian nobility were able to defeat Razin's zealous but disorganized bands of rebels. In crushing the rebellion, more than one hundred thousand rebels were slaughtered.

ABSOLUTISM AND AUTOCRACY

These campaigns were but a prelude to the deliberate and ruthless drive toward autocratic authority launched by the seventeen-year-old Peter after he overthrew the regency of his half-sister Sophia and assumed personal control of the state in 1689. Within ten years he had scandalized nobility and clergy alike by traveling to Holland and England to recruit highly skilled foreign workers and to study the craft of shipbuilding. Upon his return he distressed them still further by declaring his intention to westernize Russia, a process he began by cutting off the "eastern" beards and flowing sleeves worn by the leading noblemen at his court. Determined to "civilize" his nobility, he published a book of manners that forbade spitting on the floor and eating with one's fingers, and encouraged the cultivation of the art of polite conversation between the sexes. To promote this latter goal, he also ordered Russian women to appear, together with men, in western garb at weddings, banquets, and other public occasions.

Much as Peter wished to reshape his country in accordance with western models, his particular brand of absolutism differed from that of other European monarchs. Peter considered himself above the law and thus the absolute master of his empire to a degree that was alien even to the most thoroughgoing absolutist theories and traditions of western Europe. Autocrat of all the Russias, he ruled despotically, with a ferocious individual power that western European rulers did not possess. Armed with such arbitrary power in theory, and intent on realizing its full potential in practice, Peter brooked no opposition to his efforts to "modernize" the Russian state. When his son showed signs of resisting his father, Peter imprisoned him. Soon thereafter, the young man died in mysterious circumstances.

Peter's efforts quickly ran into opposition, however, particularly among the *streltsy*, the elite palace guard who sought to halt his innovations by restoring his half-sister Sophia to the throne. Their initial rebellion took place while Peter was touring western Europe. Peter quickly returned home from Vienna, and crushed the rebellion with a savagery that astonished even his contemporaries. Roughly twelve hundred suspected conspirators were summarily executed, many of them gibbeted outside the walls of the Kremlin, where their bodies rotted for months as a graphic reminder of the fate awaiting those who dared challenge the tsar's authority.

Peter then set out to create a large standing army, recruited from the ranks of the peasantry and scrupu-

PETER THE GREAT'S EXECUTIONS OF HIS PALACE GUARD

This graphic account of Peter's retribution against his rebellious palace guard (a group known as the streltsy) was written by an Austrian diplomat living in Moscow in 1698, when these events took place. Peter's sister Sophia was widely believed to have been behind the uprising.

How sharp was the pain, how great the indignation, to which the tsar's Majesty was mightily moved, when he knew of the rebellion of the Streltsy, betraying openly a mind panting for vengeance! He was still tarrying at Vienna, quite full of the desire of setting out for Italy; but . . . on the announcement of the troubles that had broken out in the bowels of his realm. . . . [h]e took the quick post, as his ambassador suggested, and in four weeks' time he had got over about three hundred miles [German miles, equivalent to about fifteen hundred English miles] without accident, and arrived the 4th of September, 1698—a monarch for the well disposed, but an avenger for the wicked.

His first anxiety after his arrival was about the rebellion—in what it consisted, what the insurgents meant, who dared to instigate such a crime. And as nobody could answer accurately upon all points, and some pleaded their own ignorance, others the obstinacy of the Streltsy, he began to have suspicions of everybody's loyalty. . . .

No day, holy or profane, were the inquisitors idle; every day was deemed fit and lawful for torturing. There were as many scourges as there were accused, and every inquisitor was a butcher. . . . The whole month of October was spent in lacerating the backs of culprits with the knout and with flames; no day were those that were left alive exempt from scourging or scorching; or else they were broken upon the wheel, or driven to the gibbet, or slain with the ax. . . .

To prove to people how holy and inviolable are those walls of the city which the Streltsy rashly meditated scaling in a sudden assault, beams were run out from all the embrasures in the walls near the gates, in each of which two rebels were hanged. This day beheld about two hundred and fifty die that death. There are few cities fortified with as many palisades as Moscow has given gibbets to her guardian Streltsy.

[In front of the nunnery where Peter's sister Sophia was confined] there were thirty gibbets erected in a quadrangle shape, from which there hung two hundred and thirty Streltsy; the three principal ringleaders, who tendered a petition to Sophia touching the administration of the realm, were hanged close to the windows of that princess, presenting, as it were, the petitions that were placed in their hands, so near that Sophia might with ease touch them.

J. H. Robinson. *Readings in European History*, vol. 2. (Boston: Ginn and Co., 1906), pp. 310–312.

Peter the Great's Execution of the Streltsy. This contemporary print shows scores of corpses gibbeted outside the walls of the Kremlin. Peter kept the rotting bodies on display for months to discourage his subjects from opposing his efforts to Westernize Russian society.

began his career as a cook and finished as a prince, a degree of social mobility that would have been impossible in any contemporary western European country. Instead, noble status became dependent upon governmental service, with all nobles expected to participate in Peter's army or administration. Peter was not entirely successful in enforcing this requirement upon all the *boyars*, but the administrative machinery he devised furnished Russia with its ruling class for the next two hundred years.

PETER'S FOREIGN POLICY

Peter the Great's Eurocentric world view also manifested itself in his foreign policy, as witnessed by his bold drive to gain a Russian outlet onto the Baltic Sea. Previous battles with the Turks to secure a port on the Black Sea, and thus a southern passage to the west, had failed. Now he engaged in a war with Sweden's meteoric soldier-king Charles XII (1697–1718), who devoted most of his reign to campaigns in the field against the Danes, the Poles, and the Russians. By defeating Charles decisively at the battle of Poltava in 1709, Peter was able to secure his outlet to the West. He promptly outdid his absolutist counterparts in Europe, who had moved their courts to the oustkirts of their capital cities, by moving the Russian capital from Moscow to an entirely new city he constructed on the Gulf of Finland. An army of serfs was employed to erect the baroque city of St. Petersburg around a palace intended to imitate and rival Louis XIV's Versailles.

Opposition to Peter's drastic reforms smoldered

lously loyal to the tsar. One of every twenty males was conscripted for lifelong service. He financed his army, as did other absolutists, by increasing taxes, with their burden falling most heavily on the peasantry. To equip his new military force, he fostered the growth of the iron and munitions industries. Factories were built and manned by peasant laborers whose position was little better than that of slaves. Serfs were also commandeered for other public works projects such as road and canal building.

To further consolidate his absolute power, Peter replaced the Duma—the nation's rudimentary national assembly—with a rubber-stamp senate, and appointed a procurator, or agent, dependent directly on him, to manage the affairs of the Russian Orthodox Church, which thus became an extension of the state's authority. At the same time, Peter was fashioning new, larger, and more efficient administrative machinery to cope with the demands of his modernization program. Although he preferred to draw into the bureaucracy "new" men, whose loyalty would be unswerving, he was compelled to rely on the services of the noble—or *boyar*—class as well, rewarding them by increasing their control over their serfs. Nevertheless, membership in his new bureaucracy did not depend on birth. One of his principal advisers, Alexander Menshikov,

C H R O N O L O G Y	
SEVENTEENTH-CENTURY ABSOLUTIST RULERS	
Louis XIV (France)	1643–1715
Frederick William (Brandenburg-Prussia)	1640–1688
Leopold I (Austria)	1658–1705
Peter the Great (Russia)	1689–1725

The St. Petersburg Palaces. This first of six versions of the Winter Palace (above) was erected in 1711. It quickly proved to be too modest for Peter's needs. Within a decade he had created a far more elaborate complex called the Peterhof (below), complete with fountains modeled on those in Versailles.

guard, under whom the resentful nobles reversed many of Peter's reforms. In 1762, however, the crown passed to Catherine II, a ruler whose ambitions and determination were equal to those of her great predecessor. We shall discuss her reign later in this chapter.

ALTERNATIVES TO ABSOLUTISM

What was political power according to Locke?

Peter the Great of Russia, Leopold I of Austria, Frederick William of Brandenburg-Prussia, and above all Louis XIV of France were the "great" seventeenth-century absolutists. Elsewhere in Europe, absolutism was far less successful. In Spain, the ineffectual, weak-minded Charles II found himself besieged by rebellions in Portugal and Sicily. In 1688, after years of fighting, he was forced to recognize Portuguese independence. In Sweden, Charles X and Charles XI managed to extend their territories at the expense of the Danes and to quell the independence of the aristocracy by confiscating their fiefdoms. During the reign of Charles XII, however, that legacy was dissipated by an adventurous but ultimately unproductive foreign policy, and Sweden returned to being a more obviously "limited" monarchy. In Poland, the opposition of the landed gentry—or *szlachta*—to any form of centralized government whatever produced a political stalemate that amounted to little more than anarchy. Foreign powers took advantage of this situation to intervene in Polish affairs and, during the eighteenth century, to carve up the country and distribute it among themselves.

under his imposing hand, and flared up into outright resistance in the succession struggle that followed his death, without direct heirs, in 1725. A series of ineffective tsars followed, mostly creatures of the palace   Although absolutism was the dominant model for seventeenth-century European monarchs, it was by no means the only system by which Europeans governed themselves. In Venice, a republican oligarchy continued to rule the city; while in the Netherlands, the various provinces that had won their independence from Spain in the early seventeenth century combined to form a republic, the United Provinces, the only truly new country to take shape in Europe during the early modern era. Although Holland dominated the new republic economically and politically, the deep Dutch mistrust of monarchs that had been created by the Spanish wars prevented Holland's House of Orange (which had led the wars for independence) from transforming the republic into a monarchy. Even after 1688, when William of Orange became king of England in the "Glorious Revolution," the United Provinces remained a republic, despite the leading role William undertook in organizing a Europe-wide alliance against Louis XIV of France.

LIMITED MONARCHY: THE CASE OF ENGLAND

The political history of England in the late seventeenth century provides another alternative to absolutism as a foundation for effective government. England possessed in its Parliament the longest-surviving and most highly developed representative assembly in western Europe. English political theorists had for centuries seen their government as a "mixed" monarchy, composed of monarchical, noble, and common elements. During the seventeenth century, however, these traditions had come under threat, first through Charles I's attempts to rule without summoning Parliament, and then through Oliver Cromwell's dictatorial Protectorate. The restoration of the monarchy in 1660 resolved the question of whether England would in future be a republic or a monarchy; but the sort of monarchy England would become remained an open question as the reign of Charles II began.

THE REIGN OF CHARLES II

Despite the fact that he was the son of the beheaded and much-hated Charles I, Charles II was initially welcomed by most English men and women. Upon his accession, he declared a limited religious toleration for Protestants who were not members of the official Church of England, and he promised to observe Magna Carta and the Petition of Right, declaring that he was not anxious to "resume his travels." His delight in the unbuttoned moral atmosphere of his court, with its risqué plays, dancing, and sexual licentiousness, mirrored a public desire to forget the restraints of the Puritan past. The wits of the time suggested that Charles, "that known enemy to virginity and chastity," played his role as the father of his country to the fullest; but in fact he produced no legitimate heir and only a single illegitimate son to contest the succession to his father's throne. But as Charles's admiration of things French grew to include the absolutism of Louis XIV, he came to be regarded as a threat to more than English womanhood by a great many powerful Englishmen. Desirous though they were to preserve the restored monarchy, they were not about to surrender their traditional rights to another Stuart autocrat. By the late 1670s, the country thus found itself divided politically into those who supported the king (called by their opponents "Tories," a popular nickname for Irish Catholic bandits) and those opposed to him (called by their opponents "Whigs," a similar nickname for Scottish Presbyterian rebels).

As the new party labels suggest, religion remained an exceedingly divisive national issue. Charles was sympathetic to Roman Catholicism, even to the point of a deathbed conversion in 1685. He therefore opposed the Clarendon Code, which had reestablished the official Church of England and penalized Catholics and Protestant dissenters. In 1672, Charles suspended the Clarendon Code, asserting his prerogative to set aside Parliamentary legislation, but the resulting public outcry compelled him to retreat. This controversy, along with rising opposition to the expected succession of Charles's ardently Roman Catholic brother James, led to a series of Whig electoral victories between 1679 and 1681. But when a group of radical Whigs attempted to exclude Charles's brother James by law from succeeding him on the throne, Charles stared the opposition down in the so-called Exclusion Crisis. Thereafter, Charles found that his increased revenues, combined with a secret subsidy he was receiving from Louis XIV, enabled him to govern without relying on Parliament for money. Charles further infuriated and alarmed Whig politicians by arranging the execution of several of their most promi-

> English political theorists had for centuries seen their government as a "mixed" monarchy, composed of monarchical, noble, and common elements.

Charles II.

James II.

hanced, but he left behind a political and religious legacy that was to be the undoing of his less able and adroit successor.

KING JAMES II

James II was the very opposite of his worldly brother. A zealous Catholic convert, he alienated his Tory supporters, all of whom were members of the established Church of England, by dismissing them in favor of Roman Catholics, and by once again suspending the penal laws, approved by Parliament, that barred Catholics and Protestant dissenters from holding political office. James also flaunted his own Roman Catholicism, publicly declaring his wish that all his subjects might be converted, and parading papal legates through the streets of London. When, in June 1688, he ordered all Church of England clergymen to read his decree of religious toleration from their pulpits, seven bishops refused and were promptly thrown into prison on charges of seditious libel. At their trial, however, they were declared not guilty, to the enormous satisfaction of the overwhelmingly Protestant English populace.

The trial of the bishops was one event that brought matters to a head. The other was the unexpected birth of a son in 1688 to James and his second wife, the Roman Catholic Mary of Modena. This male infant, who was to be raised a Catholic, replaced James's much older Protestant daughter Mary as heir to the British throne. Despite a rumor that the baby boy was an imposter smuggled into the royal bedchamber in a warming pan, political leaders of both parties now began to take active steps to prevent the possibility of his succession to the throne. A delegation of Whigs and Tories crossed the Channel to Holland to invite Mary and her husband William of Orange, the *stadholder* or chief executive of the United Provinces and the great-grandson of William the Silent, to cross to England with an invading army to restore English religious and political freedom. As the leader of a Continental coalition determined to thwart Louis XIV's expansionist policies, William in particular welcomed the chance such a move represented to bring England into active opposition to the French (see p. 613).

THE GLORIOUS REVOLUTION

William's conquest was a bloodless coup. James fled the country, thereby allowing Parliament to declare the throne vacant and clearing the way for the acces-

nent leaders on charges of treason, and by remodeling local government so as to make it more dependent on royal favor. Charles died in 1685 with his power en-sion of William and Mary as joint sovereigns of England. A Bill of Rights, passed by Parliament and accepted by the new king and queen in 1689, reaffirmed English civil liberties such as trial by jury, habeas corpus (guaranteeing that individuals could not be imprisoned without being charged with a crime), and the right of subjects to petition their monarch through Parliament for redress of their grievances. The Bill of Rights also declared that the monarchy was subject to the law of the land. An Act of Toleration, passed in 1689, granted Protestants who were not members of the Church of England the right to worship, though not the right to hold political office. In 1701, with Queen Mary now dead and the son of the exiled James II reaching maturity in France, an Act of Succession ordained that the English throne was to pass first to Mary's childless sister Anne, who ruled from 1702 to 1714, and then to George, elector of the German principality of Hanover, who was the Protestant great-grandson of James I. The connection was a distant one, but the Hanoverians were the nearest Protestant dynasty with even a plausible claim to the English throne. Henceforth, Parliament required that all English monarchs be members of the Church of England. If foreign born, they could not engage England in the defense of their native land, or even leave the country without the prior consent of Parliament.

The English soon referred to the events of 1688 and 1689 as the "Glorious Revolution": glorious for the English in that it occurred without bloodshed (although James is reputed to have suffered a nosebleed at the moment of crisis); glorious, too, for defenders of Parliamentary prerogative. Although William and Mary and their successors continued to enjoy a large measure of executive power, after 1688 no king or queen attempted to govern without Parliament, which met annually from that time on. Parliament strengthened its control over the collection and expenditure of public funds. Future monarchs were therefore unable to conduct the country's business without seeking from the House of Commons the funds with which to do so. The revolution was glorious, finally, for advocates of the civil liberties now guaranteed within the Bill of Rights, and for defenders of the "Protestant cause," who saw nothing less than divine will as lying behind the favorable winds that blew William and Mary so speedily to England.

Yet 1688 was not all glory. It was a revolution that consolidated the position of large property holders, magnates whose local power base had been threatened by the interventions of Charles II and James II. If it was a revolution, it was one designed to restore the status quo on behalf of a wealthy social and economic order that would soon make itself even wealthier as it drank its fill of government patronage and war profits. And it was a revolution that brought nothing but misery to the Roman Catholic minority in Scotland, which joined with England and Wales in the union of Great Britain in 1707, and to the Catholic majority in Ireland where, following the Battle of the Boyne in 1690, repressive military forces imposed the exploitive will of a self-interested Protestant minority on the Catholic inhabitants of the island.

JOHN LOCKE AND THE CONTRACT THEORY OF GOVERNMENT

Although the Glorious Revolution was an expression of immediate political circumstances, it also reflected anti-absolutist theories that had taken shape in the late seventeenth century in response to the ideas of writers such as Bodin, Hobbes, Filmer, and Bossuet. Chief among these opponents of absolutism was the Englishman John Locke (1632–1704), whose *Two Treatises of Government*, written prior to the revolution but published for the first time in 1690, was used to justify the events of the previous two years. Locke maintained that humans had originally lived in a state of nature in which absolute freedom and equality prevailed, and in which there was no government of any kind. The only law was the law of nature (which Locke equated with the law of reason), by which individuals enforced for themselves their natural rights to life, liberty, and property.

It was not long, however, before humans began to perceive that the inconveniences of the state of nature greatly outweighed its advantages. With each individual attempting to enforce his own rights, confusion and insecurity were the unavoidable results. Accordingly, people agreed among themselves first to quit the state of nature and establish a civil society based on absolute equality, and then to set up a government to act as an impartial arbiter of disputes for the society they had already created. But they did not make that government absolute. The only power society conferred upon government was the executive power of the law

> The "Glorious Revolution" reflected anti-absolutist theories that had taken shape in the late seventeenth century in response to the ideas of writers such as Bodin, Hobbes, Filmer, and Bossuet.

THE AMERICAN DECLARATION OF INDEPENDENCE

The Declaration of Independence, issued from Philadelphia on July 4, 1776, is perhaps the most famous single document of American history. But its familiarity does not lesssen its interest as a piece of political philosophy. The indebtedness of the document's authors to the ideas of John Locke will be obvious from the selections below. But Locke, in turn, drew many of his ideas about the contractual and conditional nature of human government from the conciliarist thinkers of the fifteenth and early sixteenth centuries. The appeal of absolutism notwithstanding, the Declaration shows how vigorous the medieval tradition of contractual, limited government remained at the end of the eighteenth century.

When in the course of human events, it becomes necessary for one people to dissolve the political bonds which have connected them with another, and to assume among the powers of the earth the separate and equal station to which the Laws of Nature and of Nature's God entitle them, a decent respect to the opinions of mankind requires that they should declare the causes which impel them to the separation. . . . We hold these truths to be self-evident, that all men are created equal, that they are endowed by their Creator with certain unalienable rights, that among these are Life, Liberty and the pursuit of Happiness. . . . That to secure these rights, Governments are instituted among men, deriving their just powers from the consent of the governed. . . . That whenever any form of Government becomes destructive of these ends, it is the Right of the People to alter or to abolish it, and to institute new Government, laying its foundation upon such principles and organizing its power in such form, as to them shall seem most likely to effect their Safety and Happiness. Prudence, indeed, will dictate that Governments long established should not be changed for light and transient causes; and accordingly all experience has shown, that mankind are more disposed to suffer, while evils are sufferable, than to right themselves by abolishing the forms to which they are accustomed. But when a long train of abuses and usurpations, pursuing invariably the same Object, evinces a design to reduce them under absolute despotism, it is their right, it is their duty, to throw off such Government, and to provide new Guards for their future security. . . . Such has been the patient sufferance of these Colonies; and such is now the necessity which constrains them to alter their former Systems of Government. . . .

of nature. Since the state was nothing but the joint power of all the members of society, its authority could "be no more than those persons had in a state of nature before they entered into society, and gave it up to the community." All powers not expressly surrendered to the government were therefore reserved to the people themselves. All governmental authority was thus contractual and conditional. If, therefore, a government exceeded or abused the authority granted to it, it became tyrannical, and the society had the right to dissolve it and constitute another.

Locke condemned absolutism in every form. He

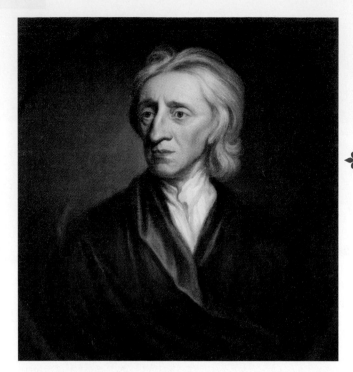

John Locke.

INTERNATIONAL RELATIONS AND THE EMERGENCE OF A EUROPEAN STATE SYSTEM

What was the "balance of power"?

As European states became more unified and centralized during the age of absolutism, contemporaries came more and more to think of them as entities with their own distinctive "interests," distinguishable, at least potentially, from the dynastic and religious interests of the monarchs who ruled over them. These were gradual developments, to be sure, but by the second quarter of the eighteenth century the abstract interests of "commerce" and "stability" were beginning to outweigh older modes of thought that had equated the interests of each state with the personal and familial interests of its ruler. The results were the emergence, for the first time, of a Europe-wide state system, and a significant redefinition of the aims and calculations of diplomacy and warfare.

DIPLOMACY AND WARFARE

The organization of diplomatic bureaucracies was one of the major accomplishments of the age of absolutism. The rationalization of diplomatic processes and the establishment of foreign ministries and embassies in European capitals, with their growing staffs of clerks and ministers, reflected a desire to bring order out of the international chaos that had gripped Europe during the early seventeenth century. To an unprecedented degree, the history of international relations from the late seventeenth century on therefore becomes a history of diplomatic coalitions, an indication of the extent to which negotiation was now a weapon in the armory of European states.

denounced despotic monarchy, but he was no less severe in his strictures against the absolute sovereignty of parliaments. Though he defended the supremacy of the law-making branch, with the executive primarily an agent of the legislature, he nevertheless refused to concede to the representatives of the people an unlimited power. Arguing that government was instituted among people for the preservation of property, he denied the authority of any political agency to invade the natural rights of a single individual. The law of nature, which embodied these rights, was thus an automatic and absolute limitation upon every branch of government.

Locke's theoretical defense of political liberty emerged in the late eighteenth century as an important element in the intellectual background of the American and French revolutions. Between 1688 and 1720, however, it served a far less radical purpose. The landed magnates responsible for replacing James II with William and Mary read Locke as a defense of their conservative revolution. James II, rather than protecting their property and liberties, had encroached upon them; hence the magnates had every right to overthrow the tyranny he had established and to replace it with a government that would, by ensuring their rights, defend their interests.

> Locke's theoretical defense of political liberty emerged as an important element in the intellectual background of the American and French revolutions.

Warfare, however, continued to play an integral and almost constant role in the international arena. The armies of the period grew dramatically. When Louis XIV came of age in 1657, the French army numbered twenty thousand men; by 1688, it stood at two hundred ninety thousand; by 1694, four hundred thousand. These armies were increasingly professional organizations, controlled directly by the state, and under the command of trained officers recruited from the nobility. In Prussia, common soldiers were mostly conscripts; in other European countries they were volunteers, either native or foreign, though often "volunteers" in no more than name, having been coerced or tricked into service. Increasingly, however, enlistment was perceived by common soldiers as an avenue to a career, one that included the possibility of promotion to corporal or sergeant, and in the case of France, the promise of a small pension at the end of one's service. However recruited, common soldiers became part of an increasingly elaborate and efficient fighting force. Above all, they were made to understand the dire consequences of disobedience, breaking ranks, or desertion. Soldiers were expected to obey instantly and unquestioningly. Failure to do so resulted in brutal punishment, often flogging, sometimes execution. Drill, not only on the battlefield but on the parade ground, in brilliant, elaborate uniforms and intricate formations, was designed to reduce individuals to automatonlike parts of an army whose regiments were moved across battlefields as a chess player moves pawns across the board.

THE FOREIGN POLICY OF LOUIS XIV

The patterns of international relations during the period from 1660 to 1715 show European monarchs making use of the new machinery of diplomacy and warfare to resolve the conflicting interests of dynasty, stability, and commerce. At the center of that pattern, as at the center of Europe, stood Louis XIV. From 1661 until 1688, in a quest for glory, empire, and even revenge, he waged war across his northern and eastern frontiers on the pretext that the lands in question belonged both to the Bourbons and to the French by tradition, by former treaty, or by dynastic inheritance. His aggressively expansionist policies, alarming to other European rulers, led William of Orange, in 1674, to form an anti-French coalition with Austria, Spain, and various smaller German states. Yet Louis continued to push his frontiers eastward, invading territories that had been Germanic for centuries, and capturing Strassburg in 1681 and Luxembourg in 1684. Louis's seizure of Strassburg (subsequently called Strasbourg by the French), completing the conquest of the German-speaking province of Alsace begun in 1634 by Richelieu, irreversibly incorporated the seeds of a Franco-German animosity centered on this region that would bear bitter fruit in the great wars of the nineteenth and twentieth centuries. A sec-

ond coalition, the so-called League of Augsburg (1686), which comprised Holland, Austria, Sweden, and further German allies, was only somewhat more successful than the first.

These allies were concerned above all to maintain some sort of European balance of power. They feared an expansionist France would prove insatiable, as it pressed its boundaries farther and farther into Germany and the Low Countries. Louis, mistakenly expecting that William would be forced to fight an English army under James to establish his right to his new throne and would therefore be too preoccupied to devote his full attention to developments on the Continent, kept up the pressure. In September 1688 he invaded the Palatinate and occupied the city of Cologne. The following year the French armies crossed the Rhine and continued their eastward drive, burning Heidelberg and committing numerous atrocities throughout the middle Rhine area. Aroused at last to effective action, the League of Augsburg, led by William and now including in addition to its original members both England and Spain, engaged Louis in a war that began in 1689 and was to last until 1697.

The major campaigns of this War of the League of Augsburg were fought in the Low Countries. William managed to drive an army under his predecessor, James II, from Ireland in 1690; from that point on, he took command of the allied forces on the Continent. By 1694 Louis was pressed hard, not only by his allied foes, but by a succession of disastrous harvests that crippled France. Fighting remained stalemated until a treaty was signed at Ryswick in Holland in 1697, which compelled Louis to return most of France's recent gains, except for Alsace, and to recognize William as the rightful king of England.

THE WAR OF THE SPANISH SUCCESSION

Ryswick did nothing, however, to resolve the dynastic tangle known as the Spanish succession. Since Charles II of Spain had no direct heirs, and since he appeared to be on his deathbed in 1699, European monarchs and diplomats were obsessed by the question of who would succeed to the vast domain of the Spanish Habsburgs: not only Spain itself, but also its overseas empire, as well as the Spanish Netherlands, Naples, Sicily, and other territories in Italy. Both Louis XIV and Leopold I of Austria were married to sisters of the decrepit, unstable Charles; and both, naturally, eyed the succession to the Spanish inheritance as an exceedingly tempting dynastic plum. Yet it is a measure of the degree to which even absolutists were willing to keep their ambitions within bounds that both Leopold and Louis agreed to William's suggestion that the lion's share of the Habsburg lands should go to six-year-old Joseph Ferdinand, the prince of Bavaria, who was Charles II's grandnephew. Unfortunately, in 1699 the child died. Though the chances of war increased, William and Louis were prepared to bargain further and arranged a second treaty that divided the Spanish empire between Louis's and Leopold's heirs. Yet at the same time, Louis's diplomatic agents in Madrid persuaded Charles to sign a will in which he stipulated that the entire Spanish Habsburg inheritance should pass to Louis's grandson Philip of Anjou. This option was welcomed by many influential Spaniards, willing to endure French hegemony in return for the protection France could provide to the Spanish empire. For a time, Louis contemplated an alternative agreement that would have given France direct control of much of Italy. When Charles finally died in November 1700, Louis decided to accept the will. As if this was not enough to drive his former enemies back to war, he sent troops into the Spanish Netherlands and traders to the Spanish colonial empire, while declaring the late James II's son—the child of the warming-pan myth—the legitimate king of England.

Once it was clear to the allies that Louis intended to treat Spain as if it were his own kingdom, they again united against him in the cause of balance and stability. William died in 1702, just as the War of the Spanish Succession was beginning. His position as first general of the coalition passed to two brilliant strategists, the Englishman John Churchill, duke of Marlborough, and his Austrian counterpart Prince Eugene of Savoy, an upper-class soldier of fortune who had been denied a commission by Louis. Under their command the allied forces engaged in fierce battles in the Low Countries and Germany, including an extraordinary march deep into Bavaria, where the combined forces under Marlborough and Eugene defeated the French and their Bavarian allies decisively at Blenheim (1704). While the allies pressed France's armies on land, the English navy captured Gibraltar and the island of Minorca, thus establishing a strategic and commercial foothold in the Mediterranean and helping to open a fourth major military theater in Spain itself.

The War of the Spanish Succession was a "professional" war that tested the highly trained armies of the combatants to the fullest. At the battle of Malplaquet in northeastern France in 1709, eighty thousand French soldiers faced one hundred ten thousand allied troops. Though Marlborough and Eugene could claim to have won that battle, in that they forced the French to retreat, they suffered twenty-four thousand casualties, twice those of the French. Neither Malplaquet nor other such victories brought the allies any closer to their final goal, which now appeared to be not the containment, but the complete destruction of the French military force. Queen Anne of England (Mary's sister and William's successor), once Marlborough's staunchest defender, grew disillusioned with the war and fired her general.

More than war weariness impelled the combatants toward negotiation, however. The War of the Spanish Succession had begun as a conflict about the balance of power in Europe and the world. Yet dynastic changes had by 1711 compelled a reappraisal of allied goals. Leopold I had died in 1705. When his elder son and successor Joseph I died in 1711, the Austrian monarchy fell to Leopold's youngest son, the archduke Charles, who had been the allies' candidate for the throne of Spain. With Charles now the Austrian and the Holy Roman emperor as Charles VI (1711–1740), the prospect of his accession to the Spanish inheritance conjured up the ghost of Charles V and threatened to give him far too much power. International stability therefore demanded an end to hostilities and diplomatic negotiation toward a solution that would reestablish some sort of general balance.

THE TREATY OF UTRECHT

The Treaty of Utrecht settled the conflict in 1713 by redistributing territory and power in equitable portions. No one emerged a major winner or loser. Philip, Louis's grandson, remained on the throne of Spain, but Louis agreed that France and Spain would never be united under the same ruler. Austria gained territories in the Netherlands and Italy. The Dutch, victims of French aggression during the war, were guaranteed protection of their borders against future invasion. The English retained Gibraltar and Minorca, as well as territory in America (Newfoundland, Acadia, Hudson Bay) and in the Caribbean (St. Kitts). Perhaps most valuable of all, the English extracted from Spain the right to supply Spanish America with African slaves. The settlement reflected the degree to which new interests had superseded old. Balance of power and stability among states were the major goals of the negotiations, goals that reflected a departure from the world of seventeenth-century turmoil when religion

HOW DID SEVENTEENTH- AND EIGHTEENTH-CENTURY FORMS OF ABSOLUTISM DIFFER?

ENLIGHTENED ABSOLUTISM AND LIMITED MONARCHY   615

had been a major factor in international conflict. The eventual "winners" were undoubtedly the English, whose dynastic concerns were limited to a general acceptance of the Hanoverian settlement, and who could therefore concentrate their efforts on amassing overseas territories that would contribute to the growth of their economic prosperity and hence their international power.

ENLIGHTENED ABSOLUTISM AND LIMITED MONARCHY IN THE EIGHTEENTH CENTURY

How did seventeenth- and eighteenth-century forms of absolutism differ?

Eighteenth-century absolutism was a series of variations on the dominant themes composed in the previous century by Louis XIV. Eighteenth-century rulers backed their sovereign claims not in the language of divine right, but in terms of their determination to act, as Frederick the Great of Prussia declared, as "first servant of the state." That phrase meant not so much service to the people as it did service to the goal of further strengthening the authority of the state over institutions that sought to challenge its corporate well-being. Enlightened rulers moved to curtail the privileges of old institutions. The Roman Catholic Church, for example, was compelled to suffer the expulsion of the Jesuits from most Catholic countries. Customary laws benefiting particular orders or interests were reformed. To strengthen the state community, innovative policies in the areas of taxation, economic development, and education were also instituted.

As we shall see in Chapter 18, rational schemes of this sort reflected the spread of Enlightenment ideals as manifested in the writings of thinkers such as Beccaria, Diderot, and Voltaire. (The last was, in fact, a guest at Frederick's court for several years.) Assisting enlightened "first servants" in the implementation of these charges was a growing cadre of lesser servants: bureaucrats, often recruited from the nobility, but once recruited, expected to declare primary allegiance to their new master, the state. Despite innovation, "enlightened" absolutists continued to insist, as their predecessors had, that state sovereignty rested with the monarchy. Authority remained their overriding concern, and to the extent that they combatted efforts by the estates of their realms to dilute that authority, they declared their descent from their seventeenth-century forebears.

CROWN AND *PARLEMENT* IN FRANCE

Louis XIV's successors, his great-grandson Louis XV (1715–1774) and that monarch's grandson Louis XVI (1774–1792), were unable to sustain the energetic drive toward centralization that had taken place under the Sun King. Indeed, during his last years, while fighting a desperate defensive war against his allied enemies, Louis XIV had seen his own accomplishments begin to crumble under the mounting pressure of military expenses. His heir was only five years old when he assumed the throne. As he grew up, Louis XV displayed less single-minded determination than had his great-grandfather to act the role of Sun King. The heroic, Baroque grandeur of the main palace at Versailles yielded to the Rococo grace of the Grand and Petit Trianons, pleasure pavillions built by Louis XV in the palace gardens.

During the minority of Louis XV, the French *parlements*, those courts of record responsible for registering royal decreees, enjoyed a resurgence of power which they retained throughout the century. No longer tame adjuncts of absolutist governmental machinery as they had been under Louis XIV, these bodies now proclaimed themselves the protectors of French "liberties." In 1770, encouraged by his chancellor René Maupeou, Louis XV issued an edict effectively ending the right of *parlements* to reject decrees. Protest on the part of the magistrates resulted in their imprisonment or banishment. The *parlements* themselves were replaced by new courts charged not only with the responsibility of rubber-stamping legislation but also with administering law more justly and less expensively. When Louis XVI ascended the throne in 1774, his ministers persuaded him to reestablish the *parlements* as a sign of his willingness to conciliate his trouble-making aristocracy. This he did, with the result that government—particularly the management of finances—developed into a stalemated battle.

THE RISE OF PRUSSIA

Stalemate was what the Prussian successors to Frederick William, the Great Elector, were determined to avoid. Frederick I (1688–1713), the Great Elector's im-

AGE OF ABSOLUTISM

What nations on this map were governed by "enlightened absolutists"? How did their competing claims to sovereignty differ from the absolutists who based their claim to rule on divine right? How did the conception of this new type of absolutism affect the relations between states and the construction of continental empires in the early eighteenth century?

mediate successor, enhanced the appearance and cultural life of Berlin. As the Roman numeral after his name attests, he also succeeded in bargaining his support to the Austrians during the War of the Spanish Succession in return for the coveted right to style himself king. (The Austrian monarch was the Holy Roman emperor and therefore had the right to create kings.)

Frederick William I (1713–1740), cared little for the embellishments his father had made to the capital city.

His overriding concern was the building of a first-rate army. So single-minded was his attention to the military that he came to be called "the sergeant king." Military display became an obsession. His private regiment of "Potsdam Giants" was composed exclusively of soldiers over six feet in height. The king traded musicians and prize stallions for such choice specimens and delighted in marching them about his palace grounds. Frederick William I's success as the builder of a military

HOW DID SEVENTEENTH- AND EIGHTEENTH-CENTURY FORMS OF ABSOLUTISM DIFFER?

ENLIGHTENED ABSOLUTISM AND LIMITED MONARCHY   617

machine can be measured in terms of numbers: thirty thousand men under arms when he came to the throne; eighty-three thousand when he died twenty-seven years later, commander of the fourth-largest army in Europe, after France, Russia, and Austria. Most of his soldiers were conscripts, drafted from the peasantry for a period of years and required to attend annual training exercises lasting three months. Conscription was supplemented by the kidnapping of forced recruits in neighboring German lands. To finance his army, Frederick William I increased taxes and streamlined their collection through the establishment of a General Directory of War, Finance, and Domains. In 1723, he instituted a system of administration by boards, hoping thereby to eliminate individual inefficiency through collective responsibility and surveillance. In addition, he created an inspectorate to uncover and report to him the mistakes and inefficiencies of his officialdom. Even then, he continued to supervise personally the implementation of state policy while shunning the luxuries of court life; for him, the "theater" of absolutism was not the palace but the office, which placed him at the helm of the state and the army. Perceiving the resources of the state to be too precious to waste, he pared costs at every turn to the point where, it was said, he had to invite himself to a nobleman's table in order to enjoy a good meal.

A hard, unimaginative man, Frederick William I had little use for his son, whose passion was not the battlefield but the flute, and who admired French culture as much as his father disdained it. Not surprisingly, young Frederick rebelled; in 1730, when he was eighteen, he ran away from court with a friend. Apprehended, the companions were returned to the king, who welcomed the fledgling prodigal with something other than a fatted calf. Before Frederick's eyes, he had the friend executed. The grisly lesson took. Thenceforward Frederick, though he never surrendered his love of music and literature, bound himself to his royal duties, living in accordance with his own image of himself as "first servant of the state," and earning himself history's title of Frederick the Great.

Frederick William I's zealous austerity and his compulsion to build an efficient army and administrative state made Prussia a strong state. Frederick the Great (1740–1786), building on the work of his father, raised his country to the status of a major power. As soon as he became king in 1740, Frederick mobilized the army his father had never taken into battle and occupied the poorly protected Austrian province of Silesia, to which Prussia had no legitimate claim. Although he had ear-

Frederick the Great and Voltaire. Although Frederick offered asylum to the French philosophe, this "enlightened despot" did not permit his own intellectual pursuits to interfere with matters of state.

lier vowed to make morality rather than expediency the hallmark of his reign, he seemingly had little difficulty in sacrificing his youthful idealism to the opportunity to make his Prussian state a leading power. The remaining forty-five years of his monarchy were devoted to the consolidation of this first bold stroke.

Such a daring course required some adjustments within the Prussian state. The army had to be kept at full strength, and to this end, Frederick staffed its officer corps with young noblemen. In expanding the bureaucracy, whose financial administration kept his army in the field, he relied on the nobility as well, reversing the policy of his father, who had recruited his civil servants according to merit rather than birth. But Frederick was not one to tolerate mediocrity; he fashioned the most highly professional and efficient bureaucracy in Europe. The degree to which both army and bureaucracy were staffed by the nobility is a measure of his determination to secure the unflagging support of the most privileged order in his realm, in order to ensure a united front against Prussia's external foes.

Frederick's domestic policies reflected that same strategy. In matters where he ran no risk of offending the nobility, he followed his own rationalist bent, prohibiting the torture of accused criminals, putting an end to the bribing of judges, and establishing a system of elementary schools. He encouraged religious toleration, declaring that he would happily build a mosque in Berlin if he could find enough Muslims to fill it. (Yet he was strongly anti-Semitic, levying special taxes on Jews and making efforts to close the professions and the civil service to them). On his own royal estates he was a model "enlightened" monarch. He abolished capital punishment, curtailed the forced labor services of his peasantry, and granted them long leases on the land they worked. He fostered scientific forestry and the cultivation of new crops. He opened new lands in Silesia and brought in thousands of immigrants to cultivate them. When wars ruined their farms, he supplied the peasants with new livestock and tools. Yet he never attempted to extend these reforms to the estates of the Junker elite, since to have done so would have alienated that social and economic group upon which Frederick was most dependent.

Maria Theresa of Austria. The empress was a formidable monarch and a match for Frederick the Great.

THE AUSTRO-HUNGARIAN EMPIRE

Although the monarchs of eighteenth-century Austria eventually proved themselves even more willing than Frederick the Great to undertake significant social reform, the energies of Emperor Charles VI (1711–1740) were concentrated on guaranteeing the future dynastic and territorial integrity of the Habsburg lineage and domain. Without a male heir, Charles worked to secure the right of his daughter Maria Theresa to succeed him as empress. By his death in 1740 Charles had managed to persuade not only his subjects but all the major European powers to accept his daughter as his royal heir—a feat known as the "pragmatic sanction." Yet his painstaking efforts were only partially successful. As we have seen, Frederick the Great used the occasion of Charles's death to seize Silesia. The French, unable to resist the temptation to grab what they could, joined the coalition against the new empress, Maria Theresa (1740–1780).

With most of her possessions already occupied by her enemies, Maria Theresa appealed successfully to the Hungarians for support. The empress was willing to play the role of the wronged woman when, as on this occasion, it suited her interests to do so. Hungary's vital troops combined with British financial assistance enabled her to battle Austria's enemies to a draw, although she never succeeded in regaining Silesia. The experience of those first few years of her reign persuaded Maria Theresa, who was both capable and tenacious, to reorganize her dominions along the tightly centralized lines characteristic of Prussia and France. Ten new administrative districts were established, each with its own "war commissar" appointed by and responsible to the central administration in Vienna—an Austrian equivalent of the French intendant. Property taxes were increased to finance an expanded army, which was modernized and professionalized so as to remain on a

HOW DID SEVENTEENTH- AND EIGHTEENTH-CENTURY FORMS OF ABSOLUTISM DIFFER?

ENLIGHTENED ABSOLUTISM AND LIMITED MONARCHY   619

Edict of Tolerance. An illustration from a pamphlet depicting Joseph II of Austria as an enlightened monarch.

par with the military establishments of the other great powers. Centralization, finances, army: once more those three crucial elements in the formula of absolute rule came into play.

Reform did not stop there, however. Together Maria Theresa and her son Joseph II, with whom she ruled jointly from 1765 to 1780, and who then succeeded her for another ten years, instituted a series of significant social reforms. Although both mother and son were devout Roman Catholics, they moved to assert their control over the church, abolishing the clergy's exemption from taxation and decreeing the state's ability to block the publication of papal bulls in Austria. In 1773, following the papal suppression of the Jesuits, they used the order's assets to finance a program of statewide primary education. Although the General Schools Ordinance of 1774 never achieved anything like a universally literate population, it did succeed in

educating hundreds of thousands, and in financing not only schools for children but schools as well for those who taught the children. Joseph followed these reforms with an "Edict on Idle Institutions" in 1780, which resulted in the closing of hundreds of monastic houses, whose property went to support charitable institutions now under state control. These reforms and others—liberalization of punishment for criminal offenses, a relaxation of censorship, the abolition of serfdom and feudal dues, and an attempt to eradicate superstition by curbing the practice of pilgrimages and celebration of saint's days—made Joseph more enemies than friends, among both the noble elite and the common people. "Enlightened" though Joseph II was, however, he nevertheless remained a staunch absolutist, as concerned with the maintenance of a strong army and an efficient bureaucracy as with the need to educate his peasantry. Joseph's brother Leopold II, who succeeded him in 1790, attempted to maintain the reformist momentum. His death two years later and the accession of his reactionary son Francis II (1792–1835) put an end to liberalizing experiments.

CATHERINE THE GREAT OF RUSSIA

Unlike Joseph II, Catherine the Great of Russia (1762–1796) felt herself compelled to curry the favor of her nobility by involving them directly in the structure of local administration, by exempting them from military service and taxation, and probably most important, by granting them absolute control over the serfs on their estates. Her policy grew out of her strong ties to powerful nobles and her involvement in the conspiracy that led to the assassination of her husband, Tsar Peter III, the last of a series of weak rulers who followed Peter the Great. Catherine was herself a German, and prided herself on her devotion to Western principles of government. Ambitious to establish a reputation as an intellectual and enlightened monarch, she corresponded with French philosophers, wrote plays, published a digest of William Blackstone's *Commentaries on the Laws of England*, and began a history of Russia. Her contributions to social reform did not extend much beyond the founding of hospitals and orphanages, and the expression of a pious hope that someday the serfs might be liberated. Although she did summon a commission in 1767 to codify Russian law, its achievements were modest: a minor extension of religious toleration, a slight restriction of the use of torture by the state. Catherine's interest in theories of reform did, however, stimulate the development of a social conscience among certain gentry intellectuals, foreshadowing a more widespread movement in the nineteenth century.

Any plans Catherine may have had for improving the lot of the peasants, however, were abruptly cancelled after their frustration with St. Petersburg's centralization efforts erupted in a violent peasant-serf rebellion in 1773–1774. Free peasants in the Volga valley region found themselves compelled to provide labor services to nobles sent by the crown to control them, Cossacks were subjected to taxation and conscription for the first time, and factory workers and miners were pressed into service in the state's industrial enterprises. These and other disparate but dissatisfied groups, including serfs, united under the rebel banner of Emelyan Pugachev, an illiterate Cossack who claimed to be the late Tsar Peter III. The hapless Peter, who had spoken as a reformer in life, in death became a larger-than-life hero for those opposed to the determined absolutism of his successor. As Pugachev marched, he encouraged his followers to strike out not only against the empress but also against the nobility and the church. More than fifteen hundred landlords and priests were murdered, and the ruling classes were terrified as the revolt spread. Catherine's

CHRONOLOGY	
EIGHTEENTH-CENTURY ABSOLUTIST RULERS	
France	
Louis XV	1715–1774
Louis XVI	1774–1792
Brandenburg-Prussia	
Frederick I	1688–1713
Frederick William	1713–1740
Frederick the Great	1740–1786
Austria	
Charles VI	1711–1740
Maria Theresa	1740–1780
Joseph II	1765–1790
Russia	
Catherine the Great	1762–1796

forces initially had little success against the rebel army, but the threat of famine plagued Pugachev's advance and finally led to disarray among his troops. Betrayed in 1774, he was captured and taken in an iron cage to Moscow, where he was tortured and killed. Catherine responded to this uprising with further centralization and tightening of aristocratic authority over the peasantry.

The brutal suppression and punishment of the rebels reflected the ease with which the German-born Catherine took to the despotic authoritarianism that characterized Russian absolutism. At the same time, Catherine continued the work of Peter the Great in introducing Russia to Western ideas; she came to terms with the nobility in a way that brought stability to the state; and she made the country a formidable power in European affairs by extending its boundaries to include not only most of Poland but also lands on the Black Sea.

Catherine the Great.

THE GROWTH OF PARLIAMENTARY GOVERNMENT IN ENGLAND

Eighteenth-century monarchs were determined to press ahead with the task, begun by their seventeenth-century predecessors, of building powerful, centralized states by continuing to attempt the elimination or harnessing of the ancient privileges of still-powerful noble

HOW DID SEVENTEENTH- AND EIGHTEENTH-CENTURY FORMS OF ABSOLUTISM DIFFER?

ENLIGHTENED ABSOLUTISM AND LIMITED MONARCHY   621

orders and provincial estates. The notion of a limited monarchy, in which power was divided between local and central authorities and shared by monarchs, nobles, and legislative assemblies, struck them as a dangerous anachronism. Yet as the century progressed, they found that conviction challenged by the emergence of England, under limited monarchy, as the world's leading commercial and naval power.

England (or Britain, as the country was called after its union with Scotland in 1707) prospered as a state in which power was divided between the king and Parliament. This division of political power was guaranteed by a constitution which, though unwritten, was grounded in common law and strengthened by precedent and by particular legal settlements such as those that had followed the restoration of the Stuarts in 1660 and the overthrow of James II in 1688. The Hanoverians George I (1714–1727) and his son George II (1727–1760) were by no means political nonentities. Though George I could not speak English, he could converse comfortably enough with his ministers in French. The first two Georges made a con-

> Britain was governed locally, not from the center as in an absolutist state.

scientious and generally successful effort to govern within their adopted kingdom. They appointed chief ministers who remained responsible to them for the creation and direction of state policy. Yet because Parliament, after 1688, retained the right to legislate, tax, and spend, its powers were far greater than those of any European *parlement*, estate, or diet. During the reign of the first two Hanoverians, politics was on most occasions little more than a struggle between factions within the Whig party, composed of wealthy—and in many cases newly rich—landed magnates who were making fortunes in an expanding economy based on commercial and agricultural capitalism.

The Tories, because of their previous association with the Stuarts, remained political "outs" for most of the century. To the Whigs, national politics was no longer a matter of clashing principles. Those principles had been settled—to Whig satisfaction—in 1688. Nor was politics a matter of legislating in the national interest. Britain was governed locally, not from the center as in an absolutist state. Aristocrats and landed gentry administered the affairs

The House of Commons. Despite its architectural division into two "sides," the House was composed of men of property whose similar economic interests encouraged them to agree on political fundamentals.

of the particular counties and parishes in which their estates lay, as lords lieutenant, as justices of the peace, as overseers of the poor, unhampered, to a degree unknown on the Continent, by legislation imposed uniformly throughout the kingdom. The quality of local government varied greatly. Some squires were as "all-worthy" as Henry Fielding's fictional character of that name in the novel *Tom Jones*. Others cared for little beyond the bottle and the hunt. A French traveler noted in 1747 that the country gentleman was "naturally a very dull animal" whose favorite after-dinner toast was "to all honest fox hunters in Great Britain." These men enforced those general laws that did exist—the Poor Law, game laws—which were drawn in such a way as to leave their administrators wide latitude, a latitude that they exercised in order to enhance the appearance of their own local omnipotence. Thus in Britain there was no attempt to pass a law establishing a statewide system of primary education. Centralizing legislation of that sort, the hallmark of absolutist states, was anathema to the British aristocracy and gentry. They argued that education, if it was to be provided, should be provided at their expense, in village schoolrooms by schoolmasters in their employ. Those instructors would make it their business to teach their pupils not only rudimentary reading, writing, and figuring, but the deferential behavior that bespoke the obligation of the poor to their rich benefactors. As the Church of England catechism had it, they were "to do their duty in that station of life unto which it shall please God to call them."

Politics, then, was neither first principles nor national legislation. It was "interest" and "influence," the weaving of a web of obligations into a political faction powerful enough to secure jobs and favors—a third secretaryship in the foreign office from a minister, an Act of Enclosure from Parliament. The greatest master of this game of politics was Robert Walpole (1676–1745), who was Britain's leading minister from the early 1720s until 1742. Walpole is sometimes called Britain's first prime minister, a not entirely accurate distinction, since officially that position did not exist until the nineteenth century. Prime minister or not, he wielded great political power. He took advantage of the king's frequent absences in Hanover to assert control over the day-to-day governance of the country. He ruled as chief officer of his cabinet, a small group of like-minded politicians whose collective name derived from the room in which they met. In time the cabinet evolved into the policy-making executive arm of the British political system; Britain is governed today by cabinet and Parliament,

the cabinet being composed of leading politicians from the majority party in Parliament.

Walpole was a member of a Norfolk gentry family who had risen to national prominence on the fortune he amassed while serving as paymaster-general to the armed forces during the War of the Spanish Succession. Adept at bribery and corruption, he used his ability to reward his supporters with appointments to ensure himself a loyal political following. By the end of his career, grossly fat and stuffed seemingly with the profits of his years in office, he was being depicted by cartoonists and balladeers as Britain's most accomplished robber. "Little villians must submit to Fate," lamented a typical lampoon, "while great ones do enjoy the world in state." Walpole was no more corrupt, however, than the political process over which he presided. Most seats in Parliament's lower House of Commons were filled by representatives from boroughs that often had no more than two or three dozen electors. Hence it was a relatively simple task to buy votes, either directly or with promises of future favors. Walpole cemented political factions together into an alliance that survived for about twenty years. During that time, he worked to ensure domestic tranquillity by refusing to press ahead with any legislation that might arouse national controversy. He withdrew what was perhaps his most innovative piece of legislation—a scheme that would increase excise taxes and reduce import duties as a means of curbing smugglers—in the face of widespread popular opposition.

Other Whig politicians succeeded Walpole in office in the 1740s and 1750s, but only one, William Pitt, later elevated to the House of Lords as the earl of Chatham, commanded public attention as Walpole had. George III (1760–1820), who came to the throne as a young man in 1760, resented the manner in which he believed his royal predecessors had been treated by the Whig oligarchy. Whether or not, as legend has it, his mother fired his determination with the constant injunction "George, be king!" he began his reign convinced that he must assert his rightful prerogatives. He dismissed Pitt and attempted to impose ministers of his own choosing on Parliament. King and Parliament battled this issue of prerogative throughout the 1760s. In 1770, Lord North, an aristocrat sastisfactory to the king and with a large enough following in the House of Commons to ensure some measure of stability, assumed the position of first minister. His downfall occured a decade later, as a result of his mismanagement of the overseas war that resulted in Britain's loss of its original thirteen North American colonies. A period of

HOW DID THE BALANCE OF POWER SHIFT IN THE EIGHTEENTH CENTURY?

WAR AND DIPLOMACY IN THE EIGHTEENTH CENTURY   623

political shuffling was followed by the king's appointment, at the age of twenty-three, of another William Pitt, Chatham's son, and this Pitt directed Britain's fortunes for the next twenty-five years—a political reign even longer than Walpole's. Although the period between 1760 and 1780 witnessed a struggle between crown (as the king and his political following were called) and Parliament, it was a very minor skirmish compared with the titanic constitutional struggles of the seventeenth century. Britain saw the last of absolutism in 1688. What followed was the mutual adjustment of the two formerly contending parties to a settlement both considered essentially sound.

WAR AND DIPLOMACY IN THE EIGHTEENTH CENTURY

How did the balance of power shift in the eighteenth century?

The history of European diplomacy and warfare after 1715 reveals that the twin goals of international stability and economic expansion remained paramount. The fact that those objectives often conflicted with one another set off further frequent wars, in which the ever-growing standing armies of absolutist Europe were matched against each other, and in which the deciding factor often turned out to be not Continental military strength but British naval power. The major conflict at mid-century, known as the Seven Years' War in Europe and the French and Indian War in North America, reflects the overlapping interests of power balance and commercial gain. In Europe, the primary concern was balance. Whereas in the past France had seemed the major threat, now Prussia loomed—at least in Austrian eyes—as a far more dangerous interloper. Under these circumstances, in 1756 the Austrian foreign minister, Prince Wenzel von Kaunitz, effected the so-called diplomatic revolution, which put an end to the enmity between France and Austria, and resulted in a formidable threat to the Prussia of Frederick the Great. Frederick, meanwhile, was taking steps to protect his flanks. Although anxious not to arouse his French ally, he nevertheless signed a neutrality treaty with the British, who were concerned with securing protection for their sovereign's Hanoverian domains. The French read Freder-

ick's act as a hostile one, and thus fell all the more readily for Kaunitz's offer of an alliance. The French indeed perceived a pressing need for trustworthy European allies, since they were already engaged in an undeclared war with Britain in North America. By mid-1756 Kaunitz could count France, Russia, Sweden, and several German states as likely allies against Prussia. Rather than await retribution from his enemies, Frederick invaded strategic but neutral Saxony and then Austria itself, thus once again playing the role of aggressor.

The configurations in this diplomatic gavotte are undoubtedly confusing. They are historically important, however, because they indicate the way in which the power balance was shifting, and the attempts of European states to respond to those shifts by means of new diplomatic alliances. Prussia and Britain were the volatile elements: Prussia on the Continent, Britain overseas. The war from 1756 to 1763 in Europe centered on Frederick's attempts to prevent the dismemberment of his domain at the hands of the French-Austrian-Russian alliance. Time and again the Prussian army's superiority and Frederick's own military genius frustrated his enemies' attacks. Ultimately, Prussia's survival against these overwhelming odds—"the miracle of the House of Brandenburg"—was ensured by the death of the Tsarina Elizabeth (1741–1762), daughter of Peter the Great, and by the accession of Peter III (1762), whose admiration for Frederick was as great as was his predecessor's hostility. Peter withdrew from the war, returning the conquered provinces of East Prussia and Pomerania to his country's erstwhile enemy. The peace that followed, though it compelled Frederick to relinquish Saxony, recognized his right to retain Silesia, and hence put an end to Austria's hope of one day recapturing that rich prize.

Overseas, battles occurred not only in North America but in the West Indies and in India, where Anglo-French commercial rivalry had resulted in sporadic, fierce fighting since the 1740s. Ultimate victory would go to that power possessing a navy strong enough to keep its supply routes open—that is, to Britain. Superior naval forces resulted in victories along the North American Great Lakes, climaxing in the battle of Québec in 1759 and the eventual surrender of all of Canada to the British. By 1762 the French sugar islands, including Martinique, Grenada, and St. Vincent, were in British hands. Around the globe in India, the defeat of the French in the Battle of Plassey in 1757 and the capture of Pondichéry four years later made Britain the dominant European presence on the subcontinent. In the Treaty of Paris in 1763, which

The Battle of Québec, 1759. Most often remembered for the fact that the British and French commanders, Generals Wolfe and Montcalm, were killed on the bluffs above the St. Lawrence River (the Plains of Abraham), this battle was even more notable for the success of the British amphibious assault, a measure of Britain's naval superiority.

brought the Seven Years' War to an end, France officially surrendered Canada and India to the British, thus affording them an extraordinary field for commercial exploitation.

THE AMERICAN REVOLUTION

The success of the British in North America in the Seven Years' War was itself a major cause of the war that broke out between the mother country and her thirteen North American colonies in 1775. To pay for the larger army the British now deemed necessary to protect their vastly expanded colonial possessions, they imposed unwelcome new taxes on the colonists. The North Americans protested that they were being taxed without representation. The home government responded that, like all British subjects, they were "virtually" if not actually represented by the present members of the House of Commons. Colonists thundered back that the present political system in Britain was so corrupt that no one but the Whig oligarchs could claim that their interests were being looked after.

Meanwhile the British were exacting retribution for rebellious acts on the part of colonists. East India Company tea, shipped to be sold in Boston at prices advantageous to the company, was dumped in Boston Harbor. The port of Boston was thereupon closed, and

representative government in the colony of Massachusetts curtailed. The British garrison clashed with colonial civilians. Colonial "minutemen" formed a counterforce. By the time war broke out in 1775, most Americans were prepared to sever ties with Britain and declare themselves an independent nation, which they did the following year. Fighting continued until 1781 when a British army surrendered to the colonists at Yorktown to the tune of a song entitled "The World Turned Upside Down." The French, followed by Spain and the Netherlands, determined to do everything possible to inhibit the further growth of Britain's colonial empire, had allied themselves with the newly independent United States in 1778. A peace treaty signed in Paris in 1783 recognized the sovereignty of the new state. Though the British lost direct control of their former colonies, they reestablished their transatlantic commercial ties with America in the 1780s. Indeed, the brisk trade in raw cotton between the slave-owning southern states and Britain made possible the industrial revolution in textiles that began in the north of England at this time, and that carried Britain to worldwide preeminence as an economic power in the first half of the nineteenth century. This ultimately profitable arrangement lay in the future. At the time, the victory of the American colonists seemed to contemporary observers to right the world

HOW DID THE BALANCE OF POWER SHIFT IN THE EIGHTEENTH CENTURY?

WAR AND DIPLOMACY IN THE EIGHTEENTH CENTURY   625

Dividing the Royal Spoils. A contemporary cartoon showing the monarchs of Europe at work carving up a hapless Poland.

balance of commercial power, which had swung so far to the side of the British. In this instance, independence seemed designed to restore stability.

THE PARTITIONING OF POLAND

In eastern Europe, however, the very precariousness of Poland's independence posed a threat to stability and to the balance of power. As an independent state, Poland functioned, at least in theory, as a buffer among the major central European powers—Russia, Austria, and Prussia. Poland was the one major central European territory whose landed elite had successfully opposed introduction of absolutist centralization and a consequent curtailment of its "liberties." The result, however, had not been anything like real independence for either the Polish nobility or the country as a whole. Aristocrats were quite prepared to accept bribes from foreign powers in return for their vote in elections for the Polish king. And their continued exercise of their constitutionally guaranteed individual veto

(the *liberum veto*) in the Polish Diet meant that the country remained in a perpetual state of weakness that made it fair game for the land-hungry absolutist potentates who surrounded it.

In 1764 Russia intervened to influence the election of King Stanislaus Poniatowski, an able enough nobleman who had been one of Catherine the Great's lovers. Thereafter Russia continued to meddle in the affairs of Poland—and of Turkey as well—often protecting both countries' Eastern Orthodox Christian minority. When war finally broke out with Turkey in 1769, resulting in large Russian gains in the Balkans, Austria made known its opposition to further Russian expansion, lest it upset the existing balance of power in eastern Europe. In the end Russia was persuaded to acquire territory in Poland instead, by joining Austria and Prussia in a general partition of that country's lands. Though Maria Theresa opposed the dismemberment of Poland, she reluctantly agreed to participate in the partition in order to maintain the balance of power, an attitude that prompted a scornful Frederick the Great to remark, "She weeps, but she takes her share." According to the agreement of 1772, Poland lost about 30 percent of its kingdom and about half of its population.

Following this first partition, the Russians continued to exercise virtual control of Poland. King Stanislaus, however, took advantage of a new Russo-Turkish war in 1788 to press for a more truly independent state with a far stronger executive than had existed previously. A constitution adopted in May 1791 established just that; but this rejuvenated Polish state was to be short lived. In January 1792, the Russo-Turkish war ended, and Catherine the Great pounced. Together the Russians and Prussians took two more enormous bites out of Poland in 1793, destroying the new constitution in the process. A rebellion under the leadership of Thaddeus Kosciuszko, who had fought in America,

CHRONOLOGY	
SEVENTEENTH- AND EIGHTEENTH-CENTURY WARS	
Glorious Revolution	1688–1689
War of the League of Augsburg	1689–1697
War of the Spanish Succession	1702–1713
Seven Years' War	1756–1763
American Revolution	1775–1783
The Russo-Turkish War	1787–1792

was crushed in 1794 and 1795. A final swallow by Russia, Austria, and Prussia in 1795 left nothing of Poland at all. After this series of partitions of Poland, each of the major powers was a good deal fatter; but on the international scales by which such things were measured, they continued to weigh proportionately the same.

The final devouring of Poland occurred at a time when the Continent was once again engaged in a general war. Yet this conflict was not just another military attempt to resolve customary disputes over commerce or problems of international stability. It was the result of violent revolution that had broken out in France in 1789, that had toppled the Bourbon dynasty there, and that threatened to do the same to other monarchs across Europe. The second and third partitions of Poland were a final bravura declaration of power by monarchs who already feared for their heads. Henceforth, neither foreign nor domestic policy would ever again be dictated as they had been in absolutist Europe by the convictions and determinations of kings and queens alone. Poland disappered as Europe fell to pieces, as customary practice gave way to new and desperate necessity.

CONCLUSION

Though absolutism met its death in the years immediately after 1789, the relevance of its history to that of the modern world is greater than it might appear. First, centralization provided useful precedents to nineteenth-century state builders. Modern standing armies —made up of soldiers or bureaucrats—are institutions whose origins rest in the age of absolutism. Second, absolutism's centripetal force contributed to an economic climate that gave birth to industrial revolution. Factories built to produce matériel, capitalist agricultural policies designed to provide food for burgeoning capital cities, increased taxes that drove peasants to seek work in rural industries: these and other programs pointed to the future. Third, in their constant struggle to curb the privileges of nobility and oligarchy, absolute monarchs played out one more act in a drama that would continue into the nineteenth century. French nobles, Prussian junkers, and Russian boyars all bargained successfully to retain their rights to property and its management while surrendering to some degree their role as governors. But as long as their property rights remained secure, their power was assured. The French Revolution would curb their power for a time, but they were survivors. Their adaptability, whether as agricultural entrepreneurs or as senior servants of the state, ensured their order an important place in the world that lay beyond absolutism.

SELECTED READINGS

Beales, Derek. *Joseph II.* New York, 1987. The standard biography of this "enlightened" Austrian despot.

Blanning, T. C. W., ed. *The Eighteenth Century: Europe 1688–1815.* Oxford and New York, 2000. Chapters by leading experts on political, economic, cultural, and religious developments.

Bossuet, Jacques-Benigne. *Politics Drawn from the Very Words of Holy Scripture.* Edited by Patrick Riley. Cambridge and New York, 1998. The standard English translation.

Brewer, John, and Eckhart Hellmuth, eds. *Rethinking Leviathan: The Eighteenth-Century State in Britain and Germany.* Oxford and New York, 1999. An innovative comparative history of state building in Britain and Prussia. All Brewer's works on eighteenth-century Britain are important.

Burke, Peter. *The Fabrication of Louis XIV.* New Haven, 1992. A study of how Louis XIV constructed a public image of himself through architecture.

Campbell, Peter R. *Louis XIV, 1661–1715.* London, 1993. A reliable recent biography; short, with primary source material and a good bibliography.

Colley, Linda. *In Defiance of Oligarchy: The Tory Party, 1714–1760.* Cambridge and New York, 1982. An influential examination of the political ideology of dissent in eighteenth-century Britain.

———. *Britons: Forging the Nation, 1707–1837.* New Haven, 1992. An illuminating study of the construction of a British (as opposed to English) national identity.

Dukes, Paul. *The Making of Russian Absolutism: 1613–1801,* 2d ed. New York, 1990. An authoritative account of the formation of the Russian state.

Finkelstein, Andrea. *Harmony and the Balance: An Intellectual History of Seventeenth-Century English Economic Thought.* Ann Arbor, 2000. A sophisticated study that traces the links between economic thought and the intellectual history of the period.

Grell, Ole Peter, Jonathan I. Israel, and Nicholas Tyacke. *From Persecution to Toleration: The Glorious Revolution and Religion in England.* Oxford and New York, 1991. An excellent collection of essays, reflecting recent research and approaches.

Harris, Ian. *The Mind of John Locke: A Study of Political Theory in its Intellectual Setting,* rev. ed. Cambridge and New York, 1998. A comprehensive, synthetic overview of Locke's thought that argues for a fundamental consistency between his philosophical and his political ideas.

Hobbes, Thomas. *Leviathan.* Edited by Richard Tuck, 2d ed. Cambridge and New York, 1996. The most recent edition, up-to-date and complete.

Hughes, Lindsey. *Russia in the Age of Peter the Great.* New Haven, 1998. An immensely detailed scholarly account by the leading British authority on Peter's reign.

Ingrao, Charles. *The Habsburg Monarchy, 1618–1815,* 2d ed. Cambridge and New York, 2000. A newly revised and updated edition of a standard work; authoritative and accessible.

Kennedy, Paul M. *The Rise and Fall of the Great Powers: Economic Change and Military Conflict from 1500 to 2000.* New York, 1987. A sweeping view of diplomatic and military history, with implications for the American military build-up during the 1980s.

Kenyon, John P. *Revolution Principles: The Politics of Party, 1689–1720.* Cambridge and New York, 1977. A study of the reception of Locke's ideas in the wake of the Glorious Revolution.

Kishlansky, Mark A. *A Monarchy Transformed: Britain, 1603–1714.* London, 1996. The best survey history of the seventeenth-century British Isles, which takes seriously its claims to be a "British" rather than merely an "English" history.

Koch, H. W. *A History of Prussia.* London, 1978. Still the best account of its subject, and especially of the Great Elector.

Ladurie, Emmanuel le Roy. *The Ancien Régime: A History of France, 1610–1774.* Oxford and Cambridge, Mass., 1996. A reliable survey by an eminent French historian.

Locke, John. *Two Treatises of Government,* rev. ed. Edited by Peter Laslett. Cambridge and New York, 1963. Laslett has revolutionized our understanding of the historical and ideological context of Locke's political writings.

Luvaas, Jay, ed. and trans. *Frederick the Great on the Art of War.* New York, 1966. A selection from the Prussian king's voluminous works on war and politics.

The Memoirs of Catherine the Great. Many editions. A fascinating autobiographical account.

Monod, Paul K. *The Power of Kings: Monarchy and Religion in Europe, 1589–1715.* New Haven, 1999. A wide-ranging study of the seventeenth century's declining confidence in the divinity of kings.

Quataert, Donald. *The Ottoman Empire, 1700–1922.* Cambridge and New York, 2000. Well balanced, up-to-date, and intended to be read by students.

Riasanovsky, Nicholas V. *A History of Russia,* 6th ed. Oxford and New York, 1999. Far and away the best single-volume textbook on Russian history: balanced, comprehensive, intelligent, and with full bibliographies.

Saint-Simon, Louis. *Historical Memoirs.* Many editions. The classic source for life at the court of Louis XIV.

Western, J. R. *Monarchy and Revolution: The English State in the 1680s.* London, 1972. Still in many ways the best account of the ideological significance of the Glorious Revolution as a check to the absolutist pretensions of Charles II and James II.

CHAPTER EIGHTEEN

THE SCIENTIFIC
REVOLUTION

BETWEEN THE EARLY 1500s and the late 1600s, new ideas about the physical world brought sweeping changes to European philosophy and, more broadly, to Europeans' view of their place in the world. What we call the "scientific revolution" entailed three changes: the emergence and confirmation of a heliocentric view of the universe, the development of a new physics that fit such a view, and the establishment of a method of enquiry. Thinkers associated with the new "natural philosophy," as science was called at the time, explained how the earth could, in defiance of common sense, be hurtling around the sun. In so doing, they also vindicated the role of reason, experiment, and observation in understanding the natural world. They established "science" as a new form of knowledge.

Eighteenth-century philosophers later hailed men such as Galileo and Newton as heroes. They championed science as humanity's greatest triumph to date. They sought to broaden the application of these new scientific methods from the physical to the "moral" or "human" sciences. These "enlightened" thinkers—for so they declared themselves to be—believed that the scientific revolution had opened a new age in which reason would become the tool by which to reform government, re-order society, purify (or in some cases, abolish) religion, and bring an end to superstition, credulity, and "irrational" custom.

The story of the scientific revolution is less heroic than its "enlightened" champions acknowledged. It was not an organized effort. Brilliant theories sometimes led to dead ends; discoveries were often accidental. Artisans grinding lenses for telescopes played as much of a role as great abstract thinkers. Most important, old and new world views often overlapped. "Science" did not necessarily undermine either religion or magic, and it did not supplant "superstition." Individual thinkers struggled to reconcile their discoveries with their faith or to make their theories (about the earth's movements, for instance) fit their everyday experiences. For all of these reasons, changes came slowly and fitfully. The new world view was, nonetheless, revolutionary, and had ramifications well beyond the small circles of scientists, theologians, and philosophers with whom it began.

FOCUS QUESTIONS

• What were the intellectual roots of the scientific revolution?

• How did the Catholic Church affect scientific thinking?

 • What were the philosphical differences between Bacon and Descartes?

• What did it mean to be a mechanist in the seventeenth century?

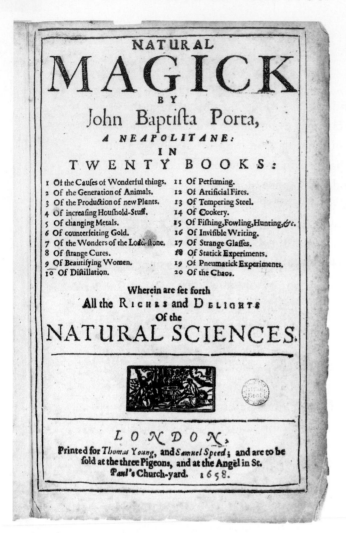

Della Porta's "*Natural Magick.*" This book, from Sir Isaac Newton's own library, testifies to the great scientist's interest in alchemy and to the links between "magik" and natural science.

THE INTELLECTUAL ROOTS OF THE SCIENTIFIC REVOLUTION

What were the intellectual roots of the scientific revolution?

Keen interest in the workings of the natural world was not new to sixteenth-century Europe. As we have seen, European artistic life had been characterized from the twelfth century on by its commitment to naturalism. Medieval sculptors carved plants and vines with such

remarkable accuracy that modern botanists can easily identify the species of the plants they represented. Medieval sculptors and painters poured their energies into accurately depicting the human face and form. Italian Renaissance painters took these techniques to new heights with their rediscovery of the principles of linear perspective. Like other intellectuals of the period, Renaissance painters were also fascinated by light. The nature of light had been a fundamental intellectual preoccupation for architects and theologians since the twelfth century. During the fourteenth century, however, some thinkers had broadened their studies of light and begun to explore the science of optics—inventing, along the way, the first reading glasses. Astrologers too were active in the fourteenth and fifteenth centuries, charting the heavens in the firm belief that the stars controlled the fates of human beings.

Behind this high medieval fascination with nature and the natural world lay a combination of Christian Neoplatonism and Aristotelianism. Thomas Aquinas, in particular, had argued that God had structured the natural world in such a way that enquiring humans, rationally investigating nature, would be led to almost all the theological truths of Christianity, without any necessary recourse to faith. Faith offered a more certain and complete road to God, but human reason was a divinely instilled attribute, and it could spur mankind toward salvation. Such ideas encouraged rational argument and investigation. At the same time, however, they subordinated natural observation to theological truths. Should the observation of nature conflict with the truths of theology, theology must necessarily triumph.

By the fourteenth century, however, confidence in the compatibility of faith and reason was collapsing. Although many intellectuals continued to argue, as Aquinas had, that the natural world was a book in which human reason could read the mind of God, so-called nominalist theologians and philosophers had begun to argue that nature did not necessarily fit the stable and certain picture drawn by the Aristotelians. (See discussion on page 411 in Chapter 11.) Nature, the nominalists asserted, was radically distinct from God the Creator. Humans could only understand God's truths through revelation and faith. They might rationally investigate nature and record its regularities. But the laws of nature did not necessarily reveal anything about the nature of God. The nominalist challenge, thus, freed the investigation of the natural world from the constraints of theology and opened the way for the emergence of the mechanistic, materialistic world view we associate with modern science.

What did the scientific revolution of the sixteenth and seventeenth centuries owe to the Renaissance humanists? The educational program of the humanists placed a low value on science because it seemed irrelevant to their aim of making people more eloquent and moral. For such humanists as Petrarch, Leonardo Bruni, or Erasmus, science was part and parcel of the "vain speculation" of the Scholastics (most of whom were nominalists), which they attacked and held up to ridicule. Accordingly, none of the great scientists of the Renaissance period belonged to the humanist movement. The scientific revolution was largely the product of a melding of the Scholastic tradition, epitomized by nominalism, and the developing study of mathematics.

Nonetheless, Renaissance humanists contributed to the developing interest in science. Perhaps the most important influence came from Neoplatonism, which led these humanists to seek out the ideal and perfect structures that, they believed, must lie behind the "shadows" of the everyday world. The Neoplatonists proposed ideas, such as the central position of the sun and the supposed divinity of certain geometrical shapes, that would help lead to crucial scientific breakthroughs. Copernicus and Kepler, for example, were both deeply influenced by Neoplatonism.

Humanism also played some role in the growing fascination with the intricate mechanisms at work in the universe. Renaissance mechanism owed its greatest impetus to the publication in 1543 of the works of the great Greek mathematician and physicist Archimedes. His concrete observations and discoveries were among the most accurate and reliable in the entire body of Greek science. Archimedes taught that the universe operates on the basis of mechanical forces, like a great machine; because this world view conflicted so directly with the search for ideal structures that the Neoplatonists pursued, it took some time for the mechanists' proposals to gain wide acceptance. Nevertheless, mechanism won some very important late Renaissance adherents, including the Italian scientist Galileo. Ultimately mechanism played an enormous role in the development of modern science because it insisted on finding observable and measurable causes and effects in the world of nature.

One other Renaissance development that contributed to the rise of modern science was the developing amalgamation between the worlds of the artisan and the intellectual. During the High Middle Ages, trained clerics theorized about the natural world, but rarely did they think of tinkering with machines—much less of dissecting corpses! On the other hand, numerous technicians who had little formal education had developed much practical expertise in various aspects of mechanical engineering. During the fifteenth century, these two worlds began to come together. One reason for this was that some highly respected Renaissance artists such as Leonardo da Vinci bridged both areas of endeavor. Not only were they marvelous craftsmen, but they also investigated the laws of perspective and optics, worked out geometric methods for supporting the weight of enormous architectural domes, studied the dimensions and details of the human body, and devised new and more effective weapons for war. Another reason was the growing interest in alchemy and astrology among the leisured classes. This vogue led some wealthy amateurs to start building laboratories and measuring the courses of the stars, assisted by telescopes made possible by the combined work of intellectuals and artisans in grinding lenses. With these developments, the modern science of astronomy was born.

One Renaissance development that contributed to the rise of modern science was the developing amalgamation between the worlds of the artisan and the intellectual.

CHRONOLOGY

ORIGINS OF THE SCIENTIFIC REVOLUTION, ELEVENTH–FIFTEENTH CENTURIES

Rediscovery of classical Greek texts	Twelfth–Fifteenth centuries
Naturalism becomes the dominant artistic aesthetic	Twelfth Century
Science of optics	Fourteenth century
Astrologers chart the heavens	Fourteenth and Fifteenth centuries
Nationalism challenges Aristotelianism	Fourteenth and Fifteenth centuries
Neoplatonism influences Copernicus and Kepler	Fourteenth–Fifteenth centuries
Growing expertise in mechanical engineering among artisans	Fourteenth and Fifteenth centuries

A REVOLUTION IN ASTRONOMY

> How did the Catholic Church affect scientific thinking?

For more than three thousand years, from the age of the pharaohs until the 1500s, people believed that the sun, the stars, and the planets moved around the earth. In the Middle Ages, this idea fitted with explanations offered by ancient authorities; with conceptions of the purposefulness of God's universe; with complex explanations of matter and physics (which showed that each fundamental element of the universe had its place, with the heaviest fundamental elements, water and earth, forming around the center); and with the common-sense observations of philosophers and peasants alike, who could watch the sun and the stars move from one horizon to the other each day and night.

To the astronomers of the Middle Ages, the most important classical authorities on natural philosophy were Aristotle and Ptolemy. Both had created frameworks that explained the whole universe, explanations rooted in notions of cosmic order that could be made to fit Europeans' deeper concerns about sin, transformation, and perfection. Aristotle had offered a complete explanation of the natural world, a vision grounded in the apparent orderliness of the cosmos. He suggested that each being or substance sought to reach its "natural place." On earth, the four fundamental elements were constantly mingled together, forever trying to sort themselves out into those natural places. This ever-changing earth sat at the center of the universe, separated from the unchanging heavens that moved in perfect, regular circles. Aristotelian physics had its critics, but most of them sought to correct minor errors of logic and to improve on its basic principles, not to dismantle them.

People had long observed problems with the perfect circles that heavenly objects were supposed to describe. The planets, Mars in particular, sometimes seemed to stop and loop backward before continuing on their paths again. The Greek mathematician Ptolemy had produced the most sophisticated mathematical formulas to account for these and other orbital irregularities. By the late Middle Ages, however, European astronomers were beginning to have doubts about Ptolemy's complicated formulas. During the late

CHRONOLOGY

THE SCIENTIFIC REVOLUTION, 1543–1637

Publication of Copernicus's *On the Revolutions of the Heavenly Spheres*	1543
Brahe sets up Uranienborg laboratory	1576
Kepler sets out his laws in Rudolphine tables	1609
Galileo publishes *The Starry Messenger*	1610
Galileo publishes *A Dialogue between the Two Great World Systems*	1632
Bacon publishes *Novum Organum*	1620
Descartes publishes *Discourse on Method*	1637
Newton publishes *Principia Mathematica*	1687

1400s several European astronomers, notably the German Johannes Müller (1436–1476), gained access to Ptolemy's texts in their original Greek. They discovered that the great astronomer's work had not been corrupted by translators, but was in fact marred by omissions and faulty mathematics.

THE COPERNICAN REVOLUTION

The problems with Ptolemy's system were particularly serious because of a developing crisis over the European calendar, which was based on it. By the early sixteenth century the old Roman calendar was significantly out of alignment with the movement of the heavenly bodies. The major saints' days, Easter, and the other holy days were more than a week off where they should have been according to the stars. Catholic authorities spent nearly a century trying to correct this fundamental problem, summoning mathematicians and astronomers from all over Europe to put their minds to this dilemma. One of these researchers was the Polish clergyman and university astronomer Nicholas Copernicus (1473–1543). Copernicus was a careful mathematician and a faithful Christian; he could not believe that God would create a universe as ramshackle and messy as Ptolemy's, with its mathematical trickery and circles within circles. His solution was as simple as it was radical. He concluded that the sun was not one of the planets orbiting a fixed earth, as Ptolemy had argued. Instead, the earth itself moved through the heavens, in the sun's old position at the third orbit out from the center. If the positions of the earth and the sun were switched, the mathematics of astronomy became simpler, the orbits of the other planets made more sense, and the calendar could be put right.

Copernicus was in many ways an extremely conservative thinker. He did not see his work as a break either with the church or the ancient authorities. He believed he had restored a pure understanding of God's design, one that had been lost over the centuries, and he cited Greek astronomers even more ancient than Ptolemy to support his claim. What he wanted was a simple explanation of heavenly perfection that did away with the clumsiness of Ptolemy's mathematical calculations. Yet the implications of the theory troubled him. His ideas contradicted many biblical passages that described a fixed earth and moving heavens, and discarded centuries of assumed astronomical knowledge. Practical problems also presented themselves. Copernicus was not a physicist. He made no observations of real objects. If the earth was moving around the sun, it had to be going at a terrifying speed. Copernicus had no way to reconcile his suggestion that the earth careened through the heavens with the fact that objects on earth fell to the ground or moved "normally." As he worked on the problem his astronomy became more cumbersome: he continued to assume that orbits were perfect circles, and he fell back on some of Ptolemy's devices to explain errors in those patterns.

These frustrations and complications dogged Copernicus through his later years. He hesitated to publish his findings until just before his death, when he consented to the release of his work *On the Revolutions of the Heavenly Spheres* (*De Revolutionibus*) in 1543. In the book Copernicus insisted that his model was physically real. To fend off scandal, his Lutheran publisher added an introduction to the book that declared that Copernicus's system was just an abstraction, another set of mathematical tools for doing astronomy—not a dangerous claim about the nature of heaven and earth. Assisted by his publisher's disclaimer, Copernicus's ideas remained politically harmless and obscure for decades, while other, less radical thinkers busied themselves with cleaning up the calendar.

TYCHO'S SYSTEM AND KEPLER'S LAWS

Copernicus's ideas were revived through the work of two astronomers who also sought a perfect explanation of the universe, but did so by observing the sky itself. Tycho Brahe (1546–1601) and Johannes Kepler (1571–1630) were each considered the greatest as-

tronomers of their day. Tycho was a high-ranking Danish nobleman, a gifted rogue endowed with lands and wealth by his king but trained in his youth as an astronomer. He first made a name for himself by observing a completely new star, which Aristotle had claimed was impossible. Tycho then set out to correct other flaws in ancient astronomy by observing the movement of the whole heavens. Before the invention of telescopes, he turned a small island that formed part of his estates into a giant laboratory, specially designed for observation. For over twenty years he spent each night carefully mapping out the motion of each significant object in the night sky, accurate to within the tiniest fraction of a degree. Before he drank himself to death, Tycho had collected the finest set of astronomical data ever seen in Europe.

Tycho did not accept Copernicus's conclusion that the earth moved around the sun. Instead he created a model in which the planets orbited the sun, and the whole system then orbited the (stationary) earth. The "Tychonic" system proved enormously successful. It allowed accurate astronomical and astrological predictions to be made more easily than in the old Ptolemaic system, and it avoided the upsetting theological implications of the Copernican system.

In his old age, Tycho moved his work and his huge tables of data to Prague, where he became court astronomer to the Holy Roman Emperor. One of Tycho's assistants in Prague, a sober young mathematician from a troubled family, was much more impressed with Copernicus's ideas than Tycho had been. That assistant, Johannes Kepler, combined Copernicus's system with his own interest in mysticism, astrology, and the religious power of mathematics. Kepler's work offered the first credible physical explanation of a moving earth and the astronomy that went with it.

Kepler believed that everything in creation, from human souls to the orbits of the planets, had been created according to mathematical laws. Understanding those laws would thus allow human beings to share God's wisdom and the inner secrets of the universe. Kepler's search for this pattern of mathematical perfection took him through musical harmonies, "nested" geometric shapes inside the planets' orbits, and numerical formulas. The driving power of Kepler's spiritual goals was matched, however, by his respect for empirical data. Relying on Tycho's astronomical tables, Kepler was able to recognize that two of Copernicus's assumptions about planetary motion simply did not fit with the observable facts. Specifically, Kepler replaced Copernicus's view that

Natural Harmonies. This illustration from Robert Fludd's *History of the Macrocosm and the Microcosm* (1617) maps the solar system as a musical octave and parallels Kepler's use of both mathematics and mysticism.

NEW HEAVENS, NEW EARTH, AND WORLDLY POLITICS: GALILEO GALILEI (1564–1642)

Galileo transformed Copernicanism from a theory about astronomy into a larger debate about the role of natural philosophy in revealing the true nature of the world. He offered evidence that the earth moved, discovered a variety of new celestial bodies, and was able to form some idea of the enormous distances between the stars. But he also made a case for a new relationship between religion and science, a proposal that challenged some of the most powerful churchmen of his day. His firm belief in his new ideas and his penchant for controversy made him the best-known natural philosopher of his day, but ultimately brought him into conflict with the authority of the Catholic Church.

By the early 1600s, Galileo was already a successful mathematician at the prestigious university at Padua, in northern Italy. He had begun work on one of his life's great scientific passions, the problem of motion, particularly the motion of objects on a moving earth. Galileo found Aristotle's explanation of motion inadequate. In its place, he developed the first rough theory of inertia, which suggested that only a change in motion required a cause; otherwise, objects either stayed in motion or remained at rest. He also began work on theories about moving objects, using a combination of small, practical experiments and ideal cases drawn up with mathematics. This work ultimately delivered the first well-defined formulas that accounted for the normal motion of objects on a moving earth.

Galileo did not make his name by mathematical skill, however. Fame and scientific opportunity came his way through his innovative use of the telescope, and through his skill as a participant in Italy's networks of courtly patronage. In 1610, after hearing of the newly invented telescope from a Flemish friend, Galileo procured one, and rather than training it on earthly sights he pointed it at the night sky. The results changed his career. He observed sunspots, which he sketched and documented as real irregularities on the surface of the sun. Likewise, he showed the craters of the moon to be features of its landscape, not shadows. Jupiter yielded the greatest prize: evidence of orbiting moons around the great planet, providing solid proof that the earth was not the only body with

planetary orbits were circular with his own "First Law" that the earth and the other planets travel in elliptical paths around the sun. He also replaced Copernicus's belief in uniform planetary velocity with his own "Second Law" that the speed of planets varies with their distance from the sun. Further, he argued that magnetic attractions between the sun and the planets keep the planets in orbital motion. That approach was rejected by most seventeenth-century mechanistic scientists as being far too magical, but in fact it paved the way for the law of universal gravitation formulated by Isaac Newton at the end of the seventeenth century.

> Galileo transformed Copernicanism from a theory about astronomy into a larger debate about the role of natural philosophy in revealing the true nature of the world.

objects in orbit around it. Galileo published these astonishing results in his book *The Starry Messenger* (1610). This book gained him entry into Italy's centers of power and patronage. By naming Jupiter's moons the "Medicean stars," and through his great skill in debating such controversial subjects, he gained the favor of the Medici rulers of Florence. With a court appointment and Medici support, Galileo was able to pursue his work on astronomy and his conviction that Copernicus's heliocentric (sun-centered) model of the universe was correct.

Before long, both of Galileo's goals—promoting Copernicanism and challenging Aristotelianism—brought him into conflict with powerful opponents. The great Jesuit astronomers of the day argued that Galileo's telescopic discoveries fitted perfectly well with Tycho's system, and so did not require that the earth be displaced from its position at the center of the universe. The most important of these critics was Cardinal Robert Bellarmine (1542–1621). Perhaps the most influential Jesuit of his day, Bellarmine was a skilled mathematician who had helped repair the calendar when he was a young man. In the decades since then, he had become the Catholic Church's champion in theological debates with Protestant critics. Copernicus's ideas were already under critical church scrutiny. Bellarmine himself argued that Copernicanism was wrong in practice, for all the reasons that had worried Copernicus himself. Other churchmen went further, however, seeing in Copernicanism a direct threat to church doctrine. Bellarmine was asked to caution Galileo about pursuing those ideas too far. Galileo had been expecting such a warning, and responded at once. In his *Letter to the Grand Duchess Christina di Medici* (1615), Galileo launched his first and most famous reply to his critics, and his clearest defense of a Copernican science.

Galileo was a sincere Catholic and a sincere Copernican. He believed that if the church refused to acknowledge the "new science" and its explanation of the natural world, the authority of the church would suffer. What Galileo wanted was a new and more equal partnership between natural philosophy and the church in finding and proving truth. The Church's senior clergy did the vital work of saving souls, but that did not mean that the church, or the university philosophers in whom it had placed too much trust, had any power to explain the physical world. The natural philosopher, who created solid mathematical explanations of the visible world, was much better qualified to offer those explanations. Any conflict between what natural philosophers revealed and a literal interpretation of the Bible was a false problem. The Bible was a notoriously difficult book, and the church's theologians, Galileo argued, would be able to reconcile the complex language of the Bible with the new conclusions of natural philosophy. Natural philosophers and theologians were therefore partners in a search for truth, but they had very different roles to play. Galileo quoted one of Bellarmine's fellow cardinals against him: the church's role was to "tell us how to go to Heaven, and not how heaven goes."

Galileo made his argument with great skill and flattery. He impressed his Medici patrons and kept the sympathy of important figures in the church, particularly the Medicis' ally Cardinal Maffeo Barberini, who was not only Galileo's patron but a close friend as well. Bellarmine, however, had been equally careful in his own arguments; he also knew that Galileo's political connections would prove fragile if they were pushed. Bellarmine also had precedent on his side. In response to the Reformation, the church had given senior clergy the right of final appeal in matters of theology. Galileo's protests notwithstanding, the church believed his work challenged its authority. In 1616, Copernicus's work was included in the Index of Prohibited Books. Galileo's friends and critics alike now suggested that he leave Copernican ideas alone and put limits on his great ambitions.

For nearly a decade after the debate with Bellarmine, Galileo did as he was asked, continuing his work while keeping his opinions to himself. During the 1620s, however, the political and philosophical climates seemed to be changing. Several of Galileo's most formidable critics, including Bellarmine, died, and Galileo's old friend Barberini became Pope Urban VIII. Seizing his chance, Galileo drafted a "dialogue," a debate between supporters of the old and new sciences. He took great care in publishing the new work. He showed this Copernican tract—for that was just what it was—to the church authorities, who edited for content, suggested the bland title *A Dialogue Between the Two Great World Systems*, and allowed its publication in 1632. In the book, Galileo's opponents won the mock debate, but along the way Galileo made a thorough case for Copernicanism, with great detail and biting wit. The book was an international success, but it created a scandal within Italy's networks of sacred and worldly patronage. Galileo was charged with two dangerous attacks on the authority of the church. The first was promoting Copernicanism. The second was that he had insulted his old patron Barberini by setting him up as the character Simplicio (the "simple-minded one"), who argues the case against

GALILEO ON NATURE, SCRIPTURE, AND TRUTH

One of the clearest statements of Galileo's convictions about religion and science comes from his 1615 letter to the Grand Duchess Christina. The grand duchess was the mother of Galileo's patron, Cosimo de Medici, and a powerful figure in her own right. Galileo knew that others had raised objections to his work. He had been warned that Copernicanism was not just inaccurate but impious: it could be disproved scientifically and it contradicted the authority of those who interpreted the Bible. Thoroughly dependent on the Medicis for support, he wrote to the grand duchess to explain his position.

In this section of the letter, Galileo reflects on the problems of interpreting both the Bible and nature. He sets out his understanding of the parallel but distinct roles of the Church and natural philosophers. He walks a fine line between acknowledging the authority of the Church and standing firm in his convictions.

They know that . . . I hold the sun to be situated motionless in the center of the revolution of the celestial orbs while the earth rotates on its axis and revolves about the sun. They know also that I support this position not only by refuting the arguments of Ptolemy and Aristotle, but by producing many counterarguments; in particular, some which relate to physical effects whose causes can perhaps be assigned in no other way. In addition there are astronomical arguments derived from many things in my new celestial discoveries that plainly confute the Ptolemaic system while admirably agreeing with and confirming the contrary hypothesis. Possibly because they are disturbed by the known truth of other propositions of mine which differ from those commonly held, and therefore mistrusting their defense so long as they confine themselves to the field of philosophy, these men have resolved to fabricate a shield for their fallacies out of the mantle of pretended religion and the authority of the Bible. . . .

Copernicus never discusses matters of religion or faith, nor does he use arguments that depend in any way upon the authority of sacred writings which he might have interpreted erroneously. He stands always upon physical conclusions pertaining to the celestial motions, and deals with them by astronomical and geometrical demonstrations, founded primarily upon sense experiences and very exact observations. He did not ignore the Bible, but he knew very well that if his doctrine were proved, then it could not contradict the Scriptures when they were rightly understood. . . .

I think that in discussions of physical problems we ought to begin not from the authority of scriptural passages, but from sense-experiences and necessary demonstrations; for the holy Bible and the phenomena of nature proceed alike from the divine Word, the former as the dictate of the Holy Ghost and the latter as the observant executrix of God's commands. It is necessary for the Bible, in order to be accommodated to the understanding of every man, to speak many things which appear to differ from the absolute truth so far as the bare meaning of the words is concerned. But Nature, on the other hand, is inexorable and immutable; she never transgresses the laws imposed upon her, or cares a whit whether her abstruse reasons and methods of operation are understandable to men. For that reason it appears that nothing physical which sense-experience sets before our eyes, or which necessary demonstrations prove to us, ought to be called in questions (much less condemned) upon the testimony of biblical passages which may have some different meaning beneath their words. For the Bible is not chained in every expression to conditions as strict as those which govern all physical effects; nor is God any less excellently revealed in Nature's actions than in the sacred statements of the Bible. . . .

Galileo, "Letter to the Grand Duchess Christina," in Stillman Drake, ed., *The Discoveries and Opinions of Galileo Galilei*, (Garden City, N.Y.: Doubleday, 1957), pp. 177–183.

Copernicanism in the *Dialogue*. Barberini was offended by Galileo's portrait; he also needed the support of church conservatives during a difficult stretch of the Thirty Years' War. His anger at Galileo's disregard for political judgment broke their relationship. Galileo was cast to his critics and charged with heresy.

The trial that followed was news across Europe. Galileo was the most famous natural philosopher of his day, the pride of one of the great intellectual centers of the continent. The church's legal arm, the Inquisition in Rome, backed its weak case against the philosopher with threats of death and excommunication. The elderly Galileo bent rather than let himself be broken. He recanted his belief in Copernicus' ideas; he was banned from working on or even discussing those ideas, and placed under house arrest for life. Yet he was not put off his life's work so easily, and continued to refine his ideas about the problems of motion. His physics for a moving earth, compiled under the title *The Two New Sciences* (1638), was smuggled out of Italy and published in Protestant Holland.

Galileo left two great legacies. He combined abstract mathematics and practical experiments to produce a new physics, one that explained how objects behaved "normally" on a moving earth. Galileo's second legacy, however, was exactly the disaster he had hoped to avoid. Galileo spent thirty years striving after a Copernican science that worked, and he hoped that Copernicanism could coexist peacefully with the religious wisdom of the Catholic Church. His trial made such coexistence impossible. The trial silenced Copernican voices in southern Europe, and the church's leadership retreated into conservative reaction. It was therefore in northwest Europe that the "new philosophy" Galileo had fought for would ultimately flourish.

METHODS FOR A NEW PHILOSOPHY: BACON AND DESCARTES

What were the philosophical differences between Bacon and Descartes?

By the early 1600s the increasingly "Copernican" sciences of mathematics and astronomy were changing quickly. At first those changes were haphazard and very loosely related. The achievements and methods of such men as Kepler and Galileo were held together only by the common problem of understanding a moving earth. What was lacking was a common set of organizing principles, and a fresh, unified set of goals for natural philosophy. As the practice of those new sciences became concentrated in Protestant northwestern Europe, several important thinkers began to produce not only new discoveries, but new philosophies of philosophy. This rethinking of natural philosophy from the ground up spelled out standards of practice, new ideas about what proved a theory correct, fresh judgments about what answers to questions about the natural world were most complete and satisfying, and what methods served best to reach those answers.

BACON AND DESCARTES

The new methods were refined by two men in particular: the Englishman Sir Francis Bacon and the Frenchman René Descartes. Both men believed they lived in a new age of profound change and great opportunities for discovery. Both also believed that the old bedrock of natural philosophy, the ideas of Aristotle, no longer met the needs of the times, and that a fresh approach would take European "moderns" well beyond the knowledge of the ancients. The methods they created were very different, but between them they shaped the practice of natural philosophy in the later seventeenth century and left a deep mark on the evolution of modern science.

Sir Francis Bacon (1561–1626), a leading judge who became lord chancellor of England, was an extremely influential theorist of the new philosophy. Bacon's view, best expressed in his *Novum Organum (New Instrument)* of 1620, was that natural science could not advance unless it cast off the inherited errors of the past. The knowledge of ancient authorities was no longer the best guide to truth; or, at least, too much reverence for accepted doctrines put up roadblocks to discovery and full understanding. The worth of knowledge could only be proven through "progressive stages of certainty," or what philosophers would term an empirical approach. For Bacon this meant coming directly to grips with nature and its mysteries, gaining knowledge through the senses, piece by piece. Using the "inductive method," philosophers would arrive at truth by combining evidence from a huge number of particular observations to draw general conclusions. What Bacon wanted was "useful knowledge," practical forms of understanding grounded in the detailed study of each part of the natural world. He further argued

Bacon's contemporary, the French philosopher René Descartes (1596–1650), agreed with him on two points. The first was that all past knowledge should be discarded. The second was that the value of ideas depended on their usefulness. Yet Descartes offered a completely different method for reaching useful knowledge. Unlike Bacon, Descartes was a rationalist and a champion of pure logic and mathematics. In his *Discourse on Method* (1637), Descartes explained how, during a period of solitude, he submitted all knowledge and ideas to a process of systematic doubt. His first rule was "never to receive anything as a truth which [he] did not clearly know to be such," and he found himself doubting everything until he accepted that the process of thought proved his own existence. Reckoning back from this famous position—*cogito ergo sum* ("I think, therefore I am")—Descartes made rationality the point of departure for his entire philosophical enterprise. By doing so he rebuilt the universe through pure speculation. Speculation, he asserted, met the highest standards of reason as expressed in the laws of mathematics.

Descartes' deductive approach, reasoning out from a set of first principles, was enormously influential for several reasons. By organizing his logic on mathematical lines, he contributed greatly to the authority of mathematics as a tool for natural philosophers. Descartes'

Title Page of Bacon's *Novum Organum*. The ship going out to sea represents the search for knowledge. The quotation below reads: "Many shall venture forth and science shall be increased."

that such knowledge was best gained through cooperation between researchers, using carefully recorded experiments. The useful knowledge that came out of such work would produce rewards for philosophers and artisans alike, in every field from astronomy to shipbuilding. It would refine skills and technology, ultimately giving humanity command over nature. Bacon's ideology is evoked vividly by two images. One is his description of "Solomon's House," a utopian factory of discovery that would turn out useful knowledge, first tested in experiments by "sifters," then compiled and understood at the highest levels. The other is the cover illustration of his *Novum Organum*, with its bold ships sailing out beyond the Straits of Gibraltar into the open sea, in pursuit of unknown but great things to come.

René Descartes.

TWO REACTIONS TO THE "NEW PHILOSOPHY"

In his poem, "An Anatomie of the World" (1609), the English poet John Donne (1572–1631) summed up the sense of loss and confusion created by new work in natural philsophy. "The element of fire" refers to Aristotle's physics. The second selection below is an excerpt from Francis Bacon's Novum Organum *(1620), a "new" Organon. The Organon was Aristotle's treatise on the elements of philosophy, one of the basic texts of a university education. Bacon's work constituted a bold summing up of the new learning and its implications. Bacon, like Donne, was English; his world view, however, is very different, and he tries to spell out the real possibilities of human knowledge. Educated English people would have had both books on their shelf.*

AN ANATOMIE OF THE WORLD

And new Philosophy calls all in doubt,
The element of fire is quite put out;
   The sun is lost, and th' earth,
And no man's wit
Can well direct him where to look for it.
'Tis all in pieces, all coherence gone,
Prince, subject,
Father, son,
All just supply,
And all relation. . . .

APHORISMS FROM *NOVUM ORGANUM*

XXXI

It is idle to expect any great advancement in science from the superinducing and engrafting of new things upon old. We must begin anew from the very foundations, unless we would revolve forever in a circle with mean and contemptible progress. . . .

XXXVI

One method of delivery alone remains to us which is simply this: we must lead men to the particulars themselves, and their series and order; while men on their side must force themselves for a while to lay their notions by and begin to familiarize themselves with facts. . . .

XLV

The human understanding is of its own nature prone to suppose the existence of more older and regularity in the world than it finds. And though there be many things in nature which are singular and unmatched, yet it devises for them parallels and conjugates and relatives which do not exist. Hence the fiction that all celestial bodies move in perfect circles. . . . Hence too the element of fire with its orb is brought in, to make up the square with the other three which the sense perceives. . . . And so on of other dreams. And these fancies affect not dogmas only, but simple notions also. . . .

Those who have handled sciences have been either men of experiment or men of dogmas. The men of experiment are like the ant, they only collect and use; the reasoners resemble spiders, who make cobwebs out of their own substance. But the bee takes a middle course: it gathers its material from the flowers of the garden and of the field, but transforms and digests it by a power of its own. Not unlike this is the true business of philosophy; for it neither relies solely or chiefly on the powers of the mind, nor does it take the matter which it gathers from natural history and mechanical experiments and lay it up in the memory whole . . . but lays it up in the understanding altered and digested. Therefore, form a closer and purer league between these two faculties, the experimental and the rational (such as has never yet been made), much may be hoped. . . .

Matthews, Michael R., ed. *The Scientific Background to Modern Philosophy: Selected Readings.* (Indianapolis/Cambridge: Hackett Publishing Company, 1989), pp. 47–48, 50–52.

work also provided a logical underpinning for a purely "mechanistic" view of the natural world. This mechanistic approach to nature was a much broader current in seventeenth-century thought. Mechanists argued that all matter, all of creation, except humans, existed solely in terms of physical laws. Each rock, plant, and living animal, was a self-operating machine propelled by a force that followed from the original motion given to the universe by God. Descartes, like many other mechanists, thought that humans themselves were machines—although, in this single exception, machines equipped with reasoning minds. Through a combination of Descartes' logical, deductive approach and mechanistic philosophy, the study of the natural world could be dispassionate as never before. If the universe were only matter in motion, the whole system could be understood objectively, leaving aside questions of meaning and purpose to concentrate on simple mechanisms and their causes. All the subjective attributes of matter, such as light, color, sound, taste, or smell, had no "extension." This meant they were only surface impressions and could be ignored. Mechanists studied the pure, rational qualities of size, speed, and direction—a universe full of machines constantly running into each other in an orderly fashion—and pondered the underlying mechanisms that made this great clockwork run.

CHRONOLOGY

THE EXPERIMENTERS OF THE SCIENTIFIC REVOLUTION

Nicholas Copernicus	1473–1543
Tycho Brahe	1546–1601
Francis Bacon	1561–1626
Galileo Galilei	1564–1642
Johannes Kepler	1571–1630
William Harvey	1578–1657
René Descartes	1596–1650
Blaise Pascal	1623–1662
Robert Boyle	1627–1691
Christian Huygens	1629–1695
Baruch Spinoza	1632–1677
Robert Hooke	1635–1703
Isaac Newton	1642–1727

THE POWER OF METHOD AND THE FORCE OF CURIOSITY: SEVENTEENTH-CENTURY EXPERIMENTERS

What did it mean to be a mechanist in the seventeenth century?

For nearly a century after Bacon and Descartes, the work of England's natural philosophers was mostly Baconian, while their colleagues in France and northern Europe were mostly Cartesian (the name given to followers of Descartes). Both groups shared a strong preference for a mechanistic view of the world, but their methods differed greatly. The English followers of Bacon concentrated on performing experiments in many different fields, which offered concrete but hotly debated results. The Cartesians turned instead toward

WHAT DID IT MEAN TO BE A MECHANIST IN THE SEVENTEENTH CENTURY?

THE POWER OF METHOD AND THE FORCE OF CURIOSITY   641

mathematics and philosophical theory. This preference for the abstract did not mean that their work had no practical applications. Several Cartesians such as the Dutchman Christian Huygens (1629–1695) combined their mathematical proofs with experiments to understand problems of orbital motion. Descartes himself pioneered analytical geometry. Blaise Pascal (1623–1662) worked on probability theory and invented a calculating machine before applying his mathematical skills to theology. Another Dutch Cartesian, the Jewish philosopher Baruch Spinoza (1632–1677), applied geometry to ethics and believed he had gone beyond Descartes by proving that the universe was composed of a single substance that was both God and nature.

While the Cartesians contributed to the objectivity of natural philosophy through deductive reasoning, English experimenters pursued the same goal by very different means. They began with practical research, putting the alchemist's tool, the laboratory, to new uses. They also sought a different kind of conclusion to their research: empirical laws, which were general conclusions based on the evidence rather than absolute statements about how the universe worked. Among the many English laboratory scientists of the era were the physician William Harvey (1578–1657), the chemist Robert Boyle (1627–1691), and the biologist Robert Hooke (1635–1703). Harvey's research continued the work of Vesalius but, unlike his predecessor, Harvey was willing to dissect living animals and was able to observe and describe the circulation of blood through the arteries and back to the heart through the veins. Boyle designed and used an air pump to establish "Boyle's law," showing that, under constant temperature, the volume of a gas decreases in proportion to the pressure placed on it. This was a classic example of an empirical law in practice. Robert Hooke was as much a physicist as a student of biology, although he is best known today for using the microscope to discover the cellular structure of plants.

Boyle and Hooke shared a long working relationship and harbored great ambitions for the power of experiments. In 1660, when England's monarchy was restored after years of civil war and religious division, the two men helped establish a formal society of natural philosophers. The group caught the eye of the newly crowned King Charles II, who voiced his approval and granted the dignified name of the Royal Society. Its founders, Boyle in particular, believed the Royal Society could play a vital role in the much larger task of restoring order and consensus to English soci-

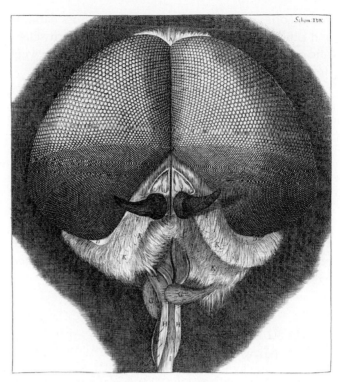

Robert Hooke's *Micrographia*. Hooke's diagram of a fly's eye as seen through a microscope seemed to reveal just the sort of intricate universe the mechanists predicted.

ety. Boyle in particular hoped the society would combine Bacon's goal of collective research and discovery with the task of offering scientific support for the restoration of royal power and the authority of the Church of England. Members of the society would conduct formal experiments, record the results, and exchange them with other researchers, who could study, reproduce, and criticize the outcome. This would give England's natural philosophers a common sense of purpose and a system of reasoned, gentlemanly agreement on "matters of fact." It was also an effort to separate systematic research into nature from the dangerous language of politics and dogma that had marked the Civil War. The society, through its newsletter *Transactions*, first published in 1666, reached out to professional scholars and gentleman experimenters in England, Scotland, and continental Europe. Similar societies appeared across Europe soon after, and together these groups of gentleman philosophers provided a new model for scientific organization and new standards of success. The natural philosopher's work became much more collective, and rough agreements about what kinds of research and explanation were legitimate developed within the societies. Information and theories could be exchanged easily across national and philosophical boundaries, and the modern scientific custom of crediting discoveries to those who were first to publish their results emerged.

Until the beginning of the 1690s both Cartesians and the English experimenters tended to be mechanists. With the authority of the new scientific societies behind it, mechanistic philosophy came to dominate the study of the physical world. A universe composed of matter in motion that operated with mathematical order and was driven by intangible "underlying" mechanisms, seemed to be the best working model for explaining nature. During the 1690s however, this philosophy, which produced much of the best science of the seventeenth century, was suddenly overturned by the work of one man: Isaac Newton.

"AND ALL WAS LIGHT": ISAAC NEWTON

Sir Isaac Newton (1642–1727), an English experimenter, empiricist, and university mathematician, is still considered the greatest single scientific mind of all time. That genius was masked by an unattractive personality—Newton was secretive, obsessive, vindictive, and petty. The son of a small landholding family, Newton received a working scholarship to Cambridge, and by dint of his skills in mathematics received a minor chair in the university's Trinity College. He had few close friends and tended to work alone. Newton was nearly as good with his hands as he was with mathematics, putting those skills to use in his study of alchemy and optics. He was also a secret Antitrinitarian (a dissident Protestant sect) and produced several books that combined his interests in alchemy and theology. To the end of his life he considered these his most important achievement.

Newton's work, like that of many mechanists, was a mix of different theories and philosophies, but he brought to it an extraordinary mind and an unmatched command of mathematics. He shared the Cartesians' belief in the power of mathematics to describe nature, but he disliked their dry logic. He also disagreed with their indifference to studying the behavior of objects in nature. His respect for observation was fueled by his obsessive personality. Once he became involved with a problem—the nature of light, for example—it consumed his efforts for

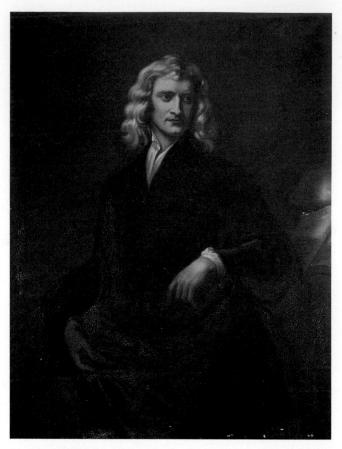

Isaac Newton.

Sir Isaac Newton is still considered the greatest single scientific mind of all time.

months or years at a time. He dismantled the larger question into its component parts and studied them to exhaustion. If he lacked the tools to do his experiments properly, Newton built his own. He improved ordinary prisms in order to understand the nature of light and color, making two important discoveries: that each "color" of light was a component of white light, and that the colors came into focus at different distances. Not only could he prove his point by splitting and recombining white light between two prisms, he was also able to build a new lens for telescopes that focused the colors accurately and produced much clearer images. When he became interested in the problem of orbits, Newton lacked the mathematics to describe heavenly objects moving in curves. He created the first form of calculus to do the job.

The work on optics brought Newton out of his sheltered obscurity at Cambridge. He presented his results to the Royal Society in 1672. These results made his name immediately and provoked the first in a series of

WHAT DID IT MEAN TO BE A MECHANIST IN THE SEVENTEENTH CENTURY?

THE POWER OF METHOD AND THE FORCE OF CURIOSITY   643

Popularization of Newton's Work. Newton's work became popular in the education of children. This 1762 English volume is from a series for children, called *Tom Telescope,* which stayed in print until the nineteenth century.

at work when any two objects came into contact. What Newton wanted was a descriptive answer to the problem of motion, one that not only explained how objects fell toward a moving earth, but also how that heavy earth and other bodies could move in such a regular way. He believed that forces were involved. Rather than offering a mechanist's explanation, based on invisible, swirling particles, Newton wanted a single, clear, mathematical description of forces at work. To achieve this he took individual examples of falling objects on a moving earth and bodies in orbit, and managed to reach a formula that covered all cases. His explanation was leaden but complete: "Every particle of matter in the universe attracts every other particle with a force varying inversely as the square of the distance between them and directly proportional to the product of their masses." This force was universal gravitation, and Newton explained it with the clarity of mathematics. It was a descriptive law, and it offered a single system for understanding motion in the heavens and on the earth.

Newton balked at showing his results. He was wary of more battles with Hooke, and arrogant enough to assume that few other philosophers would understand his theory. After much patient effort Halley persuaded Newton to publish. The result, Newton's *Principia Mathematica* (*Mathematical Principles of Natural Philosophy*), went to press in 1687. Newton did not carry the argument all at once. Many mechanistic philosophers, Cartesians in particular, admired Newton's skill but strongly objected to the prominence of "forces" in his explanations. Such explanations smacked of mysticism and seemed to lack any driving mechanism.

Newton answered his critics in two ways, redefining the methods and goals of the physical sciences in the process. The first part of Newton's response lay in the *Principia* itself. Newton used enormous geometric proofs, speaking the Cartesians' own language to show how forces worked. The second achievement marked the real transformation. Newton's geometry was backed by powerful evidence from the world of everyday observation and experience. This evidence did not just

arguments with the society's president, Robert Hooke. Several of the arguments were quite bitter—each man believed he was the brightest natural philosopher of his generation and was determined to prove himself right. Hooke was a preeminent mechanist and criticized Newton's work on those grounds. Newton had revealed the nature of light, but had nothing to say about deeper mechanical causes. Hooke challenged Newton's theories of orbital motion on the same grounds: they described but did not explain. Stung by these exchanges, Newton withdrew to his college and continued his work in alchemy and theology. Two of his few close friends—the astronomer and architect Sir Christopher Wren (1632–1723), and the physicist and astronomer Edmond Halley (1656–1742)—brought him back to his work on orbits, however, which led him to even greater fame. Halley, skeptical of Hooke's mechanical explanation of orbits, asked Newton for his thoughts on the subject. Newton claimed to have done some research on the problem, but had mislaid the papers. The lost work launched him into a fresh, five-year obsession, and brought him back to the fundamental problems of motion.

Newton had already done work on forces of attraction, refining Galileo's theory of inertia and suggesting that equal and opposite "forces" of motion were

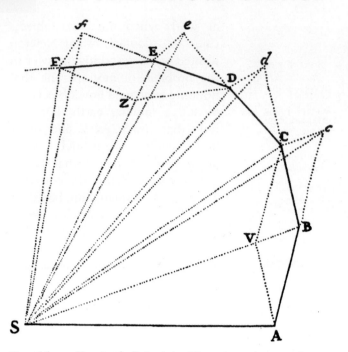

Proof from Newton's *Principia*. These complex, overlapping triangles demonstrated Kepler's "equal areas" law about the orbit of planets.

ture's law lay hid in night; / God said, 'Let Newton be!' and all was light."

Newton was more cautious about his own achievements than many of his admirers. Near the end of his life, in his *General Scholium* (1714), Newton explained the crucial difference between his own work and that of the mechanists. He enforced it sternly during his presidency of the Royal Society. It was spelled out in Latin: *hypotheses non fingo,* "I frame no hypotheses." Newton believed it vain and scientifically improper to seek out an underlying explanation for what he still saw as God's handiwork. Trying to understand why the universe was as it was would lead to futile speculation. What could be understood, with mathematical certainty, was how the universe operated as it did.

The word *scientist* was a nineteenth-century invention. Even after the designs for new methods outlined by Bacon and Descartes, the increasing importance of experiments, and the much-praised successes of Newton, natural philosophy in the eighteenth century

prove his theories—it showed that his conclusions could be applied to the everyday world. The power of Newton's synthesis was not only majestic, it was practical. Newton's laws of motion helped engineers design new kinds of working parts for machinery. The push and pull of gravitation showed geographers that the earth was not a perfect sphere, which altered the nature of map making. The mathematics of gravity could be used to predict the ebb and flow of tides, even in waters where European ships had never sailed, a gigantic leap in an age of seaborne empires and maritime trade. His comprehensive explanation of motion not only provided an orderly and comprehensible picture of the heavens and earth, it also gave humanity greater power over its environment.

Newton's theories combined mathematics, meticulous analysis, and predictive capabilities. The results were extraordinary. Modern historians of science still consider Newton's law of universal gravitation to be the greatest contribution to physics ever made by a single person. The praise was just as great in Newton's own time. He became an English national hero. He was also celebrated across Europe, particularly in France, as a well-loved and much envied icon. Newton's countryman, the poet Alexander Pope, expressed the awe that Newton inspired in a famous eulogy: "Nature and na-

Newton and Satire. The English artist and satirist William Hogarth mocking both philosophy and "Newton worship" in 1763. The philosophers' heads are being weighed on a scale that runs from "absolute gravity" to "absolute levity" or "stark fool."

NEWTON ON THE PURPOSES OF EXPERIMENTAL PHILOSOPHY

When Newton published his General Scholium in 1713, he was seventy-one, president of the Royal Society, and widely revered. He could set out his general views on science and its methods. Newton argues here against deductive reasoning and against the search for large, general causes. "Experimental philosophy" should not try to prove propositions; nor could it identify or philosophize about causes. It could, if properly conducted, discover laws and regularities based on evidence.

Hitherto we have explained the phenomena of the heavens and of our sea by the power of gravity, but have not yet assigned the cause of this power. This is certain, that it must proceed from a cause that penetrates to the very centres of the sun and planets, without suffering the least diminution of its force; that operates not according to the quantity of the surfaces of the particles on which it acts (as mechanical causes used to do), but according to the quantity of the solid matter which they contain, and propagates its virtue on all sides to immense distances, decreasing always as the inverse square of the distances. . . . [H]itherto I have not been able to discover the cause of those properties of gravity from phenomena, and I frame no hypothesis; and hypotheses, whether metaphysical or physical, whether of occult qualities or mechanical, have no place in experimental philosophy. In this philosophy particular propositions are inferred from the phenomena, and afterwards rendered general by induction. . . . And to us it is enough that gravity does really exist, and act according to the laws which we have explained, and abundantly serves to account for all the motions of the celestial bodies, and of our sea.

Matthews, Michael R., ed. *The Scientific Background to Modern Philosophy: Selected Readings.* (Indianapolis/Cambridge: Hackett Publishing Company, 1989), p. 152.

would remain as broad a field as it had been a hundred years before. Likewise, the great scientific minds of the seventeenth century were driven by goals and priorities that were not completely removed from those of their medieval predecessors. Natural philosophy did not break with religion; many mechanists, far from being atheists, argued that such an intricate universe was "evidence of design" by God. Blaise Pascal argued for God's existence on the basis of logic and probability; Robert Boyle endowed lectures and funding for research to prove the divine connection to natural processes. Classical arguments collapsed in the face of new discoveries, but natural philosophers seldom gave up on the project of restoring a picture of an orderly universe, with explanations that strove toward perfection.

What, then, had changed? Seventeenth-century natural philosophers produced different answers to fundamental questions about the physical world. Scientific work took new forms. During the seventeenth century the most innovative scientific work moved out of the universities. Natural philosophers began talking and working with each other in organizations that developed standards of research. England's Royal Society spawned imitators across Europe, in Florence, Berlin, and later in Russia. The French Royal Academy of

Enlightenment Admiration for Newton. A Frenchman's plans for a vast planetarium that would serve as a monument to the great thinker. The small objects along the concourse are mature trees.

Sciences had a much more direct relationship with the monarchy and the French state. France's statesmen wanted some control over these societies, and wanted to share in the rewards of any discoveries they made.

New, too, were beliefs about the purpose and practice of science. The practice of breaking a complex problem down into parts that could be understood, abstracted, and explained in the clear language of mathematics made it possible to tackle more and different questions in the physical sciences. Mathematical language and solutions assumed a more central role in the "new science" than classical logic and geometry had in the medieval world view. Finally, rather than simply proving established truths, the new methods could lend shape and substance to the unknown, and predict what might be found next.

CONCLUSION

The pioneering natural philosophers remained circumspect about their abilities. They also believed their science to be fully compatible with their faith. Some

natural philosophers sought to lay bare the inner mechanisms of nature, to show how the whole system worked. Others believed humans could only catalogue and order the regularities observed in nature, but never truly understand what made those regularities as they were. Newton, for instance, worked towards explanations that would reveal the logic of creation laid out in mathematics. Yet in the end he set those goals aside, and was content to have solid theories explaining actions and substances that could be observed.

The eighteenth-century heirs to Newton's success were often much more daring. Laboratory science and the work of the scientific societies largely stayed true to the experimenters' rules and limitations. But as we will see, the natural philosophers who began investigating the "human sciences" cast aside some of their predecessors' caution. Society, technology, government, religion, even the individual human mind seemed to be mechanisms or parts of a larger nature waiting for study. If they could be explained in terms of laws, like gravity, humanity itself could be perfected. The revolution in science changed Europeans' understanding of the world; it also inspired thinkers much more interested in revolutions in society.

SELECTED READINGS

Biagioli, Mario. *Galileo, Courtier.* Chicago, 1993. Emphasizes the importance of patronage and court politics in Galileo's science and career.

Cohen, I. B. *The Birth of a New Physics.* New York, 1985. Emphasizes the mathematical nature of the revolution; unmatched at making the mathematics understandable.

Drake, Stillman. *Discoveries and Opinions of Galileo.* Garden City, N.Y., 1957. The classic translation of Galileo's most important papers by his most admiring modern biographer.

Gaukroger, Stephen. *Descartes: An Intellectual Biography.* Oxford, 1995. Detailed and sympathetic study of the philosopher.

Gooding, David, Trevor Pinch, et al. *The Uses of Experiment: Studies in the Natural Sciences.* Cambridge, 1989. An important reconsideration of the motives driving seventeenth-century research.

Hall, A. R. *The Scientific Revolution, 1500–1800: The Formation of the Modern Scientific Attitude.* London, 1954. The classic formulation of the concept of a "scientific revolution"; basic and readable.

Jones, Richard Foster. *Ancients and Moderns: A Study of the Rise of the Scientific Movement in Early Modern England.* Berkeley, 1961. Still a persuasive study of the scientific revolutionaries' attempts to situate their work in relation to that of the Greeks.

Kuhn, Thomas. *The Structure of Scientific Revolutions.* Chicago, 1962. A classic and much-debated study of how scientific thought changes.

Porter, Roy, and M. Teich, eds. *The Scientific Revolution in National Context.* Cambridge, 1992. A crucial set of articles questioning the focus on northern Europe's role in the scientific revolution.

Scheibinger, Londa. *The Mind Has No Sex? Women in the Origins of Modern Science.* Cambridge, Mass., 1989. A lively and important recovery of the lost role played by women mathematicians and experimenters.

Shapin, Steven. *The Scientific Revolution.* Chicago, 1996. The best recent survey.

Shapin, Steven, and Simon Schaffer. *Leviathan and the Air Pump.* Princeton, 1985. A modern classic, on one of the most famous philosophical conflicts in seventeenth-century science.

Stephenson, Bruce. *The Music of the Heavens: Kepler's Harmonic Astrology.* Princeton, N.J., 1994. An engaging and important explanation of Kepler's otherworldly perspective.

Thoren, Victor. *The Lord of Uraniborg: A Biography of Tycho Brahe.* Cambridge, 1990. A vivid reconstruction of the scientific revolution's most flamboyant astronomer and his pathbreaking scientific center.

Westfall, Richard. *The Construction of Modern Science.* Cambridge, 1977.

———. *Never at Rest: A Biography of Isaac Newton.* Cambridge, 1980. The standard work.

Wilson, Catherine. *The Invisible World: Early Modern Philosophy and the Invention of the Microscope.* Princeton, 1995. An important study of how the "microcosmic" world revealed by technology reshaped scientific philosophy and practice.

CHAPTER NINETEEN

THE
ENLIGHTENMENT

IN 1762, THE *PARLEMENT* (law court) of Toulouse, in France, convicted Jean Calas of murdering his son. Calas was Protestant, and Catholic-Protestant tensions ran high in the region. Witnesses called before the court claimed that the young Calas had wanted to break with his family and convert to Catholicism, and they convinced the magistrates that Calas had killed his son rather than let him fall from the Protestant faith. French law stipulated the punishment. Calas was tortured twice: first in an attempt to get him to confess, and next, as a formal part of certain death sentences, to force him to name his alleged accomplices. His arms and legs were slowly pulled apart, gallons of water were poured down his throat, and his body was publicly broken on the wheel, which meant that each of his limbs was smashed with an iron bar. Then the executioner cut off his head. Throughout the trial, torture, and execution, Calas maintained his innocence. Two years later, the *Parlement* reversed its verdict, declared Calas not guilty, and offered the family a payment in compensation.

François Marie Arouet, also known as Voltaire, was one of those appalled by the verdict and punishment. At the time of the case, Voltaire was the most famous Enlightenment thinker in Europe. Well connected and a prolific writer, Voltaire took up his pen to clear Calas' name; he contacted friends, hired lawyers for the family, and wrote briefs, letters, and essays to bring the case to the public eye. Calas' case exemplified nearly everything Voltaire opposed in his culture. Intolerance, ignorance, and what Voltaire throughout his life called religious "fanaticism" and "infamy" had made a travesty of justice. "Shout everywhere, I beg you, for Calas and against fanaticism, for it is *l'infame* that has caused their misery," he wrote to his friend Jean Le Rond d'Alembert, a fellow Enlightenment thinker. Using torture to uncover truth demonstrated the power of unquestioned and centuries-old practices. Legal procedures that included secret interrogations, trials behind closed doors, summary judgment (Calas was executed the day after being convicted, with no review by a higher court), and barbaric punishments defied reason, morality, and

FOCUS QUESTIONS

• What were the basic characteristics of Enlightenment writings?

• How did the French *philosophes* differ in their critiques and styles?

• How did the Enlightenment themes influence life around Europe?

• How did the *philosophes* view the New World?

• Was the Enlightenment "revolutionary"?

• How did the "public sphere" expand during the eighteenth century?

human dignity. Any criminal, however wretched, "is a man," wrote Voltaire, "and you are accountable for his blood."

Voltaire's comments on the Calas case illustrate the classic concerns of the Enlightenment: the dangers of arbitrary and unchecked authority, the value of religious toleration, and the overriding importance of law, reason, and human dignity in all affairs. He borrowed most of his arguments from others—from his predecessor Baron Montesquieu and from the Italian writer Cesare Beccaria, whose *On Crimes and Punishments* appeared in 1764. Voltaire's reputation did not rest on his originality as a philosopher. It came from his effectiveness as a writer and advocate, his desire and ability to reach a wide audience. In this, too, he was representative of the Enlightenment project.

THE FOUNDATIONS OF THE ENLIGHTENMENT

What were the basic characteristics of Enlightenment writings?

The Enlightenment was an eighteenth-century phenomenon, lasting for close to the entire century. Not every important thinker who lived and worked in the eighteenth century rallied to the Enlightenment banner. Some, such as the Italian philosopher of history G. B. Vico (1668–1744), opposed almost everything the Enlightenment stood for, and others, most notably Jean-Jacques Rousseau, accepted certain Enlightenment values but sharply rejected others. Patterns of Enlightenment thought varied from country to country, and they changed in each country over the course of the century. Many eighteenth-century thinkers nonetheless shared the sense of living in an exciting new intellectual environment in which the "party of humanity" would prevail over customary practices and traditional thought.

Enlightenment writings shared several basic characteristics. They were marked, first, by a confidence in the powers of human reason. This self-assurance stemmed from the accomplishments of the scientific revolution (see Chapter 18). Even when the details of

Newton's physics were poorly understood, his methods provided a model for scientific inquiry into other phenomena. Nature operated according to laws that could be grasped by study, observation, and thought. Understanding and the exercise of human reason, however, required freedom from old authorities and traditions. "Dare to know!" the German philosopher Immanuel Kant challenged his contemporaries in his classic 1784 essay "What is Enlightenment?" For Kant, the Enlightenment represented a declaration of intellectual independence. He called it an escape from humanity's "self-imposed immaturity," and a long overdue break with humanity's self-imposed parental figure, namely the Catholic Church. Coming of age meant the "determination and courage to think without the guidance of someone else," as an individual. Reason needed autonomy and freedom.

Despite their declarations of independence from the past, Enlightenment thinkers recognized a great debt to their immediate predecessors. Voltaire called Bacon, Newton, and John Locke his "Holy Trinity." Indeed, much of the eighteenth-century Enlightenment consisted of translating, republishing, and thinking through the implications of the great works of the seventeenth century. Enlightenment thinkers drew heavily on Locke's studies of human knowledge, especially his *Essay Concerning Human Understanding* (1690), which was even more influential than his political philosophy. Locke's theories of knowledge gave education and environment a critical role in shaping human character. All knowledge, he argued, originates from sense perception. The human mind at birth is a "blank tablet" (in Latin, *tabula rasa*). Only when an infant begins to experience things, to perceive the external world with its senses, does anything register in its mind. Locke's starting point, which became a central premise for those who followed, was the goodness and perfectibility of humanity. Building on Locke, eighteenth-century thinkers made education central to their project; education

Building on Locke, eighteenth-century thinkers made education central to their project; education promised individual moral improvement and social progress.

promised individual moral improvement and social progress. It is worth noting that Locke's theories had potentially more radical implications: education might be able to level hierarchies of status, sex, or race. As we will see, only a few Enlightenment thinkers made such egalitarian arguments. Still, optimism and a belief in universal human progress constituted a second defining feature of nearly all Enlightenment thinking.

Third, Enlightenment thinkers were extraordinarily

HOW DID THE FRENCH *PHILOSOPHES* DIFFER IN THEIR THEMES AND STYLES?

THE WORLD OF THE *PHILOSOPHES*   651

ambitious and wide ranging. They sought nothing less than the organization of all knowledge. The "scientific method," by which they meant the empirical observation of particular phenomena in order to arrive at general laws, offered a way to pursue research in all areas—to study human affairs as well as natural ones. Thus they collected evidence to learn the laws governing the rise and fall of nations, and they compared governmental constitutions to arrive at an ideal and universally applicable political system. As the English poet Alexander Pope stated in his *Essay on Man* of 1733, "the science of human nature [may be] like all other sciences reduced to a few clear points," and Enlightenment thinkers became determined to learn exactly what those "few clear points" were. They took up a strikingly wide array of subjects in this systematic manner: knowledge and the mind, natural history, economics, government, religious beliefs, customs of indigenous peoples in the New World, human nature, and sexual (or what we would call gender) and racial differences.

Historians have called the Enlightenment a "cultural project," emphasizing Enlightenment thinkers' interest in practical, applied knowledge, and their determination to spread knowledge and to promote free public discussion. They intended, as Denis Diderot wrote, "to change the common way of thinking," and to advance the cause of "enlightenment" and humanity. While they shared many of the theoretical concerns of their predecessors, they wrote in a very different style, and for a much larger audience. Hobbes and Locke had published treatises for small groups of learned seventeenth-century readers. Voltaire, in contrast, wrote plays, essays, and letters; Rousseau composed music, published his *Confessions*, and wrote novels that moved his readers to tears; David Hume, one of the giants of the Scottish Enlightenment, wrote history for a wide audience. A British aristocrat or a governor in the North American colonies would have read Locke. But a middle-class woman might read Rousseau's fiction, and shopkeepers and artisans could become familiar with popular, Enlightenment-inspired pamphlets. Among the elite, newly formed "academies" sponsored prize essay contests, and well-to-do women and men discussed affairs of state in salons. In other words, the intellectual achievements and goals of the Enlightenment followed from cultural developments in the eighteenth century. Those developments included the expansion of literacy and growing markets for books, new networks of readers, new forms of intellectual exchange,

and the emergence of what some historians call the first "public sphere."

In sum, Enlightenment thinkers confronted their culture, exposing time-worn practices, beliefs, and authority to the shining "light" of reason. That often meant criticism and satire. They combined an irreverence for custom and tradition with a belief in human perfectibility and progress, a confidence in their ability to understand the world with a passionate interest in the relationship between "nature" and culture, or environment, history, and human character and society. Their program of reform had immediate political implications; in a remarkably short time it changed the premises of government and society throughout the Atlantic world.

THE WORLD OF THE *PHILOSOPHES*

How did the French *philosophes* differ in their themes and styles?

Enlightenment thought was European in a broad sense, including southern and eastern Europe as well as Europe's colonies in the New World. France, however, provided the stage for some of the most widely read Enlightenment books and the most closely watched battles. For this reason, Enlightenment thinkers, regardless of where they lived, are often called by the French word *philosophes*. Yet hardly any of the *philosophes*—with the exceptions of David Hume and Immanuel Kant—were philosophers in the sense of being highly original abstract thinkers. Especially in France, Enlightenment thinkers shunned forms of expression that might seem incomprehensible, priding themselves instead on their clarity and style. *Philosophe*, in French, simply meant a free thinker, a person whose reflections were unhampered by the constraints of religion or dogma in any form.

VOLTAIRE

At the time, the best known of the *philosophes* was Voltaire, born François Marié Arouet (1694–1778). As Erasmus two centuries earlier had embodied Christian humanism, Voltaire virtually personified the Enlightenment, commenting on an enormous range of subjects in a wide variety of literary forms. Educated by

Voltaire, by Jean Antoine Houdon.

the Jesuits, he emerged quite young as a gifted and sharp-tongued writer. His gusto for provocation landed him in the Bastille (a notorious prison in Paris) for libel, and soon afterward in temporary exile in England. In his three years there, Voltaire became a great admirer of British political institutions, British culture, and British science; above all, he became an extremely persuasive convert to the ideas of Newton, Bacon, and Locke. His single greatest accomplishment may have been popularizing Newton's work in France and more generally championing the cause of British empiricism and the scientific method against the more Cartesian French.

Voltaire's *Philosophical Letters* (or, Letters on the English Nation), published after his return in 1734, made an immediate sensation. Voltaire's themes were religious and political liberty, and his weapons were comparisons. His admiration for British culture and politics became a stinging critique of France—and other absolutist countries on the Continent. He praised British open-mindedness and empiricism: the country's respect for scientists and its support for research. He considered the relative weakness of the British aristocracy a sign of Britain's political health. Unlike the French, the British respected commerce and people who engage in it, Voltaire wrote. The British tax system was rational, free of the complicated exemptions for the privileged that were ruining French finances. The British House of Commons represented the middle classes and, in contrast with French absolutism, brought balance to British government and checked arbitrary power. In one of the book's more incendiary passages, he argued that in Britain, violent revolution had actually produced political moderation and stability: "the idol of arbitrary power was drowned in seas of blood. . . . The English nation is the only nation in the world that has succeeded in moderating the power of its kings by resisting them." Of all Britain's reputed virtues, religious toleration loomed largest of all. Britain, Voltaire argued, brought together citizens of different religions in a harmonious and productive culture. In this and other instances, Voltaire oversimplified: British Catholics, Dissenters, and Jews did not have equal civil rights. Yet the British policy of "toleration" did contrast with Louis XIV's intolerance of Protestants. Revoking the Edict of Nantes (1685) had stripped French Protestants of civil rights, and had helped to create the atmosphere in which Jean Calas—and others—were persecuted.

Voltaire's famous battlecry, "Écrasez l'infâme," translates as "crush infamy," and by "infamy" he meant all forms of repression, fanaticism, and bigotry. He wrote the following to an opponent, and it is a statement cited ever since as the first principle of civil liberty: "I do not agree with a word you say, but I will defend to the death your right to say it." Of all forms of intolerance Voltaire loathed religious bigotry most, and with real passion he denounced religious "fraud," faith in miracles, and superstition. "The less superstition, the less fanaticism; and the less fanaticism, the less misery." He did not oppose religion per se; rather he sought to rescue morality, which he believed to come from God, from narrow dogma—elaborate ritual, dietary laws, formulaic prayers—and from a powerful church bureaucracy. He argued for common sense and simplicity, persuaded that these would bring out the goodness in humanity and establish stable authority. "The simpler the laws are, the more the magistrates are respected; the simpler the religion will be, the more one will revere its ministers. Religion can be simple. When enlightened people will announce a single God, rewarder and avenger, no one will laugh, everyone will obey."

Voltaire relished his position as a critic, and it never

HOW DID THE FRENCH *PHILOSOPHES* DIFFER IN THEIR THEMES AND STYLES?

THE WORLD OF THE *PHILOSOPHES*   653

stopped him from being successful. He was regularly exiled from France and other countries, his books banned and burned. As long as his plays attracted large audiences, however, the French king felt he had to tolerate him. Voltaire had an attentive international public, including Frederick of Prussia, who invited him to his court at Berlin, and Catherine of Russia, with whom he corresponded about reforms she might introduce in Russia. Voltaire described himself as "contraband," but that seemed only to enhance his value. When he died in 1778, a few months after a triumphant return to Paris, he was possibly the best-known writer in Europe.

MONTESQUIEU

The baron de Montesquieu (1689–1755) was a very different kind of Enlightenment figure. Montesquieu was born to a noble family. He inherited both an estate and, since state offices were property that passed from father to son, a position as magistrate in the *Parlement*, or law court, of Bordeaux. He was not a stylist or a provocateur like Voltaire, but a relatively cautious jurist. He did write a satirical novel, *The Persian Letters* (1721), published anonymously (to protect his reputation) in Amsterdam. The novel was composed as letters from two Turkish visitors to France. The visitors detailed the odd religious superstitions they witnessed, compared manners at the French court with those in Turkish harems, and likened French absolutism to their own brands of despotism.

Montesquieu's serious treatise *The Spirit of Laws* (1748) may have been the most influential work of the Enlightenment. It was a groundbreaking study in what we would call comparative historical sociology, and very Newtonian in its careful, empirical approach. Montesquieu asked about the structures that shaped law. How had different environments, histories, and religious traditions combined to create such a variety of governmental institutions? What were the different forms of government: what "spirit" characterized each, and what were their respective virtues and shortcomings? Montesquieu proposed a threefold classification of states. A republic was governed by the many—in his view either an elite aristocracy or the people. In a monarchy, a single authority ruled in accordance with the law. "Despotism," Montesquieu's most important negative example, allowed a single ruler to govern unchecked by law or other powers, sowing corruption and capriciousness. The soul or spirit of a republic was virtue; of monarchy, honor; of despotism, where no citizen could feel secure and punishment took the place of

Montesquieu.

education, fear. Lest this seem abstract, Montesquieu devoted two chapters to the French monarchy, in which he spelled out what he saw as a dangerous drift toward despotism in his own land. Like other Enlightenment thinkers, Montesquieu admired the British system and its separate and balanced powers—executive, legislative, and judicial—which guaranteed liberty in the sense of freedom from the absolute power of any single governing individual or group. His idealization of "checks and balances" had formative influence on Enlightenment political theorists and members of the governing elites, particularly those who wrote the United States Constitution in 1787.

DIDEROT AND THE *ENCYCLOPEDIA*

Voltaire's and Montesquieu's writings represent the themes and style of the French Enlightenment. But the most remarkable French publication of the century was a collective venture: the *Encyclopedia*. The *Encyclopedia* intended to summarize and disseminate all the most advanced contemporary philosophical, scientific, and technical knowledge. In terms of sheer scope, this was the grandest statement of the *philosophes'* goals. It demonstrated how scientific analysis could be applied in nearly all realms of thought. It aimed to reconsider

Diderot. A contemporary portrait by Van Loo.

large volumes of text and eleven more of illustrations. A collaborative project, it helped create the *philosophes'* image as the "party of humanity."

The *Encyclopedia* sought to "change the general way of thinking." Diderot commissioned articles that explained recent achievements in science and technology, showing how machines worked and illustrating new industrial processes. The point was to demonstrate how the everyday applications of science could promote progress and alleviate all forms of human misery. Diderot turned the same methods to matters of religion, politics, and the foundations of the social order, including articles on economics, taxes, and the slave trade. Censorship made it difficult to write openly antireligious articles. Diderot thumbed his nose at religion in oblique ways; at the entry on the Eucharist, the reader found a terse cross reference: "See *cannibalism.*" Gibes like this aroused storms of controversy when the early volumes of the *Encyclopedia* appeared. The French government revoked permission for the *Encyclopedia* to be published, declaring in 1759 that the Encyclopedists were trying to "propagate materialism," which meant atheism, "to destroy Religion, to inspire a spirit of independence, and to nourish the corruption of morals." The volumes sold remarkably well despite such bans and their hefty price. Purchasers belonged to the elite: aristocrats, government officials, prosperous merchants, and a scattering of members of the higher clergy. That elite, though, stretched across Europe, including its overseas colonies.

an enormous range of traditions and institutions, and to put reason to the task of bringing happiness and progress to humanity. The guiding spirit behind the venture was Denis Diderot. Diderot was helped by the Newtonian mathematician Jean Le Rond d'Alembert (1717–1783), and other leading "men of letters," including Voltaire and Montesquieu. The *Encyclopedia* was published, in installments, between 1751 and 1772; by the time it was completed, it ran to seventeen

Although the French *philosophes* sparred with the state and the church, they sought political stability and

A Laboratory, from Diderot's *Encyclopedia.* Each printed number refers to a detailed discussion in the text.

Illustrating technology and industry, this engraving is from the mining section of Diderot's *Encyclopedia*.

Enlightenment thinkers admired British institutions and British scholarship, and they used both as points of reference. Great Britain also produced among the most important Enlightenment thinkers: the historian Edward Gibbon and the Scottish philosophers David Hume and Adam Smith. The *philosophes* considered Thomas Jefferson and Benjamin Franklin part of their group. Despite stiffer resistance from religious authorities, stricter state censors, and smaller networks of educated elites to discuss and support progressive thought, the Enlightenment flourished across central and southern Europe. Frederick II of Prussia housed Voltaire during one of his exiles from France, though the *philosophe* quickly wore out his welcome. Frederick also patronized a small but unusually productive group of Enlightenment thinkers. Northern Italy was an important center of Enlightenment thought. Enlightenment thinkers across Europe raised similar themes: humanitarianism, or the dignity and worth of all individuals, religious toleration, and liberty.

reform. Montesquieu, not surprisingly in light of his birth and position, hoped that an enlightened aristocracy would press for reforms and defend liberty against a despotic king. Voltaire, persuaded that aristocrats would represent only their particular narrow interests, looked to an enlightened monarch for leadership. Neither was a democrat, and neither conceived of reform from below. Still, their widely read writings were subversive. Their satires of absolutism and, more broadly, arbitrary power, stung. By the 1760s the French critique of despotism provided the language in which many people across Europe articulated their opposition to existing regimes.

INTERNATIONALIZATION OF ENLIGHTENMENT THEMES

How did the Enlightenment themes influence life around Europe?

The "party of humanity" was international. French became the lingua franca of much Enlightenment discussion, but "French" books were often published in Switzerland, Germany, and Russia. As we have seen,

ENLIGHTENMENT THEMES: HUMANITARIANISM AND TOLERATION

Among the most influential writers of the entire Enlightenment was the Italian (Milanese) jurist Cesare Beccaria (1738–1794). Beccaria's *On Crimes and Punishments* (1764) sounded the same general themes as did the French *philosophes*—arbitrary power, reason, and human dignity—and it provided Voltaire with most of his arguments in the Calas case. Beccaria also proposed concrete legal reforms. He attacked the prevalent view that punishments should represent society's vengeance on the criminal. The only legitimate rationale for punishment was to maintain social order, and to prevent other crimes. Beccaria argued for the greatest possible leniency compatible with deterrence; respect for individual dignity and humanity dictated that humans should punish other humans no more than is absolutely necessary. Above all, Beccaria's book eloquently opposed torture and the death penalty. The spectacle of public execution, which sought to dramatize the power of the state and the horrors of hell, in fact dehumanized victim, judge, and spectators. In 1766, a few years after the Calas case, another French trial provided an example of what horrified Beccaria and the *philosophes*. A nineteen-year-old French nobleman, convicted of blasphemy, had his tongue cut out and his hand cut off before being burned at the stake. Since the court discovered the blasphemer had read Voltaire, it ordered the *Philosophical Dictionary* burned along with the body. Sensational cases such as this one helped publicize Beccaria's work, and *On Crimes and Punishments* was quickly translated into a dozen languages. Owing primarily to its influence, most European countries by around 1800 abolished torture, branding, whipping, and various forms of mutilation, and reserved the death penalty for capital crimes.

Instruments of Torture. The rack and the thumbscrew, from an official Austrian governmental handbook. Beccaria's influence helped phase out the use of such instruments by around 1800.

Humanitarianism and reason also counseled religious toleration. Enlightenment thinkers spoke almost as one on the need to end religious warfare and the persecution of "heretics" and religious minorities. It is important, though, to differentiate between the church as an institution and dogma, against which many Enlightenment thinkers rebelled, and religious belief, which most accepted. Only the smallest number of Enlightenment thinkers were atheists, and very few even were avowed agnostics. Many (Voltaire, for instance) were deists, holding a religious outlook that saw God as a "divine clockmaker" who, at the beginning of time, constructed a perfect timepiece and then left it to run with predictable regularity. Enlightenment inquiry proved compatible with very different stances on religion.

"Toleration" was limited. Most Christians saw Jews as heretics and Christ killers. And although Enlightenment thinkers deplored persecution, they commonly viewed Judaism and Islam as backward religions mired in superstition and obscurantist ritual. One of the few Enlightenment figures to treat Jews sympathetically was the German *philosophe* Gotthold Lessing

(1729–1781). Lessing's extraordinary play *Nathan the Wise* (1779) takes place in Jerusalem during the Fourth Crusade and begins with a pogrom, or violent attack, in which the wife and children of Nathan, a Jewish merchant, are slain. Nathan survives to become a sympathetic and wise father figure. He adopts a Christian-born daughter and raises her with three religions: Christianity, Islam, and Judaism. At several points, authorities ask him to choose the single true religion. Nathan shows none exists. The three great monotheistic religions are three versions of the truth. Religion is authentic, or true, only insofar as it makes the believer virtuous.

Lessing modeled his hero on his friend Moses Mendelssohn (1729–1786), a self-educated rabbi and bookkeeper (and the grandfather of the composer Felix Mendelssohn). Moses Mendelssohn moved—though with some difficulty—between the Enlightenment circles of Frederick II and the Jewish community of Berlin. Mendelssohn unsuccessfully tried to avoid religion as a subject. Repeatedly attacked and invited to convert to Christianity, he finally took up the question of Jewish identity. In a series of writings, the best-known of which is *On the Religious Authority of Judaism* (1783), he defended Jewish communities against anti-

The German philosopher **Gotthold Lessing** visiting his friend **Moses Mendelssohn.**

Semitic policies and Jewish religion against Enlightenment criticism. At the same time, he also promoted reform within the Jewish community, arguing that his community had special reason to embrace the broad Enlightenment project: religious faith should be voluntary, states should promote tolerance, humanitarianism would bring progress to all.

ECONOMICS, GOVERNMENT, AND ADMINISTRATION

Enlightenment ideas had a very real currency in affairs of state. The *philosophes* defended reason and knowledge for humanitarian reasons. But they also promised to make nations stronger, more efficient, and more prosperous. Beccaria's proposed legal reforms were a good case in point; he sought to make laws not simply more just, but also more effective. In other words, the Enlightenment spoke to individuals, but also to states. The *philosophes* addressed issues of liberty and rights, but also took up matters of administration, tax collection, and economic policy.

The rising fiscal demands of eighteenth-century states and empires made these issues newly urgent. Which economic resources were most valuable to states? How could governments tap them? Enlightenment economic thinkers such as the physiocrats argued that long-standing mercantilist policies were misguided. By the eighteenth century, mercantilism had become a term for a very wide range of policies that shared a belief in government regulation of trade in manufactured goods and precious metals. The physiocrats, most of them French, held that real wealth came from the land and agricultural production. More important, they advocated simplifying the tax system and following a policy of *laissez-faire*, which comes from the French expression *laissez faire la nature* ("let nature take its course"), letting wealth and goods circulate without government interference.

The now-classic expression of laissez faire economics, however, came from the Scottish economist Adam Smith (1723–1790), and especially from Smith's landmark treatise *Inquiry into the Nature and Causes of the Wealth of Nations* (1776). Smith disagreed with the physiocrats on the value

Adam Smith.

of agriculture, but he shared their opposition to mercantilism. For Smith, the central matters were the productivity of labor and how labor was used in different sectors of the economy. Mercantile restrictions—such as high taxes on imported goods, which was one of the grievances of the colonists throughout the American empires—did not encourage the productive deployment of labor and thus did not create real economic health. For Smith, general prosperity could best be obtained by allowing the famous "invisible hand" to guide economic activity. Individuals, in other words, should pursue their own interests without competition from state-chartered monopolies or legal restraints. As Smith wrote in his earlier *Theory of Moral Sentiments,* self-interested individuals could be "led by an invisible hand . . . without knowing it, without intending it, [to] advance the interest of the society."

The Wealth of Nations spelled out, in more technical and historical detail, the different stages of economic development, how the invisible hand actually worked, and the beneficial aspects of competition. Its perspective owed much to Newton and the Enlightenment's idealization of both nature and human nature. Smith wanted to follow what he called, in classic Enlightenment terms, the "obvious and simple system of natural liberty." Smith thought of himself as the champion of justice against state-sponsored economic privilege and monopolies. He was a theorist of human feelings as well as market forces. Smith emerged as the most influential of the new eighteenth-century economic thinkers. In the following century, ironically, his work and his followers became the target of reformers and critics of the new economic world.

> For Smith, general prosperity could best be obtained by allowing the famous "invisible hand" to guide economic activity. Individuals, in other words, should pursue their own interests without competition from state-chartered monopolies or legal restraints.

EMPIRE AND ENLIGHTENMENT

How did the *philosophes* view the New World?

Smith's *Wealth of Nations* formed part of a debate about the economics of empire: *philosophes* and statesmen alike asked how the colonies could be profitable, and to whom. The colonial world loomed large in Enlightenment thinking in several other ways. The "new" world across the Atlantic offered a foil to the "old" civilization of Europe, in other words, an often idealized portrait of natural humanity and simplicity, by comparison with which Europe looked decadent or corrupt. Second, Europeans' colonial activities—especially, by the eighteenth century, the slave trade—could not help but raise pressing issues about humanitarianism, individual rights, and natural law. The effects of colonialism on Europe were a central Enlightenment theme.

"There has never been any event which has had more impact on the human race in general and for Europeans in particular, as that of the discovery of the New World, and the passage to the Indies around the Cape of Good Hope." So wrote Abbé Guillaume Thomas François Raynal. Raynal's massive *Philosophical History . . . of Europeans in the Two Indies,* published in 1770, another co-authored work, like the *Encyclopedia,* was one of the most widely read works of the Enlightenment, going through twenty printings and at least forty pirated editions. Raynal drew his inspiration from the *Encyclopedia,* and aimed at nothing less than a total history of colonization: customs and civilizations of indigenous peoples, natural history, exploration, and commerce in the Atlantic world and India. He also tried to draw up a balance sheet, asking if, in the end, colonization had made humanity happier, more peaceful, or better. The question was fully in the spirit of the Enlightenment. So was the answer. Raynal believed that industry and trade brought improvement and progress. Like other Enlightenment writers, however, he and his co-authors considered natural simplicity an antidote to the corruptions of their culture. They sought out and idealized what they considered examples of "natural" humanity, many of them in the New World. For example, they wrote that what Europeans considered "savage life" might be "a hundred times preferable to that of societies corrupted by despotism" and lamented the loss of humanity's "natural liberty." They condemned the tactics of the Spanish in Mexico and Peru, of the Portuguese in Brazil, and of the British in North America. They echoed Montesquieu's theme that good government required checks and balances against arbitrary authority. In the New World, they argued, Europeans found themselves with virtually unlimited power,

THE IMPACT OF THE NEW WORLD
ON ENLIGHTENMENT THINKERS

The Abbé Guillaume Thomas François Raynal (1713–1796) was a clergyman and intellectual who moved in the inner circles of the Enlightenment. As a senior cleric he had access to the royal court; as a writer and intellectual he worked with the Encyclopedists and other authors who criticized France's institutions, including the Catholic church of which Raynal himself was a part. Here he tries to offer a perspective on the profound effects of discovering the Americas, and ends by asking a typical Enlightenment question: will particular historical developments and institutions lead to the betterment of society, or not?

There has never been any event which has had more impact on the human race in general and for Europeans in particular, as that of the discovery of the New World, and the passage to the Indies around the Cape of Good Hope. It was then that a commercial revolution began, a revolution in the balance of power, and in the customs, the industries and the government of every nation. It was through this event that men in the most distant lands were linked by new relationships and new needs. The produce of equatorial regions were consumed in polar climes. The industrial products of the north were transported to the south; the textiles of the Orient became the luxuries of Westerners; and everywhere men mutually exchanged their opinions, their laws, their customs, their illnesses, and their medicines, their virtues and their vices. Everything changed, and will go on changing. But will the changes of the past and those that are to come, be useful to humanity? Will they give man one day more peace, more happiness, or more pleasure? Will his condition be better, or will it be simply one of constant change?

Abbé Guillaume Thomas François Raynal, *Philosophical and Political History of European Establishments and Commerce in the Two Indies* (1770), as cited in Dourinda Outram, *The Enlightenment*. (Cambridge: Cambridge Univ. Press, 1995), p. 73.

which encouraged them to be arrogant, cruel, and despotic. In a later edition, after the outbreak of the American revolution, the book went even further, drawing parallels between exploitation in the colonial world and inequality at home: "We are mad in the way we act with our colonies, and inhuman and mad in our conduct toward our peasants," asserted one author. Eighteenth-century radicals repeatedly warned that overextended empires sowed seeds of decadence and corruption at home.

SLAVERY AND THE ATLANTIC WORLD

Discussing Europe's colonies and economies inevitably raised the issue of slavery. The sugar islands of the Caribbean were among the most valued possessions of the colonial world, and the sugar trade one of the leading sectors of the Western economy. The Atlantic slave trade reached its peak in the eighteenth century. European slave traders sent at least 1 million Africans into New World slavery in the late seventeenth century, and at least 6 million in the eighteenth century. On this topic, however, even such radical thinkers as Raynal and Diderot hesitated, and their hesitations are revealing about the tensions in Enlightenment thought. Enlightenment thinking began with the premise that individuals could reason and govern themselves. Individual moral freedom lay at the heart of what they considered to be a just, stable, and harmonious society. Slavery defied natural law and natural freedom. Montesquieu, for instance, wrote that civil law created chains, but natural law would always break them. Nearly all Enlightenment thinkers condemned "slavery" in the metaphorical sense; that the "mind should break free of its chains," or that "despotism enslaved the king's subjects" were phrases that echoed through much eighteenth-century writing. It was common for the central characters of eighteenth-century fiction, such as Voltaire's hero Candide, to meet enslaved people, learning compassion as part of their moral education. Writers dealt more gingerly, however, with the actual enslavement and slave labor of Africans.

Some Enlightenment thinkers skirted the issue of slavery. Others reconciled principle and practice in different ways. Adam Smith condemned slavery as uneconomical. Voltaire, quick to expose his contemporaries' hypocrisy, wondered if Europeans would look away if Europeans—rather than Africans—were enslaved. Voltaire, however, did not question his belief that Africans were inferior peoples. Montesquieu (who came from Bordeaux, one of the central ports for the Atlantic trade) believed that slavery debased master and slave alike. But he also argued that all societies balanced their systems of labor in accordance with their different needs, and slave labor was one such system. Finally, like many Enlightenment thinkers, Montesquieu defended property rights, including those of slave holders.

The *Encyclopedia*'s article on the slave trade did condemn the slave trade in the clearest possible terms, as a violation of self-government. Humanitarian antislavery movements, which emerged in the 1760s, advanced similar arguments. From deploring slavery to imagining freedom for slaves, however, proved a very long step, and one that few were willing to take. In the end, the Enlightenment's environmental determinism—in other words the belief that environment shaped character—provided a common way of postponing the entire issue. Slavery corrupted its victims, destroyed their natural virtue, and crushed their natural love of liberty. Enslaved people, by this logic, were not ready for freedom. It was characteristic for Warville de Brissot's

Society of the Friends of Blacks to call for abolition of the slave trade and invite Thomas Jefferson, a slaveholder, to join the organization. Only a very few advocated abolishing slavery, and they insisted that emancipation be gradual. Slavery proved one of several realms where different currents in Enlightenment thought ran toward very different conclusions.

EXPLORATION AND THE PACIFIC WORLD

The Pacific world also figured prominently in Enlightenment thinking. Systematically mapping new sections of the Pacific was among the crucial developments of the age, and one with tremendous impact on the public imagination. These explorations were also scientific missions, sponsored as part of the Enlightenment project of expanding scientific knowledge. In 1767 the French government sent Louis-Anne de Bougainville (1729–1811) to the South Pacific in search of a new route to China, new lands suitable for colonization, and new spices for the ever lucrative trade. They sent along scientists and artists to record his findings. Like many other explorers, Bougainville found none of what he sought, but his travel accounts—above all his fabulously lush descriptions of the earthly paradise of Nouvelle-Cythère, or Tahiti—captured the attention and imaginations of many at home. The British captain James Cook (1728–1779), who followed Bougainville, made two trips into the South Pacific (1768–1771 and 1772–1775), with impressive results. He charted the coasts of New Zealand and New Holland, and added the New Hebrides and Hawaii to European maps. He explored the outer limits of the Antarctic continent, the shores of the Bering Sea, and the Arctic Ocean. The artists and scientists who accompanied Cook as well as Bougainville vastly expanded the boundaries of European botany, zoology, and geology. Their drawings—such as Sydney Parkinson's extraordinary portraits of the Maori—appealed to a wide public. So did the accounts of dangers overcome and peoples encountered. A misguided attempt to communicate with South Pacific islanders, perhaps with the intention of conveying them to Europe, ended in the grisly deaths of Cook and four Royal Marines on Hawaii in late January 1779, which surely added to European readers' fascination with his travels. Large numbers of people in Europe avidly read travel accounts of these voyages. When Cook and Bougainville brought Pacific islanders to the metropolis they attracted large crowds. Joshua Reynolds painted portraits of the islanders.

SLAVERY AND THE ENLIGHTENMENT

The Encyclopedists made an exhaustive and deliberate effort to comment on every institution, trade, and custom in Western culture. The project was conceived as an effort to catalogue, analyze, and improve each facet of society. Writing in an age of burgeoning maritime trade and expanding overseas empires they could not, and did not wish to, avoid the subject of slavery. These were their thoughts on plantation slavery, the African slaves who bore its brunt, and broader questions of law and liberty posed by the whole system.

Thus there is not a single one of these hapless souls—who, we maintain, are but slaves—who does not have the right to be declared free, since he has never lost his freedom; since it was impossible for him to lose it; and since neither his ruler nor his father nor anyone else had the right to dispose of his freedom; consequently, the sale of his person is null and void in and of itself: this Negro does not divest himself, indeed cannot under any condition divest himself of his natural rights; he carries them everywhere with him, and he has the right to demand that others allow him to enjoy those rights. Therefore, it is a clear case of inhumanity on the part of the judges in those free countries to which the slave is shipped, not to free the slave instantly by legal declaration, since he is their brother, having a soul like theirs.

From *Encyclopédie*, Vol. 16. Neuchâtel, 1765, p. 532 as cited in David Brion Davis, *The Problem of Slavery in Western Culture* (Ithaca, N.Y.: Cornell University Press, 1966), p. 416.

THE IMPACT OF THE SCIENTIFIC MISSIONS

Back in Europe, Enlightenment thinkers drew freely on reports of scientific missions. Since they were already committed to understanding human nature and the origins of society, and to studying the effects of the environment on character and culture, stories of new peoples and cultures were immediately fascinating. In 1772 Diderot, one of many eager readers of Bougainville's accounts, published his own reflections on the cultural significance of those accounts, the *Supplément au Voyage de Bougainville*. For Diderot, the Tahitians were the original human beings, and unlike the inhabitants of the New World, virtually free of European influence. They represented humanity in its natural state, Diderot believed, uninhibited about sexuality and free of religious dogma. Their simplicity exposed the hypocrisy and rigidity of overcivilized Europeans. Others considered the indigenous peoples of the Pacific akin to the classical civilizations of Greeks and Romans, associating Tahitian women, for instance, with Venus, the Roman goddess of love. All these views said more about Europe and European utopias than about indigenous cultures in the Pacific. Enlightenment thinkers found it impossible to see other peoples as anything other than "primitive" versions of Europeans. Even these views, however, marked a change from former times. In earlier periods Europeans had understood the world as divided between Christendom and heathen "others." In the eighteenth century religious understanding of Western identity was giving way to more secular conceptions.

One of the most important scientific explorers of the period was the German scientist Alexander von

Humboldt. Humboldt spent five years in Spanish America, aiming to do nothing less than assess the civilization and natural resources of the continent. He went equipped with the most advanced scientific instruments Europe could provide. Between 1814 and 1819, Humboldt produced an impressive multivolume *Personal Narratives of Travels* much like the lavishly illustrated reports by Cook and Bougainville. The expense bankrupted him, sending him to the Prussian court in search of financial support. Humboldt's investigations provide an important link between the Enlightenment and nineteenth-century science. Humboldt, in good Enlightenment fashion, attempted to demonstrate that climate and physical environment determined which forms of life would survive in any given region. These investigations would continue in nineteenth-century discussions of evolutionary change. Charles Darwin referred to Humboldt as "the greatest scientific traveler who ever lived," and the German scientist's writing inspired Darwin's voyage to the Galapagos Islands of the coast of Ecuador.

In sum, Europeans who looked outward did so for a variety of reasons and reached very different conclusions. For some Enlightenment thinkers and rulers, scientific reports from overseas fitted into a broad inquiry about "civilization" and "human nature." That inquiry sometimes encouraged self-criticism, and at others simply shored up Europeans' sense of their superiority. The late-eighteenth-century revolutions brought this Enlightenment discussion to a close. Yet these themes reemerged during the nineteenth century, when new empires were built and West's place in the world reassessed.

NATURE, GENDER, AND ENLIGHTENMENT RADICALISM: ROUSSEAU AND WOLLSTONECRAFT

Was the Enlightenment "revolutionary"?

Historians have asked if the Enlightenment was "revolutionary," a logical question in light of the upheavals of the late eighteenth century. Enlightenment thought did undermine central tenets of eighteenth-century culture and politics. It did have a wide resonance, well beyond a small group of intellectuals. Yet Enlightenment thinkers did not hold to any single political position. Even the most radical among them disagreed on the implications of their thought. Jean-Jacques Rousseau and Mary Wollstonecraft provide good examples of such radical thinkers.

THE WORLD OF ROUSSEAU

Jean-Jacques Rousseau (1712–1778) was an "outsider" who quarreled with the other *philosophes* and contradicted many of their assumptions. He shared the *philosophes'* search for intellectual and political freedom, attacked inherited privilege, and believed in the good of humanity and the possibility of creating a just society. Yet he introduced other strains into Enlightenment thought, especially morality and what was then called "sensibility," or the cult of feeling. He was also considerably more radical than his counterparts, one of the first to talk about popular sovereignty and democracy. He was surely the most utopian, which made his work popular at the time and has opened it to different interpretations since. In the late eighteenth century he was the most influential and most often cited of the

Jean-Jacques Rousseau.

ROUSSEAU'S SOCIAL CONTRACT

Jean-Jacques Rousseau (1712–1778) was one of the most radical Enlightenment thinkers. In his works he suggested that humans needed not only a clearer understanding of "natural laws" but also a much closer relationship with nature itself, and a thorough reorganization of society. In order to achieve the clearest expression of natural laws in practice, a "sovereign" society, formed by free association of equal citizens without patrons or factions, should be formed. This society would make laws and order itself by the genuinely collective wisdom of its citizens. This idea of a "general will" was an inspiration to the early leaders of the French Revolution. Rousseau sets out the definition of his "sovereign" society and its authority in the passages below.

BOOK I, CHAPTER 6

To find a form of association which may defend and protect with the whole force of the community the person and property of every associate, and by means of which each, coalescing with all, may nevertheless obey only himself, and remain as free as before." Such is the fundamental problem of which the social contract furnishes the solution.

BOOK II, CHAPTER 4

What, then, is an act of sovereignty properly so called? It is not an agreement between a superior and an inferior, but an agreement of the body with each of its members; a lawful agreement, because it has the social contract as its foundation; equitable, because it is common to all; useful, because it can have no other object than the general welfare; and stable, because it has the public force and the supreme power as a guarantee.

Jean-Jacques Rousseau. *The Social Contract*, trans. Victor Gourevitch. (New York: Cambridge University Press, 1997), pp. 49–50.

philosophes, the thinker who brought the Enlightenment to a larger audience.

Rousseau's milestone and difficult treatise on politics, *The Social Contract*, began with a now famous paradox. "Man was born free, and everywhere he is in chains." How had humans freely forged these chains? To ask this was to reformulate the key questions of seventeenth- and eighteenth-century thought. What were the origins of government? Was government's authority legitimate? If not, Rousseau asked, how could it become so? Rousseau argued that in the state of nature, all men had been equal. (On women, men, and nature, see below.) Social inequality, anchored in private property, profoundly corrupted "the social contract," or the formation of government. Under conditions of inequality, governments and laws represented only the rich and privileged. They became instruments of repression and enslavement. Legitimate governments could be formed, Rousseau argued. "The problem is to find a form of association . . . in which each, while uniting himself with all, may still obey himself alone, and remain as free as before." Freedom did not mean the absence of restraint, it meant that equal citizens obeyed laws they had made themselves. Rousseau hardly imagined any social leveling, and by "equality" he meant only that no one would be "rich enough to buy another, nor poor enough to have to sell oneself."

Rousseau believed that legitimate authority arose from the people alone. His argument has three parts. First, sovereignty should not be divided among different branches of government (as suggested by Montesquieu), and it emphatically could not be "usurped" by a king. In the late seventeenth century, Locke had spelled out the people's right to rebel against an errant king. Rousseau argued that a king never became sovereign to begin with. Instead, the people themselves acted together as legislators, executives, and judges. Second, exercising sovereignty transformed the nation. Rousseau argued that when individual citizens formed a "body politic," that body became more than just the sum of its parts. He offered what was to many an appealing image of a regenerated and more powerful nation, in which citizens were bound by mutual obligation rather than coercive laws and united in equality rather than divided and weakened by privilege. Third, the national community would be united by what Rousseau called "the general will." This term is notoriously difficult. Rousseau proposed it as a way to understand the common interest, which rose above particular individual demands. The general will favored equality; that made it general, and in principle at least equality guaranteed that citizens' common interests would be represented in the whole.

Rousseau's lack of concern for balancing private interests against the general will leads some political theorists to consider him authoritarian, coercive, or moralistic. Others interpret the general will as one expression of his utopianism. In the eighteenth century, *The Social Contract* was the least understood of Rousseau's works. Yet it provided influential radical arguments and, more important, extraordinarily powerful images and phrases, which were widely cited during the French Revolution.

Rousseau was better known for his writing on education and moral virtue. His widely read novel *Emile* (1762) tells the story of a young man who learns virtue and moral autonomy—and in the school of nature rather than in the academy. Rousseau disagreed with other *philosophes'* emphasis on reason, insisting instead that "the first impulses of nature are always right." Children should not be forced to reason early in life. Books, which "teach us only to talk about things we do not know," should not be central to learning until adolescence. Emile's tutor thus walked him through the woods, studying nature and its simple precepts, cultivating his conscience and, above all, his sense of independence. "Nourished in the most absolute liberty, the greatest evil he can imagine is servitude."

Such an education aimed to give men moral autonomy and make them good citizens. Rousseau argued that women should have very different educations. "All education of women must be relative to men, pleasing them, being useful to them, raising them when they are young and caring for them when they are old, advising them, consoling them, making their lives pleasant and agreeable, these have been the duties of women since time began." Women were to be useful socially as mothers and wives. In *Emile*, Rousseau laid out just such an education for Emile's wife-to-be, Sophie. At times, Rousseau seemed convinced that women "naturally" sought out such a role: "Dependence is a natural state for women, girls feel themselves made to obey." At other moments he insisted that girls needed to be disciplined, and weaned from their "natural" vices.

Rousseau's conflicting views on female nature provide a good example of the shifting meaning of "nature," a concept central to Enlightenment thought. Enlightenment thinkers used "nature" as a yardstick against which to measure society's shortcomings. "Natural" was better, simpler, uncorrupted. What, though, was "nature"? It could refer to the physical world. It could refer to "primitive" societies. Often, it was a useful invention.

Rousseau's novels sold exceptionally well, especially among women. *Julie* (subtitled *La nouvelle Heloise*), published just after *Emile*, went through seventy editions in three decades. *Julie* tells the story of a young woman who falls in love with one man but dutifully obeys her father's order to marry another. At the end, after many travails and twists of the plot, she dies of exposure after rescuing her children from a cold lake—a perfect example of domestic and maternal virtue. Rousseau's fellow *philosophes* deemed the tale "hysterical and obscene." What appealed to the public, however, was the love story, the tragedy, and Rousseau's conviction that humans were ruled by their hearts as much as their heads, that passion was more important than reason. Rousseau's novels became part of a larger cult of *sensibilité* ("sensitivity") in middle-class and aristocratic circles, an emphasis on spontaneous expressions of feeling, and a belief that sentiment was an expression of authentic humanity. Thematically, this aspect of Rousseau's work contradicted much of the Enlightenment's cult of reason. It is more closely related to the concerns of nineteenth-century romanticism.

How did Rousseau's ideas fit into Enlightenment

views on gender? As we have seen, Enlightenment thinkers considered education key to human progress. Many lamented the poor education of women, especially since, as mothers, governesses, and teachers, many women were charged with raising and teaching children. What kind of education, however, should girls receive? Here, again, Enlightenment thinkers sought to follow the guidance of nature, and they produced scores of essays and books in philosophy, history, literature, and medicine, discussing the "nature" or "character" of the sexes. Were men and women different? Were those differences natural, or had they been created by custom and tradition? Humboldt and Diderot wrote essays on the nature of the sexes; scientific travel literature reported on the family structures of indigenous peoples in the Americas, the South Pacific, and China. Histories of civilization by Adam Smith among many others commented on family and gender roles at different stages of history. Montesquieu's *Spirit of the Laws* included an analysis of how the different stages of government affected women. To speculate on the subject, as Rousseau did, was a common Enlightenment exercise.

Some disagreed with his conclusions. Diderot, Voltaire, and the German thinker Theodor Von Hippel among many others deplored legal restrictions on women. Rousseau's prescriptions for women's education drew especially sharp criticism. The English writer and historian Catherine Macaulay set out to refute his points. The marquis de Condorcet argued on the eve of the French Revolution that the Enlightenment promise of progress could not be fulfilled unless women were educated—and Condorcet was virtually alone in asserting that women should be granted political rights.

THE WORLD OF WOLLSTONECRAFT

Rousseau's sharpest critic was the British writer Mary Wollstonecraft (1759–1797). Wollstonecraft published her best known work, *A Vindication of the Rights of Woman*, in 1792, during the French Revolution. Her argument, however, was anchored in Enlightenment debates. Wollstonecraft shared Rousseau's political views and admired his writing and influence. Like Rousseau and her countryman Thomas Paine, a British writer who supported the American and French revolutionaries, Wollstonecraft was a republican. She called monarchy "the pestiferous purple which renders the progress of civilization a curse, and warps the understanding." She spoke even more forcefully than Rousseau against inequality and the artificial distinc-

Mary Wollstonecraft.

tions of rank, birth, or wealth. Believing that equality laid the basis for virtue, she contended, in classic Enlightenment language, that the society should seek "the perfection of our nature and capability of happiness." She argued more forcefully than any other Enlightenment thinker that: (1) women had the same innate capacity for reason and self-government as men; (2) "virtue" should mean the same thing for men and women; and (3) relations between the sexes should be based on equality.

Wollstonecraft did what few of her contemporaries even imagined. She applied the radical Enlightenment critique of monarchy and inequality to the family. The legal inequalities of marriage law, which among other things deprived married women of property rights, gave husbands "despotic" power over their wives. Just as kings cultivated their subjects' deference, so culture, she argued, cultivated women's weakness. "Civilized women are . . . so weakened by false refinement, that, respecting morals, their condition is much below what it would be were they left in a state nearer to nature." Middle-class girls learned manners, grace, and seductiveness in order to win a husband; they were trained to be dependent creatures. "My own sex, I hope, will excuse me, if I treat them like rational creatures instead of flattering their *fascinating* graces, and

ROUSSEAU AND HIS READERS

Jean-Jacques Rousseau's writings provoked very different responses from eighteenth-century readers—women as well as men. Many women readers loved his fiction and found his views about women's character and prescriptions for their education inspiring. Other women disagreed vehemently with his conclusions. In the first excerpt below, from Rousseau's novel Emile *(1762), the author sets out his views on a woman's education. He argues that her education should fit with what he considers her intellectual capacity and her social role. It should also complement the education and role of a man. The second selection is an admiring response to* Emile *from Anne-Louise-Gennaine Necker, or Madame de Stael (1766–1817), a well known French woman writer and literary critic. While she acknowledged that Rousseau sought to keep women from participating in political discussion, she also thought that he had granted women a new role in matters of sentiment and domesticity. The third excerpt is from Mary Wollstonecraft, who shared many of Rousseau's philosophical principles but sharply disagreed with his assertion that women and men should have different virtues and values. She believed that women like Madame de Stael were misguided in embracing Rousseau's ideas.*

ROUSSEAU'S *EMILE*

Researches into abstract and speculative truths, the principles and axioms of sciences—in short, everything which tends to generalize our ideas—is not the proper province of women; their studies should be relative to points of practice; it belongs to them to apply those principles which men have discovered . . . All the ideas of women, which have not the immediate tendency to points of duty, should be directed to the study of men, and to the attainment of those agreeable accomplishments which have taste for their object; for as to works of genius, they are beyond their capacity; neither have they sufficient precision or power of attention to succeed in sciences which require accuracy; and as to physical knowledge, it belongs to those only who are most active, most inquisitive, who comprehend the greatest variety of objects . . .

She must have the skill to incline us to do everything which her sex will not enable her to do herself, and which is necessary or agreeable to her; therefore she ought to study the mind of man thoroughly, not the mind of man in general, abstractedly, but the dispositions of those men to whom she is subject either by the laws of her country or by the force of opinion. She should learn to penetrate into the real sentiments from their conversation, their actions, their looks and gestures. She should also have the art, by her own conversation, actions, looks, and gestures, to communicate those sentiments which are agreeable to them without seeming to intend it. Men will argue more philosophically about the human heart; but women will read the heart of men better than they. . . . Women have most wit, men have most genius; women observe, men reason. From the concurrence of both we derive the clearest light and the most perfect knowledge which the human mind is of itself capable of attaining.

MADAME DE STAEL

Though Rousseau has endeavoured to prevent women from interfering in public affairs, and acting a brilliant part in the theatre of politics; yet in speaking of them, how much has he done it to their satisfaction! If he wished to deprive them of some rights foreign to their sex, how has he for ever restored to them all those to which it has a claim! And in attempting to diminish their influence over the deliberations of men, how sacredly has he established the empire they have over their happiness! In aiding them to descend from an usurped throne, he has firmly seated them upon that to which they were destined by nature; and though he be full of indignation against them when they endeavour to resemble men, yet when they come before him with all the *charms, weaknesses, virtues,* and *errors* of their sex, his respect for their *persons* amounts almost to adoration.

MARY WOLLSTONECRAFT

...Rousseau declares that a woman should never, for a moment, feel herself independent, that she should be governed by fear to exercise her *natural* cunning, and made a coquettish slave in order to render her a more alluring object of desire, a *sweeter* companion to man, whenever he chooses to relax himself. He carries the arguments, which he pretends to draw from the indications of nature, still further, and insinuates that truth and fortitude, the corner stones of all human virtue, should be cultivated with certain restrictions, because, with respect to the female character, obedience is the grand lesson which ought to be impressed with unrelenting rigour.

What nonsense! when will a great man arise with sufficient strength of mind to puff away the fumes which pride and sensuality have thus spread over the subject! If women are by nature inferior to men, their virtues must be the same in quality, if not in degree, or virtue is a relative idea; consequently, their conduct should be founded on the same principles, and have the same aim.

Jean-Jacques Rousseau, *Emile* (1762), and Madame de Stael as cited in Mary Wollstonecraft, *A Vindication of the Rights of Woman* (New York/London: Penguin Books, 1992), pp. 124–25, 203–4. Mary Wollstonecraft as cited in Susan Bell and Karen Offen, eds. *Women, the Family, and Freedom: The Debate in Documents*, Vol. 1, *1750–1880*. (Stanford: Stanford University Press, 1983). p. 58.

viewing them as if they were in a state of perpetual childhood, unable to stand alone. I earnestly wish to point out in what true dignity and human happiness consists—I wish to persuade women to endeavor to acquire strength, both of mind and body . . . " A culture that encouraged feminine weakness produced women who were childish, cunning, cruel—and vulnerable. Here Wollstonecraft echoed common eighteenth-century themes. The scheming aristocratic women in Choderlos de Laclos' *Dangerous Liaisons*, written in the 1780s, were meant to illustrate the same points. To Rousseau's specific prescriptions for female education, which included teaching women timidity, chasteness, and modesty, Wollstonecraft replied that Rousseau wanted women to use their reason to "burnish their chains rather than to snap them." Instead, education for women had to promote liberty and self-reliance.

Wollstonecraft was a woman of her time. She argued for the common humanity of men and women, but believed that they had different duties, and that women's foremost responsibility was mothering and educating children. Like many of her fellow Enlightenment thinkers, Wollstonecraft believed that a natural division of labor existed, and that it would assure social harmony. "Let there be no coercion *established* in society, and the common law of gravity prevailing, the sexes will fall into their proper places." Like others, she wrote about middle-class women, for whom education and property were issues. She only hinted that women might have political rights, and even so was considered scandalously radical.

The Enlightenment as a whole left a mixed legacy on gender, one that closely paralleled that on slavery. Enlightenment writers developed and popularized arguments about natural rights. They also elevated natural differences to a higher plane by suggesting that nature should dictate different, and quite possibly unequal, social roles. Mary Wollstonecraft and Jean-Jacques Rousseau shared a radical opposition to

CHRONOLOGY

LIVES OF ENLIGHTENMENT THINKERS

Baron de Montesquieu	1689–1755
Voltaire	1694–1778
David Hume	1711–1776
Jean-Jacques Rousseau	1712–1778
Guillaume Thomas François Raynal	1713–1796
Denis Diderot	1717–1783
Adam Smith	1723–1790
Mary Wollstonecraft	1759–1797

despotism and slavery, a moralist's vision of a corrupt society, and a concern with virtue and community. Their divergence on gender is characteristic of Enlightenment disagreements about "nature" and its imperatives, and a good example of different directions in which the logic of Enlightenment thinking could lead.

THE ENLIGHTENMENT AND EIGHTEENTH-CENTURY CULTURE

How did the "public sphere" expand during the eighteenth century?

THE BOOK TRADE

What about the social structures that produced these debates and received these ideas? To begin with, the Enlightenment was bound up in a much larger expansion of printing and print culture. From the early eighteenth century on, book publishing and selling flourished, especially in Britain, France, the Netherlands, and Switzerland. National borders, though, mattered very little. Much of the book trade was both international and clandestine. Readers bought books from stores, by subscription, and by special mail order from book distributors abroad. Cheaper printing and better distribution also helped to multiply the numbers of journals, some specializing in literary or scientific topics and oth-

ers quite general. They helped bring daily newspapers, which first appeared in London in 1702, to Moscow, Rome, and cities and towns throughout Europe. By 1780, Britons could read one hundred fifty different magazines, and thirty-seven English towns had local newspapers. These changes have been called a "revolution in communication," and they form a crucial part of the larger picture of the Enlightenment.

Governments did little to check this revolutionary transformation. In Britain, the press encountered few restrictions, although the government did use a stamp tax on printed goods to raise the price of newspapers or books and discourage buyers. Elsewhere, laws required publishers to apply in advance for the license or privilege (in the sense of "private right") to print and sell any given work. Some regimes granted more permissions than others. The French government, for instance, alternately banned and tolerated different volumes of the *Encyclopedia*, depending on the subjects covered in the volume, the political climate in the capital, and economic considerations. In practice, publishers frequently printed books without advance permission, hoping that the regime would not notice, but bracing themselves for fines, having their books banned, and finding their privileges temporarily revoked. Russian, Prussian, and Austrian censors tolerated much less dissent, but those governments also sought to stimulate publishing and, to a certain degree, they permitted public discussion. Vienna housed an important publishing empire during the reigns of Joseph and Maria Theresa. Catherine of Russia encouraged the development of a small publishing enterprise which, by 1790, was issuing three hundred fifty titles a year. In the smaller states of Germany and Italy, governed by many local princes, it was easier to find progressive local patrons, and English and French works also circulated widely through the regions. That governments were patrons as well as censors of new scholarship illustrates the complex relationship between the age of absolutism and the Enlightenment.

As one historian puts it, censorship only made banned books expensive, keeping them out of the hands of the poor. Clandestine booksellers, most near the French border in Switzerland and the Rhineland, smuggled thousands of books across the border to bookstores, distributors, and private customers. What did readers want, and what does this tell us about the reception of the Enlightenment? Many clandestine dealers specialized in what they called "philosophical books," which meant subversive literature of all kinds: stories of

HOW DID THE "PUBLIC SPHERE" EXPAND DURING THE EIGHTEENTH CENTURY?

THE ENLIGHTENMENT AND EIGHTEENTH-CENTURY CULTURE   669

languishing in prison, gossipy memoirs of life at the court, pornographic fantasies (often about religious and political figures), and tales of crime and criminals. A book smuggler would have carried several copies of *The Private Lives of Louis XIV*, or *The Black Gazette*, Voltaire's comments on *Encyclopedia* and, less frequently, Rousseau's *Social Contract*. Much of this flourishing eighteenth-century "literary underground," as the historian Robert Darnton calls it, echoed the radical Enlightenment's themes, especially the corruption of the aristocracy and the monarchy's degeneration into despotism. Less explicitly political writings, however, such as Raynal's *History*, Rousseau's novels, travel accounts, biographies, or futuristic fantasies such as Louis Sebastien Mercier's *The Year 2440* proved equally popular. Even expensive volumes like the *Encyclopedia* sold remarkably well, testifying to a keen public interest. It is worth underscoring that Enlightenment work circulated in popular form, and that Rousseau's novels sold as well as his political theory.

HIGH CULTURE, NEW ELITES, AND THE "PUBLIC SPHERE"

The "enlightenment" was not simply embodied in books; it was produced in networks of readers and new forms of sociability and discussion. Eighteenth-century elite or "high" culture was small in scale but cosmopolitan and very literate, and it took discussion seriously. A new elite joined together members of the nobility and wealthy people from the middle classes. Among the institutions that produced this new elite were "learned societies": the American Philosophical Society of Philadelphia, British literary and philosophical societies, and the Select Society of Edinburgh. Such groups organized intellectual life outside of the universities, and they provided libraries, meeting places for discussion, and journals that published members' papers or organized debates on issues from literature and history to economics and ethics. Elites also met in "academies," financed by governments to advance knowledge, whether through research into the natural sciences (the Royal Society of London, the French Academy of Science, both founded in 1660), promoting the national language (the Académie Française, or French Academy of Literature), or safeguarding traditions in the arts (the various academies of painting). The Berlin Royal Academy, for instance, was founded in 1701 to demonstrate the Prussian state's commitment to learning. Members included scholars in residence, "corresponding" members in other countries, and honorary associates, so the academy's reach was quite broad, and the Prussian government made a point of bringing in scholars from other countries. Particularly under Frederick II, who was eager to sponsor new research, the Berlin Academy flourished as a center of Enlightenment thinking. The academy's journal published members' papers every year, in French, for a European audience. In France, provincial academies played much the same role. Works such as Rousseau's *Discourse on the Origins of Inequality* were entered in academy-sponsored essay contests. Academy members included government and military officials, wealthy merchants, doctors, noble land owners, and scholars. Learned societies and academies both brought together different social groups (most from the elite) and in so doing, they fostered a sense of common purpose and seriousness.

> Eighteenth-century elite or "high" culture was small in scale but cosmopolitan, very literate, and it took discussion seriously.

CHRONOLOGY

MAJOR PUBLICATIONS OF THE ENLIGHTENMENT, 1721–1792

Montesquieu, *The Persian Letters*	1721
Voltaire, *Philosophical Letters*	1734
Montesquieu, *The Spirit of Laws*	1748
The *Encyclopedia*	1751–1772
Beccaria, *On Crime and Punishments*	1764
Smith, *Inquiry into Nature and Causes of the Wealth of Nations*	1776
Raynal, *Philosophical History*	1770
Rousseau, *The Social Contract*	1762
Rousseau, *Emile*	1762
Wollstonecraft, *A Vindication of the Rights of Woman*	1792

SALONS

"Salons" did the same, but operated informally. Usually they were organized by well-connected and learned aristocratic women. The prominent role of women distinguished the salons from the academies and universities. Salons brought together men and women of letters

Immanuel Kant.

selves to the regeneration of society, attracted a remarkable array of aristocrats and middle-class men. Mozart, Frederick II, and Montesquieu all were Masons. Behind their closed doors, the lodges were egalitarian. They pledged themselves to a common project of rational thought and benevolent action, and to banishing religion and social distinction—at least from their ranks.

Other networks of sociability were less exclusive. Coffeehouses multiplied with the colonial trade in sugar, coffee, and tea, and they occupied a central spot in the circulation of ideas. A group of merchants gathering to discuss trade, for instance, could turn to politics, and the many newspapers lying about the café tables provided a ready-to-hand link between their smaller discussions and news and debates elsewhere.

The philosopher Immanuel Kant remarked that a sharper public consciousness seemed one of the hallmarks of his time. "If we attend to the course of conversation in mixed companies consisting not merely of scholars and subtle reasoners but also of business people or women, we notice that besides storytelling or jesting they have another entertainment, namely, arguing." The ability to think critically and speak freely, without deferring to religion or tradition, was a point of pride, and not simply for intellectuals. Eighteenth-century cultural changes—the expanding networks of sociability, the flourishing book trade, the new genres of literature, and the circulation of Enlightenment ideas—widened the circles of reading and discussion, expanding what some historians and political theorists call the "public sphere." That, in turn, began to change politics. Informal deliberations, debates about how to regenerate the nation, discussions of civic virtue, and efforts to forge a consensus played a crucial role in moving politics beyond the confines of the court.

with members of the aristocracy for conversation, debate, drink, and food. Rousseau loathed this kind of ritual and viewed salons as a sign of superficiality and vacuity in a privileged and overcivilized world. Thomas Jefferson thought the influence of women in salons had put France in a "desperate state." Some of the salons reveled in parlor games. Others, such as the one organized in Paris by Madame Necker, wife of the future French reform minister, lay quite close to the halls of power, and served as testing ground for new policy ideas. Madame Marie-Thérèse Geoffrin, another celebrated French *salonière*, became an important patron of the *Encyclopedia* and exercised influence in placing scholars in academies. Moses Mendelssohn, an exception to the feminine rule, held an open house for intellectuals in Berlin. Salons in London, Vienna, Rome, and Berlin worked the same way, and like academies they promoted among their participants a sense of belonging to an active, learned elite.

Scores of similar societies emerged in the eighteenth century. Masonic lodges, organizations with elaborate secret rituals whose members pledged them-

> The ability to think critically and speak freely, without deferring to religion or tradition, was a point of pride, and not simply for intellectuals.

The eighteenth century gave birth to the very idea of "public opinion." A French observer described the changes this way: "In the last thirty years alone, a great and important revolution has occurred in our ideas. Today, public opinion has a preponderant force in Europe that cannot be resisted." Few thought the "public" involved more than the elite. Yet by the late eighteenth century, European governments recognized the existence of a civic-minded group that stretched from salons to coffee houses, academies, and circles of government, and to which they needed, in some measure, to respond.

HOW DID THE "PUBLIC SPHERE" EXPAND DURING THE EIGHTEENTH CENTURY?

THE ENLIGHTENMENT AND EIGHTEENTH-CENTURY CULTURE   671

MIDDLE-CLASS CULTURE AND READING

Enlightenment fare constituted only part of the new cultural interests of the eighteenth-century middle classes. Lower down on the social scale, shopkeepers, small merchants, lawyers, and professionals read more and more different kinds of books. Instead of owning one well-thumbed Bible to read aloud, a middle-class family would buy and borrow books to read casually, pass on, and discuss. This literature including much more science, history, biography, travel literature, and fiction. A great deal of it was aimed at middle-class women, among the fastest-growing group of readers in the eighteenth century. Etiquette books sold very well; so did how-to manuals for the household. Scores of books about the manners, morals, and education of daughters, popular versions of Enlightenment treatises on education and the mind, illustrate close parallels between the intellectual life of the high Enlightenment and everyday middle-class reading matter.

The rise of a middle-class reading public, much of it female, helps to account for the soaring popularity and production of novels, especially in Britain. Novels were the single most popular new form of literature in the eighteenth century. A survey of library borrowing in late-eighteenth-century Britain, Germany, and North America showed that 70 percent of books taken out were novels. For centuries, Europeans had read romances such as tales of the knights of the Round Table. Novels, though, did not treat quasimythical subjects, the writing was less ornate, and the setting and situations were literally closer to home. The novel's more recognizable, nonaristocratic characters seemed more relevant to common middle-class experience. Moreover, examining emotion and inner feeling also linked novel writing with a larger eighteenth-century concern with personhood and humanity. As we have seen, classic Enlightenment writers like Voltaire, Goethe, and Rousseau wrote very successful novels, and those should be understood alongside the *Pamela* or *Clarissa* of Samuel Richardson (1689–1761); the *Moll Flanders* or *Robinson Crusoe* of Daniel Defoe (1660–1731); or the *Tom Jones* of Henry Fielding (1707–1754).

Many historians have noted that women figured prominently among fiction writers. In seventeenth-century France the most widely read authors of romances had been Madeleine de Scudéry and the countess de La Fayette. Later, in England, Fanny Burney (1752–1840), Ann Radcliffe (1764–1823), and Maria Edgeworth (1767–1849) all wrote extremely popular novels. The works of Jane Austen (1775–1817), especially *Pride and Prejudice* and *Emma,* are to many readers the height of a novelist's craft. Women writers, however, were not the only ones to write novels, nor were they alone in paying close attention to the domestic or private sphere. Their work took up central eighteenth-century themes of human nature, morality, virtue, and reputation. Their novels, like much of the nonfiction of the period, explored those themes in domestic as in public settings.

POPULAR CULTURE: URBAN AND RURAL

How much did books and print culture touch the lives of the common people? Literacy rates varied dramatically by gender, social class, and region, but were generally higher in northern than in southern and eastern Europe. Not surprisingly, literacy ran highest in cities and towns—higher, in fact, than we might expect. In early eighteenth-century Paris, 85 percent of men and 60 percent of women could read. Well over half the residents of poorer Parisian neighborhoods, especially small shopkeepers, domestic servants and valets, and artisans, could read and sign their names. Even the illiterate, however, lived in a culture of print. They saw one-page newspapers and broadsides or flysheets posted on streets and tavern walls, and regularly heard them read aloud. Moreover, visual material—inexpensive woodcuts especially, but also prints, drawings, satirical cartoons—figured as prominently as text in much popular reading material. By many measures, then, the circles of reading and discussion were even larger than literacy rates might suggest, especially in cities.

To be sure, poorer households had few books on their shelves, and those tended to be religious texts: an abridged Bible, *The Pilgrim's Progress,* or an illustrated prayer book bought or given on some special occasion and read aloud repeatedly. But popular reading was boosted by the increasing availability of new materials. From the late seventeenth century on, a French firm published a series of inexpensive small paperbacks, the so-called blue books, which itinerant peddlers carried from cities to villages in the countryside for a growing popular market. The blue library included traditional popular literature. That meant short catechisms, quasireligious tales of miracles, and stories of the lives of the saints, which the church hoped would provide religious instruction. It also included almanacs, books on astrology, and manuals of medical cures for people or farm animals. In the eighteenth century, book peddlers began to carry abridged and simple novels, and to sell books on themes popular in the middle classes, such as travel and history. Books provided an incentive to read.

Neither England nor France required any primary schooling, leaving that task to sporadic local initiatives. In central Europe, some regimes made efforts to develop state-sponsored education. Catherine of Russia summoned an Austrian consultant to set up a system of primary schools, but by the end of the eighteenth century only 22,000 of a population of 40 million had attended any kind of schools. In the absence of primary schooling, most Europeans were self-taught. The varied texts in the peddler's cart—whether religious, political propaganda, or entertainment—attest to a widespread and rapidly growing popular interest in books and reading.

Like its middle-class counterpart, popular culture rested on networks of sociability. Guild organizations offered discussion and companionship. Street theater and singers mocking local political figures offered culture to people from different social classes. The difficulties of deciphering popular culture are considerable. Most testimony comes to us from outsiders who regarded the common people as hopelessly superstitious and ignorant. Still, historical research has begun to reveal new insights. It has shown, first, that popular culture did not exist in isolation. Particularly in the countryside, market days and village festivals brought social classes together, and popular entertainments reached a wide social audience. Folktales and traditional songs resist pigeonholing as either elite, middle-class, or popular culture, for they passed from one cultural world to another, being revised and reinterpreted in the process. Second, oral and literate culture overlapped. In other words, even people who could not read often had a great deal of "book knowledge": they argued seriously about points from books, and believed that books conferred authority. A group of villagers, for instance, wrote this eulogy to a deceased friend: "he read his life long, and died without ever knowing how to read." The logic and world view of popular culture needs to be understood on its own terms.

It remains true that the countryside, especially in less economically developed regions, was desperately poor. Life there was far more isolated than in towns. A yawning chasm separated peasants from the world of the high Enlightenment. The *philosophes*, well established in the summits of European society, looked at popular culture with distrust and ignorance. They saw the common people of Europe much as they did indigenous peoples of other continents. They were humanitarians, critical thinkers, and reformers; they were not democrats. The Enlightenment, while well entrenched in eighteenth-century elite culture, nonetheless involved changes that reached well beyond elite society.

EIGHTEENTH-CENTURY MUSIC

European elites sustained other forms of high culture. English gentlemen who read scientific papers aloud in clubs also commissioned architects to design classical revival country houses for the weekends. Royal courts underwrote the academies of painting, which upheld aristocratic taste and aesthetics; Austrian salons that hosted discussions of Voltaire also staged performances of Mozart. We have already noted that the *philosophes'* work crossed genres, from political theory to fiction. Rousseau not only wrote discourses and novels, he composed music and wrote an opera. A flourishing musical culture was one of the most important features of the eighteenth century.

BACH AND HANDEL

The early eighteenth century brought the last phase of Baroque music and two of the greatest composers of all time: Johann Sebastian Bach (1685–1750) and George Frideric Handel (1685–1759). Bach was an intensely pious man who remained in the backwaters of provincial Germany all his life. As a church musician in Leipzig for most of his adult career, Bach had to supply music for nearly all Sunday and holiday services, and he combined imagination and brilliance with steely self-discipline and an ability to produce music on demand. He was an ardent Protestant, entirely unaffected by the secularism of the Enlightenment: each one of his church pieces is full of such fervor that the salvation of the world appears to hang on every note. He was also prolific, writing across the entire gamut of contemporary forms (excluding opera), from unaccompanied instrumental pieces to large-scale works for vocal soloists, chorus, and orchestra. Much of his work consists of religious cantatas (over two hundred surviving), motets, and Passions, but he also wrote concertos and suites for orchestra, and composed the purest of "pure" music—subtle and complex fugues for keyboard.

Handel, by contrast, was a public-pleasing cosmopolitan, who sought out large, secular audiences. After spending his early years mastering Baroque compositional techniques in Italy, Handel established

HOW DID THE "PUBLIC SPHERE" EXPAND DURING THE EIGHTEENTH CENTURY?

THE ENLIGHTENMENT AND EIGHTEENTH-CENTURY CULTURE   673

Johann Sebastian Bach.

George Frideric Handel.

himself in London. He tried to make a living by composing Italian operas, but after initial success opera sounded foreign and flowery to British ears. Handel eventually found a more marketable genre, the oratorio: a musical drama to be performed in concert, without staging. Handel's oratorios were usually set to biblical stories but featured very worldly music, replete with ornate instrumentation and frequent flourishes of drums and trumpets. (Some music historians refer to Handel's "big bow-wow" manner.) These heroic works succeeded in packing London's halls full of prosperous Britons, who interpreted the victories of the ancient Hebrews in such oratorios as *Israel in Egypt* and *Judas Maccabaeus* as implicit celebrations of Britain's own burgeoning national greatness. Handel's greatest oratorio, *Messiah*, is still sung widely throughout the English-speaking world every Christmas; its stirring "Hallelujah" chorus remains the most popular single choral piece in the entire classical repertoire.

HAYDN AND MOZART

Bach and Handel were among the last and certainly the greatest composers of Baroque music; the Austrians Joseph Haydn (1732–1809) and Wolfgang Amadeus Mozart (1756–1791) were the leading representatives of the "Classical" style, which swept Europe in the second half of the eighteenth century. Classicism here had nothing to do with imitating music written in classical antiquity. It sought to imitate classical principles of order, clarity, and symmetry—in other words, to sound as a Greek temple looked. The Classical era brought the string quartet and, most impressively, the symphony, sometimes called the novel of music, which has proven to be the most versatile and popular of all Classical musical forms. Composers of the Classical school created music that adhered rigorously to certain structural principles. For example, nearly all Classical symphonies have four movements, and nearly all symphonies open with a first movement in sonata form, characterized by the successive presentation of theme, development, and recapitulation.

Mozart's last three symphonies (out of his total of forty-one) are unequalled in their grace, variety, and technical perfection. But Mozart's short and famously difficult life captures the problems that even prodigiously talented eighteenth-century artists faced. Wolfgang began composing at four, became known as a keyboard virtuoso at six, and wrote his first symphony at nine. Wolfgang's father promoted his son, touring him as a child prodigy (with his very gifted sister) through the courts

Two Contemporary Representations of Mozart. Above is the child prodigy, age seven; below, the composer in his twenties, wearing a badge of honor of an Italian musical society that he won at age fourteen.

of Europe: "My boy as an eight-year-old knows as much as what one expects from a man of forty. In short: whoever does not see or hear it cannot believe it." These were the 1760s, the height of the Enlighten-

ment, and Mozart senior grumbled about the climate of skepticism and disbelief. "Nowadays, people ridicule everything that is called a miracle," he wrote. "It was a great pleasure and a great victory for me to hear a Voltairian say to me, 'Now for once in my life I have seen a miracle; this is the first.'" Wolfgang gathered awards and honors from the pope and the Austrian empress Maria Theresa, attracted attention across Europe, and became a moneymaker for his family. But once he was no longer a child prodigy, like nearly all eighteenth-century artists and writers he had to rely on patronage. Mozart, a difficult person himself, suffered in the service of the cantankerous archbishop of Salzburg, a town he hated. He tried to support himself as a freelance composer and keyboard performer in Vienna. Despite his immense productivity and well-known genius, he could barely make ends meet. He lived hand to mouth, borrowing money from his fellow Masons in the Lodge of Beneficence. He was only thirty-five when he died of rheumatic fever. In keeping with eighteenth-century medical practice, his physicians bled him frequently in the last month of his life and may have hastened his death, possibly poisoning his blood with their unsterilized instruments. It is not true that he was buried, unrecognized, in a pauper's grave. His funeral was simple and cheap, in keeping with his poverty, but also with his Masonic principles and Enlightenment opposition to Catholic ritual. His fellow composer Joseph Haydn rued that "we have lost the greatest among us."

The career of Joseph Haydn (1732–1809) provides a revealing contrast. Knowing much better how to take care of himself, he spent most of his life employed by an extremely wealthy Austro-Hungarian aristocratic family that maintained its own private orchestra. But this security entailed the indignity of wearing the Esterházy uniform, like any common butler. Only toward the end of his life, in 1791, did Haydn, then famous, strike out on his own by traveling to London, where for five years (excluding a brief interval) he supported himself handsomely by writing for a paying public rather than for private patrons. Eighteenth-century London was one of the rare localities with a commercial market for culture. In this regard London was the wave of the future, for in the nineteenth century serious music would leave the aristocratic salon forever for urban concert halls all over Europe. In deeply aristocratic Austria Haydn had been obliged to wear servants' livery; in London he was greeted as a creative genius, one of the earliest composers to be regarded as such. Haydn's "Miracle" symphony, written for performance

HOW DID THE "PUBLIC SPHERE" EXPAND DURING THE EIGHTEENTH CENTURY?

THE ENLIGHTENMENT AND EIGHTEENTH-CENTURY CULTURE   675

Haydn in London. While he worked in the pay of the Esterházy family, Haydn was little more than a high-level servant. In London, on the other hand, he was portrayed as an inspired genius with a preoccupied look in his eye.

in a London concert hall, is called that because during one performance a chandelier came crashing down, narrowly missing the crowd gathered to see the "genius" conduct. Although not the first writer of symphonies, Haydn is often termed the "father of the symphony." In over one hundred works in the symphonic form—especially his last twelve symphonies, which he composed in London—Haydn formulated the most enduring techniques of symphonic composition and demonstrated the symphony's enormous creative potential.

OPERA

Finally, opera flourished in the eighteenth century. Opera was a seventeenth-century creation, developed most significantly by the Italian Baroque composer Claudio Monteverdi (1567–1643), who combined music with theater for greater dramatic intensity. Monteverdi's new form of opera appealed immediately: within one generation operas were performed in all the leading cities of Italy, and by the eighteenth century they had captured attention across Europe. Staged within magnificent settings and calling on the talents of singers, musicians, dramatists, and stage designers, opera expressed as clearly as any art form Baroque artists' dedication to grandeur, drama, and display. In the Classical period, opera's popularity was boosted by Christoph Willibald von Gluck (1714–1787). Gluck, who came to Paris from Austria as the musical tutor of the young Marie Antoinette, insisted that the texts be as important as the music. He simplified arias, emphasized dramatic action, and produced high-end entertainment for the French court. Mozart, however, was the greatest operatic composer of the Classical era. *The Marriage of Figaro, Don Giovanni,* and *The Magic Flute* remain among the best-loved operas of all time.

Eighteenth-century musicians, like eighteenth-century writers, found their careers and art shaped by changing structures of culture. Despite a trend toward secularism, the church continued to provide support for much everyday music. In a very few cases —Haydn's in London is one —composers could be supported by the market. Aristocratic and court patronage, however, remained the pillars of support for musicians. And musicians, like Enlightenment writers, had an ambivalent relationship with their patrons and culture. Rousseau, in his role as a composer, railed at the way in which the aristocracy set the tone of opera productions in his time. He deplored pretentious staging and emotional inauthenticity. In his own opera he tried to bring different themes—nature, simplicity, and virtue—to the stage. The British writer Samuel Johnson called patrons "insolent wretches." Mozart relied on the overbearing archbishop of Salzburg to commission work and, just as important, ensure that it would be performed, but he resented his position: "I did not know that I was a valet." One of Mozart's most popular operas—*The Marriage of Figaro,* based on a French play—circled around just these themes: relations between masters and servants, the abuses of privilege, and the presumptuousness of the European nobility.

The Marriage of Figaro, indeed, followed a classic eighteenth-century path to popularity. The author of the play was born Pierre Caron, the son of a watchmaker. Caron rose to become watchmaker to the king, bought noble office, married well, took the name Pierre Augustin de Beaumarchais, and wrote several comedies in an Enlightenment tone satirizing the French nobility. *Figaro* ran into trouble with French censors, but like so many other banned works, the play sold well. It was translated into Italian, was set to music by the Mason Mozart, and played to appreciative elite audiences from Paris to Prague. Satire, self-criticism, the criticism of hierarchy, optimism and social mobility, and a cosmopolitan outlook supported by what was in many ways a traditional society—all of these are key to understanding all of eighteenth-century culture as well as the Enlightenment.

Conclusion

The Enlightenment arose from the scientific revolution, from the new sense of power and possibility that science created, and from the rush of enthusiasm for new forms of inquiry. Together, the Enlightenment and the scientific revolution created science as a form of knowledge. Eighteenth-century thinkers scrutinized a remarkably wide range of topics: human nature, reason and the processes of understanding, religion, belief, law, the origins of government authority, economics, and social practices. Whether well-known *philosophes* or underground journalists, they raised problems that made regimes, their contemporaries, and even themselves uncomfortable. Ideas circulated in popular forms from plays and operas to journalism. Intellectual changes went hand in hand with social and cultural ones: government efforts to put their states on a new footing, the emergence of a new elite, and the expansion of the public sphere.

The Atlantic revolutions (the American Revolution of 1776, the French Revolution of 1789, and the Latin American upheavals of the 1830s) were steeped in the language of the Enlightenment. The constitutions of the new nations formed by these revolutions followed the basic ideas of Enlightenment liberalism: neither religion nor the state could impede individual freedom of conscience; government authority could not be arbitrary; equality and freedom were natural; humans sought happiness, prosperity, and the expansion of their potential. These arguments had been made, tentatively, earlier. But when the North American colonists declared their independence from Britain in 1776, they called these ideas "self-evident truths." That bold declaration marked both the distance traveled since the late seventeenth century and the self-confidence that was the Enlightenment's hallmark.

Selected Readings

Baker, Keith. *Condorcet: From Natural Philosophy to Social Mathematics.* Chicago, 1975. An important reinterpretation of Condorcet as a social scientist.

Bell, Susan and Karen Offen, eds. *Women, the Family, and Freedom: The Debate in Documents.* Vol. 1, *1750–1880.* Stanford, 1983. An excellent introduction to Enlightenment debates about gender and women.

Blum, Carol. *Rousseau and the Republic of Virtue: The Language of Politics in the French Revolution.* Ithaca and London, 1986. Fascinating account of how eighteenth-century readers interpreted Rousseau.

Calhoun, Craig, ed. *Habermas and the Public Sphere.* Cambridge, Mass., 1992. Calhoun's introduction is a good starting point for Habermas's argument.

Cassirer, E. *The Philosophy of the Enlightenment.* Princeton, 1951.

Chartier, Roger. *The Cultural Origins of the French Revolution.* Durham, N.C., 1991. Looks at topics from religion to violence in everyday life and culture.

Darnton, Robert. *The Business of Enlightenment: A Publishing History of the* Encyclopédie, *1775–1800.* Cambridge, Mass., 1979. Darnton's work on the Enlightenment offers a fascinating blend of intellectual, social, and economic history. See his other books as well: *The Literary Underground of the Old Regime,* Cambridge, Mass., 1982; *The Great Cat Massacre and other Episodes in French Cultural History,* New York, 1984; and *The Forbidden Best Sellers of Revolutionary France,* New York and London, 1996.

Davis, David Brion. *The Problem of Slavery in Western Culture,* Cornell. 1966. A Pulitzer-prize–winning examination of a central issue as well as a brilliant analysis of different strands of Enlightenment thought.

Gay, Peter. *The Enlightenment: An Interpretation.* Vol. 1, *The Rise of Modern Paganism.* Vol. 2, *The Science of Freedom.* New York, 1966–1969. Combines an overview with an interpretation. Emphasizes the *philosophes'* sense of identification with the classical world and takes a generally positive view of their accomplishments. Includes extensive annotated bibliographies.

———. *Mozart.* New York, 1999.

Goodman, Dena. *The Republic of Letters: A Cultural History of the French Enlightenment.* Ithaca, N.Y., 1994. Important in its attention to the role of literary women.

Hazard, Paul. *The European Mind: The Critical Years (1680–1715).* New Haven, 1953. A basic and indispensable account of the changing climate of opinion that preceded the Enlightenment.

Hildesheimer, Wolfgang. *Mozart.* New York, 1982. An exceptionally literate and thought-provoking biography.

Munck, Thomas. *The Enlightenment: A Comparative Social History 1721–1794.* London, 2000. An excellent recent survey, especially good on social history.

Outram, Dorinda. *The Enlightenment.* Cambridge, 1995. An excellent short introduction and a good example of new historical approaches.

Rendall, Jane. *The Origins of Modern Feminism: Women in Britain, France and the United States, 1780–1860.* New York, 1984.

Sapiro, Virginia. *A Vindication of Political Virtue: The Political Theory of Mary Wollstonecraft.* Chicago, 1992. A subtle and intelligent analysis for more advanced readers.

Shklar, Judith. *Men and Citizens: a Study of Rousseau's Social Theory.* London, 1969.

———. *Montesquieu.* Oxford, 1987.

Venturi, Franco. *The End of the Old Regime in Europe, 1768–1776: The First Crisis,* trans. R. Burr Litchfield. Princeton, 1989 and *The End of the Old Regime in Europe, 1776–1789.* Princeton, 1991. Detailed and wide-ranging, particularly important on international developments.

Watt, Ian P. *The Rise of the Novel.* London, 1957. The basic work on the innovative qualities of the novel in eighteenth-century England.

PART VI

THE FRENCH AND INDUSTRIAL REVOLUTIONS AND THEIR CONSEQUENCES

NO TWO EVENTS more profoundly altered the shape of Western culture than the French and Industrial Revolutions. The major developments of the nineteenth and early twentieth centuries—the decline of landed aristocracies and the rise of new social groups, the emergence of dramatically new forms of politics, changes in political and social thought, economic expansion and Europe's expanding hegemony in the world—all had their roots in these two revolutions.

The French and Industrial Revolutions took place at about the same time and affected many of the same people, though in different ways and to varying degrees. Together they brought the collapse of absolutism, mercantilism, and the last vestiges of manorialism. Together they produced the theory and practice of economic individualism and political liberalism. And together, the wrenching changes they wrought polarized Europe for several generations. What historians call the "age of revolution" lasted from the 1770s through at least half the nineteenth century.

Each revolution, of course, produced results peculiarly its own. The French Revolution helped make such terms as *citizen, nation,* and *liberty* central to the political vocabulary of modern times. It encouraged the growth of nationalism—in both liberal and authoritarian forms. The Industrial Revolution changed the economic and cultural landscape of Europe, with ramifications for the private worlds of men and women as well as the economic organization of the world. Despite their unique contributions, the two revolutions must be studied together and understood as the joint progenitors of Western history in the nineteenth and early twentieth centuries.

	POLITICS	SOCIETY AND CULTURE	ECONOMY	INTERNATIONAL RELATIONS
1750		Johann Wolfgang von Goethe (1749–1852)	British export production increases 80 percent (1750–1770)	
		William Blake (1757–1827)	British Parliament increases enclosures (1750–1860)	
	Reign of Catherine the Great of Russia (1762–1796)		Spinning jenny, water frame, and spinning mule invented (1764–1799)	Poland partitioned by Russia, Austria, and Prussia (1772, 1793, 1795)
	American Revolution (1774–1782)	William Wordsworth (1770–1850)	James Watt patents improved steam engine (1769)	
		Goethe's *Faust* (1790)		
			Industrial Revolution (1780–1880)	
	Louis XVI calls Assembly of Notables (1788)			
	The French Revolution breaks out (1789)	Jeremy Bentham's *An Introduction to the Principles of Morals and Legislation* (1789)		
	Great Fear in the French countryside (1789)			
	Declaration of the Rights of Man and of the Citizen (1789)			
	French National Assembly abolishes feudal rights and privileges (1789)			
1790	Slave revolt in St. Domingue (1791)	Edmund Burke's *Reflections on the Revolution in France* (1790)		Slave rebellion in St. Domingue sparks British and Spanish invasion (1791)
	Louis XVI of France overthrown and French Republic declared (1792)	Thomas Paine's *The Rights of Man* (1791)		France declares war on Austria and Prussia (1792)
	Reign of Terror (1793–1794)	French Convention abolishes slavery and primogeniture (1793–1794)	Eli Whitney invents cotton gin (1793)	England enters war against France (1793)
	Maximilien Robespierre executed (1794)	Edward Jenner's vaccination against smallpox (1796)		Revolutionary France occupies Low Countries, Rhineland, and parts of Spain and Italy (1794–1796)
		Heinrich Heine, German poet (1797–1856)		
		Wordsworth's and Coleridge's *Lyrical Ballads* (1798)		
		Thomas Malthus' *An Essay on the Principle of Population* (1798)		
		Eugene Delacroix, French painter (1799–1837)		
	Napoleon Bonaparte is declared temporary consul (1799)	Honoré de Balzac, French novelist (1799–1850)		
1800	President Thomas Jefferson (1800–1808)	Emergence of Romanticism (early 1800s)	Women comprise 50 percent of British textile workforce (c. 1800)	Peace of Amiens temporarily halts war between Britain and France (1801)
	Bonaparte's Concordat with the pope (1801)	Continental population doubles (1800–1850)		Napoleon unsuccessfully tries to restore slavery in St. Domingue (1801–1803)
	Bonaparte elected Consul for Life by plebiscite (1802)			Louisiana Purchase (1803)
	Bonaparte crowns himself Emperor Napoleon I (1804)	Napoleonic Code (1804)		Independent state of Haiti (formerly St. Domingue) (1804)
		George Sand, novelist (1804–1876)		Nelson's victory at Trafalgar breaks French naval power (1805)
				Napoleon defeats Austria and Russia at Battle of Austerlitz (1805)
			Napoleon's Continental System imposed (1806)	
			Serfdom abolished in Prussia (1807)	
1808	Prussian reform era begins (1808)	Johann Gottlieb Fichte's *Addresses to the German Nation* (1808)		Napoleon invades Spain (1808)

POLITICS	SOCIETY AND CULTURE	ECONOMY	INTERNATIONAL RELATIONS	
			Napoleon marries Mary Louise of the Habsburgs (1809)	1809
	Grimm's Fairy Tales by the Brothers Grimm (1813)		Napoleon's Russian campaign (1812)	
Bourbon monarchy restored in France (1815)			Napoleon exiled to Elba (1814) Congress of Vienna (1814–1815) Napoleon defeated at Waterloo (1815) German Confederation created by Congress of Vienna (1815)	
	Gustav Courbet, French painter (1819–1877)	Prussian Zollverein (customs union) founded (1818)	Quintuple Alliance formed (1818) Greek war of independence (1821–1827) Monroe Doctrine (1823)	
Decembrist Revolt in Russia (1825)			Serbia emerges from within Ottoman Empire (1828)	
Revolution in France, Belgium (1830) Mazzini founds Young Italy society (1831) Electoral Reform Act in England (1832)		First railway to carry passengers (1830)		
Poor Laws Reform in England (1834) Reign of Queen Victoria (1837–1901) English Chartist Movement (1838–1848)	Alexis de Tocqueville's *Democracy in America* (1835–1840) *The Economist* is founded (1838) Emergence of Realism in art and literature (1840s) Great Famine in Ireland (1845–1849)	Rail transport spreads across Continent (1840s) Zollverein expands to include nearly all German states (1840s) Poor harvests contribute to economic crisis across Europe (1845) Great Irish Famine (1845–1849)		
Repression of revolutionary movements in central and eastern Europe (1848–1850)	Seneca Falls Convention (1848)		Treaty of Guadalupe Hidalgo ends war between United States and Mexico (1848) United States buys western territory, including California, for $15 million (1848)	
	Florence Nightingale's medical reforms (1850s) Great Exhibit of the Works of Industry in All Nations, London (1851)	California gold rush (1849) Serfdom abolished in southern and eastern Europe (1850) Great Exhibition of the Works of Industry in All Nations, London (1851) Britain exports half of world's iron (1852) Cotton accounts for 40 percent of domestic exports from Britain (1852)		1850
Louis Napoleon Bonaparte overthrows Second Republic (1851)				
	Charles Darwin's *On the Origin of Species* (1859) John Stuart Mill's *On Liberty* (1859)	Agricultural laborers still largest occupation in Britain (1860) Britain and France sign free-trade agreement (1860)	Crimean War (1854–1856) Sardinia takes Lombardy, Papal States, and various duchies (1859)	
Reign of Kaiser William I (1861–1888) Civil War in the United States (1861–1865) Otto von Bismarck appointed prime minister of Germany (1862)	Victor Hugo's *Les Misérables* (1862)	Emancipation of serfs in Russia (1861)	Victor Emmanuel II claims title of king of Italy (1861–1878)	
Reform Bill of 1867 in England (1867)	Fyodor Dostoyevsky's *Crime and Punishment* (1866) Mill's *The Subjection of Women* (1869)	Slavery abolished in United States (1865) Railroad connects Mississippi valley with Pacific coast (1869)	Seven Week's War; Prussia takes Schleswig-Holstein (1866) Canada gains independence (1867)	
			Franco-Prussian War (1870–1871) Italians take Rome from Napoleon III's protection (1870) German Empire proclaimed (1871)	1870

CHAPTER TWENTY

THE FRENCH
REVOLUTION

IN 1789, ONE EUROPEAN out of every five lived in France. Many Europeans considered France the center of European culture. It followed that a revolution in France would immediately command the attention of Europe and assume international significance. Yet the French Revolution attracted and disturbed men and women for much more important reasons. Both its philosophical ideals and its political realities mirrored attitudes, concerns, and conflicts that had occupied the minds of educated Europeans for several decades. When the revolutionaries pronounced in favor of liberty, they spoke not only with the voice of the eighteenth-century *philosophes*, but with that of the English aristocracy in 1688 and the North American revolutionaries of 1776.

They also raised issues that resonated across Europe. Absolutism was increasingly the bane of a wide spectrum of thoughtful opinion. Aristocrats across Europe and the colonies resented monarchical inroads on their ancient freedoms. Members of the middle class, many of whom were very successful, chafed under a system of official privilege that they increasingly considered outmoded. Peasants fiercely resented what seemed to them the never-ceasing demands of central government on their limited resources. Nor were resentments focused exclusively on absolutist monarchs. Tensions existed as well between country and city dwellers, between rich and poor, overprivileged and underprivileged, slave and free. The French Revolution marked part of a crisis that shook all of late eighteenth-century Europe and its colonies, bringing revolutionary movements to the British Empire, to Belgium and the Netherlands, and to South America. The age of revolution restructured the nations of the West.

The opening of the age of revolution came in the North American colonies. The American Revolution of 1776 had been one of the last in a series of conflicts over colonial control of the New World, conflicts that had wracked England and France throughout the eighteenth century (see pages 623–25). It also became one of the first crises of the old regime at home. "The New World was where the fears and aspirations . . . were first dramatized, where extralegal associations of common citizens defied acts of a sovereign power, where abstract ideals of political philosophy were substantiated in the actions of ordinary men," as one historian recently said. Among "enlightened" Europeans, the success with which citizens of the new nation had thrown off British rule and formed a republic based on Enlightenment principles was the source of tremendous optimism. Change would come. Reform was possible. The costs would be modest.

If the American Revolution first dramatized Europeans' "fears and aspirations," the events in France deepened them. The French Revolution proved a more radical project, though it did not necessarily begin that way. It became immeasurably more costly—protracted, complex, and violent. It aroused much greater hopes and consequently, in many cases, bitter disillusionment. It raised issues that would not be settled for half a century.

THE FRENCH REVOLUTION: AN OVERVIEW

In Charles Dickens's *Tale of Two Cities* (1859), the source of many popular images of revolution, the French upheaval blurs into a frightening picture of bloodthirsty crowds watching a guillotine. The picture is memorable but misleading. The "French Revolution" is a shorthand for a complex series of events between 1789 and 1799. (Napoleon ruled from 1799 to 1814–1815.) To simplify, those events can be divided into three stages. In the first stage, running from before 1789 to 1792, the struggle was constitutional and relatively peaceful. An increasingly bold elite articulated its grievances against the king. Like the American revolutionaries, elites refused taxation without representation, attacked "despotism," or arbitrary authority, and offered an Enlightenment-inspired program to rejuvenate the nation. Reforms, many of them breathtakingly wide ranging, were instituted—some accepted or even offered by the king, and others passed over his protests. The peaceful, constitutional phase did not last. Unlike the American Revolution the French Revolution did not stabilize around one constitution or one set of political leaders, for many reasons. Reforms met with resistance, dividing the country. The threat of change in France created international tensions. In 1792, these tensions exploded into war and the monarchy fell, to be replaced with a republic. The second

CHRONOLOGY

PERIODS OF THE FRENCH REVOLUTION ERA, 1789–1815

First Stage: The First French Revolution	July 1789–August 1792
Second Stage: The Second French Revolution	August 1792–July 1794
Third Stage: The Directory	1794–1799
Fourth Stage: The Napoleonic Era	1799–1815

stage of the Revolution, which lasted from 1792–1794, was one of crisis and consolidation. A ruthlessly centralized government mobilized all the country's resources to fight the foreign enemy as well as counterrevolutionaries at home, to destroy traitors and the vestiges of the Old Regime. The Terror, as this policy was called, did save the republic, but it exhausted itself in factions and recriminations. In the third phase, from 1794 to 1799 the government, still at war with Europe, drifted into corruption and almost inevitably into military rule under Napoleon. Napoleon continued the war until his final defeat in 1815.

THE COMING OF THE REVOLUTION

What were the causes of the French Revolution?

What were the long-term causes of the revolution in France? Historians long argued that the causes and outcomes should be understood in terms of class conflict. Grounding their case on the economic and political theories of the nineteenth-century philosopher Karl Marx (see page 885) these interpreters concluded that a rising bourgeoisie (middle class), inspired by the ideology of Enlightenment philosophers and economists, overthrew the remaining vestiges of the aristocratic order.

Historians have substantially modified this bold thesis. Certainly, to understand the origins of the French Revolution, we must first analyze late-eighteenth-century French society. Yet recent studies show that far from a society in which the bourgeoisie was pitted against the aristocracy, French society was increasingly dominated by a new elite or social group that brought together aristocrats, officeholders, professionals, and, to a lesser degree, merchants and businessmen. To comprehend the Revolution, we must thus comprehend the nature of this dominant segment of French society and its serious discontents with the government of Louis XVI.

French society was divided into three Estates. (An individual's "estate" marked his standing, or status, and it determined legal rights, taxes, and so on.) The First Estate was comprised of all the clergy and the Second Estate of the nobility. The Third Estate, by far the largest, included everyone else, from wealthy lawyers and businessmen to urban laborers and very poor peasants. Within the political and social elite of the country, which was a small but very powerful group, these legal distinctions often seemed artificial and not in keeping with social realities. To begin with, in the upper reaches of society, the social boundaries between noble and nonnoble were ill defined. Noble title was accessible to those who could afford to buy an ennobling office. Approximately two thirds of the eighteenth-century French nobility had acceded to its status since 1600, and close to fifty-thousand new nobles were created between 1700 and 1789. The order depended for its vigor on a constant infusion of talent and economic power from the wealthy social groups of the Third Estate.

The case of the family of the revolutionary figure Honoré Gabriel Riqueti, the comte de Mirabeau, well illustrates the point. Mirabeau's sixteenth-century ancestors had been merchants. In 1570, however, one of them had purchased the seigneury of Mirabeau. In the following century another bought himself the title of marquis. Despite its commercial origins, the family had acquired positions in the French army. Mirabeau, a lawyer, also held a commission in the cavalry that his grandfather once commanded. Aristocrats spoke of a distinction between the nobility of the "sword" and of the "robe," the former supposedly of a more ancient and distinguished lineage derived from military service, the latter aristocrats by reason of their purchase of administrative or judicial office (hence the robe). As the example of the Mirabeau family shows, even that distinction could be illusory.

Nor did noble families disdain investment in trade and commerce, as historians long thought. In fact, noblemen financed most industry, and they also invested heavily in banking and such enterprises as ship own-

ing, the slave trade, mining, and metallurgy. The bulk of their wealth, nevertheless, was what one historian has labeled "proprietary," that is, tied to land, urban properties, purchased offices, and the like. This form of wealth was not only noble but also the fountain of riches for members of the Third Estate who also preferred to invest in secure, proprietary, holdings. Thus throughout the century, this "bourgeois" wealth was constantly being transformed into "noble" wealth as its owners were transformed into noblemen. Clearly, then, this economically important bourgeois group did not see itself as a separate class. Its members recognized themselves as different from and often opposed to the mass of men and women beneath them who worked with their hands—the populace. But they identified closely with the values of a nobility to which they frequently aspired.

At the same time, however, hostilities and frictions within the middle orders and between bourgeois and noble were both real and important. Less prosperous lawyers—and there were an increasing number of them—were jealous of the privileged position of a favored few in their profession. Over the course of the century the price of offices rose, making it more difficult to buy one's way into the nobility, and creating tensions between middling members of the Third Estate and the very rich in trade and commerce who, by and large, were the only group able to afford the degree of social advancement to which many more aspired. Not surprisingly, the more financially modest nobles resented the success of rich, upstart commoners whose income allowed them the luxury of life in the grand style that they could not have themselves. In sum, several fault lines ran through the elite and the middle classes. Despite these fissures, however, these social groups could join in attacking with mounting vehemence a government and an economy that were not serving its interests.

The new elite aired its frustrations in the widening circles of public debate (see Chapter 19). Although ideas did not "cause" the Revolution, they played a critical role in articulating the discontents experienced by the elite and middle orders. The political theories of Locke, Voltaire, and Montesquieu could appeal to both discontented nobles and members of the middle class. Voltaire was popular because of his attacks on noble privileges; Locke and Montesquieu gained widespread followings because of their defense of private property and limited sovereignty. Montesquieu's ideas were especially congenial to the noble lawyers and office holders who dominated France's powerful law

Prerevolutionary Propaganda, 1788–1789. These prints support the popular view that the third estate was carrying the burden of national taxation on its shoulders while the privileged orders enjoyed the fruits of the peasant's labors, tax free.

courts, the *parlements*. They read his doctrine of checks and balances as a defense of *parlements* as the governmental bodies that would provide a check to the despotism of the king's government. When conflicts arose, noble leaders presented themselves as defenders of a national political community threatened by the king and his ministers.

The campaign for change was also fueled by proponents of economic reform. The "physiocrats," as they were called in France, urged the government to simplify the tax system and free the economy from mercantilist regulations. They urged the government to lift its controls on the price of grain, for example, which had been imposed to keep the cost of bread low but, they argued, had interfered with the natural workings of the market.

Whether or not the public accepted the physiocrats' prescriptions, it agreed with their diagnosis: the French economy was seriously ailing. A general price rise during much of the eighteenth century, which permitted the French economy to expand by providing capital for investment, created hardship for the peasantry and for urban tradesmen and laborers. Their plight deteriorated further at the end of the 1780s, when poor harvests sent bread prices sharply higher, creating desperation among the urban poor. In 1788 families found themselves spending more than 50 percent of their income on bread, which made up the bulk of their diet. The following year the figure rose to as

much as 80 percent. Poor harvests contributed to a marked reduction in demand for manufactured goods, and contracting markets in turn created unemployment. Many peasants left the countryside for the cities, hoping to find work there, only to discover that urban unemployment was far worse than that in rural areas. Evidence indicates that between 1787 and 1789 the unemployment rate in many parts of urban France was as high as 50 percent.

Those peasants who remained behind were caught in a web of obligations to landlords, church, and state: a tithe and levy on farm produce owed to the church; fees for the use of a landlord's mill or wine press; fees, as well, to the landlord when land changed hands. In addition, peasants paid a disproportionate share of both direct and indirect taxes—the most onerous of which was the salt tax—levied by the government. (For some time the production of salt had been a state monopoly; every individual was required to buy at least seven pounds a year from the government works. The result was a commodity whose cost was often as much as fifty or sixty times its actual value.) Further grievances stemmed from the requirement to maintain public roads (the corvée) and from the hunting privileges that nobles for centuries had regarded as the distinctive badge of their order.

An inefficient tax system further weakened the country's financial position. Not only was taxation tied to differing social standings, it varied as well from

Louis XVI.

region to region—some areas, for example, were subject to a much higher rate than others. The myriad special circumstances and exemptions made the task of collectors all the more difficult. Those collectors were in many cases so-called tax farmers, members of a syndicate that loaned the government money in return for the right to collect taxes and to keep for itself the difference between the amounts it took in and the amounts it loaned. The financial system, already burdened by debts incurred under Louis XIV, all but broke down completely under the increased expenses brought on by French participation in the American Revolution. The cost of servicing the national debt of approximately 4 billion livres in the 1780s consumed 50 percent of the nation's budget.

Problems with the economy reflected weaknesses in France's administrative structure, ultimately the responsibility of the country's absolutist monarch, Louis XVI (1774–1792). Anxious to serve his people in "en-

lightened" ways, Louis wished to improve the lot of the poor, to abolish torture, and to shift the burden of taxation onto the richer classes. Yet he lacked the ability to put these reforms into effect. His well-intentioned attempts at reform ultimately undermined his own authority. He appointed such reformers as Anne-Robert-Jacques-Turgot, a philosopher, physiocrat, and former provincial intendant, and Jacques Necker, a Swiss Protestant banker, as finance ministers, only to arouse opposition among traditionalist factions within the court. He allowed his wife, the young yet strong-willed Marie Antoinette—daughter of Austria's Maria Theresa—a free hand to dispense patronage among her friends. The result was constant intrigue and frequently reshuffled administrative alliances at Versailles. In consequence, the intendants, or administrative representatives of the central government who possessed considerable power, found their power too often circumscribed by rivalries and indecision among those to whom they reported. Their administrative effectiveness was further eroded by the fact that they shared authority with provincial governors, local military authorities, and—in a third of the provinces, the pays d'états—with local tax-levying bodies.

Wrangling between the central government and the provincial parlements also slowed reform. As we have noted, the parlements had reasserted their independence during the early years of the reign of Louis XV. Throughout the century they had grown increasingly insistent on what they began to call their "constitutional" rights, or privileges. When Louis XVI pressed for new taxes to be paid by the nobility as well as the rest of the community after the expensive Seven Years' War, the parlements successfully defended the nobil-

CHRONOLOGY

ORIGINS OF THE FRENCH REVOLUTION, 1788–1789

Failure of fiscal reform	1787–1788
Louis XVI summons the Estates General	May 1788
Bread riots across France	Spring 1789
Estates General convenes in Paris	May 1789
Third Estate declares itself the National Assembly	May 1789
Oath of the Tennis Court	June 1789
Fall of the Bastille	July 14, 1789

ENGLAND

English Channel

HOLY ROMAN
EMPIRE

FLANDERS & HAINAUT

ARTOIS

• Amiens

PICARDY

AUSTRIAN
NETHERLANDS

PALATINATE

• Rouen

ÎLE DE
FRANCE

Varennes

METZ AND
VERDUN

Marne R.

NORMANDY

Paris ✦

Versailles

WÜRTTEMBERG

BRITTANY

MAINE

CHAMPAGNE
AND BRIE

LORRAINE

ALSACE

Seine R.

ORLÉANAIS

Rhine R.

ANJOU

Loire R.

TOURAINE

SAU-
MUROIS

BERRY

NIVERNAIS

FRANCHE-
COMTÉ

POITOU

AUNIS

MARCHE

BOURBONNAIS

BURGUNDY

SWISS
CONFEDERATION

ATLANTIC
OCEAN

SAINTONGE AND
ANGOUMOIS

LIMOUSIN

Lyon •

LYONNAIS

DUCHY
OF
SAVOY

• Bordeaux

AUVERGNE

Rhône R.

DAUPHINÉ

KINGDOM
OF
SARDINIA

GASCONY AND GUIENNE

BEARN

• Toulouse

LANGUEDOC

PROVENCE

Marseilles •

FOIX

ROUSSILLON

*MEDITERRANEAN
SEA*

ANDORRA

SPAIN

CORSICA

EUROPE

Area of
detail

AFRICA

0   100   200 Miles

0   100   200 Kilometers

FRANCE UNDER THE OLD REGIME

This is a map of the internal organization of France before the outbreak of revolution in 1789. Compare this map with that on page 332. How significantly had France changed in its territorial organization since the High Middle Ages? How did such a system help to perpetuate the social and political inequities of France under the Old Regime, and why? Why did the revolutionaries see the reorganization of France as vital to their overall program?

ity's right to exemption from major national taxes. In the mid-1770s this episode was reenacted when Turgot, Louis XVI's principal financial minister, proposed reducing the debted by curtailing court expenses, replacing the corvée with a small tax on landowners, and abolishing certain guild restrictions in order to

HOW DID POPULAR UPRISINGS AFFECT POLITICAL EVENTS EARLY IN THE FRENCH REVOLUTION?

THE DESTRUCTION OF THE OLD REGIME   689

stimulate manufacturing. The Paris *parlement* steadfastly opposed such innovations, claiming that Turgot was trampling on ancient prerogatives and privileges—and he was.

In the end, however, the plan failed because the king withdrew his support of Turgot. Although the *parlements* were jealous of their prerogatives, they could not indefinitely inhibit the reforms of a determined monarch. Louis XVI was not determined. By 1788, a weak monarch, together with a chaotic financial situation and severe social tensions, brought absolutist France to the edge of political disaster.

> By 1788, a weak monarch, together with a chaotic financial situation and severe social tensions, brought absolutist France to the edge of political disaster.

THE DESTRUCTION OF THE OLD REGIME

How did popular uprisings affect political events early in the French Revolution?

The fiscal crisis precipitated the Revolution. In 1787 and 1788 the king's principal ministers, Charles de Calonne and Loménie de Brienne, attempted to institute a series of reforms to stave off bankruptcy. To meet the mounting deficit, they proposed new taxes, notably a stamp duty and a direct tax on the annual produce of the soil.

Hoping to persuade the nobility to agree to these reforms, the king summoned an Assembly of Notables (last called in 1626) from among the aristocracy. Far from acquiescing, however, this group used the financial emergency to attempt to extract major constitutional reforms. Most important, they insisted that any new tax scheme must have the approval of the Estates General, the representative body of the three estates of the realm, and that the king had no legal authority to arrest and imprison arbitrarily. The dominant order, its patience with delay and inefficiency at an end, was speaking as English aristocrats had in 1688, and American revolutionaries had in 1775.

Economic hardship and financial chaos in the end compelled Louis XVI in the summer of 1788 to summon the Estates General (which had not met since 1614) to meet in May of the following year. His action appeared to many as the only solution to France's deepening problems. Long-term grievances and short-term hardships had produced bread riots across the country in the spring of 1789. Looting in Brittany, Flanders, Provence, and elsewhere was accompanied by demands that the king take measures to make bread affordable. Fear that the forces of law and order were collapsing and that the common people might take matters into their own hands spurred the delegates to the Estates General with a sense of their responsibilities and destiny. Each of the three orders elected its own deputies—the Third Estate indirectly through local assemblies. These assemblies were charged as well with the responsibility of drawing up lists of grievances (*cahiers des doléances*) further heightening expectations for fundamental reform.

The delegates of the Third Estate, though elected by assemblies chosen in turn by artisans and peasants, represented the outlook of what we have called the dominant order. Only 13 percent were men of business. About 25 percent were lawyers; 43 percent were government officeholders of some sort. Thus, despite initial disagreements between members of the second and third estates, once the Estates General convened there remained within that body a strong sense of common grievance and common purpose.

The major area of disagreement between the Second and Third Estates stemmed from the tradition that each estate met and voted as a body. In the past, this had generally meant that the First Estate (the clergy) had combined with the Second (the nobility) to defeat the Third. Now the Third Estate made it clear it would not tolerate such an arrangement. The Third's interests were articulated most memorably by the Abbé Emmanuel Sieyès, a radical member of the clergy. "What Is the Third Estate?" asked Sieyès, in his famous pamphlet of January 1789. Everything, he answered, and pointed to eighteenth-century social changes to bolster his point. In early 1789, Sieyès' views were still unusually radical. But the leaders of the Third Estate agreed that the three orders should sit together and vote as individuals. More important, they insisted that the Third Estate should have twice as many members as the First and Second.

During the months prior to May 1789, the question of "doubling the Third" was fiercely debated. After opposing the reform initially, the king agreed to it in December. His unwillingness to take a strong stand on

WHAT IS THE THIRD ESTATE?

The Abbé Emmanuel-Joseph Sieyès (1748–1836) was, by virtue of his office, a member of the First Estate of the Estates General. Nevertheless, his political savvy led him to be elected as a representative of the Third Estate from the district of Chartres. Sieyès was a formidable politician as well as a writer. His career during the Revolution, which he ended by assisting Napoleon to the imperial throne, began with one of the most important radical pamphlets of 1789. In What is the Third Estate?, *Sieyès posed fundamental questions about the rights of the Estate, which represented the great majority of the population, and helped provoke its secession from the Estates General.*

The plan of this book is fairly simple. We must ask ourselves three questions.

1. What is the Third Estate? *Everything.*
2. What has it been until now in the political order? *Nothing.*
3. What does it want to be? *Something.*

It suffices to have made the point that the so-called usefulness of a privileged order to the public service is a fallacy; that without help from this order, all the arduous tasks in the service are performed by the Third Estate; that without this order the higher posts could be infinitely better filled; that they ought to be the natural prize and reward of recognized ability and service; and that if the privileged have succeeded in usurping all well-paid and honorific posts, this is both a hateful iniquity towards the generality of citizens and an act of treason to the commonwealth.

Who is bold enough to maintain that the Third Estate does not contain within itself everything needful to constitute a complete nation? It is like a strong and robust man with one arm still in chains. If the privileged order were removed, the nation would not be something less but something more. What then is the Third Estate? All; but an "all" that is fettered and oppressed. What would it be without the privileged order? It would be all; but free and flourishing. Nothing will go well without the Third Estate; everything would go considerably better without the two others.

Emmanuel-Joseph Sieyès. *What is the Third Estate?*, trans. M. Blondel, ed. S. E. Finer. (London: Phaidon Press, 1964), pp. 53–63.

voting procedures cost him support he might otherwise have obtained from the Third Estate. Shortly after the Estates General opened at Versailles in May 1789, the Third Estate, angered by the king's attitude, took the revolutionary step of leaving the body and declaring itself the National Assembly. Now the leaders of the Third Estate acted on that belief. Locked out of the Estates General meeting hall on June 20, the Third Estate and a handful of sympathetic nobles and clergymen moved to a nearby indoor tennis court.

Here, under the leadership of the volatile, maverick aristocrat Mirabeau and the radical clergyman Sieyès, they bound themselves by a solemn oath not to separate until they had drafted a constitution for France. This Oath of the Tennis Court, sworn on June 20, 1789, can be seen as the beginning of the French

HOW DID POPULAR UPRISINGS AFFECT POLITICAL EVENTS EARLY IN THE FRENCH REVOLUTION?

THE DESTRUCTION OF THE OLD REGIME   691

The Tennis Court Oath, by Jacques Louis David (1748–1825). In June, 1789, in the hall where royalty played a game known as *jeu de paume* (similar to tennis) leaders of the Revolution swore to draft a constitution. In the center of this painting, standing on the table, is Jean Bailly, president of the National Assembly. Seated at the table below him is Abbé Sieyès. Mirabeau stands in the right foreground with a hat in his left hand.

Revolution. By claiming the authority to remake the government in the name of the people, the National Assembly was not merely protesting against the rule of Louis XVI but asserting its right to act as the highest sovereign power in the nation. On June 27 the king virtually conceded this right by ordering all the delegates to join the National Assembly.

FIRST STAGES OF THE FRENCH REVOLUTION

The first stage of the French Revolution extended from June 1789 to August 1792. In the main, this stage was moderate, its actions dominated by the leadership of liberal nobles and equally liberal men of the Third Estate. Yet three events in the summer and fall of 1789 furnished evidence that the Revolution was to penetrate to the very heart of French society, ultimately touching both the urban populace and the rural peasants.

POPULAR REVOLTS

From the beginning of the political crisis, public attention was high. It was roused not merely by interest in political reform, however, but also by the economic crisis that, as we have seen, brought the price of bread to astronomical heights. Many believed that the aristocracy and the king were conspiring to punish the upstart Third Estate by encouraging scarcity and high prices. Rumors circulated in Paris during the latter days of June 1789 that the king was about to stage a reactionary coup d'état. The electors of Paris (those who had voted for the Third Estate) feared not only a counterrevolution but also the actions of the Parisian poor, who had been parading through the streets and threatening violence. These electors included workshop masters, artisans, shopkeepers, and petty tradespeople. The men and women of the common people would soon be referred to as *sans-culottes*. The term, which translates to "without breeches," was an antiaristocratic badge of

The Fall of the Bastille, July 14, 1789. A contemporary engraving celebrating the heroic actions of the citizenry of Paris.

pride: a man of the people wore full-length trousers rather than aristocratic breeches, stockings, and gold-buckled shoes. They formed a provisional municipal government and organized a militia of volunteers to maintain order. Determined to obtain arms, they made their way on July 14 to the Bastille, an ancient fortress where guns and ammunition were stored. Built in the Middle Ages, the Bastille had served as a prison for many years but was no longer much used. Nevertheless, it symbolized hated royal authority. When crowds demanded arms from its governor, he at first procrastinated and then, fearing a frontal assault, opened fire, killing ninety-eight of the attackers. The crowd took revenge, capturing the fortress (which held only seven prisoners—five common criminals and two persons confined for mental incapacity) and decapitating the governor. At the same time the sans-culottes were es-

tablishing a revolutionary municipal government in Paris, similar groups assumed control in other cities across France. These events—dramatized by the fall of the Bastille—were the first to demonstrate the commitment of the common people to revolutionary change.

The second popular revolt occurred in the countryside, where the peasants were suffering the direct effects of economic privation. They too anticipated and feared a monarchical and aristocratic counterrevolution. Rumors flew that the king's armies were on their way, that Austrians, Prussians, or "brigands" were invading. Frightened and uncertain, peasants and villagers organized militias; others attacked and burned manor houses, sometimes looking for grain, but usually to find and destroy records of manorial obligations. This "Great Fear," as historians have labeled it, compounded the confusion abroad in rural areas through-

HOW DID POPULAR UPRISINGS AFFECT POLITICAL EVENTS EARLY IN THE FRENCH REVOLUTION?

THE DESTRUCTION OF THE OLD REGIME 693

Women of Paris Leaving for Versailles, October 1789. A crowd of women, accompanied by Lafayette and the National Guard, marched to Versailles to confront the King about shortages and rising prices in Paris.

out the summer. The news, when it reached Paris, convinced deputies at Versailles that the administration had simply collapsed. The third instance of popular uprising, the "October Days" of 1789, was brought on by economic crisis. This time Parisian women from the market district, angered by the price of bread and fired by rumors of the king's continuing unwillingness to cooperate with the Assembly, marched to Versailles on October 5 and demanded to be heard. Not satisfied with its reception by the Assembly, the crowd broke through the gates to the palace, calling for the king to return to Paris from Versailles. On the afternoon of the following day the king yielded. The National Guard, sympathetic to the agitators, led the crowd back to Paris, the procession headed by a soldier holding aloft a loaf of bread on his bayonet.

THE NATIONAL ASSEMBLY

Each of these popular uprisings decidedly affected the course of political events as they were unfolding at Versailles. The storming of the Bastille persuaded the king and nobles to acquiesce in the creation of the National Assembly. The "Great Fear" compelled the most sweeping changes of the entire revolutionary period. Trying to put an end to rural disorder, on the

night of August 4 the Assembly took a giant step towards abolishing all forms of privilege. It eliminated the church tithe, the labor requirement known as the corvée, the nobility's hunting privileges, and a wide variety of tax exemptions and monopolies. In effect, these reforms obliterated the remnants of feudalism. One week later, the Assembly abolished the sale of offices, thereby sweeping away one of the fundamental institutions of the old regime. The king's return to Paris during the October Days undercut his ability to resist further changes.

The Assembly issued its charter of liberties, the Declaration of the Rights of Man and Citizen, in September 1789. It declared property to be a natural right, along with liberty, security, and "resistance to oppression." It declared freedom of speech, religious toleration, and liberty of the press inviolable. All citizens were to be treated equally before the law. No one was to be imprisoned or otherwise punished except in accordance with due process of law. Sovereignty was affirmed to reside in the people, and officers of the government were made subject to deposition if they abused the powers conferred on them. These were not new ideas; they represented the outcome of Enlightenment discussions and revolutionary debates and deliberations. The Declaration became the preamble to the new constitution, which the Assembly finished in 1791.

Whom did the Declaration mean by "man and citizen"? The revolutionaries distinguished between "passive" citizens, guaranteed rights under law and "active" citizens, who paid a certain amount in taxes, and could thus vote and hold office. About half the adult males in France qualified as "active" citizens. Even their power was curtailed, because they could only vote for "electors," men whose property ownership qualified them to hold office. Those electors, in turn, chose delegates to the Assembly. Power, therefore, was virtually monopolized by the well-to-do. Later in the revolution, the more radical republic abolished the distinction between active and passive, and the conservative regimes reinstated it. Which men could be trusted to participate in politics and on what terms was a hotly contested issue. So, to a certain extent, were the rights of religious minorities. The revolution gave full civil rights to Protestants, though in areas long divided by religious conflict those rights were challenged by Catholics. The revolution did, hesitantly, give civil rights to Jews, again confronting protest in areas of eastern France, and only on the condition that Jews renounce any separate identity. Religious toleration, a central theme of the Enlightenment, meant eschewing persecution; it did not mean that the regime was prepared to accommodate religious difference. The Assembly abolished serfdom and banned slavery in continental France. It remained silent on colonial slavery, and although delegations pressed the assembly on political rights for free people of color, the assembly exempted the colonies from the constitution's provisions. Events in the Caribbean, as we will see, later forced the issue.

The rights and roles of women became the focus of sharp debate, though most of the discussion centered on the future of working women's guilds, or trade organizations, marriage and divorce, poor relief, and education. The Englishwoman Mary Wollstonecraft's milestone book *A Vindication of the Rights of Woman* (see Chapter 19) was penned during the revolutionary debate over national education. Should girls be educated? To what end? What did the revolutionary project of rationally reordering society, abolishing despotism and privilege, and rejuvenating the nation imply for gender roles? Wollstonecraft, as we have seen, argued strongly that it entailed nothing less than overthrowing prevailing ideas about female character, and forging a new concept of independent and equal womanhood. She carried the critique of privilege and despotism to private life. Even Wollstonecraft, however, only hinted at political representation, aware that such an idea would only "excite laughter." The marquis de Condorcet wrote a pamphlet in 1790 arguing for women's political rights.

Women's political rights found a colorful proponent in Marie Gouze, also known as Olympe de Gouges, the self-educated daughter of a butcher who had become an intellectual and playwright. Like many "ordinary" people who found in the explosion of revolutionary activity the opportunity to address the public by writing speeches, pamphlets, or newspapers, Gouges composed her own manifesto, *The Declaration of the Rights of Woman and Citizen* (1791). Beginning with the proposition that "social distinctions can only be based on the common utility," she declared that women had the same rights as men, including resistance to authority, participation in government, and naming the fathers of illegitimate children— a revealing glimpse of issues of economic distress, shame, and isolation as experienced by women of the era. Women participated in the everyday activities of the revolution, joining clubs, demonstrations, and debates; women artisans' organizations had a well-established role in municipal life; market women were familiar public figures, often central to the circulation of news and spontaneous popular demonstrations. The regime celebrated the support of women "citizens," and female figures were allegories for liberty. Those conceptions, however, were increasingly tied to an image of women as supportive mothers, educators, and tenders of the private sphere, not to be involved in public.

In this early period of the revolution, the most divisive issue to confront the Assembly involved religion. In November 1789, the National Assembly resolved to confiscate the lands of the church and to use them as collateral for the issue of assignats, interest-bearing notes that eventually circulated as paper money. The Assembly hoped—vainly, as it turned out—that this device would resolve the country's inflationary crisis. In July of the following year it enacted the Civil Constitution of the Clergy, which provided that all bishops and priests should be subject to the authority of the state. Their salaries were to be paid out of the public treasury, and they were required to swear allegiance to the new state, making it clear they served

> In this early period of the revolution, the most divisive issue to confront the Assembly involved religion.

DECLARATION OF THE RIGHTS OF MAN

One of the first important pronouncements of the National Assembly after the Tennis Court Oath was the Declaration of the Rights of Man. The authors drew inspiration from the American Declaration of Independence, but the language is even more heavily influenced by the ideals of French Enlightenment philosophers, particularly Rousseau. Following are the Declaration's preamble and some of its most important principles.

The representatives of the French people, constituted as the National Assembly, considering that ignorance, disregard, or contempt for the rights of man are the sole causes of public misfortunes and the corruption of governments, have resolved to set forth, in a solemn declaration, the natural, inalienable, and sacred rights of man, so that the constant presence of this declaration may ceaselessly remind all members of the social body of their rights and duties; so that the acts of legislative power and those of the executive power may be more respected . . . and so that the demands of the citizens, grounded henceforth on simple and incontestable principles, may always be directed to the maintenance of the constitution and to the welfare of all. . . .

Article 1. Men are born and remain free and equal in rights. Social distinctions can be based only on public utility.

Article 2. The aim of every political association is the preservation of the natural and imprescriptible rights of man. These rights are liberty, property, security, and resistance to oppression.

Article 3. The source of all sovereignty resides essentially in the nation. No body, no individual can exercise authority that does not explicitly proceed from it.

Article 4. Liberty consists in being able to do anything that does not injure another; thus the only limits upon each man's exercise of his natural laws are those that guarantee enjoyment of these same rights to the other members of society.

Article 5. The law has the right to forbid only actions harmful to society. No action may be prevented that is not forbidden by law, and no one may be constrained to do what the law does not order.

Article 6. The law is the expression of the general will. All citizens have the right to participate personally, or through representatives, in its formation. It must be the same for all, whether it protects or punishes. All citizens, being equal in its eyes, are equally admissable to all public dignities, positions, and employments, according to their ability, and on the basis of no other distinction than that of their virtues and talents. . . .

Article 16. A society in which the guarantee of rights is not secured, or the separation of powers is not clearly established, has no constitution.

Declaration of the Rights of Man, as cited in K. M. Baker, ed. *The Old Regime and the French Revolution.* (Chicago: University of Chicago Press, 1987), pp. 238–239.

OLYMPE DE GOUGES, DECLARATION OF THE RIGHTS OF WOMEN

Opposition to the Declaration of the Rights of Man did not come from conservatives alone. Some radicals did not think the Declaration went nearly far enough. In this pamphlet from 1791 Olympe de Gouges, a literate butcher's daughter and political radical, chastised the Declaration's authors for their arrogance in presuming to speak for the rights and best interests of a large part of the Third Estate—its women. Note her satirical attack on the revolutionaries' fascination with "natural laws," a legacy of Enlightenment thought.

Man, are you capable of being just? It is a woman who asks you this question; at least you will not deny her this right. Tell me! Who has given you the sovereign authority to oppress my sex? Your strength? Your talents? Observe the creator in his wisdom; regard nature in all her grandeur, with which you seem to want to compare yourself; and give me, if you dare, an example of this tyrannical empire. Go back to the animals, consult the elements, study the plants, then glance over the modifications of organized matter, and cede to the evidence when I offer you the means. Seek, search, and distinguish, if you can, the sexes in the administration of nature. Everywhere you will find them mingled, everywhere they cooperate in harmony with this immortal masterpiece.

Only man has fasioned himself a principle out of this exception. Bizarre, blind, bloated by science and degenerate, in this century of enlightenment and wisdom, he, in grossest ignorance, wishes to exercise the command of a despot over a sex that has received every intellectual faculty; he claims to rejoice in the Revolution and claims his rights to equality, at the very least.

"The Declaration of the Rights of Woman and Citizen," as cited in Susan Bell and Karen Offen, eds. *Women, the Family and Freedom: The Debate in Documents*, Vol. 1, *1750–1880*. (Stanford: Stanford University Press, 1983), pp. 104–106.

France rather than Rome. The Assembly's aim was to make the Catholic Church of France a truly national and civil institution.

Reforming the church polarized large sections of France. The church's privileged position during the old regime, including its vast monastic land holdings, had earned it the resentment of many. Bishops and other members of the higher clergy had often held several ecclesiastical appointments at the same time, had paid scant attention to their duties, and had led far from spiritual lives. Exempt from taxes itself, the church had not hesitated to extract all it could from the peasantry. Its control of the country's educational system made it a target for those men and women who, influenced by Enlightenment thinkers such as Voltaire, had turned against the doctrines of Roman Catholicism. On the other hand, the practice of centuries had made the parish church an institution of great local importance. The local priest not only baptized, married, and buried people, he helped with any written documents. The church provided poor relief and other services. In many areas peasants relied on and respected their priests. The dramatic changes embodied in the Civil Constitution of the Clergy

HOW DID POPULAR UPRISINGS AFFECT POLITICAL EVENTS EARLY IN THE FRENCH REVOLUTION?

THE DESTRUCTION OF THE OLD REGIME 697

THE REVOLUTIONARY DEPARTMENTS OF FRANCE

Compare this with the map on page 688. Why is this a more "rational" system of territorial organization? How thoroughly did the revolutionaries disguise or eliminate the older territorial distinctions of France? How did such a reorganization affect the power of the church, of nobles, and of territorial *parlements*?

thus encountered considerable resistance in some parts of rural France. When the pope threatened to excommunicate priests who signed the Civil Constitution, the stakes rose, driving many local people in the deeply Catholic areas of western France into counterrevolution.

The National Assembly made a series of economic and governmental changes with lasting effects. To

CHRONOLOGY

THE FIRST FRENCH REVOLUTION, 1789–1792

Fall of the Bastille	July 14, 1789
The "Great Fear"	Summer of 1789
Declaration of Rights of Man and of the Citizen	August 1789
The "October Days"	1789
National Assembly confiscates church lands	November 1789
National Assembly enacts the Civil Constitution of the Clergy	July 1790
Royal family tries to escape Paris	June 1791
National Assembly declares war on Austria and Prussia	April 1792

raise money, it sold off church lands, although few of the genuinely needy could afford to buy them. To encourage the growth of unfettered economic enterprise, guilds and trade unions were abolished. To rid the country of Bourbon centralization and local aristocratic power, local governments were completely restructured. France was divided into eighty-three equal departments. All towns henceforth enjoyed the same form of municipal organization. All local officials were locally elected. This reorganization and decentralization expressed a belief in the necessity of individual liberty and freedom from ancient privilege. Its principal beneficiaries were, for the most part, members of the elite, people on their way up under the previous regime who were able to take advantage of the opportunities, such as buying land or being elected to office, that the new one offered.

A NEW STAGE: POPULAR REVOLUTION

Why did the French Revolution become more radical?

In the summer of 1792, the Revolution entered a second stage. The moderate leaders were toppled and replaced by much more radical "republicans" claiming to rule on behalf of the common people. Why this abrupt and drastic change? Was the Revolution "blown off course"? These are among the most difficult questions about the French Revolution. Answers need to take account of three factors: changes in popular politics, a crisis of leadership, and international polarization.

First, the revolution produced a remarkable politicization of the common people, especially in cities. Newspapers filled with political and social commentary multiplied, freed from restrictions on printing. From 1789 forward, a wide variety of political clubs became part of daily political life. Some were formal, almost like political parties, gathering members of the elite to debate issues facing the country and influence decisions in the assembly. Others opened their doors to those excluded from formal politics, and they read aloud from newspapers and discussed the options facing the country, from the provisions of the constitution to the trustworthiness of the king and his ministers. This political awareness was heightened by the crisis of nearly constant shortages and fluctuating prices. Prices particularly exasperated those among the working people of Paris who had demanded changes in 1789 and eagerly awaited change since then. Urban demonstrations, often led by women, demanded cheaper bread, while their political leaders in clubs and newspapers called for the government to control rising inflation. Their leaders also articulated the frustrations of a mass of men and women who felt cheated by the constitution. Despite their major role in the creation of a new regime, they found themselves deprived of any effective voice in its operation.

A second major reason for the change of course was a lack of effective national leadership. Louis XVI remained the weak, vacillating monarch he had been prior to 1789. Though outwardly prepared to collaborate with the leaders of the Assembly, he proved no more than a victim of events. He was compelled to support measures personally distasteful to him, in particular the Civil Constitution of the Clergy. He was thus sympathetic to the plottings of the queen, who was in correspondence with her brother Leopold II of Austria. Urged on by Marie Antoinette, Louis agreed to attempt an escape from France in June 1791, in hopes of rallying foreign support for counterrevolution. The members of the royal family managed to slip past their palace guards in Paris, but they were apprehended near the border at Varennes and brought back to the capital. Though the Constitution of 1791 declared France a monarchy, after Varennes that declaration was more fiction than fact. From that point on, Louis was little more than a prisoner of the Assembly.

The third major reason for the dramatic turn of affairs was war. From the outset of the Revolution, men and women across Europe had been compelled, by the very intensity of events in France, to take sides in the conflict. In the years immediately after 1789, the Revolution in France won the enthusiastic support of a wide range of thinkers. The British poet William Wordsworth, later to become disillusioned by the course of revolutionary events, recalled the rapture of his initial mood: "Bliss was it in that dawn to be alive. . . ." His sentiments were echoed across the Continent by poets and philosophers, among the latter the German Johann Gottfried von Herder, who declared the Revolution the most important historical moment since the Reformation. Political societies in Britain proclaimed their allegiance to the principles of the new revolution, often quite incorrectly seeing it as nothing more than a French version of the far less momentous events of 1688. In the Low Countries, a "patriot" group organized strikes and plotted a revolution of its own against dominant merchant oligarchies. Political revolutionaries in western Germany and Italy welcomed the possibility of invasion by the French as a means of achieving radical change within their own countries.

THE COUNTERREVOLUTION

Others opposed the course of the Revolution from the start. Exiled nobles, who had fled France for sympathetic royal courts in Germany and elsewhere, did all they could to stir up counterrevolutionary sentiment. The lobbying of the exiled nobles, along with the plight of Louis XVI and his family, aroused the sympathy of conservative European monarchs, though those monarchs were not ready to lend active support. In Britain the conservative cause was strengthened by the publication in 1790 of Edmund Burke's *Reflections on the Revolution in France*. A Whig politician who had sympathized with the American revolutionaries, Burke nevertheless attacked the Revolution in France as a monstrous crime against the social order. He argued that by remodeling their government as they had, the French had turned their backs on both human nature and history. Men and women were not constitutional abstractions, endowed with an objective set of natural rights, as the Declaration of the Rights of Man had insisted. Rights—and duties as well—were the consequence of the individual histories of the countries into which men and women were born. Those histories

bound people to the past and entailed a commitment to the future, as well as the present. The French had no right to remake their country and its institutions without reference to the past or concern for the future, as Burke insisted they had. Their failure to pay proper respect to tradition and custom had destroyed the fabric of French civilization woven by centuries of national history.

Burke's famous pamphlet, in which he painted a romantic and highly inaccurate picture of the French king and queen, helped arouse sympathy for the counterrevolutionary cause. That sympathy did not turn to active opposition until France became a threat to international stability and the individual ambitions of the great powers. It was that threat which led to war in 1792, and which kept the Continent in arms for a generation. The revolutionary war polarized political and social attitudes in Europe. Once a country declared war against France, citizens who expressed sympathy with the Revolution appeared as traitors. Those who continued to support the Revolution, as did many artisans and members of the middle class, were persecuted and punished for their beliefs. To be found in Britain, for example, possessing a copy of Thomas Paine's revolutionary tract *The Rights of Man* (1791–1792), a prorevolutionary response to Burke's *Reflections*, was enough to warrant imprisonment.

The first European states to express public concern about events in revolutionary France were Austria and Prussia. They were not anxious to declare war; their interests at the time centered on the division of Poland between themselves. Nevertheless, they jointly issued the Declaration of Pillnitz in August 1791, in which they avowed that the restoration of order and of the rights of the monarch of France was a matter of "common interest to all sovereigns of Europe." The leaders of the French government at this time were a moderate faction, but they were afraid of losing political support in France. They pronounced the Declaration of Pillnitz an affront to national sovereignty, hoping that enthusiasm for a war would unite the French and strengthen the revolution. Monarchists both within and outside France played into their hands with plots and pronouncements against the government. On April 20, 1792, the Assembly declared war against Austria and Prussia.

Almost all of the various political factions in France welcomed the war. The political leadership expected an aggressive policy to shore up the people's loyalty and bring freedom to the rest of Europe. Counterrevolutionaries hoped the intervention of Austria and

DEBATING THE FRENCH REVOLUTION: EDMUND BURKE AND THOMAS PAINE

The best known debate on the French Revolution set the Irish-born conservative Edmund Burke against the British radical Thomas Paine. Burke opposed the French Revolution from the beginning. His Reflections on the Revolution in France *was published early, in 1790, when the French king was still securely on the throne. Paine responded almost immediately in a famous pamphlet defending the revolution and, more generally, the rights of man.*

EDMUND BURKE

You will observe, that from the Magna Charta to the Declaration of Right, it has been the uniform policy of our constitution to claim and assert our liberties, as an entailed inheritance derived to us from our forefathers . . . We have an inheritable crown; an inheritable peerage; and a house of commons and a people inheriting privileges, franchises, and liberties, from a long line of ancestors. . . .

You had all these advantages in your ancient states, but you chose to act as if you had never been moulded into civil society, and had every thing to begin anew. You began ill, because you began by despising every thing that belonged to you . . . If the last generations of your country appeared without much luster in your eyes, you might have passed them by, and derived your claims from a more early race of ancestors. . . . Respecting your forefathers, you would have been taught to respect yourselves. You would not have chosen to consider the French as a people of yesterday, as a nation of low-born servile wretches until the emancipating year of 1789 . . . you would not have been content to be represented as a gang of Maroon slaves, suddenly broke loose from the house of bondage, and therefore to be pardoned for your abuse of liberty to which you were not accustomed and ill fitted. . . .

. . . The fresh ruins of France, which shock our feelings wherever we can turn our eyes, are not the devastation of civil war; they are the sad but instructive monuments of rash and ignorant councel in time of profound peace. They are the display of inconsiderate and presumptuous, because unresisted and irresistible authority. . . .

. . . Nothing is more certain, than that of our manners, our civilization, and all the good things which are connected with manners, and with civilization, have, in this European world of ours, depended upon two principles; and were indeed the result of both combined; I mean the spirit of a gentleman, and the spirit of religion. The nobility and the clergy, the one by profession, the other by patronage, kept learning in existance, even in the midst of arms and confusions . . . Learning paid back what it received to nobility and priesthood . . . Happy if they had all continued to know their indissoluble union, and their proper place. Happy if learning, not debauched by ambition, had been satisfied to continue the instructor, and not aspired to be the master! Along with its natural protectors and guardians, learning will be cast into the mire, and trodden down under the hoofs of a swinish multitude.

Edmund Burke. *Reflections on the Revolution in France* (1790). (New York: Anchor Books, 1973), pp. 45, 48, 49, 52, 92.

THOMAS PAINE

Mr. Burke, with his usual outrage, abuses the *Declaration of the Rights of Man*. . . . Does Mr. Burke mean to deny that man has any rights? If he does, then he must mean that there are no such things as rights any where, and that he has none himself; for who is there in the world but man? But if Mr. Burke means to admit that man has rights, the question will then be, what are those rights, and how came man by them originally?

The error of those who reason by precedents drawn from antiquity, respecting the rights of man, is that they do not go far enough into antiquity. They stop in some of the intermediate stages of an hundred or a thousand years, and produce what was then a rule for the present day. This is no authority at all. . . .

To possess ourselves of a clear idea of what government is, or ought to be, we must trace its origin. In doing this, we shall easily discover that governments must have arisen either *out* of the people, or *over* the people. Mr. Burke has made no distinction. . . .

What were formerly called revolutions, were little more than a change of persons, or an alteration of local circumstances. They rose and fell like things of course, and had nothing in their existance or their fate that could influence beyond the spot that produced them. But what we now see in the world, from the revolutions of America and France, is a renovation of the natural order of things, a system of principles as universal as truth and the existance of man, and combining moral with political happiness and national prosperity.

Thomas Paine. *The Rights of Man*. (New York: Anchor Books, 1973), pp. 302, 308, 383.

Prussia would begin to undo all that had happened since 1789. Radicals, suspicious of aristocratic leaders and the king, believed that war would expose all "traitors" who harbored misgivings about the Revolution and flush out those who sympathized with the king and the European counterrevolutionaries. As the radicals expected, the French forces met serious reverses. By August 1792 the allied armies of Austria and Prussia had crossed the frontier and were threatening to capture Paris. Many, including soldiers enlisting in the army, believed that the military disasters had been the result of treasonable dealings with the enemy by the king and his conservative followers. On August 10, Parisian crowds, organized by their radical leadership, attacked the royal palace, killing the king's guards and driving him to seek refuge in the meeting hall of the Assembly. At the same time, radicals seized the municipal government in Paris, replacing it with a revolutionary Commune under their control. The Commune successfully demanded that the Assembly suspend the king from his duties and hand him and his family over for imprisonment. Here began a second and far more radical revolution.

THE JACOBINS

From this point, the country's leadership passed into the hands of the more egalitarian leaders of the Third Estate. These new leaders soon came to be known as Jacobins, the name of the political club to which they belonged. Although their headquarters were in Paris, their membership extended throughout France. They proclaimed themselves enemies of the country's former political leaders, the Girondins, so called after the department of the Gironde, which was centered about the commercial hub of Bordeaux. With this label, the Jacobins hoped to paint their Girondin foes as defenders of the selfish commercial classes, and to proclaim themselves spokesmen for the people and the nation. In fact little distinguished the groups from each other, and both groups contained large numbers of professionals, government officeholders, and lawyers. An increasing number of artisans joined Jacobin clubs as the movement grew, and other, more democratic clubs expanded as well.

The Assembly called for delegates to be elected by universal manhood suffrage to a national convention. This Convention became the effective governing body of the country for the next three years. It was elected in September 1792, at a time when disturbances across France reached a new height. The so-called September Massacres occurred when revolutionary Paris crowds, hearing a rumor that political prisoners were plotting to escape from their prisons, responded by hauling them before hastily convened tribunals and sentencing them to swift execution. More than one thousand supposed enemies of the Revolution were killed in less than a week.

The Execution of Louis XVI. A revolutionary displays the king's head moments after it is severed by the guillotine in January 1793.

Similar riots engulfed Lyons, Orléans, and other French cities.

When the newly elected Convention met in September, its membership was far more radical than that of its predecessor, the Assembly, and its leadership was determined to demand an end to the monarchy and the death of Louis XVI. On September 21, the Convention declared France a republic. In December it placed the king on trial, and in January he was condemned to death by a narrow margin. The heir to the grand tradition of French absolutism met his end bravely as "Citizen Louis Capet," beheaded by the guillotine, the frightful mechanical headsman that had become the symbol of revolutionary fervor.

Meanwhile, the Convention turned its attention to the enactment of further domestic reforms. Among its most significant accomplishments over the next three years were the abolition of slavery in French colonies (see below) and the repeal of primogeniture, so that property would not be inherited exclusively by the oldest son but would be divided in substantially equal portions among all immediate heirs. The Convention

also confiscated the property of enemies of the Revolution for the benefit of the government and the lower classes. Some great estates were broken up and offered for sale to poorer citizens on relatively easy terms. It abruptly canceled the policy of indemnifying, or compensating, nobles for the loss of their privileges. To curb rising prices, the government set maximum prices for grain and other necessities. Merchants who profiteered at the expense of the poor were threatened with the guillotine, as were peasants accused of "hoarding" supplies. In an astonishing effort to root out Christianity from everyday life, the Convention adopted a new calendar. The calendar year began with the birth of the republic (September 22, 1792), and divided months in such a way as to eliminate the Catholic Sunday.

Much of this program, particularly that which involved price fixing and requisitioning, did not follow from Jacobin political conviction. It was the consequence, rather, of desperate political necessity, and of pressure from the urban sans-culottes. In the three years after 1790, prices had risen staggeringly: wheat

Sans-Culottes feeding Europe with the Bread of Liberty. This counter-revolutionary cartoon shows the French revolutionaries forcing the "bread of liberty" down the throats of others: Holland, Prussia, Britain, and the papacy.

by 27 percent, beef by 136 percent, potatoes by 700 percent. While the government imposed its maximums in Paris, small armies of urban sans-culottes attacked those they considered hoarders and profiteers. Left to its own economic inclinations, the Jacobin leadership would have pursued policies in line with liberal, reformist thinking that had challenged absolutist centralization and control. Yet the dire circumstances of Continental warfare and domestic turmoil left the leadership with no choice but to acquiesce to the sans-culottes' demands.

While effecting a political revolution in France, the Convention's leadership at the same time accomplished an astonishingly successful reorganization of its armies. By February 1793, Britain, Holland, Spain, and Austria were in the field against the French. Britain's entrance into the war was dictated by both strategic and economic reasons. The British feared French penetration into the Low Countries directly across the Channel; they were also concerned that French expansion might pose a serious

> To ensure the accomplishment of their achievements, the Committee on Public Safety resorted to a bloody authoritarianism that has come to be known as the Terror.

threat to Britain's own growing economic hegemony around the globe. The allied coalition, though united only in its desire to contain this puzzling, fearsome revolutionary phenomenon, was nevertheless a formidable force. To counter it, the French organized an army that was able to win engagement after engagement during these years. In August 1793, the revolutionary government imposed a levy on the entire male population (*levée en masse*) capable of bearing arms. Fourteen hastily drafted armies were flung into battle under the leadership of young and inexperienced officers. What they lacked in training and discipline they made up for in improvised organization, mobility, flexibility, courage, and morale. (In the navy, however, where skill was of paramount importance, the revolutionary French never succeeded in matching the performance of the British.) In 1793–1794, the French armies preserved their homeland. In 1794–1795, they occupied the Low Countries, the Rhineland, parts of Spain, Switzerland, and Savoy. In 1796, they invaded and occupied key parts of Italy and broke the coalition that had arrayed itself against them.

THE REIGN OF TERROR

These achievements exacted a heavy price. To ensure their accomplishment, the rulers of France resorted to a bloody authoritarianism that has come to be known as the Terror. Although the Convention succeeded in 1793 in drafting a new democratic constitution based on male suffrage, it deferred its introduction because of wartime emergency. Instead, the Convention prolonged its own life year after year, and increasingly delegated its responsibilities to a group of twelve leaders known as the Committee of Public Safety. By this time the Girondins had lost all influence within the Convention. Complete power had passed to the Jacobins, who proclaimed themselves champions of the common man or, in Rousseauian terms, the general will.

The Death of Marat. This painting by the French artist David immortalized Marat. The note in the slain leader's hand is from Charlotte Corday, his assassin.

Foremost among the political leadership were Jean Paul Marat, Georges Jacques Danton, and Maximilien Robespierre, the latter two members of the Committee of Public Safety. Jean Paul Marat was educated as a physician, and by 1789 had already earned enough distinction in that profession to be awarded an honorary degree by St. Andrews University in Scotland. Marat opposed nearly all of his moderate colleagues' assumptions, including their admiration for Great Britain, which Marat considered corrupt and despotic. Soon made a victim of persecution and forced to take refuge in unsanitary sewers and dungeons, he persevered as the editor of the popular news sheet, *The Friend of the People*. Being exposed to infection left him with a chronic skin disease, from which he could find relief only through frequent bathing. In the summer of 1793, at the height of the crisis of the revolution, he was stabbed in his bath by Charlotte Corday, a young royalist, and became a revolutionary martyr.

Georges Jacques Danton did not achieve prominence until three years into the Revolution. But like Marat, he was a popular political leader, well known in the more plebian clubs of Paris. Elected a member of the Committee of Public Safety in 1793, he had much to do with organizing the Terror. As time went on, however, he wearied of ruthlessness and displayed a tendency to compromise that gave his opponents in the Convention their opportunity. In April 1794 Danton was sent to the guillotine. Upon mounting the scaffold he is reported to have said, "Show my head to the people; they do not see the like every day."

The most famous and perhaps the greatest of the radical leaders was Maximilien Robespierre. Born of a family reputed to be of Irish descent, Robespierre was trained for the law and speedily achieved modest success as a lawyer. A fervent Rousseauian, he presented himself as the "incorruptible," the one willing to repudiate all private interests and follow the general will. His eloquence, and his consistent, or ruthless, insistence that leaders respect the "will of the people" eventually won him a following in the Jacobin Club. Later he became president of the National Convention and a member of the Committee of Public Safety. Though he had little or nothing to do with originating the Terror, he was nevertheless responsible for enlarging its scope. He came to justify ruthlessness as a necessary and therefore laudable means to revolutionary progress.

Maximilien Robespierre.

The years of the Terror were years of stern dictatorship in France. Pressed by foreign enemies from without, the Committee faced sabotage from both the political right and left at home. In June 1793, responding to the need for absolute political control, leaders of the "Mountain," a party of Jacobins and other radicals allied with roughhousing Parisian artisans, intimidated the moderates into leaving the Convention. The purged Girondists helped fuel rebellions in the great provincial cities of Lyons, Bordeaux, and Marseilles, ruthlessly repressed by the Committee and its local representatives. The government also faced counter-revolution in the western region called the Vendée. The peasantry there resented the government's assault on its religious institutions. The government's attempts to conscript troops into the revolutionary armies fanned long-smoldering resentments into open rebellion. By the summer, the peasant forces in the Vendée posed a serious threat to the Convention. This harvest of the policies of the National Assembly was bitter fruit to the Committee. At the same time they met with the scornful criticism of revolutionaries even more radical than themselves. This latter group, known as the *enragés* ("the enraged"), was led by the journalist Jacques Hébert and threatened to topple not only the government but the country itself by its crusades. Determined to stabilize France, whatever the cost, the Committee dispatched commissioners into the countryside to suppress the enemies of the state.

During the period of the Terror, from September 1793 to July 1794, the most reliable estimates place the number of executions as high as twenty-five to thirty thousand in France as a whole, fewer than twenty thousand of whom were condemned by the courts. In addition, approximately five hundred thousand were incarcerated between March 1793 and August 1794. Few victims of the Terror were aristocrats. Many more were peasants or laborers accused of hoarding, treason, or counterrevolutionary activity. Anyone who appeared to threaten the republic, no matter what his or her social or economic position, was at risk. When some time later the Abbé Sieyès was asked what he had done to distinguish himself during the Terror, he responded dryly, "I lived."

THE LEGACY OF THE SECOND FRENCH REVOLUTION

Several points need to be made concerning this "second" French Revolution. First, for a time revolutionary enthusiasm affected the everyday life of French men, women, and children in a remarkably direct way. The city-based sans-culottes imposed their style of dress on their fellow citizens. Workers' trousers replaced the breeches that until now were a sartorial badge of the middle classes and the nobility. A red cap, said to symbolize freedom from slavery, became popular headgear, wigs having vanished. Men and women addressed each other as "citizen" or "citizeness." Public life was marked by ceremonies designed to dramatize the break with the Old Regime. In the early stages of the revolution, these festivals galvanized and expressed popular enthusiasm for new ways of living and thinking. Under the Committee of Public Safety, they became didactic and hollow. Perhaps the most famous was the Festival of Reason in November 1793. The secular ceremony was held inside the venerable Cathedral of Notre Dame, where a mountain was constructed, symbolizing the all-powerful ruling party. Atop the mountain a temple, adorned with the motto "To Philosophy," housed a troop of maidens, dressed in white and crowned with laurel. At the

The Guillotine in Paris. The mechanical executioner before and after the fall of the blade.

Meeting of a Revolutionary Committee of Surveillance during the Terror. Note the presence of women and children at the proceedings.

cal revolution of 1792–1793 is that it dramatically reversed the trend toward decentralization that had characterized the reforms of the Assembly. It replaced local officials, some of them still royalist in sympathy, with "deputies on mission," whose task was to conscript troops and generate patriotic fervor. When these deputies appeared too eager to act independently, they were in turn replaced by "national agents," with instructions to report directly to the Committee. In another effort to stabilize authority, it closed down all the women's political clubs, decreeing them a political and social danger.

Third, the domestic and foreign policies pursued with such ruthlessness by the Committee began to foster a new sense of the nation as a political community. The Revolution eroded the strength of those traditional institutions—church, guild, parish—that had for centuries given people a common bond. In their place now stood patriotic organizations and a culture that insisted on loyalty to one national cause. Those institutions started with the election campaigns, meetings, and pamphlet wars of 1788 and the interest they heightened. They included the political clubs and local assemblies, which at the height of the revolution (1792–1793) met every day of the week,

appropriate moment, they descended the mount while the audience sang a hymn that, in the words of an admiring contemporary commentator, "expressed natural truths" rather than the "mystical and chimerical adulations" of organized religion. As a finale, a woman dressed as Liberty emerged from the temple to receive the homage of the crowd.

A second point worth making concerning the radi-

Patriotic Women's Club. The members of this patriotic club wear "constitutional bonnets" to show their support for the Revolution and the reforms of the Convention.

CHRONOLOGY

THE SECOND FRENCH REVOLUTION, 1792–1794

First Republic established	Summer 1792
National Convention elected	September 1792
Execution of the king	January 1793
War between Britain, Holland, Spain and France	February 1793
Jacobins purge the Girondin	June 1793
Levée en Masse	August 1793
"Reign of Terror"	September 1793–July 1794
Purge of the Jacobins	July 27, 1794
Execution of Robespierre	July 28, 1794

THE TERROR

The "Terror" often came to the common people of the French countryside in the form of forced requisitioning. Commissioners of the "revolutionary armies," militias of sans-culottes, posted notices on walls in small villages. The text below is from a poster from the revolutionary government warning that the country is in danger and that the markets in towns have been empty since the law of the maximum, which fixed the price of grain. Peasants who fail to deliver grain to their patriotic brothers will meet revolutionary justice.

We have put your persons and your property under the responsibility [or jurisdiction] of the municipalities, and the revolutionary sword [this means the guillotine] is waiting, suspended over the head of any evil doers . . . woe be to those who do not hurry to bring to their brothers in the cities the gifts that nature has entrusted to them.

The revolutionary army will come through all the villages, and it will treat egotistical monsters as enemies even more deadly to the country than the Austrians and the Prussians.

Metz, Brumaire 14, year 2 of the French Republic, one and indivisible.

Richard Cobb. *Les armées révolutionnaires*, Vol. 2 (Paris: Mouton, 1963), pp. 436–37.

and offered an apprenticeship in politics. In addition to the national army (*fédérés*), they included the people's armies, which were vigilante groups of sans-culottes sent from the town into the countryside to requisition food and materials.

Those who sided with the revolution were not the only ones mobilized. Counterrevolutionary movements were also "popular" movements, enlisting peasants and artisans who believed their local areas were being invaded, and who fought for their local priest, or against the summons from the revolutionaries' conscription boards. The revolution divided France. But it also forged new bonds. The sense that the rest of Europe, carrying what the verses of the Marseillaise, the most famous anthem of the Revolution, called the "blood-stained flag of tyranny," would crush the new nation and its citizens unquestionably strengthened French national identity.

FROM THE TERROR TO BONAPARTE: THE DIRECTORY

Why did the Directory fail?

The Committee of Public Safety, though able to save France, could not save itself. It failed to put a stop to inflation, thereby losing the support of those commoners whose dissatisfactions had helped bring the Convention to power. The long string of military victories convinced growing numbers that the Committee's demands for continuing self-sacrifice, as well as its insistence on the necessity of the Terror, were no longer justified. By July 1794, the Committee was virtually without allies. On July 27 (9 Thermidor, according to the new calendar), Robespierre was shouted down by his enemies while attempting to speak on the floor of the Convention. The following day, along with twenty-one other conspirators, he met his death by guillotine as an enemy of the state.

"Moderation" did not follow immediately. Jacobins were driven into hiding, and hunted by vigilante groups of royalists. The repeal of the law of maximum prices, which was a form of price control, combined with the worst winter in a century, caused widespread misery. Yet other measures which had constituted the Terror, though, were gradually repealed. In 1795 the National Convention adopted a new and more conservative constitution. It granted suffrage to all adult male citizens who could read and write. They were permitted to vote for electors, who in turn would choose the members of the legislative body. Electors had to show an annual income equivalent to at least one hundred days of labor. The drafters of the constitution thus ensured that the authority of the government would actually be derived from citizens of considerable wealth. Eager to avoid personal dictatorship, it vested executive authority in a board of five men known as the Directory, chosen by the legislative body. The new constitution included not only a bill of rights but also a declaration of the duties of the citizen. Conspicuous among the latter was the obligation to bear in mind that "it is upon the maintenance of property . . . that the whole social order rests."

Although the Directory lasted longer than its revolutionary predecessor, it could not stabilize the government for several reasons. First, many leaders of the Directory were rich speculators and war profiteers who rose to prominence during the first two stages of the revolution. The Directory did not want to unravel the major accomplishments of the Revolution, but the members were continually faced with trying to appease dissatisfied elements from both the radical left and the conservative right. Their efforts to maintain this delicate balancing were partially undermined by their opulent lifestyles, which flew in the face of the more democratic legacies of the revolution. They were regularly lampooned in various newspapers for their decadent and ostentatious habits and manner of appearance—outrageously overdressed men and underdressed women.

> Although the Directory lasted longer than its revolutionary predecessor, it could not stabilize the government.

By 1797, the popular movement had all but collapsed. On the left, the Directory successfully quashed various movements to abolish private property and parliamentary-style government, including the movement led by the radical "Gracchus Babeuf," whose followers were mostly executed or deported. Dispatching threats from the right proved more challenging. Elections in March 1797—the first free elections held in France as a republic—returned a large number of constitutional monarchists to the councils of government. Leading politicians, among them some who had voted for the execution of Louis XVI, took alarm. With the support of the army, in September 1797 the Directory annulled most of the election results of the previous spring. Its bold coup did little, however, to end the nation's political irresolution. Two years later, after a series of further abortive uprisings and purges, and with the country still plagued by severe inflation, the Directors were desperate. This time they called their brilliant young general Napoleon Bonaparte to their assistance.

Bonaparte's first military victory in 1793, the recapture of Toulon from royalist and British forces, had earned him promotion from captain to brigadier general at the age of twenty-four. Though arrested as a Terrorist following the fall of Robespierre, he was subsequently patronized by Viscount Paul Barras, a Directory politician. Bonaparte had gained further public fame and the gratitude of the Directory when on October 4, 1795 (13 Vendémiaire, new calendar), he had delivered what he called a "whiff of grapeshot" that saved the Convention from attack by opponents of the new constitution. Since that time he had registered a remarkable series of victories in Italy, which had resulted in Austria's withdrawal from the war. Most recently, he had attempted to defeat Britain by attacking its colonies in Egypt and the Near East. Despite initial successes on land, Bonaparte eventually found himself trapped by the British, following the defeat of the French fleet by Admiral Horatio Nelson at Abukir Bay in 1798. A year of further fighting had brought Bonaparte no nearer decisive victory in North Africa.

It was at this point that the call came from the Directory. Bonaparte slipped away from Egypt and appeared in Paris, already having agreed to participate in a coup d'état with the leading director, that former revolutionary champion of the Third Estate, the Abbé Sieyès. On November 9, 1799 (18 Brumaire), Bonaparte was declared a "temporary consul." He was the answer to the prayers of the Directory: a strong, popular leader who was not a king. Sieyès, who had once declared for revolution in the name of the Third Estate, now declared for counterrevolution in the name of virtual dictatorship: "Confidence from below, authority from above." With those words Sieyès pronounced the end of the revolutionary period.

THE HAITIAN REVOLUTION

Throughout all of these events, the French colonies across the Atlantic were reshaping the revolution and its legacy. The Caribbean islands of Guadeloupe, Martinique, and St. Domingue occupied a central role in the French economy because of the sugar trade. Their planter elites had powerful influence in Paris. The French National Assembly (like its American counterpart) declined to discuss the matter of slavery in the colonies, unwilling to trench on the property rights of slave owners and fearful of losing the lucrative sugar islands to their British or Spanish rivals should discontented slaveowners talk of independence from France. More difficult, from the point of view of the French men in the Assembly, was the question of rights for free men of color, a group that included a significant number of wealthy owners of property (and slaves).

St. Domingue had about forty thousand whites of different social classes, thirty thousand free people of color, and five hundred thousand slaves, most of them recently enslaved in West Africa. In 1790, free people of color from St. Domingue sent a delegation to Paris, asking to be seated by the Assembly, underscoring that they were men of property and, in many cases, of European ancestry. The Assembly refused to seat them. Their refusal sparked a mulatto rebellion in St. Domingue. The colonial authorities repressed the movement quickly and brutally, capturing Vincent Ogé, a member of the mulatto delegation to Paris and one of the leaders of the rebellion, and publicly executing him and his allies by breaking on the wheel and decapitation. Radical deputies, in Paris, including Robespierre, expressed outrage but could do little to change the Assembly's policy.

In August 1791 the largest slave rebellion in history broke out in St. Domingue. How much that rebellion owed to revolutionary propaganda is unclear; like many rebellions during the period, it had its own roots

How much the Revolution of St. Domingue owed to French Revolution propaganda is unclear; like many rebellions during this period, it had its own roots and followed its own logic.

and followed its own logic. The British and the Spanish invaded St. Domingue, confident they could quash the rebellion and take the island. In the spring of 1792, the French government, on the verge of collapse and war with Europe, scrambled to win allies in St. Domingue by making free men of color citizens. Soon after the revolution of August 1792, the new French Republic dispatched commissioners to St. Domingue with troops and instructions to hold the island. The volatile combination of Spanish and British troops, and rebellious St. Domingue planters and slaves, proved more than the Republican forces could handle on their own. In this context, the local French commissioners capitulated to a successful slave revolution, and in 1793 promised freedom to slaves who would join the French. A year later, the Assembly in Paris extended to all the colonies what had already been accomplished in St. Domingue.

The new situation brought new leaders to the fore, chief among them a former slave, Toussaint Bréda, later Toussaint L'Ouverture, meaning "the one who opened the way." Over the course of the next five years, Toussaint and his soldiers, now allied with the French army, emerged victorious over the French planters, the British (in 1798), and the Spanish (in 1801). Toussaint also broke the power of his rival generals in both the mulatto and former slave armies, becoming the statesman of the revolution. In 1801, Toussaint set up a constitution, swearing allegiance to France but denying France any right to interfere in St. Domingue affairs. The constitution abolished slavery, reorganized the military, and established Christianity as the state religion (this entailed a rejection of vodoun, a blend of Christian and various West and Central African traditions) and made Toussaint governor for life. It was an extraordinary moment in the revolutionary period: the formation of an authoritarian society but also an utterly unexpected symbol of the universal potential of revolutionary ideas.

Toussaint's accomplishments, however, put him on a collision course with the other French general he admired and whose career was remarkably like his own: Napoleon Bonaparte. St. Domingue stood at the center of Bonaparte's ambitions for the New World, and in January, 1802 he dispatched twenty thousand troops to bring the island under control. Toussaint, captured when he arrived for discussions with the French, was shipped under heavy guard to a prison in the mountains of eastern France where he died in 1803. Fighting continued in St. Domingue, however, with fires now fueled by Bonaparte's determination to restore slavery. The war turned into a nightmare for the French. Yellow fever killed thousands of French troops, including one of Napoleon's best generals. Armies on both sides committed atrocities. By December 1803, the French army had collapsed. In January 1804, Jean-Jacques Dessalines, a general in the army of former slaves, declared the independent state of Haiti.

The Haitian revolution remained, in significant ways, an anomaly. It was the only successful slave revolution in history, and by far the most radical of the revolutions that occurred in this age. It suggested that the emancipatory ideas of the revolution and Enlightenment might apply to non-Europeans and enslaved peoples—a suggestion that residents of Europe attempted to ignore but one that struck home with planter elites in North and South America. Combined with later rebellions in the British colonies it contributed to the British decision to end slavery in 1838. And it cast a long shadow over nineteenth-century slave societies from the southern United States to Brazil.

> The Haitian revolution remained, in significant ways, an anomaly. It was the only successful slave revolution in history, and by far the most radical of the revolutions that occurred in this age.

NAPOLEON AND IMPERIAL FRANCE

How did Napoleon centralize his authority?

Few figures in Western history have compelled the attention of the world as Napoleon Bonaparte did during the fifteen years of his rule in France. Few men lived on with such persistence as myth, not just in their own countries, but across the West. For the great majority of ordinary Europeans, memories of the French Revolution were dominated by those of the Napoleonic wars, which devastated Europe, convulsed its politics, and traumatized its peoples for a generation. What had begun as political revolution and popular revolt ended in war and efforts to create a new kind of European empire. To many observers, that transformation seemed embodied in the career of one man. From the onset of

war in 1792, France's revolutionaries had turned to the armies of France for defense and survival. It seemed all too natural that the future of the Revolution should be bound up with the successes of its greatest general, Napoleon Bonaparte.

Bonaparte's relationship to the Revolution, however, was not simple. His regime consolidated some of the revolution's political and social changes but sharply repudiated others. He presented himself as the son of the revolution, but he also borrowed freely from very different regimes, fashioning himself as the heir to Charlemagne, or to the Roman empire. His regime remade revolutionary politics and the French state, transformed the nature of European warfare, and left a legacy of conflict and legends of French glory that lingered in the dreams, or nightmares, of Europe's statesmen and citizens for more than a century.

CONSOLIDATING AUTHORITY: 1799–1804

Napoleon's early career reinforced the claim that the Revolution rewarded the efforts of able men. The son of a provincial Corsican nobleman, he attended the Ecole Militaire in Paris. In pre-Revolutionary France, he would have been unable to rise beyond the rank of major, for doing so required buying a regimental command. The Revolution, however, had abolished the purchase of military office, and Bonaparte quickly became a general. Here, then, was a man who had risen from obscurity because of his own gifts, which he lent happily to the service of France's revolution. His character seemed suited to the age as well, at least to his early admirers, who noted his wide range of talents and intellectual interests. He pursued serious interests in history, law, and mathematics. His particular strengths as a leader lay in his ability to create financial, legal, or military plans and then to master their every detail; in his capacity for inspiring others, even those initially opposed to him; and in his belief that he was the destined savior of France. That last conviction eventually led to Napoleon's undoing. But supreme self-confidence was just what the French government had recently lacked. Napoleon believed both in himself and in France. That faith was the tonic France needed, and Napoleon administered it.

In the first five years of his reign, Bonaparte quickly consolidated personal power. When he overthrew the government in 1799, he assumed the title of First Consul and governed in the name of the Republic. A new constitution established universal white male suffrage and set up two legislative bodies. Elections, however, were indirect, and the power of the legislative bodies sharply curbed. "The government?" said one observer. "There is Bonaparte." Bonaparte instituted what has since become a common authoritarian device, the plebiscite, which put a question directly to popular vote. This allows the head of state to bypass politicians or legislative bodies who might disagree with him—as well as permitting local officials to tamper with ballot boxes. In 1802, flush with victory abroad, he asked the legislature to proclaim him consul for life. When the Senate refused to do so, Bonaparte's Council of State stepped in, offered him the title, and had it ratified by plebiscite. In 1804, his power secure, he abolished the republic, a plebiscite ratified the creation of a hereditary empire, and he crowned himself Napoleon, emperor of the French. Throughout, his regime retained the appearance of consulting with the people, but its most important feature was the centralization of authority.

That authority came from reorganizing the state. Bonaparte's regime confirmed the abolition of estates, privileges, and local liberties, thereby promising "careers open to talent." Through centralization of the administrative departments, he achieved what no recent French regime had yet achieved: an orderly and generally fair system of taxation. His plan, by prohibiting the type of exemptions formerly granted the nobility and clergy, and by centralizing collection, enabled him to budget rationally for expenditures and consequent indebtedness. More efficient tax collection and fiscal management also helped him halt the inflationary spiral that had crippled the revolutionary governments, although Bonaparte's regime relied heavily on resources from areas he had conquered to fund his military ventures. As we have seen, the revolutionaries began the work of reorganizing the administration, abolishing the ancient fiefdoms with their separate governments, making a uniform system of departments. Bonaparte continued that work, but with an accent on centralization. He replaced elected officials and local self-government with centrally appointed "prefects" and "subprefects" whose administrative duties were defined in Paris, where local government policy was made as well. Napoleon's state was a point midway between absolutism and the modern state.

Napoleon's most significant accomplishment, and one exported to the areas he conquered, was the completion of the legal reforms begun during the revolutionary period and the promulgation of a new legal code in 1804. The Napoleonic Code reflected two principles that had threaded their way through all the constitutional changes since 1789: uniformity and individualism. The code cleared through the thicket of different legal traditions, creating one uniform law. It confirmed the abolition of feudal privileges of all kinds: not only noble and clerical privileges but the special rights of craft guilds, municipalities, and so on. It set the conditions for exercising property rights: the drafting of contracts, leases, and stock companies. The code's provisions on the family, which Napoleon worked on personally, insisted on the importance of paternal authority and the subordination of women and children. In 1793, during the most radical period of the revolution, men and women had been declared "equal in marriage"; now Napoleon's code affirmed the "natural supremacy" of the husband. Married women could not sell property, run a business, or have a profession without their husbands' permission. Fathers had the sole right to control their children's financial affairs, consent to their marriages, and (under the ancient right to correction) to imprison them for up to six months without showing cause. Divorce remained legal, but under unequal conditions; a man could sue for divorce on the grounds of adultery, but a woman could only do so if her husband moved his "concubine" into the family's house. Most important to the common people, the code prohibited paternity suits for illegitimate children. The new criminal code consolidated some of the gains of the revolution, treating citizens as equals before the law and outlawing arbitrary arrest and imprisonment. Yet it, too, reintroduced harsher measures that the revolutionaries had abolished, such as branding and cutting off the hands of parricides. The Napoleonic code was more egalitarian than law under the Old Regime, but no less concerned with authority.

Bonaparte also rationalized the educational system. He ordered the establishment of *lycées* (high schools) in every major town to train civil servants and army

> Napoleon's most significant accomplishment was the completion of the legal reforms begun during the revolutionary period and the promulgation of a new legal code in 1804.

Coronation of Napoleon and Josephine, by David. Napoleon crowned himself and his wife and assumed the title of Napoleon I, emperor of France.

officers and a school in Paris to train teachers. To supplement these changes, Napoleon brought the military and technical schools under state control and founded a national university to supervise the entire system. Like almost all his reforms, this one reinforced reforms introduced during the Revolution, and it intended to abolish privilege and create "careers open to talent." Napoleon also embraced the burgeoning social and physical sciences of the Enlightenment. He sponsored the Academie Française and retained several of the revolutionaries' more practical attempts to rationalize society and commerce, such as the metric system.

Who benefited from these changes? Education did offer new opportunities to members of the middle class. Like Bonaparte's other new institutions, the new schools helped confirm the power of a new elite or group of "notables." Those "notables" came from all three estates, and included businessmen, bankers, and merchants. The new elite, however, was still composed primarily of men whose wealth and power was derived from owning land. What was more, at least half of the fellowships to the high schools went to the sons of military officers and high civil servants. Finally, like most

of Bonaparte's reforms, changes in education aimed to strengthen the power of the state: "My object in establishing a teaching corps is to have a means of directing political and moral opinion," Napoleon said bluntly.

Bonaparte's early measures were ambitious. To win support for them, he made allies without regard for their past political affiliations. He admitted back into the country exiles of all political stripes. His two fellow consuls were a regicide of the Terror and a bureaucrat of the Old Regime. His minister of police had been an extreme radical republican; his minister of foreign affairs was the aristocrat and opportunist Charles Talleyrand. The most remarkable act of political reconciliation came in 1801, with Bonaparte's concordat with the pope, an agreement that put an end to more than a decade of hostility between the French state and the Catholic Church. Although it shocked anticlerical revolutionaries, Napoleon, ever the pragmatist, believed that reconciliation would create domestic harmony and international solidarity. The agreement gave the pope the right to depose French bishops and to discipline the French clergy. In return, the Vatican agreed to forego any claims to church lands expropriated by the Revolution. That property would remain in the hands of its new middle-class rural and urban proprietors. The concordat did not revoke the principle of religious freedom established by the Revolution, but it did win Napoleon the support of conservatives who had feared for France's future as a godless state. Lest anyone think he had severed ties with the Revolution, however, in 1804 Napoleon shocked French and European conservatives by invading the independent state of Baden, where his troops arrested and summarily executed a young and well-liked relative of the Bourbons.

Such political balancing acts increased Bonaparte's general popularity. Combined with early military successes (peace with Austria in 1801 and England in 1802), they muffled any opposition to his personal ambitions. He had married Josephine de Beauharnais, a Creole from Martinique and an influential mistress of the Revolutionary period. Josephine had given the Corsican soldier-politician legitimacy and access among the revolutionary elite early in his career. Neither Bonaparte nor his ambitious wife were content to be first among equals, however, and in December of 1804, he finally cast aside any traces of republicanism. In a ceremony that evoked the splendor of medieval kingship and Bourbon absolutism, he crowned himself Emperor Napoleon I in the Cathedral of Notre Dame in Paris. Napoleon did much to create the modern state, but he did not hesitate to proclaim his links to the past.

> The nations of Europe had looked on—some in admiration, others in horror, all in astonishment—at the phenomenon that was Napoleon.

IN EUROPE AS IN FRANCE: NAPOLEON'S WARS OF EXPANSION

The nations of Europe had looked on—some in admiration, others in horror, all in astonishment—at the phenomenon that was Napoleon. A coalition of European powers led by Austria, Prussia, and Britain had fought France from 1792 until 1795, in hopes of maintaining European stability. This first coalition collapsed in disarray, defeated by the French armies and by financial exhaustion. The coalition was revived in 1798, at Britain's behest, but in the end it fared no better than the first effort. Despite Napoleon's debacle in Egypt, French victories in Europe split the alliance. Russia and Austria withdrew from the fray in 1801, and even the intransigent British were forced to make peace the following year.

Out of these victories Napoleon created his new empire and affiliated states. These included a series of small republics carved from Austria's empire and the old German kingdoms. These were presented as France's revolutionary gift of independence to patriots elsewhere in Europe, but in practice they were a military buffer and a system of client states for a new French empire. A loose federation of German states, known as the Confederation of the Rhine, seemed to glorify France's role in "liberating" Europe, but also brought the French Revolution's practical consequences—a powerful, centralizing state and an end to old systems of privilege—to Europe's doorstep. In the case of Britain, these successes stretched beyond Europe as the British were forced to return territories recently captured in colonial warfare, although they retained the important islands of Trinidad and Ceylon.

Napoleon's reign accelerated developments already underway in the territories of central Europe. The French introduced a carefully organized, deliberate system of administration, based on the notion of careers open to talent, equality before the law, and the abolition of ancient customs and privileges. The Napoleonic program of reform applied to the empire principles that had already transformed post-Revolutionary France. It eliminated manorial and church courts. It joined previously separate provinces into an enormous bureaucratic network that reached directly back to Paris. It codified laws and modernized tax systems, and freed individuals to work at whatever trade they chose. These new freedoms of law, property, and profession, however, did not extend to politics. All governmental direction emanated from Paris, and therefore from Napoleon.

The effect of these changes on the men and women who experienced them was profound. In those small principalities previously ruled by small princes—the patchwork states of Germany, for example, or the repressive kingdom of Naples—reforms that provided for more efficient, less corrupt administration, a workable tax structure, and an end to customary privileges were welcomed by most of the local population. Yet the Napoleonic presence proved a mixed blessing. Vassal states contributed heavily to the maintenance of the emperor's military power. The French levied taxes, drafted armies, and required states to support occupying armies. In Italy, the policy was called "liberty and requisitions," and the Italians, Germans, and Dutch paid an especially high price for reforms. From the

EUROPE IN 1812

- French territory
- French dependencies
- Allies with Napoleon
- Independent states

NAPOLEON'S INVASION
OF RUSSIA, 1812

→ Advance
◄- - Retreat

EMPIRE OF NAPOLEON AT ITS GREATEST EXTENT

Why did Napoleon launch his campaign of conquest? What role did the revolution in France play not only in his elevation to power, but in the wars fought by the French across Europe? Which states allied themselves to Napoleon, and why? Who opposed him? How did the geopolitical organization of central and eastern Europe aid Napoleon's aims? Why was the campaign into Russia, a weaker foe, such a disaster for the French?

point of view of the common people, the local lord and priest had been replaced by the French tax collector and army recruiting board.

This arrogance slowly but irretrievably cost Napoleon the support of revolutionaries, former Enlightenment thinkers, and liberals across the Continent. The German composer Ludwig van Beethoven originally planned to dedicate his Third Symphony, the *Eroica*, to Napoleon. Like so many European idealists, Beethoven at first hoped that the nation of revolution had found its hero, who would bring the fruits of the French experience to the whole continent. But Napoleon's empire building and his self-coronation in 1804 forced a swift and bitter change of judgment. Beethoven revoked the dedication to Bonaparte, declaring, "Now he, too, will trample on all the rights of man and indulge only his ambition."

TWO LETTERS FROM NAPOLEON

Napoleon placed his brothers on the thrones of different vassal states in conquered territories throughout Europe. The first excerpt below is from a letter to his brother Eugène, head of one of the new Italian states, in which Napoleon explains how Italy's lucrative silk trade was to be diverted in order to damage English commercial interests and bolster the French empire. It provides a revealing glimpse of Napoleon's vision of a united Europe, with the other countries' futures tied to France's.

On March 1, 1815, Napoleon landed in the south of France having escaped from his exile on the island of Elba. The restored Bourbon king abdicated, and Napoleon ruled for 100 more days, until his defeat at the battle of Waterloo in June. The second selection below is excerpted from a proclamation, addressed to the sovereigns of Europe, explaining the Emperor's return. It is an excellent illustration of Napoleon's self image, his rhetoric, and his belief that he represented the force of history itself.

LETTER TO PRINCE EUGÈNE, 23 AUGUST 1810

I have received your letter of August 14. All the raw silk from the Kingdom of Italy goes to England, for there are no silk factories in Germany. It is therefore quite natural that I should wish to divert it from this route to the advantage of my French manufacturers: otherwise my silk factories, one of the chief supports of French commerce, would suffer substantial losses. I cannot agree with your observations. My principle is *France first.* You must never lose sight of the fact that, if English commerce is supreme on the high seas, it is due to her sea power: it is therefore to be expected that, as France is the strongest land power, she should claim commercial supremacy on the continent: it is indeed our only hope. And isn't it better for Italy to come to the help of France, in such an important matter as this, than to be covered with Customs Houses? For it would be short-sighted not to recognise that Italy owes her independence to France; that it was won by French blood and French victories; that it must not be misused; and that nothing could be more unreasonable than to start calculating what commercial advantages France gets out of it.

Piedmont and Parma produce silk too; and there also I have prohibited its export to any country except France. Why should Piedmont be treated in one way, and the Kingdom of Italy in another? If any discrimination were made, it should be in favour of Piedmont; for whilst the Venetians fought against France, the Piedmontese came to her aid, taking sides against their own king. But never mind about all that. I understand Italian affairs better than anyone else. It is no use for Italy to make plans that leave French prosperity out of account; she must face the fact that the interests of the two countries hang together. Above all, she must be careful not to give France any reason for annexing her; for if it paid France to do this, who could stop her? So make this your motto too—*France first.*

If I were to lose a great battle, a million men—nay, two million men of my old France would flock to my banners, and every purse in the country would be opened for me; but my kingdom of Italy would desert me. I find it odd, then, that there should be any unwillingness to help the French manufacturers in what is only another way of damaging the English. . . .

CIRCULAR LETTER TO THE SOVEREIGNS OF EUROPE, 4 APRIL 1815

Monsieur, My Brother,

You will have learnt, during the course of last month, of my landing again in France, of my entry into Paris, and of the departure of the Bourbon family. Your Majesty must by now be aware of the real nature of these events. They are the work of an irresistable power, of the unanimous will of a great nation conscious of its duties and of its rights. A dynasty forcibly reimposed upon the French people was no longer suitable for it: the Bourbons refused to associate themselves with the natural feelings or the national customs; and France was forced to abandon them. The popular voice called for a liberator. The expectation which had decided me to make the supreme sacrifice was in vain. I returned; and from the place where my foot first touched the shore I was carried by the affection of my subjects into the bosom of my capital.

My first and heartfelt anxiety is to repay so much affection by the maintenance of an honourable peace.

The re-establishment of the Imperial throne was necessary for the happiness of Frenchmen: my dearest hope is that it may also secure repose for the whole of Europe. Each national flag in turn has had its gleam of glory: often enough, by some turn of fortune, great victories have been followed by great defeats. . . . I have provided the world in the past with a programme of great contests; it will please me better in future to acknowledge no rivalry but that of the advocates of peace, and no combat but a crusade for the felicity of mankind. It is France's pleasure to make a frank avowal of this noble ideal. Jealous of her independence, she will always base her policy upon an unqualified respect for the independence of other peoples. . . .

Monsieur my Brother,
Your good Brother,
Napoléon.

K. M. Baker, ed. *The Old Regime and the French Revolution.* (Chicago: University of Chicago Press, 1987), pp. 419–20 and 426–27.

THE RETURN TO WAR AND NAPOLEON'S DEFEAT: 1806–1815

What led to Napoleon's downfall?

Napoleon's motives in introducing radical political and administrative changes were never altruistic. He understood that the defense of his enormous domain depended on efficient government and the rational getting and spending of funds for his armies. Yet his boldest attempt at consolidation, a policy banning British goods from the Continent, was a dangerous failure. This "Continental System," established in 1806, was designed as a strategic measure in Napoleon's continuing economic war against Britain. Britain had bitterly opposed each of France's revolutionary regimes since the death of Louis XVI; now they tried to rally Europe against Napoleon with promises of generous financial loans and trade. The Continental System sought to starve Britain's trade and force its surrender. The system failed for several reasons. Throughout the war Britain retained control of the seas. The British naval blockade of the Continent, begun in 1807, effectively countered Napoleon's system. While the French empire strained to transport goods and raw materials overland to avoid the British blockade, the British successfully developed a lively trade with South America. A second reason for the failure of the system was its internal tariffs. Europe divided into economic camps, at odds with each other as they tried to subsist on what the Continent alone could produce and manufacture. The final reason for the system's collapse was that its policies hurt the Continent more than Britain. Stagnant trade in Europe's ports and unemployment in its manufacturing centers eroded public faith in Napoleon's dream of a working European empire.

The Continental System was Napoleon's first serious mistake. A second cause of his decline was his unmasterable ambition and growing sense of self-importance. Napoleon's goal was to remake Europe as a new Roman empire, ruled from Paris. The symbols of his empire—reflected in painting, architecture, and the design of furniture and clothing—were deliberately Roman in origin. This was not a novelty; the early revolutionaries, Jacobins in particular, harked back to the Roman republic as their model for political virtue, drawing on its imagery in art and political rhetoric. But the triumphal columns and arches Napoleon had erected to commemorate his victories recalled the ostentatious monuments

Napoleon Bonaparte on the Battle Field. This lithograph by F. C. Vogel shows Napoleon checking the operation of a cannon and thus emphasizes the emperor's attention to the details of battle.

of the Roman emperors. He made his brothers and sisters the monarchs of his newly created kingdoms, which Napoleon controlled from Paris while their mother allegedly sat at court, anxiously wringing her hands and repeating to herself, "If only it lasts!" In 1809 he divorced the empress Josephine, and ensured himself a successor of royal blood by marrying Marie Louise, daughter of Francis I of the powerful and respectable house of Habsburg. Even Napoleon's admirers began to wonder if his empire would reflect simply a larger, more efficient, and ultimately more dangerous absolutism than the monarchies of the eighteenth century.

War had broken out again in 1805, with the Russians, Prussians, Austrians, and Swedes joining the British in an attempt to contain France. Their efforts were to no avail. Napoleon's military superiority led to defeats, in turn, of all three Continental allies. Napoleon was a master of well-timed, well-directed shock attacks on the battlefield. He led an army that had transformed European warfare: first raised as a revolutionary militia, it was now a trained, conscript army of native Frenchmen, loyal, well supplied by a nation whose economy was committed to serving the war effort, and led by generals promoted largely on the basis of talent. This new kind of army, directed with Napoleon's lethal flair, inflicted crushing defeats on his enemies. The battle of Austerlitz,

in December 1805, was a mighty triumph for the French against the combined forces of Austria and Russia and became a symbol of the emperor's apparent invincibility. His subsequent victory against the Russians at Friedland in 1807 only added to his reputation.

Over time, however, the bitter tonic of defeat began to have an effect on Napoleon's enemies, who changed their own approach to waging war in response to his devastating victories. After the Prussian army was humiliated at Jena in 1806 and forced out of the war, a whole generation of younger Prussian officers reformed their military and their state by demanding rigorous practical training for commanders and a genuinely national army made up of patriotic Prussian citizens rather than well-drilled mercenaries.

The myth of Napoleon's invincibility worked against him as well, as he took ever greater risks with France's military and national fortunes. Russian numbers and Austrian artillery inflicted horrendous losses on the French at Wagram in 1809, although these difficulties were forgotten in the glow of another victory. Napoleon's allies and supporters shrugged off the British admiral Horatio Nelson's victory at Trafalgar in 1805 as no more than a temporary check to the emperor's ambitions. But Trafalgar broke French naval power in the Mediterranean and helped lead to a rift with Spain, which had been France's equal partner in the battle and suffered equally in the defeat. In the Americas, too, Napoleon was forced to cut growing losses, giving up on St. Domingue in the face of disaster and selling France's territories along the Mississippi to the United States for badly needed cash.

A crucial moment in Napoleon's undoing came with his invasion of Spain in 1808. The invasion aimed, eventually, toward the conquest of Portugal, which had remained a stalwart ally of the British. Napoleon overthrew the Spanish king, installed his own brother on the throne, and then imposed a series of reforms similar to those he had instituted elsewhere in Europe. But he reckoned without two factors that led to the ultimate failure of his Spanish mission: the presence of British forces

Execution of the Rebels on 3d May 1808, by Francisco Goya. This painting of the execution of Spanish rebels by Napoleon's army as it marched into Spain is one of the most memorable depictions of a nation's martyrdom.

under Sir Arthur Wellesley (later the duke of Wellington), and the determined resistance of the Spanish people. They particularly detested Napoleon's interference in the affairs of the church. The peninsular wars, as the Spanish conflicts were called, were especially long and bitter, but the British and Spanish forces found complementary means of defeating France's large occupying army. The smaller British force learned how to concentrate a devastating volume of gunfire on the French pinpoint attacks on the open battlefield, and laid siege to French garrison towns. The Spanish quickly began to wear down French numbers, supplies, and morale through what was called "guerrilla" warfare. Terrible atrocities were committed by both sides; the French military's torture and execution of Spanish guerrillas and civilians was immortalized by the Spanish artist Francisco Goya (1746–1828) with sickening accuracy in his prints and paintings. Though at one point Napoleon himself took charge of his army, he could not achieve anything more than temporary victory. The Spanish campaign was the first indication that Napoleon could be beaten, and encouraged resistance elsewhere.

The second, and most dramatic stage in Napoleon's downfall began with the disruption of his alliance with Russia. As an agricultural country, Russia had suffered a severe economic crisis when it was no longer able to trade its surplus grain for British manufactures. The consequence was that Tsar Alexander I began to wink at trade with Britain and to ignore or evade the protests from Paris. By 1811 Napoleon decided that he could endure this flouting of their agreement no longer. Accordingly, he collected an army of six hundred thousand and set out for Russia in the spring of 1812. Only a third of the soldiers in this "Grande Armée" were French: nearly as many were Polish or German, joined by soldiers and adventurers from the rest of France's client states. It was the grandest of Napoleon's imperial expeditions, an army raised from across Europe and sent to punish the autocratic tsar. It ended in disaster. The Russians refused to make a stand, drawing the French farther and farther into the heart of their country. Just before Napoleon reached the ancient Russian capital of Moscow, the Russian army drew the French forces into a bloody, seemingly pointless battle in the narrow streets of a town called Borodino, where both sides suffered terrible losses of men and supplies, harder on the French who were now so far from home. After the battle, the Russians permitted Napoleon to occupy Moscow. But on the night of his entry, Russian partisans put the city to the torch, leaving little but the blackened walls of the Kremlin palaces to shelter the invading troops.

Napoleon Bonaparte Visiting the Plague Stricken at Jaffa (1804), by Antoine-Jean Gros. This painting, commissioned by the emperor, was one of Gros's many contributions to the later legend of Napoleon. Gros showed Napoleon touching plague victims in a sick house in Jaffa (a city in the Ottoman empire), a scene meant to suggest the emperor's Christ-like compassion.

The Retreat from Russia, 1812. A much less sympathetic and idealized view, this painting simply shows the bleak horrors of war during the Russian campaign.

Hoping that the tsar would eventually surrender, Napoleon lingered amid the ruins for more than a month. On October 19 he finally ordered the homeward march. The delay was a fatal blunder. Long before he had reached the border, the terrible Russian winter was on his troops. Swollen streams, mountainous drifts of snow, and bottomless mud slowed the retreat almost to a halt. To add to the miseries of frostbite, disease, and starvation, mounted Cossacks rode out of the blizzard to harry the exhausted army. Each morning the miserable remnant that pushed on left behind circles of corpses around the campfires of the night before. On December 13 a few thousand broken soldiers crossed the frontier into Germany—a tragic fragment of what had once been proudly styled the Grande Armée. Nearly three hundred thousand of its soldiers and untold thousands of Russians lost their lives in Napoleon's Russian adventure.

Following the retreat from Russia, the anti-Napoleonic forces took renewed hope. United by a belief that they might finally succeed in defeating the emperor, Prussia, Russia, Austria, Sweden, and Britain renewed their attack. Citizens of many German states in particular saw this as a war of liberation, and indeed most of the fighting took place in Germany. The climax of the campaign occurred in October 1813 when, at what was thereafter known as the Battle of the Nations, fought near Leipzig, the allies dealt the French a resounding defeat. Meanwhile, allied armies won significant victories in the Low Countries and Spain. By the beginning of 1814, they had crossed the Rhine into France. Left with an inexperienced army of raw youths, Napoleon retreated to Paris, urging the French people to further resistance despite constant setbacks at the hands of the larger invading armies. On March 31, Tsar Alexander I of Russia and King Frederick William III of Prussia made their triumphant entry into Paris. Napoleon was forced to abdicate unconditionally, and was sent into exile on the island of Elba, off the Italian coast.

Napoleon was back on French soil in less than a year. In the interim the allies had restored the Bourbon dynasty to the throne, in the person of Louis XVIII, brother of Louis XVI. Despite his administrative abilities, Louis was less than charismatic and could not fill the void left by Napoleon's abdication. It was no surprise that, when the former emperor staged his escape from Elba, his fellow countrymen once more rallied to his side. By the time Napoleon reached Paris, he had generated enough support to cause Louis to flee the country. The allies, meeting in Vienna to conclude peace treaties with the French, were stunned by the news of Napoleon's return. They dispatched a hastily organized army to meet the emperor's typically bold offensive push into the Low Countries. At the battle of Waterloo, fought over three bloody days from June 15 to 18, 1815, Napoleon was stopped by the forces of his two most persistent enemies, Britain and Prussia, and suffered his final defeat. This time the allies took no chances and shipped their prisoner off to the bleak island of St. Helena in the South Atlantic. The once-mighty emperor, now the exile Bonaparte, lived out a dreary existence writing self-serving memoirs until his death in 1821.

CONCLUSION

The tumultuous events in France formed part of a broad pattern of late-eighteenth-century democratic upheaval. The French Revolution was the most violent, protracted, and contentious of the revolutions of the era, but its dynamics were much the same. One of the most important developments of the French Revolution was the emergence of a popular movement, which included political clubs representing people previously excluded from politics, newspapers read by and to the common people, and political leaders who spoke for the *sans-culottes*. In the French Revolution as in other revolutions, the popular movement challenged the early and moderate revolutionary leadership, pressing for more radical and democratic measures. And as in other revolutions, the popular movement in France was defeated, and authority was reestablished by a quasi-military figure. Likewise, the revolutionary ideas of liberty, equality, and fraternity were not specifically French; their roots lay in the social structures of the eighteenth century and in the culture of the Enlightenment. Yet French armies brought them, literally, to the doorsteps of many Europeans.

What was the larger impact of the Revolution and the Napoleonic era? Its legacy is partly summed up in three key concepts: liberty, equality, and nation. Liberty meant individual rights and responsibilities, and more specifically freedom from arbitrary authority. By equality, as we have seen, the revolutionaries meant the abolition of legal distinctions of rank between European men. Though their concept of equality was limited, it became a powerful mobilizing force in the nineteenth century. The most important legacy of the revolution may have been the new term *nation*. The nation was a political concept. A "nation" was formed of citizens, not a king's subjects. A nation was ruled by law and treated citizens as equal before the law. Sovereignty did not lie in dynasties or historic fiefdoms, but in the nation of citizens. Loyalty and affinity to this new kind of nation was bred in the hearts of the French people when their citizen armies repelled attacks against their newly won freedoms. By the Napoleonic period, however, this new political body of freely associated citizens was most powerfully embodied in a centralized state, its army, its greatest general turned Emperor of the French, and a kind of citizenship defined by individual commitment to the needs of "the nation" at war.

The revolutionary concept of nationhood spread throughout Europe in response to French aggression. The French did not hesitate to champion their revolutionary principles abroad. France's enemies, who learned harsh lessons from this new brand of citizenship, responded with a growing sense of their own commonality. In the German and Italian principalities a similar response occurred. Men and women, under the domination of an alien emperor and his unwelcome agents, grew increasingly conscious of an identity of their own.

When the revolutionary period closed, the three concepts of liberty, equality, and nationality were no longer merely ideas. They had taken shape in new communities and institutions. They had created new alliances between countries. They also polarized Europe and much of the world, giving rise to debates, grievances, and conflict that would shape the nineteenth century.

SELECTED READINGS

Applewhite, Harriet B., and Darline G. Levy, eds. *Women and Politics in the Age of the Democratic Revolution.* Ann Arbor, 1990. Essays cover women's activities in France, Britain, the Netherlands, and the United States.

Bergeron, Louis. *France under Napoleon.* Princeton, 1981. Concentrates on the social history of the Napoleonic period.

Best, Geoffrey. *War and Society in Revolutionary Europe, 1770–1870.* Leicester, 1982.

Blackburn, Robin. *The Overthrow of Colonial Slavery.* London and New York, 1988.

Blum, Carol. *Rousseau and the Republic of Virtue: The Language of Politics in the French Revolution.* Ithaca, N.Y., 1986. Excellent on how Rousseau was read by the revolutionaries.

Bruun, Geoffrey. *Europe and the French Imperium, 1799–1814.* Westport, Conn., 1983. Describes the impact of Napoleon upon Europe.

Cobb, Richard. *The People's Armies.* New Haven, 1987. Brilliant and detailed analysis of the sans-culottes.

Cobban, Alfred. *The Social Interpretation of the French Revolution.* Cambridge, 1964. A penetrating critique of the radical interpretation of the Revolution, more important for its questions than for its conclusions.

Doyle, William. *Oxford History of the French Revolution.* New York, 1989.

———. *Origins of the French Revolution,* 2d ed. New York, 1988. A revisionist historian surveys recent research on the political and social origins of the Revolution and identifies a new consensus.

Forrest, Alan. *The French Revolution and the Poor.* New York, 1981. An account that argues the poor fared little better under revolutionary governments than under the old regime.

Furet, Francois. *Revolutionary France, 1770–1880.* Trans. Antonia Nerill. Cambridge, Mass., 1992.

Geyl, Pieter. *Napoleon: For and Against,* rev. ed. New Haven, 1964. The ways in which Napoleon was interpreted by French historians and political figures.

Hesse, Carla. *Publishing and Cultural Politics in Revolutionary Paris 1789–1810.* Berkeley, 1991.

Hunt, Lynn. *Politics, Culture, and Class in the French Revolution.* Berkeley, 1984. An analysis of the interaction between political events and sociocultural phenomena out of which grew a new culture of democracy and republicanism.

———. *The French Revolution and Human Rights.* Boston, 1996.

Landes, Joan B. *Women and the Public Sphere in the Age of the French Revolution.* Ithaca, N.Y., 1988. Discusses the revolutionaries' exclusionary policy toward women.

Lefebvre, Georges. *The Coming of the French Revolution.* Princeton, 1947. An excellent study of the causes and early events of the Revolution.

———. *The French Revolution.* 2 vols. New York, 1962–1964. An impressive synthesis by the greatest modern scholar of the Revolution.

———. *The Great Fear of 1789.* New York, 1973. The best account of the rural disturbances.

Lewis, G., and C. Lucas. *Beyond the Terror: Essays in French Regional and Social History, 1794–1815.* New York, 1983.

O'Brien, Connor Cruise. *The Great Melody: A Thematic Biography of Edmund Burke.* Chicago, 1992.

Palmer, R. R. *The Age of the Democratic Revolution: A Political History of Europe and America, 1760–1800.* 2 vols. Princeton, 1964. Impressive for its scope; places the French Revolution in the larger context of a worldwide revolutionary movement.

———. *Twelve Who Ruled: The Year of the Terror in the French Revolution.* Princeton, 1958. Excellent biographical studies of the members of the Committee of Public Safety.

Rudé, George. *The Crowd in the French Revolution.* Westport, Conn., 1986. An important monograph that analyzes the composition of the crowds that participated in the great uprisings of the Revolution.

Schama, Simon. *Citizens: A Chronicle of the French Revolution.* New York, 1989. Particularly good on art and politics.

Soboul, Albert. *The Sans-Culottes: The Popular Movement and Revolutionary Government, 1793–1794.* Garden City, N.Y., 1972. A classic study of the pressures on the Convention in the year of the Terror.

Sutherland, D. M. G. *France, 1789–1815: Revolution and Counterrevolution.* Oxford, 1986. An important synthesis of work on the revolution, especially in social history.

Thompson, J. M. *Robespierre and the French Revolution.* London, 1953. An excellent short biography.

Tilly, Charles. *The Vendée: A Sociological Analysis of the Counter-Revolution of 1793.* Cambridge, Mass., 1964. An important economic and social analysis of the factors that led to the reaction in the Vendée.

Tocqueville, Alexis de. *The Old Regime and the French Revolution.* Garden City, N.Y., 1955. Originally written in 1856, this remains a classic analysis of the causes of the French Revolution.

Trouillot, Michel Rolph. *Silencing the Past.* Boston, 1995.

Woloch, Isser. *The New Regime: Transformations of the French Civic Order, 1789–1820.* New York, 1994. The fate of revolutionary civic reform.

Woolf, Stuart. *Napoleon's Integration of Europe.* New York, 1991.

Chapter TWENTY-ONE

THE INDUSTRIAL REVOLUTION

THE FRENCH REVOLUTION quickly transformed the political and diplomatic landscape of Europe. The transformation of industry came more slowly. Yet even contemporaries were aware of profound and unexpected changes in their economic world. By the early nineteenth century, observers spoke of an "industrial" revolution, one whose effects paralleled the revolution in politics. The term has stayed with us. There have been many periods of rapid and far-reaching changes in industry during human history, and there will be many more. What historians still call the Industrial Revolution spanned the hundred years after 1780. It represented the first breakthrough from a largely rural, handicraft economy to one dominated by urban, machine-driven manufacturing. It involved technological change, mobilized new sources of energy and power, generated new ways of organizing human labor, and triggered social changes with revolutionary consequences for the West and the world.

Why did the Industrial Revolution come to Europe? Ever since the beginning of the seventeenth century, overseas commercial exploration and development had been opening new territories to European trade. India, Africa, North and South America—all had been woven into the pattern of European economic expansion. The colonies and commercial dependencies provide the first part of an explanation, although they do not account for many of the specifics. A second factor in the origins of the Industrial Revolution was the significant population growth that occurred throughout western Europe in the eighteenth century. Increasing populations, along with overseas expansion, provided an ever-growing market for manufactured goods. It furnished, as well, an adequate pool—eventually a surplus—of laboring men, women, and children to work in the manufacture of those goods either at home or in factories.

A third factor was human and cultural. Although in the mid-eighteenth century Europe was still a predominantly agricultural continent, and although the majority of its people remained poor and illiterate, living out their lives within sight of the

FOCUS QUESTIONS

• Why did the Industrial Revolution first take hold in Britain?

• Why did the Industrial Revolution develop more slowly on the Continent?

• How did the railway boom accelerate industrialization?

 • What fueled the increase in production throughout Europe between 1850 and 1870?

• How did the Industrial Revolution affect the world economy?

place they were born—despite these conditions, which in our eyes might make Europe appear "underdeveloped," it was no such thing. Europeans had become among the world's foremost manufacturers, financiers, and traders. Governments relied on these men to maintain their economies, both in terms of flourishing commercial activity and of victorious armies and navies. More secure property rights—upheld by the written contracts that were replacing unwritten, long-acknowledged custom—helped persuade merchants, bankers, traders, and entrepreneurs that they lived in a world that was stable, rational, and predictable. Their hopes seemed ratified by success in trade, and were shared, even celebrated, by many Enlightenment thinkers. Believing the world was so, they moved out into it with self-confidence and in hopes of increasing their own, and their country's, prosperity. Only through the activities of such people could the Industrial Revolution have taken place.

Historians, however, have qualified the concept of a single industrial revolution. First, the existence of a thriving commercial class, expanding markets, and increasing populations prior to the Industrial Revolution suggests that the changes we are about to analyze had important antecedents. We have already noted, for example, the manner in which proto-industrialization was transforming rural areas into sizable manufacturing regions in the seventeenth and eighteenth centuries. Second, industrialization proceeded at very different rates and along different paths in the various regions of Europe. Beginning in northern England and western Scotland in the late eighteenth century, it took hold slowly and unevenly across continental Europe. Pockets of industry coexisted with vast areas of seemingly unchanged subsistence agriculture. Unlike the French Revolution, whose history can be measured by a decade, the Industrial Revolution occurred over the span of at least a century.

THE INDUSTRIAL REVOLUTION IN BRITAIN

Why did the Industrial Revolution first take hold in Britain?

Britain's economy had progressed further than that of any other country in the direction of abundance. In simplest terms, fewer people had to struggle just to remain alive, more people were in a position to sell a surplus of the goods they produced to an increasingly expanding market, and more people had enough money to purchase the goods that market offered. British laborers, though poorly paid, enjoyed a better and more consistent diet than did their Continental counterparts—among other things they ate meat with some regularity. Because a smaller portion of their income was spent on food, they might occasionally have some to spare for articles that were bought rather than homemade.

Further evidence of this increasing abundance was the number of bills for the enclosure of agricultural land passed by a British Parliament sympathetic to capitalism during the last half of the eighteenth century. The enclosure of fields, pastures, and waste lands into large fenced tracts of land under the private ownership and individual management of capitalist landlords meant a greater food supply to feed a growing and increasingly urban population as well as augmented wealth for a class of landed investors. Yet another sign of Britain's abundance was its growing supply of surplus capital, derived from investment in land or commerce, and available to finance new economic enterprises. London had become the leading center for international trade, and served as a headquarters for the transfer of raw material, capital, and manufactured products. Portugal alone channeled as much as fifty thousand pounds in Brazilian gold per week into London. British merchants and financiers had accumulated prodigious fortunes, with enough money on hand to underwrite and sustain an unexpected but profound industrial revolution.

But the revolution required more than money. It required habits of mind that would encourage investment in enterprises that were risky but that had an enormous potential for gain. In Britain far more than on the Continent, the pursuit of wealth was perceived to be a worthy end in life. The nobility of Europe had, from the period of the Renaissance, cultivated the notion of "gentlemanly" conduct, in part to hold the line against social encroachments from below. The British aristocrats, whose ancient privileges were meager when compared with those of Continental nobles, respected those commoners who had a talent for making money, and had never hesitated to do likewise themselves. Their scramble to enclose their lands reflected this sympathy with commercial capitalism. Below the aristocracy, an even lower barrier separated the world of urban commerce from that of the rural gentry. Most of those who pioneered as entrepreneurs in the early years of the Industrial Revolution sprang from the minor gentry or yeoman farmer class. Men from this

Moscow

RUSSIAN EMPIRE

BLACK SEA

OTTOMAN EMPIRE

St. Petersburg

Uppsala
Stockholm

NORWAY

SWEDEN

DENMARK
Copenhagen

BALTIC SEA

Lemberg

Warsaw

Cracow
Posen
Lodz
Breslau

GERMAN EMPIRE

SILESIA

AUSTRIAN EMPIRE

Budapest

Vienna

Hamburg

Berlin
Dresden
Zwickau
Prague
Pilsen

Bremen
Hannover
Kassel
Eisenach
Chemnitz
Nuremberg
Munich
Steyr

RUHR
Cologne
Frankfurt
Stuttgart

NETHERLANDS
Amsterdam

NORTH SEA

BELGIUM
Brussels
Liège
Karlsruhe
Strasbourg
Mulhouse
SAAR
Basel

Zurich
SWITZ.

ITALY

Milan
Turin

Florence

Naples

Rome

MEDITERRANEAN SEA

Lyons

Avignon

Marse.lles

Barcelona

Lille
Amiens
Paris
Orleans
Tours
FRANCE
Limoges
Nantes

Le Havre

UNITED KINGDOM

Glasgow

Darlington
Leeds
Sheffield

Liverpool
Manchester
Birmingham
Cardiff
London

Dublin

Livorno

Bilbao
Santander
Gijon
Oviedo
Seville
Jerez
Granada
Madrid

Lisbon

ATLANTIC OCEAN

Area of detail

EUROPE

AFRICA

| 0 | 100 | 200 | 300 Miles |
| 0 | 100 200 | 300 Kilometers |

PERCENT OF POPULATION LIVING IN CITIES OF 100,000 OR MORE

5 percent or less
6 to10 percent
20 percent or more

Railroads in 1850
Centers of industry ☐
Iron ore deposits •
Coal and lignite deposits •

THE INDUSTRIAL REVOLUTION

Why were the effects of the Industrial Revolution more rapidly apparent in Great Britain and in north central Europe? Compare Sweden and northern Spain to Great Britain. Was the availability of important mineral deposits the only condition for rapid industrial development? How did the presence of an extensive railroad system help to accelerate industrialization? What effects did the Industrial Revolution have on urban population densities?

sort of background felt themselves free to rise as high as their abilities might carry them on the social and economic ladder. Eighteenth-century Britain was not by any means free of social snobbery: lords looked down on bankers, as bankers looked down on artisans. But a lord's disdain might well be tempered by the fact of his own grandfather's origins in the counting house.

Britain's eighteenth-century prosperity was based on expanding markets both at home and abroad for whatever goods it manufactured. The British were voracious consumers. By the mid-eighteenth century, yearly fashions were setting styles not only for a court elite, but most of Britain's landed and professional society. "Nature may be satisfied with little," one London entrepreneur declared. "But it is the wants of fashion and the desire of novelties that causes trade." The country's small size and the fact that it was an island encouraged the development of a nationwide domestic market that could respond to increasing demand. The absence of a system of internal tolls and tariffs, such as existed on the Continent, meant that goods could be moved freely to wherever they could fetch the best price. This freedom of movement was assisted by a constantly improving transportation system. Parliament in the years just before the Industrial Revolution passed acts to finance turnpike building at the rate of forty roads per year; the same period saw the construction of canals and the further opening up of harbors and navigable streams. Unlike the government of France, whose mercantilist policies as often as not thwarted economic growth, the British Parliament believed that the most effective way in which it could help businessmen was to assist them in helping themselves.

If domestic markets promised steady growth, foreign markets promised greater returns—along with greater risks. Expansion was assisted by a favorable political climate: some members of Parliament were businessmen themselves; others had invested heavily in commerce, hence their eagerness to encourage by statute the construction of canals, the establishment of banks, and the enclosure of common lands. And hence their insistence, throughout the eighteenth century, that Britain's foreign policy respond to its commercial needs. At the end of every major eighteenth-century war, Britain wrested overseas territories from its enemies. At the same time, Britain was penetrating hitherto unexploited territo-

ries, such as India and South America, in search of further potential markets and resources. In 1759, over one third of all British exports went to the colonies; by 1784, if we include the newly established United States, that figure had increased to one half. Export production increased by 80 percent between 1750 and 1770, while production for domestic consumption gained just 7 percent over the same period. The British possessed a merchant marine capable of transporting goods around the world, and a navy practiced in the art of protecting its commercial fleets. By the 1780s, Britain's markets, together with its fleet and its established position at the center of world commerce, gave its entrepreneurs unrivaled opportunities for trade and profit. It was on these fortunate terms that Britain experienced the first great changes that would become an "industrial revolution."

> By the 1780s, Britain's markets, together with its fleet and its established position at the center of world commerce, gave its entrepreneurs unrivaled opportunities for trade and profit.

INNOVATION IN THE TEXTILE INDUSTRIES

The revolution was not an instant or universal process; it began with great technological leaps in a few well-placed industries. British entrepreneurs and inventors first grasped the opportunity by revolutionizing the production of cotton textile goods. Although fewer cotton goods were made in eighteenth-century Britain than woolen goods, the extent of cotton manufacture by 1760 was such as to make cotton more than an infant industry. Tariffs prohibiting the importation of East Indian cottons, imposed by Parliament to stimulate the sale of woolen goods, had instead served to spur the manufacture of domestic cottons. British industrialists drew on the raw materials of India and the American South, however, and many of the patterns woven on their new machines were derived from Indian spinners and weavers. Thus the revolution, when it did occur, took place in an already well-established industry. Yet without the invention of some sort of machinery that would improve the quality and at the same time dramatically increase the quantity of spun cotton thread, the necessary breakthrough would not have come. John Kay's 1733 invention of the flying shuttle, which greatly speeded the process of weaving, only made the bottleneck in the prior process of spinning more apparent. The problem was solved by the inven-

WHY DID THE INDUSTRIAL REVOLUTION FIRST TAKE HOLD IN BRITAIN?

THE INDUSTRIAL REVOLUTION IN BRITAIN   727

Spinning Jenny. James Hargreaves's invention, patented in 1770, enabled one spinner operating the vertical wheel to spin several threads at the same time.

tion of a series of comparatively simple mechanical devices, the most important of which was the spinning jenny, invented by James Hargreaves, a carpenter and hand-loom weaver, in 1764 (patented 1770). The spinning jenny, named after the inventor's wife, was a com-

pound spinning wheel, capable of producing sixteen threads at once. The threads it spun were not strong enough, however, to be used for the longitudinal fibers, or warp, of cotton cloth. It was not until the invention of the water frame by Richard Arkwright, a barber, in 1769, that quantity production of both warp and woof (latitudinal fibers) became possible. In 1799 Samuel Compton invented the spinning mule, which combined the features of both the jenny and the frame. The water frame and the spinning mule solved the problems that had heretofore curtailed the output of cotton textiles. They increased the mechanical advantage over the spinning wheel enormously. From six to twenty-four times the amount of yarn could be spun on a jenny as by hand; by the end of the century two to three hundred times as much could be produced on the mule. Just as important, the quality of the thread improved not only in terms of strength but also of fineness.

Once these machines came into general use, the revolution proceeded apace. Cotton suited the mule and the jenny because it was a tougher thread than wool; as such cotton was a fiber that could withstand the rough treatment it received at the mechanical hands of the crude early machines. In addition, the supply of cotton was expandable in a way that the supply of wool was

Cotton Mill in Lancashire, 1834. Women and girls prepare the cotton by carding, drawing, and roving the fibers.

THE FACTORY SYSTEM AND THE ENGLISH WORKING CLASS

Reactions to the Industrial Revolution and the factory system it produced ranged from celebration to horror. Dr. Andrew Ure, a Scottish professor of chemistry, was fascinated with these nineteenth-century applications of Enlightenment science. He believed that the new machinery and its products would create a new society of wealth, abundance, and, ultimately, stability through the useful regimentation of production.

This island [Britain] is preeminent among civilized nations for the prodigious development of its factory wealth, and has been therefore long viewed with a jealous admiration by foreign powers. This very pre-eminence, however, has been contemplated in a very different light by many influential members of our own community, and has even been denounced by them as the certain origin of innumerable evils to the people, and of revolutionary convulsions to the state. . . .

The blessings which physico-mechanical science has bestowed on society, and the means it has still in store for ameliorating the lot of mankind, has been too little dwelt upon; while, on the other hand, it has been accused of lending itself to the rich capitalists as an instrument for harassing the poor, and of exacting from the operative an accelerated rate of work. It has been said, for example, that the steam-engine now drives the power-looms with such velocity as to urge on their attendant weavers at the same rapid pace; but that the hand-weaver, not being subjected to this restless agent, can throw his shuttle and move his treddles at his convenience. There is, however, this difference in the two cases, that in the factory, every member of the loom is so adjusted, that the driving force leaves the attendant nearly nothing at all to do, certainly no muscular fatigue to sustain, while it produces for him good, unfailing wages, besides a healthy workshop *gratis:* whereas the non-factory weaver, having everything to execute by muscular exertion, finds the labour irksome, makes in consequence innumerable short pauses, separately of little account, but great when added together; earns therefore proportionally low wages, while he loses his health by poor diet and the dampness of his hovel.

Andrew Ure. *The Philosophy of Manufacturers: or, An Exposition of the Scientific, Moral and Commercial Economy of the Factory System of Great Britain, 1835,* as cited in J. T. Ward, *The Factory System,* v. 1. (New York: Barnes and Noble, 1970), pp. 140–41.

not. The cotton gin, invented by the American Eli Whitney in 1793, separated seeds from fiber mechanically, thereby making cotton available at a lower price. The invention kept America's slave plantations profitable, and meant that supply would meet increased demand.

The first machinery was cheap enough to be used by spinners at home. But as it increased in size it was more and more frequently housed not in the cottages of individual spinners, but in workshops or mills located near water that could be used to power the machines. Eventually, with the further development of steam-driven equipment, the mills could be built wherever they might suit the entrepreneur. Frequently those

ENGELS AND WORKING-CLASS TRANSFORMATION

Friedrich Engels (1820–1895) was one of the many socialists to criticize Dr. Ure as shortsighted and complacent in his outlook. Engels, himself part of a factory-owning family who was able to examine the new industrial cities at close range, provides a classic nineteenth-century analysis of industrialization. The Condition of the Working Class in England *is compellingly written, angry, and revealing about middle-class concerns of the time, including female labor.*

Histories of the modern development of the cotton industry, such as those of Ure, Baines, and others, tell on every page of technical innovations. . . . In a well-ordered society such improvements would indeed be welcome, but social war rages unchecked and the benefits derived from these improvements are ruthlessly monopolized by a few persons. . . . Every improvement in machinery leads to unemployment, and the greater the technical improvement the greater the unemployment. Every improvement in machinery affects a number of workers in the same way as a commercial crisis and leads to want, distress, and crime. . . .

Let us examine a little more closely the process whereby machine- continually supesedes hand-labour. When spinning or weaving machinery is installed pratically all that is left to be done by the hand is the piecing together of broken threads, and the machine does the rest. This task calls for nimble fingers rather than muscular strength. The labour of grown men is not merely unnecessary but actually unsuitable. . . . The greater the degree to which physical labour is displaced by the introduction of machines worked by water- or steam-power, the fewer grown men need be employed. In any case women and children will work for lower wages than men and, as has already been observed, they are more skillful at piecing than grown men. Consequently it is women and children who are employed to do this work. . . .

When women work in factories, the most important result is the dissolution of family ties. If a woman works for twelve or thirteen hours a day in a factory and her husband is employed either in the same establishment or in some other works, what is the fate of the children? They lack parental care and control. . . . It is not difficult to imagine that they are left to run wild.

Friedrich Engels, *The Condition of the Working Class in England in 1844*, trans. and eds. W. O. Henderson and W. H. Chaloner, (New York: Macmillan, 1958), pp. 150–51, 158, 160.

---

mills went up in towns and cities in the north of England, away from the old commercial and seafaring centers, but where local political interests were well disposed toward textile manufacturers and the money and growth they brought in their wake.

The new textile mills, which the British poet William Blake called "dark satanic mills," were among the most visible landmarks of the Industrial Revolution. At the time and in historical accounts they have come to represent either the benefits or the tyranny of industry and economic development. The employment of women in the mills provoked particularly

Cotton Mill. Cotton thread is woven into cloth on a spinning mule.

anguished cries from contemporaries, who worried about the "promiscuous mixing of the sexes" in crowded and humid workshops. Manufacturers did seek out women workers, who were paid less and considered less likely to make trouble; they sought to lure them from neighboring villages, paying good wages by comparison with other jobs open to women; in some cases they asked poor-law officials to find "needy and suitable families" for the mills. Women and children made up nearly half of the labor force in some textile manufacturing. Most began young, at ten or eleven years old; and once they had children they either put their children out to wet nurses, brought them to the mills, or continued to earn wages doing piecework (paid by the piece rather than by the hour) at home. Men, women, and children were assigned very different tasks, and one of the principal causes of labor protest was the introduction of women workers to do jobs considered the property of men. Anxious discussions of "mixing the sexes" did not necessarily reflect social realities. Instead they expressed more general fears about the effects of technology and industry on "nature."

> Men, women, and children were assigned very different tasks, and one of the principal causes of labor protest was the introduction of women workers to do jobs considered the property of men.

Factories, however, formed a small part of the industrial revolution, even in textiles. The costs of building and operating a large plant and the difficulties of recruiting a labor force were significant, and often offset the efficiencies of scale. Cotton yarn continued to be spun at home by families of workers at the same time it was being produced in mills. Weaving remained a home industry until the invention of a cheap, practical power loom convinced entrepreneurs that they could save money by moving the process from home to mill. Handloom weavers were probably the most obvious victims of the Industrial Revolution in Britain. Their unwillingness to surrender their livelihood to machinery meant that they continued to work for less and less—by 1830, no more than a pitiful six shillings a week. In 1815 they numbered about two hundred fifty thousand; by 1850, there remained only forty thousand; by 1860, only three thousand. By 1851, three fifths of those employed in cotton manufacture worked in medium- to large-size mills.

British cotton textiles flooded the world market from the 1780s. This light material was suitable for the

WHY DID THE INDUSTRIAL REVOLUTION FIRST TAKE HOLD IN BRITAIN?

THE INDUSTRIAL REVOLUTION IN BRITAIN   731

climates of Africa, India, and the more temperate zones of North America. Here was a material cheap enough to make it possible for millions who had never before enjoyed the comfort of washable clothing to do so. And here was material fine enough to tempt the rich to experiment with muslins and calicos in a way they had not done before. Figures speak eloquently of the revolutionary change wrought by the expanding industry. In 1760, Britain exported less than two hundred fifty thousand pounds worth of cotton goods; by 1800 it was exporting over £5 million worth. In 1760, Britain imported 2.5 million pounds of raw cotton; in 1787, 22 million pounds; in 1837, 366 million pounds. By 1800, cotton accounted for about 5 percent of the national income of the country;

The Steam Hammer, from a painting by James Nasmyth. This steam-powered machine was used to beat out ingots of white-hot metal into strips.

by 1812, from 7 to 8 percent. By 1815, the export of cotton textiles amounted to 40 percent of the value of all domestic goods exported from Great Britain. Although the price of manufactured cotton goods fell dramatically, the market expanded so rapidly that profits continued to increase.

COAL, IRON, AND CHEMICALS

By comparison with the extraordinary changes in the textile industry, those occurring in the manufacture of iron were not "revolutionary." But they were decisive. Britain's advanced transportation network was well supported by vast reserves of coal, which allowed the British, from the middle of the eighteenth century, to substitute coal for wood in the heating of molten metal. A series of discoveries made fuel savings possible, along with a higher quality of iron and the manufacture of a greater variety of iron products. Not only could Britain supply all the coal for its own industry: Britons could export the surplus fuel overseas. Demand rose sharply during the war years at the end of the eighteenth century. It remained high as a result of calls for plant machinery, agricultural implements, and hardware; it rose dramatically with the coming of railways in the 1830s and 1840s. Britain was exporting 571,000 tons of iron in 1814; in 1852, it exported 1,036,000 tons out of a world total of almost 2 million—more iron than was made by all the rest of the world combined.

The need for more coal required the mining of deeper and deeper veins. In 1711, Thomas Newcomen had devised a cumbersome but remarkably effective steam engine for pumping water from mines. Though of value to the coal industry, it was of less use in other industries since it wasted both fuel and power. In 1763, James Watt, a maker of scientific instruments at the University of Glasgow, was asked to repair a model of the Newcomen engine. While doing the repairs, he conceived the idea of improving the machine by adding a separate chamber to condense the steam, eliminating the need to cool the cylinder. He patented his first engine incorporating this device in 1769. Watt's genius as an inventor was far greater than his ability as a businessman. He admitted that he would "rather face a loaded cannon than settle a disputed account or make a bargain." As a consequence, he fell into debt in attempting to place his machines on the market. He was rescued by Matthew Boulton, a wealthy hardware manufacturer from Birmingham. The two men formed a partnership, with Boulton providing the capital. By 1800 the firm had sold 289 engines for use in factories and mines. Watt and Boulton made their fortune from the revolutionary quality of their product; the price for Watt's engines was a regular percentage of the increased profits from each mine that operated one. Steam power only slowly replaced water: in 1850 more than a third of the power used in woolen manufacture and an eighth of that used in cotton was still produced by water. The steam engine, nonetheless, was decisive for the industrial expansion of the early nineteenth century.

WOMEN AND CHILD LABORERS

REPORT OF THE COMMISSION ON THE LABOUR OF WOMEN AND CHILDREN IN MINES (1842)

By the 1840s, French and British governments had already conducted several studies of child and female labor. This is from a British report on the coal mines.

First Report. Tables of Proportion of Children and Young People employed in different Districts

TABLE NO. I.—ENGLAND

Districts	Adults		13 to 18		Under 13		Total of children and young persons to 1000 adult males	Proportion of children and young persons in the whole number employed	Proportion of children in the whole number under 18
	Males	*Fem.*	*Males*	*Fem.*	*Males*	*Fem.*			
Leicestershire	1000	—	227	—	180	—	407	Two-sevenths.	Much more than one third.
Derbyshire	1000	—	240	—	167	—	407	Two-sevenths.	Much more than one.third.
Yorkshire	1000	22	352	36	246	41	675	Upwards of one-third.	Much more than one-third.
Lancashire	1000	86	352	79	195	27	653	Upwards of one-third.	Upwards of one-third.
South Durham	1000	—	226	—	184	—	410	Two-sevenths.	Much more than one-third.
Northumberland and North Durham	1000	—	266	—	186	—	452	Nearly one-third.	Much more than one-third.

TABLE NO. IV.—WALES

Districts	Adults		13 to 18		Under 13		Total of children and young persons to 1000 adult males	Proportion of children and young persons in the whole number employed	Proportion of children in the whole number under 18
	Males	*Fem.*	*Males*	*Fem.*	*Males*	*Fem.*			
Monmouthshire	1000	—	302	—	154	—	456	Nearly one-third.	One-third.
Glamorganshire	1000	19	239	19	157	12	427	Approaching one-third.	Much more than one-third.
Pembrokeshire	1000	424	366	119	196	19	700	One-third.	More than one-third.

First Report: Conclusions

From the whole of the Evidence which has been collected, and of which we have thus endeavoured to give a digest, we find,—

In regard to COAL MINES—

1. That instances occur in which Children are taken into these mines to work as early as four years of age, sometimes at five, and between five and six, not unfrequently between six and seven, and often from seven to eight, while from eight to nine is the ordinary age at which employment in these mines commences.

2. That a very large proportion of the persons employed in carrying on the work of these mines is under thirteen years of age; and a still larger proportion between thirteen and eighteen.

4. That the great body of the Children and Young Persons employed in these mines are of the families of the adult workpeople engaged in the pits, or belong to the poorest population in the neighbourhood, and are hired and paid in some districts by the workpeople, but in others by the proprietors or contractors.

11. That, in the districts in which females are taken down into the coal mines, both sexes are employed together in precisely the same kind of labour, and work for the same number of hours; that the girls and boys, and the young men and young women, and even married women and women with child, commonly work almost naked, and the men, in many mines, quite naked; and that all classes of witnesses bear testimony to the demoralizing influence of the employment of females underground

13. That when the workpeople are in full employment, the regular hours of work for Children and Young Persons are rarely less than eleven; more often they are twelve; in some districts they are thirteen; and in one district they are generally fourteen and upwards.

20. That one of the most frequent causes of accidents in these mines is the want of superintendence by overlookers or otherwise to see to the security of the machinery for letting down and bringing up the work-people, the restriction of the number of persons that ascend and descend at a time, the state of the mine as to the quantity of noxious gas in it, the efficiency of the ventilation, the exactness with which the air-door keepers perform their duty, the places into which it is safe or unsafe to go with a naked lighted candle, and the security of the proppings to uphold the roof, &c.

G. M. Young and W. D. Handcock. *English Historical Documents, 1833–1874.* Vol. 12 (1). (London: Eyre and Spottiswoode, 1956), pp. 972–75.

Child Labor in the Mines. This engraving of a young worker pulling a coal cart up through the narrow shaft of a mine accompanied a British Parliamentary report on child labor.

Other industries experienced profound changes during the hundred years of the Industrial Revolution. Many of those changes came in response to the growth of textile manufacture. The chemical industry, for example, developed new methods of dyeing and bleaching, as well as improved methods of production in the fields of soap and glassmaking. Production of goods increased across the board as profits from the boom in manufacturing increased the demand for new and more sophisticated articles. Such trades as pottery and metalware expanded to meet demands, in the process adopting methods that in most instances reduced cost and speeded manufacture.

Old Hetton Colliery, Sunderland, England. Designed by Thomas Hair about 1840, this large mine was typical of those built to meet the increased demand for coal. Note the railways that connected the mines with the sea.

To understand the Industrial Revolution in Britain we must not lose sight of two important factors. First, dramatic as the revolution was, it spanned two or three generations, and changed different industries in different parts of the country at very different paces. Many men and women continued to work at home, much as their grandparents had. Old tools and old methods were not immediately replaced by new ones. Populations did not flee the countryside overnight for the city. Second, the revolution was accomplished from a very limited technological and theoretical base. Except in the chemical industry, change was not the result of scientific research. It was the product of empirical experimentation—in some cases, of little more than creative tinkering. Inventers such as Arkwright, Hargreaves, Watt, and their like were crucial. But Great

Britain did not have a national system of education. The skills that led to technological breakthroughs—practical knowledge of machinery—were handed down from artisan to artisan on the shop floor. From such everyday efforts came changes of enormous magnitude. The industrial change in Britain was a "revolution," and it reshaped the lives of the British and people across the globe. By responding as it did to the demands of its apparently insatiable markets, Britain made a revolution every bit as profound and long lasting as the political revolution which occurred simultaneously in France.

THE INDUSTRIAL REVOLUTION ON THE CONTINENT

Why did the Industrial Revolution develop more slowly on the Continent?

Continental Europe offers a different model of industrialization. As we have seen, manufacturing in eighteenth-century France and Germany clustered in regions whose proximity to raw materials, access to markets, and traditional attachment to particular skills had resulted in their development as industrial centers. Flanders and Normandy in France, and Saxony in Germany were

CHRONOLOGY

THE INDUSTRIAL REVOLUTION IN GREAT BRITAIN, 1733–1825

Invention of the fly shuttle	1733
Invention of the spinning jenny	1764
Invention of the water frame	1769
Invention of the steam engine	1769
Invention of the spinning mule	1779
Invention of the cotton gin	1793
First railroad built	1825

WHY DID THE INDUSTRIAL REVOLUTION DEVELOP MORE SLOWLY ON THE CONTINENT?

THE INDUSTRIAL REVOLUTION ON THE CONTINENT 735

centers for the manufacture of woolen cloth. Switzerland, southern Germany, and Normandy produced cottons. Wallonia (the area around Liège in Belgium), the Marne valley, and Silesia in Germany became centers for iron. Yet for a variety of reasons, changes along the lines seen in Britain did not occur until the 1830s. Britain's transportation system was highly developed; those of France and Germany were not. France was far larger than Britain; its rivers were not so easily navigable, its seaports were farther apart. Central Europe was so divided into tiny principalities, each with its own set of tolls and tariffs, as to make the transportation of raw materials or manufactured goods over any considerable distance impractical. France itself imposed regulations that thwarted easy shipments. In addition, the Continent was not so blessed with an abundance of raw materials as Britain. Continental Europe lacked an abundant supply of the fuel that was the new source of industrial energy. Few major coal deposits were known to exist, and the ready availability of timber discouraged exploration that might have resulted in its discovery. Capital was not so readily available on the Continent as in Britain. In France, the tenacity of small peasant landholders stood in the way of the concentration and commercialization of agriculture.

The Continent did not simply stand idle as Britain assumed its industrial lead. The pace of mechanization was increasing in the 1780s. But the French Revolution and the wars that followed disrupted growth that might otherwise have taken place. Although ironmaking increased to meet the demands of the wars, techniques remained what they had been. Commerce was badly hurt both by British destruction of French merchant shipping and by Napoleon's Continental System. Probably the revolutionary change most beneficial to industrial advance in Europe was the removal of previous restraints on the movement of capital and labor—for example, the abolition of trade guilds and the reduction of tariff barriers across the Continent. On balance, however, the revolutionary and Napoleonic wars clearly slowed industrial development on the Continent.

After 1815, a number of factors combined to produce a climate more generally conducive to industrialization on the Continent. Population continued to increase, not only throughout Europe, but in those areas now more and more dependent on the importation of manufactured goods—Latin America, for example. European increases, which doubled the populations of most countries between 1800 and 1850, meant that the Continent would now have a growing number of producers

and consumers. More people did not necessarily mean further industrialization. In Ireland, where other necessary factors were absent, more people meant less food. But in those countries with an already well-established commercial and industrial base—France and Germany, for example—increased population did encourage the adoption of the technologies and methods of production that were transforming Britain.

Transportation improved in western Europe both during and following the Napoleonic wars. The Austrian Empire added over thirty thousand miles of roads between 1830 and 1847; Belgium almost doubled its road network in the same period; France built, in addition to roads, two thousand miles of canals. In the United States, where industrialization was occurring at an increasingly rapid rate after 1830, road mileage jumped from twenty-one thousand miles in 1800 to one hundred seventy thousand in 1856. When these improvements were combined with the introduction of rail transport in the 1840s, the resulting increase in markets available to all Western countries encouraged them to introduce methods of manufacturing that would help meet new demands.

Governments played a considerably more direct role in the process of industrialization on the Continent than in Britain. Napoleon's legal code, which guaranteed freedom of contract and facilitated the establishment of joint-stock enterprises, encouraged other rulers to provide a similar framework for commercial expansion. In Prussia, lack of private capital necessitated state operation of a large proportion of that country's mines. All the European states, with the exception of Britain, underwrote the constructions of railroads. In the private sector, Continental governments gave much more attention to the need for government incentives to produce industrial change. It was in Belgium that the first joint-stock investment bank—the Société Générale—was founded, an institution designed to facilitate the accumulation of ready capital for investment in industry and commerce. Europeans were also willing for the state to establish educational systems whose aim, among others, was to produce a well-trained elite capable of assisting in the development of industrial technology. What Britain had produced almost by chance, the Europeans began to reproduce by design.

The growth of the textile industry in Europe was patterned by the circumstances of the Napoleonic wars. The British blockade interrupted the supply of cotton to the Continent, but the military's greater demand for woolen cloth meant that expansion occurred

A German Textile Factory, 1848. This is an unusually large manufacturing facility for this period on the Continent.

more rapidly in the woolen than in the cotton industry. By 1820, the spinning of wool by machine was the common practice on the Continent; weaving, however, was still accomplished largely by hand. Regional centers for the production of wool were located around Rheims and in Alsace in France; in what is now

Belgium; and in Saxony and Silesia in Germany. All possessed, at least in some measure, the various elements necessary to the successful growth and development of a regional economic system: transportation, resources, markets, technology, and labor supply. Mechanization, however, came slowly because manual labor was cheap; also, since Britain's market was so large, Continental profits too often depended on the manufacture of some particular specialty not made in Britain, and therefore without broad commercial appeal.

In the area of heavy industry on the Continent, the picture was much the same as in textiles: technological innovation advanced slowly against a background of more general resistance to change. Because change came later than in Britain, it coincided with an increased demand for various new products important in an industrial and urban society: iron pipe, much in use by mid-century in cities for gas, water, and drainage; metal machinery, now replacing earlier wooden prototypes. One exception was the textile industry in Catalonia, centered on Barcelona,

Silk Weavers of Lyons, 1850. The first significant working-class uprisings in nineteenth-century France occured in Lyons in 1831 and 1834. Note the domestic character of the working conditions.

where early technical and commercial advances were stalled by the absence of consistent new investment and political instability elsewhere in the country. Consequently, on the Continent the iron industry became more important than textiles and was accompanied by an increase, where possible, in the production of coal. Coal was scarce, however; in the Rhineland, wood was still used to manufacture iron. The result was an unwillingness on the part of entrepreneurs to make as extensive use of the steam engine as they might have otherwise; it consumed too much fuel. In France, as late as 1844, hydraulic (water-driven) engines were employed far more often for the manufacture of iron than were steam engines. One further aspect of Continental manufacturing should be noted: British competition forced Continental manufacturers of machines to scramble for whatever orders they could get. Responding to a variety of requests made it difficult for firms to specialize in a single product. Industrialization thus did not result in standardization, at least not until much later. Moreoever, Continental industry would long continue to produce to specific orders, remaining flexible when rationalization and specialization might have resulted in an increased volume of production.

The New Railway Age. "The Railway Juggernaut of 1845." A cartoon from the British humor magazine *Punch* satirizing speculation—often financially disastrous—in railway stocks.

THE COMING OF RAILWAYS

How did the railway boom accelerate industrialization?

By about 1840, then, Continental countries, and to some degree the United States, were industrializing gradually, producing far more than they had, yet nothing like as much as their spectacular pacesetter. Within the next ten years, the coming of the railways was to alter that situation. Though Britain by no means lost its lead, the stimulus generally provided to Western economies by the introduction of railway systems throughout much of the world carried the Continent and America far enough and fast enough to allow them to become genuine competitors with Britain.

Railways answered two needs. Manufacturers had to transport their goods as quickly and cheaply as possible across long distances. Despite already mentioned improvements in transportation during the years before 1830, the movement of heavy materials, particularly coal, remained a problem. It is significant that the first modern railway was built in England in 1825 from the Durham coal field of Stockton to Darlington, near the coast. Tramways, or tracks along which coal carts were pulled by horses, had long been used to haul coal short distances. The Stockton-to-Darlington railway was a logical extension of this device, designed to answer the transportation needs produced by constantly expanding industrialization. The man primarily responsible for the design of the first steam railway was George Stephenson, a self-educated engineer who had not learned to read until he was seventeen. He persuaded a group of investors from northern England of the merits of steam traction and was given full liberty to carry out his plans. The locomotives on the Stockton-Darlington line traveled at fifteen miles per hour, the fastest rate at which machines had yet moved people overland.

Railways also responded to other needs, namely the opportunity for capitalists to invest their money. Britishers such as those who had made sizable fortunes in textiles, once they had paid out workers' wages and

American Railway Scene in Pennsylvania. This 1874 advertisement by Currier and Ives suggests the benefits of the rail industry, such as more reliable mail delivery and the comfort of the Pullman Hotel, and conveys the fervid railway mania that swept Europe and America in this period.

plowed back substantial capital in their factories, retained a surplus profit for which they wanted a decent yet reliable return. Railways provided them with the solution to their problem. Though by no means as reliable as had been hoped, railway investment proved capable of more than satisfying the capitalists' demands. No sooner did the first combined passenger and goods service open in 1830, on the Liverpool-to-Manchester line, than plans were formulated and money pledged to extend rail systems throughout Europe, the Americas, and beyond. In 1830, there were no more than a few dozen miles of railway in the world. By 1840, there were over four thousand five hundred miles; by 1850, over twenty-three thousand. British engineers, industrialists, and investors were quick to realize the opportunities available in constructing railways overseas; a large part of Britain's industrial success in the later nineteenth century came through building other nations' infrastructures. The English contractor Thomas Brassey, the most famous, but by no means the only one of his kind, built railways in Italy, Canada, Argentina, India, and Australia.

The railway boom accelerated industrialization gen-

erally. Not only did it increase enormously the demand for coal and for a variety of heavy manufactured goods—rails, locomotives, carriages, signals, switches—but by enabling goods to move faster from factory to salesroom, railways decreased the time it took to sell those goods. Quicker sales meant, in turn, a quicker return on capital investment, money that could then be reinvested in the manufacture of more goods. Finally, by opening up the world market as it had never been before, the railway boom stimulated the production of such a quantity of material goods as to ensure the rapid completion of the West's industrialization.

The building of a railway line was a vast undertaking, much more so than building a factory. Railway construction required capital investment beyond the capacity of any single individual. In Britain, a factory might be worth anywhere from twenty thousand to two hundred thousand pounds. The average cost of twenty-seven of the more important railway lines constructed between 1830 and 1853 was 2 million pounds. The average labor force of a factory ranged from fifty to three hundred. The average labor force of a railway, after construction, was two thousand five hundred. Because a

WHAT FUELED THE INCREASE IN PRODUCTION THROUGHOUT EUROPE BETWEEN 1850 AND 1870?

INDUSTRIALIZATION AFTER 1850   739

railway crossed the property of a large number of individual landowners, each of whom would naturally demand as much remuneration as he thought he could get, the planning of an efficient and economical route was a tricky, time-consuming business. The entrepreneur and contractor had to concern themselves not only with the purchase of right-of-way. They also contended with problems raised by the destruction of sizable portions of already existing urban areas, to make room for stations and switching yards. And they had to select a route that would be as free as possible of the hills and valleys that would necessitate the construction of expensive tunnels, cuts, and embankments. Railway builders ran tremendous risks. Portions of most lines were subcontracted at fixed bids to contractors of limited experience. A spate of bad weather might delay construction to the point where builders would be lucky to bring in the finished job within 25 percent of their original bid. Of the thirty major contractors on the London-to-Birmingham line, ten failed completely.

Throughout the world, a veritable army of construction workers built the railways. In Britain, they were called "navvies," derived from "navigator," a term first used for the construction workers on Britain's eighteenth-century canals. The work that they accomplished was prodigious. Because there is little friction between a train's wheels and its tracks, it can transport heavy loads easily. But lack of friction ceases to be an advantage when a train has to climb or descend a grade, thereby running the risk of slippage. Thus railroads required comparatively level roadbeds; and the work of constructing those tunnels, cuts, and embankments that would keep the roadbeds level was enormous. Navvies worked in gangs whose migrations throughout the countryside traced the course of railway development. They were a rough lot, living with a few women in temporary encampments. Often immigrant workers, they faced local hostility. A sign posted by local residents outside a mine in Scotland in 1845 warned the Irish navvies to get "off the ground and out of the country" in a week, or else be driven out "by the strength of our armes and a good pick shaft." Later in the century railway building projects in Africa and the Americas were lined with camps of immigrant Indian and Chinese laborers, who also became targets of nativist anger.

The magnitude of the navvies' accomplishment was

> In Britain and in much of the rest of the world, mid-nineteenth-century railways were constructed almost entirely without the aid of machinery.

extraordinary. In Britain and in much of the rest of the world, mid-nineteenth-century railways were constructed almost entirely without the aid of machinery. An assistant engineer on the London-to-Birmingham line, in calculating the magnitude of that particular construction, determined that the labor involved was the equivalent of lifting 25 billion cubic feet of earth and stone one foot high. This he compared with the feat of building the Great Pyramid, a task he estimated had involved the hoisting of some 16 billion tons. But whereas the building of the pyramid had required over two hundred thousand men and had taken twenty years, the construction of the London-to-Birmingham railway was accomplished by twenty thousand men in less than five years. Translated into individual terms, a navvy was expected to move an average of twenty tons of earth per day. Railways were laid upon an almost infinite base of human muscle and sweat.

INDUSTRIALIZATION AFTER 1850

What fueled the increase in production throughout Europe between 1850 and 1870?

Until 1850 Britain remained the industrial power of the West. Individual British factories were small by the standards set later in the century, let alone those of modern times. Still, their output was tremendous and their ability to sell to home and foreign markets was unrivaled. Between 1850 and 1870, however, France, Germany, Belgium, and the United States emerged as challengers to the power and place of British manufacturers. The British iron industry grew more slowly than did its counterparts in France or Germany. (The rate of growth was 5.2 percent for Britain, as against 6.7 percent for France and 10.2 percent for Germany.) It remained the largest in the world; in 1870 Britain produced half the world's pig iron; 3.5 times more than the United States, 4 times more than Germany, and more than 5 times more than France. In the cotton industry, too, other countries' production rose quickly. The number of cotton spindles increased from 5.5 to 11.5 million in the United

States between 1852 and 1861, and by significant but not as spectacular percentages in European countries. Again, numbers capture the developments: in 1861, Britain had 31 million spindles at work; France 5.5 million, Germany 2 million, Switzerland 1.3 million, and Austria 1.8 million.

Most of the gains experienced in Europe came as a result of continuing changes in those areas we recognize as important for sustained industrial growth: transport, commerce, and government policy. The improved transportation systems that resulted from the spread of railways helped encourage an increase in the free movement of goods. International monetary unions were established, and restrictions removed on international waterways such as the Danube. The Prussian Zollverein, or tariff union, an organization designed to facilitate internal free trade, was established in 1818 and was extended over the next twenty years to include most of the German principalities outside Austria. Free trade went hand in hand with further removal of barriers to entering trades and to practicing business unhampered by restrictive regulation. The control that guilds and corporations had over artisan production was abolished in Austria in 1859 and in most of Germany by the mid-1860s. Laws against usury, most of which had ceased to be enforced, were officially abandoned in Britain, Holland, Belgium, and in many parts of Germany. Governmental regulation of mining was surrendered by the Prussian state in the 1850s, freeing entrepreneurs to develop resources as they saw fit. The formation of investment banks proceeded apace, encouraged by an important increase in the money supply, and therefore an easing of credit, following the opening of the California gold fields in 1849.

A further reason for increased European production was the growing trade in raw materials. Wool and hides imported from Australia helped diminish the consequences of the cotton shortage suffered after the outbreak of the Civil War in the United States and the Union blockade of the American South. Other imports—guano from the Pacific, vegetable oils from Africa, pyrites (sulfides) from Spain—stimulated the scale of food production and both altered and increased the manufacture of soap, candles, and finished textiles. Food production itself began to be a matter of imports as Britain drew more and more of its grain from the Americas and Australia. Later, refrigerated shipping brought fresh meat to European tables from the prairies of the United States and Argentina, while stimulating transportation and industry in those coun-

tries as well. Finally, discoveries of new sources of coal, particularly in the Pas-de-Calais region of France and in the Ruhr valley in Germany, had dramatic repercussions. Production of coal in France rose from 4.4 million to 13.3 million tons between 1850 and 1869; during the same years, German production increased from 4.2 million to 23.7 million tons.

Industrialization in eastern and southern Europe after mid-century proceeded unevenly. This was in part a result of the fact that many eastern regions played an increasingly specialized role in the economy of the Continent, providing food and agricultural materials to the West. The ever-growing demand for agricultural products from the east resulted in the development of agriculture as a major capitalist industry there. As they rationalized their operations for increased efficiency and hence profitability, entrepreneurs recognized the degree to which they were hampered by the outmoded economic practices of serfdom, a system that prevented the mobility of labor and thus the formation of an effective agricultural work force. Serfdom was abolished in most parts of eastern and southern Europe by 1850, and in Poland and Russia in the 1860s.

Although industry continued to take a back seat to agriculture, eastern Europe had several important manufacturing regions. By the 1880s, the number of men and women employed in the cotton industry in the Austrian province of Bohemia exceeded that in the German state of Saxony. In the Czech region, textile industries, developed in the eighteenth century, continued to thrive. By the 1830s, there were machine-powered Czech cotton mills and iron works. In Russia, a factory industry producing coarse textiles—mostly linens—had grown up around Moscow. At mid-century, Russia was purchasing 24 percent of the total British machinery exports to mechanize its own mills. Many workers in Russian industry remained serfs until the 1860s—about 40 percent of them employed in mines. Of the over eight hundred thousand Russians engaged in manufacturing by 1860, however, most labored not in factories but in very small workshops, where average employment numbered about 40 persons.

By 1870 Europe was by no means a fully industrialized continent. Fifty percent of France's labor force remained on farms. Agricultural laborers were the single largest occupational category in Britain during the 1860s. Great stretches of the Continent—Spain, southern Italy, eastern Europe—were almost untouched by the Industrial Revolution. We also need to underscore what *industrial* meant. Machine production initially remained confined to a few sectors of the economy. Even where it was used, technology did not in any simple way replace human toil. As machines were introduced in some sectors to do specific tasks, they usually intensified the tempo of hand work in other sectors, such as preparation or finishing. Even in the industrialized regions, much work was still accomplished in tiny workshops or at home.

INDUSTRY AND EMPIRE

How did the Industrial Revolution affect the world economy?

From an international perspective, nineteenth-century Europe was the most industrial region of the world. Moreover, Europeans, particularly Britain, jealously guarded their international advantages. They preferred to do so through financial leverage. Britain, France, and other European nations gained control of the national debts of China, the Ottoman empire, Egypt, Brazil, Argentina, and other non-European powers. They also supplied large loans to other states, which bound those nations to their European investors. If the debtor nations expressed discontent, as Egypt did in the 1830s when it attempted to establish its own cotton textile industry, they confronted financial pressure and shows of force. Coercion, however, was not always necessary or even one sided. Social change in other empires—China, Persia, and the Mughals of India, for example—created new vulnerabilities or new opportunities. Ambitious local elites often reached agreements with Western governments or trading combines such as the British East India Company. These trade agreements transformed regional economies on terms that sent the greatest profits to Europe after a substantial gratuity to the Europeans' local partners. Where agreements could not be made, force prevailed, and Europe took territory and trade by conquest.

In important respects, then, the world economy remained divided between the producers of manufactured goods—Europe itself—and suppliers of the necessary raw materials and buyers of finished goods—everyone else. Cotton growers in the southern United States, sugar growers in the Caribbean, and wheat growers in Ukraine accepted their arrangements with the industrialized West and typically profited by them. If there were disputes, however, those suppliers often found that Europe could look elsewhere for the same goods, or dictate the terms of trade down the business end of a bank ledger or a cannon barrel.

CONCLUSION

In 1851, the British government staged a great exhibition to display the benefits of industry. The exhibition followed in an Enlightenment tradition of celebrating the application of knowledge and science to the human

British Clipper Ships in Calcutta Harbor, 1860. Calcutta, a long-established city on the eastern coast of India, was one of the hubs of the British empire—a center for trade in cotton, jute, opium, and tea. The dazzling new clipper ships, first built in the 1830s and 1840s, were very fast and were central to the global economy of the nineteenth century.

The Interior of the Crystal Palace. Designed by Sir Joseph Paxton, this building of iron and glass was constructed to house the Exhibition of the Works of Industry of All Nations, held in London in 1851. The exhibition celebrated the triumph of industry, technology, and progress.

enterprise. The grandness of the Crystal Palace Exhibition, with its stained-glass galleries and long rows of machines, marked a turning point. By mid-century, industry had decisively changed the European economy. Those changes did not follow any single model. Early attention focused on Britain, and to a lesser extent on France, but changes later in the century would upset many expectations about the way industry could develop. In other countries observers asked how they might harvest the benefits of industry without reaping the inequalities and troubles that accompanied it. Britain was the first to raise these questions, and was thus a model for other industrializing nations.

Factories, steam engines, railroads, children working in mines, and women in textile mills: these were the most visible emblems of the industrial revolution. Equally important changes, however, were much less visible. New ways of organizing labor mattered as much as new technologies. Small changes in older workshops paved the way for prodigious improvements in productivity. The industrial revolution rested, in large measure, on human industriousness. In subtle as well as spectacular ways, nineteenth-century indus-

trial development reshaped Europe—and Europe's relations with the rest of the world.

SELECTED READINGS

Berg, Maxine. *The Age of Manufactures: Industry, Innovation, and Work in Britain, 1700–1820.* Oxford, 1985.

Cameron, R. E. *France and the Industrial Development of Europe.* Princeton, 1968. Valuable material on the Industrial Revolution outside Britain.

Cipolla, Carlo M., ed. *The Industrial Revolution, 1700–1914.* New York, 1976. A collection of essays that emphasizes the wide range of industrializing experiences in Europe.

Deane, Phyllis. *The First Industrial Revolution,* 2d ed. Cambridge, 1979.

Goodman, Jordan, and Katrina Honeyman. *Gainful Pursuits: The Making of Industrial Europe, 1600–1914.* London, 1988. Stresses continuity.

Hobsbawm, Eric. *Industry and Empire: The Making of Modern English Society, 1750 to the Present Day.* New York, 1968.

Kemp, Tom. *Industrialization in Nineteenth-Century Europe.* London, 1985.

Landes, David S. *The Unbound Prometheus: Technological Change and Industrial Development in Western Europe from 1750 to the Present.* London, 1969. An excellent treatment of the technological innovations and economic results of the Industrial Revolution.

Mathias, Peter. *The First Industrial Nation: An Economic History of Britain, 1700–1914,* 2d ed. London, 1988.

Mokyr, Joel. *The Lever of Riches: Technological Creativity and Economic Progress.* New York, 1992.

Price, Roger. *An Economic History of Modern France, 1730–1914.* New York, 1981. Stresses the importance of transportation and communications networks.

Sabel, Charles, and Jonathan Zeitlin. "Historical Alternatives to Mass Production" *Past and Present* 108 (August 1985): 133–176.

Schofer, Lawrence. *The Formation of a Modern Labor Force, Upper Silesia, 1865–1914.* Berkeley, 1975. Analyzes industrialization and its social consequences in Silesia.

Tilly, Louise, and Joan Scott. *Women, Work and the Family.* New York, 1978. Now the classic study.

Trebilcock, Clive. *The Industrialization of the Continental Powers, 1780–1914.* New York, 1981. Emphasizes the relationship between politics and industrialization.

Valenze, Deborah. *The First Industrial Woman.* New York, 1995. Excellent and readable on industrialization and economic change in general.

CHAPTER TWENTY-TWO

CONSEQUENCES OF INDUSTRIALIZATION: URBANIZATION AND CLASS CONSCIOUSNESS, 1800–1850

THE INDUSTRIAL REVOLUTION was more than an important event in the economic history of the West and the world. It brought in its wake far-reaching social changes, transforming the landscape of Europe and the everyday lives of men and women. Factories and railroads were among the most visible symbols of change. So were rapidly growing cities. Industrialization brought the migration of millions from the countryside. The overcrowded poor neighborhoods of cities with their accompanying problems—unsanitary living conditions, hunger, unemployment, prostitution—riveted the attention and galvanized the fears of those watching changes taking place. Political leaders, social scientists, public health officials, novelists such as Charles Dickens and Honoré de Balzac, and artists such as Honoré Daumier focused their attention on what they all saw as the new drama of modern urban life. That drama included feats of engineering such as railroads, but also the creation of new forms of wealth alongside new kinds of poverty, and an acute awareness of the disparity between social groups. Before the age of revolution, that disparity would have been described in terms of birth, rank, or privilege. In the nineteenth century, it was increasingly seen in terms of class. Not only did the Industrial Revolution change the economic and social structures of the West, combined with the French Revolution it helped to create a new language of politics.

We shall examine this range of social and cultural changes as they occurred during the first fifty years or so of the nineteenth century. We begin with the peasantry, or the bulk of the population that remained on the land, and with the less visible but important ways in which industrialization transformed the countryside. We include shifts in the private landscape of both middle- and working-class life: the family, the home, people's patterns of everyday life, and their identities. Since the Industrial Revolution came first to Britain, our focus will be on that country. Industrialization and urbanization brought very similar changes, though at different rates, to other European countries.

FOCUS QUESTIONS

• What caused widespread rural poverty in the first half of the nineteenth century?

• Did the Industrial Revolution improve the standard of living?

• What was the role of middle-class women in everyday life?

• How did the Industrial Revolution change working-class women's lives?

• How did the middle class define its interest within a new social order?

• Why did artists and writers criticize the new middle-class world view?

THE COUNTRYSIDE

What caused widespread rural poverty in the first half of the nineteenth century?

Despite the dramatic growth of industry and cities, in 1850 the population of Europe was still overwhelmingly peasant. By 1830, a sizable minority of the British population lived in towns and cities, but elsewhere society remained predominantly rural. In France and Italy, 60 percent of the population lived in the country; in Prussia, over 70 percent; in Spain, over 90 percent; in Russia, over 95 percent. Demographic pressures, which helped produce chaos in the cities, likewise caused severe hardship in the countryside. The populations of the predominantly agricultural nations leaped forward with those that were industrializing. The population of Europe as a whole, estimated roughly at 205 million by 1800, had risen to 274 million by 1850, and to 320 million by 1870. In Britain, with its comparatively high standard of living, the numbers increased from 16 million to 27 million. In rural Ireland, despite devastating famines, the population also increased from 5.5 to 8 million, and the Russian population rose from 39 to 60 million in the same period.

How do historians explain the population explosion? Some speculate that the cyclical potency of microbes made certain fatal diseases less virulent. Certainly the curbing of cholera, through the adoption of sanitary reforms, and smallpox, as Edward Jenner's technique of vaccination gained gradual acceptance after 1796, help to explain longer lives. Governments were better able and more determined to monitor and improve the lives of their people. Less expensive foods of high nutritional value—most notably the potato—and the ability to transport foodstuffs cheaply by railroad meant that most European populations were better nourished and, thus, less susceptible to debilitating illness. Men and women married earlier, which raised fertility and family size. As serfdom declined, peasants tended to set up households at a younger age. The spread of cottage industries, so important to early industrialization, also allowed more rural couples to marry and set up households—even before they inherited any land. Not only did the age of marriage fall, but more people married. A relatively small expansion in the population of a region in one generation would result in a far greater one in the next. As the population grew, the number of young and fertile people grew faster, thereby significantly increasing the ratio of births to total population.

Despite, and even because of improved life expectancy, life for the country dwellers of Europe remained bleak at best. Population growth outstripped resources and land. Farmers—or peasants, as farmers were called in Europe—still sowed and harvested by hand. Millions of tiny farms produced, at most, a bare subsistence living, and families wove, spun, made knives, and sold butter to make ends meet. Conditions in rural areas deteriorated sharply whenever there was a bad harvest. The average daily diet for an entire family in a "good" year might amount to no more than two or three pounds of bread—a total of about 3,000 calories daily. Hunger, often near-starvation, as well as epidemic disease were still common occurrences. By many measures, living conditions for rural inhabitants of many areas in Europe grew worse in the first half of the nineteenth century. Governments in some countries attempted to solve the related problems of population pressure and impoverishment by passing laws raising the age of marriage. In some of the states of southern and western Germany, as well as in Austria, men were forbidden to marry before the age of thirty, and were also required to prove their ability to support a family. Governments did their best to encourage emigration to ease the overcrowding, the majority of emigrants relocating in the Americas. Emigration from Britain rose from 57,000 in 1830, to 90,000 in 1840, to 280,000 in 1850.

The most tragic combination of famine, poverty, and population in the nineteenth century came to Ireland, in the Great Famine of 1845–1849. Potatoes, brought to Europe from the New World, had transformed the diets of European peasants, providing much more nutrition for less money than corn and grain. They also grew more densely, an enormous advantage for peasants scraping a living from small plots of land. Nowhere did they become more important than in Ireland, where the climate and soil made growing grain difficult, and both overpopulation and poverty were rising. An 1840 report from the Irish poor law commissioner in Limerick described a male laborer's daily meals as follows: "Breakfast: 4½ lbs potatoes, 1 pint skimmed milk. Dinner: The same, and in winter herrings and water instead of milk. Supper: This meal is occasionally omitted in the city of Limerick, particularly during the short days." This diet was relatively nutritious by the standards of the day, but potatoes had risks: they spoiled easily and were difficult to store. When a fungus hit the crop, first in 1845 and

WHAT CAUSED WIDESPREAD RURAL POVERTY IN THE FIRST HALF OF THE NINETEENTH CENTURY?

THE COUNTRYSIDE   747

Potato Fields. A scene from the Irish countryside in the late eighteenth century showing potatoes densely planted on a hillside.

again, fatally, in 1846 and 1847, no alternate foods were at hand. At least one million Irish died of starvation, of dysentery from spoiled foods, or of fever, which spread through villages and the overcrowded poorhouses. Irish nationalists would later charge the British governments with deliberate callousness: "The Almighty sent the potato blight, but the British created

the Famine." By all accounts, the British decision to shift all poor relief to the overburdened Irish poor-law system—a decision taken in 1847, on the mistaken assumption that the famine had run its course—made conditions worse. Before the famine, tens of thousands of Irish were already crossing the Atlantic to North America; they accounted for one third of all voluntary migration to the New World. In the ten years after 1845, 1.5 million left for good. The potato blight also struck in Germany, Scotland, and the Netherlands, but with less catastrophic results. The Irish hunger was small relative to earlier episodes; Europe had witnessed deadly famines for centuries. But this one came late, when regular subsistence crises seemed to have subsided, and it testified to the specific vulnerabilities of the nineteenth-century countryside.

The effects of population growth and rural poverty were compounded by the commercialization of agriculture. The speed with which agricultural change occurred in various parts of Europe depended on the nature of particular governments. Those more sympathetic to new capitalist impulses passed legislation making it simpler to transfer and reorganize land. They encouraged the elimination of small farms and an increase in larger, more efficient units of production. In Britain, over half the total area of the country, excluding waste land, was composed of estates of a thousand acres or more. In Spain, the fortunes of large-scale commercial agriculture fluctuated with the political tenor of successive regimes: with the coming of a liberal party to power in 1820 came a law encouraging the free transfer of land; with the restoration of absolutism in 1823 came a repeal of the law. Russia was one of the countries least affected by agricultural change in the first half of the nineteenth century. There land was worked in vast blocks; some of the largest land owners possessed over half a million acres. Until the emancipation of the serfs in the 1860s, land owners claimed the labor of dependent peasant populations for as much as several days per week. But the system of serfdom gave neither land owners nor serfs incentive to improve farming or land-management techniques.

The Gardeners' Chronicle.

SATURDAY, SEPTEMBER 13, 1845.

MEETINGS FOR THE TWO FOLLOWING WEEKS.
WEDNESDAY, Sept. 17—South London Floricultural   .   1 P.M.

COUNTRY SHOWS.
WEDNESDAY, Sept. 17—Hexham Floral and Horticultural.
FRIDAY,   Sept. 19—Devon and Exeter Botanical and Hort.
THURSDAY,   Sept. 25—Surrey Horticultural and Floral.

WE stop the Press, with very great regret, to announce that the POTATO MURRAIN has unequivocally declared itself in Ireland.   The crops about Dublin are suddenly perishing.   The conversion of Potatoes into flour, by the processes described by Mr. BABINGTON and others in to-day's Paper, becomes then a process of the first national importance ; for where will Ireland be, in the event of a universal Potato rot ?

First Potato Blight. An early glimpse of impending catastrophe: a London paper announces the first potato blight in 1845.

THE IRISH FAMINE: INTERPRETATIONS AND RESPONSES

When the potato blight appeared for the second year in a row in 1846, famine came to Ireland. The first letter excerpted below is from Father Theopold Mathew, a local priest, to Charles Edward Trevelyan, the English official in charge of Irish relief. While Father Mathew attributes the potato blight to "divine providence," he also worries that businessmen opposed to government intervention in a free market will let the Irish starve.

The second and third excerpts are from letters that Trevelyan wrote to other British officials concerned with the crisis. Trevelyan makes clear that while he does not want the government to bear responsibility for starving its people, he believes that the famine will work to correct "social evils" in Ireland, by which he means everything from families having too many children to farmers failing to plant the right crops. In the nineteenth century, reactions to food crises were reshaped by the rise of new economic doctrines, changing social assumptions, and the shifting relationship between religion and government. These letters provide a good example of those changes and how they affected government officials.

LETTER OF REV. THEOBALD MATHEW TO TREVELYAN

Cork, 7 August 1846.
. . . Divine providence, in its inscrutable ways, has again poured out upon us the viol [*sic*] of its wrath. A blot more destructive than the simoon of the desert has passed over the land, and the hopes of the poor potato-cultivators are totally blighted, and the food of a whole nation has perished. On the 27th of last month I passed from Cork to Dublin, and this doomed plant bloomed in all the luxuriance of an abundant harvest. Returning on the 3rd instant, I beheld, with sorrow, one wide waste of putrefying vegetation. In many places the wretched people were seated on the fences of their decaying gardens, wringing their hands and wailing bitterly the destruction that had left them foodless.

It is not to harrow your benevolent feelings, dear Mr. Trevelyan, I tell this tale of woe. No, but to excite your sympathy in behalf of our miserable peasantry. It is rumoured that the capitalists in the corn and flour trade are endeavoring to induce government not to protect the people from famine, but to leave them at their mercy. I consider this a cruel and unjustifiable interference.

LETTER OF TREVELYAN TO ROUTH

Treasury, 3 February 1846.
. . . That indirect permanent advantages will accrue to Ireland from the scarcity and the measures taken for its relief, I entertain no doubt; but if we were to pursue these incidental objects to the neglect of any of the precautions immediately required to save the people from actual starvation, our responsibility would be fearful indeed. Besides, the greatest improvement of all which could take place in Ireland would be to teach the people to depend upon themselves for developing the resources of their country, instead of having recourse to the assistance of the government on every occasion. Much has been done of late years to put this important matter on its proper footing; but if a firm stand is not made against the prevailing disposition to take advantage of this crisis to break down all barriers, the true permanent interest of the country will, I am convinced, suffer in a manner which will be irreparable in our time.

LETTER OF TREVELYAN TO LORD MONTEAGLE

To the Right Hon. Lord Monteagle.

My Dear Lord,

. . . I need not remind your lordship that the ability even of the most powerful government is extremely limited in dealing with a social evil of this description. It forms no part of the functions of government to provide supplies of food or to increase the productive powers of the land. In the great institution of the business of society, it falls to the share of government to protect the merchant and the agriculturist in the free exercise of their respective employments; but not itself to carry on those employments; and the condition of a community depends upon the result of the efforts which each member of it makes in his private and individual capacity . . .

I must give expression to my feelings by saying that I think I see a bright light shining in the distance through the dark cloud which at present hangs over Ireland. A remedy has been already applied to that portion of the maladies of Ireland which was traceable to political causes, and the morbid habits which still to a certain extent survive are gradually giving way to a more healthy action. The deep and inveterate root of social evil remains, and I hope I am not guilty of irreverence in thinking that, this being altogether beyond the power of man, the cure has been applied by the direct stroke of an all-wise providence in a manner as unexpected and unthought of as it is likely to be effectual. God grant that we may rightly perform our part and not turn into a curse what was intended for a blessing. The ministers of religion and especially the pastors of the Roman Catholic Church, who possess the largest share of influence over the people of Ireland, have well performed their part; and although few indications appear from any proceedings which have yet come before the public that the landed proprietors have even taken the first step of preparing for the conversion of the land now laid down to potatoes to grain cultivation. I do not despair of seeing this class in society still taking the lead which their position requires of them, and preventing the social revolution from being so extensive as it otherwise must become.

Believe me, my dear lord, yours very sincerely,

C. E. Trevelyan. Treasury, 9 October 1846.

Noel Kissane. *The Irish Famine: A Documentary History.* (Dublin: National Library of Ireland, 1995), pp. 17, 47, 50–51.

European serfdom, which bound hundreds of thousands of men, women, and children to particular estates for generations, prohibited the use of land as a negotiable commodity and therefore prevented the development of agricultural entrepreneurship. In France, despite the fact that manorialism had been abolished by the Revolution, there was no rapid movement toward large-scale capitalist farming. Peasant proprietors, direct beneficiaries of the French Revolution's sale of lands, continued to work the small farms they owned. Although French peasants were poor, they were able to sustain themselves on the land. This had important consequences. France suffered less agricultural distress, even in the 1840s, than did other European countries; migration from country to city was slower than in the other nations. Fewer peasants left France for other countries than did their counterparts in England and Germany.

Rural populations were not always isolated from urban centers, however, and the Industrial Revolution directly affected their lives. Improved communication networks not only afforded rural populations a keener sense of events and opportunities elsewhere, but also made it possible for governments to intrude into the lives of these men and women to a degree previously impossible. Central bureaucracies now found it easier to collect taxes from the peasantry and to conscript its sons into their armies. Some rural cottage industries came into direct competition from factory-produced goods, which meant less work or lower piece rates and falling incomes for families, especially during winter months. In other sectors of the economy, industry spread out into the countryside, making whole regions producers of shoes, shirts, ribbons, cutlery, and so on in small shops and workers' homes. Changes in the market could bring entire regions to the verge of starvation. In the German district of Silesia, for in-

> Rural populations were not always isolated from urban centers, and the Industrial Revolution directly affected their lives.

stance, villages of linen weavers found themselves quite suddenly thrown out of work when cotton replaced linen as the fabric of choice in the Russian and Spanish markets to which they exported. Wage rates plummeted in the villages of Silesia, unemployment rose, and in June of 1844 a crowd of several thousand attacked manufacturers' houses, demanding work and bread. The rebellion lasted for several days before being repressed. Its leaders were sentenced to prison and public whippings—news of which quickly traveled throughout the Continent.

Violent rural rebellions were common in the early nineteenth century. In southern England in the late 1820s, small farmers and day laborers joined forces to burn barns and haystacks protesting the introduction of threshing machines, a symbol of the new agricultural capitalism. They masked and otherwise disguised themselves, riding out at night under the banner of their mythical leader, "Captain Swing." Their raids were preceded by anonymous threats such as the one received by a large-scale farmer in the county of Kent: "Pull down your threshing machine or else [expect] fire without delay. We are five thousand men [a highly inflated figure] and will not be stopped." In the southwest of France, peasants, at night and in disguise, attacked local authorities who had barred them from collecting wood in the forests. Since forest wood was in demand for new furnaces, the peasants traditional gleaning rights had come to an end. Similar rural disturbances broke out across Europe in the 1830s and 1840s: insurrections against landlords, against "tithes," or taxes to the church, against laws curtailing customary rights, against unresponsive governments. In Russia, serf uprisings were a reaction to continued bad harvests and exploitation. Although many onlookers considered the nineteenth-century cities dangerous seedbeds of sedition, conditions in the countryside and frequent flare-ups of rural protest remained the greatest source of trouble for governments. It was not simply that peasants were land poor and hungry; governments' inability to contend with rural protest made them look autocratic, indifferent, or inept.

Agricultural Disturbances. Violence erupted in southern England in 1830 in protest against the introduction of threshing machines.

THE URBAN LANDSCAPE

Did the Industrial Revolution improve the standard of living?

The countryside continued to hold the bulk of Europe's population in the years between 1800 and 1850. But the growth of cities remains one of the most important facts in nineteenth-century social history. Cities grew in size and number once the steam engine made it practical to bring together large concentrations of men, women, and children to work in factories. Steam engines freed entrepreneurs from their dependence on water power and allowed them to consolidate production in large cities. In cities, transportation was more accessible than in the countryside. Hence it was less costly to import raw materials and ship out finished goods. Workers were more readily available in cities as well, attracted as they were in large numbers in the hope—often false—of finding steady work at higher wages than for agricultural labor. Industrialization was not the only reason for the growth of cities in the early nineteenth century, however. General population increases combined with industrialization, forcing cities to expand at what most considered an alarming rate.

In the ten years between 1831 and 1841 London's population, already one million, grew by 130,000, Manchester's by 70,000. Paris increased by 120,000 between 1841 and 1846. Vienna grew by 125,000 from 1827 to 1847, into a city of 400,000. Berlin had as large a population by 1848, having increased by 180,000 since 1815. The primary result in these and other fast-growing centers was dreadful overcrowding. Construction lagged far behind population growth. In Vienna, though population rose 42 percent during the twenty years before 1847, the increase in housing was only 11.5 percent. In many of the larger cities, old and new, working men and women lived in lodging houses, apart from families left behind in the country. The poorest workers in almost all European cities dwelt in wretched basement rooms, often without any light or drainage.

The rapidly growing cities were overcrowded and unhealthy, their largely medieval infrastructures unable to contend with the demands of an industrial world. The middle classes moved as far as possible from disease and factory smoke, leaving the poorest members of the community isolated and a prey to the sickness that ravaged working-class sections. Cholera, typhus, and tuberculosis were natural predators in areas without adequate sewerage facilities and fresh water, and over which smoke from factories, railroads, and domestic chimneys hung heavily. A local committee appointed to investigate conditions in the British manufacturing town of Huddersfield—not by any means the worst of that country's urban centers—reported that there were large areas without paving, sewers, or drains, "where garbage and filth of every description are left on the surface to ferment and rot; where pools of stagnant water are almost constant; where dwellings adjoining are thus necessarily caused to be of an inferior and even filthy description; thus where disease is engendered, and the health of the whole town perilled." Measures were gradually adopted by successive governments in an attempt to cure the worst of these ills, if only to prevent the spread of catastrophic epidemics. Legislation was designed to rid cities of their worst slums by tearing them down, and to improve sanitary conditions by supplying both water and drainage. Yet by 1850, these projects had only just begun. Paris, perhaps better supplied with water than any other European city, had enough for no more than two baths per person per year; in London, human waste remained uncollected in two hundred fifty thousand domestic cesspools; in Manchester, fewer than a third of the dwellings were equipped with toilets of any sort.

Women and Boys Fetching Water from Standpipe in Fryingpan Alley, London. Not until the beginning of the twentieth century did major European cities begin to provide poorer residents with an adequate water supply.

> The rapidly growing cities were overcrowded and unhealthy, their largely medieval infrastructures unable to contend with the demands of an industrial world.

Did the Industrial Revolution improve living conditions during the first half of the nineteenth century? One school of historians, the "optimists," argues that workers shared in the more general increase in living standards that occurred throughout Europe from 1800 onward. A variation on this optimistic theme maintains that whatever the hardships workers were compelled to suffer during the period of intense industrialization after 1800, they were the necessary and worthwhile price society had to pay before it could "take off" into a period of "sustained economic growth." Sacrifices, in terms of standard of living, were required to permit accumulation of a capital base sufficient to guarantee economic expansion and an eventual level of general prosperity higher than any civilization had hitherto achieved. Other historians insist that such an analysis encourages us to ignore the

NINETEENTH-CENTURY VIEWS, AND FEARS, OF THE CITIES

The 1830s and 1840s brought an outpouring of literature on the causes and dangers of urban poverty. Economic thinkers, philanthropists, urban engineers, social reformers, and politicians all watched, with increasing alarm, as nineteenth-century cities grew larger and more crowded. The passages below come from the writings of two French social scientists. These and similar writings, in turn, inspired novelists such as Honoré de Balzac, Charles Dickens, and Victor Hugo, whose subjects were crime, poverty, and the working people of nineteenth-century cities.

THE SOCIAL EVIL

The largest number of truly indigent belong to the class of the aged, the infirm, the sick and children, all of them in the circumstances of age or health least productive of crimes and felonies. The largest number of crimes are committed precisely at the age at which indigence is least common and easiest to avoid, that is to say, between the ages of twenty-five and thirty.

It is not within the walls of the cities that the most abundant, the most hideous poverty is displayed? Is it not the corrupting poison of the cities which extinguishes the bodily and mental strength of so many unfortunates by its insidious operation? Is it not there that harlotry and gambling insolently reign? . . . Look at London, they tell us, with its 118,000 thieves and fences, its 75,000 whores, its 16,000 beggars, its 20,000 persons without visible means of support.

PARIS IN THE WINTER OF 1845

A terrible scourge here, for there are an immense number of people, thousands of families, with no means of coping with it. Huddled up there in garrets under the leaking tiles, packed together, pent up between dripping, freezing walls, with no fire and no means of getting one, innumerable families, throngs of workmen, with nothing but sordid rags to clothe them, are suffering unto death in this Babylon of pleasure and luxury. As the cold came on, dense fogs shrouded Paris in an impenetrable and mysterious winding sheet. It was all that was needed to bring crime, the offspring of destitution, down into the streets and freeze the soul of the late walker with dread. In dark and lonely districts unknown even by name to the opulent inhabitant of the wealthy districts flooded with the light of innumerable lamp posts, the cutthroats, the *"escarpes,"* as this plague is called, crept closer and closer, and emboldened by the success of their nightly ventures, finally fell upon our districts. In the rue de Castiglione, at nine o'clock in the evening, at the door of the Hôtel Clarendon, right opposite the sentry outside the Ministry of Finance, a young man was very nearly murdered. . . . These dark deeds soon came up before the criminal court.

Louis Chevalier. *Laboring Classes and Dangerous Classes in Paris During the First Half of the Nineteenth Century,* trans. Frank Jellinek. (New York: H. Fertig, 1973), pp. 138, 370–71.

Soup Kitchen Run by Quakers, Manchester, England, 1862. Working people lived a precarious existence, vulnerable to seasonal unemployment, work accidents, and sickness as well as economic crises. Hard times strained the capacities of private charities like this one.

evidence of physical squalor and psychological disruption suffered by men, women, and children.

The debate is hampered by an absence of reliable evidence about wage levels, hours of work, and cost of living. Some skilled workers within the new factories, along with some artisans in older trades as yet unaffected by industrialization, appear to have benefited from a slight rise in wages and a decline in living costs. But regional variables, along with a constantly fluctuating demand for labor in all countries, suggest that the lower-paid, unskilled worker, whether in Britain or on the Continent, led a thoroughly precarious existence. Textile workers in Britain, if guaranteed something like full employment, could theoretically earn enough to support a family. Such was not the case in Switzerland, however, where similar work paid only half what was necessary, or in Saxony, where a large portion of the population was apparently dependent on either poor relief or charity.

One of the defining features of working-class life in these years was its instability. Seasonal unemployment, high in almost all trades, made it impossible to collect regular wages. Markets for manufactured goods were small and unstable, producing cyclical economic depressions; when those came, thousands of workers found themselves laid off with no system of unemployment insurance to sustain them. The early decades of industrialization were also marked by several severe agricultural depressions and economic crises. In the

crisis years of the 1840s (see page 797), half the working population of Britain's industrial cities was out of work. In Paris, eighty-five thousand went on relief in 1840. One particularly hard-pressed district of Silesia reported thirty thousand out of forty thousand citizens in need of relief in 1844. In the British manufacturing town of Bolton, a hand-loom weaver could earn no more than about three shillings per week in 1842, at a time when experts estimated it took at least twenty shillings a week to keep a family of five above the poverty line. Wages were not only low but irregular, and working-class families were vulnerable to large-scale economic crises, seasonal unemployment, and personal misfortune: accidents on the job, sickness and death, and so on. Families survived by working several small jobs, pawning their possessions, and getting credit from local wineshops and grocery stores. The optimists' generalizations do not take us very close to the everyday lives of working people and the experience of industrialization.

Prostitution flourished in nineteenth-century cities, and for scores of worried nineteenth-century observers it exemplified the dangers and corruptions of urban life. At mid-century the number of prostitutes in Vienna was estimated to be fifteen thousand; in Paris, where prostitution was a licensed trade, fifty thousand; in London, eighty thousand. London newspaper reports of the 1850s catalogued the vast underworld of prostitutes and their followers. Those included entrepreneurs with names like Swindling Sal who ran lodging houses; the pimps and "fancy men" who managed the trade of prostitutes on the street; and the relatively few "prima donnas" or courtesans who enjoyed the protection of rich, upper-middle-class lovers, who entertained lavishly and whose wealth allowed them to move on the fringes of more respectable high society. The heroines of Alexandre Dumas's novel *La Dame aux Camélias* and of Giuseppe Verdi's opera *La Traviata* ("the lost one") were prototypes of women of this sort. The vast majority of prostitutes, however, were not courtesans but women who worked long and dangerous hours in port districts of cities, or at lodging houses in the overwhelmingly male working-class neighborhoods. Often prostitutes were young women who had just arrived in the city or working women trying to manage during a period of unemployment. Some contemporaries attributed rising prostitution to poverty, others to moral squalor. As in the debate about the standard of living, both positions make more sense if understood as part of a larger discussion of the social effects and cultural responses to industrialization and urbanization.

THE LIFE OF THE URBAN MIDDLE CLASS

What was the role of middle-class women in everyday life?

The rising political and cultural power of the urban middle classes was another hallmark of nineteenth-century society. The middle class was not one homogeneous unit, in terms of occupation or income. In a general category that reaches from international bankers to humble shopkeepers, subdivisions are important. The middle class included families of industrialists, such as the Peels (cotton) in Britain and, at a later period, the Krupps (iron) in Germany. It included financiers such as the internationally famed Rothschilds, and, on a descending scale of wealth and power, bankers and capitalists throughout the major money markets of Europe: London, Brussels, Paris, Berlin. It included entrepreneurs, such as the British railway magnate Thomas Brassey and the British ironmaster John Wilkinson (who had himself buried in an iron coffin), and technicians, such as the engineer Isambard Kingdom Brunel, designer of the steamship the *Great Western*. It included bureaucrats, in growing demand when governments began to regulate the pace and direction of industrialization, and to ameliorate its harshest social and economic results. It included those in the already established professions—in law particularly, as lawyers put their expertise at the service of industrialists. It included the armies of managers and clerks necessary to the continuing momentum of industrial and financial expansion, and the equally large army of merchants and shopkeepers necessary to supply the wants of wealthier urban middle-class population. It included wives who ran elegant mansions, women who did the accounting for family businesses,

or, much more modestly, women who worked as governesses, schoolteachers, or writers.

Movement within middle-class ranks was often possible in the course of one or two generations. Very few, however, moved from the working class into the middle class. Most middle-class successes originated within the middle class itself—the children of farmers, skilled artisans, or professionals. Upward mobility was almost impossible without education; education was an expensive, if not unattainable, luxury for the children of laborers. Careers open to talents, that goal achieved by the French Revolution, frequently meant jobs for middle-class young men who could pass exams. The examination system was an important path for ascendancy within governmental bureaucracies.

If passage from working class to middle class was not common, neither was the equally difficult social journey from middle class to aristocratic, landed society. In Britain, mobility of this sort was easier to achieve than on the Continent. Sons from wealthy upper-middle-class families, if they were sent to elite schools and universities, and if they left the commercial or industrial world for a career in politics, might actually move up. William Gladstone, son of a Liverpool merchant, attended the exclusive educational preserves of Eton (a private boarding school) and Oxford University, married into the aristocratic Grenville family, and became prime minister of England. Yet Gladstone was an exception to the rule in Britain, and Britain was different from the Continent. Movement, when it occurred, generally did so in less spectacular degrees.

Nevertheless, the European middle class helped sustain itself with the belief that it was possible to get ahead by means of intelligence, pluck, and serious devotion to work. The Englishman Samuel Smiles, in his extraordinarily successful how-to-succeed book *Self-Help* (1859), preached a gospel dear to the middle class. "The spirit of self-help is the root of all genuine growth in the individual," Smiles wrote. "Exhibited in the lives of many, it constitutes the true source of national vigor and strength." A corollary to Smiles's discussion was the moral obligation to use the fruits of success in accordance with middle-class notions of respectability. The middle classes' claim to political power and cultural influence rested on arguments that they were a new and deserving social elite, superior to the common people yet sharply different from the older aristocracy, and a group that could become custodians of the nation's future. Thus middle-class "respectability," like a code, stood for many values. It meant financial independence, providing responsibly for one's family, avoiding gambling and debt. It suggested merit and character as opposed to aristocratic privilege, and hard work as opposed to living off noble estates. "Respectable" middle-class gentlemen might be wealthy, but they should live modestly and soberly, avoiding conspicuous consumption, lavish dress, womanizing and other forms of "dandyish" behavior associated with the aristocracy. These were aspirations and codes, not social realities. They nonetheless remained key to the middle-class sense of self and understanding of the world.

PRIVATE LIVES OF THE URBAN MIDDLE CLASS

Family and home played a central role in forming middle-class identity. Few themes are more common in nineteenth-century fiction than the pursuit of mobility and status through marriage. Families served intensely practical purposes: sons, nephews, and cousins were expected to assume responsibility in family firms when it came their turn, wives managed accounts, and parents-in-law provided business connections, credit, inheritance, and so on. Middle-class men's ability to command respect and organize economic activities rested concretely on their families. The family's role in middle-class thought, however, did not arise only from these practical considerations; it formed part of a larger world view. A well-governed household offered a counterpoint to the business and confusion of the world, a realm of continuity and tradition. Sheltered behind solid walls and amid the comfort of their ornate furnishings, middle-class fathers retired each evening to enjoy the fruits of their daily labors. Indeed, this retreat served as a daily reaffirmation of power and of middle-class belonging and standing.

There was no single type of "middle-class" family or home. Yet people did have powerful convictions about a respectable home life should operate, and about the rituals, hierarchies, and distinctions that should prevail. Wives and mothers were assigned to a "separate sphere" of life, in which they lived in subordination to their spouses. "Man for the field and woman for the hearth; man for the sword and for the needle she. . . . All else confusion," wrote the British

poet Alfred Lord Tennyson in 1847. Boys were educated in secondary schools; girls at home. Soon after the revolutionary and Napoleonic period, men began to dress in sober, practical clothing—and to see as "effeminate" or "dandyish" the wigs, ruffled collars, and tight breeches that had earlier been the pride of aristocratic masculinity. The nineteenth-century idea of separate spheres was paired with longer-standing traditions of paternal authority and codified in law. Throughout Europe women were legally subjugated to their husbands. The Napoleonic Code, a model for other countries after 1815, classified women, children, and the mentally ill together as legally incompetent. In Britain, a woman transferred all her property rights to her husband on marriage. Although unmarried women did enjoy a degree of legal independence in France and Austria, laws generally assigned them to the "protection" of their fathers.

WOMEN'S LIVES

Despite this legal subordination, middle-class culture often referred to equality between men and women, and took pride in marriages in which the wife was a "companion" and "helpmate." Middle-class values were often articulated in opposition to aristocratic customs on the one hand and the lives of the common people on the other. Middle-class values asserted this new elite's moral superiority and a vision of the future. Middle-class marriages, for instance, were not supposed to found aristocratic dynasties, carefully arranged to accumulate power and privilege; they were to be based on mutual respect and division of responsibilities. A "respectable" middle-class woman should be free from the unrelenting toil that was the lot of a woman of the people. She was not to sully herself by working for wages, but she should show "industriousness," thrift, and good sense. Called in Victorian Britain the "angel in the house," the middle-class woman was responsible for the moral education of her children. That being a good wife and mother was a demanding task, requiring an elevated character, was central to middle-class Victorian thinking about women. This reassessment of femininity, which marked the period, arose from roots in nineteenth-century religion and efforts to moralize society, guarding against the disorders of the French and industrial revolutions.

> Despite the legal subordination of women to men, middle class culture often referred to equality between men and women, and took pride in marriages in which the wife was a "companion" and "helpmate."

As a housewife, a middle-class woman's task was to keep the household functioning smoothly and harmoniously. She maintained the accounts and directed the activities of the servants. Having at least one servant was a mark of middle-class status, and in wealthier families governesses and nannies cared for children, idealized views of motherhood notwithstanding. The middle classes, however, included many gradations of wealth, from a well-housed banker with a governess and five servants to a village preacher with one. Moreover, the work of running and maintaining a home was enormous. Linens and clothes had to be made and mended. Only the wealthy had the luxury of running water, and others had to carry and heat water for cooking, laundry, and cleaning. Heating with coal and lighting with kerosene involved hours of cleaning, and so on. The angel in the house thus had real economic value.

Outside the home, women had very few respectable options for earning a living. Unmarried women might act as companions or governesses—the British novelist Charlotte Bronte's heroine Jane Eyre did so and led a generally miserable life until "rescued" by marriage to her not altogether pleasant employer. But nineteenth-century convictions about women's moral nature, combined as they were with middle-class aspirations to political leadership, encouraged middle-class wives to undertake voluntary charitable work or to campaign for social reform. In Britain and the United States, women played an important role in the struggle to abolish the slave trade and slavery in the British empire. Many of these movements also drew on the energies of religious, especially Protestant, organizations, committed to the eradication of social evils and moral improvement. Throughout Europe, a wide range of movements to improve conditions for the poor in schools and hospitals, for temperance, against prostitution, or for legislation on factory hours were often run by women. Florence Nightingale, who went to the Crimean Peninsula in Russia to nurse British soldiers fighting there in the 1850s, remains the most famous of those women, whose determination to right social wrongs compelled them to ignore convictions about the "women's sphere." Equally famous—or infamous, at the time—was the French female novelist George Sand (1804–1876), whose real name was Amandine Aurore Dupin Dudevant. She dressed like a man and smoked cigars. Her novels often told the tales of independent women thwarted by convention and unhappy marriage. Her notoriety gave rise to the expression "George Sandism," a term of opprobrium for those who defied middle-class convention.

Queen Victoria, who came to the British throne in 1837, labored to make her solemn public image reflect contemporary feminine virtues of moral probity and dutiful domesticity. Her court was eminently proper, a marked contrast to that of her uncle George IV, whose cavalier ways had set the style for high life a generation before. Though possessing a bad temper, Victoria trained herself to curb it in deference to her ministers and her public-spirited, ultrarespectable husband, Prince Albert of Saxe-Coburg. She was a successful queen because she embodied the traits important to the middle class, whose triumph she seemed to epitomize and whose habits of mind we have come to call Victorian.

> Victoria was a successful queen because she embodied the traits important to the middle class, whose triumph she seemed to epitomize and whose habits of mind we have come to call Victorian.

SEXUALITY

"Victorian" ideas about sexuality are among the most remarked-on features of nineteenth-century culture. They have become virtually synonymous with anxiety, prudishness, and ignorance. An English mother counseling her daughter about her wedding night is said to have told her to "lie back and think of the Empire." Etiquette apparently required that piano legs be covered. Many of these anxieties and prohibitions, however, have been caricatured. Historians have worked to disentangle the teachings of etiquette books and marriage manuals from the actual beliefs of men and women and, equally important, to understand each on its own terms. Prescriptions about sexuality followed from the firm belief in "separate spheres." Indeed one of the defining aspects of nineteenth-century ideas about men and women is the extent to which they rested on scientific arguments about nature. Codes of morality and methods of science combined to reinforce the idea that certain characteristics were inherent to each sex. Men and women had different social roles, and those differences were rooted in their bodies. The French social thinker Auguste Comte provides a good example: "Biological philosophy teaches us that, through the whole animal scale, and while the specific type is preserved, radical differences, physical and

MARRIAGE, SEXUALITY, AND THE FACTS OF LIFE

In the nineteenth century sexuality became the subject of much anxious debate, largely because it raised other issues: the roles of men and women, morality, and social respectability. Doctors threw themselves into the discussion, offering their expert opinions on the health (including sexual lives) of the population. Yet doctors did not dictate people's private lives. Nineteenth-century men and women responded to what they experienced as the facts of life more than to expert advice. The first document provides an example of medical knowledge and opinion. The second offers a glimpse of the daily realities of family life.

A French Doctor Denounces Contraception

One of the most powerful instincts nature has placed in the heart of man is that which has for its object the perpetuation of the human race. But this instinct, this inclination, so active, which attracts one sex towards the other, is liable to be perverted, to deviate from the path nature has laid out. From this arises a number of fatal aberrations which exercise a deplorable influence upon the individual, upon the family and upon society. . . .

We hear constantly that marriages are less fruitful, that the increase of population does not follow its former ratio. I believe that this is mainly attributable to genesiac frauds. It might naturally be supposed that these odious calculations of egotism, these shameful refinements of debauchery, are met with almost entirely in large cities, and among the luxurious classes, and that small towns and country places yet preserve that simplicity of manners attributed to primitive society, when the *pater familias* was proud of exhibiting his numerous offspring. Such, however, is not the case, and I shall show that those who have an unlimited confidence in the patriarchal habits of our country people are deeply in error. At the present time frauds are practiced by all classes. . . .

The laboring classes are generally satisfied with the practice of Onan [withdrawal] . . . They are seldom familiar with the sheath invented by Dr. Condom, and bearing his name.

Among the wealthy, on the other hand, the use of this preservative is generally known. It favors frauds by rendering them easier; but it does not afford complete security . . .

Case X.—This couple belongs to two respectable families of vintners. They are both pale, emaciated, downcast, sickly. . . .

They have been married for ten years; they first had two children, one immediately after the other, but in order to avoid an increase of family, they have had recourse to conjugal frauds. Being both very amorous, they have found this practice very convenient to satisfy their inclinations. They have employed it to such an extent, that up to a few months ago, when their health began to fail, the husband had intercourse with his wife habitually two and three times in twenty-four hours.

The following is the condition of the woman: She complains of continual pains in the lower part of the abdomen and kidneys. These pains disturb the functions of the stomach and render her nervous. . . . By the touch we find a very intense heat, great sensibility to pressure, and all the signs of a chronic metritis. The patient attributes positively her present state to the too frequent approaches of her husband.

The husband does not attempt to exculpate himself, as he also is in a state of extreme suffering. It is not in the genital organs, however, that we find his disorder, but in the whole general nervous system; his history will find its place in the part of this work relative to general disturbances. . . .

DEATH IN CHILDBIRTH

Mrs. Ann B. Pettigrew was taken in Labour after returning from a walk in the garden, at 7 o'clock in the evening of June 30, 1830. At 40 minutes after 11 o'clock, she was delivered of a daughter. A short time after, I was informed that the Placenta was not removed, and, at 10 minutes after 12 was asked into the room. I advanced to my dear wife, and kissing her, asked her how she was, to which she replied, I feel very badly. I went out of the room, and sent for Dr. Warren.

I then returned, and inquired if there was much hemorrhage, and was answered that there was. I then asked the midwife (Mrs. Brickhouse) if she ever used manual exertion to remove the placenta. She said she had more than fifty times. I then, fearing the consequences of hemorrhage, observed, Do, my dear sweet wife, permit Mrs. Brickhouse to remove it: To which she assented. . . . After the second unsuccessful attempt, I desired the midwife to desist. In these two efforts, my dear Nancy suffered exceedingly and frequently exclaimed: "O Mrs Brickhouse you will kill me," and to me, "O I shall die, send for the Doctor." To which I replied, "I have sent."

After this, my feelings were so agonizing that I had to retire from the room and lay down, or fall. Shortly after which, the midwife came to me and, falling upon her knees, prayed most fervently to God and to me to forgive her for saying that she could do what she could not . . .

The placenta did not come away, and the hemorrhage continued with unabated violence until five o'clock in the morning, when the dear woman breathed her last 20 minutes before the Doctor arrived.

So agonizing a scene as that from one o'clock, I have no words to describe. O My God, My God! have mercy on me. I am undone forever . . .

Cited in Erna Olafson Hellerstein, Leslie Parker Hume, and Karen M. Offen, eds. *Victorian Women: A Documentary Account of Women's Lives in Nineteenth-Century England, France, and the United States.* (Stanford: Stanford University Press, 1981) pp. 193–94, 219–20.

moral, distinguish the sexes." Comte also spelled out the implications: "Sociology will prove that the equality of the sexes, of which so much is said, is incompatible with all social existence. . . . The economy of the human family could never be inverted without an entire change in our cerebral organism." Women were unsuited for higher education because their brains were smaller, or because their bodies were fragile. "Fifteen or 20 days of 28 (we may say nearly always) a woman is not only an invalid, but a wounded one. She ceaselessly suffers from love's eternal wound," wrote the well-known French author Jules Michelet about menstruation.

Finally, scientists and doctors considered women's alleged moral superiority to be literally embodied in an absence of sexual feeling, or "passionlessness." Scientists and doctors considered male sexual desire natural, if not admirable—an unruly force that had to be channeled. Many governments legalized and regulated prostitution—which included the compulsory examination of women for venereal disease—precisely because it provided an outlet for male sexual desire. Doctors disagreed about female sexuality, but the British doctor William Acton stood among those who asserted that women functioned differently:

> I have taken pains to obtain and compare abundant evidence on this subject, and the result of my inquiries I may briefly epitomize as follows: – I should say that the majority of women (happily for society) are not very much troubled with sexual feeling of any kind. What men are habitually, women are only exceptionally.

Like others, Acton also believed that more open expressions of sexuality were disreputable and that working-class women were less "feminine." In reality, any such differences arose from the absence of privacy in small and crowded working-class homes. Most observers, though, ignored such evidence. Medical, scientific, and sociological writings joined in insisting on the ineradicable differences between men and women, and on seeing sexual mores as a mark of class belonging.

These convictions about sexuality are revealing about Victorian science and medicine, but they did not necessarily dictate people's intimate lives. As far as sexuality was concerned, much more important in people's experiences and feelings was the absence of any reliable contraception. Abstinence and withdrawal were the only common techniques. Their effectiveness was limited, since until the 1880s doctors continued to believe that a woman was most fertile during and around her menstrual period. Midwives and prostitutes knew of other forms of contraception and abortifacients (all of them dangerous and most ineffective), and surely some middle-class women did as well, but such information was not respectable middle-class fare. Concretely, then, sexual intercourse was directly related to the real dangers of frequent pregnancies. In England, one in one hundred childbirths ended in the death of the mother; at a time where a woman might become pregnant eight or nine times in her life, this was a sobering prospect. Those dangers varied with social class, but even among wealthy and better-cared-for women, they took a real toll. Not surprisingly, middle-class women's diaries and letters are full of their anticipations of childbirth, both joyful and anxious. Queen Victoria, who bore nine children, declared that childbirth was the "shadow side" of marriage—and she was a pioneer in using anesthesia!

MATERIAL SECURITY OF THE MIDDLE CLASS

The public life of families also, literally, reshaped the nineteenth-century landscape. Family vacations were a

The Beach at Trouville, by Claude Monet. Among the Impressionists' favorite subjects were the light, air, and water at new places of middle-class leisure. New railway lines made Trouville, on the English Channel northwest of Paris, a very popular nineteenth century beach resort.

particularly nineteenth-century middle-class invention. The advent of the railways made one- or two-week-long trips to the mountains or to the seashore available to families of even moderate means. Entrepreneurs built large, ornate hotels, adorned with imposing names—Palace, Beau Rivage, Excelsior—and attracted middle-class customers by offering them on a grander scale exactly the same sort of comfortable and sheltered existence they enjoyed at home. Impressionist paintings of the 1870s and 1880s chronicle a wide variety of new middle-class leisures: going to the racetracks, bathing on the beaches of northern France, and enjoying outdoor picnics and concerts. For wealthier clients, entrepreneurs such as Karl Baedeker and Thomas Cook created "packaged" versions of aristocrats' "grand tours," with visits to the great cultural landmarks of Europe and the Mediterranean.

The houses and furnishings of the middle class were an expression of the material security the middle class valued. Solidly built, heavily decorated, they proclaimed the financial worth and social respectability of those who dwelt within. In provincial cities they were often freestanding "villas." In London, Paris, Berlin, or Vienna, they might be in rows of five- or six-story townhouses, or large apartments. Whatever particular shape they took, they were built to last a long time. The rooms were certain to be crowded with furniture, art objects, carpets, and wall hangings. Chairs, tables, cabinets, and sofas might be of any or all periods; no matter, so long as they were adorned with their proper complement of fringe, gilt, or other ornamentation. The size of the rooms, the elegance of the furniture, the number of servants—all depended, of course, on the extent of one's income. A bank clerk did not live as elegantly as a bank director. Yet they shared many standards and aspirations, and those common values helped bind them to the same class, despite the differences in their material way of life.

Social class, in short, made its mark on nineteenth-century cities. Middle-class people lived far from the unpleasant sights and smells of industrialization. Their residential areas, usually built to the west of the cities, out of the path of the prevailing

Apartment Living in Paris. This print shows that on the Continent rich and poor often lived in the same buildings, the rich on the lower floors, the poor at the top. This sort of residential mixing was unknown in Britain.

THE LIFE OF THE URBAN WORKING CLASS

How did the Industrial Revolution change working-class women's lives?

Like the middle class, the working class was divided into various subgroups and categories, determined in this case by skill, wages, gender, and workplace. The working class included skilled workers in crafts that were centuries old—glassblowing and cabinetmaking, for example. This class also included mechanics equally skilled in the new industrial technology. It included the men who built textile machinery and the women and children who tended it. It included the men, women, and children who together worked in mines and quarries, where employers often hired whole families. And it included the countless millions who labored at unskilled jobs—dock workers, coal porters, seamstresses, domestic servants, and the like. The nature of workers' experiences naturally varied, depending on where they worked, where they lived, and, above all, how much they earned. A skilled textile worker lived a life far different from that of a ditch digger, the former able to afford the food, shelter, and clothing necessary for a decent existence, the latter so busy trying to keep himself and his family alive that he would have little time to think about anything but the source of their next meal.

Some movement from the ranks of the unskilled to the skilled was possible, if children were provided, or provided themselves, with at least a rudimentary education. Yet education was considered by many parents a luxury, especially since children could be put to work at an early age to supplement a family's meager earnings. Downward mobility from skilled to unskilled was also possible, as technological change—the introduction of the power loom, for example—drove highly paid workers into the ranks of the unskilled and destitute. Further variations within the working class were the result of the fact that though every year more men, women, and children were working in factories, the majority still labored either in workshops or at home. These variations mean that we cannot speak of a common European working-class experience during the years from 1800 to 1850. The life we shall be describing was most typical of British workers, during the first half century of their exposure to industrialization. Only in the years 1850 to

breeze and therefore of industrial pollution, were havens from congestion. When the members of the middle class rode into the urban centers they took care to do so on avenues lined with respectable shops, or across railway embankments that lifted them above monotonous working-class streets en route to their destination. At the same time, nineteenth-century cities were celebrated as middle-class achievements, signs of development and prosperity. The middle classes increasingly managed their cities' affairs, although this varied across Europe. And it was they who provided new industrial cities with their proud architectural landmarks: city halls, stock exchanges, museums, opera houses, outdoor concert halls, and department stores. These buildings were, in important ways, the new cathedrals of the industrial age, proclamations of rapid change in public culture and the social world.

HOW DID THE INDUSTRIAL REVOLUTION CHANGE WORKING-CLASS WOMEN'S LIVES?

THE LIFE OF THE URBAN WORKING CLASS   761

Nineteenth Century Working Class Housing. As cities grew, medieval neighborhoods with tiny narrow streets were cleared to make way for new, improved buildings such as the ones below. This process also drove many working people out of the central areas and into shantytowns on the outskirts, such as those to the right.

1900 did most Continental workers undergo this harsh process of urban acclimatization.

Life in industrial cities was, for almost all workers, uncomfortable at best and unbearably squalid at worst. Workers and their families lived in housing that failed to answer the needs of its inhabitants. In older cities single-family dwellings were broken up into apart-ments, often of no more than one room per family. In new manufacturing centers, rows of tiny houses, located close by smoking factories, were built back to back, thereby eliminating any cross-ventilation or space for gardens. Whether housing was old or new, it was generally in poor condition. Old buildings were allowed by landlords to fall into disrepair; new houses, constructed of cheap material, decayed quickly. Water often came from an outdoor tap, shared by several houses and adjacent to an outdoor toilet. Crowding was commonplace. Families of as many as eight lived in two or, at the most, three rooms. A newspaper account from the 1840s noted that in Leeds, a textile center in northern Britain, an "ordinary" worker's house contained no more than 150 square feet, and that in most cases those houses were "crammed almost to suffocation with human beings both day and night." When, after 1850, governments began to rid cities of some of their worst slums, many working-class men and women discovered that urban "improvement" meant relocation into dreary "model" tenements whose amenities were matched by their barracklike anonymity, or removal from one dilapidated structure to another in the wake of a clearance scheme. The nineteenth century called such schemes "ventilation"; they replaced ancient, overcrowded housing with a more sanitary—and, for the landlord, more profitable—railway switching yard.

Household routines, demanding in the middle classes, were grinding for the poor. The family remained a survival network, in which everyone played a crucial role. In addition to working for wages, wives were expected to house, feed, and clothe the family on the very little money different members of the family earned. A "good wife" was able to make ends meet even in bad times. Working women's daily lives involved constant rounds of carrying and boiling water, cleaning, cooking, and doing laundry—in one- and two-room crowded, unventilated, poorly lit apartments. Families could not rely on their own gardens to help supply them with food. City markets catered to their needs for cheap goods, but these were regularly stale, nearly rotten, or dangerously adulterated. Formaldehyde was added to milk to prevent spoilage. Pounded rice was mixed into sugar. Fine brown earth was introduced into cocoa.

WORKING WOMEN IN THE URBAN LANDSCAPE

Few figures raised more public anxiety and outcry in the nineteenth century than the working woman. Certainly plenty of women worked in earlier times, but industrialization made the working woman much more visible. Women and children formed at least half the labor force in some of the most "modern" industries, like textiles. Scores of early nineteenth-century writers in England and France chronicled what they considered to be the economic and moral horrors of female labor: unattended children running in the streets, small children caught in accidents at the mills or the mines, pregnant women hauling coal, or women laboring alongside men in shops. These scenes reaffirmed nineteenth-century convictions that femininity and industry were incontovertibly opposed. Still, most women did not work in factories. Many more labored at home or in small workshops—"sweatshops," as they came to be called—for notoriously low wages, paid not by the hour but by the piece for each shirt stitched or each matchbox glued. And by far the greatest number of unmarried working-class women worked, less visibly, in domestic service, a job that brought low wages and, by a great many women's testimony, coercive sexual relationships with male employers or their sons. This type of work, however, provided room and board. In a time when a single woman simply could not survive on her own wages, a young woman who had just arrived in the city had few choices: marriage, which was unlikely to happen right away; renting a room in a boarding house, many of which were often centers of prostitution; domestic service; or living with someone. Once women

started bearing children, they might give birth every two years. How women balanced the demands for money and the time for household work varied with the number and age of the children. Mothers were actually more likely to work when their children were very small, for there were more mouths to feed and the children were not yet old enough to earn wages.

Poverty, the absence of privacy, and the particular vulnerabilities of working-class women made working-class sexuality very different from its middle-class counterpart. Illegitimacy rose dramatically between 1750 and 1850. In Frankfurt, Germany, for example, where the illegitimacy rate had been a mere 2 percent in the early 1700s, it reached 25 percent in 1850. In Bordeaux, France, in 1840, one third of the recorded births were illegitimate. Reasons for this increase are difficult to establish. Increased mobility and urbanization meant weaker family ties, more opportunities for young men and women, and more vulnerabilities. Premarital sex was an accepted practice in preindustrial villages, but because of the social controls that dominated village life, it was almost always a precursor to marriage. These controls were weaker in the far more anonymous setting of a factory town. The economic uncertainties of the early industrial age meant that a young workingman's promise of marriage based on his expectation of a job might frequently be difficult to fulfill. Economic vulnerability drove many single women into temporary relationships that produced children and a continuing cycle of poverty and abandonment. Historians have shown, however, that in the city as in the countryside, many of these temporary relationships became enduring ones: the parents of illegitimate children would marry later. Again, nineteenth-century writers dramatized what they considered the disreputable sexuality of the "dangerous classes" in the cities. Some of them attributed illegitimacy, prostitution, and so on to the moral weakness of working-class people, others to the systematic changes wrought by industrialization. Both sides, however, overstated the collapse of the family and the destruction of traditional morality. Families remained crucial economic units, central to survival in an insecure world. Working-class families passed on expectations about gender roles and sexual behavior: girls should expect to work, daughters were responsible for caring for their younger siblings as well as earning wages, sexuality was a fact of life, midwives could help desperate pregnant girls, marriage was an avenue to respectabil-

> Few figures raised more public anxiety and outcry in the nineteenth century than the working woman.

HOW DID THE INDUSTRIAL REVOLUTION CHANGE WORKING-CLASS WOMEN'S LIVES?

THE LIFE OF THE URBAN WORKING CLASS   763

ity, and so on. The gulf that separated these expectations and codes from those of middle-class women was one of the most important factors in the development of nineteenth-century class identity.

THE IMPACT OF FACTORY LIFE

The new demands of factory life also created common experiences and difficulties. The factory system, emphasizing as it did standard rather than individual work patterns, denied skilled laborers the pride in craft that had previously been theirs. Many workers found themselves stripped of the protections of guilds and formal apprenticeships that had bound their predecessors to a particular trade or place, and that were outlawed or sharply curtailed by legislation in France, Germany, and Britain in the first half of the nineteenth century. Factory hours were long; before 1850 usually twelve to fourteen hours a day. Conditions were dirty and dangerous. Textile mills remained unventilated, so that minute particles of material lodged in workers' lungs. Machines were unfenced and were a particular danger to child workers, often hired, because of their supposed agility, to clean under and around the moving parts. Manufacturing processes were unhealthy. The use of poisonous lead in the making of glazed pottery, for example, was a constant hazard to men and women workers in that industry. Surveys by British physicians in the 1840s catalogued the toll that long factory hours and harsh working conditions were taking, particularly on young workers, such as spinal curvature and other bone malformations that resulted from standing hour after hour in unnatural positions at machines. One concerned doctor stated his belief that "from what I saw myself, a large mass of deformity has been produced by the factory system." And what was true of factories was true as well of mines, in which over fifty thousand children and young people were employed in Britain in 1841. Children were used to haul coal to underground tramways or shafts. The youngest were set to work—often for as long as twelve hours at a stretch—operating doors that regulated the ventilation in the mines. When they fell asleep during long shifts they jeopardized the safety of the entire work force. Lung diseases—popularly known as "black spittle"—and eye infections, not to mention the danger of explosions caused by trapped gas, were constant threats to life and limb in the mines.

Factories also imposed new routines and disciplines. Artisans in earlier times worked very long hours for very little pay. But at least to some degree, they could set their own hours and structure their own activities, to move from their home workshops to their small garden plots and back again as they wished. In a factory, all "hands" learned the discipline of the whistle. To function efficiently, a factory demanded that all employees begin and end work at the same time. Most workers could not tell time; fewer possessed clocks. None was accustomed to the relentless pace of the machine. In order to increase production, the factory system encouraged the breaking down of the manufacturing process into specialized steps, each with its own assigned time, an innovation that upset workers accustomed to completing a task at their own pace. It is no wonder that workers began to see machinery itself as the tyrant that had changed their lives and bound them to a kind of industrial slavery. A radical working-class song written in Britain in the 1840s expressed the feeling: "There is a king and a ruthless king; / Not a king of the poet's dream; / But a tyrant fell, white slaves know well, / And that ruthless king is steam."

Faced with a drastic reordering of their lives, working-class men and women reacted in various ways. New cities could be lonely places, particularly for anyone struggling to cope with an alien environment. If possible, they would live near relatives who had already made the transition and who could assist the newcomers in adjusting to their new very different existence. In many cities working-class families lived in districts inhabited primarily by others working at the same trade—weavers in one place, miners in another—and in this way achieved some sense of commonality. Some sought "the shortest way out of Manchester" by taking to drink (that city had twelve hundred public houses in 1850). Pubs, music halls, and wine shops, however, were centers of sociability for the common people, places to gather after work and on weekends, and in some cases venues for political discussion.

By mid-century, various experiences were beginning to make working people conscious of themselves as different from and in opposition to the middle classes. Changes in the workplace—whether the introduction of machines and factory labor, speedups, subcontracting to cheap labor, or the loss of guild protections—were part of the picture. The social segregation of the

> By mid-century, various experiences were beginning to make working people conscious of themselves as different from and in opposition to the middle classes.

"Capital and Labour." In its earliest years, the British magazine *Punch,* though primarily a humorous weekly, manifested a strong social conscience. In this 1843 cartoon, the capitalists are seen reveling in the rewards of their investments while the workers—men, women, and children—who toil in the mines under cruel and dangerous conditions are found crippled and starving.

rapidly expanding nineteenth-century cities also contributed to the sense that working people lived a life apart. Class differences seemed embedded in a very wide array of everyday experiences and beliefs: work, "private" life, expectations for children, the roles of men and women, and definitions of respectability. Industrialization did not simply create a class society. Yet over the course of the nineteenth century, all of these different experiences gave concrete, specific meaning to the word "class."

changes, found themselves worried about what those changes implied. Confidence was often accompanied by apprehension. No one knew what the factory system and urbanization might eventually produce. Evidence drawn from the reports of various official commissions and from the intentionally lurid writings of sensational journalists suggested that city life was already spawning an underclass of men and women who preferred a life of promiscuity and criminality to one of honest toil. French novelists such as Victor Hugo began to use the sewers as a metaphor to describe the general condition of urban existence for what was assumed to be a vast number of Parisians. Poverty and crime were linked together in the middle-class mind, until it began to seem that poverty itself was defined as criminal. That view, of course, could be used to justify middle-class ascendancy and to dismiss the demands of the poor. There was no single response to the tumultuous changes of the early nineteenth century. But the awareness that new forms of wealth had created worrisome new forms of poverty provided a tremendous spur to social and economic thought. What were the sources of change? How could governments contend with change? How could they ensure stability? What values would define the future?

THE MIDDLE-CLASS WORLD VIEW: POLITICAL ECONOMY

How did the middle class define its interest within a new social order?

Industrialization wrenched European society out of old patterns of living and thrust it into new ones. Even the new middle classes, and others who benefited from the

PROPHETS AND CRITICS: INTERPRETING INDUSTRIALIZATION

We have noted already how Adam Smith's economic ideas sustained middle-class respect for individual enterprise (see Chapter 18). Enlightenment thought in general had extolled the virtues of individualism. John Locke, for example, celebrated the reason that allowed men and women to make intelligent choices based on their own enlightened self-interest. Arguments such as these were reinforced by a second generation of economists—particularly Thomas Malthus (1766–1834) and David Ricardo (1772–1823) of Britain—whose writings

HOW DID THE MIDDLE CLASS DEFINE ITS INTEREST WITHIN A NEW SOCIAL ORDER?

THE MIDDLE-CLASS WORLD VIEW: POLITICAL ECONOMY 765

embodied principles appealing to manufacturers, merchants, and entrepreneurs who desired a free hand to remake the economies of their countries. The chief elements in the theories of these economists were:

- Economic individualism. Individuals are entitled to use for their own best interests the property they have inherited or acquired by any legitimate method. People must be allowed to do what they like so long as they do not trespass on the equal right of others to do the same.

- Laissez-faire. The functions of the state should be reduced to a minimum consistent with public safety. The government should shrink itself into the role of a modest policeman, preserving order and protecting property, but never interfering with the operation of economic processes.

- Obedience to natural law. Immutable laws operate in the realm of economics as in every other sphere of the universe: the law of supply and demand, the balance of trade, the law of diminishing returns, and so on. These laws must be recognized and respected; failure to do so is disastrous.

- Freedom of contract. Individuals should be free to negotiate the best kind of contract they can obtain from any other individuals. In particular, the liberty of workers and employers to bargain with each other as to wages and hours should not be hampered by laws or by the collective power of labor unions.

- Free competition and free trade. Competition serves to keep prices down, to eliminate inefficient producers, and to ensure the maximum production in accordance with public demand. Therefore, neither monopolies nor price-fixing laws should be tolerated. Further, in order to force each country to engage in the production of those things it is best fitted to produce, all protective tariffs should be abolished. Free international trade will also help to keep prices down.

Such views shaped the outlook of the new middle classes. They did so indirectly, for factory owners and bankers were not likely to have read the actual works on political economy. Yet members of the middle class would have encountered popular journalistic versions of these ideas, or have participated in discussions at which the conclusions, if not the reasoned arguments, of the economists were aired. Because those conclu-

sions supported their own interests, they grew familiar with them, until, in time, they could talk of the ideas of political economists as if they were their own. In England, for instance, journals like *The Economist,* founded in 1838, argued vigorously for free trade. It is important to recognize, however, that the new middle class was a composite made up of people with very different experiences, goals, and beliefs. Not surprisingly, middle-class ideas frequently drew on seemingly contradictory theories to bolster often contradictory aims.

MALTHUS AND RICARDO

Malthus and Ricardo advanced particularly important and extremely influential arguments about how conflicting interests played out in society. Malthus, in his controversial and widely cited *Essay on the Principle of Population,* first published in 1798, argued that nature had set stubborn limits to the progress of humanity. Because of the voracity of the sexual appetite, Malthus argued, there was a natural tendency for population to increase more rapidly than the supply of food. To be sure, there were powerful checks, such as war, famine, disease, and vice; but these, when they operated effectively, further augmented the burden of human misery. It followed that poverty and pain were inescapable. Even if laws were passed distributing all wealth equally, they would only temporarily improve the condition of the poor; in a very short time working people would begin to raise larger families, straining resources and returning their class to poverty. In the second edition of his work, Malthus advocated postponement of marriage as a means of relief, but he continued to stress the danger that population would outrun any possible increase in the means of subsistence.

Malthus's arguments, with their emphasis on the inevitability of poverty and misery, allowed the middle class to acquiesce in the destruction of an older society that had made some attempt to care for its poor. In Britain, for example, officials in rural parishes had instituted a system of poor relief and subsidized wages to help sustain unemployed laborers and their families. The attempt failed to prevent distress and was met with increasing resistance by taxpayers. Malthus's arguments suggested that older forms of poor relief damaged both rich and poor alike and that efforts to redistribute wealth only shifted resources from the more productive members of society to the least productive. Malthus's views helped shift the responsibility for poverty from society to the individual and provided useful arguments for groups that wished to be freed from the burden of supporting the unemployed. They helped produce an alliance between industrialists such as mill owners and smaller "squires" who were feeling economically squeezed. The private philanthropy that took the place of poor relief and was strongly influenced by an evangelical religious impulse, allowed charity to be dispensed solely to the "deserving" poor, often through the activities of middle-class women.

Malthusian assumptions played a large role in the development of the theories of the British economist David Ricardo. According to Ricardo, wages seek a level that is just sufficient to enable workers "to subsist and perpetuate their race, without either increase or diminution." This Ricardo held to be an inescapable iron law, in much the same way that Malthus had seen the interplay between population growth and the means of subsistence. According to Ricardo, if wages should rise temporarily above the subsistence standard, men and women would be encouraged to marry earlier and produce more children, the population would increase, and the ensuing competition for jobs would quickly force the rate of pay down to its former level. Ricardo devised a law of rent as well as a law of wages. He maintained that rent is determined by the cost of production on the poorest land that must be brought under cultivation. Consequently, as a country's population increases, more land is cultivated, and higher rents are charged for more productive land, an ever-increasing proportion of the national income is absorbed by landlords.

Here again, classical political economy provided arguments useful to the middle class in its attempt to define and defend itself within a new social order. The law of wages gave employers a useful weapon to protect themselves from their workers' petitions for higher pay. The "inevitability" of both population growth beyond the means of subsistence and the negative effects of overpopulation on wages and rent helped neutralize the middle class's sense of personal responsibility for the plight of the urban poor. These writings, however, could also point toward the need for reform. Ricardo's law of rent justified middle-class opposition to the continuing power of elite landed interests. Landowners, middle-class reformers argued, derived their income not from hard work but from collecting rents; they profited unfairly at the expense of the rest of society.

> If society was to function properly, it needed an organizing principle that would both acknowledge humanity's selfishness and compel people to sacrifice at least some self-interest for the good of the majority.

BRITAIN AND THE UTILITARIANS

Of all the early nineteenth-century economic and social thinkers, the one who best represented this reforming outlook of the middle classes was Jeremy Bentham, founder of the British school of "utilitarian" philosophy. Bentham's major work, *The Principles of Morals and Legislation*, was published in 1789. It argued against the eighteenth-century Enlightenment belief in the natural harmony of human interests. Bentham started from the premise that humans were basically selfish beings. To suppose that a stable social order could emerge unassisted from a body of self-interested individuals was, Bentham believed, to suppose the impossible. If society was to function properly, it needed an organizing principle that would both acknowledge humanity's selfishness and compel people to sacrifice at least some self-interest for the good of the majority. That principle, called utilitarianism, stated that every institution, every law, must be measured according to its social usefulness. And a socially useful law was one that produced the "greatest happiness of the greatest number." If a law passed this test, it could remain on the books; if it failed, it should be abandoned forthwith, no matter how long-standing.

The Utilitarians' arguments had very wide appeal and became the creed of middle-class reform movements. Utilitarians acknowledged the importance of the individual. Each individual best understood his or her own interests, and was therefore best left free, whenever possible, to pursue those interests as he or she saw fit. Only when an individual's interests conflicted with the interests—the happiness—of the greatest number were they to be curtailed. Entrepreneurs could understand this doctrine as a spur to industrial development and progress. At the same time, Bentham's doctrines plainly called for reform. Was the greatest happiness, British factory owners might ask, produced by an antiquated electoral system that denied representation to growing industrial cities? Were productive landowners best served by having their profits diverted to the pockets of unemployed laborers, who might then have no incentive to work? Reformers inspired by utilitarian logic had a simple answer: obviously not. The congenial match between utilitarian logic and reformers' practical ambitions lent weight to calls for reform, and they were expressed in an electoral reform act in 1832 and the

WHY DID ARTISTS AND WRITERS CRITICIZE THE NEW MIDDLE-CLASS WORLD VIEW?

EARLY CRITICS OF THE MIDDLE-CLASS WORLD VIEW   767

complete overhaul of the Poor Laws in 1834. Belief in laissez-faire economics and changes in the poor law also shaped the British government's response to the Irish famine, with results that are still debated today.

Utilitarianism, thus, cut two ways: in favor of laissez-faire and in favor of governmental intervention and reform. Bentham and his followers provided the theoretical basis for many of the middle-class interventionist reforms, such as the revised poor law in Britain and an expanded educational system in France, achieved between 1815 and 1848 (see Chapter 23). At the same time utilitarianism, combined with the theories of Malthus and Ricardo, fortified the position of those businessmen who believed that unfettered individualism had produced the triumphs of the Industrial Revolution. To restrain that individualism was to jeopardize the further progress of industrialization and hence the greatest happiness of the greatest number.

Political economists and philosophers in France as well as in Britain helped provide the new middle class with a congenial world view. Count Claude de Saint-Simon, though a proponent of utopian schemes for social reorganization, nevertheless preached the gospel of "industrialism" and "industrialists" (two words that he coined). Disciples of Saint-Simon were among the leading proponents in France of industrial entrepreneurship and a standardized and centralized financial system.

Far more generally influential was the positivist philosophy of Auguste Comte. Comte's philosophy, like utilitarianism, insisted that all truth is derived from experience or observation of the physical world. Comte rejected metaphysics as utterly futile. No one can discover the hidden essences of things—why events happen as they do, or what is the ultimate meaning and goal of existence. All we can really know is how things happen, the laws that control their occurrence, and the relations existing between them. Positivism derived its name from the assertion that the only knowledge of any current value was "positive," or scientific, knowledge. Comte argued that humankind's ability to analyze society scientifically and to predict its future had reached a point that would soon enable Europe to achieve a "positive" society, organized not in terms of belief but in terms of facts. Such an achievement would not be a simple matter, however; "positive" attitudes and institutions could not replace those of the "metaphysical" stage through which Europe had just passed without a struggle. By

dividing the history of the world into progressive stages (a "religious" stage had preceded the "metaphysical"), and by declaring that the achievement of the highest stage was not possible without the turmoil of industrialization, Comte assured the middle class of its leading role in the better world that was to be.

EARLY CRITICS OF THE MIDDLE-CLASS WORLD VIEW

Why did artists and writers criticize the new middle-class world view?

The middle-class world view did not go unchallenged. Among its most effective critics were writers and artists who deplored the social chaos wrought by industrialization. Others criticized the materialism and hypocrisy they saw as the hallmarks of the middle class. The Scottish writer Thomas Carlyle, though a defender of the French Revolution and a believer in the need for a new aristocracy of industrialists ("captains of industry"), had nothing but contempt for the theories of the utilitarians. In Carlyle's view, they did no more than excuse the greed and acquisitiveness of the new middle class. Equally scathing in his attacks on the middle class was the English novelist Charles Dickens. In such novels as *Oliver Twist*, *Hard Times*, and *Dombey and Son*, he wrote with sympathy for the common people, from coal miners to orphan children, and mercilessly satirized both the middle classes and what he saw as the heartlessness of political economy. The French writer Honoré de Balzac had little of Dickens's sympathy for working people, but he fully shared Dickens's disdain for the new social elites and middle-class materialism. Balzac's multivolume *Human Comedy* (which includes among other novels *Old Goriot*, *Lost Illusions*, and *A Harlot High and Low*) aimed to be a sweeping portrait of the new bourgeois world. Balzac was biting in his observations about the ruthless self-promotion of aspiring young men, the cold calculations behind romantic liaisons, and, generally, the ways in which the postrevolutionary middle classes had simply replaced

The middle-class world view did not go unchallenged. Among its most effective critics were writers and artists who deplored the social chaos wrought by industrialization.

the aristocracy. Gustave Flaubert's novels, too, especially *Madame Bovary*, chronicled the emergence of a new social class and heaped scorn on the banality of middle-class life, on women made desperate by the empty formal rituals of family life in the bourgeoisie, on the destructive search for status and respectability. Victor Hugo's *Les Misérables* treated the world of the Paris poor with genuine sympathy.

A wide variety of artists also attacked the values of industrial society in painting and sculpture. The art preferred by the European middle class in the nineteenth century was that which in some way either told a story or offered a clearly stated message. Even artists most critical of the middle class, though repudiating what they considered their culture's taste for artificial and decorative art, held to the belief that art and beauty should be moral. The Pre-Raphaelite Brotherhood of

British painters was a group of men and women, led by the painter-poet Dante Gabriel Rossetti, determined to create an alternative to contemporary aesthetic and social values. By calling themselves Pre-Raphaelites they announced their admiration for the techniques of early Renaissance artists, untainted, supposedly, by corrupted artistic taste. Such a strong strain of moralism and sentimentality runs through their work that we need to remind ourselves that they saw themselves as rebellious. The same can be said, to a lesser degree, of the work of the Frenchman Jean-François Millet. His *Man with a Hoe* is a stark, bitter statement about peasant life. As in any period, artists in the nineteenth century reproduced the assumptions and conventions of their time while criticizing many of its values. When the Great Exhibition of the Works of Industry in All Nations was held at the Crystal Palace in London in 1851 to celebrate the tri-

Man With a Hoe, by Jean-François Millet. This painting depicts a peasant, exhausted by work, standing against the backdrop of his stony, bare plot of land. When the painting was shown in Paris, its subject matter drew a storm of criticism.

WHY DID ARTISTS AND WRITERS CRITICIZE THE NEW MIDDLE-CLASS WORLD VIEW?

EARLY CRITICS OF THE MIDDLE-CLASS WORLD VIEW   769

The Greek Slave, by Hiram Powers (1805–1873). An extremely popular sculpture at the London Exhibition of 1851 and the New York Crystal Palace of 1853.

umph of industrialism, one of the most popular exhibits was *The Greek Slave*, a statue by the American sculptor Hiram Powers. The statue depicted a young Christian woman stripped bare and standing, according to the catalogue, before the gaze of an "Eastern potentate." The woman represents the Greek struggle for liberty against Ottoman rule, a cause that had many British followers and was cast by many as a Christian and anti-Islamic crusade. It was characteristic of Victorian culture to have a beautiful, helpless, vulnerable woman represent the oppressed Greeks. It was equally characteristic for the statue to combine sexual sensationalism, moral indignation, and a political lesson.

In both England and France, some of the most tal-

ented painters of the time questioned many of the values the middle class revered. The French artist Honoré Daumier was a powerful satirist of social and political evils, ridiculing the corruption of petty officials, lawyers, and political leaders. Like Balzac's *Human Comedy* or Charles Dickens's fiction, Daumier's countless prints and paintings offer a panorama of the middle-class world with its ambitions, arrogance, and uncertainties. Daumier and his fellow Frenchman Gustave Courbet both broke new ground and shook contemporaries' sensibilities by putting working-class figures and scenes from everyday life at the center of their art. Most of Daumier's and Courbet's work had a harsh bite that proscribed sentimentalizing. Gustave Doré, a French graphic artist and journalist who worked for the Illustrated London News in the 1850s and 1860s, documented the tenements of East London—and Dickens's landscape of bleak alleys, workhouses, and dark courtyards—with care and accuracy in his sketches. These sketches unsettled the middle-class audience of his newspaper.

Artists and writers could criticize middle-class values without proposing radical reform. Though they opposed the materialism of the new elite, many also opposed the idea of complete democracy. Carlyle and Balzac, for instance, criticized the present by comparing it with a much idealized past. Moreover, most had to confront a common dilemma of early nineteenth-century thought: Did the social and economic hardships that industrialization brought in its train require a return to earlier times, to a society that was harsh and confining, though probably more secure? Could one imagine an industrial future without social dislocation and new forms of poverty?

For some time, a small band of thinkers had been trying to reimagine that future. They argued that there could be no return to old times and old ways, but that society could be at the same time both industrial and humane. These radical thinkers were often explicitly utopian. Two of the most persuasive were the Scot Robert Owen and the Frenchman Charles Fourier. Owen, himself the proprietor of a large cotton factory at New Lanark in Scotland, argued against the middle-class belief that the profit motive should be allowed to shape social and economic organization. Having reorganized his own mills to provide good housing and sanitation, good working conditions, child care, free schooling, and a system of social security for his workers, he proceeded to advocate a general reorganization of society on the basis of cooperation, with communities rewarding workers solely as a result of their actual labor. Fourier urged an even more far-reaching recon-

A Lawyer, by Honoré Daumier. Lawyers with their theatrical poses, dramatic robes, and displays of power, were among Daumier's favorite subjects, and he drew countless caricatures of the courtroom.

stitution, including the abolition of the wage system, the division of work according to people's natural inclinations, and the complete equality of the sexes. The numerous followers of Owen and Fourier, women as well as men, sought escape from the confusions of the contemporary world in idealist communities founded according to the principles of their leaders. That so many took utopian visions seriously is a measure of the deep uncertainties of the early nineteenth century, and the belief, held by many, that change seemed limitless.

Other radical thinkers proposed intensely practical reforms. The 1840s, which as we will see brought recurring economic depressions and new levels of misery, galvanized opposition to the new order across Europe. The French politician and journalist Louis Blanc took a stand, like many contemporary critics, against the competitiveness of the new industrial society, and particularly opposed the exploitation of the working class. His solution was to campaign for universal male suffrage, which would give working-class men control of the state. Following their triumph, these workers would make the state the "banker of the poor" and institute "associations of production"—actually a system of workshops governed by workers—that would guarantee jobs and security for all. Once these associations became established, private enterprise would wither through competition, and with it the

state, for which there would no longer be any need. These workshops would be established, fleetingly, in Paris during the Revolution of 1848.

Another Frenchman, Pierre-Joseph Proudhon (1809–1865), condemned the profits that accrued to employers at the expense of their workers. He, too, proposed new institutions: producers' cooperatives that would sell goods at a price fairer to the workers, working-class credit unions, and so on. Proudhon's "What is Property?" was one of many early nineteenth-century socialist writings, and quite widely read among artisans, laborers, and middle-class intellectuals, including Karl Marx (see Chapter 26).

One of the most influential critics of nineteenth-century society was the English philosopher and economist John Stuart Mill. Mill's father had worked closely with Bentham, and his son began his adult life a convinced Utilitarian. For many reasons, though, including a serious psychological crisis in his twenties, Mill gradually broke with both utilitarianism and classical economic theory. First, he rejected the universality of economic laws. Though he admitted that unchangeable laws governed production, he insisted that the distribution of wealth could be regulated by society for the benefit of the majority of its members. Second, he broke with the doctrine of laissez-faire. He favored legislation, under certain conditions, for shortening the working day, and he believed that the state might properly take steps toward redistributing wealth by taxing inheritances. In the fourth book of his *Principles of Political Economy* he urged the abolition of the wage system and looked forward to a society of producers' cooperatives in which the workers would own the factories and elect the managers to run them. Mill read and was deeply influenced by the socialists, although he distrusted the state. In 1859 he wrote what many consider the classic defense of individual freedom, *On Liberty*, in which he attacked what he called "the tyranny of the majority." Finally, Mill was also a fierce critic of Victorian conceptions of womanhood. With his lover and, later, wife, Harriet Taylor Mill, he co-authored essays on political rights, marriage, and divorce; their views and their affair scandalized his contemporaries. After her death, he published *The Subjection of Women* (1869), which was immediately translated into many languages and taken by many as the founding statement for late-nineteenth-century women's suffrage movements. The *Subjection* was as important as *On Liberty* In Mill's eyes the condition of women revealed a society's conceptions about authority, coercion, and individuality.

Conclusion

An acute awareness of change was a hallmark of the first half of the nineteenth century. Artists and writers—both the defenders and the opponents of the new industrial world—tried to capture the new drama of modern life. Social thinkers sought to understand the historical processes and social forces that had been set in motion by the French and industrial revolutions. Their ideas (and for artists, images) helped shape the identities of ordinary people: the duties and roles of men and women, for instance, or the new role of the middle class as guardian of the nation's future. Champions and critics of the new order alike spoke of a "class society," and new class identities were another key feature of the period. They were embodied in the growing and overcrowded working-class districts of the new cities, in the daily experiences of work, in new conceptions of "respectability," and in middle-class homes. Those new identities would be sharpened in the political events to which we now turn.

Selected Readings

Beecher, Jonathan. *Charles Fourier: The Visionary and His World.* Berkeley, 1986. A thorough examination of the reformer in the context of his times.

Bridenthal, Renate, Claudia Koonz, and Susan Stuard, eds. *Becoming Visible: Women in European History*, 2d ed. Boston, 1987. Excellent, wide-ranging introduction.

Briggs, Asa. *Victorian Cities.* New York, 1963. A survey of British cities, stressing middle-class attitudes toward the new urban environment.

Chevalier, Louis. *Laboring Classes and Dangerous Classes during the First Half of the Nineteenth Century.* New York, 1973. An important, though controversial account of crime, class, and middle-class perceptions of life in Paris.

Davidoff, Leonore, and Catherine Hall. *Family Fortunes: Men and Women of the English Middle Class, 1780–1850.* Chicago, 1985. A brilliant and detailed study of the lives and ambitions of several English families.

Gay, Peter. *The Bourgeois Experience: Victoria to Freud.* New York, 1984. A multivolume, path-breaking study of middle-class emotional life.

Halévy, Elie. *The Growth of Philosophic Radicalism*, rev. ed. London, 1949. The best introduction to the thought of Malthus, Ricardo, Bentham, and their philosophical heirs.

Hellerstein, Erna, Leslie Hume, and Karen Offen, eds. *Victorian Women: A Documentary Account.* Stanford, 1981. An essential source, with excellent introductory essays.

Hobsbawm, Eric. *Labouring Men: Studies in the History of Labour.* London, 1964. A series of essays on workers and the working class in England.

Hobsbawm, Eric, and George Rudé. *Captain Swing: A Social History of the Great English Agricultural Uprising of 1830.* New York, 1975. Analyzes the formation of a rural working-class consciousness.

Langer, William L. *Political and Social Upheaval, 1832–1852.* New York, 1969. Comprehensive survey, with excellent analytical chapters and thorough bibliographies.

McLaren, Angus. *Sexuality and Social Order: The Debate over the Fertility of Women and Workers in France, 1770–1920.* New York, 1983. Examines the relationship between private and public morality.

O'Gráda, Cormac. *Black '47 and Beyond: The Great Irish Famine.* Princeton, 1999.

———. *The Great Irish Famine.* Cambridge, 1989. A fascinating and recent assessment of scholarship on the famine.

Sabean, David Warren. *Property, Production, and Family Neckarhausen, 1700–1870.* New York, 1990. Brilliant and very detailed study of gender roles and family.

Shorter, Edward, and Charles Tilly. *Strikes in France, 1830–1968.* New York, 1974. A valuable study of early Continental class consciousness.

Smith, Bonnie G. *Changing Lives: Women in European History since 1700.* Lexington, Mass., 1989. Analysis of patterns in the domestic and working lives of women.

Thompson, E. P. *The Making of the English Working Class.* London, 1963. Argues that the coincidence of the French and Industrial Revolutions fostered the growth of working-class consciousness. A brilliant and important work.

Tilly, Louise A., and Joan W. Scott. *Women, Work and Family.* New York, 1978.

Walker, Mack. *German Home Towns: Community, State and General Estate, 1648–1871.* Ithaca, N.Y., 1971. Attempts to explain the absence of a strong middle class in Germany.

Valenze, Deborah. *The First Industrial Woman.* New York, 1995.

Zeldin, Theodore. *France, 1848–1945*, 2 vols. Oxford, 1973–1977.

CHAPTER
TWENTY-THREE

REVOLUTION AND
LIBERAL REFORM,
1815–1870

EIGHTEEN FORTY-EIGHT was a wild and eventful year. Revolution again shook Europe. Insurgents rushed to hastily built barricades in many cities, from Paris, Berlin, and Vienna to Rome. Kings and princes, eager to avoid the fate of Louis XVI of France, beat an equally hasty—although, as it turned out, temporary—retreat. Across the Atlantic, the treaty of Guadalupe Hidalgo ended the war between Mexico and the United States with a massive territorial transaction: for a sum of $15 million, the United States acquired half a million square miles of western territory, including California. The treaty nearly completed the United States' continental expansion, but it also ushered in conflicts that would lead to the American Civil War. July of 1848 brought the Seneca Falls Convention, which marked the emergence of an organized movement for woman suffrage in the United States, a movement paralleled in Europe. The New York *Herald* nervously announced that "To whatever part of the world the attention is directed, the political and social fabric is crumbling. . . . [T]he work of revolution is no longer confined to the Old World, nor to the masculine gender." It was in 1848, too, that miners struck gold in California, starting the gold rush, an event with trans-Atlantic resonance. When news of California gold reached Paris in the fall of 1848, after a summer of bitter social conflict, the socialist writer Karl Marx acidly remarked that "golden dreams were to supplant the socialist dreams of the Paris workers."

All of these events were important turning points. They can be understood with reference to three key themes of the mid-nineteenth century: revolution, liberalism, and nation building. The revolutions of 1848 marked the high point of the "age of revolution," and their failure signaled the end of that age. Liberalism meant different things to different people and groups, as we will see below. In general, liberalism promised constitutional rule, representative government, the abolition of hierarchy and privilege, and most broadly, the value of the individual. Historians use the term *nation building* to refer to the process of creating new states and reconstructing older ones. Nation building did entail territorial changes, but territory was often less

FOCUS QUESTIONS

• What was the basis of early nineteenth-century conservatism?

• What did liberalism mean during the nineteenth century?

• What were the key themes of Romanticism?

• Who opposed the Restoration?

• Why was there no revolution in Great Britain during the 1830s?

• What issues were included in the "social question"?

• What was the impact of liberalism in France and Great Britain after 1850?

THE REVOLUTIONS OF 1848

Note the location of the major revolutionary outbreaks in 1848. How had the center of gravity for such activity shifted since the 1830s, and why? What new social and economic doctrines helped give voice to and encourage the agitation of the new working industrial classes for better living conditions? What role did the foreign regimes play in exacerbating tensions in Ireland and certain parts of eastern Europe? Why was there a revolution in Paris in 1848, but not in England, where many similar circumstances prevailed?

important than political reform, new state structures, and the emergence, among the common people, of new identities and allegiances. Scores of new nations emerged during the nineteenth century in South America, the Balkans, and continental Europe. Yet older countries, such as France and Britain, were also rebuilt: legal reforms, broader voting rights, larger bureaucra-

cies, and economic expansion transformed how states worked and their relations with their citizens. The United States was similarly reconstructed during the 1860s and 1870s, through a combination of continental expansion, civil war, and economic growth.

Why did these changes happen? The Industrial Revolution, and the social changes it brought, which we surveyed in the last chapter, provide part of the answer. But politics, ideas, and events mattered as well. We begin by returning to the aftermath of the Napoleonic wars and examining the history of the conservative order that was restored at that time. We then look at the challenges to the conservative order. This chapter is principally concerned with liberalism and revolution, and with Britain and France. The next chapter looks more closely at nationalism, nation building, and revolution, especially in central Europe.

CONSERVATIVE REACTION, 1815–1830

What was the basis of early nineteenth-century conservatism?

At the end of the Napoleonic wars, the victorious European powers met at the Congress of Vienna in 1814 to draw up a peace settlement. They sought an agreement that would satisfy their territorial ambitions and guarantee international tranquillity. As the conservative allies saw it, revolution had produced war. International peace, therefore, had to rest on blocking revolution, on avoiding the kind of political turmoil they had experienced in the aftermath of 1789. They achieved only a partial victory. In many cases, their repressive policies only made the heirs to the French revolution more determined to succeed.

Repressive conservative policies only made the heirs to the French revolution more determined to succeed.

The Congress of Vienna was attended by an array of dignitaries from nearly all the principal nations of Europe. It became a long affair, for it produced two peace treaties, one in 1814 and another in 1815, after Napoleon's hundred days and his final defeat at Waterloo. In the interim there was much conservative celebration of the defeat of the upstart revolutionary emperor: expensive banquets with elaborate aristocratic etiquette, where relieved members of European royalty jockeyed for positions at table. The principal players at the Congress, though, were the major powers, with Tsar Alexander I (1801–1825) and the Austrian diplomat Klemens von Metternich (1773–1859) in dominant roles, and the French Prince Charles Maurice de Talleyrand (1754–1838) in a surprisingly strong position

in the supporting cast. Napoleon's defeat left Russia as the most powerful Continental state. Alexander had been reared at the court of Catherine the Great, where he took in both Enlightenment doctrines from his French tutor and notions of absolutist authority from his autocratic father, Tsar Paul. In 1801 he succeeded his murdered father and during the Napoleonic wars he presented himself as the "liberator" of Europe. Many feared that he would substitute an all-powerful Russia for an all-powerful France. Talleyrand, the French representative, had been a bishop and a revolutionary, had survived the Terror by going into exile in the United States, and had returned to serve as Napoleon's foreign minister before turning on the emperor and becoming foreign minister to the restored Louis XVIII. That he was present at Vienna testified to his diplomatic skill— or opportunism.

The commanding figure at the Congress, the architect of the peace, was the Austrian foreign minister. Klemens von Metternich was the son of an Austrian diplomat and had grown up in the unstable patchwork of the small German states. As a student at the University of Strasbourg the young Metternich witnessed popular violence connected with the outbreak of the French Revolution, and to this he attributed his lifelong hatred of political innovation. He had tried to upset the 1807 alliance between Napoleon and Tsar Alexander in the interest of Austria, and had played some part in arranging the marriage of Napoleon to the Austrian archduchess Marie Louise. Metternich once declared himself an admirer of spiders, "always busy arranging their houses with the greatest of neatness in the world." At the Congress of Vienna, he attempted at every turn to arrange international affairs with equal neatness, to suit his own diplomatic designs. His central concerns, nearly obsessions, were checking Russian expansionism and preventing political and social change. He feared that the baffling Tsar Alexander would inspire revolution for the sake of establishing Russian supremacy in Europe. For this reason he favored moderate terms for France in its hour of defeat. Indeed, at one point he was ready to sponsor the restoration of Napoleon as emperor of the French under the protection and supervision of the Habsburg monarchy. Metternich was an archconservative who readily resorted to harsh repressive tactics, including secret police and spying. Yet he helped craft a peace that prevented a major European war until 1914.

The idea that guided the work of the Congress of Vienna was the principle of legitimacy. The idea had broad appeal as a general antirevolutionary policy. Reestablishing "legitimacy" across Europe meant restoring the dynasties that had reigned in prerevolutionary days and establishing for each country essentially the same territories it had held in 1789. The Congress recognized Louis XVIII as the "legitimate" sovereign of France; it also confirmed the restoration of Bourbon rulers in Spain and the two Sicilies. The other monarchs of Europe had no interest in undermining the newly restored French king: he was their bulwark against revolution. But when the French people seemed to welcome Napoleon back from exile in 1815, the allies became sterner; France was compelled to pay an indemnity of 700 million francs and support an allied army of occupation for five years. Its boundaries were to remain essentially the same as in 1789, a retreat from the greater France of the revolutionary years, but not so punitive as it might have been.

The peace also sought to ensure that the French would not again overrun their boundaries, and erected a strong barrier to contain them. Here the guiding principle was the balance of power, according to which no country should be powerful enough to destabilize international relations. The Dutch Republic, conquered by the French in 1795, was restored as the kingdom of the Netherlands. Its territory now expanded into Belgium, formerly the Austrian Netherlands. This now substantial power would discourage any future French expansion. For the same reason, the allies ceded the German left bank of the Rhine to Prussia. Austria expanded its empire in northern Italy, regaining the territories lost under Napoleon.

The peace of 1815 had particularly important consequences for Germany and Poland. Napoleon had reorganized the German states into the Confederation of the Rhine; the great powers at Vienna reduced the number of German states and principalities from over three hundred to thirty-nine, and linked them with Prussia into a loose German Confederation under the honorary presidency of Austria. Although the Confederation would later become the basis for German unification, such was not the intent of the peacemakers. Fear of an aggressive Russia led the other European nations to support the maintenance of the Confederation and the independent kingdoms of Bavaria, Wurttemburg, and Saxony. Poland, which had been partitioned into extinction by Russia, Austria, and Prussia in the 1790s, became a bone of contention. Tsar Alexander demanded that Poland be restored as a kingdom with himself as its constitutional monarch. Prussia was prepared to agree with this scheme, provided that it was allowed to swallow up Saxony. In this case, the principle of legitimacy took a backseat to the great powers' territorial ambitions. Metternich, worried by the threat to equilibrium from Russia and Prussia, brokered a peaceful solution. The wily Austrian allied himself with Talleyrand and Lord Castlereagh (the British foreign secretary), both of whom secretly agreed to go to war against Russia and Prussia, if necessary, to block the Polish-Saxon deal. The parties eventually compromised. They created a nominally independent kingdom of Poland but gave Tsar Alexander control over it. Sections of Poland also went to Prussia and Austria. Prussia took a part of Saxony. Like the other victorious powers, Britain demanded compensation for long years at war and received territories that had been under French dominion in South Africa and South America, as well as the island of Ceylon. Success in European warfare expanded Britain's commercial empire and helped to compensate for the loss of the North American colonies.

The Congress of Vienna also called for a "Concert of Europe" to secure the peace and create permanent stability. Britain, Austria, Prussia, and Russia formed the Quadruple Alliance, which became the Quintuple Alliance when France was admitted in 1818. Its members pledged to meet regularly and to cooperate in the suppression of any disturbances—either attempts to overthrow legitimate governments or to change international boundaries. At the same time, Tsar Alexander I persuaded the allies to join him in the declaration of a "Holy Alliance" dedicated to the precepts of justice, Christian charity, and peace. The only result of this second league was to sow concern among Europe's leaders about Alexander's intentions. Moreover, many of the nobles gathered at Vienna were steeped in the values of the Enlightenment and agreed with the British foreign minister that the Holy Alliance was "a piece of sublime mysticism and nonsense." Though they were conservatives and legitimists, they were wary of crusading.

What, then, was the basis of early nineteenth-century conservatism? Restoring conservative power took different forms in individual countries, but there were common themes. Edmund Burke's *Reflections on the Revolution in France* (see page 699) became more influential in this new context than they had been in the 1790s. Burke's warnings that social order had to be anchored in custom, tradition, and hierarchy were echoed by other conservatives such as Joseph de Maistre and Louis-

THE CONGRESS OF VIENNA

Note how the borders of European nations were established after the final defeat of Napoleon. How did the diplomats at the Congress attempt to reestablish the status quo insofar as that was possible? How had Napoleon's conquests irrevocably changed the political geography of Europe, and in what case did the delegates at Vienna build on some of Napoleon's ideas for organizing his own empire? Was the settlement reached at Vienna a success? What were the major social and political concerns of the diplomats, and how did they try to address them?

Gabriel-Ambroise Bonald. It was naïve, conservatives argued, to imagine that change could be decreed or that it could follow from the precepts of reason. To advocate rapid, let alone revolutionary, change not only ignored the importance of the past, it endangered social harmony and international peace. For conservatives in general and the diplomats at Vienna in particular, lib-

erty, equality, and nationality would subvert the European order they had at last reestablished. King Leopold of the Belgians, who was granted the throne by the allies, observed that war now threatened to become "a conflict of principles"—a conflict sparked by revolutionary ideas, and that set peoples against emperors. "From what I know of Europe," he continued, "such a conflict would change her form and overthrow her whole structure." Metternich and many of his fellow diplomats at Vienna dedicated the rest of their lives to seeing that such a conflict would never take place.

LIBERALISM

What did liberalism mean during the nineteenth century?

"Seen as a whole from a distance, our history from 1789 to 1830 appears to be forty-one years of deadly struggle between the Old Regime with its traditions, memories, hopes, and men [that is, the aristocrats] and the new France led by the middle class." So wrote Alexis de Tocqueville, a prominent liberal opponent of the restoration in France. Many of those who set their course against the restored Old Regime across Europe could be ranged under the broad banner of liberalism. Liberals considered themselves heirs to key principles of the revolution and standard bearers of change. For them, the conservative order represented a futile effort to turn back the clock.

Liberals considered themselves heirs to key principles of the revolution and standard bearers of change.

Liberalism is a broad term. Its nineteenth-century meaning differed sharply from our contemporary usage. Nineteenth-century liberalism had three basic components. First, in politics, liberalism promised an end to traditional privileges and the restrictive power of rank and hereditary authority. Liberals called for constitutional as opposed to hereditary monarchy; and they advocated direct representation in government—at least for those who had the property and public standing to be trusted with the responsibilities of power. Second, in economics, liberalism sought efficient government: a state that would end sectionalism, and respect and promote commercial enterprise. Liberals generally considered free trade a social as well as economic value. Third, and at the most basic level, liberals believed in individualism, in the value of well-intentioned members of society and the contributions they could make to its order and prosperity.

This framework accommodated many different views. Some liberal leaders believed in the doctrines of the classical economists and championed limited, constitutional government and unrestricted free trade above anything else. Other members of the middle classes and artisans cared more deeply about genuine democracy, calling for universal male suffrage and at least some new freedoms for women as well. Liberalism expanded, thrived, and was often thwarted by the tensions it contained. In the wake of the French Revolution, liberals were torn between desires for liberty and reform on the one hand and fear of anarchy on the other. They often parted company on economic policy, disagreeing about the government's role in sponsoring the development of industry and banking, the merits of free trade, and so on. Liberals were torn between commitments to a government of laws (and the belief that humans needed to be taught responsibility through such laws), and much more radical notions of human freedom.

The English writer John Stuart Mill, for instance, discussed in the last chapter, was the most passionate and influential defender of personal liberty. For him, liberalism meant freedom of thought, religion, and expression, and the emancipation of women (and men) from restrictive family laws and narrow notions of gender roles. Yet Mill also thought that liberalism's commitment to laissez faire conflicted with his commitment to social and economic equality, and he found himself drawn to socialism. Alexis de Tocqueville was another liberal of his time. Born into the aristocracy, he was skeptical about the merits of the middle class and at the same time deeply committed to preserving political liberties at a time of conservative reaction. At the time, the new United States fascinated liberal political thinkers. Tocqueville traveled to the United States in 1831–1832, studying government, social life, prison systems, and slavery, trying to capture what was promising and what dangerous in the American model. *Democracy in America* (1835–1840) made his reputation as a political scientist; he refurbished his noble family's chateau with the profits. *The Old Regime and the Revolution*, Tocqueville's other great work, was one of the era's first efforts to look back with some critical distance at the French revolution of 1789. Tocqueville was impressed by the tenacity of the revolutionary ideal in France. But he also showed that that the revolutionaries had not entirely broken with the past. He was one of the first to draw attention to continuities between the centralization of state power under the Bourbons and consolidation of power in the revolutionary government. The German Romantic poet

Heinrich Heine (1797–1856) was another representative of early nineteenth-century liberalism. Young, rebellious, and alienated, Heine felt stifled by the conservative spirit of postrevolutionary Europe. He charged that the Restoration promoted only "stagnation, lethargy, and yawning." He studied German philosophy and literature. He wrote political poetry. And like many Germans and Russians who faced censorship at home, he went into exile in Paris, which he considered the epicenter of contemporary history.

ROMANTICISM

What were the key themes of Romanticism?

In the early nineteenth century, liberalism was often infused with Romanticism. Romanticism was a broad and diverse intellectual movement that touched literature, painting, music—indeed all the arts. Put most simply, it marked a reaction against the Classicism of the eighteenth century and against many of the values of the Enlightenment. Eighteenth-century Classical art had aspired to reason, discipline, and harmony. Romanticism, in contrast, stressed emotion, freedom, and imagination. Romantic artists prized the individual, individuality, and subjective experience; many were personally rebellious and sought out intense experiences. In contrast to Enlightenment thinkers, they considered intuition, emotion and feelings better guides to truth—and to human happiness—than reason and logic.

Romanticism varied dramatically from one country to another. It came earliest in Germany and England, where it was fueled in part by reactions against the "French" Enlightenment; it came later to France. Romanticism had many dimensions and Romantic artists championed contradictory causes. For this reason some historians have refused to call Romanticism a movement, preferring "mood," "world view," or "cultural style." *Cultural style* may be the best term, for it captures the ways in which Romanticism mattered in the lives of men and women who were not actually artists themselves. As a cultural style, Romanticism also cut across political lines, providing images and ideas for both conservatives and liberals.

Like any intellectual or artistic movement, Romanticism did not completely break with its predecessors. Indeed, the early Romantics developed themes raised by dissenting figures of the Enlightenment, especially Jean-Jacques Rousseau (see Chapter 19). Rousseau's key themes—nature, simplicity, and feeling—ran through the very influential *Lyrical Ballads* (1798) of William Wordsworth (1770–1850) and Samuel Taylor Coleridge (1772–1834). Wordsworth considered emotions, or soul, the core of humanity; for him, poetry was "the spontaneous overflow of powerful feelings." Like Rousseau, Wordsworth also emphasized the ties of compassion and feeling that bind all of humankind, regardless of social class. "We have all of us one human heart," he wrote; "men who do not wear fine clothes can feel deeply." Like Rousseau, Wordsworth considered nature to be humanity's most trustworthy teacher, and he considered the experience of nature the source of true feeling. Poetic insights could be inspired by landscapes and the memories those evoked—in Wordsworth's case the wild hills and tumbledown cottages of England's Lake District. At the head of his poem "The Ruined Cottage," Wordsworth quoted from the Scottish romantic poet Robert Burns:

> Give me a spark of Nature's fire,
> 'Tis the best learning I desire…
> My muse, though homely in attire,
> May touch the heart.

The Lake Poets, as Wordsworth and Coleridge were sometimes called, offered one key theme of nineteenth-century Romanticism: a view of nature that rejected the abstract mechanism of eighteenth-century thought, and the belief that feeling and experience should be the starting point for art.

Like Wordsworth, William Blake (1757–1827), another early English Romantic poet, championed the individual imagination and poetic vision, and saw both as transcending the limits of the material world. Blake was a fierce and brilliant critic of industrial society and its corruptions, of the factories (which he called the "dark satanic mills") that blighted the English landscape, and of the values of a market culture in which everything was for sale. Imagination for Blake was not only poetic; its role was to awaken human sensibilities and to sustain belief in different values, breaking humanity's "mind-forged manacles," or constraints of the contemporary world. Like many Romantics Blake looked back to a past in which he thought society had been more organic, united, and humane.

With the next generation of English romantic poets—George Gordon, Lord Byron (1788–1824), Percy Bysshe Shelley (1792–1822), and John Keats (1795–1821)—

English Romanticism reached its height. In some cases, these poets' lives and loves appealed as much as their writing; their adventures seemed to personify their poetic themes. Lord Byron was not a man of the people, but an aristocrat, rich, handsome and defiant. His affairs with countless women earned him the reputation of a libertine, or a Romantic rebel against conformity and inhibition. Byron was known for his emphasis on creativity, imagination, and spontaneity. Poetry, he wrote, was the "lava of the imagination, whose eruption prevents an earthquake." His emotional extravagence was not a sign of a carefree personality; if he were alive today, he would probably be diagnosed as bipolar. He entered into an unhappy marriage with an unhappy woman, treated her brutally, and drove her away within a year. His poetic language occasionally gives glimpses of his painful inner turmoil. Byron's Romanticism went hand in hand with liberal politics: his works express a defense of liberty and a bitter disappointment with the corruptions and limitations of the world. He denounced the British government's frequent recourse to the death penalty, defended working-class protest movements, and finally sailed off to fight in the Greek movement for independence from the Ottoman Turks. When he died in Greece (of tuberculosis, not in battle) he seemed to epitomize the liberal Romantic hero.

Byron's friend Percy Shelley was also a poet and a radical. Shelley fell in love with the sixteen-year-old Mary Godwin, daughter of the British philosopher William Godwin and the feminist Mary Wollstonecraft (see Chapter 19). At the age of nineteen, Mary Shelley wrote *Frankenstein*, in some respects one of the most important Romantic novels. The novel centers on the arrogance of Enlightenment science and rationalism. Through the character of the monster, an artificially made creature who develops human feelings, Mary Shelley expressed typically Romantic concerns about emotion, human nature, and inspiration. Mary Shelley had more than her share of tragedy: only one of her four children survived, and her husband Percy drowned at the age of twenty-nine.

Romanticism stressed the power of emotion and feeling over reason. Another key theme was that every individual's experiences are unique and subjective. The mind was not a "blank tablet" on which one's sense imprinted knowledge (which was John Locke's image, and central to most Enlightenment philosophy). Instead Romantics reguarded imagination and creativity as paramount. The Romantic belief in individual creativity led in several directions. It could become a cult of artistic genius—of the "inexplicably and uniquely

creative individual," able to see things that others could not. The search for experiences that would elicit intense emotions and creative leaps of imagination encouraged a kind of living on the edge, which could entail everything from traveling to "exotic" lands to using opium. The romantic style encouraged the daring to defy conventionality, as did Lord Byron, the Shelleys, or the French women writers Germaine de Staël and George Sand (Amandine Aurore Lucile Dupin, 1804–1876). George Sand, like Lord Byron, cultivated a persona. In her case this meant earning a living as a woman writer, taking lovers as she liked, and wearing men's clothing—all in rebellion against middle-class moral codes. Other women played a prominent role in Romantic letters. Madame de Staël (1766–1817), who emigrated from France to Germany during the revolutionary period, played a key role in popularizing German romanticism in France in her *De l'Allemagne* ("Germany," 1810) and wrote many books of history.

More important, Romanticism also stimulated new thinking about men's and women's roles. In the eighteenth and nineteenth centuries it was common to assert that men were rational and women emotional, or intuitive. Romanticism, though, valued the emotional and intuitive as creative. The language of Romanticism, for instance, helped Madame de Staël describe herself as a "genius." It also suggested that men could be emotional, and that men and women shared a common human nature. In addition, by emphasizing the search for individuality, and valuing emotion and the soul as well as sensuality, the romantics forged new ways of writing—and indeed thinking—about love.

Romanticism had many conservative elements, including, for some, a return to Christianity. Writers' interest in religious feeling paralleled a more widespread revival of religion in the period after Napoleon. Many conservative Romantics also looked back with some nostalgia to medieval times. German Romanticism was often very conservative, opposed not only to French cultural style, but to what could be cast as "French" liberalism. The fiercely liberal Heinrich Heine, however, was critical of his conservative Romantic contemporaries. Much of the Romantic writing in Germany involved theories of historical development, and the distinctive individual development of nations. Romantic history will be discussed later, in conjunction with nationalism.

These were some of the components of Romanticism. As an intellectual movement, it was diverse and contradictory. It proposed a dramatically new way of looking at the world. As a cultural style, it could be picked up and reinterpreted by middle-class men and women caught up in the movement for change. Not only was the lyricism of Romantics' writing appealing, the experiences they evoked were accessible. A middle-class man or woman (a governess, teacher, or pastor) did not need either money or literary talent to walk in the countryside and to be both moved and reassured by the permanent beauty of nature. Appreciating nature's beauty did not require creating the expensive, formal, and elaborately cultivated gardens of the French aristocracy; on the contrary, nature's inspiration came out best in the wild. It was in the simple countryside that "the passions of men are incorporated with the beautiful and permanent forms of Nature." The emphasis on imagination, intense experience, radical individuality could be expressed in dress, in the frequent and ritualized duels so popular in the 1810s and 1820s among young men at universities, in the language middle-class men and women used writing letters to their friends, or in the new ways that men and women talked about falling in love.

ROMANTIC ART, LITERATURE, AND MUSIC

Painters of the early nineteenth century carried the Romantic interest in subjectivity and imagination onto their canvases. The movement is far too wide ranging to classify, but in Great Britain, romantic painting was best represented by John Constable (1776–1837) and J. M. W. Turner (1775–1851); in France by Théodore Géricault (1791–1824) and Eugène Delacroix (1799–1863). Both British painters tried to develop more

Weymouth Bay, by John Constable.

Stormy Sea Breaking on a Shore, by J. M. W. Turner.

emotional and poetic approaches to nature. "It is the soul that sees," wrote Constable, echoing Wordsworth. Constable pored over Isaac Newton's prisms, studying the properties of light, but with an eye to capturing the "poetry" of a rainbow. His landscapes emphasized the artist's way of seeing, and the artist's technique. One contemporary remarked, "It is evident that Mr. Constable's landscapes are like nature: it is still more evident that they are like paint." Turner's intensely subjective, personal, and imaginative paintings were even more unconventional and defiant. Turner experimented with technique and color to produce surprisingly abstract paintings, which were frequently assailed by critics. "I did not paint it to be understood," he retorted on one occasion. Turner's paintings are among the most remarkable of his time. His concerns—imagination, ways of seeing, the creativity of the artist and the force of nature—were those of his contemporaries. Yet his technique took Romantic painting to a new level. Although the French Romantic artist Eugène Delacroix's paintings look very different,

his ideas about subjectivity and the creative process (which he set out in detailed diaries) were much the same. The poet Charles Baudelaire, one the last representatives of French Romanticism, believed that Delacroix had shown him that "The whole visible universe is but a store-house of images and signs. . . . All the faculties of the human soul must be subordinated to the imagination . . ." In sum, Romanticism opened new ways of seeing.

What of the politics of Romanticism? In France, Romantic artists tended to focus on historical and political subjects, and Romanticism was most explicitly caught up with liberalism. For Victor Hugo (1802–1885), the Romantic movement of his time was a call to liberty. "Romanticism, so often ill-defined, is only . . . liberalism in literature. Liberty in Art, liberty in Society, behold the double banner that rallies the intelligence. . . . The Ultras [conservative royalists] of all sorts, classical and monarchical, will in vain help each other to restore the old system, broken to pieces, literary and social . . . every stride of liberty will have caused their scaffolding to give way." Hugo wrote poetry, plays, and immensely influential historical novels that focused sympathetically on the experience of the common people: *Nôtre Dame de Paris* (1831) and *Les Misérables* (1862) among others. Géricault's *Raft of the Medusa*, which portrays the aftermath of a shipwreck, and Delacroix's *Liberty Leading the People* (see page 791), also represent the liberal and political aspects of Romanticism.

Many artists of the period are hard to classify. Johann Wolfgang von Goethe (1749–1852) was enormously influential for the Romantic movement and for German writers trying to cast off the French style and develop their own language and voice. His early novel *The Sorrows of Young Werther* (1774), a Rousseau-like story of a young man's yearnings and restless love, captured readers all over Europe. Yet Goethe backed away from what he came to consider the excessiveness of Romanticism: its cult of feeling over restraint and order, which Goethe considered self-indulgent and "morbid." In 1790 Goethe published the first part of his masterpiece *Faust*, a drama in verse, which he finished one year before he died in 1832. The play retold the German legend of the man who sold his soul to the devil in return for eternal youth and universal knowledge. It was more classical in its tone than other works of the Romantic era, though it still reflected a Romantic concern with spiritual freedom and humanity's daring.

The composer Ludwig van Beethoven (1770–1827) is equally difficult to classify. Beethoven is often called a Romantic. The glorification of nature and Romantic individuality ring clearly through his work, and his insistence that instrumental music (without vocal accompaniment) could become more poetic and expressive of emotion made him the key figure for later Romantic composers. "Music is a more sublime revelation than all wisdom and all philosophy," he wrote, "[and] it is the wine that inspires and leads to fresh creations. . . ." His musical achievements did indeed help raise the standing of music as an art form, placing it at the center of the Roman-

tic movement. Yet he considered himself a Classicist and was steeped in the principles of the eighteenth century. Beethoven's political views also changed over the course of his lifetime. Like many of his contemporaries he was caught up in a burst of enthusiasm for the French Revolution. His disillusionment with the revolution began, however, when Napoleon, whom he had admired as a revolutionary, crowned himself emperor and repudiated his principles, and it continued through the Napoleonic wars. What was more, by the age of thirty-two, Beethoven knew that he was losing his hearing. He hoped the problem could be cured, but it slowly put an end to his career as a virtuoso pianist, and by 1819 he was completely deaf. As his condition worsened and his disenchantment grew, Beethoven further withdrew into composing.

Beethoven and Goethe were central transitional figures between the eighteenth and nineteenth centuries. They also illustrate the elusiveness of a simple definition of Romanticism. The Romantic movement was composed of many different currents that sometimes cut across each other: a critique of eighteenth-century classicism, a quasi-mystical view of nature, a return to history, a cult of individual heroism, defiance, and creativity, and the search for a new way of seeing. At its common core lay an insistence that the arts needed to find a new way of expressing emotion and feeling, a search that sent nineteenth-century art in a new direction.

Raft of the Medusa, by Théodore Géricault. The painting itself became a political issue because the ill-fated ship was commanded by an incompetent loyalist to the Bourbon regime who owed his commission to political favoritism.

CHALLENGES TO THE CONSERVATIVE ORDER IN SOUTHERN AND EASTERN EUROPE

Who opposed the Restoration?

With this background in mind, we can return to the course of events in the early nineteenth century, in the immediate aftermath of the Napoleonic wars. Liberals who opposed the restoration had few resources. Much of the opposition was driven underground by the legions of watchful police. In Italy, for instance, secret

Napoleon for the People. During the nineteenth century, hand-colored prints of Napoleon became increasingly popular. Book peddlers carried images such as this one through the French countryside, selling them to villagers and peasants.

brotherhoods that called themselves Carbonari met in hiding, establishing obscure rituals of recognition and taking vows to oppose the conservative allies of Vienna and their goals. In some ways, they followed the eighteenth-century model of the Masonic lodges. The name *carbonari* referred to the charcoal with which they blackened their faces at secret meetings. Their influence spread throughout Europe in the early 1820s, especially southern Europe and France. The Carbonari's political views were murky: they called for constitutions, political representation, and other liberal reforms. Some sang the praises of Bonaparte. During the 1820s and 1830s, the exiled emperor became a popular folk hero. Veterans of the Napoleonic wars played a central role in maintaining and reinterpreting what came to be called the Napoleonic legend. Military officers provided much of the membership for the Carbonari and other clandestine opponents of restoration Europe. Only a minority of those who opposed the restoration were Bonapartists, but the emperor's name was one reminder of the revolutionary legacy.

During the 1820s clandestine liberal groups with considerable popular support spearheaded revolts in Naples and Spain. In both cases, they succeeded in forcing conservative kings to establish representative government and constitutions modeled on the liberal French constitution of 1791. Spain's king, the restored Bourbon Ferdinand VII, faced several liberal uprisings at home. Worse, he had to contend with a series of revolutions in the Spanish colonies of South America from around 1810 to 1825. In Italy, similar revolts broke out in the south, in Naples and in Piedmont, a northern province governed by Austria.

The conservative powers of Europe quickly asserted their interest in these domestic skirmishes. They convened two congresses, in 1820 and 1882, to deal with the threat to international stability. In the Troppau memorandum, signed in Austria in 1820, Austria, Prussia, and Russia pledged to aid each other in suppressing revolution. France and Britain declined to sign, not because they opposed repression but because they did not want their actions hampered by commitments to detailed treaties. Metternich felt he had diplomatic permission to repress the Carbonari in northern Italy, forcing them into prison or exile.

The French took on the Spanish problem, sending two hundred thousand troops to the Iberian peninsula in 1823. This force suppressed the Spanish liberals and restored Ferdinand's authority. Ferdinand tortured and publicly executed hundreds of rebels. Despite their victory in mainland Spain, the defenders of the status quo

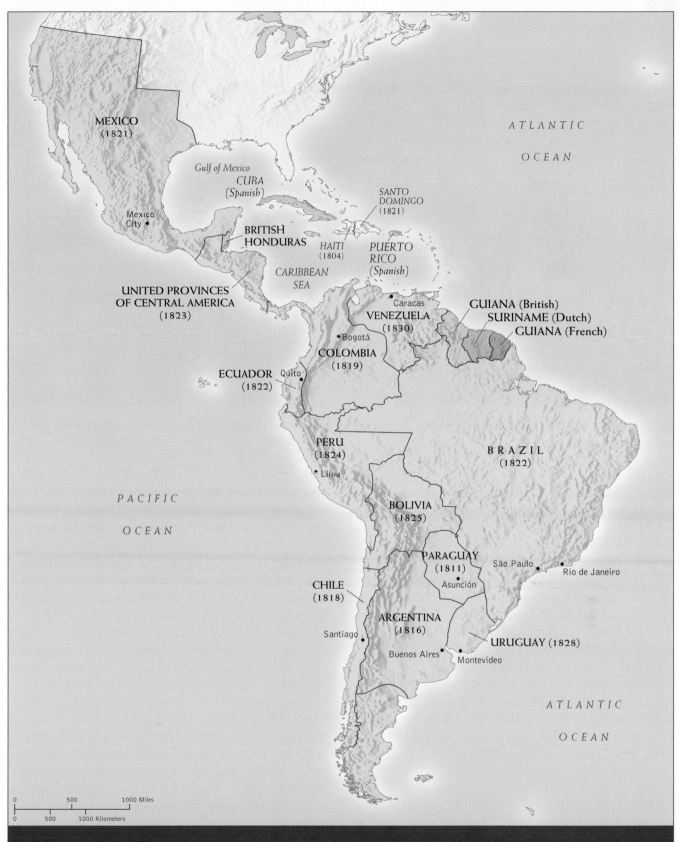

MEXICO
(1821)

ATLANTIC

OCEAN

Gulf of Mexico

CUBA
(Spanish)

Mexico
City •

SANTO
DOMINGO
(1821)

BRITISH
HONDURAS

HAITI
(1804)

PUERTO
RICO
(Spanish)

UNITED PROVINCES
OF CENTRAL AMERICA
(1823)

CARIBBEAN
SEA

• Caracas

GUIANA (British)
SURINAME (Dutch)
GUIANA (French)

VENEZUELA
(1830)

• Bogotá

COLOMBIA
(1819)

ECUADOR
(1822)

Quito •

PERU
(1824)

• Lima

B R A Z I L
(1822)

BOLIVIA
(1825)

PACIFIC

OCEAN

PARAGUAY
(1811)

• São Paulo

• Rio de Janeiro

Asunción •

CHILE
(1818)

ARGENTINA
(1816)

Santiago •

URUGUAY (1828)

Buenos Aires •

Montevideo •

ATLANTIC

OCEAN

| 0 | 500 | 1000 Miles |
| 0 | 500 | 1000 Kilometers |

NEW NATIONS OF LATIN AMERICA

Many regions of Latin America rose in revolt in the first decades of the nineteenth century. After Haiti became the western hemisphere's second independent nation, many areas of South America also broke away from colonial rule. Whereas the Americans had revolted against a vibrant and powerful empire, however, many of the Latin American revolutionaries took advantage of the disorder created by the Napoleonic wars and their aftermath. How had Napoleon's grab for the Spanish and Portuguese crowns facilitated the independence movement in South America?

Russian Revolt of 1825. This contemporary watercolor shows the formidable opposition the Decembrists faced in the disciplined troops of the government.

did not succeed in stemming liberal independence movements in the colonies of Central and South America. Efforts to prop up Spain's empire ran up against two forces: the newly ambitious United States and Britain. In 1823 President James Monroe of the United States issued the Monroe Doctrine, warning Europe's great powers that any efforts to intervene in the affairs of the New World would be regarded as an unfriendly act. Without British naval support, however, the Americans' doctrine would have remained a dead letter. Britain was ready to recognize the independence of the South American republics, since as new countries they preferred to trade with Britain rather than Spain. The British used their navy to keep Spain from intervening to protect its vanishing empire and reaped the benefits of increased trade from their threat of force.

RUSSIA

Liberal ideas also provoked hope and disruption in Russia. In 1825, Tsar Alexander died, and uncertainty about his heir sparked an uprising among a group of army officers. Many of the Decembrists, as they were called, came from noble families and were members of elite regiments. Many of them had served in the tsarist armies that drove Napoleon back to France and had

been posted there during the years while the peace was being settled. Young and idealistic, they took seriously Tsar Alexander's claim that Russia was the "liberator" of Europe. If Russia was to assume that kind of "moral greatness," though, it needed to reform. Serfdom contradicted the promise of liberation, and so did the autocratic tsar's monopoly on political power. Not only were Russian peasants enslaved; Russian nobles were "slaves to the tsar." The Decembrists had no single political program. They ranged from constitutional monarchists to Jacobin republicans. The rebels hoped to persuade Alexander's liberal-minded brother, Constantine, to assume the throne and guarantee a constitution. The attempt failed. Constantine was unwilling to usurp power from the rightful heir, a third brother, Nicholas. The officers themselves failed to attract support from the rank-and-file peasant soldiers, and without such support were doomed to fail. This does not mean that repression was easy. The new tsar, Nicholas I (1825–1855), ruthlessly interrogated hundreds of mutinous soldiers, sentencing many to hard labor and exile. The five leaders, sentenced to death, were more troublesome. Young members of the elite, they were "the cream of the cream," and attractive candidates for martyrdom. The tsar ordered them hanged at dawn inside the walls of the Peter and Paul fortress in St. Petersburg and buried in secret graves, so that neither their funerals nor their gravesites could provide occasions for unrest.

Nicholas went on to rule in the ways of his predecessor. Among his most autocratic acts was the creation of the Third Section, a political police force, to prevent further domestic disorder. Like the secret police of so many conservative powers, it was overstretched and undermanned, but its very existence contributed to a culture of fear and suspicion. Nicholas became perhaps Europe's most uncompromising conservative, but nevertheless, Russia showed signs of change. Bureaucracy became less dependent on the aristocracy, and grew more centralized and more efficient. Laws were systematically codified in 1832. European demand for Russian grain encouraged the owners of great estates to reorganize for more effective production, and railways were built to transport the grain to Western markets. Other opponents of the regime, like Alexander Herzen, who admired the Decembrists, would carry on the Decembrists' unresolved political legacy.

GREECE

Of all the liberal struggles in the 1820s, none captured the imagination of Romantics and liberals more than the Greek war of independence (1821–1827). The rebellion pitted different groups of Greeks against the Turkish Ottomans who ruled over the area. Many Europeans found it easy to recast this battle as another chapter in an ongoing struggle between Christianity and Islam. For nonreligious European liberals, the Greeks' battle was a vicarious crusade for liberty and a struggle to preserve the ancient classical heritage of the land, now appropriated as the birthplace of the West. "We are all Greeks," wrote Percy Shelley, the Romantic poet. "Our laws, our literature, our religion, our arts have their roots in Greece. But for Greece . . . we might still have been savages and idolators." Celebrating the Greeks went hand in hand with demonizing the Turks and reviving the theme of Turkish despotism, which had figured prominently in the Enlightenment. A British official remarked, "Almost the whole extent of European Turkey presents a dreadful picture of anarchy, rebellion, and barbarism."

The first Greek uprising of 1821 was led by Alexander Ypsilantis. He was a former officer in the Russian army who enjoyed close relations with Tsar Alexander, but the tsar refused to intervene. A second rising, however, drew British support and volunteers such as Lord Byron from different European countries. Philhellenic (devoted to classical Greece) committees in cities across Europe raised money and sent volunteers; men and women in Paris wore blue and white ribbons to show they had given to the Greek cause. On the ground in Greece, the cause seemed less exalted. On several occasions Greek forces laid siege to Turkish towns and massacred the inhabitants. In March of 1822, a group of Greeks invaded and proclaimed the independence of the island of Chios, then inhabited by Turks and Greeks loyal to the Ottomans. When Ottoman troops arrived, the invaders killed their Turkish prisoners and fled. The Turks took their revenge by massacring thousands of Greeks and selling forty thousand Greeks into slavery.

The Turkish-Greek fighting on the island of Chios became the subject of one of the most famous Romantic paintings of the period, Eugene Delacroix's *Massacre at Chios* (1824). Delacroix's painting only depicted atroc-

The Massacre at Chios, by Eugène Delacroix (1798–1863). Delacroix was a Romantic painter of dramatic and emotional scenes. Here he put his brush to work for the cause of liberty, eulogizing the more than 20,000 Greeks slain by the Turks during the Greek war of independence in 1822. The painting is another example of the manner in which the emotionalism of Romanticism came to the aid of reformist nationalism.

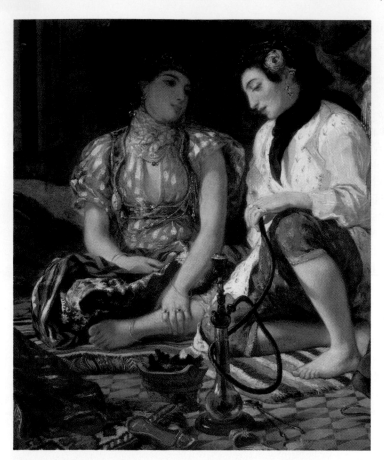

Women of Algiers, by Eugène Delacroix. This is one of many paintings done during Delacroix's trips through North Africa and a good example of the Romantics' "orientalism."

ities committed by the Turks. Like much of the writing and art about the Greek war for independence, the painting expressed decidedly western European concerns. Europeans sought to identify with a Greek heritage and returned, repeatedly, to images of "Eastern" or "Islamic" cruelty and despotism. Similar images recur throughout nineteenth-century Western painting, literature, and scholarship. Delacroix's *Massacre* and his other works, such as *Women of Algiers,* illustrate well what scholars call "Orientalism," nineteenth-century Europeans' tendency to project onto the "Orient" (and especially Islam) their fears and aspects of their own culture that they could not acknowledge: brutality, arbitrary authority, and sensuality. Orientalism runs through much Romantic painting and poetry, as well as through the work of writers and scholars who set out to study the Islamic East.

Greek independence owed little to such sentiments, which revealed more about European Romanticism than about power in the Balkans. In Greece, Great Power politics made the difference: in 1827, British,

French, and Russian troops went in against the Turks. Two London Protocols, in 1829 and 1830, established Greek autonomy and then independence. In 1831, though, the allies set on the Greek throne the son of the king of Bavaria. Great Power politics and the struggle against the Ottoman Turks also made possible the emergence of Serbia in 1828. Aided by the Russians, Serbia became semi-independent, an Orthodox Christian principality under Ottoman rule. In both Greece and Serbia, however, the new nations were small and fragile. Only eight hundred thousand Greeks actually lived in the new Greek state. Greek and Serbian overseas merchants, bankers, and administrators remained thoroughly ensconced in the Ottoman empire.

Liberal struggles of the 1820s brought conservatives closer together. But they also exposed cracks in the conservative alliance. Despite broad agreements of conservative principle, the Great Powers had their own national interests to advance. When the leaders of movements for independence could play the Great Powers off against each other, or when those movements fell in line with Europe's ongoing struggle against the Ottoman empire, as in Greece and Serbia, they were more likely to succeed. These movements were also important, as we have seen, for opponents of the restoration elsewhere. International consciousness ran high. News traveled quickly. Political exiles watched events at home and elsewhere with keen interest. For liberal thinkers, Romantic poets and painters, and ordinary people, movements such as the Greek uprising were ways to dramatize their own causes.

CHRONOLOGY

CONCERT OF EUROPE, 1815–1830

Congress of Vienna	1814–1815
Quintuple Alliance	1818
France restores King Ferdinand in Spain	1823
South American revolutions	1810–1825
Decembrist revolt in Russia	1825
Greek war of independence	1821–1827
Serbian independence	1828

WHY WAS THERE NO REVOLUTION IN GREAT BRITAIN DURING THE 1830S?

FRANCE AND BRITAIN IN THE 1830S   789

FRANCE AND BRITAIN IN THE 1830S

Why was there no revolution in Great Britain during the 1830s?

THE 1830 REVOLUTION IN FRANCE

Much international attention in the period focused on two countries: France, the "nation of revolution," and Great Britain, the home of the early Industrial Revolution. In both countries the new middle classes appeared most prominent in politics and culture. In both countries liberalism played a crucial role in the political and cultural conflicts of the age, from electoral and factory reform to outright revolution. These campaigns for change produced some real triumphs for liberal ideals and their supporters, but also exposed liberalism's contradictions and emboldened its critics.

The Congress of Vienna restored the Bourbon monarchy in France. Louis XVI's son had died in captivity, so the designated king, Louis XVIII, was the oldest of Louis XVI's surviving brothers. Louis did not forsake absolute power, and he restored the nobility of the old regime. But in the name of reconciliation he granted a "charter," and conceded some rights important to French liberals: legal equality, careers open to talent, and a two chamber parliamentary government. The franchise was based on age and property qualifications, and the vast majority of those born after 1789 could not participate directly in the government of their country. This narrowly based rule, combined with the sting of military defeat, nostalgia for a glorious Napoleonic past and, for some, memories of the revolution would undermine Louis's "restoration."

In 1824, Louis died, succeeded by his far less conciliatory brother Charles X (1824–1830). Charles once said that in the years since 1789, only two Frenchmen had not changed: the marquis de Lafayette was still a liberal, Charles still a zealous absolutist. Charles immediately set his course against the legacies of the revolutionary and Napoleonic eras. At his direction the French assembly voted to compensate members of the nobility whose land had been confiscated and sold during the revolution. Doing so appeased the ultraroyalists, as the extreme right wing was called, but it antagonized property holders who had benefited from the revolution and persuaded many that Charles sought nothing less than to turn back the clock. The regime restored the Catholic Church to its traditional place in French classrooms. These policies provoked widespread discontent, several votes of no confidence in the monarch, and a series of elections that brought liberals to the French Chamber of Deputies. The rising tide of liberal public opinion was also swollen by economic hard times. In Paris and the provinces, worried police reports flagged the extent of unemployment, hunger, and anger. Confronted with alarming evidence of the regime's unpopularity, Charles and his ministers called new elections, and when those went against them the king tried, essentially, to overthrow the parliamentary regime. The so-called July ordinances of 1830 (1) dissolved the newly elected chamber before it had even met; (2) imposed strict censorship on the press; (3) further

The July Revolution of 1830 in Paris. Workers construct street barricades in the narrow streets of Paris to ward off government troops.

POPULAR UNREST IN PARIS, 1828

Throughout Europe the police regularly reported on the mood of the common people. This police report, filed in Paris in 1828, captured the rising anger of citizens in the capital. Poor grain harvests in the years before had helped to drive up prices. In the working-class districts of Paris the economic crisis fueled criticism of the regime. The document also reflects the anxieties of the police, who were not persuaded they could enforce order.

A handwritten placard has been put up at the corner of the rue Saint-Nicolas in the quartier des Quinze-Vingts: "Long live Napoleon! War to the death against Charles X and the priests who are starving us to death!" Several workers cheered, saying that "they would make an end of it, if die they must, since there was no work for them. . . ." Similar leaflets have been distributed in the rue de Charenton and the rue de Charonne in the faubourg Saint-Marceau and the faubourg Saint-Martin. . . . People are saying in the wine shops and workshops that the people must assemble and march on the Tuileries to demand work and bread and that they do not fear the soldiery, since many of them have been won over. This exasperation on the part of the workers has been noted ever since the recent rise in prices, and professional agitators (there are plenty of them in the faubourgs) are trying to exploit it to incite the workers to indulge in excesses. Circumstances are favorable. A great many workers have been suffering for a long time and the price of bread is driving them to utter despair. . . . I have begged the Prefect of Police to get some digging and similar work started from which they can earn at least a pittance.

From Louis Chevalier, *Laboring Classes and Dangerous Classes in Paris during the First Half of the Nineteenth Century.* (Princeton: Princeton University Press, 1973), p. 266.

restricted suffrage so as to exclude anyone outside the nobility almost completely; and (4) called for new elections.

What Charles got in return for these measures was revolution. Led by republicans—most of whom were workers, artisans, students, and writers—Parisians took to the streets. Three days of intense street battles followed in which the revolutionaries, fighting behind hastily constructed barricades, defied the army and the police, neither of which was anxious to fire into the crowds. Quickly realizing that further resistance was futile, Charles abdicated. Monarchy was "no longer a religion," said one writer. The Bourbon flag "droops along its pole because no breath of life flutters it." Those who had fought on the barricades pressed for a genuine republic. But other leaders of the revolutionary movement feared a return to the domestic and international turmoil of the revolution of 1789. They brought the duke of Orléans to the throne as King Louis Philippe (1830–1848), promoting him as a thoroughly constitutional monarch and accountable to the people: king of the French, not king of France. The new regime, called the July Monarchy, doubled the franchise (number of eligible voters). Yet voting was still a privilege, not a right, and was still based on steep requirements of property ownership. The major bene-

WHY WAS THERE NO REVOLUTION IN GREAT BRITAIN DURING THE 1830S?

FRANCE AND BRITAIN IN THE 1830S   791

Liberty Leading the People (1830), by Eugène Delacroix. One of the best known images of revolution in general, this painting is characteristically Romantic: a tempestuous scene celebrating the rising of a united people and the triumph of liberty.

ficiaries of the change, and of the revolution in general, were the propertied classes. Yet the revolution of 1830 brought the common people back into politics, reviving the memories—and nightmares—of the revolution of 1789.

The most celebrated image of the July revolution, *Liberty Leading the People*, came from Delacroix, who had earlier mourned the extinction of liberty in *The Massacre at Chios*. The allegorical female figure of liberty leads a united people: a middle-class man (identified by his top hat), a worker, and a pistol-firing boy of the streets. Neither bourgeois nor children fought on the barricades, and the image of revolutionary unity was optimistic. But optimistic images of the "Three Glorious Days" of July were widespread. For liberal opponents of the restoration across Europe, such as the young Heinrich Heine, 1830 assumed enormous importance. It suggested that history was moving in a new direction, that conservative rule would not last. After 1830, Heine remarked, German liberalism suddenly acquired new troops.

THE REFORM BILL OF 1832 IN BRITAIN

The 1830s did not bring revolution to Britain, but they did bring wide-ranging and significant reforms. After an era of political conservatism that paralleled that on the Continent, British politics took a different direction, and Britain became one of the most liberal nations in Europe.

The Peterloo Massacre, 1819. A contemporary rendering of the riot. The cartoon's caption condemned the "wanton and furious attack by that brutal armed force The Manchester & Cheshire Yeomanry Cavalry."

The end of the Napoleonic wars brought with it a major agricultural depression in Britain, and the combination of low wages, unemployment, and bad harvests provoked regular social unrest. When rioting broke out after 1815, it met with repression. Spies were hired to ferret out evidence against popular agitators and legislation was adopted to stifle workers' protests. In the new industrial towns of the north, where economic conditions were especially bad, radical members of the middle class joined with workers to demand increased representation in Parliament. In 1819 a crowd of sixty thousand gathered to demonstrate peacefully for political reform in St. Peter's Field in Manchester. The militia and some soldiers on horseback charged the crowd, killing eleven and injuring four hundred, including 113 women. Public opinion condemned the massacre, which British radicals dubbed "Peterloo": a domestic Waterloo where the nation's heroes against the French had murdered innocent citizens. Parliament quickly passed legislation to stifle the reform movement. The Six Acts, passed in 1819, outlawed "seditious and blasphemous" literature, increased the stamp tax on newspapers, allowed the searching of houses for arms, and restricted the rights of public meeting.

Yet within a surprisingly short time British political leaders reversed their opposition to reform. They dis-

played an ability to compromise that kept outright revolution at bay. George Canning, the aristocratic foreign minister, and Robert Peel, the home secretary and son of a rich cotton manufacturer, led the way in government. Both men were sensitive to the interests of Britain's liberal-minded middle classes. Under their direction, the government retreated from the conservative Quintuple Alliance. At home, they began a program of wide-ranging reform. They began to liberalize the Corn Laws, which were tariffs imposed during the Napoleonic wars on imported grain. The Corn Laws protected British landlords and grain farmers from foreign competition, but they hurt consumers of bread, and they were increasingly seen as special protection for the British aristocracy. Other legal reforms allowed Catholics and dissenting Protestants (non-Anglicans, such as Baptists, Congregationalists, and Methodists) to participate in public political life.

Most of these reforms passed, ironically, under the conservative Tory party, which held the majority in Parliament. The Tories, however, refused to reform the system of representation in the House of Commons, heavily weighted on the side of the landed interests. Liberals from all walks of the population argued passionately for such reform: it would enable "responsible" citizens to play a constant and active role in shaping British policy to comply with their own interests. "Interest" was, indeed, the key word in the debate over parliamentary reform. For centuries Parliament had represented the interests of aristocratic landowners, the major propertied class in Britain. About two-thirds of the members of the House of Commons were either directly nominated by or indirectly owed their election to the patronage of the richest titled landowners in the country. Many of the parliamentary electoral districts, or boroughs, which returned members to the House of Commons, were controlled by landowners who used the pressure of their local economic power—or, in many cases, outright bribery—to return candidates sympathetic to their interests. These were the "rotten" or "pocket" boroughs, so called because they were said to be in the pockets of those men who controlled them. Defenders of the system argued that electoral corruption or inequality mattered little. What did matter, they claimed, was that Parliament looked after the interests of the nation at large, which they perceived to coincide with the interests of landed property.

Liberals in the opposing Whig party, the new industrial middle class, and radical artisans all disagreed. It is important to note, however, that the liberals in particular were not great proponents of democracy. Some leaders within the emerging working class did argue for political reform in the name of democracy, and they continued to do so, as we shall see, even after a reform bill was passed in 1832. Most of the reform spokesmen believed the middle class to be capable of representing working-class interests as well its own. Why did liberals make this argument? Some believed it. Others realized that the prospect of direct representation for the working class would frighten the more timid reformers and hence defeat their whole campaign.

Spurred by the example of liberal reformers on the Continent and by the oratory and organizational abilities of middle-class and artisan radicals at home, the movement for reform intensified after 1830. It was strong enough to topple the Tories and embolden the Whigs, under the leadership of Lord Grey, to make reform a party issue. Grey and several other Whig leaders introduced a bill to modify the outmoded electoral structure. They were able to capitalize on the fears of their political enemies and allies alike. Revolution, if it were ever to come in Britain, would arise from the kind of alliance that was forming between middle-class industrialists and the leaders of the emerging working class. In Birmingham, a middle-class banker, Thomas Attwood, organized a Political Union of the Lower and Middle Classes of the People. By July 1830, similar organizations had arisen in several provincial cities, some willing to engage in bloody clashes with army units and police. Middle-class shopkeepers announced they would withhold taxes and, if necessary, form a national guard. Also plagued by an outbreak of cholera, the country appeared to be on the verge of serious general disorder, if not outright revolution. The king, William IV (1830–1837), wrote to Lord Grey that "miners, manufacturers, colliers, and labourers" appeared ready for some sort of open rebellion. Sensing the grave danger of a possible union of the working and middle classes, the governing class once more accommodated change, as it had in the 1820s.

The Reform Bill of 1832 cleansed Parliament of the "rotten boroughs." It reallocated 143 parliamentary seats, most of them from the rural south, to the industrial north. This redistribution had the potential to increase the political power of the industrial middle classes. On the other hand, the electoral districts remained unequal. Even the expanded franchise, moreover, gave the vote to no more than 3 percent of the total male population. Whether or not men could vote depended on the amount of property they owned and the length of time they had owned it. In short, the bill granted the vote to a few men in the middle classes and to virtually none in the working classes. Produced by nearly revolutionary conditions, the bill ended as a relatively modest measure. It reduced but did not destroy the political strength of landed aristocratic interests. It admitted British liberals, including some of the industrial middle classes, into a junior partership with the landed oligarchy that had ruled Britain for centuries and was to rule it for at least one more generation.

LIBERALISM IN FRANCE AND BRITAIN: CONTRADICTION AND CONFLICT, 1830–1848

What issues were included in the "social question"?

The revolution of 1830 in France and the Parliamentary Reform Bill of 1832 in Britain dealt a blow to conservatism in both countries. The older landed interests and their supporters, however, continued to play an active role in politics. Aristocratic politicians dominated both major parties in Britain. The rather conservative Whig Lord Palmerston, for instance, was one of Britain's most influential prime ministers at mid-century and one of Europe's most authoritative diplomats. Still, the legislatures of France and Britain could no longer ignore the industrial middle classes. Their interest in liberal reforms, and the way in which they reshaped liberal ideas around their economic interests shaped politics in both countries.

What kinds of changes did the new regimes bring? In France, free trade attracted few supporters, and industrialization did not follow a liberal model. The most important changes came in education. Under the

WOMEN IN THE ANTI–CORN LAW LEAGUE, 1842

The campaign to repeal the Corn Laws enlisted many middle-class women in its ranks. For many such women, the anti–Corn Law campaign led to other causes, such as woman suffrage. The following article, hostile to the reform campaign, deplores women's participation in the endeavor. The author raises characteristically Victorian objections to women's participation in politics. The article also offers a glimpse of the reformers' arguments and tactics.

We find that the council of the Manchester Anti-Corn-Law Association had invited the inhabitants to 'an *anti-Corn-law tea-party*, to be held on the 20th of May, 1841—gentlemen's tickets, 2s.; ladies 1s. 6d.' . . . [L]adies were advertised as *stewardesses* of this assembly. So now the names of about 300 Ladies were pompously advertised as the *Patroness* and *Committee* of the *National Bazaar*. We exceedingly wonder and regret that the members of the Association . . . and still more that anybody else, should have chosen to exhibit their wives and daughters in the character of political agitators; and we most regret that so many ladies—modest, excellent, and amiable persons we have no doubt in their domestic circles—should have been persuaded to allow their names to be *placarded* on such occasions—for be it remembered, this Bazaar and these *Tea-parties* did not even pretend to be for any *charitable* object, but entirely for the purposes of *political agitation*. . . .

We have before us a letter from Mrs. Secretary Woolley to one body of workmen. . . . She 'appeals to them to stand forth and denounce as *unholy*, unjust, and cruel all restrictions on the food of the people'. She acquaints them that 'the ladies are resolved to perform *their* arduous part in the attempt to *destroy a monopoly* which, for *selfishness* and its *deadly* effects, has no parallel in the history of the world'. 'We therefore', she adds, 'ask you for contributions. . . .' Now surely . . . not only should the *poorer classes* have been exempt from such unreasonable solicitations, but whatever subscriptions might be obtainable from the wealthier orders should have been applied, not to *political agitation* throughout England, but to charitable relief at home.

J. Croker, "Anti–Corn Law Legislation," *Quarterly Review*, December, 1842, as cited in Patricia Hollis, ed. *Women in Public: The Women's Movement 1850–1900*. (London: G. Allen & Unwin, 1979), p. 287.

succession of governments dominated by France's leading politician of the period, François Guizot, the French expanded their educational system, marking their belief in the liberal doctrine of a meritocracy, or careers open to talent. A French law of 1833 provided for the establishment of elementary schools in every village. Poor children were to receive a free education; all others would pay a modest fee. In addition, larger towns were to provide training schools for trade and industry, and departments were to provide schools for teacher training. As a result, the number of pupils in France increased from about 2 million in 1831 to about 3.25 million in 1846.

In most ways the new regime differed little from the old, disappointing the high hopes that it had inspired. The new king gathered around him representatives of the banking and industrial elite. The regime often gave the impression of complacency and corruption. When confronted with demands to enfranchise more members of the middle class, Guizot quipped that everyone was free to rise into the ranks of the wealthy. "Enrich yourselves," he counseled. Construction projects and the expansion of the railway system presented ample opportunities for graft. Louis Philippe had played a minor part in the Revolution of 1830, but he was neither a revolutionary nor a Napoleon.

Liberal reforms made more significant headway in Britain during this period. There were several reasons for this. First, the Reform Bill of 1832 gave the middle class a share of political power. Second, and in part a consequence of reform, Parliament was generally sensitive to the needs of industrialists, above all their desire for policies of free trade. And third, rapid industrialization compelled legislative intervention on a number of fronts.

The most powerful symbol of British middle-class liberalism was the repeal of the Corn Laws in 1846. Although those laws had been modified in the 1820s, they continued to keep the price of bread artificially high. More than that, the Corn Laws symbolized to the industrial middle classes the unwarranted privileges of the aristocracy. The campaign to accomplish repeal was superbly orchestrated and relentless, combining the support of those who believed, in principle, in reform and free trade and those who had a direct economic stake in a new system. The Anti–Corn Law League, which drew surprisingly broad support, held large meetings throughout the north of England and lobbied members of Parliament.

In the end the League achieved a crucial victory, persuading Sir Robert Peel, now prime minister, that repealing the Corn Laws was both inevitable and necessary for Britain's economic health and global power. The widespread suffering caused by the potato famine in Ireland (see page 746) was a further argument for ending restrictions against the importation of cheap foodstuffs. Peel, a supremely self-confident (and self-important) politician, was willing to split the Tory party—or as it was now coming to be called, the Conservative party—to introduce repeal. Peel's gamble repealed the law but changed the shape of British politics as a new party, which called itself Liberal, emerged among the liberal Whigs and local interests in the industrial north. One of the central planks in the Liberal platform was described with a metaphor that invoked religious conviction about the issue: "the gospel of free trade."

BRITISH RADICALISM AND THE CHARTIST MOVEMENT

In both France and Britain, many of those who had helped the liberals to power in 1830 and 1832 grew increasingly dissatisfied with the new regimes. The British reform bill did little to increase working-class chances for political participation. In France, the July Monarchy rested on a very narrow base—less than 1 percent of the population could actually vote. In both countries, political disillusionment with the new regimes combined with the social grievances created by industrialization, urbanization, and new forms of inequality (see Chapter 22). The combination produced an upsurge of radicalism in the 1840s.

In Britain, those disappointed with the scope of liberal reform focused their energy on more significant political change, in the form of what was called the "People's Charter." This document, circulated across the country by committees of Chartists, as they were known, and signed by millions, contained six demands: universal white male suffrage, institution of the secret ballot, abolition of property qualifications for membership in the House of Commons, annual parliamentary elections, payment of salaries to members of the House of Commons, and equal electoral districts.

The fortunes of the Chartist movement waxed and waned. In some areas its strength depended on economic conditions: Chartism spread with unemployment and depression. In others it tapped into local traditions of worker self-help and organization. Such a broad movement was also divided internally over its goals and the best means for achieving them. Did Chartism imply a reorganization of industry or, instead, a return to preindustrial society? Were its goals to be accomplished by petition only, or by force if necessary? Should social groups such as immigrant Irish Catholics in England be included in the movement, or excluded as dangerous competition for scarce jobs, as many local activists preferred? Should the franchise be extended only to working men, representing their families as respectable, "interested" members of society, or to women as well? Three examples may help illustrate the convictions and contradictions bundled together in Chartism. The Chartist William Lovett, a cabinetmaker, was as fervent a believer in self-improvement as any member of the middle class. He advocated a union of educated workers to acquire their fair share of the nation's increasing industrial bounty. The Chartist Feargus O'Connor, a member of a minor Anglo-Irish landholding family but a political radical, appealed to the more impoverished and desperate class of workers. He attacked industrialization and the resettlement of the poor on agricultural allotments. Another Chartist, Bronterre O'Brien, openly admired Robespierre and shocked crowds by attacking "the big-bellied, little-brained, numbskull aristocracy." Chartism was composed of many smaller movements with different emphases, but its goal was plainly political democracy as a means to social justice.

> Chartism's goal was plainly political democracy as a means to social justice.

Democracy alone was a very radical demand in the 1840s. Not surprisingly, it met with staunch opposition. The Chartists persisted. Committees presented massive petitions for the Charter to Parliament in 1839 and 1842; on both occasions they were summarily rejected. In the north of England, political demands took place against a backdrop of strikes, trade-union demonstrations, and attacks on factories and manufacturers who imposed low wages and long hours, or who harassed unionists. The combination of political and social radicalism did not sway the government; conservatives saw anarchy and liberals repudiated any interest in revolution. The movement peaked in April of 1848. Partly inspired by revolution in continental Europe, Chartist leaders planned a major demonstration and show of force in London. A procession of twenty-five thousand workers assembled, and carried to Parliament a petition containing 6 million signatures demanding the six points. Confronted once again with the specter of open class conflict, special constables and contingents of the regular army were marshalled under the now aged duke of Wellington, hero of the battle of Waterloo, to resist this threat to order. In the end, only a small delegation of leaders presented the petition to Parliament. Rain, poor management, and unwillingness on the part of many to do battle with the well-armed constabulary put an end to the Chartists' campaign. A relieved liberal observer, Harriet Martineau, observed, "From that day it was a settled matter that England was safe from revolution."

The Great Chartist Rally of April 10, 1848. Undiscovered in the royal archives until the 1970s, this early photograph draws attention to the respectable attire of working-class radicals.

1848 AND REVOLUTION IN FRANCE

In France, the reign of Louis Philippe, which began in 1830, proved short lived. Discontent had several roots. The first cause, crucial for all the movements of the 1840s, was a Europe-wide economic crisis. Problems started in the early 1840s, with poor harvests. In 1845–1846, the crisis became acute. For two years in a row, the grain harvest failed completely. The potato blight struck, bringing starvation to Ireland (see page 746) and hunger to Germany, another potato-growing region. By 1846–1847, food prices had, on average, doubled. Bread riots broke out across Europe; city and village dwellers attacked carts carrying grain, refusing to let merchants take it to other markets; or they simply took the grain and sold it at what they considered a fair price. Compounding the problem was a cyclical industrial slowdown, which threw thousands of workers into unemployment. Starving peasants and unemployed laborers swamped public-relief organizations. The years 1846 and 1847 were "probably the worst of the entire century in terms of want and human suffering," and the decade has earned the name of "the Hungry Forties." Hunger does not cause revolution. It does, however, test governments' abilities and their legitimacy. When the inadequate public relief systems in France foundered, when troops moved to repress potato riots in Berlin, or when regimes armed middle-class citizens to protect themselves against beggars, governments looked both authoritarian and inept.

In France, economic grievances provided the background for political ones. Republicans who had fought on the barricades in 1830 quickly became disillusioned with the new regime. Republican societies proliferated, especially in older cities like Paris and Lyons, where worker and artisans associations had long political traditions. Workers' strikes and outright rebellions in 1831 and 1834 met with harsh repression, heightening the impression of class-based, authoritarian rule. In 1834, the government declared radical political organizations illegal. Rebellions broke out in Lyons and Paris, where for two days government troops massacred hundreds of insurgents and arrested some two thousand republican leaders. Radicals waged some of their most successful campaigns in the press. Honoré Daumier was only one of the caricaturists who gleefully savaged the king in print; more than once he found himself in prison. In 1835, following an attempt to assassinate Louis Philippe, the government passed a censorship law that forbade the publication of articles attempting to inspire contempt for the king and that prohibited the printing of any drawing or emblem without prior governmental approval. These repressive measures only heightened dissent.

The issue that actually sparked revolution, though, was political. Forward-looking members of legislature advised Guizot to widen the franchise slightly, extending the vote to middle-class professionals. Guizot unwisely refused, driving moderates into the camp of the republicans. By 1847, the opposition was strong enough to organize a campaign for electoral reform throughout France. Since political meetings were outlawed, the opposition organized political "banquets," where opponents of the regime drank toasts to reform—though not to outright revolution. Defying the king's threats, the opposition called a final, giant banquet for February 22, 1848. When the government banned the meeting, revolution broke out. Members of the opposition, students, and workers joined in fighting on the barricades.

Louis Philippe, King of France during the July Monarchy, 1830–1848.

LES POIRES,

Faites à la cour d'assises de Paris par le Directeur de la CARICATURE.

Vendues pour payer les 6,000 fr. d'amende du journal le *Charivari*.

Louis Philippe in Caricature. In contrast to the portrait of Louis Philippe as he wanted to appear, on p. 797, these 1833 caricatures by Charles Philipon depict the king as he increasingly appeared to his subjects. "Poire," French for pear, also means "nitwit" or "dummy."

After a short time, Louis Philippe abdicated amid increased demands for a republic.

The new provisional government was a remarkable group, consisting of a combination of liberals, republicans and, for the first time, socialists, who believed the government had to address economic inequality. It set about making a new constitution, with elections based on universal male suffrage. Yet tensions between middle-class republicans and radical socialists, which had momentarily dissolved in opposition to Louis Philippe, now emerged to shape the political events of the ensuing months in several specific ways. Many, especially those who had fought on the barricades, expected the government to take action on the "social question," the current term for economic justice and welfare. For working men and women, by far the most widely supported demand involved the "right to work," which meant the ability to earn a living wage, to be able to support oneself. As one socialist said, "The right to work has its origin and its legitimacy in the fundamental and absolute clauses of the social compact." Louis Blanc, the leading socialist in the government, proposed the government establish national workshops. These were to be organized by trades as producers' cooperatives where men and women workers would be trained if necessary, put to work, and paid two francs a day when employed and a smaller stipend when unemployed. The provisional government did make an important gesture in this direction, cautiously supporting the "right to work," and naming Blanc head of what was called the Luxembourg Commission, formed to study labor issues. The National Workshops it created, though, were more akin to a program of public works in and around Paris, where economic conditions had resulted in widespread unemployment. Initially, plans had called for the employment of no more than ten or twelve thousand in projects throughout the city. But with unemployment running as high as 65 percent in the construction trades

Gargantua, by Honoré Daumier. This illustration is one of Daumier's most biting attacks on Louis Philippe. The king's face, as usual, is drawn in the shape of a pear. He sits on his throne, swallowing bags of gold and excreting useless decrees.

The Uprising (1848), by Honoré Daumier. A worker in shirtsleeves raises a fist as a group marches to the barricades.

and 51 percent in textiles and clothing, workers began to flood into the government's so-called workshops, as many as sixty-six thousand by April, and one hundred twenty thousand by June 1848.

As before, revolution brought exhilaration, the flourishing of political activity, and growing counter-revolutionary murmurings. The provisional government removed all restrictions on freedom of speech and political activity. One hundred seventy new journals and more than two hundred clubs formed within weeks; the Central Republican Society, the club headed by the socialist Auguste Blanqui, boasted a membership of some three thousand. Delegations claiming to represent the oppressed of all European countries—Chartists, Hungarians, Poles—moved freely about the city, attracting attention, if not devoted followings. Women's clubs and newspapers appeared, with names like *The Voice of Women* or *The Opinion of*

Women, and demands ranging from real, universal suffrage to living wages for working women. This revival of popular politics, though, convinced rising numbers of middle-class onlookers that stern measures were needed to forestall further insurrectionary outbreaks. The concern for order was reinforced by the results of elections held in April. Universal male suffrage by no means guaranteed radical victory in elections. Voters in the countryside especially worried about radicals in Paris, elected moderate republicans and monarchists.

By late spring 1848, a majority of the French assembly believed that the workshop system had become a financial drain and, worse, a serious threat to social order. At the end of May, the government closed the workshops to new enrollment, excluded anyone who had resided in Paris for less than six months, and sent all members between the ages of eighteen and twenty-five to the army. On June 21, the government simply

The Revolution of 1848 in France. A contemporary broadside celebrating the triumph of the people.

The Barricade, by Ernest Meissonier (1815–1891). A very different view of 1848, one that foreshadows the defeat of revolutionary hopes.

ended the program, repudiating any responsibility for the social question. The reaction brought some of the bloodiest conflict of the period. Laborers, journeymen, unemployed, traditional manual laborers, socialists and some republican leaders once more threw up barricades across Paris. For four days, June 23–26, they defended themselves in an ultimately hopeless military battle against armed forces recruited, in part, from willing provincials eager enough to assist in the repression of the urban working class. The repression was ferocious, shocking many observers. About three thousand were killed and twelve thousand more arrested, the majority of whom were deported to Algerian labor camps.

In the aftermath of the "June Days," the French government moved quickly to bring order to the country. Assembly members arranged for the immediate election of a president. Their hope was that a strong leader might assist in bringing dissidents to heel. Four candidates ran: Alphonse de Lamartine, the moderate republican; General Louis Eugène Cavaignac, who had commanded the troops in June; Alexandre August Ledru-Rollin, a socialist; and Louis Napoleon Bonaparte, nephew of the former emperor, who polled more than twice as many votes as the other three candidates combined.

"All facts and personages of great importance in world history occur twice . . . the first time as tragedy, the second as farce." This was how Karl Marx (no admirer of Napoleon I) summarized the relationship of Louis Napoleon to his uncle. Tocqueville dubbed Louis Napoleon a "chance prince" who did not hesitate "to put an outlandish idea side by side with a good one." The upstart, rumored by yet other detractors to be illegitimate, had spent most of his life in exile. Returning to France after the Revolution of 1830, he was imprisoned a few years later for attempting to provoke a local uprising. But in 1846 he escaped to England, where both British and French conservatives supplied him with funds. By the spring of 1848 the situation in France was such that he knew it was safe to return. His name gave him a wide and suitably vague appeal. Conservatives believed he would protect property and

TWO VIEWS OF THE JUNE DAYS, FRANCE, 1848

These two passages make for an interesting comparison. The socialist Karl Marx reported on the events of 1848 in France as a journalist for a German newspaper. For Marx, the bloodshed of the June days shattered the "fraternal illusions" of February 1848, when the King had been overthrown and the Provisional Government established. That bloodshed also symbolized a new stage in history: one of acute class conflict.

The French liberal politician Alexis de Tocqueville also wrote about his impressions of the revolution. (Tocqueville's account, however, is retrospective, for he wrote his memoirs well after 1848.) For Marx, a socialist observer, the June Days represented a turning point: "the working class was knocking on the gates of history." For Tocqueville, a member of the government, the actions of the crowd sparked fear and conservative reaction. Unlike Marx, Tocqueville was not sympathetic to the revolutionaries of June. Yet he, too, underscored the historical significance of the events.

KARL MARX'S JOURNALISM

The last official remnant of the February Revolution, the Executive Commission, has melted away, like an apparition, before the seriousness of events. The fireworks of Lamartine [French Romantic poet and member of the provisional government] have turned into the war rockets of Cavaignac [French general, in charge of putting down the workers' insurrection]. *Fraternité*, the fraternity of antagonistic classes of which one exploits the other, this *fraternité*, proclaimed in February, on every prison, on every barracks—its true, unadulterated, its prosaic expression is civil war, civil war in its most fearful form, the war of labor and capital. This fraternity flamed in front of all the windows of Paris on the evening of June 25, when the Paris of the bourgeoisie was illuminated, whilst the Paris of the proletariat [Marxist term for the working people] burnt, bled, moaned. . . . The February Revolution was the beautiful revolution, the revolution of universal sympathy, because the antagonisms, which had flared up in it against the monarchy, slumbered peacefully side by side, still undeveloped, because the social struggle which formed its background had won only a joyous existence, an existence of phrases, of words. The June revolution is the ugly revolution, the repulsive revolution, because things have taken the place of phrases, because the republic uncovered the head of the monster itself, by striking off the crown that shielded and concealed it.— Order! was the battle cry of Guizot . . . Order! shouts Cavaignac, the brutal echo of the French National Assembly and of the republican bourgeoisie. Order! thundered his grape-shot, as it ripped up the body of the proletariat. None of the numerous revolutions of the French bourgeoisie since 1789 was an attack on order; for they allowed the rule of the class, they allowed the slavery of the workers, they allowed the bourgeois order to endure, however often the political form of this rule and of this slavery changed. June has attacked this order. Woe to June!"

Neue Rheinische Zeitung (New Rhineland Gazette), June 29, 1848; from Karl Marx, The Class Struggles in France. (New York: International Publishers, 1964), pp. 57–58.

ALEXIS DE TOCQUEVILLE REMEMBERS THE JUNE DAYS

Now at last I have come to that insurrection in June which was the greatest and the strangest that had ever taken place in our history, or perhaps in that of any other nation: the greatest because for four days more than a hundred thousand men took part in it, and there were five generals killed; the strangest, because the insurgents were fighting without a battle cry, leaders, or flag, and yet they showed wonderful powers of coordination and a military expertise that astonished the most experienced officers.

Another point that distinguished it from all other events of the same type during the last sixty years was that its object was not to change the form of government, but to alter the organization of society. In truth it was not a political struggle (in the sense in which we have used the word "political" up to now), but a class struggle, a sort of "Servile War" . . . One should not see it only as a brutal and a blind, but as a powerful effort of the workers to escape from the necessities of their condition, which had been depicted to them as an illegitimate depression, and by the sword to open up a road towards that imaginary well-being that had been shown to them in the distance as a right. It was this mixture of greedy desires and false theories that engendered the insurrection and made it so formidable. These poor people had been assured that the goods of the wealthy were in some way the result of a theft committed against themselves. They had been assured that inequalities of fortune were as much opposed to morality and the interests of society as to nature. This obscure and mistaken conception of right, combined with brute force, imparted to it an energy, tenacity and strength it would never have had on its own.

From Alexis de Tocqueville, *Recollections: The French Revolution of 1848.* Edited by J. P. Mayer and A. P. Kerr, translated by George Lawrence. (New Brunswick, N.J.: Transaction Books, 1987), pp. 436–437.

---

order. Some people on the left had heard of the glittering schemes for prosperity in his book *The Extinction of Pauperism* or of his correspondence with important socialists. In between these two classes was a group of voters for whom the name Napoleon evoked glory and greatness. He may have been an illegitimate nephew, but as one historian puts it, "he was very precisely the son of the Napoleonic myth." His role as an "an all purpose personage" helped secure his electoral victory. As one old peasant expressed it, "How could I help voting for this gentleman—I whose nose was frozen at Moscow?"

With dreams of emulating his uncle, Louis Napoleon was not long content to remain president of France. Almost from the first he used the power he already had to achieve the further power he desired. He enlisted the support of the Catholics by permitting them to regain control over the schools and by sending an expedition to Rome in 1849 to restore to the pope the temporal power denied him during the revolutionary struggles of 1848. (The Italian revolutions are discussed in the next chapter.) He courted the workers and the middle class by introducing old-age insurance and laws for the encouragement of business. Above all, his regime began a process of demobilizing radicals across the country: banning meetings, workers' associations, and so on. In 1851, alleging the need for extraordinary measures to protect the rights of the masses, he proclaimed a temporary dictatorship and invited the people to grant him the power to draw up a new constitution. In the plebiscite shortly thereafter an overwhelming majority (7,500,000 to 640,000) authorized his actions. The new constitution, which he put into effect in January 1852, made the president an actual dictator. After one year Louis Napoleon Bonaparte ordered another plebiscite and, with the approval of over 95 percent of the voters, established the Second Empire and assumed the title of Napoleon III (1852–1870), emperor of the French.

What was the significance of the French Revolution of 1848 and its political aftermath? First, the middle classes played a pivotal political role. Louis Philippe's regime, which seemed so proudly bourgeois, sent much of the middle class into opposition. Denied a direct political voice because of a severely limited franchise, key groups of the middle class swung to the left, allying themselves with radicals who by themselves never would have toppled the regime. Yet the desire for reform soon ran up against fears of disorder, and the desire for a strong state. This familiar dynamic led to the collapse of the republic and to the rule of Louis Napoleon Bonaparte. Second, for many observers at the time, the June Days seemed nothing less than naked class struggle. The violence of the June Days

WHAT WAS THE IMPACT OF LIBERALISM IN FRANCE AND GREAT BRITAIN AFTER 1850?

LIBERALISM IN FRANCE AND BRITAIN AFTER 1850   803

shattered many of the liberal aspirations of the earlier period. The romantic image of revolutionary unity captured in Delacroix's *Liberty Leading the People* now seemed naïve. In the aftermath of 1848, the interests and politics of middle- and working-class people were more sharply differentiated and more directly at odds. The social question, once raised, would not be banished. On the other side, liberal middle-class politics did not collapse, but they would be transformed. To thrive, liberals would not only have to pay lip service to working-class demands, but in some measure accommodate them as well.

LIBERALISM IN FRANCE AND BRITAIN AFTER 1850

What was the impact of liberalism in France and Great Britain after 1850?

Napoleon III labored hard and successfully to sell his empire to the people of France. Like his uncle, he believed that legislative assemblies only divided a nation along class lines and that consolidating power in himself would unite the country. Napoleon III modeled his constitution on that of his uncle. An assembly, elected by universal male suffrage, in fact possessed almost no power. It could do no more than approve legislation drafted at the emperor's direction by a Council of State. Elections were manipulated by the government in order to ensure the return of politically docile representatives. Control of finance, the army, and foreign affairs rested exclusively with the emperor. France was a democracy only in the sense that its people were periodically afforded a chance, through elections, to express their approval of Napoleon's regime.

In return for the gift of considerable power, Napoleon III gave the French what they appeared to want. For the powerful and propertied, and the larger middle class as well, Napoleon's regime provided political stability and important economic changes. The Crédit Mobilier, an investment banking institution, facilitated the expansion of industry by selling its shares to the public and using its income to underwrite various entrepreneurial schemes. In 1863 a limited liability law encouraged further investment by guaranteeing that stockholders could lose no more than the par value of their stock no matter how indebted the company in which they had invested. Railways, owned by the state, spread across the country and spurred further industrial expansion. So prosperous did the French economy appear that Napoleon was prepared to follow Britain's lead in pressing for tariff-free trade between the two countries. A treaty was signed in 1860. The apparent satisfaction of the middle class with Napoleon's regime provides a measure with which to assess the state of liberalism in France after 1850. The fact that the country no longer enjoyed a free press, that universities were politically controlled, and that political opposition was repressed seemed to matter very little to most, at least for the first decade.

Napoleon III, though he catered to the constituencies that had brought both Louis Philippe and himself to power, did not fail to court the favor of the workers as well. Some of the radicalism of his youth was expressed in careful measures of social reform that went beyond what French liberals might have done on their own. He encouraged the establishment of hospitals and instituted a program of free medical assistance. More important, he permitted, though did not encourage, the existence of trade unions and in 1864 introduced legislation to legalize strikes. Ultimately, he appealed to the workers much as he appealed to the middle class, as a symbol of his country's reemergence as a leading world power. The activities of his court and of his stylish empress, Eugénie, were well publicized. The reconstruction of Paris into a city of broad boulevards and grand open spaces was calculated to provide appropriate scenery for the theater of empire—as well as to decrease the chances of successful proletarian barricade building across narrow streets.

Grandeur, however, appeared to Napoleon III to demand an aggressive foreign policy. Although he declared himself in favor of international peace, he was soon at war. First came mixed results against Russia in the Crimea; then success against the Austrians in Italy; then an adventurous expedition to Mexico, where he attempted to assist in the establishment of another empire but met with costly failure. Finally and most disastrously came a war with Prussia that brought the collapse of his regime. The details of these adventures are part of the subject of the following chapter. It is

> In the aftermath of 1848, the interests and politics of middle- and working-class people were more sharply differentiated and more directly at odds.

enough at this point to remark that Napoleon III's foreign policy reflects clearly how far he had subordinated the liberal heritage of the first French Revolution to another of the Revolution's legacies: national glory.

What, meanwhile, of the aftermath of Chartism in Britain? Social changes in the working class came to alter politics. By the second half of the century, industrialization began to sustain a growing stratum of highly skilled and relatively well-paid workers (almost exclusively male). These workers—concentrated for the most part within the building, engineering, and textile industries—turned from the tradition of militant radicalism that had characterized the "Hungry Forties." They believed in collective self-help, achieved by means of cooperative societies or through trade unions, whose major function was the accumulation of funds to be used as insurance against old age and unemployment. They believed in education as a tool for advancement, and patronized the Mechanics Institutes and other similar institutions either founded by them or on their behalf.

These prosperous workers created real pressure for electoral reform. Some pressed for extension of the franchise as democrats. Others, however, adopted the arguments that middle-class candidates for the vote had used in 1832. They were responsible workers, respectable and upstanding members of society, whose social consciences extended further than those of many laissez faire liberals but whose patriotism and religious conviction was often even deeper. They were no band of revolutionaries; their loyalty to the state could not be questioned. As such, they were a bona fide "interest," as worthy of the vote and of direct representation as the middle class. They were joined in their campaign by many reformers in the Liberal party, and even some shrewd Conservatives such as the semi-aristocratic Benjamin Disraeli (1804–1881), who argued that responsible politics and social order would be improved, not disrupted, by welcoming these "aristocrats of labor" into political life. Many middle-class men and women, for example, were dissenters from the Church of England. This gave them religious links to many of the workers campaigning for reform. This community of "dissent," which crossed class lines, was vital to Liberal party politics and the campaign for reforming the vote. Dissenters were forced to pay taxes to support the Church of England, a church that was largely staffed by sons of the gentry and run in the interests of landed society. For centuries dissenters' sons had been denied the facilities of the nation's ancient universities, Oxford and Cambridge, unless those sons

CHRONOLOGY

REFORM IN GREAT BRITAIN, 1832–1867

Electoral Reform Bill	1832
Slavery abolished in British West Indies	1838
Chartist Movement	1840s
Corn Laws repealed	1846
Great Reform Bill	1867
Woman Suffrage movement grows	1860s

abandoned their parents' faith and subscribed to the articles of the Anglican church. These same ambitious young men also faced discrimination in the civil service and the military, denied posts that liberals felt should be open to talent, not used as rewards in a corrupt system of privilege.

Working-class leaders and middle-class dissidents joined in a countrywide campaign for a new reform bill and a House of Commons responsive to their interests. Disraeli, by now the Conservative leader of the House of Commons, seized on reform as an issue. Rather than being swept aside by a Liberal tide backing reform, Disraeli's about-face made him prime minister. In 1867 he steered through Parliament a bill more far-reaching than anything proposed by his political opponents. The Great Reform Bill doubled the franchise by extending the vote to any men who paid poor rates or rent of ten pounds or more a year in urban areas (this meant, in general, skilled workers), and to tenants paying rent of twelve pounds or more in the counties. As in 1832, the bill redistributed seats, with large northern cities gaining representation at the expense of the rural south. The "responsible" working class had been deemed worthy to participate in the affairs of state. The reform bill was silent on women. Yet a significant minority, including John Stuart Mill (see page 770), insisted that liberalism needed to enfranchise women, and the period saw the mobilization of a woman suffrage movement, building on the remarkable number of women who had participated in the reform campaigns of earlier years, especially the Anti–Corn Law League and the movement to abolish slavery.

The decade or so following the passage of the Reform Bill of 1867 marked the high point of British liberalism. Liberalism had opened the door to the peaceful restructuring of political institutions and social life. But it had done so under considerable pressure from below. What was more, in Britain, France, and elsewhere liberal groups demonstrated a willingness to close that door on numerous (and critical) occasions. It was one thing for men of property to champion the rule of law and representative government, and another to contend with the challenges of a truly democratic politics. These tensions made it possible for liberals to work within a variety of different political regimes, but they could also lead to heavy-handed, law-and-order politics.

CONCLUSION

The peace settlement of 1815 had aimed to inoculate Europe against revolution. It was only partially successful. Liberal revolts challenged the conservative order. The industrialization and urbanization of Europe, which we considered earlier, contributed to undermining the conservative order. Faced with rapid social transformations, conservative governments looked indifferent or crudely authoritarian. From the 1820s through the 1840s, a combination of social grievances and political disappointments created powerful movements for change. Those movements brought revolution in France, and far-reaching change, though without revolution, in Britain. Many of the same forces were at work in central Europe. There, however, all politics were more strongly infused with nationalism, to which we now turn.

SELECTED READINGS

Agulhon, Maurice. *The Republican Experiment, 1848–1852*. New York, 1983. A full treatment of the revolution in France.

Anderson, R. D. *Education in France, 1848–1870*. Oxford, 1975. Covers every level of formal education and its practical and theoretical relationship to state and society.

Briggs, Asa. *The Age of Improvement, 1783–1867*. New York, 1979. A survey of England from 1780 to 1870, particularly strong on Victorian attitudes.

Colley, Linda. *Britons: Forging the Nation, 1707–1837*. New Haven, Conn., 1992. An important analysis of the manner in which Britain gained a national consciousness in the eighteenth and early nineteenth centuries.

Coppa, Frank. *The Origins of the Italian Wars of Independence*. London, 1992.

Furet, François. *Revolutionary France, 1770–1880*. New York, 1970. An excellent and fresh overview by one of the preeminent historians of the revolution of 1789.

Hobsbawm, Eric. *The Age of Revolution: Europe 1789 to 1848*. New York, 1970. A very useful account of the period by an enthusiastic Marxist.

Johnson, Susan. *Roaring Camp*. New York, 2000. A fascinating story of one mining camp in California, and a microhistory of the larger forces changing the West and the world.

Merriman, John M., ed. *1830 in France*. New York, 1975. Emphasizes the nature of revolution and examines events outside Paris.

Pinkney, David. *Napoleon III and the Rebuilding of Paris*. Princeton, N.J., 1972. An interesting account of the creation of modern Paris during the Second Empire.

———. *The French Revolution of 1830*. Princeton, N.J., 1972. A reinterpretation, now the best history of the revolution.

Raeff, Marc. *The Decembrist Movement*. New York, 1966. Examines the uprising in Russia; contains documents.

Robertson, Priscilla. *Revolutions of 1848: A Social History*. Princeton, N.J., 1952. Old-fashioned narrative, but very readable.

Sahlins, Peter. *Forest Rites: The War of the Demoiselles in Nineteenth-Century France*. Cambridge, Mass., 1994. A fascinating study of relations among peasant communities, the forests, and the state.

Said, Edward W. *Orientalism*. New York, 1979. A brilliant and biting study of the imaginative hold of the "Orient" on European intellectuals.

Saville, John. *1848: The British State and the Chartist Movement*. New York, 1987. A detailed account of the movement's limited successes and ultimate failure.

Sperber, Jonathan. *The European Revolutions, 1848–1851*. New York, 1994. Now the best single volume on the period, with a new bibliography.

Stearns, Peter N. *1848: The Revolutionary Tide in Europe*. New York, 1974. Stresses the social background of the revolutions.

Wordsworth, Jonathan, Michael C. Jaye, and Robert Woof. *William Wordsworth and the Age of English Romanticism*. New Brunswick, N.J., 1987. Wide ranging and beautifully illustrated, a good picture of the age.

Zeldin, Theodore. *France, 1848–1945*, 2 vols. Oxford, 1973–1977. A highly individualistic synthesis of French history, remarkable for its scope and insight.

CHAPTER TWENTY-FOUR

REVOLUTION,
NATIONALISM,
AND
NATION BUILDING,
1815–1870

THE 1848 REVOLUTION in France became a catalyst for uprisings across Europe. The causes of those revolutions of 1848 lay with developments throughout Europe: simmering social antagonisms, economic crisis, and increasing impatience with conservative efforts to impede any form of change. Yet the revolutions took different forms. In southern and central Europe, where nobles retained many, if not all of their privileges, middle-class liberals had much less political power. Above all, in central and southern Europe social and political issues were complicated by the national question. Many middle-class men and women in these regions had liberal goals: representative government, an end to privilege, economic development, and so on. But for them, an equally important objective was the achievement of some form of national unity. In Germany, Italy, Poland, and the Austrian empire, reformers believed that their chances of achieving liberal goals could only be realized in a vigorous, "modern" nation-state.

If the history of nineteenth-century Britain and France can be studied against a background of liberalism, much of the rest of Europe must be understood in terms of a more complex combination of liberalism, nationalism, and nation building. We can define nationalism, broadly, as a sentiment of belonging to a community that shares historical, geographic, linguistic, or cultural traditions. Since this sentiment is diffuse, nationalism could be—and was—cultivated by intellectuals, revolutionaries, and governments for different purposes. It could serve liberal or conservative politics and goals. Nation building can be understood as the political implementation of nationalism, or the translation of sentiment into power. More concretely, it involved a combination of territorial expansion, changes in state structures (such as the military, the civil service), political reform, or social change.

The emergence of nationalism as a political force was one of the key developments of the nineteenth century. Nationalism played a critical role in the revolutions

FOCUS QUESTIONS

• What was the nineteenth-century definition of a nation?

• How did Romanticism influence nationalism?

• Which groups drove reform in early nineteenth-century Germany?

• How did Austrian and German nationalism differ?

• How did Italian and Irish nationalism differ?

• Why did the revolutions of 1848 in Germany and Austria fail?

• What forces drove nation building in the mid-nineteenth century?

of 1848. Those revolutions failed. After that failure, however, new nations were built—and often by the very statesmen who earlier had been sharp critics of nationalism. The unification of Germany and Italy changed the map of Europe and brought adjustments in the international balance of power. They also showed the enduringly unpredictable character of nationalism.

NATIONALISM AND NATIONAL IDENTITY

What was the nineteenth-century definition of a nation?

What is a nation? *Nation* comes from the Latin verb *nasci*, "to be born," and the term suggests common birth. But the meaning of *nation* has changed historically. In sixteenth-century England, for instance, the "nation" designated the aristocracy, those who shared noble birthright. The French nobility, too, referred to itself as the "nation." Those unfamiliar usages are helpful because they underscore the most important development of the late eighteenth and early nineteenth centuries: the redefinition of "nation" to mean the people, or the sovereign people. As we have seen, the French Revolution of 1789 contributed powerfully to this redefinition. The revolutionaries' boldest claim was that the nation, not the king, was the sovereign power. In the aftermath of the French Revolution of 1789, the "nation" became what one historian calls "the collective image of modern citizenry." It was a symbol of legal equality, of constitutional government, and of unity, in the sense of an end to feudal privileges and divisions.

Nationalism became an important rallying cry for liberals across Europe in the early nineteenth century precisely because it was associated with political change. It celebrated the achievements and "awakening" of the common people. In this period, too, nationalism usually went hand in hand with demands for economic modernity. Liberals sought the development of a national economy, a move from smaller, inward-turning communities to larger, stronger, and more effective systems of banking, transportation, production, and distribution. But nationalism could have conservative implications as well. For instance, the image of the Napoleonic army appealed to conservative proponents of military strength and authority as well as to liberals who wanted an army of citizens. To liberalism's readiness to welcome the future, some nationalist thinkers responded with an appreciation, if not veneration, of the past. And to the liberals' insistence on the value and importance of individualism, those committed to building nations replied that their vital task might require the sacrifice of some measure of each citizen's freedom.

Nineteenth-century writers often spoke of the awakening of peoples, as if national feeling were a natural force, inscribed in the movement of history. We read of the sudden awakening of slumbering, atavistic feelings buried deep within the collective consciousness of a "German," an "Italian," a "French," or a "British" people. This is misleading. National identity (like religious, gender, or ethnic identities) developed and changed historically. It rested on specific social bases, such as an increasingly literate population; on the creation of national institutions, such as schools or the military; and on participation in national rituals, from voting to holidays and festivals. In recent years, historians have tried to understand what national identity meant to ordinary men and women, and how it came to be so important. They have shown how nineteenth-century governments sought to develop national feeling, to link their peoples more closely to their states. State-supported educational systems taught a "national" language, fighting the centrifugal forces of traditional dialects. Italian became the official national language of the newly unified Italian nation, despite the fact that only 2.5 percent of the population spoke it. That tiny percentage, because of its dominant position, managed to define a "national" culture. Textbooks and self-consciously nationalist prose and poetry played an important role, elaborating, and sometimes inventing a national heritage. Political leaders associated the nation with specific causes. But historians have also showed how common everyday activities, such as reading a daily newspaper in the morning, help people to imagine and identify with a national community.

Liberal politicians in both Britain and France in-

> The French revolutionaries' boldest claim was that the nation, not the king, was the sovereign power.

voked nationalist imagery. When Britain's prime minister Lord Palmerston declared in 1850 that any British citizen in any part of the world had but to proclaim, like a citizen of the Roman Empire, *"Civis romanus sum"* ("I am a citizen of Rome") to protect himself, he was echoing his countrymen's pride in the powers of their nation. When the French rejoiced in 1840 at the return of the emperor Napoleon's remains from St. Helena to an elaborate shrine in Paris, they were reliving triumphs that had become part of their nation's heritage. Palmerston's boast and Napoleon's bones were both artifacts of national traditions and sentiments bound up in the lives of the British and the French.

Nineteenth-century nationalism in other areas of Europe was to be an even more assertive phenomenon than it was in Britain and France, which had for centuries existed as particular geographical, cultural, and political entities. Elsewhere, common traditions and language were more difficult to discover, let alone impose. When no state existed, nationalists tended to either look to the past, to historical institutions and traditional rights, or appeal to common religion and ethnicity. In eastern Europe, for instance, when Polish and Hungarian nobles unfurled the banner of nationalism against the Habsburg dynasty, they hoped to revive their historic privileges. Proponents of a Czech nation leaned on cultural and literary traditions. Slavic nationalism had strong currents of Orthodox Christianity. Yet national identities usually had little meaning for the common people. A Silesian peasant or a Venetian merchant had no difficulty in perceiving of themselves as such; history had provided them with those identities. But history had not provided them, except in the most general way, with identities as Germans or Italians. They had to come to think of themselves in those terms to a degree the British and French did not, before the terms themselves could have much concrete meaning.

Nationalism proved a particularly explosive force in the Austrian Empire. When the Habsburg emperor sought to create an Austrian national identity, the effort quickly elicited counternationalism from Hungarians, Czechs, and many others for whom adopting an Austrian identity would imply acknowledging the inferiority of their culture. The history of nineteenth-century Austria proved, in a specific instance, what the history of nineteenth-century Europe proved more generally: not all nationalisms could be accommodated, and nationalism, often seen as a sentiment guaranteeing order, might as easily produce disorder.

NATIONALISM, ROMANTICISM, AND HISTORY

How did Romanticism influence nationalism?

Early nineteenth-century nationalism, like other political creeds, had strong currents of Romanticism. Romantic writers and artists fueled the development of nationalism by idealizing the imagined characteristics of specific peoples and cultures. Works of art and literature could be transformed from examples of their creators' talents into symbols of national culture. In Germany especially, nationalism was linked to conservative strains in Romanticism—thinkers who idealized history and community. Instead of emphasizing the uniqueness of individuals, these thinkers insisted on the uniqueness of cultures.

One of the earliest and most influential German nationalists was Johann von Herder. Herder was a Protestant pastor and theologian whose interest in past cultures led him, in the 1780s, to set out his thoughts, at great length, in *Ideas for a Philosophy of Human History*. For Herder, real civilization could not be produced by a learned, cultivated, and international elite—a criticism of eighteenth-century thinking; it came from of the genuine culture of the common people, in German the Volk. Each culture had to express its own unique historical character, or Volksgeist, the spirit (genius) of the people. Where other romantics prized individual genius, Herder extolled the particular genius of a people. No one Volksgeist was either better or worse than any other. Herder insisted only that each nation must be true to its own particular heritage, in Germany's case its culture and language. Herder did not believe in the superiority of the German people. On the contrary, he regarded the Slavic peoples as embodying some of humanity's best and most democratic impulses—largely because they were so poorly treated by Germans. Herder's writings were especially important to the Czechs. Most educated Czechs attended German universities and read German writers; in Herder they found a call to study their own language and cultural traditions and a stimulus to Czech nationalism.

In Germany, conservative Romantics and historians such as Friedrich Schlegel and Friedrich von Savigny helped to develop Herder's ideas. They condemned any effort to implant "foreign" democratic and liberal ideas in German cultural soil. History, they argued, taught that institutions must evolve organically (a favorite word of the German Romantics), and that good laws issued from a nation's particular historical growth rather than following, rationally, from universally established first principles. Thus the development of future laws and institutions rested on understanding a nation's past. This idea was not peculiar to German Romantics. The British Romantic poet and philosopher Samuel Taylor Coleridge argued in favor of giving that ancient institution, the national church, a larger role in the shaping of society. The French conservative François Chateaubriand made much the same case in *The Genius of Christianity* (1802). The past, and in particular the religious experiences of the national past, are woven into the present, he declared. They cannot be unwoven without destroying the fabric of a nation's society.

In Germany, too, nationalists drew on the work of Georg Wilhelm Hegel, an idealist philosopher and professor of philosophy at the University of Berlin. Hegel's work on the organic evolution of society and the state was at once very difficult and enormously influential. What his students and intellectual heirs took from him was, primarily, a theory of history. Hegel wrote of history as development and change. History was not just the accumulation of precedents, it did not follow divine will or design, but it did have a meaning. Social and political institutions grew to maturity, achieved their purposes, and then gave way to others. Yet the new never entirely replaced the old, for the pattern of change was a "dialectic." When new institutions challenged established ones, there was a clash between what had been and what was becoming, producing a "synthesis," a reordering of society that retained elements from the past while adapting to the present. Hegel expected, for example, that the present disunity among the German states, which generated the idea of unity, would result in the creation of a nation-state. The state was itself a natural historic organism; only within that institution, protected by its particular laws and customs, could men and women enjoy freedom, which Hegel defined not as the absence of restraint but as the absence of social disorder.

These theories of history and of historical development played an important role in the development of nationalism in the first decades of the nineteenth century. So did the French revolution. In Germany (and in Italy), revolutionary France was both an inspiration, showing what a nation could achieve, and a negative example, against which Germany's own distinctive character could shine. The works of the philosopher J. G. Fichte are a case in point. Fichte was a young professor at the University of Jena in east central Germany during the revolution. Like the British poet Wordsworth and many others, he welcomed the French Revolution as an emancipation of the human spirit. Yet when France conquered much of Germany, Fichte's attitude changed dramatically. He adopted Herder's notion of a Volksgeist. What mattered was no longer the individual spirit, but the spirit of a whole people, expressed in its customs, traditions, and history. In 1808, Fichte delivered a series of *Addresses to the German Nation*, in which he declared the spirit of the German people to be, potentially, superior to the French and others. Though the world had not yet heard from that spirit, he predicted it soon would. The French military commander in Berlin, where Fichte spoke, considered the addresses too academic to bother censoring. Yet they were widely echoed during the Prussian campaigns to rally the people and throw out Napoleon and the French. The Prussian statesman

An Illustration from *Grimms' Fairy Tales.*

Romantic Nationalism on the Stage. Gioachinno Rossini's very popular 1829 opera, *William Tell,* retold the story of a fourteenth-century Swiss peasant who had rebelled against Austrian rule. The opera was composed by an Italian, based on an 1804 play by the German Friedrich von Schiller, and performed in Paris; Romantic accounts of the "awakening of peoples" had international appeal.

Baron Wilhelm von Humboldt seconded Fichte's insistence on a special German spirit. "Other nations do not love their country in the same way as we love Germany." That love, Humboldt said, rested on "a longing for German feeling and German spirit." German nationalism sought to fuse individuality with the collectivity of the German feeling and German spirit. Only through that fusion could the German nation assume its rightful place in history.

Nationalism was also shaped by the Romantics' new historical imagination and keen interest in historical development and destiny. The brothers Grimm, editors of *Grimms' Fairy Tales* (1812–1815), traveled across Germany to study native dialects, and collected folktales that were published as part of a national heritage. The poet Friedrich Schiller retold the drama of the Swiss hero William Tell (1804) to make it a rallying cry for German national consciousness. Ironically, the Italian composer Gioacchino Rossini later turned Schiller's

poem into an opera that was used to promote the cause of Italian nationalism. In Britain, Sir Walter Scott retold in many of his novels the popular history of Scotland; Wordsworth's *Lyrical Ballads* sought to evoke the simplicity and virtue of the English people. Among the Poles, Adam Mickiewicz wrote the national epic *Pan Tadeusz* ("Lord Thaddeus") as a vision of a recently lost way of life.

Music, too, reflected national themes, though not until a generation or so after 1815. Many of Giuseppe Verdi's operas, such as *Don Carlos,* contained musical declarations of faith in the resurgence of the Italian spirit. The operas of Richard Wagner—in particular, those based on the German epic *Song of the Nibelungs*—reinterpreted the myths of Nordic gods and goddesses. Though architects found it difficult to escape entirely from the Neoclassicism of the eighteenth century, they often tried to resurrect a "national" style in their designs. Sir Charles Barry, assigned the task of redesigning the British Houses of Parliament following their destruction by fire in 1836, managed to mask a straightforward and symmetrical classical plan behind a Gothic screen, intended to acknowledge the country's debt to its own past. All this creative activity was the spontaneous result of artists' and writers' enthusiastic response to the Romantic movement—again, a reflection of the importance of Romanticism as a "cultural style." But it should not be interpreted as evidence of deep-seated popular nationalism. For artisans and peasants in the 1840s, social, economic, and political issues mattered more than nation building.

REFORM AND NATION BUILDING IN GERMANY, 1800–1848

Which groups drove reform in early nineteenth-century Germany?

Germany as a nation-state did not exist during this period. The Congress of Vienna had created a "German Confederation," a loose organization of thirty-eight states, including Austria and Prussia, although their non-German territories (sections of Poland, and Hungary) were not included. The Confederation was intended to provide only common defense; there was no real executive power. As a practical matter, Prussia, the great power in the area, loomed large on the horizon of anyone who wanted change.

In 1806, Prussia had suffered humiliating defeat at the hands of Napoleon. Unlike the rest of the German states, which were allied directly with France in the Confederation of the Rhine, the separate kingdom of Prussia consciously avoided French "contamination." That defeat, however, mobilized both conservatives and liberals to restore their country to its former position among European powers. Many considered that defeat the logical result of the inertia that had gripped the country during the half century or so since the aggressive achievements of Frederick the Great. They saw aggressive reforms as the remedy.

The reforms that followed were imposed from above. The reformers' major task was to rebuild the country's armies. To that end, and borrowing from the Napoleonic example, they reconstituted the army. Eventually based on a system of universal military service, the army involved the country as a whole in its own defense and became a more consciously "Prussian" force than it had been before. Officers were recruited and promoted on the basis of merit, not birth, although the large majority continued to come from the Junker (aristocratic) class. Members of the middle class were encouraged to take a more active role. Old or inefficient officers, even those with noble status, were removed from positions of command; training at the royal cadet school in Berlin was modernized. These reforms were, at once, liberalizing and nation building.

Similar changes came in the political sphere under the direction of Prussia's principal minister, Baron Heinrich von Stein, and his successor, Prince Karl von Hardenberg. Stein was not himself a Prussian; he was initially less interested in achieving a Prussian nation-state than in finding a way to unite the various principalities of Germany. He had read Hegel and Fichte, and was convinced that a state must make its citizens aware of their obligations to the

GERMAN CONFEDERATION, 1815

Compare this map with the one on p. 815. What helped to bring the various states of the German Confederation together? What was their relationship with German-speaking Prussia? What factors prevented a more formally unified German state at this time?

national interest. Stein hoped to bring a "revival of patriotism and of a national honor and independence" so that Prussians would be willing "to sacrifice property and life" for king and fatherland. Citizens, however, were more likely to make sacrifices than subjects, and Stein began a reform program to build civic equality and dismantle social privilege in Prussia. The Edict of 1807 abolished serfdom and the estate system, ended the restrictions that kept nobles from selling their land to the middle class, and opened trades and professions to all classes. The Municipal Ordinance of 1808 was a conscious attempt to increase middle-class Germans' sense of themselves as citizens—a goal shared by liberals and nationalists. The ordinance required cities and towns to elect their councilmen and handle their own finances. (Justice and security continued to be administered by the central government in Berlin.) The Prussian reformers expanded facilities for both primary and secondary education and founded the University of Berlin, which numbered among its faculty such ardent nationalists as Fichte and Savigny.

The history of Prussia between 1815 and 1850 can most easily be understood in terms of its continuing struggle to establish itself as the leading independent national power among the thirty-nine states that Germany comprised after 1806, and as a successful rival to Austrian domination. The most important Prussian victory in this respect was creating the Zollverein, or customs union, in 1834, which established free trade among the German states and a uniform tariff against the rest of the world. By the 1840s, the union included almost all of German states except German Austria, and offered manufacturers a market of almost 34 million people. The spread of the railways after 1835 provided easy access within this internal market. The important economist Friedrich List justified this protectionist system to liberal free-trade economists. Whereas free trade might suit the British, List wrote, it did not suit a nation such as Prussia. Economics was not an abstract science equally applicable everywhere, but a discipline that must be grounded in the particular national experience of individual countries. Only when sheltered behind a protectionist system could Prussia build the factories and manufacture the goods that would guarantee its economic health.

In both Prussia and the smaller German states, middle-class liberal movements pressed for reforms like those that had changed France and Britain in the first half of the nineteenth century. Liberals resented both Prussian dominance within the German Confederation and the conservatism of the ruling Habsburgs

in the Austrian empire. They attacked the combination of autocracy and bureaucratic authority that stifled political life in Prussia and Austria, and they hoped that unity would bring freedom. The creation of a German nation would lead to the realization of liberal goals; it would break with the fragmentation that had haunted Germany's political past; it would end the Austrian or Prussian domination that they believed would blight Germany's future.

Students were among the earliest proponents of German nationalism. Student fraternities devoted to the emancipation of Germany (Burschenschaften) had sprung up throughout Germany following the Napoleonic wars. At an assembly in 1817 at Wartburg Castle, where three hundred years before Martin Luther had proclaimed his Ninety-Five Theses, these modern protestants on behalf of "the holy cause of union and freedom" marched to a bonfire upon which they placed the works of reactionary writers. Repressed for a time by Metternich, who was by now the Austrian chancellor, the Burschenschaften reappeared in the late 1820s and welcomed the 1830 revolution in France. Minor revolts occurred in Brunswick, Saxony, and Hesse-Cassel; unpopular monarchs were replaced by royal relatives more sympathetic to reform. At an all-German festival held at Hambach, on the French border, in 1832, twenty-five thousand men and women toasted Lafayette and denounced the Holy Alliance. The activities of the Burschenschaften expressed a form of nationalism linked to the ideals of the French Revolution, and therefore alarming to the German and Austrian political establishment. Once again, Metternich imposed a series of repressive reforms upon the German Confederation, stifling protest. German conservatives might support "the holy cause of union and freedom" if it meant opposing Austrian domination of central Europe, but conservatives feared that national sentiments might easily be joined with democratic aspirations.

In the 1840s, the liberal pulse quickened throughout the German states. Newspapers multiplied, defying censorship. Political clubs, gathering middle-class lawyers, doctors, and businessmen, pressed demands for representative government and reform. In Prussia, the reforms instituted a generation before by Stein and Hardenberg had answered only some demands. When Frederick William IV (1840–1861) succeeded to the Prussian throne in 1840, liberals' expectations rose. Frederick William did make gestures toward liberal principles. He relaxed censorship laws and encouraged participation in the central government by provincial

CHRONOLOGY

NATION BUILDING IN GERMANY, 1800–1850

Napoleon defeats Prussia	1806
Edict abolishing serfdom	1807
Municipal Ordinance of 1808	
Creation of the Zollverein	1834
Liberal protests	1820s–1840s
Revolution of 1848	
Frankfurt Assembly meets	1848
Frederick Willam grants Prussian constitution	1850

diets. Yet his authoritarian tendencies soon became apparent. The economic troubles of the 1840s tested his regime. He sent troops in to crush a revolt of the weavers of Silesia, who were protesting the importation of English yarn and cotton goods and, generally, unemployment, falling wages, and hunger. The brutality of the repression shocked many. He made plain his opposition to constitutionalism, that central doctrine in the liberal canon of beliefs. The liberals kept up their campaign, pressing in 1847 for control over legislative and budgetary matters in the recently convened assembly of diets (the Landtag). They confronted tenacious resistance from the king. Frederick William, determined to avoid revolution from below, turned his attention to a scheme whereby Prussia might play a far larger role in the German Confederation. But before his plan could receive a hearing, it was overtaken by the revolutionary movement of 1848, which, as we shall see, engulfed central Europe as it had western Europe, though with different results.

NATIONALISM IN THE HABSBURG EMPIRE

How did Austrian and German nationalism differ?

In the German states, nationalist sentiments pulled toward unification. In the sprawling and multiethnic Austrian empire, nationalism played a different, centrifugal role. The peoples of the empire, who lived within three major geographical areas—Austria, Bohemia, and Hungary—were composed of a considerable number of different ethnic and language groups: Germans, Czechs, Magyars, Poles, Slovaks, Serbs, and Italians, to name the most prominent. In some parts of the empire, these ethnic groups lived in relatively isolated clusters; elsewhere they dwelt in direct proximity, if not much harmony, with others. The Habsburgs' attempts to hold these groups and their empire together grew increasingly difficult as nationalist sentiment rose after 1815. In the Polish territories of the empire, nationalist sentiment was strongest among aristocrats, who were especially conscious of their historic role as leaders of the Polish nation. Here, the Habsburg empire successfully played the serfs against their masters, and social grievances became a way of dampening ethnic nationalism. Elsewhere within the empire the government was less adroit. Hungarian nationalism was also tied to a relatively small Magyar aristocracy, and it took both cultural and political forms. In 1827, a Hungarian national theater was established at Budapest. The year before, Magyar was substituted for Latin as the official language of government. In addition, a political movement, led by the gifted and influential radical nationalist Lajos (Louis) Kossuth, had begun to seek independence and a parliamentary government for Hungary. Kossuth came from the lower nobility; he was by turns a lawyer, publicist, newspaper editor, and political leader. To protest the closed political debates of the empire's barely representative Diet (Parliament) Kossuth published transcripts of parliamentary debates, and had the transcripts copied and distributed. He campaigned to bring politics to the people. He staged political "banquets" like those in France, where local and national personalities would make speeches in the form of toasts, and interested citizens could eat, drink, and participate in politics. Kossuth's newspaper promoted liberal causes, for instance helping to get Tocqueville's *Democracy in America* translated into Hungarian. The Hungarian political leader combined aristocratic style with rabble-rousing politics: a delicate balancing act but one that, when it worked, catapulted him to the center of Habsburg politics. He was as well known in the Habsburg capital of Vienna as he was in Pressburg and Budapest.

The most widespread of the eastern European cultural nationalist movements was Pan-Slavism. Slavs included Russians, Poles, Ukrainians, Czechs, Slovaks, Slovenes, Croats, Serbs, Macedonians, and Bulgarians. Before 1848 Pan-Slavism was almost exclusively a cultural movement. Although it was united by a general

LANGUAGES OF THE AUSTRIAN EMPIRE

This map shows the distribution of languages across the German Confederation and the Austrian Empire. Note the pattern of linguistic groups in comparison to the political boundaries. How did this disparity help encourage nationalism in central and southeastern Europe? Why was the Austrian Empire at a disadvantage in achieving some permanent unity when contrasted with the situation in the German Confederation? How did the emergence of identities based on language ultimately help redraw the map of Europe?

pro-Slavic sentiment, it was also divided by quarrels over the superiority of different Slavic languages and traditions. Pan-Slavism inspired the works of the Czech historian and leader, František Palacký, author of *History of the Bohemian People,* and the Slovak Jan Kollár, whose book *Salvy Dcera ("Slava's Daughter")* mourned the loss of identity among Slavs in the Germanic world. A renewed sense of "Slavic" uniqueness became part of the "autocracy, orthodoxy, nationality" ideology of Tsar Nicholas after 1825. Pan-Slavism did not appeal to all; as it became more closely associated with Russia, it alienated the Western-oriented Poles and other Slavs who resented oppressive Russian rule. Despite these divisions, Pan-Slavism remained a thorn in the side of the Habsburg empire. The literature of the movement—for example, the poetry of the revolutionary Pole Adam Mickiewicz—fed the desires of those who wished to rid themselves of what they considered a foreign yoke. In Russia, extreme nationalism had been held in check by the Western-turning Alexander I. After his death in 1825, however, the notion that the Russian people possessed distinctive characteristics increased in general popularity. At the same time, the many ethnic minorities within Russia began pressing for their own recognition.

Giuseppe Mazzini.

NATIONALISM IN ITALY AND IRELAND

How did Italian and Irish nationalism differ?

Two other nationalist movements developed in the years before 1848: one in Italy, the other in Ireland. At the beginning of the nineteenth century, the Italian peninsula was divided into a multitude of states, most of them poor and ineffectually governed. Austria occupied the most economically developed, industrial, and urban states of Italy, Lombardy and Venetia, but also cast its influence over semidependent provinces. At the opposite pole were the kingdom of the Two Sicilies and the Papal States. The Sicilies were governed by equally obscurantist rulers, Francis I (1825–1830), a Bourbon, and thereafter by his son, Ferdinand II (1830–1859); Pope Gregory XVI ruled the Papal States (1831–1846). Of the independent states, the most effectively run was Piedmont-Sardinia, headed by a royal family with a tradition of dynastic opposition to the Habsburgs, though

no particular commitment to nationalism. By virtue of being independent, though, the reform-minded king of Sardinia, Charles Albert (1831–1849), played a central role in nationalist and anti-Austrian politics. The year 1830 brought scattered uprisings in Modena, Parma, and Bologna, but few lasting consequences, either for local liberal reforms or for the cause of unifying the various disparate states into some sort of national whole.

The leading figure in Italian nationalism, and a prominent Romantic nationalist, was Giuseppe Mazzini. Mazzini began his political career as a member of the secret society of Carbonari, and from there went on to found, in 1831, a society of his own. Young Italy, as it was called, was dedicated to the cause of uniting the peninsula. Mazzini spoke in Romantic tones of the awakening of the Italian people, and of the common people's mission to bring democracy to the world; his brand of romantic nationalism was populist and democratic. Mazzini also had charisma and a gift for political persuasion. Under his star Young Italy clubs multiplied. Their politics, however, proved ineffective. Young Italy hatched plots for mutinies and armed rebellions, none of which produced any effect. In 1834, Mazzini launched an invasion of the kingdom of Sardinia from Switzerland. But when the rest of Italy did not rally behind him, the invasion turned into a fiasco.

WHY DID THE REVOLUTIONS OF 1848 IN GERMANY AND AUSTRIA FAIL?

THE REVOLUTION OF 1848 IN THE AUSTRIAN EMPIRE   817

Mazzini subsequently contented himself with promoting Italian nationalism and republicanism, attracting a devoted following, particularly among British liberals. Liberals in Italy, however, mistrusted him. Although they too wished to see a united Italy, as "good" liberals and members of the middle class they were dismayed by Mazzini's insistence on a republic. They hoped instead to merge existing principalities together into some sort of constitutional monarchy.

If Italian nationalism was primarily a middle-class, liberal phenomenon at this time, the same was not true of the Irish movement to repeal the union with Britain. Headed by Daniel O'Connell, the Irish movement derived its strength from the support of Irish peasants. O'Connell's remarkably successful appeal was based on the hatred all Irish felt for the British because of the centuries of oppression Irish Catholics had suffered under British Protestant rule. Both before and after the official union of 1801, the British had imposed on the Irish a foreign rule that had brought with it little but poverty and persecution. O'Connell's campaign for the repeal of the union was grounded in the hope that he would be able to negotiate some sort of moderate agreement with the British ruling class. The desires of his followers were far more radical. Neither the separatist hopes of O'Connell, called by the Irish the "Liberator," nor the more genuinely nationalist hopes of his followers, however, would be realized. Unlike the nationalist movements of central Europe, nationalism in Ireland faced a powerful and determined adversary—Britain—which would for a century deny it victory.

THE REVOLUTION OF 1848 IN THE AUSTRIAN EMPIRE

Why did the revolutions of 1848 in Germany and Austria fail?

In central and eastern Europe, the spring of 1848 brought a dizzying sequence of revolution and repression. These 1848 revolutions arose from the same combination of acute economic distress and mounting political frustration that produced revolution in France. Yet they were propelled—and pulled apart—by a different set of forces, most of which were connected with nationalism. To simplify, we can focus on two themes.

The first theme is the the struggle of various nationalities, particularly within the Austrian empire, to assert their own autonomy. The so-called springtime of peoples often lapsed into violence between different ethnic groups. The second theme is the changing relationship between the forces of liberalism and nationalism in Germany.

1848: AUSTRIA-HUNGARY

News of the February revolution in France traveled quickly eastward. By the end of March 1848 several different movements had split the Habsburg empire apart. Kossuth, in Hungary, actually provided much of the early leadership and spark. In March 1848, he pilloried the "Metternich system" of Habsburg autocracy and control, demanding representative institutions throughout the empire and, characteristically, more autonomy for the Hungarian "Magyar" nation. The Hungarian Diet prepared to draft its own constitution. In Vienna as in Paris, a popular movement combined students and artisans, who built barricades and attacked the imperial palace. A Central Committee of Citizens took shape, as did a middle-class militia, or National Guard, determined at once to maintain order and press demands for reform. The Habsburg regime made a few initial concessions, then tried to shut the movement down, closing the university. That effort only unleashed more popular anger, forcing the regime to retreat almost entirely. Metternich, veteran of a score of threats to the precarious stability he had crafted, found the pressure this time too great, and fled in disguise to Britain—a measure of the political turmoil. The government conceded to radical demands for male suffrage and a single house of representatives; it also agreed to withdraw troops from Vienna. It began the process of abolishing forced labor and serfdom in various Habsburg-run provinces. Once he had been deserted by Metternich, the Habsburg emperor, Ferdinand I, yielded to Czech demands in Bohemia, granting that kingdom its own constitution. To the south, Italian liberals and nationalists attacked Austrian-held territories in Naples and Venice; in Milan, the forces of King Charles Albert of Piedmont routed the Austrians, raising hopes of victory.

Yet the forces of national sentiment that had brought the Habsburgs to their knees later allowed the empire to recoup its fortunes. The paradox of nationalism in central Europe was that as soon as a cultural majority had declared itself an independent or semi-independent state, other cultural minorities

The "March Days" in Vienna. The revolutionary fervor of 1848 transcended class boundaries. In this watercolor a student leads armed railway workers to the center of Vienna.

within that new state rebelled against their status in the new regime. In Bohemia, for instance, Czechs and Germans who lived side by side worked in concert to pass reforms ending feudalism. Within a month, however, nationalism was splitting their alliance apart. German Bohemians wanted to attend an all-German parliament meeting in Frankfurt to create a constitution (see below); the Czech majority refused to send representatives. What was more, the Czechs countered by convening a confederation of Slavs in Prague. Some of the delegates to the Slav confederation were hostile to what the Russian anarchist Baukunin called the "monstrous Austrian empire." But the majority of delegates preferred to be ruled by the Habsburgs (though with some autonomy) than to be dominated by the Germans or the Russians. This bundle of animosities allowed the Austrians to divide and conquer. In May 1848, there was a student- and worker-led insurrection in Prague. Austrian troops

came into the city to restore order, sent the Slav congress packing, and reasserted control in Bohemia. The repression was ordered by the liberal Austrian government, the product of the March revolution in Vienna. Yet it was no less determined than its predecessor had been to prevent the total dismemberment of the empire, for economic as well as political reasons. For the same reasons, the regime sent troops to restore control in the Italian provinces of Lombardy and Venetia, and quarrels among the Italians helped the Austrians succeed.

Nationalism and counternationalism in Hungary set the stage for the final act of the drama, which restored Austrian hegemony. The March Laws, passed by the Hungarian parliament and accepted by Ferdinand I, served as a constitution to unite Hungary with Austria, though solely through a personal union. They abolished serfdom, ended noble privilege, established freedom of the press and of religion, and implemented

WHY DID THE REVOLUTIONS OF 1848 IN GERMANY AND AUSTRIA FAIL?

THE REVOLUTION OF 1848 IN THE AUSTRIAN EMPIRE   819

male suffrage with low property requirements. Fear of peasant insurrection made passing sweeping reforms urgent. These laws did find considerable support among Hungarian peasants, Jewish communities, and women. But other provisions, particularly the extension of Magyar control, also provoked opposition from the Croats, Serbs, and Romanians within Hungary. After crushing the Bohemian revolution in Prague in the spring and a second revolution in Vienna, the Austrians appointed the anti-Magyar Josip Jelacic as governor of the breakaway province of Croatia. Encouraged by the Austrians, Jelacic first broke off links with and then attacked Hungary. Kossuth defied the invaders, and by March of 1849, he had succeeded in turning the tide in the Hungarians' favor, fighting against both Austrians and Croats. On April 14 he boldly severed all ties with the Habsburgs. The new Austrian emperor, Franz Josef, now had no choice but to seek aid from Nicholas I of Russia. The Habsburgs were unable to win their "holy struggle against anarchy," but the Russian army of over three hundred thousand found this an easier task. By mid-August 1849, the Hungarian revolt was crushed.

In Vienna itself, the revolutionary movement lost ground through the fall of 1848. Economic crisis and unemployment helped spark a second popular uprising in Vienna in October. At that point, the emperor's forces, assisted by troops from Russia, descended on Vienna. On October 31, the liberal government capitulated. The regime reestablished censorship, disbanded the National Guard and student organizations, and put twenty-five revolutionary leaders to death in front of a firing squad. Kossuth went into hiding in Turkey, and lived the rest of his life in exile.

Once the imperial government had reasserted itself, it passed a series of reforms designed to strengthen the state, win support, and keep nationalist impulses at bay. German became the official language throughout the Habsburg holdings. The emperor's chief minister, Prince Felix zu Schwarzenberg, and the minister of the interior, Alexander Bach, both nation builders, together centralized the state within one united political system. Hungary and Bohemia no longer enjoyed separate rights. Peasants of all ethnic groups, liberated from serfdom as part of the general reform movement, were permitted to retain their freedom in return for loyalty to the empire. The legal code was reformed to achieve uniformity. Railways and roads were constructed to link the empire. The government imposed tariffs against foreign manufacturers, but freed trade within the empire and between Austria and Germany,

to encourage Austrian industrial development. Having done all it could to eradicate separatist movements, the Austrian government thus moved to secure its advantage by engaging in a vigorous campaign of nation building.

1848 IN GERMANY

In Germany, revolution ran a similar course. In the smaller German states, kings and princes yielded surprisingly quickly to revolutionary movements. The governments promised freedom of the press, elections, expanded suffrage, jury trials, and other liberal reforms. In Prussia, Frederick William IV, who had successfully staved off liberal reforms thus far, faced revolutionary crowds in Berlin and finally capitulated. Equally important, all of the German states—and Austria—agreed to elect delegates to an all-German Assembly in Frankfurt to discuss the issue of national unification.

At this Frankfurt Assembly, issues of nationalism and liberalism came into sharp focus. Delegates were largely from the professional classes—professors,

Procession of the German Assembly to Its Opening Session at St. Paul's Church, Frankfurt, May 1848.

FREDERICK WILLIAM IV REFUSES THE "THRONE FROM THE GUTTER"

In March 1849, after months of deliberation and constitution making, the Frankfurt Assembly offered the throne of its proposed German state to the Prussian kaiser Frederick William IV, who quickly turned it down. He had already reflected on the matter. In an earlier (December 1848) letter to one of his advisors, the diplomat Christian von Bunsen, he had set out his reasoning as follows.

I want the princes' approval of neither *this* election nor *this* crown. Do you understand the words emphasized here? For you I want to shed light on this as briefly and brightly as possible. First, *this* crown is no crown. The crown which a Hohenzoller [the Prussian royal house] could accept, *if* circumstances *permitted*, is not one *made* by an assembly sprung from a revolutionary seed in the genre of the crown of cobble stones of Louis Philippe—even if this assembly was established with the sanction of princes . . . but one which bears the stamp of God, one which makes [the individual] on whom it [the crown] is placed, after his anointment, a "divine right" monarch—just as it has elevated more than 34 princes to Kings of the Germans by divine right and just as it bonds the last of these to his predecessors. The crown worn by Ottonians, Staufens [earlier German royal houses], Habsburgs can of course also be worn by a Hohenzoller; it honors him overwhelmingly with the luster of a thousand years. But *this* one, to which you regrettably refer, overwhelmingly dishonors [its bearer] with its smell of the gunpowder of the 1848 revolution—the silliest, dumbest, worst, though—thank God!—not the most evil of this century. Such an imaginary headband, baked out of dirt and the letters of the alphabet, is supposed to be welcome to a legitimate divine right king: to put it more precisely, to the King of Prussia who is blessed with a crown which may not be the oldest but, of all those which have never been stolen, is the most noble? . . . I will tell you outright: if the thousand-year-old crown of the German nation . . . should be bestowed again, it will be *I* and my equals who will bestow it. And woe to those who assume [powers] to which they have no title.

Ralph Menning, *The Art of the Possible: Documents on Great Power Diplomacy, 1814–1914* (New York: McGraw-Hill, 1996), p. 82.

lawyers, administrators—and generally devoted to the cause of middle-class liberalism. Many had assumed that their task would resemble that of the assembly that had met in 1789 to draft a constitution for the French: that is, they would draft a constitution for a liberal, unified Germany. In France in 1789, however, a French nation-state and a centralized sovereign power already existed. The French assembly had been elected to give the nation a new shape and new direction. By contrast, the Frankfurt Assembly had no resources, no sovereign power to take, no single legal code. Even the meeting place, an old church in Frankfurt, seemed to suggest the obstacles. The church had no separate meeting rooms for committees to confer and draft legislation; for eleven months nearly all discussions were in the public room, which had bad acoustics. Although

WHAT FORCES DROVE NATION BUILDING IN THE MID-NINETEENTH CENTURY?

NATION BUILDING IN THE WEST, 1850–1870   821

the Assembly benefited from the energy, idealism, and devotion of the delegates, at times it teetered on the brink of chaos.

Almost from the start, the Assembly found itself tangled in the problems of nationality. Who, the delegates asked, were the Germans? A majority of the delegates argued that Germans were all those who, by language, culture, or geography, felt themselves bound to the enterprise now underway at Frankfurt. The German nation being created must include as many "Germans" as possible—a goal that seemed achievable in view of the disintegrating Habsburg empire. This point of view came to be known as the "Great German" position. A minority called for a "Small Germany," one that left out all lands of the Habsburg empire, including Austrian Germany. Great Germans were a numerical majority, but they found themselves stymied by other nationalities unwilling to be included in their fold. The Czechs in Bohemia, as we have seen, wanted no part of Great Germany. After a long and difficult debate, and when the Habsburg emperor repudiated the enterprise, the Assembly moved toward the "Small German" solution and offered the crown of the new German nation to Frederick William IV.

Frederick William, though tempted, refused the offer. He argued that the Assembly's proposed constitution was too liberal. The very idea that a parliament could offer a crown to a monarch was insulting to him—he called it the "crown from the gutter." Frederick William wanted the crown, and he wanted a larger German state, but on his own terms. After a brief protest, summarily suppressed by the military, the delegates went home, disillusioned by their experience, many of them convinced that their dual goals of liberalism and nationalism were impossible. Some who refused to give up emigrated to the United States, where they believed the goals had already been achieved. Many of those who stayed behind convinced themselves that half the goal was better than none, and sacrificed the immediate achievement of liberal goals to the seemingly realistic goals of nationalism. In Prussia itself, the army dispatched what remained of the revolutionary forces.

In Prussia and all the German states, liberal debates such as the Frankfurt Assembly's unrolled against a backdrop of popular revolution. Peasants tore apart tax collectors' offices and burned castles, and workers smashed machines. In towns and cities, a groundswell of political activity took the form of citizen militias, new daily newspapers, pamphleteering, and political clubs. For the first time, many of these clubs admitted women, although they refused them the right to speak. As in Paris, in Berlin and other German cities separate women's clubs also emerged, asking to be admitted to the newly expanded political world. The concept of voting rights for all males, however, was already sufficiently radical to be alarming. In Prussia and the German states as elsewhere, popular politics made many moderate reformers uneasy. Popular anger and protest had been crucial in forcing the king to make concessions in the early spring of 1848, but they quickly came to be seen as threatening. If many German moderates wanted a new nation, it was to maintain order. "In order to realize our ideas of freedom and equality, we want above all a strong and powerful government," ran one speech during the election campaigns for the Frankfurt Assembly. Popular sovereignty, "strengthened by the authority of a hereditary monarchy, will be able to repress with an iron hand any disorder and any violation of the law."

NATION BUILDING IN THE WEST, 1850–1870

What forces drove nation building in the mid-nineteenth century?

The emergence of nationalism as a political force was one of the key developments of the nineteenth century. As we have witnessed, early forms of nationalism played a critical role in the revolutions of 1848. Even though those revolutions failed, new modern nations would be built—nations that would respond to the demands for more representative government, the abolition of privilege, and land reform. The unification of Germany and Italy changed the map of Europe and brought adjustments in the international balance of power. Across the Atlantic Ocean the internal expansion of the United States would begin the slow transformation of the former colonies into a world power.

THE UNIFICATION OF GERMANY AND THE CRIMEAN WAR

The Frankfurt Assembly and the revolution of 1848 failed to unite Germany. In the aftermath of that defeat, however, a German nation would be built under authoritarian Prussian rule. German nation building owed a great deal to the diplomatic skill of one man, Otto von Bismarck. Born into the Junker class of conservative, land-owning aristocrats, Bismarck had defended the monarchy during the revolutionary period of 1848–1849. An opponent of liberalism, Bismarck was not a nationalist. He was before all else a Prussian. He did not institute domestic reforms because he favored the "rights" of a particular group, but because he thought that these policies would unify and strengthen Prussia. When he maneuvered to bring other German states under Prussian domination, he did so not in pursuit of a grand Germanic design, but because he believed that some sort of union was inevitable. If that were the case, union should benefit Prussia. He prided himself on being a realist, and he became a first-rate practitioner of what has come to be called Realpolitik—the politics of what its supporters claim to be hardheaded reality. Bismarck readily acknowledged his admiration of power. At one point he had considered a career in the military, not surprising in view of his aristocratic origins. He once wrote that he regretted that he was compelled to serve his country from behind a desk rather than at the front. But whatever his post, he intended to command. "I want to play the tune the way it sounds good to me or not at all," he declared. "Pride, the desire to command . . . I confess I am not free from these passions." Nor did he consider those passions unworthy of the man who was to undertake the task of shaping the fortunes of the German state.

Bismarck was appointed prime minister of Prussia in 1862 by Kaiser William I (1861–1888), who needed Bismarck's help in a growing conflict with his liberal Parliament. The Prussian electoral system, part of the constitution granted by Frederick William to Prussia in 1850, had aimed to preserve conservative power. The parliament was divided into two houses, the lower one elected by universal male suffrage. Voters, however, were divided into three classes, depending on the amount of taxes they paid, and their votes were apportioned accordingly. The fewer wealthy voters who together paid one third of the country's taxes elected one third of the legislators. A large landowner or industrialist exercised about a hundred times the voting power of a laborer. Contrary to the king's expectations, however, a liberal majority had nonetheless emerged, and by the 1860s was again pressing its demands. A decade of industrial growth had consolidated the economic and political power of many liberals, and they would not give way. Specifically, since 1859 it had opposed increasing military expenditures, despite pressure from the king. In Bismarck the liberals more than met their match. When they refused to levy taxes, he dissolved the parliament and collected them anyway, claiming that the constitution, whatever its purposes, had not been designed to subvert the state. When liberals argued that Prussia was setting a poor example for the rest of Germany, Bismarck replied that Prussia was admired not for its liberalism but for its power.

> A decade of industrial growth in Germany had consolidated the economic and political power of many liberals, and they would not give way.

THE CRIMEAN WAR

Whether or not the Germans—or the rest of Europe—admired Prussia's power, they soon found themselves confronted by it. Bismarck proceeded to build a nation that in the short space of eight years came into being as the German empire. Bismarck was assisted in his task by his readiness to take advantage of international situations as they presented themselves, without concerning himself particularly with the ideological or moral implications of his actions. He was aided as well by developments over which he had no initial control but which he was able to turn to his advantage.

The first of these developments, the Crimean War, had occurred in 1854–1856, well before Bismarck took office. The issue was the "Eastern Question," the term Europeans used for Ottoman-controlled provinces in southeastern Europe. Russia, constantly trying to establish a presence in the Mediterranean and always willing to take advantage of Ottoman weakness, invaded the Ottoman-governed territories of Moldavia and Walachia (later Romania). The pretext was Turkey's refusal to honor Russia's right to protect Orthodox Christians in the Ottoman empire, including Jerusalem. Austria, acting to protect its border along the Danube, drove Russia out of these territories and garrisoned Austria's own troops there. The Russians turned on the Turks and quickly won the battle, but that victory only provoked French and especially British fears of Russian expansionism in the Near East. In 1854, France and then Britain declared war on Russia and invaded Russia's Crimean peninsula. France, Britain, and the Ottomans were soon joined by the small but ambitious Italian kingdom of Sardinia, all fighting against the Russians. This was the closest Europe had come to a general war since 1815.

WHAT FORCES DROVE NATION BUILDING IN THE MID-NINETEENTH CENTURY?

NATION BUILDING IN THE WEST, 1850–1870   823

The war was relatively short, but particularly gruesome. Conditions on the Crimean peninsula were dire, and the disastrous management of supplies and hygiene by the British and French led to epidemics among the troops. At least as many soldiers died from typhus or cholera as in combat; efforts to reform the care and supply of the troops became national scandals in the popular press, and made heroes of individual doctors and nurses such as Florence Nightingale. Indeed the war was the most "public" to date, with constant reports sent back to newspapers in Britain and France via telegraph, along with grim photographs of the troops and their living conditions that lacked the elegant distortions of paintings. The fighting was bitter as well; the British "charge of the Light Brigade," the ill-advised attack by a British cavalry unit that was slaughtered by massed Russian artillery, is only the most famous example. The battles were vast, pitting tens of thousands of British and French troops against Russian formations in combat that was often settled with bayonets. Despite the sheer physical toughness of the British and French troops, and their nations' dominance of the seas around Crimea, the Russians denied them a clear victory. The French and Sardinians took away positive national feelings about the bravery of their soldiers; the British and Russians met waves of intense internal criticism about the conduct of the war; the Ottomans simply survived. The bitter, unsatisfying conflict was ended by treaty in 1856.

As far as international relations were concerned, the peace settlement was a severe setback for Russia, whose influence in the Balkans was drastically curbed. The pro-

CRIMEAN WAR

This map depicts the theater of operations and the major assaults of the Crimean War. Why did the Crimean War erupt? Who comprised the opposing sides, and what were the aims of the Allies in launching an assault here? Why would some scholars deem this war one of the most senseless in European history? In what ways was the Crimean War the first "modern war"? In what ways did the Allies achieve their objectives?

The Crimean War. The Black Sea port of Balaklava, Ukraine, was essential for getting supplies to the French, Turkish, and British forces, and therefore it was the target of a Russian offensive in 1854. The Battle of Balaklava was indecisive, but it inspired Alfred Lord Tennyson's poem "Charge of the Light Brigade."

Portrait of Florence Nightingale. Nightingale became one of the few popular figures in the unpopular Crimean War. She made a crucial contribution to changes in the delivery of medical service in the military, altering procedures and improving hygiene in order to reduce the infections that ran rampant in nineteenth-century hospitals.

vinces of Moldavia and Walachia were united as Romania and became an independent nation. Austrian military resources had been severely taxed during the invasion and occupation of Moldavia and Walachia, wearing them down for future conflicts. And Austria's refusal to come to the aid of Russia lost her the support of that powerful erstwhile ally. The Crimean War left Russia and Austria considerably weaker, and Bismarck used this weakness to his advantage in the 1860s.

THE FRANCO-PRUSSIAN WAR AND GERMAN UNIFICATION

In consolidating the German states into a union controlled by Prussia, Bismarck first moved to eliminate Austria from its commanding position in the German Confederation. As a means to this end he inflamed the long-smoldering dispute with Denmark over the possession of Schleswig and Holstein. Inhabited by Germans and Danes, these two provinces had an anomalous status. Since 1815 Holstein had been included in the German Confederation, but both were subject to the personal overlordship of the king of

WHAT FORCES DROVE NATION BUILDING IN THE MID-NINETEENTH CENTURY?

NATION BUILDING IN THE WEST, 1850–1870   825

Denmark. When, in 1864, the Danish king attempted to annex them, Bismarck invited Austria to participate in a war against Denmark. A brief struggle followed, at the end of which the Danish ruler was compelled to renounce all his claims to Schleswig and Holstein in favor of Austria and Prussia. Then the sequel for which Bismarck had ardently hoped occurred: a quarrel between the victors over division of the spoils. The conflict that followed in 1866, known as the Seven Weeks' War, ended in an easy triumph for Prussia over war-weakened Austria. Austria was forced to give up all claims to Schleswig and Holstein, to surrender Venetia, and to acquiesce in the dissolution of the German Confederation. Immediately following the war Bismarck proceeded to isolate Austria by uniting all of the German states north of the Main River into the North German Confederation.

Bismarck's adept use of the Prussian military was matched by his manipulation of public support and opinion. He willingly turned himself into a democrat to achieve the confederation. He saw that if he was to attain his end—a strong union with Prussia at its head—he would need to cultivate a constituency hitherto untapped by any German politicians: the masses. He appreciated the manner in which Napoleon III had reinforced his regime through plebiscites. And Bismarck understood that the majority of Germans were not particularly enthusiastic supporters of capitalist liberals, of the bureaucracies of their own small states, or of the Austrian Habsburgs. The constitution he devised for his confederation provided for two chambers: the upper chamber represented the individual states within the union, though not equally; the lower chamber was elected by universal male suffrage. The liberal middle class, to say nothing of the Junkers, was astonished and dismayed, as well they might be. Bismarck's intention was to use popular support to strengthen the hand of the conservative central government against the interests of both landlords and capitalists.

Bismarck's final step in the completion of German unity was the Franco-Prussian War of 1870–1871. He hoped that a conflict with France would kindle the spirit of German nationalism in Bavaria, Württemberg, and other southern states still outside the confederation; he understood, that is, how powerful a spur to national sentiment an enemy "other" could prove. Taking advantage of a diplomatic tempest concerning the right of the Hohenzollerns (Prussia's ruling family) to occupy the Spanish throne, Bismarck worked hard to foment a Franco-German misunderstanding. King William agreed to meet with the French ambassador at the resort spa of Ems in Prussia to discuss the Spanish succession. When William telegraphed Bismarck that the demands of the French for perpetual exclusion of the Hohenzollern family from the Spanish throne had been refused, Bismarck released portions of the message to the press so as to make it appear that King William had insulted the ambassador—which he had not done. Once the garbled report of what happened at Ems was received in France, the nation reacted with a call for war. The call was echoed in Prussia, where Bismarck published evidence that he claimed proved French designs upon the Rhineland. Upon the declaration of war, the south German states rallied to Prussia's side in the belief that it was the victim of aggression. The war was quickly fought. The French were no match for Prussia's professionally trained and superbly equipped forces. Nor did other European powers come to France's assistance. Austria, the most likely candidate, remained weakened by its recent war with Prussia. The Magyars, who at this time had assumed positions of influence within the Austrian government, were quite prepared to welcome a strengthened Prussia; Prussia's growing strength in Germany would further increase Austria's weakness there. And the weaker Austria was as a German power, the stronger would be the claims of the Magyars to predominance. Once more one nationalist consciousness was grinding against another. The war began in July; it ended in September with the defeat of the French and the capture of Napoleon III himself at Sedan in France.

Following the collapse of the French imperial government, insurrectionary forces in Paris continued to hold out against the Germans until the winter of 1870–1871. Bismarck meanwhile proceeded to consummate the German union toward which he had worked so assiduously. On January 18, 1871, in the great Hall of Mirrors at Versailles, the German empire

CHRONOLOGY

UNIFICATION OF GERMANY, 1854–1871

Crimean War	1854–1856
Bismarck becomes prime minister	1862
Danish War	1864
Seven Weeks' War	1866
Franco-Prussian War	1870–1871

SWEDEN

NORTH
SEA

DENMARK

BALTIC SEA

Memel

Niemen R.

Copenhagen

Königsberg

EAST
PRUSSIA

SCHLESWIG

Kiel

Danzig

WEST
PRUSSIA

HOLSTEIN

Lübeck

POMERANIA

POSEN

POLAND

Hamburg

MECKLENBURG
SCHWERIN

Stettin

OLDENBURG

Bremen

Warthe R.

Vistula R.

Warsaw

HANOVER

Berlin

Posen

RUSSIAN

Amsterdam

Hanover

BRANDENBURG

Lodz

EMPIRE

NETHERLANDS

Breslau

WESTPHALIA

Elbe R.

SILESIA

Leipzig

Antwerp

Rhine R.

Weimar

Dresden

Oder R.

Lemberg

BELGIUM

Bonn

Cologne

THURINGIAN
STATES

SAXONY

Sadowa
(1866)

RHINE
PROVINCE

Cracow

LUXEMBURG

Mainz

Frankfurt

Main R.

BOHEMIA

Prague

MORAVIA

Sedan
(1870)

HESSE

Nuremberg

Olmütz

Verdun

Metz

PALATINATE

Toul

LORRAINE

Karlsruhe

BAVARIA

AUSTRIAN

Strasbourg

Stuttgart

Danube R.

Vienna

ALSACE

Munich

BADEN

AUSTRIA

Zurich

EMPIRE

HUNGARY

FRANCE

Berne

SWITZERLAND

Trieste

Milan

Venice

ADRIATIC

Po R.

SEA

ITALY

EUROPE

Area of
detail

AFRICA

0   100   200 Miles
0   100   200 Kilometers

German Confederation boundary (1815)

Prussian acquisitions

From Austria in 1763   Prussia
                               (1815)
From partitions of Poland
in 1772, 1793, 1795

States annexed by Prussia in 1866

States joining Prussia in Confederation of 1867

North German Confederation boundary

States added to form German Empire (1871)

Territories ceded by France (1871)

✳ Battle

■ Fortifications

TOWARD THE UNIFICATION OF GERMANY

This map outlines the stages leading to the unification of the German state in the eighteenth and nineteenth centuries. How did the German state of Prussia expand at the expense of Poland and the Austrian empire? On what basis was the relatively small Baltic state of Prussia able to vie with other, larger powers in central and eastern Europe? How did the nineteenth-century wars with France ultimately strengthen the emergent Prussian state? Examine closely the fragmented nature of Prussia. What challenges did Bismarck face in making a unified Germany a reality? What cultural and historical factors could he use to his advantage?

was proclaimed. All those states, except Austria, that had not already been absorbed into Prussia declared their allegiance to William I, henceforth emperor or kaiser. Four months later, at Frankfurt, a treaty between the French and Germans ceded the border region of Alsace to the new empire, condemned the French to an

WHAT FORCES DROVE NATION BUILDING IN THE MID-NINETEENTH CENTURY?

NATION BUILDING IN THE WEST, 1850–1870   827

indemnity of 5 billion francs, and thereby broadcast to the world the remarkable success of Bismarck's nation building.

THE UNIFICATION OF ITALY

The building of the Italian nation paralleled the unification of Germany. Before 1848, Italy was a patchwork of small states. The most important ones not under Habsburg control were the kingdom of Sardinia in the north, the Papal States in the central region, and the kingdom of the Two Sicilies in the south. The former republics of Lombardy and Venetia were held by Austria, while Habsburg dependents ruled in Tuscany, Parma, and Modena. As the revolutionary fervor of 1848 swept across the peninsula, one ruler after another granted democratic reforms. Charles Albert of Sardinia outdistanced all the others by guaranteeing civil liberties and granting a parliamentary form of government. These victories raised the hopes of nationalists who spoke of a *risorgimento*, or Italian resurgence, that would restore the nation to the position of leadership it had held in Roman times and during the Renaissance. To achieve this, Italy must be welded into a single state. Opinions differed as to the form the new government should take. Young idealists for a time followed the leadership of Giuseppe Mazzini. Religious-minded patriots hoped for a federated state of Italy under the presidency of the pope. Most moderate nationalists advocated a constitutional monarchy built upon the foundations of the kingdom of Sardinia. The aims of this third group gradually crystallized under the leadership of a shrewd Sardinian nobleman, Count Camillo Benso di Cavour (1810–1861). In 1850 he was appointed minister of commerce and agriculture of his native state and in 1852, premier.

The campaign for unification of the Italian peninsula began with efforts to expel the Austrians. In 1848, the territories under Habsburg domination rebelled, and the Sardinian army marched to aid the rebels. After brief successes, the movement failed. Cavour, now considered the leader of the campaign, turned to less heroic but more practical methods. In 1858 he held a secret meeting with Napoleon III and prepared the stage for an Italian war of liberation. Napoleon agreed to cooperate in driving the Austrians from Italy in return for Sardinia ceding Savoy and Nice to France. A

> Liberal victories raised the hopes of nationalists who spoke of an Italian resurgence that would restore the nation to the position of leadership it had held in Roman times and during the Renaissance.

war with Austria was duly provoked in 1859, and for a time all went well for the Franco-Italian allies. After the conquest of Lombardy, however, Napoleon III suddenly withdrew, concerned that he might either lose or antagonize Catholics, alienated by Cavour's hostility to the pope. Deserted by the French, Sardinia could not expel the Austrians from Venetia. The campaign did make extensive gains: Sardinia annexed Lombardy and acquired by various means the duchies of Tuscany, Parma, and Modena, and the northern portion of the Papal States. Sardinia was now more than twice its original size and by far the most powerful state in Italy.

The second step in consolidating Italy was the conquest of the kingdom of the Two Sicilies, ruled by an unpopular Bourbon king, Francis II (1859–1860). In May 1860 a romantic adventurer, Giuseppe Garibaldi, set out with a regiment of one thousand "red shirts" to liberate Sicily from the Bourbon rule. Within three months he had conquered the island of Sicily and had then marched on to Naples,

Camillo di Cavour.

SWITZERLAND

AUSTRIA

EUROPE

Area of
detail

AFRICA

SAVOY
(to France in 1860)

LOMBARDY

VENETIA

KINGDOM OF
SARDINIA

Milan

Venice

Turin

Po R.

PIEDMONT

PARMA

FRANCE

Genoa

MODENA

Bologna

ROMAGNA

OTTOMAN
EMPIRE

LUCCA

Florence

Arno R.

TUSCANY

PAPAL STATES

ADRIATIC SEA

CORSICA
(to France)

UMBRIA

Tiber R.

Rome

KINGDOM
OF
SARDINIA

TYRRHENIAN
SEA

Naples

KINGDOM OF THE TWO SICILIES

MEDITERRANEAN SEA

Palermo

Messina

SICILY

The Kingdom of Sardinia at the time
of the Congress of Vienna, 1815

Territories acquired, 1859–1860

Territories acquired, 1861–1870

0   50   100 Miles

0   50   100 Kilometers

THE UNIFICATION OF ITALY

In what ways was the geography of nineteenth-century Italy still "medieval" in character? Why did the Austrian von Metternich call Italy nothing but a "geographic expression" at mid-century? Why did Cavour see French support and sympathy as crucial to the cause of unification? Why did leadership of the unification movement fall to Piedmont in great measure? Why did the Papal States oppose the unification of Italy, and why did Cavour see the crushing of papal resistance as crucial to the cause? Why did Cavour and his southern rival Garibaldi both see popular support as crucial, whereas Bismarck achieved German unification through military and diplomatic means?

BUILDING THE ITALIAN NATION: THREE VIEWS

MAZZINI AND ROMANTIC NATIONALISM

The charismatic revolutionary Giuseppe Mazzini left more than fifty volumes of memoirs and writings. In this excerpt, he sets out his vision of the "regeneration" of the Italian nation and the three Romes: ancient Rome, the Rome of the popes, and (in the future) the Rome of the people, which would emancipate the peoples of Europe. Mazzini's conception of Italian nationalism was Romantic in its interpretation of Italy's distinctive history and destiny, and revolutionary in its emphasis on the Italian people rather than on statesmen.

I saw regenerate Italy becoming at one bound the missionary of a religion of progress and fraternity. . . .

The worship of Rome was a part of my being. The great Unity, the One Life of the world, had twice been elaborated within her walls. Other peoples—their brief mission fulfilled—disappeared for ever. To none save to her had it been given twice to guide and direct the world. . . . There, upon the vestiges of an epoch of civilization anterior to the Grecian, which had had its seat in Italy . . . the Rome of the Republic, concluded by the Caesars, had arisen to consign the former world to oblivion, and borne her eagles over the known world, carrying with them the idea of right, the source of liberty.

In later days . . . she had again arisen, greater than before, and at once constituted herself, through her Popes—the accepted center of a new Unity. . . .

Why should not a new Rome, the Rome of the Italian people . . . arise to create a third and still vaster Unity; to link together and harmonize earth and heaven, right [law] and duty; and utter, not to individuals but to peoples, the great word Association—to make known to free men and equal their mission here below?

Giuseppe Mazzini, *The Life and Writings of Joseph Mazzini*. (London: Smith, Elder & Co., 1964) as cited in Denis Mack Smith, *The Making of Italy, 1796–1870* (New York: Harper & Row, 1968), pp. 48–49.

THE POLITICAL CREED OF THE NATIONAL SOCIETY, FEBRUARY, 1858

The National Society was formed in 1857 to support Italian unification. By the 1860s, the society had over five thousand members. It was especially strong in Piedmont, where it was formed, and central Italy. Giuseppe la Farina was a tenacious organizer; he drafted the society's political creed and had it printed and sold throughout Italy. The society's practical nationalism differed from Mazzini's Romantic vision.

Italian independence should be the aim of every man of spirit and intelligence. Neither our educational system in Italy, nor our commerce and industry, can ever be flourishing or properly modernized while Austria

keeps one foot on our neck. . . . What good is it to be born in the most fertile and beautiful country in the world, to lie midway between East and West with magnificent ports in both the Adriatic and Mediterranean, to be descended from the Genoese, the Pisans, the men of Amalfi, Sicily and Venice? What use is it to have invented the compass, to have discovered the New World and been the progenitor of two civilizations? . . .

To obtain political liberty we must expel the Austrians who keep us enslaved. To win freedom of conscience we must expel the Austrians who keep us slaves of the Pope. To create a national literature we must chase away the Austrians who keep us uneducated. . . .

Italy must become not only independent but politically united. Political unity alone can reconcile various interests and laws, can mobilize credit and put out collective energies to speeding up communications. Only thus will we find sufficient capital for large-scale industry. Only thus will we create new markets, suppress internal obstacles to the free flow of commerce, and find the strength and reputation needed for traffic in distant lands. . . .

Everything points irresistibly to political unification. Science, industry, commerce, and the arts all need it. No great enterprise is possible any longer if we do not first put together the skill, knowledge, capital and labor of the whole of our great nation. The spirit of the age is moving toward concentration, and woe betide any nation that holds back!

A. Franchi, ed. *Scritti politici di Giuseppe La Farina*, Vol. 2. (Milan, 1870), pp. 83–98, as cited in Denis Mack Smith, *The Making of Italy, 1796–1870* (New York: Harper & Row, 1968), pp. 224–225.

COUNT CAVOUR AS A LEADER

The unification of Italy owed as much to Cavour's hard-nosed diplomacy as it did to middle-class movements for unification. In 1862, one of Cavour's contemporaries offered the following assessment of the count and how he had found "an opening in the complicated fabric of European politics."

Count Cavour undeniably ranks as third among European statesmen after Lord Palmerston [British prime minister 1885–1858, 1859–1865] and the Emperor Napoleon. . . . Count Cavour's strength does not lie in his principles; for he has none that are altogether inflexible. But he has a clear, precise aim, one whose greatness would—ten years ago—have made any other man reel: that of creating a unified and independent Italy. Men, means, circumstances were and still are matters of indifference to him. He walks straight ahead, always firm, often alone, sacrificing his friends, his sympathies, sometimes his heart, and often his conscience. Nothing is too difficult for him. . . .

Count Cavour . . . always has the talent to assess a situation and the possibilities of exploiting it. And it is this wonderful faculty that has contributed to form the Italy of today. As minister of a fourth-rate power, he could not create situations like Napoleon III, nor has he possessed the support of a great nation like Palmerston.

Count Cavour had to seek out an opening in the complicated fabric of European politics; he had to wriggle his way in, conceal himself, lay a mine, and cause an explosion. And it was by these means that he defeated Austria and won the help of France and England. Where other statesmen would have drawn back, Cavour plunged in headlong—as soon as he had sounded the precipice and calculated the possible profit and loss. The Crimean expeditionary force . . . the cession of Nice, the invasion of the Papal States last autumn [i.e., in 1860], were all the outcome of his vigorous stamina of mind.

There in brief you have the man of foreign affairs. He is strong; he is a match for the situation, for the politicians of his time or indeed of any time.

F. Petruccelli della Gattina, *I moribundi del Palazzo Carignano* (Milan, 1862), pp. 58–65, as cited in Denis Mack Smith, *The Making of Italy, 1796–1870* (New York: Harper & Row, 1968), pp. 181–182.

WHAT FORCES DROVE NATION BUILDING IN THE MID-NINETEENTH CENTURY?

NATION BUILDING IN THE WEST, 1850–1870   831

Giuseppe Garibaldi.

already shaken by a popular uprising. By November the whole kingdom of Francis II had fallen to Garibaldi. He at first intended to convert the territory into an independent republic but was finally persuaded to surrender it to the kingdom of Sardinia. With most of the peninsula now united under a single rule, Victor Emmanuel II, king of Sardinia, assumed the title of king of Italy (1861–1878).

Venetia was still in the hands of the Austrians, but in 1866, following their defeat in the Seven Weeks' War, they were forced by the Prussians to cede it to Italy. All that remained to complete the unification of Italy was the annexation of Rome. The Eternal City had resisted conquest thus far, largely because of the military protection accorded the pope by Napoleon III. But in 1870 the outbreak of the Franco-Prussian War compelled Napoleon to withdraw his troops. In September 1870, Italian soldiers occupied Rome, and in July of the following year it was made the capital of the by now united kingdom.

The occupation of Rome brought the kingdom of

Italy into conflict with the papacy. During the first years of his reign, which began in 1846, Pope Pius IX instituted a series of "modern" improvements: gaslight, railways, vaccination. Yet Pius, who, like his conservative predecessor, Gregory XVI, continued to rule over the Papal States in the manner of a secular prince, was no friend to either liberalism or nationalism. And no wonder: the movement that had brought Italian troops to Rome had from its inception expressed hostility to the church as an impediment to unification. Following the occupation of Rome in 1870, an attempt was made to solve the problem of relations between the state and the papacy. In 1871 the Italian parliament enacted the Law of Papal Guaranties, purporting to define and limit the status of the pope as a reigning sovereign. At the same time, a Vatican council in 1870 had proclaimed the doctrine of papal infallibility in spiritual matters. The reigning pontiff, Pius IX, promptly denounced the secular law on the grounds that issues affecting the pope could be settled only by an international treaty to which he himself was a party—whereupon he shut himself up in the Vatican and refused to have anything to do with a government that had so shamefully treated Christ's vicar on earth. His successors continued this practice of voluntary imprisonment until 1929, when a series of agreements between the Italian government and Pius XI effected settlement of the dispute.

Although Italy was now a unified state, it was hardly a nation. As already noted, fewer than 3 percent of the "Italian" population in fact spoke Italian; the rest used local and regional dialects so diverse that schoolmasters sent from Rome to Sicily following unification were, because of the "foreign" language they spoke, presumed to be British. As one politician remarked, "We have made Italy; now we must make Italians." That task did not prove an easy one. The gap between

CHRONOLOGY

UNIFICATION OF ITALY, 1848–1870

Revolutions of 1848	
Italian war with Austria	1859
Conquest of the kingdom of Two Sicilies	1860
Austria cedes Venetia	1866
Occupation of Rome	1870
Law of Papal Guaranties enacted	1870

an increasingly industrialized north and a backward, rural south remained very wide. Cavour and those who succeeded him as prime minister battled not only against north-south disparities, but also against the tensions in rural regions between landlords and an increasingly embittered agricultural proletariat. Banditry in the territory of the former kingdom of the Two Sicilies compelled the central administration to dispatch troops to quell serious uprisings, killing more people than the war of unification. Regional differences and social inequalities made building the Italian nation an ongoing process.

NATION BUILDING IN RUSSIA, THE UNITED STATES, AND CANADA

The challenges of nationalism and nation building also occupied Russia, the United States, and Canada. In all three countries, nation building entailed territorial and economic expansion, the incorporation of new peoples, and, in Russia and the United States, contending with slavery and serfdom.

RUSSIA

Serfdom in Russia, which had been finalized in 1649, had begun to draw significant protest from the intelligentsia under the reign of Catherine the Great (1762–1796). After 1789, and especially after 1848, the abolition of serfdom elsewhere in Europe made the issue more urgent. Abolishing serfdom became part of the larger project of building Russia as a modern nation. How that should happen was the subject of much debate; two schools of thought emerged. The "Slavophiles," or Romantic nationalists, sought to preserve Russia's distinctive features; they idealized traditional Russian culture and the peasant commune, rejecting Western secularism, urban commercialism, and bourgeois culture. In contrast, the "westernizers" wished to see Russia adapt European developments in science, technology, and education, which they believed to be the foundation for Western liberalism and protection of individual rights. Both groups agreed that serfdom must be abolished. Russian nobles' resistance to emancipation remained tenacious, however. Tangled debates about how lords would be indemnified for the loss of "their" serfs, and how emancipated serfs would survive

without full-scale land reform and redistribution, also checked progress on the issue. The Crimean War broke the impasse. In its aftermath, Alexander II (1855–1881), later known as the tsar-liberator, forced the issue. Worried that the persistence of serfdom had sapped Russian strength and contributed to its defeat in the war, and persuaded that serfdom would only continue to create violent and protracted conflict, he ended serfdom by decree in 1861.

The emancipation decree of 1861 was a reform of massive scope, but it produced limited change. It granted legal rights to some 22 million serfs and authorized their title to at least a portion of the land they had worked. It also required the state to compensate landowners for what properties they lost. Large-scale landowners managed to retain much of the most profitable acreage for themselves, and they vastly inflated the prices they charged the state for land surrendered to emancipated serfs. Newly liberated serfs, in turn, had to pay, in installments, for the land they received. Finally, the law granted the land not to the individual peasant, but to the village commune which, in turn, was charged with collecting money from the peasants. As a result, the pattern of rural life in Russia did not change drastically. The land granted to peasants was often of poor quality and insufficient to sustain themselves and their families. The system of payment kept peasants in the villages—not as freestanding farmers, but as agricultural laborers for their previous masters.

While the Russian state was undertaking reforms it was also building its territories. After mid-century, the Russians pressed east and south. They invaded and conquered several independent Islamic kingdoms along the old "Silk Road" and expanded into Siberia in search of natural resources. Russian diplomacy wrung various commercial concessions from the Chinese and led to the founding of the Siberian city of Vladivostok in 1860. Racial, ethnic, and religious differences made the task of governance a daunting one. In most cases, the Russian state did not try to assimilate new territories. Letting ethnic particularity develop was the government's more pragmatic response to the difficulties of governing such a heterogeneous population. When the state did make sporadic efforts to impose Russian culture, the results were disastrous. Whether power was wielded by the nineteenth-century tsars or, later, the Soviet Union, powerful centrifugal forces pulled against genuine unification. Expansion helped create a

> The emancipation decree of 1861 was a reform of massive scope, but it produced limited change.

THE ABOLITION OF SERFDOM IN RUSSIA

TSAR ALEXANDER II'S DECREE EMANCIPATING THE SERFS, 1861

The abolition of serfdom was central to Tsar Alexander II's program of modernization and reform after the Crimean War. Emancipated serfs were now allowed to own their land, ending centuries of peasant bondage. The decree, however, emphasized the tsar's benevolence and the nobility's generosity—not peasant rights. The government did not want emancipation to bring revolution to the countryside; it sought to reinforce the state's authority, the landowners' power, and the peasants' obligations. After spelling out the detailed provisions for emancipation, the decree added:

And We place Our hope in the good sense of Our people.

When word of the Government's plan to abolish the law of bondage [serfdom] reached peasants unprepared for it, there arose a partial misunderstanding. Some [peasants] thought about freedom and forgot about obligations. But the general good sense [of the people] was not disturbed in the conviction that anyone freely enjoying the goods of society correspondingly owes it to the common good to fulfill certain obligations, [a conviction held] both by natural reason and by Christian law, according to which "every soul must be subject to the governing authorities." . . .

Rights legally acquired by the landlords cannot be taken from them without a decent return or [their] voluntary concession; and that it would be contrary to all justice to make use of the lords' land without bearing the corresponding obligation.

And now We hopefully expect that the bonded people, as a new future opens before them, will understand and accept with gratitude the important sacrifice made by the Well-born Nobility for the improvement of their lives.

James Cracraft, ed., *Major Problems in the History of Imperial Russia* (Lexington, Mass.: D. C. Heath, 1994), pp. 340–344.

EMANCIPATION: THE VIEW FROM BELOW

Emancipation did not solve problems in the Russian countryside. On the contrary, it unleashed a torrent of protest, including complaints from peasants that nobles were undermining attempts to reform. These petitions detail the struggles that came in the wake of emancipation in two villages.

PETITION FROM PEASANTS IN PODOSINOVKA (VORONEZH PROVINCE) TO ALEXANDER II, MAY 1863

The most merciful manifesto of Your Imperial Majesty from 19 February 1861, with the published rules, put a limit to the enslavement of the people in blessed Russia. But some former serfowners—who desire not to improve the peasants' life, but to oppress and ruin them—apportion land contrary to the laws, choose the best land from all the fields for themselves, and give the poor peasants . . . the worst and least usable lands.

To this group of squires must be counted our own, Anna Mikhailovna Raevskaia. . . . Of our fields and resources, she chose the best places from amidst our strips, and, like a cooking ring in a hearth, carved off 300 dessiatines [measures of land] for herself. . . . But our community refused to accept so ruinous an allotment and requested that we be given an allotment in accordance with the local Statute. . . . The peace arbitrator . . . and the police chief . . . slandered us before the governor, alleging that we were rioting and that it is impossible for them to enter our village.

The provincial governor believed this lie and sent 1,200 soldiers of the penal command to our village. . . . Without any cause, our village priest Father Peter—rather than give an uplifting pastoral exhortation to stop the spilling of innocent blood—joined these reptiles, with the unanimous incitement of the authorities. . . . They summoned nine township heads and their aides from other townships. . . . In their presence, the provincial governor—without making any investigation and without interrogating a single person—ordered that the birch rods be brought and that the punishment commence, which was carried out with cruelty and mercilessness. They punished up to 200 men and women; 80 people were at four levels (with 500, 400, 300 and 200 blows); some received lesser punishment . . . and when the inhuman punishment of these innocent people had ended, the provincial governor said: "If you find the land unsuitable, I do not forbid you to file petitions wherever you please," and then left. . . .

We dare to implore you, Orthodox emperor and our merciful father, not to reject the petition of a community with 600 souls, including wives and children. Order with your tsarist word that our community be allotted land . . . as the law dictates without selecting the best sections of fields and meadows, but in straight lines. . . . [Order that] the meadows and haylands along the river Elan be left to our community without any restriction; these will enable us to feed our cattle and smaller livestock, which are necessary for our existence."

Gregory L. Freeze, ed., *From Supplication to Revolution: A Documentary Social History of Imperial Russia* (New York: Oxford University Press, 1988), pp. 170–173.

PETITION FROM PEASANTS IN BALASHOV DISTRICT TO GRAND DUKE CONSTANTIN NIKOLAEVICH, JANUARY 25, 1862

Your Imperial Excellency! Most gracious sire! Grand Duke Konstantin Nikolaevich! . . .

After being informed of the Imperial manifesto on the emancipation of peasants from serfdom on 1861 . . . we received this [news] with jubilation. . . . But from this moment, our squire ordered that the land be cut off from the entire township. But this is absolutely intolerable for us: it not only denies us profit, but threatens us with a catastrophic future. He began to hold repeated meetings and [tried to] force us to sign that we agreed to accept the above land allotment. But, upon seeing so unexpected a change, and bearing in mind the gracious manifesto, we refused. . . . After assembling the entire township, they tried to force us into making illegal signatures accepting the land cut-offs. But when they saw that this did not succeed, they had a company of soldiers sent in. . . . Then [Colonel] Globbe came from their midst, threatened us with exile to Siberia, and ordered the soldiers to strip the peasants and to punish seven people by flogging in the most inhuman manner. They still have not regained consciousness.

Gregory L. Freeze, ed., *From Supplication to Revolution: A Documentary Social History of Imperial Russia* (New York: Oxford University Press, 1988), pp. 170–173.

vast empire, geographically of one piece but by no means one nation.

THE UNITED STATES AND CANADA

The American Revolution had bequeathed to the United States a loose union of slave and free states, tied together in part by a commitment to territorial expansion. The so-called Jeffersonian Revolution combined democratic aspirations with a drive to expand the nation's boundaries. Leaders of the movement under the Democratic-Republican president Thomas Jefferson (1801–1809) led the campaign to add a Bill of Rights to the Constitution and were almost exclusively

WHAT FORCES DROVE NATION BUILDING IN THE MID-NINETEENTH CENTURY?

NATION BUILDING IN THE WEST, 1850–1870   835

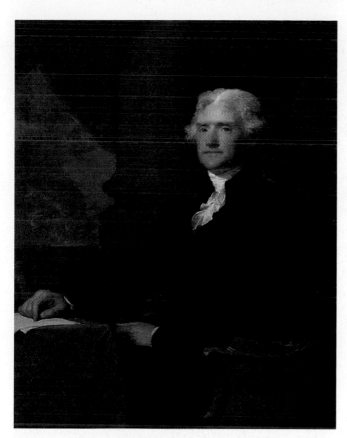

Thomas Jefferson, by Gilbert Stuart.

responsible for its success. Though they supported, in principle, the separation of powers, they believed in the supremacy of the representatives of the people and viewed with alarm attempts of the executive and judicial branches to increase their power. They supported a political system based on an aristocracy of "virtue and talent," in which respect for personal liberty would be the guiding principle. They opposed the establishment of a national religion and special privilege, whether of birth or of wealth. Yet the Jeffersonian vision of the republic rested on the independence of yeomen farmers, and the independence and prosperity of those farmers depended on the availability of new lands. This made territorial expansion, as represented by the Louisiana Purchase in 1803, central to Jeffersonian America. Expansion brought complications. The purchase of the port of New Orleans made lands in the South well worth developing. The American republic forcibly removed the Indians of the Old South west of the Mississippi River. And though expansion did provide land for many yeomen farmers in the North and South, it also added millions of acres of prime cotton land, thus extending the empire of slavery. The process of expansion and expropriation

stretched from Jefferson's administration through the age of Jackson, or the 1840s.

Under Andrew Jackson (1829–1837), the Democrats (as some of the Democratic-Republicans were now called) transformed the circumscribed liberalism of the Jeffersonians. They campaigned to extend the suffrage to all white males; they argued that all governmental officeholders should be elected rather than appointed; and they sought the frequent rotation of men in positions of political power—a doctrine that permitted politicians to use patronage to build national political parties. What was more, the Jacksonian vision of democracy and nationhood carried over into a crusade to incorporate more territories into the republic. It was the United States' "Manifest Destiny" wrote a New York editor, "to overspread the continent allotted by Providence for the free development of our yearly multiplying millions." That "overspreading" brought Oregon and Washington into the Union through a compromise with the British, and brought Arizona, Texas, New Mexico, Utah, Nevada, and California through war with Mexico, all of which led to the wholesale expropriation of Indian lands. In the North, these changes heightened belief in "democratic rule" and a free-labor ideology; in the South they fueled a sense of isolation and deepened southern whites' commitments to an economy and society based on plantation slavery. Ultimately, they pushed southern political leaders toward secession.

Territorial expansion made it impossible for the United States government to avoid the question of slavery. The Haitian revolution (see page 709) had begun the long and uneven process of dismantling slavery. Great Britain ended the slave trade in 1807 (so did the United States) and slavery in the 1830s. Spanish America abolished slavery in the first decades of the nineteenth century; France during the revolution of 1848. In the face of growing antislavery sentiment, southern planters, like Russian serf owners, continued to insist that without the slave system they would go bankrupt. Like the Russian nobility, they responded to abolitionists with arguments based on theories of inherited inferiority and warnings of the chaos they believed abolition would bring. As the country expanded west, North and South engaged in a protracted tug of war as to which new states were to be "free" and which "slave." The failure of a series of elaborate compromises led to the outbreak of the Civil War in 1861.

The protracted and costly struggle—a first look at the horrors of modern war—decisively transformed

AMERICAN EXPANSION IN THE EARLY NINETEENTH CENTURY

A crucial turning point in American westward expansion came in 1803, when the Louisiana Purchase transferred a vast expanse of land from Napoleon I's France to the United States. Napoleon had failed to reconquer St. Domingue and restore slavery there, and he urgently needed to regroup his forces for war in Europe. Both factors persuaded him to give up visions of a North American empire. How did the withdrawal of a major colonial power reshape American attitudes about the western frontier? What relationship did this new land have to the population centers of the United States? How did exploration shape the future settlement of this territory? What further issues did the Louisiana Purchase raise?

the nation. First, it abolished slavery. Second, it established the preeminence of the national government over states' rights. The Fourteenth Amendment to the Constitution stated specifically that all Americans were citizens of the United States, and not of an individual state or territory. In declaring that no citizen was to be deprived of life, liberty, or property without due process of law, it established that "due process" was to be defined by the national, not the state or territorial, government. Third, in the aftermath of the Civil War the United States' economy expanded with stunning rapidity. In 1865, there were thirty-five thousand

miles of railroad track in the United States; by 1900, there were almost two hundred thousand. Industrial and agricultural production rose, putting the United States in a position to compete with Great Britain. As we will see later on, American industrialists, bankers, and retailers introduced innovations in assembly-line manufacturing, corporate organization, and advertising that startled their European counterparts and gave the United States new power in world politics. These developments were all part of the process of nation building. They did not overcome deep racial, regional, or class divides. Though the war brought the South

WHAT FORCES DROVE NATION BUILDING IN THE MID-NINETEENTH CENTURY?

NATION BUILDING IN THE WEST, 1850–1870   837

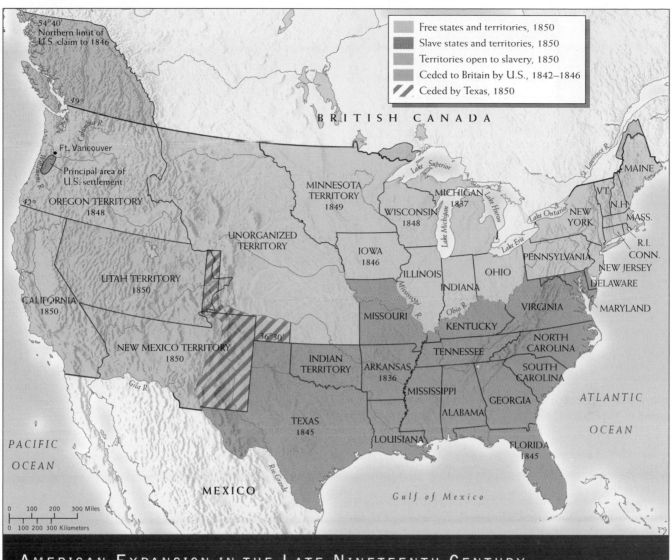

Free states and territories, 1850
Slave states and territories, 1850
Territories open to slavery, 1850
Ceded to Britain by U.S., 1842–1846
Ceded by Texas, 1850

AMERICAN EXPANSION IN THE LATE NINETEENTH CENTURY

Note the stages by which American settlement progressed across the North American continent, and the organization of newly acquired territory by the American government. How was American expansion different from European colonialism? How was it similar? What considerations informed the compromises made by the American government in establishing less ambitious northern borders? Why were the Utah and New Mexico territories opened to slavery even though the West and Southwest had previously been considered free? What role did the admission of California as a state play in such considerations?

back into the Union, the rise of northern capitalism magnified the "backwardness" of the South as an underdeveloped agricultural region whose wealth was extracted by northern industrialists. The railroad corporations, which pieced together the national infrastructure, became the classic foe of labor and agrarian reformers. The Civil War laid the foundations for the modern American nation-state.

The expansion of the United States also had an im-

portant effect on its neighbor to the north. In 1763, the Treaty of Paris had passed the territories of New France to Britain. Throughout the nineteenth century, relations between French-speaking, largely Roman Catholic inhabitants of what came to be called Québec and more recently arrived, largely Protestant British settlers, were difficult. Unity among European settlers, however fragile, was forged—as it was in the United States—by westward expansion accompanied by the

Slavery in the American South. Left: Slave pens at Pine, Birch & Co., a Virginia slave broker. Right: Cotton being prepared by slaves for the gin on a South Carolina plantation.

dispossession of Indians and their resettlement into separate native territories. The drive westward, which opened up the Canadian forests and prairies as a vast resource of wheat and timber, fueled demands for greater autonomy. The fear of falling prey to the United States' expansionist drive, however, made English-speaking Canadians less eager to break completely with British rule. In 1867, an Act of Parliament gave Canada independence, but the state remained a "dominion" within the British Commonwealth. With dominion status in place the Canadian government, like its American counterpart, pursued a policy of economic expansion and settlement. It annexed territories, offered particularly attractive homestead grants to lure European immigrants, policed settler-Indian relations, and built vast railroads. Government-encouraged economic development aimed to connect the Canadian cities with each other, developing networks independent of the United States. The railways not only joined Canadian cities; they linked the vast wheatfields of western Canada with sea ports that would ship that wheat on to Canada's major overseas buyer, Great Britain. In culture, commerce, and matters of national defense, ties between independent Canada and the "mother country," Britain, remained strong.

CONCLUSION

The twenty years between 1850 and 1870 were years of intense nation building in the Western world. The unification of Germany and Italy changed the map of Europe with, as we have seen, important consequences for the balance of power. The emergence of the United States as a major power also had international ramifications. All of these nation-states both built on and encouraged economic development and political transformation, sometimes on a very large scale. Nation building entailed responding to demands for more representative government, the abolition of privilege, and land reform. It forced a reckoning with systems of slavery and serfdom. It short, it meant transforming relations between states and their citizens.

Nationalism showed itself to be a volatile, unpredictable, and malleable force in the middle of the nineteenth century. It provided much of the fuel for revolutionary movements in 1848, but it also helped to tear them apart, undermining liberal gains. Liberals who in the 1830s and 1840s hoped that the new nations would also be more democratic political communities were disappointed. In the aftermath of the defeated revolutions, most nation-building was more conservative. Nationalism came to serve the needs of statesmen and bureaucrats who did not seek an "awakening of peoples," and who had serious reservations about popular sovereignty; for them nations represented simply modern, organized, and stronger states.

SELECTED READINGS

Anderson, Benedict. *Imagined Communities: Reflections on the Origin and Spread of Nationalism*. London, 1983. The most influential recent study of the subject, highly recommended for further reading.

Beales, Derek. *The Risorgimento and the Unification of Italy*. New York, 1971. Objective, concise survey of Italian unification.

Blackburn, Robin. *The Overthrow of Colonial Slavery*. London, 1988. Brilliant and detailed overview of the social history of slavery and antislavery movements.

Craig, Gordon. *Germany, 1866–1945*. New York, 1978. An excellent and thorough synthesis.

Deak, Istvan. *The Lawful Revolution: Louis Kossuth and the Hungarians, 1848–1849*. New York, 1979.

Eyck, Erich. *Bismarck and the German Empire*, 3d ed. London, 1968. The best one-volume study of Bismarck.

Hamerow, Theodore S. *The Social Foundations of German Unification, 1858–1871*. 2 vols. Princeton, N.J., 1969–1972. Concentrates on economic factors that determined the solution to the unification question. An impressive synthesis.

———. *The Birth of a New Europe: State and Society in the Nineteenth Century*. Chapel Hill, N.C., 1983. A discussion of political and social change, and their relationship to industrialization and the increase in state power.

Hobsbawm, Eric J. *Nations and Nationalism since 1870: Programme, Myth, Reality*, 2d ed. Cambridge, 1992. A clear, concise analysis of the historical and cultural manifestations of nationalism.

Hutchinson, John, and Anthony Smith, eds. *Nationalism*. New York, 1994. A recent collection of articles, not particularly historical, but with the merit of discussing non-European nationalisms.

Howard, Michael. *The Franco-Prussian War*. New York, 1981. The war's effect on society.

Kolchin, Peter. *Unfree Labor: American Slavery and Russian Serfdom*. Cambridge, Mass., 1987. Pioneering comparative study.

Langer, William. *Political and Social Upheaval, 1832–1851*. New York, 1969. Long the standard, and still the most comprehensive survey.

Mack Smith, Denis. *Cavour and Garibaldi*. New York, 1968.

———. *The Making of Italy, 1796–1870*. New York, 1968. A narrative with documents.

Pflanze, Otto. *Bismarck and the Development of Germany*, 2d ed. 3 vols. Princeton, N.J., 1990. An impressive analysis of Bismarck's aims and policies.

Sammons, Jeffrey L. *Heinrich Heine: A Modern Biography*. Princeton, N.J., 1979. An excellent historical biography, as well as a study of culture and politics.

Sheehan, James J. *German Liberalism in the Nineteenth Century*. Chicago, 1978. Fresh and important synthesis.

Smith, Bonnie. *The Gender of History: Men, Women, and Historical Practice*. Cambridge, Mass., 1998. On Romanticism and the historical imagination.

Sperber, Jonathan. *Rhineland Radicals: The Democratic Movement and the Revolution of 1848–1849*. Princeton, N.J., 1993. A detailed study of Germany, by the author of the most recent overview of the revolutions of 1848.

———. *The European Revolutions, 1848–1851*. New York, 1994. Now the best single volume on the period, with new bibliography.

PART VII
THE WEST AT THE WORLD'S CENTER

THE YEARS BETWEEN 1870 and 1945 have been called the "European era." Three developments run through this period. The first is the rapid and dramatic expansion of European empires. The industrial development of western Europe and the United States gave those nations unprecedented power in the world arena. The West's trade, its wars, and its methods of wielding political power were global. That newfound, worldwide power produced both confidence and crisis. Although the economic might of the Western nations enabled them to dominate the less-developed quarters of the globe, it also created new and dangerous competition among them. The old system of the "balance of power," designed to preserve peace by ensuring that no one country could dominate others, was strained to the breaking point by rivalries that grew swiftly and stretched around the world. The second development, slower and more uneven, was the emergence of "mass" politics and culture: the expansion of suffrage and of liberal and parliamentary democracy, new techniques for mobilizing (or manipulating) citizens, and modern cultural forms ranging from mass-market newspapers and advertising to radio and movies. The third theme to consider involves the wrenching transformations brought by war. Twice during the period, in 1914 and 1939, international and domestic pressures exploded. Twice during the period, war proved shockingly different from what citizens, soldiers, or political leaders expected. And twice during the period, in 1918 and 1945, Europeans awoke to a world they barely recognized. The two world wars had far reaching consequences, among them the fracturing of the European empires and the transformation of Europe's place in the world.

	POLITICS	SOCIETY AND CULTURE	ECONOMY	INTERNATIONAL RELATIONS
			Britain monopolizes opium trade in China (1830s)	British expand foothold in India (1797–1818)
				Opium Wars (1839–1842)
		Karl Marx and Friedrich Engels publish *Communist Manifesto* (1848)	Production of steel alloys revolutionized (1850–1870s)	Treaty of Nanjing (1842)
	Reign of Alexander II (1855–1881)	Gustave Flaubert's *Madame Bovary* (1856)		
	Sepoy Rebellion in India (1857–1858)	Darwin's *On the Origin of Species* (1859)		
1860	American Civil War (1861–1864)	Leo Tolstoy's *War and Peace* (1862–1869)		
	Emancipation of serfs in Russia (1861)	Fyodor Dostoyevsky's *Crime and Punishment* (1866)		
	Otto von Bismarck unifies Germany (1862–1871)			
	Reform Bill of 1867 in England (1867)			
	Pope Pius IX's pronouncement of papal infallibility (1869)		Limited liability laws change investment strategies (1870)	Franco-Prussian War (1870–1871)
	Bismarck's Kulturkampf (1871–1878)	First Impressionist salon with Claude Monet and others (1874)	Birth of vertical and horizontal monopolies (1870)	European scramble for Africa (1870–1900)
	Paris Commune repressed (1871)			Britain gains control of Suez Canal (1875)
	Third French Republic (1875)		Electricity demand rises (1880s)	Congress of Berlin redraws Balkan states (1878)
1880	The progressive movement in the United States (1880–1914)		Rockefeller's Standard Oil Company controls over 90 percent of U.S. oil (1880s)	British occupation of Egypt begins (1882)
	Alexander III and the Counter Reforms (1881–1894)	Friedrich Nietzsche's *Thus Spoke Zarathustra* (1883)	Russia launches industrialization program (1880–1890s)	France moves into Vietnam, Laos, and Cambodia (1883–1893)
	Bismarck's health and social legislation (1883–1884)	Émile Zola's *Germinal* (1885)		Berlin West Africa Conference (1884–85)
	Reform Bill expands male suffrage in Britain (1884)	Completion of the Eiffel Tower (1889)		
	Kaiser Wilhelm II ascends throne (1888)	Anti-Semitic League founded in Paris (1889)		
		Vincent Van Gogh's *The Starry Night* (1889)	Birth of the department store (1890s)	Sino-Japanese War (1894–1905)
	Bismarck resigns (1890)			Italian forces defeated by Ethiopians (1896)
				Fashoda Crisis (1898)
				Boer War (1898–1901)
	The Dreyfus Affair (1894–1899)			Spanish-American War (1898)
				United States annexes Puerto Rico and makes Cuba a Protectorate (1898)
1900	Boxer Rebellion in China (1900)	Sigmund Freud publishes *The Interpretation of Dreams* (1899)	Discovery of oil fields in Russia, Borneo, Persia, and Texas (1900)	London Pan-African Conference (1900)
	Sinn Fein party forms in Ireland (1900)			
	French laws separate church and state (1901–1905)			
	Labour party established in Britain (1901)			
	Vladimir Lenin's "What Is to Be Done?" (1902)			
	Russian Marxists split into Bolsheviks and Mensheviks (1903)			United States occupies Panama (1903)
	British House of Lords loses veto power (1911)		Sherman Anti-Trust Act in the United States (1912)	First and Second Balkan Wars (1912–1913)
				First World War (1914–1918)
				Battle of the Marne (1914)
		Albert Einstein proposes theory of relativity (1915)		*Lusitania* sunk by German U-boat (1915)
				Battles of Verdun and the Somme (1916)
	Russian Revolution in February and October (1917)		Bread riots and strikes against wartime shortages in Britain (1917)	United States enters World War I (1917)

POLITICS	SOCIETY AND CULTURE	ECONOMY	INTERNATIONAL RELATIONS	
		Vladimir Lenin's *Imperialism: The Highest Stage of Capitalism* (1917)	Treaty of Brest-Litovsk (1918)	1917
Russian Civil War (1918–1920) Britain extends vote to men and women over age thirty (1918) German (Weimar) Republic declared (1918) Nineteenth Amendment gives American women vote (1919) Separate parliaments for north and south Ireland (1920) Mussolini's fascists march on Rome (1922)	Dadaist and Surrealist artistic movements flourish (1920–1940) Marie Stopes opens birth control clinic in London (1921) T. S. Eliot's *The Waste Land* (1922) Hitler writes *Mein Kampf* in prison (1924)	Hyperinflation in Weimar Republic (1920–1924) Beginning of New Economic Policy in U.S.S.R. (1921)	Treaty of Versailles (1919–1920)	
Joseph Stalin's Revolution from Above (1927–1928)		Joseph Stalin's First Five-Year Plan for modernization of Russian economy (1928–1932) American stock market crash (1929) Great Depression (1929–1933)	Kellogg-Briand Pact (1928)	
Hitler appointed chancellor of Germany, proclaims the Third Reich (1933) Concentration camp for political prisoners opens at Dachau (1933) Popular Front government formed by Leon Blum (1936) Spanish Civil War (1936–1939) Great Terror of Stalin (1937–1938) Nazis begin deporting Jews in occupied territories to ghettos (1939)	James Chadwick discovers the neutron (1932) German laws exclude Jews from public office (1933) Leni Riefenstahl's *Triumph of the Will* (1934) Otto Hahn and Fritz Strassman split the atom (1939)	Britain abandons gold standard (1931) United States abandons gold standard (1933) One third of American workers unemployed (1933) President Franklin Roosevelt announces the New Deal (1933)	Japan invades Manchuria (1931) Italy conquers Ethiopia (1935–1936) Germany and Italy form Axis (1935) Germany annexes Austria (1938) Hitler invades Czechoslovakia (1939) Soviet Union signs nonaggression pact with Germany (1939) Soviets and Germans invade Poland (1939) Britain and France declare war on Germany (1939)	1930
Winston Churchill becomes prime minister of England (1940)	Charlie Chaplin's *The Great Dictator* (1940) Enrico Fermi stages first controlled nuclear chain reaction (1942)	Winston Churchill brokers Lend-Lease program with Franklin Roosevelt (1940)	France surrenders to Germany (1940) Battle of Britain (1940–1941) Germany invades the Soviet Union (1941) Japan strikes Pearl Harbor; United States enters World War II (1941) Japan invades Philippines (1941) American island-hopping campaigns in the Pacific (1942) Rommel and the Afrika Korps defeated in Tunisia (1942) Warsaw ghetto uprising (1943) D-Day: Allies land at Normandy (1944) Germany surrenders (1945) United States detonates nuclear bombs over Hiroshima and Nagasaki in August (1945) Conferences at Potsdam and Yalta (1945) Nuremberg trials (1945) United Nations founded (1945)	1940 1945

CHAPTER TWENTY-FIVE

CHAPTER CONTENTS

IMPERIALISM AND COLONIALISM (1870–1914)

IN 1869, THE SUEZ CANAL opened with a grandiose celebration. The imperial yacht *Eagle*, Empress Eugénie of France on board, entered the canal on November 17, followed by sixty-eight steamships carrying the rest of the party— the emperor of Austria, the crown prince of Prussia, the grand duke of Russia, and scores of other dignitaries. Flowery speeches flowed freely, as did the champagne. The ceremony cost a staggering £1.3 million. But the size of the celebration paled in comparison to the canal itself. The largest project of its kind, the canal cut through 100 miles of Egyptian desert to link the Mediterranean and Red seas. It was a masterful feat of engineering. As a fast, cheap, and efficient route to the East, the canal had instant strategic importance. It cut the trip from London to Bombay in half, becoming Britain's lifeline to India and the Pacific.

The building of the canal was the result of half a century of increasingly pervasive commercial, financial, and political involvement in Egypt on the part of two great European powers, France and Britain. France led the way, but Britain's bankers soon followed. These European financial interests developed a close relationship with those who governed Egypt as a semi-independent state inside the Ottoman empire. By 1875 the canal itself had come under the control of Britain, which had purchased 44 percent of the shares in the canal from the khedive (viceroy) of Egypt at a time when he was threatened with bankruptcy. By the late 1870s, this set of economic and political relationships had produced debt and instability in Egypt, and consternation among European investors who wanted returns on their loans. In a bid to produce both an independent state and an Egyptian nation—not so different from the European model—free of foreign "interference," a group of Egyptian army officers (led by 'Urabi Pasha) took control of Egypt's government in 1882. France found the threat to long-term investments an aggravation; Britain found the danger to the new, strategic route to India intolerable.

After much debate, the British government decided to intervene. The Royal Navy shelled Egyptian forts along the canal into rubble. A special task force of troops led by Britain's most successful colonial general, "Garnet" Wolseley, landed along the shore of the canal near 'Urabi Pasha's central base. Wolseley planned his attack down to the last detail—the order of maneuvers looked very much like a railway

FOCUS QUESTIONS

- What were the causes of the "new imperialism"?
- How was the Indian empire reorganized after the Mutiny of 1857?
- How did Western countries "open" China?
- What was the "civilizing mission"?
- What events set off the "scramble for Africa"?
- How did empire affect European identity?
- Why was the Boer War unique?

timetable—and overwhelmed the Egyptian lines just before dawn, at bayonet point. This striking success brought immediate popular support at home, but the political consequences ran much deeper and lasted for more than seventy years. Britain took over effective control of the province of Egypt. Lord Evelyn Baring (immediately nicknamed "Over" Baring by British anti-colonialists) assumed the role of "proconsul" in a power-sharing relationship with Egyptian authorities—a relationship in which all the real power rested with Britain. Britain put conditions on the repayment of loans owed by the old Egyptian government, and regulated the trade in Egyptian cotton that helped supply Britain's prolific textile mills. Most important, the route to India and the markets of the East was secured.

The convergence of technology, money, and politics involved in the Suez Canal epitomizes the interplay of economics and empire in late-nineteenth-century Europe. The years 1870 to 1914 brought both rapid industrialization throughout the West and the stunningly rapid expansion of Western power abroad. The "new imperialism" of the late nineteenth century was distinguished by its scope, intensity, and long-range consequences. It transformed cultures in addition to economies and states. Projects such as the Suez Canal changed—literally—the landscape and map of the world. Projects like the Suez Canal not only brought together newly made money and fresh desires for power, they also represented an ideology: the belief in technology and in Western superiority. The new imperialism, however, was not a one-way relationship, nor did it allow the West simply to conquer vast territories and dictate its terms to the rest of the world. The new political and economic relationships created between colonies and dependent states on the one hand and the "metropole" (the colonizing power) on the other ran both ways, bringing changes to the heart of empire. Fierce competition among nations upset the balance of power. The new imperialism was an expression of European strength, but it was also profoundly destabilizing.

IMPERIALISM

What were the causes of the "new imperialism"?

"Imperialism," or the process of extending one state's control over another, came in many forms. Colo-

nialism, the most direct form, meant annexing territories outright, and establishing new governments to subjugate and administer other states and peoples. Equally common was indirect rule, whereby Europeans reached agreements with indigenous leaders and dictated their activities without actually taking over political responsibility for their states. Imperialism also took the form of carving out zones of European sovereignty and privilege, such as treaty ports, within other states. Finally, imperialism could refer to Europeans using their considerable economic, political, and cultural power to get advantageous treaties or terms of trade.

All of these forms of imperialism expanded dramatically in the nineteenth century. The "scramble for Africa" was the most sudden and startling case of colonization: from 1875 to 1902 Europeans took up to 90 percent of the continent. The overall picture is no less remarkable: between 1870 and 1900, a small group of Western states (France, Britain, Germany, the Netherlands, Russia, and the United States) colonized about one quarter of the world's land surface. In addition to colonizing, Western states established semicolonial relationships in sections of China and Turkey. "Informal" empire expanded into South America and across South and East Asia. So striking was this expansion of European power and sovereignty that by the late nineteenth century contemporaries were speaking of the "new imperialism."

Imperialism was not new. It is more helpful to think of nineteenth-century developments as a new stage of European empire building. The "second European empires" took hold after the first empires, especially in the New World, had by and large collapsed: the British empire in North America was shattered by 1776, French imperial ambitions fell along with Napoleon, and Spanish and Portuguese domination of South America ended with the Latin American revolutions of the nineteenth century. What, then, had changed?

The nineteenth-century empires developed against the backdrop of developments we have considered: industrialization, democratic revolutions, the rise of liberalism, and nation building. These developments shaped the new empires. First, industrialization created new economic needs for raw materials. Second, industrialization, liberalism, and faith in progress created new beliefs. A distinguishing feature of nineteenth-century imperialism lay in Europeans' conviction that economic development and technological advances would inevitably bring progress to the rest of the world. Third, in the case of Britain and France, the nineteenth-century imperial powers were also in principle democratic nations, where government authority rested on consent and on the equality of most citizens. This made conquest and subjugation more difficult to justify and raised increasingly thorny questions about the status of colonized peoples. Nineteenth-century imperialists sought to distance themselves from earlier histories of conquest; they spoke not of winning souls for the church or subjects for the king, but rather of building railroads and harbors, encouraging social reform and fulfilling Europe's secular mission to bring civilization to the world.

The "new" aspects of nineteenth-century imperialism, however, resulted equally from changes and events outside Europe. Resistance, rebellion, and recognition of colonial failures obliged Europeans to develop new strategies of rule. The Haitian revolution, echoed by slave rebellions in the early nineteenth century, compelled the British and French, slowly, to end the slave trade and slavery in their colonies in the 1830s and 1840s, though new systems of forced labor cropped up to take their places. The American Revolution helped encourage the British to grant self-government to white settler states in Australia, New Zealand, and Canada. In India, as we will see, the British responded to rebellion by taking the area away from the East India Company and putting it under control of the crown, by requiring civil servants to undergo more training, and by much more careful policing of indigenous peoples. Almost everywhere, nineteenth-century empires established carefully codified racial hierarchies to organize relationships between Europeans and different indigenous groups. (Apartheid in South Africa is but one example.) In general, nineteenth-century imperialism involved less independent "entrepreneurial" activity by merchants and traders (such as the East India Company) and more "settlement and discipline." This meant that empire became a vast project, involving legions of administrators, schoolteachers, and engineers. Nineteenth-century imperialism, then, arose from new motives. It produced new forms of government and management in the colonies. Last, it created new kinds of interactions between Europeans and indigenous peoples.

THE NEW IMPERIALISM AND ITS CAUSES

All historical events have many causes. The causes of a development with the scope, intensity, and long-range importance of the "new imperialism" inevitably provoke heated controversy. The most influential and long-standing interpretation points to the economic dynamics of imperialism. As early as 1902, the British writer J. A. Hobson charged that what he named the "scramble for Africa" had been driven by the interests of a small group of wealthy financiers. British taxpayers subsidized armies of conquest and occupation, and journalists whipped up the public's "spectatorial lust of jingoism," but the core interests behind imperialism were those of international capitalists. At a time when fierce economic competition was producing protectionism and monopolies, Hobson said, and when western Europe did not provide the markets that industry needed, investors sought out secure investment opportunities overseas, in colonies. Hobson saw investors and international bankers as the central players: "large savings are made which cannot find any profitable investment in this country; they must find employment elsewhere." Yet investors were not alone. Their interests matched those of manufacturers involved in colonial trade, the military, and the armaments industry. Hobson was a reformer and social critic. His point was that conceptions of England's real national interests had been distorted by international finance and business. He hoped that genuine democracy would be an antidote to the country's imperial tendencies.

Hobson's analysis, still widely read, inspired the most influential Marxist critique of imperialism—from Russian socialist and revolutionary leader Vladimir Ilich Lenin (see Chapter 26). Lenin, like Hobson, underscored the economics of imperialism. Unlike Hobson, he considered imperialism to be an integral part of late-nineteenth-century capitalism. Competition and the monopolies that it produced had lowered domestic profits. Capitalists, Lenin argued, could only enlarge

CHRONOLOGY	
MAJOR IMPERIAL CONFLICTS, 1857–1905	
First Opium War, China	1839–1842
"Sepoy Rebellion," India	1857–1858
Siege of Khartoum, Sudan	1884–1885
Italian invasion of Ethiopa	1896
Crisis of Fashoda, Sudan	1898
Boer War, South Africa	1898–1902
Spanish-American War	1898
Boxer Rebellion, China	1900
Russo-Japanese War	1904–1905

Dredges and Elevators at Work on the Construction of the Suez Canal, 1869. The canal was one of the most massive construction jobs of its time.

benefits to the industrial sectors of European economies than it did to the financial ones. Colonial markets were generally too poor to meet the needs of European manufacturers. Africa, the continent over which Europeans frantically "scrambled," was the poorest and least profitable to investors. Regarding overseas investment, before 1914 only a very small portion of German capital was invested in German colonies; only one fifth of French capital was so invested; indeed, the French had more capital invested in Russia, hoping to stabilize that ally against the Germans, than in all their colonial possessions. Yet some of these calculations are clear

their markets at home by raising workers' wages, which would have the effect of further reducing profits. Thus the "internal contradictions" of capitalism produced imperialism, compelling capitalists to invest and to search for new markets overseas. If this was the case, it followed that Hobson's hopes for democratic reform were misplaced; only overthrowing capitalism itself could check imperialist expansion, conflict, and violence. Lenin published his book (*Imperialism: The Highest Stage of Capitalism*, 1917) at the height of World War I, a war many considered imperialist. The timing gave real urgency to his argument that revolution alone could topple capitalism, imperialism, and the forces that had brought the world to the brink of disaster.

Historians now would agree that economic pressures were one, though only one, important cause of imperialism. In the case of Great Britain, roughly half its total of £4 billion in foreign investments was at work within its empire. As Hobson, Lenin, and their contemporaries correctly noted, late-nineteenth-century London was rapidly becoming the banker of the world. In all western European countries, demand for raw materials made colonies a necessary investment and helped persuade governments that imperialism was a worthwhile policy. Rubber, tin, and minerals from the colonies supplied European industries—and foods, coffee, sugar, tea, wool, and grain supplied European consumers. Yet the economic explanation has limits. Empire offered fewer

only in retrospect. Many nineteenth-century Europeans expected the colonies to produce profits. French newspapers, for instance, reported that the Congo was "rich, vigorous, and fertile virgin territory," with "fabulous quantities" of gold, copper, ivory, and rubber. Such hopes certainly contributed to expansionism, even if the profits of empire did not match Europeans' expectations.

A second interpretation emphasizes strategic and nationalist motives over economic interests. International rivalries fueled the belief that vital national interests were at stake, and made European powers more determined to control both the governments and economies of less-developed nations and territories. French politicians supported imperialism as a means of restoring national prestige and honor, lost in the humiliating defeat by the Germans in the Franco-Prussian War of 1870–1871. The British, on the other hand, looked with alarm at the accelerating pace of industrialization in Germany and France and feared losing their existing and potential world markets. The Germans, recently unified in a modern nation, viewed overseas empire as a "national" possession and as a way of entering the "club" of Great Powers.

This second interpretation emphasizes the new links between imperialism and nineteenth-century state and nation building. That nations should be empires was not always self-evident. Otto von Bismarck, the archi-

HOW WAS THE INDIAN EMPIRE REORGANIZED AFTER THE MUTINY OF 1857?

IMPERIALISM IN SOUTH ASIA   849

tect of German unification, long considered colonialism overseas a distraction from far more serious issues on the continent of Europe. By the last decades of the century, however, Germany had joined France and England in what seemed an urgent race for territories. Advocates of colonialism—from businessmen and explorers to writers (such as Rudyard Kipling) and political theorists—spelled out why empire was important to a new nation. Colonies did more than demonstrate military power; they showed the vigor of a nation's economy, the strength of its convictions, the will of its citizenry, the force of its laws, and the power of its culture. A strong national community could assimilate others, bring progress to new lands and new peoples. One German proponent of expansion called colonialism the "national continuation of the German desire for unity." Lobby groups such as the German Colonial Society, the Committee for French Africa, and the Royal Colonial Institute argued for empire in similar terms, as did newspapers, which also recognized the attractions of sensational stories of overseas conquest. Presented in this way, as part of nation building, imperialism seemed to rise above particular interests or mundane cost-benefit analysis. Culture, law, religion, and industry were vital national products, and their value rose as they were exported and defended abroad.

Third, imperialism had important cultural dimensions. A French diplomat once described the British imperial adventurer Cecil Rhodes as "a force cast in an idea"; the same might be said of imperialism itself. Imperialism as an idea excited such explorers as the Scottish missionary David Livingston, who believed that the British conquest of Africa would put an end to the East African slave trade, and "introduce the Negro family into the body of corporate nations." Rudyard Kipling, the British poet and novelist, wrote of the "white man's burden" (see p. 870), a notorious phrase that referred to the European mission to "civilize" what Kipling and others considered the "barbaric" and "heathen" quarters of the globe. Combatting slave trading, famine, filth, and illiteracy seemed to many Europeans not only a reason to invade Africa and Asia, but also a duty and proof of a superior civilization. These convictions did not cause imperialism, but they illustrate how central empire building became to the West's self-image.

In short, it is difficult to disentangle economic, political, and strategic "causes" for imperialism. It is better to recognize how they overlapped. Strategic interests

It is difficult to disentangle the economic, political, and strategic "causes" for imperialism.

often persuaded policy makers that economic issues were at stake. Different constituencies—the military, international financiers, missionaries, colonial lobby groups at home—held different and often clashing visions of the purpose and benefits of imperialism. "Imperial policy" was less a matter of long-range planning than of a series of quick responses, often improvised, to particular situations. International rivalries led policy makers to redefine their ambitions. So did individual explorers, entrepreneurs, or groups of settlers who established claims to hitherto unknown territories that home governments then felt compelled to recognize and defend. Finally, Europeans were not the only players on the stage. Their goals and practices were shaped by social changes in the countries in which they became involved, by the independent interests of local peoples, and by resistance, which, as often as not, they found themselves unable to understand and powerless to stop.

IMPERIALISM IN SOUTH ASIA

How was the Indian empire reorganized after the Mutiny of 1857?

India was the center of the British empire, the jewel of the British crown. It was also an inheritance from eighteenth-century empire building, secured well before the period of the "new imperialism." The conquest of most of the subcontinent began in the 1750s and quickened during the age of revolution. Conquering India helped compensate for "losing" North America. General Cornwallis, defeated at Yorktown, went on to a brilliant career in India. By the mid-nineteenth century, India had become the focal point of Britain's newly expanded global power, which reached from southern Africa across South Asia and to Australia. Keeping this region involved changing tactics and forms of rule.

Until the mid-nineteenth century, British territories in the subcontinent were under the control of the British East India Company. The company had its own military, divided into European and (far larger) Indian divisions. The company held the right to collect taxes on land from Indian peasants. The company had legal

INDIA: POLITICAL DIVISIONS AND MUTINY

How and why did the British become involved in India, and why did India soon become central to the foreign policy and economic interests of Great Britain? Why did the British decide to annex directly the various parts of India,

monopolies over trade in all goods, including indigo, textiles, salt, minerals, and, most lucrative of all, opium. The British government had granted trade mo-

nopolies in its northern American colonies. Unlike North America, however, India never became a settler state. In the 1830s Europeans were a tiny minority,

HOW WAS THE INDIAN EMPIRE REORGANIZED AFTER THE MUTINY OF 1857?

IMPERIALISM IN SOUTH ASIA   851

KASHMIR

PUNJAB

1849

PUNJAB STATES

KUMAON

1815

1803

OUDH
(AWADH)

RAJPUTANA

ASSAM

NORTH WESTERN PROVINCES

1826

SIND

BIHAR

BENGAL

MANIPUR

1843

1801

1856

1765

BUNDELKHAND

Calcutta

GUJARAT

GWALIOR

SAUGOR
AND
NARBADA

1818

1800, 1818

1818

1853

1854

NAGPUR

LOWER
BURMA

Bombay

1826

1853

BERAR

ORISSA

1803

PESHWAS
TERRITORY

HYDERABAD

1765

ARABIAN

KANARA

CEDED
DISTRICTS

NORTHERN
CIRCARS

Bay of

1852

1799

1799

Bengal

1826

SEA

1801

MYSORE
(to 1831)

TENASSERIM

MALABAR

Madras

1792

1801

1792

SALIM

Cochin

TRAVANCORE

CEYLON

ASIA

Area of
detail

- Indian states bound to Britain by treaties
- Areas conquered and directly ruled by British
- ← British annexation, with dates

0   200   400 Miles

0   200   400 Kilometers

and what prevailing native political conditions made the advance of British control easier? Why did formal, direct British rule—with the appointment of a viceroy—only come in 1861?

numbering forty-five thousand in an Indian population of 150 million. The company's government was military and repressive. Soldiers collected taxes; civil ser-

vants wore military uniforms; British troops brashly commandeered peasants' oxen and carts for their own purposes. Typically, though, the company could not enforce its rule uniformly. It governed some areas directly, others through making alliances with local leaders, and others still by simply controlling goods and money. Indirect rule, here as in other empires, meant finding indigenous collaborators and maintaining their good will. Thus the British cultivated groups that had provided administrators in earlier regimes, the Rajputs and Bhumihars of North India, whom they considered especially effective soldiers, and merchants of big cities such as Calcutta. They offered economic privileges, state offices, or military posts to either groups or entire nations that agreed to ally with the British against others.

British Executing Sepoy Mutineers, 1859. The British were determined to make an example of the leaders of the Sepoy mutiny. This engraving shows executions in which the condemned were blown apart by cannons.

British policy shifted between two poles: one group wanted to "westernize" India, another believed it safer, and more practical, to defer to local culture. Christian missionaries, whose numbers rose as occupation expanded, were determined to replace "blind superstition" with the "genial influence of Christian light and truth." Indignant at such practices as child marriage and sati (in which a widow immolated herself on her husband's funeral pyre), they sought support in England for a wide-ranging assault on Hindu culture. Secular reformers, many of them liberal, considered "Hindoos" and "Mahommedans" susceptible to forms of despotism—in both the family and in the state. They turned their reforming zeal to legal and political change. But other company and British administrators warned their countrymen not to meddle with Indian institutions and practices. "Englishmen are as great fanatics in politics as Mahommedans in religion. They suppose that no country can be saved without English institutions," said one British administrator. Indirect rule, they argued, would only work with the cooperation of local powers. Conflicts such as these meant that the British never pursued any single cultural policy.

THE MUTINY

The company's rule often met resistance and protest. In 1857–1858, it was particularly badly shaken by what the British called the "Sepoy Rebellion," or simply "the mutiny." The uprising began near Delhi, when the military disciplined a regiment of sepoys (the traditional term for Indian soldiers employed by the British) for refusing to use rifle cartridges greased with pork fat—unacceptable to either Hindus or Muslims. Yet as the British prime minister Disraeli later observed, "The decline and fall of empires are not affairs of greased cartridges." The causes of the mutiny were more deep seated, and involved social, economic, and political grievances. Indian peasants attacked law courts and burned tax rolls, protesting debt and corruption. In areas such as Oudh, which had recently been annexed, rebels defended their traditional leaders, who had been summarily ousted by the British. Army officers from privileged castes resented arbitrary treatment at the hands of the British: first promoted as loyal allies and then forced to serve without what they considered titles and honors. The mutiny spread through large areas of northwest India. European troops, which counted for fewer than one fifth of those in arms, found themselves losing control. Religious leaders, both Hindu and Muslim, seized the occasion to denounce Christian missionaries sent in by the British and their assault on local traditions and practices.

At first the British were faced with a desperate situation, with areas under British control cut off from one another and pro-British cities under siege. Loyal Indian troops were brought south from the frontiers, and British troops, fresh from the Crimean War, were shipped directly from Britain to suppress the rebellion.

HOW WAS THE INDIAN EMPIRE REORGANIZED AFTER THE MUTINY OF 1857?

IMPERIALISM IN SOUTH ASIA   853

The fighting lasted more than a year, and the British matched the rebels' early massacres and vandalism with a systematic campaign of repression. Whole rebel units were either killed rather than being allowed to surrender, or else were tried on the spot and executed. Towns and villages that supported the rebels were burned, just as the rebels had burned European homes and outposts. Yet the defeat of the rebellion caught the British public's imagination. After the bloody, inconclusive mess of Crimea, the terrifying threat to British India and the heroic rescue of European hostages and British territory by British troops were electrifying news. Pictures of the Scottish highland regiments (wearing wool kilts in the sweltering heat of India) liberating besieged white women and children went up in homes across the United Kingdom. At a political level, British leaders were stunned by how close the revolt had brought them to disaster and were determined never to repeat the same mistakes.

After "the mutiny," the British were compelled to reorganize their Indian empire, developing new strategies of rule. They brought the subcontinent under direct control of the British crown. They reorganized relations between soldiers. The military separated indigenous troops to avoid the kind of "fraternization" that had proved subversive. As one British officer put

British Imperialism.
Above: This cartoon, "The Execution of 'John Company,' " appeared in *Punch* magazine in 1857. It celebrates the end of the British East India Company's corrupt rule. Note the reference to executions such as the ones on page 852.
Left: A British officer is waited on by two Indian servants, circa 1900.

LORD CURZON ON THE IMPORTANCE OF INDIA AND INDIANS TO THE BRITISH EMPIRE

Lord George Nathaniel Curzon (1859–1925) served as viceroy of India from 1898 to 1905, and foreign secretary from 1919 to 1924. He made his reputation in India, and as a prominent Tory politician he became among the most vocal proponents of the new imperialism. In this speech Curzon spells out the benefits of empire and underscores British dependence on India.

If you want to save your Colony of Natal from being over-run by a formidable enemy, you ask India for help, and she gives it; if you want to rescue the white men's legations from massacres at Peking, and the need is urgent, you request the Government of India to despatch an expedition, and they despatch it; if you are fighting the Mad Mullah in Somaliland, you soon discover that Indian troops and an Indian general are best qualified for the task, and you ask the Government of India to send them; if you desire to defend any of your extreme out-posts or coaling stations of the Empire, Aden, Mauritius, Singapore, Hong-Kong, even Tien-tsin or Shan-hai-kwan, it is to the Indian Army that you turn; if you want to build a railway to Uganda or in the Soudan, you apply for Indian labour. When the late Mr. Rhodes was engaged in developing your recent acquisition of Rhodesia, he came to me for assistance. It is with Indian coolie labor that you exploit the plantations equally of Demerara and Natal; with Indian trained officers that you irrigate and dam the Nile; with Indian forest officers that you tap the resources of Central Africa and Siam; with Indian surveyors that you explore all the hidden places of the earth . . . [Moreover,] India is a country where there will be much larger openings for the investment of capital in the future than has hitherto been the case, and where a great work of industrial and commercial exploitation lies before us.

William Roger Louis, editor in chief, *The Oxford History of the British Empire*, vol. 3, *The Nineteenth Century*, edited by Andrew Porter (Oxford: Oxford University Press, 1999), p. 403.

it, "If one regiment mutinies I should like to have the next so alien that it would fire into it." Even more than before, the British sought to rule through the Indian upper classes rather than in opposition to them. Queen Victoria, now empress of India, set out the principles of indirect rule: "We shall respect the rights, dignity and honour of native princes as our own, and we desire that they, as well as our own subjects, should enjoy that prosperity and that social advancement which can only be secured by internal peace and good government." Civil-service reform opened up new positions to members of the Indian upper classes. The domains of indigenous princes, with their bureaucracies, were incorporated as protectorates into the British "raj" or rule. The British had to reconsider their relationship to Indian cultures. Missionary activity was subdued, and the British channeled their reforming impulses into the more secular project of economic development, railways, roads, irrigation, and so on.

What changed during the period of the new imperialism? In India, its most prominent representative was Lord Curzon, a prominent conservative and the viceroy of India from 1898 to 1905. Curzon deepened British commitments to the region. Concerned about the British position in the world, he warned of the need to fortify India's borders against Russia. He urged continued economic investment. Curzon worried out loud that the British would be worn down by resistance to the raj, that confronted with their apparent inability to transform Indian culture, they would become cynical, get "lethargic and think only of home." In the same way that Rudyard Kipling urged the British and the Americans to "take up the white man's burden" (see p. 870), Curzon pleaded with his countrymen to see how central India was to the greatness of Britain.

What did India provide to Great Britain? By the eve of World War I, India was Britain's largest export market. One tenth of all the British empire's trade passed through India's port cities of Madras, Bombay, and Calcutta. Even more crucial to Great Britain were the human resources of India. Indian laborers worked on tea plantations in Assam, near Burma, and they built railways and dams in southern Africa and Egypt. British rule cast an enormous diaspora of Indian workers throughout the empire. Over a million indentured Indian servants left their country in the second half of the century. India also provided the British empire with highly trained engineers, land surveyors, clerks, bureaucrats, schoolteachers, and merchants. The nationalist leader Mohandas Gandhi, for instance, first came into the public eye as a young lawyer in Pretoria, South Africa, where he worked for an Indian law firm. The British deployed Indian troops across the empire. (They would later call up 1.2 million troops in World War I.) For all these reasons, men such as Curzon found it impossible to imagine their empire, or even their nation, without India.

How did the British raj shape Indian society? The British practice of indirect rule sought to create an Indian elite that would serve British interests, a group "who may be the interpreters between us and the millions whom we govern—a class of persons Indian in colour and blood, but English in tastes, in opinion, in morals, and in intellect," as one British writer put it. Eventually, this practice created a large social group of British-educated Indian civil servants and businessmen, well trained for government and skeptical about British claims of bringing progress to the subcontinent. This group provided the leadership for the nationalist movement that challenged British rule in India. At the same time, that group became increasingly distant from the rest of the nation. The overwhelming majority of Indians remained desperately poor peasants, many of them unable to pay taxes and thus in debt to British landlords, all struggling to subsist on diminishing plots of land, villagers working in the textile trade beaten down by imports of cheap manufactured goods from England, all residents of what would become the most populous nation in the world.

IMPERIALISM IN CHINA

How did Western countries "open" China?

In China, too, European imperialism escalated early, well before the period of the "new imperialism." Yet it took a different form. Europeans did not conquer and annex whole regions. Instead, they forced favorable trade agreements at gunpoint, set up treaty ports where Europeans lived and worked under their own jurisdiction, and established outposts of European missionary activity—all with such dispatch that the Chinese spoke of their country as being "carved up like a melon."

Since the seventeenth century European trade with China—in coveted luxuries such as silk, porcelain, art objects, and tea—had run up against resistance from the Chinese government, which was determined to keep foreign traders, and foreign influence in general, at bay. By the early nineteenth century, however, Britain's global ambitions and rising power were setting the stage for a confrontation. Free from the task of fighting Napoleon, the British set their sights on improving the terms of the China trade, demanding the rights to come into open harbors and to have special trading privileges. The other source of constant friction involved the harsh treatment of British subjects by Chinese law courts—including the summary execution of several Britons convicted of crimes. And by the 1830s, these diplomatic conflicts had been heightened by the opium trade.

THE OPIUM TRADE

Opium provided a direct link among Britain, British India, and China. The drug had been produced in India and since at least the sixteenth century traded, by the Dutch and then the British, to southeast Asia and China. In fact, opium (derived from the poppy plant)

An Opium Factory in Patna, India, c. 1851. Balls of opium dry in a huge warehouse before being shipped to Calcutta for export to China and elsewhere.

The Opium Trade, 1880s. A European merchant examines opium.

was one of the very few commodities that Europeans could sell in China, and for this reason it became crucial to the balance of East-West trade. When the British conquered northeast India, they also annexed one of the richest opium-growing areas and became deeply involved in the trade—so much so that historians do not shy from calling East India Company rule a "narco-military empire." British agencies designated specific poppy-growing regions and gave cash advances to Indian peasants who would cultivate the crop. Producing opium was a labor-intensive process: peasant cultivators collected sap from the poppy seeds, others cleaned the sap and formed it into opium balls, which were dried before being weighed and shipped out. In the opium-producing areas northwest of Calcutta, "factories" employed as many as one thousand Indian workers forming and curing the opium, as well as young boys whose job it was to turn the opium balls every four days. From India, the East India Company sold the opium to "country traders"—small fleets of British, Dutch, and Chinese shippers who carried the drug to southeast Asia and China. Silver paid for the opium came back to the East India company, which used it, in turn, to buy Chinese goods for the European market. The trade, therefore, was not only profitable, it was key to a triangular European-Indian-Chinese economic relationship. Production and export rose dramatically in the early nineteenth century. By the 1830s, when the British-Chinese confrontation was taking shape, opium provided British India with more revenues than any other source except taxes on land.

People all over the world consumed opium, for medicinal reasons as well as for pleasure. The Chinese market was especially lucrative.

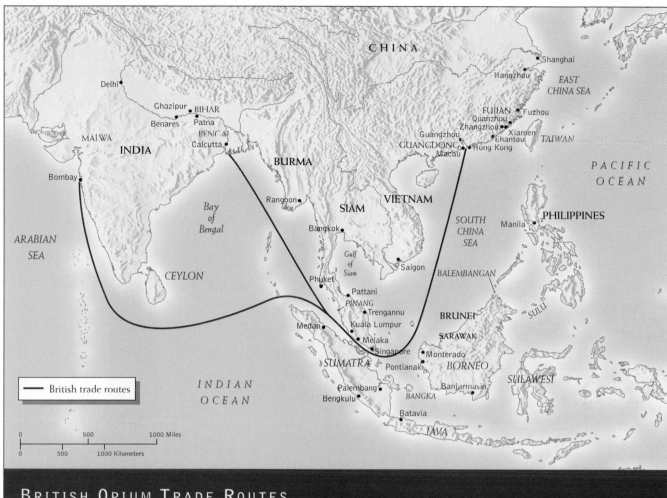

BRITISH OPIUM TRADE ROUTES

This map depicts the major trade routes used by the British in the shipment of opium in Asia. How did opium come to play such an important role in the imperial efforts of the British in this part of the world? How did the intensification of the opium trade affect the British position in this part of the world? What social and political problems did it create for both colonizer and colonized?

Eighteenth-century China had witnessed a craze for tobacco and smoking that taught users how to smoke opium. A large and wealthy Chinese elite of merchants and government officials provided much of the market, but opium smoking also became popular among soldiers, students, and Chinese laborers, and in the nineteenth century opium imports followed Chinese labor all over the world—to southeast Asia and San Francisco. In an effort to control the problem, the Chinese government banned opium imports, prohibited domestic production, criminalized smoking, and in the 1830s began a full-scale campaign to purge the drug from China. That campaign set the Chinese emperor on a collision course with British opium traders. In one confrontation the Chinese drug commissioner Lin confiscated 3 million pounds of raw opium from the British and washed it out to sea. In another the Chinese authorities blockaded British ships in port, and local citizens demonstrated angrily in front of British residences.

THE OPIUM WARS

In 1839, these simmering conflicts broke into what was called the first "Opium War." Drugs were not the core of the matter but highlighted larger issues of

SOUTH AND EAST ASIA, C. 1914

Why were European powers (and to some extent, the United States) anxious to establish treaty ports and spheres of influence in China? Why was control of Chinese markets particularly crucial to British economic interests? What was the relationship among colonial powers, capitalist investors, and the Chinese government? How did the Boxer Rebellion and the effects of the Open Door Policy encourage more intensive exploitation in other parts of Southeast Asia?

Map labels:

EUROPE

RUSSIAN EMPIRE

SAKHALIN

KURILE ISLANDS (Jap.)

Tokyo

JAPAN

Vladivostok

KOREA

Port Arthur

Hangchow

Lake Baikal

OUTER MONGOLIA

INNER MONGOLIA

REPUBLIC OF CHINA

RYUKYUS (Jap.)

FORMOSA (Br.)

PACIFIC OCEAN

PHILIPPINES

Hong Kong (Br.)

Macao (Port.)

TONKIN

COCHIN-CHINA

LAOS

CAMBODIA

TIBET

SIKKIM BHUTAN

NEPAL

BURMA

SIAM

BR. NORTH BORNEO

BRUNEI

FEDERATED MALAY STATES

Singapore (Br.)

DUTCH EAST INDIES

PORTUGUESE TIMOR

TIMOR

AUSTRALIA

Lake Balkash

ARAL SEA

AFGHANISTAN (Br. influence)

INDIA

Bay of Bengal

CEYLON (Br.)

Pondicherry (Fr.)

Bombay

Goa (Port.)

Mahé (Fr.)

MALDIVE IS. (Br.)

INDIAN OCEAN

ARABIAN SEA

CASPIAN SEA

PERSIA

(Russian influence)

OMAN

KUWAIT (Br.)

BAHRAIN (Br.)

NEJD

(Br.)

YEMEN

ADEN (Br.)

HEJAZ

RED SEA

OTTOMAN EMPIRE

BLACK SEA

MEDITERRANEAN SEA

AFRICA

BLACK SEA

Legend:

- British
- Protected states in India
- Dutch
- Ottoman Empire
- Treaty ports in China
- French
- Portuguese
- Japanese
- U.S.A.

Scale:
0   1000   2000 Miles
0   1000   2000 Kilometers

sovereignty and economic status: the Europeans' "rights" to trade with whomever they pleased, by-passing Chinese monopolies; to set up zones of European residence in defiance of Chinese sovereignty; and to proselytize and open schools. War flared up several times over the course of the century. After the first war of 1839–1842, in which British steam vessels and guns overpowered the Chinese fleet, the Treaty of Nanking (1842) compelled the Chinese to give the British trading privileges, the right to reside in five cities, and the port of Hong Kong "in perpetuity." After a second war, the British secured yet more treaty ports and privileges, including the right to send in missionaries. In the aftermath of those agreements between the Chinese and British, other countries demanded similar rights and economic opportunities. By the end of the nineteenth century, during the period of the new imperialism, the French, Germans, and Russians had claimed mining rights and permission to build railroads, to begin manufacturing with cheap Chinese labor, and to arm and police European communities in Chinese cities. In Shanghai, for instance, seventeen thousand foreigners lived with their own courts, schools, churches, and utilities. The United States, not wanting to be shouldered aside, demanded its own "open door policy." Japan was an equally active imperialist power in the Pacific, and the Sino-Japanese war of 1894–1895 forced China to concede to the Japanese trading privileges, the independence of Korea, and the Liaotung Peninsula in Manchuria.

Surrendering privileges to Europeans seriously undermined the authority of the Chinese Qing (Ching) emperor at home, and only heightened popular hostility to foreign intruders. Authority at the imperial center had been eroding for more than a century by 1900, hastened by the Opium Wars and by the vast Taiping Rebellion, an enormous conflict in which radical Christian rebels in south-central China challenged the authority of the emperors themselves. On the defensive against the rebels, the dynasty hired foreign generals, including the British commander Charles Gordon to command its forces. The war devastated China's agricultural heartland, and the death toll, never confirmed, may have reached into the millions. This sort of disorder, and the increasing inability of the emperor to keep order and collect the taxes necessary to stabilize trade and repay foreign loans, led European countries to take more and more direct control of their side of "the China trade."

THE BOXER REBELLION

From a Western perspective, the most important of the nineteenth-century rebellions against the corruptions of foreign rule came with the Boxer Rebellion of 1900. The Boxers were a secret society of young men trained in Chinese martial arts and believed to have spiritual powers. Antiforeign and antimissionary, they provided the spark for a loosely organized but widespread uprising in northern China. Bands attacked foreign engineers, tore up railway lines, and in the spring of 1900 marched on Beijing. They laid siege to the foreign legations in the city, home to several thousand Western diplomats and merchants and their families. The legations' small garrison defended their walled compound with little more than rifles, bayonets, and improvised artillery, but they withstood the siege for fifty-five days until a large relief column arrived. The rebellion, and particularly the siege at Beijing, mobilized a global response. Europe's Great Powers, rivals everywhere else in the world, drew together in response to this crisis in order to tear China apart. An expedition numbering twenty thousand troops—combining the forces of Britain, France, the United States, Germany, Italy, Japan, and Russia—ferociously repressed the Boxer movement. The outside powers then demanded indemnities, new trading concessions, and reassurances from the Chinese government.

The Boxer Rebellion was one of several anti-imperialist movements at the end of the nineteenth century. The rebellion testified to the vulnerability of Europeans' imperial power. It dramatized the resources Europeans would have to devote to maintaining their far-flung influence. In the process, too, the Europeans became committed to propping up corrupt and fragile governments in order to protect their agreements and interests, and they were drawn into putting down popular uprisings against local inequalities and foreign rule.

In China the age of the "new imperialism" capped a century of conflict and expansion. By 1900, virtually all of Asia had been divided up among the European powers. Japan, an active imperial power in its own right, alone had maintained its independence. British rule extended from India across Burma, Malaya, Aus-

The Boxer Rebellion dramatized the resources Europeans would have to devote to maintaining their far-flung influence.

tralia, and New Zealand. The Dutch, Britain's long-standing trade rivals, secured Indonesia. During the 1880s, the French moved into Indochina. Imperial rivalries (among Britain, France, and Russia, China and Japan, Russia and Japan) caused the struggle for influence and economic advantage in Asia; that struggle, in turn exacerbated nationalist feeling. Imperial expansion, the expression of European power, was showing its destabilizing effects.

RUSSIAN IMPERIALISM

Russia was a persistently imperialist power throughout the nineteenth century. Its rulers championed a policy of annexation—by conquest, treaty, or both—of lands bordering on the existing Russian state. Beginning in 1801, with the acquisition of Georgia following a war with Persia, the tsars continued to press their expansionist quest. Bessarabia and Turkestan (taken from the Turks) and Armenia (from the Persians) vastly increased the empire's size. This southward colonization brought the Russians close to war with the British twice: first in 1881, when Russian troops occupied territories in the trans-Caspian region, and again in 1884–1887, when the tsar's forces advanced to the frontier of Afghanistan. In both cases the British feared incursions into areas they deemed within their sphere of influence in the Middle East. They were concerned, as well, about a possible threat to India. The maneuvering, spying, and support of friendly puppet governments by Russia and Britain became known as the "Great Game," and was a foretaste of Western countries' jockeying for the region's oil resources in the twentieth century.

Russian expansion also moved toward the east. In 1875, the Japanese traded the southern half of Sakhalin Island for the previously Russian Kurile Islands. The tsars' eastward advance was finally halted in 1904. Russian expansion in Mongolia and Manchuria came up against Japanese expansion, and the two powers went to war. Russia's huge imperial army more than met its match in a savage, bloody conflict. Russia's navy was sent halfway round the world to reinforce the beleaguered Russian troops, but was ambushed and sunk by the better-trained and equipped Japanese fleet. This national humiliation helped provoke a revolt in Russia and led to an American-brokered peace treaty in 1905. The defeat shook the already unsteady regime of the tsar, and proved that European nations were not the only ones who could play the imperial game successfully.

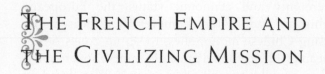

THE FRENCH EMPIRE AND THE CIVILIZING MISSION

What was the "civilizing mission"?

Like British expansion into India, French colonialism in Northern Africa began before the so-called new imperialism of the late nineteenth century. By the 1830s, the French had created a general government of their possessions in Algeria, the most important of which were cities along the Mediterranean coast. From the outset the Algerian conquest was different from most other colonial ventures: Algeria became a settler state, one of the few apart from South Africa. Some of the early settlers were utopian socialists, out to create ideal communities; some were workers the French government deported after the revolution of 1848 to be "resettled" safely as farmers; some were winegrowers whose vines at home had been destroyed by an insect infestation. The settlers were by no means all French; they included Italian, Spanish, and Maltese merchants and shopkeepers of modest means, laborers, and peasants. By the 1870s, in several of the coastal cities, this new creole community outnumbered indigenous Algerians, and within it, other Europeans outnumbered the French. With the military's help, the settlers appropriated land, and French business concerns took cork forests and established mining in copper, lead, and iron. Economic activity was for European benefit. The first railroads, for instance, did not even carry passengers; they took iron ore to the coast for export to France, where it would be smelted and sold.

The settlers and the French government did not necessarily pursue common goals. In the 1870s, the new and still fragile Third Republic (founded after Napoleon III was defeated in 1870; see Chapter 24), in an effort to ensure the settlers' loyalty, made the colony a department of France. This gave the French settlers the full rights of republican citizenship. It also gave them the power to pass laws in Algeria that consolidated their privileges and community (naturalizing all Europeans, for instance) and further disenfranchised indigenous populations, who had no voting rights at all. French politicians in Paris occasionally objected to the settlers' contemptuous treatment of indigenous peoples, arguing that it subverted the project of "lifting up" the natives. The French settlers in Algeria had little interest in such a project; although they paid lip service to republican ideals, they wanted the advantages of "Frenchness" for themselves. Colonial administrators and social scientists differentiated the "good" mountain-dwelling Berbers, who could be brought into French society, from the "bad" Arabs, whose religion made them supposedly inassimilable. In Algeria, then, colonialism was at the very least a three-way relationship, and illustrates the dynamics that made colonialism in general a contradictory enterprise.

Before the 1870s, colonial activities aroused relatively little interest among the French at home. But after the humiliating defeat in the Franco-Prussian war (1870–1871) and the establishment of the Third Republic, colonial lobby groups and, gradually, the government, became increasingly adamant about the benefits of colonialism. These benefits were not simply economic: taking on the "civilizing mission" would reinforce the purpose of the French republic and the prestige of the French people. It was France's duty "to contribute to this work of civilization." Jules Ferry, a republican political leader, successfully argued for expanding the French presence in Indochina, saying, "We must believe that if Providence deigned to confer upon us a mission by making us masters of the earth, this mission consists not of attempting an impossible fusion of the races but of simply spreading or awakening among the other races the superior notions of which we are the guardians." Those "superior notions" included a commitment to economic and technological progress and to liberation from slavery, political oppression, poverty, and disease. In what Ferry considered an attack on the racism of his contemporaries, he argued that "the superior races have a right vis-à-vis the inferior races . . . they have a right to civilize them."

Under Ferry, the French acquired Tunisia (1881), northern and central Vietnam (Tonkin and Annam; 1883), and Laos and Cambodia (1893). They also carried this "civilizing mission" into their colonies in West Africa. European and Atlantic trade with the west coast of Africa, in slaves, gold, and ivory, had been well established for centuries. In the late nineteenth century, trade gave way to formal administration. The year 1895 saw the establishment of a Federation of French West Africa, a loosely organized administration to govern an area nine times the size of France, including Guinea, Senegal, and the Ivory Coast. French control, however, was uneven. Despite military campaigns of

> In Algeria, colonialism was at the very least a three-way relationship, and illustrates the dynamics that made colonialism in general a contradictory enterprise.

pacification, resistance remained, and the French dealt gingerly with tribal leaders, at some times deferring to their authority and at others trying to break their power. They established French courts and law only in cities, leaving Islamic or tribal courts to run other areas. The federation aimed to rationalize the economic exploitation of the area, and to replace "booty capitalism" with a more careful management and development of resources. The French called this "enhancing the value" of the region, which was part of the civilizing mission of the modern republic. The federation embarked on an ambitious program of public works. Engineers rebuilt the huge harbor at Dakar, the most important on the coast, to accommodate rising exports. With some utopian zeal they redesigned older cities, tried to improve sanitation and health, improved water systems, and so on. The French republic was justifiably proud of the Pasteur Institute for bacteriological research, which opened in France in 1888; overseas institutes became part of the colonial enterprise. One plan called for a large-scale West African railroad network to lace through the region. A public-school program built free schools in villages not controlled by missionaries. Education, though, was not compulsory and was usually for boys.

Such programs plainly served French interests. "Officially this process is called civilizing, and after all, the term is apt, since the undertaking serves to increase the degree of prosperity of our civilization," remarked one Frenchman who opposed the colonial enterprise. None of these measures aimed to give political rights. As one historian puts it, "the French Government General was in the business not of making citizens, but of civilizing its subjects." More telling, however, the French were not often successful. The French government did not have the resources to carry out these plans, which proved much more expensive and complicated than anyone imagined. Transportation costs ran very high. Labor posed the largest problems. Here as elsewhere, Europeans faced massive resistance from the African peasants, whom they wanted to do everything from building railroads to working mines and carrying rubber. They resorted to forced labor, signing agreements with local tribal leaders to deliver workers, and they turned a blind eye to the continuing use of slave labor in the interior. For all of these reasons, the colonial project did not produce the profits some

Slaves in Chains, 1896. In Africa, native labor was exploited by Europeans and by other natives, as here.

expected. In important respects, however, the French investment in colonialism was cultural. Railroads, schools, and projects such as the Dakar harbor were, like the Eiffel Tower (1889), symbols of the French nation's modernity, power, and world leadership.

THE "SCRAMBLE FOR AFRICA" AND THE CONGO

What events set off the "scramble for Africa"?

French expansion in West Africa was only a small sample of European voracity on the African continent. The scope and speed with which all the major European powers entered this new wave of formal control and colonization was such that the process gained a nickname that has stuck ever since: the "scramble for Africa." The effects were obvious and profound. In 1875, 11 percent of the continent was in European hands. By 1902, the figure was 90 percent. European powers conquered disease, logistical problems of transport and communication, and the resistance of indigenous kingdoms and

> In 1875, 11 percent of Africa was in European hands. By 1902, the figure was 90 percent.

competing European powers to extend their holdings inland at terrific speed.

THE CONGO FREE STATE

In the 1870s, the British had formed new imperial relationships along the costs of south and east Africa, just as the French had been active in the north and west. The newest phase of European involvement struck right at the heart of the continent. Up until the latter part of the nineteenth century this territory had been out of bounds for Europeans. The rapids downstream on such strategic rivers as the Congo and the Zambezi made it difficult to move inland, and tropical diseases against which Europeans had little or no resistance were lethal to most explorers. But during the 1870s, a new drive into central Africa produced results. The target was the fertile valleys around the river Congo, and the European colonizers were a privately financed group of Belgians paid by their king, Leopold II (1865–1909). They followed in the footsteps of Herbert M. Stanley, an American newspaperman and explorer who later became a British subject and a knight of the realm. Stanley hacked his way through thick canopy jungle and territory where no European had previously set foot. His "scientific" journeys inspired the creation of a society of researchers and students of African culture in Brussels, in reality a front organization for the commercial company set up by Leopold. The ambitiously named International Association for the Exploration and Civilization of the Congo was set up in 1876, and set about signing treaties with local elites that opened the whole Congo River basin to commercial exploitation. The vast resources of palm oil and natural rubber, and the promise of minerals (including diamonds) were now within Europeans' reach.

The strongest resistance that Leopold's company met came from other colonial powers, particularly Portugal, which objected to this new drive for occupation. In 1884, a conference was called in Berlin to settle the matter of control over the Congo River basin. It was chaired by

ATROCITIES IN THE CONGO

George Washington Williams (1849–1891), an African American pastor, journalist, and historian, was among a handful of international observers who went to the Congo in the 1890s to explore and report back on conditions. He wrote several reports: one for the United States government, another that he presented at an international antislavery conference, several newspaper columns, and an open letter to King Léopold, from which the following is excerpted

Good and Great Friend,

I have the honour to submit for your Majesty's consideration some reflections respecting the Independent State of Congo, based upon a careful study and inspection of the country and character of the personal Government you have established upon the African Continent. . . .

I was led to regard your enterprise as the rising of the Star of Hope for the Dark Continent, so long the habitation of cruelties. . . . When I arrived in the Congo, I naturally sought for the results of the brilliant programme:—*"fostering care," "benevolent enterprise,"* an *"honest and practical effort"* to increase the knowledge of the natives *"and secure their welfare."* . . .

I was doomed to bitter disappointment. Instead of the natives of the Congo "adopting the fostering care" of your Majesty's Government, they everywhere complain that their land has been taken from them by force; that the Government is cruel and arbitrary, and declare that they neither love nor respect the Government and its flag. Your Majesty's Government has sequestered their land, burned their towns, stolen their property, enslaved their women and children, and committed other crimes too numerous to mention in detail. It is natural that they everywhere shrink from *"the fostering care"* your Majesty's Government so eagerly proffers them.

There has been, to my absolute knowledge, no *"honest and practical effort made to increase their knowledge and secure their welfare."* Your Majesty's Government has never spent one franc for educational purposes, nor instituted any practical system of industrialism. Indeed the most unpractical measures have been adopted *against* the natives in nearly every respect; and in the capital of your Majesty's Government at Boma there is not a native employed. The labour system is radically unpractical . . . recruits are transported under circumstances more cruel than cattle in European countries. They eat their rice twice a day by the use of their fingers; they often thirst for water when the season is dry; they are exposed to the heat and rain, and sleep upon the damp and filthy decks of the vessels often so closely crowded as to lie in human ordure. And, of course, many die. . . .

All the crimes perpetrated in the Congo have been done in *your* name, and *you* must answer at the bar if Public Sentiment for the misgovernment of a people, whose lives and fortunes were entrusted to you by the august Conference of Berlin, 1884–1885. . . .

George Washington Williams, "An Open Letter to His serene Majesty Leopold II, King of the Belgians, and Sovereign of the Independent State of Congo, July 1890" in John Hope Franklin, *George Washington Williams: A Biography* (Chicago: University of Chicago Press, 1985), pp. 243–254.

the master of European power politics, Otto von Bismarck, and attended by all the leading colonial nations, as well as the United States. The conference established ground rules for a new phase of European economic and political expansion. Europe's two great overseas empires, Britain and France, and the strongest emerging power inside Europe, Germany, joined forces and settled the Congo issue. Their dictates seemed to be perfectly in line with nineteenth-century liberalism. The Congo valleys would be open to free trade and commerce; a slave trade still run by some of the Islamic kingdoms in the region would be suppressed in favor of free labor; and a Congo Free State would be set up, denying the region to the formal control of any single European country.

In reality the "Congo Free State" was run by Leopold's private company, and the region was opened up to unrestricted exploitation by a series of large European corporations. The older slave trade was suppressed, but the European companies took the "free" African labor guaranteed in Berlin and placed workers in equally bad conditions. Huge tracts of land, larger than whole European countries, became plantations for the extraction of palm oil, rubber, cocoa, or diamonds. African workers labored in appalling conditions, with no real medicine or sanitation, too little food, and according to production schedules that made European factory labor look mild by comparison. Hundreds of thousands of African workers died from disease and overwork. Because European managers did not respect the different cycle of seasons in central Africa, whole crop years were lost, leading to famines. Laborers working in the heat of the dry season often simply dropped under the sun, carrying individual loads on their backs that would have been handled by heavy machinery in a European factory. Yet thousands of Africans were still pressed into work harvesting goods Europe wanted. They did so for little or no pay, under the threat of beatings and ritual mutilation for dozens of petty offenses against the plantation companies, who made the laws of the "Free State." Eventually the scandal of the Congo became too great to go on unquestioned. A whole generation of authors and journalists, most famously Joseph Conrad in his *Heart of Darkness*, publicized the arbitrary brutality and the vast scale of suffering. In 1908, Belgium was forced to take direct control of the Congo, turning it into a Belgian colony.

Africans worked for little or no pay, under the threat of beatings and ritual mutilation for dozens of petty offenses against the plantation companies, who made the laws of the Congo "Free State."

A few restrictions at least were imposed on the activities of the great plantation companies that had brought a vast new store of raw materials to European industry by using slavery in all but name.

THE PARTITION OF AFRICA

The occupation of Congo, and its promise of great material wealth, pressured other colonial powers into expanding their holdings. The guarantees made at the 1884 Berlin conference combined with stories of rubber forests or diamond mines in other parts of central and southern Africa to set off the "scramble." The French and Portugese increased their holdings. Italy moved into territories along the Red Sea, beside British-held land and the independent kingdom of Ethiopia.

Germany came relatively late to the game. Bismarck was reluctant to engage in an enterprise that he believed would do little to profit the empire either politically or economically. Yet he did not want either Britain or France to dominate Africa, and Germany seized colonies in strategic locations. The German colonies in Cameroon and most of modern Tanzania separated the territories of older, more established powers. Though the Germans were not the most enthusiastic colonialists, they were still fascinated by the imperial adventure, and jealous of their territories. When the Herero people of German Southwest Africa (now Namibia) rebelled in the early 1900s, the Germans responded with a vicious campaign of village burning and ethnic killing that nearly annihilated the Herero.

Great Britain and France had their own ambitions. The French aimed to move west to east across the continent, an important reason for the French expedition to Fashoda (in the Sudan) in 1898 (see below). Britain's part in the "scramble" took place largely in southern and eastern Africa, and was encapsulated in the dreams and career of one man: the diamond tycoon, colonial politician, and imperial visionary Cecil Rhodes. Rhodes, who made a fortune from the South African diamond mines in the 1870s and 1880s and founded the diamond-mining company DeBeers. Rhodes became prime minister of Britain's Cape Colony in 1890. (He left part of this fortune for the creation of the Rhodes scholarships to educate future leaders of the empire at Oxford.) In an uneasy alliance with the Boer

Left: **"The Rhodes Colossus."** This cartoon, which appeared in *Punch* magazine, satirized the ambitions of Cecil Rhodes, the driving force behind British imperialism in South Africa. Right: **"Now We Shant Be Long to Cairo."** So read the banner across Engine No. 1 taking the first train from Umtali to Salisbury, Rhodesia, reflecting Cecil Rhodes's vision of a Capetown-to-Cairo railway as a symbol of British domination of the African continent.

settlers in their independent republics and with varying levels of support from London, Rhodes pursued two great personal and imperial goals. The personal goal was to build a southern African empire that was founded on diamonds. This "Rhodesia" would fly the Union Jack out of pride but send its profits into Rhodes' own companies. Through bribery, double dealing, careful coalition politics with the British and Boer settlers, warfare, and outright theft, Rhodes helped carve out territories occupying the modern nations of Zambia, Zimbabwe, Malawi, and Botswana—most of the savannah of southern Africa. Rhodes had a broader imperial vision, one that he shared with the new British colonial secretary in the late 1890s, Joseph Chamberlain. The first part of that vision was a British presence along the whole of eastern Africa, symbolized by the goal of a "Cape-to-Cairo" railway. The second was that the empire should make Britain self-sufficient, with British industry able to run on the goods and raw materials shipped in from its colonies, then exporting many finished products back to those lands. Once the territories of "Zambeziland" and "Rhodesia" were taken, Rhodes found himself turning against the European settlers in the region, a brewing conflict that led to outright war in 1899 (see below).

This battle over strategic advantage, diamonds, and European pride was symbolic of the "scramble." As each European power sought its "place in the sun," in the famous phrase of the German kaiser William II, they brought more and more of Africa under direct colonial control. It created a whole new scale of plunder as companies were designed and managed to strip the continent of its resources, and African peoples faced a combination of direct European control and "indirect rule" which allowed local elites friendly to European interests literally to lord over those who

CHRONOLOGY

THE "SCRAMBLE FOR AFRICA," 1870–1908

European drive into Central Africa	1870s
French acquire Tunisia	1881
Berlin Congress	1884
Germany colonizes Cameroon and Tanzania	1884
Federation of French West Africa	1895
Congo becomes a Belgian colony	1908

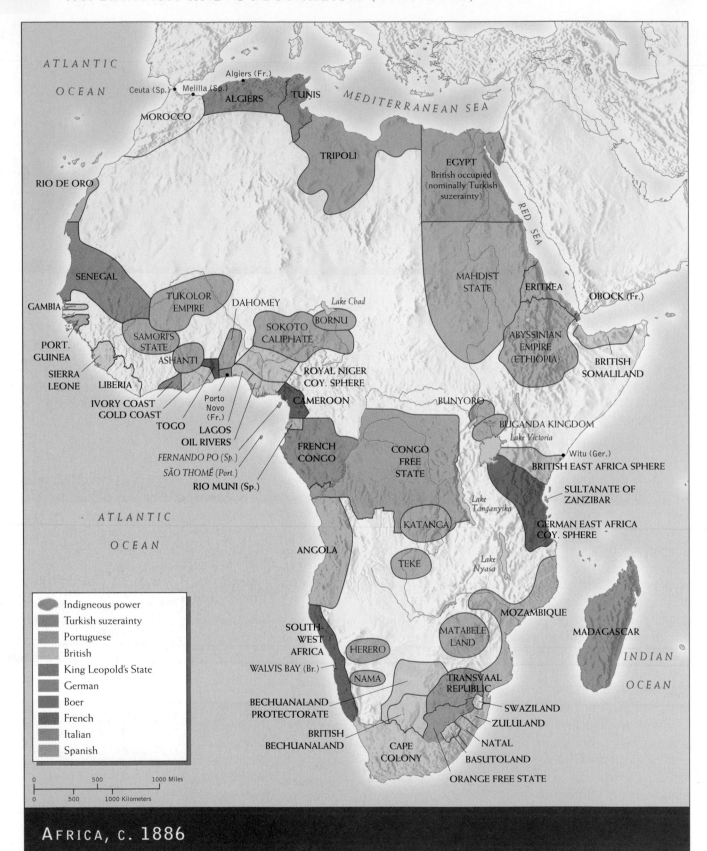

ATLANTIC
OCEAN

Ceuta (Sp.)   Melilla (Sp.)
Algiers (Fr.)
ALGIERS   TUNIS
MOROCCO
                              TRIPOLI   MEDITERRANEAN SEA

RIO DE ORO
                                                 EGYPT
                                                 British occupied
                                                 (nominally Turkish
                                                 suzerainty)

                                                                         RED SEA

SENEGAL
                   TUKOLOR   Lake Chad
GAMBIA   EMPIRE   DAHOMEY   MAHDIST   ERITREA
                                              SOKOTO   STATE   OBOCK (Fr.)
PORT.   SAMORI'S   BORNU   CALIPHATE   ABYSSINIAN
GUINEA   STATE   EMPIRE
                 ASHANTI   ROYAL NIGER   (ETHIOPIA)   BRITISH
SIERRA   COY. SPHERE   SOMALILAND
LEONE   LIBERIA
IVORY COAST   CAMEROON   BUNYORO
GOLD COAST   Porto   BUGANDA KINGDOM
   TOGO   Novo   Lake Victoria
                (Fr.)   LAGOS   Witu (Ger.)
                           OIL RIVERS   FRENCH   CONGO   BRITISH EAST AFRICA SPHERE
      FERNANDO PO (Sp.)   CONGO   FREE
      SÃO THOMÉ (Port.)   STATE   SULTANATE OF
         RIO MUNI (Sp.)   ZANZIBAR

ATLANTIC   Lake   GERMAN EAST AFRICA
                                                           Tanganyika COY. SPHERE
OCEAN   KATANGA

                                ANGOLA   TEKE   Lake
                                                            Nyasa

Indigenous power   MOZAMBIQUE
Turkish suzerainty   MATABELE   MADAGASCAR
Portuguese   SOUTH-   LAND
British   WEST   HERERO   INDIAN
King Leopold's State   AFRICA   OCEAN
German   WALVIS BAY (Br.)   NAMA   TRANSVAAL
Boer   REPUBLIC
French   BECHUANALAND   SWAZILAND
Italian   PROTECTORATE   ZULULAND
Spanish   NATAL
                    BRITISH   CAPE   BASUTOLAND
                    BECHUANALAND   COLONY
0   500   1000 Miles   ORANGE FREE STATE
0   500   1000 Kilometers

AFRICA, C. 1886

Before World War I, who had been the "winners" and "losers" in the scramble for Africa? While the French claim
was the largest, why were the British imperial gains more impressive? Given their late arrival as a unified nation
and colonial power, how had Germany fared in the race for colonial possessions? Why had Italy, despite an advan-

AFRICA, c. 1914

Legend:
- British
- French
- Belgian
- Spanish
- Portuguese
- German
- Italian
- Independent state

tageous geographical relationship to Africa, fared so poorly in carving out an African empire? What does the ultimate result of the pre-war scramble for Africa suggest to us about the ways in which European powers regarded one another, and why they felt maintaining economic and material resources were so important?

resisted. The partition of Africa was the most striking instance of the new imperialism, with international and domestic repercussions.

IMPERIAL CULTURE

How did empire affect European identity?

The relationship between the metropole and the colonies was not carried on at a distance; imperialism was thoroughly anchored in late nineteenth-century Western culture. Images of empire were everywhere in the metropole. They were not just in the propagandist literature distributed by the proponents of colonial expansion, but on tins of tea and boxes of cocoa, as background themes in posters advertising everything from dance halls to sewing machines. Museums and world's fairs displayed the products of empire and introduced spectators to "exotic peoples" who were now benefiting from European "education." Music halls rang to the sound of imperialist songs. Empire was almost always present in novels of the period, sometimes appearing as a faraway setting for fantasy, adventure, or stories of self-discovery. Sometimes imperial themes and peoples were presented as a subtly menacing presence at home. Even in the tales of Sherlock Holmes, which were set in London and not overtly imperialist, the furnishings of empire provided instantly recognizable signs of opulence and decadence. In *The Sign of Four*, Holmes visits a gentleman in a lavish apartment: "Two great tiger-skins thrown athwart [the carpet] increased the suggestion of Eastern luxury, as did a huge hookah which stood upon a mat in the corner." In "The Man with the Twisted Lip," Watson wanders into one of the supposed opium dens in the East End of London, and is waited on by a "sallow Malay attendant." The "dens" themselves were largely an invention; police records of the time show very few locations in London that supplied the drug. As a realm of fantasy, overseas empires and "exotic" cultures became part of the century's sexual culture. Photos and postcards of North African harems or "unveiled" Arab women were common in European pornography, as were colonial memoirs that chronicled the sexual adventures of their authors.

Empire, however, was not simply background; it played an important part in establishing European identity. In the case of France, the "civilizing mission" demonstrated to French citizens the grandeur of their nation. Building railroads and "bringing progress to other lands" illustrated the vigor of the French republic. Many British writers spoke in similar tones. One called the British empire "the greatest secular agency for good known to the world." Another, using more religious language, argued, "The British race may safely be called a missionary race. The command to go and teach all nations is one that the British people have, whether rightly or wrongly, regarded as specially laid upon themselves." The sense of high moral purpose was not restricted to male writers or authority figures. In England, the United States, Germany, and France, the speeches and projects of women's reform movements were full of references to empire and the civilizing mission. Britain's woman suffrage movement, for instance, was fiercely critical of the British government but often equally nationalist and imperialist. Asking that women be brought into British politics seemed to involve their taking on imperial, as well as civic, responsibilities. British women reformers wrote about the oppression of Indian women by child marriage and sati, and saw themselves taking up the "white woman's burden" of reform. The French suffragist Hubertine Auclert wrote a book entitled *Arab Women in Algeria* (1900), which angrily indicted both French colonial administrators for their indifference to the condition of women in their domains and the French republic for shrugging off the claims of women at home. Her arguments stung precisely because they rested on the assumption that European culture should be enlightened. Arab women were "victims of Muslim debauchery," wrote Auclert, and polygamy led to "intellectual degeneracy." The image of women languishing in the colonies not only dramatized the need for reform, it enabled European women in their home countries to see themselves as bearers of progress. The liberal writer and political theorist John Stuart Mill (see Chapter 22) regularly used the colonial world as a foil. When he wanted to drive home a point about freedom of speech or religion, he pointed to India as a counter example, trading in stereotypes about Hindu or Muslim "obscurantism," and appealing to British convictions that theirs was the superior civilization. This contrast between colonial backwardness or moral degeneration and European civility and stability shaped Western culture and political debate.

Imperial culture also gave new prominence to theories of race. In the 1850s, Count Arthur de Gobineau (1816–1882) had written a massive tome on *The Inequality of the Races*, but the book sparked little interest until the period of the new imperialism, when it was translated into English and widely discussed. For Gobineau, race offered the "master key" to understanding problems in the modern world. He argued, "The racial question overshadows all other problems of history . . . the inequality of the races from whose fusion a people is formed is enough to explain the whole course of its destiny." Some of Gobineau's ideas followed from earlier Enlightenment projects that compared and examined different cultures and governments. Unlike his Enlightenment predecessors, however, Gobineau did not believe that environment had any effect on politics, culture, or morals. Race was all. He argued that a people degenerated when it no longer had "the same blood in its veins, continual adulteration having gradually affected the quality of that blood." Enlightenment thinkers often argued that slavery made its victims unable to understand liberty. Gobineau, by contrast, asserted that it proved its victims' racial inferiority. Houston Stewart Chamberlain (1855–1927), the son of a British admiral, tried to improve Gobineau's theories and make them more "scientific." That meant tying racial theories to the new scientific writing about evolution, Charles Darwin's natural science, and Herbert Spencer's views about the evolution of societies. (On Darwin and Spencer, see Chapter 26.) Like other European thinkers concerned with race, Chamberlain used the concept of evolutionary change to show that races changed over time. Chamberlain's books proved extremely popular, selling tens of thousands of copies in England and Germany. Francis Galton (1822–1911), a British scientist who studied evolution, similarly explored how hereditary traits were communicated from generation to generation. In 1883, Galton first used the term "eugenics" to refer to the science of improving the "racial qualities" of humanity through selective breeding of "superior types." Karl Pearson (1857–1936), who did pioneering work in the use of statistics, turned his systematic analysis to studies of intelligence and "genius," sharing Galton's worries that only new policies of racial management would check Europe's impending decline. These theories did not, by themselves, produce an imperialist mindset, and they were closely linked with other developments in European culture, particularly renewed antagonism about social class and a fresh wave of European anti-Semitism (see Chapter 26). Yet the increasingly scientific racism of late-nineteenth-century Europe made it easier for many to reconcile the rhetoric of progress, individual freedom, and the "civilizing mission" with contempt for other peoples. It also provided a rationale for imperial conquest and a justification for the bloodshed that imperialism brought, for instance, in Africa.

Still, Europeans disagreed on these issues. Politicians and writers who championed imperialism, or offered racial justifications for it, met with opposition. Such thinkers as Hobson and Lenin condemned the imperial enterprise from the roots up as an act of greed and anti-democratic arrogance. Writers such as Joseph Conrad, who shared many of their contemporaries' prejudices, nevertheless believed that imperialism signaled deeply rooted pathologies in European culture that had to be put right. In short, one result of imperialism was serious debate on its effects and causes. Many of the anti-imperialists were men and women from the colonies themselves, who brought their case to the metropole. The British Committee of the Indian National Congress, for instance, gathered together many members of London's Indian community determined to educate British public opinion about the exploitation of Indian peoples and resources. This work involved speaking tours, demonstrations, and meetings with potentially sympathetic British radicals and socialists. Perhaps the most defiant of all anti-imperialist actions was the London Pan-African conference of 1900, staged at the height of the "scramble for Africa" and during the Boer War (see below). The conference grew out of an international tradition of African American, British, and American antislavery movements, and out of groups like the African Association (founded in 1897), which brought the rhetoric used to abolish slavery to bear on the tactics of European imperialism. They protested forced labor in the mining compounds of South Africa as akin to slavery, and asked in very moderate tones for some autonomy and representation for native African peoples. The Pan-African Conference of 1900 was small, but it drew delegates from the Caribbean, West Africa, and North America, including the thirty-two-year-old Harvard Ph.D. and leading African American intellectual W. E. B. Dubois (1868–1963). The conference issued a proclamation "To the Nations of the World," with a famous introduction written by DuBois. "The Problem of the twentieth century is the problem of the color line . . . In the metropolis of the modern world, in this the closing year of the nineteenth century," the proclamation read, "there has been assembled a congress of men and women of African blood, to deliberate solemnly the present situation and outlook of the darker races of mankind." The British government ignored the conference completely. Yet Pan-Africanism, like Indian nationalism, grew by sudden (and, for imperialists, disturbing) leaps after World War I.

RUDYARD KIPLING AND HIS CRITICS

Rudyard Kipling (1865–1936) remains one of the most famous propagandists of empire. His novels, short stories, and poetry about the British imperial experience in India were defining texts for the cause in which he believed. Kipling's poem, "The White Man's Burden," reprinted below, was published in 1899 during the Spanish-American War and the struggle for the Philippines. The poem called on the United States to shoulder the burden of empire. It became an instant classic and, as the response on the follwing page shows, it soon became part of the turn-of-the-century debate about imperialism.

Take up the White Man's burden—
   Send forth the best ye breed—
Go, bind your sons to exile
   To serve your captives' need;
To wait, in heavy harness,
   On fluttered folk and wild—
Your new-caught sullen peoples,
   Half devil and half child.

Take up the White Man's burden—
   In patience to abide,
To veil the threat of terror
   And check the show of pride;
By open speech and simple,
   An hundred times made plain,
To seek another's profit
   And work another's gain.

Take up the White Man's burden—
   The savage wars of peace—
Fill full the mouth of Famine,
   And bid the sickness cease;
And when your goal is nearest
   (The end for others sought)
Watch sloth and heathen folly
   Bring all your hope to nought.

Take up the White Man's burden—
   No iron rule of kings,
But toil of serf and sweeper—
   The tale of common things.
The ports ye shall not enter,
   The roads ye shall not tread,

Go, make them with your living
   And mark them with your dead.

Take up the White Man's burden,
   And reap his old reward—
The blame of those ye better
   The hate of those ye guard—
The cry of hosts ye humour
   (Ah, slowly!) toward the light:—
"Why brought ye us from bondage,
   Our loved Egyptian night?"

Take up the White Man's burden—
   Ye dare not stoop to less—
Nor call too loud on Freedom
   To cloak your weariness.
By all ye will or whisper,
   By all ye leave or do,
The silent sullen peoples
   Shall weigh your God and you.

Take up the White Man's burden!
   Have done with childish days—
The lightly-proffered laurel,
   The easy ungrudged praise:
Comes now, to search your manhood
   Through all the thankless years,
Cold, edged with dear-bought wisdom,
   The judgment of your peers.

Rudyard Kipling, "The White Man's Burden," *McClure's Magazine* 12 (Feb. 1899).

To the Editor of *The Nation*:

Sir: The cable informs us that "Kipling's stirring verses, the 'Call to America,' have created a . . . profound impression" on your side. What that impression may be, we can only conjecture. There is something almost sickening in this "imperial" talk of assuming and bearing burdens for the good of others. They are never assumed or held where they are not found to be of material advantage or ministering to honor or glory. Wherever empire (I speak of the United Kingdom) is extended, and the climate suits the white man, the aborigines are, for the benefit of the white man, cleared off or held in degradation for his benefit. . . .

Taking India as a test, no one moves a foot in her government that is not well paid and pensioned at her cost. No appointments are more eagerly contended for than those in the Indian service. A young man is made for life when he secures one. The tone of that service is by no means one "bound to exile," "to serve . . . captives' need," "to wait in heavy harness," or in any degree as expressed in Mr. Kipling's highfalutin lines. It is entirely the contrary: "You are requested not to beat the servants" is a not uncommon notice in Indian hotels. . . . So anxious are we, where good pay is concerned, to save Indians the heavy burden of enjoying them, that, while our sons can study and pass at home for Indian appointments, her sons must study and pass in England; and even in India itself whites are afforded chances closed to natives. . . .

There never was a fostered trade and revenue in more disastrous consequences to humanity than the opium trade and revenue. There never was a more grinding and debilitating tax than that on salt. . . .

Alfred Webb, "Mr. Kipling's Call to America," *The Nation* 68 (Feb. 23, 1899).

In recent years historians have become increasingly interested in colonial cultures, or the results of the imperial encounter across the world. Cities such as Bombay, Calcutta, and Shanghai boomed in the period, more than tripling in size. Hong Kong and other "treaty ports" run as outposts of European commerce and culture were transformed as Europeans built banks, shipping enterprises, schools, and military academies, and engaged in missionary activities. The variety of national experiences makes generalization very difficult, but we can underscore a few points. First, colonialism created new, hybrid cultures. Both European and indigenous institutions and practices, especially religion, were transformed by their contact with each other. Second, although Europeans often considered the areas they annexed "laboratories" for creating well-disciplined and orderly societies, the social changes Europeans brought in their wake confounded such plans. In both western and southern Africa, European demands for labor brought men out of their villages, leaving their families behind, and crowded them by the thousands into the shantytowns bordering sprawling new cities. Enterprising locals set up all manner of illegal businesses catering to transitory male workers, disconcerting European authorities in the process. Hopes that European rule would create a well-disciplined labor force and well-patrolled cities were quickly dashed.

Third, authorities on both side of the colonial encounter worried enormously about preserving national traditions and identity in the face of an inevitably hybrid and constantly changing colonial culture. Especially in China and India, debates about whether education should be "westernized" or continue on traditional lines set off fierce debates. Chinese elites, already divided over such customs as foot binding and concubinage (the legal practice of maintaining formal sexual partners for men outside their marriage), found their dilemmas heightened as imperialism became a more powerful force. Uncertain whether such practices should be repudiated or defended, they wrestled with great anguish over the ways in which their own culture had been changed by the corruption of colonialism. Proponents of reform and change in China or India had to sort through their stance toward "modern" Western culture, the culture of the colonizers, and "traditional" popular culture. For their part, British, French, and Dutch colonial authorities fretted that too much familiarity between colonized and colonizer would weaken European traditions and undermine European power. In Phnom Penh, Cambodia (then part of French Indochina), where French citizens lived in neighborhoods separated from the rest of the city by a moat, colonial authorities nonetheless required "dressing appropriately and keeping a distance from the natives." Scandalized by what he considered the absence of decorum among the French in the city, a French journalist asserted that French women should never be seen in the public market. "The Asians cannot understand such a fall." European women were to uphold European standards and prestige.

Not surprisingly, sexual relations provoked the most anxiety and also the most contradictory responses. "In this hot climate, passions run higher" wrote a French administrator in Algeria. "The French soldiers seek out Arab women due to their strangeness and newness." "It was common practice for unmarried Englishmen resident in China to keep a Chinese girl, and I did as others did," reported a British man stationed in Shanghai. But when he followed convention and married an English woman, he sent his Chinese mistress and their three children to England to avoid any awkwardness. European administrators fitfully tried to prohibit liaisons between European men and indigenous women, labeling such affairs as "corrupting" and "nearly always disastrous." They grew increasingly hostile to the children of such unions. But such prohibitions only drove relations underground, increasing the gap between the public façade of colonial rule and the private reality of colonial lives. In this and other spheres, colonial culture forced a series of compromises about "acceptability," and created changing, sometimes subtle, ethnic hierarchies. And such local and personal dramas were no less complex than the Great Powers' clashes over territories.

CRISES OF EMPIRE AT THE TURN OF THE TWENTIETH CENTURY

Why was the Boer War unique?

The turn of the twentieth century brought a series of crises to the Western empires. Those crises did not end European rule. They did, however, create sharp tensions between Western nations. The crises also drove imperial nations to expand their economic and military commitments in territories overseas. They shook Western confidence. In all of these ways, they became central to Western culture in the years before World War I.

FASHODA

The first crisis, in the fall of 1898, pitted Britain against France at Fashoda, in the Egyptian Sudan. Britain's establishment of a "protectorate" in Egypt after the 1880s Suez Canal confrontation had several important effects. It changed British strategy in east Africa, encouraging Rhodes's "Cape to Cairo" ideas. It also opened up the archaeological and cultural treasures of Egypt's past to British adventurers and academics, keen students—and self-aggrandizing editors—of history. It seemed that the most ancient civilization was now linked to the most successful modern one, and British explorers could trace the "source of the Nile" by rafting up waters that were governed under a British flag.

Explorers were not the only Britons to venture farther up the Nile. In the name of protecting the new, pro-British ruler, Britain intervened in an Islamic uprising in the Sudan. An Anglo-Egyptian force was sent to the Sudanese capital, Khartoum, led by the most flamboyant—and perhaps least sensible—of Britain's colonial generals, Charles "Chinese" Gordon, well known for his role in suppressing the Taiping Rebellion. The Sudanese rebels, led by a Mahdi (a religious leader who claimed to be the successor to the prophet Muhammad), besieged Gordon. British forces were ill prepared to move south on the Nile in strength; Gordon ended up dying a "hero's death" as the rebels stormed Khartoum. Avenging Gordon occupied officials in Egypt and the British popular imagination for more than a decade. In 1898, a second large-scale rebellion provided the opportunity. An Anglo-Egyptian army commanded by a methodical and ambitious engineer, General Horatio Kitchener, sailed south up the Nile and attacked Khartoum. Using modern rifles, artillery, and machine guns, they massacred the Mahdi's army at the town of Omdurman and retook Khartoum. Gordon's body was disinterred and reburied with pomp and circumstance as the British public celebrated a famous and easy victory.

That victory brought complications, however. France, which held territories in central Africa next door to the Sudan, saw the British presence along the eastern side of Africa as a prelude to Britain's dominance of the whole continent. A French expedition was sent to the Sudanese town of Fashoda to challenge British claims to the southernmost part of the territory. The French faced off with troops from Kitchener's army. For a few weeks in September 1898 the situation teetered on the brink of war. The matter was resolved, however, when

Britain not only called France's bluff but also provided guarantees against further expansion by cementing borders for the new "Anglo-Egyptian Sudan," an even greater extension of the political control that had begun with the Suez Canal.

ETHIOPIA

Traditional methods of imperial rule and notions of European military and moral superiority also faced other challenges at the turn of the century. The Boxer Rebellion in China was one of a number of indigenous revolts against the injustices of Western imperial methods and their consequences. The Russo-Japanese war was a dangerously large conflict between two imperial powers that challenged notions of inherent European superiority over all the peoples of the world.

Other complications for European powers arose as well. During the 1880s and 1890s Italy had been developing a small empire of its own along the shores of the Red Sea. Italy annexed Eritrea and parts of Somalia, and shortly after the death of Gordon at Khartoum defeated an invasion of its new colonies by the Mahdi's forces. These first colonial successes encouraged Italian politicians, still trying to build a modern industrial nation, to mount a much more ambitious imperial project. In 1896, an expedition was sent to conquer Ethiopia. Ethiopia was a mountainous, inland empire, the last major independent African kingdom. Its emperor, Menelik II, was a savvy politician and shrewd military commander. His subjects were largely Christian, and the empire's trade had allowed Menelik to invest in the latest European artillery to guard his vast holdings. The expedition, which consisted of a few thousand professional Italian soldiers and many more Somali conscripts, marched into the mountain passes of Ethiopia. Menelik let them come, knowing that by keeping to the roads the Italian commanders would have to divide their forces. Menelik's own huge army moved over the mountains themselves, and as the disorganized Italian command tried to regroup near the town of Adowa in March 1896, the Ethiopian army set on the separate columns and destroyed them completely, killing six thousand. Adowa was a national humiliation for Italy, and an important symbol for African political radicals and reformers during the early twentieth century. Menelik's prosperous kingdom seemed a puzzling and perhaps dangerous exception to European judgments about African cultures generally.

SOUTH AFRICA: THE BOER WAR

Elsewhere in Africa vaulting ambitions led to an even more troubling kind of conflict: Europeans fighting European settlers. The Afrikaners, also called Boers (an appropriation of the Dutch word for "farmer"), of South Africa, settlers from the Netherlands and Switzerland who had arrived there in the early 1800s, had a long and troubled relationship with their imperial neighbor, Great Britain. Over the nineteenth century British-held territory had gradually encircled the independent Afrikaner states. The British diamond magnate and imperialist Cecil Rhodes had actually tried to provoke war between Britain and the Boers in hopes of adding the Afrikaners' prosperous diamond mines and pastureland to his own territory of "Rhodesia." In 1898, as the result of a series of disputes, Britain did go to war with the Afrikaners. Despite the recent British victory in the Sudan, the British army was woefully unprepared for the war: supplies, communications, and medicine for the army in South Africa were a shambles. These initial problems were followed by several humiliating defeats as British columns were shot to pieces by Afrikaner forces who knew the terrain. British garrisons at the towns of Ladysmith and Mafeking were besieged. Angered and embarrassed by these early failures the British government, particularly the colonial secretary Joseph Chamberlain, refused any compromise. The new British commander, Sir Robert Roberts, used superior British resources and the railroads built to service the diamond mines to his advantage. British forces steamrolled the Boers, relieved the besieged British garrisons, and took the Afrikaner capital at Pretoria. There were celebrations in London, and hopes that the war was now over.

The Afrikaners, however, were determined never to surrender. Supplied by other European nations, particularly Germany and the Netherlands, the Afrikaners took to the wilderness in "commandos" (small raiding parties) and fought a guerrilla war that dragged on for another three years. British losses due to the commandos and disease led British generals to take most of the comprehensive and brutal steps to which later Western armies would frequently resort in the face of guerrilla warfare. Armored blockhouses were set up to guard strategic locations, shooting at anything that moved. Special cavalry units—often using Irish or Australian horsemen fighting for the "mother country," Britain—were sent in to fight the guerrillas on their own terms, each side committing its share of atrocities. Black

Boer Commandos under Louis Botha. Botha became the first prime minister of the Union of South Africa following the Boer War.

A Traction Engine in Use during the Boer War. Imperial warfare was by 1900 an increasingly mechanized business.

bred opposition in Britain itself where protesters, labeled "pro-Boers" by the conservative press, campaigned against these violations of white Europeans' rights while saying very little about the fate of native Africans in the conflict. In the end, the Afrikaners acquiesced. Afrikaner politicians signed their old republics over to a new, British "Union of South Africa" that gave them a share of political power. The poisoned relations between Britons and Afrikaners persisted for fifty years and contributed to Afrikaners' intransigence about the system of racial segregation known as apartheid.

U.S. IMPERIALISM

Another imperial power began to emerge in the 1890s: the United States. During the late nineteenth century, American governments and private interests that supported imperial expansion played a double game. The United States acted as the champion of the underdeveloped countries in the Western Hemisphere when they were threatened from Europe. Yet America was willing, whenever it suited, to prey on its neighbors either "informally" or formally. This ultimately brought conflict with another, fragile Western empire. Spain's feeble hold on its Caribbean and Pacific colonies was plagued by rebellion in the 1880s

Africans, despised by both sides, suffered the effects of famine and disease as the war destroyed valuable farmland. The British also instituted "concentration camps" —the first use of the term—where Afrikaner civilians were rounded up and forced to live in appalling conditions so that they would be unable to lend aid to the guerrillas. Nearly twenty thousand civilians died due to disease and poor sanitation over the course of two years. These measures provoked an international backlash. European and American newspapers lambasted the British as imperial bullies. The concentration camps

and 1890s. The American popular press talked up the cause of the rebels, and when an American battleship accidentally exploded in port at Havana, Cuba, American imperialists and the press clamored for a war of revenge. The administration of President William McKinley was extremely wary of going to war, but McKinley also understood the political necessity. The United States stepped in to protect its investments, to guarantee the maritime security of trade routes in the Americas and the Pacific, and to demonstrate the power of the newly built-up American navy. It de-

clared war on Spain in 1898 on trumped-up grounds and swiftly won. In Spain, the Spanish-American War provoked an entire generation of writers, politicians, and intellectuals to national soul searching. This eventually led to the end of the Spanish monarchy in 1912 and the germination of political tensions that eventually exploded in the Spanish Civil War of the 1930s.

In the same year that the United States won its "splendid little war" against Spain, it also annexed Puerto Rico, established a "protectorate" over Cuba, and fought a short but brutal war against Philippine rebels who liked American colonialism no better than the Spanish kind. In the Americas, the United States continued its interventions. When the Colombian province of Panama threatened to rebel in 1903, the Americans quickly backed the rebels, recognized Panama as a republic, and then proceeded to grant it protection while Americans built the Panama Canal on land leased from the new government. The Panama Canal, like Britain's canal at Suez, cemented American dominance of the seas in the Americas and the eastern Pacific. Interventions in Hawaii and later Santo Domingo were further proof that the United States was no less an imperial power than the nations of Europe.

CONCLUSION

In the last quarter of the nineteenth century, the long-standing relationship between European nations and the rest of the world entered a new stage. That stage was distinguished by the stunningly rapid extension of formal European control and by new patterns of discipline and settlement. It was driven by the rising economic needs of the industrial West, by territorial conflict, and by nationalism, which by the late nineteenth century linked nationhood to empire. Among its immediate results was the creation of a "self-consciously imperial" culture in the West. At the same time, however, it plainly created unease in Europe, and contributed powerfully to the sense of crisis that swept through the late-nineteenth-century West.

For all its force, this European expansion was never unchallenged. Imperialism provoked resistance and required constantly changing strategies of rule. During World War I, mobilizing the resources of empire would become crucial to victory. In the aftermath, reimposing the conditions of the late nineteenth cen-

tury would become nearly impossible. And over the longer term, the political structures, economic developments, and patterns of race relations established in this period would be contested throughout the twentieth century.

SELECTED READINGS

Adas, Michael. *Machines as the Measure of Man: Science, Technology, and Ideologies of Western Dominance.* Ithaca and London, 1989.

Burton, Antoinette. *Burdens of History: British Feminists, Indian Women, and Imperial Culture, 1865–1915.* Chapel Hill, 1994.

Clancy Smith, Julia, and Frances Gouda. *Domesticating the Empire: Race, Gender, and Family life in French and Dutch Colonialism.* Charlottesville and London, 1998. A particularly good collection of essays that both breaks new historical ground and is accessible to nonspecialists. Essays cover daily life and private life in new colonial cultures.

Conklin, Alice. *A Mission to Civilize: The Republican idea of Empire in France and West Africa, 1895–1930.* Stanford, 1997.

Cooper, Frederick, and Ann Laura Stoler. *Tensions of Empire: Colonial Cultures in a Bourgeois World.* Berkeley, 1997. New approaches, combining anthropology and history, with an excellent bibliography.

Headrick, Daniel R. *The Tools of Empire: Technology and European Imperialism in the Nineteenth Century.* Oxford, 1981. A study of the relationship between technological innovation and imperialism.

Hobsbawm, Eric. *The Age of Empire, 1875–1914.* New York, 1987. Surveys the European scene at a time of apparent stability and real decline.

Lorcin, Patricia. *Imperial Identities: Stereotyping, Prejudice and Race in Colonial Algeria.* New York, 1999.

Louis, William Roger. *The Oxford History of the British Empire.* 5 vols. Oxford, 1998. Excellent and wide-ranging collection of the latest research.

Metcalf, Thomas. *Ideologies of the Raj.* Cambridge, 1995.

Pakenham, Thomas. *The Scramble for Africa, 1876–1912.* London, 1991. A well-written narrative of the European scramble for Africa in the late nineteenth century.

Prochaska, David. *Making Algeria French: Colonialism in Bône, 1870–1920.* Cambridge, 1990.

Robinson, Ronald, and J. Gallagher. *Africa and the Victorians: The Official Mind of Imperialism.* London, 1961.

Said, Edward. *Culture and Imperialism.* New York, 1993.

Sangari, Kumkum, and Sudesh Vaid. *Recasting Women: Essays in Colonial History.* New Delhi, 1989.

Schneer, Jonathan. *London 1900: The Imperial Metropolis.* New Haven, 1999. Excellent on imperial and anti-imperial dimensions of the metropole.

Jonathan Spence. *The Search for Modern China.* New York, 1990.

Chapter
TWENTY-SIX

THE CHALLENGE
OF THE
MODERN WEST

BETWEEN 1870 AND 1914 the Great Powers of Europe faced the task of sustaining international security, domestic political stability, and rising material affluence that Western nations had enjoyed since the 1850s. Although many of their citizens were healthier and wealthier than previously, European governments struggled with new forms of political dissent and searched, with difficulty, for solid popular support. Three broad changes created new issues. The first was the emergence of the West as an industrial powerhouse. During this period the Industrial Revolution entered a second phase that was distinguished by increased production, new industries, mass consumption, and the spread of industrial wage labor. The enlarged scope and scale of economic activity enabled governments to introduce social reform and to experiment with social welfare systems, but it also created new inequalities and grievances. The second change was the expansion of the political world and the arrival of what we now call mass politics. Armed with the vote and mobilized by a widening horizon of expectations, new social groups entered the political arena. In Germany, democrats battled an imperial bureaucracy; in Russia, populist radicals rose against the authoritarian tsar. And across Europe, socialists mobilized the industrial working classes and feminists called on disenfranchised women to redraw the boundaries of political participation. Finally, new movements in science and culture undermined comfortable mid-nineteenth-century conceptions of progress. New theories, especially the theory of evolution, suggested that rational, ordered development did not necessarily produce progress; instead change was bound up with chance and anarchic struggle. Philosophers, psychologists, writers, and artists also focused their attentions on the irrationality of the individual. Indeed,

FOCUS QUESTIONS

- What developments spurred the second industrial revolution?

- How did the second industrial revolution change everyday life?

- Why did the modern corporation emerge during this period?

- What were key changes in international economics?

- What challenges did the working-class movements face?

 • Who was the "new woman" and why was she so controversial?

- How did the French republic establish itself after 1870?

- How did Darwinianism affect popular thinking?

- What were the dominant cultural trends of this period?

theories of men's and women's conflicting impulses and hidden desires redefined humankind in the modern era. Anxiety and uncertainty about an ever-changing, fractious world thus tempered the earlier faith in progress.

THE SECOND INDUSTRIAL REVOLUTION: NEW TECHNOLOGIES

What developments spurred the second industrial revolution?

The last third of the nineteenth century brought tremendous change to European manufacturing and the world economy. New technologies allowed the industrial economy to achieve new levels of growth, not only changing the scale of economic enterprises but also spurring corporate reorganization.

The first industrial revolution, which began in the late eighteenth century, had centered on coal, steam, and iron. The technologies of the second industrial revolution were more diverse. Still, the key innovations involved steel, electricity, and chemicals. Steel, for instance, had long been prized over iron. Because of its lower carbon content, steel is harder, stronger, and more malleable, and also holds a sharper edge than iron. As a construction material, it is far more adaptable than industrial iron, which must usually be cast, or poured into molds. But until the mid-nineteenth century, producing steel cheaply and in large quantities was impossible. That changed between the 1850s and 1870s, as three different processes for refining and mass producing alloy steel revolutionized the metallurgical industry—one by the Englishman Henry Bessemer, the others in tandem between the German Siemen brothers and the French engineer Pierre Martin. Although iron did not disappear overnight, steel production soared and soon moved into the lead. One of Britain's traditional industrial occupations, ship-

Annual Output of Steel (in millions of metric tons)

Year	Britain	Germany	France	Russia
1875–1879	0.90	—	0.26	0.08
1880–1884	1.82	0.99	0.46	0.25
1885–1889	2.86	1.65	0.54	0.23
1890–1894	3.19	2.89	0.77	0.54
1895–1899	4.33	5.08	1.26	1.32
1900–1904	5.04	7.71	1.70	2.35
1905–1909	6.09	11.30	2.65	2.63
1910–1913	6.93	16.24	4.09	4.20

Source: Carlo Cipolla, *The Fontana Economic History of Europe*, vol. 3(2) (London: Collins/Fontana Books, 1976), p. 775.

building, was completely transformed by the introduction of steel construction, allowing Britain to keep its lead in the industry. The rest of the steel industry was dominated by Germany and America. By 1901 Germany was producing almost half again as much steel as Britain, allowing Germany to build a massive national and industrial infrastructure.

Another important set of technological developments made electricity available for industrial, commercial, and domestic use. Like steel, electricity had been discovered prior to the first Industrial Revolution. Its advantages were similarly well known; it can be easily transmitted over long distances to be converted into heat, light, and other types of energy. But electricity could not be put to general use without a series of nineteenth-century inventions. In 1800, the Italian Alessandro Volta invented the chemical battery. In

A Bessemer Converter.

A German electrical engineering works illustrates the scale of production during the second industrial revolution.

1831, the English scientist Michael Faraday discovered electromagnetic induction, which led to the first electromagnetic generator in 1866. By the 1880s, engineers and technicians had developed alternators and transformers capable of producing high-voltage alternating current, which proved more powerful over long distances than direct current. By century's end, large power stations—which often produced electricity with cheap water power—could send electric current over vast distances, opening up opportunities for mass consumption in the household as well as for industry. In 1879 Thomas Edison and his associates invented the incandescent-filament lamp and changed electricity into light. The demand for electricity skyrocketed and soon entire metropolitan areas were electrified. The discovery gradually altered the living habits of the modern household. This electric boom furthermore transformed life inside and outside the factory. It powered subways, tramways, and, eventually, long-distance railroads. It made possible new techniques in the chemical and metallurgical industries. Electrical engineering became a leading sector in the new economy.

The chemical industry was a third sector of important new technologies. Advances in the manufacturing of alkali and organic compounds made chemicals a major industry. Europeans mastered the efficient production of alkali and sulfuric acid, thus transforming the production of paper, soaps, textiles, and fertilizer. Britain and particularly Germany became leaders in the field. German chemists developed synthetic dyes and methods for refining petroleum for use in chemical processes. The British, especially the company headed by the entrepreneur Harold Lever, led the way in production of hand soap and household cleaners. Heightened concerns for household hygiene and new techniques in mass marketing enabled Lever to market his soaps and cleansers around the world. German production, on the other hand, focused on industrial use and came to control roughly 90 percent of the world's chemical market. The chemical and dye industry became one of Germany's leading sectors in the second industrial revolution.

These growth industries demanded increasingly efficient uses of power, which spurred the invention of the liquid-fuel internal combustion engine. Improved steam turbines permitted engines to run at previously

Industrial concentration
- Cities •
- Areas

Mining
- □ Low-grade coal
- ▨ High-grade coal
- ▨ Iron ore
- ▨ Petroleum

Steel ▬
Engineering ▬
Chemicals ⬭
Electrical industry ▼
Oil production ◀

Railroad Development
- Lines completed by 1848
- Area of main railroad completed by 1870
- Lines after 1870

Area of detail
EUROPE
AFRICA

300 Miles
100   200   300 Kilometers
200
100
0

MOSCOW
RUSSIA
St. Petersburg
FINLAND
NORWAY
SWEDEN
Stockholm
BALTIC SEA
Warsaw
DENMARK
GERMANY
Berlin
Breslau
Nuremberg
Vienna
AUSTRIA-HUNGARY
Laibach
SERBIA
Belgrade
ROMANIA
BULGARIA
MONTE-NEGRO
ALBANIA
GREECE
Constantinople
TURKEY
BLACK SEA
MEDITERRANEAN SEA
ITALY
Rome
Naples
Salerno
SWITZ.
FRANCE
Paris
Limoges
St. Étienne
Toulouse
Marseilles
Barcelona
SPAIN
Madrid
PORTUGAL
Lisbon
NETHERLANDS
BELGIUM
London
GREAT BRITAIN
IRELAND
NORTH SEA
ATLANTIC OCEAN

THE INDUSTRIAL REGIONS OF EUROPE

Note the distribution of mineral resources, rail lines and other industrial activity marked on this map. What nations enjoyed a significant advantage in the development of industrial infrastructures, and why? What resources would have been most important for the burgeoning industry of mid-century Europe? Compare this map to the one on page 774; what was the relationship between industrial development and social upheaval?

unobtainable speeds, but internal combustion engines offered two significant advantages: they did not require stoking as did steam engines, and they were more efficient. By 1914 most navies had converted from coal to oil, as had domestic steamship companies, which in turn transformed the speed and efficiency of international travel, and made essential a grand strategy designed to protect oil reserves. The new engines' dependence on crude petroleum and distilled gasoline initially threatened their general application, but the discovery of oil fields in Russia, Borneo, Persia, and Texas around 1900 allayed fears. With the growing availability of oil, entrepreneurs were liberated from locating factories near rivers or coal mines, allowing regions around the world bereft of natural resources to mechanize production. The potential for world industrialization was in place. The internal combustible engine would, of course, radically change the face of transportation in the twentieth century, but the automobile and the airplane were both still in their infancies before 1914.

CHANGES IN SCOPE AND SCALE

How did the second industrial revolution change everyday life?

These technological changes were part of a much larger process—impressive increases of the scope and scale of industry. Technologies were both causes and results of the Western race toward a bigger, faster, cheaper, and more efficient world. At the end of the nineteenth century, size mattered. The rise of heavy industry and mass marketing had factories and cities growing hand in hand, while advances in media and mobility created national mass cultures. For the first time, ordinary people followed the news on national and global levels. They watched as European powers divided the globe, spreading "civilization" with prodigious feats of engineering mastery; railroads, dams, canals, and harbors grew to epic proportions. Such projects embodied the ideals of modern European industry. They also generated enormous income; canals in central Europe, railroads in the Andes, and telegraph cables covering the ocean floors reaped vast profits for builders, investors, bankers, entrepreneurs,

Population Growth in Major States between 1871 and 1911 (population in millions)

	c. 1871	c. 1911	% increase
German Empire	41.1	64.9	57.8
France	36.1	39.6	9.7
Austria-Hungary*	35.8	49.5	38.3
Great Britain	31.8	45.4	42.8
Italy	26.8	34.7	29.5
Spain	16.0	19.2	20.0

*Not including Bosnia-Herzegovina.
Source: Colin Dyer, *Population and Society in Twentieth Century France* (New York: Holmes and Meier, 1978), p. 5.

and, of course, makers of steel and concrete. Yet the most profound effects of industrialization were those that reshaped the everyday lives of working women and men.

During the second industrial revolution, Europe's population grew constantly. The general health and life expectancy of that population—with the crucial, continued exception of its poorest members—also improved drastically. Members of both the middle and working classes married later and had fewer children. They could also be confident that those children stood a good chance of survival. Scientific discoveries in medicine, along with improved standards for sanitation, nutrition, and vaccination helped to diminish significantly such dangerous diseases as cholera and typhus. The greatest increases in population came in central and eastern Europe; Russia's population increased by nearly a quarter and Germany's by half in the space of a generation. Britain's population, too, grew by nearly one third between 1881 and 1911.

Mass consumption developed rapidly in urban and industrialized areas. Department stores epitomized the new middle-class consumerism. Designed to make shopping as easy and inviting as possible, these great "cathedrals" of conspicuous consumption tempted customers with attractive displays behind large plate-glass windows. Periodic sales told householders to take advantage of "bargains"; catalogues and charge accounts made it easy for customers to spend money without leaving home. Manufacturers believed that women were now responsible for the majority of household purchases, and they designed their goods and advertising to appeal directly to perceived female interests and concerns. The rural countryside was less susceptible to the new patterns of consumption, but even there traditional thrift was challenged by the power of marketing

THE DANGERS OF CONSUMER CULTURE

By 1880 the Bon Marché in Paris, the world's first department store, was turning over the astronomical sum of 80 million francs annually and came to embody the new rhythm and tempo of mass consumer culture. The vast scale of selling sparked debate about the decline of the family store, the recreation of browsing and window shopping, and, above all, the "moral disaster" of women's limitless desire for goods. In writing the novel The Ladies' Paradise *(1883), Émile Zola noted he wanted to "write the poem of modern activity." The passage below captures the fascination for Denise, a clerk in her uncle's fabric shop, of the fictitious department store the Ladies' Paradise.*

But what fascinated Denise was the Ladies' Paradise on the other side of the street, for she could see the shop-windows through the open door. The sky was still overcast, but the mildness brought by rain was warming the air in spite of the season; and in the clear light, dusted with sunshine, the great shop was coming to life, and business was in full swing.

Denise felt that she was watching a machine working at high pressure; its dynamism seemed to reach to the display windows themselves. They were no longer the cold windows she had seen in the morning; now they seemed to be warm and vibrating with the activity within. A crowd was looking at them, groups of women were crushing each other in front of them, a real mob, made brutal by covetousness. And these passions in the street were giving life to the materials: the laces shivered, then drooped again, concealing the depths of the shop with an exciting air of mystery; even the lengths of cloth, thick and square, were breathing, exuding a tempting odour, while the overcoats were throwing back their shoulders still more on the dummies, which were acquiring souls, and the huge velvet coat was billowing out, supple and warm, as if on shoulders of flesh and blood, with heaving breast and quivering hips. But the furnace-like heat with which the shop was ablaze came above all from the selling, from the bustle at the counters, which could be felt behind the walls. There was the continuous roar of the machine at work, of customers crowding into the departments, dazzled by the merchandise, then propelled towards the cash-desk. And it was all regulated and organized with the remorselessness of a machine: the vast horde of women were as if caught in the wheels of an inevitable force. . . .

Émile Zola, *The Ladies Paradise*, translated by Brian Nelson (New York: Oxford University Press, 1995), pp. 15–16.

and merchandising. Mass-market retailers transformed annual summer fairs and traditional markets with their trinkets and wares, and when rural families journeyed by train into cities, advertisers confronted them with an array of products.

This increased scale of manufacturing often had tan-gible consequences for workers. New machinery often displaced skilled workers, a change that usually resulted in a loss of pay and status. Similarly, workers suffered from the large-scale manufacturing strategy of operating on thin profit margins. Higher standards of efficiency for bulk production were critical, making factory owners

London Dock Strike, 1911. Dockyard workers were among the semi- and unskilled workers organized for the first time by "new unions."

enterprises had been financed by individual investors through the joint-stock principle for a long time, it was during this period that the modern corporation fully emerged. To mobilize the enormous funds needed for large-scale enterprises, entrepreneurs needed to give investors stronger guarantees on their money. To provide this protection, most European countries enacted or improved their limited liability laws, which ensured that stockholders could lose their share value only in the event of bankruptcy. Insured in this way, many thousands of middle-class men and women now considered corporate investment a promising venture. After 1870, stock markets ceased to be primarily a clearinghouse for state paper and railroad bonds, attracting myriad new commercial and industrial ventures.

Limited liability was one part of a larger trend of incorporation. Whereas most firms had previously been small or middle-sized, companies now incorporated to attain the necessary size for survival. In doing so, control tended to shift from company founders and local directors to distant bankers and financiers. Because financial institutions represented the investments of clients whose primary concern was the bottom line, bankers' control over industrial growth encouraged a pattern of impersonal finance capital. Equally important, the second industrial revolution's demand for technical expertise undercut family management traditions, just as university degrees in engineering and chemistry became more valuable than on-the-job apprenticeships. The emergence of a white-collar class—middle-level salaried managers who were neither owners nor laborers—marked a significant change in work life and for society's evolving class structure.

push their older and less productive equipment to the limit if they were to remain competitive with modernized operations. Pressed to produce more, workers reacted with varying kinds of resistance, from individual factory strikes to a wave of labor reorganization often referred to as the "new unionism." These large unions stressed mass membership across whole trades and organized unskilled workers for the first time. The unions' broad organizational scope undercut the power of individual managers, companies, and even governments, giving labor new stature in negotiating wages and job conditions.

THE GROWTH OF CORPORATIONS

Why did the modern corporation emerge during this period?

Economic growth and the demands of mass consumption spurred reorganization, consolidation, and regulation of capitalist institutions. Although capitalist

The drive toward larger business enterprises was encouraged by the belief that consolidation protected against the hazards of economic fluctuation—the recurring boom-and-bust cycles that put so many undercapitalized firms in peril. Some industries combined vertically, attempting to control every step of production from the acquisition of raw materials to the distribution of finished products. Andrew Carnegie's steel company in Pittsburgh controlled costs by owning the iron and coal mines necessary for steel production as well as acquiring its own fleet of steamships and railways to transport them to the mills. A second form of corporate self-protection was horizontal alignment. Organizing into cartels, companies in the same industry would band together to control competition, if not eliminate it. Since they made the same product, they charged the same price. Coal, oil, and steel companies were especially suited to the organization of cartels. The huge expense of building, equipping, and running mines, refineries, or foundries restricted the field to a few major players—which made forming a cartel much easier. In 1894, for example, German entrepreneurs organized the Rhenish-Westphalian Coal Syndicate, which came to control 98 percent of Germany's market. Ruthless tactics were used against small producers who were given the difficult choice of joining the syndicate or facing ruin. Through similar tactics, both legal and illegal, John D. Rockefeller's Standard Oil company came to control the refined petroleum market in the United States, producing over 90 percent of the country's oil by the 1880s. The monopoly was sustained through the Standard Oil Trust, a legal innovation that enabled Rockefeller to control and manage assets of allied companies through the nation. Cartels were particularly strong in Germany and America but less so in France and Britain. France had less heavy industry, and both family firms and laborers opposed cartel behavior. British dedication to the policy of free trade made price fixing by cartels difficult well into the twentieth century. But trusts in the United States came under increasing public scrutiny. During the early twentieth century President Theodore Roosevelt began enforcing the Sherman Anti-Trust Act, signed into law some years before, and banned trusts wherever they seemed to threaten "fair competition."

Elsewhere in the West, governments were much friendlier to big business. Contrary to the laissez faire mentality of early capitalism, corporations developed close relationships with governments. In fact, most of the industrial projects in the colonies—railroads, harbors, and seafaring steamships—were so costly that they could be built and maintained only with government funds. Because nation building relied on a combination of politics and economics, European nations willingly surrendered profits to serve their larger political and strategic interests. This was underscored by the appearance of businessmen and financiers as officers of state. The German banker Bernhard Dernburg was the German secretary of state for colonies. Joseph Chamberlain, the British manufacturer and mayoral boss of industrial Birmingham, also served as colonial secretary. And in France, Charles Jonnart, president of the Suez Canal Company and the Saint-Étienne steel works, was later governor general of Algeria. The growing interdependence of government and industry, like the growth of cartels, seemed a natural development in the capitalist system which, its defenders argued, was showering its benefits on all classes of society.

INTERNATIONAL ECONOMIC COMPETITION

What were key changes in international economics?

From the 1870s on, the rapid spread of industrialization heightened international competition among nations. The search for markets, goods, and influence fueled much of the imperial expansion and, consequently, often put the nations at odds with each other. Trade barriers arose again to protect home markets. All nations save Britain raised tariffs, arguing that the needs of the nation-state trumped laissez faire doctrine. Yet changes in international economics mandated the continuing growth of an interlocking, worldwide system of manufacturing, trade, and finance. For example, the near universal adoption of the gold standard in currency exchange greatly facilitated world trade. Pegging the value of currencies, particularly Britain's powerful pound sterling, against the value of gold meant that currencies could be readily exchanged. The common standard also allowed nations to use a third country to mediate trade and exchange to mitigate trade imbalances—a common problem for the industrializing West. Almost all European countries, dependent on vast supplies of raw materials to sustain their rate of industrial production, imported more than they exported. To avoid the mounting deficits that would otherwise have resulted from this practice, they relied on "invisible" exports: shipping, insurance, and banking services. The extent of Britain's exports in these areas was far greater than that of any other country. London was the money market of the world, to which would-be borrowers looked for assistance before turning elsewhere. By 1914, Britain had $20 billion invested overseas, compared with $8.7 billion for France and $6 billion for Germany. Britain also used its invisible trade to secure relationships with food-producing nations, becoming the major overseas buyer for the wheat of the United States and Canada, the beef of Argentina, and the mutton of Australia. These goods, shipped cheaply aboard refrigerated vessels, kept down food prices for working-class families and eased pressure for increased wages.

During this period the relationship between European manufacturing nations and the overseas sources of their materials was transformed. Those changes, in turn, reshaped economies and cultures on both sides of the exchange with different degrees of expectations and benefits. This international push toward mass manufacturing and commodity production necessarily involved changes in deep-seated patterns in consumption as well as in production. It changed the landscape and habits of India as well as those of Britain. It brought new rhythms of life to women working in clothing factories in Germany, to porters carrying supplies to build railways in Senegal, to workers dredging the harbor of Dakar.

THE CHALLENGE OF SOCIALISM

What challenges did the working-class movements face?

In 1842 Friedrich Engels, the son of a textile manufacturer from the Rhineland, traveled to "the first manufacturing city of the world," Manchester, England. The two-year residence in the capital of "King Cotton" would complete Engels's apprenticeship and eventually entitle him to assume ownership of his father's mills. But his experience in Manchester led him not to the company's boardroom but to a life of political engagement on behalf of industrial workers. Having witnessed what he called "the filth, ruin, and uninhabitableness" of Manchester's slums, Engels published in 1845 *The Condition of the Working Class in England*, an empirical report on the abject misery of British workers that, in turn, served as a scathing critique of capitalism. His knowledge of British industrial life galvanized his radical political spirit, developed earlier when he was a student and through a developing friendship with Karl Marx. Marx, too, hailed from the Rhineland but lived in exile after 1844, first in

Paris until 1848 and thereafter in London. Together the two Rhinelanders collaborated closely over the next four decades to become Europe's most renowned socialists.

MARX AND ENGELS

Like Engels, Marx struggled to understand the systematic inequalities that capitalism seemed to produce. He sought to do so historically. Educated as a Hegelian philosopher, Marx saw history as a process driven by reason toward human freedom. In his early writing, Marx strove to understand the philosophical meaning of industrial society's failure to make work satisfying and its inability to create a life-affirming identity for workers. Modern forms of labor, he concluded, "alienated" workers from their capacity to realize their freedom through work and social cooperation. How had this come about? The answer lay with the history of capitalism as a mode of production. As Marx thought about this history, he began an intellectual migration; he rejected Hegel's idealism, or the view that ideas were the moving force of history, and instead embraced materialism, focusing his attention on the social

Karl Marx.

and economic forces that drove historical change. He turned away from philosophical treatises to the writings of economists. He concluded that the prime forces of historical development were the institution of property and the means of producing wealth. As the primary sources of wealth changed, from land to factories, for example, so did the groups in society who wielded the most political and economic power. Always, however, an individual's life chances were largely determined by his or her relationship to the *means of production.* To be a large landowner or an owner of tools of industry (a "capitalist") was to belong to the ruling class. To be propertyless generally was to belong to a subordinate and exploited class.

In preindustrial societies, many working people, like artisans and small farmers, worked with their hands but also owned productive property (the artisan's shop and tools of the trade, the farmer's small plot of land). However, the rise of industrial capitalism brought an increasing concentration of ownership of the means of production and of the products of workers' toil. This separation of workers from ownership and control over the processes and products of work lay at the heart of the problem of the "alienation" of labor that the young Hegelian Marx had identified. At the same time, industrial capitalism also brought mounting "class struggle," as society was increasingly divided into two contending groups, the capitalist class or bourgeoisie and the working class or proletariat.

The *Communist Manifesto* presented class conflict as the catalyst for historical change, arguing that the instability of capitalism would help destroy the bourgeois economic order.

Marx and Engels summarized the new political outlook of historical materialism in a spirited pamphlet, *The Communist Manifesto,* published in 1848 for a secret political society, the Communist League. The manifesto combined political radicalism with economic socialism. Most important, it presented class conflict as the catalyst for historical change. World history, the manifesto claimed, passed through three major stages, each stage characterized by conflict between successive social groups: master and slave in ancient slavery, lord and serf in feudalism, and bourgeois and proletariat in capitalism. According to Marx's theory, the stage of feudal or aristocratic property relations had ended in 1789 with the French Revolution's dissolution of the old order, ushering in bourgeois political power and industrial capitalism. The manifesto openly admired the accomplishments of capitalism, saying that the bourgeoisie had "created more impressive and

more colossal productive forces than had all preceding generations together." Yet Marx and Engels underscored the human costs of those accomplishments and the systematic social inequalities that capitalism created. They argued that the instability of capitalism would help destroy the bourgeois economic order. The ruling class of property owners, the manifesto prophesied, would dwindle in size through the ruthless concentration of capital. A growing army of wage workers—the necessary consequence of industrial capitalism—would come to understand its disenfranchisement and act as a political revolutionary class. Recurring economic crises, caused by capitalism's unending need for new markets and the cyclical instability of overproduction, would eventually bring about the collapse of capitalism. After the revolution, the working classes (proletariat) would seize the state, reorganize the means of production, abolish private property, and eventually create a communist society based on human needs and wants, not avarice and exploitation. Revolution, then, was an economic and a political necessity. Despite the contemporary despair of workers, the two socialists promised them the future. With winged words they proclaimed, "Workers of the World, Unite!"

Nearly twenty years later in 1867, Karl Marx published the first volume of *Capital,* a work he believed was his greatest contribution to the struggle for human emancipation. Indeed, the book was momentous. Not only did it provide the theoretical bedrock for historical materialism, but it also attacked the socioeconomic inequities of capitalism on the battlefield of economics. Claiming to offer an "objective" and "scientific" proof of capitalism's unethical core, Marx demonstrated how capitalism's wage and price system unfairly forced workers to exchange their labor —their sole commodity in the marketplace—for subsistence wages while enabling property owners to amass surplus wealth through a complex scheme of rents, dividends, and profits. Splicing together scholarly erudition on economics with exhortations for revolutionary politics, the book became the preeminent socialist critique of capitalism.

THE SPREAD OF SOCIALISM

The many new working-class movements of the late nineteenth century, however, were not necessarily

Marxist. The new confidence of the working-class movement produced an array of political parties and doctrines. The irregular pace of industrialization, the differing reactions of political states to organized labor, and the workers' varied forms of political knowledge produced a diverse range of workers' grievances and political objectives. Workers' parties, for example, differed sharply over the question of whether they should cooperate with bourgeois governments for piecemeal reform or hold out for the eventual economic collapse of capitalism. For such reasons, directing labor politics as an international movement proved to be difficult. The International Workingmen's Association, founded in 1864 by British and continental European workers, chalked up some early successes in bringing together disparate unions and associations throughout Europe. But protracted arguments between Marx, who aimed for a disciplined movement to overthrow capitalism, and such anarchists as Mikhail Bakunin, who preached random political terror and violence against the state, made it impossible to draw a clear map of political action. After the organization moved to New York in 1876, it languished and eventually died. In 1889 a second International was more successful in establishing an international tribune for coordinated, international labor activity, but here too revolutionary pronouncements often conflicted with workers' wishes to negotiate with, not overthrow, parliamentary governments.

By the turn of the century, organized labor politics in Europe had developed in several different directions. Marx's influence spread through a number of socialist and social democratic parties founded between 1875 and 1905 in Germany, Belgium, France, Austria, and Russia. Those parties were disciplined, politicized workers' organizations aimed at seizing control of the state for revolutionary change. The German Social Democratic Party became the model Marxist party the 1890s. Formed in 1875 through the union of two smaller associations, it became the largest, best organized workers' party in the world, attracting over four million voters by the outbreak of the First World War. In its first Gotha Program (1875), the party strove for political change within Germany's parliamentary political system. Following an era of oppressive antisocialist laws, however, the party rewrote its platform, and the Erfurt Progam in 1890 explicitly endorsed Marxism's call to prepare a politically conscious proletariat for the imminent collapse of capitalism.

In England, although socialism was much debated and discussed, no party calling itself socialist emerged. Its nearest equivalent was the Labour Party, formed in 1901, which housed a range of political activists, among them trade unionists, who advocated negotiation and cooperation with the capitalist state for incremental reform. Among the most influential members of this party were the Fabians, named after the ancient Roman dictator Fabius, who blocked Hannibal's conquest of Rome through delaying tactics and small-scale skirmishes. Moderate socialists such as George Bernard Shaw, H. G. Wells, and Sidney and Beatrice Webb promoted "gradualism": pragmatic reforms in public housing, urban renewal, welfare benefits, and improved wages for workers. Focused on these aims, the Labour Party and Britain's many trade unions saw Parliament as a legitimate vehicle for effecting social change.

In Italy, France, and Spain, the doctrines of syndicalism and anarchism became popular variants of socialism, often among agricultural laborers. Syndicalism, following socialist principles, demanded that workers share in the ownership of the means of production, and that production be governed by workers' syndicates. These syndicates, or trade associations, would take the place of the state, each one organizing its own members in their activities as steel producers, coal miners, railroad workers, collective farmers, and so on. Unlike socialists, however, syndicalists had no faith in the political process. The French intellectual Georges

Syndicalism. An image from a French syndicalist poster calling for a general strike.

Sorel, the most widely read theorist of syndicalism, argued that a general strike of all industrial workers would do more to bring down the capitalist state than would electoral politics. (*Reflections on Violence*, published in French in 1908, was translated into English in 1916). Sorel later moved to the extreme right, however, and practical, more grass-roots syndicalist leaders such as the Frenchman Fernand Pelloutier would prove more influential. Pelloutier's labor organizations joined with other French unions in 1902 to create a General Confederation of Labor, and in a syndicalist spirit the confederation dedicated itself to seeking solutions to economic problems outside the legally constituted framework of French politics. Anarchism shared a certain kinship with syndicalism, for it, too, sought to raze the state. Yet it put more emphasis on violence.

The anarchists believed that terrorism, or what the Italian anarchists called "propaganda by the deed," had an educational value: it would show that even powerful institutions and political leaders could be vulnerable, it would create chaos, and it would embolden the people. Peter Kropotkin and Mikhail Bakunin were anarchism's most popular propagandists. They especially influenced radical Russian student groups in the late nineteenth century, one of which, the People's Will, assassinated the tsar in 1881—one of six heads of state killed by anarchists in this period. Although there are significant differences between the two doctrines, anarcho-syndicalism nonetheless became a common designation for twentieth-century labor movements in Spain and Italy. The International Workers of the World, an American socialist organization, also identified itself as anarcho-syndicalist.

By the turn of the century, Europe's working-class parties faced serious internal conflict. Committed socialists questioned the accuracy of Marx's predictions regarding workers' impoverishment and the inevitable collapse of the bourgeois order. In Germany, a group of so-called revisionists led by Eduard Bernstein argued that party tactics ought to recognize capitalism's ability to weather economic crises and German workers' rising standard of living. Bernstein's call for moderate reform within the existing political system failed to carry majority votes at either domestic or international congresses. Yet Bernstein's pragmatism appealed to many socialists and working people, and thus set off serious debates in socialist parties across Europe. More debate and conflict came after an unexpected (and unsuccessful) revolutionary uprising in Russia in 1905. German Marxists such as Rosa Luxembourg, inspired by Russian events, advocated calling mass strikes, trying to seize the moment and ignite spontaneous revolutionary energy. These debates over strategy and tactics did not diminish the strength and appeal of turn-of-the-century socialism. They did prefigure deep splits in workers' movements just before the war, when moderates, revolutionary reformists, and orthodox Marxists would disagree about how to respond to the threat of international conflict.

By the turn of the century, working-class parties exhibited impressive organizational skills and political strength. On the eve of the First World War, governments discreetly consulted with labor leaders about the rank-and-file workers' willingness to enlist and fight. Working-class parties now affected the ability of nation-states to wage war; they had come of age.

THE CHALLENGE OF WOMEN'S WIDENING SPHERE

Who was the "new woman" and why was she so controversial?

In the last third of the nineteenth century the challenges of industrialization and an expanding civil society also weakened the Victorian view that men and women had distinctly different social roles and spheres. Not only did increasing numbers of working-class women in factories and workshops puncture the myth of female domesticity, but the expansion of governmental and corporate bureaucracies also attracted middle-class women to the work force as social workers and clerks. Equally important, the conventional roles for men and women, which assigned men to public activities in business and politics but relegated women to the domestic roles of mothers and helpmeets, came under increasing criticism, ushering in an era of educational and legal reforms. Swiss universities and medical schools began to admit women in the 1860s. In the 1870s and 1880s, British women established their own colleges at Cambridge and Oxford and further won the right to control their own property. Laws in 1884 and 1910 gave Frenchwomen the right to divorce their husbands and also control their own property. German women, too, enjoyed liberal divorce laws by 1870 and in 1900 gained full legal personhood that no longer

Changes in white-collar work. Male clerical work underwent great change at the end of the nineteenth century to accommodate the cadres of women office workers.

characterized as gradual and uneven, and it varied from one country to another. Overall, though, the movement grew out of the same ideological forces that imbued the middle classes with the confidence and aspiration to remake society. The reform movements of the early nineteenth century depended on women, thus increasing their public presence by mid-century. First with charity work in religious associations and later with hundreds of secular associations, women throughout Europe directed their energies toward such causes as poor relief, prison reform, emancipation of slaves, Sunday school, prostitution, temperance, and expanded educational opportunities for women. Associational life allowed women to gather outside the home, speak their minds as free-thinking equals, and pursue causes under the legal person of an association—a right denied them as individual females. Women in such associations, however, did not necessarily endorse political emancipation. Their engagement and recruitment was often grounded in a sense of moral superiority over men, and they argued that women's public activities were merely an extension of womanly and feminine domestic duties. Nonetheless such associational activity had brought women's lives beyond the home and widened the scope of possibilities for subsequent generations.

Political rights for women remained deeply controversial throughout the nineteenth century. When Mary Wollstonecraft argued for women's rights, most men could not vote. Even after Britain's momentous Reform Bill of 1832, only one of five Englishmen had this right. Yet between 1866 and 1884, Germany, France, and Britain promulgated broad enfranchisement laws for men; the exclusion from suffrage now became based solely on sex. As women's associations demanded women's property rights and more vocational possibilities, reforming the franchise crystallized as the next logical goal. Its symbolism cannot be underestimated. For suffragists enfranchisement meant not merely political progress but economic, spiritual,

subordinated them to traditional paternalism. As compulsory primary schooling became prevalent in Europe, women campaigned for vocational education and training. In the sphere of professional work, change also occurred. In Prussia, for instance, 14,600 full-time women teachers were staffing schools by 1896. By the turn of the century, European legislatures had introduced legal and economic reforms to accommodate women's widening participation in the public sphere.

The term *feminism* had been coined in the 1830s, but the advocacy of women's rights during the nineteenth century did not simply follow one doctrine or program of ideas. The process by which women came to claim greater social, economic, and political rights is better

Organized anti-feminism. Male students demonstrate against opening some universities to women.

and moral advancement as well. By the last third of the century, middle-class women throughout western Europe had founded clubs, published journals, organized petitions, sponsored assemblies, and initiated other public activities to press for the vote. In the 1870s, the French League of Women's Rights as well as the Society to Improve the Condition of Women and Claim Their Rights launched the French women's movement. In 1865 Louise Otto-Peters founded the General German Women's Association, whose advocacy of women's education led to a proliferation of new organizations. The need to coordinate the extensive network of societies led in 1894 to the formation of the League of German Women's Associations, an umbrella organization that attempted to direct the women's movement. In 1902, different views on woman suffrage split the organization, and the League of Women's Voting Rights was founded solely to advocate enfranchisement. These middle-class movements were flanked by organizations of feminist socialists—women such as Clara Zetkin and Lily Braun who believed that only a socialist revolution would free women from economic as well as political exploitation.

In Britain political agitation was particularly pronounced. Millicent Fawcett, a distinguished middle-class woman with connections to the political establishment, organized sixteen different organizations in 1897 as the National Union of Women's Suffrage Societies, striving for reform through consti-

tutional means. But British suffragists lacked the political or economic clout to sway a male legislature. They became increasingly exasperated by their inability to win over either the Liberal or Conservative party, each of which feared that female suffrage would benefit the other. For this reason Emmeline Pankhurst founded the Women's Social and Political Union in 1903, which adopted tactics of militancy and civil disobedience. WSPU women chained themselves to the visitors' gallery in the House of Commons; slashed paintings in museums; inscribed "VOTES FOR WOMEN" in acid on the greens of golf courses; disrupted political meetings; burned politicians' houses; and smashed department store windows. The government countered violence with repression. When arrested women went on hunger strikes in prisons, wardens proceeded to feed them forcibly, tying them down, holding their mouths open with wooden and metal clamps, and running tubes down their throats. In 1910 the attempt of

Violent Suffragist Protest. Emmeline Pankhurst is arrested during a violent demonstration at Buckingham Palace in 1911.

Militant Martyrdom for Women's Suffrage. Emily Davison throwing herself under the king's horse at the Derby in 1913.

suffragists to enter the House of Commons set off a six-hour riot with policemen and bystanders, shocking and outraging a nation unaccustomed to such kinds of violence from women. The intensity of suffragists' moral claims eventually led in 1913 to the martyrdom of Emily Wilding Davison, who wearing a "Votes for Women" sash, threw herself in front of the king's horse on Derby Day and was trampled to death.

The development of the woman suffrage movement was paralleled by the emergence of a new social type, dubbed the "new woman." A "new" woman demanded education and a job, she refused to be escorted by chaperones when she went out, she rejected the restrictive corsets of mid-century fashion. In other words, she claimed the right to a physically and intellectually active life, and refused to conform to the norms that defined nineteenth-century womanhood. The new woman was an image—in part the creation of artists and journalists, who filled newspapers, magazines, and advertising billboards with pictures of women riding bicycles in bloomers (voluminous trousers with a short skirt), smoking cigarettes, and enjoying the cafes, dance halls, tonic waters, soaps, and other emblems of consumption. Very few women actually fit this image —among other things, most were too poor. Yet many middle- and working-class women were demanding great social freedom and redefining social norms. For opponents, such independence amounted to an abdication of womanly domestic responsibilities. Critics disparaged their ideals, painting them as ugly "half-men" unable to marry. For supporters, though, new women

symbolized a new era of social emancipation. Indeed, new women and suffragists marked an unmistakable shift in the conception of women's social roles.

Because a greater public presence of women challenged the fundamental, middle-class principle of separate spheres of activities for men and women, opposition to change was intense. Not only did men scorn the women who threatened their elite preserves in universities, clubs, and public offices, but a wide array of female antisuffragists also denounced the movement. Conservatives such as Mrs. Humphrey Ward maintained that women in the political arena would sap the virility of the English empire, whereas Octavia Hill, a noted social worker, stated that women should "temper this wild struggle for place and power." Christian commentators criticized suffragists for the moral decay that their selfish individualism would bring about. Still others stressed feminism's dissolution of the family, a theme that fed into a larger discussion on the decline of the West. Bound up in the criticism of women's rights was a larger anxiety about a general cultural crisis. Because political rights for women capped a century's ongoing effort to redefine political community, and, ultimately, civilization, the issue remained controversial. The "woman question" threatened to undermine the consensus and order that nineteenth-century middle-class people so ardently desired.

THE DELICATE EQUILIBRIUM OF POLITICS

How did the French republic establish itself after 1870?

Over the first three quarters of the nineteenth century, middle-class liberal society had recast European politics, mixing landed lords with new industrial magnates, monarchical rule with constitutional freedoms, and bourgeois political elites with popular constituencies. In the final decades of the nineteenth century, however, the delicate balance struck between traditional elites and the middle classes came under new strain with the pressures of mass politics. From both the right and the left, groups strove to deploy universal male suffrage to their best advantage—either to broaden political representation or reverse the advances of the last half century. Having championed doctrines of individual rights throughout the century, moderate liberals now found themselves on the defensive. Democrats, unionists, socialists, and feminists challenged liberals' claims of an open society based on merit, demanding that the door to political participation be opened to all.

FRANCE: THE EMBATTLED REPUBLIC

In September 1870, during the Franco-Prussian war, Napoleon III had been captured and his government, the Second Empire, had come to an end. The French proclaimed a republic and established a provisional government. Creating a durable republican government, however, proved a difficult and protracted process, producing bloody conflict and pitched political contests between right and left.

The new government's immediate crisis, in the fall of 1870, involved bringing Paris under control. During the war, the city had appointed its own municipal government, the Commune. Not only did the city refuse to surrender to the Germans, it proclaimed itself the true government of France. Throughout a four-month siege by the Germans, a starved Paris held on, declared itself independent, and refused to recognize the French government sitting in Versailles and negotiating the terms of an armistice with the Germans. The armistice signed, the French government turned its attention to the city. After long and fruitless negotiations, in March 1871, the government sent troops to the capital. Their attempt to disarm the Commune led to a civil war, and since the Commune's strongest support came from the workers of Paris (most middle-class people had left during the siege), the conflict became a class war. For a week, the Communards fought tenaciously against the government's troops, building barricades to stop the invaders, taking and shooting hostages, and retreating very slowly into the northern working-class neighborhoods of the city. The French government's repression was brutal. At least twenty-five thousand Parisians were executed, killed in fighting, or consumed in the fires that raged through the city. The government deported thousands more to the penal colony of New Caledonia in the South Pacific. Al-

though the Commune's existence was brief, the incident, coupled with the swift defeat by Germany, opened up old wounds of political division that poisoned political debate for decades. Socialists, including Karl Marx, interpreted the Commune as the beginning of modern class warfare.

While the fratricide of the Commune revealed to many the pressing need for political consensus, France's three intertwined political legacies of monarchism, Bonapartism, and republicanism lived on and militated against any easy solutions. When the French elected a National Assembly in 1871, monarchists formed the majority but could not agree on whether the king should be a Bourbon or an Orleanist. This stalemate—a critical missed opportunity for royalists—led to the eventual passage in 1875 of a series of constitutive laws that created the Third Republic. These laws established a parliament with a lower house elected by universal male suffrage (the Chamber of Deputies), an upper house elected indirectly (the Senate), a premier who directed a cabinet of ministers, and a president. In 1879, the Chamber of Deputies passed a law that made ministers responsible to the Chamber, thus securing the power of the legislature over the cabinet. Between 1870 and 1914 there would be no fewer than fifty cabinets.

THE DREYFUS AFFAIR AND ANTI-SEMITISM

In the 1880s and 1890s, conservative parties found it increasingly important to attract votes from a broader electorate, coupling the "little man" to right-wing politics. Anti-Semitism became one way to do so. Édouard Drumont, an anti-Semitic journalist, linked all of late-nineteenth-century France's problems to the baneful influence of an international Jewish conspiracy and labeled all the right wing's enemies "Jewish." "Jews in the army" subverted the national interest; financial scandals came from "international conspiracies"; mass culture, the women's movement, dance halls, and all the developments that were corrupting French culture simply demonstrated the strength of "cosmopolitan and international Jewish interests"; "wealthy Jewish bankers" or "greedy Jewish socialists and trade unionists" preyed on the peasants and small shopkeepers of France. Drumont pounded at these themes in his newspaper, *La Libre Parole* ("*Free Speech*") founded in 1892, through his Anti-Semitic League, and in his massive, five-hundred-page

Socialists interpreted the Paris Commune as the beginning of modern class warfare.

bestseller, *Jewish France* (1886), which sold one hundred thousand copies in the first two months. Drumont brought together three strands of anti-Semitism: (1) long-standing Christian anti-Semitism, which damned the Jewish people as Christ killers; (2) economic anti-Semitism, which insisted that the wealthy banking family of Rothschild was representative of all Jews; and (3) late-nineteenth-century racial thinking, which opposed the Aryan (Indo European) race to the (inferior) Semitic race. Drumont and others across Europe brought together these themes in a powerful ideology of hatred. Political anti-Semitism as they developed it insisted that social and political issues should be seen as racial ones. The mayor of Vienna in 1897 was elected on an anti-Semitic campaign. The Russian secret police forged and published a book called *The Protocols of the Learned Elders of Zion* (1903 and 1905) which detailed an allegedly Jewish plot to dominate the world. Anti-Semitism became a prominent aspect of politics all across Europe.

In France, this politicized anti-Semitism furnished the foundation for the Dreyfus Affair, a pivotal politi-

> Political anti-Semitism insisted that social and political issues should be seen as racial ones.

cal moment in the life of the French Republic. In 1894 a clique of monarchist officers in the French army accused Alfred Dreyfus, a Jewish captain on the French general staff, of selling military secrets to Germany. Tried by court-martial, he was convicted, stripped of his rank, and deported for life to Devil's Island, a ghastly prison in the Atlantic Ocean. In 1896 Colonel Georges Picquart, a new head of the Intelligence Division, questioned the initial verdict of guilty and, after an initial probe, announced that the trial documents were forgeries.

When the War Department rebuffed attempts to give Dreyfus a new trial, the French public embraced the affair as a cause célèbre of higher principles, polarizing the nation into royalist and republican camps. At issue was the definition of the modern French nation. Backing Dreyfus were republicans, socialists, liberals, and such figures as the writer Emile Zola. Zola blasted the French establishment in a provocative newspaper essay that accused the government, the courts, and the military of falsifying documents, covering up treason, and blatantly ignoring basic issues of justice and right. As the Dreyfusards saw it, the survival of the republic was at stake, and they stood for progress and justice against reaction and prejudice. The anti-Dreyfusards included monarchists, some members of the clergy, militarists, and some members of the working class, who considered the affair a distraction from more important economic issues. As one Catholic newspaper insisted, the question was not whether Dreyfus was guilty or innocent but whether Jews and unbelievers were not the "secret masters of France." Such pronouncements only fueled the Dreyfusards' anticlericalism, or hostility toward the Catholic church. Their opposition to the church had been honed in debates during the 1870s and 1880s on secular compulsory public education. After six years of controversy, an executive order in 1899 set Dreyfus free; in 1906, the Supreme Court cleared him of all guilt, reinstating him in the army as a major and inducting him into the Legion of Honor. The fate of Dreyfus furnished republicans with

The January 1, 1895 edition of *Le Petit Journal* depicts the military degradation of Alfred Dreyfus.

ANTI-SEMITISM IN LATE-NINETEENTH-CENTURY FRANCE

Over the course of the nineteenth century, European (though not Russian) Jews slowly gained more legal and political rights: access to occupations from which they had been barred, the right to vote and hold political office, the right to marry non-Jews, and so on. France, the land of the revolution of 1789, appeared to many European Jews the beacon of liberty. But in the late nineteenth century, France also proved the birthplace of new forms of anti-Semitism. This excerpt from Éduoard Drumont's best-selling Jewish France *(1885) illustrates some themes of that ideology: the effort to displace economic grievances, conservative hatred of the republic, parliamentary government, and the legacy of 1789, and conservative nationalism.*

The only one who has benefitted from the Revolution [of 1789] is the Jew. Everything comes from the Jew; everything returns to the Jew.

We have here a veritable conquest, an entire nation returned to serfdom by a minute but cohesive minority, just as the Saxons were forced into serfdom by William the Conqueror's 60,000 Normans.

The methods are different, the result is the same. One can recognize all the characteristics of a conquest: an entire population working for another population, which appropriates, through a vast system of financial exploitation, all of the profits of the other. Immense Jewish fortunes, castles, Jewish townhouses, are not the fruit of any actual labor, of any production: they are the booty taken from an enslaved race by a dominant race.

It is certain, for example, that the Rothchild family, whose French branch alone possesses a declared fortune of three billion [francs], did not have that money when it arrived in France; it has invented nothing, it has discovered no mine, it has tilled no ground. It has therefore appropriated these three billion francs from the French without giving them anything in exchange. . . .

Thanks to the Jews' cunning exploitation of the principles of '89, France was collapsing into dissolution. Jews had monopolized all of the public wealth, had invaded everything, except the army. The representatives of the old [French] families, whether noble or bourgeois . . . gave themselves up to pleasure, and were corrupted by the Jewish prostitutes they had taken as mistresses or were ruined by the horse-sellers and money-lenders, also Jews, who aided the prostitutes. . . .

The fatherland, in the sense that we attach to that word, has no meaning for the Semite. The Jew . . . is characterized by an *inexorable universalism.*

I can see no reason for reproaching the Jews for thinking this way. What does the word "Fatherland" mean? Land of the fathers. One's feelings for the Fatherland are engraved in one's heart in the same way that a name carved in a tree is driven deeper into the bark with each passing year, so that the tree and the name eventually become one. You can't become a patriot through improvization; you are a patriot in your blood, in your marrow.

Can the Semite, a perpetual nomad, ever experience such enduring impressions? . . .

Édouard Drumont, *La France juive. Essai d'histoire contemporaine* (Paris: C. Marpon and E. Flammarion, 1885), excerpt translated by Cat Nilan, 1997.

concrete evidence that the church and the army were hostile toward the republic. In this respect, the affair had long-term consequences for church-state relations. Laws passed between 1901 and 1905 prohibited religious orders in France not authorized by the state, forbade clerics from teaching in either public or private schools, and, finally, dissolved the union of church and state. For the first time since 1801, the adherents of all creeds were place on an equal basis.

With the threat from the right quelled, the Third Republic emerged stronger in the first decade of the new century. As noted above, subsequent governments would have to address the growing militancy of the country's labor movement and face the threat of a number of debilitating strikes, but the republican tradition—so gravely threatened in the late nineteenth century—had solidified into a political force.

Among the many people to watch with alarm as the Dreyfus Affair unfolded was Theodor Herzl (1860–1904), a Hungarian-born journalist working in Paris. The rise of virulent anti-Semitism in France, often considered the most liberal of European countries, troubled Herzl deeply. He considered the Dreyfus Affair "only the dramatic expression of a much more fundamental malaise." Despite Jewish emancipation, Herzl came to believe Jewish people might never be assimilated into liberal Western culture, and that staking the Jewish community's hopes on acceptance and tolerance was dangerous and illusory. Herzl endorsed a different strategy of Jewish nationalism, or Zionism, a doctrine that blended strains of nineteenth-century nationalism, liberalism, and socialism. Concretely, it called for building a separate Jewish homeland outside of Europe (though not necessarily in Palestine). Herzl was not the first to voice these goals: a small movement of Jewish settlers, most of them refugees from Russia, had already begun to establish settlements. But he was the most effective advocate of political Zionism. He argued that Zionism should be recognized as a modern nationalist movement, capable of negotiating with other states. In 1896 Herzl published *The State of the Jews* (1896); a year later he convened the first Zionist Congress in Switzerland; throughout he was involved in high politics, meeting and negotiating with British and Ottoman heads of state. Herzl's vision of a Jewish homeland had strong utopian elements, for he believed that building a new state had to be based on a new and transformed society, dealing with issues of inequality and rights. Herzl's writing created a wave of enthusiasm among Jews and non-Jews in Europe, but nothing happened in politics

or diplomacy until the turmoil of World War I, when specific wartime needs prompted the British to become involved in the issue (see Chapter 27).

GERMANY'S SEARCH FOR IMPERIAL UNITY

Through deft foreign policy, three short wars, and a groundswell of national sentiment, Otto von Bismarck united Germany under the banner of Prussian conservatism in the years 1864 to 1871. In constructing a federal political system, Bismarck sought to safeguard the political privileges of the Prussian aristocracy and court, preserve the deep-seated traditions of regional dynastic governance, and create centralizing institutions to serve a modern nation-state. His constitution assigned administrative, educational, and juridical roles to local state governments while creating a bicameral parliament to oversee Germany's national interests. The lower house, the Reichstag, was made up of officials elected through universal male suffrage, and was thus the most democratic. Although lacking the power to initiate legislation, the Reichstag possessed budgetary powers and thus the ability to obstruct any government. The upper house, the Bundesrat, made up of appointed delegates from the empire's twenty-five state governments, served as a conservative counterbalance. The Bundesrat could veto any law passed by the lower house and, furthermore, Prussia alone possessed enough seats to veto any bill it wished. William I, the Prussian king and German kaiser (emperor), embodied the executive branch. He wielded full control of foreign and military affairs, and furthermore appointed a cabinet that answered solely to him. Unlike in France or Britain ministers had no responsibility to the parliament. Neither genuinely federal nor democratic, Bismarck's mixed system of powers aimed to secure the political dominance of Prussia. Prussia's social and political conservatism set the tone in German political life until the end of the First World War.

Creating a national polity with a sense of common purpose was no easy task. The German government successfully created imperial agencies for banking, coinage, federal courts, and railroads, all of which fostered administrative and economic union. But the question of political unity remained. Many states had, after all, sided with Austria in 1866, and had only acquiesced in Germany unity under the threat of French conquest. Three fault lines in Germany's political landscape especially threatened to crack the national

Contemporary Cartoon depicting Bismarck stuffing the antisocialist law of 1878 down the throat of the German parliament. The caption read: "Devour it, Bird, or die!"

framework: the confessional divide between Catholics and Protestants; a growing Social Democratic party; and the potentially divisive economic interests of agriculture and industry.

Between 1866 and 1876, Bismarck governed principally with liberal factions interested in promoting free trade and economic growth. To strengthen the bond between him and these liberal coalitions, Bismarck unleashed an anti-Catholic political campaign in Prussia in the period 1871–1878, known as the Kulturkampf, or the Cultural Struggle. Pope Pius IX's criticism of liberal secular society in 1864 and his encyclical on papal infallibility in 1871 exacerbated long-standing tension between the two religions, sharpening anew Protestant and liberal biases about secular public education, civil marriage, and the influence of clerics in a modern civil society. Questioning the loyalty of Catholics whose allegiance was allegedly undercut by their "ultramontanism," or need to look "beyond the mountains" for papal guidance, Bismarck and the majority of Protestant liberals passed laws between 1872 and 1875 that imprisoned priests for political sermons, banned Jesuits from Prussia, and curbed the church's control over education and marriage. Bismarck's campaign, however, backfired. The Catholic Center party appealed to the electorate so effectively on behalf of the persecuted clergy that it won fully one quarter of the seats in the Reichstag in 1874. By 1878, recognizing that he needed Catholic support for new economic legislation, Bismarck took the occasion of the election of the more

conciliatory Pope Leo XIII in that year to make his peace with the Vatican and to negotiate an alliance of convenience with the Catholic Center party.

Bismarck needed socially conservative Catholics to create a new political and economic alliance in 1878, an alliance that endured beyond Bismarck's tenure. The onset of a downward business cycle in 1873 soured both agrarians' and industrialists' earlier support for free trade. Cheap grain from Argentina and North America made it difficult for Prussian estates to compete on an open market and sustain their socioeconomic position. Similarly, the English sale of iron at cost in German markets—called "dumping"—angered German industrialists. A new coalition of interests emerged that enabled Bismarck to introduce both grain tariffs for Prussian lords and protective duties on iron and steel for industrialists. Agriculture and industry were coupled in a political-economic alliance that insured the future of Bismarck's class of landed elites. This coalition of "rye and iron" was opposed by commercially minded liberals, who wanted open markets for trading, and by the Social Democratic Party, the representative of German workers, who would pay more for their bread with few offsetting benefits.

To build this new majority, Bismarck found a new "enemy of the empire"—Social Democrats. Couching the protectionist and antisocial legislation in loftier terms of defending a "Christian moral order," Bismarck browbeat factions of Liberal and Center party deputies to pass a series of antisocialist laws. In 1878, Bismarck molded two separate attempts on the life of the emperor into a national crisis to secure legislation that abolished the rights of Social Democrats to assemble or distribute their literature. Additional legislation further expelled socialists from major cities. In effect, these laws obliged the Social Democratic party to become a clandestine organization, fostering a workers' subculture that increasingly viewed socialism as the sole answer to their political needs.

Having made the stick to beat down organized labor politics, Bismarck now offered a carrot to German workers—social legislation. Bismarck's program of national health legislation was initiated in 1883–1884 with the enactment of laws insuring workers against sickness and accidents. These acts were followed by others providing rigorous factory inspection, limited working hours for women and children, a maximum workday for men, public employment agencies, and workers' old-age pensions. By 1890, Germany had put together a raft of social legislation, with the exception of unemployment insurance, that later became a prototype for the majority of Western nations in the decades to come. Yet, significantly, the laws failed to achieve Bismarck's short-term political goal of winning state loyalty among workers. In spite of all legal hindrances, votes for the Social Democratic party rose from 311,961 in 1881 to 1,427,298 in 1890.

> Germany put together a raft of social legislation that became a prototype for the majority of Western nations in the decades to come.

The embittered atmosphere of Bismarck's domestic politics—amply confirmed by a violent general strike of miners, carpenters, and textile workers in May 1889—would be one reason for the new kaiser, William II, to distance himself from Bismarck's policies when coming to the throne in 1888, following the one-hundred-day reign of his father, Frederick III. Additional conflicts over Bismarck's attempts to rein in the new kaiser, especially in his views on imperial expansion, resulted in Bismarck's resignation in 1890. To signal a new era, William II suspended the antisocialist legislation, hoping for a wider base of political support. The full legalization of the Social Democratic party was merely a cosmetic reform, however, for William steadfastly refused to extend any sort of meaningful political participation beyond the powerful industrial, military, and agricultural classes. The country was administered by a cabinet and influential court circles but not governed by elected officials. With the exception of Count Leo von Caprivi, a military officer, all of William's chancellors were civil servants, a fact that underscored his determination to keep the administration of the country as far removed as possible from parliamentary control.

By 1912, German politics approached a stalemate. The Social Democrats polled a third of the votes cast, and elected the largest single bloc—110 members—to the Reichstag. And because of a liberal bloc of commercial interests that opposed maintaining tariffs and duties that had benefited heavy industry and agriculture since 1878, nearly all legislation foundered on a three-way deadlock. Any meaningful resolution of the country's domestic constitutional crisis was preempted by the profound international crisis of the First World War.

BRITAIN: FROM MODERATION TO MILITANCE

During the half century before 1914, the British prided themselves on what they believe to be an orderly and workable system of government. Following the passage of the Second Reform Bill in 1867, which extended suffrage to more than a third of the nation's adult males, the two major political parties, Liberal and Conservative, vied with each other to provide an increasingly larger proportion of the population the chance to lead fuller and healthier lives. During this period Parliament passed laws that demonstrated its ability to respond to pressing issues. It recognized the legality of trade unions, commissioned the rebuilding of large urban areas, provided elementary education for all children, and permitted male religious dissenters to attend the elite universities of Oxford and Cambridge. In 1884, suffrage was once more widened, to include more than three fourths of adult males, which allowed rural workingmen the chance to vote for the first time. Coupled with a previous act that instituted the secret ballot, this electoral reform bill brought Britain closer to representative democracy.

The Conservative Benjamin Disraeli and the Liberal William Gladstone dominated parliamentary politics. Disraeli, a converted Jew and the author of a best-selling novel on poverty, and Gladstone, a devout Anglican and moral reformer, were remarkably different men. Whereas Disraeli stressed his pragmatism and referred to politics as a "greasy pole," Gladstone viewed

CHRONOLOGY	
GERMANY'S QUEST FOR POLITICAL UNITY, 1871–1890	
Bismarck's Kulturkampf	1871–1878
Conciliation with the Vatican	1878
Bismarck's antisocialist legislation	1878–1884
Bismarck launches social legislation	1883–1890
Bismarck resigns	1890

politics as "morality writ large." Despite these leaders' different sensibilities, British parties shared similar political outlooks. Managed by cabinet ministers drawn from either the upper middle class or the landed gentry, they offered moderate programs that appealed to the widening electorate. Cabinet ministers prepared legislative bills but acknowledged the ultimate authority of the House of Commons, which could topple a government with a vote of no confidence. When differences of opinion did arise—as with the issue of imperialism—both parties generally agreed on a course steered by men whose similar education and outlooks promised middling solutions. Both Conservatives and Liberals prided themselves on the stability and "reasonableness" of their political system.

Not everyone was content. Prosperity, though widespread, did not extend to dockers, transport workers, seamen and other unskilled and semiskilled laborers. These groups formed trade unions to press their claims, which encouraged other unions to assume a more militant and demanding stance. In reaction to these "new unions," employers in the 1890s formed antitrade associations that successfully lobbied to limit the unions' right to strike. Laborers, in turn, worked with middle-class socialist societies to create an independent Labour party in 1901. With James Kier Hardie as its principal spokesman, within five years the new political party managed to send twenty-nine members to the House of Commons. Sensitive to this pressure from the left, the Liberals, during a ministry that began in 1906, passed sickness, accident, old-age, and unemployment insurance acts, hoping to set decent standards of living for those who had previously known little security. Labor interests also successfully negotiated minimum wages in certain industries and also established labor exchanges to help unemployed men and women find new jobs. The Liberal government, in turn, relaxed restrictions on strikes and on trade unions' right to raise money for political purposes.

Much of this legislation was the work of David Lloyd George, a radical lawyer from Wales, much feared by many within the political establishment. Lloyd George was chancellor of the exchequer (finance minister) in the Liberal cabinet of Prime Minister Herbert Asquith. Together with another young Liberal, Winston Churchill, he hammered together legislation that was both a reflection of his own political philosophy and a practical response to the growing political power of the

> British Conservatives and Liberals prided themselves on the stability and "reasonableness" of their political system.

working class. To pay for these programs—and for a larger navy to counter the German buildup—Lloyd George proposed a budget in 1909 that included progressive income and inheritance taxes, designed to make wealthier taxpayers pay at higher rates. His proposals so enraged the aristocratic members of the House of Lords that they vowed to throw out the budget, an action contrary to constitutional precedent. Asquith countered with a threat to use his influence to create enough new peers (titled noblemen) sympathetic to the budget to ensure its passage. The House of Lords eventually surrendered, leading to an act of Parliament in 1911 that prohibited the House of Lords from vetoing legislation passed by the House of Commons.

The rancor of this debate, including angry threats from self-proclaimed gentlemen in the House of Lords, was characteristic of the intensity of politics and the rising militancy of British public life in the early twentieth century. Despite reforms designed to appease laborers, a decline in real wages after 1900 kept the working class in a militant mood and produced an unusually severe series of strikes in 1911 and 1912. A Liberal plan to grant home rule (self-government) to Ireland produced not only panic in the Protestant-majority counties of the north (Ulster) but also the arming and drilling of private militias that seemed to forecast civil war. Perhaps the most alarming—because the most unexpected—of the militant revolts that seized Britain in the years before 1914 was the campaign for woman suffrage, discussed earlier. Britain, once so self-confident, was proving no more stable than other European nations.

RUSSIA: THE ROAD TO REVOLUTION

In the era of modern nation building, Russia was beset with conflicts. Its autocratic political system sustained the power of the tsar and the nobility, but it poorly equipped Russian society to handle the growing pressures of modern society. Western industrialization challenged Russia's military might, but Western political doctrines—liberalism, democracy, socialism—threatened its internal political stability.

In the 1880s and 1890s Russia launched a program of industrialization that made it the world's fifth largest economy by the early twentieth century. The state largely directed this industrial development, for despite the creation of a mobile work force for wage labor after the emancipation of the serfs in 1861, no independent middle class capable of raising capital and stewarding industrial enterprises emerged. In fact, the Russian state financed more domestic industrial development than other major European government during the nineteenth century. In the 1890s the tsar increased taxes on the peasantry, forced Russia to adopt the gold standard, constructed rail and telegraph lines, and supported the expansion of the iron, steel, and other heavy industries. Russia's annual economic growth averaged 8 percent through the 1890s, and between 1880 and 1913, exports rose sevenfold.

Rapid industrialization heightened social and legal tensions in tsarist Russia. The transition from country to city life was sudden and harsh. Men and women left agriculture for factory work, straining the fabric of village life and rural culture. Many of Russia's factory workers coped by leaving their villages only temporarily; though they migrated to cities they returned home to their farms for planting or the harvest. In the industrial areas, workers lived in large barracks and were marched, military style, to and from the factories, where working conditions—sanitation, safety, hours—were among the worst in Europe. These new social realities also strained Russia's legal system, whose codes were incapable of recognizing such institutions as trade unions or employers' associations. Laws still distinguished among nobles, peasants, clergy, and town dwellers, categories that did not correspond to an industrializing society. Similarly, outdated banking and financial laws failed to serve the needs of a modern economy.

Real legal reform, however, would threaten the stability of the tsarist regime and its traditional social order. Alexander II (1855–1881) had grown fearful of the path of change. Far from loosening restrictions, the tsar tightened them. In 1864 the regime had set up a system of provincial and county assemblies, or zemstvos, elected by all social classes (though dominated by the nobility). By 1875 the government had passed laws forbidding the zemstvos to discuss general political issues, and it extended censorship to the press and schools as well. When the "Tsar Liberator" was killed by a radical assassin in 1881, his successor, Alexander III (1881–1894), reversed Russia's political direction and instituted a period of reaction known as the "Counter Reforms." Russia had nothing in common with western Europe, Alexander III claimed; his people had been nurtured on mystical piety for centuries and would be utterly lost without a strong autocratic system. With this guiding principle, he enforced a regime

of stern repression. He curtailed all powers of the zemstvos, increased the authority of the secret police, and subjected villages to the governmental authority of nobles appointed by the state.

Nicholas II (1894–1917) continued his father's counterreforms, though less rigorously. Both tsars ardently advocated Russification, government policies attempting to extend the language, religion, and culture of Greater Russia over all non-Russian subjects of the empire. Russification amounted to coercion, expropriation, and physical oppression: Finns lost their constitution; Poles studied their own literature in Russian translation; and Jews perished in *pogroms*. (*Pogrom* is a Russian term for violent attacks, which in the late nineteenth century were usually aimed at Jewish communities.) The Russian government did not organize pogroms, but it was openly anti-Semitic, and made a point of looking the other way when villagers massacred Jews and destroyed their homes, businesses, and synagogues. Other groups whose repression by the state led to long-lasting undercurrents of anti-Russian nationalism included the Georgians, Armenians, and Azerbaijanis of the Caucasus Mountains. Tensions between Christians and Muslims within these groups augmented interethnic tensions that even a common hatred of forced Russification could not defuse.

Russia's autocratic political system left some room for moderate opposition, but radical alternatives were more common. Members of the middle class, primarily enterprising landowners, came together in 1905 to form a Constitutional Democratic party whose program included the creation of a nationally elected parliament, or Duma, to determine and carry out policies that would advance the twin goals of liberalization and modernization. But the reactionary politics of Alexander II and Alexander III harvested bitter resentment among middle-class Russians and disaffected students. Since any political activity was by definition illegal, those who opposed the government were often driven to extreme politics, both utopian and violent in nature. Prominent among clandestine political groups stood the nihilists, many of whom followed Mikael Bakunin's anarchist teachings, which claimed that political renewal could only begin with the utter destruction of the state (see page 888).

The most important radical political group in late-nineteenth-century Russia, however, was a large, loosely knit group of men and women who called themselves populists. Populists believed that Russia needed to modernize on its own terms, not the West's. They envisioned an egalitarian Russia based on the ancient institution of the village commune (*mir*). Advocates of populism sprang primarily from the middle class; many of its adherents were young students, and women made up about 15 percent—a significantly large proportion for the period. They formed secret bands, plotting the overthrow of tsarism through anarchy and insurrection. They dedicated their lives to "the people," attempting wherever possible to live among common laborers so as to understand and express the popular will. Populism's historical importance lies not so much in what it accomplished, which was little, but in what it promised for the future. It acted as a seedbed of organized revolutionary agitation in Russia, which would in time produce general revolution. Populists read Marx's *Capital* and revised his ideas and those of other major revolutionaries to produce a doctrine suited to Russia. Populists' emphasis on peasant socialism subsequently influenced the Social Revolutionary party, formed in 1901, which also concentrated on increasing the political power of the peasant and building a socialist society based on the agrarian communalism of the mir.

The emergence of industrial capitalism and a new, desperately poor working class brought into existence Russian Marxism. Organized as the Social Democratic party, Russian Marxists concentrated their efforts on behalf of urban workers and saw themselves as part of the international working-class movement. Although they made little headway in a peasant-dominated Russia before the First World War, they provided disaffected urban factory workers and intellectuals alike with a powerful ideology, one that stressed the necessity of overthrowing the tsarist regime and the inevitability of a better future. Autocracy would give way to capitalism and capitalism to an egalitarian, classless society. Russian Marxism blended radical, activist opposition with a rational, scientific approach to history, furnishing revolutionaries with a set of concepts with which to understand the upheavals of the young twentieth century.

In 1903 the leadership of the Social Democratic party split over an important disagreement on revolutionary strategy. One group, temporarily in the majority and quick to name itself the Bolsheviks ("majority group"), believed that the Russian situation called for a strongly centralized party of active revolutionaries. The Bolsheviks also insisted that the rapid industrialization of Russia meant that they did not have to follow Marx's model for the West. Instead of working for liberal capitalist reforms, Russian revolutionaries could skip a stage, and immediately begin to build a socialist state. The Mensheviks ("minority group") were more

cautious, or "gradualist," seeking slow changes and reluctant to depart from Marxist orthodoxy. When the Mensheviks regained control of the Social Democratic party, the Bolsheviks formed a splinter party under the leadership of the young, dedicated revolutionary Vladimir Ilyich Ulanov, who lived in political exile in western Europe between 1900 and 1917. He wrote under the pseudonym of N. Lenin.

Lenin's zeal and skills as both a theoretician and a political activist commanded respect, enabling him to retain leadership of his wing of the Social Democrats even while residing abroad. From his foreign perch Lenin preached unrelenting class struggle, the need for a coordinated revolutionary socialist movement throughout Europe, and, most important, the belief that Russia was passing into an economic stage that made it ripe for revolution. It was the Bolsheviks' responsibility to organize a revolutionary party on behalf of workers, for without the party's discipline, workers' could not effect change. Lenin's treatise *What Is to Be Done?* (1902) set out his vision of Russia's special destiny, and it denounced those gradualists who had urged collaboration with moderate parties. Lenin considered revolution the only answer to Russia's problems, and he argued that organizing for revolution needed to be done, soon, by "vanguard" agents of the party acting in the name of the working class.

THE FIRST RUSSIAN REVOLUTION

The revolution that came in 1905, however, took all of these radical movements by surprise. Its unexpected occurrence was the result of Russia's resounding defeat in the Russo-Japanese War of 1904–1905. On land and sea the Japanese armed forces proved themselves superior. But the revolution had deeper roots. Rapid industrialization had transformed Russia unevenly; certain regions were heavily industrial, while others were less integrated into the market economy. The economic boom of the 1880s and 1890s turned to bust in the early 1900s, as demand for goods tapered off, prices plummeted, and the nascent working class suffered high levels of unemployment. At the same time, low grain prices resulted in a series of peasant uprisings which, combined with student's energetic radical organizing, became overtly political.

As dispatches reported the defeats of the tsar's army and navy, the Russian people grasped the full extent of the autocracy's inefficiency. Hitherto apolitical middle-class subjects clamored for change, and radical workers organized strikes and held demonstrations in

LENIN'S VIEW OF A REVOLUTIONARY PARTY

At the turn of the century, Russian revolutionaries debated political strategy. How could Russian autocracy be defeated? Should they follow the programs of their counterparts in the West? Or did the Russian situation require different tactics? In What is To Be Done? *(1902) Lenin (Vladimir Ilyich Ulyanov, 1870–1924) argued that Russian socialists needed to revise the traditional Marxist view, according to which a large and politically conscious working class would make revolution. In Russia, Lenin argued, revolution required a small but dedicated group of revolutionaries to lead the working class. Lenin's vision was important, for it shaped the tactics and strategies of the Bolsheviks in 1917 and beyond.*

[T]he national tasks of Russian Social-Democracy are such as have never confronted any other socialist party in the world. We shall have occasion further on to deal with the political and organisational duties which the task of emancipating the whole people from the yoke of autocracy imposes upon us. At this point, we wish to state only that the *role of vanguard fighter can be fulfilled only by a party that is guided by the most advanced theory.* . . .

I assert: (1) that no revolutionary movement can endure without a stable organisation of leaders maintaining continuity; (2) that the broader the popular mass drawn spontaneously into the struggle, which forms the basis of the movement and participates in it, the more urgent the need for such an organisation, and the more solid this organisation must be (for it is much easier for all sorts of demagogues to side-track the more backward sections of the masses); (3) that such an organisation must consist chiefly of people professionally engaged in revolutionary activity; (4) that in an autocratic state, the more we *confine* the membership of such an organisation to people who are professionally engaged in revolutionary activity and who have been professionally trained in the art of combating the political police, the more difficult will it be to unearth the organisation; and (5) the *greater* will be the number of people from the working class and from the other social classes who will be able to join the movement and perform active work in it. . . .

. . . Social-Democracy leads the struggle of the working class, not only for better terms for the sale of labour-power, but for the abolition of the social system that compels the propertyless to sell themselves to the rich. Social-Democracy represents the working class, not in its relation to a given group of employers alone, but in its relation to all classes of modern society and to the state as an organised political force. Hence, it follows that not only must Social-Democrats not confine themselves exclusively to the economic struggle . . . We must take up actively the political education of the working class and the development of its political consciousness.

Vladimir Lenin, "What is To Be Done?" from *Collected Works of V. I. Lenin*, vol. 5 (Moscow: Progress Publishers, 1964), pp. 369–70, 373, 375.

Bloody Sunday. Demonstrating workers who sought to bring their grievances to the attention of the tsar were met and gunned down by government troops, January 1905.

every important city. Trust in the benevolence of the tsar was severely shaken on January 22, 1905—known ever since as "Bloody Sunday"—when a group of two hundred thousand workers and their families, led by a priest, Father Gapon, went to demonstrate their grievances at the tsar's winter palace in St. Petersburg. When guard troops shot 130 demonstrators dead and wounded several hundred more, the government seemed not only inefficient, but arbitrary and brutal. Over the course of 1905 general protest grew. Merchants closed their stores, factory owners shut down

CHRONOLOGY

THE RUSSIAN ROAD TO REVOLUTION, 1861–1905

Emancipation of the serfs	1861
State-directed industrialization begins	1880s–1890s
Alexander II assassinated	1881
Alexander III launches counterreforms	1881–1894
Nicholas II continues "Russification" policies	1894–1905
Russo-Japanese War	1904–1905
The first Russian revolution: "Bloody Sunday" and October Manifesto	1905

their plants, lawyers refused to plead cases in court. The autocracy lost control of entire rural towns and regions as local authorities were ejected and often killed by enraged peasants. Forced to yield, Tsar Nicholas II issued the October Manifesto, pledging guarantees of individual liberties, a moderately liberal franchise for the election of a Duma, and genuine legislative veto powers for the Duma. Although the 1905 revolution brought the tsarist system perilously close to collapse, it failed to convince the tsar that fundamental political change was necessary. Between 1905 and 1907 Nicholas revoked most of the promises made in the October Manifesto. Above all, he deprived the Duma of its principal powers and decreed that it be elected indirectly on a class basis, which ensured a legislative body of obedient followers.

Nonetheless, the revolt of 1905 persuaded some of the tsar's more perceptive advisers that some reform was urgent. The agrarian programs sponsored by the government's leading minister, Peter Stolypin, were especially significant. Between 1906 and 1911 the Stolypin reforms provided for the sale of five million acres of royal land to peasants, granted permission to peasants to withdraw from the *mir* and form independent farms, and canceled peasant property debts. Further decrees legalized labor unions, reduced the working day (to ten hours in most cases), and established sickness and accident insurance. Liberals could reasonably hope that Russia was on the way to becoming a progressive nation on the Western model, yet the tsar remained stubbornly autocratic. Russian agriculture remained suspended between an emerging capitalist system and the traditional peasant commune; Russian industry, though powerful enough to allow Russia to maintain its status as a world power, had hardly created a modern, industrial society capable of withstanding the enormous strains that Russia would face during the First World War.

THE OTTOMAN EMPIRE DECLINES FURTHER

In southeastern Europe rising nationalism continued to divide the ever disintegrating Ottoman Empire. Before 1829 the entire Balkan peninsula—bounded by the Aegean, Black, and Adriatic seas—was controlled by the Turks. Over the course of the next eighty-five years, however, the Turkish empire ceded territories to rival European powers, especially Russia and Austria, as well as to nationalist revolts by the empire's Christian

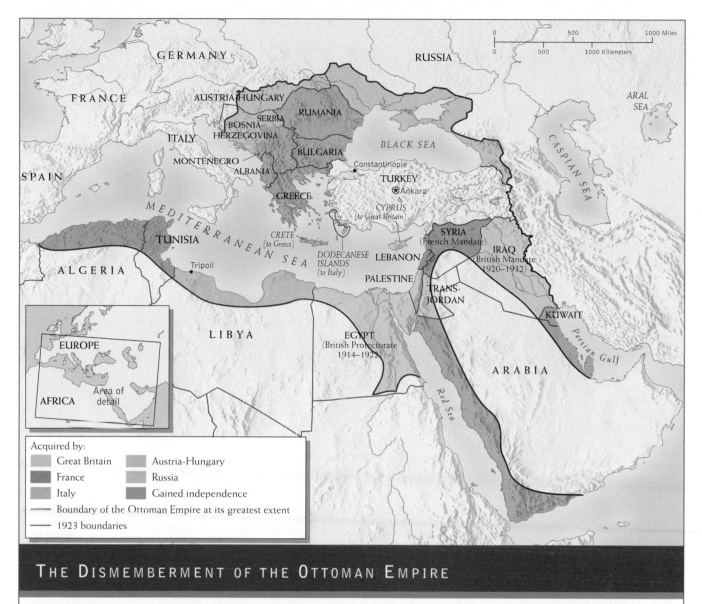

THE DISMEMBERMENT OF THE OTTOMAN EMPIRE

How had the Ottoman empire reached such power by the late seventeenth century? What helps to explain the slow decline of that power in relationship to Europe and the emerging global economy? How did the discovery by Europeans of trade routes around Africa—as well as the acquisition of overseas empires— adversely affect the Ottoman economy? How did the rising tide of nationalism in eastern Europe undermine Ottoman control there, and what did European governments do to encourage this trend?   Why did Britain and France have an interest in placing certain portions of the Ottoman empire under "protectorates" following World War I?

subjects. Once a formidable world power, the Ottoman empire was now dubbed the "sick man of Europe." In 1829, at the conclusion of a war between Russia and Turkey, Sultan Abdul Hamid II (1876–1909) acknowledged the independence of Greece and granted autonomy to both Serbia and the provinces that later became Romania. As the years passed, resentment against Ottoman rule spread through other Balkan territories. In

1875–1876 there were uprisings in Bosnia, Herzegovina, and Bulgaria, which the sultan suppressed with effective ferocity. Reports of atrocities against Christians gave Russia an excuse for renewal of its age-long struggle for domination of the Balkans. In this Russo-Turkish War (1877–1878) the armies of the tsar won a smashing victory. The Treaty of San Stefano, which terminated the conflict, forced the sultan to

Bosnia and Herzegovina placed under Austrian control (not annexed)

Serbia, Montenegro and Romania become independent (had been under Ottoman control)

Bulgaria as amended by Congress of Berlin, 1878

Ottoman Empire

EUROPE AFTER THE CONGRESS OF BERLIN, 1878

What events precipitated the Congress of Berlin? What issues did the delegates hope to resolve? How did the Congress strengthen the German position within Europe, and why? What national groups won sovereignty and independence, and at whose expense? How did the settlement complicate matters for supranational empires, such as Austria-Hungary?

surrender nearly all of his territory in Europe, except for a remnant around Constantinople. But at this juncture the Great Powers intervened. Austria and Great Britain were especially opposed to granting Russia jurisdiction over so large a portion of the Near East. In 1878 a congress of the Great Powers, meeting in Berlin, trans-ferred Bessarabia to Russia, Thessaly to Greece, and Bosnia and Herzegovina to the control of Austria. Montenegro, Serbia, and Romania also became independent states, thus launching the modern era of Balkan nationalism. Seven years later the Bulgars, who had been granted some degree of autonomy by the

Congress of Berlin, seized the province of Eastern Rumelia from Turkey. In 1908 they established the independent kingdom of Bulgaria. In 1908 Austria annexed the provinces of Bosnia and Herzegovina, which it had administered since 1878, and in 1911–1912 Italy entered into war with Turkey. The power vacuum in the Orient significantly strained Europe's imperial balance of power.

In this period, Turkey fell prey to its own nationalist movement. For some time informed Turks had grown increasingly impatient with the sultan's weakness and his government's incompetence. Those who had been educated in European universities advocated national rejuvenation through the introduction of Western science and democratic reforms. Invoking a Western liberal variant of nationalism, these reformers called themselves "Young Turks" and in 1908 successfully forced the sultan to establish a constitutional government. The following year, in the face of a reactionary movement, they deposed Sultan Abdul Hamid II and placed on the throne his brother, Mohammed V (1909–1918). The real powers of government were now entrusted to a grand vizier and ministers responsible to an elected parliament. The new representative government did not, however, extend liberties to the empire's non-Turkish inhabitants. On the contrary, the Young Turks launched a vigorous effort to "Ottomanize" all their imperial subjects, trying to bring both Christian and Muslim communities under more centralized control and to spread Turkish culture. That effort, intended to compensate for the loss of territories in Europe, undercut the popularity of new reformist regime.

THE UNITED STATES: LABOR UNREST AND PROGRESSIVISM

Of all the major nations of the West, the United States probably underwent the least domestic turmoil during the several decades before 1914. Not only had the Civil War exhausted the country, but the frontier —both as myth and reality—also provided an alternative for those discontented with their present lot. Yet the United States did not entirely avoid the pressures that made stability so hard to sustain in Europe. Though the Civil War had ended, the complex moral problem of racism continued to block all attempts to heal the nation. An economic depression in the 1890s, which brought about the collapse of agricultural prices and the closing of factories, caused great suffering and aroused anger at capitalist adventurers—"robber barons"—who seemed to be profiting at the expense of the country as a whole. Many grew convinced that a restricted money supply had produced the depression. The Greenback and Populist parties, which attracted large followings, demanded the issue of paper money and the increased coinage of silver as well as an income tax and government ownership of railways.

European socialists often asked, "Why is there no socialism in America?" As in Europe, socialist politics attracted a following. Eugene V. Debs's Socialist party offered a vigorous brand of reform. But for many reasons, it failed to win the majority of American workers away from the Democrats and Republicans. Most trade unionists remained wary of ambitious plans for using state power; they simply wanted a free arena for union organizing. The new immigrants and their children, who formed the bulk of the industrial working class, felt excluded from national politics. They depended instead on local patronage and ethnic associations.

The romantic Industrial Workers of the World or "Wobblies" did try to organize the unskilled new immigrant workers. They too mistrusted the state and programs of legislative reform. Instead theirs was a radical vision of seizing the factories, mines, and mills in the name of workers' power. National, state, and local governments joined in repressing the Wobblies, denouncing them as "foreign agitators."

If socialism never appealed to a broad band of American voters, the Progressives captured the imagination of countless middle- and working-class Americans. Progressive politicians such as Presidents Theodore Roosevelt and Woodrow Wilson voiced these voters' anger at trusts and large corporations and at the corrupt political machines that dominated urban politics. The advent of the First World War, however, eclipsed many of the Progressives' projects for reform.

THE CHALLENGE OF SCIENCE AND PHILOSOPHY

How did Darwinism affect popular thinking?

While democrats, socialists, and suffragists invoked middle-class beliefs in progress and social reform, other forces challenged the notion of "progress" altogether. Science, which had for decades largely bolstered middle-class notions of progress, gradually undermined deeply held beliefs about humanity's place in the universe.

DARWIN AND EVOLUTIONARY THEORY

Evolutionary theory became an area of science that unsettled Victorian minds. Although as old as the sixth century B.C.E., evolutionary theory was revived in the eighteenth century by the scientists Buffon and Linnaeus (see Chapter 18) and systematized by the French biologist Jean Lamarck. The essential principle in Lamarck's hypothesis, published in 1809, was the inheritance of acquired characteristics. He maintained that an animal subjected to changes in environment acquired new habits, which in turn became structural changes. These acquired characteristics of body structure, he argued, were passed on to offspring, and over generations a new species of animal could potentially result. Lamarck's hypothesis was widely attacked, for it raised serious problems concerning nature's role as a manifestation of the divine plan.

The British naturalist Charles Darwin formulated a much more convincing hypothesis of organic evolution, published in 1859. The son of a small-town physician, Darwin obtained in 1831 an appointment as a naturalist without pay to a government-sponsored expedition aboard the H.M.S. *Beagle*, a ship that had been chartered for scientific exploration on a trip around the world. The voyage lasted nearly five years and gave Darwin an unparalleled opportunity to study at first hand the manifold variations of animal life. He noted the differences between animals inhabiting islands and related species on nearby continents, and observed the resemblances between living animals and the fossilized remains of extinct species in the same locality. His prior knowledge of pigeon breeding (a popular hobby in the Victorian era), including the unique characteristics that breeders could select through controlled mating, prompted him to seek a "natural" mechanism for the selection of characteristics. Darwin believed his hypothesis of natural selection fit with Thomas Malthus's earlier *Essay on the Principle of Population* (1798), which argued that in nature many more individuals are born than can survive. Consequently, the weaker ones must perish in the struggle for food. In Darwin's explanation, competition led to adaptation and, if adaptation was successful, to survival. The fruits of his years of observation, research, and hypothesizing were eventually published in 1859 as the *Origin of Species.*

Darwin's theory of natural selection argued that the natural environment selects those variants among offspring that are to survive and reproduce. Because no two offspring are exactly alike, some will have variations such as longer horns or sharper claws or body coloration that will enable them to win out in the struggle for existence and survive as the "fittest" of their generation. By contrast, other genetic variants would generally be eliminated before they lived long enough to reproduce. Darwin regarded variation and natural selection as the primary factors in the origin of new species. He believed that individual plants and animals with favorable characteristics would transmit their inherited qualities to their descendants over generations, and that successive eliminations of the least fit would eventually produce a new species. Darwin applied his concept of evolution not only to plant and animal species but also to humans. In his second great work, *The Descent of Man* (1871), he attempted to show that the human race originally sprang from some apelike ancestor, long since extinct, but probably a common ancestor of the existing anthropoid apes and humans.

POPULARIZATION OF DARWINIAN THEORY

Darwin's impact, however, went far beyond the domain of the evolutionary sciences. For instance, the implications of Darwin's writings for Christian religion disturbed many Victorians. Although popularizers denounced Darwin for contradicting literal interpretations of the Bible, those contradictions were not what made religious middle class readers uncomfortable. David Friedrich Strauss, a German theologian, had earlier cast doubt on the Bible's inaccuracies and inconsistencies. A body of works had, in fact, already helped people adapt their faith. They did not need to abandon either Christianity or faith simply because Darwin showed (or argued) that the world and its life forms had developed over millions of years and had not been created in six days. Religious readers in the nineteenth century found it much more difficult to situate God in Darwin's picture of the natural world, a world in which the governing principles were not order and harmony but constant and undirected struggle. By Darwin's account, chance, not a divine plan, ruled the universe. Nothing was fixed, nothing perfect; all was in a state of flux. More important, good and bad were defined only in terms of an ability to survive. The "best" of a species were those that triumphed over their weaker rivals. The Darwinian universe was a harsh and uncompromising place, deprived of critical moral certainties. Belief in a benevolent God and a morally-guided universe was now much harder to sustain.

Darwin's writings sparked an important public discussion on the existence and knowability of God. It was not Darwin but one of his defenders, the philosopher Thomas Henry Huxley, who found himself unable to reconcile science with a belief in God. Huxley earned himself the nickname of "Darwin's bulldog" because of his fierce attacks on orthodox Christians who were appalled by the implications of Darwinian theory. Though he did not reject the possibility of a supernatural power, Huxley asserted that "there is no evidence of the existence of such a being as the God of the theologians." He pronounced Christianity to be "a compound of some of the best and some of the worst elements of Paganism and Judaism, moulded in practice by the innate character of certain people of the Western World." Huxley called himself an *agnostic* (from the Greek *agnostos*, or "unknowable"), a person who believed that neither the existence nor the nature of God could be known. Opposed to all forms of rigid dogma and certainty, Huxley argued that the thinking person should simply follow reason "as far as it can take you," and recognize that the ultimate character of the universe lay beyond his or her grasp.

THE RISE OF THE SOCIAL SCIENCES

The theory of natural selection also spilled over into the social sciences, influencing intellectuals in search of an ordering principle for human behavior consistent with current scientific and philosophical developments. The so-called Social Darwinists, whose most famous proponent was the English philosopher Herbert Spencer (1820–1903), adapted Darwinian thought to the "science" of human society in a way that would have shocked Darwin himself. Spencer, who coined the phrase "survival of the fittest," used evolutionary theory to ground his defense of the virtues of competition. As a political philosopher, Spencer championed individualism. He condemned collectivism as a relic of primitive society, as a feature of the earliest stage of social evolution. Any state programs that aimed to lessen economic and social hardships, he argued, were primitive and counterproductive. State assistance to individuals would not only undermine the individual's natural

> The idea of Social Darwinism was used to support a number of political doctrines.

tendency to adapt, it also undermined what Spencer considered society's general goal—to develop vigorous, prosperous citizens and to advance civilization. Other thinkers quickly seized on Social Darwinism for their own political purposes.

The idea of Social Darwinism was used to support a number of political doctrines. Proponents of laissez faire capitalism and opponents of socialism used Social Darwinism to justify marketplace competition and the "natural order" of rich and poor. Nationalists embraced Social Darwinism to rationalize imperialism and the violence and warfare that accompanied it. In the late nineteenth century, Spencer's doctrine was closely tied to theories of racial superiority. The white race, so went this line of thinking, had proved itself superior to other races and thus earned the right to dominate and rule (see Chapter 25). Nature was a matter of competition, and so was society. Victory went to the class, nation, or race that could demonstrate its fitness by controlling others.

If Social Darwinists asserted the biological right of Western civilization to survive as the "fittest" within the contemporary world, some anthropologists—pioneers in what was essentially a new scientific discipline—borrowed evolutionary theory to argue the contrary. No culture, they claimed, could be perceived as "better" than any other; all societies were adaptations to a particular environment. Social customs could not be declared "good" or "bad," but only successful or unsuccessful, according to how well they helped that society survive. This notion of cultural "relativism" was a theme in the influential work of the Scottish anthropologist Sir James Frazer (1854–1941).

Frazer's masterpiece, *The Golden Bough* (1890), aimed to set out a theory and history of "primitive" cultures. Frazer argued that thought had evolved through various stages: magic, religion, and science. Other anthropologists turned their attention to family forms and sexuality, arguing that familiar forms of patriarchy (literally, rule of the father) and monogamy (the practice of having only one sexual partner at a time) were not universal, but culturally specific.

EARLY PSYCHOLOGY: PAVLOV AND FREUD

Other attempts to explore the various and sometimes contradictory implications of evolutionary theory helped to chip away at the comforting notion that humanity was essentially superior to the rest of the animal

DARWIN AND HIS READERS

Charles Darwin's Origin of Species *(1859) and his theory of natural selection transformed Western knowledge of natural history. The impact of Darwin's work, however, extended well beyond scientific circles. It assumed a cultural importance that exceeded even Darwin's scholarly contribution. How Darwinism was popularized is a complex question, for writers and readers could mold Darwin's ideas to fit a variety of political and cultural purposes. The first excerpt below comes from the conclusion to* The Origin of Species *itself, and it sets out the different laws that Darwin thought governed the natural world. The second excerpt, on the next page, comes from the autobiography of Nicholas Osterroth (1875–1933), a clay miner from western Germany. Osterroth was ambitious and self-educated. The passage recounts his reaction to hearing about Darwin and conveys his enthusiasm for late-nineteenth-century science.*

The natural system is a genealogical arrangement, in which we have to discover the lines of descent by the most permanent characters, however slight their vital importance may be.

The framework of bones being the same in the hand of a man, wing of a bat, fin of the porpoise, and leg of the horse,—the same number of vertebrae forming the neck of the giraffe and of the elephant,—and innumerable other such facts, at once explain themselves on the theory of descent with slow and slight successive modifications. The similarity of pattern in the wing and leg of a bat, though used for such different purposes,—in the jaws and legs of a crab,—in the petals, stamens, and pistils of a flower, is likewise intelligible on the view of the gradual modification of parts or organs, which were alike in the early progenitor of each class. . . .

It is interesting to contemplate an entangled bank, clothed with many plants of many kinds, with birds singing on the bushes, with various insects flitting about, and with worms crawling through the damp earth, and to reflect that these elaborately constructed forms, so different from each other, and dependent on each other in so complex a manner, have all been produced by laws acting around us. These laws, taken in the largest sense, being Growth with Reproduction; Inheritance which is almost implied by reproduction; Variability from the indirect and direct action of the external conditions of life, and from use and disuse; a Ratio of Increase so high as to lead to a Struggle for Life, and as a consequence to Natural Selection, entailing Divergence of Character and the Extinction of less-improved forms. Thus, from the war of nature, from famine and death, the most exalted object which we are capable of conceiving, namely, the production of the higher animals, directly follows. There is grandeur in this view of life, with its several powers, having been originally breathed into a few forms or into one; and that, whilst this planet has gone cycling on according to the fixed law of gravity, from so simple a beginning endless forms most beautiful and most wonderful have been, and are being, evolved.

Charles Darwin, *The Origin of Species.* (Harmondsworth: Penguin, 1968), pp. 450–51, 458–60.

The book was called *Moses or Darwin?* . . . Written in a very popular style, it compared the Mosaic story of creation with the natural evolutionary history, illuminated the contradictions of the biblical story, and gave a concise description of the evolution of organic and inorganic nature, interwoven with plenty of striking proofs.

What particularly impressed me was a fact that now became clear to me: that evolutionary natural history was monopolized by the institutions of higher learning; that Newton, Laplace, Kant, Darwin, and Haeckel brought enlightenment only to the students of the upper social classes; and that for the common people in the grammar school the old Moses with his six-day creation of the world still was the authoritative world view. For the upper classes there was evolution, for us creation; for them productive liberating knowledge, for us rigid faith; bread for those favored by fate, stones for those who hungered for truth!

Why do the people need science? Why do they need a so-called Weltanschauung [world view]? The people must keep Moses, must keep religion; religion is the poor man's philosophy. Where would we end up if every miner and every farmhand had the opportunity to stick his nose into astronomy, geology, biology, and anatomy? Does it serve any purpose for the divine world order of the possessing and privileged classes to tell the worker that the Ptolemaic heavens have long since collapsed; that out there in the universe there is an eternal process of creation and destruction; that in the universe at large, as on our tiny earth, everything is in the grip of eternal evolution; that this evolution takes place according to inalterable natural laws that defy even the omnipotence of the old Mosaic Jehovah; . . . Why tell the dumb people that Copernicus and his followers have overturned the old Mosaic creator, and that Darwin and modern science have dug the very ground out from under his feet of clay?

That would be suicide! Yes, the old religion is so convenient for the divine world order of the ruling class! As long as the worker hopes faithfully for the beyond, he won't think of plucking the blooming roses in this world. . . .

The possessing classes of all civilized nations need servants to make possible their godlike existence. So they cannot allow the servant to eat from the tree of knowledge.

Alfred Kelly, ed., *The German Worker: Working-Class Autobiographies from the Age of Industrialization* (Berkeley: University of California Press, 1987), pp. 185–86.

kingdom. The work of the Russian physician Ivan Pavlov (1849–1936) resulted in the discovery of classical conditioning, a form of learning in which a reflex reaction is produced by an originally neutral stimulus. Pavlov showed that if dogs were fed immediately following the ringing of a bell, they would eventually respond to the sound of the bell alone and secrete saliva exactly as if they smelled and saw food. What was more, Pavlov insisted that his conclusions applied equally to human beings, and suggested that conditioning is a critically significant element in human behavior. Physiological experiments, which could establish connections between body and mind, promised an entirely new way to comprehend the psychological makeup of humans. This type of physiological psychology is known as behaviorism. Behaviorists often consider concepts such as mind and consciousness to be vague and meaningless and focus their attention instead on the reaction of muscles, nerves, glands, and visceral organs. Every complex emotion and idea is a group of physiological responses produced by some stimulus in the environment.

The most powerful alternative to this mechanistic understanding of human nature was psychoanalysis, the other important school of psychology to appear after the turn of the century. Founded by Sigmund Freud (1856–1939), an Austrian physician, psychoanalysis interprets human behavior as motivated by a variety of hidden and unconscious drives and desires. Freud's model of the mind or psyche might be likened to an iceberg: most of the psyche is submerged, and only occasional partings of the waves—dreams, for instance, slips of the tongue, or neurotic behaviors—allow the psychoanalyst to glimpse what lies below the surface. Freud's most important early work, *The Interpretation of Dreams*, set out this theory in 1899. As Freud refined his theory, he described a model of the psyche with three parts: (1) the id, or undisciplined desires for pleasure, sexual gratification, aggression, and so on; (2) the superego, or conscience, which registers the prohibitions of morality and culture; and (3) the ego, the arena in which the conflict between id and superego worked itself out. The human psyche, in other words, is a constant conflict between id and

Sigmund Freud and his Family.

PHILOSOPHY AND RELIGION

The German philosopher Friedrich Nietzsche (1844–1900) did embrace the irrational. He shared with Freud the desire to understand humanity's illusions and the self-deceptions of respectable, middle-class society. But he was more profoundly critical of Western culture. He considered faith in progress, science, democracy, religion, or morality misplaced. He assailed the moral certainties of Judaism and Christianity. For Nietzsche, accepted notions of good and evil merely trapped men and women in a fruitless search for security and "truth," which he denied existed. Humans, said Nietzsche, must abandon the idea of obedience and conformity which he labeled the "slave morality" of Christianity, and instead master the world through the "will to power," which elevated individuals and their struggle against the chaos of the universe. The individual who abandons the burdens of cultural conformity was, for Nietzsche, a "dionysian man," a "superman," who creates his own values based on artistic vision and strength of character. Nietzsche here scorned the egalitarian principles of democracy and the Judeo-Christian values of tolerance and charity. In a process roughly akin to natural selection, the "supermen" would triumph over the moral weaklings who lacked the strength and courage to face the chaos of the universe and overcome it. Before any such process of natural selection could operate, however, religious obstacles would have to be removed. Nietzsche therefore demanded that the moral supremacy of Christianity and Judaism be overthrown. Nietzsche's cultural criticism crystallized in works such as *Thus Spake Zarathustra* (1883), *Beyond Good and Evil* (1886), and *On the Genealogy of Morals* (1887).

Nietzsche's writing and criticism covered so many topics (from morals to music to university teaching) that his themes could be adapted by any number of political leaders, writers, or artists. Interpreted selectively, Nietzsche's ideas could be made to support doctrines that the philosopher would have opposed. Since Nietzsche never made a system of his ideas and never concretely addressed social and political organization—he preferred wide-ranging and provocative essays—his ideas were easily distorted. The most notorious distorters were the German Nazis, who quoted from the influen-

superego, or desire and repression. Drives are too strong to be overcome, yet culture brands them as sinful, forcing them into the unconscious, where they linger, repressed, indefinitely. Freud believed that most cases of mental and nervous disorder result from violent conflict between natural drives and cultural restraints, that those disorders allow scientists to understand how "normal" behavior works. Freud did stress the irrational element of human behavior. He shocked his contemporaries by questioning the concept of childhood innocence, arguing that even tiny infants had powerful and unfocused sexual drives. But he did not exalt the irrational and he saw himself as a nineteenth-century scientist, seeking a rational and all-inclusive theory of the mind and behavior. His dream theory was scientific, ascribing dreams to the unconscious mind working through specific experiences. His theory of the unconscious aimed to discern predictable patterns in seemingly "irrational" human activity. Some of his most enduring insights concern "man with all his contradictions," simultaneous feelings of love and hate, and humanity's conflicted relationship with the restraints of civilization (spelled out later, in *Civilization and its Discontents* [1930]). He sometimes came to melancholy conclusions about humanity's ability to master its own destructive instincts. Yet Freud remained a practitioner of nineteenth-century science, and his work represented the rising prestige of science in the late nineteenth century.

tial German thinker to justify anti-Semitism and racial violence, both of which Nietzsche abhorred.

Faced with these various scientific and philosophical challenges, the institutions responsible for the maintenance of traditional faith found themselves on the defense. Protestantism had based its revolt against Roman Catholic orthodoxy on the belief that men and women should seek to understand God with the aid of not much more than the Bible and a willing conscience. In consequence, Protestants had little in the way of doctrine to support them when their faith was challenged. Some fundamentalists chose to ignore the implications of scientific and philosophical inquiry altogether, and continued to believe in the literal truth of the Bible. Some were willing to agree with the school of American philosophers known as Pragmatists (principally Charles Peirce and William James), that if belief in a personal god produced mental peace or spiritual satisfaction, that belief must therefore be true. For Pragmatists, truth was whatever provided useful, practical results. Other Protestants sought solace from religious doubt in founding missions, laboring among the poor, and other good works. Many adherents to this "social gospel" were also "modernists," who accepted the ethical teachings of Christianity but discarded beliefs in miracles and original sin.

Similarly, the Roman Catholic Church was compelled to counsel its followers in a changing world, appealing to its dogma and venerated traditions to counter the cultural, intellectual, and political changes of nineteenth-century secular civil society. In 1864 Pope Pius IX issued a Syllabus of Errors condemning what he regarded as the principal religious and philosophical "errors" of the time. Among them were materialism, free thought, and "indifferentism," or the idea that one religion is as good as another. In 1869 he convoked a church council, the first to be summoned since the Catholic Reformation. Out of this First Vatican Council came in 1871 the pronouncement of papal infallibility, the dogma that when the pope speaks in his capacity "as pastor and doctor of all Christians," he is infallible in regard to all matters of faith and morals. Though generally accepted by pious Catholics, the claim of papal infallibility evoked a storm of protest in many circles. Governments of several Catholic countries denounced it, including those of France, Spain, and Italy. The death of Pius IX in 1878 and the accession of Pope Leo XIII, however, brought a more accommodating climate to the Church. The new pope acknowledged, for example, that there was "good" as well as "evil" in modern civilization. Responding to modern times, he also added a scientific staff to the Vatican and opened archives and observatories. However, he made no further concessions to liberalism in the political sphere. He would go no further than to urge capitalists and employers to be more generous in recognizing the rights of organized labor.

The effect of various scientific and philosophical challenges upon the men and women who lived at the end of the nineteenth century cannot be measured precisely. Millions undoubtedly went about the business of life untroubled by the implications of evolutionary theory, content to believe as they had believed before. Certainly, for most members of the middle class, the challenge of socialism was understood as "real" in a way that the challenges of science and philosophy probably were not. Socialism threatened specific interests. Darwinism, relativism, and behaviorism, though "in the air" and troubling, did not matter to the same degree. Men and women could postpone thoughts about their origins and ultimate destiny. Furthermore, as we have seen, many religious men and women could reconcile faith and religion with the new science. Yet the changes we have been discussing eventually had a profound impact. Darwin's theory was not too complicated to be popularized. If educated men and women had neither the time nor inclination to read the *Origin of Species*, they read magazines and newspapers that summarized its implications. They encountered some of its central concepts in other places, from political speeches to novels and crime reports. Later events would make them more plausible.

THE CHALLENGE OF LITERATURE AND THE ARTS

What were the dominant cultural trends of this period?

Artists and writers used literature and art to question and rethink the dominant views of the age. Much artistic endeavor continued to focus on challenging middle-class values, especially the alleged virtues of industrial society and its culture. But in the last quarter of the century, intellectuals confronted the new development of mass culture and the increasingly broad and segmented audiences of the modern era. Between 1750 and 1870,

The New Power of the Press. With the spread of literacy, newspapers adapted to the needs and desires of the new mass audience. Here British railway passengers scramble for the latest edition.

readership had expanded from the aristocracy to include middle-class circles and, thereafter, to an increasingly literate general population. In 1850 approximately half the population of Europe was illiterate. In subsequent decades, country after country introduced state-financed elementary and secondary education—an institution to provide opportunities for social advancement, to diffuse of technical and scientific knowledge, and to inculcate civic and national pride. Britain instituted elementary education in 1870, Switzerland in 1874, Italy in 1877. France expanded its existing system between 1878 and 1881. After 1871 Germany instituted a state system modeled on Prussia's. By 1900, approximately 85 percent of the population in Britain, France, Belgium, the Netherlands, Scandinavia, and Germany could read. The era of mass readership had arrived. Elsewhere, however, the percentages were far lower, ranging between 30 and 60 percent.

In those countries where literacy rates were highest, commercial publishers such as Alfred Harmsworth in Britain and William Randolph Hearst in the United States hastened to serve the new reading public. Middle-class readers had for some time been well supplied by newspapers catering to their interests and point of view. The *Times* of London had a readership of well over fifty thousand by 1850; the *Presse* and the *Siècle* in France, a circulation of seventy thousand. By 1900, however, other newspapers were appealing to the newly literate, and doing so by means of sensational journalism and

spicy easy-to-read serials. Advertisements drastically lowered the costs of the mass-market newspapers, enabling even workers to purchase one or two newspapers a day. The "yellow" journalism of the penny presses operated on the premise of attracting readers to increase circulation figures for more lucrative advertising sales. Entertainment and sensationalism were as important as the news.

These new developments in mass culture prompted some intellectuals to distance themselves from what seemed to them a vulgar, materialistic culture. They agreed with critics of the mid-century who had insisted that the purpose of art and literature was not to pander or sentimentalize. They went further, however, by declaring that art had no business preaching morality to a public that, in any event, had proved itself unwilling to heed the sermon. This generation of artists and writers argued that one did not look at a painting or read a poem to be instructed in the difference between good and evil, but to understand what was eternally true and beautiful—to appreciate art for its own sake. Spurning the idea of reaching a wider audience, many artists aspired instead to address and influence other intellectuals. This self-conscious desire not only to live apart but to think apart from society encouraged less accessible forms of artistic expression. In 1850, educated men and women could read a Charles Dickens novel or examine an Honoré Daumier print and understand it, even if they did not admire it or agree with its message. In 1900, men and women found it much harder to understand, let alone admire, a painting by Paul Cézanne or a poem by Paul Valéry. Artists of the "avant garde" often refused to speak the same language as the general public.

REALISM

These new perceptions of the artist's relationship to society did not surface to any measurable degree before the 1890s. Until that time, the arts were dominated by what has come to be called realism. The artists and writers identifying themselves as realists were predominantly critics of contemporary society. Swayed by a fervor for social reform, they depicted the inequities of the human condition against the sordid background of industrial society and the hypocrisies of the political establishment. Like the Romantics, the realists affirmed the possibility of human freedom, although realists put more emphasis on obstacles that prevented its achievement. Realists differed most markedly from Romantics in their disdain of sentiment and emotional extravagance. Borrowing from natural science the idea of life as a struggle for survival, they tried to portray human existence in accordance with hard facts, often insisting that their characters were the hapless victims of heredity, environment, or their own animal passions.

Realism as a literary movement made its initial appearance in France. Its leaders included the novelists Honoré de Balzac and Gustave Flaubert, whose work, as we have already noted, meticulously recorded the dullness and greed of modern life. Balzac's portrayal of the effects of social conditions on the individual earned him a place as Marx's favorite novelist. Émile Zola (1840–1902), another Frenchman, is often called a naturalist rather than a realist, to emphasize his interest in an exact, scientific presentation of society without the intrusion of personal philosophy. Zola, however, did have a definite moral viewpoint. His early years of wretched poverty imbued him with a deep sympathy for common people and with a passion for social justice—as evinced by his role in the Dreyfus Affair. Though in novels such as *Nana* (1880) he portrayed human nature as weak and prone to vice and crime, he remained optimistic about the future. In *Germinal* (1885), one of his most widely read novels, Zola confronted the many social problems of working-class industrial life—alcoholism, poverty, hunger, strikes—but held out the hope of a better future for workers through unions and political organization.

Realism in the writings of the Briton Charles Dickens (1812–1870) was overlaid with layers of sentimentality. Dickens was a master at depicting the evils of society, as in *Great Expectations* (1860–1861) and *Little Dorrit* (1855–1857). But the invariably happy endings of his novels testify to his determined—and unrealistic—unwillingness to allow wrong to triumph over right. No such ambivalence marked the works of the later British novelist Thomas Hardy (1840–1928). In such well-known novels as *The Return of the Native* (1878), *Tess of the D'Urbervilles* (1891), and *Jude the Obscure* (1896), he expressed his conception that humans are the playthings of an inexorable fate. He depicted the universe as devoid of a relationship to humanity, and the struggle of individuals with nature as a pitiless battle against almost impossible odds. If God existed, he watched with indifference while humankind lurched helplessly toward suffering and death. Yet Hardy rendered his fictive characters with endearing pathos, regarding them not as depraved animals but as the victims of cosmic forces beyond their control.

Pity for humanity was also a central theme in the work of the German dramatist Gerhart Hauptmann (1862–1946). Like Zola, he identified himself as a naturalist, and he too embodied a concern for suffering and the downtrodden. His plays, like Zola's novels, show the influence of a simplified Darwinism in their emphasis on the determining power of the environment and the hereditary character traits of the working classes. *The Weavers* (1892), which depicts the suffering of Silesian weavers in the 1840s, is probably his most outstanding work.

The best-known playwright among realists and naturalists, however, was the Norwegian Henrik Ibsen. In such plays as *A Doll's House* (1879), *An Enemy of the People* (1882), *The Wild Duck* (1884), and *Hedda Gabler* (1890), he satirized the conventions and institutions of respectable life, especially the condition of women. *A Doll's House*, the drama of a woman who manages to break out of the constraints of a suffocating domesticity, was both enormously popular and wildly scandalous. It played to full houses in London and Paris in the 1890s, with some of Europe's leading actresses in the role of Nora, the young rebel who rails at both her father and her husband for their paternalism and refuses to be a "plaything" in their "dollhouse." Accompanied as it was by the rise of women's political movements, the play helped make the theme of marriage and women's rights central to late-nineteenth-century culture. Ibsen not only scorned hypocrisy and social tyranny, he profoundly distrusted majority rule. Ibsen despised democracy as the enthronement of unprincipled leaders who would do anything for the sake of votes to perpetuate their power. As one of his characters in *An Enemy of the People* says, "A minority may be right—a majority is always wrong."

Russian literature flourished during this period, and Russian writers created their own distinctive hybrid of romanticism and realism. Realism in their hands became more philosophical. Russian writers felt compelled to take on social and political issues such as poverty, crime, or the roles of men and women, but they joined those topics to larger themes of love, spirituality, or the individual's role in history.

The literature of the Russians comprises themes that are both Romantic and idealist. Russia's three outstanding novelists of the late nineteenth century were Ivan Turgenev, Feodor Dostoevsky, and Leo Tolstoy. They were preceded by the equally talented Alexander Pushkin, who between 1820 and his death in a duel seventeen years later, established himself as one of Russia's greatest writers. Though his early work was Romantic in tone, his verse epic *Eugene Onegin* (1825–1831) demonstrated his sympathy with realist themes.

Turgenev, who spent much of his life in France, was the first of the Russian novelists to become known to western Europe. His chief work, *Fathers and Sons* (1861), describes in brooding terms the struggle between the older and younger generations. The hero is a nihilist (a term first used by Turgenev), who is convinced that the whole social order has nothing in it worth preserving. The novel inspired a group of young Russian intellectuals, who sought to reform society by abandoning their parents' emphasis on status, wealth, and leisure and turning instead to serve "the people."

Dostoevsky was almost as tragic a figure as any he projected in his novels. Condemned at the age of twenty-eight on a charge of revolutionary activity, he was exiled to Siberia, where he endured four horrible years of imprisonment. His later life was harrowed by poverty, family troubles, and epileptic fits. As a novelist, he chose to explore the anguish of people driven to shameful deeds by their raw emotions and by the intolerable meanness of their lives. He was a master of psychological analysis, probing into the motives of distorted minds with an intensity that bordered on morbidity. At the same time, though, he filled his novels with a broad sympathy and with a mystic conviction that humanity can be purified only through suffering. His best-known works are *Crime and Punishment* (1866) and *The Brothers Karamazov* (1879–1880).

As an earnest champion of the simple life of the peasant, Tolstoy was somewhat less deterministic than Dostoevsky. Yet in *War and Peace* (1862–1869), a majestic epic of Russian conditions at the time of the Napoleonic invasion, he explores the fate of individuals caught up in the powerful movements of history. His *Anna Karenina* (1873–1876) is a study of the conflict between urban and rural life, Russian aristocratic culture, the plight of women caught in loveless marriages and, most generally, the tragedy that can come of pursuing individual desire. As Tolstoy grew older he became prone to use the novel to preach a social gospel. In such novels as *The Kreutzer Sonata* (1889) and *Resurrection* (1899–1900) he condemned most of the institutions of civilized society and called on men and women to renounce selfishness and greed, to earn their living by manual toil, and to cultivate the virtues of poverty, meekness, and nonresistance. His last years were devoted to attacks on such evils as war and capital punishment and to the defense of victims of political persecution.

The works of all these realists and naturalists, whatever their individual differences, shared two features: they contained vigorous moral criticism of present-day middle-class society, and they were written in direct, forceful, and accessible language. Such realist painters as Courbet and Daumier, discussed in Chapter 21, were equally direct; their style and message were neither difficult to comprehend nor easy to ignore. Realist artists were still anxious to address the public.

ART FOR ART'S SAKE: TWENTIETH-CENTURY ARTISTIC MOVEMENTS

The advent of the impressionist movement in painting in the 1870s marks the first significant break in this tradition. At this point artists began to turn away from the public and toward each other. The movement started in France, among a group of young artists whose work had been refused a place in the annual exhibitions of the traditional-minded French Royal Academy. They had been labeled "impressionists" in derision by critics who took them to task for painting not an object itself, but only their impression of that object. The name in fact suited the philosophical nature of their work. They were painting to pursue new ideas about perceiving material reality and capturing the glints of life's fleeting moments of beauty in an art form.

In the sense that impressionists were determined to paint only what they saw, they were realists. But im-

Iris Beside a Pond by Claude Monet (1840–1926). Monet called some of his paintings impressions, and the name soon came to designate a school.

Probably the greatest of the impressionists were the Frenchmen Claude Monet (1840–1926) and Pierre-Auguste Renoir (1841–1919). Monet was perhaps the leading exponent of the new mode of interpreting landscapes. His paintings have little structure or design in the conventional sense; they suggest, rather than depict, the outlines of cliffs, trees, mountains, and fields. Intensely interested in the effects of light, Monet would go out at sunrise with an armful of canvases in order to paint the same subject in a dozen momentary appearances. It has been said of one of his masterpieces that "light is the only important person in the picture." Renoir's subjects include not only landscapes but portraits and scenes from contemporary life. He is famous for his pink and ivory nudes with their expressions of frank sexuality.

The freedom explicit in the work of the impressionists encouraged other painters to pursue fresh techniques and to define different

pressionists and their techniques were different from that of the realist painters. Vitally interested in the scientific rendering of natural and material phenomena, impressionists sought to reveal immediate sense impressions, leaving it to the mind of the observer to fill in additional details. A few significant details were made to represent an entire object; dabs of primary color were placed side by side without a trace of blending. For example, the effect of the green in nature was achieved by placing dabs of pure blue and yellow side by side, allowing the viewer's eye to mix them and "finish" the painting. Impressionists attempted to apprehend the world and its beauty not with the solid, finished representations of the realists but, rather, through a diametrically opposed approach to color theory and presentation of subject. Appearing at first glance to be nonnaturalistic, the style was initially scorned as amateurish. In fact, it marked an important departure from representation that helped launch other avant-garde modernist movements. Modern abstraction had been launched.

goals. The expressionists turned against the impressionists, objecting to their preoccupation with the composition of surface perception and their indifference to the internal subjectivity of both nature and people. They insisted that a painting must render the artist's particular subjective grasp of the world. Here again, art was less about the masterful re-presentation of the world on canvas but an exploration into a new realm of self-expression. The artist who laid the foundations of expressionism was the Frenchman Paul Cézanne (1839–1906), who labored to express a sense of order in nature that he believed the impressionists had ignored. To achieve this end, he painted objects as a series of planes, each plane expressed in terms of a color change. While Cézanne was in this way equating form with color, he also began to reduce natural forms to their geometrical equivalents, hoping thereby to express the basic shapes of existence itself. He distorted form into geometrical regularity until abstraction became reality. In all this Cézanne was declaring the painter's right to recreate nature in such a way as to express an intensely

Mont Sainté-Victoire by Paul Cézanne (1839–1906). Cézanne's reduction of the exterior world to forms and planes of color provided an important bridge between impressionism and cubism.

personal vision. In the decades before the First World War, German and Russian artists especially embraced expressionism's innovation of using color and dimensionality to articulate internal subjectivity. Ernst Ludwig Kirchner, Erich Heckel, and Franz Marc but also Wassily Kandinsky and Marc Chagall all manifest the tendencies of employing color and form for synthesizing worldly phenomena with the subjective vitality of the human psyche.

Art as personal expression was the hallmark of two other painters in the so-called post-impressionist period, the Frenchman Paul Gauguin and the Dutchman Vincent Van Gogh. Both, through their lives and their art, declared war on traditional nineteenth-century values. Dismayed by the artificiality and complexity of

Western culture, Gauguin fled to the Pacific islands and spent the last decade of his life painting the luscious colors of an unspoiled, primitive society. Van Gogh harbored passionate sympathies for the sufferings of his fellow humans. He poured out the full intensity of his feelings in paintings such as *The Starry Night* (1889), which seems to swirl off the canvas.

In the years between 1900 and the First World War, art underwent still further revolutionary development. Henri Matisse greatly extended Cézanne's use of distortion, thereby declaring once again the painter's right to create according to an individual definition of aesthetic merit. This declaration was given its most ringing prewar endorsement by Pablo Picasso. Picasso, a Catalan Spaniard who came to Paris in 1903, devel-

Ia Orana Maria by Paul Gauguin (1848–1903). Gauguin's striking use of vibrant color and bold shading greatly influenced modernist painting.

pose. The symbolist poets Paul Verlaine, Arthur Rimbaud, Stéphane Mallarmé, and Paul Valéry strove less to articulate coherent expression than to evoke intensity of image, sensuality, color, and the darker corners of the human soul. Artists such as the Norwegian Edvard Munch and the Austrian Gustav Klimt also alarmed middle-class viewers by exploring the darker and erotic dimensions to the human condition.

In music, as well, there was a break from the Romantic tradition that had dominated the nineteenth century and that had been expressed in the works of composers such as Robert Schumann, Felix Mandelssohn, and Franz Liszt. The late Romantic operas of Richard Wagner had already taken vast liberties with harmony and departed from stereotypical melodic patterns, producing music that was not subject to the "tyranny" of form but beholden to sensitive, personal expression. In the subsequent works of composers such as the Austrian Richard Strauss and the Frenchman Claude Debussy, music moved even further in the direction of the intensely personal. Strauss's opera *Der Rosenkavalier* (1911), although based externally on the conventions of late-eighteenth-century plot, is nevertheless a musical expression of the inner realities of its characters, written

oped the style known as cubism, which attempts to carry Cézanne's fascination with geometrical form to its logical conclusion. Cubists went beyond distortion, actually separating the various parts of a figure and rearranging them in other than their natural pattern. The purpose is to express defiance of traditional notions of form, space, and time—to repudiate once and for all the conception of art as representational prettiness.

Symbolism was another artistic movement that flourished during the last decade of the nineteenth century and the beginning years of the twentieth. Its practitioners, both artists and writers, attempted to intensify personal experience and psychological perception by heightening the importance of formal aesthetics and symbolic structures, transcending reality in a way that, once again, challenged traditional roles of artistic pur-

CHRONOLOGY

THE CHALLENGE OF SCIENCE AND PHILOSOPHY

Darwin, *Origin of Species*	1859
Tolstoy, *War and Peace*	1862–1869
Pius IX issues Syllabus of Errors	1864
Dostoyevsky, *Crime and Punishment*	1866
Darwin, *Descent of Man*	1871
Pius IX's pronouncement of papal infallibility	1871
Ibsen, *A Doll's House*	1879
Zola, *Germinal*	1885
Nietzsche, *Beyond Good and Evil*	1886
Nietzsche, *On the Genealogy of Morals*	1887
Van Gogh, *The Starry Night*	1889

to express those realities more directly than before. Both Strauss and Debussy were, like the impressionists, determined to convey atmosphere; Debussy's piano compositions and his symphonic work *La Mer* (1905) are musical manifestations of the impressionists' regard for association rather than formal structure.

Whether in painting, literature, or music, artists developed manifold attempts to move art beyond the form and content of conventional representation. The heterodoxy of modern art defies simple explanation, but we nonetheless see a common interest in taking subjectivity and individualism further than before.

CONCLUSION

Many Europeans who had grown up in the period from 1870 to 1914, but lived through the hardship of the First World War, looked back on the prewar period as a golden age of European civilization. In one sense this retrospective view is apt. The continental powers had successfully avoided major wars, enabling a second phase of industrialization to provide better living standards for the growing populations of mass society. An overall spirit of confidence and purpose pervaded Europe's perceived mission to exercise political, economic, and cultural dominion in the far reaches of the world. Yet European politics and culture also registered the presence of powerful forces of change. Industrial expansion, relative abundance, and rising literacy produced a political climate of rising expectations. As the age of mass politics arrived, democrats, socialists, and feminists clamored for access to political life, threatening violence, strikes, and revolution. Marxist socialism especially changed radical politics, redefining the terms of debate for the next century. Western science, literature, and the arts explored new perspectives on the individual, undermining some of the cherished beliefs of nineteenth-century liberals. The competition and violence central to Darwin's theory of evolution, the subconscious urges that Freud found in human behavior, and the rebellion against representation in the arts all pointed in new and baffling directions. These experiments, hypotheses, and nagging questions accompanied Europe into the Great War of 1914. They would help to shape Europeans' responses to the enormity of mass death and destruction that devastated the continent. After the war, the political changes and cultural unease of the period from 1870 to 1914 would reemerge in the form of mass movements and artistic developments that would define the modern age.

SELECTED READINGS

Berlanstein, Lenard. *The Working of Paris, 1871–1914*. Baltimore, 1984. A social history of the workplace and its impact on working men and women.

Berlin, Isaiah. *Karl Marx: His Life and Environment*, 4th ed. New York, 1996. An excellent short account, especially for Marx's early intellectual life.

Blackbourn, David. *The Long Nineteenth Century: A History of Germany, 1780–1918*. New York, 1998. The best current survey of German society and politics.

Bredin, Jean-Denis. *The Affair: The Case of Alfred Dreyfus.* New York, 1986. Detailed, up to date, and readable.

Burns, Michael. *Dreyfus: A Family Affair.* New York, 1992. Follows the story Dreyfus through the next generations.

Clark, T. J. *The Painting of Modern Life: Paris in the Art of Manet and His Followers.* New York, 1985. Argues for seeing impressionism as a critique of French society.

Gay, Peter. *The Bourgeois Experience: Victoria to Freud*, 5 vols. New York, 1984–2000. Imaginative and brilliant study of private life and middle class culture.

———. *Freud: A Life of Our Time.* New York, 1988. Beautifully written and lucid about difficult concepts; now the best biography.

Herbert, Robert L. *Impressionism: Art, Leisure, and Parisian Society.* New Haven, 1988. An accessible and important study of the impressionists and the world they painted.

Hughes, H. Stuart. *Consciousness and Society.* New York, 1958. A classic study on late-nineteenth-century European thought.

Jones, Gareth Stedman. *Outcast London.* Oxford, 1971. Studies the breakdown in class relationships during the last half of the nineteenth century.

Joyce, Patrick. *Visions of the People: Industrial England the Question of Class, 1848–1914*. New York, 1991. A social history of the workplace.

Kelly, Alfred. *The German Worker: Autobiographies from the Age of Industrialization.* Berkeley, 1987. Excerpts from workers' autobiographies provide fresh perspective on labor history.

Kern, Stephen. *The Culture of Time and Space.* Cambridge, Mass., 1983. A cultural history of the late nineteenth century.

Landes, David. *The Unbound Prometheus: Technological Change and Industrial Development in Western Europe from 1750 to the Present.* New York, 1969. Includes a first-rate analysis of the second industrial revolution.

Lidtke, Vernon. *The Alternative Culture: Socialist Labor in Imperial Germany.* New York, 1985. A probing study of working-class culture.

Lindemann, Albert. *Esau's Tears: Modern Anti-Semitism and the Rise of*

Jews. New York, 1997. A solid analysis of Jews and European anti-Semitism from the French Revolution to the twentieth century.

Marrus, Michael Robert. *The Politics of Assimilation: A Study of the French Jewish Community at the Time of the Dreyfus Affair.* Oxford, 1971.

Micale, Mark S. *Approaching Hysteria: Disease and Its Interpretations.* Princeton, N.J., 1995. Important study of the history of psychiatry before Freud.

Rupp, Leila J. *Worlds of Women: The Making of an International Women's Movement.* Princeton, N.J., 1997.

Silverman, Deborah L. *Art Nouveau in Fin-de-Siècle France: Politics, Psychology, and Style.* Berkeley, 1989. A study of the relationship between psychological and artistic change.

Smith, Bonnie. *Changing Lives: Women in European History since 1700.* New York, 1988. A useful overview of European women's history.

Tickner, Lisa. *The Spectacle of Women: Imagery of the Suffrage Campaign, 1907–14.* Chicago, 1988. A very engaging study of British suffragism.

Verner, Andrew. *The Crisis of Russian Autocracy: Nicholas II and the 1905 Revolution.* Princeton, N.J., 1990. A detailed study of this important event.

Weber, Eugen. *Peasants into Frenchmen: The Modernization of Rural France, 1870–1914.* Stanford, 1976. A study of how France's peasantry was assimilated into the Third Republic.

Wynn, Charters. *Workers, Strikes, and Pogroms: The Donbass-Dnepr Bend in Late Imperial Russia, 1870–1905.* Princeton, N.J., 1992. Excellent on Russian industrialization and Russian workers' politics.

CHAPTER TWENTY-SEVEN

WOMEN
MUNITION
WORKERS

Enrol at once

THE FIRST
WORLD WAR

IN SEVERAL CRUCIAL RESPECTS, the twentieth century began in August 1914, with the outbreak of the First World War. Soldiers marched into battle with the confidence and ambition bred by nineteenth-century successes. The leading nations of Europe were at the height of their power. Europe was the center of the world economy and commanded far-flung empires. Many Europeans entered the war with faith in modernity, in its ability to deliver not only prosperity but all the advantages of "civilization," especially peace and progress.

Despite those expectations, many people harbored fears about the future. The war justified that quiet dread. The "Great War" introduced the ugly face of industrial warfare and the grim capacities of the modern world. It caught Europeans unprepared not only militarily, but economically and politically. In a catastrophic combination of old mentalities and new technologies, the war left 9 million dead soldiers in its wake.

But by the war's end in 1918, soldiers were not the only casualties. World War I was waged against entire nations, not just armies. Devastation stretched across the countryside. Four years of fighting left Europe exhausted and anxious to avoid further bloodshed. Those years also exposed the weaknesses of European society; divisions among classes, nations, and generations intensified under the strains of battle. Victory and defeat created new ambitions and antagonisms that made stability impossible, and that would eventually lead to the Second World War. Postwar Europe faced more problems than peace could manage.

FOCUS QUESTIONS

- What were the causes of World War I?
- Why did the Schlieffen Plan fail?
- Why did the war become a stalemate?
- Why did the Allies persist with an offensive strategy?

 • What was the role of empire in World War I?
- How did the war change women's lives?
- How did the Bolsheviks seize power?
- How did the Allies win the war?

THE JULY CRISIS

What were the causes of World War I?

In 1914 Europe had built a seemingly stable peace. The Great Powers had divided themselves into two rival alliances: the Triple Entente (later the Allied Powers) of Britain, France, and Russia; and the Triple Alliance (later the Central Powers) of Germany, Austria-Hungary, and Italy. Within this balance of power, reasonable diplomacy could resolve international conflicts, such as the disputes over African colonies in 1905 and 1911 and the Balkan wars of 1912–1913. But when diplomacy failed, as it did in the summer of 1914, the alliance system could hasten the outbreak of a wider war. Domestic conflict and international suspicions also threatened the long-preserved peace. Muscling for their own interests abroad, the European nations engaged in a fierce arms race, confident that superior technology and larger armies would result in a quick victory if war occurred. Indeed, war seemed inevitable to many political and military leaders—a question of when, not if. None of the diplomats, spies, military planners, or cabinet ministers of Europe—nor any of their critics—predicted the war they eventually got. Nor did many expect that the Balkan crisis of July 1914 would touch off that conflict, engulfing all of Europe in just over a month's time.

The Great Powers had long been involved in the affairs of southeast Europe. The Balkans lay between two venerable but unsteady empires, the Austro-Hungarian and the Ottoman. The region was also home to newly formed states under the sway of ambitious nationalist movements, "Pan-Slavic" ethnic crusaders, and local power brokers. Balkan politics were a traditional focus for Russian intervention in European affairs, and also for German and British diplomacy. Despite these entanglements, the Great Powers tried to avoid direct intervention, seeking instead to bring the new Balkan states into the web of alliances. In 1912 the independent states of Serbia, Greece, Bulgaria, and Montenegro launched the First Balkan War against the Ottomans; in 1913, the Second Balkan War was fought over the spoils of the first. The Great Powers steered clear of entanglement, and these wars remained localized.

The link between Balkan conflict and continental war would be the Austro-Hungarian Empire, which was struggling to survive amid increasing nationalist ambitions. The "dual monarchy," as it was called after reforms in 1876, had frustrated many ethnic groups excluded from the arrangement. Czechs and Slovenes protested their second-class status in the German half of the empire; Poles, Croats, and ethnic Romanians chafed at Hungarian rule. The province of Bosnia was particularly volatile, home to several Slavic ethnic groups and formerly part of the Ottoman empire. In 1878, the Austrians had occupied and then annexed Bosnia, drawing hatred and resistance from most of Bosnia's ethnic groups. Bosnian Serbs, in particular, had hoped to secede and join the independent kingdom of Serbia. But now the Austrians blocked their plans. So with the support of Serbia, the Bosnian Serbs began an underground war against the empire to achieve their goals. Bosnia would be the crucible of European conflict.

On June 28, 1914, Franz Ferdinand (1889–1914), archduke of Austria and heir to the Austro-Hungarian Empire, paraded through Sarajevo, the capital of Bosnia. As a hotbed of Serb resistance, Sarajevo was an admittedly dangerous place for the head of the hated empire to parade in public. The archduke had escaped an assassination attempt earlier in the day, with a bomb barely missing his

Franz Ferdinand and His Wife, Sophie. The Austrian archduke and archduchess, in Sarajevo on June 28, 1914, approaching their car just minutes before they were assassinated.

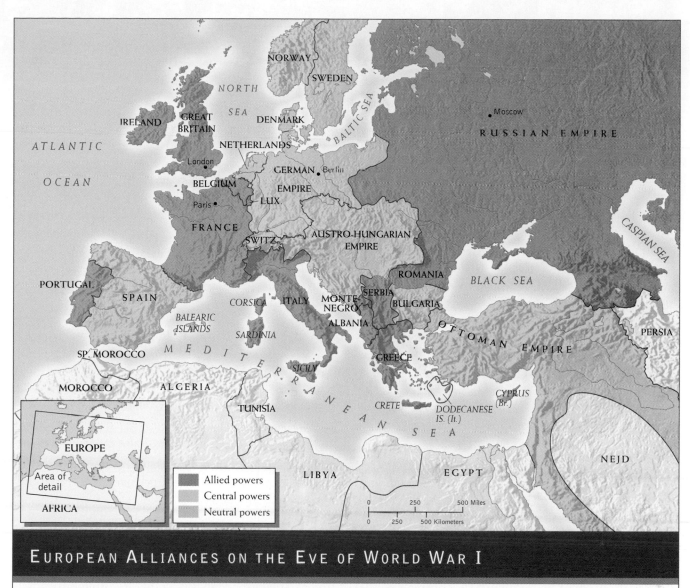

EUROPEAN ALLIANCES ON THE EVE OF WORLD WAR I

Study the pattern of alliances shown in this map. How had the alliance system emerged to protect the varied interests and the integrity of the balance of power in Europe? Why were Germany and the Austro-Hungarian empire allied? Why would the Ottoman empire join such an alliance? Why would the Russian empire gravitate toward Great Britain and France? Did colonial rivalries inform this pattern at all? How did such a system of alliances contribute to global conflict?

automobile; but when his car made a wrong turn and stopped to back up, a nineteen-year-old Bosnian student named Gavrilo Princip shot Ferdinand and his wife at point-blank range. Princip was a member of the Young Bosnian Society, a national liberation group with close links to Serbia. He undoubtedly saw his violent act as a part of a struggle for his people's independence—we see it as the start of World War I.

Shocked by Ferdinand's death, the Austrians saw the assassination as a direct attack from the Serbian gov-

ernment. Eager for retribution, Austria issued an ultimatum to Serbia three weeks later, demanding that the Serbian government denounce the aims and activities of the Bosnian Serbs, prohibit further propaganda and subversion, and allow Austro-Hungarian officials to prosecute and punish Serbian officials who the Austrians believed were involved in the assassination. The demands were deliberately unreasonable. Austria wanted war, a punitive campaign to restore order in Bosnia and crush Serbia. The Serbs recognized the

TOWARD WORLD WAR I: DIPLOMACY IN THE SUMMER OF 1914

The assassination of Franz Ferdinand in Sarajevo on June 28, 1914, set off an increasingly desperate round of diplomatic negotiations. As the following exchanges show, diplomats and political leaders on both sides swung from trying to provoke war to attempting to avert or, at least, contain it.

EMPEROR FRANZ JOSEPH OF AUSTRIA-HUNGARY TO KAISER WILLIAM II OF GERMANY, JULY 5, 1914

A week after his nephew, the heir to the throne, had been shot, Franz Joseph set out his interpretation of the longstanding conflict with Serbia and its larger implications.

The plot against my poor nephew was the direct result of an agitation carried on by the Russian and Serb Pan-Slavs, an agitation whose sole object is the weakening of the Triple Alliance and the destruction of my realm.

So far, all investigations have shown that the Sarajevo murder was not perpetrated by one individual, but grew out of a well-organized conspiracy, the threads of which can be traced to Belgrade. Even though it will probably be impossible to prove the complicity of the Serb government, there can be no doubt that its policy, aiming as it does at the unification of all Southern Slavs under the Serb banner, encourages such crimes, and that the continuation of such conditions constitutes a permanent threat to my dynasty and my lands. . . .

This will only be possible if Serbia, which is at present the pivot of Pan-Slav policies, is put out of action as a factor of political power in the Balkans.

You too are [surely] convinced after the recent frightful occurrence in Bosnia that it is no longer possible to contemplate a reconciliation of the antagonism between us and Serbia and that the [efforts] of all European monarchs to pursue policies that preserve the peace will be threatened if the nest of criminal activity in Belgrade remains unpunished.

AUSTRO-HUNGARIAN DISAGREEMENTS OVER STRATEGY

The following comes from an account of a meeting of the Council of Ministers of the Austro-Hungarian empire on July 7, 1914. The ministers disagreed sharply about diplomatic strategies and about how crucial decisions should be made.

[Count Leopold Berchtold, foreign minister of Austria-Hungary] . . . both Emperor Wilhelm and [chancellor] Bethmann Hollweg had assured us emphatically of Germany's unconditional support in the event of military complications with Serbia. . . . It was clear to him that a military conflict with Serbia might bring about war with Russia. . . .

[Count Istvan Tisza, prime minister of Hungary] . . . We should decide what our demands on Serbia will be [but] should only present an ultimatum if Serbia rejected them. These demands must be hard but not so that they cannot be complied with. If Serbia accepted them, we could register a noteworthy diplomatic success and our prestige in the Balkans would be enhanced. If Serbia rejected our demands, then he too would favor military action. But he would already now go on record that we could aim at the down-sizing but not the complete annihilation of Serbia because, first, this would provoke Russia to fight to the death and, second, he—as Hungarian premier—could never consent to the monarchy's annexation of a part of Serbia. Whether or not we ought to go to war with Serbia was not a matter for Germany to decide. . . .

[Count Berchtold] remarked that the history of the past years showed that diplomatic successes against Serbia might enhance the prestige of the monarchy temporarily, but that in reality the tension in our relations with Serbia had only increased.

[Count Karl Stürgkh, prime minister of Austria] . . . agreed with the Royal Hungarian Prime Minister that we and not the German government had to determine whether a war was necessary or not . . . [but] Count Tisza should take into account that in pursuing a hesitant and weak policy, we run the risk of not being so sure of Germany's unconditional support. . . .

[Leo von Bilinsky, Austro-Hungarian finance minister] . . . The Serb understands only force; a diplomatic success would make no impression at all in Bosnia and would be harmful rather than beneficial. . . .

AUSTRO-HUNGARY'S ULTIMATUM TO SERBIA

The British foreign secretary Sir Edward Grey, for one, was shocked by Austria's demands, especially its insistence that Austrian officials would participate in Serbian judicial proceedings. The Serbian government's response was more conciliatory than most diplomats expected, but diplomatic efforts to avert war still failed. The Austrians' ultimatum to Serbia included the following demands:

The Royal Serb Government will publish the following declaration on the first page of its official *journal* of 26/13 July:

"The Royal Serb Government condemns the propaganda directed against Austria-Hungary, and regrets sincerely the horrible consequences of these criminal ambitions.

"The Royal Serb Government regrets that Serb officers and officials have taken part in the propaganda above-mentioned and thereby imperiled friendly and neighbourly relations.

"The Royal Government . . . considers it a duty to warn officers, officials and indeed all the inhabitants of the kingdom [of Serbia], that it will in future use great severity against such persons who may be guilty of similar doings.

The Royal Serb Government will moreover pledge itself to the following:

1. to suppress every publication likely to inspire hatred and contempt against the Monarchy;

2. to begin immediately dissolving the society called *Narodna Odbrana**; to seize all its means of propaganda and to act in the same way against all the societies and associations in Serbia, which are busy with the propaganda against Austria-Hungary.

3. to eliminate without delay from public instruction everything that serves or might serve the propaganda against Austria-Hungary, both where teachers or books are concerned;

4. to remove from military service and from the administration all officers and officials who are guilty of having taken part in the propaganda against Austria-Hungary, whose names and proof of whose guilt the I. and R. Government [Imperial and Royal, that is, the Austro-Hungarian empire] will communicate to the Royal Government;

5. to consent to the cooperation of I. and R. officials in Serbia in suppressing the subversive movement directed against the territorial integrity of the Monarchy;

6. to open a judicial inquest [*enquête judiciaire*] against all those who took part in the plot of 28 June, if they are to be found on Serbian territory; the I. and R. Government will delegate officials who will take an active part in these and associated inquiries;

The I. and R. Government expects the answer of the Royal government to reach it not later than Saturday, the 25th, at six in the afternoon. . . .

*Narodna Odbrana, or National Defense, was pro-Serbian and anti-Austrian, but nonviolent. The Society of the Black Hand, to which Franz Ferdinand's assassin belonged, considered Narodna Odbrana too moderate.

Ralph Menning, *The Art of the Possible: Documents on Great Power Diplomacy, 1814–1914* (New York: McGraw Hill, 1996), pp. 400, 402–403, and 414–415 (source for all three document excerpts).

Declaration of War, August, 1914. In Berlin, an officer reads the Kaiser's order to mobilize troops before a crowd of civilians and soldiers.

provocation and mobilized their army three hours before sending a reply, which agreed to all but the most important Austrian demands. Austria responded with its own mobilization and declared war three days later, on July 28, 1914.

For a brief moment, it seemed possible to avoid a wider war. At first diplomats and politicians hoped to write the confrontation off as another crisis in the Balkans. Austria's steady escalation, coupled with Russia's traditional ties to Serbia, ultimately made that impossible. For Austria, the conflict was a matter of prestige and power politics—a chance to reassert the fraying empire's authority. For Russia, too, the emerging conflict was an opportunity to regain some of the tsar's authority by standing up for the rights of "brother Slavs." Initially, Russia planned to respond to Austria's threat with a partial mobilization, but when the orders came down on July 30, Russia mobilized fully—its troops were readied to fight both Austria and Germany.

The crisis spread, and the Germans were prepared. Sitting in the most precarious geographic position, Germany had the most detailed plans for fighting a war of necessity. Its military planners were among those who saw war as inevitable, an opportunity to settle the nation's future in continental Europe. As Russia began to mobilize, Kaiser William II (1888–1918) sent an ultimatum to St. Petersburg demanding that Russian mobilization cease within twelve hours; the Russians refused. Meanwhile, the German ministers demanded to know France's intentions. Premier René Viviani (1914–1915) replied that France would act "in accordance with her interests"—which meant an immediate mobilization against Germany. Finally facing the dual threat it had long anticipated, Germany mobilized on August 1 and declared war on Russia—two days later, on France. The next day, the German army invaded Belgium on its way to take Paris.

This invasion of neutral Belgium galvanized public and parliamentary support for war in Great Britain. The British had secret pacts that obligated them to help France, but they also had an old, public agreement to guarantee Belgium's neutrality. Moreover, Britain wanted to keep any Continental power from dominating the Low Countries, which lay directly across the English Channel, and to stop the threat of the growing German navy. So on August 4, Britain entered the war against Germany. Other nations were quickly drawn into the struggle. On August 7 the Montenegrins joined with the Serbs in fighting Austria. Two weeks later the Japanese declared war on Germany, mainly to attack German possessions in the Far East. On August 1 Turkey allied with Germany, and in October began the bombardment

WORLD WAR I BEGINS

Assassination of Archduke Franz Ferdinand of Austria	June 28, 1914
Austria and Russian mobilize for war	July 28, 1914
Germany declares war on Russia and France	August 1–3, 1914
Britain enters war against Germany	August 4, 1914

of Russian ports on the Black Sea. Italy had been allied with Germany and Austria before the war, but at the outbreak of hostilities, the Italians cited a strict interpretation of their obligations and declared neutrality. They insisted that since Germany had invaded neutral Belgium, they owed Germany no protection.

The diplomatic maneuvers during the five weeks that followed the assassination at Sarajevo have been characterized as "a tragedy of miscalculation." Diplomats' hands were tied, however, by the strategic thinking and rigid timetables set by military leaders. Speed was of prime importance to generals. To them, once war seemed certain, time spent on diplomacy was time lost on the battlefield. Historians continue to debate whether Germany pressured Austria to attack Serbia in order to precipitate a continental war. A number of factors contributed to the outbreak of war when it came. Austria negotiated about its ultimatum for three weeks, and during the delay both Russia and Germany felt obliged to make shows of strength. Reasoned debate about the problem never occurred. During the crisis government officials had little contact with each other, and even less with the diplomats and ambassadors of other countries. Several heads of state, including the kaiser and the president of France, along with many of their ministers, spent most of July on vacation; they returned to find their generals holding orders for mobilization,

waiting for signature. Austria's mismanagement of the crisis and Russia's inability to find a way to intervene without mobilizing its army contributed greatly to the spiraling confrontation. It is clear, however, that powerful German officials were arguing that war was inevitable. It seemed clear to them that Germany should fight before Russia recovered from its 1905 loss to Japan, and before the French army could benefit from its new three-year conscription law that would put more men in uniform. The same sense of urgency characterized the strategies of all combatant countries. The lure of a bold, successful strike against one's enemies, and the fear that too much was at stake to risk losing the advantage, created a rolling tide of military mobilization that carried Europe into battle.

THE MARNE AND ITS CONSEQUENCES

Why did the Schlieffen Plan fail?

Declarations of war were met with public fanfare. Europeans imagined a romantic war, a great adventure of national glory, a ritual purification of the body politic. Young men enlisted with excitement: the war would be "over by Christmas." If less idealistic, the expectations of the politicians and generals in charge were equally

A Hopeful Beginning. French women send soldiers off to war in 1914.

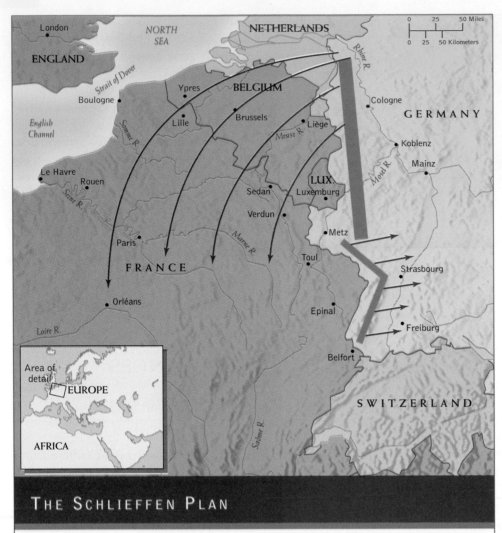

THE SCHLIEFFEN PLAN

This map details the plan developed by Prussian strategist and general Alfred von Schlieffen years before the outbreak of World War I. Schlieffen outlined the plan as part of what he believed was inevitable conflict with Russia. Why did Schlieffen seek to send German military resources to France in the event of a war with Russia? Why would he wish to defeat France first? What does the willingness of the German high command to commit to the violation of neutral territory (in this case Belgium) suggest about the breakdown of the diplomatic system carved out over the previous two generations?

achieved "through improvisation, not planning."

The Germans based their offensive on the plans of Count Alfred von Schlieffen. The Schlieffen Plan was designed to suit Germany's efficient, well-equipped but outnumbered army. It called for attacking France first to secure a quick victory that would neutralize the Western Front, and free the German army to fight Russia in the east. With France expecting an attack through Alsace-Lorraine, the Germans would instead invade through Belgium and sweep down through northwestern France to fight a decisive battle near Paris. The German plan came close to succeeding, but the achievement was in spite of itself. Schlieffen's plan required knowing how many men could be marshalled at what rail heads, how many horses would be required to haul how much equipment, how fast soldiers carrying a certain amount of equipment could move, how many pairs of boots could tramp on the surface of Belgian roads without causing them to give way—all without any unexpected surprises. As soon as the German army

disproved on the battlefield. Military planners foresaw a short, limited, and decisive war—a tool to be used where diplomacy failed. They thought that a modern economy simply could not function amid a sustained war effort, and that modern weaponry made protracted war impossible. They placed their bets on size and speed: bigger armies, more powerful weapons, and faster offensives would win the war. But for all of their planning, they were unable to respond to the uncertainty and confusion of the battlefield. In the Great War, one historian has noted, military success was

entered Belgium it faced the mud, mess, and exhaustion of reality. There were also changes of plan. Fearing the Russians would move faster than expected, German commanders first altered Schlieffen's plan by dispatching some troops to the east instead of committing them all to the assault on France. Second, they chose to attack Paris from the northeast instead of completely circling to the southwest.

For over a month, the German army advanced swiftly. Yet the plan overestimated the army's physical and logistical capabilities. The speed of the operation

THE GERMAN OFFENSIVE

In what ways was the Schlieffen plan a success? How did the French Plan XVII help to frustrate the Schlieffen Plan despite leaving Paris dangerously vulnerable? Note how close the German advance came to Paris. How did the German command staff's decision not to commit the entire German military to the defeat of France undermine the success of the Schlieffen Plan?

collapsed the German front into a single major thrust towards Paris. The French commander, Jules Joffre, who was immensely calm under pressure and almost callously indifferent to casualties, reorganized his armies and slowly drew the Germans into a trap. In September, with the Germans just thirty miles outside of the capital, Britain and France launched a counteroffensive at the battle of the Marne. The German line retreated to the Aisne river, and the Schlieffen Plan was dead. Unable to advance, the armies tried to outflank one another to the north, creating a "race to the sea" that neither side won. After four months of swift charges across open ground, Germany set up a fortified, defensive position that the Allies could not break. Along an immovable front, stretching over four hundred miles from the northern border of Switzerland to the English Channel, the Great Powers dug fortifications for a protracted battle. By Christmas, trench warfare was born and the war had just begun.

—advancing twenty to twenty-five miles a day—was simply too much for soldiers and supply lines to keep up with. They were also slowed by the poorly armed but determined resistance of the Belgian army, and by the intervention of Britain's small but highly professional field army, whose trained marksmen caused terrible losses among the advancing Germans. Nevertheless, German plans seemed to be working during August. French attacks into Alsace-Lorraine were a chaotic failure, and casualties mounted as the French lines retreated toward Paris. Yet those successes began to erode. The Belgian and British defense, which cost the defenders terribly in casualties and exhaustion as they too fled south and west just ahead of the Germans,

The Marne proved to be the most strategically important battle of the entire war. This single battle shattered Europe's expectations of war and dashed hopes of a quick finish. The war of movement had stopped dead in its tracks, where it would remain for four years. Europeans learned after the Marne that the war would be long, costly, and deadly. Politicians and generals began a continual search for ways to break the stalemate and to bring the war out of trenches, seeking new allies, new theaters, and new weapons. But they also remained committed to offensive tactics on the Western Front. Whether through ignorance, stubbornness, callousness, or desperation, military leaders continued to order their men to go "over the top."

Part of the success of the Marne resulted from an unexpectedly strong Russian assault in the east, which pulled some German units away from the war in the west. But Russia's initial gains were obliterated at the battle of Tannenberg, August 26–30. Plagued with an array of problems, the Russian army was tired and half-starved; the Germans devastated it, taking one hundred thousand prisoners and virtually destroying the Russian Second Army. The Russian general killed himself on the battlefield. Two weeks later, the Germans won another decisive victory at the battle of the Masurian Lakes, forcing the Russians to retreat from German territory. Despite this, Russian forces were able to defeat Austrian attacks to their south, inflicting terrible losses and thereby forcing the Germans to commit more troops to face the poorly armed but enormous Russian army. Through 1915 and 1916, the Eastern Front remained bloody and indecisive, with neither side able to capitalize on its gains.

STALEMATE, 1915

Why did the war become a stalemate?

In the search for new points of attack, both the Allies and the Central Powers added new partners. The Ottoman empire (Turkey) joined Germany and Austria at the end of 1914. In May 1915, Italy joined the Allies, persuaded by the popular support of its citizens and by the lure of land and money. The Treaty of London of April 1915 promised Italy financial reparations, parts of Austrian territory, and pieces of Germany's African colonies. Bulgaria also hoped to gain territory in the Balkans and joined the war on the side of the Central Powers a few months later. The entry of these new belligerents expanded the geography of the war and introduced the possibility of breaking the stalemate in the west by waging offensives on other fronts.

GALLIPOLI AND NAVAL WARFARE

Turkey's involvement, in particular, altered the dynamics of the war, for it threatened Russia's supply lines and endangered Britain's control of the Suez Canal. To defeat Turkey quickly—and in hopes of bypassing the western stalemate—the British first lord of the Admiralty, Winston Churchill (1911–1915), argued for a naval offensive in the Dardanelles, the narrow strait

separating Europe and Asia Minor. Under particularly incompetent leadership, however, the Royal Navy lacked adequate planning, supply lines, and maps to mount a successful campaign. Thus, the Allied attack began with a series of ineffective naval bombardments and mine sweeps, resulting in the loss or damage of six Allied ships. The Allies then attempted a land invasion of the Gallipoli peninsula, beginning on April 25, 1915. The combined force of French, British, Australian, and New Zealand troops made little headway, however. The Turks defended the narrow coast from positions high on fortified cliffs, and the shores were covered in nearly impenetrable barbed wire. During the disastrous landing, a British officer recalled, "the sea behind was absolutely crimson, and you could hear the groans through the rattle of musketry." The battle became entrenched on the beaches at Gallipoli, and the casualties mounted for seven months before the Allied commanders admitted defeat and ordered a withdrawal in December. The Gallipoli campaign—the first large-scale amphibious attack in history—was a major defeat for the Allies. It brought death into London's neighborhoods and the cities of Britain's industrial north. Casualties were particularly devastating in the "white dominions"—practically every town and hamlet in Australia and New Zealand lost young men, sometimes all the sons of a single family. The campaign cost the Allies two hundred thousand soldiers and did little to shift the war's focus away from the deadlocked Western Front. In fact, the failure of "going around" simply reinforced the logic of fighting in the trenches.

By 1915 both sides realized that fighting this prolonged and costly "modern" war would require countries to mobilize all of their resources. As one captain put it in a letter home, "It is absolutely certainly a war of 'attrition,' as somebody said here the other day, and we have got to stick it out longer than the other side and go on producing men, money, and material until they cry quits, and that's about it, as far as I can see."

The Allies started to wage war on the economic front. Germany was vulnerable, dependent as it was on imports for at least one third of its food supply. The Allies' naval blockade against all of central Europe aimed to slowly drain their opponents of food and raw materials. Germany responded with a submarine blockade, threatening to attack any vessel in the seas around Great Britain. On May 7, 1915, the German submarine *U-20*, without warning, torpedoed the passenger liner *Lusitania*, which was secretly carrying war supplies. The attack killed 1,198 people, including 128 Americans. The attack provoked the animosity of the

United States, and Germany was forced to promise that it would no longer fire without warning. (This promise proved only temporary: in 1917 Germany would again declare unrestricted submarine warfare, drawing America into the war.) Although the German blockade against Britain destroyed more tonnage, the blockade against Germany was far more devastating in the long run, as the continued war effort placed increasing demands on the national economy.

TRENCH WARFARE

While the war was escalated economically and politically, life in the trenches remained largely the same: a cramped and uncomfortable existence of daily routines and continual killing. "When all is said and done," an English officer later wrote, "the war was mainly a matter of holes and ditches." Indeed, some twenty-five thousand miles of trenches snaked along the Western Front, normally in three lines on each side of "No Man's Land." The front line was the attack trench, lying anywhere from fifty yards to a mile away from the enemy. Behind the front was the second line, a support trench; and behind that, a third trench for reserves. But despite the similar layouts, the two sides' trenches were remarkably different. The Germans saw their position as permanent, and they built elaborate bunkers—fully enclosed rooms with electric light, running water, and overstuffed furniture. Some even had kitchens, wallpaper, curtains, and doorbells. These comforts contrasted sharply with the ramshackle constructions of the French and British, who refused to abandon their offensive strategy, and so saw little value in fortifying a defensive position. "The result," one soldier realized, was "that we lived a mean and impoverished sort of existence in lousy scratch holes."

The British trenches were wet, cold, and filthy. Rain turned the dusty corridors into squalid mud pits, and flooded the floors up to waist level. Soldiers lived with lice and large black rats, which fed on the dead soldiers and horses that cast their stench over everything. Cadavers could go unburied for months, and were often just embedded in the trench walls. It was little wonder that soldiers were rotated out of the front lines frequently—after only three to seven days—to be relieved from what one soldier called "this present, ever-present, eternally present misery, this stinking world of sticky, trickling earth ceilinged by a strip of threatening sky." Indeed, there was a constant threat of enemy fire: seven thousand British men were killed or wounded daily. This "wastage," as it was called, was part of the routine, along with the inspections, rotations, and mundane duties of life on the Western Front.

As the war progressed, new weapons added to the frightening dimensions of daily warfare.

The Lines of Battle on the Western Front. A British reconnaissance photo showing three lines of German trenches (right), No Man's Land (the black strip in the center), and the British trenches (partially visible to the left). The upper right hand quadrant of the photo shows communications trenches linking the front to the safe area.

Besides artillery, machine guns, and barbed wire, the instruments of war now included exploding bullets, liquid fire, and poison gas. Gas, in particular, brought visible change to the battlefront. First used effectively by the Germans in April 1915 at the second battle of Ypres, poison gas was not only physically devastating—especially in its later forms—but also psychologically disturbing. The deadly cloud hung frequently over the trenches, although the quick appearance of gas masks limited its effectiveness. Like other new weapons, poison gas solidified the lines and took more lives, but could not end the stalemate. The war dragged through its second year, bloody and stagnant. Soldiers grew accustomed to the stalemate, while their leaders plotted ways to end it.

SLAUGHTER IN THE TRENCHES: THE GREAT BATTLES, 1916–1917

Why did the Allies persist with an offensive strategy?

The bloodiest battles of all—those that epitomize the First World War—occurred in 1916–1917. Massive campaigns in the war of attrition, these assaults produced hundreds of thousands of casualties and only minor territorial gains. These battles encapsulated the military tragedy of the war: a strategy of soldiers in cloth uniforms marching against machine guns. The result, of course, was carnage. The common response to these staggering losses was to replace the generals in charge. But though commanders changed, commands did not. Military planners continued to believe that their original strategies were the right ones, and that their plans had simply been frustrated by bad luck and German determination. The "cult of the offensive" insisted that a breakthrough was possible with enough troops and enough weapons.

But the manpower they needed could not be moved efficiently or protected adequately. Railroad networks made it possible to bring large numbers of troops to the front, but mobility ended there. Heavy mud,

The "cult of the offensive" insisted that a breakthrough was possible with enough troops and enough weapons.

labyrinthine trenches, and tangles of barbed wire made movement arduous, if not impossible. More important, the new technologies of killing made movement deadly. Unprotected soldiers armed with rifles, grenades, and bayonets were simply no match for machine guns and deep trenches. Another major problem of military strategy—and another explanation for continued slaughter—was the lack of effective communication between the front lines and general headquarters. If something went wrong at the front (which happened frequently) it was impossible for the leaders to know in time to make meaningful corrections. As the great battles of the Great War illustrate, firepower had outpaced mobility, and the Allied generals simply did not know how to respond.

VERDUN

The first of these major battles was the German attack on the French stronghold of Verdun, near France's eastern border, in February 1916. Verdun had little strategic importance, but it quickly became a symbol of France's strength and was defended at all costs. Germany's goal was not necessarily to take the city, but rather to break French morale—France's "remarkable devotion"—at a moment of critical weakness. As the German general Erich von Falkenhayn (1914–1916) said, the offensive would "compel the French to throw in every man they have. If they do so the forces of France will bleed to death." One million shells were fired on the first day of battle, inaugurating a ten-month struggle of back-and-forth fighting: offensives and counteroffensives of intense ferocity, enormous costs, and zero gains. Led by General Henri Pétain (1914–1918), the French pounded the Germans with artillery and received heavy bombardment in return. The Germans relied on large teams of horses, seven thousand of which were killed in a single day, to drag their guns through the muddy, cratered terrain. The French moved supplies and troops into Verdun continually: twelve thousand delivery trucks were employed for service, as were 259 of 330 regiments of the French army (including the future president Charles de Gaulle, who was captured during a raid on a German fort). Neither side could gain a real advantage—one small village on the front changed hands thirteen times in one month alone—but both sides incurred devastating losses of life. By the end of June, over four hundred

Verdun, 1916. French soldiers look out from their trenches during a round of shelling. A dead body lies at the right.

thousand French and German soldiers were dead. "Verdun," writes on historian, "had become a place of terror and death that could not yield victory." In the end, however, the advantage fell to the French. They had simply survived, and bled the Germans as badly as they suffered themselves.

THE SOMME

Meanwhile, the British opened their own offensive against Germany farther west; beginning the battle of the Somme on June 24. The Allied attack began with a fierce five-day bombardment, blasting the German lines with a massive amount of artillery. Over fourteen hundred guns delivered nearly 3 million shells; the blasts could be heard all the way across the English Channel. The British assumed that this preliminary attack would break the mesh of German wire, destroy Germany's trenches, and clear the way for Allied troops to advance forward and upright, virtually unprotected. They were tragically wrong. The shells the

British used were designed for surface combat, not to penetrate the deep, reinforced trenches dug by the Germans, The wire and trenches withstood the bombardment. When the British soldiers were ordered "over the top" toward enemy lines, they found themselves snared in wire and facing fully operational German machine guns. Each man carried sixty pounds of supplies that were to be used during the expected fighting in the German trenches. A few British commanders who had disobeyed orders and brought their men forward before the shelling ended were able to break through German lines. Elsewhere it was hardly a battle; whole British divisions were simply mowed down. Those who made it to the enemy trenches faced bitter hand-to-hand combat with pistols, grenades, knives, bayonets, and bare hands. On the first day of battle alone, a stunning twenty thousand British soldiers died, and another forty thousand were wounded. The carnage continued from July until mid-November, resulting in massive casualties on both sides: five hundred thousand German, four hundred thousand

British, and two hundred thousand French. The losses were unimaginable, and the outcome was even harder to fathom: for all their sacrifices, neither side had made any real gains. The first lesson of the Somme was offered later, by a war veteran: "Neither side had won, nor could win, the War. The War had won, and would go on winning."

The futility of offensive war began to take its toll on army morale. Military commanders, however, maintained their strategy and pushed for victories on the Western Front again in 1917. The French general Robert Nivelle (1914–1917) promised to break through the German lines with overwhelming manpower, but the "Nivelle Offensive" (April–May 1917) failed immediately, with first-day casualties like those at the Somme. The British also reprised the Somme at the third battle of Ypres (July–October 1917) where a half million casualties earned Great Britain only insignificant gains—and no breakthrough. The one weapon with the potential to break the stalemate, the tank, was finally introduced into battle in 1916, but with such reluctance by tradition-bound commanders that its half-hearted employment made almost no difference. Other innovations were equally indecisive. Airplanes were used almost exclusively for reconnaissance, though occasional "dogfights" did occur between German and Allied pilots. And though the Germans sent zeppelins to raid London, they did little significant damage.

Of the battle of the Somme, one veteran later said "Neither side had won, nor could win, the War. The War had won, and would go on winning."

Off the Western Front, fighting produced further stalemate. The Austrians continued to fend off attacks in Italy and Macedonia, while the Russians mounted a successful offensive against them on the Eastern Front. The initial Russian success brought Romania into the war on Russia's side, but the Central Powers quickly retaliated and knocked the Romanians out of the war within a few months.

The war at sea was equally indecisive, with neither side willing to risk the loss of enormously expensive battleships. The British and German navies fought only one major naval battle early in 1916, which ended in stalemate. Afterward they used their fleets primarily in the economic war of blockades.

As a year of great bloodshed and growing disillusionment, 1916 showed that not even the superbly organized Germans had the mobility or fast-paced communications to win the western ground war. Increasingly, warfare would be turned against entire nations, including civilian populations on the "home front" and in the far reaches of the European empires.

WAR OF EMPIRES

What was the role of empire in World War I?

Coming as it did at the height of European imperialism, the Great War quickly became a war of empires, with far-reaching repercussions. As the demands of warfare rose, Europe's colonies provided soldiers and material support. Britain, in particular, benefited from its vast network of colonial dominions and dependencies, bringing in soldiers from Canada, Australia, New Zealand, India, and South Africa. These colonial troops fought with the Allies on the Western Front, as well as in Mesopotamia and Persia against the Turks and in East Africa against Germany. They suffered eight hundred thousand casualties, with one-fourth fatalities—losses double those of the United States. Colonial recruits were also employed in industry. In France, where even some French conscripts were put to work in factories, the international labor force numbered over two hundred fifty thousand—including workers from China, Vietnam, Egypt, India, the West Indies, and South Africa.

With the stalemate in Europe, colonial areas also became strategically important theaters for armed engagement. Although the campaign against Turkey began poorly for Britain with the debacle at Gallipoli, beginning in 1916 Allied forces won a series of battles, pushing the Turks out of Egypt and eventually capturing Baghdad, Jerusalem, Beirut, and other cities throughout the Middle East. The British commander in Egypt and Palestine was Edmund Allenby (1919–1925), who led a multinational army against the well-drilled Turks. Allenby was a shrewd general and an excellent manager of men and supplies in desert conditions, but in his campaigns the support of different Arab peoples seeking independence form the Turks proved crucial. Allenby allied himself to the successful Bedouin revolts that split the Ottoman empire; British officer T. E. Lawrence (1914–1918) popularized the Arab's guerrilla actions. When one of the senior Bedouin aristocrats, the emir Abdullah, captured the strategic port of Aqaba in July

1917, Lawrence took credit and entered popular mythology as "Lawrence of Arabia."

Britain encouraged Arab nationalism for its own strategic purposes, offering a qualified acknowledgment of Arab political aspirations. At the same time, for similar but conflicting strategic reasons, the British declared their support of "the establishment in Palestine of a national home for the Jewish people." Britain's foreign secretary Arthur Balfour made the pledge. European Zionists, seeking a Jewish homeland, took the Balfour Declaration very seriously. The conflicting pledges to Bedouin leaders and Zionists sowed the seeds of future Arab-Israeli conflict. The war drew Europe more deeply into the Middle East, where conflicting dependencies and commitments created numerous postwar problems.

The conflicting pledges to Arabian Bedouin leaders and Zionists sowed the seeds of future Arab-Israeli conflict.

IRISH REVOLT

Britain's own empire was also vulnerable, and the demands of war strained precarious bonds to the breaking point. Before the war, long-standing tensions between Irish Catholics and the Protestant British government had reached fever pitch, and civil war was likely. The Sinn Fein ("Ourselves Alone") party had formed in 1900 to fight for Irish independence, and a home rule bill had passed Parliament in 1912. But with the outbreak of war in 1914, national interests took precedence over domestic politics: the "Irish question" was tabled, and two hundred thousand Irishmen volunteered for the British army. The problem festered, however, and on Easter Sunday, 1916, a group of nationalists revolted in Dublin. The insurgents' plan to smuggle in arms from Germany failed, and they had few delusions of achieving victory. The British army arrived with artillery and machine guns; they shelled parts of Dublin and crushed the uprising within a week.

The revolt was a military disaster but it was a striking political success. Britain shocked the Irish public by executing the rebel leaders. Even the British prime minister David Lloyd George (1916–1922) thought the military governor in Dublin exceeded his authority with these executions. The martyrdom of the "Easter Rebels" seriously damaged Britain's relationship with its Irish Catholic subjects. The deaths galvanized the cause of Irish nationalism and touched off guerrilla violence that kept Ireland in turmoil for years. Finally, a new home rule bill was enacted in 1920, establishing separate parliaments for the Catholic south of Ireland and for Ulster, the northeastern counties where the majority population was Protestant. The leaders of the so-called Dáil Éireann (Irish Assembly), which had proclaimed an Irish Republic in 1918 and therefore been outlawed by Britain, rejected the bill, but accepted a treaty that granted dominion status to Catholic Ireland in 1921. Dominion was followed almost immediately by civil war between those who abided by the treaty and those who wanted to absorb Ulster, but the conflict ended in an uneasy compromise. The Irish Free State was established, and British sovereignty was partially abolished in 1937. Full status as a republic came, with some American pressure and Britain's exhausted indifference, in 1945.

THE HOME FRONT

How did the war change women's lives?

When the war of attrition began in 1915, the belligerent governments were completely unprepared for the strains of sustained warfare. The costs of war—in both money and manpower—were staggering. In 1914 the war cost Germany 36 million marks per day (five times the cost of the war of 1870), and by 1918 the cost had skyrocketed to 146 million marks per day. Great Britain had estimated it would need one hundred thousand soldiers but ended up mobilizing 3 million. The enormous task of feeding, clothing, and equipping the army became as much of a challenge as breaking through enemy lines; civilian populations were increasingly asked or forced—to shoulder the burden. Bureaucrats and industrialists led the effort to mobilize the "home front," focusing all parts of society on the single goal of military victory. The term "total war" was introduced to describe this intense mobilization of society: it meant that civilians were practically as important to the war as soldiers, and that they were, therefore, equally vulnerable to enemy action.

The demands of industrial warfare led first to a transition from general industrial manufacturing to munitions production, and then to increased state control of all aspects of production and distribution. The govern-

American Poster, 1918. This poster also calls for workers (in this case, machinists) to show their solidarity with the military effort. The emphasis on industrial production and the close connections between labor and army were central to "total war."

German Poster, 1917. "Through Work to Victory! Through Victory to Peace!" A soldier from the front shakes hands with a munitions worker—an image calling for solidarity between the army and the "home front." Following a series of strikes in 1917, the German government responded to labor's rising discontent with posters such as this.

ments of Britain and France managed to direct the economy politically, without serious detriment to the standard of living in their countries. Germany, however, put its economy in the hands of army and industry; under the Hindenburg Plan, named for Paul von Hindenburg (1916–1919), the chief of the imperial staff of the German army, pricing and profit margins were set by individual industrialists. The result was a chaotic conflict of personal interests that permanently impaired the Germany war economy and led to deteriorating social conditions throughout the nation. The Allied blockade compounded Germany's problems, eliminating imports and driving up the price of food,

while open supply lines and naval superiority kept the Allies better supplied on both the front lines and at home.

WOMEN IN THE WAR

As Europe's adult men left farms and factories to become soldiers, the composition of the work force changed: thousands of women were recruited into fields that had previously excluded them. Young people, foreigners, and unskilled workers were also pressed into newly important tasks; in the case of colonial workers, their experiences had equally critical repercussions. But because they were more visible, it was women who became symbolic of many of the changes brought by the Great War. In Germany, one third of the labor force in heavy industry was female by the end of the war, and in France, 684,000 women worked in the munitions industry alone. In England the "munitionettes," as they

Women at Work. The all-out war effort combined with a manpower shortage at home brought women into factories across Europe in unparalleled numbers. Right: Men and women work side-by-side in a British shell factory. Below: Women toil in a German gun factory.

were dubbed, numbered nearly a million. Women also entered the clerical and service sectors. In the villages of France, England, and Germany, women became mayors, school principals, and mail carriers. Hundreds of thousands of women worked with the army as nurses and ambulance drivers, jobs that brought them very close to the front lines. With minimal supplies and under squalid conditions, they worked to save lives or patch bodies together.

In some cases, war offered new opportunities. Middle-class women often said that the war broke down the restrictions on their lives; those in nursing learned to drive and acquired rudimentary medical knowledge. At home they could now ride the train, walk the street, or go out to dinner without an adult present to chaperone them. In terms of gender roles, an enormous gulf sometimes seemed to separate the wartime world from nineteenth-century Victorian society. In one of the most famous autobiographies of the war, Vera Brittain's *Testament of Youth*, Brittain (1896–1970) recorded the dramatic new social norms that she and others forged during the rapid changes of wartime. "As a generation of women we were now sophisticated to an extent which was revolutionary when compared with the romantic ignorance of 1914. Where we had once spoken with polite evasion of 'a certain condition,' or 'a certain profession,' we now unblushingly used the words 'pregnancy' and 'prostitution.'" For every Vera Brittain who celebrated the changes, however, journalists, novelists, and other observers grumbled that women were now smoking, refusing to wear the corsets that gave Victorian dresses their hourglass shape, or cutting their hair into the new fashionable bobs. The "new woman" became a symbol of profound and disconcerting cultural transformation.

How long lasting were these changes? In the after-

ONE WOMAN'S WAR

Vera Brittain (1893–1970) was talented, ambitious, and privileged. She was among the few women to attend Oxford University the year before the war. When war broke out, her fiancé enlisted in the British army. Brittain later joined the Voluntary Aid Detachment and served as a nurse in Europe and in the Mediterranean. In the following excerpt from her memoir, Testament of Youth, *Brittain writes home to her family from France in 1917, worrying about morale on the home front. She also reflects on women's different and often conflicting duties, and on what the war meant to her as a sheltered girl from a well-to-do family.*

"Conditions . . . certainly seem very bad," I wrote to my family on January 10th [1917] . . . "But do if you can," I implored, "try to carry on without being too despondent and make other people do the same . . . for the great fear in the Army and all its appurtenances out here is not that it will ever give up itself, but that the civil population at home will fail us by losing heart—and so of course morale—just at the most critical time. . . .

This despondency at home was certainly making many of us in France quite alarmed: because we were women we feared perpetually that, just as our work was reaching its climax, our families would need our youth and vitality for their own support. One of my cousins, the daughter of an aunt, had already been summoned home from her canteen work in Boulogne; she was only one of many, for as the War continued to wear out strength and spirits, the middle-aged generation, having irrevocably yielded up its sons, began to lean with increasing weight upon its daughters. . . .

What exhausts women in wartime is not the strenuous and unfamiliar tasks that fall upon them, nor even the hourly dread of death for husbands or lovers or brothers or sons; it is the incessant conflict between personal and national claims which wears out their energy and breaks their spirit. . . .

When I was a girl . . . I imagined that life was individual, one's own affair; that the events happening in the world outside were important enough in their own way, but were personally quite irrelevant. Now, like the rest of my generation, I have had to learn again and again . . . about the invasion of personal preoccupations by the larger destinies of mankind, and at last to recognise that no life is really private, or isolated, or self-sufficient. People's lives were entirely their own, perhaps . . . when the world seemed enormous, and all its comings and goings were slow and deliberate. But this is so no longer, and never will be again, since man's inventions have eliminated so much of distance and time; for better, for worse, we are now each of us part of the surge and swell of great economic and political movements, and whatever we do, as individuals or as nations, deeply affects everyone else.

Vera Brittain, *Testament of Youth: An Autobiographical Study of the Years 1900–1925* (London, New York: Penguin Books, 1989), pp. 401, 422–423, 471–472.

math of the war, governments and employers scurried to send women workers home, in part to give jobs to veterans, in part to deal with male workers' complaints that women were undercutting their wages. Efforts to demobilize women faced real barriers. Many women wage earners —widowed, charged with caring for relatives, or faced with inflation and soaring costs—needed their earnings more than ever. It was also difficult to persuade women workers who had grown accustomed to the relatively higher wages in heavy industry to return to their poorly paid traditional sectors of employment: the textile and garment industries, and domestic service. The demobilization of women after the war, in other words, created as many dilemmas as had their mobilization. Governments passed "natalist" policies to encourage women to go home, marry, and most important, have children. These policies did make maternity benefits—time off, medical care, and some allowances for the poor—available to women for the first time. Nonetheless, birth rates had been falling across Europe by the early twentieth century, and they continued to do so after the war. One upshot of the war was the increased availability of birth control—Marie Stopes (1880–1958) opened a birth-control clinic in London in 1921—and a combination of economic hardships, increased knowledge, and the demand for freedom made men and women more likely to use it. Universal suffrage, and the vote for all adult men and women, and for women in particular, had been one of the most controversial issues in European politics before the war. At the end of the fighting it came in a legislative rush. Britain was first off the mark, granting the vote to all men and women over thirty with the Representation of the People Act in 1918; the United States gave women the vote with the Nineteenth Amendment the following year. Germany's new republic and the Soviet Union did likewise. France was much slower to offer woman suffrage (1945), but did provide rewards and incentives for the national effort.

> The demobilization of women after the war created as many dilemmas as had their mobilization.

MOBILIZING RESOURCES

Along with mobilizing the labor front, the wartime governments had to mobilize men and money. All the belligerent countries had conscription laws before the war, except for Great Britain. Military service was seen as a duty, not an option. Bolstered by overwhelming public support for the war, this belief brought millions of young Europeans into recruitment offices in 1914.

The French began the war with about 4.5 million trained soldiers, but by the end of 1914—just four months into the war—three hundred thousand were dead and six hundred thousand injured. Conscripting citizens and mustering colonial troops became increasingly important. Eventually, France called up 8 million citizens: almost two thirds of Frenchmen aged 18 to 40. In 1916, the British finally introduced conscription, dealing a serious blow to civilian morale; by the summer of 1918, half its army was under nineteen.

Government propaganda, while part of a larger effort to sustain both soldier and civilian morale, was also important to the recruitment effort. From the out-

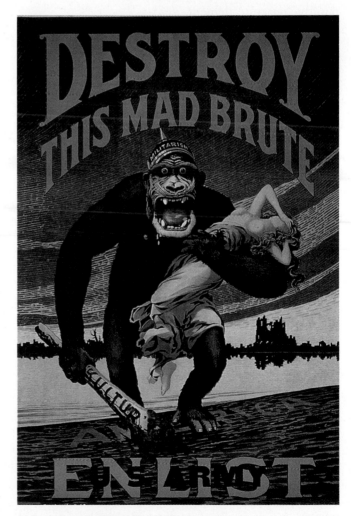

British Propaganda Poster, World War I. The mad beast, meant to represent Germany, with "militarism" on his crown threatens British civilization with a club of "Kultur" (culture). All the warring countries produced similar propaganda.

set, the war had been sold to the people on both sides of the conflict as a moral and virtuous crusade. In 1914, the French president Raymond Poincaré (1913–1920) assured his fellow citizens that France had no other purpose than to stand "before the universe for Liberty, Justice and Reason." Germans were presented with the task of defending their superior *Kultur* against the wicked encirclement policy of the Allied nations: "May God punish England!" was practically a greeting in 1914. By the middle of the war, massive propaganda campaigns were underway. Film, posters, postcards, newspapers—all forms of media proclaimed the strength of the cause, the evil of the enemy, and the absolute necessity of total victory. The success of these campaigns is difficult to determine, but it is clear that they had at least one painful effect—they made it more difficult for any country to accept a fair, non-punitive peace settlement.

Financing the war was another heavy obstacle. Countries had to borrow money, or print more of it. The Allied nations borrowed heavily from the British, who borrowed even more from the United States. American capital flowed across the Atlantic long before the United States entered the war. American economic aid was a decisive factor in the Allies' victory, but it left Britain with a $4.2 billion debt and hobbled the United Kingdom as a financial power after the war. The situation was far more disastrous for Germany, which faced a total economic blockade of money and goods. In an effort to get around this predicament, and lacking an outside source of cash, the German government simply issued more money. The amount of paper money in circulation increased by over 1,000 percent during the war, triggering a devastating rise in inflation. During the war, prices in Germany rose about 400 percent, double the inflation in Britain and France. For middle-class people living on pensions or fixed incomes, soaring prices were a push into poverty.

THE STRAINS OF WAR, 1917

The demands of total war grew increasingly unbearable as the war dragged into 1917. On the front lines, morale fell as war-weary soldiers began to see their commanders' strategy as futile. After the debacle of the Nivelle Offensive, the French army recorded acts of mutiny in two thirds of its divisions; similar resistance arose in nearly all major armies in 1917, if not before. Military leaders portrayed the mutineers as part of a dangerous pacifist movement, but most were nonpolitical. As one soldier put it: "All we wanted was to call

the government's attention to us, make it see that we are men, and not beasts for the slaughterhouse." Resistance within the Germany army was never organized or widespread, but existed in subtler forms. Self-mutilation rescued some soldiers form the horror of the trenches; many more were released because of various emotional disorders. Over six hundred thousand cases of these "war neuroses" were reported among German troops—an indication, if not of intentional disobedience, of the severe physical and psychological trauma that caused the mutinies.

The war's toll also mounted for civilians, who often suffered from the same shortages of basic supplies that afflicted the men on the front. In 1916–1917, the lack of clothing, food, and fuel was aggravated in central

German Poster, 1918. "Collect women's hair that has been combed out. Our industry needs it for drive belts." This poster calls on women to donate their hair, which was used to replace leather and hemp, to the war effort.

Desperation at Home, 1918. A German photograph of women digging through garbage in search of food. The last year of the war brought starvation to cities in Germany and Austria-Hungary, sending many people into the countryside to forage for provisions.

who needed supplies the most—soldiers at the front, workers in the munitions industry, or hungry and cold families.

Like other nations, Germany moved from encouraging citizens to restrain themselves—"those who stuff themselves full, those who push out their paunches in all directions, are traitors to the Fatherland"—to direct control, issuing ration cards in 1915. Britain was the last to institute control, rationing bread only in 1917 when Germany's submarines sank an average of 630,000 tons per month and brought British food reserves within two weeks of starvation level. But rations indicated only what was allowed, not what was available. Hunger continued despite mass bureaucratic control. Governments regulated not only food but also working hours and wages, and unhappy workers directed their anger at the state, adding a political dimension to labor disputes and household needs. The bread lines, filled mainly by women, were flash points of political dissent, petty violence, even large-scale riots. Likewise, the class conflicts of prewar Europe had been briefly muffled by the outbreak of war and mobilization along patriotic lines, but as the war ground on, political tensions reemerged with new intensity. Thousands of strikes erupted throughout Europe, involving millions of frustrated workers. In April of 1917, three hundred thousand in Berlin went on strike to protest ration cuts. In May, a strike of Parisian seamstresses touched off a massive work stoppage that included even white-collar employees and munitions workers. Shipbuilders and steelworkers in Glasgow went on strike as well, and the British government replied by sending armored cars to "Red Glasgow." Stagnation had given way to crisis on both sides.

Europe by abnormally and unbearably cold and wet weather. These strains provoked rising discontent on the home front. Although governments attempted to solve the problem with tighter controls on the economy, their policies often provoked further hostilities from civilians. "The population has lost all confidence in promises from the authorities," a German official reported in 1917, "particularly in view of earlier experiences with promises made in the administration of food."

In urban areas, where undernourishment was worst, people stood in lines for hours to get food and fuel rations that scarcely met their most basic needs. The price of bread and potatoes—still the central staples of working-class meals—soared. Prices were even higher in the thriving black market that emerged in cities. Consumers worried aloud that speculators were hoarding supplies and creating artificial shortages, selling tainted goods, and profiting from others' miseries. They decried the government's "reckless inattention" to families. Governments, however, were concentrated on the war effort and faced difficult decisions about

> The strains of total war and the resulting social upheavals threatened political regimes throughout Europe.

The strains of total war and the resulting social upheavals threatened political regimes throughout Europe. Governments were pushed to their limits. The Russian Revolution, which resulted in the overthrow of the tsar and the rise of Bolshevism, was only the most dramatic response to widespread social problems.

THE RUSSIAN REVOLUTION

How did the Bolsheviks seize power?

The first country to break under the strain of total war was tsarist Russia. The outbreak of war temporarily united Russian society against a common enemy, but Russia's military effort quickly turned sour. All levels of Russian society became disillusioned with Tsar Nicholas II; unable to provide leadership, he nonetheless refused to open government to those who could. The political and social strains of war brought two revolutions in 1917. The first, in February, overthrew the tsar and established a transitional government. The second, in October, was a communist revolution that marked the emergence of the Soviet Union.

WORLD WAR I AND THE FEBRUARY REVOLUTION

Like the other participants in World War I, Russia entered the war with the assumption that it would be over quickly. Autocratic Russia, plagued by internal difficulties before 1914 (see Chapter 25), was unable to sustain the political strains of extended warfare. In all the warring countries success depended on leaders' ability not only to command, but also to maintain social and political cooperation. Tsar Nicholas II's political authority had been shaky for many years, severely undermined by his unpopular actions following the October Revolution of 1905 and his efforts to erode the minimal political power he had grudgingly granted to the Duma, Russia's parliament. Corruption in the royal court further tarnished the tsar's image. The best Nicholas' supporters could say about him was that he was morally upright and devoted to his family. Once war broke out the tsar insisted on personally commanding Russian troops, leaving the government in the hands of his court, especially his wife Alexandra and her eccentric spiritual mentor and faith healer, Grigorii Rasputin (1872?–1916). Rasputin won the tsarina's sympathy by treating her hemophiliac son, and he used his influence to operate corrupt and self-aggrandizing schemes. His presence only added to the image of a court mired in decadence, incompetent to face the modern world.

In 1914 the Russians advanced against the Austrians into Galicia in the south, but during 1915 Russia suffered terrible defeats. All of Poland and substantial territory in the Baltics fell to the Germans at the cost of a million Russian casualties. Although the Russian army was the largest in Europe, it was poorly trained and, at the beginning of the war, undersupplied and inadequately equipped. In the first battles of 1914 generals sent soldiers to the front without rifles or shoes, instructing them to scavenge supplies from fallen comrades. By 1915, to the surprise of many, Russia was producing enough food, clothing, and ammunition, but political problems blocked the supply effort. The tsarist government distrusted public initiatives and tried to direct all provisioning itself. Tsarist officials insisted on making crucial decisions about the allocation of supplies without any consultation. Another major offensive in the summer of 1916 brought hope for success, but turned into a humiliating retreat. Demoralized and poorly supplied, the hastily trained peasants in the Russian armies found their will to fight disappearing fast. When word came that the government was requisitioning grain from the countryside to feed the cities, peasants began to desert en masse, returning to their farms to guard their families' holdings. By the end of 1916, a combination of political ineptitude and military defeat brought the Russian state to the verge of collapse.

The same problems that hampered the Russian war effort also crippled the tsar's ability to override domestic discontent and resistance. As the war dragged on, the government faced not only liberal opposition in the Duma, soldiers unwilling to fight, and an increasingly militant labor movement, but also a rebellious urban population. City dwellers were impatient with inflation and shortages of food and fuel. In February 1917, these forces came together in Petrograd (now St. Petersburg). The revolt began on International Women's Day, February 23, an occasion for a loosely organized march of women—workers, mothers, wives, and consumers—demanding food, fuel, and political reform. The march was the latest in a wave of demonstrations and strikes that had swept through the country during the winter months. This time, within a few days the unrest spiraled into a mass strike of three hun-

> The Russian army was the largest in Europe, but it was poorly trained and, at the beginning of the war, undersupplied and inadequately equipped.

dred thousand people. Nicholas II sent in police and military forces to quell the disorder. When nearly sixty thousand troops in Petrograd mutinied and joined the revolt, what was left of the tsar's power evaporated. Nicholas II abdicated the throne on March 2. This abrupt decision brought a century-long struggle over Russian autocracy to a sudden end.

After the overthrow of the tsar, two parallel centers of power emerged. Each had its own objectives and policies. The first was the provisional government, organized by leaders in the Duma and composed mainly of middle-class liberals. The new government hoped to establish a democratic system under constitutional rule. Its main task was to set up a national election for a constituent assembly, and it also acted to grant and secure civil liberties, release political prisoners, and redirect power into the hands of local officials. The other center of power lay with the *soviets*, a Russian term for local councils elected by workers and soldiers. Since 1905, socialists had been active in organizing these councils, which claimed to be the true democratic representatives of the people. A Soviet, organized during the 1905 revolution and led by the well-known socialist Leon Trotsky, reemerged after February 1917 and asserted claim to be the legitimate political power in Russia. The increasingly powerful soviets pressed for social reform, the redistribution of land, and a negotiated settlement with Germany and Austria. Yet the provisional government refused to concede military defeat and desert the Allies. Continuing the war effort made domestic reform impossible and cost valuable popular support. More fighting during 1917 was just as disastrous as before and this time the provisional government paid the price. By the autumn desertion in the army was rampant, administering the country was nearly impossible, and Russian politics balanced on the edge of chaos.

THE BOLSHEVIKS AND THE OCTOBER REVOLUTION

The Bolsheviks, a branch of the Russian social democratic movement, had little to do with the events of February 1917. Over the course of the next seven months, however, they became enough of a force to overthrow the provisional government. The chain of

events leading to the October revolution surprised most contemporary observers, including the Bolsheviks themselves. Marxism had been quite weak in late-nineteenth-century Russia, although it made small but rapid inroads during the 1880s and 1890s. In 1903 the leadership of the Russian Social Democrats split over revolutionary strategy and the steps to socialism. One group, which won a temporary majority (and chose to call itself the Bolsheviks, or "members of the majority"), favored a centralized party of active revolutionaries. They believed that revolution alone would lead directly to a socialist regime. The Mensheviks ("members of the minority"), like most European socialists, wanted to move toward socialism gradually, supporting "bourgeois" or liberal revolution in the short term. The Mensheviks regained control of the party, but the Bolshevik splinter party survived under the leadership of the young, dedicated revolutionary Vladimir Ilyich Ulyanov, who adopted the pseudonym Lenin.

Lenin was a member of the middle class; his father had been an inspector of schools and a minor political functionary. Lenin himself had been expelled from university for engaging in radical activity after his elder brother was executed for being involved in a plot to assassinate Tsar Alexander III. Lenin spent three years as a political prisoner in Siberia. After that, from 1900 until 1917, he lived and wrote as an exile in western Europe.

Lenin believed that the development of Russian capitalism made socialist revolution possible. To bring revolution, he argued, the Bolsheviks needed to organize on behalf of the new class of industrial workers. Without the party's disciplined leadership, Russia's factory workers could not accomplish the change on the necessary scale. Lenin's Bolsheviks remained a minority among Social Democrats well into 1917. But their dedication to the singular goal of revolution, and their tight, almost conspiratorial organization gave them tactical advantages over larger and more loosely organized opposition parties. The Bolsheviks merged a peculiarly Russian tradition of revolutionary zeal with Western Marxism and endowed the mix with a sense that their goals could be achieved immediately. Lenin and his followers created a party capable of seizing the moment that history presented when the tsar left the scene.

Throughout 1917 the Bolsheviks consistently

The Bolsheviks merged a peculiarly Russian tradition of revolutionary zeal with Western Marxism, seizing the moment that history presented when the tsar left the scene.

TOWARD THE OCTOBER REVOLUTION: LENIN TO THE BOLSHEVIKS

In the fall of 1917, Lenin was virtually the only Bolshevik leader who believed that an insurrection should be launched immediately. As the Provisional Government faltered, he attempted to convince his fellow Bolsheviks that the time for revolution had arrived.

Having obtained a majority in the Soviets of Workers' and Soldiers' Deputies of both capitals, the Bolsheviks can and *must* take power into their hands.

They can do so because the active majority of the revolutionary elements of the people of both capitals is sufficient to attract the masses, to overcome the resistance of the adversary, to vanquish him, to conquer power and to retain it. For, in offering immediately a democratic peace, in giving the land immediately to the peasants, in re-establishing the democratic institutions and liberties which have been mangled and crushed by Kerensky [leader of the provisional government], the Bolsheviks will form a government which *nobody* will overthrow. . . .

The majority of the people is *with* us. . . .the majority in the Soviets of the capitals is the *result* of the people's progress *to our side*. The vacillation of the Socialist-Revolutionaries and Mensheviks . . . is proof of the same thing . . .

To "wait" for the Constituent Assembly would be wrong. . . . Only our party, having assumed power, can secure the convocation of the Constituent Assembly; and, after assuming power, it could blame the other parties for delaying it and could substantiate its accusations. . . .

It would be naive to wait for a 'formal' majority on the side of the Bolsheviks; no revolution ever waits for *this* . . . History will not forgive us if we do not assume power now.

No apparatus? There is an apparatus: the Soviets and democratic organisations. The international situation *just now,* on the *eve* of a separate peace between the English and the Germans, is *in our favour*. It is precisely now that to offer peace to the peoples means to *win*.

Assume power *at once* in Moscow and in Petrograd . . .; we will win *absolutely and unquestionably*.

Lenin, *Bol'sheviki dolzhny vzyat'vlast'* (The Bolsheviks Must Seize Power), 12–14 (25–7) September 1917, PSS, vol. 34, pp. 239, 240, 241–2. From Richard Sakwa, *The Rise and Fall of the Soviet Union, 1917–1991* (New York and London: Routledge, 1999), p. 45.

---

demanded an end to the war, improvement in working and living conditions for workers, and redistribution of aristocratic land to the peasantry. Popular discontent with the provisional government shot up after the government's disastrous military offensives against the Germans. The provisional government tried to enlist a conservative military leader, General Kornilov, to bring order to Petrograd by military force. While the provisional government struggled to hold together the Russian war effort, Lenin led the Bolsheviks on a bolder course, shunning any collaboration with the "bourgeois" government and condemning its imperialist war policies. Even most Bolsheviks considered Lenin's approach too radical. Yet as conditions in Russia deteriorated, his uncompromising calls for "Peace, Land, and Bread, Now" and "All Power to the Soviets,"

Street fighting in St. Petersburg, summer 1917.

Russian soldiers join the Bolsheviks in front of the Winter Palace, fall 1917.

ernment on October 24–25, 1917. On October 25, Lenin appeared from hiding to announce to a stunned meeting of Soviet representatives that "all power had passed to the Soviets." The head of the provisional government fled to rally support at the front lines, and the Bolsheviks took over the Winter Palace, the seat of the provisional government. The initial stage of the revolution was quick and relatively bloodless. In fact, many observers believed they had seen nothing more than a coup d'état, one that might quickly be reversed. Life in Petrograd went on as normal.

The Bolsheviks took the opportunity as they found it and rapidly consolidated their position. First, they moved against all political competition, beginning with the soviets. They immediately expelled parties that disagreed with their actions, creating a new government in the soviets comprised entirely of Bolsheviks. Trotsky, sneering at moderate socialists who walked out protesting what they saw as an illegal seizure of power, scoffed: "You are a mere handful, miserable, bankrupt; your role is finished, and you may go where you belong—to the garbage heap of history." The Bolsheviks did follow through on the provisional government's promise to elect a Constituent Assembly. But when they did not win a majority in the elections, they dispersed the Assembly by force. From that point on, Lenin's Bolsheviks ruled socialist Russia, and later the Soviet Union, as a one-party dictatorship.

won the Bolsheviks support from workers, soldiers, and peasants. As many ordinary people saw it, the other parties could not govern, win the war, or achieve an honorable peace. While unemployment continued to climb, and starvation and chaos reigned in the cities, the Bolsheviks' power and credibility was rising fast.

In October 1917, Lenin convinced his party to act. He goaded Trotsky, better known among workers, into organizing a Bolshevik attack on the provisional gov-

In the countryside, the new Bolshevik regime did little more than ratify a revolution that had been going on since the summer of 1917. When peasant soldiers on the front heard that a revolution had occurred, they streamed home to take land they had worked for generations and believed was rightfully theirs. The provisional government had set up commissions to deal, deliberately, with the legal issues surrounding the redistribution of land, a process that threatened to become as complex as the emancipation of the serfs in 1861. The Bolsheviks simply approved the spontaneous redistribution of the nobles' land to peasants without compensation to former owners. They nationalized banks and gave workers control of factories.

Most important, the new government immediately took Russia out of the war. They negotiated a separate treaty with Germany, signed at Brest-Litovsk in March 1918. The Bolsheviks surrendered vast Russian territories: the rich agricultural region of Ukraine, Georgia, Finland, Russia's Polish territ-ories, the Baltic states, and more. However humiliating, the treaty ended Russia's role in the fighting and saved the fledgling communist regime from almost certain military defeat at the hands of the Germans. The treaty enraged Lenin's political enemies, both moderates and reactionaries, who were still a force to be reckoned with—and who were prepared to wage a civil war rather than accept the revolution. Withdrawing from Europe's war only plunged the country into a vicious civil conflict (see Chapter 28).

Russian autocracy had fended off opposition for the better part of a century. After a long struggle, the regime, weakened by the war, collapsed with little resistance. By the middle of 1917, Russia was not suffering a crisis of government, but rather an absence of government. In June, at the First All-Russian Congress of Soviets a prominent Menshevik declared, "At the present moment, there is not a political party in Russia that would say: Hand the power over to us, resign, and we will take your place. Such a party does not exist in Russia." Lenin shouted back from the audience, "It does exist!" Indeed, seizing power was easy for the Bolsheviks, but building the new state proved vastly more difficult.

John Reed, an American journalist covering the Russian Revolution, called the events of October "ten days that shook the world." What had been shaken? First, the Allies, for the revolution allowed the Germans to win the war on Eastern Front. Second, conservative governments, who in the aftermath of the war worried about a wave of revolution sweeping away other regimes. Third, the expectations of many socialists, startled to see a socialist regime gain and hold power in what many considered a backward country. Over the long run, 1917 was to the twentieth century

what the French Revolution had been to the nineteenth century. It was a political transformation, it set the agenda for future revolutionary struggles, and it created the frames of mind on the right and the left for the century that followed.

THE ROAD TO GERMAN DEFEAT, 1918

How did the Allies win the war?

Russia's withdrawal dealt an immediate strategic and psychological blow to the Allies. Germany could soothe domestic discontent by claiming victory on the Eastern Front, and it could now concentrate its entire army in the west. The Allies feared that Germany would win the war before the United States, which entered the conflict in April 1917, could make a difference. It almost happened. With striking results, Germany shifted its offensive strategy to infiltration by small groups under flexible command. On March 21, Germany initiated a major assault on the west and quickly broke through the Allied lines. The British were hit hardest. Some units, surrounded, fought to the death with bayonets and grenades, but most recognized their plight and surrendered, putting tens of thousands of prisoners in German hands. The British were in retreat everywhere and their commander, Sir Douglas Haig, issued a famous order warning that British troops "now fight with our backs to the wall." The Germans advanced to within fifty miles of Paris by early April. Yet the British—and especially troops from the overseas empire—did just as they were asked and stemmed the tide. As German forces turned southeast instead the French, who had refused to participate in the foolish attacks "over the top," showed stubborn courage on the defensive bogged down in heat, mud, and casualties. It had been a last great try by the well-organized German army; exhausted, they now waited for the Allies to mount their own attack.

When it came in July and August, the Allied counterattack was devastating and quickly gathered steam. New offensive techniques had finally materialized.

> However humiliating, the treaty of Brest-Litovsk saved the fledgling communist regime from almost certain military defeat at the hands of the Germans.

The Allies improved their use of tanks and the "creeping barrage," in which infantry marched close behind a rolling wall of shells to overwhelm their targets. In another of the war's ironies these new tactics were pioneered by the conservative British, who launched a crushing counterattack in July, relying on the survivors of the armies of the Somme reinforced by troops from Australia, Canada, and India. The French made use of the burgeoning numbers of American troops, whose generals attacked the Germans with the same harrowing indifference to casualties shown in 1914. Despite their lack of experience the American troops were tough and resilient. When combined with more experienced French and Australian forces, they punched several large holes through German lines, crossing into the "lost provinces" of Alsace and Lorraine by October. At the beginning of November, the sweeping British offensive had joined up with the small Belgian army and was pressing towards Brussels.

The Allies' material advantage had finally come to bear on the Germans, who were suffering acutely by the spring of 1918. This was not only because of the continued effectiveness of the Allied blockade, but also because of growing domestic conflict over war aims. On the front lines, German soldiers were exhausted, their morale crumbling. German troops faced one shattering blow after another, forcing them deep into Belgium. Popular discontent mounted, and the government, which was now largely in the hands of the military, seemed unable either to win the war or to meet basic household needs.

Germany's network of allies was also coming undone. By the end of September, the Central Powers were headed for defeat. In the Middle East, Allenby's army, which combined Bedouin guerrillas, Indian sepoys, Scottish highlanders, and Australian light cavalry, decisively defeated Ottoman forces in Syria and Iraq. In the Balkans, France's capable battlefield commander, Louis Franchet d'Esperey (1914–1921), completely reorganized the Allied war effort. He transformed the Allied expedition that had been sent to Greece and with the help of sympathetic Greek politicians drew Greece into the war. The results were remarkable. In September, a three-week offensive by the Greek and Allied forces knocked Bulgaria out of the war. Franchet d'Esperey's army, which included many exiled Serbs, pushed on to defeat Austrian forces and a number of exhausted German divisions. Austria-Hungary faced disaster on all sides, collapsing in Italy as well as the Balkans. Czech and Polish representatives in the Austrian government began pressing for self-government. Croat and Serb politicians proposed a "kingdom of Southern Slavs" (soon known as Yugoslavia). When Hungary joined the chorus for independence the emperor, Karl I, accepted reality and sued for peace. The empire that had started the conflict surrendered on November 3, 1918, and disintegrated soon after.

Germany was now left with the impossible task of carrying on the struggle alone. By the fall of 1918, the country was starving and at the verge of civil war. German forces in Belgium stemmed the British attack short of Brussels but were still reeling from French and American attacks to the south. A plan to use the German surface fleet to attack the combined British and American navies only produced a mutiny among German sailors at the start of November. Revolutionary tremors swelled into an earthquake. On November 8 a republic was proclaimed in Bavaria, and the next day nearly all of Germany was in the throes of revolution. The kaiser's abdication was announced in Berlin on November 9; he fled to Holland early the next morning. Control of the German government fell to a provisional council headed by Friedrich Ebert (1912–1923), the socialist leader in the Reichstag. Ebert and his colleagues immediately took steps to negotiate an armistice. The Germans could do nothing but accept the Allies' terms, so at five o'clock in the morning of November 11, 1918, two German delegates met with the Allied army commander in the Compiègne forest and signed papers officially ending the war. Six hours later the order "cease fire" was given across the Western Front. That night thousands of people danced through the streets of London, Paris, and Rome, engulfed in a different delirium from that four years before, a joyous burst of exhausted relief.

THE UNITED STATES AS A WORLD POWER

The final turning point of the war had been the entry of the United States in April 1917. Although America had supported the Allies financially throughout the war, its official intervention undeniably tipped the scales. The United States created a fast and efficient wartime bureaucracy, instituting conscription in May 1917. Ten million men were registered, and by the next year, three hundred thousand soldiers a month were being shipped "over there." Large amounts of food and supplies also crossed the Atlantic, under the armed protection of the U.S. Navy. This system of convoys effectively neutralized the threat of German submarines to Allied merchant ships: the number of ships sunk fell from 25 to 4 percent. America's entry—though not immediately decisive—gave an immediate, colossal boost to British and French morale, while nearly crushing Germany's.

The direct cause of America's entry into the war was the German U-boat. Germany had gambled that unrestricted submarine warfare would cripple Britain's supply lines and win the war. But by attacking neutral and unarmed American ships, Germany only provoked an opponent it could not afford to fight. Germany correctly suspected that the British were clandestinely receiving war supplies from U.S. passenger ships; and on February 1, 1917, the kaiser's ministers announced that they would sink all ships on sight, without warning. The American public was further outraged by an intercepted telegram from Germany's foreign minister, Arthur Zimmerman (1916–1917), stating that Germany would support a Mexican attempt to capture American territory if the United States entered the war. The United States cut off diplomatic relations with Berlin, and on April 6 President Woodrow Wilson (1913–1921) requested and received a declaration of war by Congress.

Wilson vowed that America would fight to "make the world safe for democracy," to banish autocracy and

> America's primary interest was maintaining the international balance of power.

militarism, and to establish a league or society of nations in place of the old diplomatic maneuvering. The Americans' primary interest was maintaining the international balance of power. For years, U.S. diplomats and military leaders believed that American security depended on the equilibrium of strength in Europe. As long as Britain could prevent any one nation from achieving supremacy on the Continent, the United States was safe. But now Germany threatened not only the British navy—which had come be seen as the shield of American security—but also the international balance of power. American involvement stemmed those threats in 1918, but the monumental task of establishing peace still lay ahead.

THE PEACE SETTLEMENT

Making peace was a tenuous process, complicated by the conflicting ambitions and interests of the victor nations. Negotiations were held in Paris in 1919 and 1920. In all, five separate treaties were signed, one with each of the defeated nations: Germany, Austria, Hungary, Turkey, and Bulgaria. (The settlement with Germany was called the Treaty of Versailles, after the town in which it was signed.) The peace conference involved representatives from many nations, including small, newly formed states and even non-European ones. Yet both the conference and the treaties were controlled almost entirely by the so-called Big Four: the U.S. president Woodrow Wilson (1913–1921), the British prime minister David Lloyd George (1916–1922), the French premier Georges Clemenceau (1917–1920), and the Italian premier Vittorio Orlando (1917–1919).

The peace progress began in a spirit of idealism, expressed in Wilson's widelypublicized Fourteen Points, which he had promoted as the foundation of a permanent peace. Based on the principle of "open covenants of peace, openly arrived at," Wilson's plan called for an end to secret diplomacy, freedom of the seas, removal of international tariffs, and reduction of national armaments "to the lowest point consistent with safety." It also called for the "self-determination of peoples" and for the establishment of a League of Nations to settle international conflicts. Thousands of copies of the Fourteen Points had been scattered by Allied planes over the German trenches and behind the lines in an attempt to convince both soldiers and civilians that the Allied nations were striving for a just and durable peace.

CHRONOLOGY

MAJOR EVENTS OF WORLD WAR I AND ITS AFTERMATH, 1914–1920

Battle of the Marne	September 1914
Gallipoli campaign	April–December 1915
Sinking of the *Lusitania*	May 1915
Battle of Verdun	February–July 1916
Battle of the Somme	July–November 1916
Russian Revolution:	
Tsar Nicholas II overthrown	February 1917
Communist Revolution	October 1917
Treaty of Brest-Litovsk	March 1918
Russian Civil War	1918–1920
United States enters the war	April 1917
Final offensives	March–November 1918
Germany surrenders	November 11, 1918
Paris negotiations	1919–1920

Crowds Greet President Wilson in Paris after the War. Despite public demonstrations of this sort, Wilson's attempt to shape the peace was a failure.

of East Prussia was cut off from the rest of its territory. The port of Danzig, with a majority German population, was put under the administrative control of the League of Nations and the economic domination of Poland. Germany was also disarmed. It was forbidden to build an air force, while its navy was reduced to a token force to match an army capped at the strength of one hundred thousand volunteers. To protect France and Belgium, all German soldiers and fortifications were to be removed from the Rhine valley.

The most important part of the Versailles treaty, and the part most at odds with Wilson's original plan, was the "war-guilt" provision in Article 231. Versailles held Germany and its allies responsible for the loss and damage suffered by the Allied governments and their citizens "as a consequence of the war imposed upon them by the aggression of Germany and her allies." Germany would be forced to pay reparations on a crippling scale. The exact amount was left to a Reparations Commission, which set the total at $33 billion in 1921. These harsh demands were deeply resented by Germans, but others outside Germany also warned of the dangers of punitive reparations. In *The Economic Consequences of the Peace*, the noted British economist John Maynard Keynes (1883–1946) argued that reparations would doom Europe's most important task: repairing the world economy.

The negotiations, however, followed other dictates. Throughout the war, Allied propaganda led soldiers and civilians to believe that their sacrifices to the war effort would be compensated by payments extracted from the enemy; total war demanded total victory. Lloyd George had campaigned during the British election of 1918 on the slogan "Hang the Kaiser!" Clemenceau had twice in his long lifetime seen France invaded and its existence imperiled. With the tables turned, he believed that the French should take full advantage of their opportunity to place Germany under strict control. The devastation of the war, and the fiction that Germany could be made to pay for it, made comprise impossible. The settlement with Germany reflected this desire for punishment.

The Versailles treaty required Germany to surrender the "lost provinces" of Alsace and Lorraine to France, and to give up territories in the north to Denmark and a large part of Prussia to the new state of Poland. The treaty gave Germany's coal mines in the Saar basin to France for fifteen years, at which point the German government could buy them back. Germany's province

The most important part of the Treaty of Versailles was the "war-guilt" provision.

The treaties signed by the other Central Powers were based partly on the Allies' strategic interests, but also on the principle of national self-determination. The experience of the prewar years convinced leaders that they should draw nations' boundaries to conform to the ethnic, linguistic, and historical traditions of the people they were to contain. This combined with Wilson's idealism about freedom and equal representation, and seemed sensible to most factions at Versailles. It was more difficult to accomplish in practice. National boundaries did not follow ethnic divisions; they were created according to political

TERRITORIAL CHANGES IN EUROPE AND THE NEAR EAST AFTER WORLD WAR I

Note the changes in geography as a result of World War I. What areas were most affected by the changes within Europe, and why? What geographical problems were solved after the war? Can you see any obvious difficulties created by the redrawing of the map of Europe? What historical circumstances and/or new threats guided the victors to create such geopolitical anomalies?

Map labels

Legend:
- 1914 boundaries
- New boundaries as a result of postwar treaties
- To Great Britain
- To France
- To Italy
- To Rumania
- To Denmark
- To Yugoslavia (Serbia and Montenegro)
- To Belgium
- To Greece
- Became independent

GREENLAND

ICELAND

ARCTIC OCEAN

ATLANTIC OCEAN

FAEROES (Denmark)

SHETLANDS

ORKNEYS

HEBRIDES

UNITED KINGDOM
- Dublin
- London

NORTH SEA

NORWAY
- Christiania

SWEDEN
- Stockholm

FINLAND
- Helsinki

SOVIET RUSSIA
- Archangel
- Leningrad
- Lake Ladoga
- Moscow
- Kazan
- Samara
- Stalingrad
- Kiev
- Odessa
- Volga R.
- Don R.

ARAL SEA

CASPIAN SEA

ESTONIA
- Tallinn

LATVIA
- Riga

LITHUANIA
- Kaunas

GOTLAND

BALTIC SEA

DENMARK
- Copenhagen

NETHERLANDS
- Amsterdam

BELGIUM
- Brussels

GERMANY
- Berlin

EAST PRUSSIA
- Danzig

POLAND
- Warsaw
- Brest-Litovsk

CZECHOSLOVAKIA
- Prague

AUSTRIA
- Vienna

HUNGARY
- Budapest

RUMANIA
- Bucharest

YUGOSLAVIA
- Belgrade

SERBIA

MONTENEGRO

BULGARIA
- Sofia

ALBANIA
- Tirana

GREECE
- Athens

TURKEY
- Ankara
- Constantinople

BLACK SEA

LUX

SWITZ
- Berne

FRANCE
- Paris

LORRAINE

ALSACE

Rhine R.

ITALY
- Rome

CORSICA (Fr.)

SARDINIA (It.)

SICILY (It.)

CRETE (Gr.)

DODECANESE IS. (It.)

CYPRUS (U.K.)

MEDITERRANEAN SEA

SPAIN
- Madrid

PORTUGAL
- Lisbon

BALEARIC IS. (Sp.)

MOROCCO
- Rabat
- Tangier

ALGERIA
- Algiers

TUNISIA
- Tunis

LIBYA
- Tripoli

SPANISH SAHARA

PERSIA

ARMENIA
- Tifis

SYRIA
- Damascus
- Beirut

LEBANON

PALESTINE
- Jerusalem

TRANS-JORDAN

IRAQ
- Mosul
- Tigris R.
- Euphrates R.

KUWAIT

Persian Gulf

ARABIA

RED SEA

EGYPT
- Cairo
- Alexandria

Suez Canal

Nile R.

Scale:
0   250   500 Miles
0   250   500 Kilometers

dictates of the moment. The frustrated expectations of eastern and central European nationalists, combined with other factors, would produce dangerous challenges to European stability during the 1930s.

The treaties also reflected European ambitions to shore up, or even expand, their overseas empires. The settlement with Turkey marked the end of the Ottoman empire. It also created an opportunity for Allied leaders to haggle over the spoils of the dismantled state. It did not, however, create the truly independent kingdoms that Bedouin leaders had hoped for during the war. Accompanied by their advocate T. E. Lawrence, the emirs attended the Versailles conference and listened as their independence was circumscribed. Choice pieces of land were divided up as "mandates" held by Britain and France. Lawrence was bitterly disillusioned. The more pragmatic emirs began to turn these new colonial commitments to their advantage by playing Britain and France off one another. The peoples of the Allies' already existing colonies were less fortunate. Ho Chi Minh, a young student from Indochina attending a Parisian University, was one of many colonial activists who attended the conference to protest conditions in the colonies, and to ask that the rights of nations be extended to their homelands. Well-organized deputations from French West Africa and the Congress Party of India, who favored dominion status in return for the wartime efforts of millions of sepoys who had fought for the British Empire, were also snubbed. Although the European powers spoke about reforming colonial rule, little was done. Many nationalists in the colonies who had favored moderate, legislative change decided that active struggle might be the only answer to the injustices of colonialism.

The end of the Ottoman empire also produced two other results: the creation of the modern Turkish state, and a new set of systems for British and French colonial rule. As territories were taken from the Ottomans, Greece chose to seize some by force. The effort was successful at first but the Turks counterattacked, driving out Greek forces by 1923 and creating the modern state of Turkey under the charismatic leadership of General Mustafa Kemal Attaturk (1923–1938). Ottoman territories placed under French and British control were part of the colonial "mandate system" that legitimized Europe's dominance over territories in the Middle East, Africa, and the Pacific. Territories were officially placed under the supervision of the League of Nations and divided into groups on the basis of their location and level of development.

Incorporated in each of the five peace treaties was the Covenant of the League of Nations, an organization envisioned as the arbiter of world peace but that never achieved the idealistic aims of its founders. The League was handicapped from the start by a number of changes to its original design. The arms-reduction requirement was watered down, and the League's power to enforce it almost nonexistent. Japan would not join unless it was allowed to keep former German concessions in China. France demanded that both Germany and Russia be excluded from the League, which contradicted Wilson's goals but had already been legitimized by the Paris peace conference, where neither Soviet Russia nor the defeated Central Powers were allowed at the table. The League received an even more debilitating blow when the United States Congress, citing the long-standing national preference for isolation, refused to approve U.S. membership of the League. Hobbled from the start, the international organization had little potential to avert conflicts. Indeed, the League of Nations' failures originated in, and reflected, the larger problems of power politics that emerged after the war.

The League of Nations' failures originated in the larger problems of power politics that emerged after the war.

CONCLUSION

Europe fought the First World War on every front possible—military, political, social, and economic. Consequently, the war's effects extended far beyond the devastated landscapes of the Western Front. Statistics can only hint at the enormous loss of human life: of the 70 million men who were mobilized, nearly 9 million were killed. Russia, Germany, France, and Hungary recorded the highest number of deaths, but the smaller countries of southeast Europe had the highest percentages of soldiers killed. Almost 40 percent of Serbia's soldiers died in battle. With the addition of war-related deaths cause by privation and disease, Serbia lost 15 percent of its population. In comparison, Britain, France, and Germany lost only 2 to 3 percent of their populations. But the percentages are much more telling if we focus on the young men of the war generation. Germany lost one third of men aged 19–22 in 1914. France and Britain sustained similar losses, with mortality among young men reaching eight to ten times the normal rate. This was the "lost generation."

The war planted seeds of political and social discontent around the globe. Relations between Russia and western Europe grew sour and suspicious. The Allies had attempted to overthrow the Bolsheviks during the war and had excluded them from the negotiations afterward; these actions instilled the Soviets with a mistrust of the West that lasted for generations. The Allied nations feared that Russia would dominate the new states of eastern Europe, building a "Red Bridge" across the continent. Elsewhere, the conflicting demands of colonialism and nationalism struck only a temporary balance, while the redrawn maps left ethnic and linguistic minorities in every country. The fires of discontent raged most fiercely in Germany, where the Treaty of Versailles was decried as outrageously unjust. Nearly all national governments agreed that it would have to be revised. Neither war nor peace had ended the rivalries that caused the First World War.

The war also had powerful and permanent economic consequences. Beset by inflation, debt, and the difficult task of industrial rebuilding, Europe found itself displaced from the center of the world economy. The war had accelerated the decentralization of money and markets. Many Asian, African, and South American nations benefited financially as their economies became less dependent on Europe, and they were better able to profit from Europeans' needs for their natural resources. The United States and Japan reaped the biggest gains and emerged leaders in the new world economy. Europe was chronically unable to restore the relative economic stability that existed before the war.

In social and political terms, the war's most potent legacy was death. Its most powerful cultural legacy was disillusionment. A generation of men had been sacrificed to no apparent end. Surviving soldiers—many of them permanently injured, both physically and psychologically—were sickened by the useless slaughter they had participated in. They were disgusted by the greedy abandonment of principles by the politicians at Versailles. In the postwar period many younger men and women mistrusted the "old men" who had dragged the world into the war. These feelings of loss and alienation were voiced in the vastly popular genre of "war literature," memoirs and fiction that commemorated the experience of soldiers on the front lines. The German writer and ex-soldier Erich Maria Remarque captured the disillusion of a generation of his novel *All Quiet on the Western Front*: "Through the years our business has been killing; —it was our first calling in life. Our knowledge of life is limited to death. What will happen afterwards? And what shall come out of us?"

That was the main question facing postwar Europe. The German novelist Thomas Mann recognized that 1918 had brought "an end of an epoch, revolution and the dawn of a new age," and that he and his fellow Germans were "living in a new and unfamiliar world." The struggle to define this new world would increasingly be conceived in terms of rival ideologies—democracy, communism, and fascism—competing for the future of Europe. The eastern autocracies had fallen with the war, but liberal democracy was soon on the decline as well. While militarism and nationalism remained strong, calls for major social reforms gained force during worldwide depression. Entire populations had been mobilized during the war, and they would remain so afterward—active participants in the age of mass politics. Europe was about to embark on two turbulent decades of rejecting and reinventing its old social and political institutions. As Thomas Masaryk, the first president of newly formed Czechoslovakia, described it, postwar Europe was "a laboratory atop a graveyard."

SELECTED READINGS

Chickering, Roger. *Imperial Germany and the Great War, 1914–1918.* New York, 1998. An excellent new synthesis.

Eksteins, Modris. *Rites of Spring: The Great War and the Birth of the Modern Age.* New York, 1989. Fascinating, though impressionistic, on war, art, and culture.

Ferro, Marc. *The Great War, 1914–1918.* London, 1973. Very concise overview.

Figes, Orlando. *A People's Tragedy: A History of the Russian Revolution.* New York, 1997. Excellent, detailed narrative.

Fischer, Fritz. *War of Illusions.* New York, 1975. Deals with Germany within the context of internal social and economic trends.

Fitzpatrick, Sheila. *The Russian Revolution, 1917–1932.* New York and Oxford, 1982. Concise overview.

Fussell, Paul. *The Great War and Modern Memory.* New York, 1975. A brilliant examination of British intellectuals' attitudes toward the war.

Higonnet, Margaret Randolph, et al., eds. *Behind the Lines: Gender and the Two World Wars.* New Haven, 1987.

Hynes, Samuel. *A War Imagined: The First World War and English Culture.* New York, 1991. The war as perceived on the home front.

Jelavich, Barbara. *History of the Balkans: Twentieth Century.* New York, 1983. Useful for an understanding of the continuing conflict in Eastern Europe.

Joll, James. *The Origins of the First World War.* London, 1984. Comprehensive and very useful.

Keegan, John. *The First World War.* London, 1998. The best overall military history.

Mazower, Mark. *Dark Continent: Europe's Twentieth Century.* New York, 1999. An excellent new survey, attentive to the Balkans and Eastern Europe.

Rabinowitch, Alexander. *The Bolsheviks Come to Power.* New York, 1976. A well-researched and carefully documented account.

Roberts, Mary Louise. *Civilization without Sexes: Reconstructing Gender in Postwar France, 1917–1927.* Chicago, 1994. A prize-winning study of the issues raised by the "new woman."

Smith, Leonard. *Between Mutiny and Obedience: The Case of the French Fifth Infantry Division During World War I.* Princeton, N.J., 1994. An account of mutiny and the reasons behind it.

Stites, Richard. *Revolutionary Dreams: Utopian Visions and Experimental Life in the Russian Revolution.* New York, 1989. The influence of utopian thinking on the revolution.

Williams, John. *The Home Fronts: Britain, France and Germany, 1914–1918.* London, 1972. A survey of life away from the battlefield and the impact of the war on domestic life.

Winter, J. M. *The Experience of World War I.* New York, 1989. Comprehensive illustrated history viewing the war from different perspectives.

Chapter Twenty-Eight

Chapter Contents

Turmoil Between the Wars

THE GREAT WAR TOPPLED four empires and left 9 million dead in its wake. Death reached across borders, ideologies, classes, and generations; it touched ancient mansions, industrial cities, towns, and farmsteads across Europe and its overseas dominions. It destroyed lives and futures, shook cherished standards and pillars of stability, and produced haunting revelations of brutality. Coming to terms with the war's incalculable losses produced a wide range of reactions, from dogged efforts to return to prewar "normalcy," to cultural experimentation, repudiation of the past, or the splintering of older political regimes and arrangements. From the perspective of the late 1930s, the most striking development of the interwar period was the near collapse of democracy. At that time, few Western democracies remained. Even in those that did, most notably Great Britain, France, and the United States, regimes were frayed by the same pressures and strains that in other countries wrecked democracy entirely.

The reasons for the decline of democracy varied according to particular national circumstances. We can, however, identify some general causes. The foremost was a series of continuing disruptions in the world economy. These were brought about by dislocations that followed in the wake of the First World War and the Versailles reparations settlements, and second, by the Great Depression of 1929–1933. A second source of the crisis of democracy lay in increased social conflict. Across the West, the strains of war deepened long-standing social rifts, and the disappointments of the postwar period created serious polarization. Many expected the peace to bring change. After the sacrifices of the war years, most citizens had been rewarded with the vote. It was far from clear, however, that their votes counted, or that the traditional elites who dominated the economy and seemed to hold the reins of politics had lost any of their power. Broad swaths of the electorate became increasingly attracted to political parties, many of them extremist, that promised to represent their interests. Finally, nationalism, sharpened by the war, provided a key source of discontent in its aftermath. In Italy and Germany, frustrated nationalist sentiment turned against governments. In new countries such as Czechoslovakia,

FOCUS QUESTIONS

- How did the Soviet Union industrialize during the 1930s?
- What were the components of Italian fascism?
- Why did German democracy fail?

- How did the Nazis come to power?
- How did the Western democracies deal with the Great Depression?
- How did the mass media change everyday life?

and across eastern and southern Europe, friction among national minorities posed enormous problems for relatively fragile democratic regimes.

The most dramatic instance of democracy's decline came with the rise of new authoritarian dictatorships, especially in the Soviet Union, Italy, and Germany. As we shall see, the experiences of those three countries differed significantly as a result of varying historical circumstances and personalities. Yet in each case, many citizens allowed themselves to be persuaded that only drastic measures could bring order from chaos. Those measures, including the elimination of parliamentary government, strict restrictions on political freedom, and increasingly virulent repression of the "enemies" of the state were implemented with a combination of violence, intimidation, and propaganda. That so many citizens seemed willing to sacrifice their freedoms was a measure of their alienation, impatience, or desperation.

THE SOVIET UNION UNDER LENIN AND STALIN

How did the Soviet Union industrialize during the 1930s?

THE RUSSIAN CIVIL WAR

The Bolshevik takeover in October of 1917 was only the beginning of revolutionary events in Russia. After signing a separate peace with Germany in March of 1918, the Bolsheviks, under Lenin's leadership, moved to consolidate their internal political power (see pp. 943–46). But the Bolshevik seizure of power and withdrawal from the war polarized Russian society and ignited a civil war that was far more costly than conflict with Germany. The peace treaty galvanized the enemies of the Bolsheviks, especially those associated with the ousted tsarist regime, who began to attack the new government from the periphery of the old empire. Known collectively as "Whites," the Bolsheviks' opponents were a varied lot, only loosely bound by their common goal of removing the "Reds" from power. Their military force came

mainly from supporters of the old regime, including tsarist military officers, reactionary monarchists, the old nobility, and disaffected liberal supporters of the monarchy. The Whites were joined by groups as diverse as liberal supporters of the provisional government, Mensheviks, Social Revolutionaries, and anarchist peasant bands known as "Greens" who opposed all central state power. The Bolsheviks also faced insurrections from strong nationalist movements in some parts of the former Russian empire, including Ukraine, Georgia, and the north Caucasus regions. Finally, several foreign powers, including the United States, Great Britain, and Japan, launched small but threatening interventions on the periphery of the old empire. Outside support for the Whites proved to be an insignificant threat to the Bolsheviks, but it served them as a propaganda device; they claimed that the Whites were trying to assist foreign powers in invading Russia. The intervention also solidified Bolshevik mistrust of the capitalist world powers, which would, in the Marxist view, naturally oppose the existence of the world's first "socialist" state.

The Bolsheviks eventually won the civil war because they gained greater support—or at least tacit acceptance—from the majority of the population, and because they were better organized for the war effort itself. The Bolsheviks quickly mobilized to fight, foregoing many of their radical concerns about egalitarian-

Lenin Speaking to Crowds in Moscow. To the right of the platform, in uniform, is Trotsky.

THE SOVIET UNION, 1918–1945

How did the civil war of 1917–1920 affect the new Soviet state? How did the possession of Moscow and Leningrad (St. Petersburg) aid the Bolsheviks in their victory over the "Whites"? How was Stalin's dictatorship instrumental in modernizing and uniting the Soviet Union's vast and diverse landscape?

Map labels

Legend:
- Area of Russia under Bolshevik (Red) control: 1919
- Area of Russia under anti-Bolshevik (White) control: 1919
- Area lost by Russia, 1914–1921
- White Russian attacks
- Non-Russian attacks
- Movements of Allies

RUSSIAN SOVIET FEDERATIVE SOCIALIST REPUBLIC

ARCTIC OCEAN

SEA OF OKHOTSK

SAKHALIN I.

PACIFIC OCEAN

SEA OF JAPAN

JAPAN

KOREA

MANCHURIA

MONGOLIA

CHINA

SINKIANG

INDIA

AFGHANISTAN

IRAN

IRAQ

SYRIA

TURKEY

Yakutsk

Khabarovsk

Vladivostok

Chita

Lake Baikal

Irkutsk

Ulan-Bator

Krasnoyarsk

Novosibirsk

Omsk

URAL MOUNTAINS

Ob R.

Yenisei R.

Lena R.

Amur R.

Lake Balkhash

Alma-Ata

KAZAKH S.S.R.

ARAL SEA

Tashkent

UZBEK S.S.R.

Frunze

KIRGIZ S.S.R.

TADZHIK S.S.R.

Dushanbe

Ashkabad

TURKMEN S.S.R.

CASPIAN SEA

Baku

AZERBAIDZHAN S.S.R.

Yerevan

ARMENIAN S.S.R.

Tbilisi

GEORGIAN S.S.R.

CAUCASUS MTS.

Pyatigorsk

Novorossisk

Krasnodar

Rostov

BLACK SEA

Odessa

UKRAINIAN S.S.R.

Kiev

MOLDAVIAN S.S.R.

RUMANIA

HUNGARY

CZECHOSLOVAKIA

POLAND

Warsaw

Brest-Litovsk

Danzig

GERMANY

Minsk

BELORUSSIAN S.S.R.

LITHUANIAN S.S.R.

LATVIAN S.S.R.

ESTONIAN S.S.R.

Kronstadt

Leningrad

FINLAND

Helsinki

Gulf of Bothnia

SWEDEN

NORWAY

BALTIC SEA

Murmansk

Archangel

Moscow

Yaroslavl

Ivanovo

Gorki

Volga R.

Kazan

Perm

Sverdlovsk

Chelyabinsk

Orenburg

Kuibyshev

Saratov

Stalingrad

Orenburg

Persian Gulf

1000 Miles

1000 Kilometers

500

500

ism and political self-control in favor of strong bureau-cratic and military structures. Leon Trotsky, the revolutionary hero of 1905 and 1917, became the new commissar of war and created a hierarchical, disciplined military machine that grew to some 5 million men by 1920. Trotsky's Red Army triumphed over White armies by the end of 1920, and then put down the nationalist uprisings on the periphery in 1920–1921. When the conflict was over, the country had suffered some one million combat casualties, several million deaths from hunger and disease caused by the war, and one hundred thousand to three hundred thousand executions of noncombatants as part of Red and White terror. The barbarism of the war engendered permanent hatreds within the emerging Soviet nation, especially among ethnic minorities, and it brutalized the fledgling society that came into existence under the new Bolshevik regime.

The civil war also shaped the Bolsheviks' approach to economic aspects of "socialism." On taking power in 1917, Lenin expected to create, for the short term at least, a state-capitalist system that resembled the successful European wartime economies. The new government took control of large-scale industry, banking, and all other major capital concerns while allowing small-scale private economic activity, including agriculture, to continue. The civil war pushed the new government toward a more radical economic stance known as "war communism." The Bolsheviks began to requisition grain from the peasantry, outlawed private trade in consumer goods as "speculation," militarized production facilities, and abolished money. Most of these innovations were improvised responses to deteriorating economic conditions beyond the regime's control. The idea of war communism, however, was attractive to radical Bolsheviks. Indeed, many believed that war communism would replace the capitalist system that had collapsed in 1917.

Such hopes were largely unfounded. War communism, though it sustained the civil war effort, further disrupted the already war-ravaged economy. The civil war devastated Russian industry and emptied major cities. The population of Moscow fell by 50 percent between 1917 and 1920; that of Kiev by 25 percent. The masses of urban workers, who had strongly supported the Bolshevik revolution, melted back into the countryside; only 1.5 million of the 3.5 million workers employed in major industries before 1917 remained on the job by the end of 1920. Industrial output had

> The civil war shaped the Bolsheviks' approach to economic aspects of "socialism."

fallen by 1920–1921 to only 20 percent of prewar levels. Most devastating were the effects of war communism on agriculture. On the one hand, the civil war had solved the "land question" to the benefit of peasants, who spontaneously seized and redistributed noble lands. By 1919 peasants held almost 97 percent of the land in small plots, generally fewer than twenty acres. Nonetheless, the agricultural system was severely disrupted by the civil war, by the grain requisitioning of War Communism, and by the outlawing of all private trade in grain. Large-scale famine resulted in 1921 and claimed some 5 million lives.

As the civil war came to a close, urban workers and soldiers became increasingly impatient with the Bolshevik regime, which had promised socialism and workers' control but had delivered something more akin to a military dictatorship. Large-scale strikes and protests broke out in late 1920, but the Bolsheviks moved swiftly and effectively to subdue the "popular revolts." In crushing dissent, the Bolshevik regime that emerged from the civil war had made a clear statement that internal competition would not be tolerated.

THE NEP PERIOD

In response to these political and economic difficulties, the Bolsheviks abandoned war communism and in March 1921 embarked on a radically different course known as the New Economic Policy (NEP). The NEP was a reversion to the state capitalism that had been attempted right after the Revolution: the state was to continue to own all major industry and monetary concerns (which Lenin called the "commanding heights" of the economic system), while individuals were to be allowed to own private property, trade freely within limits, and most important, farm their land for their own benefit. Grain requisitioning was replaced by fixed taxes on the peasantry; what peasants grew beyond the tax requirements was theirs to do with as they saw fit. The Bolshevik most identified with the NEP was Nikolai Bukharin (1888–1938), a young and brilliant Marxist theoretician who argued that the Bolsheviks could best industrialize the USSR by taxing private peasant economic activity. Peasants were encouraged to "enrich themselves" so that their taxes could support urban industrialization and the working class. Lenin himself described the NEP as "one step backward in order to take two steps forward."

Lenin and Stalin. Under Stalin this picture was used to show his close relationship with Lenin. In fact, the photograph has been doctored.

The NEP was undeniably successful in allowing Soviet agriculture to recover from the civil war; by 1924 agricultural harvests had returned to prewar levels. It was a prosperous time for peasants—what one historian describes as the "golden age of the Russian peasantry." Peasants were largely left alone to do as they pleased, and they responded by redividing noble lands among themselves to level wealth discrepancies between rich and poor, by reinforcing traditional social structures in the countryside (especially the peasant commune) and by producing enough grain to feed the country, though they continued to use very primitive farming methods to do so. The NEP was less successful, however, in encouraging peasants to participate in markets to benefit urban areas. The Bolsheviks found it difficult in the 1920s to produce manufactured goods cheaply enough to get peasants to trade their grain for them. Peasants responded to these price difficulties by simply abstaining from the market and keeping excess grain for themselves, their livestock, or their illegal moonshine stills. The result was a series of shortages in grain deliveries to cities, a situation that prompted many Bolsheviks to call for revival of the radical economic practices of war communism. The fate of these radical proposals, however, was tied to the fate of the man who would, contrary to all expectations, replace Lenin as the leader of the USSR and become one of the most notorious dictators of all time: Joseph Stalin.

STALIN AND THE "REVOLUTION FROM ABOVE"

The rise of Stalin as undisputed dictator of the USSR was swift and unpredicted. Stalin's political success was cemented in intraparty conflicts in the 1920s, but it was also closely tied to the abrupt end of the NEP period in the late 1920s and the beginning of a massive program of social and economic transformation designed to modernize the still agricultural nation in just a few years. This "revolution from above," as it has come to be called, was the most rapid social and economic transformation any nation has seen in modern history. It was carried out, however, at unprecedented human cost.

Stalin (1879–1953) was a Bolshevik from the Caucasus nation of Georgia; his real name was Iosep Jughashvili. The son of a poor shoemaker, Stalin, at his mother's insistence, originally studied at an Orthodox seminary to become a priest. Rejecting the priesthood, he participated in revolutionary activity in the Caucasus and spent many years in Siberian exile before the Revolution. He was an important member of the Bolshevik party before and during the Russian Revolution. Yet Stalin was not one of the central figures of the early Bolshevik party, and he was certainly not a front runner for party leadership. The question of Lenin's successor arose with the leader's poor health

CHRONOLOGY	
THE EARLY SOVIET UNION, 1917–1929	
Bolsheviks seize power	October 1917
Treaty of Brest-Litovsk	March 1918
Russian civil war	1918–1920
Bolsheviks suppress nationalist rebellions	1920–1921
Launch of the NEP	1921
Lenin dies	1924
Stalin, Trotsky, Bukharin vie for power	1924–1928
Stalin seizes full power	1928–1929

STALIN'S INDUSTRIALIZATION OF THE SOVIET UNION

"THE TASKS OF BUSINESS EXECUTIVES"

Stalin gave the following speech at a Conference of Managers of Socialist Industry in 1931. In his usual style, he invoked fears of Soviet backwardness and Russian nationalism while summoning all to take up the task of industrial production.

It is sometimes asked whether it is not possible to slow down the tempo somewhat, to put a check on the movement. No, comrades, it is not possible! The tempo must not be reduced! On the contrary, we must increase it as much as is within our powers and possibilities. This is dictated to us by our obligations to the workers and peasants of the USSR. This is dictated to us by our obligations to the working class of the whole world.

To slacken the tempo would mean falling behind. And those who fall behind get beaten. But we do not want to be beaten. No, we refuse to be beaten! One feature of the history of old Russia was the continual beatings she suffered because of her backwardness. She was beaten by the Mongol khans. She was beaten by the Turkish beys. . . . She was beaten by the British and French capitalists. She was beaten by the Japanese barons. All beat her—for her backwardness: for military backwardness, for cultural backwardness, for political backwardness, for industrial backwardness, for agricultural backwardness. . . .

We are fifty or a hundred years behind the advanced countries. We must make good this distance in ten years. Either we do it, or we shall be crushed . . . .

In ten years at most we must make good the distance which separates us from the advanced capitalist countries. We have all the 'objective' possibilities for this. The only thing lacking is the ability to take proper advantage of these possibilities. And that depends on us. *Only* on us! . . . It is time to put an end to the rotten policy of non-interference in production. It is time to adopt a new policy, a policy adapted to the present times—the policy of interfering in everything. If you are a factory manager, then interfere in all the affairs of the factory, look into everything, let nothing escape you, learn and learn again. Bolsheviks must master technique. It is time Bolsheviks themselves became experts . . . .

There are no fortresses which Bolsheviks cannot capture. We have assumed power. We have built up a huge socialist industry. We have swung the middle peasants to the path of socialism. . . . What remains to be done is not so much: to study technique, to master science. And when we have done that we will develop a tempo of which we dare not even dream at present.

"The Tasks of Business Executives," speech at the First All-Union Conference of Managers of Socialist Industry, February 4, 1931, in Joseph Stalin, *Problems of Leninism* (New York: International Publishers, c. 1934), pp. 350, 354–5, 355–5, 357–8. As found in Richard Sakwa, *The Rise and Fall of the Soviet Union, 1917–1991* (New York and London: Routledge, 1999), pp. 187–188.

STALIN'S INDUSTRIAL DEVELOPMENT: THE VIEW FROM BELOW

How did the Soviet people experience Stalin's industrialization drive? New archives have helped historians glimpse what the common people lived through and how they responded. The following letters come from several hundred that workers and peasants sent to Soviet newspapers and authorities recounting their experiences and offering their opinions. Both were sent to the Soviet paper Pravda.

It should not be forgotten that many millions of workers are participating in the building of socialism. A horse with its own strength can drag seventy-five poods,[*] but its owner has loaded it with a hundred poods, and in addition he's fed it poorly. No matter how much he uses the whip, it still won't be able to move the cart.

This is also true for the working class. They've loaded it with socialist competition, shock work, over-fulfilling the industrial and financial plan, and so forth. A worker toils seven hours, not ever leaving his post, and this is not all he does. Afterward he sits in meetings or else attends classes for an hour and a half or two in order to increase his skill level, and if he doesn't do these things, then he's doing things at home. And what does he live on? One hundred fifty grams of salted mutton, he will make soup without any of the usual additives, neither carrots, beets, flour, nor salt pork. What kind of soup do you get from this? Mere "dishwater."

—B.N. Kniazev, Tula, Sept. 1930.

Comrade Editor, Please give me an answer. Do the local authorities have the right to forcibly take away the only cow of industrial and office workers? What is more, they demand a receipt showing that the cow was handed over voluntarily and they threaten you by saying if you don't do this, they will put you in prison for failure to fulfill the meat procurement. How can you live when the cooperative distributes only black bread, and at the market goods have the prices of 1919 and 1920? Lice have eaten us to death, and soap is given only to railroad workers. From hunger and filth we have a massive outbreak of spotted fever.

—Anonymous, from
Aktybinsk, Kazakhstan

[*]A pood is a Russian unit of weight, equal to 36.11 pounds.

Lewis Siegelbaum and Andrei Sokolov, *Stalinism as a Way of Life: A Narrative in Documents* (New Haven and London: Yale University Press, 2000), pp. 39–41.

---

after 1922 and his death in 1924, but the civil war hero Leon Trotsky was widely assumed to be the best candidate for Lenin's position. Other top Bolsheviks, however, also exhibited some aspirations for a leading role.

Stalin, though not a brilliant orator like Trotsky or a respected Marxist theoretician like Bukharin, was nonetheless a master political strategist, and he played the game of internal party politics almost without fault after Lenin's death. Stalin sidelined his opponents within the Bolshevik party, many of whom supported the Leninist principle of collective leadership within the top ruling circle, by isolating and expelling each of them successively. Trotsky was the first to go, driven out of top party circles by a coalition of Stalin and others who, ironically, feared Trotsky's desire to take control of the party himself. Stalin then turned on his former allies and removed them in turn, culminating in the removal of Bukharin from the Politburo in 1928–1929.

Stalin's campaign against Bukharin, however, was not just political. It was also connected to Stalin's desire to discard the NEP system and to launch an all-out industrialization drive. By the late 1920s, Stalin had begun to agree with those critics of the NEP who had argued that the USSR could not hope to industrialize by relying on taxes generated from small-scale peasant agriculture. Stalin began to push for an increase in the tempo of industrialization as early as 1927, prompted by fears of "falling behind" the West and by the perceived threat of another world war. Almost all of the top-level Bolshevik leaders supported Stalin's plan to step up the tempo of industrialization. But hardly anybody supported what happened next: an abrupt turn toward forced industrialization and total collectivization of agriculture.

In 1927 a poor harvest (several tons below that of 1926) caused yet another crisis in the grain-collection system. Low prices for agricultural goods and high prices for scarce industrial goods led peasants to hoard grain, resulting in food shortages in cities and difficulties in collecting taxes from the peasantry. In early 1928 Stalin ordered local officials in the distant Urals and Siberian areas, which supposedly had bumper crops but were nonetheless behind in tax payments, to begin requisitioning grain in the civil war style. He soon applied this revival of war communism to the entire country. In 1929 he broke with the NEP completely by announcing the complete collectivization of agriculture. Peasants were to be convinced, by force if necessary, to give up private farmlands and join collective farms. Collective farms were supported by the state, and peasants in them worked, in effect, as employees.

The "liquidation of the kulaks as a class" magnified the disruptive effects of agricultural collectivization, and the two together produced one of the most devastating famines in modern European history.

COLLECTIVIZATION

Collectivization was initially expected to be a gradual process, but by 1929 Stalin decided to promote total collectivization of agriculture within a few months. The process that ensued was brutal and chaotic. Local party and police officials forced peasants to give up their private land, farming implements, and livestock and to join collective farms. Peasants resisted, often violently. There were some sixteen hundred large-scale rebellions in the USSR between 1929 and 1933; some involved several thousand people, and quelling them required military intervention, including the use of artillery. Peasants also resisted collectivization by slaughtering their livestock instead of turning it over to the farms, a loss that hampered agricultural production for years to follow. Sensing a possible crisis, Stalin deftly called the process to a temporary halt in early 1930, but soon thereafter ordered the process to proceed more gradually, and by 1935 collectivization of agriculture was complete in most areas of the USSR.

To facilitate collectivization, Stalin also launched an all-out attack on peasants designated as kulaks (a derogatory term for well-to-do farmers, literally meaning "tight-fisted ones"). Most kulaks, though, were not any better off than their neighbors, and the term was soon used for all peasants hostile to collectivization. Between 1929 and 1933, some 1.5 million peasants were uprooted, dispossessed of their property, and resettled from their farmlands to either inhospitable reaches of the Soviet east and north or to poor farmland closer to

their original homes. The land and possessions of these unfortunate peasants were distributed to collective farms or, just as often, to the local officials and peasants participating the liquidation process. The "liquidation of kulaks as a class" magnified the disruptive effects of agricultural collectivization, and the two together produced one of the most devastating famines in modern European history. Peasants who were forced into collective farms had little incentive to produce extra food, while the exile of the majority of the more productive members of peasant society not surprisingly enfeebled the agricultural system. In 1932–1933, famine spread across the southern region of the Soviet Union. This was the most productive agricultural area in the country, and the famine that struck there was thus particularly senseless. The 1933 famine cost some 3 to 5 million lives and is recorded in history as the only famine in modern times to occur without any natural causes. During the famine, the Bolsheviks maintained substantial grain reserves in other parts of the country, enough to save many hundreds of thousands of lives at a minimum, but they refused to send this grain to the affected areas, preferring instead to seal off famine-stricken regions and allow people to starve. Grain reserves were instead sold overseas for hard currency and stockpiled in case of war. After 1935 there would never again be any large-scale resistance to Soviet power in the countryside. Yet resistance had forced the state to cede small private plots of land to peasant families; this land provided as much as 50 percent of the nation's produce from a tiny fraction of the land.

THE FIVE-YEAR PLANS

In Stalin's view, collectivization provided the resources for the other major aspect of his "revolution from above": a rapid campaign of forced industrialization. The roadmap for this industrialization process was the first Five-Year Plan (1928–1932), an ambitious set of goals that Stalin and his cohorts drew up in 1927 and continued to revise upward. The plan called for truly herculean industrialization efforts, and its results rank as one of the most stunning periods of economic growth the modern world has ever seen. The industrial output of the USSR increased by 50 percent in five years; the annual rate of growth during the first Five-Year Plan was between 15 and 22 percent. This

"The Five-Year Plan in Four Years." Stalin faces down capitalist enemies in this Soviet propaganda poster of the 1930s. The caption translates as "Under the banner of Lenin, we triumphed in the battles of the October Revolution. Under the banner of Lenin, we achieved decisive successes in the battle for the victory of socialist construction. Under this banner, we will triumph in the proletarian revolution in all the world."

rate of growth seemed even more impressive when contrasted with the economic depression that was shaking the foundations of Western economies in the late 1920s and early 1930s. The Bolsheviks built entirely new industries in entirely new cities. The factory town of Magnitogorsk, for example, emerged from absolutely barren, uninhabited steppes in 1927 to become a steel-producing factory town of some two hundred fifty thousand residents in 1933; at least in scale, it rivaled anything that the West had built. The industrialization drive transformed the nation's landscape and population as well. Cities such as Moscow and Leningrad doubled in size in the early 1930s, while new cities sprang up across the USSR. In 1926, only one fifth of the population lived in towns. Fifteen years later, in 1939, roughly a third did. The urban population had grown from 26 million to 56 million in under fifteen years. The USSR was well on its way to becoming an urban, industrial society.

This rapid industrialization came at enormous human cost. Many large-scale projects were carried out with prison labor, especially in the timber and mining industries. The labor camp system, known as the *gulag*, became a central part of the Stalinist economic system. People were arrested and sent to camps for a bewilder-

ing array of reasons, ranging from petty criminal infractions to contact with foreigners to having the ill fortune to be born of bourgeois or kulak parents. The camp system spread throughout the USSR in the 1930s: by the end of the decade, roughly 3.6 million people were incarcerated by the regime. This army of prisoners was used to complete the most arduous and dangerous industrialization tasks, such as the Moscow–White Sea canal. To save money, the canal connecting Moscow to the seaports of the north was constructed without the use of any machinery. It was dug by hand, with human labor used to power everything from conveyor belts to pile drivers. Tens of thousands of individuals lost their lives during construction. One of Stalin's pet projects, it never functioned properly, froze over in winter, and was bombed early in the Second World War.

The economic system created during this "revolution from above" was also fraught with structural problems that would plague the USSR for its entire history. The "command" economy, with each year's production levels entirely planned in advance in Moscow, never functioned in a rational way. Heavy industry was always favored over light industry, and the emphasis on quantity made quality practically meaningless. A factory that was charged with producing a certain number of pairs of shoes, for example, could cut costs by producing all one style and size. The consumer would be left with useless goods, but the producer would fulfill the plan. Stalin's industrialization drive did transform the USSR from an agrarian nation to a world industrial power in the space of a few short years, but in the longer run, the system would become an economic disaster.

The Stalin revolution also produced fundamental cultural and economic changes. The "revolution from above" altered the face of Soviet cities and the working class populating them. New cities were largely made up of first-generation peasants who brought their rural traditions to the cities with them, diluting the fragile urban culture that had existed in the 1920s. Women, too, entered the urban work force in increasing numbers in the 1930s—women went from 20 percent to almost 40 percent of the work force in one decade, and in light industry they made up two thirds of the labor force by 1940.

At the same time, Stalin promoted a sharply conservative shift in all areas of culture and society. In art, the radical modernism of the 1920s was crushed by socialist realism, a deadening aesthetic that celebrated the drive toward "socialism" and left no room for experimentation. Family policy and gender roles underwent a similar reversal. Early Bolshevik activists had promoted a utopian attempt to rebuild one of the basic structures of pre-Revolutionary society—the family—and to create a genuinely new proletarian social structure. The Bolsheviks in the 1920s legalized divorce, expelled the Orthodox Church from marriage ceremonies, and legalized abortion. Stalin abandoned these ideas of communist familial relations in favor of efforts to strengthen traditional family ties: divorce became more difficult, abortion was outlawed in 1936 except in cases that threatened the life of the mother, and homosexuality was declared a criminal offense. State subsidies and support for mothers, which were progressive for the time, could not change the reality that Soviet women were increasingly forced to carry the "double burden" of familial and wage labor to support Stalin's version of "Soviet" society. All areas of Soviet cultural and social policy experienced similar reversals.

THE GREAT TERROR

The apogee of Stalinist repression came with the "Great Terror" of 1937–1938, which left nearly a million people dead and as many as a million and a half more in the labor camps. As Stalin consolidated his personal dictatorship over the country, he eliminated enemies—real and imagined—along with individuals and groups he considered superfluous to the new "Soviet" society. As we have seen, repression was central to the Stalinist system from the early 1930s, yet the years 1937–1938 brought a qualitative and quantitative change—a whirlwind of mass repression unprecedented in scale.

The Terror was aimed at various categories of internal "enemies," from the top to the very bottom of Soviet society. Former and current political elites were perhaps the most visible victims. The top level of the Bolshevik party itself was purged almost completely; some one hundred thousand party members were removed, most facing prison sentences or execution. Many top party officials including Bukharin were condemned at carefully staged show trials and then shot. The purge also struck—with particular ferocity—nonparty elites, industrial managers, and intellectuals. In 1937, Stalin purged the military of people he deemed a potential threat, arresting some forty thousand officers and shooting at least ten thousand among them. These purges disrupted the government and the economy but allowed Stalin to promote a new, young cadre of officials who had no experience in the pre-Stalinist era and who owed their careers, if not their lives, to Stalin personally. Whole ethnic groups were also targeted, including Poles, Ukrainians, Lithuanians, Latvians, Koreans, and others with supposed cross-border ties that, in Stalin's mind, represented a national security threat. From the "bottom," some two hundred to three hundred thousand "dekulakized" peasants, petty criminals, and other social misfits were arrested, and many shot.

The Great Terror remains one of the most puzzling aspects of Stalin's path to dictatorial power. The Terror succeeded, with a certain twisted kind of logic, in solidifying Stalin's personal control over all aspects of social and political life in the USSR, but it did so by destroying the most talented elements in Soviet society. The Terror was to some extent the result of Stalin's personal paranoia, but it was also a fitting end to the "Stalin revolution" that began in 1927–1928 with the end of the NEP.

The results of the Stalin revolution were profound. No other regime in the history of western Europe had ever attempted to reorder completely the politics, economy, and society of a major nation. The Soviets had done so in a mere ten years. By 1939 private manufacturing and trade had been almost entirely abolished. Factories, mines, railroads, and public utilities were exclusively owned by the state. Stores were either government enterprises or cooperatives in which consumers owned shares. Agriculture had been almost completely socialized. The decade saw certain advances as well, especially in the area of social reform. Illiteracy was reduced from at least 50 percent to about 20 percent, and higher education was made available to increasingly large numbers. Government assistance for working mothers and free hospitalization did a great deal to raise the national standard of health. The society that emerged from this terrible

> The Great Terror disrupted the government and the economy but allowed Stalin to promote a new, young cadre of officials who owed their careers, if not their lives, to Stalin personally.

CHRONOLOGY

THE STALINIST REVOLUTION, 1927–1938

Launch of collectivization	1927
Launch of the first Five-Year Plan	1928
Stalin breaks with the NEP	1929
Stalin halts collectivization	1930
Liquidation of the kulaks	1929–1933
The Great Terror	1937–1938

decade was industrial, more urban than rural, and more modern than traditional. But it was a society badly pummeled in the process, one in which the most productive peasants, the most gifted among the intellectuals, and the most experienced among the economic and social elites had been removed from society in the name of total dictatorial power. The USSR that emerged from this tumultuous period would barely be able to withstand the immense strains placed on it when the Germans struck less than three years after the end of the Terror.

THE EMERGENCE OF FASCISM IN ITALY

What were the components of Italian fascism?

Like many European nations, Italy emerged from the First World War as a democracy in distress. Italy was on the winning side and had been among the Big Four nations (with France, Great Britain, and the United States) that put together the postwar settlement. Yet the war had cost Italy nearly seven hundred thousand lives and over $15 billion. These sacrifices were no greater than those of France or Britain but were hard to bear for a much poorer nation. Moreover, Italy had received secret promises of specific territorial gains during the war, only to find those promises withdrawn when they conflicted with principles of self-determination. Italian claims to the west coast of the Adriatic, for instance, were bitterly disputed and in the end denied by Yugoslavia. Italy received most of the Austrian territories it demanded, but many maintained that these were inadequate rewards for

their sacrifices. Groups of militant nationalists seized Fiume, a port city on the Adriatic, and held it for a year before being disbanded by the Italian army. At first the nationalists blamed the "mutilated victory" on President Wilson, but after a short time they turned on their own rulers and what they considered the weaknesses of parliamentary democracy.

Italy had long-standing problems that were made worse by the war. Since unification, the Italian nation had been rent by an unhealthy economic split—divided into a relatively prosperous industrialized north and a extremely poor agrarian south. Social conflict over land, wages, and local power caused friction in the countryside as well as in urban centers. Governments were often seen as corrupt, indecisive, and defeatist. This was the background for the more immediate problems that Italy faced after the war.

Inflation and unemployment were perhaps the most destructive effects of the war. Inflation produced high prices, speculation, and profiteering. And though normally wages would have risen also, the postwar labor market was glutted by returning soldiers. Furthermore, business elites were shaken by strikes, which became increasingly large and frequent, and by the closing of foreign markets. The parliamentary government that was set up after the war failed to ease these dire conditions, and increasingly Italians wanted radical reforms. For the working class, this meant socialism. The Italian socialists embraced a philosophy akin to Bolshevism and voted to join the Third International in 1919. In November of that year, the socialists won about a third of the seats in the Chamber of Deputies. The movement grew increasingly radical: in 1920, the socialist and anarchist workers took over about a hundred factories, most in the metallurgy sector, and tried to run them for the benefit of the workers themselves. In the countryside, most peasants were land poor, and many had no land at all, but instead worked for wages as rural laborers on large estates. Demands for land reform grew increasingly militant. In some rural areas, so-called Red Leagues tried to break up large estates and force landlords to reduce their rents. In all these actions, the model of the Russian revolution, although it was only vaguely understood, encouraged the development of well-rooted, local, radical traditions. In large numbers, voters abandoned the poorly organized parties of the center and the moderate left. They supported two more radical groups: the Socialists and the Catholic People's party (newly formed with the pope's blessing) which appealed to the common people, especially in the countryside. Neither party preached revolution, yet both urged wide-scale social and economic reforms.

The rising radical tide, especially seen against the backdrop of the Bolshevik revolution, worried other social groups. Industrialists and landowners feared for their property. Small shopkeepers and white-collar workers—social groups that did not think the working-class movement supported their interests—found themselves alienated by business elites on the one hand and by apparently revolutionary radicals on the other. The threat from the left provoked a strong surge to the right: fascism appeared in the form of vigilante groups breaking up strikes, fighting with workers in the streets, or ousting the Red Leagues from lands occupied in the countryside.

THE RISE OF MUSSOLINI

"I am fascism," said Benito Mussolini, and indeed, the success of the Italian fascist movement depended heavily on his leadership. Mussolini (1883–1945) was the son of a socialist blacksmith. His mother was a schoolteacher, and he deferentially followed in her footsteps. But he was restless and dissatisfied, soon leaving Italy for further study in Switzerland. Here he gave part of his time to his books and the rest to writing articles for socialist newspapers. Expelled from the country for fomenting strikes, he returned to Italy, where he became a journalist and eventually the editor of *Avanti*, the leading socialist daily.

Mussolini did not hold to any particular doctrine, and he reversed himself at several points. When war broke out in August 1914, Mussolini insisted that Italy should remain neutral. He had scarcely adopted this position when he began urging participation on the Allied side. Deprived of his position as the editor of *Avanti*, he founded a new paper, *Il Popolo d'Italia*, and dedicated its columns to arousing enthusiasm for war. He regarded the Italian government's decision the following spring to go in on the side of the Allies as a personal victory.

As early as October 1914, Mussolini had organized groups, called *fasci*, to help drum up support for the war. Members of the *fasci* were young idealists, fanatical nationalists. After the war, these groups formed the base of Mussolini's Fascist movement. (The word *fascism* derives from the Latin *fasces*: an ax surrounded by a bundle of sticks that represented the authority of the Roman state. The Italian *fascio* means "group" or "band.") In 1919 Mussolini drafted the original platform of the Fascist party. It had several surprising elements, including universal (including woman) suffrage, an eight-hour workday, and a tax on inheritances. A new platform, adopted in 1920, abandoned all references to economic reforms. Neither platform earned the fascists much political success.

What the fascists lacked in political support, they made up for with aggressive determination. They gained the respect of the middle class and landowners, and intimidated many others, by forcefully repressing radical movements of industrial workers and peasants. They attacked socialists, often physically, and succeeded in taking over some local governments. As the national regime weakened, Mussolini's coercive politics made him look like a solution to the absence of leadership. In September 1922, he began to negotiate with other parties and the king for fascist participation in government. On October 28 an army of about fifty thousand fascist militia, in black-shirted uniforms, marched into Rome and occupied the capital. The premier resigned, and the following day the king, Victor Emmanuel III, reluctantly invited Mussolini to form a cabinet. Without firing a shot the Black Shirts had gained control of the Italian government. The explana-

Mussolini Reviews a Fascist Youth Parade. Mobilizing youth was central to fascism and Nazism; it demonstrated the vigor of the movements.

tion of their success is to be found less in the strength of the fascist movement itself than in the disappointments after the war and the weakness of the older governing classes.

The parliamentary system had folded under pressure. And though Mussolini had "legally" been granted his power, he immediately began to establish a one-party dictatorship. The doctrines of Italian fascism had three components. The first was statism. The state was declared to incorporate every interest and every loyalty of its members. There was to be "nothing above the state, nothing outside the state, nothing against the state." The second was nationalism. Nationhood was the highest form of society, with a life and a soul of its own apart from the lives and souls of the individuals who composed it. The third was militarism. Nations that did not expand would eventually wither and die. War ennobled man and regenerated sluggish and decadent peoples.

Mussolini began to rebuild Italy in accordance with these principles. The first step was to change electoral laws so they granted his party solid parliamentary majorities, and to intimidate the opposition; he then moved to close down parliamentary government and other parties entirely. He abolished the cabinet system and all but extinguished the powers of the Parliament. He made the Fascist party an integral part of the Italian constitution. The king was compelled to select a prime minister from a list compiled by the party's Great Council. Voters, as well, selected their candidates from lists prepared by the party. Mussolini assumed the dual position of prime minister and party leader (*duce*), and he used the party's militia to eliminate his enemies by violent means. Mussolini's government also controlled the police, muzzled the press, and censored academic activity.

Meanwhile, Mussolini preached the end of class conflict and its replacement by national unity. He began to reorganize the economy and labor, taking away the power of the country's labor movement. The Italian economy was placed under the management of twenty-two corporations, each responsible for a major industrial enterprise. In each corporation were representatives of trade unions, whose members were organized by the Fascist party, the employers, and the government. Together, the members of these corporations were given the task of determining working conditions, wages, and prices. Unsurprisingly, however,

the decisions of these bodies were closely managed by the government and favored the position of management. Indeed, the government quickly aligned with big business, creating more of a corrupt bureaucracy than a revolutionary economy.

Mussolini secured some working-class assent with state-sponsored programs including massive public-works projects, library building, vacations, and social security. In 1929, he settled Italy's sixty-year-old conflict with the Roman Catholic Church. He signed a treaty granting independence to the papal residence in the Vatican City and promising restitution for expropriations that occurred during Italian unification. The treaty also established Roman Catholicism as the official religion of the state, guaranteed religious education in the nation's schools, and made religious marriage ceremonies mandatory. The agreement with the church was part of Mussolini's campaign to "normalize" relations with other Italian institutions—army, industry, church, monarchy—in order to maintain stability.

> The fascist government quickly aligned with big business, creating more of a corrupt bureaucracy than a revolutionary economy.

In fact, Mussolini's regime did much to maintain the status quo. Party officers exercised a degree of political supervision over bureaucrats, yet did not infiltrate the bureaucracy in significant numbers. Moreover, Mussolini remained on friendly terms with the elites who had assisted his rise to power, insuring that whatever he might proclaim about the distinctions between fascism and capitalism, the economy of Italy would remain dependent on private enterprise.

The Italian dictator boasted that fascism had pulled the country back from economic chaos. Like other European economies, the Italian economy did improve in the late 1920s. The regime did a great deal to create the appearance of efficiency, and Mussolini's admirers famously claimed that he had at last "made the trains run on time." Fascism, however, did little to lessen Italy's plight during the worldwide depression of the 1930s.

Like Nazism later, fascism had contradictory elements. It sought to restore traditional authority and, at the same time, mobilize all of Italian society for economic and nationalist purposes—a process that inevitably undercut older authorities. It brought new authoritarian organizations and activities that comported with these goals: exercise programs to make the young fit and mobilized, youth camps, awards to mothers of large families, political rallies, and parades in small towns in the countryside. Activities like these offered people a feeling of political involvement without any political rights. This mobilized but essentially passive citizenship was a hallmark of fascism.

WEIMAR GERMANY

Why did German democracy fail?

On November 9, 1918—two days before the armistice ending the First World War—thousands of Germans swarmed the streets of Berlin in a nearly bloodless overthrow of the imperial government. A massive and largely unexpected uprising, the demonstration converged on the Reichstag in the city center, where a member of the Social Democratic Party (SPD) announced the birth of the new German republic. The kaiser had abdicated only hours before, turning the government over to the Social Democratic leader Friedrich Ebert. The revolution spread quickly through the war-ravaged country; councils of workers and soldiers controlled most major cities within a couple of days, and hundreds of cities by month's end. The "November Revolution" was fast and far reaching, though not as revolutionary as many middle- and upper-class conservatives feared. The majority of socialists steered a cautious, democratic course: they wanted reforms, but were willing to leave much of the existing imperial bureaucracy intact. Above all, they

wanted a popularly elected national assembly to draft a constitution for the new republic.

It was two months, however, before elections could be held—a period of crisis that verged on civil war. Once in control, the Social Democratic leadership made order its top priority. The revolutionary movement that had brought the SPD to power now threatened it. Independent socialists and a nascent Communist party wanted radical reforms, and in December 1918 and January 1919, they staged armed uprisings in the streets of Berlin. Fearful of a Bolshevik-style revolution, the Social Democratic government turned against its former allies and sent militant bands of workers and volunteers to crush the uprisings. During the conflict, the government's fighters executed Rosa Luxemburg and Karl Liebknecht—two German communist leaders who became instant martyrs for the left. Violence continued into 1920, creating a lasting bitterness among groups on the left.

More important, the revolutionary aftermath of the war gave rise to bands of militant counterrevolutionaries. Veterans and other young nationalists joined so-called *Freikorps* (free corps). Such groups developed throughout the country, drawing as many as several hundred thousand members. Former army officers who led these militias continued their war experience by fighting against "Bolsheviks," Poles, and communists calling themselves "Spartacists" well into the 1920s. The politics of the *Freikorps* were fiercely right wing. Anti-Marxist, anti-Semitic, and antiliberal, they had scant affection for the new German republic or its parliamentary democracy. Many of the early Nazi leaders had fought in World War I and participated in Freikorps units.

Germany's new government—known as the Weimar Republic for the city where its constitution was drafted—rested on a coalition of socialists, Catholic centrists, and liberal democrats, a necessary compromise since no single party won a majority of the votes in the January 1919 election. The Weimar constitution was based on the values of parliamentary liberalism, and set up an open, pluralistic framework for German democracy. Through a series of compromises, the constitution established universal suffrage (for both

The German Election of 1919. Here German women line up to vote for the first time.

women and men) and a bill of rights that guaranteed not only civil liberties but also a range of social entitlements. On paper, at least, the revolutionary movement had succeeded.

Yet the Weimar government lasted just over a decade. By 1930 it was in crisis, and in 1933 it collapsed. What happened? The failure of German democracy was not a forgone conclusion. It resulted from a confluence of social, political, and economic crises that were singly manageable but collectively disastrous.

Many of Weimar's problems were born out Germany's defeat in the First World War, which was not only devastating but also humiliating. The ignominious loss to the Allies shocked many Germans, who soon latched on to rumors that the army hadn't actually been worsted in battle, but instead had been "stabbed in the back" by socialists and Jewish leaders in the German government. Army officers cultivated this story even before the war was over, and though untrue, it helped to salve the wounded pride of German patriots. In the next decade, those in search of a scapegoat also blamed the seemingly lax republican regime, epitomized by what they considered the modern decadence of 1920s Berlin. What was needed, many critics argued, was authoritative leadership to guide the nation and regain the world's respect.

The Treaty of Versailles magnified Germany's sense of dishonor. Germany was forced to cede a tenth of its territory, accept responsibility for the war, and slash the size of its army to a mere one hundred thousand men—a punishment that riled the politically powerful corps of officers that remained in charge. Most important, the treaty saddled Germany with crippling reparations. Negotiating the $33 billion debt created problems for the government and provoked nothing but anger from the public. Some opponents of the reparations settlement urged an obstructionist policy of nonpayment, arguing that the enormous sum would doom Germany's economy for the foreseeable future. Indeed, by one estimate, the debt would not have been paid off until 1987. In January 1923, the French accused the Germans of falling behind in payments and sent soldiers into the Ruhr valley, fruitlessly trying to force German miners to produce for France. In 1924 Germany accepted a new schedule of reparations designed by an international committee headed by the American financier Charles G. Dawes. The German chancellor Stresemann had successfully moved Germany toward a foreign policy of cooperation and rapprochement that lasted throughout the 1920s. Many German people, however, continued to resent reparations, Versailles, and the government that continued to accommodate the treaty.

Major economic crises also played a central role in Weimar's collapse. The first period of emergency occurred in the early twenties. Still reeling from wartime inflation, the government was hard pressed for revenues. Funding postwar demobilization programs, social welfare, and reparations forced the government to continue to print money. Inflation became nearly unstoppable. By 1923, as one historian writes, the economic situation had "acquired an almost surrealistic quality." A pound of potatoes cost about nine marks in January, 40 million marks by October. Beef went for almost 2 trillion marks per pound. The government finally took drastic measures to stabilize the currency in 1924, but millions of Germans had already been ruined. For those on fixed incomes, such as pensioners and stockholders, savings and security had vanished. According to one German, life was "madness, nightmare, desperation, and chaos." Middle-class employees, farmers, and workers were all hard hit by the economic crisis, and many of them abandoned the traditional political parties in protest. In their eyes, the parties that claimed to represent the middle classes had created the problems and proved incapable of fixing them.

Beginning in 1925, however, Germany's economy and government seemed to be recovering. By borrowing money, the country was able to make its scaled-down reparations payments and to earn money by selling cheap exports. In large cities, socialist municipal governments sponsored building projects that included schools, hospitals, and low-cost worker housing. But such economic and political stability was misleading. The economy remained dependent on large infusions of capital from the United States set up by the Dawes plan as part of the effort to settle reparations. That dependence made the German economy especially vulnerable to American economic developments. When the U.S. stock market crashed in 1929, beginning the Great Depression (see below), capital flow to Germany virtually stopped.

The Great Depression pushed Weimar's political system to the breaking point. In 1929, there were two million unemployed; in 1932, six million. In those

> The failure of German democracy resulted from a confluence of social, political, and economic crises that were singly manageable but collectively disastrous.

three years production dropped by 44 percent. Artisans and small shopkeepers lost both status and income. Farmers fared even worse, having never recovered from the crisis of the early twenties. Peasants staged mass demonstrations against the government's agricultural policies even before the depression hit. For white-collar and civil service employees, the depression meant lower salaries, poor working conditions, and a constant threat of unemployment. The government drifted toward crisis itself, facing opposition from all sides. Burdened with plummeting tax revenues and spiraling numbers of Germans in need of relief, the government repeatedly cut welfare benefits, which further demoralized the electorate. Finally, the crisis created an opportunity for Weimar's opponents. Many leading industrialists supported a return to authoritarian government, and they were allied with equally conservative landowners, united by a desire for protective economic policies to stimulate the sale of domestic goods and foodstuffs. Those conservative forces wielded considerable power in Germany, beyond the control of the government. So too did the army and the civil service, which were staffed with opponents of the republic—men who rejected the principles of parliamentary democracy and international cooperation that Weimar represented.

HITLER AND THE NATIONAL SOCIALISTS

How did the Nazis come to power?

Adolf Hitler was born in 1889 in Austria, not Germany. The son of a petty customs official in the Austrian civil service, Hitler dropped out of school and went to Vienna in 1909 to become an artist. Rejected from the academy and temporarily homeless, he eked out a dismal existence doing manual labor and painting cheap watercolors in Vienna. Meanwhile he developed the violent political prejudices that would become the guiding principles of the Nazi regime. He ardently admired the Austrian politicians preaching anti-Semitism, anti-Marxism, and Pan-Germanism. When war broke out in 1914, Hitler was among the jubilant crowds in the streets of Munich;

and though he was an Austrian citizen, he enlisted in the German army, where he claimed to have finally found meaning in his life. After the war, he joined the newly formed German Workers' Party, whose name changed in 1920 to the National Socialist Workers' Party (abbreviated in popular usage to Nazi). The Nazis were but one among many small, militant groups of disaffected Germans devoted to racial nationalism and to the overthrow of the Weimar Republic. They grew out of the political milieu that refused to accept the defeat or the November Resolution, and that blamed both on socialists and Jews.

Ambitious and outspoken, Hitler quickly moved up the rather short ladder of party leadership as a talented stump orator. By 1921 he was the *Führer*—the leader—to his followers in Bavaria. The wider public likely saw him as a "vulgar demagogue"—if they noticed him at all. In November of 1923, during the worst days of the inflation crisis, the Nazis made a failed attempt (the Beer Hall putsch in Munich) at overthrowing the state government of Bavaria. Hitler spent the next seven months in prison, where he wrote his autobiography and political manifesto *Mein Kampf* ("*My Struggle*") in 1924. Combining anti-Semitism with anticommunism, the book set out at great length the popular theory that Germany had been betrayed by its enemies and that the country needed strong leadership to regain international prominence. The failed 1923 putsch proved an eye-opening experience for Hitler; he recognized that the Nazis would have to play politics if they wanted to gain power. Released from prison in 1924, Hitler resumed leadership of the party. In the next five years, he consolidated his power over a growing membership of ardent supporters. Actively cultivating the image of the Nazi movement as a crusade against (Jewish) Marxism and capitalism, he portrayed himself as the heroic savior of the German people.

An equally important factor in Hitler's rise to power was the Nazis' ambitious and unprecedented campaign program. In the "inflation election" of 1924, the Nazis polled 6.6 percent of the vote as a protest party at the radical fringe. With the economic stabilization of the mid-twenties, their meager share dropped to below 3 percent. But during this time of seeming decline, the Nazis were building an extensive organization of party activists that helped to lay the foundation for the party's electoral gains later.

The 1928 election was a pivotal moment for both

> An important factor in Hitler's rise to power was the Nazis' ambitious and unprecedented campaign program.

Nazism and the Rural Myth. To stress the rural roots of Aryan Germany, Hitler appeared in lederhosen in the 1920s.

Weimar and for the Nazis for two reasons. First, from this point on, politics became polarized between right and left, making it virtually impossible to put together a coalition that would support the continuation of Weimar democracy. Second, it was apparent that alienated voters, especially peasants, were deserting their traditional political parties and voting for other interest-group organizations that would voice their grievances and push their demands. The Nazis quickly learned how to benefit from this splintering of the electorate. Previously they had tried, with little success, to win the large German working-class vote away from the left. Now, guided by its chief propagandist, Joseph Goebbels, the party stepped up its efforts to attract members of the urban and rural middle classes. The party's most consistent message, hammered home in propaganda, speeches, and rallies, was that the Nazis opposed everything about Weimar: the political system, economic organizations, the left and the labor movement, looser postwar moral codes, women wearing "decadent" flapper fashions, and "cosmopolitan" movies such as *All Quiet on the Western Front*. (Nazi gangs

started a street riot outside the first showing of the film in Berlin; Goebbels broke up a later showing by tossing stench bombs and mice into the theater.) The answers to Germany's problems, the Nazis argued, could only be found by breaking with Weimar. Presenting itself as young and dynamic, the party built a national profile as an alternative to the parties of middle-class conservatives. In 1930, bolstered by the economic crisis, the Nazis were better funded and better organized than ever, and they won 18.3 percent of the vote.

Who voted for the Nazis? Recent analysis of election results and campaign materials suggests that different groups supported the Nazis at varying times and for varying reasons. The Nazis polled highly with small property holders and the rural middle class long before the depression. The Nazis offered these voters economic protection and renewed social status. Other segments of the middle class—notably pensioners, the elderly, and war widows—came to support the Nazis during the economic crisis, when they feared reduction of insurance or pension benefits, and when the older conservative parties failed to meet their needs. The Nazis also courted the traditionally elitist civil service. And though they failed to win votes from industrial workers, the Nazis found some of their strongest support among workers in handicrafts and small-scale manufacturing.

In 1930, the Nazi party won 107 of 577 seats in the Reichstag, second only to the Social Democrats, who controlled 143. No party could gain a majority. No governing coalition was possible without Nazi support. And the Nazis refused to join any cabinet that was not headed by Hitler. The chancellor, Heinrich Brüning of the Catholic Center party, continued to govern by emergency decrees, but his deflationary economic policies were disastrous. Industrial production continued to crash and unemployment continued to climb. In 1932, Hitler ran for president and narrowly lost, although he staged an unprecedented campaign by airplane, visiting twenty-one cities in six days. When another parliamentary election was called in July 1932, the Nazis won 37.4 percent of the vote, which, though not a majority, was a significant plurality. The Nazis could claim that they were the party able to draw support across class, geographic, and generational lines. They benefited from their position as outsiders, untainted by involvement in unpopular parliamentary coalitions. Indeed, the failure of the traditional parties was key to the success of the Nazis.

Despite its electoral success in 1932, the Nazi party had not won a majority; Hitler was not in power. He was appointed chancellor in January 1933 by President

NAZI PROPAGANDA

JOSEPH GOEBBELS, "WHY ARE WE ENEMIES OF THE JEWS?"

The Nazis promised many things to many people. As the following document shows, anti-Semitism allowed them to blend their racial nationalism, vaguely defined (and anti-Marxist) socialism, and disgust with the state of German culture and politics. Joseph Goebbels, one of the early members of the party, became director of propaganda for the party in 1928. Later Hitler appointed him head of "National Ministry for Public Enlightenment and Propaganda."

We are NATIONALISTS because we see in the NATION the only possibility for the protection and the furtherance of our existence.

The NATION is the organic bond of a people for the protection and defense of their lives. He is nationally minded who understands this IN WORD AND IN DEED. . . .

Young nationalism has its unconditional demands, BELIEF IN THE NATION is a matter of all the people, not for individuals of rank, a class, or an industrial clique. The eternal must be separated from the contemporary. The maintenance of a rotten industrial system has nothing to do with nationalism. I can love Germany and hate capitalism; not only CAN I do it, I also MUST do it. The germ of the rebirth of our people LIES ONLY IN THE DESTRUCTION OF THE SYSTEM OF PLUNDERING THE HEALTHY POWER OF THE PEOPLE.

WE ARE NATIONALISTS BECAUSE WE, AS GERMANS, LOVE GERMANY. And because we love Germany, we demand the protection of its national spirit and we battle against its destroyers.

WHY ARE WE SOCIALISTS?

We are SOCIALISTS because we see in SOCIALISM the only possibility for maintaining our racial existence and through it the reconquest of our political freedom and the rebirth of the German state. SOCIALISM has its peculiar form first of all through its comradeship in arms with the forward-driving energy of a newly awakened nationalism. Without nationalism it is nothing, a phantom, a theory, a vision of air, a book. With it, it is everything, THE FUTURE, FREEDOM, FATHERLAND! . . .

WHY DO WE OPPOSE THE JEWS?

We are ENEMIES OF THE JEWS, because we are fighters for the freedom of the German people. THE JEW IS THE CAUSE AND THE BENEFICIARY OF OUR MISERY. He has used the social difficulties of the broad masses of our people to deepen the unholy split between Right and Left among our people. He has made two halves of Germany. He is the real cause for our loss of the Great War.

The Jew has no interest in the solution of Germany's fateful problems. He CANNOT have any. FOR HE LIVES ON THE FACT THAT THERE HAS BEEN NO SOLUTION. If we would make the German people a unified community and give them freedom before the world, then the Jew can have no place among us. He has the best trumps in his hands when a people lives in inner and outer slavery. THE JEW IS RESPONSIBLE FOR OUR MISERY AND HE LIVES ON IT.

That is the reason why we, AS NATIONALISTS and AS SOCIALISTS, oppose the Jew. HE HAS CORRUPTED OUR RACE, FOULED OUR MORALS, UNDERMINED OUR CUSTOMS, AND BROKEN OUR POWER. . . .

NATIONAL SOCIALIST CAMPAIGN PAMPHLET, 1932

The Nazis worked hard to win the rural vote, as evidenced by the Nazi campaign pamphlet reprinted below. The Nazis tried to appeal to farmers' economic grievances, their fears of socialism on the one hand and big business on the other, and their more general hostility to urban life and culture.

GERMAN FARMER YOU BELONG TO HITLER! WHY?

The German farmer stands between two great dangers today:

The one danger is the American economic system—Big capitalism!

   it means "world economic crisis"
   it means "eternal interest slavery" . . .
   it means that the world is nothing more than a bag of booty for Jewish finance in Wall Street, New York, and Paris
   it enslaves man under the slogans of progress, technology, rationalization, standardization, etc.
   it knows only profit and dividends
   it wants to make the world into a giant trust
   it puts the machine over man
   it annihilates the independent, earth-rooted farmer, and its final aim is the world dictatorship of Jewry [. . .]
   it achieves this in the political sphere through parliament and the swindle of democracy. In the economic sphere, through the control of credit, the mortgaging of land, the stock exchange and the market principle [. . .]
The farmer's leagues, the Landvolk and the Bavarian Farmers' League all pay homage to this system.

The other danger is the Marxist economic system of bolshevism:

   it knows only the state economy
   it knows only one class, the proletariat
   it brings in the controlled economy
   it doesn't just annihilate the self-sufficient farmer economically—it roots him out [. . .]
   it brings the rule of the tractor
   it nationalizes the land and creates mammoth factory-farms
   it uproots and destroys man's soul, making him the powerless tool of the communist idea—or kills him
   it destroys the family, belief, and customs [. . .]
   it is anti-Christ, it desecrates the churches [. . .]
   its final aim is the world dictatorship of the proletariat, that means ultimately the world dictatorship of Jewry, for the Jew controls this powerless proletariat and uses it for his dark plans
   Big capitalism and bolshevism work hand in hand; they are born of Jewish thought and serve the master plan of world Jewry.

Who alone can rescue the farmer from these dangers?

NATIONAL SOCIALISM!

Anton Kaes, Matin Jay, and Edward Dimendberg, *The Weimar Republic Sourcebook* (Los Angeles: University of California Press, 1994), pp. 137–38, 142. (Source for both documents.)

Hindenburg, who hoped to create a conservative coalition government by bringing the Nazis into line with the less radical parties. But Hindenburg and others in the government had underestimated the Nazis' power and popularity. Legally installed in office, Hitler immediately made the most of it. When a Dutch anarchist with links to the communist party set fire to the Reichstag on the night of February 27, Hitler seized the opportunity to suspend civil rights "as a defensive measure against Communist acts of violence." He convinced Hindenburg to dissolve the Reichstag and to order a new election on March 5, 1933. Under Hitler's sway, the new parliament legally granted him unlimited powers for the next four years. Hitler proclaimed his new government the Third Reich. (The first Reich was the German empire of the Middle Ages; the second was that of the kaisers.)

NAZI GERMANY

By the fall of 1933, Germany had become a one-party state. The socialist and communist left was crushed by the new regime. Almost all non-Nazi organizations

DER ARBEITER IM REICH DES HAKENKREUZES!

DARUM WÄHLT **LISTE 1 SOZIALDEMOKRATEN!**

Anti-Nazi Poster, 1932, reads "The worker in the Reich of the Swastika" at top, and "Vote Social Democratic" at bottom.

had been either abolished or forced to become part of the Nazi system. Nazi party leaders took over various government departments, and party *Gauleiters*, or regional directors, assumed administrative responsibility throughout the country. Loyal functionaries had a virtual free hand to expand and exploit their power. Party propaganda sought to impress citizens with the regime's "monolithic efficiency." But in fact, the Nazi government was a tangled bureaucratic maze, with both agencies and individuals vying fiercely for Hitler's favor.

Ironically, at the end of the party's first year in power, the most serious challenges to Hitler came from within the party. Hitler's paramilitary Nazi "storm troopers" (the SA) had been formed to maintain discipline within the party and impose order in society. SA membership soared after 1933, and many in the SA hailed Hitler's appointment as the beginning of a genuinely Nazi revolution. Such radicalism was alarming

to the more traditional conservative groups who had helped make Hitler chancellor. If Hitler were to maintain power, then, he needed to tame the SA. On the night of June 30, 1934, more than a thousand high-ranking SA officials, including several of Hitler's oldest associates, were executed in a bloody purge known as the Night of Long Knives. The purge cleared the way for a second paramilitary organization, the *Schutzstaffel* (bodyguard), or SS. Headed by the fanatical Heinrich Himmler, the SS became the most dreaded arm of Nazi terror. As Himmler saw it, the SS was to fight political and racial enemies of the regime, which included building the system of concentration camps. The first camp, at Dachau, opened in March 1933. The secret state police, known as the Gestapo, were responsible for the arrest, incarceration in camps, and murder of thousands of Germans. But the police force was generally understaffed and deluged with paperwork—as one historian has shown, anything but "omniscient, omnipotent, and omnipresent." In fact, the majority of arrests was based on voluntary denunciations made by ordinary citizens against each other, often as petty personal attacks. It was not lost on the Gestapo leadership that these denunciations created a level of control that the Gestapo itself could never achieve.

Despite—or perhaps because of—these efforts to quash opposition, Hitler and the Nazis enjoyed a sizable amount of popular support. Many Germans approved of Hitler's use of violence against the left. The Nazis could play on deep-seated fears of communism, and they spoke a language of intense national pride and unity that had broad appeal. Many Germans saw Hitler as a symbol of a strong, revitalized Germany. Propagandists fostered a Führer cult, depicting Hitler as a charismatic leader with the magnetic energy to bring people to their knees. Hitler's appeal also rested on his ability to give the German people what they wanted: jobs for workers, a productive economy for industrialists, a bulwark against communism for those who feared the wave of revolution. His appeal lay not so much in the programs he championed, many of which were ill conceived or contradictory, but in his revolt against politics as they had been practiced in Germany. Finally, he promised to lead Germany back to national greatness and to "overthrow" the Versailles settlement, and through the 1930s he seemed to be doing so with a series of bloodless diplomatic triumphs.

Hitler's plans for national recovery called for full-scale rearmament and economic self-sufficiency. With policies similar to those of other Western nations, the Nazis made massive public investments, set strict

Nazi Parade, 1933. The Nazis understood the propaganda value of parades, rituals, and uniforms.

market controls to stop inflation and stabilize the currency, and sealed Germany off from the world economy. The regime launched state financed construction projects—highways, public housing, reforestation. Late in the decade, as the Nazis rebuilt the entire German military complex, unemployment dropped from over 6 million to under two hundred thousand. The German economy looked better than any other in Europe: Hitler claimed this as his "economic miracle." Such improvements were significant, especially in the eyes of Germans who had lived through the continual turmoil of war, inflation, political instability, and economic crisis.

As for promises to unite the German people in a national community free of divisions, the Nazis made little headway. Like Mussolini, Hitler moved to abolish class conflict by stripping working-class institutions of their power. He outlawed trade unions and strikes, froze wages, and organized workers and employers into a National Labor Front. At the same time, the Nazis increased workers' welfare benefits, generally in line with the other Western nations. Class distinctions were somewhat blurred by the regime's attempts to infuse a new national "spirit" into the entire society. Popular organizations cut across class lines, especially among the youth. The Hitler Youth, a club modeled on the Boy Scouts, was highly successful at teaching children the values of

Hitler's Reich; the National Labor Service drafted students for a term to work on state-sponsored building and reclamation projects. Government policy encouraged women to withdraw from the labor force, both to ease unemployment and to conform to Nazi notions of a woman's proper role. "Can woman," one propagandist asked, "conceive of anything more beautiful than to sit with her husband in her cozy home and listen inwardly to the loom of time weaving the weft and warp of motherhood . . . ?"

CHRONOLOGY

THE RISE OF NAZISM, 1920–1934

National Socialist Workers' Party founded	1920
Beer Hall Putsch in Munich	1923
Hitler writes *Mein Kampf* in prison	1924
Hitler consolidates power	1924–1929
Hitler loses presidential election	1932
Hitler appointed chancellor of Germany	1933
Nazi party rules Germany	1933
Night of Long Knives	1934

NAZI RACISM

At the core of Nazi ideology lay a particularly virulent racism. Much of this racism was not new. Hitler and the Nazis drew on a revived and especially violent form of nineteenth-century social Darwinism, according to which nations and people struggled for survival, with the superior peoples strengthening themselves in the process. By the early twentieth century, the rise of the social sciences had taken nineteenth-century prejudices and racial thinking into new terrain. Just as medical science had cured bodily ills, doctors, criminologists, and social workers sought ways to cure social ills. Across the West, scientists and intellectuals worked to purify the body politic, improve the human race, and eliminate the "unfit." Even progressive-minded individuals sometimes subscribed to eugenics, a program of racial engineering to improve either personal or public fitness. Eugenic policies in the Third Reich began with a 1933 law for the compulsory sterilization of "innumerable inferior and hereditarily tainted" people. This "social-hygienic racism" became the systematic murder of mentally and physically ill patients. Social policy was governed by a basic division between those who possessed "value" and those who did not, with the aim of creating a racial utopia.

The centerpiece of Nazi racism was anti-Semitism. This centuries-old phenomenon was part of Christian society from the Middle Ages on. By the nineteenth century, traditional Christian anti-Semitism was joined by a current of nationalist anti-Jewish theory. A great many of the theorists of European nationalism saw the Jewish people as permanent outsiders who could only be assimilated and become citizens if they denied their Jewish identity. At the end of the nineteenth century, during the Dreyfus affair in France (see Chapter 26), French and European anti-Semites launched a barrage of propaganda against Jews—scores of books, pamphlets, and magazines blamed Jews for all the troubles of modernity, from socialism to international banks and mass culture. The late nineteenth century also brought a wave of pogroms—assaults on Jewish communities—especially in Russia. Racial anti-Semitism drew the line between Jews and non-Jews on the basis of erroneous biology. Religious conversion, which traditional Christian anti-Semites encouraged, would not change biology. Nor would assimilation, which was counseled by more secular nationalist thinkers.

It is important not to generalize, but anti-Semitism in these different forms was a well-established and open political force in most of the West. By attacking Jews, anti-Semites attacked modern institutions—from socialist parties and the mass press to international banking—as part of a "international Jewish conspiracy" to undermine traditional authority and nationality. Conservative party leaders told shopkeepers and workers that "Jewish capitalists" were responsible for the demise of small businesses, for the rise of giant department stores, and for precarious economic swings that threatened their livelihoods. In Vienna, middle-class voters supported the openly anti-Semitic Christian Democrats. In Germany, in 1893, sixteen avowed anti-Semites were elected to the Reichstag, and the Conservative party made anti-Semitism part of its official program. Hitler gave this anti-Semitism an especially murderous twist by tying it to doctrines of war and social-hygienic racism.

To what extent was the Nazis' virulent anti-Semitism shared? Although the "Jewish Question" was clearly Hitler's primary obsession during the early 1920s, he made the theme less central in campaign appearances as the Nazi movement entered mainstream politics, shifting instead to attacks on Marxism and the Weimar democracy. Moreover, anti-Semitic beliefs would not have distinguished the Nazi from any other party on the political right; it was likely of only secondary importance to people's opinions of the Nazis. Soon after Hitler came to power, though, German Jews faced discrimination, exclusion from rights as citizens, and violence. Racial laws excluded Jews from public office as early as April 1933. The Nazis encouraged a boycott of Jewish merchants, while the SA created a constant threat of random violence. In 1935, the Nuremberg Decrees deprived Jews (defined by bloodline) of their German citizenship and prohibited marriage between Jews and other Germans. Violence escalated. In November 1938, the SA attacked some seventy-five hundred Jewish stores, burned nearly two hundred synagogues, killed ninety-one Jews, and beat up thousands more in a campaign of terror known as *Kristallnacht*, the Night of Broken Glass. Violence like this did raise some opposition from ordinary Germans. Legal persecution, however, met only silent acquiescence. And from the perspective of Jewish people, *Kristallnacht* made it plain that there was no safe place for them in Germany. Unfortunately, only one year remained before the outbreak of war made it possible for Jews to escape.

What did national socialism and fascism have in common? Both arose in the interwar period as responses to World War I and the Russian Revolution. Both were violently antisocialist and anticommunist, determined to "rescue" their nations from the threat of Bolshevism. Both were intensely nationalistic; they

HOW DID THE WESTERN DEMOCRACIES DEAL WITH THE GREAT DEPRESSION?

THE GREAT DEPRESSION IN THE DEMOCRACIES   977

believed that national solidarity came before all other allegiances and superseded all other rights. Both opposed parliamentary government and democracy as cumbersome and divisive. Both found their power in mass-based authoritarian politics. Similar movements existed in all the countries of the West, but only in a few cases did they actually form regimes. Nazism, however, distinguished itself by making a racially pure state central to its vision, a vision that would lead to global struggle and mass murder.

THE GREAT DEPRESSION IN THE DEMOCRACIES

How did the Western democracies deal with the Great Depression?

The histories of the three major Western democracies—Great Britain, France, and the United States run roughly parallel during the years after the First World War. In all three countries governments put their trust in prewar policies and assumptions until the Great Depression forced them to make major social reforms, laying the foundations of the modern welfare state. These nations weathered the upheavals of the interwar years, but they did not do so easily.

France continued to fear Germany and took every opportunity to keep the Germans as weak as possible. Under the leadership of the moderate conservative Raymond Poincaré during the 1920s, France tried to keep the price of manufactured goods low by restraining wages. This policy of deflation kept businessmen happy but put a heavy burden on the working class. Édouard Herriot interrupted Poincaré's service as premier, serving for two years in the mid-1920s. A radical socialist by affiliation, Herriot was a spokesman for small-business owners, farmers, and the lower middle class. Herriot said he supported social reform, but refused to raise taxes in order to pay for it. Meanwhile, class conflict simmered just below the surface. As industries prospered, employers refused to bargain with labor unions. A period of major strikes immediately after the war was followed by a sharp decline in union activity. And even though the government passed a modified social insurance program in 1930—insuring against sickness, old age, and death—workers remained dissatisfied.

Social conflict flared in Britain as well. Anxious to regain its position as the major industrial and financial power in the world, Britain also pursued a policy of deflation, hoping to make its manufactured goods cheaper and more attractive on the world market. The result was a reduction in wages that undermined the standard of living of many British workers. Their resentment helped to elect the first Labour party government in 1924, and a second in 1929. The Labour party accomplished little, however, because of its minority position in Parliament. Besides, its leader, Prime Minister J. Ramsay MacDonald, was a rather timid socialist. The Conservative government returned to power in 1925 under Stanley Baldwin and refused to abandon its deflationary policy, which continued to drive down wages. British trade unions grew increasingly militant in response, and in 1926, the unions staged a nationwide general strike. The strike's only appreciable effect was to heighten middle-class antipathy toward workers.

The United States was the bastion of conservatism among the democracies. The presidents elected in the 1920s Warren G. Harding, Calvin Coolidge, and Herbert Hoover—upheld a social philosophy formulated by the barons of big business in the nineteenth century. The Supreme Court used its power of judicial review to nullify progressive legislation enacted by state governments and occasionally by Congress.

The conservative economic and social policies of the prewar period were dealt their deathblow by the Great Depression of 1929. This worldwide depression peaked during the years 1929–1933, but its effects lasted a decade. For those who went through it, the depression was perhaps the formative experience of their lives and the decisive crisis of the interwar period. It was an important factor in the rise of Nazism, but in fact, it forced every country to forge new economic policies, and to deal with unprecedented economic turmoil.

THE ORIGINS OF THE GREAT DEPRESSION

What caused the Great Depression? Its deepest roots lay in the instability of national currencies, and in the interdependence of national economies. Throughout the 1920s, Europeans had seen a sluggish growth rate. A major drop in world agricultural prices hurt the countries of southern and eastern Europe, where agriculture was small in scale and high in cost. Unable to make a profit on the international market, these agri-

The Stock Market Crash, October 24, 1929. Crowds milling outside the New York Stock Exchange on the day of the big crash.

third of the workforce. By then, per capita income in the United States had fallen 48 percent. In Germany, too, the drop was brutal. In 1929, 2 million were unemployed; in 1932, 6 million. Production dropped 44 percent in Germany, 47 percent in the United States. This was not an economic slowdown, or even a severe recession. The stock-market collapse led to widespread bank failure, and brought the economy virtually to a standstill.

The depression took a profound psychological and cultural toll. One of the distinctive features of the crisis was that the decline continued; there seemed to be no bottom for the market to hit and no way to revive the economy. The lines at soup kitchens and at flophouses where the suddenly homeless could sleep for a few hours were not just signs of poverty and misery, but of government's helplessness. As governments flailed about for solutions, people grew increasingly pessimistic, bewildered by economic forces that no one seemed to understand. They were easily disillusioned with politics. For the depression generation, no experience had the permanent, searing effect of "the calvary of unemployment and the dole," writes one economic historian.

The governments of the West initially responded to the depression with monetary measures. In 1931 Great Britain abandoned the gold standard; the United States followed suit in 1933. By no longer pegging their currencies to the price of gold, these countries hoped to make money cheaper, and thus more available for economic recovery programs. This action was the forerunner of a broad program of currency management, which became an important element in a general policy of economic nationalism. In another important move, Great Britain abandoned its time-honored policy of free trade in 1932, raising protective tariffs as high as 100 percent. But monetary policy alone could not end the hardships of ordinary families: governments were increasingly forced to address their concerns with a wide range of social reforms.

Britain was the most cautious in its relief efforts. A national government composed of Conservative, Liberal, and Labour party members came to power in 1931. To underwrite effective programs of public assistance, however, the government would have to spend

cultural countries bought fewer manufactured goods from the more industrial sectors of northern Europe, causing a widespread drop in industrial productivity. Restrictions on free trade crippled the economy even more. Although debtor nations needed open markets to sell their goods to, most nations were raising high trade barriers to protect domestic manufacturers from foreign competition.

Then in October of 1929, prices on the New York Stock Exchange collapsed. On October 24, "Black Thursday," 12 million shares were traded amid unprecedented chaos. Even more surprising, the market kept falling. Black Thursday was followed by Black Monday and then Black Tuesday: falling prices, combined with an enormously high number of trades, made for the worst day in the history of the stock exchange to that point. The rise of the United States as an international creditor during the Great War meant that the crash had immediate, disastrous consequences in Europe. When the value of stocks dropped, banks found themselves short of capital and then, when not rescued by the government, forced to close. International investors called in their debts. A series of banking houses shut their doors, among them Credit Anstalt, the biggest bank in Austria, with significant interests in two thirds of Austrian industry. Workers did not simply lose their jobs, manufacturers laid off virtually entire work forces. In 1930, 4 million Americans were unemployed, in 1933, 13 million—nearly a

HOW DID THE WESTERN DEMOCRACIES DEAL WITH THE GREAT DEPRESSION?

THE GREAT DEPRESSION IN THE DEMOCRACIES   979

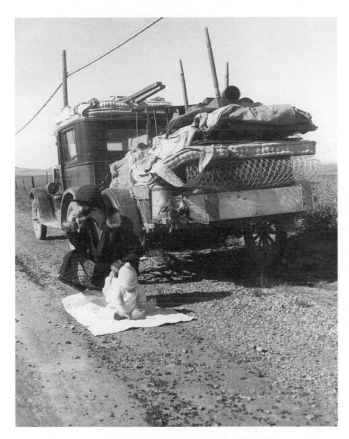

U.S. Farmers on Their Way West in the 1930s. Forced from their land by depression, debts, and drought, thousands of farmers and their families headed to California, Oregon, and Washington in search of employment.

beyond its income—something it was reluctant to do. France, on the other hand, adopted the most advanced set of policies to combat the effects of the depression. In 1936, responding to a threat from ultraconservatives to overthrow the republic, a Popular Front government under the leadership of the socialist Léon Blum was formed by the Radical, Radical Socialist, and Communist parties, and lasted for two years. The Popular Front nationalized the munitions industry and reorganized the Bank of France to break the largest stockholders' monopolistic control over credit. The government also decreed a forty-hour week for all urban workers and initiated a program of public works. For the benefit of the farmers it established a wheat office to fix the price and regulate the distribution of grain. Although the Popular Front temporarily quelled the threat from the political right, conservatives were generally uncooperative and unimpressed by the attempts to aid the French working class. Both a socialist and Jew, Blum faced fierce anti-Semitism in France. Fearing that Blum was the forerunner of a French

Lenin, conservatives declared, "Better Hitler than Blum." They got their wish before the decade was out.

The most dramatic response to the depression came in the United States for two reasons. First, the United States had clung longer to nineteenth-century economic philosophy. Prior to the depression, the business classes adhered firmly to the dogma of freedom of contract. The "barons" of industry insisted on their right to form monopolies, and they used the government as a tool to frustrate the demands of both workers and consumers. Second, the depression was more severe in the United States than in the European democracies. America had survived the First World War unscathed—and indeed, had benefited enormously—but now its economy was ravaged even more than Europe's. In 1933, Franklin D. Roosevelt succeeded Herbert Hoover as president and announced the New Deal, a program of reform and reconstruction to rescue the country.

The New Deal aimed to get the country back on its feet without destroying the capitalist system. The government would manage the economy, sponsor relief programs, and fund public-works projects to increase mass purchasing power. These policies were shaped by the theories of the British economist John Maynard Keynes, who had already proved influential during the 1919 treaty meetings at Paris. Keynes argued that capitalism could create a just and efficient society if governments would play a part in its management. First, Keynes abandoned the sacred cow of balanced budgets. Without advocating continuous deficit financing, he would have the government deliberately operate in the red whenever private investments weren't enough. Keynes also favored the creation of large amounts of venture capital—money for high-risk, high-reward investments—which he saw as the only socially productive form of capital. Finally, he recommended monetary control to promote prosperity and full employment.

Along with Social Security and other programs, the United States adopted a Keynesian program of "currency management," regulating the value of the dollar according to the needs of the economy. The New Deal helped both individuals and the country to recover, but it left the crucial problem of unemployment unsolved. In 1939, after six years of the New Deal, the United States still had more than 9 million jobless workers—a figure that exceeded the combined unemployment of the rest of the world. Only with the outbreak of a new world war—which required millions of soldiers and armament workers—did the United States reach the full recovery that the New Deal had failed to deliver.

INTERWAR CULTURE: ARTISTS AND INTELLECTUALS

How did the mass media change everyday life?

We have seen how governments and their citizens responded to social, political, and economic crises. The interwar period brought equally dramatic upheavals in the arts and sciences. Revolutionary artistic forms that were pioneered at the turn of the century moved from the margins to the mainstream. Artists, writers, architects, and composers rejected traditional aesthetic values and experimented with new forms of expression. Further affronts to tradition came from scientists and psychologists, whose work challenged deeply held beliefs about the universe and about human nature. Finally, mass culture, in the form of radio, movies, and advertising sharpened many anxieties, and stood as a stark example of the promise and peril of modern times.

INTERWAR INTELLECTUALS

Like many other people, novelists, poets, and dramatists were disillusioned by the brute facts of world war and by the failure of victory to fulfill its promises. Much of the literature of the interwar period reflected themes of frustration, cynicism, and disenchantment; but many writers were also fascinated by revolutionary developments in science, including the probing of psychoanalysts into the hidden secrets of the mind. The works of several writers came to represent the mood of the era: the early novels of the American Ernest Hemingway, for example, along with the poetry of the Anglo-American T. S. Eliot, and the plays of the German Bertolt Brecht. In *The Sun Also Rises* (1926), Hemingway gave the public a powerful description of the so-called lost generation and set a pattern that other writers, such as the American F. Scott Fitzgerald, were soon to follow. In his monumental poem *The Waste Land* (1922), Eliot presented a philosophy that was close to despair: life is a living death, to be endured as boredom and frustration. Eliot's themes were echoed by William Butler Yeats, an Irish nationalist poet who, like Eliot, deplored the superficiality of modern life. In plays written for the working-class patrons of cabarets, Brecht decried the corruption of the state and the pointlessness of war. Like many artists, he rebelled against high culture and bourgeois values, but he also protested against the pretentious elitism of his contemporaries.

Other writers focused their attention on consciousness and inner life, often experimenting with new forms of prose. The Irish writer James Joyce was much renowned for his experiments with language and literacy forms—especially with the "stream of consciousness" technique, which he perfected in *Ulysses* (1922). The same was true, though to a lesser extent, of the novels of the Frenchman Marcel Proust and the Englishwoman Virginia Woolf (1882–1941). Woolf's essays and novels, among them *Mrs. Dalloway* (1925), *To The Lighthouse* (1927), and *A Room of One's Own* (1929), offered an eloquent and biting critique of Britain's elite institutions, from the universities who isolated women in separate, underfunded colleges to the suffocating decorum of middle-class families and relationships.

The depression of the 1930s forced many writers to reexamine the style and purpose of their work. Amid threats of economic devastation totalitarianism, and war, literature became increasingly politicized, along with most areas of society. Authors felt themselves called to indict injustice and cruelty, and to point the way to a better society. Moreover, they no longer directed their work to fellow intellectuals alone, but to common men and women as well. In *The Grapes of Wrath* (1939), for example, the American writer John Steinbeck depicted the sorry plight of impoverished farmers fleeing from the Dust Bowl to California only to find that all the land had been monopolized by companies that exploited their workers. Young British writers such as W. H. Auden, Stephen Spender, and Christopher Isherwood were communist sympathizers who believed that it was their duty as artists to politicize their work to support the revolution. They rejected the pessimism of their immediate literary forebears in favor of optimistic commitment to their cause.

INTERWAR ARTISTS

Trends in art tended to parallel those in literature. The innovations of the prewar avant-garde thrived in the postwar period, and in fact, continued to dominate art through much of the twentieth century. Artists continued to focus on subjective experiences, multiplicities of meaning, and personal expression. Numerous and varied styles emerged, though all were characteristically modern in their rejection of traditional forms and values. Visual art responded to the rapid transformations of twentieth-century society

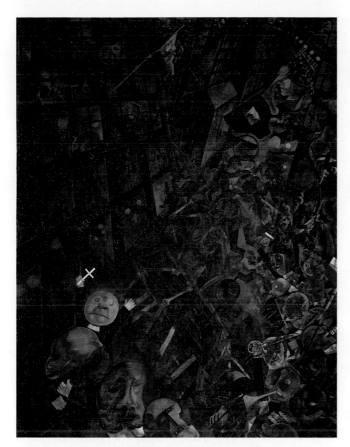

The Funeral Procession, by Grosz. Painted in the late stages of the First World War, this painting of a funeral procession gone mad shows death triumphant as humanity is swept into a hell of its own making.

—changes brought about by new technologies, scientific discoveries, the abandonment of traditional beliefs, and the influence of non-Western cultures. Like writers of the period, visual artists pushed the boundaries of aesthetics, moving far from the conventional tastes of average men and women.

Pablo Picasso followed his particular genius as it led him further into cubist variations and inventions. So did others, such as the Frenchman Fernand Léger, who combined devotion to cubist principles and a fascination with the artifacts of industrial civilization. Another group, known as expressionists, argued that color and line express inherent psychological qualities all by themselves, and so a painting need not have a "subject" at all. The Russian Wassily Kandinsky carried this position to its logical conclusion by calling his untitled paintings "improvisations" and insisting that they meant nothing. A second group of expressionists rejected intellectuality for what they called "objectivity," by which they meant a candid appraisal of the state of

the human mind. They were frequent attackers of the greed and decadence of postwar Europe. Chief among this group was the German George Grosz, whose cruel, satiric line has been likened to a "razor lancing a carbuncle." His scathing images became the most popular portraits of the despised Weimar government.

Another school rebelled against the very idea of aesthetic principle. Principles were based on reason, their argument went, and the world had proved beyond all doubt—by fighting itself to death—that reason did not exist. Calling themselves dadaists (allegedly after a name picked at random from the dictionary), these artists were led by the Frenchman Marcel Duchamp, the German Max Ernst, and the Alsatian Jean (Hans) Arp. Rejecting all formal artistic conventions, dadaists concocted haphazard "fabrications" from cutouts and juxtapositions of wood, glass, and metal, and gave them bizarre names, for example, *The Bride Stripped Bare by her Bachelors, Even* (Duchamp). The artists claimed their works were meaningless and playful, but critics thought otherwise, seeing them instead as expressions of the subconscious. Dadaism influenced surrealist artists such as the Italian Giorgio de Chirico and the Spaniard Salvador Dali, who explored the interior of the mind and produced irrational, fantastic, and generally melancholy paintings. Dadaism also took on political undertones, especially in Germany, by offering a nihilistic social critique that bordered on anarchism. Extending their attacks on rationalism to theater and print, these artists challenged the very basis of national culture. John Heartfield's sharply critical photomontages attacked Hitler and the Nazis well into the 1930s.

Some artists responded to the sense of international crisis much as writers did. During the thirties, their paintings expressed pain and outrage directly to a mass audience. The most important members of this new movement were the Mexican muralists Diego Rivera and José Clemente Orozco, and the Americans Thomas Hart Benton and Reginald Marsh. These men sought to depict the social conditions of the modern world, presenting in graphic detail the hopes and struggles of ordinary people. Though they scarcely adhered to the conventions of the past, there was nothing unintelligible about their work. It was art intended for everyone. Much of it bore the sting of social satire. Orozco, in particular, delighted in pillorying the hypocrisy of the church and the greed and cruelty of plutocrats and plunderers.

Architects, too, rejected sentimentality and tradition. Between 1880 and 1890 designers in Europe and

The Persistence of Memory, by Salvador Dali (1904–1989). The Spaniard Dali is the outstanding representative of the surrealist school. Many objects in his paintings are Freudian images.

Detroit Industry (detail), by Diego Rivera (1886–1957). Painted between 1931 and 1933, this work aimed to depict the social conditions of the modern world, especially the struggles and triumphs of the working class.

Architectural Style in Germany between the Wars. The Bauhaus, by Walter Gropius (1883–1969). This school in Dessau, Germany, is a starkly functional prototype of the interwar "international style."

Fallingwater, by Frank Lloyd Wright (1867–1959). This most famous example of Wright's "organic architecture" is perched atop a waterfall. The pattern of the house conforms to the natural surroundings.

America announced that the prevailing architectural styles were out of harmony with the needs of modern civilization. Modern architects pioneered a style known as "functionalism"; this group included Otto Wagner in Austria, Charles Édouard Jeanneret (known as Le Corbusier) in France, and Louis Sullivan and Frank Lloyd Wright in the United States. The basic principle of functionalism was that the appearance of a building should proclaim its actual use and purpose. "Form ever follows function" was Sullivan's maxim. Ornamentation was designed to reflect an age of science and machines. A leading European practitioner of functionalism was the German Walter Gropius, who in 1919 established a school—the Bauhaus—in Dessau to serve as a center for the theory and practice of modern architecture. Gropius and his followers declared that their style of design, which in time came to be called "international," was the only one that permitted an honest application of new materials—chromium, glass, steel, and concrete.

INTERWAR SCIENTIFIC DEVELOPMENTS

One powerful influence on the artists and intellectuals of the day was neither social nor political, but scientific. The pioneering work of the German physicist Albert Einstein revolutionized not only the entire structure of physical science, it also challenged ordinary people's most basic beliefs about the universe. Quickly recognized as one of the greatest intellects of all time, Einstein began to question the very foundations of traditional physics early in the twentieth century. By 1915, he had proposed entirely new ways of thinking about space, matter, time, and gravity. His most famous theory, the principle of relativity, states that space and motion are relative to each other instead of being absolute. To the familiar three dimensions, Einstein added a fourth —time—and represented all four as fused in the space-time continuum. This meant that mass depends on motion, so that bodies in motion (especially at very high velocities) have a different shape and mass than they would at rest. Einstein also posited the conception of a finite universe—that is, finite in space. The region of matter does not extend into infinity, he suggested: the universe has limits. Though these boundaries are indefinite, there is at least a region beyond which nothing exists. In his view, space curves back on itself so as to make the universe a gigantic sphere within which are contained all the galaxies, solar systems, stars, and planets.

Einstein's theories paved the way for another revolutionary development in physics—the splitting of the atom. As early as 1905 Einstein became convinced of the equivalence of mass and energy and worked out a formula for the conversion of one into the other. Expressed as $E = mc^2$, the equation states that the amount of energy locked within the atom is equal to the mass multiplied by the square of the velocity of light. The formula had no practical application for years. Then in 1932, when the Englishman Sir James Chadwick discovered the neutron, which carries no electric charge, scientists had an ideal weapon for bombarding the atom—that is, a way to split it. In 1939 two German physicists, Otto Hahn and Fritz Strassman, successfully split atoms of uranium by bombarding them with neutrons. The initial reaction produced a chain of reactions: each atom that was split shot off more neutrons, which split even more atoms. Scientists in Germany, Great Britain, and the United States were spurred on by governments anxious to turn these discoveries into weapons during the Second World War. American scientists soon prepared an atomic bomb, the most destructive weapon ever created. The legacy was ironic for Einstein, a man who devoted much of his life to promoting pacifism, liberalism, and social justice.

Another important contribution to physics that quickly entered popular culture was the "uncertainty principle" posited by the German physicist Werner Heisenberg in 1927. Heisenberg, who was strongly influenced by Einstein, showed that it is impossible—even in theory—to measure both the position and the speed of an object at the same time. The theory was of consequence only when dealing with atoms or subatomic particles, because of the interconnected nature of waves and particles on such a small scale. Though the public had little to no understanding of these ground-breaking scientific concepts, metaphorical invocations of "relativity" and the "uncertainty principle" fit right in line with the ambiguities of the modern world. For many people, nothing was definite, everything was changing—and science seemed to be proving it.

MASS CULTURE AND ITS POSSIBILITIES

Cultural change, however, extended far beyond circles of artistic and intellectual elites. The explosive rise of mass media in the interwar years transformed popular culture and the lives of ordinary people. New mass media—especially radio and films—reached audiences of unprecedented size. Political life incorporated many of these new media, setting off worries that the common people, increasingly referred to as the "masses," could be manipulated by demagogues and propaganda. In 1918, mass politics was rapidly becoming a fact of life: that meant nearly universal suffrage (varying by country), well-organized political parties reaching out to voters, and in general, more participation in political life. That change was accompanied by the rise of mass culture: books, newspapers, films, and fashions were produced in large numbers and standardized formats, which were less expensive and more accessible, appealing not only to more, but to more kinds of people. Older forms of "popular culture" were often local and class specific; mass culture, at least in principle, cut across lines of class and ethnicity, and even nationality. The term, however, can easily become misleading. The world of culture did not suddenly become homogenous. No more than half the population read newspapers regularly. Not everyone listened to the radio, and

The explosive rise of mass media in the interwar years transformed popular culture and the lives of ordinary people, and showed that it held both democratic and authoritarian potential.

those who did certainly did not believe everything they heard. The pace of cultural change, however, did quicken suddenly. And in the interwar years, mass culture showed that it held both democratic and authoritarian potential.

The expansion of mass culture rested on widespread applications of existing technologies. Wireless communication, for instance, was invented before the turn of the century, and saw limited use in the First World War. With major financial investment in the 1920s, though, the radio industry boomed. Three out of four British families had a radio by the end of the 1930s, and in Germany, the ratio was even higher. In every European country, broadcasting rights were controlled by the government; in the United States, radio was managed by corporations. The radio broadcast soon became the national soapbox for politicians, and it played no small role in creating new kinds of political language. President Franklin Roosevelt's reassuring "fireside chats" took advantage of the way that radio bridged the public world of politics with the private world of the home. Hitler cultivated a different kind of radio personality, barking his fierce invectives; he made some fifty addresses in 1933 alone. In Germany, Nazi propagandists beamed their messages into homes or blared them through loudspeakers in town squares, constant and repetitive. Broadcasting created new rituals of political life—and new means of communication and persuasion.

So did advertising. Advertising was not new, but it was newly prominent. Businesses spent vastly more on advertising than they had before. Hard-hitting visual images replaced older ads that simply announced products, prices, and brand names. Many observers considered advertising the most "modern" of art forms. Why? It was efficient communication, streamlined and standardized, producing images that would appeal to all. It was scientific, drawing on modern psychology; advertising agencies claimed to have a science of selling to people. In a world remade by mass politics, and at a moment when the purchasing power of the common people was beginning to rise, however slowly, the high stakes in advertising (as in much of mass culture) were apparent to many.

The most dramatic changes came on movie screens. The technology of moving pictures came earlier; the 1890s were the era of nickelodeons and short action pictures. And in that period, France and Italy had strong film industries. Further popularized by news shorts during the war, film boomed in the war's aftermath. When sound was added to movies in 1927, costs soared, competition intensified, and audiences grew rapidly. By the 1930s, an estimated 40 percent of British adults went to the movies once a week, a strikingly high figure. Many went more often than that. The United States' film industry gained a competitive edge in Europe, buoyed by the size of its home market, by huge investments in equipment and distribution, by aggressive marketing, and by Hollywood's star system of long-term contracts with well-known actors who, in a sense, standardized the product and guaranteed a film's success.

Germany, too, was home to a particularly talented group of directors, writers, and actors, and to a major production company, UFA (Universum Film AG), which ran the largest and best equipped studios in Europe. The UFA's history paralleled the country's: it was run by the government during World War I, devastated by the economic crisis of the early twenties, rescued by wealthy German nationalists in the late twenties, and finally taken over by the Nazis. During the Weimar years, UFA produced some of the most remarkable films of the period, including *Der letzte mann* ("*The Last Man*," released as *The Last Laugh* in English), a universally acclaimed film directed by F. W. Murnau, one of the two great masters of German expressionism. Fritz Lang was the other, directing such masterpieces as the science-fiction film *Metropolis* (1926) and his most famous German film, *M* (1931). After Hitler's rise to power, the Nazis took control of UFA, placing it under the control of Joseph Goebbels and the Ministry of Propaganda. Though production continued unabated during the Third Reich, many of the industry's most talented members fled from the oppressive regime, ending the golden age of German cinema.

Many found the new mass culture disturbing. As they perceived it, the threat came straight from the United States, which deluged Europe with cultural exports after the war. Hollywood westerns, cheap dime novels, and jazz music—which became increasingly popular in the 1920s—introduced Europe to new ways of life. Advertising, comedies, and romances disseminated new and often disconcerting images of femininity. With bobbed haircuts and short dresses, "new women" seemed assertive, flirtatious, capricious, and materialistic. The "Wild West" genre was popular with teenage boys, much to the dismay of their parents and teachers, who saw westerns as an inappropriate, lower-class form of entertainment. In Europe, the cross-class appeal of American popular culture grated against long-standing social hierarchies. Conservative critics abhorred the fact that "the parson's wife sat nearby his maid at Sunday matinees, equally rapt in the gaze of Hollywood stars." American critics expressed many of the same concerns. Yet the United States enjoyed more social and political stability than Europe. War and revolution had shaken Europe's economies and cultures, and in that context "Americanization" seemed a handy shorthand for economic as well as cultural change. One critic expressed a common concern: "America is the source of that terrible wave of uniformity that gives everyone the same [sic]: the same overalls on the skin, the same book in the hand, the same pen between the fingers, the same conversation on the lips, and the same automobile instead of feet."

Authoritarian governments, in particular, decried these developments as decadent threats to national culture. Fascist, communist, and Nazi governments tried to control not only popular culture, but also high culture and modernism, which were typically out of line with the designs of the dictators. Stalin much preferred "socialist realism" to the new Soviet avant garde. Mussolini had a penchant for classical kitsch, though he was far more accepting of modern art than Hitler, who despised its "decadence." Nazism had its own cultural aesthetic, promoting "Aryan" art and architecture and rejecting the modern, "international" style they associated with the "international Jewish conspiracy." Modernism, functionalism, and atonality were banned: the hallmarks of Weimar Germany's cultural preeminence were replaced by a state-sponsored revival of an alleged mystical and heroic past. Walter Gropius's acclaimed experiments in modernist architecture, for example, stood as monuments to everything the Nazis hated. The Bauhaus school was closed in 1933, and Hitler hired Albert Speer as his personal architect, commissioning him to design grandiose neoclassical buildings, including an extravagant plan to rebuild the entire city of Berlin.

The Nazis, like other authoritarian governments, used mass media as efficient means of indoctrination and control. Movies became part of the Nazis' pioneering use of "spectacular politics." Media campaigns, mass rallies, parades and ceremonies: all were designed to display the strength and glory of the Reich, and to impress and intimidate spectators. In 1934 Hitler commissioned the filmmaker Leni Riefenstahl to record a political rally staged by herself and Albert Speer in Nuremberg. The film, entitled *Triumph of the Will*, was a visual hymn to the

CINEMA: FRITZ LANG ON THE FUTURE OF THE FEATURE FILM IN GERMANY, 1926

Fritz Lang (1890–1976), came from Austria to Berlin after World War I and became one of the German Weimar Republic's most brilliant movie directors, best known for Metropolis *(1926) and* M *(1931). In this essay, Lang reflects on the technological, artistic, and human potential of film. Like all European filmmakers he was fascinated by American movies. In 1932 Joseph Goebbels (see p. 972), dazzled by Lang's work, asked him to work on movies for the Nazis. Lang immediately left Germany for Paris, and from there for the United States, where he continued to make films in Hollywood.*

There has perhaps never before been a time so determined as ours in its search for new forms of expression. Fundamental revolutions in painting, sculpture, architecture, and music speak eloquently of the fact that people of today are seeking and finding their own means of lending artistic form to their sentiments. . . .

The speed with which film has developed in the last five years makes all predictions about it appear dangerous, for it will probably exceed each one by leaps and bounds. Film knows no rest. What was invented yesterday is already obsolete today. This uninterrupted drive for new modes of expression, this intellectual experimentation, along with the joy Germans characteristically take in overexertion, appear to me to fortify my contention that film as art will first find its form in Germany. . . .

Germany has never had, and never will have, the gigantic human and financial reserves of the American film industry at its disposal. To its good fortune. For that is exactly what forces us to compensate a purely material imbalance through an intellectual superiority. . . .

The first important gift for which we have film to thank was in a certain sense *the rediscovery of the human face*. Film has revealed to us the human face with unexampled clarity in its tragic as well as grotesque, threatening as well as blessed expression.

The second gift is that of visual empathy: in the purest sense the expressionistic representation of thought processes. No longer will we take part purely externally in the workings of the soul of the characters in film. We will no longer limit ourselves to seeing the effects of feelings, but will experience them in our own souls, from the instant of their inception on, from the first flash of a thought through to the logical last conclusion of the idea. . . .

The internationalism of filmic language will become the strongest instrument available for the mutual understanding of peoples, who otherwise have such difficulty understanding each other in all too many languages. To bestow upon film the double gift of ideas and soul is the task that lies before us. . . .

Anton Kaes, Matin Jay, and Edward Dimendberg, *The Weimar Republic Sourcebook* (Los Angeles: University of California Press, 1994), pp. 622–23.

Nordic race and the Nazi regime. Everything in the film was on a huge scale: masses of bodies stood in parade formation, flags rose and fell in unison; the film invited viewers to surrender to the power of grand ritual and symbolism. The comedian Charlie Chaplin riposted in his celebrated lampoon *The Great Dictator* (1940), an enormously successful parody of Nazi pomposities.

The Nazis also tried to eliminate the influences of American popular culture, which even before 1933 had been decried as an example of biological and cultural degeneracy. For instance, critics associated American dances and jazz music (which were increasingly popular in German cities) with what the Nazis deemed "racially inferior" blacks and Jews. With culture, however, the Nazis were forced to strike a balance between party propaganda and popular entertainment. The regime allowed many cultural imports, including Hollywood films, to continue, while consciously cultivating German alternatives to American cinema, music, fashions, and even dances. Joseph Goebbels, the minister of propaganda who controlled most film production, placed a high value on economic viability. During the Third Reich, the German film industry turned out comedies, escapist fantasies, and sentimental romances. It developed its own star system and tried to keep audiences happy; meanwhile it became a major competitor internationally. For domestic consumption, the industry also produced vicious anti-Semitic films, such as *The Eternal Jew* (1940) and *Jew Suss* (1940), a fictional tale of a Jewish moneylender who brings the city of Württemberg to ruin in the eighteenth century. In the final scene of the film, the town expels the entire Jewish community from its midst, asking that "posterity honor this law." Goebbels reported that the entire Reich cabinet had viewed the film and considered it "an incredible success."

CONCLUSION

The strains of World War I created a world that few recognized—transformed by revolution, mass mobilization, and loss. In retrospect, it is hard not to see the period that followed as a succession of failures. Capitalism foundered in the Great Depression, democracies collapsed in the face of authoritarianism, and the Treaty of Versailles proved hollow. Yet we come closer to the experience of ordinary people if we do not treat the failures of the interwar period as inevitable. By the late 1920s, many were cautiously optimistic that the Great War's legacy could be overcome and that problems were being solved. The Great Depression (1929–1933) wrecked these hopes, bringing economic chaos and political paralysis. Paralysis and chaos, in turn, created new audiences for political leaders who offered authoritarian solutions and more voters for their political parties. Finally, economic troubles and political turmoil made contending with rising international tensions, to which we now turn, vastly more difficult. By the 1930s, even cautious optimism had given way to apprehension and dread.

SELECTED READINGS

Carr, E. H. *The Bolshevik Revolution, 1917–1923*. London and New York, 1950–1953. One of the classics.

Cohen, Stephen F. *Bukharin and the Bolshevik Revolution: A Political Biography, 1888–1938*. New York, 1973.

Conquest, Robert. *The Great Terror: A Reassessment*. New York, 1990.

Crew, David F. *Nazism and German Society, 1933–1945*. New York, 1994. An excellent and accessible collection of essays.

Figes, Orlando. *Peasant Russia, Civil War: The Volga Countryside in Revolution, 1917–1921*. Oxford, 1989.

Friedlander, Saul. *Nazi Germany and the Jews*. New York, 1998. Excellent; the first of a projected two-volume study.

Gay, Peter. *Weimar Culture*. New York, 1968. Concise and elegant overview.

Getty, J. Arch and Oleg V. Naumov. *The Road to Terror: Stalin and the Self-Destruction of the Bolsheviks, 1932–1939*. New Haven, 1999. Combines analysis with many newly discovered documents.

Gilbert, Felix and David C. Large, *The End of the European Era, 1890 to the Present*. New York, 2001.

Goldman, Wendy Z. *Women, the State, and Revolution: Soviet Family Policy and Social Life, 1917–1936*. New York, 1993.

Kershaw, Ian. *The Hitler Myth: Image and Reality in the Third Reich*. New York, 1987.

Klemperer, Victor. *I Will Bear Witness: A Diary of the Nazi Years, 1933–1941*. New York, 1999. First of a two-volume memoir, certain to be a classic.

Lewin, Moshe. *The Making of the Soviet System: Essays in the Social History of Interwar Russia*. New York, 1985. One of the best to offer a view from below.

Rentschler, Eric. *The Ministry of Illusion: Nazi Cinema and Its Afterlife*. Cambridge, Mass., 1996. For the more advanced student.

Suny, Ronald Grigor. *The Revenge of the Past: Nationalism, Revolution, and the Collapse of the Soviet Union*. Stanford, Calif., 1993.

Tucker, Robert C. *Stalin as Revolutionary, 1879–1929*. New York, 1973.

——— . *Stalin in Power: The Revolution from Above, 1928–1941*. New York, 1990.

CHAPTER TWENTY-NINE

THE SECOND WORLD WAR

IN SEPTEMBER 1939, Europe was consumed by another world war. The peace of 1919–1920 was fleeting, and the devastation of 1914–1918 paled in comparison to this new, global conflict. The Second World War was not simply a continuation of the First. Both were triggered by threats to the European balance of power. Yet even more than the Great War, the Second World War was a conflict among nations, whole peoples, and fiercely opposing ideals. The methods of warfare in the Second World War had little in common with those of the First. In 1914 military firepower had outmatched mobility, resulting in four years of static, mud-sodden slaughter. In 1939, mobility was joined to firepower on a massive scale. The results were terrifying. On the battlefield, the tactics of high-speed armored warfare (*Blitzkrieg*), aircraft carriers sinking ships far below the horizon, and submarines used in vast numbers to dominate shipping lanes changed the scope and the pace of fighting. This was not a war of trenches and barbed wire but a war of motion, dramatic conquests, and terrible destructive power.

The other great change was not one of tactics, but of targets. Much of the unprecedented killing power now available was aimed directly at civilians. Cities were laid waste by artillery and aerial bombing. The countryside of whole regions was put to the torch, while towns and villages were systematically cordoned off and leveled. Whole populations were targeted as well, in ways that continue to appall. The Nazi regime's systematic murder of gypsies, homosexuals, and other "deviants," along with the effort to exterminate the Jewish people completely, made the Second World War a horrifyingly unique event. So did the United States' use of a weapon whose existence would dominate politics and society for the next fifty years: the atomic bomb. The naive enthusiasm that had marked the outbreak of the Great War was absent from the start. Terrible memories of the first conflict lingered. Yet those who fought against the Axis Powers (and many of those who fought for them) found that their determination to fight and win grew as the war went on. Unlike the seemingly meaningless killing of the Great War, the Second World War was cast as a war of absolutes, of good and evil, of national and global survival. Nevertheless the scale of destruction brought with it a profound weariness. It also provoked deep-seated questions about the value of Western "civilization" and the terms on which it, and the rest of the world, might live peaceably in the future.

THE CAUSES OF THE WAR: UNSETTLED QUARRELS, ECONOMIC FALLOUT, AND NATIONALISM

What were the long-term causes of World War II?

The causes of the Second World War were rooted in the peace settlement of 1919–1920. That peace, understandable in view of the hatreds engendered by the First World War, created as many problems as it solved. The senior Allied heads of state yielded to demands that involved annexing German territory and creating satellite states out of the eastern European empires. By meeting those demands, the peacemakers created fresh bitterness and conflict. The Versailles treaty and its champions such as President Woodrow Wilson proclaimed the principle of self-determination for the peoples of eastern and southern Europe. Yet the new states created by the treaty crossed ethnic boundaries, involved political compromises, and frustrated many of the expectations they had raised. The unsteady new boundaries would be redrawn by force in the 1930s. The Allied powers also kept up the naval blockade against Germany after the end of the fighting. This forced the new German government to accept harsh terms that deprived Germany of its political power in Europe, and saddled the German economy with the bill for the conflict in a "war guilt" clause. The blockade and its consequences created grievances that many angry, humiliated Germans considered legitimate.

Power politics persisted after the peace conference, just as it did in the treaties. Although Woodrow Wilson and other sponsors of the League of Nations acclaimed the League as a means of eliminating power struggles, it did nothing of the sort. The signatures on the peace treaties were hardly dry when the victors began carving out new alliances to maintain their supremacy, interfering in the new central European states and the "mandate" territories added to the British and French empires in the Middle East. Even the League itself was fundamentally an alliance of the victors against the vanquished; it was natural that politicians feared disturbances in this imbalance of power.

A second cause of World War II was the failure to create lasting, binding standards for peace and security. Diplomats spent the ten years after Versailles trying to restore such standards. Some put their faith in the legal and moral authority of the League. Others saw disarmament as the most promising means of guaranteeing peace. Throughout the 1920s, a number of important European statesmen—the German and French foreign ministers Gustav Stresemann and Aristide Briand, and the British prime ministers Stanley Baldwin and Ramsay MacDonald—tried to reach a set of agreements that would stabilize the peace and prevent rearmament. In 1925 an effort was made to secure the frontiers on the Rhine established at Versailles. In 1928, the Kellogg-Briand Pact attempted to outlaw war as an international crime. Despite the good faith of many of the statesmen involved, none of these pacts carried any real weight. Each nation involved tried to include special provisions and exceptions for "vital interests" that compromised the treaties from the start. Had the League of Nations been better organized, it might have relieved some of the tensions or at least prevented clashes between nations. But the League was never a league of all nations. Essential members were absent, since Germany and the Soviet Union were excluded for most of the interwar period, and the United States never joined.

Economic conditions were a third important cause of renewed conflict. The huge reparations imposed on the Germans, and France's occupation of much of Germany's industrial heartland, helped slow Germany's recovery. German and French stubbornness about the pace of repayments combined disastrously to bring on the German inflation of the 1920s. The spiraling inflation made German money nearly worthless, damaging the stability and credibility of Germany's young republic almost beyond repair.

The depression of the 1930s contributed to the coming of the war in several ways. It intensified economic nationalism. Baffled by problems of unemployment and business stagnation, governments imposed high tariffs in an effort to preserve the home market for their own producers. The collapse of investment and terrible unemployment at home caused the United States to withdraw even further from world affairs. While France suffered less than some other countries, the depression still inflamed tensions between management and labor. This exacerbated France's political battles between left and right, making it difficult for either side to govern the country. Britain turned in on its empire, raising tariffs for the first time and guarding its financial investments jealously.

These inward-looking policies among the old Allies left the door open to more aggressive tactics elsewhere. In Germany, the depression was the last blow to the Weimar Republic. There was physical conflict between left and right, as there had been in 1919–1920. A series of right-wing governments tried and failed to deal with the crisis. In 1933 power passed to the Nazis, who promised a total program of national renewal. In the fascist states (and, exceptionally, the United States) public works projects of one kind or another were prescribed as an answer to mass unemployment. This produced highways, bridges, and railroads; it also produced a new arms race.

Despite the misgivings of many inside the governments of Britain and France, Germany was allowed to ignore the terms of the peace treaties and rearm. Armaments expansion on a large scale first began in Germany about 1935, with the result that unemployment was reduced and the effects of the Depression eased. Other nations followed the German example, not simply as a way of boosting their economies, but in response to growing Nazi military power. In the Pacific, the decline of Japanese exports meant that the nation did not have enough foreign currency to pay for vital raw materials from overseas. This played into the hands of Japan's military regime. Japanese national ambitions, and Japanese leaders' perception of the political and cultural inferiority of the Chinese, led them to fresh imperial adventures in the name of establishing economic stability in East Asia. They began in 1931 with the invasion of Manchuria, and moved from there to create a "Greater Pacific Co-Prosperity Sphere" that involved seizing other territories as Japanese colonies. Raw materials could then be bought with Japanese money, and more of Asia would serve the needs of Japan's empire.

Imperial success could serve as consolation when economic methods failed. As the depression dragged on in fascist Italy, Mussolini tried to distract his public with national conquests overseas, culminating in the invasion of Ethiopia in 1935.

In sum, the tremendous economic hardship of the depression and the political difficulties of building a lasting peace shook international stability. But the decisive factor in the crises of the 1930s, and the trigger for another world war, lay in a blend of violent nationalism and modern ideologies that glorified the nation and national destiny. This blend, particularly in the forms of fascism and militarism, appeared around the world in many countries. By the middle of the 1930s, recognizing common interests, fascist Italy and Nazi Germany formed an "Axis," an alliance binding their goals of national glory and international power. They were later joined by Japan's military regime. In Spain, the ultranationalist forces that tried to overthrow the Spanish Republic, setting off the Spanish Civil War (see below) believed they were reviving the stability, authority, and morality of the nation. Fascist or semifascist regimes spread in Eastern Europe, in Yugoslavia, Hungary, and Romania. One exception to this sobering trend was Czechoslovakia. Czechoslovakia boasted no ethnic majority. Although the Czechs practiced an enlightened policy of minority self-government, and though their government was remarkably stable, questions of nationality remained a potential source of friction. Those questions became a key factor as international tensions mounted in the late 1930s.

> The trigger for another world war lay in a blend of violent nationalism and modern ideologies that glorified the nation and national destiny.

THE 1930S: CHALLENGES TO THE PEACE, APPEASEMENT, AND THE "DISHONEST DECADE"

What was the policy of "appeasement"?

The 1930s brought the tensions and failures caused by the treaties of 1919–1920 to a head. Fascist and nationalist governments flouted the League of Nations by launching new conquests and efforts at national expansion. With the memories of 1914–1918 still fresh, these new crises created a deepening atmosphere of fear and apprehension. Each new conflict seemed to warn that another, much wider war would follow unless it could somehow be averted. Ordinary people— particularly in Britain, France, and the United States —were divided. Some saw the actions of the aggressors as a direct challenge to civilization, one that had to be met with force if necessary. Others hoped to avoid premature or unnecessary conflict. Their governments tried instead at several points to negotiate with the fascists and keep a tenuous peace. Writers, intellectuals, and politicians on the left vilified these acts of "appeasement." The 1930s were not just a time of renewed warfare and global crisis; many saw the period as a series of missed opportunities to prevent the larger war to come. In 1939, on the first day of the Second World War, the British poet and leftist W. H. Auden condemned the behavior of Western governments, calling the 1930s "a low, dishonest decade."

The object of Auden's venom was the policy of "appeasement" pursued by Western governments in the face of German, Italian, and Japanese aggression. Appeasement was neither simple power politics nor pure cowardice. It was grounded in three deeply held assumptions and geared toward two very different but rational ends. The first assumption was that the outbreak of another war was unthinkable. With the memory of the slaughter of 1914–1918 fresh in their minds, many in the West embraced pacifism, or at any rate adopted an attitude that kept them from facing up to the uncompromising aggression of the fascist governments, especially Nazi Germany. Second, many in Britain and the United States argued that Germany had been mistreated by the Versailles treaty and harbored legitimate grievances that should be acknowledged and resolved. Finally, many appeasers were staunch anticommunists. They believed that the fascist states in Germany and Italy were an essential bulwark against the advance of Soviet communism, and that division among the major European states only played into the hands of the USSR. Yet this last point divided the appeasers. All were concerned with maintaining Europe's balance of power. One group, however, believed that the Soviets posed the greater threat, and that accommodating Hitler might create a common interest against a common enemy. The other faction believed that Nazi Germany presented the true threat to European stability; never-

> Appeasement was neither simple politics nor pure cowardice.

theless, they believed, Hitler would have to be placated until Britain and France finished rearming. At that point greater military power would deter Hitler or Mussolini from risking a general European war. It took most of the 1930s for the debate between appeasers to come to a head. In the meanwhile, the League of Nations faced more immediate and pressing challenges.

The 1930s brought three crucial tests for the League: the crises in China, Ethiopia, and Spain. In China, the Japanese invasion of Manchuria in 1931 turned into an invasion of the whole country. Chinese forces were driven before the Japanese advance, and the Japanese deliberately targeted civilians in order to break the Chinese will to fight. In 1937, the Japanese laid siege to the strategic city of Nanjing. Their orders on taking the city were simple: "kill all, burn all, destroy all." More than two hundred thousand Chinese citizens were slaughtered in what came to be known as the "Rape of Nanjing." The League voiced shock and disapproval but did nothing. In 1935 Mussolini began his efforts to make the Mediterranean an Italian empire by returning to Ethiopia to avenge the defeat of 1896. This time the Italians came with tanks, bombers, and poison gas; the Ethiopians fought bravely but hopelessly, and this imperial massacre aroused world opinion. The League attempted to impose sanctions on Italy and condemned Japan. But for two reasons, no enforcement followed. The first was British and French fear of communism, and their hope that Italy and Japan would act as counterweights to the Soviets. The second reason was practical. Enforcing sanctions would involve challenging Japan's powerful fleet or Mussolini's newly built battleships. Britain and France were unwilling, and dangerously close to unable, to use their navies to those ends.

THE SPANISH CIVIL WAR

The third challenge came closer to home. In 1936 civil war broke out in Spain. A series of weak republican governments, committed to large-scale social reforms, could not overcome opposition to those measures and political polarization. War broke out as extreme right-wing military officers rebelled. Although Hitler and Mussolini had signed a pact of nonintervention with the other Western powers, both leaders sent troops and equipment to assist the rebel commander, Francisco Franco (1936–1975). The Soviet Union countered with aid to communist troops serving under the banner of the

"Help Spain." This poster calls for volunteers and funds to support the Spanish republican government against the fascists during the Spanish Civil War. The poster was designed by Juan Miró, a Spanish artist in exile in Paris.

Spanish Republic. Again, Britain and France failed to act decisively. Thousands of volunteers from England, France, and the United States, including many working-class socialists and writers such as George Orwell and Ernest Hemingway, took up arms as private soldiers for the Republican government. They saw the war as a test of the West's determination to resist fascism and military dictatorships. Their governments were much more hesitant. For the British, Franco was anticommunist at least, just like Mussolini and the Japanese. The French prime minister Léon Blum, a committed antifascist, stood at the head of a Popular Front government—an alliance of socialists, communists, and republicans. The Popular Front had been elected on a program of social reform and opposition to Hitler abroad and fascism. Yet Blum's margin of support was limited. He feared that intervening in Spain would further polarize his country, bring down his government, and make it impossible to follow through on any commitment to the conflict. In Spain, despite some heroic fighting, the Republican camp degenerated into a hornet's nest of competing factions: republican, socialist, comunist, and anarchist.

The Spanish Civil War itself was brutal. Both the German and Soviet "advisors" saw Spain as a "dress rehearsal" for a later war between the two powers. They each brought in their newest weapons and practiced their skills in destroying civilian targets from the air. In April 1937, a raid by German dive bombers utterly

Guernica (1937), by Pablo Picasso. One of Picasso's most influential paintings, *Guernica* was painted as a mural for the Spanish republican government as it fought for survival in the Spanish Civil War. The Basque town of Guernica had been bombed by German fighters just a few months earlier, in April, 1937. Near the center a horse writhes in agony; to the left a distraught woman holds her dead child.

destroyed the town of Guernica in northern Spain, in an effort to cut off Republican supply lines and terrorize civilians. It shocked public opinion, and was commemorated by Pablo Picasso in one of the most famous paintings of the twentieth century. Both sides committed atrocities. The Spanish Civil War lasted three years, ending with a complete victory for Franco in 1939. In the aftermath, Britain and France proved extremely reluctant to admit Spanish Republicans as refugees, even though they faced recriminations from Franco's regime; Franco sent one million of his Republican enemies to prison or concentration camps. Hitler in particular took two lessons from Spain. The first was that if Britain, France, and the Soviet Union ever tried to contain fascism, they would have a hard time coordinating their efforts. The second was that Britain and France were deeply averse to fighting another European war. This meant that the Nazis could use every means short of war to achieve their goals.

GERMAN REARMAMENT AND THE POLITICS OF APPEASEMENT

Hitler took advantage of this combination of international tolerance and war weariness to advance his ambitions. As Germany rearmed, Hitler played on Germans' sense of shame and betrayal, proclaiming their right to regain their former power in the world. In 1933, he removed Germany from the League of Nations to which it had finally been admitted in 1926. In 1935 he tore up the disarmament provisions of the Treaty of Versailles, and revived conscription and universal military training. Hitler's stated goals were the restoration of Germany's power and dignity inside Europe, and the unification of all ethnic Germans inside his "Third German Reich." As the first step in this process, Germany reoccupied the Rhineland in 1936. It was a risky move, chancing war with the much more powerful French army. But France and Britain did not mount a military response. In retrospect, this was an important turning point; the balance of power tipped in Germany's favor. While the Rhineland remained demilitarized and German industry in the Ruhr valley was unprotected, France had held the upper hand. Now it no longer did so.

In March of 1938, Hitler annexed Austria, reaffirming his intention to bring all Germans into his Reich. Once more, no official reaction came from the West. The Nazis' next target was the Sudetenland in Czechoslovakia, which had a large ethnic German population.

The Munich Conference, 1938. Prime Minister Chamberlain of Britain and Hitler during the Munich conference.

With Austria now a part of Germany, Czechoslovakia was almost entirely surrounded by its hostile neighbor. Hitler declared that the Sudetenland was a natural part of the Reich and that he intended to occupy it. The Czechs did not want to give way. Hitler's generals were wary of this gamble. Czechoslovakia had a strong, well-equipped army and a line of fortifications along the border. Many in the French and Polish governments were willing to come to the Czechs' aid. According to plans already being laid for a wider European war, Germany would not be ready for another three to four years. But Hitler did gamble, and the British prime minister, Neville Chamberlain, obliged him. Chamberlain decided to take charge of international talks about the Sudetenland, on Hitler's terms. Chamberlain's logic was that this dispute was about the balance of power in Europe. If Hitler were allowed to unify all Germans in one state, he reasoned, then German ambitions would be satisfied. Chamberlain also believed that his country could not commit to a sustained war. Finally, defending Eastern European boundaries against Germany ranked low on Great Britain's list of priorities, at least in comparison to ensuring free trade in Western Europe and protecting the strategic centers of the British empire.

On September 29, 1938, Hitler met with Chamberlain, Premier Édouard Daladier (1938–1940) of France,

WHAT ACCOUNTS FOR THE EARLY GERMAN SUCCESSES IN WORLD WAR II?

THE OUTBREAK OF HOSTILITIES AND THE FALL OF FRANCE   995

and Mussolini in a four-power conference in Munich. The result was another capitulation by France and Britain. The four negotiators bargained away a major slice of Czechoslovakia, while Czech representatives were left to await their fate outside the conference room. Chamberlain returned to London proclaiming "peace in our time." Hitler soon proved that boast hollow. In March 1939 Germany invaded what was left of Czechoslovakia and established a puppet regime in its capital, Prague. This was Germany's first conquest of non-German territory, and it sent shock waves across Europe. It convinced public and political opinion outside Germany of the futility of appeasement. Chamberlain was forced to shift his policies completely. British and French rearmament sped up dramatically. Together with France, Britain guaranteed the sovereignty of the two states now directly in Hitler's path, Poland and Romania.

Meanwhile, the politics of appeasement had fueled Stalin's fears that the Western democracies might strike a deal with Germany at Soviet expense, thus diverting Nazi expansion eastward. The Soviet Union had not been invited to the Munich conference, and, suspicious that Britain and France were unreliable allies, Stalin became convinced that he should look elsewhere for security. Tempted by the traditional Soviet desire for territory in Poland, Stalin was promised a share of Poland, Finland, the Baltic states, and Bessarabia by Hitler's representatives. In a cynical reversal of their anti-Nazi proclamations, the Soviets signed a nonaggression pact with the Nazis in August 1939. By going to Munich, Britain and France had put

their interests first; the Soviet Union would now look after its own. In accordance with its agreement with Nazi Germany, the Soviet Union invaded Poland in September 1939.

THE OUTBREAK OF HOSTILITIES AND THE FALL OF FRANCE

What accounts for the early German successes in World War II?

After his success in Czechoslovakia, Hitler demanded the abolition of the Polish Corridor. This was a narrow strip of land connecting Poland with the Baltic Sea. The corridor also divided East Prussia from the rest of Germany, separating yet another large German population from union with the Reich. Judging Britain and France by past performance, Hitler believed their pledges to Poland were worthless. With the Soviets now in his camp, he expected that Poland would consent and the Western allies would back down again. When Poland stood firm instead, Hitler attacked. On September 1, 1939, German troops crossed the Polish border. Britain and France sent a joint warning to Germany to withdraw. There was no reply. On September 3, Britain and France declared war.

The conquest of Poland was shockingly quick. It demanded great resources—Germany committed nearly all of its combat troops and planes to the invasion—but the results were remarkable. Well-coordinated attacks by German panzers (tanks) and armored vehicles, supported by devastating air power, cut the large but slow-moving Polish army to pieces. German infantry still moved on foot or via horse-drawn transport, but their disciplined advance followed the devastating work of the panzers. The Poles fought doggedly, but were so stunned and disorganized that they had little hope of mounting an effective defense. The "lightning war" (*Blitzkrieg*) for which the German officer corps had trained so long was a complete success. Within three weeks German troops were laying siege to Warsaw. The Soviets invaded from the east, taking their share of Polish territory. German terror bombing, designed to destroy the heart of Warsaw from the air and frighten the population into surrender, was successful. Poland, a

CHRONOLOGY	
THE ROAD TO WORLD WAR II, 1931–1940	
Japanese Invasion of Manchuria	1931
Germany leaves the League of Nations	1933
Germany begins remilitarization	1935
Spanish Civil War	1936–1939
Germany reoccupies the Rhineland	1936
Germany annexes Austria	1938
Munich Conference	1938
Nazi-Soviet Pact	1939
Germany invades Poland	1939
Germany invades the Low Countries and France	1940

The Beginning of the Second World War. A German armored division invades Poland.

large country with a large army, was dismembered in four weeks.

After that the war resolved itself into a kind of siege, a "phony war" or "sitzkrieg," as it was sometimes called. The fighting in Poland was followed by a winter of anxious nonactivity with occasional headlines about naval skirmishes. In the spring of 1940 that calm was broken by a terrible storm. The Germans struck first in Scandinavia, taking Denmark in a day and invading Norway. Britain and France tried to aid the Norwegian defense and sank a large number of German ships, but the Allied expedition failed. Then the real blow was struck. On May 10, German forces swarmed through Belgium and the Netherlands on their way to France. The two nations were conquered in short order. When the Dutch succeeded in flooding canals that protected their major cities and defended that line with hard-fighting marines, Hitler ordered his air force to bomb the city of Rotterdam. More than eight hundred Dutch civilians died, and the Netherlands surrendered the next day. The Belgians' stubborn and effective defense of their nation was cut short when King Albert suddenly surrendered after two weeks of fighting, fearing similar destruction. In turn Albert stayed on as a figure-head for the Nazis, reviled by Belgians who found other ways to carry on the fight against Germany.

The large French army was carved up by the *Blitz-krieg*. Its divisions were isolated, outflanked, and over-whelmed by German aircraft and armored columns

working according to an exacting plan. French units either fought fierce battles until they were hopelessly surrounded, or simply collapsed. French armor and artillery, much of it better built than the German equivalents, were poorly organized and rendered useless in the face of rapid German maneuvers. The defeat turned quickly into a rout. Hundreds of thousands of civilians, each carrying a few precious possessions loaded on carts, fled south. They were joined by thousands of Allied soldiers without weapons, and these columns of refugees were attacked constantly by German dive-bombers. The disorganized British made a desperate retreat to the port of Dunkirk on the English Channel, where many of Britain's best troops were sacrificed holding off the panzers. Despite heavy German air attacks, Britain's Royal Navy evacuated more than three hundred thousand British and French troops, with the help of commercial and pleasure boats that had been pressed into emergency service.

After Dunkirk, the conflict was bitter but the outcome inevitable. French reservists fought, as their commanders asked, "to the last cartridge," killing thousands of Germans. Without proper organization and more firepower, however, this bravery was useless. The Germans swept through the northwest and the heart of the country, reaching Paris in mid-June. The political will of France's government collapsed along with its armies. Rather than withdrawing to Britain or French colonies in North Africa, the French surrendered on June 18. The armistice cut France in two. The Germans occupied all of northern France, including Paris and the Channel ports. The south lay under the jurisdiction of a deeply conservative government formed at the spa town of Vichy under the leadership of an elderly First World War hero, Marshal Henri Philippe Pétain. France had fallen. One of Germany's historic enemies, the victor of the previous war, an imperial power and nation of almost 60 million citizens, was reduced to chaos and enemy occupation in forty days.

The penalties exacted on France did not end with defeat. Many liberals within France, and most of the "Free French" movement quickly established in London, soon felt they had two enemies to fight: Germany and

French Refugees. These French refugees were driven from their homes by the Nazi advance.

Britain, thousands of planes dropped millions of tons of bombs on British targets. Docks, working-class neighborhoods, and city centers burned in nightly bombing. More than forty thousand British civilians died. Yet the British stood firm. This was possible in part because of a German mistake. After a daring British bombing raid on Berlin, Hitler angrily told his generals to concentrate on civilian targets. This spared the Royal Air Force, whose bases had been steadily devastated up to that point. The R.A.F. was not a large organization, but it had outstanding planes and determined pilots, drawn not just from Britain but from all over the British empire and occupied Europe. Given the chance to keep fighting, the British forced a costly stalemate in the air. Hitler scrapped the invasion plans, turning his attention east toward Russia.

Pétain's regime. The Vichy government proposed to cooperate with the Germans in return for retaining a small measure of sovereignty. The regime also instituted its own "National Revolution," which came very close to fascism. Vichy repudiated the republic, accusing it of sapping France's strength. The state proceeded to reorganize French life and political institutions, strengthening the authority of the Catholic Church and the family and helping the Germans to crush any resistance. "Work, Family, and Country"—this was Vichy's call to order.

NOT ALONE: THE BATTLE OF BRITAIN AND THE BEGINNINGS OF A GLOBAL WAR

What made World War II a global war?

Before launching an invasion across the Channel, the Nazis decided to break Britain's will with massive air raids. From July 1940 to June 1941, in the Battle of

Another important reason for the determined British resistance was a change of political leadership. In May 1940, Chamberlain's catalogue of failures finished his career. He was toppled by a coalition government that brought together Conservative, Liberal, and Labour politicians for the sake of national unity. It was led by the most unlikely of the choices offered to replace him: Winston Churchill (1940–1945, 1951–1955). Churchill was a political maverick who had changed parties more than once. He was extremely talented, and also arrogant. He had a wicked temper and sometimes seemed unstable, and before 1939 his political career was judged to be over. As prime minister he was not much of an administrator, constantly proposing wild schemes, but he had two genuine gifts. The first was language. Churchill spoke extraordinary words of courage and defiance just when the British public wanted and needed to hear them. He was utterly committed to winning the war. The second was personal diplomacy. He convinced the American president Franklin Roosevelt (1933–1945), who supported the Allies, to break with American neutrality and send massive amounts of aid and weapons to Britain free of charge, under a program called Lend-Lease. Churchill also allowed the new government coalition to work to best effect. The ablest Conservative ministers stayed, but Labour politicians were allowed to take positions of genuine power. Most of the Labour representatives turned out to be excellent administrators

ICELAND

EUROPE
Area of
detail

AFRICA

NORWAY

FINLAND

SWEDEN

SOVIET UNION

NORTH
SEA

DENMARK

ESTONIA
LATVIA
LITHUANIA

Leningrad
besieged
Sept. 1941–Jan. 1944

• Moscow

IRELAND

GREAT
BRITAIN
NETHERLANDS

BALTIC SEA

Gdansk
EAST
PRUSSIA
(Ger.)

Battle of Britain
Aug. 1–Oct. 12, 1940   London •

GERMANY   Berlin

POLAND

Germany invades
Soviet Union
June 1941

Stalingrad
Aug. 21, 1942–
Jan. 31, 1943

ATLANTIC
OCEAN

BELGIUM
D-Day
June 6, 1944
Paris
liberated
Aug. 25, 1944

LUX.

Battle of the Bulge
Dec. 16, 1944–
Jan. 31, 1945

FRANCE

• Kiev

UKRAINE

SLOVAKIA

VICHY
FRANCE
(occupied
Nov. 1942)

SWITZ.

HUNGARY

ROMANIA

ITALY

YUGOSLAVIA

PORTUGAL

SPAIN

CORSICA
(Fr.)

Rome
liberated
June 4, 1944

BULGARIA

BLACK SEA

SARDINIA
(It.)

ALBANIA
(It.)

GREECE

TURKEY

SPANISH
MOROCCO

SICILY

Athens •

CYPRUS
(Br.)

SYRIA
(Fr.)

MOROCCO
(Fr.)

ALGERIA
(Fr.)

TUNISIA
(Fr.)

MALTA
(Br.)

CRETE

DODECANESE
IS. (It.)

LEBANON

MEDITERRANEAN SEA

PALESTINE
(Br.)

TRANS-
JORDAN

Axis powers, August 1939

Extent of Axis control, May 1941

Allies

Neutral nations

Axis offenses

Allied offenses

★ Major battles

LIBYA
(It.)

El Alamein
June–Nov. 1942

EGYPT

SAUDI
ARABIA

RED SEA

0   250   500 Miles
0   250   500 Kilometers

WORLD WAR II IN EUROPE

This map shows the alliance systems and major offensives of the European Theater in World War II. What helps to explain the rapid expansion of Axis control by May 1941? In what ways did geography both aid and potentially hinder the Axis effort to conquer Europe? Why did Adolf Hitler hope to neutralize either the Soviet Union or Great Britain early in the war? How did the sieges at Leningrad and Stalingrad prove instrumental in sustaining the Allied effort?

London during the Blitz. A vivid impression of the devastation that the British capital suffered during the Battle of Britain, which lasted from August 1940 to June 1941.

and were directly in touch with Britain's huge working class, which now felt fully included in the war effort.

With Britain's survival, the European war quickly became a global war in four ways. The first was Germany's submarine campaign to starve out the British. The second came with fighting in North Africa, which threatened the Suez Canal and the Allies' access to Middle Eastern oil. The third was Japan's attack on the Allies in the Pacific and its stunning early success. The fourth was the great conflict Hitler had always imagined, a war of annihilation against Soviet Russia and Europe's Jewish population.

The first of these, the battle of the Atlantic, was a dire threat to the Allies. Learning from the Great War, the Germans sent hundreds of submarines (U-boats) out in "wolf packs" to stalk the major sea lanes to Britain. German submarines sank millions of tons of merchant shipping, as far away as the coasts of Brazil and Florida; Britain's supplies of weapons, raw materials, and food hung in the balance. The British devoted a huge naval effort and great technical resourcefulness to saving their convoys. They developed modern sonar and new systems of aerial reconnaissance, and cracked the Germans' codes for communicating with the "wolf packs." Despite continued losses, these efforts kept supplies coming. When the United States entered the war, the British

supplied experience and technology, the Americans the numbers and firepower to sink many more U-boats. By late 1942 the threat receded.

The war in North Africa began because Britain had to protect the Suez Canal and needed public victories, but was drawn into a larger conflict in the process. Indian troops led the liberation of Ethiopia from Italy and invaded Iran to keep its shah (ruler) from making a deal with Germany over Iranian oil. A small, well-led British army in Egypt humiliated a much larger Italian invasion force. The British nearly captured Italy's colony of Libya, and this forced Germany to intervene. An elite armored force called the Afrika Korps, led by Germany's most daring tank commander, Erwin Rommel, drove the British back and started a grudging two-year war in the desert. The British fielded an international army that included as many Australians, Indians, and New Zealanders as it did Britons, pitted against the Germans and Italians. The fighting swung back and forth for eighteen months with the British taking the worst of it. Then the momentum shifted. Despite heavy losses from German planes and submarines, the British defeated the Italian navy and took control of the Mediterranean. They also established domination in the air over the desert. When Rommel tried to invade Egypt, his forces were stopped and badly defeated near the town of El Alamein in the autumn of 1942, then driven back through Libya. The United States intervened in November, landing in the French territories of Algeria and Morocco.

A conference was held at Casablanca, Morocco, among the Allied powers to discuss the future course of the war and the fate of French territories in North Africa. French administrators in Algeria and Morocco, who had supported Vichy in public at least, surrendered peacefully or joined the Allied side. Rommel still defended Tunisia against the Allies for four months but a joint offensive broke the German lines in March 1943, ending the fighting.

Pearl Harbor, December 7, 1941. This photo shows an aerial view of the harbor following the Japanese raid on what President Franklin D. Roosevelt declared was "a date that will live in infamy."

The war became truly global when Japan struck the American naval base at Pearl Harbor, Hawaii, on the morning of December 7, 1941. The Japanese had been involved in a costly war in China since the 1930s. In order to win and to establish a Japanese empire throughout Asia, they would have to destroy America's Pacific fleet and seize the colonies of the British, Dutch, and French empires. Like Germany, Japan began with lightning blows. The attack on Pearl Harbor was a brilliant act of surprise that devastated the American fleet and shocked the American public. It was not, however, the success that the Japanese wanted. Eight U.S. battleships were sunk and more than two thousand lives lost, but much of the American fleet, including its aircraft carriers, submarines, and many smaller ships, were safely at sea on the day of the strike. The unprovoked attack galvanized American public opinion in a way the war in Europe had not. When Germany rashly declared war on the United States as well, America declared itself ready to take on all comers and joined the Allies.

Despite the mixed results at Pearl Harbor the Japanese enjoyed other, stunning successes. For the European colonial powers, Japan's entry into the war was a catastrophe. Japanese troops swept through the British protectorate of Malaya in weeks, sinking the Pacific squadrons of both the British and Dutch navies in the swift attacks. Britain's fortified island port at Singapore, the keystone of British defenses in the Pacific, fell at the end of December 1941. The shock of the loss nearly took Churchill's government with it. Thousands of British and Australian troops were captured and sent off to four years of torture, forced labor, and starvation in Japanese prison camps. The Japanese also invaded the Philippines in December, and while American soldiers and marines held out on the island of Corregidor for some time, they too were forced to surrender. Some took to the hills to fight as guerrillas; the rest were forced on a "Death March" to Japanese labor camps. The Dutch East Indies fell next, and it seemed there would be no stopping Japanese ships and soldiers before they reached Australia.

Reeling from Japan's blows, the Allies finally reorganized during 1942. After taking Singapore, Japanese troops pressed on into Burma. Several famous British generals tried and failed to defend Burma, with disastrous losses of men and matériel. After these failures, command fell to an obscure Indian Army officer, William Slim. For a British officer, Slim had quite humble origins. He was a career soldier, a minor hero in the First World War, and perhaps the best strategist in the British Army. Even more importantly, the millions of nonwhite imperial troops from India and Africa who were under his command liked and respected him as an honest, unbigoted man. He reorganized imperial defenses, and a joint force of British and Indian troops defeated an attempted Japanese invasion of India at the border near the end of 1942. After that, with an army drawn from around the world, Slim began to push the Japanese back. In New Guinea, Australian troops fresh from North Africa were first to defeat the Japanese on land in bitter hand-to-hand fighting, and staged a counterattack through the high mountain jungles. At sea, America's navy benefited from a rapidly increased production schedule that turned out new ships and planes to outnumber the Japanese, and two gifted admirals, Chester Nimitz and William Halsey, who outfought them. In 1942 America

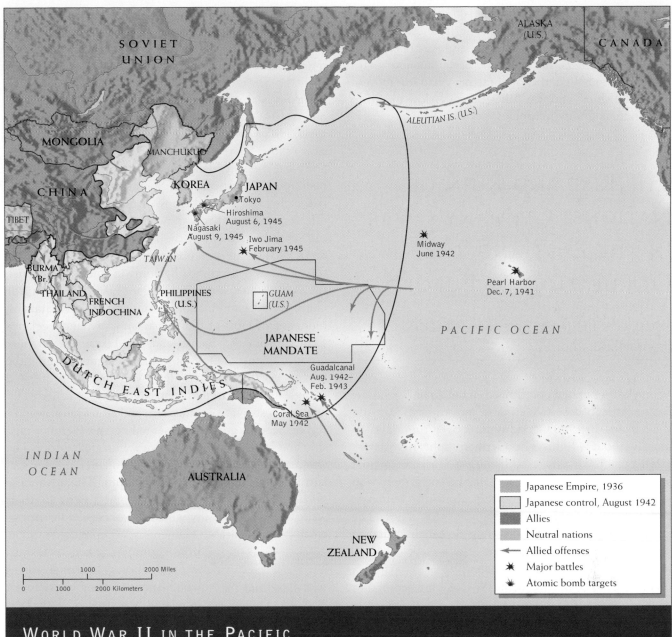

WORLD WAR II IN THE PACIFIC

This map shows the major operations and important geographical features of the Pacific Theater during World War II. Why did the Japanese strategy depend on destroying the American Pacific Fleet simultaneously with their assaults on the Philippines, Dutch East Indies, and Southeast Asia? How did the fact that American aircraft carriers were not at Pearl Harbor affect the next major battles of the war in the Pacific: Coral Sea and Midway? What factors led the Americans to decide that the dropping of atomic bombs on Hiroshima and Nagasaki was the most expeditious way to end the war?

won crucial victories in the Coral Sea and at Midway, a battle fought at sea but won and lost by aircraft flown from each side's carriers. American marines landed on the island of Guadalcanal in early 1942, and captured this strategic Japanese base after months of bitter fighting. This began a campaign of "island hopping" as the marines destroyed Japan's network of island bases throughout the Pacific. This was brutal warfare, often settled with grenades and bayonets; both sides considered the other racially inferior. The Japanese often refused to surrender; the Americans and Australians also took few prisoners. By 1943, the early Japanese victories had been halted, the Japanese navy had lost most of its capital ships, and the Allies began a slow march to Singapore and the Philippines.

THE RISE AND RUIN OF NATIONS: GERMANY'S WAR IN THE EAST AND THE OCCUPATION OF EUROPE

How were the Nazis able to rule over a continental empire?

While battles ebbed and flowed in the Atlantic and the North African desert, Germany moved eastward into the Balkans. In 1940 Germany took over Yugoslavia almost without a fight. The Germans split Yugoslavia's ethnic patchwork by establishing a Croatian puppet state, pitting Croats against their Serb neighbors who were ruled directly by the Nazis. Romania, Hungary, and Bulgaria joined the Nazis' cause as allies. The Greeks, who had dealt a crushing defeat to an Italian invasion, were suddenly confronted with a massive German force that overran the country. The Greeks stubbornly refused to surrender. An unexpected combination of Greek, British, and New Zealand troops nearly defeated the German paratroopers sent to capture the island of Crete in June of 1940. Many Greeks also took to the mountains as guerrillas, but in the end the country fell. By the summer of 1941, with the exception of Sweden and Switzerland, the whole European continent was either allied with the Nazis or subject to their rule. These victories, and the economy of plunder that enriched Germany with forced labor and other nations' money, won Hitler considerable popularity at home. But these were only the first steps in a larger plan.

Hitler's ultimate goals, and his conception of Germany's national destiny, lay to the east. Beyond occupied Poland lay the vast plains and wheat fields of Russia and Ukraine, inhabited by what the Nazis considered ethnically inferior Slavs and Jews and governed by communists. Hitler had always seen the nonaggression pact with the Soviet Union as an act of convenience, until Germany was ready for this final conflict. By the summer of 1941, it seemed Germany was ready. On June 22, 1941, Hitler authorized Operation Barbarossa, the invasion of the Soviet Union. The cream of the German army led the way, defeating all the forces the Russians could put in front of them. Stalin's purges of the 1930s had exiled or executed many of his most capable army officers, and the effects showed in Russian disorganization and disaffection in the face of the panzers. Hundreds of thousands of prisoners were taken as German forces pressed deep into Byelorussia (modern Belarus), the Baltic states, and the Ukraine. Like Napoleon, the Germans led a multinational army that included Italians, Hungarians, most of the Romanian army, and freelance soldiers from the Baltics and the Ukraine who bore grudges against Stalin's authoritarian regime. During the fall of 1941, the Nazis destroyed much of the Red Army's fighting strength and vigorously pursued their goals of destroying communism and racial purification.

The second goal was essential to the German mission and Hitler's vision of the new European order. The war against the Soviets was a war of ideologies overlaid loosely on a war of racial hatred. The advancing Nazi forces left burning fields and towns in their wake and methodically wiped the occupied territories clean of "undesirable elements." When Russian guerrillas counterattacked with sniping and sabotage, German forces would shoot or hang hundreds of innocent hostages at a time in reprisal, often torturing their victims first. The Russian guerrillas quickly chose to deliver the same punishment to any captured Germans. By the end of 1941 it was clear that the war in the East was a war of destruction, and that both sides believed that only one side would be allowed to survive. By that same time, it seemed the victors would be German. Their forces were on the march towards the capital at Moscow. On orders from Berlin, however, German forces pushing toward Moscow were diverted south to attack Russia's industrial heartland in an effort to destroy the Soviets' ability to resist before the Russian winter set in. This left the Soviet capital free, and the Russian population, its leaders, and its armies, began to organize a much more determined resistance.

> By the end of 1941 it was clear that the war in the East was a war of destruction, and that both sides believed that only one side would be allowed to survive.

AXIS EUROPE, 1941

How had Hitler and Mussolini come to dominate the bulk of mainland Europe by the eve of the German invasion of the Soviet Union? Why did Hitler choose to annex certain conquests to Germany but settle for occupation in others?

Hitler nonetheless managed to piece together an empire that stretched across the entire continent of Europe. "We come as the heralds of a New Order and a new justice," his regime announced. The New Order had no place for nations as they had been created in the nineteenth century. "Nation states would have to give way to much larger political entities." Hitler specifically compared his rule to a "new Indian empire," and claimed to have studied British imperial techniques. Much of the New Order was improvised and rested on a patchwork of provisional regimes: military government in Poland and the Ukraine, collaborators in France, allied fascists in Hungary, and so on. The clearest principle was German supremacy. The loyalty of fellow Nazis or fascists was usually suspect to Hitler, for he worried that their adherence to the cause might lead them to lay some claim to power. "The emphatic German decision to organize Europe hierarchically, like a pyramid with Germany at the top, is known to all," said an Italian diplomat at the time. The empire was meant to feed German citizens, and maintain their morale and support for the war, which would prevent the "stab in the back" that Hitler believed had undone a German victory in 1914–1918. "I will pump every last thing out of this country," said the administrator of Ukraine. "I intend to plunder, and plunder copiously," wrote Hermann Goering of his occupation policy. Occupied countries paid inflated "occupation costs" in taxes, food, industrial production, and manpower. More than 2 million foreign workers were brought into Germany in 1942–1943 from France, Belgium and Holland, and the Soviet Union. As they conscripted workers, the Nazis spoke of uniting Europe to save it from the "red menace" of communism. That propaganda seems to have had little effect. To the contrary, at least in France, deporting citizens to labor in Germany did more than any other policy to drive individuals into the resistance.

The demands of enemy occupation, and the political and moral questions of "collaboration" and resistance, were issues across occupied Europe. The Nazis set up puppet regimes in a number of occupied territories. In Norway, the leader of that government, Vikdun Quisling, lent his name to the idea of what it meant to be a true "collaborator," someone in league with the Nazis. Both Norway and the Netherlands were deeply divided by the occupation. In each country a relatively small but dedicated party of Nazis governed in the name of the Germans, while at the same time well-organized and determined resistance movements gathered information for the Allies and carried out acts of sabotage. In Denmark, the population was much more united against their German occupiers, engaging in regular acts of passive resistance that infuriated German administrators. They also banded together as private citizens to smuggle most of the country's Jewish population out to the safety of neutral Sweden.

Elsewhere the relationship between collaboration, resistance, and self-interested indifference was more complex and troubling. In France, split between German occupation and the pro-German Vichy government, collaboration ranged from simple survival tactics under occupation to active support for Nazi ideals and goals. The worst example of this was the Vichy regime's active anti-Semitism and the aid given by French authorities in isolating, criminalizing, and deporting French Jews to the concentration camps. Individual citizens made daily choices when living peacefully with the German conquerors was simply a matter of getting by. Many chose to protect their own interests by sacrificing those of others, particularly such "undesirables" as Jews and communists. At the same time in France, communist activists, some members of the military, and ordinary citizens, such as the people of France's central mountains who had a long tradition of smuggling and resisting government, became active guerrillas (*maquis*) and saboteurs. They established links with the Free French movement in London, led by the charismatic, stiff-necked general Charles de Gaulle, and supplied important intelligence to the Allies. In eastern Europe, resistance movements provoked both open warfare with the fascists and civil war inside their own countries. The Germans' system of occupation in Yugoslavia pitted a fascist Croat regime against most Serbs; the Croatian fascist guard, the Ustasha, massacred hundreds of thousands of Orthodox Catholic Serbs. Ironically, a Croat, Josip Broz (Tito), emerged as the leader of the most powerful Yugoslavian resistance movement—militarily the most significant resistance in the war. Tito's troops were communists, strong enough to form a guerrilla army. They fought Germans, Italians, and Croat fascists, and they gained support and supplies from the Allies. But the Allies became increasingly discouraged by infighting in the Yugoslavian resistance between Tito's partisans and violently anticommunist Serbian resisters under the command of royalists. Greece's resistance was, likewise, strong enough to cause grief to the German occupiers. That resistance, too, was divided between those royalists and communists, which led to political strife later on. When British troops liberated Greece in 1944 they ended up in street fighting with the royalists against the communist partisans—the start of a civil war that went on beyond 1945.

Perhaps the most important moral issue facing citizens of occupied Europe was not their national allegiance, but rather their personal attitude to the fate of the Nazis' sworn enemies: Jews, communists, gypsies, homosexuals, and political "undesirables." Some French Jews along the Riviera found Italian, Catholic army officers who occupied the area more willing to save them from deportation than their fellow Frenchmen. This deeply personal dilemma— whether to risk family, friends, and careers to aid the deportees, or simply look the other way and allow mass murder—was one of the most powerful of the war.

RACIAL WAR, ETHNIC CLEANSING, AND THE HOLOCAUST

In what ways was World War II a "racial war"?

From the beginning, the Nazis had seen the conflict as a racial war. In *Mein Kampf* Hitler had already outlined his view that war against the *Untermenschen*, or "subhuman" Jews, Gypsies, and Slavs, was natural and necessary. Not only would it purify the German people, it would also conquer territory for their expansion. Thus as soon as the war broke out, the Nazis began to implement ambitious plans for redrawing the racial map of the Reich, or what is now called ethnic cleansing. In the fall of 1939, with Poland conquered, the SS, under directives from Heinrich Himmler, began massive population transfers. Ethnic Germans were moved from elsewhere into the borders of the Reich, while Poles and Jews were deported to specially designated areas in the east. Over two hundred thousand ethnic Germans from the Baltic states were resettled in Western Prussia. Welcoming ethnic Germans went hand in hand with a brutal campaign of terror against the Poles, especially Polish Jews. All sources of potential resistance were to be rooted out. Professors at the University of Cracow, considered dangerous intellectuals, were deported to concentration camps, where they died. The SS shot "undesirables," like the inmates of Polish mental asy-

It is certain that the invasion of the Soviet Union marked a turning point in the deadly path to the Holocaust.

lums, partly to allow SS troops to occupy the asylums' barracks. Poles were deported to forced labor camps. The Nazis began to transport Jews by the thousands to the region of Lublin, south of Warsaw. Special death squads also began to shoot Jews in the streets and in front of synagogues. These Polish campaigns took one hundred thousand Jewish lives in 1940.

The elimination of European Jewry stood at the center of the Nazis' *Rassenkampf*, or "racial struggle." We have seen the role of anti-Semitism in Hitler's rise to power and the escalating campaign of terror against the Jewish community inside Germany in the 1930s, including the Night of the Broken Glass (see Chapter 28). The war radicalized that campaign. Historians disagree about whether or not the Nazis had a "blueprint" for the extermination of Europe's Jews. Most now emphasize that Nazi priorities shifted according to the war's rhythms and Hitler's wildly changing moods. Between 1938 and 1941 Nazi plans had no single focus. They ranged from forcing German Jews to emigrate to deporting all Europe's Jews to Madagascar, a former French colony off the southern coast of Africa. All these schemes took shape against the background of daily terror and frequent massacres, especially in Poland. It is certain, however, that the invasion of the Soviet Union in June, 1941 marked a turning point in the deadly path to the Holocaust. Operation Barbarossa, as the invasion was called, brought several changes. First, it was animated by the Nazis' intense ideological and racial hatreds, directed against Slavs, Jews, and Marxists. Goebbels, for example, called the Russians "not a people but an agglomeration of animals." The regime barraged civilians as well as soldiers with such propaganda. The invasion of Poland had been vicious; the invasion of the USSR was openly a "war of extermination." Second, the invading German army succeeded more quickly than it expected. The huge gains created euphoria in the Nazi hierarchy; Hitler seemed very close to realizing his dreams of an eastern empire. But success also bred fear, or worry at the prospect of controlling the millions of Soviet prisoners, Soviet civilians, and Soviet Jews who had now fallen into Nazi hands. The combination of elation and anxiety was deadly. It led, quickly, from systematic brutality to atrocities, and then to murder on a scale few could have imagined.

As the Nazi army swept into the Soviet Union, captured communist officials, political agitators, and any hostile civilians were imprisoned, tortured, or shot.

THE HOLOCAUST: MASSACRES IN UKRAINE

The following account of a mass shooting in the Ukraine comes from a German engineer testifying at the Nuremberg trials in 1946. Events like these happened so often that his is but one of many such descriptions. Note that the SS allowed him to witness these events.

From September 1941 until January 1944, I was the manager and chief engineer of a branch of the construction firm, Josef Jung of Solingen with its headquarters in Sdolbunow, Ukraine. In this capacity I had to visit the firm's building sites. The firm was contracted by an Army construction office to build grain silos on the former air field near Dubno in the Ukraine.

When I visited the site office on 5 October 1942 my foreman, Hubert Moennikes of Hamburg–Harburg, Aussenmühlenweg 21, told me that Jews from Dubno had been shot near the site in three large ditches which were about thirty metres long and three metres deep. Approximately 1,500 people a day had been killed. All of the approximately 5,000 Jews who had been living in Dubno up to the action were going to be killed. Since the shootings had taken place in his presence he was still very upset.

Whereupon I accompanied Moennikes to the building site and near it saw large mounds of earth about thirty metres long and two metres high. A few lorries were parked in front of the mounds from which people were being driven by armed Ukrainian militia under the supervision of an SS man. The militia provided the guards on the lorries and drove them to and from the ditch. All these people wore the prescribed yellow patches on the front and back of their clothing so that they were identifiable as Jews.

Moennikes and I went straight to the ditches. We were not prevented from doing so. I could now hear a series of rifle shots from behind the mounds. The peo-ple who had got off the lorries—men, women, and children of all ages—had to undress on the orders of an SS man who was carrying a riding or dog whip in his hand. They had to place their clothing on separate piles for shoes, clothing and underwear. I saw a pile of shoes containing approximately 800–1,000 pairs, and great heaps of underwear and clothing.

Without weeping or crying out these people undressed and stood together in family groups, embracing each other and saying good-bye while waiting for a sign from another SS man who stood on the edge of the ditch and also had a whip. During the quarter of an hour in which I stood near the ditch, I did not hear a single complaint or a plea for mercy. . . .

I walked round the mound and stood in front of the huge grave. The bodies were lying so tightly packed together that only their heads showed, from almost all of which blood ran down over their shoulders. Some were still moving. Others raised their hands and turned their heads to show they were still alive. The ditch was already three quarters full. I estimate that it already held about a thousand bodies. I turned my eyes towards the man doing the shooting. He was an SS man; he sat, legs swinging, on the edge of the ditch. He had an automatic rifle resting on his knees and was smoking a cigarette. The people, completely naked, climbed down steps which had been cut into the clay wall of the ditch, stumbled over the heads of those lying there and stopped at the spot indicated by the SS man. They lay down on top of the dead or wounded; some stroked those still living and spoke quietly to them. Then I heard a series of rifle shots. I looked into the ditch and saw the bodies contorting or, the heads already inert, sinking on the corpses beneath. Blood flowed from the nape of their necks. I was surprised not to be ordered away, but I noticed three postmen in uniform standing nearby. Then the next batch came up, climbed down into the ditch, laid themselves next to the previous victims and were shot.

On the way back, as I rounded the mound, I saw another lorry load of people which had just arrived. This one included the sick and infirm. An old and very emaciated woman with frightfully thin legs was being undressed by others, already naked. She was being supported by two people and seemed paralysed. The naked people carried the woman round the mound. I left the place with Moennikes and went back to Dubno by car. . . .

I am making the above statement in Wiesbaden, Germany on 10 November 1945. I swear to God that it is the whole truth.

Fred. Gräbe

J. Noakes and G. Pridham, *Nazism: A History in Document and Eyewitness Accounts, 1919–1945*, Vol. 2 (New York: Schocken, 1988), pp. 1100–1101.

Five and one half million military prisoners were taken and marched to camps. Over half of them died of starvation or were executed. Poles from regions that had been under Soviet rule, Jews, and Russians were deported to Germany to work as slave labor in German factories. On the heels of the army came special battalions of *Einsatzgruppen,* or death squads. Under the commissar order, issued by Reinhard Heydrich on July 2, 1941, the death squads were to kill party officials and civilians who resisted, but this quickly turned into rounding up and murdering Jews—men, women, and children. Joined by eleven thousand extra SS troops, they stormed through Jewish villages and those of "difficult" Russian or Polish populations. The men of the villages were shot; the women and children either deported to labor camps or massacred along with the men. German troops had butchered or sent Jewish or gypsy (Romani) refugees on forced marches that caused many to die of disease or starvation. By September, 1941, the *Einsatzgruppen* reported that in their efforts at "pacification" they had killed eighty-five thousand persons, most of them Jews. By April, 1942, the number was five hundred thousand. This killing began before the gas chambers had gone into operation and continued through the campaigns on the eastern front. As of 1943, the death squads had killed roughly 2.2 million Jews.

As Operation Barbarossa progressed, German administrations of occupied areas herded local Jewish populations even more tightly into the "ghettos" some Jewish communities had occupied for centuries: Warsaw and Lodz in Poland were the largest. There, administrators, persuaded that the Jews were hoarding supplies, refused to allow food to go in, making the ghettos centers of starvation and disease. Those who left the ghetto were shot rather than returned. A German doctor summarized the regime's logic about killing this way: "One must, I can say it quite openly in this circle, be clear about it. There are only two ways. We sentence the Jews in the ghetto to death by hunger or we shoot them. Even if the end result is the same, the latter is more intimidating." The point was not just death, but terror.

Through the late summer and fall of 1941, Nazi officials discussed and put together plans for mass killings in death camps. The ghettos had already been sealed; now orders came down that no Jews were to leave any occupied areas. That summer the Nazis had experimented with vans equipped with poison gas, which could kill thirty to fifty people at a time. Those experiments and the gas chambers were designed with the help of scientists from the T-4 euthanasia program, which had already killed eighty thousand racially, mentally, or physically "unfit" persons in Germany. By October, 1941, the SS was building camps with gas chambers and deporting people to them. At the Wannsee Conference in January, 1942, near Berlin, top Nazi officials met with administrators of different territories to plan the systematic annihilation of Europe's Jews—"transporting them to the east," as official documents phrased it. Auschwitz-Birkenau, which had been built to hold Polish prisoners, was built up to be the largest of the camps. Auschwitz eventually held many different types of prisoners— "undesirables" like Jehovah's Witnesses and homosexuals, Poles, Russians, and even some British POWs, but

As of 1943, the death squads had killed roughly 2.2 million Jews.

Jews and gypsies were the ones systematically annihilated there. Between the spring of 1942 and the fall of 1944 over a million people were killed at Auschwitz-Birkenau alone. The opening of the death camps set off the greatest wave of slaughter from 1942 to 1943. Freight cars hauled people to the camps, first from the ghettos of Poland, then from France, Holland, Belgium, Austria, the Balkans, and later from Hungary and Greece. Bodies were buried in pits dug by prisoners or burned in crematoria.

The death camps have come to symbolize the horrors of Nazism as a system of modern mass murder. Yet it is worth emphasizing that much of the slaughter was not anonymous, industrialized, or routine, and that it took place in face-to-face encounters outside the camps. Jews and other victims were not simply killed. They were tortured, beaten, and executed publicly while soldiers and other onlookers recorded the executions with cameras—and sent photos home to their families. During the last phases of the war, inmates still in the concentration camps were taken on "death marches" whose sole purpose was suffering and death. Nor was the killing done by the specially indoctrinated SS and *Einsatzgruppen*. The Nazi regime called up groups of conscripts such as Reserve Police Battalion 101 from duty in its home city of Hamburg and sent it into occupied territories. Once there, the unit of middle-aged policemen received and obeyed orders to kill, in one day, fifteen hundred Jewish men, women, and children in one village. The commander offered to excuse men who did not feel they could carry out this assignment; only a few asked for a different task. In one Polish town, occupied first by the Soviets and then retaken by the Nazis, the Polish villagers themselves, with minimal guidance or help from German soldiers, turned on their Jewish neighbors and killed hundreds in a day.

> The death camps have come to symbolize the horrors of Nazism as a system of modern mass murder.

How many knew of the extent of the Holocaust? No operation of this scale could be carried out without the cooperation or knowledge of many: the Nazi hierarchy; architects who helped build the camps; engineers who designed the gas chambers and crematoria; municipal officials of cities from which people were deported; train drivers; residents of villages near the camps, who reported the smell of bodies burning; and so on. Not surprisingly, most who suspected the worst were terrified and powerless. Not surprisingly, many people did not want to know, and did their best to ignore evidence and carry on with their lives. Many who continued to support the Nazis did so for other reasons, out of personal opportunism, or because they opposed communism and wanted order restored. Yet mere popular indifference does not provide a satisfactory explanation for the Nazis' ability to accomplish the murder of so many people. Many Europeans—German, French, Dutch, Polish, Swiss, and Russian—had come to believe that there was a "Jewish problem" that had to be "solved." The Nazis tried to conceal the death camps. Yet they knew they could count on vocal support for requiring Jews to be specially identified, for restrictions on marriage and property ownership and for other kinds of discrimination. For reasons that had to do with both traditional Christian anti-Semitism and modern, racialized nationalism, most Europeans had come to see Jewish people as "foreign," no longer members of their national communities.

What of other governments? Their level of cooperation with the Nazis' plans varied. The French Vichy regime,

Polish Jews, evicted from the Warsaw Ghetto, being deported. Most of their trains led to death camps.

THE HOLOCAUST:
TWO PERSPECTIVES FROM THE SS

THE DEATH CAMPS

An SS officer charged with inspecting the death camps wrote this account of his visit to Belzec, a camp in occupied Poland, near the former Russian border. He opposed the regime. Shortly after leaving this description, in 1945, he committed suicide.

Next morning, shortly before seven, I was told: 'the first transport will arrive in ten minutes'. And, in fact, after a few minutes, the first train arrived from the direction of Lemberg (Lvov). 45 wagons with 6,700 people, of whom 1,450 were already dead on arrival. Behind the barred hatches stared the horribly pale and frightened faces of children, their eyes full of the fear of death. Men and women were there too. . . .

The chambers fill up. 'Pack them in'—that is what Captain Wirth has ordered. People are treading on each others' toes. 700–800 in an area of twenty-five square metres, in forty-five cubic metres! The SS push them in as far as possible. The doors shut; in the meantime, the others are waiting outside in the open, naked. 'It is the same in winter', I was told. 'But they could catch their death of cold', I say. 'But that's just what they are there for', replied an SS man in dialect. Now at last I understood why the whole apparatus is called the Heckenholt Foundation. Heckenholt is the driver of the diesel engine, a little technician who constructed the installation. The people are going to be killed by the diesel exhaust gases. But the diesel engine won't start! Captain Wirth arrives. He is clearly embarrassed that this should happen just on the day when I am here. Yes indeed, I can see the whole thing. And I wait. My stop watch faithfully records it all. Fifty minutes, 70 seconds [*sic!*]. Still the diesel won't start. The people wait in their gas chambers. In vain. One can hear them crying, sobbing . . . Captain Wirth hits the Ukrainian who is responsible for helping *Unterscharführer* Heckenholt with the diesel engine twelve or thirteen times in the face with his riding whip. After two hours forty-nine minutes—the stop watch has recorded it all—the engine starts. Up to this moment, the people have been living in these four chambers, four times 750 people in four times forty-five cubic metres. A further twenty-five minutes pass. That's right, many are now dead. One can see through the little peepholes when the electric light illuminates the chambers for a moment. After twenty-eight minutes, only a few are still alive. At last, after thirty-two minutes, they are all dead. . . .

HIMMLER'S INSTRUCTIONS TO THE SS

Heinrich Himmler (1900–1945), one of the founding members of the Nazi party and head of the SS, became one of the most powerful members of the Nazi government. He directed the purge of the rebellious SA in 1934, expanded the SS, supervised the network of death camps, and by 1943, when this speech was given, had become Minister of the Interior for the administration of the Reich. Few represent better the combination of ambition, ideology, and ruthlessness that characterized Nazi leaders. Himmler committed suicide when captured by Allied troops in 1945.

...I also want to talk to you quite frankly about a very grave matter. We can talk about it quite frankly among ourselves and yet we will never speak of it publicly. Just as we did not hesitate on 30 June 1934 to do our duty as we were bidden, and to stand comrades who had lapsed up against the wall and shoot them, so we have never spoken about it and will never speak of it. It appalled everyone, and yet everyone was certain that he would do it the next time if such orders should be issued and it should be necessary.

I am referring to the Jewish evacuation programme, the extermination of the Jewish people. It is one of those things which are easy to talk about. 'The Jewish people will be exterminated', says every party comrade, 'It's clear, it's in our programme. Elimination of the Jews, extermination and we'll do it.' And then they come along, the worthy eighty million Germans, and each one of them produces his decent Jew. It's clear the others are swine, but this one is a fine Jew. Not one of those who talk like that has watched it happening, not one of them has been through it. Most of you will know what it means when a hundred corpses are lying side by side, or five hundred or a thousand are lying there. To have stuck it out and—apart from a few exceptions due to human weakness—to have remained decent, that is what has made us tough. This is a glorious page in our history and one that has never been written and can never be written. For we know how difficult we would have made it for ourselves if, on top of the bombing raids, the burdens and the deprivations of war, we still had Jews today in every town as secret saboteurs, agitators and troublemakers. We would now probably have reached the 1916–17 stage when the Jews were still part of the body of the German nation.

We have taken from them what wealth they had. I have issued a strict order, which SS *Obergruppenführer* Pohl has carried out, that this wealth should, as a matter of course, be handed over to the Reich without reserve. We have taken none of it for ourselves. . . . All in all, we can say that we have fulfilled this most difficult duty for the love of our people. And our spirit, our soul, our character has not suffered injury from it. . . .

J. Noakes and G. Pridham, *Nazism: A History in Document and Eyewitness Accounts, 1919–1945*, Vol. 2 (New York: Schocken, 1988), pp. 1151–1152, 1199–1200.

on its own initiative, passed laws that required Jews to wear identifying stars and strictly limited their movements and activities. When the German government demanded roundups and deportations of Jews, Vichy cooperated. On the other hand, Italy, though a fascist country, participated less actively; not until the Germans occupied the north of Italy in 1943 were drastic anti-Semitic measures implemented. The Hungarian government, also fascist and allied with the Nazis, persecuted Jews but dragged its heels about deportations. Thus the Hungarian Jewish community survived—until March, 1944, when Germans, disgusted with their Hungarian collaborators, took direct control and immediately began mass deportations. So determined were the Nazis to carry out their "final solution" that they killed up to twelve thousand Hungarian Jews a day at Auschwitz in May of 1944, contributing to a total death toll of six hundred thousand.

In the face of this determination, little resistance was possible. The concentration camps were designed to numb and incapacitate their inmates, making them acquiesce in their own slow deaths even if they were not killed right away. In his famous account, survivor Primo Levi writes: "Our language lacks words to express this offence, the demolition of a man. . . . It is not possible to sink lower than this; no human condition is more miserable than this, nor could it conceivably be so. Nothing belongs to us any more; they have taken away our clothes, our shoes, even our hair; if we speak, they will not listen to us, and if they listen, they will not understand." A few rebellions in Auschwitz and Treblinka were repressed with savage efficiency. In the

DEPORTATION RAILWAYS

Between March 1942 and November 1944, Jews are known to have been deported from every location on this map—as well as from numerous other locales—to Auschwitz, where most were killed. Note the effort made by the Nazis to transport Jews from the very frontiers of the empire at the height of a two-front war. Consider what this says about the Nazi regime in particular, and about other states willing to collaborate with the Nazis.

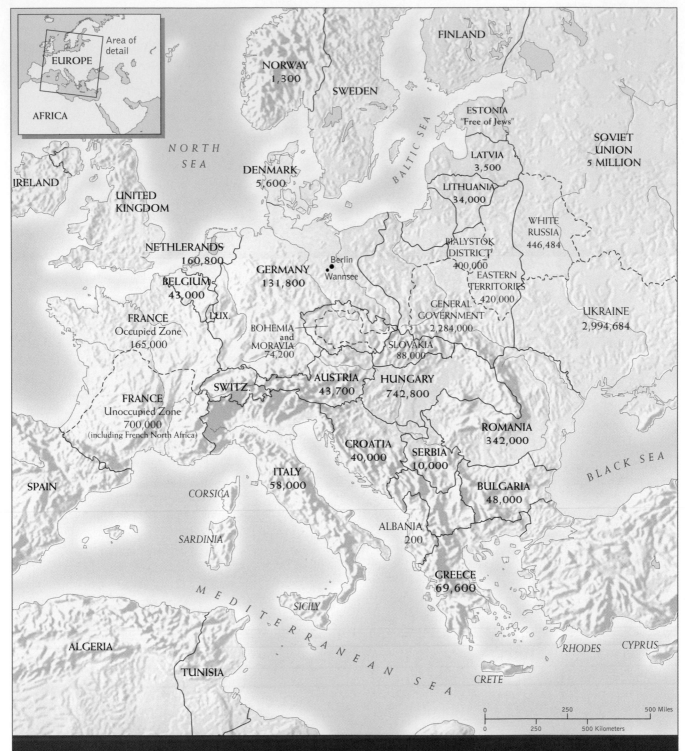

NORTH
SEA

FINLAND

NORWAY
1,300

SWEDEN

ESTONIA
"Free of Jews"

BALTIC SEA

SOVIET
UNION
5 MILLION

LATVIA
3,500

DENMARK
5,600

LITHUANIA
34,000

IRELAND

UNITED
KINGDOM

WHITE
RUSSIA
446,484

NETHERLANDS
160,800

BIALYSTOK
DISTRICT
400,000

Berlin
Wannsee

GERMANY
131,800

EASTERN
TERRITORIES
420,000

BELGIUM
43,000

LUX.

GENERAL
GOVERNMENT
2,284,000

UKRAINE
2,994,684

FRANCE
Occupied Zone
165,000

BOHEMIA
and
MORAVIA
74,200

SLOVAKIA
88,000

AUSTRIA
43,700

HUNGARY
742,800

SWITZ.

FRANCE
Unoccupied Zone
700,000
(including French North Africa)

ROMANIA
342,000

CROATIA
40,000

SERBIA
10,000

SPAIN

ITALY
58,000

BLACK SEA

BULGARIA
48,000

CORSICA

SARDINIA

ALBANIA
200

GREECE
69,600

MEDITERRANEAN SEA

SICILY

RHODES

CYPRUS

ALGERIA

CRETE

TUNISIA

EUROPE

Area of
detail

AFRICA

0   250   500 Miles
0   250   500 Kilometers

HITLER'S "FINAL SOLUTION": JEWS MARKED FOR DEATH

On January 20, 1942, German officials met at Wannsee (just outside Berlin) to discuss the "final solution" to the "Jewish problem." They also discussed what they believed to be the remaining number of Jewish people in territories they controlled or soon hoped to control. Examine these figures closely. How many millions of innocent people did the Nazis propose to slaughter?

The Flying Carriage (1913), by Marc Chagall. One of Chagall's many paintings of violence against Jews in the Russian countryside. A man with a carriage flees as a store is burned.

The Holocaust. These German civilians were compelled to view the bodies of concentration camp victims at the Landesburg camp in 1945.

dren or parents, which very few could do. The countryside offered no shelter; local populations were usually either hostile or too terrified to help. Reprisals horrified all. Families of Jews and gypsies were ordinary people whose lives could not have prepared them for the kind of violence that rolled over them. The largest Jewish resistance came in the Warsaw ghetto, in the spring of 1943. The previous summer, the Nazis had deported 80 percent of the ghetto's residents to the camps, making it clear that those left behind had little hope of survival. These people had virtually no resources, yet, when deportations started again, a small Jewish underground movement—a thousand fighters, perhaps, in a community of seventy thousand—took on the Nazis with a tiny arsenal of gasoline bombs, pistols, and ten rifles. The Nazis responded by burning the ghetto to the ground and executing and deporting to the camps nearly everyone who was left. "The Warsaw Ghetto is no more," reported the SS commander at the end; some fifty-six thousand Jews died. Word of the rising did spread, but the repression made it clear that the targets of Nazi extermination could choose only between death in the streets or death in the camps. Sustained resistance, as one person remarked, would have required "the prospect of victory."

The Holocaust claimed between 4.1 and 5.7 million Jewish lives. Even those numbers do not register the nearly total destruction of some cultures. In the Baltic states (Latvia and Lithuania), Germany, Czechoslovakia, Yugoslavia, and Poland, well over 80 percent of the long-established Jewish communities were annihilated. Elsewhere, the figures

villages, people rounded up to be deported or shot had to make split-second decisions in order to escape. Saving oneself nearly always meant abandoning one's chil- were closer to 50 percent. The Holocaust was unique. It occurred, however, in a period of racial war and the liquidation of undesirables, and within an even longer period of ethnically motivated mass murder. Through both world wars and afterward ethnic and religious groups—Armenians, Poles, Serbian Orthodox, ethnic Germans—were hunted, massacred, and legally deported en masse. Hitler's government had planned to build a "new Europe," safe for ethnic Germans and their allies and secure against communism, on the graveyards of whole cultures.

TOTAL WAR: HOME FRONTS, THE WAR OF PRODUCTION, BOMBING AND "THE BOMB"

How did the war transform the home fronts?

The Second World War was a "total war," involving the combined efforts of whole populations, on a grander scale than the First. Larger armed forces were moving much more swiftly across territory, locked in constant battle with equally well-armed opponents. This demanded massive resources and national commitment to industry, drawing in the whole economies of the combatants. Standards of living changed around the world. In the neutral nations of Latin America, which supplied vast amounts of raw materials to the Allies, wartime profits led to a wave of prosperity known as the "dance of the millions." In the lands occupied by Germany or Japan, economies of forced extraction robbed local areas of resources, workers, and even food. In East Asia this caused rising resentment of the Japanese, who were often seen initially as liberators ending the rule of the old colonial powers. In America, Detroit produced no new models of car or truck between 1940 and 1945. Work schedules were grueling. Women and the elderly, pressed back into wage work or working for the first time, put in long shifts (in Britain and Russia these sometimes ran over twelve hours) before returning home to cook, clean, and care for families and neighbors also affected by enemy bombing and wartime shortages. Diets changed. Through Germany lived comfortably off the farmlands of Europe for several years, and the United States could lean on its huge agricultural base, food, gasoline, and basic household goods were still rationed. In occu-

"Just a Good Afternoon's Work!" A British poster mobilizing women for part-time factory work.

pied Europe and the Soviet Union rations were just above starvation level, and sometimes fell below in areas near the fighting. Britain, dependent on its empire and other overseas sources for food and raw materials, ran a comprehensive rationing system that kept up production and ensured a drab but consistent diet on the table.

Production—the industrial ability to churn out more tanks, tents, planes, bombs, and uniforms than the other side—was essential to winning the war. Britain, the Soviet Union, and America each launched comprehensive, well-designed propaganda campaigns that encouraged the production of war equipment on an unmatched scale. Appeals to patriotism, to communal interests, and to a common stake in winning the war struck a chord. The Allied societies proved willing to regulate themselves and commit to the effort. Despite strikes and disputes with government officials, the three great Allied powers devoted more of their economies to war production, more efficiently, than any nations in history. Not only did they build tanks, ships, and planes capable of competing with advanced German and Japanese designs, they built them by the tens of thousands, swamping the enemy with constant reinforcements and superior firepower. Japan nearly reached comparable levels of production but then slowly declined, as Allied advances on land and American submarines cut off overseas sources of vital supplies. Germany, despite its reputation for efficiency and its access to vast supplies of slave labor, was less efficient in its use of workers and materials than the Allied nations. The Germans' ability to produce devastatingly successful weapons led to a damaging side effect—vast amounts of money and time spent developing the pet projects of high-ranking Nazi officials, or trying to make unsuccessful designs work. Rather than losing time and resources pursuing perfection, the Allies developed working, standard designs and produced them in overwhelming numbers.

Since industry was essential to winning the war, centers of industry became vital military targets. The Allies began bombing German ports and factories almost as soon as the Germans started their own campaigns. Over time, American and British planners became equally ruthless on an even larger scale. Both of these Allied nations made a major commitment to "strategic bombing," developing new planes and technology that allowed them to put thousands of bombers in the air both night and day over occupied Europe. As the war wore on and Germany kept fighting, the Allies expanded their campaign. They moved from pinpoint bombing of the military and industry in Germany to striking such targets across all of occupied Europe, and bombing Germany's civilian population in earnest. For the British, despite a public debate about the morality of bombing, it was a war of retribution; for the Americans, it was an effort to grind the Germans down without sacrificing too many Allied lives. That turned out to be a false premise. The Allies killed tens of thousands of German civilians as they struck Berlin, ports such as Hamburg, and the industrial cities of the Ruhr, but German war production persisted. At the same time German fighter planes shot down hundreds of Allied bombers, causing heavy losses. After the Allied invasion of Europe, bombing expanded well beyond targets of military value. The German city of Dresden, a center of culture and education that lacked heavy industry, was firebombed with a horrifying death toll. This gave Allied generals

and politicians pause, but strategic bombing continued. German industry was slowly degraded but the German will to keep fighting, like that of Britain or Russia, remained intact.

THE RACE TO BUILD THE BOMB

While the Allies carried out their bombing campaigns over Germany and Japan, Allied scientists in America were at work on the most powerful bomb ever designed. It was an unlikely weapon suggested from an obscure scientific field: atomic physics. British physicists—leaders in the field along with German scientists—believed that it would be possible to split the structure of an atom. The process, called fission, would rend the subatomic particles apart in a huge burst of energy. The British scientists believed that, given the resources, they could stage a chain reaction, causing the fission of one atom to trigger splits in others, as though unraveling a thread in the structure of the universe. This would produce an explosion of awesome scope and power. British scientists began work on the idea, but lacked the resources and enough radioactive material to stage a controlled chain reaction. The United States had those resources, and as America entered the war the British passed on their theories and technical information to American scientists. A group of physicists, some native-born Americans, many refugees from the fascist regimes of Europe, were set to work creating a chain reaction. Enrico Fermi, an Italian physicist and a dedicated antifascist, was put in charge of designing the world's first nuclear reactor, built on the campus of the University of Chicago. In December 1942 Fermi staged the first controlled chain reaction at the site.

Meanwhile, the governments of the United States and Germany were both racing toward a military application of fission. The Germans were hampered in their efforts from the start. Many of their best specialists were Jewish or anti-Nazi refugees now working for the Americans. The Germans also lacked crucial bits of technical information and had fewer resources. When specially trained Norwegian commandos destroyed the Germans' "heavy water" facility (used to separate out the uranium needed for the bomb) at Telemark, Norway, the German project went with it. Yet American officials feared that it had not been destroyed, and they also sensed the enormous power of the new weapon. Before Fermi's chain reaction a government project, code-named "Manhattan," had already been set up to manage an all-out effort at building an American atomic bomb. Massive facilities were built in Tennessee and Washington State to separate out the radioactive particles needed for the most effective explosion, an investment of hundreds of millions of dollars. The project went on under the tightest security of the war; most of President Roosevelt's cabinet, and the United States Congress, did not know the real purpose of "Manhattan." Once the separating facilities were finished the necessary materials were quickly produced.

Now what was needed was a bomb itself. In 1943 a laboratory was established at Los Alamos, New Mexico, bringing together the most capable nuclear physicists in the country, citizens and immigrants, old and young, to come up with a working design for a bomb. The physicist J. Robert Oppenheimer was placed in charge of the project, along with a U.S. Army Air Corps supervisor. The team devised methods for turning the radioactive material into ammunition and developed triggering devices. After nearly two years they came up with a working design whose prototype would be dropped by plane and detonated in midair above the target, for maximum effect. The first test of the device was held on July 16, 1945 near Los Alamos. The wave of heat and the roar of the explosion were indescribable. The test tower was vaporized. The ball of fire that rose in a mushroom shape overhead was the physical expression of a blast equal to twenty thousand tons of dynamite. "Manhattan" was a success. America now possessed the most destructive weapon ever devised. After watching the blast, Oppenheimer was moved to recite a phrase from an ancient Hindu text, a bitter commentary on his own work: "I am become Death, and the destroyer of worlds."

GREAT CRUSADES: THE ALLIED COUNTERATTACK AND THE DROPPING OF THE ATOMIC BOMB

How did the Soviets defeat the Germans?

Hitler had invaded the Soviet Union in June 1941. Within two years the war in the East had become his undoing; within four years it brought about his destruction.

The early successes of the German-led invasion were crippling. Nearly 90 percent of the Soviets' tanks, most of their aircraft, and huge stores of supplies were destroyed or captured. Nazi forces penetrated deep into European Russia. The Soviets fought regardless. By late 1941 German and Finnish forces had cut off and besieged Leningrad (St. Petersburg). Yet the city held out for 844 days—through three winters, massive destruction by artillery and aircraft, and periods of starvation—until a large relief force broke the siege. Russian partisans stepped up their campaigns of ambush and terrorism, and many of the Germans' former allies in the Ukraine and elsewhere turned against them in reaction to Nazi "pacification" efforts.

THE EASTERN FRONT

Most important, the character of the war on the Eastern Front changed. What had begun as a struggle between Nazi invaders and Stalin's regime became a war to save the *rodina*, the Russian motherland, as Russians fought for their own homes and families. Stalin, a shrewd politician, understood this; the message of Soviet propaganda changed to include a healthy dose of praise for Mother Russia. The courage and stamina of Soviet soldiers—many of them teenagers or men in their forties, some of them women who became particularly famous as sharpshooters—seemed boundless, despite constant defeats at the hands of German forces. After surviving the winter of 1941–1942, the Russian public became convinced that they could indeed survive the war and became committed to driving the Germans from their homeland, whatever the cost. The second change in the war was a Russian victory won by what Stalin called "General Winter." Successive winters, followed by hot, muddy summers, took a steady toll in Nazi lives and supplies, sapping German morale. The third change was the astonishing recovery of Soviet industry. The Soviets received some American and British aid, delivered at great risk over Arctic routes, but most of their achievement was self-sufficient. Whole industries were rebuilt behind the safety of the Ural Mountains, and entire populations of cities were displaced to work in them, turning out tanks, fighter planes, machine guns, and ammunition. Once the Russians achieved the same aerial stalemate that existed over Britain, their seemingly endless labor reserves were backed with boundless reserves of equipment. The fourth change in the war had more to do with the Germans, who became victims of their own success. The *Blitzkrieg*, at first a brilliantly inventive way of fighting a war, became a predictable set of maneuvers run according to a checklist. The Russians were eager students of that routine. They learned each stage of the process well, exploited its weaknesses, and became particularly good at lulling the Germans into a false sense of success before overwhelming them from unexpected angles.

The crucial year on the Russian Front came in 1943, as German efforts to break the back of Soviet industry resulted in the largest, most destructive battles the world has ever seen. The first of these began in 1942, with a massive German-led offensive in the Volga River valley, aimed at the city of Stalingrad. The Germans hoped to split Soviet forces and destroy valuable factories. But once German, Romanian, and Italian troops entered the suburbs of the city they were drawn into bitter house-to-house fighting by Russian defenders. The outnumbered Soviet forces fought beyond the "last cartridge," using rocks and knives when they had to. Germany's panzers were rendered useless with grenades and firebombs in the narrow streets. The city was reduced to rubble, which only gave the Russians cover to surprise German and Romanian units. Russian forces were pushed back to the Volga River as winter came on, but the Nazis' supplies began to run low. In November large Russian armies encircled the enemy forces inside the city itself. The attackers were now besieged, in a battle that went on through a cruel winter.

Infuriated, Hitler demanded that his commanders relieve the embattled troops. Every attempt to break through was defeated, and at the end of January 1943 the German commander in Stalingrad defied orders and surrendered the haggard survivors of his army. More than a quarter of a million German, Romanian, and Italian bodies were dragged from the wrecked city. Three times that many German troops died in the whole course of the battle. Barely six thousand of two hundred fifty thousand of the German soldiers sent into Stalingrad came home; over a million Russians died. Despite the unparalleled casualties—the battle dwarfed even Verdun in the Great War, or the fighting between China and Japan—the Russians had won a crucial victory. After Stalingrad Hitler appeared less and less often in public, and his worst tendencies to gloom and paranoia grew as the Russian front turned against his dreams.

Following Stalingrad, the Soviets mounted a series of offensives that turned German forces back from the heart of Russia. In the summer of 1943 German tank commanders launched a massive counterattack near the city of Kursk in the center of the front lines. Their early

CHRONOLOGY

THE EASTERN FRONT

Germans invade Soviet Union	June 1941
Siege of Leningrad	1941–1942
Battle of Stalingrad	1942–1943
Battle of Kursk	1943
Germans abandon Ukraine	1943
Soviet forces reach Berlin	April 1945
Germany surrenders	May 1945

victories were a baited trap; several Russian armies were waiting, with masses of men and the newest Russian tanks, specially designed to destroy the panzers. The result may have been the largest battle ever fought, lasting six weeks and involving over six thousand tanks and more than 2 million men between the two sides. Bogged down amid snipers and minefields and raked by Russian artillery and rocket launchers, the German army group, nearly a million strong, was crushed. The Russians, led by their commander at Stalingrad and the shrewdest opponent of the *Blitzkrieg*, Grigorii Zhukov, then launched a major offensive into Ukraine. By the spring of 1944 Ukraine was back in Soviet hands. With the relief of Leningrad and attacks into Byelorussia that reached the Polish border, the Russians turned the tables. Romania was knocked out of the war during 1944, and Soviet armies poured into the Balkans, eventually meeting up with Tito's victorious partisans in Yugoslavia. Zhukov, who had taken charge of most of the Soviet armies, ground down German resistance in Poland during the winter of 1944. Several German armies collapsed, and Soviet forces, joined by communist partisans from the eastern European countries, retook large parts of Czechoslovakia. It was these battles, along with the fighting in Italy and Yugoslavia, that destroyed the German army. Hitler's most ambitious goal had brought the downfall of the Nazi regime and death to a generation of German soldiers.

THE WESTERN FRONT

During the campaigns in the East, Stalin continually pressured his allies to open a second front in the West. The American-led attack on Italy was a response to that plea. Allied forces first invaded Sicily and then the Italian mainland. Italy's government deposed

D-Day. Cargo ships are seen pouring supplies ashore during the invasion of France on June 6, 1944. Balloon barrages float overhead to protect the ships from low-flying enemy planes.

April 28, 1945. Mussolini's government collapsed in the summer of 1943, but he was protected by Hitler and survived until April, 1945, when the Allies crushed German defenses and moved into northern Italy. Italian partisans captured Mussolini and his mistress trying to cross the border, shot them, and hung their bodies in a public square in Milan.

Mussolini and surrendered in the summer of 1943. A civil war ensued, for most Italians, especially Communist partisans, sided with the Allies, while dedicated fascists continued to fight for their exiled leader. Italy was invaded by both sides; large Allied armies and more than a dozen elite German divisions occupied the country. The result was eighteen months of bitter fighting on Italy's muddy hillsides, in high mountains and bombed-out towns, consuming vast resources and tens of thousands of lives on each side. Nevertheless, the fighting in Italy cost Germany much more than it did the Allies, who liberated all the major Italian cities and entered Austria by the spring of 1945.

The German Surrender. British Field Marshal Bernard Montgomery (seated, in beret) accepts the surrender of Germany's northern forces on May 4, 1945. Three days later, the entire German army surrendered.

May, 1945. A Soviet soldier raises the flag over the Reichstag in Berlin after the Germans are defeated.

The major "second front" was opened on June 6, 1944, with the massive Allied landings in Normandy. Though deadly in places, the landings were a masterpiece of planning and deception. The Germans fiercely defended the dense hedgerows of Normandy, but Allied

air superiority and a vast buildup of men and matériel led to a breakthrough. An American landing on the Riviera in August had much more immediate success, aided by the French resistance. In late July and August the Allies swept through France, liberating Paris on August 14 and pushing into Belgium. After that it was rough going. Allied commanders in the West were gifted organizers, but their skills as strategists were mixed. A British airborne invasion of the Netherlands and an American thrust into the forests of the Rhineland were bloody failures. The Germans mounted their own devastating attack in December 1944, under cover of winter storms, in the Battle of the Bulge. It was a last effort with their best men and equipment; they captured thousands of prisoners and nearly broke through Allied lines. Nevertheless, several elite American units beat off much larger German forces at key points until the snow cleared and the Allies mounted a crushing counterattack. Over the winter they destroyed German forces in the Rhineland and Holland. In April 1945, the Allies crossed the Rhine—in one of the war's ironies, French troops were the first to do so. The Germans collapsed. American tanks swept south, British and Canadian forces north. The Allies had learned the tactics of the *Blitzkrieg* on the receiving end, and now the Americans used them to overwhelm resistance. This genuine military success was helped by the fact that most Germans preferred to surrender to Americans or Britons than face the Russians to the east.

At the same time, those Soviet troops were approaching fast. By late April they had taken Prague and Vienna. On April 21, 1945, Zhukov's forces hammered their way into the suburbs of Berlin. During the next ten days a savage battle raged amid the ruins and heaps of rubble; more than a hundred thousand Russians and Germans

CHRONOLOGY

THE WESTERN FRONT

Germany invades the Low Countries	May 1940
French surrender	June 1940
Battle of Britain	July 1940–June 1941
D-Day invasion	June 1944
Liberation of Paris	August 1944
Battle of the Bulge	December 1944
Allies invade Germany	April 1945
Germany surrenders	May 1945

died. Adolf Hitler killed himself in a bomb-proof shelter beneath the Chancellery on April 30. On May 2 the heart of the city was captured, and the Soviets' red banner flew from the Brandenburg Gate. On May 7 the German high command signed a document of unconditional surrender. By the next day the war in Europe was over.

THE WAR IN THE PACIFIC

The war in the Pacific came to an end four months later. The Japanese were rolled back on all fronts. Slim's international army in Burma had waged a wily campaign to drive out the Japanese. British, Indian, and Nepalese troops liberated the Burmese capital, Rangoon, at the same time the Germans were surrendering in the West. That same spring, Australian forces recaptured the Dutch East Indies, while an Anglo-Australian attack on Singapore was planned for the autumn. The United States Navy had won one of its greatest victories the previous fall, when William Halsey's task force destroyed most of Japan's surviving surface ships in the gulfs of the Philippine islands. American forces landed and within weeks the Philippine capital of Manila fell, taken house by house in bloody fighting. The remaining battles, amphibious assaults on a series

of islands running toward the Japanese mainland, were just as brutal. Japanese pilots, hopelessly outnumbered in the air, mounted suicide attacks on American ships, while American marines and Japanese soldiers fought over every inch of the shell-blasted rocks in the middle of the Pacific. In June 1945, the Japanese island of Okinawa fell to American forces after eighty-two days of desperate fighting. American forces now had a foothold less than five hundred miles from the Japanese mainland. Chinese forces, Nationalist and Communist alike, combined to force the Japanese back on Hong Kong. The Soviets chose this moment to enter the fray. Their forces marched rapidly through Manchuria and into the colonial territory of Korea. The government in Tokyo awaited an invasion and called on its citizens for supreme endeavors to meet the crisis.

On July 26 the heads of the United States, British, and Chinese governments issued a joint proclamation calling on Japan to surrender or be destroyed. The United States had already begun that process of destruction by using its most advanced bomber, the B-29, which could fly above Japanese efforts to shoot it down, in the systematic bombing of Japanese cities. Many of the wooden Japanese cities were hit with firebombs, which created storms of flame and killed hundreds of thousands of civilians. Yet the Japanese refused to surrender. In the absence of that surrender the United States planned to increase the pace of destruction. They chose to use the atomic bomb.

View of Hiroshima after the First Atom Bomb Was Dropped, August 6, 1945. This photo, taken one month later, shows the utter devastation of the city. Only a few steel and concrete buildings remained intact.

THE ATOMIC BOMB AND ITS IMPLICATIONS

A PETITION TO THE PRESIDENT OF THE UNITED STATES

In July 1945, scientists associated with the Manhattan Project became involved in debates about how the atomic bomb could be deployed. Members of the Scientific Panel of the Secretary of War's Interim Advisory Committee agreed that a bomb could be used militarily, but disagreed about whether it could be used without prior warning and demonstration. Other groups of scientists secretly began to circulate petitions, such as the one below, in which they set out their views. The petitions never reached the president, but they raised issues that did emerge in the postwar period.

July 17, 1945

A PETITION TO THE PRESIDENT OF THE UNITED STATES

We, the undersigned scientists, have been working in the field of atomic power. Until recently we have had to fear that the United States might be attacked by atomic bombs during this war and that her only defense might lie in a counterattack by the same means. Today, with the defeat of Germany, this danger is averted and we feel impelled to say what follows:

The war has to be brought speedily to a successful conclusion and attacks by atomic bombs may very well be an effective method of warfare. We feel, however, that such attacks on Japan could not be justified, at least not unless the terms which will be imposed after the war on Japan were made public in detail and Japan were given an opportunity to surrender. . . .

[I]f Japan still refused to surrender our nation might then, in certain circumstances, find itself forced to resort to the use of atomic bombs. Such a step, however, ought not to be made at any time without seriously considering the moral responsibilities which are involved.

The development of atomic power will provide the nations with new means of destruction. The atomic bombs at our disposal represent only the first step in this direction, and there is almost no limit to the destructive power which will become available in the course of their future development. Thus a nation which sets the precedent of using these newly liberated forces of nature for purposes of destruction may have to bear the responsibility of opening the door to an era of devastation on an unimaginable scale.

If after this war a situation is allowed to develop in the world which permits rival powers to be in uncontrolled possession of these new means of destruction, the cities of the United States as well as the cities of other nations will be in continuous danger of sudden annihilation. . . .

The added material strength which this lead [in the field of atomic power] gives to the United States brings with it the obligation of restraint and if we were to violate this obligation our moral position would be weakened in the eyes of the world and in our own eyes. It would then be more difficult for us to live up to our responsibility of bringing the unloosened forces of destruction under control.

In view of the foregoing, we, the undersigned, respectfully petition: first, that you exercise your power as Commander-in-Chief, to rule that the United States shall not resort to the use of atomic bombs in this war unless the terms which will be imposed upon Japan have been made public in detail and Japan knowing these terms has refused to surrender; second, that in such an event the question of whether or not to use atomic bombs be decided by you in the light of the considerations presented in this petition as well as all the other moral responsibilities which are involved.

Michael B. Stoff, Jonathan F. Fanton, and R. Hal Williams, eds., *The Manhattan Project: A Documentary Introduction to the Atomic Age* (New York: McGraw-Hill, 2000), p. 173.

PRESIDENT TRUMAN'S MEMOIRS

In this section of his memoirs, President Harry S. Truman sets out the views of other scientists on the Secretary of War's Advisory Committee. He explains the logic of his decision to use the atomic bomb against Hiroshima (August 6, 1945) and Nagasaki (August 9, 1945) and the events as they unfolded.

I had realized, of course, that an atomic bomb explosion would inflict damage and casualties beyond imagination. On the other hand, the scientific advisers of the committee reported, "We can propose no technical demonstration likely to bring an end to the war; we see no acceptable alternative to direct military use." It was their conclusion that no technical demonstration they might propose, such as over a deserted island, would be likely to bring the war to an end. It had to be used against an enemy target.

The final decision of where and when to use the atomic bomb was up to me. Let there be no mistake about it. I regarded the bomb as a military weapon and never had any doubt that it should be used. The top military advisers to the President recommended its use, and when I talked to Churchill he unhesitatingly told me that he favored the use of the atomic bomb if it might aid to end the war.

In deciding to use this bomb I wanted to make sure that it would be used as a weapon of war in the manner prescribed by the laws of war. That meant that I wanted it dropped on a military target. I had told Stimson that the bomb should be dropped as nearly as possibly upon a war production center of prime military importance.

Stimson's staff had prepared a list of cities in Japan that might serve as targets. Kyoto, though favored by General Arnold as a center of military activity, was eliminated when Secretary Stimson pointed out that it was a cultural and religious shrine of the Japanese.

Four cities were finally recommended as targets: Hiroshima, Kokura, Niigata, and Nagasaki. They were listed in that order as targets for the first attack. The order of selection was in accordance with the military importance of these cities, but allowance would be given for weather conditions at the time of the bombing. Before the selected targets were approved as proper for military purposes, I personally went over them in detail with Stimson, Marshall, and Arnold, and we discussed the matter of timing and the final choice of the first target. . . .

On August 6, the fourth day of the journey home from Potsdam, came the historic news that shook the world. I was eating lunch with members of the *Augusta's* crew when Captain Frank Graham, White House Map Room watch officer, handed me the following message:

> TO THE PRESIDENT
> FROM THE SECRETARY OF WAR
>
> Big bomb dropped on Hiroshima August 5 at 7:15 P.M. Washington time. First reports indicate complete success which was even more conspicuous than earlier test.

I was greatly moved. I telephoned Byrnes aboard ship to give him the news and then said to the group of sailors around me, "This is the greatest thing in history. It's time for us to get home."

Harry S. Truman, *Memoirs*, Vol. 1 (Garden City, NY: Doubleday, 1955), pp. 419–21.

Many senior military and naval officers argued that use of the bomb was not necessary, on the assumption that Japan was already beaten. Some of the scientists involved, who had done their part hoping to counter the Nazis, believed that using the bomb for political ends would set a deadly precedent. Harry Truman, who had succeeded Roosevelt following the latter's death in April 1945, decided otherwise. On August 6, a single atomic bomb was dropped on Hiroshima, obliterating about 60 percent of the city. Three days later a second bomb was dropped on Nagasaki. President Truman warned that the United States would use as many atom bombs as necessary to bring Japan to its knees. On August 14, Japan surrendered unconditionally.

The decision to drop the bomb, and its consequences, were extraordinary. It did not greatly alter the scope or the plans for the American destruction of Japan. Many more Japanese died in the earlier fire

CHRONOLOGY

THE WAR IN THE PACIFIC

Japanese bomb Pearl Harbor	December 1941
Singapore falls to Japan	December 1941
Battles of Midway, Coral Sea, and Guadalcanal	1942
Invasion of the Philippines	Fall 1944
Battle of Okinawa	June 1945
Soviets invade Manchuria and Korea	June–July 1945
Atomic bombs dropped on Hiroshima and Nagasaki	August 6 and 9, 1945
Japan surrenders	August 14, 1945

bombings than in the two atomic blasts. Yet the bomb was an entirely new kind of weapon, built with untried technology; some of its designers feared that the test blast might split *every* atom in the universe. It was one of the most terrifying results of the new relationship between science and political power. The nature of the bomb mattered as well. The instant, total devastation of the blasts, along with the cancerous radiation that lingered for years and claimed victims decades later, was something terribly new. The world now had a weapon that could destroy not just cities and peoples, but humanity itself.

THE PEACE SETTLEMENT AND INTERNATIONAL SECURITY

What were the major outcomes of World War II?

The war had two very different sets of consequences. The first was a profound falling out among the major Allied powers. These disagreements gathered steam during the years immediately after the war and soon degenerated in to the long "cold war" that lasted for nearly the rest of the century. Competing national goals that had been papered over in the name of defeat-

ing Nazism and fascism came out into the open, and none of the powers involved found ways to resolve those differences on friendly terms. The other set of consequences resulted when the Allies tried to follow the opposite course—founding a much larger, more durable international organization than the League of Nations to ensure peace and security. This was the United Nations; though it was created by political bargaining and has enjoyed mixed success at best, it has been a durable forum for international diplomacy and efforts to resolve conflicts without a repeat of 1939.

TENSION AMONG THE ALLIES

During the war the Allied leaders met several times to discuss war aims and postwar goals. The public rhetoric spoke of the need for a world without conflict and of the right of all people to political self-determination. Those objectives were expressed in the Atlantic Charter issued by Roosevelt and Churchill in August 1941, and in a declaration signed by twenty-six nations, including Britain, the United States, the Soviet Union, and China the following year. These were worthy ideals, but they were easy victims of the realities of international politics.

During the war Stalin, Churchill, and Roosevelt put aside important differences among them in the name of presenting a united front to the enemy and their own publics. By the time of the meetings at Yalta in 1944 and Potsdam, held in occupied Germany during July 1945, unavoidable rifts began to surface. Some of the most important involved central Europe. The Soviets wanted a buffer against future German aggression and started by demanding to keep the territory they had taken from Poland in 1939. After the war this land was overtaken by Stalin's brutally direct approach to occupying eastern Europe. The Soviets steadily deposed independent governments and set up client states that offered a defense against invasion as well as an opportunity to develop a communist empire in half of Europe.

The Americans were equally determined to shape in their own image as much of the world as they could. The American occupations of southern Germany and Japan—particularly Japan, where General Douglas MacArthur ruled virtually alone and carried the colonial "civilizing mission" to new political heights—were opportunities to set up liberal constitutions and local governments bound to the United States, and to revive powerful economies that could benefit America's global trade. America tightened its reins on trade with Latin America. As a supplier of food and currency to the world, the United States shaped international

The Yalta Conference, 1945. From the left, Winston Churchill, Franklin Roosevelt, and Joseph Stalin, gathered for a press conference.

The situation enflamed relations between the wartime allies, who were rapidly becoming rival imperial blocs.

Returning displaced peoples and bringing Nazi criminals to justice also became important issues. The repatriation of Poles, Germans, and Russians who had fought for the Germans became political bargaining points. So did American authorities' willingness to look the other way when former Nazis assumed positions of authority in the government and economy of western Germany. The Allies had held the Nazi leadership to account before the world, putting senior officials on trial in a special international court at Nuremburg. In November 1945, twenty-two senior Nazis were tried for "war crimes" and, in a legal innovation that would endure through the century, "crimes against humanity." Eighteen were sentenced to punishments ranging from ten years' imprisonment to death. Several of their co-defendants committed suicide. But in the interest of establishing a stable, economically viable, defensible German state outside Soviet control, many former Nazis were allowed to "forget" their past and reenter society.

agreements that stabilized money and commerce on advantageous terms. The British, operating at more disadvantages, still defended their imperial and financial privileges around a "sterling area" of trade, and hoped to develop their African colonies as a source of raw materials that could compete with the United States in world markets. Churchill and several of the Labour politicians who succeeded him after the war, particularly Foreign Secretary Ernest Bevin, were deeply suspicious of the Soviets, especially Soviet involvement in the Middle East, that might threaten India or Britain's oil interests.

Dividing up the conquered territories and resettling displaced peoples brought the tensions among the Allies to a head. Germany was divided into four zones of occupation held by the United States, the Soviet Union, Britain, and France. Yet the Soviet zone was largely separate from the start, and Stalin diverted the breadbasket of Prussia to feed starving Russians, leaving Germans in the British and French zones to go hungry instead. In Berlin, also divided into four zones, the Soviets tried the same methods as a deliberate tactic. In 1948 they closed off all roads to the former capital of Germany, in an effort to absorb Berlin entirely into the Soviet zone. American and Britain met that Berlin blockade with an airlift of food and supplies.

At the same time many of the war's victims, Jewish refugees from the concentration camps, reshaped the politics of the Middle East. During World War I, with the Balfour declaration (see Chapter 27), the British had promised a "Jewish homeland" in Palestine. One of several contradictory promises, it soon led to rising conflict between Jewish settlers and Arabs in the British "mandate" of Palestine. In 1939, attempting to prevent escalating conflict, the British strictly limited further Jewish immigration. After the war, they tried to maintain that limit but were now faced with tens of thousands of Jewish refugees. The conflict quickly became a three-way war: among Palestinian Arabs fighting for what they considered their land and their independence, Jewish settlers and fighters trying to break British restrictions, and British administrators trying without success to mediate, in the name of holding onto this outpost of empire. After three years of conflict that included terrorist tactics on all sides,

the British withdrew in 1948, chafing at the United Nations' willingness to recognize the new state of Israel. Israel survived an immediate attack by neighboring Arab states, emerging as a new nation and a permanent change to the culture and balance of power in the region.

Within three years after the war, the friction between the major Allied powers had degenerated into open hostility. Many diplomats and military planners in Washington and London feared that the Soviets planned another war in Europe. Communist parties in France and Italy and other parties of the left were discouraged or covertly suppressed. A terrible new arms race slowly began, this time centering on Russian and British efforts to develop their own atomic bombs, with the Americans responding in turn. Each side mistrusted the other. As the Soviets and Americans divided the conquered territory of Korea, a former Japanese colony, into two client states, friction between them led to a bitter, bloody war in 1950. By this time the lines were drawn, in Europe, the Middle East, and Asia, for what became known as the cold war. War-weary citizens throughout the West feared another open conflict. Instead the cold war brought four decades of political brinkmanship, a tense standoff with nuclear weapons, and a multitude of smaller wars in client states.

THE UNITED NATIONS

Yet the cold war was not the only outcome of the peace talks of 1945. After each of the world wars the victorious powers set out to create an organization that would bind the nations of the world together, ensuring stability and security. The League of Nations had failed to avert the outbreak of war in 1939; in April 1946 it was formally dissolved. But Allied statesmen believed that an international organization was even more necessary after this war than the last. In February 1945 at Yalta, they agreed to hold an international conference in San Francisco to address the issue. The new body was named the United Nations. It was founded on the principle of the "sovereign equality of all peace-loving states" and would accept any member state willing to recognize its standards for human rights and proper international behavior. The UN was to be divided between a General Assembly of all members and a Security Council that had five permanent seats reserved for the most powerful Allied nations (the United States, the Soviet Union, Britain, France, and China). The charter also provided for a general secretariat and agencies for economic, social, and cultural issues, along with an International Court of Justice. After terse negotiations between the United States and the Soviets about the Security Council's power over the actions of states, and between the United States and Britain over the UN's attitude toward colonial territories, the charter was drafted and signed.

Although the United Nations has failed to live up to the hopes of its founders, it continues to function as the world's longest-lived international assembly of nations. The most important functions of the organization were assigned by the charter to the Security Council. This agency has the "primary responsibility for the maintenance of international peace and security." It has authority to investigate any dispute between nations, to recommend methods for settlement and, in order to preserve the peace, to employ diplomatic or economic measures against an aggressor. In practice, however, the Security Council gave a monopoly of authority to its permanent members. No action of any kind could be taken without the unanimous consent of all of them plus four other members. The absolute veto given to each of the principal states did not bolster the peace of the world. Instead, it has frequently left the council crippled in the face of emergencies. It was powerless in the face of any major power's efforts to have its own way, as in the case of the Soviets' repression of revolts in Hungary and Czechoslovakia, or the massive American intervention in Vietnam in the 1960s. The UN also failed to gain control of the atomic bomb, leading to the nuclear standoff between the national "superpowers." Although the UN has acted on occasion to defuse explosive situations or restore peace, the results—in Korea in the 1950s, in the Congo in the 1960s, and in the Balkans in the 1990s—have been decidedly mixed.

The UN has enjoyed more success in the work of its Economic and Social Council. The council has authority to initiate studies and make recommendations with respect to all social, economic, medical, educational, and cultural issues, and perform services in those fields at the request of UN members. Humanitarian relief and cultural exchange have both been important to the continued relevance of the UN and its mission to promote standards of health, human rights, and mutual understanding. During its first half century the work of various UN agencies produced several major failures, but also a modestly impressive record of success. Even if it has failed to meet all the lofty goals set in 1945, it still exists, and it has flexibility that its predecessor, the League of Nations, lacked to face the hopes and needs of a new century.

CONCLUSION

After World War I, many Europeans awoke to find a world they no longer recognized. In 1945 many Europeans came out from shelters or began the long trips back to their homes, faced with a world that hardly existed at all. The products of industry—tanks, submarines, strategic bombing—had destroyed the structures of industrial society—factories, ports, and railroads. The tools of mass culture—fascist and communist appeals, patriotism proclaimed via radios and movie screens, mobilization of mass armies and industry—had been put to full use. In the aftermath, much of Europe lay destroyed and, as we will see, vulnerable to the rivalry of the postwar superpowers: the United States and the Soviet Union.

The two world wars profoundly affected Western empires. Nineteenth-century imperialism had made twentieth-century war a global matter. In both conflicts the warring nations had used the resources of empire to their fullest. Key campaigns—in North Africa, Burma, Ethiopia, the Pacific—were fought in and over colonial territories. Hundreds of thousands of colonial troops—sepoys and Gurkhas from India and Nepal, Britain's King's African Rifles, French from Algeria and West Africa—served in armies on both sides of the conflict. After two massive mobilizations, many anticolonial leaders found renewed confidence in their own peoples' courage and resourcefulness, and they seized the opportunity of European weakness to press for independence. In many areas that had been under European or Japanese imperial control—sections of China, Korea, Indochina, Indonesia, Palestine—the end of World War II only paved the way for a new round of conflict. This time, the issue was when imperial control would be ended, and by whom.

The Second World War also carried on the Great War's legacy of massive killing. Historians estimate that nearly 50 million people died. The killing fields of the East took the highest tolls: perhaps 20 million Soviet soldiers and civilians; 20 percent of the Polish population and nearly 90 percent of the Polish Jewish community; 1 million Yugoslavs, including militias of all sides; 4 million German soldiers and five hundred thousand German civilians, not including the hundreds of thousands of ethnic Germans who died while being deported west at the end of the war, in one of the many acts of ethnic cleansing that ran through the period. Even the United States, shielded from the full horrors of total war by two vast oceans, lost over one hundred fifty thousand soldiers in battle and more to accidents or disease.

Why was the war so murderous? The advanced technology of modern industrial war and the openly genocidal ambitions of the Nazis offer part of the answer. The global reach of the conflict offers another. Finally World War II overlapped with, and eventually devolved into, a series of smaller, no less bitter conflicts: a civil war in Greece; conflicts between Orthodox, Catholics, and Muslims in Yugoslavia; and political battles for control of the French resistance. Even when those struggles claimed fewer lives, they left deep political scars. So did memories of the war. Hitler's empire could not have lasted as long as it did without active collaboration or passive acquiescence from many, a fact that produced bitterness and recrimination for years.

In this and many other ways, the war haunted the second half of the century. Fifty years after the battle of Stalingrad, a journalist discovered that hundreds of skeletons still lay, in the open, on the fields outside the city. Many bodies had never been buried. Others had been left in shallow, mass graves. As wind and water eroded the soil, farmers plowed the fields, and teenagers dug for medals and helmets to sell as curiosities, more bones kept rising to the surface. One of the supervisors charged with finding permanent graves and building memorials responded to the task by voicing more than simple weariness. "This job of reburying the dead," he said, "will never be done."

SELECTED READINGS

Bartov, Omer. *Hitler's Army: Soldiers, Nazis, and War in the Third Reich.* New York, 1991.

Burrin, Philippe. *France under the Germans: Collaboration and Compromise.* New York, 1996.

Browning, Christopher R. *The Path to Genocide: Essays on Launching the Final Solution.* Cambridge, 1992.

Carr, Raymond. *The Spanish Tragedy: The Civil War in Perspective.* London, 1977. A thoughtful introduction to the Spanish Civil War and the evolution of Franco's Spain.

Dawidowicz, Lucy S. *The War against the Jews, 1933–1945.* New York, 1975. A full account of the Holocaust.

Divine, Robert A. *Roosevelt and World War II.* Baltimore, 1969. A diplomatic history.

Gilbert, Martin. *The Appeasers.* Boston, 1963. Excellent study of British pro-German sentiment in the 1930s.

———. *The Second World War: A Complete History.* Rev. ed. New York, 1991. An up-to-date general account.

Hilberg, Raul. *The Destruction of the European Jews*, 2d ed. 3 vols. New York, 1985. Another excellent treatment of the Holocaust, its origins, and its consequences.

Kedward, Roderick. *In Search of the Maquis: Rural Resistance in Southern France, 1942–1944*. Oxford, 1993.

Keegan, John. *The Second World War*. New York, 1990. A classic.

Marrus, Michael R. *The Holocaust in History*. Hanover, N.H., 1987. Thoughtful analysis of central issues.

Michel, Henri. *The Shadow War: The European Resistance, 1939–1945*. New York, 1972. Compelling reading.

Milward, Alan S. *War, Economy, and Society, 1939–1945*. Berkeley, 1977. Analyzes the impact of the war on the world economy and the ways in which the economic resources of the belligerents determined strategies.

Noakes, Jeremy, and Geoffrey Pridham. *Nazism: A History in Documents and Eyewitness Accounts, 1919–1945*. New York, 1975. An excellent combination of analysis and documentation.

Overy, Richard. *Russia's War*. New York, 1998.

Paxton, Robert O. *Vichy France: Old Guard and New Order, 1940–1944*. New York, 1982.

Stoff, Michael B. *The Manhattan Project: A Documentary Introduction to the Atomic Age*. New York, 1991.

Weinberg, Gerhard L. *A Global History of World War II*. New York, 1995. Now the most comprehensive history.

Wilkinson, James D. *The Intellectual Resistance in Europe*. Cambridge, Mass., 1981. A comparative study of the movement throughout Europe.

Wright, Gordon. *The Ordeal of Total War, 1939–1945*. New York, 1968. Particularly good on the domestic response to war and the mobilization of the resources of the modern state.

PART VIII
THE WEST AND THE WORLD

THE SECOND WORLD WAR was perhaps the great watershed of the twentieth century. Its legacies were many and pervasive. The "hot war" between the Allies and the Axis was superseded by a rivalry between the most powerful of the Allies: the United States and the Soviet Union. The superpowers possessed nuclear weapons, global reach, and networks of alliances that gave them the authority of empires. The "cold war" between these powers dominated the recovery from the world war, and global politics in general, for four decades. The rise and fall of cold-war politics is a fundamental theme in twentieth-century history; it is one of the two historical trends followed here.

The other trend is more important but more diffuse. While the cold war seemed to centralize the political, cultural, and economic life of the world around the twin poles of the superpowers, the other key theme of the later twentieth century involves the decentralizing effects of globalization. This began with the breaking apart of Europe's old colonial empires and the emergence of new nations. New forms of politics and protest emerged as well, based on social movements of women, ethnic "minorities," and peoples denied a political voice in the age of imperialism. The Western European empires were not the only ones to collapse. With the end of the cold war, the unofficial empire of the Soviet Union collapsed as well, producing new nations and new hopes, but uncertain means of achieving those aspirations. These events seemed to leave the United States as the world's leading power, but the rest of the world would not simply become an American empire by default or consent to being "Americanized" on the United States' terms. Instead, it may be more useful to see all the various Western civilizations operating in a much tighter network of world civilizations in which the center of power and direction of change remains unclear. We can, however, understand the circumstances in which this "globalized" world emerged, and those circumstances are the focus of this last section.

	POLITICS	SOCIETY AND CULTURE	ECONOMY	INTERNATIONAL RELATIONS
				Mohandas Gandhi (1869–1948)
	Malcolm X (1925–1965)	Alexander Fleming discovers first antibiotic, penicillin (1928)		
	Martin Luther King Jr. (1929–1968)			
1940		Albert Camus's *The Stranger* (1942)		Gandhi leads independence movement in India (1940s)
				Soviet Union creates Iron Curtain over eastern Europe (1945–1948)
				Chinese Communist Revolution (1945–1949)
				India gains independence, formation of Pakistan (1947)
				Truman Doctrine (1947)
				Vietnam War, French phase (1947–1954)
	Germany divided; Berlin airlift (1948–1949)		Marshall Plan (1948)	Civil war in Greece (1948)
				Josip Tito declares Yugoslavia independent of Soviet Union (1948)
				State of Israel formed (1948)
	Konrad Adenauer, chancellor of West Germany (1949–1963)	George Orwell's *1984* (1949)		Formation of NATO (1949)
		Simone de Beauvoir's *The Second Sex* (1949)		
1950	Mao Zedong's Great Leap Forward (1950s)		European Coal and Steel Community created (1951)	Korean War (1950–1953)
				Abdel Nasser becomes president of Egypt (1952)
	Joseph Stalin dies (1953)	Samuel Beckett's *Waiting for Godot* (1953)		United States and Soviet Union test hydrogen bombs (1953)
	Khrushchev's regime (1953–1964)	Francis Crick and James Watson discover structure of DNA (1953)		Algerian war ends with Algerian independence (1954–1962)
		Jonas Salk develops polio vaccine (1953)		Formation of Warsaw Pact (1955)
				Vietnam War, U.S. phase (1955–1975)
	Nikita Khrushchev begins de-Stalinization (1956)	Boris Pasternak's *Dr. Zhivago* (1957)		Suez Crisis (1956)
				Hungarian rebellion repressed by Soviets (1956)
	Charles de Gaulle forms Fifth Republic in France (1958)		European Economic Community (EEC, Common Market) formed (1958)	
1960	Cultural Revolution in China (1960s)	Günter Grass's *The Tin Drum* (1959)	Inflation rates rise across western Europe (late 1960s–1970s)	Castro to power in Cuba (1959)
	John F. Kennedy, president (1961–1963)	Joseph Heller's *Catch-22* (1961)		
	Berlin Wall built (1961)	Frantz Fanon's *The Wretched of the Earth* (1961)		
		Rachel Carson's *Silent Spring* (1962)		Cuban Missile Crisis (1962)
	Martin Luther King Jr. leads March on Washington (1963)	Betty Friedan's *The Feminine Mystique* (1963)		Vietnam War (1963–1975)
	Leonid Brezhnev leads Soviet Union (1964–1982)	Herbert Marcuse's *One-Dimensional Man* (1964)		
		The Beatles play in New York (1964)		
		Birth control pill becomes available (mid-1960s)		
				Six-Day War between Israel and Arab nations (1967)
	Student protests and worker strikes in Paris (1968)			
	Czech revolt; Prague Spring (1968)			
1970	Willy Brandt, chancellor of West Germany (1970–1974)			SALT treaties (1970s and early 1980s)
				Gradual détente between Soviet Union and Western powers (1970s)
	Watergate scandal (1972–1974); President Richard Nixon resigns		Western European citizens elect representatives to EEC parliament (1972)	Nixon visits China (1972)

POLITICS	SOCIETY AND CULTURE	ECONOMY	INTERNATIONAL RELATIONS	
		Oil prices rise steadily, worsening widespread recession (1973–1980s)	OPEC embargo against Western powers (1973)	1973
			Arab-Israeli War (1973)	
			Camp David Accords (1978)	
Margaret Thatcher, prime minister of England (1979–1990)			Soviet military intervention in Afghanistan (1979–1989)	
Polish Solidarity workers movement organizes strikes (1980)		Computer revolution begins (1980s)		1980
Ronald Reagan, president (1980–1988)				
Helmut Kohl becomes chancellor of West Germany (1982)				
Mikhail Gorbachev, leader of Communist party (1985–1991)	Asian population reaches 3 billion (1986)			
Renewed Solidarity strikes in Poland, demonstrations across Eastern bloc (1988)	Nuclear reactor accident at Chernobyl (1986)			
Break-up of Soviet power in eastern Europe (1989)				
Berlin Wall falls (1989)				
Tiananmen Square massacre (1989)				
Germany reunifies (1990)		Eastern European economies in crisis (1990s)	Persian Gulf War (1991)	1990
Boris Yeltsin elected president of Russian Federation (1990)		Internet revolution begins (1990s)	Yugoslavian civil wars (1991–1992, 1992–1995)	
Soviet Union dissolved (1992)				
Nelson Mandela elected president of South Africa; end of apartheid (1994)		NAFTA signed by Canada, Mexico, and United States (1993)	Genocide in Rwanda (1994)	
			Russia's war with Chechnya begins (1994)	
			Pakistan and India test nuclear weapons (late 1990s)	
	Scientists in Scotland clone a sheep (1997)		War in Kosovo (1999)	
	Global population exceeds 6 billion (2001)		United States declares War on Terrorism (2001)	2001

CHAPTER THIRTY

COLD WAR POLITICS, ECONOMIC BOOM, AND CULTURAL CHANGE

"THE WAR ENDED the way a passage through a tunnel ends," wrote Heda Kovály, a Czech woman who survived the concentration camps. "From far away you could see the light ahead, a gleam that kept growing, and its brilliance seemed ever more dazzling to you huddled there in the dark the longer it took to reach it. But when at last the train burst out into the glorious sunshine, all you saw was a wasteland." The war left Europe a land of wreckage and confusion. Refugees trekked hundreds or thousands of miles on foot to return to their homes. Housing was scarce everywhere—in some areas it was practically nonexistent. Food remained in dangerously short supply; a year after the war, roughly 100 million people in Europe were still forced to live on less than 1,500 calories per day. Families had to scrape a few vegetables from the ground or trade smuggled goods on the "black market" to feed and clothe themselves. Food rationing remained a dreary fact of life everywhere, and without it a large portion of the Continent's population would have starved. During the winter of 1945–1946, many regions had little or no fuel for heat. What coal there was—less than half the prewar supply—could not be transported to the areas most in need of it. In 1945, many European men and women found it all but impossible to imagine their continent's rising from the ashes of total conflict.

It was no wonder that Europeans felt overwhelmed by the trauma of war. The wonder, indeed, was that the period of trauma lasted such a relatively short time. Ten years later, Europe had been transformed, though not restored. Two key developments mark the immediate postwar period. The first was the emergence of the cold war, a standoff between the United States and the Soviet Union that reflected the dramatically altered balance of international power. The cold war produced a divided continent, with Eastern Europe under the control of the Soviet Union, and Western Europe dominated by the military and economic presence of the United States. The second change, a consequence of human determination and favorable economic trends, produced a period of tremendous economic growth, buoyant optimism, and lively creativity, more expansive than even the most optimistic forecaster might have deemed possible in 1945.

FOCUS QUESTIONS

- What were the causes of the cold war?
- What caused the economic renaissance in Western Europe?

- What were de Gaulle's political aims?
- What themes defined postwar culture?

THE COLD WAR AND A DIVIDED CONTINENT

What were the causes of the cold war?

In the closing years of the war, relations between the Allied powers frayed over issues of power and influence in central and eastern Europe. After the war, they quickly descended into mutual distrust and conflict. The United States and Soviet Union rapidly formed the centers of two imperial blocs whose influence and rivalry shaped world politics for four decades.

THE IRON CURTAIN

The Soviet Union had insisted during the wartime negotiations at Teheran and Yalta that it had a legitimate claim to control Eastern Europe, an assertion that Western leaders willingly acknowledged. When visiting Moscow in 1944, Churchill and Stalin bargained over their spheres of influence and over the fate of several supposedly free nations. Stalin, however, grew increasingly mistrustful of Western leadership and believed that bargains with the West, no matter how attractive they might seem on paper, were worthless. "Churchill," he remarked, "is the kind who, if you don't watch him, will slip a kopek out of your pocket. . . . Roosevelt . . . dips his hands only for bigger coins."

Berlin, 1945. The rubble from which the German "miracle" was created.

A siege mentality, generated by Stalin himself, pervaded the authoritarian Soviet regime. Nearly everyone could be presented as a potential threat or enemy of the state. The same state of mind shaped Stalin's foreign policy. Anti-Western policy, however, did not rest on personal paranoia alone. The Soviets' enormous industrial losses and fears of further invasion made them determined to maintain political, economic, and military control of the Eastern European countries they had liberated from Nazi rule. When their wartime allies remonstrated, the Soviets grew suspicious, remembering American and British anticommunism between the wars.

Across Eastern Europe, a combination of Soviet diplomatic pressure, political infiltration, and military power quickly established "people's republics" sympathetic to the Soviet regime. The same process occurred in country after country: first, states established coalition governments from which only former Nazi sympathizers were excluded; next came coalitions in which communists predominated; finally, one party took hold of all the key positions of power. It was this process that prompted Winston Churchill, speaking in Fulton, Missouri in 1946, to say that "an Iron Curtain" had "descended across Europe." By 1948, governments dependent on Moscow had been established in Poland, Hungary, Romania, Bulgaria, and Czechoslovakia, and they were referred to as the Eastern bloc. The Soviets had hoped to include Greece in their sphere of influence, and the country was torn by civil war until 1949. Significant military aid from the British and Americans, however, restored the Greek monarchy. In 1948, the Soviets crushed a Czechoslovakian coalition government headed by the liberal leaders Eduard Beneš and Jan Masaryk—a direct challenge to the Yalta guarantee of free, democratic elections.

Germany rapidly became the center of gravity of the new cold war. The four occupied zones devolved into two hostile states: the Soviet zone became a semi-independent Socialist republic; the French, English, and American zones formed a liberal, capitalist state under the watchful eye of other Western nations. Increasingly anxious about the way in which the

Western allies were merging their territories, passing economic reforms, and introducing a new currency, the Soviets retaliated by blockading Berlin. The blockade, which cut West Berlin off from the rest of the Western zone, lasted nearly a year, from June 1948 to May 1949. Western resistance was tenacious, and for eleven months the "Berlin airlift" carried supplies to the Western zone of the city, breaking the siege. When the crisis ended, the two Germanies looked strikingly like armed camps.

In 1949, the USSR tested its first atom bomb; in 1953 both superpowers demonstrated a new weapon, the hydrogen bomb. All of these developments—the "satellization" of Eastern Europe, the Berlin blockade, the arms race and, across the Pacific, the Chinese Revolution and the Korean War (see Chapter 32) fueled Western fears and fed Western determination to stem the spread of communist governments, particularly where the old European empires were slowly giving way.

The Soviet campaign for control over Eastern Europe, however, met a series of obstacles and sporadic resistance. Yugoslavia defied Soviet ambitions in 1948, when the wartime hero Marshal Tito declared his government independent of Moscow. Tito fought to steer a middle course, unattached to either East or West. Unlike most Eastern European communist leaders, Tito had risen to power on his own, and his wartime record gave him political authority rooted in his own country. Yugoslavia's rebelliousness, however, sparked reaction from Moscow. Determined to reassert control elsewhere, the Soviets demanded purges in the parties and administrations of various satellite governments. These began in the Balkans and extended to Poland, Czechoslovakia, and East Germany; in several areas those purging the governments attacked their opponents as Jewish. Anti-Semitism, far from being crushed, remained a potent political force—for as Heda Kovály explained, it became common to blame Jews for bringing the horrors of war.

Winston Churchill Denounces Soviet Tyranny. In a speech at Fulton, Missouri, in March 1946, Churchill coined the phrase "Iron Curtain" to characterize the separation of Eastern from Western Europe.

The Berlin Airlift, 1948. For eight and a half months the United States, Britain, and France airlifted over two million tons of supplies into West Berlin, defying a Russian blockade of the city.

THE WAR THAT REFUSES
TO BE FORGOTTEN

Heda Margolis Kovály was born in Prague and returned to her city after surviving the concentration camps. Like many refugees and survivors, she received an uncertain welcome home. In Czechoslovakia and elsewhere, the Nazi occupation left a legacy of bitterness and division which persisted for decades. Survivors reminded other Europeans of the war and made them defensive. Paradoxically, as Kovály shows, it was common to blame the victims for the war's troubles.

And so ended that horrible long war that refuses to be forgotten. Life went on. It went on despite both the dead and the living, because this was a war that no one had quite survived. Something very important and precious had been killed by it or, perhaps, it had just died of horror, of starvation, or simply of disgust—who knows? We tried to bury it quickly, the earth settled over it, and we turned our backs on it impatiently. After all, our real life was now beginning and what to make of it was up to us.

People came crawling out of their hide-outs. They came back from the forests, from the prisons, and from the concentration camps, and all they could think was, "It's over; it's all over." . . . Some people came back silent, and some talked incessantly as though talking about a thing would make it vanish . . . While some voices spoke of death and flames, of blood and gallows, in the background, a chorus of thousands repeated tirelessly, "You know, we also suffered. . . . nothing but skimmed milk. . . . No butter on our bread. . . . "

Sometimes a bedraggled and barefoot concentration camp survivor plucked up his courage and knocked on the door of prewar friends to ask, "Excuse me, do you by any chance still have some of the stuff we left with you for safekeeping?" And the friends would say, "You must be mistaken, you didn't leave anything with us, but come in anyway!" And they would seat him in their parlor where his carpet lay on the floor and pour herb tea into antique cups that had belonged to his grandmother. . . . He would say to himself, "What does it matter? As long as we're alive? What does it matter?". . .

It would also happen that a survivor might need a lawyer to retrieve lost documents and he would remember the name of one who had once represented large Jewish companies. He would go to see him and sit in an empire chair in a corner of an elegant waiting room, enjoying all that good taste and luxury, watching pretty secretaries rushing about. Until one of the pretty girls forgot to close a door behind her, and the lawyer's sonorous voice would boom through the crack, "You would have thought we'd be rid of them finally, but no, they're impossible to kill off—not even Hitler could manage it. Every day there're more of them crawling back, like rats. . . ." And the survivor would quietly get up from his chair and slip out of the waiting room, this time not laughing. On his way down the stairs his eyes would mist over as if with the smoke of the furnaces at Auschwitz."

Heda Margolius Kovály, *Under A Cruel Star: A Life in Prague 1941–1968.* Translated from the Czech by Franci Epstein and Helen Epstein with the author. (Cambridge, Mass.: Plunkett Lake Press, 1986), pp. 45–46.

THE MARSHALL PLAN

The United States countered these moves with massive programs of economic and military aid to Western Europe. In 1947, President Harry Truman proclaimed the Truman Doctrine, which cast the Soviet-American conflict as a choice between "two ways of life." Truman vowed to support the resistance of "free peoples" to communist infiltration in general and granted aid to the governments of Greece and Turkey. In 1948, the European Recovery Program, or the Marshall Plan—named for Secretary of State George Marshall, who first proposed it—provided funds for the reconstruction of Western European industry. Vast amounts of American money and goods—tractors, train engines, food, and technical equipment—were supplied to the states of Western Europe. The Marshall Plan quickened the pace of those nations' recovery from the ravages of war, and helped raise standards of living. The aid, however, came with a price: political alliance with the United States and its anti-Soviet interests, restraints on wages and other fiscal measures, and the tacit suppression of left-leaning

> The United States countered Soviet moves with massive programs of economic and military aid to Western Europe.

George Marshall.

politicians and movements who might be sympathetic to communism.

The United States also moved to shore up the military defenses of the West. In April 1949, a group of representatives of Western European states, together with Canada and the United States, signed an agreement providing for the establishment of the North Atlantic Treaty Organization (NATO). Greece, Turkey, and West Germany were later added as members. The treaty declared that an armed attack against any one of the members would be regarded as an attack against all, and that they would combine their armed strength to repel the aggressor. The joint military command of NATO was established in 1950, with Dwight Eisenhower as its senior military commander. The force began with thirty divisions in 1950, and by 1953 had nearly sixty, including a dozen divisions from the young state of West Germany. West German rearmament had been the subject of agonizing debate, particularly in Britain and France, but American pressure and a sense of strategic necessity led to its acceptance within Western Europe.

From the Soviet point of view, NATO, the Marshall Plan, and especially the United States' persistent involvement in Europe's affairs were cause for alarm. The Soviets rejected an original offer of Marshall Plan aid and instead organized an Eastern European version of the plan, the Council for Mutual Economic Assistance, or Comecon. In 1947 the Soviets organized an international political arm, the Cominform (Communist Information Bureau), responsible for coordinating worldwide communist policy and programs. They responded to NATO with the establishment of their own military alliances, confirmed by the Warsaw Pact of 1955. This agreement set up a joint command among the states of Albania, Bulgaria, Czechoslovakia, Hungary, Poland, Romania, and East Germany, and guaranteed the continued presence of Soviet troops in all those countries.

The cold war arose from misperceptions on both sides. Concerned about economic weakness throughout postwar Western Europe, U.S. leaders believed that the Soviets were hatching a vast plan to take advantage of that weakness by establishing communist regimes throughout the West, as they had in the East. Americans were unwilling to give up the power—military, economic, and political—they had acquired during the war. The United States was convinced that it offered a model for mediating conflicts, and with a

The Cold War: A Soviet View. "Nyet!" or "No!" and an arm raised in protest and fear.

where. On both sides of the Iron Curtain, the cold war brought everyday anxiety, air raid drills, spy trials, and appeals to defend family and home against the other.

KHRUSHCHEV AND THE "THAW"

With Stalin's death in 1953, the relentless barrage of anti-Western propaganda gradually abated. Although relations between East and West remained wary, tensions eased considerably during the late 1950s and 1960s. The United States continued to adhere to a policy of Soviet "containment," seeking as allies those most willing to oppose by military force, if necessary, the spread of international communism. By the mid-1950s, however, Western European nations had begun to wonder whether U.S. intervention in their affairs might not, in fact, represent as much an American power play as an attempt to protect the West from Soviet aggression. American claims to this role of "protector of the free world" began to sound hollow, particularly after U.S. Secretary of State John Foster Dulles negotiated a diplomatic and military understanding with the aging Spanish dictator Francisco Franco in 1955.

combination of idealism and arrogance tried to establish that model elsewhere. On the Soviet side, Stalin's personal suspicions and his autocratic style combined with genuine worries about Soviet security to exacerbate the cold war mentality.

What did the cold war mean on the ground? In the Soviet Union writers and artists were attacked for deviation; the party disciplined economists for suggesting that European industry might recover from the damage it had sustained. The radio blared news that Czech or Hungarian leaders had been exposed as traitors. In the United States, congressional committees launched campaigns to root out "communists" every-

Nikita Khrushchev. Premier (1958–1964) and First Secretary of the Communist party (1953–1964) of the Soviet Union, Khrushchev visited the United States in 1959. Here he is shown joking with an Iowan farmer.

THE COLD WAR: SOVIET AND AMERICAN VIEWS

The excerpt below is a speech titled "The Sinews of Peace" that was delivered by Winston Churchill at Westminster College in Fulton, Missouri in early 1946. In it, he coined the phrase "Iron Curtain," warning of the rising power of the Soviet Union in Eastern Europe.

The excerpt on the following page is from an address by Nikita Khrushchev, who became first secretary of the Communist party in 1953. Three years later, his power secure, he began publicly to repudiate the crimes of Joseph Stalin. Khrushchev presided over a short-lived thaw in Soviet-American relations. Yet, as can be seen in his address, Khrushchev shared Winston Churchill's conception of the world divided into two mutually antagonistic camps.

WINSTON CHURCHILL'S "IRON CURTAIN" SPEECH

A shadow has fallen upon the scenes so lately lighted by the Allied victory. Nobody knows what Soviet Russia and its Communist international organization intend to do in the immediate future, or what are the limits, if any, to their expansive and proselytizing tendencies. I have a strong admiration and regard for the valiant Russian people and for my wartime comrade, Marshal Stalin. There is deep sympathy and goodwill in Britain . . . towards the people of all the Russias and a resolve to persevere through many differences and rebuffs in establishing lasting friendships. We understand the Russian need to be secure on her western frontiers by the removal of all possibility of German aggression. We welcome Russia to her rightful place among the leading nations of the world. We welcome her flag upon the seas. Above all, we welcome constant, frequent and growing contacts between the Russian people and our own people on both sides of the Atlantic. It is my duty however . . . to place before you certain facts about the present position in Europe.

From Stettin in the Baltic to Trieste in the Adriatic, an iron curtain has descended across the Continent. Behind that line lie all the capitals of the ancient states of Central and Eastern Europe. Warsaw, Berlin, Prague, Vienna, Budapest, Belgrade, Bucharest and Sofia, all these famous cities and the populations around them lie in what I must call the Soviet sphere, and all are subject in one form or another, not only to Soviet influence but to a very high and, in many cases, increasing measure of control from Moscow. . . .

From what I have seen of our Russian friends and Allies during the war, I am convinced that there is nothing they admire so much as strength, and there is nothing for which they have less respect than for weakness, especially military weakness. For that reason the old doctrine of a balance of power is unsound. We cannot afford, if we can help it, to work on narrow margins, offering temptations to a triad of strength. If the Western Democracies stand together in strict adherence to the principles of the United Nations Charter, their influences for furthering those principles will be immense and no one is likely to molest them. If however they become divided or falter in their duty and if these all-important years are allowed to slip away then indeed catastrophe may overwhelm us all.

Winston Churchill, *Winston S. Churchill: His Complete Speeches, 1897–1963*, vol. 7, 1943–1949, edited by Robert Rhodes James. (New York: Chelsea House Publishers, 1983), pp. 7290–7291.

Nikita Khrushchev, "Report to the Communist Party Congress (1961)"

Comrades! The competition of the two world social systems, the socialist and the capitalist, has been the chief content of the period since the 20th party Congress. It has become the pivot, the foundation of world development at the present historical stage. Two lines, two historical trends, have manifested themselves more and more clearly in social development. One is the line of social progress, peace and constructive activity. The other is the line of reaction, oppression and war.

In the course of the peaceful competition of the two systems capitalism has suffered a profound moral defeat in the eyes of all peoples. The common people are daily convinced that capitalism is incapable of solving a single one of the urgent problems confronting mankind. It becomes more and more obvious that only on the paths to socialism can a solution to these problems be found. Faith in the capitalist system and the capitalist path of development is dwindling. Monopoly capital, losing its influence, resorts more and more to intimidating and suppressing the masses of the people, to methods of open dictatorship in carrying out its domestic policy and to aggressive acts against other countries. But the masses of the people offer increasing resistance to reaction's acts.

It is no secret to anyone that the methods of intimidation and threat are not a sign of strength but evidence of the weakening of capitalism, the deepening of its general crisis. As the saying goes, if you can't hang on by the mane, you won't hang on by the tail! Reaction is still capable of dissolving parliaments in some countries in violation of their constitutions, of casting the best representatives of the people into prison, of sending cruisers and marines to subdue the "unruly." All this can put off for a time the approach of the fatal hour for the rule of capitalism. The imperialists are sawing away at the branch on which they sit. There is no force in the world capable of stopping man's advance along the road of progress.

Current Soviet Policies IV, edited by Charlotte Saikowski and Leo Gruliow, from the translations of the Current Digest of the Soviet Press. Joint Committee on Slavic Studies, 1962, pp. 42–45.

Nikita Khrushchev's slow accession to power, finally secure in 1956, signaled a change of direction. Khrushchev possessed a kind of earthy directness that, despite his hostility to the West, helped for a time to ease tensions. Stalin had secluded himself in the Kremlin; Khrushchev traveled throughout the world. On a visit to the United States in 1959, he traded quips with Iowa farmers and was entertained at Disneyland. Khrushchev was a shrewd politician, switching quickly between angry anti-American rhetoric and diplomatic reconciliation. Showing his desire to reduce international conflict, Khrushchev soon agreed to a summit meeting with the leaders of Britain, France, and the United States. This led to a series of understandings that eased the frictions in heavily armed Europe and produced a ban on testing nuclear weapons above ground in the early 1960s.

Cuba

Cold War conflict flared up, however, over the United States' closest Caribbean neighbor, Cuba. A communist-led revolution in 1958 brought the charismatic figure of Fidel Castro to power. Rejected by the United States, Castro turned immediately to the Soviets for aid. At the same time, the United States immediately began to work with exiled Cubans on the losing side of the revolution to depose Castro. An attack by American-backed Cuban exiles in 1961 failed, but Castro made a bargain with the Soviets to base Soviet nuclear missiles on Cuban soil, only a few minutes' flying time from targets in the heart of the United States. American spy planes identified the missiles and related military equipment in 1962, and in October of that year President Kennedy confronted the Soviets over the issue. After deflecting pressure from some military advisors to invade Cuba, Kennedy imposed a blockade. The Soviet government was alarmed by the threat of war, and Khrushchev was able to contain his own hard-liners and arrange a bargain for which Kennedy would be allowed to take credit. The Soviets agreed to withdraw and to remove the bombers and missiles already on Cuban soil. The incident posed an extremely difficult question for the superpowers: how could one nation convince another of its determination to brook no further interference with its plans, if its adversary could be fairly certain that because of the fear of nuclear war the threat was no more than a bluff? The crisis brought about much more direct channels of communication between the superpowers, in an effort to reduce the chance of an accidental war, but the confrontation over Cuba continued.

Khrushchev's determination to lower international tensions grew out of the need to consolidate his regime at home and to prevent the threatened crumbling of the communist bloc in Eastern Europe. The harsh demands of Stalin's regime had generated discontent among the Soviet people. Dissenters, their voices no longer silenced by the Stalinist police, began to demand a shift from the production of heavy machinery and armaments to the manufacture of consumer goods, and, in the arts, a return to a

> Khrushchev's determination to lower international tensions grew out of the need to consolidate his regime at home and in the Eastern bloc.

measure of freedom. Their voices were heard in essays and in books such as Ilya Ehrenburg's novel *The Thaw* (1954), whose title came to stand for the period. In 1956, in a now-famous speech, Khrushchev denounced the excesses of Stalin's regime, and allowed the "rehabilitation" of some of Stalin's victims. Ethnic minorities in the Soviet Union were allowed some scope to express themselves, and cultural expression was freer than it had been in the Soviet Union since the 1920s.

REPRESSION IN EASTERN EUROPE

Despite the thaw, Eastern European demands for greater autonomy and freer expression brought repression. In the East, Soviet demands for rapid industrialization and collectivization generated growing resentment. By 1953, the East German government, burdened by reparations payments to the Soviet Union, faced an economic crisis. The successes of West German recovery, of which East Germans were acutely aware, made matters worse. Tens of thousands of East German citizens fled to the West—fifty-eight thousand in March 1953 alone. In June, the government called for steep increases in industrial productivity, setting off strikes in East Berlin and spreading unrest throughout the country. The East German uprising was put down by the Soviet army, and hundreds were executed in the subsequent purge. In the aftermath, the East German government, under the leadership of Walter Ulbricht, used fears of disorder to solidify one-party rule. The flight of East Germans to

the West, however, continued to be a substantial problem until the building of the Berlin Wall in 1961.

In 1956 Poland and Hungary followed suit, demanding more independence in the management of their domestic affairs. In Poland, strikes broke out. The government responded first with military repression and then with a promise of liberalization. The anti-Stalinist Polish leader Wladyslaw Gomulka was able to win Soviet permission for his country to pursue its own "ways of Socialist development" by pledging Poland's continued loyalty to the terms of the Warsaw Pact.

Events in Hungary produced a different result. The charismatic leader of Hungary's communist government, Imre Nagy, was as much a Hungarian nationalist as a communist. Under his government, protests against Moscow's policies developed into a much broader anti-communist struggle and, even more important, attempted secession from the Warsaw Pact. Khrushchev's government was willing to allow looser ties between Eastern Europe and Moscow, but an end to the pact was unthinkable. On November 4, 1956, Soviet troops occupied Budapest, arresting and executing leaders of the Hungarian rebellion. The Hungarians took up arms, and street fighting continued for several weeks. The Hungarians had hoped that vague promises of Western aid would produce military intervention but Dwight Eisenhower, newly elected to a second term as president, steered clear of supporting the Hungarians. Soviet forces installed a new government under the staunchly communist Janos Kadar, the repression continued, and tens of thousands of Hungarian refugees fled for the West. Khrushchev's efforts at presenting a gentler, more conciliatory Soviet Union to the West had been shattered by revolt and repression.

Despite these events, Khrushchev held to his policy of "peaceful coexistence" with the West. Soviet leaders nonetheless remained determined to reduce any possible German military threat to Eastern Europe. Still persuaded that Germany might launch a new war, abetted by its capitalist allies, they staunchly opposed the reunification of the country. In 1961 the East German government built a high wall separating the two sectors of Berlin to prevent any more East Germans from escaping to West Berlin and thence to West Germany. The wall brought a dangerous show of force on both sides, as the Soviets and Americans mobilized reservists for war. The new American president, John Kennedy, visited Berlin to proclaim that "all free men"

EUROPE DURING THE COLD WAR

Examine the membership of NATO and the Warsaw Pacts, respectively. What type of government characterized the member states of each? Why did the membership of each alliance stay relatively stable for nearly half a century? Why did certain socialist governments (Sweden, France) and federal democracies (Switzerland) remain neutral rather than join either pact? Why did Yugoslavia, under a communist government, not join the Warsaw Pact?

The Berlin Wall, 1961. Thirteen years after the blockade, the East German government built a wall between East and West Berlin to stop the flow of escapees to the West. This manifestation of the "Iron Curtain" was dismantled in 1989.

The Occupation of Czechoslovakia. In 1968 the liberalized regime of Alexander Dubček was suppressed by the Soviets. Protesting citizens faced military force and tanks like these in the streets of Prague.

and a powerful and dark monument to the communist German state in the East.

In 1964, Khrushchev fell prey to political rivals and was deposed. The reins of Soviet power passed to Leonid Brezhnev as secretary of the Communist party. Brezhnev was more conservative and less politically savvy than Khrushchev, less inclined to bargain with the West and more prone to defensive actions to safeguard the Soviet sphere of influence. Among the most significant challenges to Soviet authority came in 1968, with the "Prague spring." Another liberal Communist government emerged, this time in Czechoslovakia, headed by Alexander Dubček. Dubček preached "socialism with a human face"; he encouraged self-criticism within the party, relaxed censorship, and permitted a variety of subversive artists and youth movements. The Soviets tolerated Dubček as a political eccentric until 1968, when he was visited by both Tito and Nicolae Ceausescu of Romania—two of the most independent-minded communist leaders in Eastern Europe. The Soviets feared another attempt to undermine the Warsaw Pact, pointing to the American war in Vietnam as an example of heightened anticommunist activities around the world. Again, Moscow answered rebellion with repression. When Dubček attempted to democratize the Communist party, the Soviets sent tanks and troops into Prague. Again the world watched as streams of refugees left the country and a repressive government, picked by Soviet security forces, took charge. Dubček and his allies were subjected to imprisonment or "internal exile." After the destruction of the "Prague spring," Soviet diplomats consolidated their position according to the new "Brezhnev doctrine." The doctrine stated that no socialist state should permit itself to adopt policies detrimental to the interests of

should claim allegiance with the citizens of non-communist West Berlin. For almost thirty years, until 1989, the wall remained a symbol of Soviet determination to prevent the formation of a united Germany,

LUDVÍK VACULÍK, "TWO THOUSAND WORDS"

During the Prague Spring of 1968, a group of Czech intellectuals published a document titled "Two Thousand Words that Belong to Workers, Farmers, Officials, Scientists, Artists, and Everybody" that has become known simply as the "Two Thousand Words." This manifesto called for further reform, including increased freedom of the press. Seen as a direct affront by Moscow, the manifesto heightened Soviet-Czech tensions. In August 1968, Warsaw Pact tanks rolled into Prague, overthrowing the reformist government of Alexander Dubček.

Most of the nation welcomed the socialist program with high hopes. But it fell into the hands of the wrong people. It would not have mattered so much that they lacked adequate experience in affairs of state, factual knowledge, or philosophical education, if only they had enough common prudence and decency to listen to the opinion of others and agree to being gradually replaced by more able people. . . .

The chief sin and deception of these rulers was to have explained their own whims as the "will of the workers". Were we to accept this pretense, we would have to blame the workers today for the decline of our economy, for crimes committed against the innocent, and for the introduction of censorship to prevent anyone writing about these things. The workers would be to blame for misconceived investments, for losses suffered in foreign trade, and for the housing shortage. Obviously no sensible person will hold the working class responsible for such things. We all know, and every worker knows especially, that they had virtually no say in deciding anything. . . .

Since the beginning of this year we have been experiencing a regenerative process of democratization. . . .

Let us demand the departure of people who abused their power, damaged public property, and acted dishonorably or brutally. Ways must be found to compel them to resign. To mention a few: public criticism, resolutions, demonstrations, demonstrative work brigades, collections to buy presents for them on their retirement, strikes, and picketing at their front doors. But we should reject any illegal, indecent, or boorish methods. . . .

Let us convert the district and local newspapers, which have mostly degenerated to the level of official mouthpieces, into a platform for all the forward-looking elements in politics; let us demand that editorial boards be formed of National Front representatives, or else let us start new papers. Let us form committees for the defense of free speech. . . .

There has been great alarm recently over the possibility that foreign forces will intervene in our development. Whatever superior forces may face us, all we can do is stick to our own positions, behave decently, and initiate nothing ourselves. We can show our government that we will stand by it, with weapons if need be, if it will do what we give it a mandate to do. . . .

The spring is over and will never return. By winter we will know all.

Originally published as "Dva Tisice Slov," *Literarny Listy* (Prague) June 27, 1968. Translated by Mark Kramer, Joy Moss, and Ruth Tosek. From Jaromir Navratil, *The Prague Spring 1968* (Budapest: Central European Press, 1998), pp. 177–181.

CHRONOLOGY

THE EARLY COLD WAR IN EUROPE, 1946–1968

Churchill's "Iron Curtain" speech	1946
Truman Doctrine	1947
Soviets launch Cominform and Comecon	1947
Eastern bloc established	1948
Marshall Plan	1948
Berlin Blockade	1948–1949
Formation of NATO	1949
Stalin dies	1953
Formation of the Warsaw Pact	1955
Revolts in East Germany, Poland, and Hungary	1953–1956
Khrushchev visits the U.S.	1959
Building of the Berlin wall	1961
"Prague spring"	1968

international socialism and that the Soviet Union could intervene in the domestic affairs of any Soviet-bloc nation if communist rule was threatened.

EAST-WEST RELATIONS IN THE 1970S

Western leaders remained concerned about a divided Europe and sought ways to bring the two halves into closer association. The politician most effective in bridging the gap between East and West was Willy Brandt, chancellor of West Germany in the early 1970s. Brandt was a lifelong socialist, an outspoken enemy of Hitler who had been forced to flee Germany for Norway in the 1930s. He had joined the anti-Nazi resistance movement and worked actively for the Allies. Eastern Europeans respected his resistance credentials; though they chafed under Soviet control, they had just as much historical reason to fear Germany. Brandt also had credibility in the West as a moderate socialist who continued Germany's economic "miracle" (discussed below) and as the heroic mayor of West Berlin during the building of the Wall. Brandt's talents led him to take action to heal several important rifts, and to define West Germany's place in Europe more clearly. He recognized the need to accept the division of Germany into two nations, and moved to regularize relations with West Germany's eastern neighbors (Ost-

politik). A complex series of diplomatic negotiations with the Soviet Union, East Germany, and Poland established East and West Germany as separate states within one nation, guaranteed unimpeded Western access to Berlin, and recognized Poland's claim to a western frontier along the Oder and Neisse Rivers. Brandt also acted to heal relations between Germans and Jews. He improved relations with Israel and, during a symbolic visit to the old Warsaw Ghetto, scene of the Nazis' massacres, fell to his knees in an act of national penance. Brandt's government was unexpectedly undone by one of the features of the cold war—a spy scandal—in 1974. Until then, however, he helped lead the way towards a new kind of diplomacy between East and West, and offered a new approach to healing the wounds of the Second World War.

SOLIDARITY IN POLAND

Tensions between East and West, which eased during the 1960s and 1970s, arose once more in the next decade, this time in response to Polish defiance. In 1980, calling their movement "Solidarity," Polish workers organized strikes that brought the government of the country to a standstill. The strikers formulated several key demands. First, they objected to working conditions imposed by the government to combat a severe economic crisis. Second, they protested high prices and, especially shortages, both of which had roots in government policy and priorities. Above all, though, the Polish workers in Solidarity demanded truly independent labor unions—not organizations sponsored by the government. The conviction that society had the right to organize itself and, by implication, create its own government, stood at the core of the movement. The strikers were led by an electrician from the Gdansk shipyards, Lech Walesa. Walesa's charismatic personality appealed not only to the Polish citizenry but to sympathizers in the West. Again, however, the Soviets assisted a military regime in reimposing authoritarian rule. The Polish president, General Wojciech Jaruzelski, had learned from Hungary and Czechoslovakia and played a delicate game of diplomacy to maintain the Polish government's freedom of action while repressing Solidarity itself. But the implied Soviet threat remained. The presence of Soviet troops on the Polish border, along with the deployment of a new generation of American nuclear missiles in Europe, damaged détente (the policy of avoiding direct military confrontation between the superpowers) and Ostpolitik almost beyond repair. The actions of Brandt and other leaders on each

Defiance in Poland. Thousands of striking workers take part in religious services in the Lenin Shipyards in Gdansk on August 24, 1980. This was the scene of the first in a series of strikes that paralyzed an already troubled economic and political system and challenged Soviet domination of Polish governmental policy.

side had marked a step forward in East-West relations. The start of the 1980s brought unsettling steps back.

ECONOMIC RENAISSANCE

What caused the economic renaissance in Western Europe?

Despite the ongoing tensions of a global superpower rivalry, the postwar period also brought a remarkable recovery in Western Europe: the economic "miracle." The "miracle" actually rested on predictable economic forces. First, the war had encouraged a variety of technological innovations with direct and important peacetime applications: improved communications (the invention of radar, for example), the manufacture of synthetic materials, the increasing use of aluminum and alloy steels, and advances in the techniques of prefabrication. Second, wartime manufacturing had added significantly to nations' productive capacity. Despite the wartime devastation, European manufacturing plants survived to sustain a postwar boom, and the Marshall Plan aided the recovery. This boom was fueled by a third set of factors: the continued buoyancy of consumer demand and the consequent high

level of employment throughout the 1950s and 1960s. These in turn encouraged continued capital investment and technological innovation. Brisk foreign demand for Europe's goods also served to convince politicians to remove obstacles to international trade and payments. The fortunate combination of circumstances made possible a remarkable period of dynamic economic growth.

Governments resorted to a variety of devices to facilitate economic expansion: West Germany provided tax breaks to encourage business investment; Britain and Italy offered investment allowances to their steel and petroleum industries. Virtually all of Western Europe experimented with the nationalization of industry and services in an effort to enhance efficiency and productivity. The result was a series of "mixed" economies combining public and private ownership. France, Britain, Italy, and Austria took the lead in the move toward state-controlled enterprise. In France, where public ownership was already well advanced in the 1930s, railways, electricity and gas, banking, radio and television, and a large segment of the automobile industry were brought under state management. In Britain, the list was equally long: coal and utilities; road, railroad, and air transport; and banking. Though nationalization was less common in West Germany, the railway system (state owned since the late nineteenth century); some electrical, chemical, and metallurgical concerns; and the Volkswagen company—the remnant of Hitler's attempt to produce a "people's car"—were all in state hands, though the latter was largely returned to the private sector in 1963.

These government policies and programs contributed to astonishing growth rates. Between 1945 and 1963 the average yearly growth of West Germany's gross domestic product (gross national product minus income received from abroad) was 7.6 percent; in Austria, 5.8 percent; in Italy, 6 percent; in the Netherlands, 4.7 percent; and so on. This was a remarkable reversal of the economic patterns of an interwar period that had been beset by slack demand, overproduction, and insufficient investment. In the face of reconstruction and recovery, production facilities were hard pressed to keep up with soaring demand.

West Germany's recovery was particularly spectacular. Production increased sixfold between 1948 and 1964. Unemployment fell to record lows, reaching 0.4 percent in 1965, when there were six jobs for every unemployed person. Though prices rose initially, their subsequent leveling off provided an opportunity for most citizens to participate in a domestic buying spree that caused production to soar. In the 1950s, an average of half a million housing units were constructed annually. They were to accommodate those whose homes had been destroyed, new resident refugees from East Germany and Eastern Europe, and transient workers from Italy, Spain, Greece, and elsewhere who were attracted by West Germany's demand for labor. German cars, specialized mechanical goods, optics, and chemicals returned to their former role leading world markets. West German women were included in the process: during the 1950s, German politicians encouraged women to take up a role as "citizen consumers," as active but prudent buyers of goods that would keep the German economy humming.

In France the major economic problem following the war was the need to modernize the nation's industries, many of which remained small family enterprises resistant to technological change. Under the direction of a minister for planning, Jean Monnet, a special office—the General Commissariat for Planning—was established to initiate and execute a program for national economic recovery. Using money provided by the Marshall Plan, the French government played a direct and active role in industrial revival and reform, contributing not only capital but expert advice, and facilitating shifts in the national labor pool to place workers where they were most needed. The plan gave priority to basic industries, with the result that the production of electricity doubled, the steel industry was thoroughly modernized, and the French railway system became the fastest and most efficient on the Continent. Other sectors of the economy, especially agriculture, tended to stagnate. Nevertheless, France's gross national product (GNP) increased at the rate of about 5 percent per year in the 1950s.

Italy's industrial "miracle" was even more impressive than those of West Germany and France, given the woe-

ful state of the nation's economy immediately following the war. Stimulated by infusions of capital from the government and from the Marshall Plan, Italian companies soon began to compete with other European international giants. The products of Olivetti, Fiat, and Pirelli became familiar in households around the world to an extent that no Italian goods had in the past. Electric power production—particularly important in Italy because of its lack of coal—had by 1953 increased 100 percent over that in 1938. By 1954 real wages were 50 percent higher than they had been in 1938. Yet Italy's success was marred by the enduring poverty of the country's southern regions, where illiteracy remained high and land continued to be held by a few rich families.

Elsewhere on the Continent, nations with little in common in terms of political traditions or industrial patterns all shared in the general prosperity. Spain's economy changed markedly in the late 1950s, when a combination of rising foreign investment and the lifting of government controls spurred higher levels of production. Tourism was for Spain, as for all European countries, an increasingly important industry. Seventeen million visitors came to Spain in 1966, making it second only to Italy as a tourist attraction. Holland, Belgium, Austria, Greece, and the Scandinavian countries all enjoyed booms in the late 1950s. Although each country succeeded in increasing its GNP significantly, marked differences remained in the levels of prosperity across the Continent. The per capita GNP in Sweden, for example, was almost ten times that of Turkey.

Throughout, Britain remained a special case. Although it shared in the economic prosperity of the postwar years, it did so to a lesser extent than other European countries. The British rise in GNP averaged 2.5 percent per year between 1948 and 1962—a respectable enough figure when compared with past performance but nothing like the spectacular achievements recorded during the same period across the Channel. The Conservative prime minister, Harold Macmillan, campaigned successfully for reelection in 1959 with the slogan "You've never had it so good"—an accurate enough boast. Yet the British economy remained sluggish. The country was burdened with obsolete factories and methods, the legacy of its early industrialization, and by an unwillingness to adopt new techniques in old industries or invest sufficiently in more successful new ones. It was plagued as well by a series of balance-of-payments crises precipitated by an inability to sell more goods abroad than it imported.

Throughout Europe, nations with little in common shared in the general prosperity of the postwar period.

Heating Fuel Shortage in Great Britain. This scene of British householders lining up for coal during the bitterly cold winter of 1948 shows that "winners" as well as "losers" suffered in the immediate aftermath of the Second World War.

The Western European renaissance was the sum of more than the work of individual nations. From the late 1940s on, they took steps to bind themselves together as an effective economic third force between the superpowers. In 1951 the European Coal and Steel Community was created, which placed the management of those industries in France, West Germany, Belgium, Holland, and Luxembourg under a joint High Authority. Consisting of experts from each of the participating countries, the authority possessed the power to regulate prices, to increase or limit production, and to impose administrative fees. Britain declared itself unwilling to participate, fearing the effects of European economic union on its declining coal industry and on its relationship with long-time trading partners such as Australia, New Zealand, and Canada.

European economic integration quickened during the mid-1950s. The period saw the establishment of Euratom, for example, a research organization in the field of nuclear development, and it culminated in 1958 with the founding of the European Economic Community (EEC), or Common Market. The EEC declared its goals to be the abolition of all trade barriers among the initial six members: France, West Germany, Italy, Belgium, Holland, and Luxembourg. In addition, the organization pledged itself to common external tariffs, the free movement of labor and capital among the member nations, and the establishment of uniform wage structures and social security systems, so as to foster similar working conditions throughout the EEC. A commission with headquarters in Brussels was charged with the administration of this ambitious program.

Despite inevitable difficulties, particularly in the area of agricultural policy and prices, the European Economic Community was a remarkable success. By 1963, it had become the world's largest importer. Its steel production was second only to that of the United States, and total industrial production was over 70 percent higher than it had been in 1950. Even critics who complained about constant interference of EEC "Eurocrats"—more than three thousand in Brussels by 1962—conceded that centralized European planning and decision making had brought the continent extraordinary and unheralded prosperity. The Common Market operated increasingly as a semiautonomous political unit. In 1972 citizens of member nations voted directly for representatives to an EEC parliament, and economic and political integration continue.

Although economic development in Eastern Europe was not nearly as dramatic as that of the West, significant advances occurred there as well. National incomes rose and output increased. Poland and Hungary, in particular, strengthened their economic connections with the West, primarily with France and West Germany. By the late 1970s, about 30 percent of Eastern Europe's trade was conducted outside the Soviet bloc. Nevertheless, the Soviet Union required its satellites to design their economic policies to serve more than their own national interests. Regulations governing the Eastern European equivalent of the Common Market—Comecon—insured that the Soviet Union could sell its exports at prices well above the world level, while other members were compelled to trade with the Soviet Union to their disadvantage. Emphasis initially was on heavy industry and collectivized agriculture, though political tension in countries such as Hungary and Poland compelled the Soviets eventually to moderate their policies so as to permit the manufacture of more consumer goods and the development of a modest trade with the West. Like the Western nations, those in the East demonstrated a continuing determination to free themselves from economic dependence on a single power.

Economic growth in Western Europe went hand in hand with an expanded welfare state. Women and men demanded more from their governments in the form of social services. Robust economies, coupled with a determination to strengthen democracy, encouraged governments to provide for their citizens to a greater degree than ever before. State welfare programs had existed throughout the twentieth century, and their roots extended back to the insurance schemes for old age, sickness, and disability introduced by Bismarck in Germany in the late 1880s. Postwar Western European governments considered these obligations just as compelling as keeping the peace. The preamble of the French constitution explicitly stated: "The nation guarantees the condition necessary for the development of the individual and the family. It guarantees every individual . . . the protection of health, material security, rest and leisure." In 1957, public spending on health, pensions, family allowances and assistance (not including housing and education), accounted for 20.8 percent of the national income in West Germany, 18.9 percent in France, and 12.1 percent in Britain. In Sweden, money spent on social services was six times higher in 1957 than in 1930; in Italy, it was fourteen times higher.

> Economic growth in Western Europe went hand in hand with an expanded welfare state.

THE POLITICS OF EUROPEAN RECOVERY

What were de Gaulle's political aims?

The governments responsible for these remarkable economic and social changes were almost all middle-of-the-road. After World War I, "old men" had resumed power throughout Europe; after World War II new men, unwilling to see Europe return to business as usual, moved into positions of authority. In Britain the Labour party, led by the socialist Clement Attlee, enacted the social legislation that produced a welfare state. In 1951, the Labour government gave way to the Conservatives. Led most notably by Harold Macmillan from 1957 to 1963,

the Conservatives also embraced the promise of economic growth and continued welfare policies. The Labour party returned to power in the mid-1960s under the prime ministership of Harold Wilson, who pledged to forge a more prosperous nation in the "white heat" of a new technological revolution. Though Labour and Conservatives fought partisan campaigns, they agreed on fundamentals: a mixed economy and extended welfare benefits. Labour politicians still called themselves socialists, but most defined socialism, as the party's mainstream always had, as centralization and state administration, rather than as the workers' control of the means of production.

Moderates dominated the politics of continental Europe as well. In Germany, France, and Italy, centrist parties held power throughout most of the two decades after 1945: the German Christian Democratic Union; the French Mouvement Républicain Populaire (M.R.P.); and the Italian Christian Democrats. Postwar political leaders were no-nonsense men, committed to the achievement of practical economic and social agendas. Konrad Adenauer, the West German chancellor from 1949 to 1963, was a former mayor and a devout Roman Catholic. He despised German militarism and blamed that tradition for Hitler's rise to power, but he was apprehensive about the problems of German parliamentary democracy. He tended to govern in a paternalistic, if not authoritarian, manner. His determination to see an end to the centuries-old hostility between France and Germany contributed significantly to the movement toward economic union. Alcide De Gasperi, the Italian premier from 1948 to 1953, likewise stood firmly against demands from the socialists and communists for more radical reforms.

Recognizing the political popularity of economic prosperity, socialists throughout Western Europe toned down their rhetoric and their demands, speaking less about the inevitability of class war and more about the contributions workers were making to the European postwar renaissance. The program adopted by the German Socialist party (the Social Democrats) in 1959, for example, abandoned orthodox Marxism by declaring the need to leave economic planning as much as possible to individual enterprise, rather than in the hands of the state.

France's political situation during the early 1950s was much more tangled. Party strength was fragmented. Twenty-five percent of the voting population regularly

Charles de Gaulle.

supported the French Communist party. Conservative parties of the right existed as well. The political middle, which had been strong in France, gradually eroded after 1945. Matters reached a crisis over the issue of Algerian independence. A series of centrist governments found it impossible to govern in the face of growing divisions. Disgruntled French army officers threatened to overthrow the government if the regime did not take decisive action against the independence movement (see Chapter 32). Desperate, the political leaders of the republic invited the Resistance hero General Charles de Gaulle to step in. De Gaulle had played a brief role in French politics immediately after the war, but had retired from politics in 1946, stung by the French voters' refusal to accept his proposals for strengthening the executive branch of the government.

De Gaulle accepted the offer to return—but on the condition that he be permitted to rule by decree for six months and to draft a new constitution for France. The constitution, adopted by referendum in September 1958, created the Fifth Republic. It strengthened the executive branch of the government, trying to avoid parliamentary deadlocks that had weakened the country earlier. The president was granted power to appoint the premier and dissolve the National Assembly—whose powers to dismiss a premier were considerably weakened. Armed with new authority, de Gaulle set out to

restore France's power and prestige. "France is not really herself unless in the front rank," he wrote in his memoirs. "France cannot be France without greatness." De Gaulle believed that French greatness involved reorienting its world affairs, including ending its grip on Algeria. Concerned about U.S. influence in Europe, he withdrew French troops from NATO in 1966. He cultivated better relations with the Soviet Union and, with Adenauer, he worked towards closer cooperation between France and West Germany. He accelerated French economic and industrial expansion by building a modern military establishment, complete with atomic weapons. A nuclear *force de frappe,* or independent strike force whose objectives were primarily political and diplomatic, became part of de Gaulle's effort to reclaim France's Great Power status. De Gaulle's independent stand largely rested on his conviction that the Soviet leadership did not contemplate an invasion of the West.

Like De Gasperi and Adenauer, de Gaulle was not, by nature, a democrat. Like his counterparts he steered a centrist course, working hard to produce "practical" solutions to political problems and thereby undermine radicalism of any form. Most other Western European nations followed suit. Holland, Belgium, and the Scandinavian countries initiated economic and social policies that echoed those of the British, French, Germans, and Italians. In Spain and Portugal, however, different political, economic, and social agendas were pursued under the dictatorships of General Francisco Franco and António Salazar. In Greece, political instability in the 1950s and early 1960s opened the way for a coup by right-wing generals in 1967. Yet these were exceptions to a two-decade history of domestic tranquillity and economic prosperity—a sharp contrast to the tragic failures of the 1920s and 1930s.

INTELLECTUAL AND CULTURAL ACTIVITY

What themes defined the postwar culture?

The postwar period brought a remarkable burst of cultural production. Much of the literature and art during the era treated what were cast as dilemmas of the human condition. That theme, however, has to be understood against the specific backdrop of the war.

Aleksandr Solzhenitsyn.

War, occupation, resistance, and the moral dilemmas they created gave much of this writing its real resonance and appeal. The French existentialist writers, above all Jean-Paul Sartre and Albert Camus, wrote about the politics of commitment and choice. That meaning was not given but created was the existentialist premise: humanity is "condemned to be free." Humans give their lives meaning by becoming "engagés," or involved: making choices and accepting responsibility. To fail to accept freedom and responsibility is to act in "bad faith." In an important sense, the existentialists revived traditional humanist traditions in the face of the horrors of World War II. They did so in very accessible form. Although Sartre wrote philosophical treatises, he also published plays and short stories. Camus's own experience in the resistance gave him tremendous moral authority. His novels (including *The Stranger* [1942], *The Plague* [1947], and *The Fall* [1956]) often revolved around metaphors for the war, showing humanity's own responsibility for its dilemmas and, with a series of antiheroes, exploring the limited ability of men and women to help each other. The German Günter Grass's first and probably most important novel, *The Tin Drum* (1959), was written in a very different style, but it likewise portrayed the Nazi and war experience in a semi-autobiographical genre, and many considered Grass "the conscience of his generation." The American Joseph Heller's wildly

popular *Catch-22* (1961) represented a form of popular existentialism, concerned with the absurdity of war and a biting commentary on the toll of regimentation on individual freedom.

The theme of individual helplessness in the face of state power ran through countless works of the period, beginning, most famously, with George Orwell's *Animal Farm* (1946) and *1984* (1949). The Russian Boris Pasternak, in his novel *Doctor Zhivago* (1957), condemned the Soviet campaign to shape all its citizens to the same mold. His countryman Aleksandr Solzhenitsyn attacked the brutal methods employed by the Soviet Union in its rapid climb to world power. His *Gulag Archipelago*, published in 1974, is the fictionalized account of the fate of those whose willingness to stand in the way of Soviet "progress" sentenced them to life in Siberian labor camps. Both Pasternak and Solzhenitsyn were awarded the Nobel Prize for literature, the former in 1958 and the latter in 1970. Herbert Marcuse, a naturalized American, charged that authoritarianism was just as much a fact of life under capitalism as under communism. He argued that industrial capitalism had produced a "one-dimensional" society, in which the interests of individual citizens had been ruthlessly subordinated to those of

Boris Pasternak.

the powerful corporate interests that were the true governors of the world.

Some authors believed the human condition too hopeless to warrant direct attack. They expressed their despair by escaping into the absurd and fantastic. In such plays as *Waiting for Godot* (1953) by Samuel Beckett, an Irishman who wrote in French, and *The Caretaker* (1960) and *Homecoming* (1965) by the Briton Harold Pinter, nothing happens. Characters speak in the banalities that have become the hallmark of modern times. Other authors ventured into the realms of hallucination, science fiction, and fantasy. The novels of the American William Burroughs and Kurt Vonnegut carry readers from interior fantasies to outer space. The writings of the Czech author Milan Kun-

dera, who fled the repressive Czech government to live in Paris, capture the bittersweet efforts to resist senseless bureaucracy. Significantly, one of the most popular books among the young people of the sixties and seventies was *The Lord of the Rings* (1954–1955), a pseudo-saga set in the fantasy world of Middle Earth, written before and during the Second World War by the Briton J. R. R. Tolkien.

Film flourished. The Swede Ingmar Bergman, the Frenchmen Jean-Luc Godard and François Truffaut, the Italians Federico Fellini and Michelangelo Antonioni, to name but a few of the most gifted directors, dealt in their films with the same themes that marked the literature of the period: loneliness, war, and corruption. One important factor in the development of artistic films was the censors'—state or industry—willingness to let filmmakers handle themes such as racism, violence, and sexuality. Lifting taboos cleared the way for extraordinary powerful film statements, such as the American Arthur Penn's *Bonnie and Clyde* (1967) and the Italian Bernardo Bertolucci's *Last Tango in Paris* (1972). But film also flourished as entertainment. The international popularity of the British rock and roll group the Beatles was translated, for example, into equally successful films—slapstick comedies that proclaimed the emancipation of youth from the confining formalities and conventions of their elders.

Painting followed a different pattern. Following trends established by the cubists and surrealists, postwar painters experimented with color, texture, and technique, searching for new forms of expression. The enormously influential New York school of abstract expressionism was represented by the American painters Jackson Pollock, Willem de Kooning, and Franz Kline. Pollock in particular pioneered the use of new techniques; he poured and even threw paint on the canvas, creating powerful images of personal and physical expressiveness. His huge scale canvasses, which defied conventional artistic structures, gained immediate attention. Critics called the drip paintings "unpredictable, undisciplined, and explosive," and saw in them the youthful exuberance of postwar American culture. Frank Stella, an abstract expressionist and "minimalist," created abstract works by playing extremely simple

Abstract Expressionism. *Sea Change,* by Jackson Pollock (1912–1956). Pollock, one of the new American "moderns," improvised with new techniques to express gesture, movement, and feeling.

Three Flags, by Jasper Johns (1930–). Johns' flag paintings were among many that made familiar, everyday objects into icons of modern "art."

shapes and colors off each other. Mark Rothko created a series of remote yet extraordinarily compelling abstractions with glowing or somber rectangles of color imposed upon other rectangles, saying they represented "no associations, only sensation." Postwar American painters also turned a new eye to popular culture, lavishing painterly attention on instantly recognizable, commonplace images, and redefining art in the process. Jasper Johns' paintings of the American flag formed part of this trend. So did "Pop" art, associated with the Americans Andy Warhol and Roy Lichtenstein, who took objects such as soup cans and comic-strip heroes as their subjects. Warhol did not see his work as a protest against the banality of modern culture. Instead, he argued that he was continuing to experiment with abstractions. Treating popular culture with this tongue-in-cheek seriousness became one of the central themes of 1960s art.

The generally educated public was larger than ever before, due partly to the dramatic expansion of universities and partly to the ongoing democratization or ac-

cessibility of culture. Attendance at museums increased; so did middle-class concert going, which made culture bigger business and buoyed the careers of internationally acclaimed stars, such as the soprano Maria Callas, and the tenor Luciano Pavarotti. By 1965, television had found its way into 62 million homes in the United States, 13 million in Britain, 10 million in West Germany, and 5 million each in France and Italy. American programs were exported with the same ease as American cars, money, and military equipment. Like America's motion pictures and movie stars, they were integrated into the cultures of Western Europe alongside local celebrities, while critics fought about "Americanization" in Europe's newspapers and magazines. In Britain, the first European nation to see private ownership of more than one million television sets, the state-owned British Broadcasting Company (BBC) led the way in developing programs that competed with and sometimes surpassed the quality of American programming. Writers and producers on both sides of the Atlantic "borrowed" from one another regularly in

Gran Cairo, by Frank Stella (1936–). Stella, in his minimalist phase, experimented with extremely simple symmetrical forms and patterns.

developing ideas. Despite the great unease of many cultural critics, television, with its "American" overtones, became a fixture of Western European homes by the 1960s, like the family car and the washing machine.

Another American import was much more directly related to a developing postwar youth culture—the musical style known as rock and roll. During the 1930s and 1940s, the synthesis of music produced by whites and African Americans in the American South found its way into Northern cities. After World War II, black rhythm and blues musicians and white Southern "rockabilly" performers found much wider audiences through the use of new technology—electric guitars, better equipment for studio recording, and wide-band radio stations in large cities. The blend of styles and sounds, and the cultural daring of listening to what recording studios called "race" music came together to create rock and roll. The music was exciting, sometimes aggressive, and full of energy—all qualities that galvanized young listeners, eager to buy the latest records by their favorite performers. The music found its way to Europe, particularly into working-class neighborhoods in Britain and Ireland. There, local youths took the American sounds, echoed the inflections of poverty and defiance, and added touches of music-hall showmanship to produce successful artists and bands. The "British invasion" of bands suddenly popular in the United States had, by the late 1960s, blended with American sounds and stars. By the early 1970s recording studios had latched on to the earning potential of the music. It not only became the sound of worldwide youth culture, absorbing Eastern influences such as the Indian sitar and the political agenda of a folk-music revival, but also generated enormous income. Recording studios became corporations as powerful as car manufacturers or steel companies. Rock and roll became a bridge across the cold war divide.

Conclusion

No peace treaties provided a blueprint for the post–World War II world. Instead, the war gave way to a long series of conflicts and negotiations about borders, governments, and economic systems, particularly in central and eastern Europe. The intense rivalry between the superpowers, or the cold war, became the principle structure of international relations. It shaped the development of both the Soviet and American states. In his farewell address, President Eisenhower warned that a "military-industrial complex" had taken shape, and that its "total influence— economic, political, even spiritual—is felt in every city, every statehouse, every office of the federal government." The cold war became an important facet of everyday life: reflected in textbooks, advertisements, radio programs and television news in both blocs. George Orwell, a keen observer of new forms of state power, considered the power of "totalitarian" regimes like the Soviet system nearly insuperable. As we have seen, however, the Eastern European countries did not passively accept Soviet rule. And across the West, on both sides of the Iron Curtain, economic development and the social and cultural changes it brought in its wake were beginning to undermine the cold war settlement.

Selected Readings

Aron, Raymond. *The Imperial Republic: The United States and the World, 1945–1973.* Lanham, Md., 1974. World analysis by a leading French political theorist.

Carter, Erica. *How German Is She?: Postwar West German Reconstruction and the Consuming Woman.* Ann Arbor, 1997. A thoughtful examination of gender and the reconstruction of the family in West Germany during the 1950s.

Childs, David. *Britain Since 1945: a Political History,* 2d ed. London, 1986. A clear, concise account of Britain after the Second World War.

Deák, István, Jan T. Gross, and Tony Judt, eds. *The Politics of Retribution in Europe: World War II and Its Aftermath.* Princeton, N.J., 2000. Collection focusing on the attempt to come to terms with the Second World War in Eastern and Western Europe.

Fulbrook, Mary. *Europe since 1945.* Oxford, 2001. A recent, useful, and brief survey of postwar Europe.

Garton Ash, Timothy. *The Polish Revolution: Solidarity,* rev. ed. New York, 1991. The best account.

Gilbert, Felix, and David Clay Large. *The End of the European Era, 1890 to the Present,* 5th ed. New York, 2002. Comprehensive overview of political developments.

Jarausch, Konrad Hugo, ed. *Dictatorship as Experience: Towards a Socio-Cultural History of the GDR.* New York, 1999. A survey of the newest research on the former East Germany.

Kolko, Gabriel. *The Politics of War: The World and United States Foreign Policy 1943–1945.* New York, 1990. Argues that the blame for the cold war rests with the Western Allies.

Laqueur, Walter. *Europe In Our Time: A History, 1945–1992.* New York, 1992. A useful, thorough survey.

Medvedev, Roy. *Khrushchev.* New York, 1983. A perceptive biography of the Soviet leader by a Soviet historian.

Milward, Alan S. *The Reconstruction of Western Europe, 1945–1951.* Berkeley, 1984. The "miracle," which the author argues took place in the years immediately after the war.

Reynolds, David. *One World Divisible: A Global History Since 1945.* New York, 2000. A new survey of postwar politics that focuses on state building and nationalism.

Schissler, Hanna, ed. *The Miracle Years: A Cultural History of West Germany, 1949–1968.* Princeton, N.J., 2001. A new account of cultural change during the "economic miracle."

Schneider, Peter. *The Wall Jumper: A Berlin Story.* Chicago, 1998. A fascinating novel about life in divided Berlin.

Swain, Geoff, and Nigel Swain. *Eastern Europe Since 1945,* 2d ed. New York, 1998. Covers the often overlooked countries of Eastern Europe.

Wheeler, Daniel. *Art since Mid-Century, 1945 to the Present.* New York, 1991. A thorough examination of recent trends.

Williams, Kieran. *The Prague Spring and Its Aftermath: Czechoslovak Politics, 1968–1970.* Cambridge, 1997. An analysis of politics and diplomacy during and after the Czechoslovakian revolt in 1968.

CHAPTER THIRTY-ONE

FRAGMENTATION AND CHANGE IN CONTEMPORARY EUROPE

THE YEAR 1960 SEEMED golden and full of promise. The cold war rivalry between the United States and Soviet Russia created a backdrop of nearly constant international tension. Yet everyday life in Europe and North America seemed to be improving. Economies grew, many standards of living rose, and new forms of culture flourished. Citizens might worry during air raid drills, but the economic horizon looked bright and full of promise. By 1990, most of that familiar landscape had been dramatically transformed. Western Europeans could no longer be so certain of their prosperity or of their leaders' ability to provide the sort of life they took for granted. Societies had fragmented in unexpected ways. With the sudden dissolution of the Soviet bloc, the cold war ended, raising hopes for peace and fear of conflict from unexpected quarters.

How can we explain this transformation? By the middle of the 1960s, social and economic tensions were undermining the consensus that postwar prosperity created in the West. The economic expansion after 1945 ushered in dramatic changes: new industries, new economic values, new social classes, and a newly acute sense of generational difference. Governments faced demands from new social groups, and were frequently baffled in the effort to respond. Tensions exploded in the late 1960s. In 1968 uprisings and strikes broke out across the West, from Czechoslovakia to Germany, France, the United States, and Mexico. Problems were compounded after 1975 by a continuing economic crisis that threatened the security a generation had labored so hard to achieve. Economic stagnation combined with social protest in Europe and the United States for at least a decade after "the Sixties" ended. The challenges proved even more fundamental in the Soviet sphere. Economic decay combined with political and social stagnation to produce another wave of revolt. The year of 1989 marked the beginning of an extraordinarily rapid and surprising series of events. Communist rule collapsed in Eastern Europe, the Soviet Union itself disintegrated, and the cold war no longer seemed to matter. What these changes meant for the future of democracy, and the political stability of a vast region stretching from the borders of China in the east to the borders of Poland in the west, remained an open question.

FOCUS QUESTIONS

• How was daily life transformed during this period?

• What spurred the social movements of the 1960s?

 • What caused the economic stagnation of the 1970s and 1980s?

• What caused the collapse of communism?

SOCIAL CHANGE AND CULTURAL CHANGE: 1945–1968

How was daily life transformed during this period?

Across Europe, the major economic changes that occurred during the decades after the Second World War brought social change as well. Prosperity brought with it population growth and shifts. The population of Western Europe in 1940 was 264 million; rising birthrates brought that figure to 320 million by 1982. Population growth was sustained by social welfare policies such as family allowances, which encouraged parents to have children and enabled them to care adequately for them, and by health programs, which extended longevity considerably. Populations also shifted across the Continent. Both West Germany and France found it necessary to import workers in order to sustain their production booms. By the mid-1960s, there were 1.3 million foreign workers in West Germany and 1.8 million in France. Most came from the south, particularly from the agrarian areas of southern Italy, where unemployment remained high. Workers from former colonies emigrated to Britain, often to take low-paid, menial jobs and encounter pervasive discrimination at work and in the community. Migrations of this sort, not to mention the movement of political refugees that occurred during and immediately after the war, contributed to a breakdown of national barriers that was accelerated by the advent of the Common Market.

Economic expansion changed patterns and perceptions of social class. Many commentators noted the striking growth in the number of middle-class, white-collar employees—the result, in part, of the bureaucratic expansion of the state. By 1964, the total number of men and women employed in government service in most European states exceeded 40 percent of the labor force, significantly higher than the number in the 1920s and 1930s. In business and industry, the number of "middle-management" employees grew as well. This "managerial class" tended to be more innovative and adventurous than owner-managers of businesses in previous generations. More often than not, these managers possessed university degrees. In the mid-1950s, for example, over 72 percent of a sample of five thousand French industrialists were university graduates, more than half of them with degrees in engineering. This stood in marked contrast to the prewar situation, when managers far more frequently moved directly from secondary education into family-run concerns. This new class was not "bourgeois" in the Marxist sense of that term. The technocrats were not "owners of the means of production" or capitalist tycoons. To some degree they saw themselves less as the servants of the company that employed them than as servants of the general public who purchased the goods or services they were providing. What was true of the West was true of the Soviet Union as well, where, following educational reforms instituted by Nikita Khrushchev in 1958, programs encouraged bright children to pursue a course of study leading eventually to managerial positions.

If the nature of the middle class was changing, so was that of the working class. The introduction of complex machinery effectively altered the shape of the factory work force. The proportion of salaried employees—supervisors, inspectors, technicians, and drafters—grew significantly. In West Germany, for example, the number of such workers increased by 95 percent between 1950 and 1961. And manual labor tended to mean something far different from what it had in the nineteenth century. Skills were specialized to a greater degree than ever, based on technological expertise rather than custom and routine. "Skill" meant the ability to monitor automatic controls, to interpret abstract signals, and to make precise mathematically calculated adjustments.

These changes led some observers in the mid-1960s to declare class antagonism a matter of the past. Although men and women earned more money than ever before, and lived more secure lives, they did not lose their sense of themselves as workers. Trade unions remained powerful institutions: the largest of the French general unions had a membership of 1.5 million; of the Italian, 3.5 million; of the German, 6.5 million. Britain's Trades Union Congress, an affiliation of separate unions, boasted close to 8 million members.

Workers did, however, lead lives that more closely resembled those of the prewar middle class than those of their own parents and grandparents. They and their children went to school longer. All Western nations passed laws providing for the extension of compulsory secondary education—up to the age of sixteen in France, West Germany, and Britain. As a consequence of new legislation and increased birthrates, school populations increased dramatically. Secondary school enrollment in France, Holland, and

Belgium doubled between 1950 and 1960. In Britain and West Germany it grew by more than 50 percent. Higher education was used in the Soviet Union as a means of unifying a nation that remained culturally heterogeneous. Turkish Muslims, for instance, constituted a sizable minority in the Soviet Union. Concern lest the pull of ethnic "nationality" tear at the none-too-solid fabric of the Soviet "union" increased the government's desire to impose one unifying culture by means of education, not always with success.

These changes formed part of a striking transformation of everyday life, with profound cultural implications. The economic "miracle" of the postwar period (see Chapter 30) changed the organization of households, leisure, and culture. Household appliances are among the most dramatic emblems of the change. In Britain in 1956, 8 percent of households had refrigerators; by 1979 that figure had skyrocketed to 69 percent. Vacuum cleaners, washing machines, and telephones all became more common features of everyday life. They did not simply save labor or create free time, for household appliances came packaged with more demanding standards of housekeeping and new investments in domesticity—"more work for mother," in the words of one historian.

Between 1948 and 1965 car ownership increased in Western Europe from 5 million to 44 million. Automobiles alone did not make it possible for workers to take inexpensive holidays; it was more important that the work week contracted from forty-eight hours to about forty-two and that workers in most countries received over thirty days of paid vacation per year. Yet automobiles certainly captured imaginations throughout the world; in magazines, advertisements, and countless films, the car was central to new images of romance, movement, and freedom. It is worth underscoring that these changes in consumption and ownership came more slowly in Western Europe than in the United States and only very unevenly in Eastern Europe. Comparison with the rest of the world nonetheless highlights the scope of the change. In China in 1970, only a tiny minority of people (8 percent) had a radio, and most cities had no television stations at all.

These changes, which helped to create a "consumer culture," came accompanied by new industries devoted to marketing, advertising, and credit payment. They also entailed shifts in values. In the nineteenth century, a responsible middle-class family did not go into debt;

discipline and thrift were hallmarks of "respectability." By the second half of the twentieth century, banks and retailers, in the name of mass consumption and economic growth, were persuading middle- and working-class people alike not to be ashamed of debt. Abundance, credit, consumer spending, and standards of living—all these terms became part of the vocabulary of everyday economic life. The new vocabulary gradually came to reshape how citizens thought about their needs, desires, and entitlements. Standards of living, for instance, created a yardstick for measuring—and protesting—glaring social inequalities. Politicians, economists, and marketing experts paid much closer attention to the spending habits of ordinary people. Finally, changes in consumption also changed generational politics. As household incomes rose, more money was spent by and on young people. Much of the new "mass culture" of the 1960s depended on the spending habits and desires of the new generation. It is not surprising that young people, and especially students, so central to the new developments, paid special attention to critics of the "society of consumption," with its culture of seemingly relentless selling and spending. Young people felt that human values could not be reduced to market concerns; "freedom" had to mean more than being able to choose between different brands of detergent. These themes ran through popular books such as Herbert Marcuse's *One-Dimensional Man* (1964). In 1968, the heightened cultural influence of students both allowed and encouraged them to take up new political roles.

> Changes in consumption also changed generational politics. As household incomes rose, more money was spent by and on young people.

SOCIAL MOVEMENTS DURING THE 1960S

What spurred the social movements of the 1960s?

The social unrest of the "sixties" was international and deeply rooted. Its origins lay with anticolonial and civil rights movements. The liberation of colonial peoples in the decades following the Second World War rested on and also heightened racial consciousness and racial conflict, not only in Africa and Asia but in the

West as well (see Chapter 32). On guard against revivals of colonialism, newly independent African and Caribbean nations remained understandably sensitive to their continuing economic dependence on the predominantly white nations of Western Europe and America. Black and Asian immigration into those nations produced tension and frequent violence. In the Western nations, particularly in the United States, black peoples identified with these social and economic grievances and drew strength from the political force of independence movements elsewhere in the world.

> Martin Luther King, Jr. embraced the philosophy of nonviolence promoted by Indian social and political activist Mohandas Gandhi.

THE CIVIL RIGHTS MOVEMENT

The growth of insurgency among African Americans paralleled the rise of black nations in Africa and the Caribbean. The Second World War brought a significant African American migration from the American South to northern cities, intensifying a drive for rights, dignity, and independence began in the prewar era by organizations such as the National Association for the Advancement of Colored People (NAACP) and the National Urban League. By 1960, various civil rights groups, led by the Congress of Racial Equality (CORE), had started to organize boycotts and demonstrations directed at private businesses and public services that discriminated against blacks in the South.

The leader of these protests, and the undoubted leader of the civil rights movement in the United States during the 1960s, was Martin Luther King, Jr., (1929–1968) a Baptist minister. King embraced the philosophy of nonviolence promoted by the Indian social and political activist Mohandas Gandhi. King's personal participation in countless demonstrations, his willingness to go to jail for a cause that he believed to be just, and his ability as an orator to arouse both blacks and whites with his message led to his position as the most highly regarded—and widely feared—defender of black rights. His inspiring career was tragically ended by assassination in 1968.

Martin Luther King, Jr. and organizations like CORE aspired to a fully integrated nation. Other charismatic and important black leaders sought complete independence from white society, fearing that integration would leave African Americans without the spiritual or material resources necessary for a community's pride, dignity, and autonomy. The most influential of the black nationalists was Malcolm X (1925–1965), who assumed the "X" after having discarded his "white" surname (Little). For most of his adult life a spokesman for the Black Muslim movement, Malcolm X urged blacks to renew their commitment to their own heritage—the Muslim religion, for example—and to establish black businesses as a way of maintaining economic and psychological distance from white domination. Like King he was assassinated, in 1965 while addressing a rally in Harlem.

Civil rights laws enacted under the administration of President Lyndon B. Johnson in the 1960s did bring African Americans some measure of equality with regard to voting rights—and, to a much lesser degree, school desegregation. In other areas, such as housing and job opportunities, African Americans continued to suffer disadvantage and discrimination as a result

Opposition to the American War in Vietnam. The Reverend Martin Luther King, Jr. marching with Dr. Benjamin Spock, one of the country's best known pediatricians, in a 1967 protest against American involvement in Vietnam.

of white racism, patterns of economic development, and subsequent administrations' reluctance to continue the innovative programs of the Johnson era. These problems are not confined to the United States. Immigrants to Britain from former colonies in the West Indies and from India and Pakistan, for example, meet with discrimination in jobs, housing, and everyday interaction with the authorities—with the result that racial disturbances are not an uncommon occurrence in major British cities. France has witnessed hostility toward Algerian immigration, Germany toward the importation of cheap Turkish labor. In Western Europe, as in the United States, struggles for racial and ethnic integration are central to the postcolonial world.

STUDENT MOVEMENTS

The civil rights movement had enormous significance for the twentieth century, and it proved a catalyst for other movements as well. It dramatized as perhaps no other movement could the chasm between the egalitarian promises of American democracy and the real inequalities at the core of the American social and political life. African American claims were morally as well as politically compelling; and the civil rights movement sharpened others' criticisms of a complacent, one-dimensional culture. The United States' growing involvement in Indochina (see Chapter 32) further raised the stakes. As Martin Luther King, Jr. pointed out, the war in Vietnam—which relied on disproportionate number of black soldiers to conduct a war against a small nation of color—echoed and magnified racial inequality at home. And from other countries' points of view, the Vietnam War became a spectacle: one in which the most powerful, wealthiest nation of the world seemed intent on destroying a land of poor peasants in the name of anticommunism, democracy, freedom, and so on. The tarnished image of Western values stood at the center of 1960s protest movements in the United States and Western Europe.

The student movement itself also had roots in postwar changes in education and university life. In France, the number of students in high school rose from four hundred thousand in 1949 to 2 million in 1969; in universities, over the same period, enrollments skyrocketed, from one hundred thousand to six hundred thousand. Much the same happened in Italy, Britain, and West Germany. Universities, which had been created to educate a small elite, found both their teaching staffs and their facilities overwhelmed: lecture halls were packed, university bureaucracies did not respond

to requests, thousands of students took exams at the same time. More philosophically, students raised questions about the role and meaning of elite education in a democratic society, and about the relationship between the university as a "knowledge factory," consumer culture, and neocolonial ventures such as the Vietnam and, for the French, Algerian wars. Conservative traditions made intellectual reform difficult. Student demands for relaxed standards—for instance, permission to have a member of the opposite sex in a dormitory room—provoked authoritarian reactions from university representatives.

Finally, the student movement in the United States and Western Europe took inspiration from the Prague spring and the revolt against Soviet oppression in Czechoslovakia. On both sides of the Iron Curtain, protest movements attacked bureaucracy and the human costs of the cold war: on the one side the Soviet state, with its Eastern European satellites; on the other American imperialism, the "military-industrial complex," monopolies in the news media, and so on. The Soviet regime, as we have seen, responded with repression. In the United States and Western Europe, traditional political parties had little idea what to make of these new movements and those who participated in them. In both cases, events rapidly overwhelmed political systems.

SPRING 1968

Nineteen sixty-eight was an extraordinary year, quite similar to 1848 and its wave of revolution (see Ch. 24). The most serious outbreak of student unrest in Europe came in Paris in the spring. French students at the University of Paris demanded reforms that would modernize their university. University authorities, facing rising disorder and protest, closed down the university, sending students into the streets and into uglier confrontations with the police. Sympathy with the students' cause expanded, bringing in other opponents of President de Gaulle's regime, leading to massive trade union strikes. By mid-May, 10 million French workers had walked off their jobs. The government was able to satisfy the strikers with wage increases, thereby isolating the students, who grudgingly agreed to resume university life. De Gaulle had no sympathy for the students: "Reform, yes—bed wetting, no," he reportedly declared at the height of the confrontation. Though the regime recovered, the "events" of 1968 helped weaken de Gaulle's position as president and contributed to his retirement from office the following year.

Paris was not the only city to explode in 1968. Student protest broke out in West Berlin, targeting the government's close ties to the autocratic shah of Iran and the power of media corporations. In Italy, undergraduates staged a lengthy series of demonstrations to draw attention to university overcrowding. In Mexico City a confrontation with the police ended with the death of hundreds of protesters, most of them students—on the

Student Uprising at the University of Paris, May 1968. Following demonstrations calling for sweeping reforms at the university, French students took to the streets to make their case more forcefully and violently at the barricades.

Paris, May, 1968. The morning after a night of street fighting near the Sorbonne. The cars had been overturned and used as barricades against the police.

May 1968 poster. This poster was one of hundreds produced by a group of students who took over the École des Beaux Arts in Paris. It mocks "free radio," or the French government's control over the media.

1968: WORD AND IMAGE

In 1957, a small group of European artists and writers formed a group called the Situationist International. The movement combined the artistic traditions of dada and surrealism with anarchism and Marxism. Unlike traditional Marxists, the Situationists did not focus on the workplace. Instead they developed a broad critique of everyday life, protesting the stifling of art, creativity, and imagination in contemporary society. They denounced the "tyranny" of consumer culture, which constantly invented new needs and desires in order to fuel consumption. Capitalism, they said, had "colonized" everyday life. The Situationists' ideas and especially their unorthodox, surrealist style, became very influential during the events of May 1968 in France. All around Paris students painted Situationist slogans such as those printed below.

The social movements of 1968 cut across cold war boundaries, attacking Western consumerism as well as Soviet authoritarianism. A group of students and Situationists sent a telegram (second excerpt below) to the Politburo of the Communist Party of the USSR in May, 1968.

SITUATIONIST SLOGANS

OCCUPY THE FACTORIES

POWER TO THE WORKERS COUNCILS

ABOLISH CLASS SOCIETY

DOWN WITH THE
SPECTACLE-COMMODITY SOCIETY

ABOLISH ALIENATION

ABOLISH THE UNIVERSITY

HUMANITY WON'T BE HAPPY TILL THE
LAST BUREAUCRAT IS HUNG WITH THE GUTS
OF THE LAST CAPITALIST

DEATH TO THE COPS

FREE ALSO THE 4 GUYS CONVICTED FOR
LOOTING DURING THE 6 MAY RIOT

—OCCUPATION COMMITTEE OF THE
AUTONOMOUS AND POPULAR
SORBONNE UNIVERSITY

ANTI-COMMUNIST SLOGANS FROM 1968

17 MAY 1968 / To the Politburo of the Communist party of the USSR the Kremlin Moscow / Shake in your shoes bureaucrats. The international power of the workers councils will soon wipe you out. Humanity won't be happy till the last bureaucrat is hung with the guts of the last capitalist. Long live the struggle of the Kronstadt sailors and of the Makhnovshchina against Trostky and

Lenin. Long live the 1956 Councilist insurrection of Budapest • Down with the state • Long live revolutionary Marxism. Occupation committee of the Autonomous and Popular Sorbonne

"Slogans to be Spread Now by Every Means," in Situationist International Anthology, edited and translated by Ken Knabb (Berkeley: Bureau of Public Secrets, 1981), pp. 334–345.

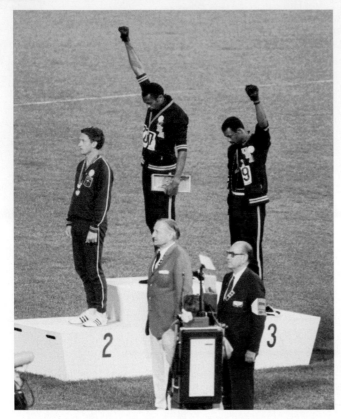

Civil Rights and the 1968 Olympics. Tommie Smith and John Carlos, American medalists in the 200-meter run, raise their fists in the black power salute, protesting the continuing discrimination against African Americans at home.

eve of the 1968 Olympics, hosted by the Mexican government. Those Olympics reflected the political contests of the period: African nations threatened to boycott if South Africa, with its apartheid regime, participated. Two African American medalists raised their hands in a black power salute during an awards ceremony—and the Olympic Committee promptly sent them home. In the United States, the spring Tet offensive brought the highest casualties rates to date in the Vietnam War, setting off intense antiwar demonstrations and student rebellions across the country; the year also brought the assassinations of Martin Luther King, Jr. and Robert F. Kennedy, as well as riots at the Democratic National Convention in Chicago. Some saw the flowering of protest as another "springtime of peoples." Others saw it as a long nightmare.

Like the revolutions of 1848, the events of 1968 shook regimes but did not topple them. De Gaulle's government recouped; the Republican Richard M. Nixon won the U.S. election of 1968. In Czechoslovakia, Warsaw Pact tanks put down risings, and the Soviet regime reiter-

ated its right to control its satellites in the Brezhnev Doctrine. Over the long term, however, changes proved more difficult to contain. Eastern European and Soviet dissent was defeated but not eliminated; the events of 1968 prefigured the collapse of Soviet control in 1989. In Western Europe and the United States new social movements eventually became part of the political scene.

WOMEN'S MOVEMENTS

Women formed one of these new social movements. Neither feminist thought nor organized women's movements were new, but the 1970s did represent a historical moment when gender consciousness became especially marked—among working-class as well as middle-class women. Since World War II the assumption that the middle-class woman's place was in the home had been challenged by the ever-increasing demand for women workers. The increased availability and social acceptance of birth-control devices meant that despite the "baby boom" most families were having fewer children and that women could exercise more control over their childbearing as well as their sexuality. Yet society seemed unwilling to acknowledge the implication of these changes: that women are equal to men. Women were paid much less than men for similar work. Women with many qualifications

Simone de Beauvoir.

THE "WOMAN QUESTION" ON BOTH SIDES OF THE ATLANTIC

How did Western culture define "femininity" and did women internalize those definitions? These questions were central to postwar feminist thought, and they were sharply posed in two classic texts: Simone de Beauvoir's The Second Sex *(1949) and Betty Friedan's* The Feminine Mystique *(1963). Beauvoir (1908–1986) started from the existentialist premise that humans were "condemned to be free" and to give their own lives meaning. Why, then, did women accept the limitations imposed on them and, in Beauvoir's words, "dream the dreams of men?" Although dense and philosophical,* The Second Sex *sent shock waves through Catholic France and was published throughout the world. Betty Friedan's equally influential bestseller took up much the same issue, trying to find the origins of the "feminine mystique," Friedan's term for the model of femininity promoted by experts, advertised in women's magazines, and seemingly accepted by middle-class housewives in the postwar United States. As Friedan points out in the excerpt below, the new postwar "mystique" was in many ways more conservative than prewar ideals had been, despite continuing social change, a greater range of careers opening up to women, the expansion of women's education, and so on. Friedan (1921–) co-founded the National Organization for Women in 1966 and served as its president until 1970.*

SIMONE DE BEAUVOIR, *THE SECOND SEX*

But first we must ask: what is a woman? . . .

All agree in recognizing the fact that females exist in the human species; today as always they make up about one half of humanity. And yet we are told that femininity is in danger; we are exhorted to be women, remain women, become women. . . . Although some women try zealously to incarnate this essence, it is hardly penetrable. It is frequently described in vague and dazzling terms that seem to have been borrowed from the vocabulary of the seers. . . .

If her functioning as a female is not enough to define woman, if we decline also to explain her through "the eternal feminine," and if nevertheless we admit, provisionally, that women do exist, then we must face the question: what is a woman?

To state the question is, to me, to suggest, at once, a preliminary answer. The fact that I ask it is in itself significant. A man would never get the notion of writing a book on the peculiar situation of the human male. But if I wish to define myself, I must first of all say: "I am a woman"; on this truth must be based all further discussion. A man never begins by presenting himself as an individual of a certain sex; it goes without saying that he is a man. The terms *masculine* and *feminine* are used symmetrically only as a matter of form, as on legal papers. In actuality the relation of the two sexes is not quite like that of two electrical poles, for man represents both the positive and the neutral . . . whereas woman represents only the negative, defined by limiting criteria, without reciprocity. . . .

A man is in the right in being a man; it is the woman who is in the wrong. Woman has ovaries, a uterus; these peculiarities imprison her in her subjectivity, circumscribe her within the limits of her own nature. . . .

For him she is sex—absolute sex, no less. She is defined and differentiated with reference to man and not he with reference to her; she is the incidental, the inessential as opposed to the essential. He is the subject, he is the Absolute—she is the Other.

Simone de Beauvoir, *The Second Sex*, translated and edited by H. M. Parshley (New York: Random House, 1974), p. xix.

BETTY FRIEDAN, *THE FEMININE MYSTIQUE*

In 1939, the heroines of women's magazine stories were not always young, but in a certain sense they were younger than their fictional counterparts today. They were young in the same way that the American hero has always been young: they were New Women, creating with a gay determined spirit a new identity for women—a life of their own. There was an aura about them of becoming, of moving into a future that was going to be different from the past. . . .

These stories may not have been great literature. But the identity of their heroines seemed to say something about the housewives who, then as now, read the women's magazines. These magazines were not written for career women. The New Woman heroines were the ideal of yesterday's housewives; they reflected the dreams, mirrored the yearning for identity and the sense of possibility that existed for women then. . . .

In 1949 . . . the feminine mystique began to spread through the land. . . .

The feminine mystique says that the highest value and the only commitment for women is the fulfillment of their own femininity. It says that the great mistake of Western culture, through most of its history, has been the undervaluation of this femininity. . . . The mistake, says the mystique, the root of women's troubles in the past, is that women envied men, women tried to be like men, instead of accepting their own nature, which can find fulfillment only in sexual passivity, male domination, and nurturing maternal love.

But the new image this mystique gives to American women is the old image: "Occupation: housewife." The new mystique makes the housewife-mothers, who never had a chance to be anything else, the model for all women; it presupposes that history has reached a final and glorious end in the here and now, as far as women are concerned. . . .

It is more than a strange paradox that as all professions are finally open to women in America, "career woman" has become a dirty word; that as higher education becomes available to any woman with the capacity for it, education for women has become so suspect that more and more drop out of high school and college to marry and have babies; that as so many roles in modern society become theirs for the taking, women so insistently confine themselves to one role. Why . . . should she accept this new image which insists she is not a person but a "woman," by definition barred from the freedom of human existence and a voice in human destiny?

Betty Friedan, *The Feminine Mystique* (New York: W. W. Norton & Company, Inc., 2001), pp. 38, 40, 42–43, 67–68.

---

were turned down because of their gender when they applied for jobs. Women with excellent employment records were forced to rely on their husbands to establish credit. Political action helped alleviate some of these inequities in the late 1960s and the 1970s. The U.S. government instituted programs of "affirmative action," which mandated the hiring of qualified women as well as members of racial minority groups. In Britain an Equal Pay Act, passed in the late 1960s, established that wages for women should be equal to those of men holding the same job. In France a ministry for the status of women was created in the mid-1970s, and in Germany government agencies were established to deal with family and youth affairs. By 1990, despite the failure in the United States to pass a constitutional Equal Rights Amendment, the campaigners for women's equality had a good many successes to their credit.

A particularly volatile subject in the area of women's rights was abortion. Feminists argued that reproductive freedom was both a private matter and a basic right—a key to women's control over their lives. A ban on abortion, like earlier bans on contraception, they argued, formed part of a larger agenda to subordinate women in the name of morality, making women alone bear responsibility for the consequences of sweeping changes in Western sexual life. Their opponents, including many women in the "right-to-life" movement, countered with the argument that abortion encouraged sexual irresponsibility; as they saw it, abortion was inextricable from moral bankruptcy, the collapse of family structures, and, for some, the murder of unborn children. In this debate—as in the Enlightenment debate about women's humanity, the late-nineteenth-century suffrage battles, and postwar worries about the "new woman"—questions about gender or women's roles became focal points for discussion of much larger questions sparked by rapid social change. In the postwar world, those issues included individuality and its limits, the disciplines of family and traditional gender roles, clashing moral codes, and the relationship between public life and private matters. More than ever before, however, women, as citizens, participated in these discussions. During the 1960s, then, the politics of gender, private life, and the household began to transform traditional electoral politics.

ECONOMIC STAGNATION: THE PRICE OF SUCCESS

What caused the economic stagnation of the 1970s and 1980s?

Economic as well as social problems plagued Europe during the 1970s and 1980s. The stagnation that overtook the Continent was the product of trends that had their roots in the prosperous 1960s. By the middle of that decade, for example, the West German growth rate had slowed. Demand for manufactured goods declined and in 1966 the country suffered its first postwar recession. Volkswagen, that mythic symbol of the German "miracle," introduced a shortened work week; almost seven hundred thousand West Germans were thrown out of work altogether. In France a persistent housing shortage increased the cost of living. Though new industries continued to prosper, the basic industries—coal, steel, and railways—began to run up deficits. Unemployment was rising in tandem with prices. Prime Minister Harold Wilson's pledge to revive Britain's economy by introducing new technology foundered on crises in the foreign-exchange value of the pound, which were compounded by continued low levels of growth. The Common Market—expanded in 1973 to include Britain, Ireland, and Denmark, and again in the early 1980s to admit Greece, Spain, and Portugal—struggled to overcome problems stemming from the conflict between the domestic economic regulations characteristic of many European states and the free-market policies that prevailed among the EEC countries.

The first very dramatic rise in oil prices compounded these difficulties. In 1973, the Arab-dominated Organization of Petroleum Exporting Countries (OPEC) instituted an oil embargo against the Western powers. By 1975 the cost of one barrel of oil had risen to $10.46, as compared with $1.73 two years before, and it continued to rise to over $30 by the early 1980s. This increase produced an inflationary spiral; interest rates rose and

with them the price of almost everything else Western consumers were used to buying. Wage demands calculated to meet rising costs produced strikes. The calm industrial relations that had characterized the 1950s and early 1960s were a thing of the past. At the same time, European manufacturers encountered serious competition, not only from such highly developed countries as Japan but also from the increasingly active economies of Asia and Africa, in which the West had invested capital eagerly in the previous decades. By 1980 Japan had captured 10 percent of the automobile market in West Germany and 25 percent in Belgium. By 1984, unemployment in Western Europe had reached about 19 million. The lean years had arrived.

Meanwhile the Soviet Union and its satellites were also experiencing the stagnation that accompanies the maturing of an economy. The Soviet Communist party proclaimed in 1961 that by 1970 the USSR would exceed the United States in per capita production. By the end of the 1970s, however, Soviet per capita production was not much higher than in the less industrialized countries of southern Europe. During the same period its rate of economic growth was on a sluggish par with that of other Western nations. The Soviet economy did get a boost from the OPEC oil price hikes of 1973 and 1979. (The Organization of Petroleum Exporting Countries was founded in 1961; the USSR did not belong but as the world's largest producer of oil benefited from rising prices.) Without this boost, the situation would have been far grimmer.

Following an impressive economic performance during the early 1970s, the Eastern European nations encountered serious financial difficulties. Their success had rested in part on capital borrowed from the West. By 1980 those debts weighed heavy on their national economies. Poland's hard-currency indebtedness to Western countries, for example, was almost four times as great as its annual exports. The solution to this problem, attempted in Poland and elsewhere, was to cut back on production for domestic consumption in order to increase exports. Yet this policy encountered strong popular opposition. Although there was virtually no unemployment in Eastern Europe, men and women were by no means happy with their economic situation. Working hours were longer than in Western Europe, and goods and services, even in prosperous times, remained far from abundant.

Western governments struggled for effective reactions to the abrupt change in their economic circumstances. Politicians of both the right and the left reached to rediscover the magic that had produced

Margaret Thatcher, Prime Minister of Great Britain, 1979–1990.

prosperity, but with little success. In Britain, the Labour and Conservative parties alternately governed through the 1970s, unable to meet either the demands of trade unionists who were angry as they saw their real wages eroded by inflation, or the demands of international bankers who were impatient with Britain's inability to bring its trade figures into balance. The new, radically conservative leader of the Conservative party, Margaret Thatcher, claimed to have the answer. She was elected prime minister in 1979—and reelected in 1983 and 1987—on the basis of that claim. Yet despite curbs on trade union power, tax cuts designed to stimulate the economy, and the return of many publicly owned enterprises to private hands, the economy remained weak, with close to 15 percent of the work force unemployed by 1986.

West Germany, like Britain, veered to the right in the 1980s. The Social Democratic party, headed in the late 1960s and early 1970s by Willy Brandt, had remained in power after Brandt's resignation as chancellor in 1974 under the leadership of his successor, Helmut Schmidt. During the early 1980s, Schmidt's coalition government attempted to combat economic recession with job-training programs and tax incentives, both financed by higher taxes. These programs did little to assist economic recovery, and Schmidt was replaced in 1982 by the Christian Democrat Helmut Kohl, who, like

Margaret Thatcher in Britain, proposed cuts in social programs and unemployment compensation.

France fared better than its neighbor in the struggle to maintain economic momentum. De Gaulle resigned in 1969, his prestige eroded by the protests and strikes of the previous year. His successors in the 1970s, George Pompidou and Valéry Giscard d'Estaing, pursued a middle course that did no more than keep the country on an even keel. In 1981, Giscard was ousted by a socialist, François Mitterrand, whose record as an escaped prisoner of war and Resistance fighter in the Second World War made him a popular figure (a record challenged by evidence of collaboration revealed just before his death). Among the array of reforms promptly undertaken by the new government was the further nationalization of major industries and private financial institutions. Yet these bold moves, bitterly opposed by conservative interests, did not resolve the nation's economic malaise. Inflation and unemployment rose, along with budget and balance-of-trade deficits. Newly nationalized enterprises drained government resources. These difficulties led to a devaluation of the franc, a temporary freeze on wages and prices, and in 1986 to a return to power of more conservative political forces committed to a policy of "privatization" of companies and industries that had been nationalized under the socialists.

Spain and Italy moved left in the early 1980s. Spain,

Helmut Kohl, Chancellor of the Federal Republic of Germany, 1982–1991.

François Mitterrand, French President, 1981–1995.

freed from the rule of General Franco by his death in 1974, and under the nominal rule of his hand-picked successor, King Juan Carlos, saw the Socialists Workers party score a major upset in 1982. Intent on modernizing rather than radicalizing Spain, the socialists eschewed widespread government ownership of industry in favor of selective nationalization, which included the nation's electric-power grid. Similarly, Italy for a time witnessed increasing victories by parties of the left at the expense of the previously indomitable Christian Democratic party.

The fact that governments of right and left were unable to recreate the sort of economic climate that had characterized Europe's unprecedented postwar prosperity suggests the degree to which economic forces remain outside the control of individual states, prey to the far from predictable vagaries of international finance, trade cycles, and human miscalculation. The economic malaise afflicting Europe led to renewed efforts to address common problems through the increasingly dominant organization of European states. By the end of the 1980s, the EEC, today known as the European Union (EU), embarked on an ambitious program of integration. Long-term goals, agreed on in 1991, included a monetary union, with a central European bank and a single currency, and unified social policies to reduce poverty and unemployment. As the twenty-first century opened, the European member states had begun to institute several of these steps. It remained unclear whether that new European "federal" state would overcome its members' claims of national sovereignty or whether it would develop the economic and political strength to counter the global domination of the United States, which became the crucial structural feature of the post-cold-war world.

EUROPE RECAST: THE COLLAPSE OF COMMUNISM AND THE END OF THE SOVIET UNION

What caused the collapse of communism?

One of history's fascinations is its unpredictability. There has been no more telling example of this than the sudden collapse of the Eastern European communist regimes in 1989 and the subsequent disintegration of the once-powerful Soviet Union.

The beginning of the end came with the accession of Mikhail Gorbachev to the leadership of the Soviet Communist party in 1985. In his mid-fifties, Gorbachev was significantly younger than his immediate predecessors and less prey to the habits of mind that had shaped Soviet domestic and foreign affairs. He was

The Euro became the official currency of the EU in 2002.

Gorbachev and the Old Guard. Gorbachev is pictured here at the height of his power in 1986, with KGB chief Victor Chebrikov, President Andrei Gromyko, and Premier Nikolai Rzyhkov. Perestroika aimed at the privileges of the political elite and would eventually lead to the fall from power of all these men.

frankly critical of the repressive aspects of communist society as well as its sluggish economy, and he did not hesitate to voice those criticisms openly. His twin policies of *glasnost* (intellectual openness) and *perestroika* (economic restructuring) held out hope for a freer, more prosperous Soviet Union. Under Gorbachev, a number of imprisoned dissidents were freed, among them Andrei Sakharov, the scientist known as the "father of the Soviet hydrogen bomb."

The policies of perestroika took aim at the privileges of the political elite and the immobility of the state bureaucracy by instituting competitive elections to official positions and limiting terms of office. Gorbachev's program of perestroika called for a shift from the centrally planned economy instituted by Stalin to a mixed economy combining planning with the operation of market forces. In agriculture, perestroika accelerated the move away from cooperative production and instituted incentives for the achievement of production targets. Gorbachev called for the integration of the Soviet Union into the international economy by participation in organizations such as the International Monetary Fund.

Even these dramatic reforms, however, were prov-

> Gorbachev was frankly critical of the repressive aspects of communist society as well as its sluggish economy, and he did not hesitate to voice those criticisms openly.

ing to be too little too late by the late 1980s. Ethnic unrest, a legacy of Russia's nineteenth-century imperialism, threatened to split the Soviet Union apart, while secession movements gathered steam in the Baltic republics and elsewhere. From 1988 onward, fighting between Armenians and Azerbaijanis over an ethnically Azerbaijani region located inside Armenia threatened to escalate into a border dispute with Iran; only the presence of Soviet troops temporarily quelled the conflict.

Spurred on by these events in the Soviet Union, the countries of Eastern Europe began to agitate for independence from Moscow. Gorbachev encouraged open discussion—glasnost—not only in his own country but also in the satellite nations. He revoked the Brezhnev Doctrine's insistence on single-party socialist governments and made frequent and inspiring trips to the capitals of neighboring satellites.

Glasnost rekindled the flame of opposition in Poland, where Solidarity had been defeated but not destroyed by the government in 1981. In 1988 the union launched a new series of strikes. These disturbances culminated in an agreement between the government and Solidarity that legalized the union and promised open elections. The results, in June 1989, astonished the world: virtually all of the government's candidates lost; the Citizen's Committee, affiliated with Solidarity, won a sizable majority in the Polish parliament.

In Hungary and Czechoslovakia, events followed a similar course during 1988 and 1989. As a result of continuing demonstrations, Janos Kadar, the Hungarian leader since the Soviet crackdown of 1956, resigned in May 1988 and was replaced by the reformist government of the Hungarian Socialist Workers' party. By the spring of 1989 the Hungarian regime had been purged of Communist party supporters. At the same time, the government had begun to dismantle its security fences along the Austrian border. A year later the Hungarian Democratic Forum, proclaiming its dedication to the reinstatement of full civil rights and to the restructuring of the economy, secured a plurality of seats in the National Assembly.

The Czechs, too, staged demonstrations against Soviet domination in late 1988. Brutal beatings of student demonstrators by the police in 1989 led to the radicalization of the nations' workers and to mass demonstrations. Civic Forum, an opposition coalition, called for the installation of a coalition government to include noncommunists, for free elections, and for the resignation of the country's communist leadership. It reinforced its demands with continuing mass demonstrations and threats of a general strike that resulted in the toppling of the old regime and the election of the playwright and Civic Forum leader Václav Havel as president.

The most significant political change in Eastern Europe during the late 1980s was the collapse of communism in East Germany and the unification of East and West Germany. Although long considered the most prosperous of the Soviet satellite countries, East Germany suffered from severe economic stagnation and environmental degradation. Waves of East Germans registered their discontent with worsening conditions by massive illegal emigration to the West. This movement combined with evidence of widespread official corruption to force the resignation of East Germany's longtime, hard-line premier, Erich Honecker. His successor, Egon Krenz, promised reforms, but he was nevertheless faced with continuing protests and continuing mass emigration.

On November 4, 1989, the government, in a move that acknowledged its powerlessness to hold its citizens captive, opened its border with Czechoslovakia. This move effectively freed East Germans to travel to the West. In a matter of days, the Berlin Wall—embodiment of the cold war, the Iron Curtain, and the division of East from West—was demolished by groups of ordinary citizens. Jubilant throngs from both sides walked through the gaping holes that now permitted men, women, and children to take the few steps that symbolized the return to freedom and a chance for national unity. Free elections were held throughout Germany in March 1990, resulting in a victory for the Alliance for Germany, a coalition allied with the West German chancellor Helmut Kohl's Christian Democratic Union. With heavy emigration continuing, reunification talks quickly culminated in the formal proclamation of a united Germany on October 3, 1990.

Throughout the rest of Eastern Europe, single-party governments in the countries behind what was left of

The Fall of the Berlin Wall, 1989. When East German officials announced that citizens could leave the country through any border crossing, rendering the Berlin Wall obsolete, people gathered at the wall to celebrate and to tear it down with picks, axes, and small hammers.

the tattered Iron Curtain—Albania, Bulgaria, Romania, and Yugoslavia—collapsed in the face of democratic pressure for change. Meanwhile, in the Soviet Union itself, inspired by events in Eastern Europe, the Balkan republics of Lithuania and Latvia strained to free themselves from the Soviet yoke. In 1990 they unilaterally proclaimed their independence from the Soviet Union, throwing into sharp relief the tension between "union" and "republics." Gorbachev reacted with an uncertain mixture of armed intervention and promises of greater local autonomy. In the fall of 1991 Lithuania and Latvia, along with the third Baltic state of

Estonia, won international recognition as independent republics.

The Soviet Union's unproductive economy continued to fuel widespread dissatisfaction. With the failure of perestroika—largely the result of a lack of resources and an inability to increase production—came the rise of a powerful political rival to Gorbachev, his erstwhile ally Boris Yeltsin. The reforming mayor of Moscow, Yeltsin was elected president of the Russian Federation—the largest Soviet republic—on an anti-Gorbachev platform in 1990. Pressure from the Yeltsin camp weakened Gorbachev's ability to maneuver independently of reactionary factions in the Politburo and the military, undermining his reform program and his ability to remain in power.

The Soviet Union's increasingly severe domestic problems led to mounting protests in 1991, when Gorbachev's policies failed to improve—indeed diminished—the living standard of the Soviet people. Demands increased that the bloated government bureaucracy respond

Soviet Forces Seizing Control of Lithuania's Main Television Broadcast Station in January 1991. By fall 1991 Lithuania, Estonia, and Latvia had successfully seceded from the Soviet Union.

with a dramatic cure for the country's continuing economic stagnation. Gorbachev appeared to lose his political nerve, having first ordered and then canceled a radical "five-hundred-day" economic reform plan, at the same time agreeing to negotiations with the increasingly disaffected republics within the union, now clamoring for independence. Sensing their political lives to be in jeopardy, a group of highly placed hard-line Communist party officials staged an abortive coup in August 1991, incarcerating Gorbachev and his wife and declaring a return to party-line orthodoxy. In response, the Soviet citizenry defied their self-proclaimed saviors. Led by Boris Yeltsin, who at one point mounted a tank in a Moscow street to rally the people, they successfully called the plotters' bluff. Within two weeks, Gorbachev was back in power, and the coup leaders were in prison.

Gorbachev's power was diminished by the August events, however, whereas Yeltsin's was dramatically in-

On December 8, 1991, the presidents of the republics of Russia, Ukraine, and Byelorussia declared that the Soviet Union was no more.

creased. Throughout the fall of 1991, as Gorbachev struggled to hold the nation together, Yeltsin capitalized on the discontent throughout the union, which was no longer united by the force of a powerful one-party state. On December 8, 1991, the presidents of the republics of Russia, Ukraine, and Byelorussia (now called Belarus) declared that the Soviet Union was no more: "The USSR as a subject of international law and geopolitical reality is ceasing to exist." Though the prose was flat, the message was momentous. The once-mighty Soviet Union, founded seventy-five years before in a burst of revolutionary fervor and violence, had evaporated nearly overnight, leaving in its wake a collection of eleven far from powerful nations loosely joined together as the Commonwealth of Independent States. On December 25, 1991, Gorbachev resigned the leadership of the now nonexistent union. The Soviet flag—the hammer and sickle that had symbolized the nation

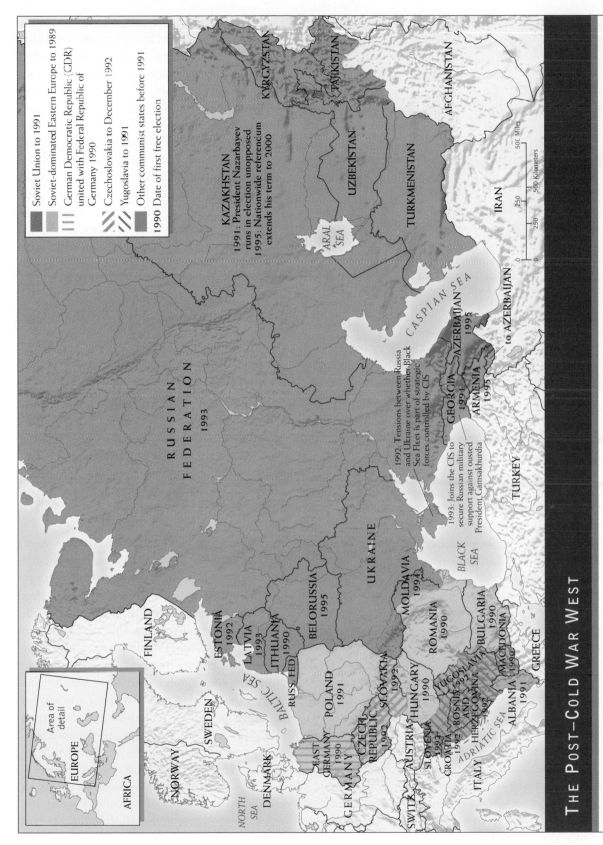

THE POST–COLD WAR WEST

How did the collapse of the Soviet Union and the end of the cold war allow for the reemergence of certain forces in the political landscape of Europe? Examine closely the geography of southeastern and central Europe. What happened here in terms of the reorganization of political boundaries?

Legend

- Soviet Union to 1991
- Soviet-dominated Eastern Europe to 1989
- German Democratic Republic (GDR) united with Federal Republic of Germany 1990
- Czechoslovakia to December 1992
- Yugoslavia to 1991
- Other communist states before 1991
- 1990 Date of first free election

Map labels

NORWAY

SWEDEN

FINLAND

DENMARK

NORTH SEA

BALTIC SEA

EAST GERMANY 1990

GERMANY

CZECH REPUBLIC 1990

SWITZ.

AUSTRIA

SLOVENIA 1992

ITALY

CROATIA 1992

ADRIATIC SEA

SLOVAKIA 1992

HUNGARY 1990

BOSNIA AND HERZEGOVINA 1992

YUGOSLAVIA 1992

MACEDONIA 1990

ALBANIA 1991

GREECE

POLAND 1991

RUSS. FED.

LITHUANIA 1990

LATVIA 1993

ESTONIA 1992

BELORUSSIA 1995

UKRAINE

MOLDAVIA 1994

ROMANIA 1990

BULGARIA 1990

TURKEY

BLACK SEA

1993: Joins the CIS to secure Russian military support against ousted President Gamsakhurdia

GEORGIA 1991

ARMENIA 1995

AZERBAIJAN 1995

to AZERBAIJAN

1992: Tensions between Russia and Ukraine over whether Black Sea Fleet is part of strategic forces controlled by CIS

RUSSIAN FEDERATION 1993

CASPIAN SEA

ARAL SEA

KAZAKHSTAN

1991: President Nazarbayev runs in election unopposed 1995: Nationwide referendum extends his term to 2000

UZBEKISTAN

TURKMENISTAN

KYRGYZSTAN

TAJIKISTAN

AFGHANISTAN

IRAN

Inset map

Area of detail

EUROPE

AFRICA

Scale

500 Kilometers
250
250
500 Miles

Boris Yeltsin Faces Down the Coup, August 1991. Russian president Boris Yeltsin stood his ground at the Russian parliament building against the hardliners who attempted to overthrow Mikhail Gorbachev. Here Yeltsin is encouraging the people to fight the takeover of the central government.

percent. The president's position was also threatened from the right. Vladimir Zhirinovsky, a xenophobic nationalist, played on the anxieties of a populace increasingly willing to blame the West for the country's difficulties.

Meanwhile, ethnic and religious conflict plagued the republics. In the first years following the dissolution of the Soviet Union, warfare flared in Georgia, Armenia, and Azerbaijan. The most serious conflict arose in the predominantly Muslim area of Chechnya, bordering Georgia in the Caucasus, which had declared its independence from Russia in late 1991. Three years later the Russian government, weary of this continuing challenge to its authority, launched a concerted effort to quash resistance. The attempt failed, demonstrating Russia's military vulnerability in a conflict that led to atrocities on both sides. A truce signed on July 30, 1995, was short lived. The Chechen war dragged on into the new century, a repeat of the Afghanistan conflict for the Russian government (see Chapter 32).

that for fifty years had kept half of Europe in thrall—was lowered for the last time over the Kremlin.

The mighty fall left mighty problems in its wake. Food shortages worsened during the winter of 1992. The value of the ruble plummeted. The republics could not agree on common military policies or resolve difficult and dangerous questions concerning the control of nuclear warheads. Yeltsin's pleas for economic assistance from the West resulted in massive infusions of private and public capital, which nevertheless failed to prevent serious economic hardship and dislocation. Free enterprise brought with it unemployment and encouraged profiteering with crime. Yeltsin's determination to press ahead with his economic program met with stiff resistance from a parliament and citizenry alarmed by the ruthlessness and rapidity of the change they were experiencing. When the parliament balked at Yeltsin's proposals in September 1993, he dissolved it. Elections in the fall of 1995 were a measure of continuing discontent. The resurgent communists captured the largest block of parliamentary seats—roughly one third. Yeltsin's party, though second in terms of representation, could claim no more than 10

The Iron Curtain had established one of the most rigid borders in European history; the collapse of the Soviet Union opened up both Russia and its former imperial dominions. That transformation brought the cold war to an end. It also created a host of unforeseen problems throughout Eastern Europe and the advanced industrial world: ethnic conflict, diplomatic uncertainty about the new Russian government, and single superpower domination, sometimes called American "unilateralism." Within the Russian and several of the former Soviet republics there emerged a new era that some called the Russian "Wild West." Capitalist market relations began to develop with clearly defined property relations or a stable legal framework. Former government officials profited from their position of power to take over whole sectors of the economy. Corruption ran rampant. Even the most energetic Russian government found itself faced with enormous problems. Post-Soviet "openness" could lay the groundwork for a new democratic Russia; it could also set into motion the resurgence of older forms of tyranny.

POSTREVOLUTIONARY TROUBLES: EASTERN EUROPE AFTER 1989

The "velvet revolutions" of central and Eastern Europe raised high hopes: local hopes that an end to authoritarian government would produce economic prosperity and cultural pluralism, and Western hopes that these countries would join them as capitalist partners in an enlarged European Community. The reality was slower and harder than the optimism of 1989 foresaw. The largest struggle, one with continuing implications for the continent, has been the reunification of Germany. The euphoria of reunification masked uncertainty even among Germans themselves about reunifying a country that had been divided in the name of preventing another European war. Practical and cultural difficulties have been even greater. Despite legal unity after 1990, the financial price for rescuing the foundering East German economy has been high. Piled onto other economic difficulties in the old West Germany during the 1990s it has produced much resentment of the need to "rescue" the East. What the writer Günter Grass has described as the "Wall in the mind" long divided the countries. Though there has been great progress in integrating elections and the bureaucracies of the two German states, economic and cultural unity has been much harder to come by.

Adapting to change has been difficult throughout Eastern Europe. Attempts to create free-market economies have brought inflation, unemployment, and—in their wake—anticapitalist demonstrations. Inefficient industries, a work force resistant to change, energy shortages, lack of venture capital, and a severely polluted environment have combined to hinder progress and dash hopes. Uprisings in Bulgaria and Albania in early 1997 were fueled by the inability of those governments to resolve basic economic and social problems. In addition, racial and ethnic conflicts have continued to divide newly liberated democracies, recalling the divisions that led to the First World War and that have plagued Eastern Europe throughout its history. Minorities waged campaigns for autonomous rights or outright secession that often descended into violence. Czechoslovakia's "velvet revolution" collapsed into a "velvet divorce," as Slovakia declared itself independent from the Czechs, forcing Havel's resignation and slowing down the promising cultural and economic reforms begun in 1989. Poland enjoyed an upswing in its economy during the 1990s, after many years of hardship, but most of the rest of Eastern Europe contin-

ues to find transformation rough going. This has been accompanied by revived ethnic tensions suppressed by centralized communist governments. There has been violence against non-European immigrants throughout Eastern Europe, against gypsies (Romani) in the Czech Republic and Hungary, and against ethnic Hungarians in Romania.

The most extreme example of these conflicts came with the implosion of the state of Yugoslavia. After the death of Tito in 1980 the government that had held Yugoslavia's federalist ethnic patchwork together began to come undone. Economic growth during the 1960s and 1970s was uneven, benefiting the capital Belgrade and the provinces of Croatia and Slovenia the most, while heavy industrial areas in Serbia, Bosnia-Hercegovina, and the tiny district of Kosovo began to lag far behind. At the same time a number of Serb politicians, most notably Slobodan Milosevic, began to redirect Serbs' frustration with economic hardship toward subjects of national pride and sovereignty. Milosevic's nationalism catapulted him to several positions of authority, alienating representatives from the non-Serb republics in the process. Inspired by the peaceful transformations of 1989, representatives of the small province of Slovenia declared that the Serbs denied them adequate representation and economic support inside the republic. In 1991, on a tide of nationalism and reform, the Slovenes seceded from Yugoslavia.

The large republic of Croatia, once part of the Habsburg empire and an independent state (allied with the Nazis) during World War II, cited injustices by Serb officials in the Yugoslav government and declared independence as a free, capitalist state. War broke out between federal Yugoslav forces and the well-armed militias of independent Croatia, a conflict that ended in arbitration by the United Nations. The religious nature of the conflict—between Catholic Croats and Orthodox Serbs—and the legacies of fighting in the Second World War produced violence on both sides. Towns and villages where Serbs and Croats had lived together since the 1940s were torn apart, as each ethnic group rounded up and massacred members of the other.

The next conflict came in the same place that in 1914 had sparked a much larger war: the province of Bosnia-Hercegovina. Bosnia was the most ethnically diverse republic in Yugoslavia. Its capital, Sarajevo, was home to several major ethnic groups and had often been praised as an example of peaceful coexistence. When Bosnia joined the round of secessions from

Yugoslavia in 1992, ethnic coexistence came apart. Bosnia began the war with no formal army: armed bands equipped by the governments of Serbian Yugoslavia, Croatia, and Bosnia battled each other throughout the new country. The Serbs and Croats, who both had reason to dislike the Muslim Bosnians, were especially well equipped and organized. They rained shells and bullets on towns and villages, burned houses with families inside, rounded up Muslim men in detention camps where they were allowed to starve to death, and raped thousands of Bosnian women. All sides committed atrocities. The Serbs however, were judged to have been responsible for the worst crimes. These included what came to be called "ethnic cleansing." This involved sending irregular troops on campaigns of terror through Muslim and Croat territories in order to

Ethnic Cleansing. The 1995 massacre of civilians in Srebrenca, a Muslim enclave of Bosnia, was one of the worst atrocities of the Yugoslavian wars. This mass grave was discovered in 1999.

encourage much larger populations to flee the area. During the first eighteen months of the fighting as many as one hundred thousand people were killed, including eighty thousand civilians who were mostly Bosnian Muslims. Although the campaigns appalled Western governments, those countries considered the Balkan conflict a civil war more complex than that in Spain during the 1930s and worried that intervention would only result in another Vietnam or Afghanistan (see Chapter 32) with no clear resolution of the horrific ethnic slaughter itself. The outside forces, mostly European troops in UN "blue helmets," concentrated on humanitarian relief, separating combatants, and creating "safe areas" for persecuted ethnic populations from all parties.

The crisis came to a head in the autumn of 1995. Sarajevo had been under siege for three years; but a series of mortar attacks on public marketplaces in Sarajevo produced fresh Western outrage and moved the United States to act. Already Croat forces and the Bosnian army had turned the war on the ground against the Serb militias, and now they were supported by a rolling wave of American air strikes. The American bombing, combined with a Croat-Bosnian offensive, forced the Bosnian Serbs to negotiate. Elite

French troops supported by British artillery broke the siege of Sarajevo. Peace talks were held at Dayton, Ohio. The agreement divided Bosnia, with the majority of land in the hands of Muslims and Croats, and a small, autonomous "Serb Republic" in areas that included land "ethnically cleansed" in 1992. Stability was restored, but three years of war had killed over two hundred thousand people.

The legacy of Bosnia flared into conflict again over Kosovo, the medieval homeland of the Orthodox Christian Serbs, now occupied by a largely Albanian, Muslim population. Milosevic accused the Albanians of plotting secession and of challenging the Serb presence in Kosovo. In the name of a "greater Serbia," Serb soldiers fought Albanian guerrillas rallying under the banner of "greater Albania." Western nations were anxious lest the conflict might spread to the strategic, ethnically divided country of Macedonia and touch off a general Balkan conflict. Talks between Milosevic's government and the Albanian rebels fell apart in early 1999, followed by a fresh and overwhelming wave of American-led bombing against Serbia itself, as well as against Serbian forces in Kosovo. A new round of ethnic cleansing drove hundreds of thousands of Albanians from their homes. The United States and its

European allies, unwilling to fight a war on the ground in the mountainous, unforgiving terrain of the southern Balkans, concentrated on strategic bombing of bridges, power plants, factories, and Serbian military bases. The Russian government, bothered by this unilateral attack on fellow Slavs, nonetheless played an important part in brokering a cease-fire. Milosevic was forced to withdraw from Kosovo, leaving it in the hands of another force of armed NATO peacekeepers.

At the same time, Serb-dominated Yugoslavia, worn by ten years of war and economic sanctions, turned against Milosevic's regime. Wars and corruption had destroyed Milosevic's credentials as a nationalist and populist. After he attempted to reject the results of a democratic election in 2000, his government fell to popular protests.

As we gain perspective on the twentieth century, however, it is clear that the Yugoslavian wars of the 1990s were not an isolated instance of "Balkan" violence. The issues are thoroughly Western. The Balkans form one of the West's borderlands, where cultures influenced by Roman Catholicism, Eastern Orthodoxy, and Islam meet, overlap, and contend for political domination and influence. Since the nineteenth century, this region of great religious, cultural, and ethnic diversity has struggled with the implications of nationalism. We have seen how conflicts regarding new nation states and ethnic minorities were worked out in central Europe, with many instances of tragic violence. The Yugoslavian wars fit into some of the same patterns.

Conclusion

The Eastern European revolutions of 1989 and ensuing the subsequent collapse of the Soviet Union were a revolutionary turning point. Like the French revolution of 1789, they brought down not only a regime, but an empire. Like the French revolution of 1789, they gave way to violence; the events are far too fresh for historians to predict what new forces and states will emerge. Like the French revolution of 1789, they had sweeping international consequences. These revolutions and the fall of the Soviet Union marked the end of the cold war, which had structured international politics and shaped the everyday lives of millions of people since the end of World War II. In the last chapter of this book, we consider how cold war politics shaped the postwar decolonization, of the nineteenth-century European empires, and how the cold war itself has given way to more complex global relations.

Selected Readings

Beschloss, Michael, and Strobe Talbott. *At the Highest Levels: The Inside Story of the End of the Cold War.* Boston, 1993. An analysis of the relationship between presidents Gorbachev and Bush, and their determination to ignore hard-liners.

Caute, David. *The Year of the Barricades: A Journey through 1968.* New York, 1988. A well-written global history of 1968.

Echols, Alice. *Daring to be Bad: Radical Feminism in America, 1967–1975.* Minneapolis, 1989. Good narrative and analysis.

Fink, Carole, Phillipp Gassert, and Detlef Junker, eds. *1968, The World Transformed.* Cambridge, 1998. A transatlantic history of 1968.

Garton Ash, Timothy. *In Europe's Name: Germany and the Divided Continent.* New York, 1993. An analysis of the effect of German reunification on the future of Europe.

Glenny, Misha. *The Balkans, 1804–1999: Nationalism, War and the Great Powers.* London, 1999. Good account by a journalist who covered the fighting.

Horowitz, Daniel. *Betty Friedan and the Making of the Feminine Mystique: The American Left, the Cold War, and Modern Feminism.* Amherst, 1998. An excellent new account.

Hosking, Geoffrey. *The Awakening of the Soviet Union.* Cambridge, Mass., 1990. The factors that led to the end of the Soviet era.

Hughes, H. Stuart. *Sophisticated Rebels: The Political Culture of European Dissent, 1968–1987.* Cambridge, Mass., 1990. The nature of dissent on both sides of the disintegrating Iron Curtain in the years 1988–1989.

Hulsberg, Werner. *The German Greens: A Social and Political Profile.* New York, 1988. The origins, politics, and impact of environmental politics.

Jarausch, Konrad. *The Rush to German Unity.* New York, 1994. The problems of reunification analyzed.

Judah, Tim. *The Serbs: History, Myth, and the Destruction of Yugoslavia.* New Haven, 1997.

Kaplan, Robert D. *Balkan Ghosts: A Journey through History.* New York, 1993.

Kennedy, Paul. *Preparing for the Twenty-First Century.* New York, 1993. A critical and generally pessimistic appraisal of the current state of world politics.

Lewin, Moshe. *The Gorbachev Phenomenon,* expanded ed., Berkeley, 1991. Written as a firsthand account, tracing the roots of Gorbachev's successes and failures.

Wright, Patrick. *On Living in an Old Country: The National Past in Contemporary Britain.* New York, 1986. The culture of Britain in the 1980s.

Young, Hugo. *One of Us: A Biography of Margaret Thatcher.* New York, 1989. A perceptive, thorough examination of Britain's first woman prime minister, her character, and her policies.

Chapter THIRTY-TWO

Decolonization and the Twenty-first-century World

FROM THE PERSPECTIVE of the West and the world, the most significant legacy of the world wars was the rapid disintegration of Europe's empires. In the decades after the war, the populations of entire continents regained self-government and entered into new kinds of relationships with the Western nations—relationships that we call postcolonial. Previously colonized nations have gained at least formal independence and new kinds of economic, political, and cultural authority. In other respects, however, very little has changed for peoples of those former colonies. The term *postcolonial*, indeed, is meant to underline that the legacy of colonial rule has extended well beyond independence.

Between 1947 and 1975, the European empires that had been built in the nineteenth century disintegrated. Imperialism had always provoked resistance. Anticolonial resistance stiffened after World War I, and war-weakened European states tried to renegotiate the terms of empire. After World War II, older forms of empire quickly became untenable. The process of decolonization was uneven. In some regions, their financial and human resources depleted, European states simply sought to cut their losses and withdraw. In others, well-organized and tenacious nationalist movements successfully demanded new constitutional arrangements and independence. In a third set of cases, Western powers helped create and were drawn into complicated, multifaceted, and extremely violent struggles between rival local powers and European representatives and settlers.

The relationships that followed the end of colonialism have been equally varied. New networks of political influence, economic power, and cultural exchange have evolved. In many cases the former imperial power—or its local clients—exercise such control that independence seems like a formality. In others the postcolonial relationship has been more fluid. Former colonies have absorbed Western goods, money, and culture and used them for their own ends. Waves of immigration from former colonies to the west have changed everyday life, diet, social relations, and culture; they have created new economic relationships and political demands. The independent postcolonial nations, able to use the natural resources that made them attractive colonies in the first place, have confronted difficult questions about

FOCUS QUESTIONS

• How did French and British decolonization differ?

• Why did the United States enter the Vietnam War?

• What is the "new world order"?

• What are the major challenges for the twenty-first century?

self-sufficiency, economics, and political and cultural values. These debates are often linked to the continuing economic relationship with the West, the many-sided struggles over resources (from oil and rubber to forests and beaches), and to the industrialization of the postcolonial world.

Decolonization has been part of the process of globalization, a term for increasing international economic, political, and technological integration. That process has a long history, but it has quickened in the last half century. Thus the first part of this chapter deals with decolonization and the complex, often violent legacies it has left to a globalized world. The second part of the chapter takes on several important developments in science, medicine, society, and economics in an effort to take stock of trends that may influence the course of what future generations will also call "history."

GLOBAL DECOLONIZATION AND POSTCOLONIAL RELATIONS IN THE BRITISH AND FRENCH EMPIRES

How did French and British decolonization differ?

Great Britain and France were the major colonial powers of the nineteenth century. In both countries, the combined strains of two world wars eventually shook the imperial structures beyond repair. The wars amplified nationalist resistance to colonial power, and they depleted French and British economic and military resources. At the same time, however, the wars also seemed to demonstrate just how crucial the colonies were to France and Britain: they provided millions of soldiers, essential strategic bases, and food. These conflicting imperatives made decolonization a difficult and sometimes violent process.

THE BRITISH EMPIRE UNRAVELS

The first major British colony to win self-government after the war was India. As we have seen, rebellions such as the Sepoy Mutiny challenged the representatives of

Britain in India throughout the nineteenth century. During the early stages of the Second World War, nationalist bodies such as the Indian National Congress (founded 1885), the umbrella party for the independence movement called on Britain to "quit India." The most famous Indian nationalist, Mohandas K. Gandhi (1869–1948), did not approve of armed attacks on anyone. His methods were noncooperation and civil disobedience. By 1945 anti-British sentiment had reached such a pitch that the country seemed ripe for revolution. By 1947 Gandhi and his fellow nationalist Jawaharlal Nehru (1889–1964, prime minister 1947–1964), the leader of the pro-independence Congress party, had gained such widespread support that the British found it impossible to continue in power. The Labour party government elected in Britain in 1945 had always favored independence. Now independence was a political necessity. At the same time that talks secured procedures for independence, however, India was torn by conflict between the vast diversity of ethnic and religious groups in the former raj. A Muslim League, led by Mohammed Ali Jinnah (1876–1948), wanted autonomy in largely Muslim areas and feared the predominantly Hindu Congress party's authority in a single united state. British India was therefore "partitioned" into the nations of India and Pakistan, a process that brought further violence and mass migrations of Hindus and Muslims.

Despite the conflicts over partition, the transfer of power in British India was generally smooth. Relations between the independent states were not. Disorders, stemming from religious conflicts between Hindus, Muslims, and Sikhs, continued to plague the two countries. These disorders resulted in three bloody wars between independence and 1971, one major Sikh rebellion within India during the 1980s, and continued conflict in the disputed region of Kashmir. An important outcome of the conflict was the establishment of the independent republic of Bangladesh, formerly the province of East Pakistan, the result of an independence struggle supported by India in 1971.

India was the first and largest of the colonies surrendered by colonial powers following the war. Important as India was to Great Britain, the move to independence did not come as a surprise. Indian nationalism, and reformers' sympathy for Indian claims in Britain, had a long history. In Africa and Southeast Asia, the British hoped to hold on for much longer. The Labour government launched carefully targeted efforts at "colonial development." These efforts were intended to develop local natural resources Britain hoped to sell on world markets. They were also part

MOHANDAS GANDHI AND NONVIOLENT ANTICOLONIALISM

After leading a campaign for Indian rights in South Africa between 1894 and 1914, Mohandas K. Gandhi (1869–1948), known as Mahatma ("great-souled") Gandhi, became a leader in the long battle for home rule in India. This battle was finally won in 1947 and brought with it the partition of India and Pakistan. Gandhi's insistence on the power of nonviolent noncooperation brought him to the forefront of Indian politics and provided a model for many later liberation struggles, including the American civil rights movement. Gandhi argued that only nonviolent resistance, which dramatized the injustice of colonial rule and colonial law, had the spiritual force to unite a community and end colonialism.

Passive resistance is a method of securing rights by personal suffering; it is the reverse of resistance by arms. When I refuse to do a thing that is repugnant to my conscience, I use soul-force. For instance, the Government of the day has passed a law which is applicable to me. I do not like it. If by using violence I force the Government to repeal the law, I am employing what may be termed body-force. If I do not obey the law and accept the penalty for its breach, I use soul-force. It involves sacrifice of self.

Everybody admits that sacrifice of self is infinitely superior to sacrifice of others. Moreover, if this kind of force is used in a cause that is unjust, only the person using it suffers. He does not make others suffer for his mistakes. Men have before now done many things which were subsequently found to have been wrong. . . . It is therefore meet that he should not do that which he knows to be wrong, and suffer the consequence whatever it may be. This is the key to the use of soul-force. . . .

It is contrary to our manhood if we obey laws repugnant to our conscience. Such teaching is opposed to religion and means slavery. If the Government were to ask us to go about without any clothing, should we do so? If I were a passive resister, I would say to them that I would have nothing to do with their law. But we have so forgotten ourselves and become so compliant that we do not mind any degrading law.

A man who has realized his manhood, who fears only God, will fear no one else. Man-made laws are not necessarily binding on him. Even the Government does not expect any such thing from us. They do not say: "You must do such and such a thing." But they say: "If you do not do it, we will punish you." We are sunk so low that we fancy that it is our duty and our religion to do what the law lays down. If man will only realize that it is unmanly to obey laws that are unjust, no man's tyranny will enslave him. This is the key to self-rule or home-rule.

M. K. Gandhi, "Indian Home Rule (1909)," in *The Gandhi Reader: A Source Book of His Life and Writings*, edited by Homer A. Jack (Bloomington: Indiana University Press, 1956), pp. 104–121.

Leaders of Indian Nationalism—Nehru and Gandhi. Mohandas Gandhi was assassinated in 1948. Jawaharlal Nehru served as prime minister of India from 1947 to his death in 1964.

Violence in Calcutta, 1946. A dead Hindu surrounded by armed Muslims. Such scenes were not uncommon on the eve of Indian independence, when tensions exploded between Hindu and Muslim segments of the population.

of a larger effort to make a continued British military presence acceptable and to maintain British power and prestige in the postwar world. "Development," however, was underfunded and largely disregarded in favor of fulfilling cold war commitments elsewhere. As a number of West African colonies established assertive independence movements, the British government moved hesitantly to meet their demands. By the middle of the 1950s, Britain agreed to a variety of terms for independence in these territories, leaving them with written constitutions and a British legal system, but little else in terms of modern infrastructure or economic support. Defenders of British colonialism claimed that these formal institutions would give advantages to the independent states. Without other resources, however, even the most promising—such as Ghana, the first to gain independence and seen in the late 1950s as a model for free African nations—foundered in corruption and lack of economic opportunity. In the Middle East, where Britain had relatively little formal control, the British government was much more active. It protected several oil-rich states with its military and helped overthrow a nationalist government in Iran, to ensure that the oil states invested their money in British financial markets.

Elsewhere, violence erupted. In Malaya, British forces, with the help of the majority Malay population, repressed a revolt by ethnic Chinese communists in the late 1940s. Britain then helped support the independent states of Singapore and Malaysia, which allowed British companies and bankers to maintain ties with Malaysia's lucrative rubber and oil reserves. In Kenya, the populist revolt by the majority Kikuyu population known as the Mau Mau rebellion quickly became bloody. British troops fired freely at targets in rebel-occupied areas, sometimes killing civilians. Internment camps set up by security forces became sites of atrocities that drew public investigations and condemnation by even the most conservative politicians and army officers. Britain began to withdraw from naval and air bases around the world because they had become too expensive to maintain. Empire was not only politically complicated after the war, it also cost too much. For each of those reasons, anticolonial movements gathered steam during the late 1950s. More than half of the remaining British possessions gained their independence in the space of five years near the end of that decade.

In Egypt, however, the British refused to yield a traditional point of imperial pride. In 1951 nationalists compelled the British to agree to withdraw their troops from Egyptian territory within three years. In 1952 a group of nationalist army officers deposed Egypt's King Farouk, who had close ties to Britain, and proclaimed a republic. Shortly after the final British withdrawal an Egyptian colonel, Gamal Abdel Nasser (1918–1970), became president of the country (1956–1970). His first major public act as president was to nationalize the Suez Canal Company. So doing would help finance the construction of the Aswan Dam on the Nile, and both the dam and nationalizing the canal represented economic independence and Egyptian national pride. Nasser also helped to develop the anticolonial ideology of pan-Arabism, proposing that Arab nationalists throughout the Muslim world should create an alliance of modern nations, no longer beholden to the West. Finally, Nasser was also willing to take aid and support from the Soviets in order to achieve that goal, which made the canal issue part of the cold war.

Three nations found Nasser and his pan-Arab ideals threatening. Israel, surrounded on all sides by unfriendly neighbors, was looking for an opportunity to seize the strategic Sinai Peninsula and create a buffer against Egypt. France, already fighting a war against Algerian nationalists (see below), hoped to destroy what it considered the Egyptian source of Arab nationalism. Britain depended on the Canal as a route to its strategic bases and was stung by this blow to imperial dignity. Though the British were reluctant to intervene, they were urged on by their prime minister, Sir Anthony Eden, who had developed a deep personal hatred of Nasser. In the autumn of 1956, the three nations colluded in an attack on Egypt. Israel occupied the Sinai while the British and French destroyed Egypt's air force on the ground and landed troops at the mouth of the Nile. Yet the war left Nasser in power, and made him a hero to the Egyptian public for holding the imperialists at bay. The attack was condemned around the world. The United States inflicted severe financial penalties on Britain and France, which

were forced to withdraw their expeditions. Suez destroyed Britain's claims as a true imperial power. Britain was soon faced with financial problems, rationed oil (after an embargo by the oil-producing nations on Nasser's behalf), and international outrage. For policy makers in the 1950s, Suez was the end of an era.

During the 1960s, the most difficult case of British decolonization involved Rhodesia, in southern Africa. White Rhodesians had long resisted any concessions to black representation and rights, instituting a system of rigid racial segregation. This system was enforced by Afrikaaner settlers before the Second World War and reaffirmed after the war by two hundred thousand new English immigrants. Britain, which had mediated transfers of power to black African politicians in Rhodesia's neighbors, insisted on a measure of racial equality as a condition for Rhodesian independence. In 1965 white Rhodesians rejected this demand and unilaterally declared independence. Rhodesian defiance infuriated the liberal Labour government in Britain and nearly resulted in a dangerous confrontation between Britain and its former colony. The white Rhodesian government held firm in its determination to resist indigenous African rule until 1977, when the cumulative effect of U.S. and British pressure, economic sanctions, fierce guerrilla warfare, and the withdrawal of South African assistance caused the government to open negotiations. In 1980 negotiations created a new state, Zimbabwe, dominated by African nationalists and ultimately governed by Robert Mugabe. Mugabe's populist and nationalist commitments faded over the years, and he became increasingly autocratic, exploiting his nation's finances and resources for personal and regional power.

Some former British colonies have reached economic and political stability—Canada, India, and Australia, for example—and have fared reasonably well. Others have collapsed into disorder or, like Nigeria, have seen periods of civil war and repressive military government. The Commonwealth of Nations—a voluntary association of Britain and some of its dependencies first organized in 1931—once foreseen as a means to maintain British influence throughout the world, has had little political or international impact. For Great Britain, the strongest imperial legacy has come with immigration. Particularly in London and the other large British cities, immigration from all parts of the former empire, particularly India, the West Indies, West Africa, and Hong Kong has turned the United Kingdom into the most

> Empire was not only politically complicated after the war, it also cost too much.

ethnically diverse nation in Western Europe. There has been racism and division, but also sweeping cultural change, economic development, and rich hybrids of food, music, and popular culture. Two generations of black or Asian Britons have now lived their whole lives in Britain, with ties to their homelands but roots in London or Manchester. The lasting effects of this transformation of British society are not yet clear.

FRENCH DECOLONIZATION

France's experience of decolonization differed from Britain's in two central respects. First, France long resisted giving up relationships with its former colonies. French officials maintained close contact with the new countries and the heads of state they had supported, however autocratic those new leaders turned out to be. French soldiers trained new rulers' security forces, and French companies kept a strong hold on lucrative contracts for local resources. These relationships between new states and a former imperial power have often been described as neocolonialism. France's active support of particular factions in local politics often made it seem that independence was little more than a formality. The French presence decreased during the 1990s, however, and former French colonies were among the first sub-Saharan nations to establish genuinely democratic governments, beginning with Benin in 1991.

Second, in two particular instances, France's experience of decolonization was bloodier, more difficult, and more damaging to French prestige and domestic politics than any in Britain's experience, with the possible exception of Northern Ireland. The first was Indochina, where French efforts to restore imperial authority after losing it in World War II only resulted in military defeat and further humiliation. The second case, Algeria, became not only a violent colonial war but a struggle with serious political ramifications at home.

VIETNAM

Indochina had been one of France's last major imperial acquisitions in the nineteenth century. During World War II a local independence movement grew up around the communist-led resistance to the Vichy government of the colony and later Japanese occupiers. During the war, the Allies actively supported the communist independence movement headed by Ho Chi Minh, who had earlier tried to represent Indochinese interests at Versailles (see Chapter 27). In 1945, the United States and

Ho Chi Minh.

Britain rejected their wartime relationship with Ho's movement, allowing the French to reclaim their colonies throughout Southeast Asia. The Vietnamese communists, who were fierce nationalists as much as they were Marxists, renewed their guerrilla war, this time against the French. The fighting was protracted and bloody; France saw in it a chance to redeem its national pride. After one of France's most capable generals, Jean de Lattre de Tassigny, finally achieved a military advantage against the rebels in 1952, the French government might have decolonized on favorable terms. Instead, it decided to press on for total victory, sending troops deep into Vietnamese territory to root out the rebels. One major base was established in a valley bordering modern Laos, at a hamlet called Dien Bien Phu. Ringed by high mountains, this vulnerable spot became a base for thousands of elite French paratroopers and colonial soldiers from Algeria and West Africa—the best of France's troops. The rebels besieged the base. Tens of thousands of Vietnamese nationalist fighters hauled heavy artillery by hand up the mountainsides and bombarded the network of forts set up by the French. The siege lasted for months, becoming a protracted national crisis in France.

THE VIETNAM WAR: FROM FRANCE TO THE UNITED STATES

At the end of World War II, the French government sought to recoup its prestige and empire by reasserting control of the former colony of Indochina. They faced fierce resistance from nationalist forces under the French-educated leader Ho Chi Minh. Within a few years, American advisors were beginning to shore up the faltering French army. Cold war ideology, anxiety about China and Korea, and a conviction that they could do what the French could not, combined to draw the Americans more deeply into the war. In 1950, the Central Intelligence Agency drew up this analysis of the strategic situation.

For more than three years, an intense conflict has been in progress in Indochina in which nationalistic Vietnamese forces under the leadership of the Moscow-trained revolutionist, Ho Chi Minh, have opposed the reimposition of French authority. Within Vietnam . . . a precarious military balance exists between the French and their Vietnamese followers on the one hand and Ho's resistance forces on the other. Thus far, French progress toward both political and military objectives has been substantially less than is necessary to eliminate the threat to French tenure posed by the resistance.

The French position and Bao Dai's [emperor of Vietnam since 1926] prospects have recently been further weakened: politically by Chinese Communist and Soviet recognition of Ho Chi Minh, and militarily by the ability of the Chinese Communist forces to make military supplies available to Ho's forces. Unless the French and Bao Dai receive substantial outside assistance, this combined political and military pressure may accelerate a French withdrawal from all or most of Indochina which, previous to the Chinese Communist and Soviet recognition of Ho, had been estimated as probably occurring within two years. . . .

The fighting in Indochina constitutes a progressive drain on French military resources which is weakening France as a partner in the Western alliance. If France is driven from Indochina, the resulting emergence of an indigenous Communist-oriented regime in Vietnam, in combination with the pressures which will be exerted by the new government of China and the Soviet Union, can be expected to cause adjacent Thailand and Burma to yield to this Communist advance. Under these conditions Malaya and Indonesia would also become highly vulnerable.

The French are trying to halt the present unfavorable trend by according certain aspects of sovereignty to Emperor Bao Dai. . . . The French political aim is to attract non-Communist nationalists from the leadership of Ho Chi Minh to that of Bao Dai.

Meanwhile, Soviet and Chinese Communist recognition of Ho's regime has made it clear that the Kremlin is now prepared to exert greater pressure to achieve its objective of installing a Communist regime in Indochina. France alone is incapable of preventing such a development and can turn only to the US for assistance in thwarting this Communist strategy. Having already publicly proclaimed support of Bao Dai, the US is now faced with the choice of bolstering his weak and vulnerable position or of abandoning him and accepting the far-reaching consequences of Communist control of Indochina.

From the National Archives, College Park, Md. Record Group 263 (Records of the Central Intelligence Agency), *Estimates of the Office of Research Evaluation, 1916–1950,* box 4.

DIEN-BIEN-PHU
...ILS SE SONT SACRIFIÉS POUR LA LIBERTÉ

PAIX ET LIBERTÉ   PAUL COLIN

"Dien-Bien-Phu: . . . they sacrificed themselves for liberty." The sentiments expressed in this poster, which was intended to commemorate the French soldiers who died at Dien-Bien-Phu in May 1954, helped to deepen French commitments to colonial control in Algeria.

When Dien Bien Phu fell in May 1954, the French government began peace talks in Geneva. The talks were conducted among France, Vietnamese politicians including the communists, Britain, and the United States. The Geneva accords divided Indochina into four countries and Vietnam into two states. North Vietnam was taken over by Ho Chi Minh's party; South Vietnam by a succession of pro-Western politicians. Corruption, repression, and instability in the south, coupled with Ho Chi Minh's nationalist desire to unite Vietnam, led to another war by the end of the 1950s. Another Western power was drawn in to fight communism and restore stability: the United States.

ALGERIA

Just as France reeled from the humiliation of Dien Bien Phu it faced a complex colonial problem closer to home, in Algeria. Since the 1830s, the colony had evolved into a settler society of three social groups. First, in addition to a small class of French soldiers and administrators, there were also one million European settlers. They typically owned farms and vineyards near the major cities, or were working-class and small merchant residents of those cities. All of them were citizens of the three administrative districts in Algeria that were legally part of France. In the small towns and villages of Algeria lived a second group of (largely Muslim) Berbers, whose long history of service in the French army entitled them to certain formal and informal privileges within the colony. Finally, there were millions of Muslim Arabs, some living in the desert south but most crowded into impoverished neighborhoods in the cities. The Arabs were the largest and most deprived group in Algerian society. Between the world wars the French government had offered small reforms to increase their rights and representation, and it had hoped to meld the three groups into a common Algerian society. Reforms came too late, and were also undercut by European settlers anxious to maintain their privileges.

At the end of the Second World War, Algerian nationalists called on all the Allies to recognize Algeria's independence in return for good service during the war. Public demonstrations became frequent, and in several cases turned into attacks on settler-landowners. In one rural town, Setif, celebrations of the defeat of Germany flared into violence against settlers. French repression was harsh and immediate: security forces killed several thousand Arabs. After the war the French government approved a provincial assembly for all of Algeria, elected by two pools of voters, one made up of settlers and mostly Berber Muslims, the other of Arabs. This very limited enfranchisement gave Arab Algerians no political power. The more important changes were economic. All of Algeria suffered in the difficulties after the war. Many Arabs had few economic alternatives to immigration; several hundred thousand went to work in France. As citizens of mainland France read their papers and frowned over the war in Indochina, the situation in Algeria grew more serious. By the middle of the 1950s, a younger generation of Arab activists, unhappy with the leadership of moderates, had taken charge of a movement dedicated to independence by force. The National Liberation Front (FLN) was organized, which leaned towards socialism and demanded equal citizenship for all.

The war in Algeria became a civil war on three fronts. The first was a guerrilla war between the

ANTICOLONIALISM AND VIOLENCE

Born in the French Caribbean colony of Martinique, Frantz Fanon (1925–1961) studied psychiatry in France before moving on to work in Algeria in the early 1950s. Fanon became a member of the Algerian revolutionary National Liberation Front (FLN) and an ardent advocate of decolonization. Black Skin, White Masks, *published in 1952 with a preface by Jean Paul Sartre, was a study of the psychological effects of colonialism and racism on black culture and individuals.* The Wretched of the Earth *(1961) was a revolutionary manifesto, one of the most influential of the period. Unlike Gandhi, Fanon believed that violence lay at the heart of both the colonial relationship and anticolonial movements. Fanon attacked nationalist leaders for their ambition and corruption. He believed that revolutionary change could only come from poor peasants, those who "have found no bone to gnaw in the colonial system." Diagnosed with leukemia, Fanon sought treatment in the Soviet Union and then in Washington, D.C., where he died.*

In decolonization, there is therefore the need of a complete calling in question of the colonial situation. If we wish to describe it precisely, we might find it in the well-known words: "The last shall be first and the first last." Decolonization is the putting into practice of this sentence. . . .

The naked truth of decolonization evokes for us the searing bullets and blood-stained knives which emanate from it. For if the last shall be first, this will only come to pass after a murderous and decisive struggle between the two protagonists. That affirmed intention to place the last at the head of things, and to make them climb at a pace (too quickly, some say) the well-known steps which characterize an organized society, can only triumph if we use all means to turn the scale, including, of course, that of violence.

You do not turn any society, however primitive it may be, upside down with such a program if you have not decided from the very beginning, that is to say from the actual formation of that program, to overcome all the obstacles that you will come across in so doing. The native who decides to put the program into practice, and to become its moving force, is ready for violence at all time. From birth it is clear to him that this narrow world, strewn with prohibitions, can only be called in question by absolute violence.

Frantz Fanon, *The Wretched of the Earth,* translated by Constance Farrington (New York: Grove Press, 1963), pp. 35–37.

regular French Army and the FLN, fought in the mountains and deserts of the country. This war continued for years, a clear military defeat for the FLN but never a clear-cut victory for the French. The second war, fought out in Algeria's cities, began with an FLN campaign of bombing and terrorism. European civilians were killed, and the French administration retaliated with its own campaign. French paratroopers hunted down and destroyed the networks of FLN bombers. The information that allowed the French to break the FLN network was extracted through systematic torture conducted by French security forces. The torture became an international scandal, bringing waves of protest in France. This third front of the

Algerian war divided France, wrecked governing coalitions, and eventually brought down the government. De Gaulle, called in to contend with the crisis in 1958, proposed constitutional reforms. Those reforms ended the Fourth French Republic and created the Fifth, with the former general and Free French leader as its powerful president.

De Gaulle visited Algiers to wild cheering from settlers and declared that Algeria would always be French. After another year of violence, he and his advisors had changed their minds. By 1962 talks had produced a formula for independence: a referendum would be held, voted on by the whole population of Algeria. On July 1, 1962, the referendum passed by a landslide vote. Arab political groups and guerrillas from the FLN entered Algiers in triumph. Settlers and Berbers who had fought for the French army fled Algeria for France by the hundreds of thousands. Later, these refugees were joined in France by another influx of Arab economic migrants.

The relationship between France and independent Algeria was relatively cordial. Racism and economic discrimination, however, continued to complicate the lives of Arab immigrants in France, although they have made important contributions to France's economy and enriched French culture.

ANTICOLONIAL MOVEMENTS IN ASIA: FROM THE CHINESE REVOLUTION TO THE VIETNAM WAR

Why did the United States enter the Vietnam War?

The cold war complicated decolonization. Both the Soviet Union and the United States saw anticolonial struggles through the lens of cold war ideology. Doing so often blurred the specific issues at stake in local struggles and made these conflicts appear to be high-stakes contests between the superpowers. This cold war perspective did not take shape immediately after the war. It was sharpened, however, by two crucial events in Asia: the Chinese Revolution and the Korean War. These developments, and the way the superpowers interpreted them, cast a long shadow over most subsequent events in the area.

THE CHINESE REVOLUTION

The single most radical change in the developing world after World War II was the Chinese Revolution. A civil war had raged in China since 1926, when the forces of the Nationalists under Jiang Jeishi (Chiang Kai-shek, 1887–1975) had engaged in battle first in the south, then in the north, with communist insurgents under the leadership of Mao Zedong (Mao Tse-tung, 1893–1976). A truce in 1937 had allowed both sides to wage a common battle against the Japanese. At the end of the war, however, the communists, still led by Mao, refused to surrender the northern provinces under their control. Civil

Algerian Soldiers Protecting Shopping Areas in Algiers during Fight for Independence from France, 1963.

Chairman Mao Zedong.

war broke out again. The United States intervened, first as mediator and then with massive military assistance for the Nationalists. But the Nationalists, corrupt and unrepresentative, were defeated in the field and surrendered in 1949. Even more than the Russian Revolution, the Chinese Revolution was the act of a nation of peasants. Their new bureaucratic leaders were bent on turning the country into a modern, industrial nation within a generation. The human cost was high, and diversions from party policy were met with repression. During the 1960s, the commitment of a younger generation of Chinese communists to the cause resulted in the excesses of the Cultural Revolution, when the government partially lost control of radical students who condemned and sometimes killed "traitors to the party." After Mao's death in 1976 the Chinese party moderated its stance. Under the leadership of Deng Xiaoping, the Chinese concentrated on population control and economic modernization, run by a strong centralized state China. There were signs of a return to more conservative policies at the end of the century, however, notably the bloody repression of democratic protests in Tienanmen Square in 1989.

The Chinese Revolution transformed not only

A Red Guard Demonstration. Middle-school students display their solidarity with Mao Zedong's revolution by waving copies of a book of his quotations. The slogan proclaims, "Not only are we able to destroy the old world, we are able to build a new world instead— Mao Zedong."

China, but politics in Asia. The "loss of China" provoked fear and consternation in the West, particularly in the United States. Despite the personal distrust between Mao and Stalin and the uneasy relationship between the two largest communist countries, the United States, like other Western countries, considered these two nations a "communist bloc" until the early 1970s. Ultimately the United States was able to reach accommodations with China, culminating in the famous visit by President Richard Nixon in 1972, part of an effort to capitalize on the rivalry with the Soviets. In the shorter run, however, the Chinese Revolution intensified Western military and diplomatic anxiety about governments throughout Asia. The revolution seemed to tip the balance in a standoff between communism and capitalism. To Western powers it represented a dangerous possible outcome of decolonization, and this successful peasant revolt stood as a model to anticolonial activists the world over.

THE KOREAN WAR

The Chinese revolution raised the stakes in Korea, which in 1950 became one of the "hot spots" of the cold war. Korea lay under Japanese control during the war, and at surrender was divided between Russian troops, liberating (and occupying) the north, and their American counterparts in the South. In June of 1950, troops of communist North Korea attacked across the border, crushing resistance in the south and forcing noncommunist forces and a small American garrison to retreat to the far end of the peninsula. The United States took advantage of a temporary Russian boycott of the United Nations and brought the invasion before the Security Council. The council passed a resolution permitting an American-led "police action" to defend South Korea and counter the communists.

General Douglas MacArthur, a hero of the Second World War and the military governor of occupied Japan, took charge of operations. He mounted an audacious amphibious attack behind North Korean lines and cut northern forces to pieces. MacArthur drove the Korean communists to the Chinese border and pressed for the authority to attack them as they retreated into China, hoping to punish China and help reverse the Chinese Revolution. President Harry S. Truman (1945–1953) denied the request and relieved MacArthur of command for exceeding his authority. The price had already been paid, however; more than a million Chinese troops flooded across the border in support of the North Koreans, and the international

troops were forced into a bloody, headlong retreat in the dead of winter. During that difficult winter the able and patient American general Matthew Ridgeway stemmed the retreat. The war, however, ended in a stalemate. Chinese and North Korean troops dug in against the United Nations force, composed largely of American and South Korean troops but drawn from around the world—small contingents from Britain, Australia, Ethiopia, the Netherlands, and Turkey distinguished themselves in the fighting. The conflict dragged on for two years as peace talks began. It was a bitter war of artillery battles, hand-to-hand fighting, attacks up well-defended hillsides, and bitter cold. The end, decreed in June of 1953, was inconclusive. Korea remained divided roughly along the original line drawn in 1945. With fifty-three thousand Americans and over a million Koreans and Chinese dead, South Korea had not been "lost," but neither had China or the United States won a decisive victory. As in Germany, the inability of major powers to achieve their ultimate goals resulted in a divisive settlement and a divided nation.

The existence of communist China and the stalemate in Korea caused mounting concern among Western nations, particularly the United States. In 1961, President John F. Kennedy (1917–1963) promised to "bear any burden" necessary to fight communism and to ensure the victory of American models of representative government and free-market economics in the developing nations. Kennnedy's plan entailed massive increases in foreign aid, much of it in weapons. It provided the impetus for humanitarian institutions such as the Peace Corps, intended to improve local conditions and show the Americans' benevolence and good intentions. Bearing burdens, however, also meant fighting guerrillas who turned to the Soviets for aid. This involved covert interventions in Latin America, the Congo, and, most important, Vietnam.

THE VIETNAM WAR

Why did the United States go into Vietnam? The intensifying cold war provides most of the answer. But American confidence and the assurance that the United States would succeed where the French had failed were also factors in the decision. Many American policy makers saw France as an old, tarnished colonial power; they saw the United States as a model of economic and political vigor. By comparison with other covert anticommunist operations, Vietnam seemed a good bet. By the time of Kennedy's death in 1963, nearly fifteen thou-

CHRONOLOGY

MAJOR DEVELOPMENTS IN ASIA, 1947–PRESENT

India gains independence	1947
Chinese Communist Revolution	1949
Korean War	1950–1953
Vietnamese defeat the French	1954
Chinese Cultural Revolution	1960s
Vietnam War	1964–1975
United States recognizes Communist China	1972
Tiananmen Square	1989

sand American "advisors" were on the ground alongside South Vietnamese troops; more than four hundred had already died. Kennedy's successor, Lyndon B. Johnson, began the strategic bombing of North Vietnam and rapidly drew hundreds of thousands of American troops into combat in South Vietnam. The rebels, known as the Viet Cong, were solidly entrenched, highly experienced guerrilla fighters, and were backed by the professional, well-equipped North Vietnamese army under Ho Chi Minh. The South Vietnamese government resisted efforts at reform, losing popular support. Massive efforts by the United States produced only stalemate and mounting American casualties.

The Viet Cong were solidly entrenched, highly experienced guerrilla fighters, and were backed by the professional, well-equipped North Vietnamese Army under Ho Chi Minh.

After early American enthusiasm, the war became increasingly unpopular. With a military designed to fight "open" wars against foes like the Soviets and a public still attuned to the total victory of 1945, a long colonial war became difficult to sustain. Vietnam did much to cause the political turmoil of the 1960s in the United States. Two events—an expansion of the involuntary draft of young American men and a massive Viet Cong offensive during the Vietnamese lunar new year in early 1968, at a time when the United States claimed it had turned the tide—polarized the public. The war created increasingly bitter rifts within the country and even within the American establishment. For example, the government brought criminal conspiracy charges against Benjamin Spock, the nation's leading pediatrician, and William Sloane Coffin, the chaplain of Yale University, for encouraging young people to resist the draft.

Exasperated by troubles in the field, American planners continued to escalate, with no effect. Peace talks in Paris stalled and the death toll on all sides increased. In 1968 criticism forced President Johnson to abandon his plans to run for a second term. Johnson's successor, Richard M. Nixon, who won a narrow victory on the basis of promises to end the war, expanded it instead. Student protests now ended in violence more often and avoiding the draft became so widespread that the system was changed in 1970.

After further talks in Paris, negotiations for a U.S. withdrawal were completed. The last American ground troops left by late 1972. Following cold war policy, the United States continued to back the South Vietnamese with aid and strategic bombing. In 1975, however, a major North Vietnamese offensive broke southern forces. The United States evacuated thousands of Americans and Vietnamese from the southern capital, Saigon, in April 1975. The refugee crisis of South Vietnam was not the only human disaster at the end of the war. The pro-Western government of Cambodia fell to a much more extreme communist movement, the Khmer Rhouge, which began a horrific campaign against its own people that left more than 5 million Cambodians dead. The Khmer Rhouge were overthrown only when the communist Vietnamese intervened in the name of political rivalry and regional stability. America's effort to contain Asian communism and prop up pro-Western governments in a variety of Southeast Asian states proved a failure.

A NEW WORLD ORDER

What is the "new world order"?

The early 1990s seemed to offer the opportunity for a new system of international relations. Western pundits hailed a "new world order" in which communism had collapsed because of the endurance and virtues of Western representative democracy and capitalism. Western states and the former communist world would now cooperate to build a more stable system of global politics, and to export the virtuous Western model to all corners of the world.

GEOPOLITICAL INTERVENTIONS

This vision was first tested in the most favorable circumstances. During the long Iran-Iraq War (1980–1990), Iraq's brutal dictator Saddam Hussein had committed thousands of political murders and used poison gas on rebellious populations inside Iraq, but received diplomatic support, financial backing, and military intelligence from both the Soviet Union and the United States in return for fighting against the Iranian revolutionary (and Shi'ite Islamic) government. After the end of that war, Iraq faced economic and social exhaustion. In an effort to revive his regime, Hussein sent his large, heavily armored army rolling into the small and oil-rich principality of Kuwait. Kuwait was taken in a day and Hussein, who possessed chemical weapons, plans for nuclear devices, and a large army, threatened to destabilize the entire region. Led by the United States, the oil dependent Western world and the threatened Arab states responded. Hussein was abandoned by his former Soviet patrons; the old opportunity to play one superpower off the other had disappeared. The United States succeeded in mobilizing an international coalition under the auspices of the United Nations to evict Iraq from Kuwait. After Vietnam, the professional American military had been reequipped with the most advanced weapons and trained intensively to defeat the well-equipped and organized Soviet forces in Europe. They had also been expecting a war over oil in the Middle East since at least 1973, when OPEC (the Organization of Petroleum Exporting Countries) had sharply increased oil prices, and 1974, when OPEC placed an embargo on petroleum exports to the West. Half a million American soldiers, sailors, and marines were sent to Saudi Arabia, backed by the Saudi army, armored divisions from Britain, France, and Egypt, and small contingents from many other nations. In a display of meticulous planning and superior firepower, they decimated the Iraqis from the air and destroyed the occupying army in four days. It did seem that there was a new order, based on a commonality of international interest, cooperation between the old superpowers, and the military leadership of the United States.

The next serious test of this model came in the East African state of Somalia. Endemic famines in the country were the direct result of its collapse into localized warlordism and clan warfare. The United Nations, led

The Iraqi Threat to Stability in the Middle East: The Case of Jordan. Left: In the wake of the Iraqi invasion and occupation of Kuwait, thousands of refugees fled from Kuwait to Jordan where they were stranded in tent cities. Added to the existing Palestinian refugee problem, this latest wave of displaced people placed an enormous burden on Jordan's fragile economy. Right: Large numbers of Jordanians and Palestinians rallied to Saddam Hussein's call for a "holy war" to free Arab soil of Western imperialists and their agents. Caught between Iraq and an international force led by a U.S. army of over 400,000 men and women, the government of King Hussein of Jordan faced the specter of revolution.

by the U.S. marines, intervened by force. Their first mission, feeding millions of starving peasants and ending banditry of the food supply, was a success. After that point, the international community exceeded its grasp. United Nations officials and a number of Western politicians and military leaders decided that Somalia needed a stable government on the Western model. Therefore the complex and ingrained warfare in the capital Mogadishu had to be stopped. The effort to do so produced anger among Somalis and resulted in a series of political failures and military ambushes that left dozens of peacekeepers dead, the United Nations humiliated, and the United States leery of using force for any purpose other than the defense of narrow American interests. This failed effort at nation building made both the UN and the United States hesitate in the face of the much more centralized, politically motivated genocide in Rwanda six months later, a clear betrayal of the principles of human rights and security on which the UN was founded.

> The nuclear threat of world destruction did not disappear with the breakup of the Soviet Union.

At the same time peacekeeping operations elsewhere foundered in Bosnia (see Chapter 31) and several African countries. Despite occasional successes such as the rebuilding of the shattered nation of Cambodia, the stationing of military observers to supervise parties who are unwilling to stop fighting has produced mixed results. The United Nations achieved more success by encouraging local nations to intervene directly—as did several West African countries, led by Nigeria, in Liberia in the 1990s, or Australia in newly independent East Timor in 1999—or by standing aside as the UN did during the conflict over Kosovo (see Chapter 31). Some local approaches have shown mixed results themselves; for example, Russia's failed effort to assert its Great Power authority in Chechnya. A more effective approach to resolving local conflicts, fought by militia bands that often include children, punctuated by atrocities, and fueled by smuggling such desirable goods as illegal drugs or diamonds to Western nations, has yet to be found. An approach that stems such conflicts before they start seems even further away.

NUCLEAR DISARMAMENT

Looming above all these issues and circumstances is the continuing threat of nuclear destruction. During the 1960s and 1970s, both the United States and the Soviet Union vacillated in their willingness to discuss arms control, let alone reduce their arsenals. Henry Kissinger, U.S. secretary of state under presidents Richard Nixon and Gerald Ford during the 1970s, proclaimed détente with the Russians as his goal and devoted much time to negotiations aimed at defusing potentially explosive areas of conflict between the two nations. Both countries hoped to curb the spread of nuclear weapons and to limit, if possible, the expansion of their own stockpiles. The Strategic Arms Limitation Treaty (SALT) talks, in which the Russians and Americans engaged during the 1970s and early 1980s, indicated mutual willingness to recognize and tackle the problem. Yet the talks produced little in the way of concrete agreement. President Ronald Reagan, who took office in 1981, denounced a second stage of the SALT negotiations during his campaign and pressed for dramatic increases in military budgets for sophisticated armaments, even as he proclaimed his devotion to the cause of nuclear disarmament. Yet in December 1987, despite continuing disagreement on other issues, the Soviet leader Mikhail Gorbachev and President Ronald Reagan signed a treaty in Washington eliminating all short-and medium-range nuclear missiles based in Europe.

The nuclear threat did not disappear with the breakup of the Soviet Union, although both the United States and the former Soviet states agreed to reduce their nuclear-arms stocks. China and Israel in particular continued to expand both their arsenals and the range of these deadliest weapons. Other countries, notably Iraq and Iran, also developed nuclear technology, and other nations have hoped to draw on resources freed up by the collapse of the Soviet Union to achieve a short route to a nuclear power. At the turn of the twenty-first century, both India and Pakistan conducted public nuclear tests, and border skirmishes between the two generated threats to use their growing nuclear arsenals. Each of these conflicts renewed the specter of general nuclear war that had seemed to subside in the 1990s.

THE POLITICAL AND ECONOMIC CRISIS IN AFRICA

Another region laboring with the legacies of colonialism was sub-Saharan Africa. A litany of troubles began with decolonization itself. Belgium, another colonial power, granted independence to the Congo (later Zaire) in 1960. The Belgian withdrawal left the colony a shambles, with crumbling roads and railroads and barely two dozen citizens with a university education. Competing political factions, choosing to play the United States and the Soviet Union off one another, began a civil war that raged for more than five years before a tenuous peace was reached. This fighting between the newly formed central government and the mineral-rich southeastern province of Katanga (later known as Shaba) continued to smolder into the 1980s with assistance from Angola-based Katangan refugees. The use of mercenaries, the murder of political figures, regular massacres of civilians, and the plundering of Zaire's tremendous mineral wealth in the name of local and international power politics became symbols for the pitfalls and cynical manipulation of the newly independent African states.

Political turmoil in Africa was compounded by massive economic decline in the 1970s; mounting oil prices and attendant inflation drove up the cost of Western technology, seed, and fertilizer. Recurring droughts in the 1980s and 1990s struck nearly every part of the continent, bringing starvation to many areas. African states had no choice but to shift priorities from development projects to importing goods for their swelling populations. But at the same time, falling world prices for agricultural commodities and metals diminished the market value of Africa's major exports. Devastating famines exacerbated tensions in drought-stricken areas, and the distribution of famine relief became an area for local power politics. Many government-sponsored corporations were inefficiently managed and became financial liabilities. Economic decline made it virtually impossible for these nations to maintain payments to Western financial institutions on debts incurred for development projects during the 1960s. Defaulting, in turn, limited their access to further loans.

These and other factors combined to make Africa at the end of the twentieth century an impoverished and strife-torn continent. Conflicts erupted in the Sudan and Chad between a Muslim north and a Christian and animist south. In Ethiopia war between the Marxist central government and the Islamic Eritreans led to Eritrean independence but also to hundreds of thousands of deaths: forced relocation of peoples exacerbated famines caused by drought and worsened by disease. In Angola and Zimbabwe there has been long-lasting con-

> Political turmoil in Africa was compounded by massive economic decline in the 1970s.

flict between the government and ethnic or regional revolutionary movements that fought in the independence struggle but were denied representation afterward. The early 1990s witnessed the further weakening of states that collapsed under the weight of failed economies and ethnic and clan warfare. In Somalia the fall of the dictatorship of Siad Barre plunged the country into anarchy and civil war. By mid-1992, more than three hundred thousand Somalians had died of starvation or war wounds. Similar political chaos prevailed in Liberia, where civil war claimed one hundred fifty thousand lives, and many more fled the country. In Rwanda and Burundi, ethnic slaughter left perhaps a million dead.

Those who fled to safety in neighboring Zaire (now called the Congo) were confronted in early 1997 by the collapse of that country's social and economic structure as well, and by political instability following the forced resignation of long-time dictator Mobutu Sese Seko. Mobutu's regime had been one of the most corrupt on the continent, backed unquestioningly by Western governments because of Zaire's vital uranium and industrial diamonds. Mobutu, famous for diverting foreign aid into his personal bank accounts, gave exiled African intellectuals and academics a word to define many of the regimes that replaced colonial rule—"kleptocracy," or government by theft of the nation's resources. After Mobuto's overthrow, those resources produced widespread fighting in Congo. This soon became the largest African conflict since the war in the same country during the 1960s, with half a dozen African states backing various factions, battling each other throughout the enormous country, looting its mineral resources, and producing only confusion, more bloodshed, and millions of refugees.

THE END OF APARTHEID

Undoubtedly the most explosive area of conflict on the African continent was the former British colony of South Africa, whose all-white minority government tenaciously fought off appeals from all quarters to relax its racial policy of apartheid. This policy enforced a separate and desperately inferior existence for the country's black and "colored" (or mixed-race) populations. Initially, nonwhite South Africans responded to apartheid with campaigns of passive resistance. Government-sponsored repression and violence, however, drove the African National Congress

Police Action in Johannesburg. In downtown Johannesburg the authorities disperse a group of black and white demonstrators who were protesting police actions in the huge Soweto ghetto. Over one thousand blacks were killed by police in Soweto in June 1976.

Change in South Africa. President F. W. de Klerk of the Republic of South Africa and Nelson Mandela, deputy president of the African National Congress, as they meet in May 1990 to open negotiations on the future of South Africa.

(ANC), led by Nelson Mandela, to adopt a more radical and violent strategy after 1960. The government responded by banning the ANC as a terrorist organization, hunting down and prosecuting militants, imprisoning Mandela in 1962, and clamping down on the personal liberties of all nonwhites.

Seeking ways to defuse domestic tensions and improve the South African image abroad, the government of Pieter W. Botha in the early 1980s began to liberalize social and economic policies. It authorized African labor unions to bargain collectively, desegregated some public facilities, and raised wages. Nearly 3 million blacks, however, were deprived of citizenship and sent to live in overcrowded "ethnic homelands." A new constitution adopted in 1984 conferred near-dictatorial powers on the president and continued to exclude black South Africans from political participation. As black South African opposition rose, Botha declared a state of emergency in mid-1985. By 1986 a wide range of nations, fearing a disastrous confrontation between the white minority and the black majority, joined in imposing severe economic sanctions upon South Africa, pressuring the government to reach a peaceful settlement with the black majority. Mandela's release from prison in 1990 (after more than twenty-seven years of

imprisonment) by Botha's successor, F. W. De Klerk, prompted the lifting of some of these sanctions. In March 1992 De Klerk and Mandela began to negotiate an end to apartheid. In May 1994, following elections in which all races participated, Mandela was chosen South Africa's first black president.

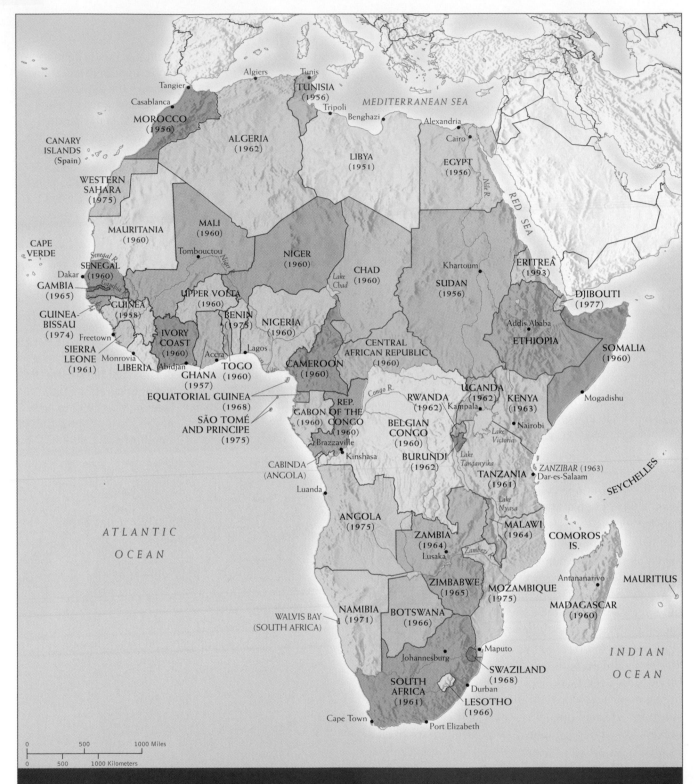

AFRICA IN 1997

How do the modern borders of African nations still bear the stamp of European colonization? What effect do you suspect this has had on ethnic tensions within these nations?

CHRONOLOGY

MAJOR DEVELOPMENTS IN AFRICA, 1952–PRESENT	
Egypt gains independence	1952
Congo gains independence	1960
Algeria gains independence	1962
Rhodesia gains independence	1965
Ethnic and tribal conflicts throughout Africa	1960s–present
Massive economic decline	1970s–1990s
Apartheid ends in South Africa	1992–1994

THE ARAB-ISRAELI CONFLICT

Achieving regional order has often seemed an impossible task in the most persistent trouble spot of the postwar world: the Middle East. The major conflicts have centered on the state of Israel, and on the volatile political mixture of lucrative oil reserves and an Islamic religious revival in some of the Arab countries. Many roots of the present troubles can be found in European imperialism during the nineteenth and early twentieth centuries—although a lasting solution to them can only lie with the peoples of the region itself.

Israel's independence was recognized in 1948 by a number of Western states that saw it as an outpost of Western culture that would counterbalance the large new Arab nations and the oil-rich states of the Southwest Asian desert. The nation was founded in warfare: first a three-way conflict among Jewish settlers, the Palestinian Arabs who had previously been the dominant population, and the British forces who had governed Palestine as a "mandate" since the First World War; next a war between the new state of Israel and its Arab neighbors in 1948–1949 (see Chapter 29). The 1956 war with Egypt, which gave Israel a strategic buffer in the Sinai desert, exacerbated tensions; Israel's defensiveness and Nasser's Pan-Arabism were a volatile mix. With Western aid, Israel embarked on a concerted program of industrialization to strengthen its economy. Yet conflicts with Israel's Arab neighbors continued. The 1967 Six-Day War ended in a decisive Israeli victory and Israeli occupation of the West Bank of the river Jordan. Years of border skirmishes followed until war erupted under the leadership of the Egyptian president Anwar Sadat. With the latest Soviet equipment, Egypt and Syria attacked in October 1973 during the Jewish high holy days. At first their assault was a well-planned, devastating success. A few Israeli armored units, however, held the line until massive supplies of replacement weapons were provided by the United States. The Israeli counterattack defeated the Syrians and pushed the Egyptians back to the Suez Canal, nearly provoking a conflict between the two sides' patrons, the United States and the Soviet Union. Within four years of the 1973 war, however, Sadat had decided that coexistence rather than the destruction of Israel was the long-term answer. In 1978, aided by the American president Jimmy Carter, Sadat and the conservative Israeli prime minister Menachem Begin brokered a peace. The Camp David accords ended the thirty year state of war between Israel and Egypt and produced an Israeli withdrawal from the Sinai, which

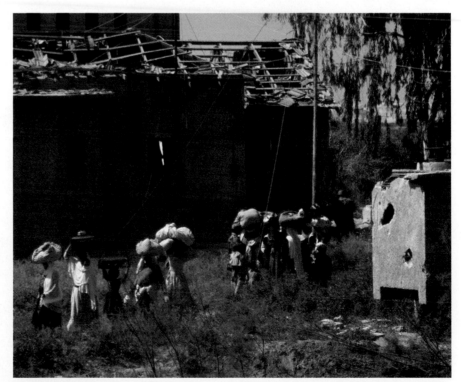

Palestinian Refugees. After the Six-Day War in 1967, more than 1.5 million Palestinians came under Israeli rule. Some refugees are seen here trying to escape the fighting, carrying whatever belongings they can.

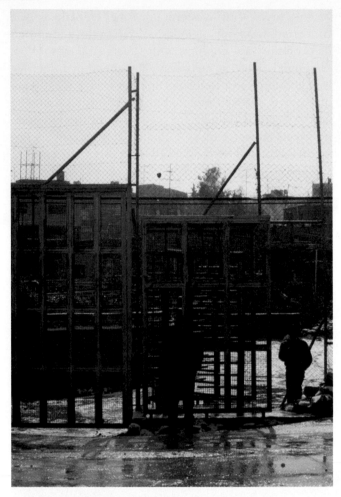

Checkpoint on the West Bank. Controlled by Jordan before passing to Israel after the Six-Day War, the West Bank is occupied primarily by Palestinians. Travel between the West Bank and Israel proper is limited by Israeli checkpoints.

had it occupied since 1967. Sadat was assassinated in 1981, partly for his role in the peace process.

The Camp David accords, however, did not end the longstanding conflict between Israelis and Palestinians. During the battles surrounding Israeli in 1948, many Palestinian Arabs, previously the dominant population of the region, had been displaced from their land and territory. The expulsions were a grim process, bringing massacres by both sides. Palestinians received a mixed reception from their Arab neighbors. Hostility sent them into refugee camps, where wretched living conditions heightened their grievances against the Israelis. Since the 1950s, Palestinians had been making guerrilla raids into Israel—raids often sponsored by the neighboring states. After the Six-Day War of 1967, the majority of Palestinians were moved into temporary residence in Jordan. It was there that the Palestine

Liberation Organization and the more radical Popular Front for the Liberation of Palestine were founded. After a 1968 attempt, aided by Syria, to overthrow the moderate Jordanian government of King Hussein, Hussein's forces expelled the Palestinians to Lebanon and Syria. There, for two decades, Palestinian and Israeli forces engaged in border raids and attempted assassinations.

The dynamic changed in the later 1980s, when the overcrowded and desperately impoverished Palestinians still living in Israeli-occupied territory on the West Bank and the Gaza Strip along the Mediterranean rebelled. (This rebellion came to be called the Intifada, or "shaking off," which lasted from 1987 to 1992. A second Intifada began in 2000.) The Palestinians were moved to anger by poverty and discrimination, by Israeli repression, and above all by the desire for statehood and the ongoing conflict over the Israeli conquest and expropriation of Palestinian land. This conflict between rock- and bomb-throwing Palestinian youths and Israeli security forces continued for years. In 1995, U.S. President Bill Clinton hosted a ceremony at which Arafat and the Israeli reformist prime minister Yitzak Rabin signed a peace agreement permitting self-rule for the Palestinians in the Gaza Strip and in Jericho on the West Bank. Promises to honor the agreements reached were undermined by the assassination of Rabin in 1995. The truce has been a fragile one. At the turn of the twenty-first century it appeared to collapse again, into a war of riots and bombings fought between neighbors.

CHRONOLOGY

MAJOR DEVELOPMENTS IN THE MIDDLE EAST, 1948–PRESENT

Israeli state formed	1948
First Arab-Israeli War	1948–1949
Egypt gains independence	1952
Israeli-Egyptian War	1956
Formation of OPEC	1960
Six-Day War; Israel occupies West Bank	1967
Second Arab-Israeli War	1973
Camp David peace accords	1978
The Iran-Iraq War	1980–1990
The Persian Gulf war	1991
Palestinians granted self-rule	1995
Israeli-Palestinian conflict continues	present

THE ARAB-ISRAELI WARS OF 1967 AND 1973

This map shows the changes in the political geography in the Middle East as a result of the Arab-Israeli conflicts of 1967 and 1973. What factors led to the Arab attacks on Israel in these two wars? Why did the Israelis wish to occupy the Sinai and West Bank regions at the end of the 1967 war? What problems did this create, and how might it have led to the conflict in 1973? Study the distribution of Israeli-occupied and Egyptian-occupied territory at the end of the 1973 war. Why was the resolution of the Sinai problem considered a top priority by many political figures in the West?

OPEC AND WORLD OIL

The other tension in the region has centered on Western dependence on oil. After the Second World War, it became much less costly for the West to tap the vast oil reserves of the Middle East, either through Western companies or arrangements with local nations, than to fuel the West's growing dependence on oil from other sources. The world's major oil producers, most of them former colonies or client states of the Western empires, banded together in a cartel to take advantage of this resource so necessary to the industrial world. The Organization of Petroleum Exporting Countries (OPEC) was formed in 1960 to regulate the production and pricing of crude oil. During the 1970s, it assumed an increasingly militant posture under the leadership of its Middle

Eastern Arab members. There had already been a brief embargo of oil to Europe after the Suez invasion of 1956 (see above), and Arab politicians understood that their "black gold" was a powerful bargaining tool in dealing with Europe and the superpowers. After the 1973 Arab-Israeli war, another embargo sparked spiraling inflation and economic troubles in Western nations, demonstrating again the power of oil as political leverage. Western nations tempered their support of Israel and designed their policies toward the PLO at least in part because of their continuing need for oil.

The mid-1980s brought new difficulties for OPEC. Overproduction, coupled with a decreasing demand for oil caused by economic recession in Western Europe and the United States, made it impossible for the OPEC countries to maintain uniformly high prices. But the resulting price reductions did not necessarily benefit Western economies. Many oil-producing nations had borrowed large sums of money from Western financial institutions in the 1970s—and used oil as collateral. Falling oil prices created financial crises for some of those nations—Mexico, for example—which threatened to default on loans. In the Middle East, as in the other OPEC regions, the wealth generated by oil produced power struggles and resentments within and between nations with oil reserves. It also fueled debate within the Arab world about the consequences of modernization. The central question was whether Middle Eastern nations should pursue ideals based on nationalism and self-sufficiency—one aim of Pan-Arabism—or whether they should strive for industrialization and modernization on the Western model. As far as the West and the world are concerned, however, the problems of oil production and pricing illustrate how the problems of the world economy and postcolonial diplomacy are linked.

The armed conflicts that spread around the globe after 1945 had two origins. The first was decolonization, or the emergence of new, independent nations. The second lay with the cold war. Often the two were intertwined as the superpowers sought to arm and influence rival groups in local conflicts. Despite the local origins of these conflicts, they almost always produced international consequences. That dynamic has not ended with the collapse of the Soviet Union and the crumbling of the cold war edifice. But the international consequences of local struggles are now less predictable. Nor is it clear what overarching structures of international relations will replace superpower rivalry. This is but one question about the future of a globalizing world.

TROUBLES AND TRANSFORMATIONS AFTER THE TURN OF A CENTURY

What are the major challenges for the twenty-first century?

Historians are loath to single out moments or trends in the present, even more so to pronounce them significant in terms of the future. Nevertheless, a number of important issues—the global environment, science and technology, genetics, the effects of population growth and new patterns of trade—can be identified as important in the moment. Taken together, they may give some sense of where the world at the twenty-first century has come from, if not necessarily where it is going. These developments arise from historical trends—industrialization, imperialism, urbanization, and globalization—that we have discussed in the preceding chapters.

THE GLOBAL ENVIRONMENT

"We still talk in terms of conquest," said the pioneering writer and scientist Rachel Carson in 1962 of Americans' relationship to nature. "We still haven't become mature enough to think of ourselves as only a tiny part of a vast and incredible universe." Carson's *Silent Spring* (1962) stands among the most influential books of the postwar world. Carson herself was an unusual woman: She grew up poor in rural Pennsylvania, supported her parents through the Great Depression, and attended a women's college and then Johns Hopkins University only by dint of her mother's scrambling to get her scholarships. She was both a gifted scientist and an eloquent writer. She gathered much of the material for her several books by working with the government's Fish and Wildlife Service and with other naturalists studying the effects of DDT and pesticides on birds and other wildlife. The title *Silent Spring* warned of a future in which the warbling of birds would not be heard. Carson not only dramatized the issues, she also insisted that the public be educated, so that environmental questions could become public political matters. She borrowed a phrase from a French biologist: "The obligation to endure gives us the right to know."

Carson's sense of urgency, and that of the international environmental movement, grow out of assess-

The Exxon *Valdez* Oil Spill, Prince William Sound, 1989. Above: the contents of 270,000 barrels of crude oil coat the water and shoreline of southern Alaska. Below: a loon, smothered by oil.

Environmental Degradation. Intentional flooding makes it easier for rainforest trees to be felled and logged, but causes severe environmental damage.

ments of the environmental damage wrought by industry and development. That damage includes poisoning the atmosphere and contaminating oceans, rivers, and lakes with toxic wastes—all of which, simply, devalue the land and sea. The excessive construction of dams causes the silting of rivers and the accumulation of nitrates at a faster rate than the sur-

rounding soil can absorb. Modern technology has also introduced an abundant variety of wastes: carbon monoxide, sulfur dioxide, and nitrogen oxide. In addition to pesticides, Carson's subject, there is the fallout of nuclear weapons testing. As the nature and gravity of these problems have become apparent, governments have been pressured to take preventive and remedial action.

Other environmental issues commanding attention in the 1990s include the continued destruction of global rain forests, with the threatened extinction of plant and animal species, and the problem of global warming due to depletion of the ozone layer of the atmosphere. In May 1990 a panel of thirty-nine nations concluded that, if the warming trend is not checked, rising sea levels will inundate Bangladesh, the Netherlands, and numerous other coastal areas and islands. This slow but detectable climatic change is directly linked to the accumulation of carbon dioxide gas. Some 5.6 billion tons of CO_2 are discharged into the atmosphere every year as a result of the burning of fossil fuels and of the annual destruction of more than 40 million acres of tropical forest. A parallel hazard lies in the depletion of the ozone layer through chemical reaction with chlorofluorocarbons (CFCs), used in acrosol sprays and refrigerants. Destruction of the ozone layer would expose living creatures to damaging radiation from the sun's ultraviolet rays. Environmentally induced changes in wind patterns have also produced catastrophic effects. New transatlantic stratospheric currents annually dump millions of tons of rich West African topsoil in Brazil. This uncontrollable phenomenon is enlarging the desert area of West Africa. Despite an international conference on such issues in June 1992 in Rio de Janeiro, international response to these problems continues to be tentative and conservative.

POPULATION GROWTH

A close link exists between the problems of environment and the population explosion occurring throughout the world. It has been accompanied by vast and rapid urbanization in Latin America, India, China, and Southeast Asia, among

Erosion and Overpopulation in Brazil. The houses and shacks crammed together on this hillside not only are overcrowded with families, but also are causing the soil to erode. Neither humans nor wildlife can survive long under such precarious conditions.

other areas. Indeed, if population and the growth of centralized cities had not increased alarmingly in recent years, environmental problems might have passed unnoticed. Calcutta now has a population of 12.9 million, compared with 3 million in 1961. Tokyo has grown from 5 million to over 28.5 million in little more than thirty years. The total population of the earth two thousand years ago was roughly 250 million. More than sixteen centuries passed before another quarter billion were added to the total. The human population of the globe did not touch 1 billion until 1860. From then on the increase became dangerously rapid. By 2001 the earth's population had passed 6 billion.

The effects of the demographic revolution have been most conspicuous in the underdeveloped nations of Central and South America, Africa, and Asia. Whereas the population of the world as a whole will double, at present rates of increase, in thirty-five years, that of Central and South America will double in only twenty-six years. The population of Asia (excluding the USSR) grew from 813 million in 1900 to approximately 2.9 billion in 1986—approximately 60 percent of the world's population. A situation in which the poorest nations are also the most populated promises enormous inequalities in the distribution of wealth and resources.

SCIENTIFIC FRONTIERS

Perhaps the single most important discovery ever made about human biology occurred in 1953, when the Englishman F. H. C. Crick and the American James D. Watson further unlocked the mysteries of genetic inheritance that had been first explored by Gregor Mendel at the end of the nineteenth century. Crick and Watson successfully analyzed deoxyribonucleic acid, or DNA, the chemical molecular structure that occurs in the nuclei of cells. They discovered that DNA is composed of smaller molecules of four different kinds, linked together in spiral chains. The arrangement of these molecules in each cell forms a distinct chemical message that determines the character of the genes and therefore of the human organism of which they are a part. The knowledge gained through analysis of DNA has enabled scientists and doctors to understand the causes of hereditary disease and also, by altering a patient's body chemistry, to prevent it. Despite the great benefits that have resulted from this recent discovery, scientists and others have warned that an understanding of the workings of DNA could lead to dangerous tampering with the genetic processes, as, for example, in attempts to produce artificially a breed of more "perfect" human beings. Indeed, in 1997, scientists in Scotland revealed the successful cloning of a sheep. Since then, several competing groups of scientists have completed the first important steps in mapping the human genome, the complete patchwork of genetic chemistry laid out in human DNA. The cloning of a sheep and the "road map" of human genetics are tentative first steps, the beginnings of a profound change in our understanding of, and power over, the human body. Genetic research may produce advances, revolutions, disasters, and transformations that we simply cannot foresee. It is, however, likely to produce slow but steady alterations in human politics, culture, and society, the likes of which have not been seen since the Industrial Revolution. Indeed, retooling the body chemistry of humans and other animals may far outstrip the steel mill and the steam engine.

Medicine has made tremendous advances since the turn of the twentieth century; several discoveries of great importance have enabled scientists to understand more clearly the ways in which the human body receives and transmits disease. The discovery of viruses was the result of experimentation conducted chiefly by the American biochemist Wendell Stanley in the 1930s. Viruses, microscopic organisms that show signs of life only when inside living cells, cause many human diseases, including measles, poliomyelitis (infantile paralysis), and rabies. Not until the nature of viruses was understood could scientists begin to develop means of treating and preventing the virus-induced illnesses in human beings.

In the 1930s, too, the Englishman Sir Alexander Fleming discovered the first of the antibiotics, penicillin. Penicillin turned out to be a drug that could produce spectacular results in the treatment of pneumonia, syphilis, peritonitis, tetanus, and countless other previously fatal sicknesses. Yet new bacterial strains have proved resistant to treatment; tuberculosis has resurfaced as a major world health threat and the Ebola virus has thus far been immune to effective treatment.

Vaccines, a way of preventing disease, have been available for centuries—indeed the French philosophe Voltaire considered the smallpox vaccine one of the "enlightened" aspects of English everyday life. Edward Jenner (1749–1823) did much of the work in improving that vaccine. But not until the 1950s were vaccines found that could protect people from diseases such as mumps, measles, and cholera. One of the most exciting breakthroughs occurred with the development of an inoculation against poliomyelitis by the American Dr. Jonas Salk in 1955. Still to be discovered are effective agents for the successful treatment of two of the world's most deadly killers, heart disease and cancer, and of a recent and potentially more dangerous worldwide plague, acquired immune deficiency syndrome (AIDS). The AIDS virus attacks the body's immune system, thus making it prey to any number of deadly diseases and infections. Unlike the victims of heart disease and cancer, no AIDS patient has ever been cured.

Science has brought alternative sources of energy, and with them both hope and unease. Some progress has been made in the development of atomic power as an alternative source of domestic and industrial fuel. But the dangers of radiation and nuclear waste as byproducts suggest that this scheme may prove of limited value. During the late 1970s, when the West's supplies of oil were threatened, heated debate continued between proponents of atomic power and those who argued in favor of other energy forms—among them solar—as safer and cheaper alternatives. Nuclear power has proven expensive and sometimes dangerous in practice. In 1986, a poorly maintained reactor at Chernobyl, in the former Soviet Union, produced the worst nuclear accident ever recorded, poisoning animals as far away as Norway with radioactive waste carried on wind currents. Other alternatives, such as more extensive use of solar power and liquid natural gas, have remained underdeveloped. Fuel cell technology combining gasoline and electric or water power is in its infancy.

Meanwhile, scientists working for private industry made use of discoveries in atomic physics to pioneer the field of electronics. Electronics derives from that branch of physics that deals with the behavior and effects of electrons, or negatively charged constituents within the atom. Electronic devices have multiplied in staggering profusion since the Second World War. Undoubtedly the electronic invention that has produced the greatest change in the everyday lives of men and women around the world has been the combination of the personal computer and the Internet, which have, with no exaggeration, revolutionized communication and social interactions, giving new meaning to the term "global village." When Chinese demonstrators rallied against the repressive Chinese regime in Tiananmen Square in 1989 they learned of the global response to their resistance by means of fax machines. The world's systems of communication and storehouses of knowledge have been transformed by links between personal, corporate, and public centers of information stored electronically and kept constantly in motion along phone lines. How the Internet will restructure economic transactions is the source of much speculation, and the rise and fall of considerable fortunes.

ECONOMIC TRANSFORMATIONS

New technologies and scientific discoveries have usually had varying and often contradictory effects. Technological unemployment has become an important problem for the modern world. Though new industries have absorbed many workers, others were displaced by automation. The demand for skilled labor remained high, but so-called entry-level jobs performed by the unskilled were fast disappearing. The mechanization of agriculture also eliminated thousands of jobs for unskilled and uneducated workers. In those industries where human beings are still required—clothing, furniture, and the assembling and packaging of machinery, for example—transnational corporations continue to shift their operations to countries of the developing world, where labor remains cheap. This creates unemployment and consequent worker resentment in the traditional manufacturing centers of Western Europe and North America. At the same time, corporations channel profits into more technology and financial investments, rather than increased pay for their employees.

At the same time, the governments of most developing countries have attempted with varying degrees of success to pursue the twin goals of industrialization and modernization. They have been encouraged in this by the governments of the West. Transnational corporations with headquarters in western Europe or the United States have also been more than willing to invest capital in parts of the world where manufacturing costs can be kept to a minimum because labor is cheap, or where valuable natural resources can be extracted and processed profitably for the same reason. Such practices have brought prosperity to an increasingly large middle class in countries such as Indonesia, South Korea, and Venezuela, at a cost. In 1984, for example, a gas plant owned by the U.S. chemical company Union Carbide in Bhopal, India, leaked toxic material that killed more than eight thousand people and injured a further one hundred fifty thousand. As a consequence of the North American Free Trade Agreement (NAFTA), signed in 1993 by Canada, the United States, and Mexico, factories financed by transnationals sprang up in northern Mexico, where demand for employment guaranteed a low wage scale. The rapid construction of those factories was not matched by the provisions of adequate environmental safeguards or decent housing, health, and educational facilities for workers and their families. International oil and mining corporations and fast-food giants have not hesitated to destroy vast areas of tropical rain forest or to threaten the very existence of ancient tribal civilizations as they have moved into parts of the world hitherto untouched by the West.

In one area of manufacture, however, the developing world has continued to respond to a steady and immensely profitable market in the West: the production of opium, heroin, and cocaine is a thriving industry in countries such as Colombia, Myanmar (formerly Burma), and Malaysia. Though the trade in drugs is illegal, the fragile economies of those countries where they are produced have encouraged governments to turn a blind eye to the devastation such multibillion-dollar trafficking brings in its wake. As nations attempt to organize and regulate the terms of truly global trade through such institutions as the World Trade Organization, they are assailed by critics on all sides: environmentalists, trade unionists, economists, nationalists, and activists for displaced indigenous

Bhopal. This Union Carbide factory in Bhopal, India, was the site of a catastrophic poisonous-gas leak in 1984.

peoples. Agreeing on acceptable ground rules for a global economy, much less building a working framework for its daily operation, is a volatile and complicated subject.

CONCLUSION

Science and technology provide no easy answers to the problems of the world. Neither does history. History does not repeat itself, and it teaches no simple lessons. The untidy and contradictory evidence that historians discover in the archives rarely yields unblemished heroes or unvarnished villains. Instead, good history reveals to us the complex process and dynamics of change over time. Though it cannot enable us to predict the future, it helps us understand that many layers of the past that formed and constrain us and our present world. At the same time, history shows again and again that these constraints never preordain what happens next or how we can make the history of the future.

SELECTED READINGS

Achebe, Chinua. *Things Fall Apart.* Expanded edition with notes. Portsmouth, N.H., 1996. An annotated edition of the now classic novel about postcolonial Africa.

Aust, Stefan. *The Baader-Meinhof Group: The Inside Story of a Phenomenon.* London, 1987. Thorough and engaging account of the history of the Red Army Faction terrorist organization in Germany.

Bates, Robert H. *Essays on the Political Economy of Rural Africa.* Cambridge, 1983. An excellent study of the problems of food production in contemporary Africa.

Betts, Raymond. *France and Decolonization.* London, 1991.

Brown, Judith. *Modern India: Origins of an Asian Democracy,* 2d ed. New York, 1994. The standard work on the development of the modern Indian state and politics.

Bhatia, Krishan. *The Ordeal of Nationhood: A Social Study of India since Independence, 1947–1970.* New York, 1971. Informed and objective account of India's problems.

Butterfield, Fox. *China: Alive in the Bitter Sea,* rev. ed. New York, 1990. Poignant and critical.

Caputo, Philip. *A Rumor of War.* New York, 1977. The best memoir of the American experience in the Vietnam War.

Clayton, Anthony. *The Wars of French Decolonization.* London, 1994.

Cooper, Frederick, and Ann Laura Stoler, eds. *Tensions of Empire: Colonial Cultures in a Bourgeois World.* Berkeley, 1997.

Coetzee, J. M. *Waiting for the Barbarians.* London, 1980. A searing critique of South Africa by a brilliant Afrikaaner novelist.

Darwin, John. *Britain and Decolonization: The Retreat from Empire in the Postwar World.* New York, 1988. Best overall survey.

Ehrlich, Paul R. *The Population Bomb.* New York, 1968. Discusses the threat of overpopulation.

FitzGerald, Frances. *Fire in the Lake: The Vietnamese and the Americans in Vietnam.* Boston, 1972.

Gamow, George. *Thirty Years that Shook Physics.* New York, 1966. A lucid account by a physicist.

Heilbroner, Robert L. *An Inquiry into the Human Prospect.* New York, 1980. Optimistic assessment of the durability of Western cultural values.

Horne, Alistair. *A Savage War of Peace: Algeria, 1954–1962.* New York, 1978. A very dated analysis, but still one of the few introductions in English.

Laqeur, Walter. *The Age of Terrorism.* Boston, 1987. A look at the way terrorism spread across the world in the 1970s and 1980s.

Lukacs, John. *The End of the Twentieth Century and the End of the Modern Age.* New York, 1991. Populism, nationalism, and state authority as they clash in contemporary society.

Lyotard, Jean-François. *The Postmodern Condition: A Report of Knowledge.* Minneapolis, 1984. Important analysis of the effects of communications technology.

Mandela, Nelson. *Long Walk to Freedom: The Autobiography of Nelson Mandela.* Boston, 1994. By the long-imprisoned leader of the African National Congress.

Medvedev, Zhores. *The Legacy of Chernobyl.* New York, 1990. A study of the disaster and its aftermath.

Myrdal, Gunnar. *Against the Stream: Critical Essays on Economics.* New York, 1972. Offers pertinent comments on the problems of the developing world.

Ngugi wa Thiong'o. *Petals of Blood.* New York, 1977. A scathing critique of neocolonialism in Kenya by Africa's best-known novelist.

Penley, Constance, and Andrew Ross, eds. *Technoculture.* Minneapolis, 1991. Essays on the technological world of the 1980s and 1990s.

Proctor, Robert. *Cancer Wars: The Politics Behind What We Know and Don't Know about Causes and Trends.* New York, 1994. The relationship among industrialism, the environment, politics, and disease.

Ross, Kristin. *Fast Cars, Clean Bodies: Decolonization and the Reordering of French Culture.* Boston, 1996. Explores the relationship between Americanization and decolonization.

Shilts, Randy. *And the Band Played On: Politics, People, and the AIDS Epidemic.* New York, 1987. An impassioned attack on the individuals and governments that refused to come to grips with the AIDS epidemic.

Yang, Rae. *Spider Eaters: A Memoir.* Berkeley, 1997. Recollections of a woman who lived through the Chinese Cultural Revolution.

Young, Marilyn B. *The Vietnam Wars, 1945–1990.* New York, 1991. Excellent account of the war and its repercussions.

Rulers of Principal States

The Carolingian Dynasty

Pepin of Heristal, Mayor of the Palace, 687–714
Charles Martel, Mayor of the Palace, 715–741
Pepin III, Mayor of the Palace, 741–751; King, 751–768
Charlemagne, King, 768–814; Emperor, 800–814
Louis the Pious, Emperor, 814–840

West Francia
Charles the Bald, King, 840–877; Emperor, 875–877
Louis II, King, 877–879
Louis III, King, 879–882
Carloman, King, 879–884

Middle Kingdoms
Lothair, Emperor, 840–855
Louis (Italy), Emperor, 855–875
Charles (Provence), King, 855–863
Lothair II (Lorraine), King, 855–869

East Francia
Ludwig, King, 840–876
Carloman, King, 876–880
Ludwig, King, 876–882
Charles the Fat, Emperor, 876–887

Holy Roman Emperors

Saxon Dynasty
Otto I, 962–973
Otto II, 973–983
Otto III, 983–1002
Henry II, 1002–1024

Franconian Dynasty
Conrad II, 1024–1039
Henry III, 1039–1056
Henry IV, 1056–1106
Henry V, 1106–1125
Lothair II (Saxony), 1125–1137

Hohenstaufen Dynasty
Conrad III, 1138–1152
Frederick I (Barbarossa), 1152–1190
Henry VI, 1190–1197
Philip of Swabia, 1198–1208 } Rivals
Otto IV (Welf), 1198–1215
Frederick II, 1220–1250
Conrad IV, 1250–1254

Interregnum, 1254–1273

Emperors from Various Dynasties
Rudolf I (Habsburg), 1273–1291
Adolf (Nassau), 1292–1298
Albert I (Habsburg), 1298–1308
Henry VII (Luxemburg), 1308–1313
Ludwig IV (Wittelsbach), 1314–1347
Charles IV (Luxemburg), 1347–1378
Wenceslas (Luxemburg), 1378–1400
Rupert (Wittelsbach), 1400–1410
Sigismund (Luxemburg), 1410–1437

Habsburg Dynasty
Albert II, 1438–1439
Frederick III, 1440–1493
Maximilian I, 1493–1519
Charles V, 1519–1556
Ferdinand I, 1556–1564
Maximilian II, 1564–1576
Rudolf II, 1576–1612

Matthias, 1612–1619
Ferdinand II, 1619–1637
Ferdinand III, 1637–1657
Leopold I, 1658–1705
Joseph I, 1705–1711
Charles VI, 1711–1740

Charles VII (not a Habsburg), 1742–1745
Francis I, 1745–1765
Joseph II, 1765–1790
Leopold II, 1790–1792
Francis II, 1792–1806

RULERS OF FRANCE FROM HUGH CAPET

CAPETIAN DYNASTY
Hugh Capet, 987–996
Robert II, 996–1031
Henry I, 1031–1060
Philip I, 1060–1108
Louis VI, 1108–1137
Louis VII, 1137–1180
Philip II (Augustus), 1180–1223
Louis VIII, 1223–1226
Louis IX (St. Louis), 1226–1270
Philip III, 1270–1285
Philip IV, 1285–1314
Louis X, 1314–1316
Philip V, 1316–1322
Charles IV, 1322–1328

VALOIS DYNASTY
Philip VI, 1328–1350
John, 1350–1364
Charles V, 1364–1380
Charles VI, 1380–1422
Charles VII, 1422–1461
Louis XI, 1461–1483
Charles VIII, 1483–1498
Louis XII, 1498–1515
Francis I, 1515–1547

Henry II, 1547–1559
Francis II, 1559–1560
Charles IX, 1560–1574
Henry III, 1574–1589

BOURBON DYNASTY
Henry IV, 1589–1610
Louis XIII, 1610–1643
Louis XIV, 1643–1715
Louis XV, 1715–1774
Louis XVI, 1774–1792

AFTER 1792
First Republic, 1792–1799
Napoleon Bonaparte, First Consul, 1799–1804
Napoleon I, Emperor, 1804–1814
Louis XVIII (Bourbon dynasty), 1814–1824
Charles X (Bourbon dynasty), 1824–1830
Louis Philippe, 1830–1848
Second Republic, 1848–1852
Napoleon III, Emperor, 1852–1870
Third Republic, 1870–1940
Péain regime, 1940–1944
Provisional government, 1944–1946
Fourth Republic, 1946–1958
Fifth Republic, 1958–

RULERS OF ENGLAND

ANGLO-SAXON DYNASTY
Alfred the Great, 871–899
Edward the Elder, 899–924
Ethelstan, 924–939
Edmund I, 939–946
Edred, 946–955
Edwy, 955–959
Edgar, 959–975
Edward the Martyr, 975–978
Ethelred the Unready, 978–1016

Canute, 1016–1035 (Danish Nationality)
Harold I, 1035–1040
Hardicanute, 1040–1042
Edward the Confessor, 1042–1066
Harold II, 1066

HOUSE OF NORMANDY
William I (the Conqueror), 1066–1087
William II, 1087–1100

Henry I, 1100–1135
Stephen, 1135–1154

HOUSE OF PLANTAGENET
Henry II, 1154–1189
Richard I, 1189–1199
John, 1199–1216
Henry III, 1216–1272
Edward I, 1272–1307
Edward II, 1307–1327
Edward III, 1327–1377
Richard II, 1377–1399

HOUSE OF LANCASTER
Henry IV, 1399–1413
Henry V, 1413–1422
Henry VI, 1422–1461

HOUSE OF YORK
Edward IV, 1461–1483
Edward V, 1483
Richard III, 1483–1485

HOUSE OF TUDOR
Henry VII, 1485–1509
Henry VIII, 1509–1547
Edward VI, 1547–1553
Mary, 1553–1558
Elizabeth I, 1558–1603

HOUSE OF STUART
James I, 1603–1625
Charles I, 1625–1649

COMMONWEALTH AND PROTECTORATE, 1649–1659

HOUSE OF STUART RESTORED
Charles II, 1660–1685
James II, 1685–1688
William III and Mary II, 1689–1694
William III alone, 1694–1702
Anne, 1702–1714

HOUSE OF HANOVER
George I, 1714–1727
George II, 1727–1760
George III, 1760–1820
George IV, 1820–1830
William IV, 1830–1837
Victoria, 1837–1901

HOUSE OF SAXE-COBURG-GOTHA
Edward VII, 1901–1910
George V, 1910–1917

HOUSE OF WINDSOR
George V, 1917–1936
Edward VIII, 1936
George VI, 1936–1952
Elizabeth II, 1952–

RULERS OF AUSTRIA AND AUSTRIA-HUNGARY

*Maximilian I (Archduke), 1493–1519
*Charles V, 1519–1556
*Ferdinand I, 1556–1564
*Maximilian II, 1564–1576
*Rudolf II, 1576–1612
*Matthias, 1612–1619
*Ferdinand II, 1619–1637
*Ferdinand III, 1637–1657
*Leopold I, 1658–1705
*Joseph I, 1705–1711
*Charles VI, 1711–1740
Maria Theresa, 1740–1780

*also bore title of Holy Roman Emperor

*Joseph II, 1780–1790
*Leopold II, 1790–1792
*Francis II, 1792–1835 (Emperor of Austria as Francis I after 1804)
Ferdinand I, 1835–1848
Francis Joseph, 1848–1916 (after 1867 Emperor of Austria and King of Hungary)
Charles I, 1916–1918 (Emperor of Austria and King of Hungary)
Republic of Austria, 1918–1938 (dictatorship after 1934)
Republic restored, under Allied occupation, 1945–1956
Free Republic, 1956–
*Frederick I, 1701–1713
*Frederick William I, 1713–1740
*Frederick II (the Great), 1740–1786

RULERS OF PRUSSIA AND GERMANY

*Frederick William II, 1786–1797
*Frederick William III,1797–1840
*Frederick William IV, 1840–1861
*William I, 1861–1888 (German Emperor after 1871)
Frederick III, 1888
*William II, 1888–1918
Weimar Republic, 1918–1933
Third Reich (Nazi Dictatorship), 1933–1945

*Kings of Prussia

Allied occupation, 1945–1952
Division into Federal Republic of Germany in west and
    German Democratic Republic in east, 1949–1991
Federal Republic of Germany (united), 1991–

RULERS OF RUSSIA

Ivan III, 1462–1505
Vasily III, 1505–1533
Ivan IV, 1533–1584
Theodore I, 1534–1598
Boris Godunov, 1598–1605
Theodore II,1605
Vasily IV, 1606–1610
Michael, 1613–1645
Alexius, 1645–1676
Theodore III, 1676–1682
Ivan V and Peter I, 1682–1689
Peter I (the Great), 1689–1725
Catherine I, 1725–1727
Peter II, 1727–1730

Anna, 1730–1740
Ivan VI, 1740–1741
Ellzabeth, 1741–1762
Peter III, 1762
Catherine II (the Great), 1762–1796
Paul, 1796–1801
Alexander I,1801–1825
Nicholas I, 1825–1855
Alexander II,1855–1881
Alexander III, 1881–1894
Nicholas II, 1894–1917
Soviet Republic, 1917–1991
Russian Federation, 1991–

RULERS OF SPAIN

Ferdinand { and Isabella, 1479–1504
          { and Philip I, 1504–1506
          { and Charles I, 1506–1516
Charles I (Holy Roman Emperor Charles V), 1516–1556
Philip II, 1556–1598
Philip III, 1598–1621
Philip IV, 1621–1665
Charles II, 1665–1700
Philip V, 1700–1746
Ferdinand VI, 1746–1759
Charles III, 1759–1788
Charles IV, 1788–1808

Ferdinand VII, 1808
Joseph Bonaparte, 1808–1813
Ferdinand VII (restored), 1814–1833
Isabella II, 1833–1868
Republic, 1868–1870
Amadeo, 1870–1873
Republic, 1873–1874
Alfonso XII, 1874–1885
Alfonso XIII, 1886–1931
Republic, 1931–1939
Fascist Dictatorship, 1939–1975
Juan Carlos I, 1975–

RULERS OF ITALY

Victor Emmanuel II, 1861–1878
Humbert I, 1878–1900
Victor Emmanuel III, 1900–1946

Fascist Dictatorship, 1922-1943 (maintained in northern
   Italy until 1945)
Humbert II, May 9–June 13, 1946
Republic, 1946–

PROMINENT POPES

Silvester I, 314–335
Leo I, 440–461
Gelasius I, 492–496
Gregory I, 590–604
Nicholas I, 858–867
Silvester II, 999–1003
Leo IX, 1049–1054
Nicholas II, 1058–1061
Gregory VII, 1073–1085
Urban II, 1088–1099
Paschal II, 1099–1118
Alexander III, 1159–1181
Innocent III, 1198–1216
Gregory IX, 1227–1241
Innocent IV, 1243–1254
Boniface VIII, 1294–1303
John XXII, 1316–1334
Nicholas V, 1447–1455
Pius II, 1458–1464

Alexander VI, 1492–1503
Julius II, 1503–1513
Leo X, 1513–1521
Paul III, 1534–1549
Paul IV, 1555–1559
Sixtus V, 1585–1590
Urban VIII, 1623–1644
Gregory XVI, 1831–1846
Pius IX, 1846–1878
Leo XIII, 1878–1903
Pius X, 1903–1914
Benedict XV, 1914–1922
Pius XI, 1922–1939
Pius XII, 1939–1958
John XXIII, 1958–1963
Paul VI, 1963–1978
John Paul I, 1978
John Paul II, 1978–

TEXT CREDITS

Chapter 1: 23 (top): from *The Epic of Gilgamesh*. Copyright 1997, Bolchazy-Carducci Publishers. 35: from *The Egyptian Book of the Dead*. Copyright 1967, Dover Books. 40: from *Readings in Ancient History: Thought and Experience from Gilgamesh to St. Augustine*. Copyright 1995, Houghton Mifflin.

Chapter 2: 53: from *Law: A Treasury of Art and Literature*. Copyright 1990, Beaux Arts Editions. 66: from *History and the Homeric Iliad*. Copyright 1959, University of California Press. 76 (top): from *Ancient Near Eastern Texts Relating to the Bible* (3rd Edition). Copyright 1969, Princeton University Press.

Chapter 3: 87: from *Ancient Near Eastern Texts Relating to the Bible* (3rd Edition). Copyright 1969, Princeton University Press. 99: from *Ancient Records of Assyria and Babylonia*. Copyright 1926-1927, University of Chicago Press.

Chapter 4: 116: from *Iliad*. Copyright 1990, Penguin Books. 124: from *Herodotus*. Copyright 1987, University of Chicago Press. 145: from *The Clouds*. Copyright 1973, Penguin Books. 146: from *The Landmark Thucydides*. Copyright 1995, Landmark Press.

Chapter 5: 159 (top): from *Isocrates*. Copyright 1995, Harvard University Press. 159 (bottom): from *Demosthenes*. Copyright 1930, Harvard University Press. 171: from *The Idylls of Theocritis*. Copyright 1988, Carcanet.

Chapter 6: 187: from *The Early History of Rome*. Copyright 1960, Penguin Books. 197: from *Life of Lucullus*. Copyright 1992, Modern Library. 204: from *Roman Civilization, Sourcebook II: The Empire*. Copyright 1966, Harper and Row. 205: from *Tacitus: The Annals of Imperial Rome*. Copyright 1989, Penguin Books. 209: from *Juvenal. The Sixteen Satires*. Copyright 1974, Penguin Books.

Chapter 7: 238: from *Didascalia Apostolorum Corpus Scriptorum Christianorum Orientalium*. Copyright 1979, Peters. 239: from *Western Societies: A Documentary History*. Copyright 1984, Knopf 243: from *Sidonius, Poems and Letters*. Copyright 1980, Harvard University Press.

Chapter 8: 274: from *The Jews of Arab Lands: A History and Source Book*. Copyright 1979, Philadelphia Jewish Publication Society. 293: from *The Reign of Charlemagne*. Copyright 1975, Edward Arnold.

Chapter 9: 315: from *Byzantium: Church, Society, and Civilization Seen through Contemporary Eyes*. Copyright 1984, University of Chicago Press. 317: from *Christianity, Social Tolerance, and Homosexuality*. Copyright 1980, University of Chicago Press. 320: from *Chronicles of the Crusades*, Copyright 1963, Penguin Books. 340: from *The Chronicle of Salimbene de Adam*. Copyright 1986, Medieval and Renaissance Texts and Studies.

Chapter 10: 348: from *Readings in Medieval History*. Copyright 1997, Broadview Press. 360: from *The Birth of Popular Heresy*. Copyright 1975, Edward Arnold Publishers. 373: from *The Wandering Scholars*. Copyright 1934, Constable.

Chapter 11: 390: from *Froissart: Chronicles*. Copyright 1968, Penguin Books. 397: from *The Council of Constance*. Copyright 1962, Columbia University Press. 398: from *Execrabilis: Defensorum Obedientae et alia Documenta*. Copyright 1968, Harvard University Press. 404: from *Women and Writing in Medieval Europe*. Copyright 1995, Routledge.

Chapter 12: 431: from *The Travels of Marco Polo*. Copyright 1926, Random House. 435: from *Memoirs of a Janissary*. Copyright 1975, Michigan Slavic Publications. 443: from *Mandeville's Travels*. Copyright 1967, Clarendon Press. 448: from *The Compendium and Description of the West Indies*. Copyright 1968, Smithsonian Institution Press.

Chapter 13: 456 (middle): from *University of Chicago Readings in Western Civilizations*. Copyright 1986, University of Chicago Press. 460: from *The Family in Renaissance Florence*. Copyright 1969, University of South Carolina Press. 463: from *The Prince*. Copyright 1947, AHM Publishing Corporation.

Chapter 14: 495: from *Selections from Conrad Celtis*. Copyright 1948, Cambridge University Press. 510: from *What Luther Says*. Copyright 1959, Concordia Publishing House. 513: from *Documents of the Christian Church*. Copyright 1967, Oxford University Press.

Chapter 15: 528: from *Simplicissimus*. Copyright 1995, Daedalus. 532: from *The Political Testament of Cardinal Richelieu*. Copyright 1961, University of Wisconsin Press. 539: from *Montaigne: Selections from the Essays*. Copyright 1971, AHM Publishing Corporation. 541 (top): from *Divine Right and Democracy: An Anthology of Political Writing in Stuart England*. Copyright 1986, Viking Penguin. 541 (bottom): from *The English Civil War: A Fight for Lawful Government*. Copyright 1967, Random House.

Chapter 16: 559: from *The Ancien Regime. French Society, 1600-1750*. Copyright 1973, Widenfeld and Nelson. 569: from *The Renaissance: University of Chicago Readings in Western Civilization*. Copyright 1995,

ILLUSTRATION CREDITS

Museum of Art; 176 (bottom): University Prints; 177 (center right): Giraudon/Art Resource, NY

Chapter 6: 182: Etruscan Musician (Scala/Art Resource); 185 (top): Villa Giulia Museum, Rome/The Warder Collection, NY; 185 (bottom): Musei Capitolini, Rome, Italy; Photo: Scala/Art Resource, NY; 187, 197, 204, 209: Rehearsal for a Satyr Play (© Archive Iconografico, S.A./Corbis); 191: Scala/Art Resource, NY; 192: American Numismatic Society; 198 (top): Scala/Art Resource, NY; 198 (bottom): American Numismatic Society; 201: Scala/Art Resource, NY; 202: Scala/Art Resource, NY; 207: SEF/Art Resource, NY; 208: Scala/Art Resource, NY; 210: Scala/Art Resource, NY; 211 (top): Alinari/Art Resource, NY; 211 (bottom): Art Resource, NY; 212: Italian State Tourist Office; 215 (top): Scala/Art Resource, NY; 215 (bottom): Gift of Martin A. Ryerson, 1922.4883. Photograph © 1997, The Art Institute of Chicago. All rights reserved; 216: Scala/Art Resource, NY

Chapter 7: 222, 235: St. Simeon Stylites on his Pillar (The Louvre, Paris. Photo: Herve Lewandowski, Réunion des Musées Nationaux/Art Resource, NY); 224: Ny Carlsberg Glyptotek; 225 (top): The Warder Collection, NY; 225 (bottom): The Warder Collection, NY; 226: Scala/Art Resource, NY; 230: The Warder Collection, NY; 231, 238, 243, 251 (top): Mosaic of Justinian (Scala/Art Resource, NY); 233: Art Resource, NY; 237: Scala/Art Resource, NY; 245: By permission of the Houghton Library, Harvard University; 246: The Warder Collection, NY; 249 (top): Biblioteca Medicea Laurenziana, Florence; 249 (bottom): The Warder Collection, NY; 251 (bottom): Scala/Art Resource, NY; 252: Scala/Art Resource, NY

Part III
256–257: A Late Medieval Funeral Scene (© Photo RMN, Paris)

Chapter 8: 260: Muslim Pilgrims on Their Way to Mecca (Bibliothèque Nationale de France, Paris); 263: Biblioteca Nacionale, Madrid; 264: cliché Bibliothèque Nationale de France, Paris; 266: Scala/Art Resource, NY; 267, 274, 281, 285, 293: Book cover (Scala/Art Resource, NY); 268: Giraudon/Art Resource, NY; 269: The Warder Collection, NY; 270: Arab Information Bureau; 272 (top): Scala/Art Resource, NY; 272 (bottom): Erich Lessing/Art Resource, NY; 276: Art Resource, NY ; 282: cliché Bibliothèque Nationale de France, Paris; 288: Kunsthistorisches Museum, Vienna; 291: cliché Bibliothèque Nationale de France, Paris; 292: Vatican Library: MS. Reg. Ret. 762, fol. 82r, written at Tours 800 A.D. (detail); 295: Courtesy of the British Museum; 296: Kunsthistorisches Museum, Vienna

Chapter 9: 300: Illustration from the Trés Riches Heures (Bibliothèque Nationale de France, Paris); 303: Biblioteca Riccardiana, Florence, Manuscript Ricc. 492 c. 18, with the permission of the Ministero per I Beni Culturali e Ambientali; 304: Bodleian Library, Division of Western Manuscripts, University of Oxford, MS. Bodley. 264, fol 81r; 305: The Warder Collection, NY; 306: By permission of the British Library; 307: Pierpont Morgan Library, New York/Art Resource, NY; 308: The Bettmann Archive; 310, 315, 317, 321, 340: View of Paris (cliché Bibliothèque Nationale de France, Paris); 312: Diebold Schilling, Official Bernese Chronicle, vol. 1, Burgerbibliothek, Berne, Ms.h.h.I.1, 289; 314: Photo by Zindman/Fremont; 324: cliché Bibliothèque Nationale de France,

Paris; 329: Giraudon/Art Resource, NY; 330: The Walters Art Gallery, Baltimore; 334: cliché Bibliothèque Nationale de France, Paris; 335: Art Resource, NY; 339: MS. Pal. Lat. 1071, fol. 1v, Foto Biblioteca Vaticana

Chapter 10: 344, 368: A Lecture Class in a Medieval University (The Bettmann Archive); 348, 360, 373: The Poet Dante Driven into Exile (Montpelliar, Faculté de Medicine); 349: Treasury, Abbey Ste. Foy, Conques, France. Photo: Giraudon/Art Resource, NY; 351: Thüringer Universität–Und Landesbibliothek, Jena; 354: The Bettman Archive; 355: Scala/Art Resource, NY; 356: Bettman/Corbis; 358: copyright Otto Muller Verlag, Salzburg, Austria; 359: Bayerische Staatsbibliothek, München; 362: Scala/Art Resource, NY; 363: Bayerische Staatsbibliothek, München; 364: cliché Bibliothèque Nationale de France, Paris; 369: Bibliotheque Nationale, Paris; 374: Foto Marburg/Art Resource, NY; 375: The Bodleian Library, Oxford: MS Bodley. 264, fol. 81v (detail); 376: cliché Bibliothèque Nationale de France, Paris; 377 (top): Richard List/Corbis; 377 (bottom): Richard List/Corbis; 378: Giraudon/Art Resource, NY

Chapter 11: 382: Burial of Plague Victims (Scala/Art Resource); 385: The Walters Art Gallery, Baltimore; 388: Réunion des Musées Nationaux/Art Resource, NY; 390, 392, 397, 404: A Party of Late Medieval Aristocrats (cliché Bibliothèque Nationale de France, Paris); 393: Musée Unterlinden, Colmar, France. Photo: Giraudon/Art Resource, NY; 394: cliché Bibliothèque Nationale de France, Paris; 395: Chris Hellier/Corbis; 398: Bayerische Staatsbibliothek, München; 406: Museo del Prado, Madrid; 407: The Warder Collection, NY; 413: By permission of the British Library; 414: Scala/Art Resource, NY; 415: Reproduced by courtesy of the Trustees, The National Gallery, London. Photograph © The National Gallery, London; 416: Bibliothèque Royale Albert I, Brussels; 417: © Bibliothèque Royale Albert I, Brussels, ms. 11209, fol. 3 recto; 418: The New York Public Library: Astor, Lenox, and Tilden Foundations; 419: Gutenberg Museum

Part IV   422–423:   A Portuguese galleon (National Maritime Museum, London)

Chapter 12:   426, 433: Mehmet II (Werner Forman Archive/Topkapi Palace Library, Istanbul/Art Resource, NY); 430: John Massey Stewart Picture Library; 434: Erich Lessing/Art Resource, NY; 435, 437 (bottom), 443, 448: The Battle of Lepanto, by Vicentino (Leabharlann Chester Beatty Library); 437 (top): Mansell/TimePix; 442: Royal Armouries Museum; 444 (left): José Pessoa, Arquivo Nacional de Fotografia, Instituto Português de Museus; (right): The Warder Collection, NY; 446 (top): Österreichesche Nationalbibliothek, Wien; (bottom): Det kongelige Bibliotek: Gl. kgl Saml. 2232. Side 527; 449: cliché Bibliothèque Nationale de France, Paris

Chapter 13:   452, 469: The School of Athens, by Raphael (Scala/Art Resource); 456, 460, 463, 470: The Creation of Adam, by Michelangelo (Scala/Art Resource); 458: Art Resource, NY; 461: © Photo RMN, Paris; 464: Erich Lessing/Art Resource, NY; 465: Erich Lessing/Art Resource, NY; 466 (top left): © Photo RMN, Paris; (top right): National Gallery of Art. Ailsa Mellon Bruce Fund, Photograph © Board of Trustees, National Gallery of Art, Washington; (bottom): Scala/Art Resource, NY; 467: Art Resource, NY/Thyssen-Bornemisza

Giraudon/Art Resource, NY; 693: Giraudon/Art Resource, NY; 702: Giraudon/Art Resource, NY; 703: The Hulton Deutsch Collection; 705: The Hulton Deutsch Collection; 706 (top): cliché Bibliothèque Nationale de France, Paris; (bottom): Giraudon/Art Resource, NY: Musée de la Ville de Paris, Musée Carnavalet, Paris, France; 712: Photo Bulloz, Louvre; 717: Dawson Collection, Morrab Library of Penzance; 718: Museo del Prado, Madrid; 719 (top): Giraudon/Art Resource, NY; (bottom): Museum of Fine Arts, Boston. S. A. Denio Collection, 47.1059. Photo: © 2001 Museum of Fine Arts, Boston

Chapter 21: 722, 727 (bottom): A cotton mill in Lancashire, 1834 (The Granger Collection, New York); 727 (top): Bettman/Corbis; 728, 729, 731, 732: *The Steam Hammer* (The Hulton Deutsch Collection); 730: The Granger Collection, New York; 732: The Granger Collection, New York; 733: The Hulton Deutsch Collection; 734: John R. Freeman & Co; 736 (top): Staatliche Museen zu Berlin—Preußischer Kulturbesitz; (bottom): City Archives of Lyons; 737: The New York Public Library: Astor, Lenox, and Tilden Foundations; 738: Scala/Art Resource, NY; 741: Hulton Deutsch Collection/Corbis

Chapter 22: 744: *The Third Class Carriage,* by Honoré Daumier (Giraudon/Art Resource, NY); 747 (both): National Library of Ireland; 748, 752, 753, 757: A soup kitchen in Manchester, England (The Warder Collection, NY); 750: The Hulton Deutsch Collection; 751: Wellcome Institute Library, London; 759: © National Gallery, London; 760: cliché Bibliothèque Nationale de France, Paris; 761: Giraudon/Art Resource, NY; 764: The Granger Collection, New York; 768: © The J. Paul Getty Museum; 769: Hiram Powers, Greek Slave. Marble. In the Collection of the Corcoran Gallery of Art. Gift of William Wilson Corcoran; 770: Roger-Viollet

Chapter 23: 772, 791: *Liberty Leading the People,* by Eugene Delacroix (Erich Lessing/Art Resource, NY); 781: Victoria & Albert Museum, London. Photo: Victoria & Albert Museum/Art Resource, NY; 782: Yale Center for British Art, Paul Mellon Collection. Photo: Bridgeman Art Library, International; 783: Scala/Art Resource, NY; 784: Bettman/Corbis; 786: Josse/Art Resource, NY; 787: © Photo RMN, Paris; 788: Archivo Iconografico, S.A./Corbis; 789, 790, 794, 801: The July Revolution of 1830, in Paris (Giraudon/Art Resource); 791: © Photo RMN, Paris; 792: Manchester and Cheshire Library; 796: Reproduced by the Gracious Permission of Her Majesty the Queen; 797: Roger-Viollet; 798 (top): cliché Bibliothèque Nationale de France, Paris; (bottom): The Armand Hammer Daumier and Contemporaries Collection, UCLA Hammer Museum, Los Angeles; 799: The Phillips Collection; 800: Giraudon/Art Resource, NY

Chapter 24: 806, 811: William Tell (Austrian Archive/Corbis); 810: BAL2594 *Little Red Riding Hood* by Arthur Rackham (1867–1939). Private Collection/Bridgeman Art Library, London/New York. The Arthur Rackham pictures are reproduced with the kind permission of his family; 811: Austrian Archive/Corbis; 816: Scala/Art Resource, NY; 818, 820, 829, 833: *The March Days* (Erich Lessing/Art Resource, NY); 819: The Warder Collection, NY; 827: Giraudon/Art Resource, NY; 831: Scala/Art Resource, NY; 835: Bowdoin College Museum of Art, Brunswick, Maine. Bequest of the Honorable James Bowdoin III; 838 (right): Library of Congress

Part VII: 840–841: *The Funeral Procession,* by George Grosz (VAGA/Art Resource, NY)

Chapter 25: 844, 856: An opium factory in Patna, India, c. 1851 (The British Library); 848, 854, 863, 870: Construction of the Suez Canal (The Warder Collection, NY); 852: Bettman/Corbis; 853 (top): From Punch magazine, 1857/Warder Collection, NY; (bottom): The Hulton Deutsch Collection; 856 (bottom): The British Library; 862: The Hulton Deutsch Collection; 865 (left): The Bettmann Archive; (right): The Warder Collection, NY; 874 (top): The New York Public Library: Astor, Lenox, and Tilden Foundations; (bottom): Courtesy of the Director, National Army Museum, London

Chapter 26: 876, 887: Poster proclaiming a general strike (Archives de la Préfecture de Police de la Ville de Paris); 878: Corbis; 879: AKG London; 882, 894, 901, 908, 912: Newspapers for sale in a British railway station (The Warder Collection, NY); 883: The Warder Collection, NY; 885: Corbis-Bettmann; 889 (top): Library of Congress; (center): Corbis; (bottom): The Hulton Deutsch Collection/Corbis; 890: The Hulton Deutsch Collection/Corbis; 891: The Hulton Deutsch Collection/Corbis; 893: Bettman/Corbis; 896: Bildarchiv Preussischer Kulturbesitz, Berlin; 902: Staatliche Museen zu Berlin—Preußisher Kulturbesitz; 910: Library of Congress/Corbis; 912: The Warder Collection, NY; 915: © The Art Institute of Chicago; 916: The Metropolitan Museum of Art, H. O. Havemeyer Collection, Bequest of Mrs. H. O. Havemeyer, 1929. (29.100.64) Photograph © 1984 The Metropolitan Museum of Art; 917: The Metropolitan Museum of Art, Bequest of Sam A. Lewisohn, 1951. (51.112.2) Photograph © 1986 The Metropolitan Museum of Art

Chapter 27: 920: A World War I poster encouraging British women to work in munitions factories (The Hulton Deutsch Collection/Corbis); 922: Staatliche Museen zu Berlin—Preußischer Kulturbesitz; 924, 927, 938, 944: French soldiers (Imperial War Museum); 926: Bildarchiv Preussischer Kulturbesitz; 931: Trustees of the Imperial War Museum, London; 933: Getty Images, Inc; 936 (left): Hoover Institution Archives, Stanford University; (right): Hoover Institution Archives, Stanford University; 937 (top): The Imperial War Museum, London; (bottom): The Warder Collection, NY; 939: Hoover Institution Archives, Stanford University; 940: Hoover Institution Archives, Stanford University; 941: Bildarchiv Preussischer Kulturbesitz; 945 (top): Staatliche Museen zu Berlin—Preußischer Kulturbesitz; (bottom): The Warder Collection, NY; 949: The National Archives

Chapter 28: 954: *Mural of Kansas City, Missouri,* by Thomas Hart Benton (© T.H. Benton and R. Benton Testamentary Trusts/Licensed by VAGA, New York, NY); 956: The Warder Collection, NY; 959: Staatliche Museen zu Berlin—Preußischer Kulturbesitz; 960, 972, 982, 986: *Detroit Industry,* by Diego Rivera (Gift of Edsel B. Ford. © 1998 Institute Nacional de Bellas Artes, Mexico City. Photograph © The Detroit Institute of Arts); 963: The Fotomas Index, London/The Warder Collection, NY; 966: Brown Brothers; 968: Stefan Lorant/The Warder Collection, NY; 971: Stefan Lorant/The Warder Collection, NY; 974: The New York Public Library: Astor, Lenox, and Tilden Foundations; 975: The Hulton Deutsch Collection; 978: UPI/Corbis-Bettmann; 979: Library of Congress; 981: © Estate of George Grosz/Liscensed by VAGA, New York, NY. Photograph Erich Lessing/Art Resource, NY; 982:

(top): Dali, *The Persistence of Memory*. 1931. Oil on canvas, 9½" x 13" (24.1 x 33 cm). The Museum of Modern Art, New York. Given anonymously. Photograph © 1997 The Museum of Modern Art, New York. © 1998 Demart Pro Arte (R), Geneva/Artists Rights Society (ARS), New York; **982**: The Museum of Modern Art, New York. Photograph Courtesy The Museum of Modern Art, New York; **983**: Western Pennsylvania Conservancy/Art Resource, NY

Chapter 29: **988, 1024**: Winston Churchill, Franklin Roosevelt, and Joseph Stalin at the Yalta Conference, 1945 (Snark/Art Resource, NY); **993 (top)**: © 2001 Artists Rights Society (ARS), New York/ADAGP, Paris; **993 (bottom), 1006, 1009, 1021**: *Guernica*, by Pablo Picasso (Giraudon/Art Resource, NY. © 1998 Estate of Pablo Picasso/Artists Rights Society (ARS), New York); **994**: The National Archives/Corbis; **996**: Library of Congress/Corbis; **997**: The National Archives; **999**: Hulton Deutsch Collection/Corbis; **1000**: The National Archives/Corbis; **1008**: The Warder Collection, NY; **1013 (top)**: Burstein Collection/Corbis; **(bottom)**: AP/World Wide Photos; **1014**: Public Record Office Image Library; **1018 (top)**: The National Archives/Corbis; **(bottom)**: Photos12.com/ARJ; **1019**: The Imperial War Museum, London; **1019**: Corbis; **1020**: Hulton Deutsch Collection/Corbis; **1024**: Snark/Art Resource

Part VIII: **1028–1029**: A scene from the fall of the Berlin Wall (© David and Peter Tumley/Corbis)

Chapter 30: **1032, 1035 (bottom)**: The Berlin airlift (UPI/Corbis-Bettman); **1034**: UPI/Corbis-Bettmann; **1035 (top)**: AP/Wide World Photos; **1036, 1039, 1043 (bottom), 1044**: A scene from the Soviet occupation of Czechoslovakia (Hulton Deutsch Collection/Corbis); **1037**: Library of Congress/Corbis; **1038 (top)**: Yerevan, Armgosizdat, 1958; **(bottom)**: AP/Wide World Photos; **1043 (top)**: German Information Center/The Warder Collection, NY; **1046**: UPI/Corbis-Bettmann; **1048**: AP/Wide World Photos; **1050**: Corbis; **1051**: **(top)**: Hulton

Deutsch Collection/Corbis; **(bottom)**: Hulton Deutsch Collection/Corbis; **1052**: Seattle Art Museum/Corbis. © 1998 Pollock-Krasner Foundation/Artists Rights Society (ARS), New York; **1053**: © Jasper Johns/Licensed by VAGA, New York, NY, Photograph © The Whitney Museum of American Art, New York; **1054**: Photograph © The Whitney Museum of American Art, New York. © 1998 Frank Stella/Artists Rights Society (ARS), New York

Chapter 31: **1056**: A French student protest poster from May, 1968 (Photos12.com); **1062 (top)**: Roger-Viollet; **(bottom right)**: Photos12.com - DR; **1062 (bottom left), 1063, 1065**: A scene from the student uprisings in Paris, May, 1968. (Bettman/Corbis); **1064 (bottom)**: Hulton Deutsch Collection/Corbis; **1068 (top)**: Adam Woolfitt/Corbis; **(bottom)**: Ronald Reagan Library/Corbis; **1069 (top)**: Owen Franken/Corbis; **(bottom)**: MTB Banking Corporation/Warder Collection, NY **1070**: AP/World Wide Photos; **1071**: © Alexandra Avakian/Woodfin Camp; **1072**: AP/Wide World Photos; **1074**: AP/Wide World Photos; **1076**: AFP/Corbis

Chapter 32: **1078**: A computer model of a DNA molecule (Corbis); **1081, 1085, 1087, 1104**: The Union Carbide factory in Bhopal, India (Chris Rainier/Corbis); **1082 (top)**: The Warder Collection, NY; **(bottom)**: Hulton Deutsch Collection/Corbis; **1084**: Hulton Deutsch Collection/Corbis; **1086**: Corbis; **1088**: The Bettmann Archive; **1089 (top)**: Hulton Deutsch Collection/Corbis; **(bottom)**: Sovfoto/Eastfoto; **1092 (left)**: Reuters/Corbis-Bettmann; **(right)**: Reuters/Corbis-Bettmann; **1095 (top)**: AP/Wide World Photos; **(bottom)**: AP/Wide World Photos; **1097**: Tim Page/Corbis; **1098**: Howard Davies/Corbis; **1101 (top right)**: Natalie Fobes/Corbis; **(bottom)**: © Kennan Ward Photography/Corbis; **1101**: Ecoscene/Corbis; **1102**: Dave G. Houser/Corbis

Every effort has been made to contact the copyright holders of the selections. Any corrections should be forwarded to W. W. Norton & Company, Inc., 500 Fifth Avenue, New York, NY 10110.

INDEX

The sounds represented by the diacritical marks used in this Index are illustrated by the following common words:

āle　　ēve　　īce　　ōld　　ūse
ăt　　ĕnd　　ĭll　　ŏf　　ŭs　　fŏŏt
câre　　　　　　　　fôrm　　ûrn
ärm

Vowels that have no diacritical marks are to be "neutral," for example: Aegean = à-je'an, common = kŏm' on, Alcaeus = ăl-sē' us. The combinations *ou* and *oi* are pronounced as in "out" and "oil."